ADVERTISING AND PUBLIC RELATIONS

PEARSON

We work with leading authors to develop the strongest learning experiences, bringing cutting-edge thinking and best learning practice to a global market. We craft our print and digital resources to do more to help learners not only understand their content, but to see it in action and apply what they learn, whether studying or at work.

Pearson is the world's leading learning company. Our portfolio includes Penguin, Dorling Kindersley, the Financial Times and our educational business, Pearson International. We are also a leading provider of electronic learning programmes and of test development, processing and scoring services to educational institutions, corporations and professional bodies around the world.

Pearson Custom Publishing enables our customers to access a wide and expanding range of market-leading content from world-renowned authors and develop their own tailor-made book. You choose the content that meets your needs and Pearson Custom Publishing produces a high-quality printed book.

Every day our work helps learning flourish, and wherever learning flourishes, so do people.

To learn more please visit us at: www.pearsoncustom.co.uk

PEARSON CUSTOM PUBLISHING

ADVERTISING AND PUBLIC RELATIONS

Compiled from:

Advertising & IMC: Principles and Practice
Global Edition, Ninth Edition
by Sandra Moriarty, Nancy Mitchell and William Wells

Integrated Advertising, Promotion, and Marketing Communications
Global Edition, Fifth Edition
by Kenneth E. Clow and Donald Baack

Digital Marketing: Strategy, Implementation and Practice
Fifth Edition
by Dave Chaffey and Fiona Ellis-Chadwick

Global Marketing
Seventh Edition
by Warren J. Keegan and Mark C. Green

Exploring Public Relations
Second Edition
by Ralph Tench and Liz Yeomans

PEARSON

Harlow, England • London • New York • Boston • San Francisco • Toronto • Sydney • Auckland • Singapore • Hong Kong
Tokyo • Seoul • Taipei • New Delhi • Cape Town • Sao Paulo • Mexico City • Madrid • Amsterdam • Munich • Paris • Milan

Pearson Education Limited
Edinburgh Gate
Harlow
Essex CM20 2JE

And associated companies throughout the world

Visit us on the World Wide Web at:
www.pearsoned.co.uk

This Custom Book Edition © Pearson Education Limited 2012

Compiled from:

Advertising & IMC: Principles and Practice
Global Edition, Ninth Edition
by Sandra Moriarty, Nancy Mitchell and William Wells
ISBN 978 0 27 37 5292 9
© Pearson Education Limited 2012

Integrated Advertising, Promotion, and Marketing Communications
Global Edition, Fifth Edition
by Kenneth E. Clow and Donald Baack
ISBN 978 0 273 75328 5
© Pearson Education Limited 2012

Digital Marketing: Strategy, Implementation and Practice
Fifth Edition
by Dave Chaffey and Fiona Ellis-Chadwick
ISBN 978 0 273 74610 2
© Pearson Education Limited 2000, 2003, 2006, 2009, 2012

Global Marketing
Seventh Edition
by Warren J. Keegan and Mark C. Green
ISBN 978 0 13 271915 5
© 2013, 2011, 2008, 2005, 2003 by Warren J. Keegan. Published by
Pearson Education, Inc

Exploring Public Relations
Second Edition
by Ralph Tench and Liz Yeomans
ISBN 978 0 27 371594 8
© Pearson Education Limited 2006

ISBN 978 1 78134 708 9

Printed and bound in Italy

CONTENTS

CHAPTER 1

The World of Advertising

1 The New World of Marketing Communication

WHOPPERFREAKOUT.COM

It's a Winner

Campaign:
"Whopper Freakout"

Company:
Burger King

Agency:
Crispin Porter + Bogusky

Award:
Grand Effie and Gold Effie in Restaurants category

CHAPTER KEY POINTS

1. What is advertising, how has it evolved, and what does it do in modern times?
2. How have the key concepts of marketing communication developed over time?
3. How is the industry organized—key players, types of agencies, and jobs within agencies?
4. How is the practice of advertising changing?

Ingredients for a Burger Freakout

Imagine the reaction store managers would receive if they announced to their customers, "Today this Burger King is a Whopper-free zone." No more Whoppers. That's precisely what happened in a Las Vegas Burger King. The announcement was part of a social experiment designed to see how consumers would react if they couldn't get their beloved burgers. In the process it showed the power of advertising to be relevant and effective in confirming that the Whopper is "America's favorite burger," and it increased sales. Here's the inside scoop.

Ad agency Crispin Porter + Bogusky (CPB) faced this challenge: the Crispin team had to "take a product that has been around for 50 years and sells more than a billion units annually and make it interesting enough that the campaign would increase sales during a highly competitive period." And they had to do it using no marketing tools other than advertising. Adding to the challenge, CPB had to accomplish this in a competitive environment: McDonald's consistently outspends Burger King three to one.

The solution: CPB knew that America loves the Whopper. The agency figured it wasn't enough to just announce that BK's burger is the best. Who would care? Instead of telling facts about the product, the agency figured it had to demonstrate that it was the best burger in a compelling manner. *Here's your first advertising lesson:* To convince consumers, show them the truth about the product—don't just tell them about it—and do it memorably.

Just who eats Whoppers? Burger King knows its core demographic (its biggest group of consumers) is 18- to 24-year-old males, and it sure knows how to connect with those dudes. Past promotional efforts included sponsorships with the National Football League and NASCAR and tie-ins with *The Simpsons Movie.* Its chicken sandwich was launched with the "Subservient Chicken" website. Who could forget the creepy King mascot who shows up in weird places? The Whopper commands a loyal and passionate following from those who love the weird—and who aren't counting calories.

To grab the attention of Whopper lovers, CPB came up with a big idea, a prank. It devised an experiment that deprived consumers of their beloved Whopper—something that hadn't been done before in the burger war. To enact the deprivation strategy, the agency took over a Burger King in Las Vegas for a single day and video-taped with hidden cameras the reactions of consumers who were either told that Whoppers had been permanently removed from the BK menu or given a competitor's burger such as a Big Mac or Wendy burger instead of a Whopper.

Actors were used as Burger King employees, but real consumers —not actors— reacted to the bad burger news. TV commercials created from these scenes drove viewers to *www.whopperfreakout.com*, where they could watch an 8-minute documentary about the experiment. The agency hoped that this would catch on with consumers who would then pass the word and generate more web traffic. Ad Lesson #2: The best advertising is word-of-mouth endorsements from friends.

Did it work? Customers freaked out. Turn to the end of the chapter to find out how wildly successful this campaign has been. And if you want to see more of this campaign, check out *www.bk.com/en/us/campaigns/whopper-freakout.html.*

Sources: Effie brief provided by New York American Marketing Association; Eleftheria Parpis, "BK's 'Whopper Freakout' Wins Grand Effie," June 3, 2009, www.adweek.com; Li Evans, "Whopper Freakout Shows Burger King Is King of Viral Marketing," January 13, 2008, www.searchmarketinggurus.com; Suzanne Vranica, "Hey, No Whopper on the Menu?! Hoax by Burger King Captures Outrage," *The Wall Street Journal,* February 8, 2008, www.wsj.com; Andrew Martin, "Gulp! Burger King Is on the Rebound," *The New York Times,* February 10, 2008, www.nytimes.com; www.whopperfreakout.com.

The Burger King "Whopper Freakout" campaign is an example of an award-winning effort that proved how much America loves the Whopper. But what made it successful? In the Part 1 opener we made the point that, in spite of economic downturns, the basic principles remain important. The Burger King story demonstrates the importance of a dramatic idea, as well as the power of word of mouth. In this chapter we'll define advertising and its role in marketing communication, explain how its basic concepts and practices evolved, and describe the agency world. We'll conclude by analyzing the changes facing marketing communication.

WHAT IS ADVERTISING?

You've seen thousands, maybe millions of commercial messages, so how would you define advertising, which is the most visible of all the forms of marketing communication that we will be discussing in this book? It may sound silly to ask such an obvious question. But where would you start if your instructor asked you for a definition of advertising?

At its most basic, the purpose of advertising has always been to sell a *product,* which can be *goods, services,* or *ideas.* Although there have been major changes in recent years from dying print media to merging and converging digital forms, the basics of advertising, as we said in the Part 1 opener, are even more important in turbulent times. To better understand advertising's development as a commercial form of communication, it helps to understand how advertising's definition and its basic roles have evolved over the years.

- *Identification Advertising identifies a product and/or the store where it's sold.* In its earliest years, and this goes back as far as ancient times, advertising focused on identifying a product and where it was sold. Some of the earliest ads were simply signs with the name or graphic image of the type of store—cobbler, grocer, or blacksmith.
- *Information Advertising provides information about a product.* Advances in printing technology at the beginning of the Renaissance spurred literacy and brought an explosion of printed materials in the form of posters, handbills, and newspapers. Literacy was no longer the badge of the elite and it was possible to reach a general audience with more detailed information about products. The word **advertisement** first appeared around 1655, and by 1660 publishers were using the word as a heading in newspapers for commercial information. These messages announced land for sale, runaways (slaves and servants), transportation (ships arriving, stagecoach schedules), and goods for sale from local merchants.

Because of the importance of commercial information, these ads were considered news and in many cases occupied more space in early newspapers than the news stories.

- **Persuasion** *Advertising persuades people to buy things.* The Industrial Revolution accelerated social change, as well as mass production. It brought the efficiency of machinery not only to the production of goods, but also to their distribution. Efficient production plus wider distribution meant that manufacturers could offer more products than their local markets could consume. With the development of trains and national roads, manufacturers could move their products around the country. For widespread marketing of products, it became important to have a recognizable brand name, such as Ivory or, more recently, Burger King. Also large groups of people needed to know about these goods, so along with industrial mechanization and the opening of the frontier came even more use of new communication media, such as magazines, catalogs, and billboards that reached more people with more enticing forms of persuasion. P. T. Barnum and patent medicine makers were among the advertising pioneers who moved promotion from identification and information to a flamboyant version of persuasion called *hype*—graphics and language characterized by exaggeration, or hyperbole.

Over the years, identification, information, and persuasion have been the basic elements of marketing communication and the focus of advertising. So how do we define it now realizing that advertising is dynamic and constantly changing to meet the demands of society and the marketplace? We can summarize a modern view of advertising with the following definition:

> **Advertising** is a paid form of persuasive communication that uses mass and interactive media to reach broad audiences in order to connect an identified sponsor with buyers (a target audience), provide information about products (goods, services, and ideas), and interpret the product features in terms of the customer's needs and wants.

This definition has a number of elements and as we review them, we will also point out where the definition is changing because of new technology, media shifts, and cultural changes. (Another source for definitions in the advertising and marketing area is the American Marketing Association Dictionary, which you can find at *www.marketingpower.com/_layouts/Dictionary.aspx*.)

Advertising is usually *paid* for by the advertiser (Burger King, for example) who has a product to *sell* (the Whopper), although some forms of advertising, such as public service announcements (PSAs), use donated space and time. Not only is the message paid for, but the sponsor is identified. Advertising began as *one-way* communication—from an advertiser to a targeted audience. Digital media, however, have opened the door to interesting new forms of *two-way* and *multiple-way* brand-related communication such as word-of-mouth conversations among friends or consumer-generated messages sent to a company. The viral video of Whopper customers' disbelieving responses became a hit on YouTube when shared among friends.

Advertising generally reaches a *broad audience* of *potential customers,* either as a *mass audience* or in smaller *targeted* groups. However *direct-response* advertising, particularly those practices that involve digital communication, has the ability to address individual members of the audience. So some advertising can deliver *one-to-one* communication but with a large group of people.

In traditional advertising, the message is conveyed through different kinds of *mass media,* which are largely *nonpersonal* messages. This nonpersonal

CLASSIC

P. T. Barnum was a pioneer in advertising and promotion. His flamboyant circus posters were more than just hype. What are the other roles they performed?

characteristic, however, is changing with the introduction of more *interactive* types of media, as the Whopper case demonstrates. Richard Edelman, CEO of the Edelman agency, emphasizes the emerging importance of *word of mouth,* which is personal communication through new media forms rather than what he describes as "scripted messages in a paid format."[1]

Most advertising has a defined strategy and seeks to *inform* consumers and/or make them *aware* of a brand, company, or organization. In many cases, it also tries to *persuade* or influence consumers to do something, such as buy a product or check out a brand's website. Persuasion may involve *emotional* messages as well as information. In an unusual use of messages tied to feelings, the Burger King "deprivation strategy" was designed to elicit negative responses to competitors' burgers that were substituted for the Whopper.

Keep in mind that, as we have said, a *product* can be a *good, service,* or *idea.* Some nonprofits, for example, use ads to "sell" memberships, get volunteers and donations, or advocate controversial positions.

Is Advertising the Only Tool in the Promotional Toolkit?

It's not the only tool, although it may be the biggest. In the United States, advertising is a $30 billion industry.[2] Advertising often is seen as the driving force in marketing communication because it commands the largest budget, as well as the largest number of agencies and professionals.

To get an idea of the scope of the advertising industry, consider Tables 1.1 and 1.2, which give some indication of the size of the advertising industry by breaking out the top 10 advertising categories and advertisers. In Table 1.1 look at how spending changed in the course of a year from 2008 to 2009 based on Third Quarter (January to September) figures. Which categories and advertisers were on the increase and which decreased and what do you think accounts for those changes?

As we said, advertising's original purpose was to sell something, but over the years, other promotional tools, with different sets of strengths, have developed to help meet that objective. For example, providing information, particularly about some new feature or a new product, is sometimes better handled through *publicity* or public relations. *Direct-response* advertising, such as catalogs and flyers sent to the home or office, can also provide more information in more depth than traditional ads that are limited in space and time. *Specialties* that carry brand logos as reminders or incentives to buy are handled by *sales promotion* companies. Communication with employees and shareholders about brands and campaigns is usually handled by *public relations.*

In other words, a variety of promotional tools can be used to identify, inform, and persuade. Professionals see differences in all of these areas, but many people just see them all as

Table 1.1   Top Ten Advertising Categories by Ad Expenditure

Category	2009 Advertising Spending ($m)	% Change Since 2008
1. Automotive	$7,492	−30.8
2. Telecom	6,190	.4
3. Financial services	5,673	−23.7
4. Local services & amusements	5,610	−15.0
5. Direct response	4,916	−12.0
6. Miscellaneous retail	4,751	−17.4
7. Food and candy	4,550	−2.2
8. Restaurants	4,204	2.4
9. Personal care products	4,082	−9.2
10. Pharmaceuticals	3,484	−.6

Source: TNS Media Intelligence Reports U.S. Advertising Expenditures Declined 14.7 Percent in First Nine Months of 2009, TNS Media Intelligence, December 8, 2009, *www.tns-mi.com/news/2009-Ad-Spending-Q3.htm.*

Table 1.2   Top Ten U.S. Advertisers

Company	2009 Advertising Spending ($m)	% Change Since 2008
1. Procter & Gamble	$1,941	−15.9
2. Verizon	1,892	−5.8
3. General Motors	1,353	−15.5
4. AT&T	1,339	−6.1
5. Johnson & Johnson	1,037	−1.3
6. News Corp	947.8	−9.4
7. Sprint Nextel	913	51.1
8. Pfizer Inc	897	11.9
9. Time Warner	875	−10.7
10. General Electric	764	−12.9

Source: TNS Media Intelligence Reports U.S. Advertising Expenditures Declined 14.7 Percent in First Nine Months of 2009, TNS Media Intelligence, December 8, 2009, *www.tns-mi.com/news/2009-Ad-Spending-Q3.htm.*

promotion, or lump them together and call them *advertising*. The proper name for this bundle of tools, however, is **marketing communication (marcom),** an umbrella term that refers to all forms of communication about a brand that appear in a variety of media. Although we are focusing on advertising in this initial chapter, the book will focus on this expanded concept of marketing communication. Chapter 2 will provide more information about this wider world of brand communication.

Why Advertising?

Advertising obviously plays a role in both communication and marketing as we've been discussing. In addition to marketing communication, advertising also has a role in the functioning of the economy and society. Consider the launch of the Apple Macintosh in 1984, which was successful because of the impact of one advertisement, a television commercial generally considered to be the greatest ever made. As you read about this "1984" commercial in the *A Matter of Practice,* note how this commercial demonstrated all four functions—marketing, communication, social, and economic.

Marketing and Communication Roles   In its marketing communication role, advertising transforms a product into a distinctive brand by creating an **image** and personality that goes beyond straightforward product features. The "1984" commercial demonstrated how a personality could be created for a computer (innovative), one that showcased it as a creative tool that breaks through the rigid systems of other computer brands (IBM?). As advertising showcases brands, it also creates consumer demand (lines of customers the following day at stores where the Macintosh was sold) and makes statements that reflect social issues and trends (opening up the new category of personal computers for non-experts). So in addition to marketing and communication, advertising has economic and social roles.

Economic and Societal Roles   Advertising flourishes in societies that enjoy economic abundance, in which supply exceeds demand. In these societies, advertising extends beyond a primarily informational role to create a demand for a particular brand. In the case of the "Whopper Freakout" campaign, the decision was to make the product disappear in order to generate **buzz,** as well as reinforce a high level of demand for the brand by loyal customers.

    Most economists presume that, because it reaches large groups of potential consumers, advertising brings cost efficiencies to marketing and, thus, lower prices to consumers. The more people know about a product, the higher the sales—and the higher the level of sales, the cheaper the product. Think about the high price of new products, such as a computer, HDTVs, and cell phones or other new technology. As demand grows, as well as competition, prices begin to drop.

Principle
Advertising *creates* cost efficiencies by increasing demand among large groups of people resulting in higher levels of sales and, ultimately, lower prices.

The Greatest Commercial Ever Made

The advertiser was Apple, the product was its new Macintosh, and the client—the person handling the advertising responsibility and making decisions—was Steve Jobs, Apple's CEO, who wanted a "thunderclap" ad. The agency was California-based Chiat/Day (now TBWA\Chiat\Day). The medium was the Super Bowl. The "supplier" was legendary British film director Ridley Scott of *Alien* and *Blade Runner* fame. The audience was the 96 million people watching Super Bowl XVIII that winter day in January 1984, and the target audience was all those in the audience who were trying to decide whether to buy a personal computer.

It's a basic principle in advertising: The combination of the right product at the right time in the right place with all the right people involved can create something magical—in this case, Jobs' thunderclap. It also required a cast of 200 and a budget of $900,000 for production and $800,000 for the 60-second time slot. By any measure, it was a big effort.

The storyline was a takeoff on George Orwell's science fiction novel about the sterile mind-controlled world of *1984*. An audience of mindless, gray-skinned drones (who were actually skinheads from the streets of London) watches a massive screen image of "Big Brother" spouting an ideological diatribe. Then an athletic young woman in bright red shorts runs in, chased by helmeted storm troopers, and throws a sledgehammer at the screen. The destruction of the image is followed by a burst of fresh air blowing over the open-mouthed drones as they "see the light." In the last shot the announcer reads the only words in the commercial as they appear on screen:

On January 24th, Apple Computer will introduce Macintosh. And you'll see why 1984 won't be like "1984."

Was it an easy idea to sell to the client?

First of all, some Apple executives who first saw the commercial were terrified that it wouldn't work because it didn't look like any commercial they had ever seen. After viewing it, several board members put their heads down in their hands. Another said, "Who would like to move on firing Chiat/Day immediately?" Legend has it

that Apple's other founder, Steve Wozniak, took out his checkbook and told Jobs, "I'll pay for half if you pay for the other half." The decision to air the commercial finally came down to Jobs, whose confidence in the Chiat/Day creative team gave him the courage to run the ad.

Was it effective?

On January 24, long lines formed outside computer stores carrying the Macintosh, and the entire inventory sold out in one day. The initial sales goal of 50,000 units was easily surpassed by the 72,000 units sold in the first 100 days. More would have been sold if production had been able to keep up with demand.

The "1984" commercial is one of the most talked-about and remembered commercials ever made. Every time someone draws up a list of best commercials, it sits at the top, and it continues to receive accolades more than two decades later. If you haven't seen it, check it out at *www.apple-history.com* or *http://s153506479 .onlinehome.us/1984.html* and decide for yourself.

Remember, the commercial only ran once—an expensive spot on the year's most-watched television program. The commercial turned the Super Bowl from just another football game into the advertising event of the year. What added to its impact was the hype before and after it ran. People knew about the spot because of press coverage prior to the game, and they were watching for it. Coverage after the game was as likely to talk about the "1984" spot as the football score. Advertising became news and watching Super Bowl commercials became an event. That's why *Advertising Age*'s critic Bob Garfield calls it "the greatest TV commercial ever made."

The debate continues about whether the "Big Brother" character was designed to represent IBM. What do you think?

Watch "1984" on:" *www.youtube.com/watch?v=OYecfV3ubP8* or *http://video.google.com/videoplay?docid=-715862862672743260* About TBWA\Chiat\Day: *https://www.tbwachiat.com/* An interview with Ridley Scott about making "1984": *www.youtube.com/watch?v=BjiRErZBC8I*

Sources: Kevin Maney, "Apple's '1984' Super Bowl Commercial Still Stands as Watershed Event," *USA Today*, January 28, 2004: 3B; Liane Hansen (Host), "Steve Hayden Discusses a 1984 Apple Ad Which Aired During the Super Bowl," National Public Radio Weekend Edition, February 1, 2004; Bradley Johnson, "10 Years after '1984': The Commercial and the Product That Changed Advertising," *Advertising Age*, June 1994: 1, 12–14; Curt's Media, "The 1984 Apple Commercial: The Making of a Legend," *www.isd.net/cmcalone/cine/1984.html*.

Two contrasting points of view explain how advertising creates economic impact. In the first, the rational view, advertising is seen as a vehicle for helping consumers assess value through price cues and other information, such as quality, location, and reputation. Advocates of this viewpoint see the role of advertising as a means to objectively provide price/value information, thereby creating more *rational economic decisions*. By focusing on images and emotional responses, the second approach appeals to consumers making a decision on *nonprice, emotional appeals*. This emotional view explains how images and psychological appeals influence consumer decisions. This type of advertising is believed to be so persuasive that it decreases the likelihood a consumer will switch to an alternative product, regardless of the price charged.

In addition to informing us about new and improved products, advertising also mirrors fashion and design trends and adds to our aesthetic sense. Advertising has an educational role in that it teaches about new products and their use. It may also expose social issues—some say the "1984" commercial symbolically proclaimed the value of computer literacy "for the rest of us," those who weren't slaves to the hard-to-operate PC systems of the time. It helps us shape an image of ourselves by setting up role models with which we can identify (a woman athlete liberating the gray masses), and it gives us a way to express ourselves in terms of our personalities (smash the screen image of Big Brother) and sense of style (red shorts—the only color in the drab environment) through the things we wear and use. It also presents images capturing the diversity of the world in which we live. These social roles have both negative and positive dimensions, which we will discuss in Chapter 3.

What Are the Most Common Types of Advertising?

There isn't just one kind of advertising. In fact, advertising is a large and varied industry. Different types of advertising have different roles. Considering all the different advertising situations, we can identify seven major types of advertising:

1. *Brand advertising,* the most visible type of advertising, is referred to as *national* or *consumer* advertising. Brand advertising, such as that for the Apple Macintosh in the classic "1984" commercial, focuses on the development of a long-term brand identity and image.
2. *Retail* or *local advertising* focuses on retailers, distributors, or dealers who sell their merchandise in a certain geographical area; retail advertising has information about products that are available in local stores. The objectives focus on stimulating store traffic and creating a distinctive image for the retailer. Local advertising can refer to a retailer, such as T. J. Maxx, or a manufacturer or distributor who offers products in a fairly restricted geographic area.
3. *Direct-response advertising* tries to stimulate an immediate response by the customer to the seller. It can use any advertising medium, particularly direct mail and the Internet. The consumer can respond by telephone, mail, or over the Internet, and the product is delivered directly to the consumer by mail or some other carrier.
4. *Business-to-business (B2B) advertising,* also called *trade advertising,* is sent from one business to another. It includes messages directed at companies distributing products as well as industrial purchasers and professionals such as lawyers and physicians. Advertisers place most business advertising in professional publications.
5. *Institutional advertising,* also called **corporate advertising,** focuses on establishing a corporate identity or winning the public over to the organization's point of view. Tobacco companies, for example, run ads that focus on the positive things they are doing. The ads for a pharmaceutical company showcasing leukemia treatment also adopt that focus.
6. *Nonprofit advertising* is used by not-for-profit organizations, such as charities, foundations, associations, hospitals, orchestras, museums, and religious institutions, to reach customers (hospitals, for example), members (the Sierra Club), and volunteers (Red Cross). It is also used to solicit donations and other forms of program participation. The *"Truth"*® campaign for the American Legacy Foundation, which tries to reach teenagers with anti-smoking messages, is an example of nonprofit advertising.
7. *Public service advertising* provides messages on behalf of a good cause, such as stopping drunk driving (as in ads from Mothers Against Drunk Driving) or preventing child abuse. Also called **public service announcements (PSAs),** advertising and public relations professionals usually create them **pro bono** (free of charge) and the media donate the space and time.

Cool leather.
Soft suede.
Hot savings. Hurry.

Fashion never waits. That's why
now's the time to shop T.J.Maxx
for the latest leather and suede
at simply incredible prices.
Think jackets, shirts, and skirts
in all the coolest colors, plus
classic browns and blacks.
Fashion forward to T.J.Maxx.

Starts Sunday, August 8

Leather and suede are always tough to resist.
At these prices, you won't have to.

Arrives Sunday, August 8... hurry in for best selection.

T·J·maxx

T·J·maxx
you should go

Retailers sometimes advertise nationally, but much of their advertising is targeted to a specific market, such as this direct-mail piece for T. J. Maxx.

LEUKEMIA MADE HIM A PATIENT. WE HELPED HIM BECOME A KID AGAIN.

"Your child has leukemia." The most devastating news a parent could hear. It used to mean there was little chance of survival. Now, 80 percent of kids diagnosed with leukemia not only survive—but lead normal lives. How? New breakthrough medicines, discovered and developed by pharmaceutical company researchers, have given many leukemia patients and their parents a second chance. The new medicines our researchers are discovering are giving families hope—and patients a chance to be kids again.

America's Pharmaceutical Companies
Leading the way in the search for cures

www.searchforcures.org

This institutional ad for a pharmaceutical trade association uses a heart-tugging visual and copy to show consumers the value of the organization's activities—producing pharmaceutical drugs that help save lives.

Most people get their Aflac policies through payroll deduction at their workplace. This B2B ad explains to businesspeople how Aflac insurance can be part of an employee benefit package at no direct cost to the company.

Although these categories identify characteristics of various types of advertising, there are many commonalities. In practice, all types of advertising demand creative, original messages that are strategically sound and well executed, and all of them are delivered through some form of media. Furthermore, advertisements can be developed as single ads largely unrelated to other ads by the same advertiser or as a **campaign,** a term that refers to a set of related ads that are variations on a theme. They are used in different media at different times for different segments of the audience and to keep attracting the **attention** of the target audience. Let's now consider the development of key advertising concepts and practices.

HOW DID CURRENT PRACTICES AND CONCEPTS DEVELOP?

As illustrated in the timeline in Figure 1.1 the advertising industry is dynamic and is affected by changes in technology, media, and the economic and social environment. But this history is far more than names and dates. The timeline reflects how the principles and practices of a multibillion-dollar industry have evolved.[3]

Eras and Ages

The timeline divides the evolution of advertising into five stages, which reflect historical eras and the changes that lead to different philosophies and styles of advertising. As you read through this, note how changing environments, in particular media advancements, have changed the way advertising functions. (For more historical information check out the extensive timeline at *http://adage.com/century/timeline/index.html* or Duke's John W. Hartman for Sales, Advertising & Marketing History at *http://library.duke.edu/digitalcollections/eaa*. Another source for classic ads is *www.vintageadbrowser.com*.)

This ad promotes a brand, Crest White Strips, and provides information about the product, as well as reasons to buy it.

The Early Age of Print   Industrialization and mechanized printing spurred literacy, which encouraged businesses to advertise beyond just their local place of business. Ads of the early years look like what we call **classified advertising** today. Their objective was to *identify products* and *deliver information* about them including where they were being sold. The primary medium of this age was *print*, particularly newspapers, although handbills and posters were also important, as well as hand-painted signs. The first newspaper ad appeared in 1704 for Long Island real estate, and Benjamin Franklin's *Pennsylvania Gazette* ran the first advertising section in 1729. The first *magazine* ads appeared in 1742 in Franklin's *General Magazine*.

The Early Age of Agencies   The 19th century brought the beginning of what we now recognize as the advertising industry. Volney Palmer opens the *first ad agency* in 1848 in Philadelphia. The J. Walter Thompson agency is formed in 1864, the oldest advertising agency still in existence. P.T. Barnum brings a Swedish singer to the United States and uses a blitz of newspaper ads, handbills, and posters, one of the first *campaigns.* In 1868 the N.W. Ayer agency begins the *commission system* for placing ads—advertising professionals initially were agents or brokers who bought space and time on behalf of the client for which they received a commission, a percentage of the media bill. The J. Walter Thompson agency invents *the account executive* position, a person who acts as a liaison between the client and the agency.

As advertisers and marketers became more concerned about creating ads that worked, professionalism in advertising began to take shape. Here, also, is when it became important to have a definition or a theory of advertising. In the 1880s, advertising was referred to by advertising legend Albert Lasker as *"salesmanship in print* driven by a *reason why."* Those two phrases became the model for stating an ad *claim* and explaining the *support* behind it.

On the retail side, department store owner John Wanamaker hired John E. Powers in 1880 as the store's full-time *copywriter* and Powers crafted an advertising strategy of *"ads as news."* The McCann agency, which began in 1902, also developed an agency philosophy stated as *"truth well told"* that emphasized the agency's role in crafting the ad message. *Printer's Ink,* the advertising industry's first trade publication, appeared in 1888. In the early 1900s, the J. Walter Thompson

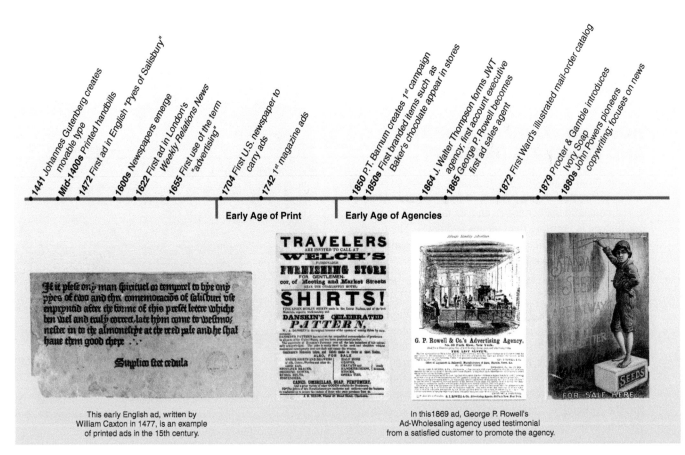

FIGURE 1.1
Advertising Timeline

agency begins publishing its "Blue Books," which explained how advertising works and compiled media data as an industry reference.

By the end of the 19th century advertisers began to give their goods brand names, such as Baker's Chocolate and Ivory Soap. The purpose of advertising during this period was to create demand, as well as a visual identity, for these new brands. Inexpensive brand-named products, known as *packed goods,* began to fill the shelves of grocers and drug stores. The questionable ethics of hype and *puffery,* which is exaggerated promises, came to a head in 1892 when *Ladies Home Journal* banned patent medicine advertising. But another aspect of hype was the use of powerful graphics that dramatized the sales message.

In Europe, the visual quality of advertising improved dramatically as artists who were also *illustrators,* such as Toulouse-Lautrec, Aubrey Beardsley, and Alphonse Mucha, brought their craftsmanship to posters and print ads, as well as magazine illustrations. Because of the artistry, this period is known as the *Golden Age.* The artist role moved beyond illustration to become the **art director** in 20th-century advertising.

The Scientific Era   In the early 1900s professionalism in advertising was reflected in the beginnings of a professional organization of large agencies, which was officially named the American Association of Advertising Agencies (known also as 4As) in 1917 (*www.aaa.org*). In addition to getting the industry organized, this period also brought a refining of professional practices. As 19th-century department store owner John Wanamaker commented, "Half the money I spend on advertising is wasted and the trouble is I don't know which half." That statement partly reflected a need to know more about how advertising works, but it also recognized the need to better target the message.

In the early 20th-century, modern professional advertising adopted scientific *research* techniques. Advertising experts believed they could improve advertising by blending science and art. Two leaders were Claude Hopkins and John Caples. At the height of Hopkins' career, he was Lord & Thomas's best-known copywriter. Highly analytical, he conducted *tests of his copy* to refine his advertising methods, an approach explained in his 1923 book, *Scientific Advertising.* John Caples, vice president of Batten, Barton, Durstine and Osborn (BBDO), published *Tested Advertising Methods* in 1932. His theories about the *pulling power of headlines* also were based on extensive tests. Caples was known for changing the style of advertising writing, which had been

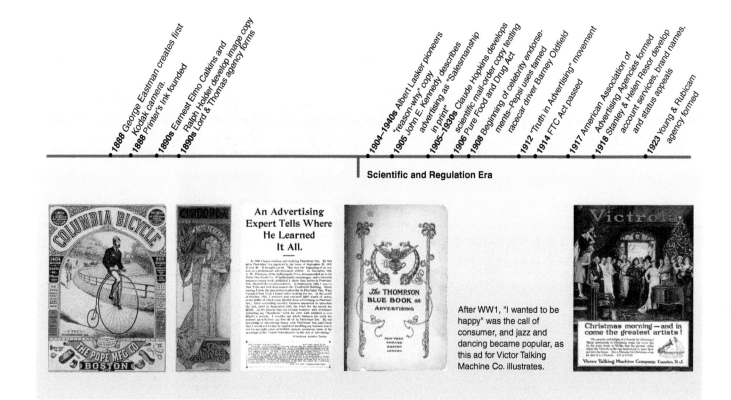

Timeline:

1888 George Eastman creates first Kodak camera.

1888 Printer's Ink founded

1890s Earnest Elmo Calkins and Ralph Holden develop image copy

1890s Lord & Thomas agency forms

1904–1940s Albert Lasker pioneers "reason-why" copy

1905 John E. Kennedy describes advertising as "Salesmanship in print"

1905–1930s Claude Hopkins develops scientific mail-order copy testing

1906 Pure Food and Drug Act

1908 Beginning of celebrity endorsements–Pepsi uses famed racecar driver Barney Oldfield

1912 "Truth in Advertising" movement

1914 FTC Act passed

1917 American Association of Advertising Agencies formed

1918 Stanley & Helen Resor develop account services, brand names, and status appeals

1923 Young & Rubicam agency formed

Scientific and Regulation Era

An Advertising Expert Tells Where He Learned It All.

The THOMPSON BLUE BOOK on ADVERTISING

NEW YORK
CHICAGO
BOSTON
LONDON

After WW1, "I wanted to be happy" was the call of consumer, and jazz and dancing became popular, as this ad for Victor Talking Machine Co. illustrates.

Christmas morning—and in come the greatest artists!

Victor Talking Machine Company, Camden, N.J.

wordy and full of exaggerations. During the 1930s and 1940s, Daniel Starch, A. C. Nielsen, and George Gallup founded research organizations that are still part of today's advertising industry.

During and after the Great Depression, Raymond Rubicam emerged as an advertising power and launched his own agency with John Orr Young, a Lord & Thomas copywriter under the name of Young and Rubicam. Their work was known for intriguing headlines and fresh, original approaches to advertising ideas.

Targeting, the idea that messages should be directed at particular groups of prospective buyers, evolved as media became more complex. Advertisers realized that they could spend their budgets more efficiently by identifying those most likely to purchase a product, as well as the best ways to reach them. The scientific era helped media better identify their audiences. In 1914 the Audit Bureau of Circulation (ABC) was formed to standardize the definition of paid circulation for magazines and newspapers. Media changes saw print being challenged by *radio advertising* in 1922. Radio surpassed print in ad revenue in 1938.

The world of advertising agencies and management of advertising developed rapidly in the years after World War II. The J. Walter Thompson (JWT) agency, which still exists today, led the boom in advertising during this period. The agency's success was due largely to its *creative copy* and the *management* style of the husband-and-wife team of Stanley and Helen Resor. Stanley developed the concept of *account services* and expanded the account executive role into strategy development; Helen developed innovative copywriting techniques. The Resors also coined the **brand name** concept as a strategy to associate a *unique identity* with a particular product as well as the concept of *status appeal* to persuade nonwealthy people to imitate the habits of rich people (*www.jwt.com*).

Television commercials came on the scene in the early 1950s and brought a huge new revenue stream to the advertising industry. In 1952 the Nielsen rating system for TV advertising became the primary way to measure the reach of *TV commercials.*

This period also saw marketing practices, such as *product differentiation* and *market segmentation* incorporated into advertising strategy. The idea of *positioning,* carving out a unique spot in people's minds for the brand, was developed by Al Ries and Jack Trout in 1969.

The Creative Revolution The creative power of agencies exploded in the 1960s and 1970s, a period marked by the resurgence of art, inspiration, and intuition. Largely in reaction to the

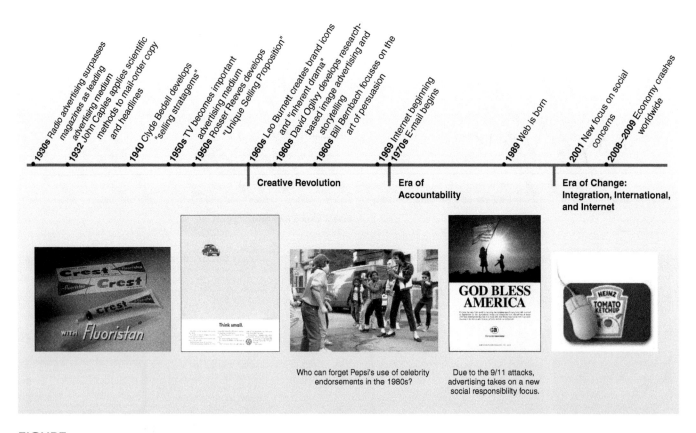

Who can forget Pepsi's use of celebrity
endorsements in the 1980s?

Due to the 9/11 attacks,
advertising takes on a new
social responsibility focus.

FIGURE
1.1 (continued)

emphasis on research and science, this revolution was inspired by three creative geniuses: Leo Burnett, David Ogilvy, and William Bernbach.

Leo Burnett was the leader of what came to be known as the *Chicago school of advertising.* He believed in finding the *"inherent drama"* in every product. He also believed in using *cultural archetypes* to create mythical characters who represented American values, such as the Jolly Green Giant, Tony the Tiger, the Pillsbury Doughboy, and his most famous campaign character, the Marlboro Man (*www.leoburnett.com*).

Ogilvy, founder of the Ogilvy & Mather agency, is in some ways a paradox because he married both the *image school* of Rubicam and the *claim school* of Lasker and Hopkins. He created enduring brands with *symbols,* such as the Hathaway Man and his mysterious eye patch for the Hathaway shirt maker, and handled such quality products as Rolls-Royce, Pepperidge Farm, and Guinness with product-specific and information-rich claims (*www.ogilvy.com*).

The Doyle, Dane, and Bernbach (DDB) agency opened in 1949. From the beginning, William Bernbach—with his acute sense of words, design, and creative concepts—was considered to be the most innovative advertising creative person of his time. His advertising touched people—and persuaded them—by focusing on *feelings and emotions.* He explained, "There are a lot of great technicians in advertising. However, they forget that advertising is persuasion, and persuasion is not a science, but an art. Advertising is the art of persuasion."[4] Bernbach is known for the understated Volkswagen campaign that ran at a time when car ads were full of glamour and bombast. The campaign used headlines such as "Think Small" with accompanying picture of a small VW bug (*www.ddb.com*).

The Era of Accountability and Integration   Starting in the 1970s, the industry-wide focus was on *effectiveness*. Clients wanted ads that produced sales, so the emphasis was on research, testing, and measurement. To be accountable, advertising and other marketing communication agencies recognized that their work had to prove its value. After the dot.com boom and economic downturn in the 1980s and 1990s, this emphasis on accountability became even more important, and advertisers demanded proof that their advertising was truly **effective** in accomplishing its *objectives* as stated in the strategy.

Social responsibility is another aspect of accountability. Although advertising regulation has been in place since the early 1900s with the passage of the Pure Food and Drug Act in 1906 and

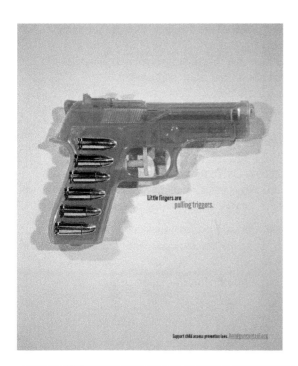 

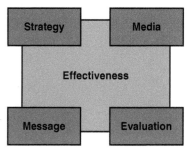

the creation of the **Federal Trade Commission** in 1914, it wasn't until 1971 that the National Advertising Review Board was created to monitor questions of *taste and social responsibility*. Charges of using sweatshops in low-wage countries and an apparent disregard for the environment concerned critics such as Naomi Klein, who wrote the best-selling book *No Logo* and Marc Gobe who wrote *Citizen Brands*. One highly visible campaign that demonstrates this commitment is the "Truth" campaign developed by Crispin Porter + Bogusky along with Arnold Worldwide to provide informative documentary-style print ads and television commercials that inform youth about the dangers of smoking without preaching to them.

As the *digital era* brought nearly instantaneous means of communication, spreading *word of mouth* among a social network of consumers, companies became even more concerned about their practices and **reputation.** The recession that began in December 2007 and subsequent headlines about bad business practices, such as the Bernard Madoff "Ponzi" scheme, made consumers even more concerned about *business ethics.*

We also characterize this as the era when integrated marketing communication became important. **Integrated marketing communication (IMC)** is another technique that managers began to adopt in the 1980s as a way to better coordinate their brand communication. Integration and consistency makes marketing communication more efficient and thus more financially accountable.

So What Are the Key Components of Advertising?

In this brief review of how advertising developed over some 300 years, a number of key concepts were introduced all of which will be discussed in more detail in the chapters that follow. But let's summarize these concepts in terms of a simple set of key components that describe the practice of advertising: strategy, message, media, and evaluation (see Figure 1.2):

* *Strategy* The logic behind an advertisement is stated in objectives that focus on areas such as sales, news, psychological appeals, emotion, branding and brand

FIGURE 1.2

Four Components of Advertising

reputation, as well as the position and differentiation of the product from the competition, and segmenting and targeting the best prospects.

- *Message* The concept behind a message and how that message is expressed is based on research and consumer insights with an emphasis on creativity and artistry.
- *Media* Various media have been used by advertisers over the centuries including print (handbills, newspapers, magazines), outdoor (signs and posters), broadcast (radio and television), and now digital media. Targeting ads to prospective buyers is done by matching their profiles to media audiences. Advertising agency compensation was originally based on the cost of buying time or space in the media.
- *Evaluation* Effectiveness means meeting objectives and in order to determine if that has happened, there must be testing. Standards also are set by professional organizations and companies that rate the size and makeup of media audiences, as well as advertising's social responsibility.

This section briefly identified how various jobs and professional concepts emerged over time. Let's now put the agency world under a microscope and look deeper at the structure of the industry.

THE AGENCY WORLD

In the discussion of definitions and the evolution of advertising practices, we briefly introduced agencies, but as a student of advertising and marketing communication you need to know more about how agencies are organized and how they operate.

Who Are the Key Players?

As we discuss the organization of the industry, consider that all the key players also represent job opportunities you might want to consider if you are interested in working in advertising or some area of marketing communication. The players include the advertiser (referred to by the agency as the *client*) who sponsors the message, the agency, the media, and the **suppliers** who provide expertise. The *A Matter of Practice* box about the greatest television commercial ever made introduced a number of these key players and illustrated how they all make different contributions to the final advertising.

The Advertiser   Advertising begins with the **advertiser,** which is the company that sponsors the advertising about its business. In the "1984" story, Apple Computer was the advertiser, and Steve Jobs, the company's CEO, made the final decision to run the then-controversial commercial. The advertiser is the number one key player. Management of this function usually lies with the marketing department but in smaller companies, such as Urban Decay Cosmetics, the advertising decisions may lie with the owner, founder, or partners in the business. Wende Zomnir is not only a founding partner of Urban Decay Cosmetics, she is also an advertising graduate and a marketing communication professional.

Most advertisers have a marketing team that initiates the advertising effort by identifying a marketing problem advertising can solve. For example, Apple executives knew that the Macintosh easy-to-use computer platform needed to be explained and that information about the launch of the new computer would need to reach a large population of potential computer buyers. Advertising was essential to the success of this new product.

The marketing executive (with input from the corporate officers and others on the marketing team) also hires the advertising agency—for Burger King this was Crispin Porter + Bogusky—and other marketing communication agencies as needed. In professional jargon, the advertiser (Burger King) becomes the agency's *client*. As the client, the advertiser is responsible for monitoring the work and paying the agency for its work on the account. That use of the word *account* is the reason agency people refer to the advertiser as *the account* and the agency person in charge of that advertiser's business as the *account manager.*

The marketing team makes the final decisions about strategy including the target audience and the size of the advertising budget. This team approves the advertising or marketing communication plan, which contains details outlining the message and media strategies. In Chapter 2 we'll explain more about how this marketing team functions.

A Passion for the Business

Wende Zomnir, *Creative Director and Founding Partner, Urban Decay Cosmetics*

Being the creative force behind a brand like Urban Decay makes me responsible for cranking out great ideas. And in the 13 years I've been doing this, I've figured out a few things about how to generate creative ideas with which people connect. It begins with a passion for the business. Here are my seven principles about how to run a business creatively:

1. *Feel a passion for your brand.* Everyone in product development, design, PR, merchandising, sales, and marketing at Urban Decay loves our makeup and deeply connects to our position as the counterculture icon in the realm of luxury makeup.

2. *Spot emerging trends.* Our best ideas don't start from analysts telling us what the trends are. My creative team and I talk about what kinds of colors, visual icons, textures, and patterns we are craving and start from there. Our job at Urban Decay is to lead graphically with our product design and formulation. Recently we launched a volumizing mascara called Big Fatty and played off the connotations in the name, infusing the formula with hemp oil and wrapping the mascara vial in an Age of Aquarius–inspired print. Shortly after the product's release, a supplier to the cosmetics industry came in to show us a version of our own mascara, giving us a presentation on the

coming trends. It's annoying, but when this happens, we know we're doing our job.

3. *Cultivate your inner voice.* You also need to develop a gut instinct for what will work. I felt that skulls were going to be huge because everyone in the office was craving them on T-shirts, shoes, key rings, and so forth. We decided to put them on our seasonal holiday compacts in 2005. And the same season that Marc Jacobs launched them, so did we. We had distributors begging us to sell them a version without the skull, but we stood firm and wouldn't change it because we knew it was right. And you know what? The same distributors who balked placed the biggest reorders and complained that we couldn't stock them fast enough.

4. *Check your ego.* Listening to that inner voice IS something you can cultivate, but you've got to check your ego at the door in order to do it. That can be hard, because being a creative leader means you've probably generated a lot of great ideas that work. So, you've got confidence in your concepts and your ability to deliver, but you have to be able to admit others have great ideas, too.

5. *Cherry-pick the best ideas.* Gut instinct is important, BUT—and this is big—even more crucial is being able to listen to all the ideas and sort out the junk. After you sort through everything, then pick the very best concept, even if it's NOT your idea.

6. *Little ideas are important, too.* You've got to rally everyone behind your Big Idea, but realize that all those little ideas that prop up the big one are great, too. That's what makes so many of our products work in the marketplace: a big idea supported by little ideas—and the people who develop them.

7. *Be flexible.* My final important creative principle is flexibility. Knowing when to be flexible has resulted in some of the best work we've created here. While working on a body powder for summer that was to be impregnated with water for a cooling sensation on the skin, we ran into production problems. We wanted a powder, but I decided to add flavor instead. That edible body powder became a huge subbrand for us, spawning multiple flavors and generating huge amounts of press and revenue. The cooling powder would have been late, had quality control issues, and probably would have lasted a season.

Wende Zomnir (aka Ms. Decay) graduated from the University of North Texas where she was a student of Professor Sheri Broyles.

Check out Urban Decay at *www.urbandecay.com/*; *www.myspace.com/urbandecaycosmetics*; and *http://twitter.com/UrbanDecay411.*

The distinctive personality of Urban Decay Cosmetics is seen in its packaging, as well as its products' names, such as the Ammo Group, and colors: "Smog," "Mildew," and "Oil Slick."

Big companies may have hundreds of agencies working for them, although they normally have an **agency-of-record (AOR)** that does most of their business and may even manage or coordinate the work of other agencies.

The Agency   The second player is the **advertising agency** (or other types of marketing communication agencies) that creates, produces, and distributes the messages. The working arrangement between advertiser and agency is known as the *agency–client partnership.* Both the "1984" story and the BK deprivation scheme demonstrated how important it is to cultivate a strong sense of trust between the agency and its clients because these were both risky ideas.

An advertiser uses an outside agency because it believes the agency will be more efficient in creating advertising messages than the advertiser would be on its own. Successful agencies such as Crispin Porter + Bogusky typically have strategic and creative expertise, media knowledge, workforce talent, and the ability to negotiate good deals for clients. The advertising professionals working for the agency are experts in their areas of specialization and passionate about their work.

Not all advertising professionals work in agencies. Large advertisers, either companies or organizations, manage the advertising process either by setting up an **advertising department** (sometimes called **marketing services**) that oversees the work of agencies or by setting up their own in-house agency, as we see in Figure 1.3. Tasks performed by the company's marketing services department include the following: select the agencies; coordinate activities with vendors, such as media, production, and photography; make sure the work gets done as scheduled; and determine whether the work has achieved prescribed objectives.

The Media   The third player in the advertising world is the media. The emergence of mass media has been a central factor in the development of advertising because mass media offers a way to reach a widespread audience. In traditional advertising, the term **media** refers to all of the channels of communication that carry the message from the advertiser to the audience and from consumers back to companies. We refer to these media as **channels** because they deliver messages, but they are also companies, such as your local newspaper or radio station.

Some of these media conglomerates are huge, such as Time Warner and Viacom. Time Warner, for example, is a $40 billion company with some 38,000 employees. It owns HBO, Time Inc., Turner Broadcasting, and Warner Brothers, among other media companies. You can learn more about this media conglomerate at *www.timewarner.com.* **Media vehicles** are the specific programs, such as *60 Minutes* or *The Simpsons,* or magazines—*The New York Times, Advertising Age, Woman's Day.*

Note that **media** is plural when it refers to various channels, but singular—**medium**—when it refers to only one form, such as newspapers.

Each medium (newspaper, radio or TV station, billboard company, etc.) has a department that is responsible for selling ad space or time. These departments specialize in assisting advertisers in

FIGURE 1.3
Two Advertising Organization Structures

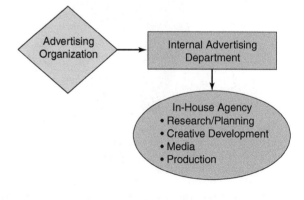

comparing the effectiveness of various media as they try to select the best mix of media to use. Many media organizations will assist advertisers in the design and production of advertisements. That's particularly true for local advertisers using local media, such as a retailer preparing an advertisement for the local newspaper.

The primary advantage of advertising's use of **mass media** is that the costs to buy time in broadcast media, space in print media, and time and space in digital media are spread over the tremendous number of people that these media reach. For example, $3 million may sound like a lot of money for one Super Bowl ad, but when you consider that the advertisers are reaching more than 100 million people, the cost is not so extreme. One of the big advantages of mass-media advertising is that it can reach a lot of people with a single message in a very cost-efficient form.

Professional Suppliers and Consultants   The fourth player in the world of advertising include artists, writers, photographers, directors, producers, printers, and self-employed freelancers and consultants. In the "1984" story, the movie director Ridley Scott was a supplier in that Chiat/Day contracted with him to produce the commercial. This array of suppliers mirrors the variety of tasks required to put together an ad. Other examples include freelance copywriters and graphic artists, songwriters, printers, market researchers, direct-mail production houses, telemarketers, and public relations consultants. Why would the other advertising players hire an outside supplier? There are many reasons. The advertiser or the agency may not have expertise in a specialized area, their people may be overloaded with work, or they may want a fresh perspective. They also may not want to incur the overhead of full-time employees.

Types of Agencies

We are primarily concerned with advertising agencies in this chapter, but other areas such as public relations, direct marketing, sales promotion, and the Internet have agencies that provide specialized promotional help, as well.

The A-List awards by *Advertising Age* recognize cutting-edge agencies that rank high in three areas: First they are creative—*Ad Age* calls them "widely imaginative"—in developing brand strategies and executions. Second, they are fast growing and winners of some of the biggest new business pitches. Finally, they are recognized for their effectiveness. In other words, their work leads to measurable results. Note that the agencies in the following list represent big and small agencies, as well as full-service and specialized agencies. At the top of the list is the agency of the year, Crispin Porter + Bogusky, the agency behind the Burger King "Whopper Freakout" campaign.

A-List of Advertising Agencies
1. *Crispin Porter + Bogusky* This agency used to be a medium-size, independent Miami hotshop, but now it's a big national creative power from Miami and Boulder, Colorado, known for its provocative work for Burger King, Old Navy, and Coke Zero, among other powerhouse clients (*www.cpbgroup.com*).
2. *TBWA/Chiat/Day* This L.A.-based agency creates what it calls its "disruptive ideas" for global clients such as Visa and Adidas. This is the agency behind the legendary "1984" ad for Apple's Macintosh (*www.tbwa.com*).

Advertising relies on the expertise of many different people, such as television producers, graphic designers, photographers, printers, and musicians.

3. *Goodby, Silverstein & Partners* The previous year's Agency of the Year, San Francisco–based Goodby continues to be recognized not only for its creative efforts, but also for building big brands, such as Doritos and General Electric, as well as the classic "Got Milk" campaign (*www.goodbysilverstein.com*).

4. *R/GA* Originally a specialized digital agency, R/GA now operates more like a full-service agency that prides itself on forging deep, lasting connections with consumers for its clients, which include Nike and Apple's iTunes (*www.rga.com*).

5. *Tribal DDB* Primarily a digital agency, New York–based Tribal is also creative, collaborative, and brand savvy. Its work includes an award-winning TV commercial for Deutsche Telekom, as well as other new media and viral projects for Philips, Wrigley, and McDonald's (*www.tribalddb.com*).

6. *Mindshare* Mindshare is a global media network that offers media and communication planning, interactive marketing, branded entertainment, sports marketing, and marketing effectiveness analyses to such clients as IBM, Unilever, and American Express (*www.mindshareworld.com*).

7. *The Martin Agency* More than a regional shop from Richmond, Virginia, this agency continues to be recognized for great creative spots, such as those for Geico (*www.martinagency.com*).

8. *Vidal Partnership* The largest independent Hispanic agency in the United States, Vidal operates as an integrated full-service marketing communication agency and handles campaigns for Wendy's, Home Depot, JCPenney, and Johnson & Johnson (*www.vidal-partnership.com*).

9. *Rapp* A giant in direct marketing, Rapp is redefining relationship marketing for its customers, such as Macy's, Audi, ExxonMobile, and General Electric (*www.rapp.com*).

10. *Deutsch* The New York–based Deutsch full-service agency believes in connecting with and motivating an audience on behalf of clients such as Evian, GM, and PlayStation (*www.deutschinc.com*).

Source: Adapted from Parekh Rupal, "Agency of the Year: Crispin Porter + Bogusky," *Advertising Age,* January 19, 2009, *http://adage.com/agencya-list08/article?article_id=133815.*

In addition to agencies that specialize in advertising and other areas of marketing communication, there are also consulting firms in marketing research and branding that offer specialized services to other agencies, as well as advertisers. Since these various types of marketing communication areas are all part of an integrated marketing communication approach, we cover many of these functions in separate chapters later in the book.

Full-Service Agencies   In advertising, a **full-service agency** includes the four major staff functions of account management, creative services, media planning, and account planning, which includes research. A full-service advertising agency also has its own finance and accounting department, a **traffic department** to handle internal tracking on completion of projects, a department for broadcast and **print production** (sometimes organized within the creative department), and a human resources department.

Let's take a minute to look inside one full-service agency, Crispin Porter + Bogusky, which was named Agency of the Year by *Adweek* and *Advertising Age,* as well as *Ad Age*'s sister publication *Creativity.* CPB celebrates some $140 million in revenue and employs nearly 900 in its two offices in Miami and Boulder, Colorado. The agency is known for its edgy, pop-culture approach to strategy. You probably know Burger King's weird "king" character, and you read about its "Whopper Freakout" campaign at the beginning of this chapter. Maybe you have been introduced to some of Old Navy's "SuperModelquins," the talking mannequins in the opening story you'll read later in Chapter 5. That's the kind of provocative work that *Ad Age* calls "culturally primal."[5] It infiltrates the social scene and creates buzz. Although known for its creative work, CPB also has an innovative product design think tank that has come up with such ideas as a public bike rental program, a portable pen version of WED-40, and BK's popular Burger Shots sliders.

In-House Agencies   Like a regular advertising agency, an **in-house agency** produces ads and places them in the media, but the agency is a part of the advertiser's organization, rather than an outside company. Companies that need closer control over their advertising have their own internal in-house agencies. An in-house agency performs most, and sometimes all, of the functions of an outside advertising agency and produce materials, such as point-of-sale displays, sales team literature, localized ads and promotions, and coupon books, that larger agencies have a hard time producing cost effectively. Retailers, for example, find that doing their own advertising and media placement provides cost savings, as well as the ability to meet fast-breaking deadlines. Some fashion companies, such as Ralph Lauren, also create their own advertising in house to maintain complete control over the brand image and the fashion statement it makes. Check out this in-house agency at *http://about.ralphlauren.com/campaigns/default.asp.*

Specialized Agencies   Many agencies do not follow the traditional full-service agency approach. They either specialize in certain functions (writing copy, producing art, or media buying), audiences (minority, youth), industries (health care, computers, agriculture, business-to-business communication), or markets (minority groups such as Asian, African American, or Hispanic). In addition, some agencies specialize in other marketing communication areas, such as branding, direct marketing, sales promotion, public relations, events and sports marketing, packaging, and point-of-sale promotions. Sometimes one-client agencies are created to handle the work of one large client. Let's take a look at two special types of agencies:

- **Creative boutiques** are ad agencies, usually small (two or three people to a dozen or more), that concentrate entirely on preparing the creative execution of the idea, or the creative product. A creative boutique has one or more writers or artists on staff, but generally no staff for media, research, or strategic planning. Typically, these agencies can prepare advertising to run in print and broadcast media, as well as in out-of-home (such as outdoor and transit advertising), Internet, and alternative media. Creative boutiques usually serve companies directly, but are sometimes retained by full-service agencies that are overloaded with work.
- **Media-buying services** specialize in the purchase of media for clients. They are in high demand for many reasons, but three reasons stand out. First, media has become more complex as the number of choices has grown—think of the proliferation of new cable channels, magazines, and radio stations. Second, the cost of maintaining a competent media department has escalated. Third, media-buying services often buy media at a low cost because they can group several clients' purchases together to get discounts from the media because of the volume of their media buys.

Agency Networks and Holding Companies   Finally let's talk about **agency networks,** which are large conglomerations of agencies under a central ownership. Agency networks are all of the offices that operate under one agency name, such as DDB Worldwide (200 offices in 90 countries) or BBDO Worldwide (287 offices in 79 countries). You can read more about these agencies and their networks at *www.ddb.com* and *www.bbdoworldwide.com.*

   Holding companies include one or more advertising agency networks, as well as other types of marketing communication agencies and marketing services consulting firms. The four largest are WPP Group, Interpublic, Omnicom, and Publicis. WPP, for example, includes the J. Walter Thompson Group, Ogilvy & Mather Worldwide, Young & Rubicam, Grey Global Group, and Bates advertising networks, as well as the Berlin Cameron creative agency, public relations agencies Hill and Knowlton, Ogilvy Public Relations, and Burson-Marsteller; direct-response company Wunderman; research firms Millward Brown and Research International; media firms Mindshare and Mediaedge:cia; and branding and corporate identity firms Landor and Lambie-Naim, to name a few. Most of those firms are also networks with multiple offices. For an inside look at a big holding company, check out WPP at *www.wpp.com.*

How Are Agency Jobs Organized?

In addition to the chief executive officer, if the agency is large enough, it usually has one or more vice presidents, as well as department heads for the different functional areas. We will concentrate on five of those areas: account management; account planning and research; creative development and production; media research, planning, and buying; and internal services.

Account Management   The **account management** (sometimes called **account services**) function acts as a liaison between the client and the agency. It ensures that the agency focuses its resources on the client's needs. The account team summarizes the client's communication needs and develops the basic "charge to the agency," which the account manager presents to the agency's team. The **account executive** (called the *content manager* at the Crispin Porter + Bogusky agency) is responsible for interpreting the client's marketing research and strategy for the rest of the agency. The *Day in the Life* story focuses on the work of an account executive at CPB.

Once the client and agency together establish the general guidelines for a campaign, the account management team supervises the day-to-day development. Account management in a major agency typically has three levels: the *management supervisor,* who provides leadership on strategic issues and looks for new business opportunities; the *account supervisor,* who is the key executive working on a client's business and the primary liaison between the client and the

A DAY IN THE LIFE

Tweets from the Front Line

Jennifer Cunningham, *Content Manager, Crispin Porter + Bogusky*

As a content manager (account executive) at Crispin Porter + Bogusky's Boulder office, I never know what's in store for me on any given day. What I DO know is that the days will never be boring. From presenting creative to clients, to going on late-night caffeine runs for teams pulling all-nighters . . . anything goes.

Though tasks vary from day to day, part of my job is to constantly stay up to date on the latest and greatest technologies and trends. Now, I'm no tech expert but if a client asks for my opinion on brand integration on Twitter, for example, I better know what they're talking about.

And since Twitter is all the rage right now, here's a day in my shoes at CP+B via real-time tweets:

- Parking. Better hustle, have a 9:30 meeting and need some coffee first! (Had a late night last night sending a print ad to the printer—when ads are due, I stay in the office and help make sure everyone has approved it before it goes out.) *9:08*
- Reading all my morning e-mails—my clients are on East Coast time so their workday started 2+ hours ago. *9:19*
- Content team status—this is an informal weekly meeting to ensure everyone knows what's up on the account. *9:32*
- Confirming teams are ready for an 11 A.M. client presentation. Creatives here don't let ANY work out the door unless it's perfect. But sometimes perfection doesn't sync with the client call times. . . . *9:55*
- Writing setup slides for the presentation—this includes recapping our assignment, thoughts on the work, and background info. *10:08*
- Don't have the creative yet—checking in with teams, starting to get a little nervous. *10:30*
- Talked with my creative director—they're making the last few tweaks on the presentation, but they're running 10 to 15 minutes behind. *10:41*
- Calling my client. She's running behind too—starting late will be "just fine." Whew. *10:49*
- Call from another client—the publisher is saying they didn't receive our print ad last night. Asking if we can look into it . . . oh boy. *10:53*

- E-mailing my print producer to check in with the publisher. *10:55*
- E-mailing my media planner to ensure we won't miss our insertion deadline. *10:56*
- Got the presentation! Looks awesome—have a feeling the clients will love these ideas. *11:10*
- On the call—reinforcing the strategy and schedules as the creatives present ideas. *11:22*
- Recapping the presentation call to make sure the creative teams have clear feedback for revisions and to ensure our clients had the same take-aways from the call. *12:01*
- Hopping on a media call—gathering info for Production, so we can start work once ideas from the presentation are approved. *1:11*
- Reviewing invoices over lunch—have to make sure our billing is accurate and that we stay on budget for projects. *2:03*
- Call with Business Affairs—just finalized legal approvals on scripts and the contracts for celebrity talent for our next TV spot. Pretty exciting! *3:15*
- Whew—lost track of time. Rereleased the print ad for the publication. Confirmed teams are working on feedback. Put together a post-campaign analysis to see how we met our goals number-wise on our last project. Participated in a brainstorming session for another account—gotta help where you can. *6:08*
- Wrapping up—need to walk my dog at home. *6:31*
- Hopping back on my computer for a couple more e-mails and prep for tomorrow. All in all a pretty good day. *8:15*
- Finishing up this day-in-the-life—hope you enjoyed reading it. Good luck should you pursue a career in advertising! There's never a dull moment. *9:01*

To learn more about Crispin Porter + Bogusky, check out *www.cpbgroup .com.*
Jennifer Cunningham is a graduate of the advertising program at the University of Colorado. She was a student of Professor Kendra Gale.

agency; and the *account executive* (as well as *assistant account executives*), who is responsible for day-to-day activities and operates like a project manager. A smaller agency will combine some of these levels. Of course, individual agencies also have their own titles for these positions, such as the "content manager" title used at CPB.

Account Planning and Research   Full-service agencies usually have a separate department specifically devoted to planning and sometimes to research as well. Today the emphasis in agency research is on developing an advertising message concept that focuses on the consumer's perspective and relationship with the brand. The **account planning** group gathers all available intelligence on the market and consumers and acts as the voice of the consumer. Account planners are strategic specialists who prepare comprehensive information about consumers' wants, needs, and relationship to the client's brand and recommendations on how the advertising should work to satisfy those elements based on insights they derive from consumer research.

Creative Development and Production   A creative group includes people who write (*copywriters*), people who design ideas for print ads or television commercials (*art directors*), and people who convert these ideas into television or radio commercials (*producers*). Many agencies build a support group around a team of an art director and copywriter who work well together. In addition to these positions, the broadcast production department and art studio are two other areas where creative personnel can apply their skills.

Media Research, Planning, and Buying   Agencies that don't rely on outside media specialists have a media department that recommends to the client the most efficient means of delivering the message to the target audience. That department has three functions: research, planning, and buying. Because the media world is so complex, it is not unusual for some individuals to become experts in certain markets or types of media.

Internal Operations   The departments that serve the operations within the agency include the traffic department and print production, as well as the more general financial services and human resources (personnel) departments. The traffic department is the lifeblood of the agency, and its personnel keep track of everything that happens.

How Are Agencies Paid?

Advertising agencies are a big business. Procter & Gamble, for example, spends nearly $5 billion annually on global advertising. With that kind of money on the table, you can imagine that the agency–client relationship is under pressure from both sides. Agencies want to get more work and get paid more; clients want to cut costs and make their advertising as cost effective as possible.

Agencies derive their revenues and profits from three main sources: commissions, **fees,** and retainers. For years, a 15 percent **commission** on media billings was the traditional form of compensation. That's actually how agencies got started back in the 19th century. For those few accounts still using a commission approach, the rate is rarely 15 percent; it is more likely lower and subject to negotiation between agency and client.

Many advertisers now use a fee system either as the primary compensation tool or in combination with a commission system. The **fee system** is comparable to the system by which advertisers pay their lawyers and accountants. The client and agency agree on an hourly fee or rate or may negotiate a charge for a specific project. This fee can vary by department, or it may be a flat hourly fee for all work regardless of the salary level of the person doing the work. Charges are also included for out-of-pocket expenses, travel, and other standard items.

An agency also may be put on a monthly or yearly **retainer.** The amount billed per month is based on the projected amount of work and the hourly rate charged. This system is most commonly used by public relations agencies.

A more recent trend in agency compensation is for advertisers to pay agencies on the basis of their performance. One consultant recommends that this arrangement be based on paying the agency either a percentage of the client's sales or a percentage of the client's marketing budget. Procter & Gamble is a pioneer in trying to apply this system. Another version of this idea is that agencies share in the profits of their client when they create a successful campaign, but that also means they have a greater financial risk in the relationship should the advertising not create the intended impact.

Another innovation in agency compensation is called **value billing,** which means that the agency is paid for its creative and strategic ideas, rather than for executions and media placements.

Sarah Armstrong, Coke's director of worldwide media and communication, has urged the industry to shift to "value-based" forms of compensation that reward agencies based on effectiveness—whether they make the objectives they set for their advertising.[6]

HOW IS THE PRACTICE OF ADVERTISING CHANGING?

We would like to end this review of advertising basics by talking about the future of advertising. Because of the recent Great Recession, Mike Carlton, an industry commentator, says, "[C]learly we are at a point in time when things will never be quite the same again for our industry." But there are still some exciting changes that open up opportunities for new professionals entering the field.

Consumer in Charge

As Jim Stengel, Procter & Gamble's former global marketing officer, has said, "[I]t's not just about doing great TV commercials: The days of pounding people with images, and shoving them down their eyeballs are over. The consumer is much more in control now."[7] This change is causing some shifts in the way the advertising business operates.

In 2009 CareerBuilder dismissed one of the most creative agencies—Portland-based Wieden + Kennedy, who had created five great Super Bowl ads for the job-posting website—and took its advertising in house. The reason is that the company wants ordinary consumers to create 25-second commercials for the brand. That will not only bring publicity, but also save bucks. CareerBuilder, through its in-house agency, will still pay for production of the winning ad and buy the ad time. Not only will this move bring more opportunities for *consumer-generated advertising* (at the expense of advertising agencies), the company estimates it will save around 15 to 20 percent of its annual marketing costs.[8]

Other brands that have used consumer-generated ads include Frito-Lay, Converse, Master-Card, and L'Oreal. Frito-Lay received thousands of media mentions for its Super Bowl ad contest on such programs as *The Tonight Show, The View,* and *Good Morning America.* You can check out Doritos' collection of consumer-generated Super Bowl ads in the "Crash the Super Bowl" contest at *www.crashthesuperbowl.com/#/winners.*

Consumer involvement in advertising is a bigger issue than just ad agencies losing their clients. In fact, consumers have been taking control of media and marketing for a number of years through Wikipedia, Twitter, and other newly democratized information sources. YouTube, MySpace, and Facebook have invited everyone into the ad distribution game. The Internet is a new world of interaction and consumer-initiated contacts that are creating entirely new ways of communicating with potential customers. That's why in 2006, *Time* magazine spotted the trend and named "You the Consumer" as its Person of the Year and then in 2007 *Advertising Age* named the consumer its "Agency of the Year."

Blurring Lines and Converging Media

One of the biggest changes impacting the advertising industry is the changing media environment. Television used to be the big gun, and it still eats up the biggest part of the budget, but the old networks (CBS, NBC, ABC, FOX) are only half as important as they used to be as the number of cable channels has exploded.

The big bomb that has fragmented the media world is digital media, which appear in so many different forms that it's impossible to keep up with them. The newspaper industry has been particularly hurt as it has realized that much, if not most, of its content can be accessed more easily and quickly in a digital format. So are newspapers dead?

Traditional media are trying to adjust by transforming themselves into new digital formats, as well. So what do you call online versions of newspapers and magazines? Are they still print when they appear on a screen? And new personal media—iPhones, iPods, iPads, BlackBerries, Kindles—are real shape-changers. They can be phones, music players, calendars, and sources of local and national information, as well as cameras, video viewers, book readers, Web surfers, and video game players. Changes such as these need to be considered when putting together media plans, a challenge that will be discussed in Part 3.

Advertising agencies make most of their money from television spots and print media. However, as we've mentioned, both of those revenue streams are threatened by economics and the changing media landscape. As Mike Carlton explains, "TV spots and other traditional work as the economic backbone of the agency business will just not work much longer."[9] However, Carlton also calls for agencies to take a stronger leadership role in the development of brand strategy, particularly for the more complex forms of marketing communication with their blurred, merged, and converged media.

Accountability and Effectiveness

Given the recent recession, you can guess that efficiency is an advantage in this new advertising world, which has been emphasizing accountability for a couple of decades. The other critical client concern is effectiveness, which is another way to look at accountability in marketing communication.

We mentioned that CareerBuilder had taken its advertising in house partly to drive a consumer-generated advertising program, but also to save costs, which is critical in an economic downturn. The need for efficiency is complicated by crack-ups in the agency–client relationships. Agencies that are creative in finding new ways to deliver cost efficiencies have a real advantage in their client dealings.

Effectiveness   Along with the ongoing need for efficiencies, there's always a concern about effectiveness, or accountability as it's sometimes called, but this has become even more important in difficult times. The recent recession forced the advertising industry to become even more serious about creating advertising that delivers results and then proving the effectiveness of the advertising work once it's completed. Effectiveness is a theme that you will see discussed throughout this book.

So what is **effectiveness?** Effective ads are ads that work. That is, they deliver the message the advertiser intended and consumers respond as the advertiser hoped they would. Ultimately, advertisers such as Burger King want consumers to buy and keep buying their goods and services. To get to that point, ads must first effectively communicate a message that motivates consumers to respond.

The most important characteristic of advertising is that it is purposeful: Ads are created to have some effect, some impact on the people who read or see their message. We refer to this as advertising's **effects,** the idea being that effective advertising messages will achieve the advertiser's desired impact and the target audience will respond as the advertiser intended. This desired impact is formally stated as a set of **objectives,** which are statements of the measurable goals or results that the advertising is intended to achieve. In other words, advertising works if it achieves its objectives.

Principle
Advertising is effective if it achieves its objectives.

Award Shows   This chapter opened with the Burger King campaign, which was identified as award-winning advertising. The Effie award, named for a shortened form of the word *effective,* is given by the New York Chapter of the American Marketing Association (AMA) to advertising and other forms of marketing communication that have been proven to be not only creative, but more importantly, effective. That means the campaigns were guided by measurable objectives, and evaluation after the campaign determined that the effort did, in fact, meet or exceed the objectives. (Check out the Effies at *www.effie.org*.) Other award shows that focus on effectiveness are the Advertising and Marketing Effectiveness (AME) awards by the New York Festivals company, Canada's Cassie Awards, and the London-based Institute of Practitioners (IPA) Award. Check out these award programs at *www.ameawards.com, www.cassies.ca,* and *www.ipa.co.uk*.

Other award shows judge factors such as creative ideas, for example, the Clios by a private award-show company, a New York–based advertising association's One Show, and the Cannes Lions Awards by a French award-show company. Awards are also given for media plans (*Adweek*'s Media Plan of the Year) and art direction (New York–based Art Directors Club award show). These awards can be found at *www.clioawards.com, www.canneslions.com, www.adweek .com,* and *www.adcglobal.org/awards/annual*.

Other professional areas also have award shows that reward such things as clever promotional ideas. For example, the Reggies are given by the Promotion Marketing Association, and outstanding public relations efforts are recognized by the Public Relations Society of America's Silver Anvil Award.

Integrated Marketing Communication (IMC)

We mentioned that effectiveness is a central theme for this book, but another concept that we will discuss throughout is *integration*. As we mentioned earlier in our timeline, the search for effective communication has led many companies to focus on the consistency of their brand communication in order to more efficiently establish a coherent brand perception. We call that practice *integrated marketing communication* or *IMC*. In other words, everything that sends a brand message is a point of concern for those managing brand communication. To be effective, these messages need to complement one another and present the same basic brand strategy.

*First Principle
of IMC*
Everything
communicates.

The point is that brand communication involves more than just advertising. We refer to the **First Principle of IMC** as *everything communicates.* And that means all marketing communication *media* (print, broadcast, out-of-home, and digital), as well as all marketing communication *platforms* (advertising, public relations, events and sponsorships, and direct response) and other new forms, such as guerilla marketing and online social media. All communication efforts are planned for maximum synergy.

Looking Ahead

This chapter has provided an introduction to many of the basic concepts of advertising, as well as IMC. We'll continue that introduction of principles and practices in Chapter 2 as we explain the bigger picture of advertising and its role in marketing communication and marketing. Marketing communication agencies play an important role in puzzling out new ways to interact with customers and cement brand relationships.

WHOPPER*FREAKOUT*.COM

IT'S A WRAP

Best Burger, Best Campaign, Best Practices

The focus on effectiveness and results is the theme of this textbook, and throughout the book we will introduce you to practices that generate effectiveness. We'll end each chapter with the results of the campaign that introduced the chapter—in this case, the Grand Effie–winning "Whopper Freakout" campaign for Burger King. The freakout campaign for Whopper's 50th anniversary demonstrates the power of having a brand identity so strong that customers not only remember it, but demand it.

So here's the rest of the Whopper story. It's a story of consumer shock and outrage: "If Burger King doesn't have the Whopper, they might as well change their name to Burger Queen," and "What are you going to put on the logo now—home of the 'whatever we got'?" griped outraged customers. When one stunned would-be Whopper eater was given a Big Mac instead, he said, "I hate McDonald's."

These comments were all captured on tape and played and replayed on the special website by intrigued viewers 5 million times. Fourteen million more watched it and the TV spots on YouTube. The agency figures this all led to a 300+ percent increase in Web chatter about Burger King, which it estimates was about a fifth of the paid media. That means it received about 20 percent of the media for free as consumers spread the word. Burger King successfully captured its audience with a viral hit. *Ad lesson #3:* Smart thinking can help you compete with competitors with bigger budgets.

Was the campaign effective? Did the captivated audience buy the burgers? The answer: the quarterly sales increased by double digits. At the beginning of this case, you read about two goals for the campaign. One was to reaffirm that the Whopper is America's most-loved burger, and the other was to increase the sales of the burger. This campaign achieved both of these measurable objectives.

What a way to celebrate the 50th anniversary of the Whopper. To make the golden anniversary more golden, the campaign was awarded a Gold Effie in the Restaurants category and the coveted Grand Effie, the top award given to acknowledge effectiveness for the campaign's "boldness and creativity across multiple media platforms, delivering real cultural relevance and above all, outstanding business results." *Ad lesson #4:* Awards mean nothing if they don't achieve the business goals.

Key Points Summary

1. **What is advertising, how has it evolved, and what does it do in modern times?** The definition of advertising has evolved over time from identification to information and persuasion, as well as selling. In modern times, advertising is persuasive communication that uses mass and interactive media to reach broad audiences in order to connect an iden-

tified sponsor with buyers and provide information about products. It performs communication, marketing, economic, and societal roles. Seven types of advertising define the industry: brand, retail or local, direct response, B2B, institutional, nonprofit, and public service.

2. **How have the key concepts of marketing communication developed over time?** A review of the evolution of advertising practice identifies the source of many of the key concepts currently used in advertising. These concepts can be grouped into the four key components of advertising: strategy (objectives, appeals, branding, positioning and differentiation, and segmenting and targeting), message (creative concept based on research and consumer insight, creativity and artistry), media (the evolution of print, broadcast, outdoor, and digital, as well as the practice of matching targets to media audiences and compensation based on the media buy), and evaluation (effectiveness in terms of meeting objectives, testing, standards).

3. **How is the industry organized—key players, types of agencies, and jobs within agencies?** The key players begin with the advertiser, the organization or brand behind the advertising effort. Other players include the agency that prepares the advertising, the media that run it, and the professional suppliers and consultants who contribute expertise. The three types of agencies are full-service, in-house, and specialized agencies. There are also networks of agencies with many offices, as well as holding companies that own many different kinds of agencies. Agency jobs are varied in expertise and provide a number of career opportunities for all kinds of skill sets: account management, planning and research, creative (writing, art direction, production), and media (research, planning, buying). Agencies are paid in different ways, including by commission based on a percent of media costs, with a fee system based on estimated project costs or hourly billing, or with a monthly retainer. Value billing is based on creative and strategic ideas rather than media costs.

4. **How is the practice of advertising changing?** A number of changes are creating new forms of advertising, such as consumer-initiated ideas and advertising executions, blurring lines between marcom areas and tools, media that are changing shape and merging with other media forms, new forms of client–agency relationships, and value-marketing practices that emerged from the recession.

Words of Wisdom: Recommended Reading

Jaffe, Joseph, *Life after the 30-Second Spot: Energize Your Brand with a Bold Mix of Alternatives to Traditional Advertising,* Hoboken, NJ: John Wiley, 2005.

Ogilvy, David, *Ogilvy on Advertising,* New York: Vintage Books, 1985.

Othmer, James, *Adland: Searching for the Meaning of Life on a Branded Planet,* New York: Doubleday, 2009.

Steel, Jon, *Perfect Pitch: The Art of Selling Ideas and Winning New Business,* Hoboken, NJ: John Wiley, 2007.

History

Applegate, Edd, *Personalities and Products: A Historical Perspective on Advertising in America,* Westport, CT: Greenwood Press, 1998.

Fox, Stephen, *The Mirror Makers: A History of American Advertising and its Creators,* Champaign, IL: University of Illinois Press, 1997.

Twitchell, James, *Twenty Ads That Shook the World: The Century's Most Groundbreaking Advertising and How It Changed Us All,* New York: Three Rivers Press, 2000.

Tungate, Mark, *Adland: A Global History of Advertising,* Philadelphia: Kogan Page, 2007.

Key Terms

account executive, p. 52
account management, p. 51
account planning, p. 53
account services, p. 51
advertisement, p. 34
advertiser, p. 46
advertising, p. 35
advertising agency, p. 48
advertising department, p. 48
agency networks, p. 51
agency-of-record (AOR), p. 48
art director, p. 42

attention, p. 41
brand advertising, p. 39
brand name, p. 43
business-to-business (B2B) advertising, p. 39
buzz, p. 37
campaign, p. 40
channels (media), p. 48
classified advertising, p. 41
commission, p. 53
corporate advertising, p. 39
creative boutique, p. 51

direct-response advertising, p. 39
effective, p. 44
effectiveness, p. 55
effects, p. 55
Federal Trade Commission (FTC), p. 45
fee, p. 53
fee system, p. 53
full-service agency, p. 50
holding companies, p. 51
image, p. 37

in-house agency, p. 50
institutional advertising p. 39
integrated marketing communication (IMC), p. 45
local advertising, p. 39
marketing communication (marcom), p. 37
marketing services, p. 48
mass media, p. 49
media, p. 48
media-buying services, p. 51
media vehicles, p. 48

Review Questions

1. Analyze the Burger King campaign discussed in this chapter and compare it to key aspects of the modern definition of advertising.

2. Advertising plays four general roles in society. Define and explain each one in the context of the "1984" commercial featured in this chapter.

3. What are the four components of advertising and what key concepts and practices do they represent?

4. Trace the evolution of advertising and the current developments that shape the practice of advertising. What are the most important periods in the development of advertising and what changes did they bring?

5. Who are the four key players in the world of advertising, and what are the responsibilities of each?

6. We discussed five categories of agency jobs. Explain each one and identify where your own personal skills might fit.

7. What challenges are affecting the current practice of advertising? In particular, why is effectiveness important to advertisers?

Discussion Questions

1. Look through the ads in this textbook and find examples that focus on each of the three definitional orientations—identification, information, and persuasion. Explain how each ad works and why you think it demonstrates that focus. Which do you think is most effective and why do you feel that way?

2. Many industry experts feel that Apple's "1984" commercial is the best television commercial ever made. Watch it online at *www.youtube.com/watch?v=OYecfV3ubP8* and analyze how it works. How many of the basic advertising practices and concepts that we introduced in the historical timeline of Figure 1.1 does it demonstrate? Why do you think the experts are so impressed with this ad?

3. You belong to an organization that wants to advertise a special event it is sponsoring. You are really concerned that the group not waste its limited budget on advertising that doesn't work. Outline a presentation you would make to the group's board of directors that explains advertising strengths and why advertising is important for this group. Then explain the concept of advertising effectiveness. In this situation, what would be effective and what wouldn't be? How would you determine whether an ad works or not?

4. *Three-Minute Debate:* In class, Mark tells the instructor that all this "history of advertising" stuff is irrelevant. The instructor asks the class to consider why it is important to understand the historical review of advertising definitions and practices. What would you say either in support of Mark's view or to change his mind? Organize into small teams with pairs of teams taking one side or the other. Develop a three-minute presentation for the class that explains the position your team has taken on this issue.

Take-Home Projects

1. *Portfolio Project:* Leo Burnett, a giant of the advertising industry, always kept a file he called "Ads Worth Saving," ads that struck him as effective for some reason. This was his portfolio of ideas. He explained that he would go through that file, not looking for ideas to copy, but because these great ads would trigger thoughts about how to solve some problem. So throughout this book, we will invite you to start your own portfolio. In some cases the assignments will ask you to find good (or bad) work and explain why you evaluate them as you do. In other cases, we'll ask you to actually do something—write, design, propose—or create something that you could take to an interview that demonstrates your understanding of the principles we talk about in this book.

   A Facebook Profile: For this first assignment, choose one of the people from the historical discussions in this chapter, someone you believe influenced the development of modern marketing communication. Research this person on the Internet and build a personal profile including samples of work if you can find some. Present your report as if it were a Facebook page. Make sure your presentation explains why you believe this person was important.

2. *Mini-Case Analysis:* Every chapter in this textbook opens with an award-winning case. For this assignment you will be asked to analyze why it was effective and, in many cases, come up with ideas for how that campaign could be extended to another year or another market.

Burger King Freakout: Reread the Burger King "Whopper Freakout" campaign that was introduced at the beginning of this chapter and wrapped up at the end of the chapter. Go online and see if you can find any other information about this campaign. What are the strong points of this campaign? Why has it won awards and why was it deemed effective? If you were on the BK team, would you recommend that this campaign be continued or is it just a one-time idea? In other words, what happens next? Is there a spin-off? Develop a one-page analysis and proposal for the next year.

Team Project: The BrandRevive Campaign

There are a number of brands that have been somewhat forgotten by consumers, or maybe never had much of a brand presence in consumer minds because of a lack of marketing communication effort. These are brands that need revitalization, rebranding, or repositioning. Some of those brands, listed below, are consumer goods but there are also services, a business-to-business marketer, a couple of nonprofit organizations, and an event. All of these could use some help building or rebuilding their brands. In other words, there are a variety of brands and types of categories from which you can choose:

- *Post's Grape Nuts* cereal, at over 110 years old, has been a mainstay on grocery shelves for more than a century and has a small band of dedicated and loyal fans. Unfortunately, the brand has been in decline for many years.
- *Ramen* noodles are based on a popular Japanese product. In the United States the packaged noodles are a low-budget dish on which college students are known to subsist.
- *Goody Beauty Products* are big in discount and drugstores, but the company has never run a national brand campaign and the brand name is largely unknown.
- *Bag Balm,* a hand lotion in a distinctive green tin, is good for farmers and others with dry, beat-up skin. You can find this product on the bottom shelf in many drugstores.
- *Ovaltine,* like Grape Nuts, is another very old brand that may have a small group of loyal customers, but has been largely forgotten by most consumers.
- *Laura Ashley,* a brand of apparel and a retailer, has been struggling since the 1990s and has lost a lot of its popularity.
- *Avaya* is a large B2B company that has a small presence in the mind of general consumers and, like Geico demonstrated, could benefit by becoming better known to a more general audience.
- Other services that could all use brand rejuvenation include *A&W Restaurants, Zale Jewelers, Discover Card, Ask.com, Amtrak,* and *TraveLodge.*
- The *Anti-Defamation League* is a nonprofit that promotes respect for cultural differences.
- *Goodwill* collects and sells used clothing and household goods.
- The *Mardi Gras* in New Orleans needs a new position and marketing strategy that will reach a broader audience and bring people back to New Orleans.

So here's your chance to work as a member of a BrandRevive team and develop a full-blown campaign to reinvigorate one of these brands. We'll be using this brand revitalization project throughout this book as an end-of-chapter exercise. By the time you have finished the book, you will have developed a complete marketing communication campaign to revitalize one of these old, fading, or largely unknown brands.

So where do you begin? For this first chapter assignment, your objective is to get organized and do some background research to determine which brand your team would like to revitalize.

How to Get Started

- After forming your team (we recommend three or four people), choose three brands from the previous list to consider for this BrandRevive assignment.
- To help you narrow your three choices down to the one your team wants to focus on, split your team up and explore the history of the three brands and their companies. Go online and visit your library for historical, as well as current, background information.
- In a paragraph, develop a short profile for each brand and identify its key problems.
- After reviewing this preliminary background information, as a team choose the brand your group wants to spend the semester working on.
- For your chosen brand, do more research and build a brand history, as well as a corporate history.
- Write up your findings in a review that is no longer than one double-spaced page. Convert your key findings into a PowerPoint presentation that is no longer than three slides. Prepare and practice to give this presentation to your class.

Hands-On Case

The Century Council

Read the Century Council case in the Appendix before coming to class.

1. In class, discuss the following:
   a. In what ways does the Century Council case reflect the expanded definition of what advertising is?
   b. How does the case illustrate the various roles that advertising campaigns can perform?
2. Write a one-page explanation of the campaign.

CHAPTER 2

Advertising Management

5 Advertising Management

THE RICHARDS GROUP

"Some companies push products. Some sell ads. We sell the truth." This guiding principle may be found on the Web site for The Richards Group, America's largest independent advertising agency, based in Dallas, Texas; an agency so distinguished that it has been listed as one of the six most influential agencies in the United States by *Graphic Design USA*.

The firm, which at one point consisted of fewer than 60 employees, all located on one floor of an office building, has expanded to a major office building on the North Central Expressway. The company has received many awards, including *Adweek* magazine's "Agency of the Year" numerous times.

The Richards Group generates billings exceeding $1 billion annually. The organization employs more than 650 marketing professionals. Its list of current and former clients includes a variety of well-known companies, Orkin, Fruit of the Loom, T.G.I. Friday's, Zales, Red Lobster, Farmer's Insurance, and others.

Beyond these simple statistics rests a story that owner-founder Stan Richards once described as "a rocket ride," which has taken him to being named as one of *The Wall Street Journal*'s "Giants of Our Time." Many of the tactics employed by The Richards Group have been emulated by other agencies. Richards notes that his company did them first and does them best.

Richards prefers hiring new employees straight out of college, because, he says with a smile, "We don't want them picking up bad habits in other agencies, before they join us." These individuals quickly discover that the offices are all completely open, with no doors or walls. More significant, Richards notes, "What we do is commingle all the disciplines, so that in every cluster of spaces we will have an art director who sits next to a brand manager, who, for example, sits next to a print production manager, so that, in those interdisciplinary villages that everyone here occupies, nobody's next door neighbor does the same thing that he or she does. What you don't get

Stan Richards

Source: Author Supplied Image.

CHAPTER OBJECTIVES

After reading this chapter, you should be able to answer the following questions:

1 What are the essential ingredients in advertising campaign management, including the role of advertising?

2 When should a company employ an external advertising agency rather than completing the work in-house?

3 How do companies choose advertising agencies?

4 What roles are played within advertising agencies and client companies?

5 What steps are completed as part of advertising campaign management?

6 What are the primary goals of advertising?

7 What are the key elements of an advertising budget?

8 What are the issues in the media-selection process?

9 How does a creative brief facilitate effective advertising?

Source: Author Supplied Image.

▲ **Employees of The Richards Group**

CHAPTER 5

is all the creative people sitting on this floor, then all the account management people on the next floor, and the media people on the floor above that."

"The reason I did that in the first place," Richards continues, "was that when we were 50 or 60 people, there was an extraordinary level of energy and electricity that just flowed through the place. You could just walk in and feel it. A lot of it was created by the casual contact people had with each other. When you have 50 or 60 people packed into a tight space, you see everybody every day.

"What agencies have always done, is when they reach that 120- to 130-person size, they then have to move to multiple floors. And the minute they do, they take a tight-knit bunch of people who really liked each other and understood each other, because they saw each other every day, and divide them up into tribes. These tribes don't always get along.

"There are lots of occasions where a creative will butt heads with a planner, because they have a different point of view. When you are packed into a tight space, and when you have a great deal of casual contact going on all day, every day, you get over that stuff, because they are your friends. When you're on a different floor, you seldom see them, and you decide, 'That's a different tribe up there, and they drive me crazy.'"

Richard's approach clearly works. "When we are hired by a client," Richards notes, "it's not just to make ads. We do so many things that are extremely important. That ad is what the consumer ultimately sees, but in order to get there, you have to have a dead-on strategy, if you're going to be successful. You go through the strategic process, you get to the right answer, and then you can execute against that answer."

Some of the success stories created by The Richards Group are relayed in various places in this textbook, including the long-standing Chick-fil-A cow campaign, the fascinating "ride" with Motel 6 described in this chapter, the company's 2010 Super Bowl commercials, and its relationships with Firestone and The Home Depot.

In the meantime, the next time you view a commercial for Corona Beer, featuring a laid-back setting on a beach in the Caribbean somewhere, and you leave the cares of the world behind you, Richards suggests, you are viewing another company success story. Corona has become the number one imported beer in the United States, passing Heineken, due, in part, to a successful advertising management program assisted by The Richards Group.[1]

OVERVIEW

① What are the essential ingredients in advertising campaign management, including the role of advertising?

The average person encounters more than 600 advertisements per day, delivered by an expanding variety of media. Television and radio have long been the advertising staples, along with newspaper and magazine ads, billboards, signs, direct-mail campaigns, and other traditional channels. Recently, advertisements presented on the Internet, social networks, and cell phones have generated new ways to contact and interact with customers.

Today's marketers face a challenge. A company simply cannot afford to prepare advertisements for every medium. Further, the message should be designed to create an advantage in a highly cluttered world in which people are becoming increasingly adept at simply tuning ads out.

To be effective, an advertisement first must be noticed. Next, it must be remembered. Then, the message of the advertisement should incite some kind of action, such as a purchase, a shift in brand loyalty, or, at the very least, find a place in the buyer's long-term memory.

Part 2 of this textbook describes the role advertising plays in an integrated marketing communications program. Figure 5.1 portrays the overall IMC approach. The three chapters in this section focus on developing an effective IMC advertising program.

FIGURE 5.1 ▶
Overview of Integrated Marketing Communications

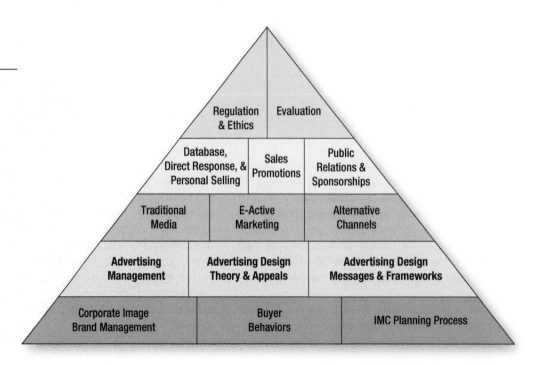

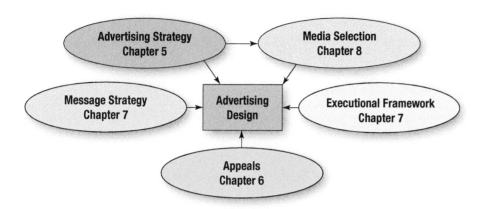

Three ingredients create effective advertisements: (1) development of a logical advertising management scheme for the company, (2) thoughtful design of advertisements, and (3) careful selection of media. Media tools and media-selection processes will be described in the next section of this textbook (Part 3); however, media selection and advertising design go hand in hand: One cannot be performed without the other. Thus, although they are presented separately in this textbook, they occur at the same time.

This chapter focuses on advertising management, which lays the groundwork for the total advertising program. One element is developing the **message theme**, which is an outline of the key idea(s) the advertising campaign conveys.

Chapters 6 and 7 describe advertising design processes. The primary issues include deciding on the leverage point to use, the major appeal in the advertising campaign, and the type of executional framework to use. A **leverage point** is the key element in the advertisement that taps into, or activates, a consumer's personal value system (a value, idea, or concept). The **appeal** is the approach used to design the advertisement that attracts attention or presents information to consumers through the use of humor, fear, sex, logic, or emotions. The **executional framework** explains how the message will be delivered. Methods include the slice-of-life approach, fantasies, dramatizations, and ads featuring animation. Figure 5.2 displays the advertising design elements.

▼ Creating eye-catching ads plays a vital role in advertising management.

OVERVIEW OF ADVERTISING MANAGEMENT

An **advertising management program** is the process of preparing and integrating a company's advertising efforts with the overall IMC message. The program consists of four activities:

1. Review the role of advertising in the IMC effort.
2. Select an in-house or external advertising agency.
3. Develop an advertising campaign management strategy.
4. Complete a creative brief.

Consistency will be the guiding principle of these four efforts. The company's goods or services and methods of doing business should match the advertising agency chosen, the strategy of the campaign, and the work of the advertising creatives. The result should be a coherent message stating the theme of the entire IMC program.

"Hey, there's a blue one."

Drivers wanted. Ⓥ

ADVERTISING AND THE IMC PROCESS

Advertising continues to be a major component of integrated marketing communications. It remains part of the "traditional" promotions mix of advertising, consumer and trade promotions, and personal selling. These functions, along with other activities, such as direct marketing, digital content, public relations efforts, and alternative marketing strategies, form the basis for communicating with customers.

The role advertising plays varies by company, product, and the firm's marketing goals. For some products and companies, advertising continues to be the central focus, and the other components (trade promotions, consumer promotions, and personal selling) support the advertising program. In other situations, advertising plays a secondary role, such as supporting the national sales force and a firm's trade promotion program. In the business-to-business sector, advertising often assists other promotional activities, including trade shows and personal sales calls. In the consumer sector, the reverse is often true. Advertising will be the primary communication vehicle, and other promotional tools (contests, coupons, sampling) reinforce the campaign.

Recently, Oscar Mayer launched an integrated campaign entitled "It Doesn't Get Better Than This," which featured new advertisements for all Oscar Mayer products (Deli Fresh, Bologna, Deli Creations, Hot Dogs, and Bacon). The campaign emphasized an altruistic effort called "Good Mood Mission." Consumers were encouraged to share their good moods. For each good mood shared, Oscar Mayer donated 1 pound of food to families in need. The goal was to donate 2 million pounds of food. Advertising launched the campaign through TV spots on the *Golden Globe Awards* as well as sponsorship of the show. The message was strengthened using print ads, video ads, package redesigns, public relations efforts with Kristin Chenoweth, digital and consumer-generated content on the Internet, and local event marketing featuring the Wienermobile (see Figure 5.3). The Oscar Mayer campaign illustrates the key role advertising continues to play in communications.

IN-HOUSE VERSUS EXTERNAL ADVERTISING AGENCIES

❷ When should a company employ an external advertising agency rather than completing the work in-house?

When beginning an advertising program, the first issue is whether to use an in-house advertising group or an external advertising agency. Figure 5.4 compares the advantages of an in-house facility to an outside agency.

Approximately 40 percent of companies use some type of in-house facility, due to its potential advantages. Managers believe this approach *lowers costs* and gives the company better control of the message, which can be *aligned* with the brand and other company communications.[2] The *CEO can work closely* with the marketing team to make sure this

FIGURE 5.3 ▶
Oscar Mayer's "Mission to Spread Good Mood Food" Campaign

Source: Adapted from Tom Lopez, Senior Director of Marketing, Oscar Mayer, Good Morning Headquarters, January 16, 2010.

Advantages of In-House	Advantages of Outside Agency
• Lower costs	• Reduce costs
• Consistent brand message	• Greater expertise
• Better understanding of product and mission	• Outsider's perspective
• Faster ad production	• Access to top talent
• Works closer with CEO	
• Lower turnover rate in the creative team	

Source: Adapted from Rupal Parekh, "Thinking of Pulling a CareerBuilder? Pros and Cons of Bringing an Account In-House," *Advertising Age,* http://adage.com/print?article_id136701, May 18, 2009.

◀ **FIGURE 5.4**
Advantages of In-House versus Outside Agencies

occurs. Consequently, members of the marketing department may conclude they have a *better understanding of the firm's products and mission.* They may also think they can more *quickly produce* advertisements. Finally, an in-house program will be more consistent because of a *lower turnover rate in the creative team.*

As a result, some firms, such as CareerBuilder and Skyjacker, perform all advertising functions in-house. Others hire marketing and advertising experts to assist in the effort. Some contract specific functions, such as writing, filming, recording, and editing advertisements. Most utilize media companies to plan and purchase media time (on television and radio) and space (in magazines, in newspapers, and on billboards).

At times, an outside agency *reduces costs* when compared to less efficient in-house facilities. This occurs when in-house employees spend more time on campaigns and ad designs than an agency would. The agency offers *greater expertise* and may have *access to top talent* in the industry. Advertising agencies offer an *outside perspective* not influenced by internal corporate politics and personal biases. Agency professionals often have a better understanding of consumers and trends, because they work with a number of clients over an array of products. Often knowledge gained from one product can be transferred to other, even unrelated products.

▼ Skyjacker is one of a number of firms that performs all advertising functions in-house.

Cost Considerations

Another factor affecting the choice of an in-house team versus an external advertising agency is the size of the account. A small account may not be attractive to an advertising agency. Smaller accounts generate lower revenues. If the agency charges a higher fee to compensate, it becomes too costly for the small firm.

Smaller accounts create other challenges for agencies. Less money is available to spend on purchasing media time and space, because the majority of the advertising budget will be spent on production of the advertisement.

One rule of thumb used by agencies is the *75–15–10* breakdown, where 75 percent of the money spent on advertising should be used to purchase media time or space, 15 percent to the agency for the creative work, and 10 percent for the actual production of the ad. In contrast, for smaller accounts, the breakdown may be 25–40–35. This means that only 25 percent of expenditures are for media purchases. The other 75 percent of the funds goes to the creative and production work.

Unless the majority of the company's advertising budget can be spent on media purchases, it may be wise either to perform the work in-house or to develop contracts with smaller specialty firms to prepare various aspects of an advertising campaign.

Crowdsourcing

A new alternative has recently emerged. **Crowdsourcing** is the process of outsourcing the creative aspect of an advertisement to the public. Unilever used this approach for its meat snack brand Peperami. Company leaders announced a creative competition on the brand's Web site. More than 1,100 entries were

Source: Courtesy of Volkswagen.

▲ Creatives at advertising agencies tend to have greater expertise and objectivity in creating ads, such as this one designed by Crispin, Porter & Bogusky for Volkswagen.

❸ How do companies choose advertising agencies?

submitted. Peperami marketing manager Noam Buchalter stated, "We were so overwhelmed with the level of entries and range of high-quality creative ideas pitched for brief that we found it impossible to pick one." Two ideas were chosen: one by Kevin Baldwin, a copywriter from London, and the other by Rowland Davies, an ex-creative director from Germany. The two ideas cost about $15,000 in prize money. They were combined into print and television campaigns produced by Smartworks, a marketing production company from South Africa.[3]

Doritos used a similar approach when creating Super Bowl ads in 2009 and 2010. Fans were invited to submit ideas for ads. An MSNBC.com poll reported that the Doritos ads were voted as the best of the Super Bowl in both years. The winning ad for 2010 triumphed over 4,000 other submissions.[4]

It may seem that crowdsourcing would be a cheaper way to create a Super Bowl commercial. In reality, the total cost was about the same as it would have been to hire a professional agency. The costs of running the contest, paying the prize money, creating the microsite to host the contest, and producing the commercial and the time spent by Doritos and the agency in choosing from the 4,000 entries were about equal to what would have been spent on an agency. The primary advantage of the crowdsourcing approach was getting fans involved and the subsequent buzz that surrounded the contest for the consumer-generated advertisement.[5]

EXTERNAL ADVERTISING AGENCIES

Most companies hire advertising agencies to perform some or all of the advertising functions. When the decision is made to retain an external advertising agency, the company commits substantial resources to the goal of expanding its audience.

Many options are available when choosing an advertising agency. All sizes and types of agencies exist. At one end of the spectrum are the highly specialized, boutique-type agencies offering only one specific service (e.g., making television ads) or serving only one type of client. G+G Advertising of Albuquerque, New Mexico, specializes in advertising to Native Americans, a market of an estimated 10 million people.[6]

At the other end of the spectrum are the full-service agencies, including The Richards Group, that provide every type of advertising and promotional activity. These companies offer advice and assistance in working with the other components of the IMC program, including consumer and trade promotions, direct-marketing programs, digital programs, and alternative media. Figure 5.5 lists the services that full-service advertising agencies typically provide.

In addition to advertising agencies are other closely associated types of firms. *Media service companies* negotiate and purchase media packages (called *media buys*) for companies. *Direct-marketing agencies* handle every aspect of a direct-marketing campaign, either through telephone orders (800 numbers), Internet programs, or by direct mail. Some companies focus on either *consumer promotions, trade promotions,* or both. These

FIGURE 5.5 ▶
Services Provided by Full-Service Agencies

- Advice about how to develop target markets
- Specialized services for business markets
- Suggestions about how to project a strong company image and theme
- Assistance in selecting company logos and slogans
- Preparation of advertisements
- Planning and purchasing media time and space

companies assist in developing promotions such as coupons, premiums, contests, and sweepstakes. A new group of agencies specialize in developing *online and digital services*. Boxcar Creative designs *interactive Web sites* and widgets that can be used on multiple sites. Other companies offer *social media services* to reach consumers and businesses through a wide array of Internet techniques. *Public relations* firms provide experts to help companies and individuals develop positive public images and for damage control when negative publicity arises.

One approach to advertising management, developed by the Young & Rubicam Advertising Agency, is the *whole-egg theory*. The program moves from only selling a client's products to instead helping the client attain total success in the marketplace. It requires a more fully integrated marketing approach that includes a wider array of services. As client companies began to move to more integrated marketing approaches, agencies such as Young & Rubicam and The Richards Group captured more accounts.[7]

CHOOSING AN AGENCY

The next advertising management function is choosing an agency. The process includes developing effective selection criteria for the process of hiring an advertising agency. Figure 5.6 lists the steps involved in this process.

Goal Setting

Before making any contact with an advertising agency, company leaders identify and prioritize corporate goals. Goals provide a sense of direction designed to prevent personal biases from affecting decisions. Without clearly understood goals, it becomes more difficult to know which agency to choose, because company leaders do not have a clear idea of what they want to accomplish. It also makes it difficult for agencies to react when companies submit requests for proposals. They will not be certain about what the company wants from an advertising campaign.

Selection Criteria

Stating the selection criteria constitutes the second step. Even firms with experience set criteria in advance in order to reduce any biases that might affect the decision. Emotions and other feelings can lead to poor decisions. Figure 5.7 identifies some of the major issues to be considered as part of the process. The list can be especially useful during the initial screening, when the field narrows to the top five (or fewer) agencies.

Agency Size
The size of the agency should be considered, especially as it compares to the size of the company hiring the agency. If a large firm hires a small agency, the small agency may be overwhelmed. A small firm hiring a large agency may find that the company's account could be lost or could be treated as being insignificant. A good rule of thumb to follow regarding the size of the agency is that the account should be large enough for the agency so that it is important to the agency but small enough that, if lost, the agency would not be badly affected.

Relevant Experience
When an agency has experience in a given industry, the agency's employees are better able to understand the client firm, its customers, and the structure of the marketing channel. At the same time, the client company will make sure the agency does not have any *conflicts of interest*. An advertising firm that has been hired by one manufacturer of

◄ **FIGURE 5.6**

Steps in Selecting an Advertising Agency

- Set goals.
- Select process and criteria.
- Screen initial list of applicants.
- Request client references.
- Reduce list to two or three viable agencies.
- Request creative pitch.

FIGURE 5.7 ▶

Evaluation Criteria in Choosing
an Advertising Agency

- Size of the agency
- Relevant experience of the agency
- Conflicts of interest
- Creative reputation and capabilities
- Production capabilities
- Media purchasing capabilities
- Other services available
- Client retention rates
- Personal chemistry

automobile tires would experience a conflict of interest if another tire manufacturer attempted to hire the agency.

An advertising agency can have relevant experience without representing a competitor. Such experience can be gained when an agency works for a similar company operating in a different industry. For example, when an agency has a manufacturer of automobile batteries as a client, the experience is relevant to selling automobile tires.

The agency should also have experience with the business-to-business side of the market, so that retailers, wholesalers, and any other channel party are considered in the marketing and advertising of the product. All of the milk advertisements in this textbook were created by Bozell Worldwide, which has become Lowe Worldwide. In addition to the milk advertisements, Lowe Worldwide's clients include Rexona, Saab, Axe, Johnson & Johnson, and Electolux. Note that the list does not include competing firms within the same industry.

▼ The milk industry is just one of the accounts being handled by Lowe Worldwide.

Creative Reputation and Capabilities

One method of assessing an agency's creativity would include asking for a list of awards the company has received. Although awards do not always translate into creating effective advertisements, in most cases there is a positive relationship between winning awards and writing effective ads. Most creative awards are given by peers. As a result, they are good indicators of what others think of the agency's creative efforts.

Production and Media Purchasing Capabilities

These capabilities should be examined if these services are needed. A firm that needs an agency to produce a television commercial and also buy media time should check on these activities as part of the initial screening process. Many agencies either employ subsidiary companies to perform the media work or subcontract it to a media firm. The advertising agency does not necessarily need to make media buys, but it should have the capacity to make sure they are made and fit with the ads being designed.

The type of information involved in selecting an advertising agency can be difficult to obtain. The company hiring the agency should engage in thorough research. It helps to access each agency's Web page and annual report and to search for news articles about the agency. Most advertising agencies provide prospectus sheets describing company capabilities.

Other Criteria

The final three selection criteria—*other services available, client retention rates,* and *personal chemistry*—are revealed as the final steps of selection take place. These criteria help make the final determination in the selection process.

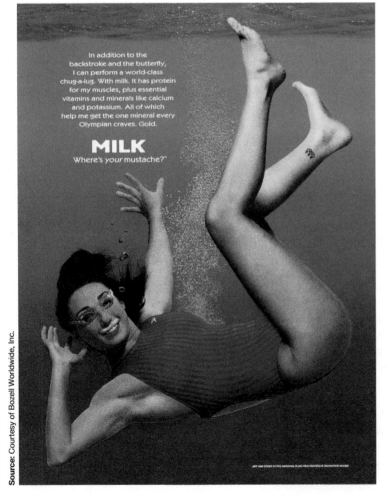

In addition to the backstroke and the butterfly, I can perform a world-class chug-a-lug. With milk. It has protein for my muscles, plus essential vitamins and minerals like calcium and potassium. All of which help me get the one mineral every Olympian craves. Gold.

MILK
Where's *your* mustache?"

Reference Requests

After completion of the initial screening, the company requests references from the agencies still in the running. Most agencies post major clients on company Web sites and provide additional client information when requested. A company can obtain references of firms with similar needs. Also, when possible, the company can contact former clients of the agency. Finding out why they switched often provides valuable information, even when changes were made for legitimate reasons.

Discovering an agency's *client retention rate* reveals how effective the firm has been working with various clients, although poor service is not the only reason a firm changes agencies. Sometimes the move was made because an agency became too small to handle an account that has increased in size due to a merger or purchase of another company.

Background checks start with finding firms that have dealt with each agency. Also, talking to media agents who sell media time provides insights as to how an agency buys time and deals with customers. Companies that have formed contracts with individual agencies for production facilities or other services are excellent sources of information. Background checks help the client company make sure the agency can provide quality professional services.

Creative Pitch

When the list has been reduced to two or three finalists, the company's selection team asks each for a creative pitch. The advertising agencies chosen to compete provide a formal presentation that addresses a specific problem, situation, or set of questions, a process which is also called a *shootout*. The presentations reveal how each agency would deal with specific issues that might arise during preparation of a campaign. This helps a client company choose the agency that best understands the issues at stake and offers a comprehensive approach to solving the problem or issue.

▼ During the creative pitch for the Oscar Mayer account, mcgarrybowen demonstrated an ability to transform the brand to bring the emotional spark sought by the client.

Preparing a pitch takes time and is costly for advertising agencies; therefore, agencies only want to prepare pitches that have a decent chance of being accepted. Spending time preparing a pitch only to find out later the company had no desire to switch agencies, but were told by upper management to solicit pitches, is frustrating.[8] A company seeking to retain an advertising agency should provide sufficient time for the competing finalists to prepare the pitch. Pink Jacket Creative's Bill Breedlove reports, "I would prefer at least 30 days to prepare a pitch. Even 45 to 60 days would be wonderful sometimes, and for some companies."

Recently, Oscar Mayer, a brand under the Kraft umbrella, was looking for ways to unify its portfolio of products and contemporize its image with consumers. The mcgarrybowen agency demonstrated how Oscar Mayer could contemporize the brand and build emotional ties with customers. The agency's ideas were fresh, contemporary, and had the emotional spark the organization desired.[9]

When Kraft launched its Oscar Mayer Deli Creations sandwiches, the initial print ad developed by the brand's previous agency depicted a woman in a suit, standing with her arm bent eating one of the Deli Creation sandwiches. Karen Adams, senior director of advertising at Kraft Foods, stated, "People don't eat sandwiches that way." Instead, new ads were created showing real people in real-life situations eating sandwiches.[10] The Oscar Mayer ad in this section depicts a construction worker ready to enjoy a Deli Creation sandwich with the tagline "Oh goody, it's Monday."

Oh goody, it's Monday.

A hot, melted sandwich that tastes so fresh, it's the perfect way to kick off your week.

it doesn't get better than this

FIGURE 5.8 ▶
Pitching Do's and Don'ts

- Do listen. Allow the client to talk.
- Do your preparation. Know the client and its business.
- Do make a good first impression. Dress up, not down.
- Do a convincing job of presenting. Believe in what you are presenting.
- Don't assume all clients are the same. Each has a unique need.

- Don't try to solve the entire problem in the pitch.
- Don't be critical of the product or the competition.
- Don't overpromise. It will come back to haunt you.
- Don't spend a lot of time pitching credentials and references.

Source: Based on Heather Jacobs, "How to Make Sure Your Pitch Is Heard," *B&T Weekly* 57, no. 2597 (February 2, 2007), pp. 14–16.

Successful creative pitches result from hard work and thorough planning. Figure 5.8 highlights some of the do's and don'ts for advertising agencies in making pitches.

Agency Selection

During the presentation phase, the opportunity exists to meet with creatives, media buyers, account executives, and other people who will work on the account. *Chemistry* between employees of the two different firms becomes critical. The client company's leaders should be convinced that they will work well together. Chemistry can break or make the final decision.[11]

After completing the selection process the agency and the company work together to prepare the advertising campaign. The account executive, account planner, and advertising creative all plays key roles in the process.

ROLES OF ADVERTISING PERSONNEL

4 What roles are played within advertising agencies and client companies?

Personnel within advertising agencies perform a wide variety of roles. In small agencies, an individual may perform multiple roles. In a large agency, multiple individuals will be employed in the various departments and perform similar functions. The primary roles within the agency consist of the account executives, creatives, traffic managers, and account planners.

Account Executives

The account executive will be the key go-between for both the advertising agency and the client company. This individual stays actively involved in soliciting the account, finalizing details of the contract, and working with personnel within the agency to make sure the advertising campaign is produced according to the client's specifications. An account executive often helps the company define the theme of the overall IMC program and provides other support, as needed.

Creatives

The persons who develop and design advertisements are called creatives. They are either members of advertising agencies or freelancers. Some smaller companies provide only creative advertising services without becoming involved in other marketing programs and activities. Creatives may appear to hold the "glamour" jobs in advertising, because they get to actually create ads and marketing materials. At the same time, creatives work long hours and face enormous pressures to design effective advertisements that produce tangible results.

Traffic Managers

The traffic manager works closely with the advertising agency's account executive, creatives, and production staff. The manager's responsibilities include scheduling the various aspects of the agency's work to make sure it is completed on time. During production, the traffic manager will be responsible for making sure props, actors, and whatever else is needed has been ordered and is in place at the time of the filming or recording.

Account Planners

The account planner becomes the voice or advocate for the consumer in the advertising agency. The planner makes sure the creative team understands the consumer (or business). Account planners interact with the account executive and the client to understand the target audience of the ad campaign. The planner then works to make sure creative messages reach the right customers.

The account planner assists the client in developing long-term communication strategies and provides direction for individual advertising campaigns. In small agencies, the role may be performed by the account executive. Larger firms employ separate individuals and or departments to conduct the account planning role.

The Role of Quality Communication

Quality communication will be a vital part of the relationship between a client company and an advertising agency. A recent survey of 250 senior executives of marketing and advertising agencies revealed that these managers believed that at least 30 percent of their staff's time was wasted or used ineffectively because of poor communications from clients. Issues such as poor competitive information and lack of clarity about the company or brand's position in the marketplace were common. More disturbing was that 75 percent of the ad agencies indicated that clients go through at least five significant changes in directions given to agencies and about what they want the agencies to do. The agencies reported that, on average, they dealt with five different individuals from the client company, each with a different agenda and different directions for the agency.[12]

The company's marketing department manager works closely with the advertising agency's account manager to overcome these obstacles. The manager remains aware that missteps and changes to an advertising program are costly in terms of additional advertising agency fees as well as the less effective campaign that might result.

Clients want to know if they are getting a good value. Many clients worry that they do not understand the relationship between an agency's cost and the actual value it renders. Ron Cox, a vice president at Wrigley Jr. Company, suggests that agencies update clients regularly on the work they are doing and the results obtained. *Stewardship reports* help clients review the process and the outcome. Updating clients will be critical, especially when large amounts of money are being spent on advertising.[13]

THIS TEA HAS MANY HEALTH BENEFITS, NONE OF WHICH HAVE TO BE FOLLOWED BY PAGES OF POSSIBLE SIDE EFFECTS.

Since 1969, our teas have been a source of wellness, all while staying 100% natural. Celestial Seasonings Green Tea contains healthful antioxidants and antioxidants have been shown to help support a healthy heart and immune system. So, be good to yourself and enjoy a cup of our Green Tea. We guarantee you'll be able to drive a car and operate heavy machinery afterwards.

celestialseasonings.com

▲ The account planner represents the consumer's viewpoint so that creatives can design effective advertisements, such as this one by Celestial Seasonings for Green Tea.

ADVERTISING CAMPAIGN MANAGEMENT

Advertising campaign management is the process of preparing and integrating a specific advertising program. Whether the work is done in-house or with an external agency, the marketing manager oversees the development of the advertising campaign. An effective campaign consists of following five steps:

1. Conduct and review the advertising research.
2. Establish advertising objectives consistent with the overall IMC program.
3. Review the advertising budget.
4. Select the appropriate media based on the viewing habits of the target market.
5. Prepare a creative brief.

5 What steps are completed as part of advertising campaign management?

The advertising program should be consistent with every part of the IMC program as well as the company's mission to make sure the firm presents a clear message to key target markets. Advertising efforts are refined to gain the maximum benefit from promotional dollars.

ADVERTISING RESEARCH

When an advertising agency is hired, the team immediately seeks to understand the client's company and products. Clients try to provide accurate and timely information that assist the agency in the preparation of the campaign. To create an effective advertising program, the advertising agency's creative personnel requires information about customers, why they purchase the product, and what exactly they seek to purchase.

Products are not typically purchased solely for attributes. Customers also consider the benefits they provide. Individuals purchasing makeup, cologne, perfume, and other beauty products may not care about the ingredients and attributes, but care very much about how these items will make them look or smell. Advertising research goes beyond identifying demographic profiles or target markets. It also identifies the brand's competitors and the communications used in the industry.

To best understand a company's customers, their purchasing habits, and the other key ideas about them, various forms of advertising research are available. Key insights about how products are used, when they are used, and why can emerge from effective research. Two primary approaches exist.

Product-specific research involves identifying key product characteristics that become selling points. For example, the marketing team might try to discover the most desirable features are "apps" for a cell phone. The team may find that certain apps are used when customers are bored and are just passing time, whereas others provide specific functional information, such as the location of a restaurant while the customer drives to dinner. One feature or the other may become the focal point of a commercial.

Consumer-oriented research will be used to understand the context of a product's use. A team may discover that a pizza restaurant's clientele tends to stay longer, because the establishment offers quality family time. This more *anthropological* approach involves direct observation of consumers using the good or service. Other customer-oriented research may feature a *sociological* analysis of social class issues, trends, and family life cycle changes. Ralph Lauren may match with upper class, richer families. Another product may appeal most to empty-nest couples looking to enrich their lives in some way. A third customer-oriented approach analyzes *psychological* motives for product purchases, such as feeling sexy, powerful, or intelligent.

▼ Consumer-oriented research provides valuable information, such as why some individuals enjoy riding motorcycles.

Sometimes a company's marketing team becomes so close to products and customers that they do not see these issues. Consequently, agencies often seek out more information than is provided by clients. One common approach used by agencies to understand a client's customers is a **focus group**, which consists of consumers who are retained to talk about a particular topic, product, or brand.

Motel 6 and The Richards Group

During the interview with Stan Richards that was conducted for the opening vignette in this chapter, he talked about a "perfect example" of understanding a client's customers using focus groups. "We've worked with Motel 6 for 24 years," he said, "and the beginning of that relationship was a remarkable insight."

Let's just say tailgaters aren't a problem.

BMW
Motorcycles

"The insight came out of our research, which was primarily qualitative. We sat behind a glass window in a focus room setting. Our account planner sat at the head of the table, moderating the session. We've got a dozen people in the room whom we recruited by phone. They don't know why they're in the room. We know that they all use Motel 6. The moderator asks, 'Where do you stay when you're on the road?' They go around the table and nobody says, 'Motel 6.'

"The moderator pushes further and says, 'Well, where else do you stay?' They go around the table again, and nobody says, 'Motel 6.' Now, why is that? They didn't know who the other people in the room were, and they didn't want to be perceived as being poor or cheap.

"Now, finally, you get somebody, by going around the table again, to say, 'You know, if it's late at night, I'll stop at a Motel 6, and I can save enough money to buy a tank of gas.' And then, somebody else across the table would say, 'I do the same thing, and I save enough money to bring a gift home to the grandkids.' And all of a sudden, the character of the room changed, because everybody had a story like that. What happened was a move from embarrassment to pride in the benefits of frugality.

"That's what the insight was all about. I am a frugal person, and if my eyes are closed, all hotel rooms look alike. I don't see any reason to overspend for lodging, when I can find a perfectly good place like Motel 6."

From this insight, The Richards Group developed the theme, tagline, and advertising approach for Motel 6 that are still used today. Richards noted that the phrase, "A clean, comfortable room, at the lowest price of any national chain," appears in every spot.[14]

Richards argues that this approach highlights the difference between simply creating an advertisement through a technique such as crowdsourcing and conducting the type of quality research that leads to a better outcome. "Let's suppose that Motel 6 has cast a wide net, that 1,000 people are working on creative, and then we're going to run the one they like best. Just run a contest. It is so unlikely that they would have gotten to the insight that really propelled their business. The insight was a really simple one, but it wouldn't have come out if people were simply just trying to sell Motel 6."

When you're sleeping, we look
just like those big fancy hotels.
Motel 6

▲ This ad for Motel 6 was inspired by a focus group and a comment made by one of the participants: "If my eyes are closed, all hotel rooms look alike."

ADVERTISING GOALS

The second step of advertising planning is establishing and clarifying advertising goals, which are derived from the firm's overall communication objectives. Several advertising goals are central to the IMC process. Several of these are listed in Figure 5.9.[15]

⑥ What are the primary goals of advertising?

Building Brand Awareness

A strong global brand and corporate image should be a key advertising goal. Building a brand's image begins with developing brand awareness. *Brand awareness* means the consumers recognize and remember a particular brand or company name when they consider purchasing options. Advertising can increase brand awareness.

• To build brand awareness	• To support other marketing efforts
• To inform	• To encourage action
• To persuade	

◀ **FIGURE 5.9**
Advertising Goals

In business-to-business marketing, brand awareness leads to being considered by members of the buying center, because business customers recognize the brand name of the goods or services the company offers. Brand awareness becomes especially important in modified rebuy situations, when a firm looks to change to a new vendor or evaluates a product that has not been purchased recently. In new buy situations, members of the buying center spend more time seeking prospective vendors than they will for modified rebuys. Consequently, brand equity creates a major advantage for any company with such recognition.

Successful brands possess two characteristics: (1) the top of mind and (2) the consumers' top choice. When consumers are asked to identify brands that quickly come to mind from a product category, one or two particular brands are nearly always mentioned. These names are the **top-of-mind brands**. For example, when asked to identify fast-food restaurants, McDonald's and Burger King almost always head the list. The same may be true for Nike and Reebok athletic shoes, and may occur both in the United States and in other countries.

The term **top choice** suggests exactly what the term implies: A top-choice brand is the first or second pick when a consumer reviews her evoked set of possible purchasing alternatives. Many products become top of mind or top choice due to *brand equity*, the set of characteristics that cause consumers or businesses to believe that a brand is different and better. Advertising can help strengthen brand equity.

Providing Information

▼ This advertisement informs consumers that GameStop workers are also players and can provide tips on how to get out of a jam.

Advertising serves other goals, including providing information to both consumers and business buyers. Typical information for consumers includes a retailer's store hours, business location, or sometimes more detailed product specifications. Information may make the purchasing process appear to be simple and convenient, which can entice customers to travel to the store and finalize the purchase.

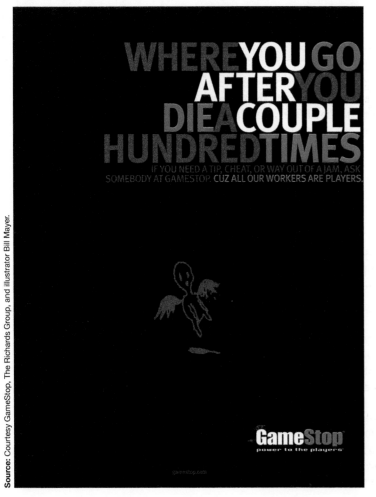

In business-to-business situations, information from some advertisements may lead various members of the buying center to consider a particular company. Information that reaches members of the buying center during the search stage of the purchasing process will be the most valuable. For high-involvement purchases, in which members of the buying center have strong vested interests in the success of the choice, informative advertisements are the also beneficial. Low-involvement decisions usually do not require the same level of detail.

Persuasion

Persuasion has taken place when an advertisement convinces consumers that a particular brand is superior. Changing consumer attitudes and persuading them to consider a new purchasing choice is a challenging task. Advertisers can utilize several methods of persuasion. One method is to show consumers the negative consequences of failing to use a particular brand. Persuasive advertising is used more in consumer marketing than in business-to-business situations.

Supporting Marketing Efforts

Advertising can be used to support other marketing functions. Manufacturers use advertising to support trade and consumer promotions, such as theme packaging or combination offers. Contests, such as the McDonald's Monopoly game, require additional advertising to be effective.

Retailers also advertise to support marketing programs. Any type of special sale (white sale, buy-one-get-one-free, pre–Christmas sale) requires effective advertising to attract customers to the store. Both manufacturers and retail outlets run advertisements in conjunction with coupons or other special offers. Del Monte placed a 30-cent coupon in the advertisement shown in this section. The ad highlights a smaller-size container with a pull-top lid. These features match the advertisement's target market: senior citizens. The first magazine featuring this advertisement was *Modern Maturity*. Manufacturer coupons are regularly redeemed at grocery stores (sometimes at double their face values), and in-store coupons are part of many retail store print advertisements. When ads are combined with other marketing efforts into a larger, more integrated effort revolving around a theme, the program is called a **promotional campaign**.

Encouraging Action

Many firms set behavioral goals for advertising programs. A television commercial encouraging viewers to take action by dialing a toll-free number to make a quick purchase is an example. Everything from ShamWow to Snuggies has been sold using action tactics. Infomercials and home shopping network programs rely heavily on immediate consumer purchasing responses.

Action-oriented advertising may be used in the business-to-business sector. When it is, generating leads becomes the primary the goal. Many business advertisements provide Web addresses or telephone numbers buyers can use to request more information or make a purchase.

Source: Courtesy of Del Monte Foods.

▲ A Del Monte advertisement directed to senior citizens offering a smaller can with a pull-off lid.

The five advertising goals of building image, providing information, being persuasive, supporting other marketing efforts, and encouraging action are not separate from each other. They work together in key ways. For instance, awareness and information are part of persuasion. The key is to emphasize one goal without forgetting the others.

THE ADVERTISING BUDGET

Once the major goals of the advertising campaign have been established, a review of the advertising budget follows. Chapter 4 described the various methods for developing marketing communication budgets. After establishing the total amount of dollars to be allocated to advertising, the challenge becomes choosing the proper media approach to reach the advertising goal. Three basic tactics used to allocate advertising funds are:

7 What are the key elements of an advertising budget?

- Pulsating schedule
- Flighting schedule
- Continuous schedule

A **pulsating schedule of advertising** involves continuous advertising during the year with bursts of higher intensity at specific times (more ads in more media). Companies can also select what is called a **flighting** approach or schedule, whereby ads are presented only during peak times, and not at all during other times of the year.

Firms often advertise more during peak seasons such as Christmas, because this involves sending messages during the times when customers are most inclined to buy, which is termed *being on the hot spot*. Weight Watchers, Diet Centers, and others advertise heavily during the first weeks of January. Many New Year's resolutions include going on a diet.

▲ Weight loss companies such as Weight Watchers tend to budget more for advertising after the Christmas Holiday, when individuals make New Year's resolutions to start dieting.

8 What are the issues in the media-selection process?

Advertising during slow sales seasons focuses on "drumming up business" when people do not regularly buy. In retail sales, slow seasons occur during January and February. Some companies advertise more during those periods to sell merchandise left over from the Christmas season and to encourage customers to shop. Manufacturers also realize that many retailers are not advertising and hope that the ads will gain greater attention as a result.

Many marketing experts believe it is best to advertise in level amounts to keep the brand name always in front of consumers, which is a **continuous campaign schedule**. Durable goods, such as washing machines and refrigerators, are purchased on an "as needed" basis. A family ordinarily buys a new washing machine only when the old one breaks down or when they remodel a home. Level advertising increases the odds that the buyer will see an advertisement or remember a given name (Kenmore, Whirlpool, or General Electric) at the right time.

The objective is to match the pacing of advertisements with the message, the media, and the nature of the product. Some media make it easier to advertise for longer periods of time. Contracts for billboards are normally for a month or a year. They can be rotated throughout a town or city to present a continuing message about a company or products. At the same time, budgetary constraints can influence the strategies and tactics used in any advertising program.

MEDIA SELECTION

Selecting the appropriate media requires an understanding of the media-usage habits of the company's target market and then matching that information with the profile of each medium's audience. Volkswagen positioned the Tiguan crossover as a fun vehicle aimed at young, active individuals who love the outdoors. Although television commercials were used in the campaign, the more unique component of the campaign was the outdoor segment. The theme "people want an SUV that parks well with others" was featured in a series of outdoor ads placed at bike racks and trail heads at 150 national parks and resorts. According to Brian Martin, CEO of Brand Connections Active Outdoor, which placed the ads, over 30 million impressions were made with hikers, bikers, and other outdoor-lovers.[16]

The advertising team carefully identifies the media a target market uses. Teenagers surf the Web and watch television. Only a small percentage reads newspapers and newsmagazines. Various market segments exhibit differences in when and how they view various media. Older African Americans watch television programs in patterns that are different from those of older Caucasians. Males watch more sports programs than females, and so forth.

In business-to-business markets, knowing the trade journals or business publications that various members of the buying center most likely read assists in the development of a print advertising campaign. Engineers, who tend to be the influencers, may have different media viewing habits than do vice presidents, who may be the deciders.

Although media buys are guided by the advertising agency and the client company, media companies typically make the purchases. A trend toward involving media companies at an earlier stage in the campaign process has evolved in recent years. Previously, most media companies were contacted after a campaign became ready or was nearly complete, with the specific task of purchasing media space or time. Instead of this approach, Procter & Gamble invited 40 media companies to a conference to solicit ideas about how to market company products and asked for new product suggestions. Companies such as Johnson & Johnson, Clorox, Kimberly-Clark, Verizon, and HP have enlisted media companies as strategic partners in developing advertising and marketing campaigns.[17] Media companies are being invited to participate in the strategy development stage because many have a good understanding of the target audience. They are able to provide valuable information to the creative staff about how to best reach the client's target market employing the primary media that target consumers use.

▲ Selecting the right media ensures that consumers who are the most likely to purchase Gold Bond Body Lotion will see this advertisement.

THE CREATIVE BRIEF

Typically, creatives work with a document prepared by the client and account executive called the *creative strategy* or *creative brief.* Although various forms exist, the basic components of a standard creative brief are provided in Figure 5.10. The creative takes the information provided to produce advertisements that convey the desired message. A quality creative brief can be extremely helpful. When prepared properly, the brief saves the agency considerable time and effort and results in a stronger advertising campaign for the client.

As mentioned earlier, ineffective communications with clients is a common difficulty agencies experience. The creative brief may part of the problem. A survey of senior executives of advertising agencies suggests that fewer than 40 percent of client briefs are clear.[18] Agency leaders reported that many briefs are weak in the areas of providing competitive information and statements about how the brand should be positioned within the competitive landscape. Consequently, attention should be given to clarifying these issues before creating advertisements.

⑨ How does a creative brief facilitate effective advertising?

The Objective

The first step in preparing the creative strategy is to identify the objective of the ad campaign. Some of the most common advertising objectives include:

- Increasing brand awareness
- Building brand image
- Increasing customer traffic
- Increasing retailer or wholesaler orders
- Responding to inquiries from end users and channel members
- Providing information

The creative reviews the main objective before designing advertisements. The objectives guide the advertising design and the choice of an executional framework. For instance, when increasing brand awareness is the goal, the *name* of the product will be prominently displayed in the advertisement. Building brand image normally results in the *actual product* being more prominently displayed.

• The objective • The support
• The target audience • The constraints
• The message theme

◄ **FIGURE 5.10**
The Creative Brief

▲ This advertisement for Playtex used additional target market profile information to help design a message directed to active teenagers and young women.

▼ An advertisement for Sub-Zero illustrating the message theme of keeping foods fresh.

The Target Audience

A creative then examines the target audience. An advertisement designed to persuade a business to inquire about new computer software will be different from a consumer advertisement created for the same company. The business advertisement focuses on the type of industry and a specific member of the buying center. The more detail that is known about the target audience, the easier it becomes for a creative to design an effective advertisement.

Target-market profiles that are too general are not helpful. Rather than specifying "males, ages 20 to 35," more specific information will be needed, such as "males, ages 20 to 35, college educated, and professionals." Other information, including hobbies, interests, opinions, and lifestyles, makes it possible to more precisely target an advertisement. The Playtex advertisement in this section was prepared for young females who enjoy playing sports and have active lifestyles. The additional information helped the creative design an advertisement that appealed to the right group of females.

The Message Theme

The message theme presents an outline of key idea(s) that the advertising program conveys. The message theme represents the benefit or promise the advertiser uses to reach consumers or businesses. The promise, or *unique selling point*, describes the major benefit the good or service offers customers. A message theme for an automobile could be oriented toward luxury, safety, fun, fuel efficiency, or driving excitement. A message theme for a hotel could focus on luxury, price, or unusual features, such as a hotel in Paris, France, noting the ease of access to all of the nearby tourist attractions. The message theme matches the medium selected, the target market, and the primary IMC message.[19]

In the advertisement for Sub-Zero refrigerators in this section, the message theme features the "freshness of food" being kept in the Sub-Zero refrigerator. This message targets consumers, but also may influence managers of restaurants, cafeterias, and catering services.

Message themes can be oriented toward either rational or emotional processes. A "left-brain" ad oriented toward the logical, rational side informs individuals using numbers, letters, words, and concepts. Left-brain advertising should be logical and factual, with a rational appeal. A number of logical features (size, price, special features) are part of the decision to buy a car. At the same time, many cars are purchased for emotional reasons. The right side of the brain contains emotions. It works with abstract ideas, images, and feelings. A car may be chosen for its color, sportiness, or other less rational reasons.

Most advertising focuses on either the right brain or the left brain. Advertising can also be effective by balancing the two sides. Rational, economic beings have difficulty defending the purchase of an expensive sports car such as a Porsche. Many product purchases are based on how a person feels about the good or service, combined with rational information.[20]

The Support

Support should be provided in the fourth component of the creative strategy. **Support** takes the form of facts that substantiate the message theme. When Aveeno products won "Best of Beauty" awards from *Allure* magazine, the *Allure* "Best of Beauty" seal was placed on the company's products. It was also used in company advertising to support Aveeno's claims of superiority. In the Pearle Vision advertisement in this section, various statements provide support. These include the idea that microTHINS are 30 percent thinner, 40 percent lighter, 4 times more scratch resistant, 10 times more impact resistant, antireflective, and have 99.9 percent UV protection. Supporting evidence allows creatives to design advertisements that attract attention to the materials that substantiate claims made about products.

The Constraints

Constraints are any legal and mandatory restrictions placed on advertisements. Constraints include legal protections for trademarks, logos, and copy registrations. Constraints also include disclaimers about warranties, offers, and claims. For warranties, a disclaimer specifies the conditions under which they will be honored. For example, tire warranties often state that they apply *under normal driving conditions with routine maintenance*, so that a person cannot ignore tire balancing and rotation and expect to get free new tires when the old ones wear out quickly. Disclaimer warranties notify consumers of potential hazards associated with products. Tobacco advertisements must contain a statement from the Surgeon General about the dangers of smoking and chewing tobacco. Disclaimers about offers spell out the terms of financing agreements, as well as when bonuses or discounts apply. Claims identify the exact nature of the statement made in the advertisement. This includes nutritional claims as well as statements about serving sizes and other information describing the product.

After these steps have been completed, the creative brief is ready. From this point forward, the message and the media match, and actual advertisements can be produced. Effective creative briefs take the overall IMC message and tailor it to a specific advertising campaign. This, in turn, gives the company a better chance of reaching customers with messages that return measurable results and help guarantee success. Recent research suggests that campaigns designed in 2 months or less have the greatest likelihood of being "highly effective." Those that take longer tend not to be as effective. The goal is to move forward without rushing. A campaign designed in 2 weeks or less is also likely to be ineffective.[21]

INTERNATIONAL IMPLICATIONS

Advertising management now involves major expenditures overseas. The top 100 global advertisers spent an average of 62 percent of advertising budgets outside

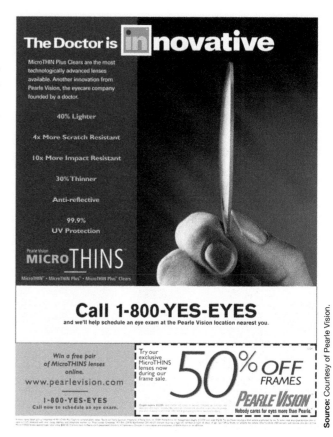

▲ This advertisement for Pearle Vision presents support information to substantiate the message claim.

▼ The Surgeon General's warning is an example of a constraint.

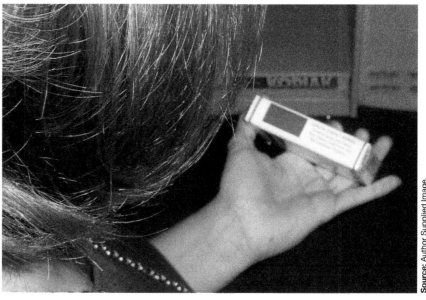

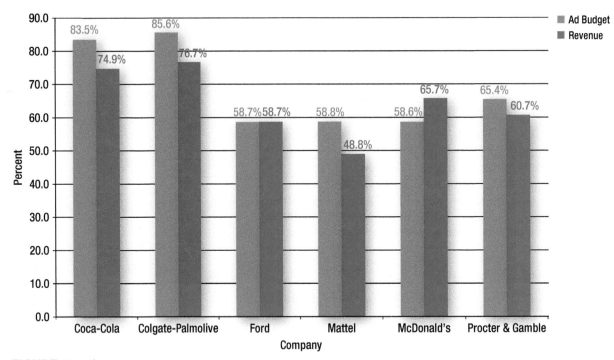

FIGURE 5.11 ▶
Non-U.S. Ad Budgets and Sales Revenues for Major Corporations

Source: Adapted from Laurel Wentz and Bradley Johnson, "Top 100 Global Advertisers Heap Their Spending Abroad," *Advertising Age,* http://adage.com/print?article_id=140723, November 30, 2009.

the United States. Figure 5.11 compares the non-U.S. advertising budget to non-U.S. sales revenue for six major corporations. As illustrated, Coca-Cola spends 83.5 percent of company advertising dollars outside the United States, where 74.9 percent of its total revenues are generated. Colgate-Palmolive spends 85.6 percent of its advertising dollars on non-U.S. ads and generates 76.7 percent of its revenues outside the United States. Data for Ford, Mattel, McDonald's, and Procter & Gamble are also provided.[22]

Two major differences emerge when advertising management is considered from an international perspective. The first is in regard to the process itself. The second concerns preparing international advertising campaigns.

The general processes used to prepare advertising campaigns are fairly uniform. Some of the most important differences are in the areas of availability of qualified advertising agencies and how those agencies are selected. For example, in many Asian cultures the beginning of a face-to-face meeting would include an exchange of gifts. Also, business cards have differing uses and meanings across cultures. In some countries, cards are only presented to highly trusted allies. In others, they are freely passed out. The marketing team in any company should carefully study the nuances of business meetings, including the use of formal titles, eye contact, who speaks first, and other variables, before beginning a relationship with an advertising agency in another country.

Agencies in other countries might not follow typical procedures such as a shootout or the preparation of a creative brief. Forms of preplanning research may also vary. In some countries, it is not possible to conduct the same types of research as in the United States and other Western cultures.

Advertising campaigns that are designed for an international audience require an understanding of the various languages and cultures that might be involved. In Europe, French, Spanish, Portuguese, Italian, and other languages would require translation and back-translation of advertising themes and messages to make certain the idea can be clearly presented in various countries. Media-selection processes may also require adjustment; some countries have state-run television networks and others place restrictions on what can be shown in an advertisement.

! INTEGRATED CAMPAIGNS IN ACTION

Oscar Mayer

Jane Hilk, senior vice president of marketing at Oscar Mayer, told the agency team at mcgarrybowen, "Oscar Mayer is everyday food that makes you feel good. It's about real joy, real moments. Living life and loving every minute of it." The ambition of the new campaign was to take Oscar Mayer to a place that is:

- Energetic
- Culturally relevant
- Contemporary
- Iconic
- Able to capture the spirit of the brand

Focus group and consumer research revealed several ideas that impacted the Oscar Mayer brand, which the agency termed the *brand idea.* The consumer insight was that the world is often too negative and uptight. You have to bring your own good times. The product category motivation was that consumers hunger for meal times that do more than just fill them up. That is where Oscar Mayer can make a brand difference. The company offers quality meats that never disappoint and always leave a smile. The brand idea, that Oscar Mayer is "good mood food," was born.

In producing the print ads, the goal of the agency was to capture real moments. The person in each photo never looks directly at the camera. The person should not be perfect. The person's hair may be slightly out of place, there might be a spot of mustard on the chin, and the ketchup on the hot dog looks natural. It was important that the photo not look stock or posed. Instead, it should portray the joy of the moment. The snapshot should capture real life, as people enjoy "good mood food."[23]

Several television commercials were also developed featuring the phrase "It doesn't get better than this," which matched the print and video ads, as well as the digital effort, "Mission to Spread Good Mood Food." The entire multimillion-dollar campaign was launched with three spots and a sponsorship of the *Golden Globes*, which was chosen because of the large number of people who watch the awards show. Jane Hilk

Source: Courtesy of Kraft Foods. Oscar Mayer is a registered trademark of Kraft foods and is used with permission.

▲ The goal of the Oscar Mayer print ads was to make consumers feel the moment.

noted, "It was an ideal setting to launch Oscar Mayer's new contemporary, energetic, look."[24]

Your instructor has additional information about the ads, visuals, and displays used in this campaign.

66 SUMMARY

Effective advertising requires matching a noticeable message with the appropriate media. This chapter reviews the advertising management process. Effective advertising occurs when the firm has a well-defined mission statement and targets its energies in the direction of creating goods or services to meet the needs of a target market.

Advertising management begins with deciding whether an in-house department should develop advertisements or whether an external advertising agency should be retained. When choosing an external agency, the company's leaders establish clear steps to lead to the optimal agency being selected. The steps include: (1) spelling out and prioritizing organizational goals, (2) carefully establishing quality selection criteria, (3) screening firms based on those criteria, (4) requesting references from firms that are finalists, (5) performing background checks, (6) requesting creative pitches, (7) making an on-site visit to get to know those in the agency, and (8) offering and finalizing a contract.

Common selection criteria used in selecting agencies include: (1) the size of the agency matching the size of the company, (2) relevant experience, (3) no conflicts of interest, (4) production capabilities, (5) quality creative capabilities, (6) suitable media-purchasing skills, (7) other services that can be rendered as needed, (8) client retention rates, and (9) a good chemistry between those in the company and those in the agency. Carefully utilizing these criteria increases the odds of a good match between the company and the agency will exist, which increases the chance of success.

Within the advertising agency, the account manager performs the functions of soliciting accounts, finalizing contracts, and selecting creatives to prepare advertising campaigns. Account executives are go-betweens who mediate between the agency and the client company. Account executives also help client organizations refine their IMC messages and programs.

Creatives prepare advertisements and are guided by the creative brief. This document spells out: (1) the objective of the promotional campaign, (2) the target audience, (3) the message theme, (4) the support, and (5) the constraints. The message theme is an outline of the key idea(s) that the program is supposed to convey. The constraints include logos, warranties, disclaimers, or legal statements that are part of various advertisements.

The creative, account executive, and company should agree about which media to use in a campaign. Media are selected based on costs, types of messages, target market characteristics, and other criteria. The creatives then complete the final elements of the ad, and the campaign is prepared.

Advertising management is an important ingredient in the success of an integrated marketing communications program. A quality ad that garners the attention of people in the target audience, makes a key memorable point, and moves buyers to action is difficult to prepare. At the same time, company officials and market account executives know that designing effective ads with tangible results is a challenging but necessary activity. It is important to go through every step of the process carefully to help the company achieve its marketing goals in both the short and long term.

KEY TERMS

message theme   An outline of key idea(s) the advertising campaign conveys.

leverage point   The key element in the advertisement that taps into, or activates, a consumer's personal value system (a value, idea, or concept).

appeal   The approach used to design the advertisement that attracts attention or presents information to consumers, through the use of humor, fear, sex, logic, or emotions.

executional framework   Method used to deliver the advertising message.

advertising management program   The process of preparing and integrating a company's advertising efforts with the overall IMC message.

crowdsourcing   Process of outsourcing the creative aspect of an advertisement to the public.

advertising campaign management   The process of preparing and integrating a specific advertising program in conjunction with the overall IMC message.

product-specific research   Research that identifies key product characteristics that become selling points.

consumer-oriented research   Research that is used to understand the context of a product's use.

focus group   A set of consumers or businesspeople who are retained to talk about a particular topic, product, or brand.

top-of-mind brands   The brands that quickly come to mind when consumers are asked to identify brands from a product category.

top choice   The first or second pick when a consumer reviews his or her evoked set of possible purchasing alternatives.

promotional campaign   Combining advertisements with other marketing efforts into a larger, more integrated effort revolving around a central idea or theme.

pulsating schedule of advertising   Continuous advertising with bursts of higher intensity (more ads in more media) during the course of the year.

flighting schedule of advertising   A schedule whereby companies present ads only during specific times and not at all during other times of the year.

continuous campaign schedule of advertising   When the company advertises in level amounts throughout the year.

support   The facts that substantiate the unique selling point of a creative brief.

constraints   The company, legal, and mandatory restrictions placed on advertisements. They include legal protection for trademarks, logos, and copy registrations.

REVIEW QUESTIONS

1. Describe the following terms: message theme, leverage point, appeal, and executional framework.

2. Define advertising management. What are the four main steps involved?

3. What four main company activities are involved in the advertising management process?

4. What is the relationship between advertising and the overall IMC process?

5. What factors influence the decision of whether to use an in-house advertising group or an external advertising agency?

6. Besides advertising agencies, what other types of organizations play roles in the communication process?

7. What steps should be taken in selecting an advertising agency?

8. What evaluation criteria should be used in selecting an advertising agency?

9. What is a creative pitch?

10. Describe the role of an advertising agency account executive.

11. Describe the role of the advertising creative.

12. Describe the role of a traffic manager.

13. Describe the role of an account planner.

14. What are the steps of an advertising campaign management process?

15. What are the two main forms of research for the purposes of creating advertisements?

16. What is a focus group, and how can such a group help to create more effective advertisements?

17. Describe the terms top of mind and top choice.

18. What elements are included in a creative brief?

CRITICAL THINKING EXERCISES

Discussion Questions

1. Pick up a magazine that you read on a regular basis. Examine 10 advertisements and identify the major selling point in each. Was the major selling idea clear, or was it difficult to ascertain?

2. Look through the ads in this chapter. Which ad to you like the best? Why? Which ad is the least appealing to you? Why? Discuss what makes a print ad appealing and what creates the opposite effect.

3. Review the responsibilities of each of the jobs under "Roles of Advertising Personnel." Which one is most appealing to you? Why? Which one is least appealing? Why?

4. Print off or open the textbook to Figure 5.9, the list of advertising goals. Create a table with three columns. In the first column, you will record the brand being advertised. In the second column, you will write down which advertising goal you think the ad was designed to meet. In the third column, you will assign a score based on your evaluation of each ad's effectiveness, with 10 being effective and 1

being completely ineffective. Once you have created the table, watch a 1-hour television program and record and evaluate every commercial you see. When you are finished, write a paragraph discussing which goals were used the most and which ads were the most effective at accomplishing their goal.

5. Follow the instructions given in question 4, but instead of a television program gather a group of 20 advertisements from a magazine. Make sure the ads are in a sequence and not ones that you randomly picked or chose.

6. Choose one of the following. Using the information in this chapter, prepare a creative brief. You can pick a brand from within the product category.
   a. Energy drink
   b. Frozen apple juice
   c. Fast-food restaurant
   d. Museum
   e. Dress shoes

INTEGRATED LEARNING EXERCISES

1. Making the decision to use an external advertising agency as opposed to an in-house program for advertising or some other aspect of the advertising function is difficult. Access the American Association of Advertising Agencies Web site at **www.aaaa.org**. From the "News and Views" section, examine articles that might help identify benefits of using

an advertising agency. What type of information is available at this Web site?

2. A number of agencies assist business organizations with integrated marketing communication programs. Whereas some firms try to provide a wide array of services, others are more

specialized. Access the following association Web sites. What type of information is available on each site? How would the information provided be useful in building an IMC program?

   a. International Social Media Association (**www.ismaconnects.org**)

   b. Promotion Marketing Association (**www.pmalink.org**)

   c. Outdoor Advertising Association of America (**www.oaaa.org**)

   d. Direct Marketing Association (**www.the-dma.org**)

3. Part of a communication marketing analysis includes understanding the media usage habits of consumers and their attitudes toward various media. An excellent source of information in Canada is the Media Awareness Network at **www.media-awareness.ca**. Review the types of information available at the Web site. Examine the news articles. What type of information is available at this Web site and how could it be used in developing an advertising campaign?

4. Many advertisers tend to direct ads toward the right side of the brain and develop advertisements based entirely on emotions, images, and pictures. Companies often advertise auto parts and tools with a scantily clad woman to attract the attention of men. The woman has nothing to do with the product, but garners attention. The rationale for using a sexy woman is that if consumers like her, they will like the product and then purchase that brand. Effective advertisements integrate elements from both the left side of the brain as well as the right. They contain elements that appeal to emotions but also have rational arguments. A laundry detergent can be advertised as offering the rational benefit of getting clothes cleaner but also contain the emotional promise that your mother-in-law will think more favorably of you. For each of the following Internet sites, discuss the balance of left-brain versus right-brain advertising appeal.

   a. Pier 1 Imports (**www.pier1.com**)

   b. Pig O' My Heart Potbellies (**www.potbellypigs.com**)

   c. Volkswagen of America (**www.vw.com**)

   d. Discount Cheerleading.com (**www.discountcheerleading.com**)

   e. Backcountry.com (**www.backcountry.com**)

5. You have been asked to select an advertising agency to handle an account for Red Lobster, a national restaurant chain. Your advertising budget is $30 million. Study the Web sites of the following advertising agencies. Follow the selection steps outlined in the chapter. Narrow the list down to two agencies and justify your decision. Then choose between the two agencies and justify your choice.

   a. The Richards Group (**www.richards.com**)

   b. Leo Burnett (**www.leoburnett.com**)

   c. BBDO Worldwide (**www.bbdo.com**)

   d. Lucas Design & Advertising (**www.aladv.com**)

   e. Grey Group (**www.grey.com**)

   f. DDB Worldwide Communications Group (**www.ddb.com**)

6. A marketing manager has been placed in charge of a new brand of jeans to be introduced into the market. The company's corporate headquarters are in Atlanta, and the firm's management team has already decided to use one of the local advertising agencies. Two primary objectives in choosing an agency are: (1) the agency must have the capability to develop a strong brand name and (2) the agency must be able to help with business-to-business marketing to place the jeans into retail stores. Type "advertising agencies in Atlanta" into your favorite search engine. Identify an initial list of six ad agencies. Follow the steps outlined in the chapter to narrow the list to two agencies. Then design a project for the agencies to prepare as part of an oral and written presentation to the company's marketing team.

STUDENT PROJECT

Creative Corner

Use the following creative brief for this exercise.

Creative Brief for Ford Motor Company	
Product:	Ford Mustang.
Objective:	To reverse lagging sales.
Target audience:	25- to 35-year-old consumers, split evenly between males and females, college educated, with annual incomes of approximately $40,000. Psychographically, the targeted market is a group known as individualists. They tend not to buy mainstream products. In automobile selection, they place greater emphasis on design elements, distinctiveness, and utility.
Message theme:	An automobile is like a fashion accessory. A car is selected because of the statement it makes to others.

1. As an account executive for an advertising agency, discuss the creative brief in terms of the completeness of the information provided and whether the objective is realistic. What additional information should Ford provide before a creative can begin working on the account?

2. The media planner for the Ford Mustang account suggests a media plan consisting of cable television, print advertising, Internet ads, and network advertising on Fox shows *Family Guy, House, The Wanda Sykes Show, The Simpsons*, and *American Idol.* Evaluate this media plan in light of the creative brief's objectives. Can these shows reach the target audience? What information does a creative and the account executive want from the media planner before starting work on actual commercials?

3. From the viewpoint of the creative assigned to this account, do the creative brief and the media plan (see question 2) contain sufficient information to design a series of advertisements? What, if any, additional information is necessary?

4. Using the information provided in the creative brief, prepare a magazine advertisement. Which magazines might match the target audience?

CASE 1   NAME YOUR HERO

In the Fall 2009 holiday season, the crowded fantasy and gaming world gained several products designed to entice new sets of buyers. The entire Guitar Hero brand faced stiff competition from other gaming products. One highly touted release was the new The Beatles: Rock Band game released early in the season. Other competitors included the Madden NFL product line and the Halo 3: ODST product.

In response, three new Guitar Hero titles were released: Guitar Hero 5, Band Hero, and DJ Hero. Each focused on a specific set of players.

Guitar Hero 5, the most recent version of the original product released in 2005, expands on the innovative technology that allows users to play real songs, real chords, and an almost-real guitar, integrating music, interactivity, and gameplay in a totally new way. The game offers the opportunity to play lead guitar, bass guitar, or drums or to sing the vocals of a variety of tunes. The primary attraction remains the ability to play great guitar riffs from the past. Guitar Hero 5 drew grumbles from Nirvana and Kurt Cobain fans, who did not like the intrusion into the band's well-established image.

Band Hero is a more family-oriented product. The music was selected to attract females and younger "tween" users. At one point, the opening page of the Guitar Hero Web site featured a music video by the youthful Taylor Swift, the most recent CMA Music Awards "Best Artist" winner. Many industry observers believe that Band Hero's design is an obvious response to The Beatles: Rock Band, which has many similar features.

The final new entry, DJ Hero, seeks to capture the hip-hop/rap connoisseur. The game features a turntable. According to Game Hero CEO Dan Rosensweig, "It's really cool. It's got 100 songs and 94 mixes that no one has ever mixed before. This is going to be one of those transformational games. You have this generation's iconic piece of equipment—the turntable—and some fantastic mixes that really give you a chance to release your inner DJ. I think that's going to be one of the hottest selling games this holiday season."

Additional trends should also be considered. When asked about mobile gaming on handheld devices, Rosensweig replied, "We're going to focus on making sure that our consumers can access games wherever it makes sense for them to access it—mobile is one of those environments which is always with you. And obviously, we're taking a look at that."

Part of the challenge in promoting both ongoing and new games is finding ways to capture the attention of the target audience. In the case of the Guitar Hero brand, consumers have somewhat differing viewing and media habits. Guitar Hero 5's audience is likely to be more of a classic music, hard rock crowd; Band Hero needs to reach younger females and families; and DJ Hero should find ways to access the hip-hop crowd.

Rosensweig notes, "Like anything else, we have to continue to remain fresh. You have to really understand that technology makes the game more interesting, more expansive, and more fun." He believes the future is bright. "I think we have an opportunity to redefine the way people interact with music. They want to listen to music, they want to play music, they want to contribute music, they want to create music. The more people and consoles are connected, the more opportunity we have to remain in consumers' lives."

1. Should Guitar Hero retain an advertising agency or develop its own ads in-house? Justify your answer.

2. If Guitar Hero's marketing team retains an advertising agency, what type should it be, and which decision variables should guide the choice?

3. Search online for five advertising agencies that you think would be a good fit for Guitar Hero. Choose the best one. Justify your choice.

4. What type of advertising planning and research should be used for each Guitar Hero product?

5. Should the marketing team develop one set of advertisements for each Guitar Hero product, or an overall campaign for the entire company?

6. Should the company use a pulsating, flighting, or continuous schedule of advertising? Explain.

Sources: Kim Thai, "'Guitar Hero' Amps up for the Holidays," *CNNMoney.com* (http://money.cnn.com/2009/10/23/technology/guitar_dj_hero_activision. fortune/index.ht, accessed November 17, 2009), October 23, 2009; www.guitarhero.com (accessed November 17, 2009); Seth Colter Wells, "Nirvana Heaven and Hell," *Newsweek.com* (www.newsweek.com/id/220978, accessed November 17, 2009), November 3, 2009.

Source: Getty Images–Thinkstock.

▲ Guitar Hero 5 allows users to play real songs, real chords, and an almost-real guitar.

CASE 2 ADVERTISING STEW

Luis Arroyo was about to begin the most exciting job assignment of his life. He had been named the brand manager for the Dinty Moore Beef Stew line of products, which is sold by Hormel Foods. His first assignment was to develop an advertising campaign for the entire line, which would be produced in the summer. The ads were scheduled to run on a pulsating schedule, with the first burst commencing in October.

The Dinty Moore brand has been in existence since 1935. Canned products in the line include Beef Stew, Chicken & Dumplings, Chicken Noodle, Chicken Stew, Meatball Stew, and Turkey Stew. A second, current set of products are microwaveable, featuring Beef Stew (7.5 ounce cup), Beef Stew (10 ounce tray), Chicken & Dumplings (7.5 ounce cup), Noodles & Chicken (7.5 ounce cup), Rice with Chicken (7.5 ounce cup), and Scalloped Potatoes & Ham (7.5 ounce cup).

The Dinty Moore page of Hormel's Web site states that its name is, "Synonymous not only with beef stew, but with a convenient and satisfying meal. Through innovations in packaging, we've made it even easier for you to enjoy by offering cups and trays for microwave cooking. And while convenience is definitely the order of the day, Dinty Moore stew meets the standards of contemporary shoppers because it has no preservatives and only 240 calories per 8-ounce serving."

Health consciousness is a major trend in the food market. Consumers are concerned about the fat, sodium, and calorie content of the foods they purchase. The Dinty Moore line clearly meets standards set by the Food and Drug Administration; however, it is possible that food producers will be required to provide more information about products in the future.

The primary competitors in the canned beef stew marketplace can be placed into four major categories:

- Direct competitors
- Substitute products
- Other foods made at home
- Restaurants

Direct competitors include Castleberry's and Armour. Both companies offer directly competing cans of stew as well as others that might compete with the Dinty Moore line. For example, Armour offers a line of chili and chili beans. Castleberry sells barbeque pork and canned tamales through its American Originals line.

Substitute products are sold by Campbell's and other soup manufacturers. Soup can easily be substituted for stew. Also, a series of private label stews are available.

Home cooking presents an additional source of competition. Many health food trends include cooking at home with natural ingredients. Many consumers now enjoy creating meals at home as a form of social activity and relaxation.

Many restaurants vend products that compete with both homemade and canned stew. The most threatening competitors are restaurants featuring home-style, hearty foods.

▲ Dinty Moore Stew meets the standards of contemporary shoppers because it has no preservatives and only 240 calories per 8-ounce serving.

Luis decided that he needed more information before moving forward with the advertising campaign. He wanted to know more about the role price plays in purchasing decisions as well as consumers' perceptions of the quality of the Dinty Moore line as compared to Armour and Castleberry's. He also sought information about consumer promotions, especially coupons and price-off programs. He also wanted to investigate possibilities for cooperative advertising with grocery stores as well as tie-ins with other food products. He wanted to begin a new era in his company, where Dinty Moore moved to the strongest position in the marketplace as the top of mind and top choice brand.

1. Should Luis look to hire an external advertising agency or perform most of the tasks in-house? Why?

2. If an external agency is chosen, what relevant experiences would be most helpful to Luis and the Dinty Moore brand?

3. What types of advertising planning and research should be conducted to identify Dinty Moore's most loyal customers and potential new customers?

4. Design a creative brief for the upcoming Dinty Moore advertising campaign.

5. Using the list of advertising agencies provided under question 5 of the Integrated Learning Exercises and the procedure outlined in this chapter, choose an outside advertising agency for the Dinty Moore account. Justify your selection.

Sources: www.hormelfoods.com, www.castelberrys.com, and www.pinnaclefoodscorp.com (accessed January 4, 2008).

CHAPTER 3

Campaign Planning 1

Strategic Research

CHAPTER KEY POINTS

1. What are the basic types of strategic research and how are they used?
2. What are the most common research methods used in advertising?
3. What are the key challenges facing advertising researchers?

Cheesy Fun. It's Not Just for Kids.

What do you think of when you think of Cheetos? The crunch and maybe orange fingers? A product that's been marketed to kids for its 60-year history, Cheetos is a brand long-associated with fun.

But it wasn't so funny when competitors Goldfish and Cheez-It started spending double the amount that Cheetos did on media.

The competitive problem was complicated by some social responsibility issues. Growing concerns about childhood obesity and the ethical concern of marketing to kids were serious challenges to Pepsico/Frito Lay, which is Cheetos' parent company. A commitment to be socially responsible led Pepsico to voluntarily sign the Children's Food & Beverage Advertising Initiative in 2007, which restricted advertising of not-so-healthy foods to children under age 12.

The result? Cheetos chose to abandon its position as a favorite kids' snack and target a new audience. That's a scary new strategy for any brand. It started its quest to find a new direction by setting specific objectives to help focus its research efforts:

1. Discover if an alternate adult target could be identified for Cheetos.
2. Develop a better understanding of the Cheetos' consumption experience.
3. Understand the overlaps between kids and the new adult target so that existing brand equities could be carried forward.
4. Develop and evaluate compelling new message strategies for the new target audience.

Findings from this research might surprise you. Even though Cheetos had been marketed as a children's snack, adults ate them too. Several studies revealed fascinating insights that eventually led to a new campaign for adults.

One study investigated attitudes of adults and children (ages 10 to 13) who claimed to be Cheetos brand lovers. Interestingly, both the adults and the kids communicated feelings of stress. A key insight from the research revealed that the playfulness associated with Cheetos could help these consumers escape some of their daily pressures.

Researchers also listened to what Cheetos fans said about the experience of eating Cheetos and watched how they acted when they ate Cheetos. Group members loved eating them and licking their fingers as if to say they were looking for permission *not* to act their age or conform to expected adult behavior.

Cheetos spokes-animal Chester Cheetah related well to kids. But would he appeal to adults? To test this idea, someone dressed up in a Chester Cheetah costume and walked the hot spots in San Francisco. Grown adults embraced the mascot by hugging and posing for pictures with him, proving this icon was up to the job no matter what the age of the Cheetos' fan.

Another study asked 1,000 adults about their attitudes to play. The respondents answered questions about when they played hooky from work and when they last skinny dipped and so on. Findings from this survey were telling. About half of those labeled "very playful" were most likely to eat a lot of Cheetos, and the "least playful" were also least likely to consume the product.

From literature on cultural trends, the agency was able to define an emerging group of people who were likely to be passionate for Cheetos. A book by Christopher Noxon[1] identified a new breed of adults called "rejuveniles." These are the folks who think playing isn't just for kids. Yankelovich, a leading consumer research firm, confirmed the emerging trend of adults who liked being just a tad naughty and child-like regardless of their age. These people identified with brands such as Disney, Wii, Lego, and, not surprisingly, Cheetos.

Cheetos' agency, Goodby, Silverstein & Partners synthesized information from these research efforts and came up with a Big Idea. The new adult target, "rejuveniles," could "bend the rules with mischievous fun." The tone of the campaign was edgy fun for adults rather than the sweet fun that had been used for kids. The big idea played out in a campaign that might not appeal to everyone, but it sure did to the target audience. Three TV spots illustrated how the inner child could be released with pranks involving Cheetos. One spot featured a woman at a laundromat who'd been berated by another woman. To get revenge and encouraged by mascot Chester Cheetah, the young woman put a bag of orange Cheetos in the other woman's white load of wash.

The online component of the campaign, OrangeUnderground.com, encouraged adults to play mischievous pranks with the orange snacks by creating Random Acts of Cheetos. The only rule: the pranks had to be "benign and harmless, never malicious or hurtful." Cheetos partnered with Comedy Central for a promotion that encouraged fans to make mischief, video it, and post it to the website. The interactive website itself features oddball humor with games, the Legend of Cheetocorn, a giant Cheetos pet, and all sorts of crazy stuff.

The ad lessons from this Cheetos story? Sometimes what looks like bad news about your product can lead to new opportunities that research can help you identify. A more important lesson: stay true to your brand. To see if the lessons learned from research paid off, go to the end of the chapter and read the *It's a Wrap* feature.

Sources: "Advertising Research Foundation Case Study: 'Mischievous Fun with Cheetos,'" *http://thearf.org/assets/ogilvy-09;* Bob Garfield, "Cheetos Ads That Promote 'Random Acts' Are Irresponsible," May 26, 2008, *http://adage.com;* Steve Centrillo and Dave Tutin, "Cheetos Offers How-to-Guide for Reaching Look-at-Me Gen," January 28, 2008, *www.brandweek.com;* Eric Newman, "Strategy: Cheetos on the Prowl for Adult Consumers," January 7, 2008, *www.brandweek.com;* Bruce Horovitz, "Don't Worry, Buy Happy: Cheerful Stuff Is Selling Well," March 30, 2009, *www.usatoday.com.*

In our previous chapters on how to plan marketing communication that has a real impact on consumers, we noted that marketers such as Frito-Lay need to do brand, market, and consumer research. This research effort becomes the foundation for objective setting, segmenting the market and targeting the audience, and developing the brand communication plan. So now that we understand the need for research, let's talk about how to do it. This chapter presents some key research concepts, beginning with an explanation of the two most basic categories of research, primary and secondary; the basic categories of research tools, quantitative and qualitative; and the most common research methods used in planning marketing communication. We also discuss the key challenges facing advertising researchers.

HOW DO YOU FIND CONSUMER INSIGHTS?

In the previous chapter we talked about insight—in fact, an effective marketing communication program is totally dependent on consumer insight. Know your customer—and listening is the first step in understanding customers.

What does that mean? It means that brand strategy begins with consumer research—the tools of listening. Consumer research investigates the topics we discussed in the previous chapter on segmentation and targeting, including attitudes, motivations, perceptions, and behaviors. The research findings then lead to planning decisions based on these insights. But first we must understand the principles and practices of advertising research and how to listen effectively to consumers.

In-house researchers or independent research companies hired from outside the company usually handle a client's market and consumer research. The objective at all stages of the planning process is to answer the question: What do we need to know in order to make an informed decision? Here are the various types of research used in planning advertising and marketing communication, such as the Cheetos campaign:

- **Market research** compiles information about the product, the product category, competitors, and other details of the marketing environment that will affect the development of advertising strategy.
- **Consumer research** identifies people who are in the market for the product in terms of their characteristics, attitudes, interests, and motivations. Ultimately, this information is used to decide who the targeted audience for the advertising should be. In an integrated marketing communication (IMC) plan, the consumer research also acquires information about all the relevant stakeholders and their points of contact with the brand.
- **Advertising research** focuses on all elements of advertising, including message development research, media planning research, evaluation, and information about competitors' advertising. **IMC research** is similar, except that it is used to assemble information needed in planning the use of a variety of marketing communication tools. IMC is particularly concerned with the interaction of multiple messages from a variety of sources to present the brand consistently.
- **Strategic research** uncovers critical information that becomes the basis for strategic planning decisions for both marketing and marketing communication. In advertising, this type of research covers all of the factors and steps that lead to the creation of message strategies and media plans. Think of strategic research as collecting all relevant background information needed to make a decision on advertising and marketing communication strategy. The importance of finding an adult target audience who appreciated having fun was important to the Cheetos campaign.

Knowledge about consumers' needs and wants is at the heart of all marketing communication plans. The foundation for all strategic decisions about segmentation, targeting, and positioning is consumer research.

In another example, whether you knew it or not, you were engaged in strategic research when you looked for an

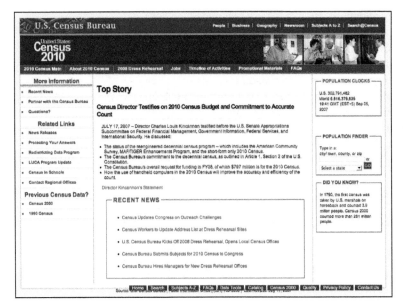

Demographic information, such as that available from the U.S. Census Bureau, is fundamental to marketing and communication planning.

Source: *www.census.gov/ 2010census.*

acceptable college to attend. You conducted market research (what information is available?), strategic research (what factors are most important in making a decision and how do the schools stack up?), and evaluative research (how will I know I made the best decision?). An advertising plan goes through similar stages of development with research as the first step.

What Are the Basic Types of Research?

New advertising assignments always begin with some kind of informal or formal background research into the marketing situation. This is called *secondary research*, and we'll compare it with *primary research*, which is original research conducted by the company or brand.

Secondary Research Background research that uses available published information about a topic is **secondary research.** When advertising people get new accounts or new assignments, they start by reading everything they can find on the product, company, industry, and competition: sales reports, annual reports, complaint letters, and trade articles about the industry. They are looking for important facts and key insights. This kind of research is called secondary, not because it is less important, but because it has been collected and published by someone else.

A typical advertising campaign might be influenced, directly or indirectly, by information from many sources, including in-house agencies and outside research suppliers. The use of secondary information for the Cheetos case—finding the information about the "rejuvenile" market in Christopher Noxon's book—underscores the importance of reading widely.

Here are a few of the more traditional sources of secondary information that are available to advertisers doing backgrounding:

- *Government Organizations* Governments, through their various departments, provide an astonishing array of statistics that can greatly enhance advertising and marketing decisions. Many of the statistics come from census records on the population's size, geographic distribution, age, income, occupation, education, and ethnicity. As we explained in Chapter 5, U.S. Census Bureau demographic information of this kind is fundamental to decision making about advertising targets and market segmentation. An advertiser cannot aim its advertising at a target audience without knowing that audience's size and major dimensions. In addition to census information, other government agencies generate reports that help advertisers make better decisions, such as the *Survey of Current Business* from the U.S. Department of Commerce (*www.bea.gov/scb*).
- *Trade Associations* Many industries support trade associations—professional organizations whose members all work in the same field—that gather and distribute information of interest to association members. For instance, the American Frozen Food Institute or the Game Manufacturers Council are both organizations that assist members in conducting their business. The trade associations for marketing communication include the American Association of Advertising Agencies (AAAA), which issues reports that help ad agencies monitor their performance and keep tabs on competitors; the Radio Advertising Bureau publishes *Radio Facts,* an overview of the commercial U.S. radio industry; the Account Planning Group (APG) conducts seminars and training sessions for account planners; and the American Association for Public Opinion Research (AAPOR) serves the professional needs of opinion researchers.
- *Secondary Research Suppliers* Because of the overwhelming amount of information available through secondary research, specialized suppliers gather and organize that information around specific topic areas for other interested parties. Key secondary research suppliers are FIND/SVP, Off-the-Shelf Publications, Dialog Information Services, Lexis-Nexis, and Dow Jones' Factiva.

• *Secondary Information on the Internet* For any given company, you're bound to find a website where you can learn about the company's history and philosophy of doing business, check out its complete product line, and discover who runs the company. These sites offer credible information for account planners and others involved in market research. Other sources of Internet information are blog sites and chat rooms where you can learn about people's reactions to brands and products. There are also many industry-related sites for marketing that report on research, essays, and best practices:

BrandEra (*www.brandera.com*) offers information by product category.

MarketPerceptions (*http://marketperceptions.com*) represents a research company that specializes in health care research. The site has information about its focus group capabilities.

Forrester Research (*www.forrester.com*) provides industry research into technology markets.

Greenbook.org (*www.greenbook.org*) is a worldwide directory of marketing research focus group suppliers.

Cluetrain (*www.cluetrain.com*) publishes new ways to find and share innovative marketing information and ideas.

Primary Research   Information that is collected for the first time from original sources is called **primary research.** To obtain primary research, companies and their agencies do their own tracking and monitoring of their customers' behavior. An example of a company that took on its own research is Perdue Farms and its classic "tough man" campaign. In contemporary times, companies usually hire specialized firms to do this type of research.

In another example of a company doing its own primary research, Toyota undertook a huge two-year study of ultra-rich consumers in the United States to better market its upscale Lexus brand. A team of nine Lexus employees from various departments was designated the "super-affluent team" and sent on the road to interview wealthy car buyers about why they live where they do, what they do for enjoyment, what brands they buy, and how they feel about car makes and models. One surprising finding was that these consumers don't just buy a car, they buy a fleet of cars because they have multiple homes and offices.[2]

Primary research suppliers (the firms clients hire) specialize in interviewing, observing, recording, and analyzing the behavior of those who purchase or influence the purchase of a particular good or service. The primary research supplier industry is extremely diverse. Companies range from A.C. Nielsen, the huge international tracker of TV viewing habits, which employs more than 45,000 workers in the United States alone, to several thousand entrepreneurs who conduct focus groups and individual interviews, prepare reports, and provide advice on specific advertising and marketing problems for individual clients.

Many advertising agencies subscribe to large-scale surveys conducted by the Simmons Market Research Bureau (SMRB) or by Mediamark Research, Inc. (MRI). These two organizations survey large samples of American consumers (approximately 30,000 for each survey) and ask questions about the consumption, possession, or use of a wide range of products, services, and media. The products and services covered in the MRI survey range from toothbrushes and dental floss to diet colas, camping equipment, and theme parks.

Both SMRB and MRI conduct original research and distribute their findings to their clients. The resulting reports are intended primarily for use in media planning, but because these surveys are so comprehensive, they also can be mined for unique consumer information. Through a computer program called Golddigger, for example, an MRI subscriber can select a consumer target and ask the computer to find all other products and services and all of the media that members of the target segment use. This profile provides a vivid and detailed description of the target as a person—just the information creative teams need to help them envision their audiences. To give you an idea of what the media data look like, check out Figure 6.1 for a sample MRI report of the types of TV programs adults ages 18 to 34 watch.

CLASSIC

"It takes a tough man to make a tender chicken" was the signature line for a long-running campaign that began in 1971 for Perdue Farms. It featured the owner, Frank Perdue, as the plain-spoken farmer who cared about the quality of his chickens. Scali, McCabe, Sloves was the agency behind the campaign that created the first recognizable brand for an unlikely commodity product—chickens. But the reason the campaign was successful wasn't just the iconic, perhaps ironic, "tough man" line, but rather Frank Perdue's knowledge of his market. When he decided in the 1960s to eliminate brokers and sell directly to stores, he spent months on the road talking to butchers about what they wanted in chickens and identified 25 quality factors. Then he modified his operations to produce chickens that delivered on those 25 factors—a tough man who was obsessed with tender chickens.

Base: Adults	Total U.S. 000	Respondent 18–34 1-Person Household				Respondent 18–34 and Married, no children				Respondent 18–34 and Married, Youngest Child <6				Respondent 18–34 and Married Youngest Child 6+			
		A 000	B % Down	C % Across	D Index	A 000	B % Down	C % Across	D Index	A 000	B % Down	C % Across	D Index	A 000	B % Down	C % Across	D Index
All Adults	184274	5357	100.0	2.9	100	7559	100.0	4.1	100	18041	100.0	9.8	100	4978	100.0	2.7	100
Program-Types: Average Show																	
Adven/Sci Fi/West-Prime	19969	590	11.0	3.0	102	875	11.6	4.4	107	2303	12.8	11.5	118	694	13.9	3.5	129
Auto Racing-Specials	6590	*226	4.2	3.4	118	*242	3.2	3.7	90	634	3.5	9.6	98	*251	5.0	3.8	141
Awards-Specials	16490	397	7.4	2.4	83	514	6.8	3.1	76	1576	8.7	9.6	98	*451	9.1	2.7	101
Baseball Specials	28019	806	15.0	2.9	99	1128	14.9	4.0	98	2671	14.8	9.5	97	*506	10.2	1.8	67
Basketball-Weekend-College	7377	*222	4.1	3.0	104	*244	3.2	3.3	81	531	2.9	7.2	74	*183	3.7	2.5	92
Basketball Specials-College	17096	529	9.9	3.1	106	694	9.2	4.1	99	1459	8.1	8.5	87	*423	8.5	2.5	92
Basketball Specials-Pro.	32470	1057	19.7	3.3	112	1369	18.1	4.2	103	3128	17.3	9.6	98	886	17.8	2.7	101
Bowling-Weekend	16808	312	5.8	1.9	654	744	9.8	4.4	108	1476	8.2	8.8	90	*386	78	2.3	85
Comedy/Variety	26254	930	17.4	3.5	122	1150	15.2	4.4	107	3257	18.1	12.4	127	999	20.1	3.8	141
Daytime Dramas	7621	*192	3.6	2.5	87	*287	3.8	3.8	92	845	4.7	11.1	113	*343	6.9	4.5	167
Daytime Game Shows	7747	*97	1.8	1.3	43	*194	2.6	2.5	61	734	4.1	9.5	97	*235	4.7	3.0	112
Documen/Information-Prime	22514	532	9.9	2.4	81	504	6.7	2.2	55	1739	9.6	7.7	79	*454	9.1	2.0	75
Early Morning News	12226	280	5.2	2.3	79	*429	5.7	3.5	86	1065	5.9	8.7	89	*330	6.6	2.7	100
Early Morning Talk/Info/News	14681	258	4.8	1.8	60	580	77	4.0	96	1291	7.2	8.8	90	*268	5.4	1.8	68
Early Eve. Netwk News-M-F	25946	596	11.1	2.3	79	836	11.1	3.2	79	1822	10.1	7.0	72	*594	11.9	2.3	85
Early Eve. Netwk News-Wknd	11338	*197	3.7	1.7	60	*208	2.8	1.8	45	795	4.4	7.0	72	*187	3.8	1.6	61
Entertainment Specials	19630	408	76	2.1	71	701	9.3	3.6	87	1719	9.5	8.8	89	*494	9.9	2.5	93
Feature Films-Prime	17232	371	6.9	2.2	74	*538	7.1	3.1	76	1209	6.7	70	72	*475	9.5	2.8	102
Football Bowl Games-Specials	13322	369	6.9	2.8	95	*381	5.0	2.9	70	1512	8.4	11.3	116	*245	4.9	1.8	68
Football Pro.-Specials	44804	1471	27.5	3.3	113	1766	23.4	3.9	96	4555	25.2	10.2	104	1104	22.2	2.5	91
General Drama-Prime	19880	581	10.8	2.9	101	571	76	2.9	70	2095	11.6	10.5	108	*555	11.1	2.8	103
Golf	5161	*102	1.9	2.0	68	*152	2.0	2.9	72	*324	1.8	6.3	64	*15	.3	.3	11
Late Evening Netwk News Wknd	5146	*146	2.7	2.8	98	*114	1.5	2.2	54	*293	1.6	5.7	58	*104	2.1	2.0	75
Late Night Talk/Variety	9590	313	5.8	3.3	112	*297	3.9	3.1	75	1009	5.6	10.5	107	*198	4.0	2.1	76
News-Specials	14508	234	4.4	1.6	55	510	6.7	3.5	86	1297	7.2	8.9	91	*212	4.3	1.5	54
Pageants-Specials	22025	439	8.2	2.0	69	952	12.6	4.3	105	2503	13.9	11.4	116	547	11.0	2.5	92
Police Docudrama	23575	726	13.6	3.1	106	1179	15.6	5.0	122	2309	12.8	9.8	100	731	14.7	3.1	115
Pvt Det/Susp/Myst/Pol.-Prime	28183	673	12.6	2.4	82	763	10.1	2.7	66	1739	9.6	6.2	63	*493	9.9	1.7	65
Situation Comedies-Prime	19097	598	11.2	3.1	108	919	12.2	4.8	117	2737	15.2	14.3	146	688	13.8	3.6	133
Sports Anthologies-Weekend	4847	*218	4.1	4.5	155	*232	3.1	4.8	117	*403	2.2	8.3	85	*108	2.2	2.2	82
Sunday News/Interview	5809	*70	1.3	1.2	41	*116	1.5	2.0	49	*214	1.2	3.7	38	*97	1.9	1.7	62
Syndicated Adult General	10444	*271	5.1	2.6	89	462	6.1	4.4	108	766	4.2	7.3	75	*221	4.4	2.1	78
Tennis	10033	338	6.3	3.4	116	380	5.0	3.8	92	826	4.5	8.2	84	*105	2.1	1.0	39

FIGURE 6.1

MRI Consumer Media Report

This MRI report breaks down the 18–34 age market into four market segments based on size of household and age of children, if any, and describes their television viewing patterns. Here's a question: Where would you advertise to reach single adults in the 18–34 category? First look at the Index column under that category heading and find the two highest percentages. Then, for each high rating, look across to column A and determine the size of that group. As a point of comparison, do the same analysis for the Married with the Youngest Child over 6 category. How do the two groups differ in the television viewing patterns?

Source: Mediamark Research, Inc.

Quantitative Research   Primary research can be both quantitative and qualitative. **Quantitative research** delivers numerical data such as number of users and purchases, their attitudes and knowledge, their exposure to ads, and other market-related information. The MRI page is an example of data obtained through quantitative research. It also provides information on reactions to advertising and motivation to purchase, sometimes called *purchase intent*. Quantitative methods that investigate the responses of large numbers of people are useful in testing ideas to determine if their market is large enough or if most people really say or behave in a certain way.

Two primary characteristics of quantitative research are (1) large sample sizes, typically from 100 to 1,000 people, and (2) random sampling. The most common quantitative research methods include surveys and studies that track such things as sales and opinions. Quantitative research is usually designed either to accurately count something, such as **sales levels,** or to predict something, such as attitudes. To be predictive, however, this type of research must follow careful scientific procedures. The Cheetos campaign used a study with a sample of 1,000 adults to find out about their frequency of game playing in order to correlate that information with their levels of Cheetos consumption.

One of the biggest problems in using quantitative methods to study consumer decision processes is that consumers are often unable to articulate the reasons they do what they do because their reasons may not fit into answers provided in a survey. Furthermore, most people aren't tuned in to their own thoughts and thinking process so that they are comfortable saying yes or no or checking a space on a rating scale. Respondents also have a tendency to give the answers that they think the researcher wants to hear. These are all reasons why qualitative research has become much more important in brand communication in the last 20 years. It offers the ability to probe and move beyond the sometimes superficial responses to a survey.

Qualitative Research   The goal of qualitative research methodologies, therefore, is to move beyond the limitations of what consumers can explain in words or in responses to preplanned questions. **Qualitative research** provides insight into the underlying reasons for how consumers behave and why. Common qualitative research methods include such tools as observation, ethnographic studies, in-depth interviews, and case studies. They trade large sample sizes and scientific predictions for greater depth of insight. These exploratory research tools are useful for probing and gaining explanations and understanding of such questions as these:

* What type of features do customers want?
* What are the motivations that lead to the purchase of a product?
* What do our customers think about our advertising?
* How do consumers relate to the brand? What are their emotional links to the brand?

Qualitative methods often are used early in the process of developing a brand communication plan or message strategy for generating insights, as well as questions and hypotheses for additional research. They are also good at confirming hunches, ruling out bad approaches and questionable or confusing ideas, and giving direction to the message strategy. However, because qualitative research is typically done with small groups, researchers cannot project their findings to the larger population.

Rather than drawing conclusions, qualitative research is used to answer the question why, as well as generate hypotheses that can be tested with quantitative methods.[3] As Sally Reinman, worldwide market planner at Saatchi & Saatchi, wrote for this book, research is more than numbers. She explains:

> Research processes are more varied and exciting than ever before. Examples include asking consumers to draw pictures, create collages, and produce home videos to show how they use a product.
>
> As consumers around the world become better informed and more demanding, advertisers that target different cultures need to find the "commonalities" (or common ground) among consumer groups from these cultures. Research for Toyota's sports-utility vehicle (SUV), the RAV 4, showed that consumers in all the targeted countries had three common desires: They wanted an SUV to have style, safety, and economy.
>
> To find these commonalities, I work with experts to learn the cultural meaning of codes and symbols that people use to communicate. The experts I work with include cultural and

Principle
Quantitative research investigates the attitudes, opinions, and behaviors of large numbers of people in order to make conclusions that can be generalized to the total population; qualitative research provides insight into how and why consumers think and behave.

Principle
Quantitative research can be used to draw conclusions about how much and how often; qualitative research answers questions about why and generates questions for quantitative methods.

cognitive anthropologists, psychologists, interior decorators, and Indian storytellers. Anyone who can help me understand consumers and the consumer decision-making process is fair game.

Experimental Research Tightly controlled scientific studies are sometimes used to puzzle out how people think and respond to messages and incentives. **Experimental research** is designed using formal hypothesis-testing techniques that compare different message treatments and how people react to them. The idea is to control for all factors except the one being tested; if there is a change in the results, then the researcher can conclude that the variable being tested caused the difference. Experimental research is used to test marketing factors as well as advertising appeals and executions in such areas as product features and design, price, and various creative ideas.

Do your professors and instructors talk about the research they conduct? Here's an example of one professor's research about cigarette advertising that has practical implications for the tobacco industry and policy makers. It tests the idea that cigarette advertising can prime (or prepare) teens to think that smoking is cool. The *A Matter of Principle* box explains how this researcher used experimental studies to determine the impact of advertising on behavior.

Sometimes in experimental research the measurements are electronically recorded using such instruments as MRI or EEG machines or eye-scan tracking devices. Electrodes can be used to monitor heart rate, pulse, and skin temperature to determine if people have a physical response to a message that they may not be able to put in words. Emotional responses, in particular, are hard to verbalize but may be observable using these types of sensors. Hewlett-Packard Company, for example, wired a group of volunteers with electrodes to see how they reacted to photos of people smiling. The study found that there were obvious differences in brain activity in people looking at photos of smiling people, particularly pictures of children smiling.

A MATTER OF PRINCIPLE

Does Advertising Make Smoking Cool?

Cornelia (Connie) Pechmann, *Professor of Marketing, University of California, Irvine*

In 1991, I began a program of research on tobacco-use prevention through advertising and the mass media. I wondered how often people saw advertisements for products shortly before experiencing the products. It occurred to me that advertising exposure and product experience were perhaps most likely to occur concurrently in the case of cigarette advertising and encounters with smokers. In 1991, cigarette advertising on billboards was ubiquitous and 20 percent of high school seniors smoked daily, so I reasoned that adolescents might see cigarette advertisements and peers smoking concurrently. I also reasoned that encounters with smokers would often be ambiguous.

Looking at the literature, I could find few controlled experiments on cigarette advertising. However, surveys indicated there was a strong association between adolescents' perceptions of smokers and smoking initiation. With the assistance of coauthors, I completed two research projects that documented that cigarette adver-

tisements can prime adolescents' positive beliefs about smokers and thus alter their social encounters with smokers. Specifically, cigarette advertisements serving as primes can favorably bias adolescents' perceptions of peers who smoke and thus increase their intent to smoke. One of our papers on this topic received the Best Paper Award from the *Journal of Consumer Research*. I continue to conduct research in this area.

I am told that my tobacco-related research has been cited by expert witnesses in legal cases such as the federal tobacco case, in legislative hearings, and in U.S. Attorney General meetings. I believe that some academic research should be conducted to inform public policy and that if research is not designed for this purpose, it likely will not have this effect.

Sources: J. A. Bargh, M. Chen, and L. Burrows, "Automaticity of Social Behavior: Direct Effects of Trait Construct and Stereotype Activation on Action," *Journal of Personality & Social Psychology*, 71, No. 2 (1996): 230–244; C. Pechmann and S. J. Knight, "An Experimental Investigation of the Joint Effects of Advertising and Peers on Adolescents' Beliefs and Intentions about Cigarette Consumption," *Journal of Consumer Research*, 29, No. 1 (2002): 5–19; C. Pechmann and S. Ratneshwar, "The Effects of Antismoking and Cigarette Advertising on Young Adolescents' Perceptions of Peers Who Smoke," *Journal of Consumer Research*, 21, No. 2 (1994): 236–251.

The Uses of Research

Agencies and clients use research to make strategic decisions, as we have just discussed, but agencies rarely *conduct* research. Most research has become so specialized that separate research companies, as well as in-house client research departments, are the most likely research sources. These firms and departments collect and disseminate secondary research data and conduct primary research that ultimately finds its way into brand communication efforts. DDB is one of the few large agencies that still does its own in-house research. Its annual Life Style Survey, which we discussed in Chapter 5, is a major source of consumer information.

As markets have become more fragmented and saturated, and as consumers have become more demanding, the need for research-based information in advertising planning has increased. Figure 6.2 summarizes the seven ways research is used in marketing communication planning:

1. Market information
2. Consumer insight research
3. Brand information
4. Media research
5. Message development research
6. Advertising or IMC plan
7. Evaluation research

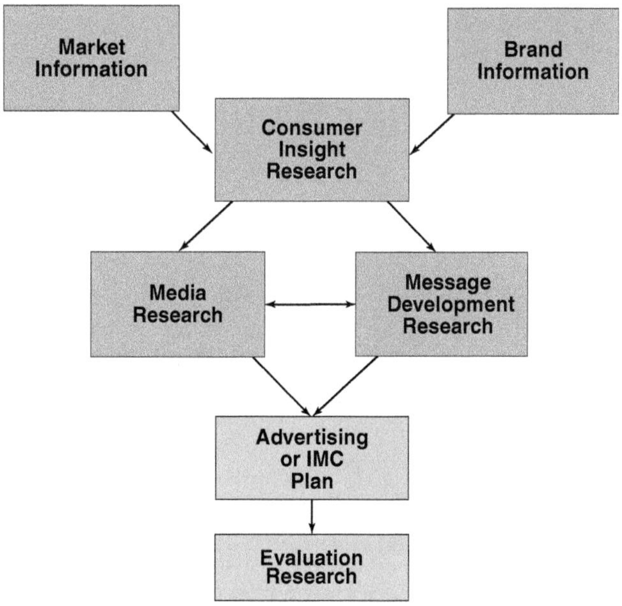

FIGURE 6.2

The Use of Research
in Marketing
Communication Planning

Market Information   Formal research used by the marketing department for strategic planning is called **marketing research.** It includes surveys, in-depth interviews, observational methods, focus groups (which are like in-depth interviews with a group rather than individuals), and all types of primary and secondary data used to develop a marketing plan and ultimately provide information for a brand communication plan. A subset of marketing research, *market research* is research used to gather information about a particular market.

An example comes from Iceland, a country hard hit by the global economic downturn that started in 2007. As explained by Ingvi Logason, principal in his own advertising firm in Reykjavik, "Iceland, with its overexpanded banking sector, was hit worse than any other Westernized country." With all of its banks except one going into bankruptcy or only barely being saved by serious rescue activities by the government, national debt outweighed gross national production by 2 to 1. Iceland was on the brink of national bankruptcy. *The Inside Story* details how Logason and his agency guided his client, the lamb industry, through this difficult time.

Market information includes everything a planner can uncover about consumer perceptions of the brand, product category, and competitors' brands. Planners sometimes ride with the sales force and listen to sales pitches, tour manufacturing plants to see how a product is made, and work in a store or restaurant to evaluate employee interaction with customers. In terms of marketing communication, planners test the brand's and its competitors' advertisements, promotions, retail displays, packaging, and other marketing communication efforts.

Brand information includes an assessment of the brand's role and performance in the marketplace—is it a leader, a follower, a challenger, or a subbrand of a bigger and better known brand? This research also investigates how people perceive brand personalities and images. Here are some common methods used to gather information about a brand and the marketplace:

- *The Brand Experience* When an agency gets a new client, the first thing the agency team has to do is learn about the brand through brand research. That means learning where the brand has been in the past in terms of the market, its customers, and competitors, as the Cheetos campaign demonstrated. Also important is eliciting the corporate point of view regarding the brand's position within the company's line of products, as well as corporate goals and plans for the brand. Another critical area of brand research is the brand's relationships with its customers. Researchers, for example, may go through all of the experiences

THE INSIDE STORY

How the Lamb Industry in Iceland Survived the Economic Downturn

Ingvi Logason, *Principal, H:N Marketing Communication, Reykjavik, Iceland*

In 2009 (when this was written) the whole world was facing probably its greatest economic crisis since the early 20th century. This recession hit the Icelandic public suddenly and it hit hard—obliterating purchasing power. Overnight the situation changed the way Icelanders search and shop, as well as what they want from their brands. In this market planners had to truly understand the role a brand plays in the lives of its target audience clarifying "what's in it for me" in all communication.

One brand that my marketing communication firm has handled and had to adapt to the changed market is Icelandic Lamb. Traditionally lamb had been around a 29 percent share of Icelandic meat consumption with heavy and almost exclusive emphasis on the prime (and more expensive) parts of the lamb. That left farmers with a high percentage of the lamb unsold. Now lamb was down to a 26 percent share and falling.

Anyone could see that this was not a good situation with the sharp decrease in purchasing power leading to fewer sales in luxury and expensive food items. Furthermore, sales figures showed that consumers were not going for the less expensive cuts of lamb, but rather opting for other cheaper meat products. Although we were quick to catch the trend and see the possible sales decline, we were not sure why sales hadn't moved to less expensive lamb cuts.

We assembled focus groups to determine the underlying problem. With clever probing, the main problem became clear: consumers simply did not know how to prepare the less costly parts—it was a forgotten art. Lamb had become such a luxury item that it was easier for our target group to increase their consumption of less costly meat than learn new recipes. Our extensive consumer research showed that:

- Our target group liked lamb meat but didn't know how to cook it.
- Lamb meat had the highest top-of-mind (TOM) awareness of all meat products in Iceland.
- Our target group was always looking for ways to find economic and quick solutions to the question "What's for dinner?"
- Our research also found up to 25 percent better engagement in food advertising when recipes were included.

So how do you connect with your target group and teach time-pressed people new tricks in a world with ever-expanding media options and less time for anything domestic like cooking?

We developed a strategy to counter the trend away from lamb. Fast dissemination of information for a fast-moving world became our goal.

The big idea we developed was "micro-cooking" shows—we would teach you to cook in 90 seconds or less. The recipes were tasty, simple, and easy. In addition, the lamb website carried the cooking shows, which also became viral ads. We created and recruited a Facebook group interested in lamb who passed the shows on, extending their reach to new customers.

By researching and understanding the role that our brand played in the lives of our target group, we were able to come up with a campaign that matched our target group's needs and pace of life. These insights resulted in a strategy that connected with consumers and delivered the sales figures we needed to help the lamb industry survive the downturn.

that a typical consumer has in buying and using the product. If you were taking on a pizza restaurant account, for example, you might work in the store or visit it as a customer. Brand buying is also a form of commitment to the client: the parking lots of agencies that have automotive accounts are usually full of cars made by their clients.

- *Competitive Analysis* It's also important to do a competitive analysis. If you handle a soap account, you obviously want to use that brand of soap, but you may also buy the competing brands and do your own comparative test just to add your experiences to your brand analysis.
- *Marketing Communication Audit* Either formally or informally, most planners will begin an assignment by collecting every possible piece of advertising and other forms of marketing communication by the brand, as well as its competitors and other relevant categories that may have lessons for the brand. Often these pieces are attached to the walls in a "war room" where team members can immerse themselves in messages to stimulate new ideas. This includes compiling a historical collection as well. There's nothing more embarrassing than proposing a great new advertising idea only to find out that it was used a couple of years ago by a competitor or, even worse, by your client.
- *Content Analysis* The marketing communication audit might include only informal summaries of the slogans, appeals, and images used most often, or it might include more formal and systematic tabulation of competitors' approaches and strategies, called a **content analysis.** By disclosing competitors' strategies and tactics, analysis of the content of competitive advertisements provides clues about how competitors are thinking and suggests ways to develop new and more effective campaigns. Planners also try to determine what mental territories or positions competitors claim and which are still available and relevant to the brand.

Principle
Do your homework about your brand. There's nothing more embarrassing than proposing a great new advertising idea only to find out that it was used a couple of years ago by a competitor or, even worse, by your client.

Consumer Insight Research A basic principle in this book is that effective marketing communication rests on truly understanding the consumer. As Regina Lewis, a member of this book's Advisory Board, explained in the Part 2 opener, brands have to be true to the consumers who buy them. Consumers, even brand loyal ones, are more loyal to themselves and their own interests than they are to brands. Both the creative team members (who create messages) and the media planners (who decide how and when to deliver the messages) need to know as much as they can, in as much depth and detail as possible, about the people they are trying to reach. That's the point of *The Inside Story* about selling Icelandic lamb during the recession. To turn the sales pattern around, the agency had to really know how its target market was adapting to the new economic situation.

We mentioned in the discussion of the communication role of marketing communication that feedback can be obtained from customers as a part of a research program that uses customer contact as an information source—systematically recording information from customer service, technical service, inbound telemarketing calls, and online sites. Some businesses use the Internet to involve customers in making decisions about product design, distribution, price, and company operations using online surveys, blogs, online communities, and other social media.

You've probably heard the phrase "This call may be monitored for quality assurance." These recordings are used for training, but they also can be analyzed for marketing intelligence.[4] If customers say they are confused or ask the representative to repeat a phrase, then it could indicate that the sales offer or technical explanation isn't working right. These calls can provide instant feedback about the strength of a brand's offering as well as competitors' offers. Specific questions such as "Where did you hear about this?" are used to monitor brand contact points and media performance.

More importantly, as we explained in Chapter 5, researchers try to determine what motivates people to buy a product or become involved in a brand relationship. But a note of caution, sometimes the biggest consumer research projects may not give reliable results. A classic example is the New Coke reformulation introduced in 1985 after some 200,000 consumers participated in blind taste tests. Based on this huge $4 million research effort, Coke managers decided to dump the old Coca-Cola formula, which had been in use since 1886, because researchers concluded that Coke drinkers preferred a new sweeter taste. The reaction was overwhelming from loyal Coke drinkers who wanted the "Real Thing," an emotional bond that wasn't revealed in the consumer research.

Principle
Insight research is designed to uncover the whys of the buys, as well as the why nots.

The objective of **consumer insight research** is to puzzle out a key consumer insight that will help move the target audience to respond to the message. Insight research, in other words, is basically about asking and listening, and then asking more questions to probe deeper into thoughts, opinions, attitudes, desires, and motivations.

Researchers often try to uncover the *whys of the buys,* but insight research may also uncover reasons why people don't want to try or buy a product. For example, Dunkin' Donuts found in its consumer research several reasons why its customers were uncomfortable ordering fancy coffee drinks. Mostly they were intimidated by the whole "barista" thing and the fancy coffee names.

The DDB agency regularly conducts "Barriers to Purchase" research[5] realizing that these barriers often create an opportunity for advertising messages to present information or change perceptions. The American Dairy Association, for example, asked DDB to find out why cheese consumption was declining. A study identified one barrier that was most easily correctable through a marketing communication effort: the absence of simple cheese recipes for home cooks. Ads and the association's website (*www.ilovecheese.com*) offer many such recipes.

Emotions are elicited by asking consumers what they think people in various photos and situations are feeling. Associations are investigated by asking people what comes to mind when a word or brand is mentioned. In **association tests,** people are asked what they think of when they hear a cue, such as the name of a product category or a brand. They respond with all of the things that come to mind, and, as we have said, that forms a **network of associations.** Brand perceptions are tested this way to map the structure and logic of these association networks, which lead to message strategies. For example, what do you think of when you think of Taco Bell? Wendy's? Arby's? Each restaurant should bring to mind some things in common (fast food, cheap food), but they also have distinct networks of associations based on type of food (Mexican, hamburgers, roast beef), restaurant design, logo and colors, brand characters, healthfulness, and so forth. Each restaurant, then, has a distinctive profile that can be determined from this network of associations.

To get inside consumers' minds to see what they are really thinking, marketers have turned to the tools of neuroscience, which uses highly technical equipment to scan the brain as it processes information and makes decisions. Neuromarketing, which we have mentioned in previous chapters, is the application of this research technology to consumer behavior. One study by a UCLA researcher, for example, mapped how viewers responded to Super Bowl ads below the level of their awareness. In the *A Principled Practice* feature at *www.pearsonglobaleditions.com/moriarty,* Professor Ann Marie Barry explains how this research works and raises some ethical questions about just how private our thinking should be.

Campbell's Soup used neuromarketing and biometrics to analyze consumer responses to brand communication. As part of a major two-year study and

The DDB agency found that a barrier to purchasing cheese was the lack of good recipe ideas using cheese products. The American Dairy Association responded by getting more recipes distributed through advertising and its website.

redesign of the labels on its iconic red and white soup cans, Campbell's used neuromarketing techniques to see how consumers reacted to everything from pictures of bowls, to the use of a spoon, and other graphic cues, such as steam rising from the bowl. The objective was to find ways to help consumers connect on a deeper and more emotional level with the brand. Changes included color coding the different varieties; depict steam to make the soup in the picture look warm; remove the spoon, which consumers said served no purpose; update the look of the bowl; and move the Campbell's logo to the bottom in order to better identify the varieties.[6]

Media Research   Media planning begins with consumer research and questions about media behavior that help with the media selection decision. Media planners often work in conjunction with the information account planners uncover to decide which media formats make the most sense to accomplish the objectives. The goal is to activate consumer interest by reaching them through some medium that engages their interest.

Next, **media research** gathers information about all the possible media and marketing communication tools that might be used in a campaign to deliver a message. Media researchers then match that information to what is known about the target audience. The MRI data shown earlier in Figure 6.1 illustrates the type of information media researchers consult to develop recommendations.

Message Development Research   As planners, account managers, and people on the creative team begin to develop a message strategy, they involve themselves in various types of informal and formal **message development research.** They read all of the relevant secondary information provided by the client and the planners to become better informed about the brand, the company, the competition, the media, and the product category. As Jackie Boulter,[7] head of planning at the London-based Abbott Mead Vickers-BBDO agency, explained, creative development research is focused on refining message ideas prior to production. It uses qualitative research to predict if the idea will solve the business problem and achieve the objectives.

Sometimes called **concept testing,** it can help evaluate the relative power of various creative ideas. It's a "work-in-progress" type of evaluation. The idea is to test the big idea that communicates the strategy behind the message—or various types of *executions* of the concept. These interviews are often conducted in malls and downtown areas where there are lots of people who can be asked to look at a rough sketch of the idea or ad and respond to it. They can also be conducted over the phone, by mail, or online.

As writers and art directors begin working on a specific creative project, they almost always conduct informal research of their own. They may do their own personal observational research and visit retail stores, talk to salespeople, and watch customers buy. They may visit the agency information center or library, browse through reference books, and borrow subject and picture files. They will look at previous advertising, especially that of competitors, to see what others have done, and in their hearts they will become convinced that they can create something better than, and different from, anything that has been done before. This informal, personal research has a powerful influence on what happens later in the message development process.

Another technique used to analyze the meaning of communication is **semiotic analysis,** which is a way to take apart the signs and symbols in a message to uncover layers and types of meanings. The objective is to find deeper meanings in the symbolism that might be particular to different groups of consumers. Its focus is on determining the meanings, even if they are not obvious or highly symbolic, that might relate to consumer motivations.

For example, the advertising that launched General Motors' OnStar global positioning system (GPS) used a Batman theme. By looking at this commercial in terms of its signs and symbols, it was possible to determine if the obvious, as well as hidden, meanings of the message are on strategy. For example, the decision to use a comic book hero as the star created a heroic association for OnStar. However, Batman is not a superhero, but rather more of a common person with a lot of great technology and cool gadgets—remember Jack Nicholson as the Joker and his famous comment: "Where does he get all those wonderful toys?" The "bat beacon" then becomes OnStar for the average person. Batman is also ageless, appealing to young people who read comic books and watch movies today as well as older people who remember

Batman from their youth.[8] A highly successful effort, this Batman OnStar campaign won a David Ogilvy Research Award.

Evaluation Research   Concept testing is actually the first level of evaluation. After an advertisement or other type of marketing communication (marcom) message has been developed and produced, it can be evaluated for its effectiveness both before and after it runs as part of a campaign. **Pretesting** is research on an execution in its finished stages but before it appears in media. While creative development research looks at the power of the advertising idea, pretesting looks at the way the idea is presented. The idea can be strong, but the target might hate the execution. This type of test elicits a go or no-go decision for a specific advertisement. Sometimes pretesting will also call into doubt the strength of the advertising idea, forcing the creative team to rethink its strategy.

Evaluative research, often referred to as **copytesting,** is done during a campaign and afterward. If it's used during a campaign, the objective is to adjust the ad to make it stronger. Afterward, the research determines the effectiveness of the ad or campaign.

We will explore many different types of evaluation methods in Chapter 19, but let's just mention two common forms here. Memory can be measured using **aided recognition** (or recall). A researcher might page through a magazine (or use some other medium) and ask respondents whether they remember seeing a particular ad. **Unaided recognition** (or recall) means respondents are asked to tell what they remember without being prompted by seeing the magazine (or other medium) to refresh their memories. These tools are used both in developmental research and also in evaluation. Strategic, developmental, and evaluative research share some common tools and processes and we briefly describe some of these in the following section.

WHAT ARE THE MOST COMMON RESEARCH METHODS?

This section focuses on the types of research used in message development and the research situations where these methods are typically used.

Ways of Contact: Quantitative Methods

Consumer research methodologies are often described in terms of the ways researchers contact their respondents. The contact can be in person, by telephone, by mail, through the Internet or cable TV, or by a computer kiosk in a mall or store. Most quantitative research in marketing communication is survey based, however, consumers can also be contacted in malls where they are invited to participate in experimental research.

Survey Research   In a survey, questionnaires are used to obtain information about people's attitudes, knowledge, media use, and exposure to particular messages, and this was an important part of the Cheetos retargeting campaign. **Survey research** is a quantitative method that uses structured interviews to ask large numbers of people the same set of questions. The questions can deal with personal characteristics, such as age, income, behavior, or attitudes. The surveys can be conducted in person, by phone, by mail, or online. There are two big questions to consider: how to build a representative sample of people to be interviewed and what method is best to collect the data.

Sampling is used because in most cases, it is cost prohibitive to try to interview everyone in the population or target market. Instead the people interviewed are a representative **sample** of the larger group, a subset of the population that is representative of the entire population.[9] For survey research to be an accurate reflection of the population, those who participate must be selected at random, which means every person who belongs to the population being surveyed has an equal likelihood (probability) of being chosen to participate. For a classic example of how nonrandom sampling can create inaccurate results, consider the *Literary Digest* presidential election polling of Landon versus Roosevelt in 1936, which produced incorrect results for the presidential election, even though it had a sample size of more than 2 million households. Why? Analysis of the poll results indicates that both the magazine's sample and the response were biased and did not accurately predict voter behavior.[10]

Incentives are important when doing surveys. As Karl Weiss, a member of this book's Advisory Board and president of a marketing research company explains, choose an incentive that

Principle
Careful scientific procedures are used in survey research to draw a representative sample of a group in order to accurately reflect the population's behavior and attitudes.

Survey research can be conducted in person and is often conducted in malls, supermarket aisles, or other public places.

Phone surveys are commonly used. Often they come from commercial call centers where many people hired by a research company staff a bank of phones. In recent years the contact is made through electronic dialing and when respondents answer, the call is transferred to an interviewer.

is appropriate for your audience—perhaps $5 or $10 in cash, a drawing for a Wii or iPhone, or even a summary of the results. Different audiences have different interests so make your incentive appealing to them. Be careful, however, not to bias your results in the process. If you are studying airline travel behavior and your incentive is a PlayStation, don't be surprised to find that most of those who complete the survey are males under 35 years old.

Since survey research first began, the way researchers have gone about collecting data from respondents has seen almost constant change as new technologies have made such research more cost efficient:

- *Door-to-Door Interviews* In the 1950s and 1960s, marketing researchers literally roamed the streets knocking on people's doors with clipboards in hand in order to gather their survey data. Following complex sampling strategies, they made their way through everything from apartment buildings to rural farm areas, with their sampling road map designed to maximize the randomness and representativeness of the population they studied. It wasn't surprising to see this laborious and oftentimes even dangerous approach to collecting survey data replaced by telephone interviewing by the 1970s.
- *Phone Interviews* As access to telephones increased after World War II, calling soon became the survey mode of choice, as it was much less expensive and far less invasive than sending interviewers out to people's homes. The listing of phone numbers in phone directories gave researchers the perfect source from which they could draw a **random sample,** which means each person in the population has an equal chance of being selected to be in the sample. Although telephone interviewing was more practical than going from door to door, researchers lost the ability to interact directly with their participants when communicating just by telephone, especially when there was a need to show pictures or samples of what they were evaluating. However, telephone surveys were not only more cost effective but necessary as people stopped answering their doors due to solicitation efforts (door-to-door sales were very common at that time) and concerns over personal safety.

But over time, telephone interviewing too faced its challenges. In the late 1980s and early 1990s, telemarketing efforts became so pervasive that consumers sought ways to make it stop, from the use of call-screening devices such as answering machines and Caller ID to signing up on the National Do Not Call Registry, which put legal ramifications behind unsolicited phone calls. Although marketing research calls were exempt from this legislation, because nothing is being sold, research calls were screened out with the rest as consumers fortified their privacy efforts. Today it is not uncommon for up to 60 percent of households to not answer their phones when called for a survey. Just as door-to-door surveying met its end as more cost-effective and acceptable alternatives became available, researchers once again need to look for new alternatives for gathering survey data.

- *Mail Surveys* As household addresses became readily available after the Second World War, mail surveys increased in use because researchers could pull addresses from city directories. Specialized research companies sold lists of addresses to direct marketers and these lists also were used by researchers. Mail surveys were popular because they didn't use live interviewers and thus were even less expensive than telephone surveys. In terms of survey design, the mail surveys have to be extremely easy to understand and all of the questions need to be carefully tested because an interviewer won't be present to clarify respondents' questions. Many variables determine the response rate, such as the interest level of the topic to the respondent, personalization of the message, the quality of the paper, the design of the envelope, and the inclusion of a prepaid return envelope. In spite of all the testing that has been done on mail survey design, the problem continues to be a low return rate, in addition to the loss of direct contact with the respondent.

- *Internet Surveys* Today, the world of data collection is changing again. Landline telephones are on the decline as cell phones become more popular and are beginning to be used for research. Unlisted phone numbers are becoming more common. Mail surveys have become largely ineffective, with response rates sometimes as low as the 1 to 3 percent range, which can fail to meet the statistical criteria necessary for valid random sampling. Researchers have been forced by these changes to find new ways to collect data from respondents. Telephone and mail surveys are gradually being replaced by online survey methods.

The Internet has opened up new opportunities for collecting data (see the *A Matter of Practice: Part 1* feature). In Chapter 7 you'll read about the Billings, Montana, rebranding campaign in which the campaign was launched with an online survey of more than 1,000 people. We have printed here the screen download, "Take the Survey," from this effort.

The rebranding campaign for Billings began with a broad survey of people involved in the business of supporting the city. For online surveys to work, they need to be supported by an invitation to participate that showcases the easy-to-use message.

In addition to survey research, the Internet can also be a useful tool for monitoring online behavior. Jason Cormier, co-founder of social-media agency Room 214, explains that marketing communication research can be based on the data provided by members of social networks such as Facebook. One example of this type of research is pay per click. In this method, when a user clicks on an ad in Facebook, the advertiser is charged a fee based on each click of the ad. This method is extremely targeted due to the volumes of data being collected.

Ways of Contact: Qualitative Methods

Various types of surveys are the most common quantitative research methods, but certain types of surveys can also be used for probing and to gather more insightful responses.

In-Depth Interviews   One qualitative method used to survey consumers is the **in-depth interview,** which is conducted one-on-one using **open-ended questions** that require respondents to generate their own answers. In a personal interview the researcher asks questions to the consumer directly. The primary difference between an interview and a survey is the interviewer's use of a more flexible and unstructured questionnaire. This is the type of research method used by the Lexus "super-affluent team" we discussed earlier. Interviewers use a discussion guide, which outlines the areas to be covered during the session.

The discussion guides tend to be longer than surveys with questions that are usually very broad. Examples include "What do you like or dislike about this product?" and "What type of television programs do you like to watch?" Interviewers probe by responding to the answer with "Why do you say that?" or "Can you explain in more detail?" Interviews are considered qualitative because they typically use smaller sample sizes than surveys, their results cannot be generalized, and they are subjected to statistical tests.

A MATTER OF PRACTICE: PART 1

Online Survey Research

Karl Weiss, *President/CEO, Market Perceptions Inc., Denver, CO*

Without a doubt, the Internet has forever changed the world in which we live, and the way in which we do marketing research. Online surveys are much less intrusive than phone surveys, allowing participants to complete them whenever they like. Also, the self-administered approach provides a greater sense of privacy than answering these questions with a stranger over the phone (or in your home!).

In their most basic form, online surveys look and feel pretty much like paper-based surveys, with radio buttons or check boxes for people to click or check instead of filling in a bubble on a computer-readable form. But the online environment allows researchers to do much more. They can not only ask questions and request answers, but they can share sound, pictures, video, and even other websites with the participant. Photos or images can be dragged and dropped into various categories or "buckets" to indicate preference, scales can be continuous sliders, and written product descriptions can be replaced or enhanced with video, audio, and images. If desired, a live interviewer can even "join" the survey midstream or at the end to ask additional questions based on the participant's responses.

Of course, the Internet has not proven to be a replacement for phone and mail surveys because two concerns still limit this approach. First, not everyone has a computer and access to the Internet, and those who do not are demographically different from those who do, making online results skewed to the more educated and affluent. Although the digital divide is shrinking every day, the bigger problem remains—that of obtaining a random sample. With telephone and mail surveys, it is possible to obtain listings of almost everyone with a physical address or to use random digit dialing to include every possible phone number.

For online surveys, however, we must reach our participants by e-mail (exceptions are panels of prerecruited respondents and survey solicitation through online banner ads or even print ads to sign up to do research surveys on a website), but there is no universal listing of e-mail addresses like there is of physical addresses. Furthermore, even when a list of a population can be obtained (such as a customer database of e-mail addresses), typically more than 90 percent of the e-mail survey requests are deleted or ignored by the user, or never make it to the user's in-box because of spam or junk mail filters. So, although Internet surveys are even more cost effective than telephone and mail surveys, the lack of representativeness of those who participate leaves us uncertain as to whether the results are projectable to the population or just to those who like to do surveys.

Online surveys can be created easily using free services such as SurveyMonkey.com and SurveyGizmo .com. But just because these services are free (or very low cost) and easy to use, that should not be a license to send out questionnaires every time a question arises or to spend less time thinking about the quality or necessity of questions. Survey participants are not an easily renewable resource. Overuse them, especially with poorly constructed questionnaires, and participants won't help again when you might really need them.

Boring surveys equal poor results. One of the greatest challenges with online surveys is getting quality data. Most people today do online surveys to get something, from cash to frequent flyer miles to a chance to win something. Their goal is less about giving you the best answers they can and more about finishing the task at hand to get to the carrot at the end of the stick. Long online surveys, especially those with long lists of attributes to rate on the same scale (such as "Extremely Important" to "Not At All Important") are easy sections to randomly pick answers without reading the questions. Make your surveys interesting so that participants *want* to read them and provide the best answers.

Check your online data for speeders and cheaters. Look at how long it took to complete the survey and discard those that were done so quickly that you know they probably didn't really give the questions much attention. Let people know you are watching for speeders by asking them to provide a certain response to a question to make sure they are paying attention. For example, a question early in the survey could be, "To make sure only real people are completing this questionnaire and that they are paying attention, please mark "Somewhat Agree" to this question."

Focus Groups   Another qualitative method is a **focus group**, which is a group interview of 6 to 10 users and potential users of a product who are gathered around a table to have a discussion about some topic, such as the brand, product category, or marketing communication. The objective is to get participants talking in a conversational format so researchers can observe the dialogue and interactions among the group. It's a directed group interview. A moderator supervises the group, providing direction through a set of carefully developed questions that stimulate conversation and elicit

In-depth interviews are conducted one on one with open-ended questions that permit the interviewee to give thoughtful responses. The informal structure of the questions allows the interviewer to follow up and ask more detailed questions to dig deeper into attitudes and motivations.

Focus groups are conducted around a conference table with a researcher serving as the moderator working from a list of prepared discussion questions. The session is usually held in a room with one-way glass so the other team members from the agency and client can observe the way respondents answer the questions.

the group members' thoughts and feelings in their own words. Other qualitative tools can also be used with groups such as asking participants to create posters, diaries, or poems or complete exercises in day mapping or memory associations (what comes to mind when you think of something, such as a brand, situation, or location).

Focus groups can be used at any step in the planning process, but they are often used early in information gathering to probe for patterns of thought and behavior that are then tested using quantitative research tools, such as surveys. For example, the Cheetos team conducted focus groups with adult heavy-users of Cheetos. Information from focus groups can uncover, as it did in this case, answers to "how" and "why" questions. The Cheetos participants said they gave themselves permission to lick their fingers and not act like adults. Focus groups are also useful in testing creative ideas or exploring various alternatives in message strategy development.

A **friendship focus group**[11] takes place in a comfortable setting, usually a private home, where the host has recruited the participants. This approach is designed to break down barriers and save time in getting to more in-depth responses. For example, one study of sensitive and insensitive visuals used in advertising directed to black women found that a self-constructed friendship group was easier to assemble and yielded more honest and candid responses than a more traditional focus group where respondents are recruited by a research company.[12]

The Web is not only a tool for online surveys, but also for online focus groups based on the idea of getting a group of brand loyalists together as a password-protected online community. Online research company Communispace has created some 225 online communities for marketers, including Kraft Foods, Unilever for its Axe brand, and Charles Schwab. You can read more about this technique at *www.communispace.com*. In the *A Matter of Practice: Part 2* feature, Karl Weiss continues his discussion of the various ways the Internet can be used to conduct qualitative research.

A broad-based approach to online focus groups is available through the new practice called **crowdsourcing**, a term coined by Jeff Howe in *Wired* magazine in 2006.[13] It refers to aggregating the wisdom of Internet users in a type of digital brainstorming. In a search for "collective intelligence," crowdsourcing collects opinions and ideas from a digital community.

Suggestions and Comments Informal feedback has always been available in stores through suggestion boxes and customer satisfaction cards. Target took that idea online by publishing an ad in the *Wall Street Journal* asking customers to "Tell us what more we can do for you." Some 627 respondents e-mailed suggestions. Target then published the suggestions and the company's responses to them in two-page ads. It was a novel way of eliciting comments, listening to them, and

A MATTER OF PRACTICE: PART 2

Online Qualitative Research

Karl Weiss, *President/CEO, Market Perceptions Inc., Denver, CO*

Qualitative research methods have benefited from the new technologies of the Internet, allowing researchers and respondents to see one another using webcams, and online focus groups provide a way for people across the state or globe to easily come together to discuss a topic.

But the Internet has provided the marketing research community with more than just a new method for collecting and reporting data; its mark on the industry is truly much more profound. With the massive explosion of the Internet and all that we can do on it, researchers now have a new *kind* of data, data that they can obtain without asking a single question. This shift is far more significant than the transition from telephone to online surveying.

The Internet allows today's researchers to observe consumer behavior in many ways previously not only unimaginable but impossible. The most obvious of these are Web surfing patterns, seeing where people go on the Web, what they are looking for, and what they choose to buy and not buy. But that's really just scratching the surface. With social media networking sites such as Facebook, Twitter, MySpace, and LinkedIn, not to mention other user-generated content through blogs, **vlogs,** podcasts, wikis, forums, chats, and discussion boards, researchers are now able to "listen" to what people are saying and see how consumers might be reacting to a competitor's new product or even what they are saying about a television ad. They can troll through millions of pages of blogs and discussion groups in seconds to find key words or phrases and perform content analysis to even classify the age and gender of the author.

Combining the data of the Internet with other electronic forms of information, such as credit card transactions, phone call records, and even GPS tracking, the amount of knowledge that can be surmised about *individuals* provides a whole new playing field for marketers, not to mention a growing area of concern for privacy organizations.

We don't need to look too far into the future to imagine how easy it would be to learn that Chris, a 19-year-old male college student who holds a season pass to an area ski resort, has been researching different brands of snowboards although has yet to purchase one. We could even know from the GPS information transmitted from his cell phone that he is about to walk past a ski and snowboard shop that just happens to be having a sale on one of the boards he has been considering. A message to his phone with a photo of the board, address of the store, and the sale price of the product he was considering, reaching him at exactly the right time, completely redefines "target marketing."

While privacy concerns certainly come to mind (not to mention that it's a bit creepy to have someone, even a computer, know that much about us), these types of systems are already in development and in some shape or form will become a significant piece of marketing research of the future. (For more on this topic, see *The Numerati* by Stephen Baker listed In the Recommended Readings section at the end of this chapter.)

But for now, the Internet provides us with a new way of surveying people, a new way of reporting back results to those who need them, and endless possibilities for making research less like a test laboratory and more like the real world.

---

then responding. Starbucks, and many other companies, use an online suggestion box incorporating the practices of *crowdsourcing.* MyStarbucks Idea is a website for Starbucks customers to contribute ideas, join the discussion, and vote on the ones they like best. Check it out at *http://mystarbucksidea.force.com/ideaHome.*

The Internet has made it even easier to track comments about a brand. Many marketers, such as IBM and Microsoft, monitor chats and blogs, and also do more general scanning for key words to find out what people are saying about their brands and products. These findings can be incorporated back into other methods, such as focus groups, to verify and explain the sentiments expressed online.[14]

Panels   An **expert panel** gathers experts from various fields into a focus group setting. This research tool can stimulate new ways of looking at a brand, product, or customer pattern. More commonly, however, a marketing or **consumer research panel** is an ongoing group of carefully selected people interested in a topic or product category. A standing panel can be maintained over time by a marketer as a proprietary source of information or by a research company whose clients provide topics for the panel members' consideration. Panels can gather in person or be contacted by phone, mail, or the Internet. An example of this type of research comes from cool hunters and trend watchers who may use proprietary panels to track fashions and fads.

A Stopwatch, Codesheet, and Curiosity

Kate Stein, *University of Florida*

I interned as a consumer-behavior researcher in grocery stores for Brian Wansink, director of the Cornell University Food and Brand Lab, and got an eyeful of insight about how people select the products they buy. I observed shoppers in the aisles as they checked the freshness of produce, compared prices, and read package labels.

Collecting data and running studies like these require observing thousands of supermarket customers in situ as they complete their shopping expeditions. The goal is to collect data that will be descriptive of reality without interfering with it. So I'm a participant, as well as a researcher.

My observations were made across several different types of grocery stores to obtain data about a wide variety of shopper types and of products available to select. I spent between 5 and 10 hours a day in grocery stores, pacing the tiled floors as I conducted my research. Setting up a study requires creating a detailed map of the grocery store, complete with measurements of the width of the grocery aisles.

To remain unnoticed and observe real behavior, researchers must appear to be supermarket shoppers themselves, blending in with their surroundings as just another innocuous grocery store patron. Using a cart and pretending that your data sheet is a grocery list are two useful measures to enhance the credibility of an undercover researcher.

Much like people watching in an airport, the appeal of observational research is easy to understand. One can feel like a true spy as you attempt to blend in with the surroundings and pose as a neutral participant in an environment where you are actually conducting research.

Observational research requires a sharp eye and a curiosity into the actions of others. Anyone with a natural interest in human nature should find consumer behavior research to be a rewarding pursuit. For more on this study, check out Professor Wansink's website: *www.mindlesseating.org.*

When this research project was undertaken, Kate was a finance and mass communication major at the University of Florida and a student of Professor Richard Lutz.

Observation Research   Like anthropologists, observation researchers study the actual behavior of consumers in settings where they live, work, shop, and play, acting as what Shay Sayre refers to as "professional snoops."[15] Direct **observation research** is closer and more personal than most other types of research. Researchers use video, audio, and disposable cameras to record consumers' behavior at home (with consumer consent), in stores, or wherever people buy and use their products. A marketer may rely on observation in the aisles of grocery, drug, and discount stores to watch people as they make product selections. Grocery shopping might seem like a mundane, mechanical activity, but look around next time you're in a store and watch how your fellow shoppers make their product choices. An example of this type of experience comes from a *New York Times* article written by Kate Stein, a University of Florida student, who describes what it's like to participate in observational research.

Cool watchers, researchers who keep tabs on trends, also use observational research when visiting places and events where their target market gathers. The Cheetos team used observational research to discover how adults respond to Chester Cheetah, the brand's character. They determined that Chester still appealed to adults because when he showed up on the street in big cities such as San Francisco, adults came up to him and gave him hugs or had their pictures taken with him.

The Consumer Behavior Odyssey was a classic observational research project that opened the door for this type of research in marketing. The Odyssey put a team of researchers in a Winnebago on a trip from Los Angeles to Boston. Along the way, the researchers used a variety of observational techniques to watch and record people behaving as consumers.[16]

A variation on observational research is **participant observation.** In this research method, the observer is a member of the group being studied. For example, research into television viewing behaviors sometimes uses friendship groups of the researcher who unobtrusively records his or her friends' behavior as part of the viewing session. The idea is that by immersing themselves in the activity, observers have an inside view—perhaps a more empathetic view—of their groups' experiences.

Ethnographic Research   Related to observation, **ethnographic research** involves the researcher in living the lives of the people being studied. Ethnographers have elevated people watching to a science. In ethnographic research, which combines anthropology and marketing, observers immerse themselves in a culture to study the meanings, language, interaction, and behavior of the people in the group.[17] The idea is that people's behavior tells you more than you can ever get in an interview or focus group. This method is particularly good at deriving a picture of a day in the life of a typical consumer. An example comes from a Walgreen's vice president who wore glasses that blurred his vision, taped his thumbs to his palms, and wore shoes containing unpopped popcorn. The exercise was designed to help him and other retail executives understand the difficulties facing elderly shoppers—confusing store layouts, eyesight problems, arthritis, and the inability to reach or stoop.[18]

Major companies like Harley-Davidson and Coca-Cola hire marketing experts trained in social science research to observe and interpret customer behavior. These participant observers then meet with the company's managers, planners, and marketing staff to discuss their impressions.[19] The case of Eight O'Clock coffee is an example of the use of a videotaped ethnographic study. The brand's agency, New York–based Kaplan Thaler, got 14 families in Pittsburgh and Chicago to use video cameras to record their typical mornings in order to identify the various roles that coffee played in their morning rituals.[20]

Direct observation and ethnographic research have the advantage of revealing what people actually do, as distinguished from what people say they do. It can yield the correct answer when faulty memory, a desire to impress the interviewer, or simple inattention to details would cause an interview answer to be wrong. The biggest drawback to direct observation is that it shows what is happening, but not *why*. Therefore, the results of direct observation often are combined with personal interviews afterward to provide a more complete and more understandable picture of attitudes, motives, and behavior.

The McCann agency is dedicating a $2.5 million research effort to understanding the lives of low-income Latinos from Mexico to Chile.[21] A new division named "Barrio" studies the marketing efforts of its clients, such as Nestlé and Danone. It has transformed conference rooms into "bodegas" (corner grocery shops) and sent employees to live with families amassing some 700 hours of video recordings. The reason is that practical insights into low-income groups are hard to find, yet these people are consumers, too, and marketers need to understand their needs as emerging economies bring new lifestyles to the disadvantaged.

Diaries   Sometimes consumers are asked to record their activities through the use of diaries. These **diaries** are particularly valuable in media research because they tell media planners exactly what programs and ads the consumers watched. If comment lines are provided, then the activities can also be accompanied by thoughts. *Beeper diaries* are used as a way to randomize the recording of activities. Consumers participating in the study are instructed to grab the diary and record what they are doing when the beeper goes off. Diaries are designed to catch the consumer in a more realistic, normal life pattern than you can derive from surveys or interviews that rely on consumers to remember their activities accurately. This can also lead to a helpful reconstruction of a typical day in the life of a consumer.

An example comes from Dunkin' Donuts. Regina Lewis, formerly vice president of consumer and brand insights, explained that she used a young adult diary study to determine when this target audience starts drinking coffee. She recruited 20 people in five cities. From their records, Lewis and her team had hundreds of points of observations. At research centers, the participants were then asked to explain what was going on when they thought about having coffee—what day, what time, why are they thinking about coffee, and so forth. From that research, the team learned that many young adults want "chuggable" coffee, particularly because they want an immediate caffeine hit. As a result, they drink iced coffee because hot coffee is too hot and they can't get their caffeine shot fast enough. Dunkin' responded with "Turbo Ice" coffee with an extra shot of espresso.[22]

Principle
Direct observation and ethnographic research methods reveal what people actually do, rather than what they say they do, but they also lack the ability to explain *why* these people do what they do.

Other Qualitative Methods Marketing communication planners are always probing for reasons, feelings, and motivations behind what people say and do. To arrive at useful consumer insights, they use a variety of interesting and novel research methods. In particular, they use stories and pictures. Cognitive psychologists have learned that human beings think more in images than in words. Most research continues to use words to ask questions and obtain answers, but recent experiments with visual-based research opens up new avenues of expression that may be better able to uncover people's deep thoughts.

Researchers use pictures, as well as other tools to uncover mental processes that guide consumer behavior. Professor Larry Soley refers to these methods as **projective techniques,** which means they ask respondents to generate impressions rather than respond to more controlled quantitative surveys and rating systems. He describes projective techniques as psychoanalytic.[23]

Harvard Business School professor Gerald Zaltman believes that the conventional wisdom about consumer research, such as using interviews and focus groups that rely on talking to people and grilling them about their tastes and buying habits, is only good for getting back predictable answers. If you ask people what they think about Coke, you'll learn that it is a "high-energy, thirst-quenching, fun-at-the-beach" kind of drink. But that may not be an adequate description of how people really feel about the soft drink.[24]

Here is a collection of some of the more imaginative ways qualitative researchers use projective techniques as games to gather insights about people's relationships with the brands they buy:

- *Word association* is a projective technique that asks people to respond with thoughts or other words that come to mind when they are given a stimulus word. The idea is to uncover the networks of connections in their thought patterns. These are used to test brand personalities, as well as other types of meanings that govern consumer behavior.
- *Fill in the blanks* is a form of attitude research in which people literally fill in the blanks in a story or balloons in a cartoon. Perceptions can come to the surface in the words participants use to describe the action or situations depicted in the visuals.
- *Sentence completion* tests give respondents the beginning of a sentence and ask them to finish it. These are good at eliciting descriptions, causes, results, as well as the meanings in personal experiences.
- *Purpose-driven games* allow researchers to see how people solve problems and search for information.[25] Games can make the research experience more fun and involving for participants. They also uncover problem-solving strategies that may mirror the participants' approach to information searching or the kinds of problems they deal with in certain product situations.
- *Theater techniques* use games in a theater setting where researchers have people experience a variety of exercises to understand how they think about their brand. Some of these games have people tell stories about products or simulations where they have to convince others to use a brand.
- *Sculpting and movement techniques,* such as positioning the body as a statue, can be a source of insight in brainstorming for creative ideas and new product ideas. Sculpting involves physically putting product users in static positions that reflect how they think about or use a brand. Physical movements, such as dance movements and martial arts, can be added to increase the range of insight.
- *Story elicitation* asks consumers to explain the artifacts of their lives, such as the photos displayed in their homes and the objects they treasure. These stories can provide insights into how and why people use or do things.
- *Artifact creation* is a technique that uses such ideas as life collages, day mapping (tracking someone's activities across a day), and the construction of instruction books as ways to elicit stories that discuss brands and their role in daily life. These projects are also useful later in explaining to others—clients, the creative team, or other agencies—the triggers behind consumer insights.[26]
- *Photo elicitation* is similar to artifact research except it uses visuals to elicit consumer thoughts and opinions. A form of photo-based interviewing, consumers are asked to look at a set of visuals or instructed to visually record something with a camera, such as a shopping trip. Later in reviewing the visuals, they are asked to explain what they were thinking or doing.

- *Photo sorts,* which is yet another visual technique, asks consumers to sort through a deck of photos and pick out visuals that represent something to them, such as typical users of the product or situations where it might be used. In identifying typical users, they may be asked to sort the photos into specific piles, such as happy, sad, angry, excited, or innovative people.
- *Metaphors* is a tool used by researchers to enrich the language consumers use to talk about brands. (Remember your grammar: A **metaphor** compares one thing to another without using the actual words *like* or *as.*) The Evian ad, for example, uses a strong metaphor to define its product. The insight into how people perceive brands through such connections comes from exploring the link between the two concepts. Metaphor games are used in creativity to elicit new and novel ideas, but they can also be used to analyze cognitive patterns in people's thinking.

L'original

These methods can be combined. Harvard professor Zaltman is the creator of ZMET (pronounced ZEE-MET), the Zaltman Metaphor Elicitation Technique, which uses metaphors and visual images to uncover patterns in people's thinking. For a typical session, the respondents bring images that they think relate to the product category or brand being studied. Then they make up stories that describe their feelings about the product or brand.[27] The Cheetos research team used the ZMET and uncovered the unexpected finding about stress and how Cheetos was an escape from those pressures.

For Coca-Cola in Europe, Zaltman asked volunteers to collect at least a dozen pictures that captured their feelings about Coca-Cola. Then they discussed the images in personal interviews. Finally, the volunteers created a summary image—a digital collage of their most important images and recorded a statement that explained its meaning. The ZMET team found that Coke is not just about feelings of high energy and good times; it also has an element of calm, solitude, and relaxation.[28]

This metaphoric ad equating Evian sparkling water with a mermaid tries to add a touch of originality, as well as meaning, to the Evian brand image.

Choosing a Research Method

Determining the appropriate research method to use is an important planning decision. It might help to understand two basic research criteria, validity and reliability, that are derived from what researchers call the "scientific method." **Validity** means that the research actually measures what it says it measures. Any differences that are uncovered by the research, such as different attitudes or purchasing patterns, really reflect differences among individuals, groups, or situations. **Reliability** means that you can run the same test again and get the same answer.

Quantitative researchers, particularly those doing experiments and surveys, are concerned about being faithful to the principles of science. Selecting a sample that truly represents the population, for example, increases the reliability of the research. Poorly worded questions and talking to the wrong people can hurt the validity of surveys, as well as focus groups. The problem with experiments is twofold: (1) experiments are limited by a small number of people in the experimental group, and (2) they are conducted under artificial conditions.

The information you get from surveys of a broad cross section of a population is limited to your ability to develop good clear questions that everyone can understand and answer. This tight control makes it harder to ask questions around the edges of a topic or elicit unexpected or unusual responses. On the other hand, focus groups and in-depth interviews that permit probing are limited by small numbers and possible problems with the representativeness of the sample.

Generally, quantitative methods are more useful for gathering data (how many do this or believe that?), and qualitative methods are better at uncovering reasons and motives (why do they do or believe?). For these reasons, most researchers use a variety of research methods—quantitative and qualitative and occasionally experimental designs. Which method should you choose when you conduct research? The answer depends on what questions you need to answer.

RESEARCH TRENDS AND CHALLENGES

Marketing communication researchers face a number of challenges: **globalization** and new media technology are reshaping the industry. Practices are also changing as the industry searches for ways to more naturally embed research as feedback, as well as gain more insightful analysis and move into IMC planning. Let's examine each challenge briefly.

Global Issues

The key issues that global researchers face include how to manage and communicate global brands in widely different localities and how to shift from studying differences to finding similarities around the world. The biggest problem is cross-cultural communication and how to arrive at an intended message without cultural distortions or insensitivities. Researchers are becoming more involved in puzzling out cultural meanings and testing marketing communication messages for cultural sensitivity in different countries. They struggle to determine how other cultures will interpret the elements of a campaign so that they convey the same brand message across cultures. Cultural differences complicate planning as account planner Susan Mendelsohn, who is a member of this book's Advisory Board, discovered in planning for a new analgesic that contained caffeine. In test markets the agency discovered that perceptions about caffeine vary positively and negatively in different cultures.

IMC Research Challenges

The deluge of data is only complicated by IMC planning, which requires research into many stakeholder groups and contact points. Instead of campaign planning where messages are tweaked slightly to fit different media, *strategic consistency* in IMC planning suggests that different audiences, as well as media, need different messages. Susan Mendelsohn calls this a more radical trend in planning research and points to "companies that are experimenting with multi-message strategies that fit each vehicle uniquely and yet might be radically different from each other." She cautions that the company needs to be clear about the goals for its brand, recognizing that there might be multiple goals—a set of integrated goals—rather than one big underlying goal and that suggests multiple measurements of effectiveness, as well.

Planning for Feedback

Learning how to better listen to consumers has become an important factor in effective marketing communication. Earlier we mentioned the use of customer contact to elicit feedback; there are also ways to structure feedback into message strategies. In **embedded feedback research,** the research method is built into the response, including the contact point, purchase activity, and use situations. Campaigns that encourage interested prospects to contact a company, for example, are setting up response monitoring as part of the message strategy. *Call centers*, both inbound (customer calls to complain or get assistance) and outbound (telemarketing), can also be used as research centers to gain real-time feedback about the brand and its marketing and advertising strategies. In other words, whenever a call is made, for whatever purpose, that contact provides an opportunity to ask a brand-related question. Marketers also monitor blogs, chat rooms, and social media (Facebook, MySpace, Twitter) for clues about what people are saying about a brand.

An example of a structured feedback program comes from Nordstrom's Personal Touch Program, which uses a team of *personal shoppers* who are fashion consultants on one level but on another level are trained to gather information from their clients to feed back into the company's business planning and marketing.

Looking Ahead

Research, analysis, and new techniques such as crowdsourcing, lead to marketing communication plans and strategic decisions, which will be the topic of the next chapter. The research findings also lead to message strategies, which we introduce in Part 3, and media strategies, which will follow in Part 4.

IT'S A WRAP

Comfort Food for Thought

Cheetos' research shifted the focus of its strategy from kids to "rejuvenile" adults as a target audience. Key insights from research efforts shaped the creative direction to create edgy humor that spoke to those current and would-be Cheetos lovers. The message became "It's all about fun"—and that appealed to a certain segment of the adult audience, who just happened to be fans of Cheetos.

Consultant Howard Papush, aka Dr. Play, said, "When we're stressed, we revert back to the things that comforted us as kids. We want to play our way through stress." It seems to be a universal truth, at least for some of us, that comfort food, aka Cheetos, can occasionally be a good way to relieve stress. And orange fingers are fun.

Interestingly, little in the campaign speaks about the product. Yet, the campaign seems to succeed, maybe because the audience it seeks rejects a direct push about the product. Besides, who doesn't know what Cheetos are? Did the campaign work to accomplish the objective of repositioning the brand for a new target market? Several indicators suggest the success of the Cheetos campaign.

First, and most importantly, Cheetos' sales rose significantly, almost doubling the targeted rate. In a tracking study about the best-regarded snack brands, Cheetos improved from 41st position to 34th, and this improvement was mainly from households without children.

The repositioning strategy created energy for the brand by connecting the message that this snack could help consumers lighten up with its audience in a variety of traditional and digital media. Disregarding your mother's admonition not to play with your food, this campaign tells you it's okay in ways that speak effectively to the target audience. The new Cheetos campaign created more than mischievous fun. It made award-winning advertising communication. In 2009 the Advertising Research Foundation awarded this campaign its best of show, the Grand Ogilvy Winner.

Key Points Summary

1. **What are the basic types of strategic research and how are they used?** Secondary research is background research that gathers already published information, and primary research is original research findings collected for the first time from original sources. Quantitative research is statistical and uses numerical data to investigate how people think and behave; qualitative research is exploratory and uses probing techniques to gain insights and identify questions and hypotheses for further quantitative research. Experimental research tests hypotheses using carefully designed experiments.

   Research is used to (1) develop an analysis of the marketing situation, (2) acquire consumer information and insights for making targeting decisions, (3) identify information about available media to match the media to the target audience, and (4) develop message strategies and evaluate their effectiveness.

2. **What are the most common research methods used in advertising?** Survey research is used to amass quantities of responses from consumers about their attitudes and behaviors. In-depth interviews probe the reasons and motivations consumers give to explain their attitudes and behavior. Focus groups are group interviews that operate like a conversation directed by a researcher. Panels are long-running consumer groups that permit tracking of attitude and behavior changes. Observation research happens in the store or home where researchers watch how consumers behave. Ethnographic research is an anthropological technique that involves the researcher in participating in the day-to-day lives of consumers. Diaries are records of consumers' behavior, particularly their media use. A number of other qualitative methods are used to creatively uncover patterns in the way consumers think and act.

3. **What are the key challenges facing advertising researchers?** Globalization complicates the way research is conducted for global products because it adds a cultural dimension and varied legal restrictions. Media fragmentation and convergence complicate the process of

determining media effects. New research techniques are being created as a result of new media technology as well as the Internet, which offers opportunities for virtual interviews. Embedded research is a way to get immediate feedback that comes from the process of buying or using the product. Beyond the accumulation of numbers and information, the search for insight is a driving force in advertising research.

Words of Wisdom: Recommended Reading

Baker, Stephen, *The Numerati,* New York: Houghton Mifflin, 2008.

Edmunds, Holly, *Focus Group Research Handbook,* New York: McGraw-Hill, 2000.

Howe, Jeff, *Crowdsourcing,* New York: Crown Business, 2008.

Hubbard, Douglas, *How to Measure Anything: Finding the Value of "Intangibles" in Business,* Hoboken, NJ: John Wiley, 2007.

Jones, John Philip (Ed.), *How Advertising Works: The Role of Research,* Thousand Oaks, CA: Sage, 1998.

Morrison, Margaret, Eric Haley, Kim Sheehan, and Ronald Tayler (Eds.), *Using Qualitative Research in Advertising: Strategies, Techniques and Applications,* 2nd ed., Thousand Oaks, CA: Sage, 2008.

Sayre, Shay, *Qualitative Methods for Marketplace Research,* Thousand Oaks, CA: Sage, 2001.

Young, Charles, *The Advertising Research Handbook,* Seattle, WA: Ideas in Flight, 2005.

Key Terms

advertising research, p. 191
aided recognition, p. 202
association tests, p. 200
concept testing, p. 201
consumer insight
    research, p. 200
consumer research, p. 191
consumer research panel, p. 207
content analysis, p. 199
copytesting, p. 202
crowdsourcing, p. 206
diaries, p. 209
embedded feedback
    research, p. 212

ethnographic research, p. 209
evaluative research, p. 202
experimental research, p. 196
expert panel, p. 207
focus group, p. 205
friendship focus group, p. 206
globalization, p. 212
IMC research, p. 191
in-depth interview, p. 204
market research, p. 191
marketing research, p. 197
media research, p. 201

message development
    research, p. 201
metaphors, p. 211
network of associations, p. 200
observation research, p. 208
open-ended questions, p. 204
participant observation, p. 209
pretesting, p. 202
primary research, p. 193
projective techniques, p. 210
qualitative research, p. 195
quantitative research, p. 195

random sample, p. 203
reliability, p. 211
sales levels, p. 195
sample, p. 202
secondary research, p. 192
semiotic analysis, p. 201
strategic research, p. 191
survey research, p. 202
unaided recognition, p. 202
validity, p. 211
vlogs, p. 207

Review Questions

1. Explain the difference between primary and secondary research and between quantitative and qualitative research.

2. What are the four uses of research in advertising? Give an example of each one.

3. How many different ways are there to contact people to gain information for use in advertising planning?

4. What is survey research and how is it conducted? How do in-depth interviews differ from surveys?

5. Explain when to use the following research methods: focus group, in-depth interviews, observational research, ethnographic research, and diaries.

6. Explain the difference between validity and reliability and explain how these concepts affect advertising research.

7. What are two ways to gather feedback? Explain how to acquire this information and why feedback is important.

Discussion Questions

1. Suppose you are developing a research program for a new bookstore serving your college or university. What kind of exploratory research would you recommend? Would you propose both qualitative and quantitative studies? Why or why not? What specific steps would you take?

2. Consult the MRI data reproduced on p. 194 and do the following analysis: Look first at the four Index columns and find the highest viewing category of late evening weekend news and compare that with the highest viewers of early evening weekend news. If you were advertising a new hybrid car, which category and time slot would deliver the greatest *percentage* of viewers who might be in the market? Now analyze the size of the category to determine which of the high viewing categories delivers the greatest *number* of viewers.

3. Bottled water is an outgrowth of the health and fitness trend. It has recently moved into second place in the beverage industry behind wine and spirits, beating out beer and coffee. The latest twist on bottled water is the "enhanced" category with designer waters that include such things as extra oxygen, vitamins, or caffeine. You have a client with a product that fits this new category. Go online and find secondary data about this market. Indicate how you would use this information to design a branding program for this product.

4. *Three-Minute Debate* You have been hired to develop and conduct a research study for a new upscale restaurant chain coming into your community. Your client wants to know how people in the community see the competition and what they think of the restaurant's offerings. It uses an unusual concept that focuses on fowl—duck, squab, pheasant, and other elegant meals in the poultry category. A specialty category, this would be somewhat like a seafood restaurant. One of your colleagues says the best way to do this study is with a carefully designed survey and a representative sample. Another colleague says, no, what the client really needs is insight into the market; she believes the best way to help the client with its advertising strategy is to use qualitative research. As a team, choose one side in this debate and identify its strengths in terms of this campaign problem. Prepare your point of view and a brief presentation to your class that will convince them.

Take-Home Projects

1. *Portfolio Project* Assume you are working for Gerber Baby Foods. You have been asked to identify the relevant trends that are forecasted for U.S. birth rates between 2012 and 2015. Identify Internet sources that would provide that information. Gather as much information as you can from these sites and write a one-page report on the trends you find.

2. *Mini-Case Analysis* What were the key research findings that led to the Cheetos repositioning campaign? You have just been assigned to the Cheetos team for the next year of the campaign. What research would you want to do before planning the next year's efforts? Identify a list of key research questions that have to be answered before the campaign can move forward.

Team Project: The BrandRevive Campaign

For the BrandRevive campaign, we need to know what people interested in this category think about the brand. All team members should identify friends and family members who would be willing to be interviewed. Identify those among your pool of interviewees who are users of your brand or the category. Also identify those in your group category users who are *not* users of your brand. (For Avaya, consider the category to be business hardware and software, similar to IBM offerings.)

- Interview both groups about their attitudes to the category and specific brands. Build a profile of the brand users—what characteristics distinguish them from the nonusers?

- What are their perceptions of the brand (of both users and nonusers)?
- What brands compete with your brand in the minds of your interviewees?
- What other research would you propose doing to better understand this market and brand?
- Present your findings in a one-page report and a PowerPoint presentation that is no longer than three slides.

Hands-On Case

The Century Council

Read the Century Council case in the Appendix before coming to class.

1. How did "The Stupid Drink" campaign team use research to better understand the problem they were trying to solve?

2. How did "The Stupid Drink" campaign team use research to inspire a creative solution to the problem of underage binge drinking on college campuses?

3. What other methodologies would you recommend to the team to better understand the success of its program in the market?

Strategic Planning

It's a Winner

Campaign:	Company:	Agencies:	Award:
"Coke/Coke Zero Taste Infringement"	Coca-Cola	Crispin Porter + Bogusky, Mediavest USA	2009 Silver Effie Winner

CHAPTER KEY POINTS

1. What is the difference between objectives, strategies, and tactics in strategic planning and how are the three levels of planning connected?
2. How is a campaign plan constructed, and what are its six basic sections?
3. What is account planning, and how is it used in advertising?
4. In what ways does an IMC plan differ from an advertising plan?

How to Sell Diet Drinks to People Who Don't Like the Idea of Diet Drinks

How many guys do you know who admit they are on a diet? Probably not many. Diets are kind of a girl thing. So you can imagine the job Coca-Cola had when it wanted to convince young men ages 18 to 34 to try its no-calorie Coke Zero. The very dudes Coca-Cola wanted to appeal to said that diet sodas tasted bad and were far too feminine for them.

Although Coke Zero had been around for three years and was gaining acceptance, Coca-Cola wanted to grow its share of market by adding the 18- to 34-year-old male demographic. This wouldn't be an easy sell. Enter Crispin Porter + Bogusky (CP+B), an agency that has made its award-winning reputation on edgy work that reaches the target market.

CP+B knew from Coca-Cola's research that these guys liked the taste of regular sugary sodas, but as they aged they began to drink more lower calorie options like energy drinks, water, or sports drinks and less pop. To accomplish the client's three main objectives—increase brand awareness, motivate the target audience to try Coke Zero, and convince men 18–34 that Coke Zero tastes like Coke—CP+B relied on consumer research, which indicated that those who tried Coke Zero really thought it tasted like Coke.

Knowing that young men had a negative perception of anything "diet," CP+B proposed to the client that the advertising should focus on the taste similarity of the two products in a funny campaign that would appeal to the skeptical audience. CP+B thought Coke Zero would be a great alternative if, and it's a big if, these young 18–34 men could be convinced it tasted as good as regular Coca-Cola. CP+B's strategy then was to convince guys that calorie-free (note they don't say "diet") Coke Zero was as good as "the real thing." But how?

The communication strategy focused on appealing to the male target through wide-reaching media such as out-of-home media and cinema (a whopping 87 percent of all U.S. theaters) to build awareness, and print, TV, digital, and radio to encourage product trial. Where Coke had big brand presence, such as with NASCAR, the NCAA, and Fantasy Football, there too went Coke Zero. And why there?

The creative strategy was based on the self-deprecating humor you recognize from *The Daily Show* and *The Office*. The gist of the big idea was that the legal department from Coca-Cola wanted to sue Coke Zero for taste infringement. The company made fun of itself proposing imaginary lawsuits and provided a nontraditional campaign for Coke Zero. In one commercial, an unsuspecting real attorney warns actors portraying Coke Classic executives not to sue Coke Zero, lest the suit be dismissed and they be utterly humiliated.

So where you might expect to see a Coke message, you might also see the lawyers ranting about Coke Zero stealing its taste. Here's a fun example. At the NCAA Final Four event in San Antonio, passersby could see a "Stop Coke Zero" rally and sample the taste similarity, providing an opportunity to prove to the targeted males that Coke Zero really did taste like Coke. CP+B even created an advergame, called *Rooftop Racer*. The object of this NASCAR game was to invite players to step into a virtual car and race with other fellow drivers to the finish line while balancing a Coke Zero bottle on top of their car. Visitors to the CokeZero.com site could "Sue a Friend."

This campaign signifies a shift in thinking about media strategy for Coca-Cola products, according to Katie Bayne, senior vice president for Coco-Cola brands in North America at Coca-Cola in Atlanta. "It's not just about a television spot," she said. That is especially true for Coke Zero as we look at where we need to be to connect with the target audience. So what lesson do we learn from Coke Zero? Sometimes you've got to take calculated risks, and sometimes they pay off, especially when you use well-conceived message and media strategies to connect with a carefully targeted audience.

To see more of this campaign, check out the Coke Zero website, *www.cokezero .com*. To see how well this oddball campaign connected with young males, turn to the end of this chapter and read the *It's a Wrap* feature.

Sources: "Coke/Coke Zero Taste Similarity," Effie Awards Brief of Effectiveness, *www.nyama.org*; Stuart Elliott, "Can't Tell Your Cokes Apart? Sue Someone," March 5, 2007, *www.nytimes.com*; Paul van Veenendaal, "CP+B Launches Rooftop Racer for Coke Zero," *www.viralblog.com*; "Coke v. Coke Zero: A Winning Case," *www.adforum.com*.

Marketing and advertising strategies are chosen from an array of possible alternatives. In most cases, there is no one completely right way to do anything in advertising, but if you understand how advertising works, you may be able to identify the best strategy to accomplish the objectives. This chapter explains the concept of strategic planning as it is used in business, marketing, and advertising and integrated marketing communication (IMC) plans. It covers key planning decisions, such as identifying critical problems and opportunities, targeting the right audience, positioning or repositioning the brand against the competition, and making implementation decisions. It also introduces the concept of account planning and explains its critical role in determining the consumer insights that lead to message and media strategies.

WHAT IS STRATEGIC PLANNING?

For marketing communication, **strategic planning** is the process of identifying a problem that can be solved with marketing communication, then determining **objectives** (what you want to accomplish), deciding on **strategies** (how to accomplish the objectives), and implementing the **tactics** (actions that make the plan come to life). This process occurs within a specified time frame. Objectives are usually long-term propositions, strategies are more medium term in focus, and tactics are more short term.

Even those experienced in advertising sometimes have a hard time telling the difference between an objective and a strategy. Remember, an *objective* is a goal to be accomplished; in advertising, objectives are determined by the effects you want to achieve. A *strategy* is the means, the design or plan, by which the objective is accomplished—the advertising message and media strategies, for example. In advertising, *tactics* are the way the ads and other marketing communication efforts are executed—how they are designed and what they say.

In the Coke Zero case, the objective was to position Coke Zero as tasting like regular Coke. The strategy was to use taste tests so the young male target could experience how similar the tastes were. The tactic was to use the idea of "taste infringement" complete with lawyers, actors, and imaginary lawsuits.

We talk a lot about creativity in this book and we'd like to emphasize that strategic thinking is just as creative as coming up with a Big Idea for a marketing communication campaign. Both processes involve searching for ideas to solve problems, whether they are found in marketing situations or communication challenges. Pat Fallon and Fred Senn, cofounders of the legendary agency Fallon Worldwide, explain that principle in their book, *Juicing the Orange: How to Turn Creativity into a Powerful Business Advantage.* They have identified seven principles that link creative thinking and strategic planning to business results[1]:

1. ***Always Start from Scratch*** Simplify the problem. You know too much. There's a good chance that you know so much that you can't see how the problem could be solved in a fresh way.
2. ***Demand a Ruthlessly Simple Definition of the Business Problem*** Smart people tend to make things too complicated. Be a relentless reductionist. Einstein said, "Make things as simple as possible, but no simpler."
3. ***Discover a Proprietary Emotion*** The key component of any communication program is a powerful consumer insight that leads to a ruthlessly smart strategy executed brilliantly across all platforms. It all starts with the insight, which is the central truth of what you are going to say and how you are going to operate. Once you find an emotional truth, you can make it proprietary through execution.
4. ***Focus on the Size of the Idea, Not the Size of the Budget*** It's our credo that it's better to outsmart than outspend.
5. ***Seek Out Strategic Risks*** Understand the benefits of prudent risk. Great big ideas in the early stages are often scary ideas. When Darwin taught us about the survival of the fittest, he didn't mean the strongest. He meant that it's the most nimble—the quickest to adapt to a changing environment—who prosper both in nature and in a capitalist economy.
6. ***Collaborate or Perish*** This is more than "getting along"; it is about recognizing that the rules of engagement have changed. We live in an era in which victory goes to the best collaborators. This means teams from different disciplines and different corporate cultures will be working together. Teams that are aligned and motivated can make history.
7. ***Listen Hard to Your Customers (Then Listen Some More)*** Listening is often step Number One on the road to understanding. Listening often yields that precious insight that gives you a competitive advantage; something your competitors have overlooked.

Pat Fallon (top) and Fred Senn were cofounders of Fallon Worldwide, the agency behind NBC, Holiday Inn Express, Travelers Insurance, Sony, and many other major brands.

The Business Plan

Strategic planning is a three-tiered process that starts with the business plan and then moves to functional areas of the company such as marketing where a marketing plan is developed that outlines objectives, strategies, and tactics for all areas of the marketing mix. As illustrated in Figure 7.1, both the business plan and the marketing plan provide direction to specific plans for specialist areas, such as advertising and other areas of marketing communication.

A business plan may cover a specific division of the company or a **strategic business unit (SBU)**, which is a line of products or all the offerings under a single brand name. These divisions, or SBUs, share a common set of problems and factors. Figure 7.2 depicts a widely used framework for the strategic planning process in business. The objectives for planning at this level tend to focus on maximizing profit and **return on investment (ROI)**. ROI is a measurement that shows whether, in general, the costs of conducting the business—the investment—are more than matched by the revenue produced in return. The revenue above and beyond the costs is where profit lies.

**Strategic Planning from
Top to Bottom**
Business planning involves a
set of cascading objectives
and strategies. Corporate objectives and strategies are
achieved through planning at
the level of marketing (and
other areas, such as production), and marketing objectives and strategies give
direction to marketing communication programs.

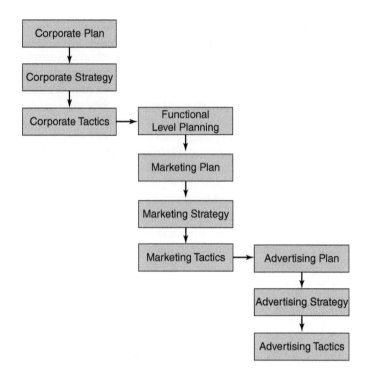

Note that the business planning process starts with a business **mission statement,** a concise expression of the broad goals and policies of the business unit. The mission statement is unique, focused, and differentiating. Tom's of Maine states its mission clearly on its website:

"Through the years, we have been guided by one simple notion—do what is right, for our customers, employees, communities, and environment. We call this Natural Care—a philosophy that guides what we make and all that we do."

The Marketing Plan

A **marketing plan** is developed for a brand or product line and evaluated annually, although sections dealing with long-term goals might operate for a number of years. To a large extent, the marketing plan mirrors the company's business plan and contains many of the same components, although they are focused on a specific brand rather than the larger organization or corporation. Figure 7.3 illustrates the steps involved in creating a marketing plan.

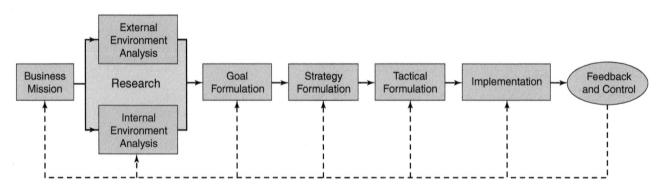

FIGURE 7.2

Steps in the Development of a Business Plan
The business planning process begins with a mission statement and moves through research, goal setting, strategy statements, identifications
of tactics, implementation processes, and controls (meeting the budget and quality standards, for example). The entire process is monitored through feedback.

Source: Philip Kotler, *Marketing Management*, 13th ed., Upper Saddle River, NJ: Prentice Hall, 2009: 48. Reproduced by permission of Pearson Education, Inc., Upper Saddle River, NJ.

A *market situation analysis* is based on extensive market research that assesses the external and internal environments that affect marketing operations—the company's history, products, and brands, as well as the competitive environment, consumer trends, and other marketplace trends that have some impact on the product category. A set of "what's going on" questions helps structure this market analysis. Answers to these questions help define the key marketing problem and, ultimately, the SWOTs, which stands for strengths, weaknesses, opportunities and threats:

- What is happening with the brand and the category?
- How is it happening?
- Where is it happening?
- When is it happening?
- To whom is it happening?

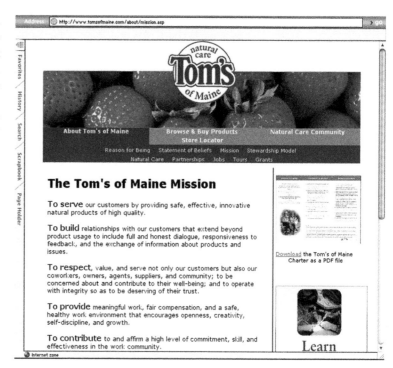

This mission statement for Tom's of Maine helps its managers develop specific business objectives and goals. It also guides all of the company's marketing communication efforts.

We could answer those questions for Coke Zero by summarizing the market situation and the key problem facing Coke Zero as a marketplace for diet drinks that appealed primarily to women, thus leaving out the large number of young male pop drinkers who make up the largest portion of the soft drink market.

The objectives at the marketing level tend to be focused on sales levels and **share of market,** measurements referring to the percentage of the category purchases that are made by the brand's customers. Other objectives deal with specific areas of the marketing mix, such as distribution, where an objective might detail how a company will open a new territory.

For marketing communication (marcom) managers, the most important part of the marketing plan is the *marketing mix strategy,* which includes decisions about the target market, brand position, product design and performance, pricing, and distribution, as well as marketing communication. Product design and formulation decisions are sometimes responses to consumer trends, such as the increase in the number of packaged foods making high-fiber claims (think Fiber One with its expanded line of cereals and snack bars). Other challenges to marketing planners came from the competition. When McDonald's began advertising its Angus burger in 2009, the Hardee's and Carl's Jr. chains responded with taste challenges, mail-in refund promotions, and parodies of Big Mac advertisements.[2]

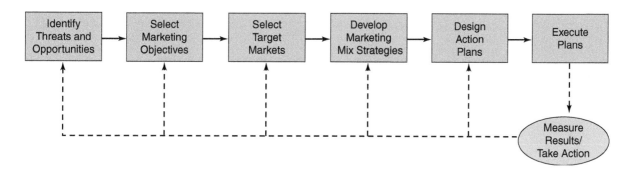

FIGURE 7.3

Steps in the Development of a Marketing Plan

A marketing plan begins with an analysis of the marketing situation in terms of strengths, weaknesses, opportunities, and threats. Setting objectives is the next step. Target markets are selected and marketing strategies are developed, as well as action plans and specific executions of ideas and programs. The plan is evaluated and that information feeds back into the next generation of planning.

This marketing analysis—and the marketing mix strategy derived from it—link the overall strategic business plan with specific marketing programs, including advertising and other IMC areas. Whether to use a frequency club, an advertising campaign, or a sales promotion strategy to increase brand loyalty, for example, are marketing communication decisions that support marketing strategies.

A new contributor to this process is crowdsourcing, which we mentioned in the previous chapter. This practice mobilizes a digital crowd to provide collective intelligence. For example, consider how Wikipedia operates with experts contributing and reviewing entries. In a marketing environment, crowdsourcing can be used to channel the latent wisdom of online crowds including experts as well as average citizens. John Fluevog Open Source Footwear is a company that invites anyone to contribute ideas for shoes. Decisions about the best ideas are made through peer voting, feasibility, and admittedly what the owner John Fluevog likes. The design ideas become public domain but the company adds the winners to its line of shoes. Check out this interesting company at *www.fluevog.com/files_2/os-1.html*. Procter & Gamble uses InnoCentive.com, a digital think tank for innovation, to engage some 140,000 scientists and engineers worldwide to help with its research and development.[3]

The Advertising or IMC Plan

Advertising and marketing communication planning operates with the same concern for objectives, strategies, and tactics that we've outlined for business and marketing plans. It outlines all of the communication activities needed to deliver on the business and marketing objectives in terms of communication objectives, strategies, tactics, timing, costs, and evaluation. In general, an advertising plan seeks to match the right audience to the right message and present the message in the right medium to reach that audience. These three elements—audience insight, message, and medium—are at the heart of an advertising plan.

An example of how all of these elements come together in a plan comes from a brand identity campaign for the city of Billings, Montana. *The Inside Story* feature gives you a look inside the planning of a branding campaign for a place. Pay particular attention to the "Brand Standards" online guidebook at the website *www.brandbillings.com*. This online guidebook explains how the campaign is designed to create a unified voice for the community with a consistent image and message, one that reinforces Billings' unique geography, resources, and heritage.

Let's now look at how an advertising or marketing communication plan is developed. The following discussion outlines the basic steps in planning a campaign, as well as the critical strategic decisions planners must make.

WHAT'S IN A CAMPAIGN PLAN?

In addition to or instead of an annual marketing plan, a firm may develop a **campaign plan** that is more tightly focused on solving a particular marketing communication problem in a specified time. Such a plan typically includes a variety of marcom messages carried in different media and sometimes targeted to different audiences. The following outline traces the steps, and the decisions they represent, in a typical campaign plan.

Typical Campaign Plan Outline

I. Situation Analysis
   • Background research
   • SWOTs: strengths, weaknesses, opportunities, threats
   • Key communication problem(s) to be solved

II. Key Strategic Campaign Decisions
   • Objectives
   • Target audience (or stakeholder targets in an IMC plan)
   • Brand position: product features and competitive advantage
   • Campaign strategy: key strategic approach and marcom tools

III. Media Strategy (or Points of Contact in an IMC Plan)
   • Media objectives
   • Media selection

Branding Billings

John Brewer, *President & CEO, Billings (Montana) Chamber of Commerce/Convention & Visitors Bureau*

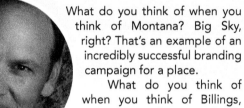

What do you think of when you think of Montana? Big Sky, right? That's an example of an incredibly successful branding campaign for a place.

What do you think of when you think of Billings, Montana? . . . uh . . . , probably not much, right?

That's the problem I faced in 2007 when our steering committee took on the problem of branding Billings. So this is a story of our two-year effort to create a brand identity campaign for the city.

You can check out the results of this plan at the website *www.brandbillings.com.* In addition to beautiful scenery, the first thing you may notice on the site is a logo with the slogan: "Billings—Montana's Trailhead." Here's how the city arrived at that theme line.

The campaign began with research including more than a thousand online surveys, community workshops, and presentations to clubs and service groups followed by countless hours of strategic envisioning sessions. The research and analysis determined that Billings is a very special place that merges its location with an attitude—a position that combines "open space" and "western pace."

The important brand characteristics begin with its location—shaped by the Yellowstone River and sheltered by the Rims geographic formation. The community is progressive and a regional center for finance, health care, transportation, arts and culture, and diverse educational opportunities. Its hard-working citizens have a unique Montana perspective that combines warmth with an appreciation of scenery and history. But what also defines them most is a lifestyle that loves the adventure of an untamed wilderness right outside the door.

Those characteristics translated into a statement of Billings brand essence as "Montana's city connects you to the authentic historical west." The "trailhead" idea springs from the recognition that Billings is a starting point for business growth and development, as well as a gateway for opportunities to explore the wonders of Montana. The starting point idea was supported in the "trail" graphic with its "X marks the spot" symbol. The "Where Ya Headin'?" tagline expresses the idea that Billings is the gateway for adventure.

The campaign's objective was to create a position that expresses this brand essence and to create a consistent and cohesive brand message that unifies the city's efforts to encourage business and workforce development, individual and family relocation, tourism, and community pride.

An ongoing identity development project, the campaign is spreading out to local businesses and community events. For example, the airport etched the brand logo into its five main terminal entryways. Newspaper ads by local merchants proclaimed billings as the trailhead for great shopping. The local Walmart carries Trailhead apparel with the new logo. Pepsi branded half a million Pepsi cans with a picture of Trailhead hats for a joint promotion with the Chamber of Commerce.

To sustain the campaign, a Trailhead Marketing Committee meets regularly. Using the brand standards website and tool kit as a guide, this committee encourages:

1. Businesses to adopt the brand
2. General local awareness
3. Individual and family relocation
4. Community pride through public relations and other marketing opportunities.

Success will be determined on an annual basis from media clips, and the increased number of businesses that are using the brand in their messaging and the frequency of that use. In terms of results as of this writing, in the first eight months of the campaign following the brand launch, the site (*www.brandbillings.com*) has had 7,913 visitors and a daily average total of 33 per day.

The Travel Planner is the primary piece sent to visitors by the Billings Chamber of Commerce/Convention & Visitors Bureau. Its cover uses an appealing photo of Billings, as well as the new logo and Trailhead slogan, and the "trail" graphics.

> IV. Media planning and buying:
> > • Vehicle selection
> > • Budget allocation
> > • Scheduling

IV. Message Strategy
- Key consumer insight (brand relationship insight in IMC)
- Message objectives
- Selling premise
- Big idea
- Message design and executions

V. Other Marcom Tools Used in Support
- Public relations
- Direct marketing
- Sales promotion
- Personal selling
- Sponsorships
- Merchandising, packaging, point-of-purchase
- Integration strategy (maximize synergy)

VI. Campaign Management
- Evaluation of effectiveness
- Campaign budget

This outline is useful as a guide for the planning document, but more importantly, it identifies the key strategic decisions that guide various sections of a campaign plan. Decisions include (1) identifying the key problem to be solved based on analysis of the SWOTs, (2) stating objectives, (3) targeting the audience, (4) creating or reinforcing a position, (5) identifying the key strategic approach that will deliver the objectives, and (6) using management controls to determine efficiency in budgeting and effectiveness through evaluation. Let's look at these strategic planning decisions in more detail.

Situation Analysis

The first step in developing an advertising plan, just as in a marketing plan, is not planning but *backgrounding*—researching and reviewing the current state of the business that is relevant to the brand and gathering all pertinent information. After the research is compiled, planners try to make sense of the findings, a process sometimes referred to as a **situation analysis.** The goal is to identify a problem that can be solved with communication. As Fallon and Senn explained in their "Juicing the Orange" list, you have to start by simplifying the problem. The information collection will probably be huge, but the problem statement should simplify the task.

Principle
SWOT analysis is the process of finding ways to address a brand's weaknesses and threats and leverage its strengths and opportunities.

SWOT Analysis   The primary tool used to make sense of the information gathered and identify a key problem related to a brand or product is a **SWOT analysis,** which, as we have said, stands for strengths, weaknesses, opportunities, and threats. The strengths and weaknesses are *internally focused,* and the opportunities and threats lie in the *external* marketing environment. In strategic planning the idea is to *leverage* the strengths and opportunities and *address* the weaknesses and threats, which is how the key problems and opportunities are identified.[4]

- The *strengths* of a business are its positive traits, conditions, and good situations. For instance, being in a growth industry is a strength. Planners ask how they can leverage this strength in the brand's advertising.
- The *weaknesses* of a business are traits, conditions, and situations that are perceived as negatives. Losing market share is a weakness. If this is an important weakness, then planners ask how they can address it with advertising.
- An *opportunity* is an area in which the company could develop an advantage over its competition. Often, one company's weakness is another company's opportunity. Planners strive to identify these opportunities and leverage them in the brand's advertising.
- A *threat* is a trend or development in the environment that will erode business unless the company takes action. Competition and economic downturns are common threats. Advertis-

ing planners ask themselves how they can address a threat if it is a critical factor affecting the success of the brand.

In the Coke Zero case, the strength of the brand lies with the Coca-Cola tradition as "the real thing." The opportunity existed to transfer that Coke magic to a calorie-free version of the flagship brand. The weakness is the association of diet drinks with women. The threat lies with the idea that "diet drinks" have an unpleasant taste.

Key Problem(s)   The key word in the title of this section is *analysis,* or making sense of all the data collected and figuring out what the information means for the future success of the brand. Advertising planners must analyze the market situation for communication problems that affect the successful marketing of a product, as well as opportunities the advertising can create or exploit. Analyzing the SWOTs and identifying any problems that can be solved with an advertising message are at the heart of strategic thinking. An example of locating a timing opportunity is illustrated by the Special K "2-Week Challenge" that capitalized on consumers' goals to lose weight after the holidays.

Advertising can solve only message-related problems such as image, attitude, perception, and knowledge or information. It cannot solve problems related to price, availability, or quality, although it can address the perception of these marketing mix factors. For example, a message can speak to the perception that the price is too high, or it can portray a product with limited distribution as exclusive. In other words, advertising can affect the way consumers perceive price, availability, and quality. The advertiser's basic assumption, however, is that the campaign works if it creates an impression, influences people to respond, and separates the brand from the competition.

Principle
Advertising can only solve message-related or perception problems.

SHOWCASE

This two-week Kellogg's Special K challenge promises customers they will lose up to six pounds in two weeks by replacing two meals a day with Special K and eating a sensible third meal. Reaching consumers at the moment they are in need of a weight-loss solution and delivering a simple diet in the context of their environment—in this case posters in department store dressing rooms, health clubs, doctor's offices, hair or nail salons, and bridal salons—was very effective. Business results included an overall increase in the poster markets of 20 percent over nonposter markets.

These two posters for Special K were contributed by Amy Hume, communications consultant in the Integrated University Communications office at the University of Colorado–Denver. Hume is a graduate of the University of Colorado–Boulder and was an associate media director at Starcom Worldwide where she handled this mini-campaign for Special K. She and her work were nominated for inclusion in this book by professor Tom Duncan.

Objectives

After planners have examined the external and internal environments and defined the critical areas that need to be addressed, they can develop specific objectives to be accomplished during a specified time period. Objectives are formal statements of the goals of the advertising or other marketing communication. They outline what the message is designed to achieve in the long term and how it will be measured.

Main Effects and Objectives   Remember from Chapter 4 the six categories in The Facets Model of Effects: perception, emotion, cognition, persuasion, association, and behavior. These main effects also can be used to identify the most common consumer-focused objectives. For example, here are some sample objectives for each category, as well as sample ads and campaigns that we have discussed in this or previous chapters:

- *Perception Objectives* Grab attention; create awareness; stimulate interest; stimulate recognition of the brand or the message; create brand reminder.

  Example: "1984" ad for Macintosh launch

- *Emotional/Affective Objectives* Touch emotions; cue the psychological appeal; create brand or message liking; stimulate brand loyalty; stimulate desire.

  Example: Burger King "Whopper Freakout" campaign

- *Cognition Objectives* Establish brand identity; establish or cue the brand position; deliver information; aid in understanding features, benefits, and brand differences; explain how to do or use something; stimulate recall of the brand message; stimulate brand loyalty; brand reminder.

  Example: "Wii would like to play" launch

The Facets Model of Effects

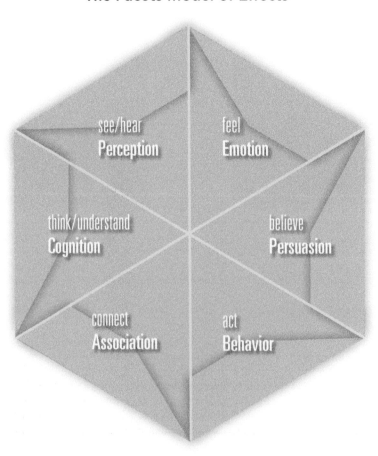

- *Association Objectives* Establish or cue the brand personality or image; create links to symbols and associations; connect to positive brand experiences.

  Example: Old Navy's "SuperModelquins"

- *Persuasion Objectives* Stimulate opinion or attitude formation; change or reinforce opinion or attitude; present argument and reasons; counterargue; create conviction or belief; stimulate brand preference or intent to try or buy; reward positive or desired response; stimulate brand loyalty; create buzz or word of mouth; energize opinion leaders; create advocacy and referrals.

  Example: Coke Zero "Taste Infringement"

- *Behavior Objectives* Stimulate trial, sample, or purchase; generate other types of response (coupon use, attendance, test drive, visit store or dealer, volunteering, sign up, call in, visit website, clicks, attend, participate); create word-of-mouth buzz; create advocacy and referrals.

  Example: Special K "2-Week Challenge," campaigns encouraging participation in the 2010 census

Given the huge amounts of money spent on advertising, it is important for advertisers to know what to expect from a campaign or ad. Although a rule of thumb for advertising is that it should be single minded, we also know from Chapter 4 that multiple effects are often needed to create the desired impact. Some ads may use an emotional strategy while others are informational, but sometimes the message needs to speak to both the head and the heart. That was particularly true for the Coke Zero campaign: customers needed to understand that the taste of Coke Zero was similar to regular Coke but it had to do it with a style and attitude that twenty-something males would like.

Although some objectives are tightly focused on one particular effect, others, such as brand loyalty, call for a more complex set of effects. To create brand loyalty, for example, an advertising campaign must have both cognitive (rational) and affective (emotional) effects, and it must move people to repeat buying. That's one reason brand loyalty is considered a type of long-term impact developed over time from many experiences that a consumer has with a brand and brand messages.

Note also that communication objectives may be important, even if they aren't focused directly on a sale. For example, Expedia.com, a travel consulting company, views its advertising as a way to draw attention to itself, create name recognition, and create understanding of the products and services it sells.

Measurable Objectives   We cannot overstate the importance of writing focused and measurable advertising objectives. Every campaign, and the ads in it, must be guided by specific, clear, and measurable objectives. We say *measurable objectives* because that's how the effectiveness of advertising is determined. It is also critical that an objective be **benchmarked,** which means the planner uses a comparable effort, such as a similar product or prior brand campaign, to predict a logical goal. A measurable objective includes five requirements:

1. A *specific effect* that can be measured
2. A *time frame*
3. A *baseline* (where we are or where we begin)
4. The *goal* (a realistic estimate of the change the campaign can create; benchmarking is used to justify the projected goal)
5. *Percentage change* (subtract the baseline from the goal; divide the difference by the baseline).

A hypothetical objective, then, would read like this: *The goal of this campaign is to move the target's awareness of Coke Zero's taste similarity with regular Coke from 18 to 23 percent within 12 months, an increase of 28 percent.*

Targeting

We discussed targeting and segmenting in Chapter 5, which are strategic decisions made possible because of a deep knowledge of consumers. In particular, this research-based knowledge identifies what makes specific groups of consumers different from people in other groups. These characteristics also identify how consumers are similar to others in ways that characterize a specific type of viewpoint or lifestyle, such as the student partying lifestyle on many campuses, a problem addressed by the Navigators' posters.

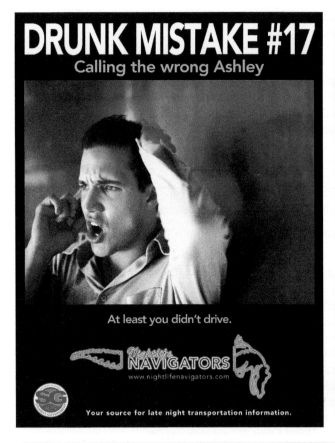

As we discussed in Chapter 5, segmenting and targeting are important because marketing communication strategy is based on accurately targeting an audience that will be responsive to a particular type of message, one that will deliver the objectives.

There is more to targeting than just identifying and profiling a possible audience. How does the target audience relate to the brand? General Mills, for example, during the recent recession was able to maintain significant marketing increases by concentrating on its big-name brands, but also on its multicultural consumers, which the marketer saw as a "high ROI area."[5] Advertising planners also want to know what's going on in people's heads and hearts—what motivates them to attend to a message and respond to it. Getting deeper insight into consumers is the responsibility of the account planning function. We'll return to that role later in this chapter.

We want to emphasize that understanding a target audience demands an appreciation of diversity—and the empathy that results from such an appreciation. Professor Peggy Kreshel defines diversity as "the acknowledgment and inclusion of a wide variety of people with differing characteristics, attributes, beliefs, values, and experiences." In advertising, diversity tends to be discussed primarily in terms of *representations of gender, race,* and *ethnicity in advertising content,* although as she points out in the *A Principled Practice* feature, diversity goes beyond the images used in ads. This is the heart of the issue raised in the excerpt in Chapter 5 from *Madison Avenue and the Color Line* by historian Jason Chambers, which Kreshel references in her essay.

In recognition of the importance of this diversity issue, the American Advertising Federation (AAF) sponsors multicultural programs such as the Most Promising Minority Students and the AAF Mosaic Awards. The leader of those programs, Constance Cannon Frazier, is on this book's Advisory Board and the work of some of the Most Promising Minority Students are featured in this book. Another effort is the AdColor Industry Coalition and its AdColor

A PRINCIPLED PRACTICE

What Is Diversity and Why Is It Important?

Peggy Kreshel, Associate Professor, Department of Advertising, University of Georgia

Sometimes we forget that diversity isn't only about gender, race, and ethnicity. Consider, for example, language use, spiritual practices, sexual orientation, socioeconomic status, and age. Nor is diversity simply about images. Certainly ads and the professionals who create them frequently are criticized for lack of inclusiveness and reliance on denigrating stereotypes. However, diversity affects every aspect of the advertising profession: professional culture, production of content, content itself, the manner in which that content is placed and received, and the ways in which the profession is regulated.

One of the most visible barometers of diversity in the advertising industry is hiring and promotion practices. In *Madison Avenue and the Color Line*, historian Jason Chambers examines African American participation in the advertising industry. He found that African Americans positioned themselves as experts on the black consumer market and worked from *outside* the industry because the doors to most advertising agencies were closed to them. A 1978 New York City Commission on Human Rights report concluded that minority employees continued to be excluded from significant participation in advertising jobs. Nearly thirty years later, the commission again challenged the industry's record of minority hiring, calling it "an embarrassment for a diverse city."[6]

The advertising industry has attempted to address the diversity problem in a variety of ways. In 2005, the AdColor Industry Coalition of advertisers, agency professionals, and trade associations was formed to increase diversity in the industry and celebrate the accomplishments of diverse role models and leaders. The AAAA has partnered with Howard University's School of Communication to create a professional development and research center at that historically black university. The industry has made progress, but diversity in hiring and retention remains a highly charged issue.

Who creates the ads we see? The industry's troubled, largely unsuccessful efforts to create a racially and ethnically diverse workplace tell part of the story. Minority-owned advertising agencies provide opportunities for diversity but are frequently viewed as being capable of speaking only to minority audiences. Women comprise the majority of the advertising workforce, yet an *Adweek* study a few years ago found only four female creative directors in the top 33 advertising agencies. We can only guess at the impact, knowing that creative directors are chiefly responsible for an agency's output.

Content reflects those who create it and their perceptions of audiences. Advertisers' persistent emphasis on 18- to 34-year-olds, a group they view to be impressionable trendsetters who haven't yet formed brand loyalties, has occurred largely to the exclusion of other demographic groups. This preoccupation shapes our business (which constructs itself as youthful, rebellious, and cutting edge), media (where reality programming, the "entertainmentization" of news, and technological wizardry target 18- to 34-year-olds), and culture (reinforcing our celebration of the young, beautiful, and white).

Similarly, marketers routinely define the Hispanic market primarily as "Spanish speaking." The richness and diversity of the many cultures that comprise that group—from Puerto Rico, to Mexico, to Central and South America—have been lost in the desire to construct a homogeneous market large enough to be economically viable. It is only recently that a conversation about the complexity of the Latino market—a complexity that goes beyond merely language or ethnic predilections—has begun to appear in the trade press.

As our lives, professional and personal, become increasingly global, diversity will continue to develop and its influence will be experienced in increasingly complex, sometimes tangled ways. It is essential that advertising professionals adopt broad interpretations of advertising's impact on diversity, and diversity's impact on advertising. Creating an inclusive advertising industry is not only a social responsibility; it is a social and economic necessity.

Awards,[7] which are sponsored by the Association of National Advertisers (ANA), the Advertising Club of New York, the American Association of Advertising Agencies (4As), Arnold Worldwide, Omnicom Group, and AAF. In addition to the AAF and AdColor programs, many local advertising and marketing groups are sponsoring diversity programs in their communities.

Positioning

Principle

The goal of positioning is to locate a product in the consumer's mind based on its features and advantages relative to its competition.

Another reason we revisit targeting here is because understanding the target is the first step in understanding the brand's position within the competitive marketplace. The objective is to establish in the consumer's mind what the brand offers and how it compares with the competition. A **position,** then, is how consumers define the product or brand in comparison to its competitors. A position is based on two things: first, a particular feature or attribute—Coke Zero is low calorie but tastes like regular Coke. The feature also can be psychological, such as heritage (Kodak or Hallmark). Secondly, that feature must be important to the consumer.

A classic example of positioning is the campaign for Avis, which used the line "We Try Harder" to describe how it competes against category leader Hertz. The line was not only a good positioning statement, it also was named as one of the Top 10 Slogans of the 20th Century. The campaign was described by the fathers of positioning, Jack Trout and Al Ries, in their groundbreaking book *Positioning: The Battle for Your Mind.*[8]

A position is based on some notion of comparison. Is the brand more expensive or less; is it a status product or a symbol of frugality; is it sporty, functional, safe or extremely risky? Walmart's position, for example, is encompassed in its slogan, "Always Low Prices." Positioning, then, is about locking the brand in consumers' minds based on some quality relevant to them where the brand stands out. Compare the positioning strategies of the various arms of the U.S. military as they represent themselves in their ads.

Positions are difficult to establish and are created over time. Once established, they are difficult to change, as Kodak discovered with its ownership of the film category when the market moved to digital pictures. Category dominance is important, as Al Ries, one of the founders of the positioning concept, argues, but sometimes the category changes and the brand has to change as well or get left behind. To better understand positioning strategy, let's consider related concepts used to define the competitive situation—product features and attributes, differentiation, and competitive advantage. Then we'll return to how advertising establishes a position in a competitive marketplace.

Principle

Positioning identifies the features that make a brand different from its competitors and relevant to consumers.

Product Features and Attributes   An initial step in crafting a position is to identify the **features** of the brand, as well as those of the competition, to determine where the brand has an advantage over its competitors. A marketer carefully evaluates the product's tangible features (such as size, color, design, price, and ease of use) and other intangible attributes (such as quality, status, value, fashion, and safety) to identify the dimensions of the product that are relevant to its customers and that make it different from its competitors.

An interesting twist on features developed when the electric hybrid cars, such as GM's Volt, were introduced to the market. The standard MPG estimate of fuel efficiency was turned upside down with projections of 230 MPG for Volt and 367 MPG for the Nissan Leaf. Of course, these cars use very little gas as long as they are running on their batteries—gas is only used when the charge runs out. If you only use the car to run around town, theoretically you could get unlimited gas mileage.[9] So what does this changing standard do to traditional car-buying marketing and decision making?

Differentiation and Competitive Advantage   Most markets involve a high level of competition. How does a company compete in a crowded market? It uses **product differentiation,** a strategy designed to focus attention on product differences that are important to consumers and that distinguish the company's product from that of its competitors. We refer to products that really are the same (examples include milk, unleaded gas, and over-the-counter drugs) as undifferentiated or **parity products.** For these products marketers often promote intangible, or psychological, differences, particularly through branding.

The creation of a unique brand image for a product (think Swatch) is the most obvious way to differentiate one product from another. Internet-based Mozilla and Craigslist are small companies but big brands that are strong because they have the support of dedicated users. This strong customer–brand relationship reflects a leadership position—a brand that has defined or created

In these four ads for the Navy, Army, Air Force, and Marines, can you perceive a difference in their positioning strategies? How do they communicate their positions in the style, copy, and graphics? Which do you think would be most effective in recruiting volunteers?

its category. But it's not just hot Internet companies that have achieved this type of leadership—McIlhenny's Tabasco Sauce, which was launched in 1868, created and still owns the hot sauce category.

A technique called **feature analysis** helps structure an assessment of features relative to competitors' products to identify where a brand has an advantage. To conduct a feature analysis, first, make a chart of the product and competitors' products, listing relevant features, as the following table illustrates. Then evaluate how well the product and the competitors' products perform on those features. What are the brand's strong points or weak points? Next, evaluate how important each feature is to the target audience using opinion research. In other words, how much do consumers care about various features (which ones are most important to them) and how do the various brands compare on these features?

How to Do a Feature Analysis

Feature	Importance to Prospect	Product Performance			
		Yours	*X*	*Y*	*Z*
Price	1	+	−	−	+
Quality	4	−	+	−	+
Style	2	+	−	+	−
Availability	3	−	+	−	−
Durability	5	−	+	+	+

Using the two factors of importance and performance, **competitive advantage** is found where (1) the product has a strong feature (2) in an area that is important to the target and (3) where the competition is weaker. The product in the preceding table would compete well on both price and style against X, on price against competitor Y, and on style against competitor Z. Competitor X seems the most vulnerable on two features, price and style, that consumers rate as the most important decision points.

An example of a product launch that was built on a competitive advantage strategy was Sprint's Palm Pre, which was launched in direct competition with Apple's iPhone. The Pre's advantage was multitasking, especially the ability to switch between several open applications and websites.

Locating the Brand Position Let's return now to the concept of a position to see how it is created. In addition to specific product attributes, a number of factors can be used to locate a position for a brand including the following:

- *Superiority Position* Jack Trout suggests that positioning is always easy if something is faster, fancier, safer, or newer.
- *Preemptive Position* Being first in the category often creates category leadership and dominance.
- *Value Position* Walmart's "Always Low Prices" is the epitome of offering good value for the money. Hyundai rode that position through the economic downturn and picked up market share faster than its competitors, passing both Honda and Ford to become the 4th largest automaker in the world.[10]
- *Psychological Position* Often brands are designed around nonproduct differences. For psychological positions, consider these examples: Volvo owns the safety position, Coke owns a position of authenticity for colas ("It's the real thing"), and Hallmark a quality position ("When you care enough to send the very best").
- *Benefit Position* How does the product help the consumer?
- *Usage Position* How, where, and when is the product used and who is using it?
- *Competitor's Strategy* How can the product go head to head with or move completely away from the competition?
- *Category Factors* Is the competition coming from outside the category and, if so, how does the brand compare to these other categories and how does that change the analysis of strengths and weaknesses?

Principle
Strong brands are known for one thing—the test is "What do you think of when you mention the brand's name?"

As we've mentioned the differences have to be distinctive to the brand, as well as important to the consumer. The point is that strong brands become well known for one thing. When you think of Google or eBay, what's the first thing that comes to mind? (Google = search engine; eBay = online auctions.)

James Stengel, former global marketing chief at Procter & Gamble, has developed a new positioning approach that he calls "purpose-based marketing." He points to P&G's Pampers brand, which moved from just keeping babies' bottoms dry to a higher purpose—helping moms nurture healthy, happy babies. The company created new programs offering parenting advice and conducted research on infant-related problems such as sleeping that led to product redesigns.[11]

Many ad campaigns are designed to establish the brand's position by giving the right set of cues about these decision factors to help place the brand in the consumer's mind. If a position is a point in a consumer's mind, planners can map that—in fact, the way planners compare positions is by using a technique called a **perceptual map** that plots all of the competitors on a matrix based on the two most important consumer decision factors. Figure 7.4 illustrates how positions can be mapped for automobiles.

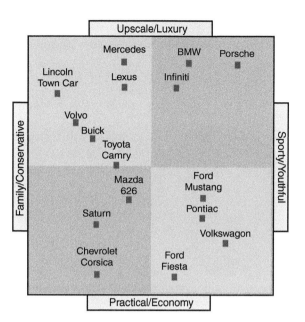

FIGURE 7.4

Perceptual Map
Perceptual maps illustrate the positions occupied by competitors relative to important decision factors. These positions are determined by research into the perceptions of the target market.

Repositioning   Positions are difficult to establish and take years of marketing communication but experts Al and Laura Ries recommend the difficult challenge of **repositioning** when the market changes. Kodak, for example, has always stood for pictures and over the years has owned the moment of capturing an image with a photo: "the Kodak moment." But Kodak also stands for film (think yellow box) and that was the reason for its recent marketplace problems as the camera industry moved to digital formats. Kodak's agency, Ogilvy, developed a repositioning strategy to adapt Kodak's position from "the Moment" to "the gallery"—a place where pictures are kept. This place, of course, can be a digital photo album and that builds on Kodak's tradition and understanding of the importance of pictures in people's lives.

Repositioning, in the view of the Ries's, can only work if the new position is related to the brand's core concept. They are wary of Kodak's move and wonder if the link between the Kodak brand and film is too strong to stretch to digital products. Instead, they recommend using a new brand name for the line of digital products.[12] It will be interesting to see how this repositioning strategy turns out and if Kodak's position can be redefined as galleries of pictures rather than film and photo albums.

For an example of an effective repositioning effort, Ries and Ries point to IBM as a company that repositioned itself from a computer manufacturer to a provider of services. Even though the market for mainframe computers has been declining, they observe that the connection with IBM's brand essence is still there in IBM's new position as a global computer service company. An example comes from China where IBM is marketing an urban-planning tool called Smart City that connects public services and infrastructure projects through information technology. IBM sees China, with its huge public sector and infrastructure projects, as a huge market for its services.

Advertising may express the position, but personal experiences anchor it in the target audience's mind. The role of the brand communication strategy, then, is to relate the product's position to the target market's life experience and associations. The principle in repositioning is to move ahead while at the same time retaining the brand essence. A classic example of an effective repositioning campaign that retains the brand essence as it carves out a new location in consumers' minds is 7-Up, which is described in the *A Matter of Principle* feature.

But sometimes the repositioning strategy may not work. How will it work, for example, when Rolls-Royce unveils an economy car, or at least one that costs a third less than its $380,000 flagship Phantom. Can Rolls use a cheaper car to pump up volume sales or will that strategy dilute the brand's exclusive image?

Brand Communication Strategy

After the objectives, targeting, and positioning have been stated, the next step is to decide the key strategic approach that will deliver the objectives. We'll discuss this in more detail later in this chapter as we explain the "communication brief" created by the account planner to give direction to the creative team. It will also be discussed in more depth in the Chapter 8 on message strategy.

For now, however, consider that the six main effects outlined in the Facets Model all lead to different communication objectives and, therefore, to different strategies. Let's just consider the two

A MATTER OF PRINCIPLE

7-Up: The Uncola Story

Bill Barre, *Lecturer, Department of Communication/Journalism, University of Wisconsin-Eau Claire*

How do you turn what was originally a medicinal product (intended to cure hangovers) and then a mixer with whisky into a soft drink without changing anything about the product or its packaging?

If you said "magic," you'd be correct. But it's not the kind of magic you might think. This is branding magic. It's called positioning. And it created magical results for 7-Up in 1967 when the company repositioned the brand as the Uncola.

Preceding 1967, during the first 37 years that 7-Up was marketed, consumers didn't think of 7-Up as a soft drink, just as we don't think of club soda and tonic water as soft drinks. In 1967, a soft drink was a cola, and a cola was a soft drink.

Four people were in the room when the term "uncola" was first uttered. Three of them are deceased—Orville Roesch, 7-Up's ad manager; Bill Ross, creative director at JWT; and Bob Taylor, senior art director at JWT. Charlie Martell was the fourth person and just a young writer at JWT at the time of the meeting.

"I remember the meeting to this day," recalls Martell. "We realized that we had to be a lot more specific if we hoped to change people's minds about 7-Up. We had to find a way to pick up that green bottle (7-Up), pick it up mentally in consumers' minds, and move it over to here, where Coke and Pepsi were. And until we did that, anything we did that smacked of soft-drink advertising was going to be rejected by consumers."

The objective was clear, yet getting there proved to be completely perplexing. "They had to find a way to attach the word *cola* to 7-Up. Nobody had ever done that before. This was before the word *positioning* was even used in advertising and marketing," says John Furr, a management supervisor at JWT at the time.

Martell remembers that the strategy meeting started as it always started for 7-Up. "We got to talking about how to get somebody to move this green bottle from here to there. And I think Orville said something like we had to associate ourselves with the colas. And Bill Ross started talking about, 'Well, how about, maybe, we call ourselves the non-cola.' And Orville nodded. Thought that sounded good. And I chimed in with 'Maybe we could call it the uncola.' And everyone nodded and said that was an interesting thought. Didn't blow anybody away at that point. They filed it away in their collective consciousness. Few days later, came back and said, 'Maybe we just got something here.' Uncola—it did everything we had been wanting to do. In one word, it did it all. It positioned 7-Up as a cola, yet not a cola. We said, 'Hey . . . let's make some advertising.'"

Today, the 7-Up Uncola campaign is regarded as perhaps the classic example of brand repositioning—and a classic example of how the right brand positioning can lead to marketing magic.

---

most basic approaches, which we sometimes refer to as appealing to the head or the heart. **Hard-sell approaches** use reasons to *persuade* consumers, whereas **soft-sell approaches** build an *image* for a brand and touch consumers' emotions. An ad trumpeting a special reduced price on a tire or claims about its performance is an example of a hard-sell approach. On the other hand, the long-running Michelin ad campaign that shows a baby sitting inside a tire is a soft sell; it symbolizes the brand's safety and reliability with an image that touches your emotions. Go back to the four military ads in the positioning discussion and decide which are hard sell and which are soft sell.

In addition to brand position, let's also consider how a consumer response to messages creates a brand perception. Brand managers use many terms to explain how they think branding works, but they all relate in some way to communication. To better understand how a brand can be linked to a perception, we propose an outline of the communication dimensions of branding using the same six effects we presented in the Facets Model in Chapter 4:

Advertiser's Brand Objective	*Consumer's Response*
Create **brand identity**	**See/Hear**
Cue **brand personality, liking**	**Feel**
Cue **brand position, understanding**	**Think/Understand**
Cue **brand image**	**Connect**
Create **brand promise, preference**	**Believe**
Inspire **brand loyalty**	**Act/Do**

- *Brand Identity* A brand identity must be distinctive. In other words it only represents one particular product within a category, and it must be recognizable and, therefore, memorable. Recognizing the brand means that the consumer knows the brand's identification markers—name, logo, colors, typeface, design, and slogan—and can connect those marks with a past experience or message. All of these can be controlled by the advertiser. The Billings brand identity campaign described earlier in *The Inside Story* included brand reminders in places, as well as conventional marketing communication materials.

- *Brand Personality and Liking* Brand personality—the idea that a brand takes on familiar human characteristics, such as loving (Hallmark, Kodak), competent (IBM), trustworthy (Volvo, Michelin), or sophisticated (Mercedes, Hermes, Rolex)—contributes an affective dimension to the meaning of a brand. Green Giant, for example, built its franchise on the personality of the friendly giant who watches over his valley and makes

The Billings airport used the new "Trailhead" identity campaign in its interior architecture as a welcome to the community and a statement of the Billings brand identity.

sure that Green Giant vegetables are fresh, tasty, nutritious, and appealing to kids. Larry Kelley and Donald Jugenheimer explain in their account planning textbook that it is important to measure the way these personality traits are associated with a brand or a competitor's brand. They observe, "Sometimes it is as important to understand what your brand isn't as much as what it is."[13] The point is to profile the brand as if it were a person, someone you like.

- *Brand Position and Understanding* What does it stand for? Brand strategists sometimes focus on the *soul* or *essence* of the brand. This is related to position, but it goes deeper into the question of what makes the brand distinctive. As Jack Trout explained, "You have to stand for something," and it has to be something that matters to consumers.[14] Kodak is a classic example of a brand with a soul, one deeply embedded in personal pictures and memories. Hallmark's soul is found in the expression of sentiment. Brand essence is also apparent when a brand dominates or defines its category. Category leadership often comes from being the first brand in the market—and with that comes an ownership position. ESPN, for example, owns sports information, Silk is *the* soy milk drink, Starbucks created the high-end coffeehouse, and eBay owns the world of online auctions.

- *Brand Image* Understanding brand meaning involves understanding the symbolism and associations that create **brand image,** the mental impression consumers construct for a product. The richness of the brand image determines the quality of the relationship and the strength of the associations and emotional connections that link a customer to a brand. Advertising researchers call this **brand linkage.**

- *Brand Promise and Brand Preference* A brand is sometimes defined as a promise because it establishes an expectation based on familiarity, consistency, and predictability. And believing the brand promise leads to brand preference and intention to buy. That's what has driven McDonald's to its position as a worldwide leader in the fast-food category. You know what to expect when you walk into a McDonald's anywhere in the world—quality fast food at a reasonable price.

- *Brand Loyalty* A personal experience with a brand can develop into a brand relationship, which is a connection over time that results in customers preferring the brand—thus brand loyalty—and buying it over and over. People have unique relationships with the brands they buy and use regularly, and this is what makes them brand loyal. The company's attitude toward its customers is another factor in loyalty.

Principle
A brand is an integrated perception that includes fragments of information, feelings, and personal experience, all of which come together to give the brand meaning.

To put all this together, a brand perception is created by a number of different fragments of information, feelings, and personal experiences with a brand. You could say that a brand is an *integrated perception*[15]—in other words, all of these different aspects of brand communication work together to create brand meaning. In the best of all worlds, these meanings would be

ALLY's ALLEY.

Carl Ally. Tough manager, persuasive salesman, creative rebel. Founder of Carl Ally, Inc., an agency noted for clear and to-the-point advertising that works with devastating effectiveness. Here, from a recent interview, are some verbal ten-strikes that went rolling right down Ally's alley.

On ad effectiveness:

"You have to satisfy three groups of people if you want an ad to work. The people who make the ad. The people who pay for the ad. And the people who read the ad. If you aren't smart enough to satisfy all three groups, the whole thing will be a bummer."

On what makes a great agency:

"Great clients make great agencies, not vice-versa. If you have an agency that produces great work, but the clients won't publish the work, you're not going to get anywhere. We've been lucky. We've had some very bright, very tough, very talented, very daring clients. They've given us our head. And that's what's made us. Clients make agencies -- good or bad. It's easy for some agency guy to come up with a wild idea. If it bombs, he can go and get another job. But it takes a lot of courage for a client to put his money behind that idea. Because if it bombs, the whole company can go down the drain."

On manipulation:

"Advertising doesn't manipulate society. Society manipulates advertising. Advertisers respond to social trends. Agencies respond to advertisers. It's that simple. The advertising business only reflects the moods of advertisers -- and their moods only reflect the moods of the people they want to sell."

On making great ads:

"Look, it's easy to say water is wet and fire is hot. But it takes something special to figure out that if you put water on fire, the fire will go out. That's what I really enjoy about this business, the whole thing of figuring out what you can do that will make a real difference. Then there's execution, the technical stuff. We're great, technically -- but so are a lot of people. The real trick is figuring out what the substance of an ad should be, and then in handling that substance in the best way possible."

On budgets:

"Good work begets good results. Results beget bigger budgets. Federal Express started with us at $300,000. This year, they'll spend $3 million. Next year, maybe $5 million. Why? Because they know that the money they put into advertising comes back to them multiplied. That's what the advertising business is all about."

On greatness:

"There's a tiny percentage of all the work that's great. And a tiny percentage that's lousy. But most of the work -- well, it's just there. That's no knock on advertising. How many great restaurants are there? Most aren't good nor bad, they're just adequate. The fact is, excellence is tough to achieve in any field. But you have to try."

On The Wall Street Journal:

"I'm a writer, a wordsmith I started as a copywriter. I was a creative director. I began by writing tons -- literally -- tons of copy. So I like The Journal because it is great copy. I use The Journal because I'm in business. And if you're trying to run a business, make it grow, you need The Journal. I put a lot of advertising in The Journal because I know advertising has to make things happen. The Journal gives me the kind of platform I need. The kind of advertising we do -- plain, honest, no nonsense, but with flair and imagination -- works like crazy in The Journal. The Journal's helped us build an advertising agency because it's helped us build the business of the people for whom we work."

CLASSIC

This ad that features Carl Ally is one in a campaign series that the *Wall Street Journal* placed in advertising trade publications. The long-running campaign began in 1975 and featured leaders in advertising explaining their views on how advertising works and why the *Wall Street Journal* is a good medium in which to advertise.

consistent from one customer to another, but because of the vagaries of personal experience, different people have different impressions of a brand.

Emotional branding is one way to anchor a brand perception. As we have said, emotion is a powerful tool in marketing communication and brand liking leads to trust and loyalty. Branding expert John Williams explains, "Research shows that reason and emotions differ in that reason generates conclusions but not necessarily actions, while emotions more frequently lead to actions."[16] Brand liking is the most powerful differentiator.

The challenge to advertisers is to manage their communication efforts so the fragments fit together to form a coherent and integrated brand impression. An example of creating a brand meaning that connects with its audience is the classic *Wall Street Journal* campaign that ran for 25 years in advertising trade publications and established the *Journal* as a premier medium for advertising. You can find many of the ads from this campaign at *www.aef.com/industry/careers/2026.*

Campaign Strategies and Management

Once the situation has been analyzed and the objectives stated, planners decide *how to achieve* the objectives. That calls for a general statement of strategy. The general strategy that guides a campaign can be described in several ways. For example a strategy can focus on branding, positioning, countering the competition, or creating category dominance. Maybe the strategy is designed to change consumers' perception of the brand's price or price–value relationship. The strategy may also seek to increase the size of the market or what marketers call **share of wallet,** the amount customers spend on the brand. Other marketing efforts might involve launching a new brand or a brand extension or moving the brand into a new market.

The important thing to remember, as marketing professor Julie Ruth explains,[17] is that planners have to first analyze the situation to arrive at a great strategy before racing ahead to think about tactics. The decision to expand the market (strategy) by increasing share of wallet (objective) is implemented through promotional tactics ("buy four and get one free").

Another factor in the brand communication strategy is determining the role and importance of the brand's competitive position and how to respond to competitor's messages. During the recession, for example, a number of major brands, such as Dunkin' Donuts, Burger King, and Campbell's Soup developed highly competitive advertising. Domino's Pizza, for example, used an aggressive campaign comparing its oven-baked sandwiches as tasting better than Subway's hoagies. This is a strategy often seen in economic downturns, which analysts describe as "a dogfight" for market share.[18]

Other strategy decisions involve the use of a celebrity spokesperson who becomes the face of the brand. A crisis in emotional branding happened when celebrity superstar Tiger Woods was caught up in a sex scandal. That event moved him from one of the most respected celebrity endorsers to a flawed figure with questionable integrity. His sponsors, including Nike and Accenture, among others, had to decide how to relate their brands not only to his long-time dominance of golf, but also his loss of honor. It's not just the brand images that were threatened by Tiger's infidelities; economists estimate the loss to shareholders of his nine corporate sponsors as close to $12 billion.[19]

For another example, American Express sponsored a four-minute humorous online commercial featuring comedian Jerry Seinfeld and an animated Superman that was designed to create *brand liking.* The two sidekicks play the role of neurotic New Yorkers complaining about such earth-shaking topics as the amount of mayonnaise on their tuna sandwiches. They also relate the benefits of using an American Express card. The message is soft sell and embedded in a gag, which makes the commercial feel more like cinema than advertising. Seinfeld jokes that it isn't going to be interrupted by a commercial because it is a commercial.[20]

Once the strategies have been identified, the next step is implementation. Next we discuss the budgeting and evaluation aspects of implementation. The budget is a critical part of planning an advertising campaign.

An online mini-film commercial for American Express featuring Jerry Seinfeld was designed to entertain and create brand liking. It also generated buzz, which extended its impact through the power of word of mouth.

Budgeting A $50,000 budget will only stretch so far and probably will not be enough to cover the costs of television advertising in most markets. Microsoft, for example, used a $300 million ad blitz to launch its Windows 7 operating system in 2009. The budget also determines how many targets and media plans a company or brand can support and the length of time the campaign can run.

Determining the total appropriation allocated to advertising is not an easy task. Typically, a dollar amount, say $370,000, is budgeted for advertising during the budget planning process (just before the end of the fiscal year). The big budgeting question at the marketing mix and marketing communication mix level is: How much do we need to spend? Let's examine five common budgeting methods used to answer that question:

- *Historical Method* Historical information is the source for this common budgeting method. A budget may simply be based on last year's budget, with a percentage increase for inflation or some other marketplace factor. This method, although easy to calculate, has little to do with reaching advertising objectives.
- *Objective-Task Method* The **objective-task method** looks at the objectives for each activity and determines the cost of accomplishing each objective. For example, what will it cost to make 50 percent of the people in the market aware of this product? This method's advantage is that it develops the budget from the ground up so that objectives are the starting point.
- *Percentage-of-Sales Method* The **percentage-of-sales method** compares the total sales with the total advertising (or marketing communication) budget during the previous year or the average of several years to compute a percentage. This technique can also be used across an industry to compare the expenditures of different product categories on advertising. For example, if a company had sales of $5 million last year and an advertising budget of $1 million, then the *ratio* of advertising to sales would be 20 percent. If the marketing manager predicts *sales* of $6 million for next year, then the ad budget would be $1.2 million. How can we calculate the percentage of sales and apply it to a budget? Follow these two steps:

    Step 1: $\dfrac{\text{Past advertising dollars}}{\text{Past sales}} = \%$ of sales

    Step 2: % of sales $\times$ Next year's sales forecast = New advertising budget

- *Competitive Budgets* This method uses competitors' budgets as benchmarks and relates the amount invested in advertising to the product's share of market. This suggests that the advertiser's share-of-advertising voice—that is, the advertiser's media presence—affects the share of attention the brand will receive, and that, in turn, affects the market share the brand can obtain. Here's a depiction of these relationships:

    $$\frac{\text{Share of}}{\text{media voice}} = \frac{\text{Share of}}{\text{consumer mind}} = \frac{\text{Market}}{\text{share}}$$

    Keep in mind that the relationships depicted here are only a guide for budgeting. The actual relationship between *share-of-media voice* (an indication of advertising expenditures) and **share of mind** or share of market depends to a great extent on factors such as the creativity of the message and the amount of clutter in the marketplace.
- *All You Can Afford* When a company allocates whatever is left over to advertising, it is using the "all you can afford" budgeting method. It's really not a method, but rather a philosophy

about advertising. Companies using this approach, such as high-tech start-ups driven by product innovation, don't value advertising as a strategic imperative. For example, a company that allocates a large amount of its budget to research and has a superior product may find the amount spent on advertising is less important.

Evaluation: Determining Effectiveness   Evaluation is an important part of an advertising plan because it is the process of determining the effectiveness of a campaign. Evaluation is impossible if the campaign has not established measurable objectives, so this part of the campaign plan specifies how exactly those objectives will be measured. In effect, it is a research proposal. All of these procedures and techniques for post-campaign evaluation will be discussed in more detail in Chapter 19. A tool for setting these measurable objectives is account planning, which provides information about what consumers think and feel in order to determine what the plan needs to do to have impact on the market.

ACCOUNT PLANNING: WHAT IS IT?

As Fallon and Senn outlined in one of their principles earlier in this chapter, the key to effective advertising is a powerful consumer insight, a central emotional truth about a customer's relationship with a brand.

When the Eight O'Clock coffee brand, for example, wanted to know more about its audience to better target its message, it used videotaped observational research to identify key insights into how people relate to coffee. Rather than a rosy sunrise, the tapes showed that it was a struggle to get moving. "In real life," the strategic planner concluded, "people stumble around, trying to get kids out of bed. Coffee is the fuel that gets them dressed, fed, and out the door." On other tapes, it also showed that coffee was the reward for mom after the kids are out the door. "I have my cup of coffee when the kids leave," one mom observed. "It's my first moment to take a breather. And it gives me energy."[21]

Account planning is the tool that analyzes the research to uncover these consumer insights. Insight—that's what happens when the light bulb goes off and the planner sees something in a new way. As in the Eight O'Clock coffee example, the planner struck gold by finding out that coffee is the fuel that gets adults, particularly moms, through the morning rush—and it's also the reward for surviving that busy routine. From this insight come clues about how and when to reach the target audience and what to say to her. Here's the planner's mission:

- *Who?* Who are you trying to reach and what insight do you have about how they think, feel, and act? How should they respond to your advertising message?
- *What?* What do you say to them? What directions from the consumer research are useful to the creative team?
- *Where?* How and where will you reach them? What directions from the consumer research are useful to the media team?

Account planning is the research and analysis process used to gain knowledge of the consumer that is expressed as a key *consumer insight* about how people relate to a brand or product. An **account planner,** then, is a person in an agency who uses a disciplined system to research a brand and its customer relationships to devise advertising (and other marketing communication) message strategies that are effective in addressing consumer needs and wants. Account planning agencies are based in research but focus on deriving meanings about consumers. Hall & Partners, for example, has noted that with the new social media, the walls between private life and public life have been breached. (Check the company out at *www.hall-and-partners.com.*) In case you're interested in account planning as a career, here is an actual job description for a vice president for global consumer insights for a major apparel company:

The role of the VP, Global Consumer Insights, is to create competitive advantage by delivering fact-based consumer/customer understanding and insights that facilitate speed and accuracy of strategic and tactical decision-making across all critical parts of the organization. In short, turning data into Insights, and then into Action. The planner will accomplish this by placing consumers first, integrating their "voices" into the planning process, and creating sustaining value at the corporate and brand levels.

As the job description suggests, the account planning function develops the marketing communication strategy with other members of the client and agency team and guides its implementation in the creative work and media planning. Here's an example from Dunkin' Donuts of how account planning works to uncover, in this case, the barriers to purchasing fancy coffee drinks. This mini-case was provided by Regina Lewis, a member of this book's Advisory Board and former vice president of consumer and brand insights at Dunkin':[22]

We found through our research that people wanted to try espresso drinks like lattes and cappuccinos, but they were intimidated and thought such fancy coffee drinks were an ordeal to order. Dunkin' Donuts, of course, is known for its coffee and we felt that to be a great coffee player, we had to have an espresso line. But our brand has always been hot regular coffee for average Joe. What we realized was that there was a place in the marketplace for espresso-based drinks for everybody. It doesn't have to be a fancy treat. We learned that a lot of people like the milky steamed beverages, but they were intimidated by whether they would know how to order them.

When we launched our new line, we used the positioning umbrella of the *democratization of espresso*. We dramatically changed the way our customers view a latte and eliminated the whole barista thing. With push-button machines, we created a world where you can get espresso through the drive-through in less than two minutes. We made espresso available for everybody and we also priced our drinks under Starbucks. We launched with a big public relations campaign titled "The Espresso Revolution—a Shot Being Fired in New England."

In contrast to account managers who are seen as the voice of the client, account planners are described as the voice of the consumer. As London's Account Planning Group (APG) explains it, "The job is to ensure that an understanding of consumer attitudes and behavior is brought to bear at every stage of communications development via continuous involvement in the process."[23]

Account planners don't design the creative strategy for an ad, because this is usually a team process with the participation of the creative people. Rather, the planner evaluates consumers' relationships with the brand to determine the kind of message to which they might respond. Ultimately, the objective is to help the creative team come up with a better idea—making their creative process easier and faster. Susan Mendelsohn, a leader in the U.S. account planning industry and another member of this book's Advisory Board, explains the account planner's task as the following[24]:

Principle
The account manager is seen as the voice of the client, and the account planner is seen as the voice of the consumer.

1. Understand the meaning of the brand.
2. Understand the target audience's relationship to the brand.
3. Articulate communication strategies.
4. Prepare creative briefs based on an understanding of the consumer and brand.
5. Evaluate the effectiveness of the communication in terms of how the target reacts to it (so that planners can keep learning more about consumers and brand communication).

The Research Foundation

As we said at the beginning of this chapter, understanding begins with consumer research, which is at the core of account planning. Some advertisers, such as Johnson & Johnson, insist that consumer researchers and creative teams need to work closely together.[25] That is the role, if not the goal, of most account planners.

Planners use a wide variety of research tools to do "insight mining." In a sense they are social anthropologists who are in touch with cultural and social trends and understand how they take on relevance in people's lives. To do that, the account planner is an *integrator* (who brings all of the information together) and a *synthesizer* (who expresses what it all means in one startlingly simple statement). The *A Matter of Practice* feature about anti-smoking campaigns provides insight about the role research plays in strategic decision-making for campaigns.

" *Just Give Me My One Vice:* "
College Students and Smoking

Joyce M. Wolburg, Professor and Associate Dean, Marquette University

A few years ago, I asked the students in my research class to bring in samples of magazine ads. One student came with anti-smoking messages, which prompted a classmate to say defiantly, "Those ads make me so mad, they just make me want to light up a cigarette." One ad was from the Lorillard Tobacco Company's Youth Smoking Prevention Program and used the slogan, "Tobacco is Whacko." The other was from the American Legacy Foundation's "truth" campaign and told readers, "Your pee contains urea. Thanks to tobacco companies, so do cigarettes. Enjoy." The student's response made me realize that if this reaction is common among other college students, millions of dollars devoted to changing attitudes and behavior toward smoking are missing the mark. As a qualitative researcher, I wanted to find out and decided to investigate what's going on.

Using individual interviews among students, my first revelation was that college student smokers and non-smokers have dramatically different views of anti-smoking messages. Among other findings, non-smokers championed the ads—in fact, the more insulting the better. Many expressed feelings that they have suffered the effects of cigarette smoke long enough, and "it's about time someone took responsibility for the deadly addiction that kills so many people." Anti-smoking messages also reinforced their decision not to smoke. Smokers, on the other hand, rarely championed the ads and frequently showed defiance toward the ads. "I am going to die from something someday, so why shouldn't this be my cause of death?" Students also felt a sense of entitlement toward smoking. "All I'm doing is smoking. I'm not doing heavy drugs or robbing banks or murdering people. This is as bad as I get. Let me have my cigarette. "

Psychologists have long known that when people are told to change their behavior, they will dig in their heels and resist change if they feel their freedom is at stake. And initiatives against smoking and binge drinking have been known to backfire— the so-called "dark side" of social marketing campaigns. Although many smokers believe that the messages are effective for others, the fact that they started smoking proves to them that anti-smoking messages don't work. When they started smoking, they were well aware of the health risks—"you would have to be a moron to not know that it kills"—and they didn't find the ads persuasive— "there isn't an ad out there that would get me to quit." Two things they didn't count on were how addictive smoking is and how quickly people become addicted.

I was convinced that anti-smoking messages were not connecting with this audience and special cessation strategies were needed. I began to wonder how students who have succeeded in quitting were able to accomplish the task. A second qualitative study explored their decisions about quitting and examined the strategies that worked versus those that failed. By far the most common reason for quitting was a personal health scare, which convinced them that they were vulnerable to the risks after all; however, others quit because they no longer identified with smokers or were afraid they were losing control to nicotine. Unfortunately, they were so optimistic that quitting would be easy that they weren't prepared for failure. Every student interviewed made multiple attempts before eventually succeeding

Every student also had a quit date in mind—"by my next birthday, by the time I graduate, by the time I get my first job, by the time I get married, by the time I have children . . . " But they didn't have a plan for how to do it. One of the most common problems was not anticipating the times and places that triggered smoking, and bars seemed to be at the top of everyone's list of places that triggered the impulse to smoke. The association between drinking and smoking was so strong that more than one student had to avoid bars for a period of time until they could handle the temptation.

Most students wanted to quit "cold turkey" without any help from others because they saw it as a badge of honor. However, this strategy only worked for a few. Other students sought support from various sources including the campus health facility. One met regularly with a physician's assistant, who provided support and held him accountable. "Once a week, I would go see this guy and it gave me a sense of accountability. I knew that if I smoked,

I would have to tell him. Not only would I disappoint myself, but I would disappoint him."

Given these insights, I began to wonder if existing cessation programs are addressing the needs of students. I examined various online cessation programs—one from a non-profit organization, one from a government organization and one from the tobacco industry—and found that most offered tips based on the same strategies that worked with these students, but few communicated in a style that students could relate to. Many used testimonials from older smokers, who quit for reasons that were not relevant to most students, such as wanting to avoid exposing their children to secondhand smoke. One program offered targeted materials to groups including smokers over the age of 50, recent quitters, African-American smokers, and Hispanic smokers, but not college students.

So why do college students need a campaign specifically designed for them? One reason is that they operate on a different calendar than others.

Holidays, such as Halloween and St. Patrick's Day, are heavy drinking occasions on most campuses, and with heavy drinking comes heavy smoking. Events that could encourage them to quit smoking are not well timed either. The Great American Smokeout traditionally takes place on the third Thursday in November, days before they are leaving campus to go home for the Thanksgiving holiday.

So, what's the next step? Certainly, it is to implement these findings into a campus-wide campaign. I don't yet know the exact message, but the strategy will have to include storytelling about what worked and what didn't to engage students' interest. Messages must also originate from students in order to achieve relevance and gain credibility.

Sources: Joyce Wolburg, 2006, "College Students' Responses to Antismoking Messages: Denial, Defiance, and Other Boomerang Effects," *Journal of Consumer Affairs, 40* (2) 294-323; Joyce Wolburg, 2009, "Misguided Optimism among College Student Smokers: Leveraging their Quit Smoking Strategies for Smoking Cessation Campaigns," *Journal of Consumer Affairs, 43* (2) 305-331..

Consumer Insight: The Fuel of Big Ideas

Advertising is sometimes thought to be an idea factory, but account planners look at advertising as an insight factory. As Mendelsohn says, "Behind every famously great idea, there is a perhaps less flashy, but immensely powerful insight." Insights are the fuel that fires the ideas. A great insight always intersects with the interests of the consumer and the features of the brand by identifying the value that the brand has for the consumer.

Through the process of strategic and critical thinking, the planner interprets consumer research in terms of a key consumer insight that uncovers the relevance factor—the reason why consumers care about a brand message. Consumer insights reveal the inner nature of consumers' thinking, including such things as mind-sets, moods, motivations, desires, aspirations, and motives that trigger their attitudes and actions.

Finding the "a-ha" in a stack of research reports, data, and transcripts, which is referred to as **insight mining,** is the greatest challenge for an account planner. The Account Planning Group (APG) association describes this process on its website (*www.apg.org.uk*) as "peering into nooks and crannies without losing sight of the big picture in order to identify a key insight that can transform a client's business."

Mendelsohn describes insight mining as "a deep dive" into the meaning of a brand looking for "major truths." She explains that the planner engages in unearthing the relationship (if there is any) that a target audience has with a brand or product and what role that brand plays in their lives. Understanding the brand/consumer relationship is important because account planners are taking on the position of the agency's brand steward. As Abigail Hirschhorn, chief strategic planning officer at DDB explains, "Our work puts our clients in touch with the souls of their brands."[26]

The account planning tool kit is made up of questions that lead to useful insights culled from research. Here is a set of questions that can lead to useful insights:

- What is a realistic response objective (perception, knowledge, feelings, attitudes, symbolic meanings, behavior) for this target group?
- What are the causes of their lack of response?
- What are the barriers to the desired response?
- What could motivate them to respond in the desired way?
- What is the role of each element in the communication mix to motivate them or remove a barrier?

Principle
A great insight intersects with the interests of the consumer and the features of the brand.

Here's an example of how data analysis works: Imagine you are working on a cookie account. Here's your brand share information:

	2009 Share (%)	*2010 Share (%)*
Choco Nuts (your brand)	50	40
Sweet 'n Crunchy (your main competitor)	25	30

What's the problem with this situation? Obviously your brand is losing market share to your primary competitor. As a result, one of your goals might be to use a marketing communication mix to drive higher levels of sales. But that goal is so broad that it would be difficult to determine whether communication is sufficient to solve the problem. Let's dig deeper and consider another set of data about household (HH) purchases in a year.

	2009 HH Purchases	*2010 HH Purchases*
Choco Nuts	4	3
Sweet 'n Crunchy	2.5	3

What problem can you identify here? It looks like your loyal brand users are reducing their purchases at the same time Sweet 'n Crunchy customers are increasing their purchases. It may even be that some of your customers are switching over to Sweet 'n Crunchy. A strategy based on this information might be to convince people that your brand tastes better and to remind your loyal customers of the reasons they have preferred your brand. Those goals can be accomplished by marketing communication.

When you combine the two pieces of information and think about it, another insight might explain this situation. Perhaps people are simply eating fewer cookies. If that's a problem, then the communication opportunity lies in convincing people to return to eating cookies. That is more of a *category sell* problem (sell cookies) rather than a *competitive sell* (set the brand against the competition). In the Choco Nuts example, it would take more research to know which situation applies here. Here's a summary of these two different strategic approaches.

	Competitive/Brand Sell	*Category Sell*
What?	Challenger brand	Leader brand
Who?	Loyal buyers	Medium/light/lapsed buyers
What effect?	Compare cookie brands	Compare against other snacks
Objective?	Increase share of wallet	Increase total category sales
Message?	"Our cookies are better than theirs"	"Cookies are better than candy or salty snacks"

The important dimensions account planners seek to understand in planning brand strategies include relationship, perceptions, promise, and point of differentiation. Most importantly, planners are looking for clues about the brand's *meaning,* which is usually phrased in terms of the brand essence (core, soul), personality, or image, as the SeaPort outdoor boards illustrate.

The Communication Brief

The outcome of strategic research usually reaches agency creative departments in the form of a strategy document called a **communication brief** or **creative brief,** which explains the consumer insight and summarizes the basic strategy decisions. Although the exact form of this document differs from agency to agency and from advertiser to advertiser, the brief is an outline of the message strategy that guides the creative team and helps keep its ideas strategically sound. As the planner's main product, it should be clear, logical, and focused. Here is an outline of a typical communication brief:

- *Problem* What's the problem that communication can solve? (establish position, reposition, increase loyalty, get people involved, increase liking, etc.)
- *Target Audience* To whom do we want to speak? (brand loyal, heavy users, infrequent users, competition's users, etc.)

WELCOME TO THE FAST CLASS. SEA✦PORT AIRLINES

DEPART FROM THE HASSLE. SEA✦PORT AIRLINES

SHOWCASE

These outdoor boards are for SeaPort Airlines, which serves Seattle, Juneau, Portland, and other West Coast cities. They make a statement about the SeaPort target audience—influential business travelers—and their lifestyle.

These ads were contributed by Karl Schroeder, copywriter at Coates Kokes in Portland, Oregon. A graduate of the University of Oregon advertising program, he was nominated by Professor Charles Frazer.

- *Consumer Insights* What motivates the target? What are the "major truths" about the target's relationship to the product category or brand?
- *Brand Imperatives* What are the important features? What's the point of competitive advantage? What's the brand's position relative to the competition? Also, what's the brand essence, personality, and/or image. Ogilvy & Mather says, "What is the unique personality for the brand? People use products, but they have relationships with brands."
- *Communication Objectives* What do we want customers to do in response to our messages? (perception, knowledge, feelings, symbolic meanings, attitudes and conviction, action)
- *The Proposition or Selling Idea* What is the single thought that the communication will bring to life in a provocative way?
- *Support* What is the reason to believe the proposition? Ogilvy & Mather explains, "We need to give consumers 'permission to believe'—something that allows them to rationalize, whether to themselves or others, what is in reality an emotionally driven brand decision. The support should be focused on the insight or proposition, the truths that make the brand benefit indisputable."
- *Creative Direction* How can we best stimulate the desired response? How can we best say it?
- *Media Imperatives* Where and when should we say it?

Source: This outline was compiled from one contributed by Susan Mendelsohn, as well as from the creative brief outline developed by the Ogilvy agency and presented on its website (*www.ogilvy.com*).

The brief is strategic, but it also should be inspirational. It is designed to ignite the creative team and give a spark to their idea process. A good brief doesn't set up limitations and boundaries but rather serves as a springboard. It is the first step in the creative process. Charlie Robertson, an account planner and brand consultant, likens the brief to a fire starter: "The match is the brief, the ignition is the inspiring dialogue [in the briefing], and the flare is the creative."[27]

PLANNING FOR IMC CAMPAIGNS

An IMC plan follows the same basic outline as an advertising plan. The difference, however, lies with the scope of the plan and the variety of marketing communication areas involved in the effort. The more tools used, the harder it is to coordinate their efforts and maintain consistency across a variety of messages. The objective in IMC planning is to make the most effective and consistent use of all marketing communication functions and to influence or control the impact of other communication elements. Account planner Susan Mendelsohn, who is also a member of this book's Advisory Board, explains the intersections of IMC and account planning in the *A Matter of Practice* feature.

IMC Campaign Planning

Effective IMC plans lead to profitable long-term brand relationships. The emphasis on brand building is one reason account planning is moving beyond advertising and being used in IMC campaign planning. Jon Steel, author of a book on advertising and account planning, says planning works best as it is integrated into the entire communication mix.[28] The three main areas where an IMC plan differs from an advertising plan are objectives, stakeholders, and contact points.

Objectives   IMC objectives are tied to the effects created by the various forms of marketing communication. All marketing communication tools have strengths and weaknesses. You use public relations, for example, to announce something that is newsworthy, whereas you use sales promotion to drive immediate action. Therefore, an IMC plan operates with a set of interrelated objectives that specify the strategies for all of the different tools. Each area has a set of objectives similar to those outlined earlier for advertising; these will be presented in more detail in chapters later in the book that relate to those areas. For discussion at this point, however, the following list presents the main IMC areas in terms of their primary effects:

- *Public Relations* Announce news; affect attitudes and opinions; maximize credibility and likability; create and improve stakeholder relationships.
- *Consumer Sales Promotion* Stimulate behavior; generate immediate response, intensify needs, wants, and motivations; reward behavior; stimulate involvement and relevance; create pull through the channel.
- *Trade Sales Promotion* Build industry acceptance; push through the channel; motivate cooperation; energize sales force, dealers, distributors.
- *Point-of-Purchase* Increase immediate sales; attract attention at decision point; create interest; stimulate urgency; encourage trial and impulse purchasing.
- *Direct Marketing* Stimulate sales; create personal interest and relevance; provide information; create acceptance, conviction.
- *Sponsorship and Events* Build awareness; create brand experience, participation, interaction, involvement; create excitement.
- *Packaging* Increase sales; attract attention at selection point; deliver product information; create brand reminder.
- *Specialties* Reinforce brand identity; continuous brand reminder; reinforce satisfaction; encourage repeat purchase; reward loyal customers.

Stakeholders   We introduced the concept of stakeholders in the IMC introduction in Chapter 2, but let's look a little deeper into this concept. The target in an IMC plan includes more than just consumers. The term **stakeholder** refers to any group of people who have a stake in the success of a company or brand. These audiences include all those who might influence the purchase of

A MATTER OF PRACTICE

The Crossover between Account Planning and IMC

By Susan Mendelsohn, Ph.D., President, Susan Mendelsohn Consultants

The distinction between account planning and IMC is becoming blurred. In today's multifaceted business world, account planners have to become immersed in all aspects of a client's business in order to address their numerous stakeholders, not just their consumers. To accomplish this, account planners first need to learn about most aspects of a company as possible using the techniques described earlier in this book. Second, planners must address every part of a business that could influence and impact the brand/product. Finally, the planner must craft meaningful communication messages and programs for each constituent.

Getting to know the unique components of each business and then understanding the interplay of these components is the account planners' new challenge. The planner must use multiple sources to uncover useful brand/product information about each business.

Example one: with nonprofits such as a museum, an account planner might need to examine the appropriate scientific community, government agencies and foundations, donors/board of trustees/friends of the museum, and the public. It might be necessary to alter the communication messages for these different groups from the overarching main message of the museum in order to address the needs of each individual constituent.

Example two: when working with packaged-good companies, planners have to address industry specific business issues and develop an appropriate contact point mix. Here, the account planner typically considers the different needs and perspectives of consumer brands, marketing, cafés/kiosks, retail, sales force, and food service (restaurants, hotels, convenience stores).

Example three: addressing insurance or financial institutions, the mix changes again. Planners in the insurance area often examine consumers (current and prospective policy holders), corporate decision makers, sales agents, stockholders, and the financial community (including Wall Street).

It's an exciting time to be involved in the field of account planning. The planner's role is expanding and becoming more complex is order to address the new challenges of of business, branding, and fragmented communication.

products and the success of a company's marketing program, as the table below shows. Employees are particularly important and their support or buy-in for marketing, advertising, and marketing communication programs is managed through an activity called **internal marketing.** Susan Mendelsohn, for example, describes the targets for one of her snack clients as brand marketing consumers, café and kiosk customers, food service operations, and sales staff.

Types of Stakeholder Audiences

Corporate Level	Marketing Level	Marcom Level
Employees	Consumers	Target audiences
Investors, financial community (analysts, brokers, and the financial press)	Customers	Target stakeholders
	Stakeholders	Employees
	Market segments	Trade audiences
Government bodies and agencies	Distributors, dealers, retailers, and others in the distribution channel	Local community
Regulatory bodies	Suppliers and vendors, including agencies	Media (general, special interest, trade)
Business partners	Competitors	Consumer activist groups
		General public
		Opinion leaders

An important thing to remember is that people don't simply line up in one box or another. Here's a new principle: the **Sixth Principle of IMC,** which states that *stakeholders overlap.* Not

Sixth Principle of IMC

Stakeholders overlap.

only do they play different roles, they also talk to one another. Employees, for example, may also be customers, shareholders, and members of the local community, perhaps even elected officials. Their primary medium is word of mouth, which is another reason why this type of communication is so important in IMC programs. The fact of overlapping membership complicates message strategy and demands that there be a certain core level of consistency in all brand messages both from a company but also within stakeholder conversations.

Contact Points   IMC programs are designed to maximize all the contacts that a consumer and other stakeholders might have with a brand. As we explained in Chapter 2, **contact points,** also called **touch points,** are all the ways and places where a person can come into contact with a brand, all the points where a message is delivered about the brand. Contact points can be advertising and traditional marketing communication messages, but they can also include all of the other ways a brand communicates through personal experiences. This leads to the **Seventh Principle of IMC:** *all contact points deliver brand messages.* These messages can be both good and bad, creating positive or negative feelings. Marcom managers hope to maximize and leverage the good ones and minimize the bad ones.

Seventh Principle of IMC
All contact points deliver brand messages.

Synergy and Strategic Consistency

Given that an IMC plan involves a lot of messages delivered through multiple media at many different contact points, as well as interactive communication, the marcom planner's biggest concern is creating consistent messages. The ultimate difference between an advertising campaign and an IMC campaign is the creation, development, delivery, and evaluation of multiplatform messages. For that reason, IMC planners are looking for ways to intensify the synergy of the messages so that the brand impact is greater than what can be delivered by any one type of message. This leads to the **Eighth Principle of IMC:** *consistency drives synergy.*

Eighth Principle of IMC
Consistency drives synergy.

Synergy is particularly important for marketers concerned about the efficiency of their marketing communication who are looking for ways to maximize the cost efficiency of their budgets. Andy Polansky, president of the Weber Shandwick agency, cautions managers to be efficient by making all communication efforts align with audience interests "so there is strategic consistency across how you are marketing online, in-person and in traditional media."[29]

The problem is that we know various stakeholders have different types of bonds with a brand, so the message, by necessity, will be different for different audiences. Kellogg's doesn't talk to moms the same way it talks to kids about a kid's cereal, such as Froot Loops. And it certainly has a different message for regulators at the Food and Drug Administration and activists concerned about children's health, as well as those messages for the investment community including its own shareholders. It isn't that the messages are inconsistent, they are just different in that they address different concerns and issues of the various stakeholder audiences. What is common, however, is faithfulness to the brand image and position. That's what we mean by **strategic consistency**—messages vary with the interest of the stakeholder but the brand strategy remains the same.

Synergy is an organizational problem, one that calls for **cross-functional planning.** In other words, everyone involved in delivering messages or responding to consumer messages needs to be involved in planning the campaign so no off-strategy messages undercut the consistency of the effort.

Looking Ahead

Strategic consistency is the result of carefully researched marketing communication plans. The actual messages that bring the strategy to life are also a result of strategic planning, but also creative thinking. Part 3 of this book will review the creative side of marketing communication beginning with Chapter 8, which continues the strategy discussion in terms of message strategy.

IT'S A WRAP

Winning the Coke Zero Infringement Case

So how well did the Coke Zero campaign strategies work in exciting the interest of young males in a lower calorie soft drink and delivering the message that Coke Zero tastes similar to real Coke?

To evaluate the effectiveness, return to the three measurable objectives: increase brand awareness, motivate the target audience to try Coke Zero, and convince men ages 18 to 34 that Coke Zero tastes like Coke. Within a year Coke Zero's overall brand awareness far exceeded the goal, achieving awareness with more than 90 percent of its target audience. It succeeded in not only getting the men to know about Coke Zero, nearly half of the target audience of young men 18–34 tried it, too. The campaign was able to increase consumer recognition of the taste similarity message. Four out of 10 people who were interviewed recognized the message that Coke Zero tastes like Coke. The success of achieving the campaign goals is evident.

You might ask if this campaign was beneficial for the Coca-Cola company overall. Could it be that it cannibalized its audience by shifting Coke drinkers to Coke Zero drinkers? John D. Sicher, Jr., editor and publisher at *Beverage Digest*, believes the campaign's effects have been positive. He said, "Forty-five percent of Coke Zero sales are incremental rather than borrowed from Diet Coke."

Based on the evidence, this nontraditional campaign, and its unconventional message, Coke Zero was awarded a Silver Effie for effectiveness.

Case closed.

Key Points Summary

1. **What is the difference between objectives, strategies, and tactics in strategic planning and how are the three levels of planning connected?** Objectives are what you want to accomplish, or goals; strategies are how you will accomplish the objectives, or the design or plan; and tactics are the ways in which you implement the strategies, or the execution. The three-tiered process of strategic planning involves a set of cascading objectives and strategies. Corporate objectives and strategies as spelled out in a business plan are achieved through planning at the level of marketing (and other business areas, such as production), and marketing objectives and strategies give direction to marketing communication programs including advertising.

2. **How is a campaign plan constructed, and what are its six basic sections?** An advertising or IMC plan summarizes the strategic decisions in the following areas: situation

analysis (background research, SWOTs, key communication problem), objectives, targeting, positioning (features, attributes, differentiation, competitive advantage), strategic approach (branding, positioning, category dominance, marketing mix support, consumer response), and campaign management (budgeting, evaluation).

3. **What is account planning, and how is it used in advertising?** Account planning matches the right message to the right audience and identifies the right media to deliver that message. The three key factors are consumer insight, message strategy direction, and media strategy direction.

4. **In what ways does an IMC plan differ from an advertising plan?** The three additional factors you find discussed in an IMC plan are the stakeholders, the contact points, and a wider set of objectives that identify the interwoven effects of the various marketing communication tools.

Words of Wisdom: Recommended Reading

Avery, Jim, *Advertising Campaign Planning,* Chicago: The Copy Workshop, 2000.

Fallon, Pat, and Fred Senn, *Juicing the Orange: How to Turn Creativity into a Powerful Business Advantage,* Boston: Harvard Business School Press, 2006.

Kelley, Larry, and Donald Jugenheimer, *Advertising Account Planning,* Armonk, NY: M.E. Sharpe, 2006.

Parente, Donald, *Advertising Campaign Strategy: A Guide to Marketing Communication Plans,* 4th ed., Florence, KY: South-Western, 2005.

Ries, Al, and Jack Trout, *Positioning: The Battle for Your Mind,* New York: McGraw-Hill, 1981 (20th anniversary ed., 2000).

Schultz, Don, and Beth Barnes, *Strategic Advertising Campaigns,* 4th ed., Lincolnwood, IL: NTC, 1995.

Steel, Jon, *Truth, Lies and Advertising: The Art of Account Planning,* Hoboken, NJ: Wiley, 1998.

Weichselbaum, Hart (Ed.), *Readings in Account Planning,* Chicago: The Copy Workshop, 2000.

Key Terms

account planner, p. 238

account planning, p. 238

benchmarked, p. 227

brand image, p. 235

brand linkage, p. 235

campaign plan, p. 222

communication brief, p. 242

competitive advantage, p. 232

contact points, p. 246

creative brief, p. 242

cross-functional planning, p. 246

feature analysis, p. 232

features, p. 230

hard-sell approaches, p. 234

insight mining, p. 241

internal marketing, p. 245

marketing plan, p. 220

mission statement, p. 220

objectives, p. 218

objective-task method, p. 237

parity products, p. 230

percentage-of-sales
   method, p. 237

perceptual map, p. 233

position, p. 230

product differentiation, p. 230

repositioning, p. 233

return on investment
   (ROI), p. 219

share of market, p. 221

share of mind, p. 237

share of wallet, p. 236

situation analysis, p. 224

soft-sell approaches, p. 234

stakeholder, p. 244

strategic business unit
   (SBU), p. 219

strategic consistency, p. 246

strategic planning, p. 218

strategies, p. 218

SWOT analysis, p. 224

tactics, p. 218

touch points, p. 246

Review Questions

1. Define objectives, strategies, and tactics, and explain how they differ.

2. What information does an advertising plan derive from the business plan? From the marketing plan?

3. What is a situation analysis, and how does it differ from a SWOT analysis?

4. What are the requirements of a measurable objective?

5. Explain how the facets model of advertising effects can be used to structure a set of advertising objectives.

6. What is a position, and how is it established?

7. What is account planning, and what does the account planner bring to an advertising plan?

8. What are the key differences between an advertising plan and an IMC plan?

Discussion Questions

1. Think of a product you purchased recently after seeing an advertisement. Which strategies can you discern in the advertising? Did the advertising help to convince you to purchase the product? How did that work?

2. Luna Pizza is a regional producer of frozen pizza. Its only major competitor is Brutus Bros. The following is a brief excerpt from Luna's situation analysis for the next fiscal year. Estimate the next year's advertising budgets for Luna under each of the following circumstances:

    a. Luna follows an historical method by spending 40 cents per unit sold in advertising, with a 5 percent increase for inflation.

    b. Luna follows a fixed percentage of projected sales method, using 7 percent.

    c. Luna follows a share-of-voice method. Brutus, the primary competitive pizza brand, is expected to use 6 percent of sales for its advertising budget in the next year.

	Actual *Last Year*	*Estimated* *Next Year*
Units sold	120,000	185,000
$ sales	420,000	580,000
Brutus $ sales	630,000	830,000

3. The owners of the Vico brand of organic coconut water believe that it is the next big trend in the bottled water category, except it uses the clear liquid inside young, green coconuts (not coconut milk that is derived from pressing the coconut pulp). Healthy and natural, the product is popular in South America and is becoming a niche market in New York City and other cities with South American immigrant populations. Outline a preliminary situation analysis, objectives, targeting, positioning, and branding strategies. In each section, explain what other information you would need to fully develop this plan.

4. *Three-Minute Debate* You are in a meeting about the strategy for an automotive client who is proposing a new upscale luxury version of an electric car. One of your team members says positioning is an old strategy and no longer useful for modern products because the market is so complex and changes so fast. Another person argues strongly that you need to understand the position in the consumer's mind before you can even begin to develop an advertising strategy. As a team, take one side of this issue, for the launch of this new product and develop your position to present and defend in a class debate.

Take-Home Projects

1. *Portfolio Project* Examine the following websites: *www.lexus.com, www.infiniti.com,* and *www.mercedes-benz.com*. Based on what you find on these sites, compare the positioning strategies for these top-of-the-line SUV models. Analyze the product features, competitive advantage, and points of differentiation.

2. *Mini-Case Analysis* Review the "Coke/Coke Zero Taste Infringement" case that opened and closed this chapter. Assume you are working on this account and have been asked to pull together a presentation for the brand team for the next year of this campaign. What research would you recommend conducting in order to decide if the campaign should be continued? What do you need to find out in order to make this decision?

Team Project: The BrandRevive Campaign

After compiling as much information as you can for your BrandRevive campaign on your brand, the category, and consumers, the next step is to draft a campaign plan for the brand's revitalization.

- Review your research and develop a set of SWOTs and from that analysis the key communication problem to be solved with this campaign.
- Develop a set of objectives for this campaign and explain them.
- Identify the target audience for your campaign and explain your decision.

- Develop a brand positioning strategy for your brand and explain it. In particular, consider the wisdom and feasibility of a repositioning effort.
- Identify the key insight(s) that would make your brand more relevant and explain how you arrived at that conclusion. Summarize your findings about the target market in a creative brief.
- Present your findings in a two-page report and a PowerPoint presentation that is no longer than four slides. In the presentation explain and justify your recommendations.

Hands-On Case

The Century Council

Read the Century Council case in the Appendix before coming to class.

1. Create an outline of what you believe "The Stupid Drink" campaign plan looked like based on this chapter and the case study. Keep it to one page.

2. Develop at least three business objectives and strategies, three communications objectives and strategies, and three media objectives and strategies based on the case study.

CHAPTER 4

Campaign Planning 2

Media Planning and Buying

CHAPTER KEY POINTS

1. What is a media plan and what is the role of media research in developing media plans?
2. What are the four steps in media planning and why are they important?
3. How do IMC and global marketing affect media plans?
4. What are the responsibilities of media buyers?

Dove Audiences Redefine Beauty

So far you've read a lot about effective brand communication. You've seen how Burger King successfully kept its Whopper in the minds of the hungry, how Wii became a cultural phenomenon, and how Chick-fil-A consistently conveys its quirky "Eat Mor Chikin" message delivered by cows on billboards. As these cases demonstrate, one of the fundamental principles of successful communication is the ability to understand how best to connect with the consumer.

Unilever's campaign for Dove, which won a Grand Effie and Festival of Media Award for "branding bravery," provides another example of great advertising that recognized a truth held by consumers and then connected on a personal level with those consumers. The "Campaign for Real Beauty" touched a nerve and punctured the cultural obsession with stick-thin bodies and Barbie doll images. The Dove campaign was risky because it sought to literally redefine beauty in advertising and to acknowledge a change in the way women see themselves. It could have been a bomb, but it was a winner because it spoke to every woman's need to look and feel her best without promising or reinforcing impossible standards of beauty.

Unilever commissioned research that eventually drove the marketing campaign. Some startling statistics from the study included these findings:

- Only 2 percent of the respondents believed they were beautiful.
- Of the respondents, 68 percent indicated they strongly believed that the media and advertising set an unrealistic standard of beauty most women can't achieve.

Here's how the Dove "Campaign for Real Beauty" unfolded.

Dove recognized it needed to reach every woman, and to do that it strategically placed messages in many different media. The message of the Dove "Campaign for Real Beauty" provided a deliberate contrast with that of the competition in beauty and women's magazines like *Glamour*, *Allure*, and *Vogue*. Heavy emphasis was placed on print rather than television because of print media's ability to stop the audience and make them really look at the models in the ad and contemplate the meaning of beauty.

Dove didn't ignore broadcast media, however—they even ran an ad during the Super Bowl. They also established a website (*campaignforrealbeauty.com*), which urges a boost in self-esteem by defying stereotypes that define beautiful as perfect—and skinny. Part of the campaign, a Web video titled *Evolution*, was a viral phenomenon that reached millions.

Spending a fifth of the normal amount for a personal-care product launch, the Dove advertising was concentrated in the top 10 cities where it would have the most immediate impact. Outdoor and transit advertisements were plastered on billboards and buses to generate public debate.

A similar strategy was used in 2007 to launch Dove's *ProAge* line, which continues the counterintuitive strategy by celebrating older women with their silver hair, wrinkles, and age spots. In Canada, the campaign found its voice in *Finding Body and Soul*, a play celebrating beauty through the ages by well-respected Canadian playwright Judith Thompson. Its cast of 12 real women (not actresses) are ages 45 and older, and auditioned by writing a letter that started "Dear Body. . . ." Dove devotees also were invited to host *ProAge* parties, complete with a party kit.

Although we live in a culture that worships physical perfection, Dove is trying valiantly to broaden that definition. At the end of the chapter you'll read about the results of the Dove efforts.

Sources: Effie brief supplied by Ogilvy & Mather; "Dove Campaign for Real Beauty Case Study: Innovative Marketing Strategies in the Beauty Industry," June 2005, *www.datamonitor.com*; Molly Prior, "Most Innovative Ad Campaign: Dove Campaign for Real Beauty," *Women's Wear Daily*, 190, Issue 122, December 9, 2005: 36–39; Ann-Christine Diaz, "Book of Tens: Best Non-TV Campaigns of the Decade," December 14, 2009, *http://adage.com*; Michael Bush, "Unilever Wins Two Awards for Axe, Dove Media Campaigns," April 20, 2009, *http://adage.com*.

As Unilever knows, media planning is a problem-solving process. The problem: How can media choices help meet the marketing and advertising objectives? The ultimate goal is to reach the target audience with the right message in the best possible way at the best possible time in the most efficient way possible. In this chapter, we review how a media plan is developed—how media planners set objectives and develop media strategies. We then explore the media-buying function and explain how media buyers execute the plan.

HOW ARE MEDIA PLANS CREATED?

Media planners are in the connection business, as the Dove case illustrates. Their work connects brand messages with customers and other stakeholders. They identify and activate the points of contact where brand messages touch consumers. The Dove plans included traditional media, particularly print and outdoor, but also websites, Internet videos, viral marketing, a theatrical play, and party hosting. Note that this media plan involved a lot more than advertising, which supports the point we made in Chapter 11 that all forms of marketing communication use media.

Making connections that resonate with the audience is the hallmark of effective marketing communication, wherever that may occur. Think about the U.S. Army's power to connect with recruits using the video game–based experience and event you read about in Chapter 13, as well as the emotional connections created in the Dove "*Real Women*" and "*ProAge*" campaigns. Another example features embedded ads in video games as described in *The Inside Story* feature. Not only was this an interesting ad placement, it also generated great publicity.

We mentioned in Chapter 11 that traditionally, the advertising agency's media department has been responsible for developing the media plan with input from the agency's account and creative teams and the marketer's brand management group. More recently, media-buying companies have moved into the planning stage as well, bringing the expertise of their media researchers and negotiators. Some major agencies have spun off the media function as a separate company; then they contract with that company for their media planning and buying services. Others have

THE INSIDE STORY

Campaign Ads in Video Games

Holly Duncan Rockwood, *Director of Corporate Communications, Electronic Arts*

In the fall of 2008, President Obama made advertising history when his political campaign ran ads in video games. The ads were highly targeted, intended to reach a typically hard-to-reach demographic—males ages 18 to 34—and ran for just a few weeks before the election in a half dozen games from Electronic Arts. The ads were dynamically served via the Internet to gamers who resided in swing states, coveted votes that had the potential to make or break the election. For example, a gamer might drive down a freeway in *Burnout* and pass a billboard advertising that "Early Voting Has Begun" and a similar message could be found inside the stadium of an *NBA LIVE* basketball game. The campaign was considered groundbreaking for several reasons. For starters, it was a first that such a prominent political candidate would build a marketing strategy that included advertising in video games. This type of advertising is an emerging medium for reaching consumers that has frequently been touted as the next big opportunity for marketers. From a corporate communications perspective, the Obama campaign seemed to suggest that video game advertising had finally arrived, and the novelty provoked an unprecedented level of interest from news organizations.

The first media calls we received were simply fact checking that the campaign ads were running and actually real, not a hoax. However, when we received calls from the *New York Times*, the Associated Press, and National Public Radio early on a Tuesday morning, we realized this might be the tip of a major news story. Our corporate message quickly evolved from one of just acknowledging the campaign, to one that proactively supported EA's corporate messaging around in game advertising. We stressed that EA did not side with one party or another, and emphasized the effectiveness of reaching a highly engaged target audience that plays the games that ran the ads.

Like political campaigns, this rapid response approach to corporate communications strategy is not uncommon in video games, an industry that is highly competitive and often in the public eye with topics ranging from mature content and video game ratings to the unveiling of hotly anticipated titles. Corporate communications professionals often act as spokespeople for timely and occasionally controversial issues.

There are many lessons to be found by working in public relations in the video games industry, like being creative in finding opportunities to drive a story when others might shy away. It's exciting to work for a company like EA, and there are a lot of opportunities for the people who speak on behalf of it. There is never a dull moment and it's one of the best jobs I've ever had.

Holly Duncan Rockwood earned her B.S. in advertising from the University of Colorado and an M.S. in integrated marketing communication from Northwestern University.

FIGURE 14.1

The Central Role of Media Research
Media planners look for data from creative, marketing, and media sources. All of this information is used in both media planning and buying.

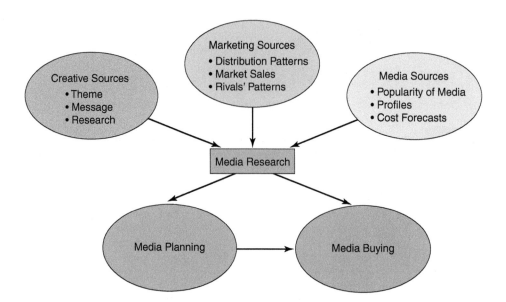

kept the planning in house but contract with an outside media-buying service. Once the media plan is developed, a media-buying unit or team, either in the ad agency or external in a separate media company, executes it.

Given the industry trends, the hot media shops have specialties in new media. For example, the long-established Ogilvy agency launched neo@Ogilvy as a digital-media group to help advertisers figure out how to allocate their ad budgets in the vast array of new media, such as online video, social networking sites, and search advertising. *The Inside Story* by David Rittenhouse in Chapter 5 explained how agencies such as neo@Ogilvy approach the new arena of online behavioral targeting.

Media Research: Information Sources

Some people believe media decisions are the hub in the advertising wheel because media costs are often the biggest element in the marketing communication budget. Not only are media decisions central to advertising planning, media research is central to media planning. That realization stems from not only the large amount of money that's on the line, but also the sheer volume of data and information that media planners must gather, sort, and analyze before media planning can begin. Figure 14.1 illustrates the wide range of media information sources and the critical role media research plays in the overall advertising planning process.

- *Client Information* The client is a good source for various types of information media planners use in their work, such as demographic profiles of current customers (both light and heavy users), response to previous promotions, product sales and distribution patterns, and, most importantly, the budget of how much can be spent on media. Geographical differences in category and brand sales also affect how the media budget is allocated. With consumer goods and services especially, rates of consumption can differ greatly from one region to another.
- *Market Research* Independently gathered information about markets and product categories is another valuable tool for media planners. Mediamark Research, Inc. (MRI), Scarborough (local markets), and Mendelsohn (affluent markets) are research companies that provide this service. This information is usually organized by product category (detergents, cereals, snacks, etc.) and cross-tabulated by audience groups and their consumption patterns. Accessible online for a fee, this wealth of information can be searched and compared across thousands of categories, brands, and audience groups. Although the reports may seem intimidating, they are not that difficult to use. Figure 14.2 is a page from an MRI report showing how to read MRI data. Media planners use MRI data to check which groups, based on demographics and lifestyles, are high and low in category use, as well as where they live and what media they use.
- *Competitive Advertising Expenditures* In highly competitive product categories, such as packaged goods and consumer services, marketers track how much competing brands spend

How to Read an MRI CrossTab

The CrossTab format is a standard research display format that allows multiple variables of related data to be grouped together. Below is a screen capture of an MEMRI² CrossTab, complete with explanations of key numbers. Please note that all the numbers are based on the 2004 Spring MRI study, and that the projected numbers (000) are expressed in thousands.

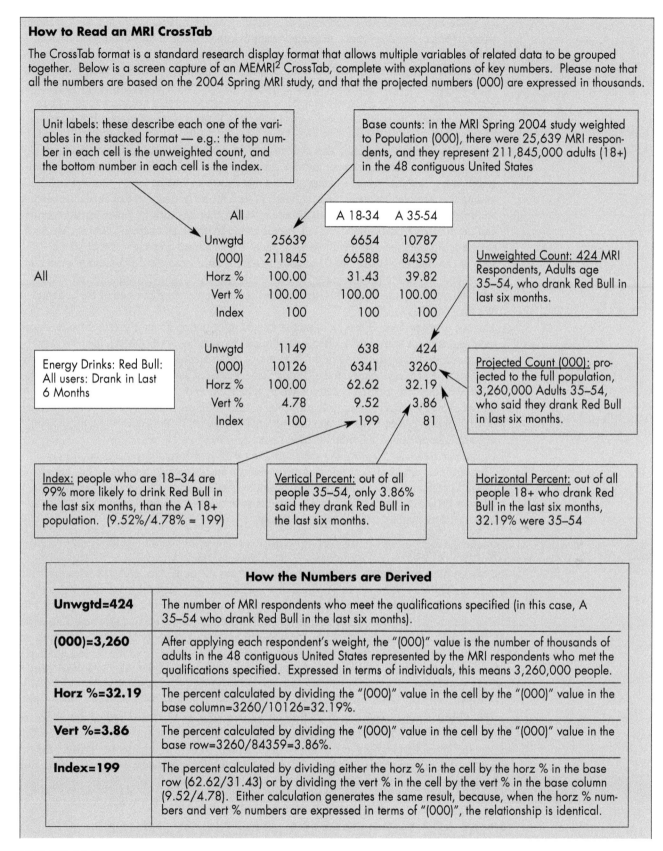

How the Numbers are Derived

Unwgtd=424	The number of MRI respondents who meet the qualifications specified (in this case, A 35–54 who drank Red Bull in the last six months).
(000)=3,260	After applying each respondent's weight, the "(000)" value is the number of thousands of adults in the 48 contiguous United States represented by the MRI respondents who met the qualifications specified. Expressed in terms of individuals, this means 3,260,000 people.
Horz %=32.19	The percent calculated by dividing the "(000)" value in the cell by the "(000)" value in the base column=3260/10126=32.19%.
Vert %=3.86	The percent calculated by dividing the "(000)" value in the cell by the "(000)" value in the base row=3260/84359=3.86%.
Index=199	The percent calculated by dividing either the horz % in the cell by the horz % in the base row (62.62/31.43) or by dividing the vert % in the cell by the vert % in the base column (9.52/4.78). Either calculation generates the same result, because, when the horz % numbers and vert % numbers are expressed in terms of "(000)", the relationship is identical.

FIGURE 14.2

How to Read MRI CrossTabs

The MRI market research service provides information on 4,090 product categories and services, 6,000 brands, and category advertising expenditures, as well as customer lifestyle characteristics and buying style psychographics.

Source: Courtesy of Mediamark Research Inc. All rights reserved.

on media compared to how much they are spending on their particular brand. This is called **share of voice**. In other words, marketers want to know which, if any, competing brands have louder voices (i.e., are spending more) than they do. For example, if the total spent on airline advertising last year was $200 million, and $50 million of that was spent by United Airlines, UA's share of voice would be 25 percent ($50 \div 200 = 25\%$). Most agencies recommend that a brand's share of voice be at least as high as its share of market. For a new brand, obviously its share of voice needs to be more than its share of market if it wants to grow.

- *Media Kits* The various media and their respective media vehicles provide media kits, which contain information about the size and makeup of their audiences. Although media-supplied information is useful, keep in mind that this is an "inside job"—that is, the information is assembled to make the best possible case for advertising in that particular medium and media vehicle. For that reason, outside research sources, such as media rep companies and the Nielsen reports, are also used. As discussed in previous chapters, Nielsen Media Research audits national and local television, and Arbitron measures radio. Other services, such as the Auditing Bureau of Circulations (ABC), Simmons, and MRI monitor print audiences, and Media Metrix measures Internet audiences. All of these companies provide extensive information on viewers, listeners, and readers in terms of the size of the audience and their profiles.

- *Media Coverage Area* One type of media-related information about markets is the broadcast coverage area for television. Called a **designated marketing area (DMA),** the coverage area is referred to by the name of the largest city in the area. This is a national market analysis system, and every county in the United States has been assigned to a DMA. The assignment of a county to a DMA is determined by which city provides the majority of the county households' TV programming. Most DMAs include counties within a 50- to 60-mile radius of a major city center. Even though this system is based on TV broadcast signals, it is universally used in doing individual market planning.

- *Consumer Behavior Reports* We mentioned some of the consumer research sources in Chapter 5 that are used in developing segmentation and targeting strategies. They are also useful in planning media strategies. For example, media planners use such services as the Claritas PRIZM system, Nielsen's ClusterPlus system, and supermarket scanner data to locate the target audience within media markets.

The Media Plan

The **media plan** is a written document that summarizes the objectives and strategies that guide how media dollars will be spent. The goal of a media plan is to find the most effective and efficient ways to deliver messages to a targeted audience. Media plans are designed to answer the following questions: (1) who (target audience), (2) what for (objectives), (3) where (the media vehicles used), (4) where (geography), (5) when (time frame), (6) how big (media weight), and (7) at what cost (cost efficiency). The first three are media objectives and the second group represents media strategies. To see where media planning and buying fit into the overall advertising process, see Figure 14.3, which outlines the primary components of a media plan.

When IMC planners develop a media plan, they also take into consideration *contact points*. These include exposure to traditional mass media, as well as word of mouth, place-based media, in-store brand exposures, and the new, interactive media. We'll discuss the IMC dimension of media planning at the end of this chapter. To help you better understand the role of media planners, read the discussion of a week in the life of a media planner in the accompanying feature.

WHAT ARE THE KEY STEPS IN MEDIA PLANNING?

Media planning is more than just choosing from a long list of media options. Traditional **measured media** are chosen based on such metrics as GRPs and CPMs, which are explained later in this chapter, but the new media lack similar metrics and are characterized more by such considerations as the quality of the brand experience, involvement, and personal impact. Old-line advertising media planners are intent on buying reach and frequency, but the problem is that many of their clients are looking for more effective outcomes, such as engaging experiences and brand-

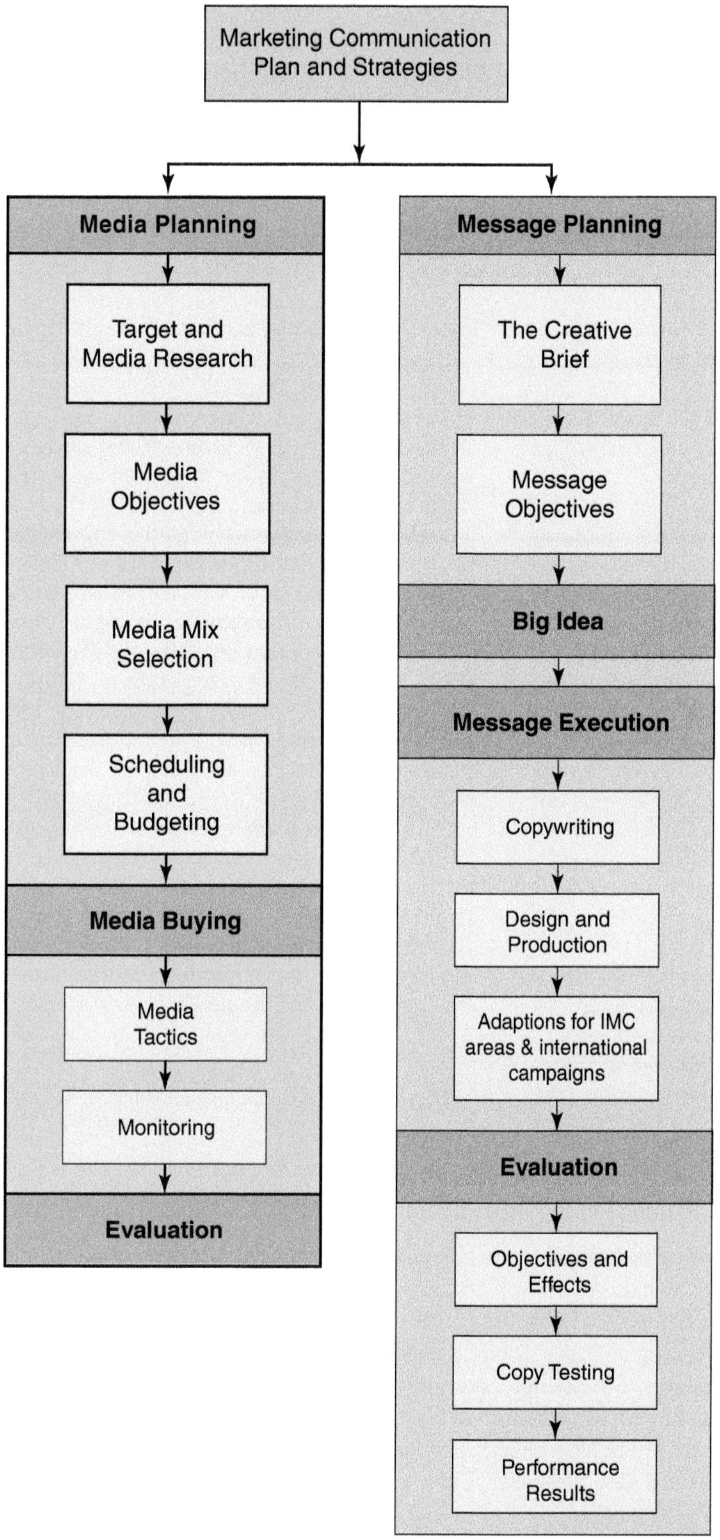

FIGURE 14.3
The Components of a
Media Plan

building relationships. Thus, the framework for making media-planning decisions is changing along with the list of media options.

The four basic steps in media planning are targeting, setting media objectives, developing media strategies, and analyzing the metrics of a media plan.

Step 1: Target Audience

A key strategic decision is identifying a target audience. In media planning, the challenge is to select media vehicles that (1) are compatible with the creative executions and (2) whose audiences

What Do I DO as a Media Planner?

Heather Beck, *Senior Media Planner, Melamed Riley Advertising, Cleveland, Ohio*

People often ask me what it is that I **DO** all day at work. There are 12 media planners in my office, and each of us would have a different answer to that question. But here's a general outline of week's worth of work.

Monday morning there is a conference call involving everyone who works on an account. The client shares information such as sales numbers from the past week, as well as budget changes or which markets are going to run a test campaign. The agency shares results from market research and the status of current projects. During the next couple of hours I **DO** *media research*—requesting and researching information from media sources for new projects.

It's lunch time now! Once or twice a week, media reps either bring in a deli tray for the office, or they take us out for a lunch meeting to pitch their media products. It is the job of the media planner to **DO** *media analysis*, by which I mean analyzing all the options and determining what is best for the client. So we don't let a nice lunch or fancy gift basket sway our judgment.

After lunch, I return phone calls and reply to e-mails. I spend the rest of the day gathering and organizing any information I have received and analyzing the data—that's when I **DO** *media planning*. Actually I do this all week long.

The rest of the week is similar. Tuesday morning conference calls are split up so that groups can talk specifics about their projects with their counterparts on the client side. This is the time to share detailed feedback. What works best in one market might not work well in another so these results are essential in tailoring the media plans.

On Wednesday mornings the agency has informal status meetings or conference calls on Thursday—this is a good time to check in with clients and **DO** *evaluations* of our media plans. Then the day is spent finalizing projects.

Fridays are when all of the agency players on an account put their projects together and determine the best way to **DO** *presentations* of the results to clients. Another typical Friday task is to **DO** *media buying*—that is, place the planned media buys for the following week or month.

This is a generalized example of a typical week in the life of a media planner. Some days you might work until midnight, and other days you'll take long lunch breaks. It might seem like the same thing day to day, but the actual projects vary enough to keep it interesting and challenging. And if you need a break, you can always catch up on the latest issues of *Media Week* or *Ad Age*.

A graduate of the advertising program at Middle Tennessee State, Heather Beck is a media planner at Cleveland-based Melamed Riley Advertising.

best match those of the brand's target audience. In other words, does the group of people who read this magazine, watch this television program, or see these posters include a high proportion of the advertiser's ideal target audience? If so, then these media vehicles may be a good choice for the campaign, depending on other strategic factors, such as timing and cost.

Media planners, for example, are unlikely to run ads for women's products on the Super Bowl, which is skewed 56 percent male; instead, they buy time on the Oscars, which has a much higher percentage of female viewers. However, in 2010 Dove used the Super Bowl to launch its Men+Care personal care products.[1] These are the kinds of decisions that make media planning both fun and challenging.

The breadth of the target, as defined in the marketing communication plan, determines whether the media planner will be using a broad mass media approach or a tightly targeted and highly focused approach. The tighter the focus, the easier it is to find appropriate media to deliver a relevant and focused message that connects with audience interests and engages them personally in a brand conversation.

As you can imagine, every media vehicle's audience is different and therefore varies regarding what percentage of its audience is in the brand's target audience. For example, Mercury Marine, which makes outboard boat motors, targets households (HHs) that own one or more boats. It prefers to advertise in magazines where it can feature beautiful illustrations of its products as well as room to explain the many benefits of its motors. Should it advertise in *Time* or *Boating* magazine? *Time* magazine reaches 4 million HHs, of which 280,000 HHs have boats; in

Principle
The tighter the focus on a target market, the easier it is to find appropriate media to deliver a relevant message.

comparison, *Boating* has only 200,000 HH subscribers. If you said *Time,* sorry, you're not being very cost efficient. This is because even though *Time* reaches 80,000 more boat-owning households, it also reaches 3.7 million HHs that don't own boats. Mercury would have to pay to reach all readers, even those not in its target audience. By advertising in *Boating,* it can pretty well assume that subscribers either own a boat or at least are interested in boating.

In addition to information compiled by the team's media researchers, consumer insight research also is used to identify and analyze the target audience's media use patterns. Industry research helps. For example, in a 2009 study, Harris Interactive Research found that 37 percent of Americans said TV ads are most helpful in making a purchase decision. Newspapers (19 percent) came in second; only 14 percent said Internet search engines were most helpful. In fact, nearly half of the respondents said they ignored Internet banner ads.[2]

This type of research that asks consumers what they think influences their behavior is best used when combined with other consumer behavior findings. Why? Because most consumers don't really know what influences them. (Just ask some of your friends how much advertising impacts what they buy. Most will probably say that "it doesn't" or "just a little.")

For the launch of the Audi A3, the McKinley + Silver media team knew it needed an in-depth understanding of its target audience of young males to develop a media plan that would work for this difficult-to-reach group. From research they found that young males typically don't read or watch traditional media. They're busy and skeptical about commercial messages. From these findings the team came up with a profile of the target, which they described as "intelligent, independent, and innovative" and heavy users of new media. This target audience for this product category is made up of opinion leaders who influence their peers. They are not as interested in buying an entry-level car as they are in getting "what's next."

Step 2: Communication and Media Objectives

Although creative decisions are sometimes made before media planning, this is changing. With the increasing variety of media options available, smart clients and agencies are having up-front cross-functional planning meetings that include creatives, media planners, and account executives. The point is that the media and message strategies are interdependent and decisions in one area affect decisions in the other.

Marketing communication objectives, as you will recall, describe what a company wants target audiences to think, feel, and most importantly, do. **Media objectives** describe what a company wants to accomplish regarding the delivery of its brand messages and their impact on the target audience.

The communication objectives provide guidance to media planners. For example, why would brands want to spend some $3 million to advertise on the Super Bowl unless the buy fits with its brand communication objectives? Pepsi, a long-time Super Bowl advertiser, pulled out in 2010 deciding that expensive brand reminder ads in front of an audience that already knows the brand don't make sense. On the other hand, brands that are building their images, launching new products, or who want to use messages to shape public perceptions on a mass scale—the Super Bowl reaches some 100 million viewers—might see the investment as a good one. Two advertisers during the 2010 Super Bowl illustrate reasons corporations might want to make the investment. Hyundai, for example, wants to change its image from a maker of small, cheap cars to a upscale image and Career Builder believes its job search services are appropriately communicated to a broad population as the United States comes out of a recession.[3]

As we mentioned in Chapter 11, the two basic media objectives are reach and frequency. Let's consider how planners create strategies that deliver on those objectives.

The Reach Objective   The percent of people exposed to a brand message one or more times within a specified period of time is called **reach.** A campaign's success is due in part to its ability to reach as many of the targeted audience as possible within a stated budget and time period. Consequently, many planners feel that reach is the most important objective and that it's the place to start when figuring out a media plan.

Using demographic and lifestyle data, planners can focus on reaching specific types of households (e.g., empty nesters, homes with two+ children under age 18, single-parent households, HHs with incomes over $100,000) or individuals (males ages 25 to 49, people who rent). This enables planners to better match media profiles with the characteristics of the campaign's target audience.

Principle
Reach is the first place to start when setting objectives for a media plan.

Because most media reach large numbers of people who are not in the target market, however, most marketers are more interested in **targeted reach**, which is the percentage of a vehicle's audience that matches the brand's target market. An estimate of targeted reach can be developed assuming the brand's target market can be identified in the vehicle's audience profile. Targeted reach is particularly important to calculate in order to estimate the amount of **wasted reach,** which is the number of people in the vehicle's audience who are neither customers nor prospects. We mentioned this problem in our discussion of network television, which is particularly susceptible to this criticism because of its mass audience.

Assessing the media for target audience opportunities is a major challenge for media planners. The evening news on television, for example, reaches a broad mass-market audience; if your target is women ages 25 to 49, then you have to consider the *targeted reach* of that news program. Obviously both men and women watch news, so you know that your audience would probably be half or less of that, especially since you are targeting a specific age group. Maybe the evening news isn't a good option to reach this target because there would be so much waste. Outdoor, as the *Court TV* posters illustrate, are a location-bound medium and posters are particularly good at targeting a specified population.

The Frequency Objective   As we explained in Chapter 11, **frequency** refers to the repetition of message exposure. You should keep in mind that the frequency number for a media buy is actually the average number of exposure opportunities of those reached.

Because frequency is an *average,* it can be misleading. The range of frequency is often large: Some people see a particular brand message once, while others may see it 10 times within a given period. **Average frequency,** then, can give the planner a distorted idea of the plan's performance because all of those people reached vary in the number of times they have the opportunity to be exposed to a message.

Suppose a media mix includes four magazines and each magazine carries one ad a week for four weeks. The total number of message insertions would be 16 (4 magazines × 1 insertion a

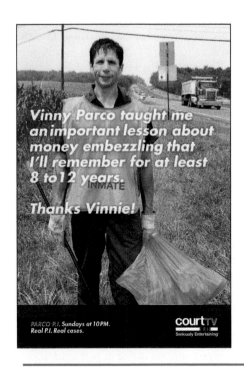

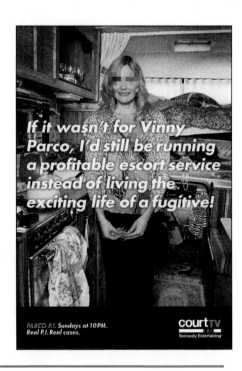

SHOWCASE

These two posters for the *Court TV* television program were created by Aaron Stern when he was an award-winning copywriter at Venables Bell & Partners in San Francisco.

A graduate of the University of Colorado, Stern is now in New York where he recently completed his MFA in Creative Writing at New York University and now works as a freelance copywriter. He and his work were nominated for inclusion in this book by Professor Brett Robbs.

week $\times$ 4 weeks = 16 total insertions). It is possible that a small percentage of the target audience could be exposed to all 16 insertions. It is also possible that some of the target would not have the opportunity to be exposed to any of the insertions. In this case the frequency ranges from 0 to 16. Thus, because the average frequency equals 8, you can see how misleading this average frequency number can be.

For this reason planners often use a **frequency distribution** model that shows the percentage of audience reached at each level of repetition. A **frequency quintile distribution analysis** divides an audience into five groups, each containing 20 percent of the audience. Employing media-usage modeling, it is then possible to estimate the average frequency for each quintile as shown in the following table. For example, this table shows that the bottom 20 percent has an average frequency of 1, whereas the top 20 percent has an average frequency of 10. In this hypothetical distribution, the average frequency is 6.

Quintile	Frequency (Average Number of Exposure Opportunities)
Top 20% of universe	10
20%	7
20%	5
20%	3
Bottom 20%	1

If the media planner feels it is necessary that 80 percent of those reached should have an average frequency of 8, then a more intensive media plan would be needed to raise the overall number of exposures; in other words, to shift the average from 6 to 8.

Effective Frequency   Because of the proliferation of information and clutter, there should be a threshold, or minimum frequency level, that produces some type of effect, such as a request for more brand information, a change in attitude toward the brand, or the most desired effect—purchase of the brand.

A standard rule of thumb is that it takes 3 to 10 exposures to have an effect on an audience. Obviously this frequency range is extremely wide. The "right" frequency number is determined by several factors, including level of brand awareness, level of competitive "noise," content of the message, and sophistication of the target audience. Because so many different things can impact a response (i.e., an effect), audience response research is necessary. If the desired effect/response is not achieved, you may need to increase frequency of exposure or change the message. Research diagnostics, such as tracking studies, provide direction. The principle of **effective frequency** is that you add frequency to reach until you get to the level where people respond.

Principle
Effective frequency means you add frequency to reach until you get to the level where people respond.

Media Waste   In the discussion of targeted reach we mentioned waste as a result of targeting too wide of a target market. Actually, there are two sides to waste—both reach and frequency. The goal of media planning is to maximize media efficiency, which is to eliminate excessive overlap or too much frequency. Efficiency is achieved, therefore, by reducing media waste. Media professionals use their own experience, as well as audience research and computer models, to identify media efficiency. The point is, when additional media weight ceases to increase the response, it produces waste.

Writing Media Objectives   Given this discussion of the relationship between reach and frequency, it should be clear that usable media objectives would focus on those dimensions ideally including both factors. Here are some examples of media objectives:

1. Reach 60 percent of target audience with a frequency of 4 within each four-week period in which the advertising runs.
2. Reach a maximum percentage of target audience a minimum of five times within the first six months of advertising.
3. Reach 30 percent of the target audiences where they have an opportunity to interact with the brand and users of the brand.
4. Reach category thought leaders and influencers in a way that will motivate them to initiate measurable word of mouth (WOM) and other positive brand messages.

The first of these objectives is the most common. It recognizes that you can seldom ever reach 100 percent of your target audience. It also acknowledges that a certain level of frequency will be necessary for the brand messages to been seen/heard/read. The second objective would be for a product where the message is more complex; through research (and judgment) it has been decided that prospects need to be exposed to the message at least five times to be effective. In this case frequency is more important than reach. Put another way, it is more important to reach a small portion of the audience five or more times and have them respond than it is to reach a major portion fewer than five times and have little or no response.

Objectives 3 and 4 deal directly with impact. To achieve these objectives, media buyers will have to find media vehicles and contact points, such as events and sponsorships, where interaction with the brand and its users is possible as opposed to using more passive media such as traditional mass media. Note that objective 4 is not measurable as stated.

Step 3: Media Strategies

Strategic thinking in media involves a set of decision factors and tools that help identify the best way to deliver the brand message. Regardless of whether a company spends a few hundred dollars on one medium or millions of dollars on a variety of media, the goal is still the same: to reach the right people at the right time with the right message.

Media strategy is the way media planners determine the most cost-effective way to reach the target audience and satisfy the media objectives. Specific media strategies are based on analyzing and comparing various ways to accomplish the media objectives, and then selecting the approach that is estimated to be the most effective alternative. The idea is that there are always multiple ways to reach an objective, but which way is the best?

Strategies That Deliver Reach and Frequency   In certain situations, for example, when the objectives call for high reach, the strategies used would involve creating broad exposure using many media vehicles. For example, high-reach strategies might be used in order to provide reminders for a well-known brand or to introduce a new product that has a broadly defined target market.

If the objectives specify high frequency, then the media strategies will probably be narrower in focus with a more limited list of media vehicles. That would be the case for niche products with tightly defined target markets (low reach) or for products that need a high level of information and explanation. High-frequency strategies are also used to counter competitive offers and to build the brand's share of voice in a highly cluttered category. Sometimes a low-frequency objective is specified when there is less need for repetition. If you are advertising a two-liter Coke for 89 cents, you don't need to repeat the message a lot, but if you are trying to explain how DVR systems work, then you may need more frequency.

Media Mix Selection   The reach and frequency objectives also lead to decisions about the media mix. We mentioned earlier that you can rarely generate an acceptable reach level with just one media vehicle. Most brands use a variety of targeted media vehicles, called a **media mix,** to reach current and potential customers. ESPN, for example, uses TV, magazines, radio, and the Internet, as well as original programming on its own ESPN channel, to promote its programs.

Media mixes are used for a number of reasons. The first is to reach people not reached by the first or most important medium. Using a variety of media vehicles distributes the message more widely because different media tend to have different audience profiles. Of course, these different audience groups should generally fit within the brand's target market.

Some people even reject certain media: television advertising, for example, is considered intrusive and Internet advertising is irritating to some people. Other reasons for spreading the plan across different media include adding exposure in less expensive media and using media that have some attractive characteristics that enhance the creative message. On the other hand, an *Ad Age* columnist believes media planners shouldn't give up traditional media just because digital media have become "sexy" and are seen as having lower costs.[4]

Still, the reason for choosing a particular medium or a set of media vehicles depends on the media objectives. What media will best deliver what effects—and can you reinforce and extend those effects with a mix of media? If audience reach is an objective, then television still reaches the largest audience; if frequency is important, then radio may be the best media vehicle to use. Print and television are considered more trustworthy, so they might be used by a media planner for a campaign that seeks to establish credibility for a brand or believability for a product claim. The *Practical Tips* box summarizes the reasons media planners choose various media.

An analysis of one industry's media mix choices presents an interesting argument about the logic of the media mix. The telecom industry (AT&T, Verizon, Sprint) was critiqued by BIGresearch and a team of media researchers from Northwestern University. Based on consumer research and a customized analytical model, the team was able to develop an idealized set of media allocations. In comparison to actual expenditures, the team concluded that the industry overspends on television at the expense of others, such as the Internet, radio, magazines, and outdoor. In particular, the consumer-based research determined an underuse of the Internet based on amount of time, its ability to influence purchase, and its lower costs.[5]

Media choices are sometimes designed to deliver the strategy of using one medium to deliver an audience to another medium or marketing communication tool. For example, mass media have frequently been used to promote special events and sales promotions. The emergence of the Internet has intensified what you might call a two-step media platform. Print and broadcast, which are basically informative and awareness building media forms, are often used to drive traffic to a brand's website, which is more interactive and experiential. The Frontier "Web" ad is an example of this use.

This ad demonstrates the use of a creative print ad to drive traffic to a website.

Geographical Strategies   Another factor planners use in analyzing the target audience is geography. Are potential customers found all over the country, therefore calling for a national campaign, and does the client have the budget to afford such an extensive media plan? In most cases, the media plan will identify special regions or DMAs to be emphasized with a **heavy-up schedule,** which means proportionately more of the budget is spent in those areas. The company's sales coverage area (i.e., geography) is a major factor used to make this decision. There's no sense advertising in areas where the product isn't available. Most national or regional marketers divide their market geographically. The amount of sales produced in each geographic market will vary, and marketers try to match advertising investments with the amount of forecasted sales or the sales potential.

To determine which geographical areas have the highest (and lowest) rate of consumption for a particular product category, marketers compute a **category development index (CDI)** for each market in which they are interested. Then they calculate a **brand development index (BDI),** which estimates the strength of their brand in the various geographical areas. If General Mills were to bring out a new line of grits, for example, it wouldn't advertise nationally because most grits are consumed in the South.

When to Use Various Media

Use newspapers if . . .

- You are a local business and want extensive local market coverage.
- You sell a product that has a news element, such as new features or formulation.
- You are creating a news element through a sale or some other event.
- You want to reach an upscale, well-educated audience.
- You need to explain how something works, but it doesn't need to be demonstrated.
- The quality of the image is not a factor.

Use magazines if . . .

- You have a target audience defined by some special interest.
- You have a product that needs to be shown accurately and beautifully and a high-quality image is important.
- You need to explain how something works, but it doesn't need to be demonstrated.

Use out-of-home media if . . .

- You are a local business and want to sell to a local market.
- You want to remind or reinforce a brand image or message.
- You need a directional message.
- You need a situational, place-based message.
- Your product requires little information.

Use directories if . . .

- You are a local business or can serve local customers.
- You want to reach people who are searching for your type of business.
- You need to provide basic inquiry and purchase information.
- You need to provide directional information.
- You have a small to moderate budget.

Use radio if . . .

- You are a local business and want to reach a local market.
- You want to build frequency.
- You have a reminder message.
- You know the timing when your audience is considering the purchase.
- Your audience's interests align with certain types of music or talk shows.
- You have a message that works well in a musical form or one that is strong in mental imagery.

Use national television if . . .

- You need to reach a wide audience.
- You have a message that benefits from motion, sight, and sound.
- Your message calls for action or drama.
- You need product demonstration—how to use it, how it works.
- Your audience's interests align with a certain type of program (particularly on cable TV).
- You want to prove or demonstrate something so people in your audience can see it with their own eyes.
- You want the halo effect of a big TV ad to impress other stakeholders, such as dealers and franchisees.

Use local or spot television if . . .

- Your product is not distributed nationally.
- You want to "heavy up" in certain cities or regions where sales are higher.

Use movie ads if . . .

- Your brand can benefit from being associated with a movie's story and stars.
- The people in the audience match your brand's target audience.

Use product placement if . . .

- You want your brand to be associated with a movie or program's story and stars.
- The people in the audience match your brand's target audience.
- There is a natural fit between the product and the movie's storyline.
- There is an opportunity in the storyline for the brand to be a star.
- The placement will appeal to the brand's stakeholders.
- You have the budget for a campaign to support the placement.

Use the Internet if . . .

- Your target audience is difficult to reach with traditional media.
- You want to create buzz.
- You want your target audience to engage in dialogue with others.
- You want to provide information.
- You want to collect customer information.
- You want to engage your audience in an online activity, such as a game.
- You want to reach people on their own time.

Now taking reservations for Octber.

BERTUCCI'S
brick oven ristorante

SHOWCASE
A billboard located at Kenmore Square above the Bertucci's restaurant is just two blocks from Fenway Park. Developed by the Boston University AdLab group, this billboard illustrates a message delivered at the right time and the right place.

A CDI is calculated for product categories. It is an index number showing the relative consumption rate of a product in a particular DMA or region as compared to the total universe (national or regional). A BDI is an index of the consumption rate of a brand in a particular market. The CDI tells you where the category is strong and weak, and the BDI tells you where your brand is strong and weak. CDI data can be found in industry and government sources, and BDI information is available through such services as Simmons and Scarborough, as well as company data.

Different strategies are used to deal with these levels, and they have implications for the media mix and schedule. Planners typically don't make heavy allocations in weak sales areas unless strong marketing signals indicate significant growth potential. Conversely, strong sales markets may not receive proportional increases in advertising unless clear evidence suggests that company sales can go much higher with greater advertising investment. When there is a lot of competitive activity, a heavy-up strategy may be used to defend the brand's market share.

Scheduling Strategies   When should a potential customer be exposed to a brand message? Scheduling strategies are designed to identify the best times for consumers to come in contact with a brand message.

For many product categories, prospective customers have one or more ideal times or places at which they are most receptive to receiving and paying attention to a brand message. This ideal time/place is called an **aperture,** and becomes an important factor in scheduling media placements. Movies and restaurants advertise on Thursdays and Fridays, knowing these are the days when potential customers are planning for the coming weekend. Ads for sporting goods, beer, and soft drinks pop up at athletic venues because sports fans are thinking about those products as they watch the game.

Regardless of whether a company spends a few hundred dollars on one medium or millions of dollars on a variety of media, the goal is still the same: to reach the right people at the right time with the right message. If advertising budgets were unlimited, most companies would advertise every day. Not even the largest advertisers are in this position, so media planners manipulate schedules in various ways to create the strongest possible impact given the budget. Three scheduling strategies involve timing, duration of exposure, and continuity of exposure.

- *Timing Strategies: When to Advertise?* Timing decisions relate to factors such as seasonality, holidays, days of the week, and time of day. These decisions are driven by how often the product is bought and whether it is used more in some months than in others. Timing also encompasses the consumers' best aperture and competitors' advertising schedules. Another consideration is **lead time,** or the amount of time allowed before the beginning of the sales period to reach people when they are just beginning to think about seasonal buying. Back-to-school advertising is an example. Advertising typically starts in July or early August for a

Principle
The CDI tells where the category is strong and weak, and the BDI tells where the brand is strong and weak.

Principle
Advertising is most effective when it reaches the right people at the right time and place with the right message.

school calendar that begins in late August or September. Lead time also refers to the production time needed to get the advertisement into the medium. There is a long lead time for magazines, but it is shorter for local media, such as newspapers and radio.

- *Duration: How Long?* For how many weeks or months of the year should the advertising run? If there is a need to cover most of the weeks, advertising will be spread rather thin. If the amount of time to cover is limited, advertising can be concentrated more heavily. Message scheduling is driven by use cycles. For products that are consumed year-round, such as fast food and movies, advertising is spread throughout the year. In general, if you cannot cover the whole year, you should heavy up the schedule in higher purchase periods. For example, movie marketers do most of their newspaper advertising on the weekends, when most people go to movies.

  Another question is how much is enough. At what point does the message make its point? If the advertising period is too short or there are too few repetitions, then the message may have little or no impact. If the period is too long, then ads may suffer from **wearout,** which means the audience gets tired of them and stops paying attention.

- *Continuity: How Often?* **Continuity** refers to the way the advertising is spread over the length of a campaign. A **continuous strategy** spreads the advertising evenly over the campaign period. Two other methods to consider, pulsing and flighting, are shown in Figure 14.4.

A **pulsing strategy** is used to intensify advertising before a buying aperture and then to reduce advertising to lower levels until the aperture reopens. The pulse pattern has peaks and valleys, also called *bursts.* Fast-food companies such as McDonald's and Burger King often use pulsing patterns as they increase media weight during special promotional periods. Although the competition for daily customers suggests continuous advertising, they will greatly intensify activity to accommodate special events such as new menu items, merchandise premiums, and contests. Pulsed schedules cover most of the year, but still provide periodic intensity.

After a media schedule has been worked out in terms of what media will run when and for how long, these decisions are plotted on a **media flow chart.** Across the top is the calendar for the period of the campaign and down the side is the list of media to be used in this campaign. Bars are then drawn across the calendar that identify the exact timing of the use of various media. When the chart is complete, strategies such as pulsing and flighting are easy to observe. You can also see where reminder advertising in less expensive media (in-store signs) may fill in between bursts and pulsing in more expensive media such as television. You can see a flow chart in the media plan example that follows later in the chapter.

A **flighting strategy** is the most severe type of continuity adjustment. It is characterized by alternating periods of intense advertising activity and periods of no advertising, called a *hiatus.* This on-and-off schedule allows for a longer campaign. The hope in using nonadvertising periods is that the consumers will remember the brand and its advertising for some time after the ads have stopped. Figure 14.5 illustrates this awareness change. The jagged line represents the rise and fall of consumer awareness of the brand. If the flighting strategy works, there will be a **carryover effect** of past advertising, which means consumers will remember the product across the gap until the next advertising period begins. The critical decision involves analyzing the *decay* level, the rate at which memory of the advertising is forgotten.

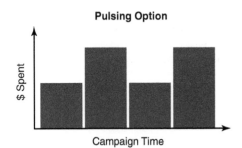

Pulsing Option

$ Spent

Campaign Time

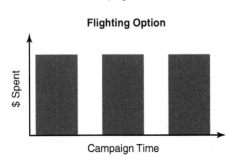

Flighting Option

$ Spent

Campaign Time

FIGURE 14.4

The Strategies of Pulsing and Flighting

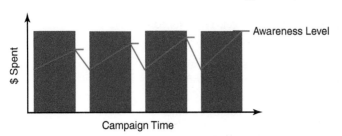

Awareness Level

$ Spent

Campaign Time

FIGURE 14.5

Consumer Awareness Levels in a Flighting Strategy

Size and Position Strategies In addition to selecting the media mix, a media planner works with the creative team to determine the appropriate size and length of the message for each medium. This question of scope and scale applies to all media—even transit advertising, as the Yellow Cab ad illustrates.

Media Weighting   Media planners often use decision criterion called **weighting** to help them decide how much to budget (we have referred to this as "heavy up") in each DMA or region and for each target audience when there is more than one. For example, if a media planner is advertising disposable contact lenses, there might be two target segments to consider: consumers who need help with their eyesight and the eye doctors who make the recommendations. You may recall the discussion of push and pull strategies in Chapter 2, which is also relevant here. If the strategy is to encourage the consumer to ask the doctor about the product, the planner might recommend putting more emphasis on consumer publications to execute a **pull strategy** rather than focusing on professional journals for eye doctors, which would represent a **push strategy.** A weighting strategy might be to put 60 percent of the budget on consumers and 40 percent on doctors.

In the case of DMAs, weak markets may be given more than their share of media weight in the hopes of strengthening the brands in these markets, a practice known as *investment spending*. On the other hand, if competition is extremely heavy in a brand's strong markets, the strategy may be to give them more than their proportional share of media dollars to defend against competitors. Weighting strategies are also used in terms of seasonality, geography, audience segments, and the level of brand development by DMA.

This photo illustrates the use of transit advertising—in this case a panel on the top of a taxi—to advertise the *Wall Street Journal*. The media plan would give direction to the decisions about the size of the sign and the duration of its appearance.

Step 4: Media Metrics and Analytics

Like every other aspect of marketing communication, media plans are driven by questions of accountability. And because media decisions are based on measurable factors, identifiable costs, and budget limitations, media planners are engrossed in calculating the impact and efficiency of their media recommendations. As a MediaBank executive said, "Media departments are no place for guessing. With millions—even tens or hundreds of millions—of dollars at stake, clients want hard data showing that their budgets are being well spent."[6]

Impact: GRPs and TRPs   Among the most important tools media planners use in designing a media mix is a calculation of a media schedule's gross rating points and targeted rating points. As we've suggested, reach and frequency are interrelated concepts that, when combined, generate an estimate called gross rating points. **Gross rating points, or GRPs,** indicate the weight, or efficiency, of a media plan. The more GRPs in a plan, the more "weight" the media buy is said to deliver.

To find a plan's GRPs, you multiply each media vehicle's rating by the number of ads inserted into each media vehicle during the designated time period and add up the total for the vehicles.

Once the media vehicles that produce the GRPs have been identified, computer programs can be used to break down the GRPs into reach and frequency (R&F) numbers. These R&F models are based on consumer media use research and produce data showing to what extent audiences, viewers, and readers overlap.

To illustrate how GRPs are determined and the difference in R&F from one media plan to another (using the same budget), look at the two media mixes that follow. Both are for a simple TV media plan for a pizza brand. As you will remember from Chapter 12, a *rating point* is 1 percent of a defined media universe (country, region, DMA, or some other target audience description) of households unless otherwise specified. *Insertions* are the number of ads placed in each media vehicle/program within a given period of time (generally four weeks). For example, in Table 14.1, if the plan delivered a household rating of 6 with eight insertions, the program *Survivor* would achieve an estimated 48 GRPs.

Using the same budget, the two different media mixes produce different GRP totals. A good media planner will look at several different mixes of programs that reach the target audience, figure the GRPs for each, and then break this calculation into R&F estimates for each plan. Because ratings are in percentages, the GRPs in both the plans in these tables indicate they reach more than 100 percent. Of course, this is impossible, just as it's impossible to eat 156 percent of a pie. This is why these numbers are called *gross* rating points; they include exposure duplication. Nevertheless, knowing the GRPs of different plans is helpful in choosing which plan delivers more for the money budgeted.

How would computer models calculate reach and frequency numbers based on achieving 208 GRPs in plan A? The media mix model would estimate something close to the following: R = 35, F = 6.9. (Even though reach is a percent, industry practice is to not use the percent sign for reach numbers.) For plan B where the number of GRPs is 176, the estimated R&F would be R = 55, F = 3.2.

Table 14.1A   Calculating GRPs for Plan A (R = 35; F = 6.9)

Program	HH Rating	Insertions	GRPs
Survivor	6	8	48
Lost	7	8	56
American Idol	9	8	72
24	4	8	32
		Total	208

Table 14.1B   Calculating GRPs for Plan B (R = 55; F = 3.2)

Survivor	6	8	48
Desperate Housewives	7	8	56
Boston Legal	5	8	40
Monday Night Football	4	8	32
		Total	176

How do you decide which is best? If a brand has a tightly targeted audience and wants to use repetition to create a strong brand presence, then plan A might be a wise choice because it has a higher frequency (6.9 vs. 3.2). If, however, a brand has a fairly simple message where frequency is less important, a planner would probably choose plan B because it has significantly higher reach. The reason for the higher reach (55 vs. 35) with plan B, even though it has fewer GRPs, is that plan B has a much more diverse set of programs that attract a more diverse audience than plan A. But because plan B has a higher reach, it also has a lower frequency.

It is important to remember that GRPs are a combination of R × F. When R increases, F decreases, and vice versa. Once experienced planners are given budgets, they generally have a good feel for how many GRPs those budgets will buy. The planning challenge is to decide whether to find a media mix with more reach or more frequency. This depends, of course, on media objectives.

Principle
Reach and frequency are interrelated: when reach increases, frequency decreases, and vice versa, within the constraints of the advertising budget.

The two media mixes shown previously are based on HH rating points. For products that have a mass-market appeal, HHs are often used in targeting. However, for more specialized products, such as tennis racquets, sports cars, and all-natural food products, target audiences can be more narrowly defined. For example, let's say that those consuming the most natural food products are females, ages 25 to 49, with a college degree; in addition, we know that they participate in at least one outdoor sport. This would be the target audience for most brands in this category. Therefore, when developing a media plan for a natural food brand, a media planner would be interested not so much in a media vehicle's total audience, but on the percentage of the audience that can be defined as being in the campaign's target audience. Those not in the target are called waste coverage.

Since the total audience obviously includes waste coverage, the estimate of **targeted rating points (TRPs)** adjusts the calculation to exclude the waste coverage so it more accurately reflects the percentage of the target audience watching a program. Because the waste coverage is eliminated, the TRPs are lower than the total audience GRPs. Targeted rating points are, like R&F, determined by media usage research data, which is available from syndicated research services like MRI and from the major media vehicles themselves.

To illustrate the difference between HH GRPs and TRPs, we'll use media plan A, shown previously. As shown in Table 14.2, the first column is HH rating points, while the new second column shows targeted rating points, or the percent of homes reached that include a female, age 25 to 49, with a college degree and an affinity for at least one outdoor sport. The insertions remain the same, but the TRPs are greatly reduced, as you can see when you multiply targeted ratings by insertions. When the 80 TRPs are compared to the 208 HH GRPs, you can see that 128 GRPs (208 − 80 = 128) were of little or no value to a natural food brand. The less waste, the more efficient the media plan.

Table 14.2   Calculating TRPs for Plan A

Program	HH Rating	Targeted Rating	Insertions TRPs	Total TRPs
Survivor	6	3	8	24
Lost	7	3	8	24
American Idol	9	1	8	8
24	4	3	8	24
			Total	80

Another reason to tightly describe a target audience, especially in terms of lifestyle, is to take advantage of the many media vehicles—magazines, TV programs and channels, and special events—that connect with various types of lifestyles. Examples of media that offer special interest topics are *Runners World,* which features topics of interest to runners; *This Old House,* the TV program that describes home improvement and remodeling; *Self* magazine, which focuses on health and fitness; and *Budget Travel* for those looking for interesting but economical trips and vacations.

We've been discussing the basic steps in media planning. Let's now consider the tools and techniques of media strategy.

Cost Efficiency

As mentioned earlier, one way to compare budgets with the competition is called *share of voice.* It sets the budget relative to your brand's and your competitors' market share. For example, if your client has a 40 percent share of the market, then you may decide to spend at a 40 percent share of voice in order to maintain your brand's competitive position. To calculate this budget level, you need to find the total ad spending in your category, as well as the share of market owned by your brand and your key competitors.[7] For example, if the category ad spending totals $10 million, and you want your share of voice to be 40 percent, then you would need to spend $4 million ($10 million × 0.40 = $4 million).

At the end of the planning process, after the media mix has been determined, the media planner will prepare a pie chart showing *media allocations,* a term that refers to allocating the budget among the various media chosen. The pie chart shows the amount being spent on each medium as a proportion of the total media budget. The pie chart visualizes the media mix and the relative importance of each vehicle in the mix.

Although much of the discussion in this book has been focused on measured advertising media and their objectives, it's useful to note that the other IMC disciplines are also concerned about proving their efficiency. Public relations, for example, has established metrics comparable to those used in evaluating advertising media. The *A Matter of Principle* box explains how important it is to integrate not only media planning, but also evaluations of efficiency comparing these other areas with advertising media planning. The author also explains the concept of *earned media,* in contrast to purchased (and measured) media.

CPMs, TCPMs, and CPPs   Advertisers don't make decisions about the media mix solely in terms of targeting, geography, and schedule considerations. Sometimes the decision comes down

Integrating Advertising and PR Media Planning

Clarke Caywood, *Professor and Director of the Graduate Program in Public Relations, Medill Graduate School, Northwestern University*

Ask advertising directors in a company or agency what profitable target media they have chosen for message delivery for their new corporate or product/service brand strategy. They will probably give a list of traditional mass media advertising vehicles.

Then ask the PR director in the same company or company PR agency what the targeted media will be for the same program. It will often be a list of news and feature story outlets.

In an integrated approach to media planning, the communication leaders should be targeting the same media to reach similar readers, viewers, and listeners. If not, the C-Suite—chief executive officer, chief financial officer, and chief marketing officer—in the client company would want to know why not.

These newer models of media planning seem to be aligned with the growth of the large holding companies that contain advertising, direct database marketing, e-commerce, public relations, and, now, media buying agencies where coordination and cross-functional planning are essential.

In the IMC program at Medill, we define integrated media planning as "coordinated research, planning, securing, and evaluation of all purchased and earned media." **Earned media** is used by marketing and PR practitioners to differentiate paid media about a product, service, or company (advertising, promotions, direct mail, Web ads, etc.) from positive or negative broadcast, print, and Internet media articles and simple mentions about the product, service, or company. The term *earned* is used to avoid the term *free*, which accurately suggests the company does not pay the media for the placement, but it does not address the fact that the publication of such stories requires hours of effort or years of experience by PR professionals to persuade journalists to cover the product, service, or company for the benefit of their readers or viewers.

Just as selecting media for advertising has become a science and management art, the field of selection and analysis of earned media (including print, broadcast, and blogs) for public relations is now more of a science. Today the existence of far richer database systems assists media managers who want to know which reporters, quoted experts, trade books, new publications, broadcasts, bloggers, and more are the most "profitable" targets for public relations messages. In other words, when we refer to *media planning*, we mean coordinating and jointly planning the earned media of public relations along with advertising and other purchased media.

Using the new built-in media metric systems, PR directors can calculate return on investment on advertising versus PR. With PR, they can read and judge a range of positive, neutral, or negative messages, as well as share-of-mind measures of media impact, advertising equivalency estimates, and other effectiveness indicators (see www.biz360.com).

Now, when the chief marketing officer and other C-Suite officers ask the integrated agency directors of advertising, public relations, or IMC if the media are fully planned to reach targeted audiences, they can answer affirmatively.

to cold, hard cash. The advertiser wants prospects, not just readers, viewers, or listeners; therefore, they compare the cost of each proposed media vehicle with the specific vehicle's ability to deliver the target audience. The cheapest vehicle may not deliver the highest percent of the target audience, and the highest priced vehicle may deliver exactly the right target audience, so the selection process is a balancing act between cost and reach.

The process of measuring a target audience's size against the cost of reaching that audience is based on calculations of efficiency as measured by two commonly used metrics: cost per thousand and cost per point.

The term **cost per thousand (CPM)** is industry shorthand for the cost of getting 1,000 impressions. CPM is best used when comparing the cost of vehicles within the same medium (comparing one magazine with another or one television program with another). This is because different media have different levels of impact. To be more precise and determine the efficiency of a potential media buy, planners often look at the **targeted cost per thousand (TCPM).**

To calculate a CPM for a broadcast commercial, you need only two figures: the cost of an ad and the estimated audience reached by the vehicle. Multiply the cost of the ad by 1,000 and divide that number by the size of the broadcast audience. You multiply the cost of the ad by 1,000 to calculate a "cost per thousand."

In the case of print, CPMs are based on circulation or number of readers. *Time* magazine has a circulation of 4 million but claims a readership of 19.5 million. The difference between circulation and readership is due to what is called **pass-along readership.** In the case of *Time,* this means each issue is read by about five people. As you would suspect, media vehicles prefer that agencies use readership rather than circulation for figuring CPM because this produces a much lower CPM.

- *Calculating CPM* In the following example, CPM is calculated based on *Time* readership and the price of a one-page, four-color ad, $240,000. Remember, you want to know what it costs to reach 1,000 readers.

$$CPM = \frac{Cost\ of\ ad\ \times\ 1,000}{Readership}$$

$$CPM = \frac{\$240,000\ \times\ 1,000}{19,500,000} = \$12.31\ CPM$$

- *Calculating TCPM* To figure the TCPM, you first determine how many of *Time's* readers are in your target audience. For the sake of discussion, we'll say that only 5 million of *Time's* readers fall into our target audience profile. As you can see from the following calculation, the TCPM greatly increases. This is because you still have to pay to reach all the readers, even though only about one-fourth of them are of value to you.

$$TCPM = \frac{Cost\ of\ ad\ \times\ 1,000}{Readers\ in\ target\ audience}$$

$$TCPM = \frac{\$240,000\ \times\ 1,000}{5,000,000} = \$48.00\ TCPM$$

- *Calculating CPP* Now we'll look at how to determine **cost per point (CPP),** which estimates the cost of reaching 1 million households based on a program's rating points. Divide the cost of running one commercial by the rating of the program in which the commercial will appear. If a 30-second spot on *Lost* costs $320,000, and it has a rating of 8, then the cost per rating point would be $40,000:

$$CPP = \frac{\$320,000}{8\ rating} = \$40,000\ CPP$$

- *Calculating TCPP* To figure the *targeted cost per point (TCPP),* the rating points based on the target audience you want to reach, determine what percentage of the audience is your target. In the case of *Lost,* we will estimate that half of the audience is our target. Thus, the overall rating of 8 is reduced to 4 (50% $\times$ 8 = 4 rating). Now we divide the one-time cost of $320,000 by 4 and find the TCPP is $80,000:

$$TCPP = \frac{\$320,000}{4\ target\ rating} = \$80,000\ TCPP$$

We can do this calculation to compare several different programs and identify those with lower costs.

CPMs have a wide range. A media planner may calculate a CPM of $56 to reach some 44 million viewers of the Super Bowl.[8] In contrast, in the real estate example given earlier, *iMapp.com* might charge a CPM of $125 to reach a small, but select group of realtors. iMapp is twice as expensive as the Super Bowl ad (not in real dollars, but in CPM), but the higher CPM is justified because of the tight targeting. Media planners are constantly balancing cost with audience characteristics to decide if the media vehicle makes sense given the target audience size and characteristics.

A MATTER OF PRINCIPLE

When Is Too Many Too Much?

Tom Duncan, IMC Founder and Director Emeritus, University of Colorado and Daniels School of Business at the University of Denver

The questions advertisers have to ask themselves when approving a plan that involves nontraditional media is whether they are using this tool effectively and with respect for consumers. Are advertisers trying to find every possible contact point they can identify or are they creating logical associations that consumers will appreciate?

The fact is that we are inundated with commercial messages from advertising of all sorts in all kinds of unexpected places that we routinely encounter. Message clutter is overwhelming every aspect of our daily lives.

Think about something as noncommercial as attending a symphony. You may find a new car in the lobby as well as promotional signs for any number of products—not to mention the symphony itself, which is promoting concerts and season subscriptions. Of course, there are ads in the program, but there may also be ads in the bathrooms and around the snack counter you visit at intermission. When you leave, you'll probably see more posters in windows adjoining the concert hall. You might even find a flyer tucked under the windshield wiper on your car.

There is a difference between "buying eyeballs" and delivering messages in a context that will intersect with a target audience's interests.

Wilson Sporting Goods, for example, sponsors Tennis Camps by furnishing practice balls and making racquets available that participants can try for free. Even though the camp may be surrounded by Wilson, the message is relevant and the brand experiences are positive.

The point is that the less relevant the messages, the more irritating they become.

Why is this a problem?

The tipping point in impact is when the percentage of irrelevant messages is so high that people respond by tuning out ALL commercial messages—the relevant along with the irrelevant.

One reason TiVo became popular is because viewers can time-shift programs and zip through commercials. In what ways will consumers create defense mechanisms to protect themselves from nontraditional media that assault them in unwanted ways in inappropriate times?

How many messages can we surround them with before they rebel?

Media Optimization   In our earlier discussion of media mix strategy, we looked at the efficiency of various media plans. Tools that help estimate the most optimum use of various media plans using computer models involve calculating the weight of a media schedule and optimizing the schedule for the greatest impact. These **optimization** techniques enable marketers to determine the relative impact of a media mix on product sales and optimize the efficiency of the media mix.

Generally the models can create an unlimited number of media combinations and then simulate the sales produced by each. Chrysler's digital agency, Organic, has designed a system to determine the best way to allocate the marketing communication budget. Here's how it works: "The system calculates how much ad spending is needed to meet certain sales targets and then analyzes how both online and offline ads affect Web activity and, ultimately, sales."[9] Using optimization models, the media planner can make intelligent decisions, given factors such as budget, timing, and so forth. Other optimization services are CPM Advisors (*www.cpmadvisors.com*), Aggregate Knowledge (*www.aggregateknowledge.com*), and Telmar (*www.telmar.com*).

The issue of media optimization, however, is bigger than just numbers and estimates of efficiency. It also involves questions of media overload and consumer irritation, as the *A Matter of Principle* feature argues.

A Sample Media Plan

Media plans do not have a universal form, but there is a common (and logical) pattern to the decision stages as we have outlined in this chapter. To illustrate one style of presentation in a real-life setting, we use an actual media plan for a Women's Health Services program based in hospitals. This media plan example was contributed by Amy Hume, who was media director

WOMEN'S HEALTH SERVICES MEDIA PLAN

Launched in winter 2009–10 in hospitals throughout the central United States, the Women's Health Services Program (WHSP) combines the health care services that women may be exposed to throughout their lives under one roof. It brings together services beyond just gynecology, like oncology, dermatology, cardiology, and more. It aids women by providing one central point of contact—a concierge—to coordinate their appointments.

Communication Objectives
- Establish awareness of a new Women's Health Services Program opening in select local hospitals throughout the Heartland of the U.S.
- Generate buzz and word of mouth
- Drive requests for information via Web and phone

Strategic Plan Development
While "all women" were the target, we knew that the best opportunity started with wealthy, more educated women who would act as influencers in the market. As a result, we focused, demographically, on,—Working Women Ages 30–54 with HHI $75M+, with or without kids.

It was important for us to gain further insight into their behaviors and attitudes relating to health care, communication and everyday routines. Via both syndicated research and primary research we uncovered many insights that helped direct the plan:

Activities/Behaviors
- They work out?—either at home, in a club, or outdoors.
  - They exercise to manage their weight, be more relaxed, reduce health problems.
  - While most women are not passionate about working out, many say it is an essential part of their lives.
- They travel to/from work an average of 7.5 miles—either in car or public transportation (depending on the market).
- They go to a coffee shop usually 1x/day—both independents and chains.
- They use the Internet for e-mail, social networking and to research just about anything.
  - But particularly health-related issues—2/3 of online health site users are female.
- Women make 75% of health care decisions, spend 2/3 of health care $, and account for 2/3 of hospital procedures.

Attitudes
- Women's most influential source of information or advice is their circle of friends:
  - Women rely on advice and opinions of those individuals around them who have proven themselves in the past.
  - They respond to anecdotes/storytelling—they will connect to an engaging narrative relating the lives and experiences of other women.
  - Through our primary research we found that many women have phone conversations with female relatives once/day.
    - Conversation serves many purposes in women's lives: recharging, validation, and learning.
- Women focus on the emotional—happiness, peace of mind, fulfillment, self-confidence—vs. more traditional, material, outward manifestations of success.
- When choosing health care they are looking for:
  - "Someone who knows me," "Ability to help with issues," "Treat me as an individual."
    - It's important for women to be communicated to on a personal level.
  - They believe it's stressful and hard to find a physician who's interested in their overall health.

(continued)

at the Denver-based Barnhart Communications when she prepared this plan. Let's briefly explore each major section in this plan:

- *Objectives* Media objectives are designed to deliver on the campaign's overall communication objectives. The primary communication objective for this Women's Health Services campaign was to build awareness. The media-related objectives that would deliver this awareness involved two tasks: generating buzz among the target audience and creating

A graduate of the University of Colorado, Amy Hume was nominated by Professor Tom Duncan.

With this background and research, we were able to establish our key strategies.

Strategies
- Overall, we determined that we would be most effective by using a combination of traditional and non-traditional vehicles that intersect women in relevant, yet respectful places—and in non-traditional ways.
- We knew that it was important to seek contacts that increase relevance—that tie into her perception of healthy living—nutrition, fitness, and relaxation—and into her passions—family and hobbies.
- Also, we needed to recommend contacts that would help provide impact, and thus increased receptivity of the message. Those that would signal "for me" (personal, part of my world), be trustworthy, and provide opportunity for narrative/storytelling.
- Finally, it was important to get out of the traditional health care mold and get her to react and engage.

Who (Target)
Active Female Health Managers
- Working women, married, ages 30–54, with or without kids
- More likely to ask their doctor to send them to a preferred specialist or hospital
- Indirectly, their knowledge, experience, and passion for updated health information makes them a valuable resource?—they have a large sphere of influence.

Where (Geography)
While the program itself was launching in 10 cities, we decided to focus on the more efficiently priced, mid-sized metro areas in the Central U.S. —Minneapolis, Denver, Kansas City, St. Louis, and Kansas City.

When (Timing/Seasonality)
Launch September 2009 to lead up to multi-city opening. Also coincides with time of "renewal" with the back-to-school mentality.
Provide additional support in January as people are making resolutions—mostly in the area of health.
Follow up with an effort in May tied into Women's Health month.

SAMPLE MEDIA PLAN FOR WOMEN'S HEALTH SERVICES

	2005						2006						BUDGET
	JULY	AUGUST	SEPTEMBER	OCTOBER	NOVEMBER	DECEMBER	JANUARY	FEBRUARY	MARCH	APRIL	MAY	JUNE	
Magazines													$ 720,000
Radio													$ 600,000
Out of Home													$ 300,000
Place-Based													
Health Clubs													$ 180,000
Coffee Sleeves													$ 90,000
Produce Section													$ 45,000
Mall boards													$ 45,000
Online													
Media													$ 300,000
Website													tbd
Events													$ 200,000
GRAND TOTAL													$ 2,480,000

How Much (Weight Levels/Budget)
We analyzed competitive advertising pressure of other hospitals and health centers in these markets as well as prominent women's programs like Brigham & Women's, Oregon Health & Science University Center for Women's Health, and the Iris Cantor Women's Health Center. We determined that there was little consistent mass media pressure in any market by these entities.

enough interest that the campaign would cause the target to search for information using the website and phone number provided in the campaign materials.

- ***Strategic Plan Development: Consumer Insights*** The key to this media plan is understanding the consumer market for the Women's Health Services Program (WHSP). Background research from the campaign's situation analysis is used to describe the women in this market in terms of their activities and behaviors, as well as their attitudes and feelings.

Due to the absence of substantive competitive reach and frequency benchmarks by competition or like programs, based weight level objectives on history and experience:
- During launch, generate 85% reach/4.0 frequency per month
  - For follow-up months, 65%/3.0 as budget allows

We were working with a Year One budget of $3.0MM to cover all markets.

What (Vehicle Selection)

Magazines: Be where they're searching for health care information—62% of women ranked magazines as their #1 source of information for healthy eating habits, fitness, health, and overall well-being. They will provide the opportunity for long-form messaging. Recommend use of local magazines as well as regional editions of national magazines to provide reach.

Radio: Close to 50% of active health managers listen to the radio everyday; and 50% always listen when they're in their car; they rely on radio to keep them informed. But, they tend to change the station when commercials come on. Thus, we need to use radio in a non-traditional manner. Recommended using 1–2 top-reaching stations per market and establish relationships with key DJs. Bring them to the Center's pre-opening to experience the staff, the atmosphere, and expose them to the services so that they will then talk about the Center during their shows. This will allow women to hear from a trusted source, yet via a good reaching medium, while not immediately turning the dial.

Out-of-Home: Use traditional billboards and transit advertising to intersect women during their daily routine. Helps create a surround-sound approach.

Place-Based: Based on their daily routines and behaviors, we recommended placements in Health Clubs, Coffee Shops, Grocery Stores, and Mall/Retail Centers. The messaging would need to be specially tailored to these environments and placements.

Internet:
- Other websites: Determine key sites within each city and talk with top-rated health sites nationally to gain a presence—particularly contextually via articles. Research blogs and chat rooms to determine other electronic avenues for contact.
- Social media: Use social networking technologies like Twitter to push out news about the doctors and other specialists working in the programs, information on events .
- WHSP website: Develop a website that will provide resources and links for women including the opportunity for community such as: blogging, chat rooms, message boards, as well as a feedback and research tool. Aggregate content that affects all women, but be specific when it comes to each community to ensure the local flavor and expertise. Also recognize that women will need to be pulled into the site via news, information—important to first go where they are first.
- Hospital websites: Tie into the partner hospital websites to create a special women's corner that links to the WHSP site.

Events/Seminars: Invite women in each community to a grand opening celebration with 2–3 key speakers. Follow up with quarterly seminars, which will encourage women to spread the word—"bring your sister or your mom." Develop a membership program that will provide an opportunity for Brand Ambassadors, creating a women's health care "community."

- ***Key Media Strategies*** Identifying the appropriate media involved locating those apertures where messages about the WHSP would be most welcome. That involves understanding the patterns in the target audiences' lives and the intersection of their activities with media opportunities. Another important aspect of media strategy is spelling out the media mix, which includes the various media to be used and strategies that drive how they support and reinforce one another. For the WHSP, the key decision was to use both traditional media and nontraditional vehicles that are specific to their lives and personal activities. The key strategic decisions in this media plan can be summarized as who, where, when, how much, and what.

WHAT IS THE BIG PICTURE OF MEDIA PLANNING?

As we have noted previously, when most people think about media, they think about traditional mass media and advertising. Media planning in an IMC context is complicated by the ways media interact in integrated programs. We'll discuss two of these practices that add complexity to the process: IMC planning and global media planning.

IMC and Contact Point Planning

When IMC planners think about media, they think about message delivery systems and that includes all of the media used in various types of marketing communication. Direct response, for example, which is the topic of Chapter 16, can appear in traditional media (print with fill-in-blanks to get more information about a brand or place an order; infomercials on TV), but also in letters mailed directly to the home or office, telemarketing (phone calls to the home or office), and in digital forms, such as e-mail and Twitter. Public relations places stories in all of the traditional media including trade media, but also uses publicity tours, speeches and interviews with executives, special events, corporate videos, blogs, and websites, to name a few.

As DePaul University marketing professor Steve Kelly says, "Because the Internet allows marketers to make their marketing dollars measurable and accountable, much like the direct marketers have done for years, the goal now is to make all marketing communications measurable. Thus, integrated marketing communications becomes the goal." He explains, "IMC tries to tie it all together. IMC is the goal of most marketers, but multichannel is what they actually do."[10]

An example of IMC multimedia planning comes from *The Today Show*, which launched a new recipe website and mobile application in sponsorship with Unilever. The "Cooking School" website contains previously aired segments of "Today's Kitchen" and streaming video *webisodes*, as well as recipes, cooking tips, and promotions for Unilever brands such as Bertolli, Country Crock, Hellmann's, and Ragu. The recipes can be downloaded at home or to a mobile device. A Smartphone app allows users to compile recipes and build shopping lists. The "Cooking School" partnership links mobile, online, and broadcast media.[11]

Another distinctive feature of IMC media plans is its emphasis on contact points. Media planning in an IMC campaign focuses on every important contact point. These can include a variety of experiential media, as well as conventional media. Think about all the ways you come in contact with a brand message when you fly on an airline—reservations, check in, baggage checking, the gate, the cabin attendants and officer's messages over the loudspeaker, the seats and food and other cabin features, departure and arrival times, deplaning, baggage again, not to mention customer service when you miss a plane or a bag gets lost. That's just a brief list and you can probably add to it. A list of contact points an IMC planner might consider would be endless, but a sample list is available online on this book's website (*www.pearsonglobaleditions.com/moriarty*).

Dentsu's ContactPoint Management   Tokyo-based Dentsu, which is the world's largest individual agency, has a strong IMC orientation, which shows up in the way Dentsu planners create IMC media plans. Dentsu's ContactPoint Management offering is a section in its IMC 2.0 model that identifies a wide diversity of contact points, including but not limited to such separate communication functions as public relations, sponsorship, direct-response marketing, events, word of mouth (WOM), in-store (signage, POP, personnel), sales promotion, traditional advertising media (broadcast, print, out-of-home), sports, entertainment, interactive (Web, podcasting), mobile media, and new out-of-home (OOH) media. Let's take a closer look at Dentsu's approach to IMC media planning.[12]

The objective of Dentsu's ContactPoint Management planning is to select the most effective contact points required to achieve the desired communication goals and to implement optimum integrated communication programs that eliminate waste. ContactPoint Management focuses on two strategies that are critical in delivering effective integrated communication:

1. Identify the value contact points, that is, the emotion-driving points at which or during which consumers come in contact with a brand.
2. Move away from the traditional B2C model, in which business targets a consumer with a message, to a more interactive B2C2C model, in which a business talks to consumers who talk to other consumers. This approach uses mass media to stimulate interconsumer communications, or word of mouth, which delivers messages more persuasively.

Media selection recognizes that (1) contact points that work well must differ depending on the communication goal and (2) contact point effectiveness will differ from product category to product category and from target to target.

An example of how Dentsu manages a full set of brand contact points comes from an automotive campaign where two target audiences have been identified as Fathers (male, 50s) and Daughters (female, 20s). The communication objective is to position the new subcompact car model as "fun driving for grown men" and "a small cute model for young women."

The various contact points considered are evaluated and ranked using a proprietary contact point planning system called VALCON (Value ContactPoint Tracer). Dentsu planners also have access to hundreds of media-related databases with vast volumes of contact point information to consult in this process. The final decisions about media usage are based on the roles and effects of the various media.

For the new subcompact, contact points were evaluated based on three objectives: their ability to launch a new product (recognition, build awareness), arouse interest (evaluation), and make the target feel like buying (intention, attitude). Here are the results by points assigned to various options:

	Father	*Both*			*Daughter*
Awareness	1. Newspaper 2. OOH ads				1. Train poster 2. TV ad
		3.	Direct mail	4.	3. Magazine ad
Interest	1. Car on display at event	3.	Car on streets	1.	
		4.	TV ad	2.	3. Automaker's website
		2.	Catalog	5.	
		5.	Newspaper insert	8.	4. Cars owned by friends
Intention	3. Car magazine story	2.	Catalog	1.	
		1.	Car on display	2.	
		6.	Test drive	3.	
					4. TV ad

As you can see, the plan calls for contact points that reach both audiences (TV ads, catalogs, street media, newspaper inserts, and direct mail). Newspaper ads, OOH ads, the car on display at the dealer's showroom, and car magazine stories were added or emphasized for the Father audience. For the Daughter audience, magazine ads, a website, transit ads, radio ads, family WOM, and TV ads were added. Here is how this complex media plan is diagrammed in terms of its effects.

	Recognition	*Evaluation*	*Attitude*
Father	Newspaper and OOH ads, car display at dealer		Car magazine stories
Both	TV ads, catalogs, street media, newspaper inserts, direct mail	TV ads, friends WOM	Catalog, car display at dealer, test drive
Daughter	Magazine and transit ads, website	Radio ads, family WOM	TV ads

Cross-Media Integration   Media selection also considers message needs. Here is where media planning and message planning intersect. Brand reminders, for example, are often found in television commercials and in OOH media. More complex information-laden messages are more likely to be found in magazines, direct mail, or publicity releases. If you want to stimulate immediate action, you might use daily newspapers, radio, or sales promotion.

With the increasing push into digital media, the chief marketing officer at a digital media company reminds planners that "Brand advertising is about telling a story, not just directing traffic."

The *Atlantic Monthly* magazine used a multiplatform campaign that integrated messages from neon signs to create an event that was filmed for videos that were seen on a website.

He calls for refocusing on media basics: "Interactivity has given us new options to tell a story, social media have given us tools to make it spread, and digital more broadly has forced advertisers to consider utility to the user." But he insists: "The basics persist—find paths to the consumers where you can get scale, buy attention, and repeat."[13]

The challenge is to create *cross-media integration*, which means the various media work together to create coherent brand communication. Planners seek to create a synergistic effect between the messages delivered in different media. In traditional media, this is sometimes called **image transfer** and refers to the way radio, in particular, reinforces and re-creates the message in a listener's mind that was originally delivered by other media, particularly TV.

An example of cross-media integration comes from the revitalization campaign for the *Atlantic Monthly* magazine. To reinforce its position as an intellectual leader, the campaign used the slogan: "Think. Again." To bring that idea to life, the campaign presented 14 of *Atlantic's* most thought-provoking questions as 14 huge neon signs placed around New York. At night the creative team taped interviews with viewers as they wondered about the brightly lit messages. These videos, which showcased the personal, profound, and sometimes hilarious responses, were housed on a website and used as a hub for a debate of these great issues. So it was OOH marketing that created an event that turned into videos that enlivened a website (see *http://thinkagain.theatlantic.com*). In this case, to quote media scholar Marshall McLuhan, media became the message. Was it successful? The magazine saw a double-digit increase in readership and the number of visitors to *TheAtlantic.com* increased by 27 percent over the previous year.

Global Media Planning

Advertising practitioners can debate global theories of advertising, but one fact is inescapable: a true global medium does not currently exist, which means global media plans have to piece together worldwide coverage using a variety of media tools. Television can transmit the Olympics around the globe, but no one network controls this global transmission. An advertiser seeking global exposure, therefore, must deal with different networks and different vehicles in different countries.

Satellite transmission now places advertising into many homes, but its availability is not universal because of the *footprint* (coverage area of the satellite), technical limitations, and regulations of transmission by various governments. Satellites beam signals to more than one country in Europe, the Asian subcontinent, North America, and the Pacific, but they are regional, not global, in coverage. Despite its regional limitation, satellite transmission is still an enormous factor in the changing face of international advertising. Star TV, with an audience spanning 38 countries, including Egypt, India, Japan, Indonesia, and Russia's Asian provinces, reaches a market of some 2.7 billion people. It is closely followed by CNN and ESPN. Sky Channel, a U.K.-based network, offers satellite service to most of Europe, giving advertisers the opportunity to deliver a unified message across the continent.

The North American, European, Asian, and Latin American markets are becoming saturated with cable TV companies offering an increasing number of international networks. Such broadcasters include the hugely successful Latin American networks of Univision and Televisa, whose broadcasts can be seen in nearly every Spanish-speaking market, including the United States. One of Univision's most popular programs, *Sabado Giganta*, is seen by tens of millions of viewers in 16 countries.

HOW DOES MEDIA BUYING WORK?

So far in this chapter, you've read about media plans and the key steps you would take to develop a media plan, and you looked at some important big picture issues related to media planning. As you recall, the media plan is a recommendation that the client must approve before any further steps are taken. In fact, planning is only the first stage in advertising media operations. Once the plan directions are set, media buyers convert objectives and strategies into tactical decisions. They select specific media vehicles and negotiate and contract for the time and space in media. In this section we explain how the media buyer makes the media plan come to life. A media buyer has distinct responsibilities as outlined in Figure 14.6.

Media Buying Complexities

Buying is a complicated process. The American Association of Advertising Agencies lists no fewer than 21 elements of a media buy. The most important one, however, is matching the media vehicle to the strategic needs of the message and the brand. In this section, we examine the most important buyer activities: providing information to media planners, selecting the media vehicles, negotiating costs, monitoring the media choices, evaluating the media choices after the campaign, and handling billing and payment.

Principle
Media buyers should be consulted early in planning as they are a good source of information on changes in media.

- ***Provide Inside Information*** Media buyers are important information sources for media planners. They are close enough to day-to-day changes in media popularity and pricing to be an important source of inside current information. For example, a newspaper buyer discovers that a key newspaper's delivery staff is going on strike, or a magazine buyer's source reveals

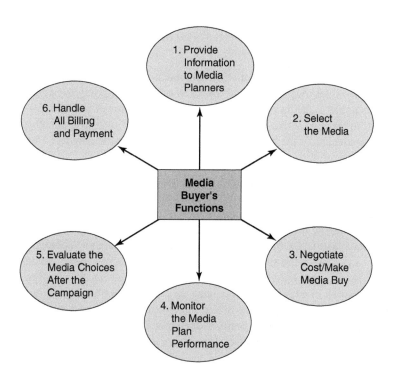

FIGURE 14.6
The Functions of a Media Buyer

The physical characteristics of a magazine can affect its ability to deliver the desired message. For example, this V8 ad, which appeared in *Reader's Digest*, uses simple visuals and minimal copy to accommodate the smaller page size. *Reader's Digest* may not be the best choice for a complex ad.

that the new editor of a publication is going to change the editorial focus dramatically. All of these things can influence the strategy and tactics of current and future advertising plans.

• **Select Media Vehicles** The media planner determines the media mix, but the buyer is responsible for choosing the specific media vehicles. A *Mediaweek* article, for example, identifies patterns in media buyers' decision making. A study reported in 2010 found that ESPN was the top cable choice of media buyers, followed by Disney, TNT, TBS, the Food Network, USA, HGTV, Comedy Central, and Bravo. In terms of buys on network TV, the study found that ABC was best, followed by Fox, NBC, and CBS.[14] In terms of programs, *American Idol* has been the most-watched show on TV since 2007, even though its numbers started dropping in 2009. More than 25 million watched the show in 2009.[15] Online media buying is usually handled through ad networks and the big portals. AOL, Yahoo, Google, and Microsoft are four of the five biggest online ad networks; the Microsoft Media Network is the fastest growing service.[16]

Armed with the media plan directives, the buyer seeks answers to a number of difficult questions as various media vehicles are considered. Does the vehicle have the right audience profile? Will the program's current popularity increase, stabilize, or decline? How well does the magazine's editorial format fit the brand and the message strategy (see the V8 ad example)? The answers to those questions bear directly on the campaign's success.

• **Negotiate** Just as a person buying a car often negotiates for the best price, so does a media buyer negotiate for the best prices. The key questions are whether the desired vehicles are available and whether a satisfactory schedule and rates can be negotiated. Aside from finding the aperture of target audiences, nothing is more crucial in media buying than securing the lowest possible price for placements.

Every medium has a published rate card, but media buyers often negotiate special prices for volume buys. The buyer must understand the trade-off between price received and audience objectives. For example, a media buyer might be able to get a lower price for 30 commercials on ESPN, but part of the deal is that half the spots are scheduled with programs that don't reach the primary target audience. So the price may not be a good deal in the long run. Here are some other negotiation considerations:

• **Bargain for Preferred Positions** Media buyers must bargain for **preferred positions,** the locations in magazines and other print media that offer readership advantages (see Chapter 12). Imagine the value a food advertiser would gain from having its message located in a special recipe section that the homemaker can detach from the magazines for permanent use. How many additional exposures might that ad get? Because they are so visible, preferred positions often carry a premium surcharge, usually 10 to 15 percent above standard space rates.

• **Demand Extra Support Offers** With the current trend toward using other forms of marketing communication in addition to advertising, buyers often demand additional promotional support. These activities, sometimes called **value-added media services,** can take any number of forms, including contests, special events, merchandising space at stores, displays, and trade-directed newsletters. The "extra" depends on what facilities each media vehicle has and how hard the buyer can bargain.

- *Monitor Performance* A media buyer's responsibility to a campaign does not end with the signing of space and time contracts. The media buyer is responsible for tracking the performance of the media plan as it is implemented and afterward as part of the campaign evaluation. Buys are made in advance, based on forecasted audience levels. What happens if unforeseen events affect scheduling? What if newspapers go on strike, magazines fold, or a television show is canceled? Buyers must fix these problems. Underperformance and schedule problems are facts of life. Poorly performing vehicles must be replaced, or costs must be modified. Buyers also check the publication issues to verify whether advertisements have been placed correctly. Buyers also make every attempt to get current audience research to ensure that schedules are performing according to forecast. Media buyers are even found out "riding the boards," which means they check the location of the outdoor boards to verify that the client is receiving the outdoor exposure specified in the plan.
- *Postcampaign Evaluation* Once a campaign is completed, the planner's duty is to compare the plan's expectations and forecasts with what actually happened. Did the plan actually achieve GRP, reach, frequency, and CPM objectives? Did the newspaper and magazine placements run in the positions expected? Such analysis is instrumental in providing guidance for future media plans.
- *Monitor Billing and Payment* Bills from the various media come in continuously. Ultimately, it is the responsibility of the advertiser to make these payments. However, the agency is contractually obligated to pay the invoice on behalf of the client. Keeping track of the invoices and paying the bills are the responsibility of the media buyer in conjunction with the accounting department.

In addition to negotiating, bargaining, buying, and monitoring the execution of a media plan, media buyers also have to deal with situations that crop up and complicate the planning. In effect, they are also troubleshooters. Buyers deal with the temporary snags in scheduling and in the reproduction of advertising messages that are sometimes unavoidable. Buyers must be alert for missed positions or errors in handling the message presentation and ensure that the advertiser is compensated appropriately when they occur. A policy of compensating for such errors is called "making good on the contract," known as **make goods**. Here are some of the common problems they may run into:

- *Program Preemptions* Special programs or news events sometimes interrupt regular programming and the scheduled commercials. In the case of long-term **program preemptions,** such as war coverage, buyers may have difficulty finding suitable replacements before the schedule ends.
- *Missed Closings* Magazines and newspapers have clearly set production deadlines, called **closings**, for each issue. Sometimes the advertising materials do not arrive in time. If the publication is responsible, it will make good. If the fault lies with the client or the agency, the publication makes no restitution.
- *Technical Problems* Technical difficulties are responsible for numerous goofs, glitches, and foul-ups that haunt the advertiser's schedule. **Bleed-throughs** (the printing on the back side of the page is visible and conflicts with the client's ad on the front side) and **out-of-register color** (full-color printing is made from four-color plates, which sometimes are not perfectly aligned) for newspapers, torn billboard posters, broken film, and tapes out of alignment are typical problems.

The media buyer's life got even more complicated in 2010 with the live broadcast of the Academy Awards where E! Entertainment and Google worked feverishly to make real-time placements that would match the drama playing out onstage. The E! online channel was able to alter its Oscar-related ads within minutes to reflect not just the winners, but also the content of the speeches, the onstage events, what the presenters were wearing, and other features of the coverage.[17]

Multichannel Buying (and Selling) It should be clear from this review of media buyers' responsibilities that this is a challenging job. A number of media services are available to help make buying for complicated media plans easier.

General Electric and its media arm, NBC Universal, for example, promoted its media opportunities using a multichannel plan that includes broadcast, cable, and the Internet, as well as original programming on its own channels. But the difference is that the media deals are packaged around a cause, such as the environment or wellness. Campbell Soup, for example, sponsored health segments on NBC's *The Today Show*, as well as Dr. Nancy Snyderman's MSNBC health program.[18] The idea is to match the media use of the target audience in all its complexity.

Newspapers have long offered simplified buys through such companies as Nationwide Newspapers, which can handle classified and display advertising in more than 21,000 newspapers. The Newspaper National Network is a trade association representing some 9,000 newspapers that also handles ad placement. In the digital world, DoubleClick's DART for Advertisers (DFA) service helps advertisers manage online display and search marketing campaigns across online channels. All of these services not only place ads, but also provide performance data to help optimize a buy, as well as report on the effectiveness of a marketer's specific plan.

On the other side of that coin is the *cross-media buy,* which is made easier by media companies that sell combinations of media vehicles in a single buy. This approach makes it easier to buy media across all of these platforms with a single deal rather than six phone calls. These **multichannel** deals are also a result of media convergence. As content moves across these various forms of new media, so also does advertising. Giant media groups, such as Viacom and Disney, are packaging "deals" based on the interests of the target audience. ESPN, for example, serves the sports market and can provide media integration that includes TV, magazines, radio, and the Internet. The media conglomerate Disney created a one-stop buying opportunity for advertisers targeting kids. To create this opportunity, Disney reorganized its ad sales staff to create one sales force for its various properties that reach children—two cable networks Disney Channel and Toon Disney, kids' programming on ABC, Radio Disney, *Disney.com,* and Disney Adventures magazine.

Global Media Buying   The definition of global media buying varies widely, but everyone agrees that few marketers are doing it yet. However, many are thinking about it, especially computer and other information technology companies that are being pursued by media such as CNN. Today, the growth area is media buys across a single region. As media become more global, however, some marketers are beginning to make the leap across regions. About 60 percent of ad buys on CNN International are regional, and 40 percent are global.

In Europe, the rise of buying "centrals" came about with the emergence of the European Union and the continuing globalization of trade and advertising. *Buying centrals* are media organizations that buy across several European countries. Their growth also began with the development of commercial broadcasting and the expansion of media choices. These firms have flourished in an environment of flexible and negotiated rates, low inflation, and a fragmented advertising market. The buying centrals have nearly three-fourths of the media market in France, nine-tenths in Spain, and about two-fifths in Britain, Holland, Italy, and Scandinavia.

The important thing, however, is to be able to consider cultural implications in media use. For that reason media planning and buying companies are also specializing or buying companies that know specific cultures, such as the Hispanic market in the United States and the Chinese market in Asia. Zenithoptimedia, for example, is a global media-buying company that has created ZO Multicultural, a multicultural unit that helps clients trying to reach ethnic markets.

Media Planning and Buying Trends

Advertising experts have been proclaiming the demise of mass media advertising for a number of years. It reached a high buzz level when Bob Garfield, an *Advertising Age* columnist, got industry-wide attention with his book, *The Chaos Scenario,* in which he speculated about the media landscape in coming years when over-the-air network TV is gone and everyone accesses their news, entertainment, and advertising any way they wish: TV, phone, camera, laptop, game console, or MP3 player. His concept of "listenomics" emphasizes the importance of consumer-in-charge media choices.[19]

The truth is that the media landscape is dynamic and changing so fast that it's hard to keep track of how the media business is practiced. All of these changes create new ways of operation and new opportunities for innovative media planners and buyers.

Unbundling Media Buying and Planning   We've mentioned before the growth of media-buying services, such as the media megashop Starcom MediaVest, as separate companies that specialize in media buying. This is a shift in the way the media industry is organized, a change referred to as **unbundling media services.** This happens when an agency transforms its media department into a separate profit center, apart from the agency. This then allows the media group to work for clients who may be competitors to some of those handled by the agency. Because these companies control the money, they have become a powerful force in the advertising industry, leading to a tug of war over control of planning. Faced with competition from these independent media companies, many large agencies have set up or bought their own buying services to compete with the independents and go after outside business.

Some of these media companies are now offering **consolidated services,** which means bringing the planning and buying functions back together. To take advantage of this consolidation argument, some media companies are also adding special planning teams for other related areas such as events, product placement, Internet, and guerilla marketing programs. WPP's MindShare created an agency-within-the-agency called the Wow Factory to develop ideas for nontraditional media.[20] For a major presentation to Coca-Cola, Starcom MediaVest pulled a team together that represented basic media planning and buying, research, consumer insights, programming, product placement, entertainment marketing, and integration solutions.[21] At this point, these big media companies begin to look more like traditional agencies.

Online Media Buying   A bigger threat to agencies than media-buying services comes from Google and Yahoo!, which, although not ad agencies, are making inroads into media buying and selling. Google is using its website to sell ads primarily to small advertisers and publishers who find its automated advertising network, Google Adworks, to be a cost-effective way to connect with one another. Agencies are trying to figure out if Google and Yahoo! are friends or enemies and what their move into online media buying will do to the revenue stream. Google, however, is betting that its expertise in search advertising, which matches ads to user interests, will give it an advantage over traditional ad media services.

New Forms of Media Research   As we mentioned earlier, one challenge media planners face is the lack of reliable audience research and measurement metrics for the new media. The traditional "measured" media with their CPMs were at least somewhat predictable in level of impact. But the metrics for online media—hits and clicks—don't really tell us much about impact. Comparing TRPs and clicks is like comparing apples and oranges.

We also know that exposure does not equal attention, which is a huge problem for evaluating the impact of television. In other words, just because the television is on does not mean anyone is watching; and just because a program is on does not mean anyone is watching the ads.

Search advertising on the Internet is also complicating things because, if it's successful, it steals viewers away from the original site. Does ESPN benefit when viewers leave its site to click on the banner ad for StubHub Ticket Center? As one critic observed, search advertising may make sense as a form of direct marketing, but it is a nightmare for content publishers who sell advertising on their pages. In such a situation, how do you evaluate efficiency of the publisher's site? Of the search advertising? If one is a winner, doesn't that automatically mean the other is a loser?

Viral marketing is equally difficult to measure, although YouTube is developing analytic data to help media planners assess the impact of the video-sharing site. Other companies such as Visible Measures, Unruly Media, and Millward Brown's Link provide viral monitoring services that assess the impact not only of YouTube, but also of multiple online platforms. As such services mature, marketers will become smarter about selecting marketing communication messages with the most viral video potential.[22]

Another problem is that media research is based on each medium as a silo—separate studies for separate media. Most of the research services are unable to tell you much about the effectiveness of combined media; the impact such as seeing the same message on television and then reading about it in a newspaper story or ad is difficult to evaluate.

Looking Ahead

That point leads to the next part of the book in which we review specific areas of marketing communication, such as public relations, direct response, sales promotion, and sponsorships—all of which are important aspects of multiplatform IMC programs. Then we'll apply this wider world of IMC to specific situations, such as retail, business-to-business, nonprofit, and international marketing. We'll end Part 5 with a discussion of evaluation and wrap up the effectiveness theme that is so important in today's brand communication.

Beauty of a Campaign

This chapter identified media strategies that are relevant to advertisers as they decide how to reach their audience effectively. The point is that the key to effective customer-focused advertising is staying sensitive to consumers and understanding how they think, act, and feel—and where they'll be able connect with the brand message.

The provocative copy in the Dove "Campaign for Real Beauty" challenges the audience to reconsider how they define beauty and to love their bodies, no matter what their age or shape. The campaign generated a huge buzz. But did it work to sell the product?

According to Unilever, the campaign resulted in a 24 percent sales increase during the advertising period across the entire Dove brand.

The brand also fared well globally. When it was launched in the United Kingdom, sales of Dove Firming Lotion reportedly increased by 700 percent in the first seven months after the posters appeared. It generated a substantial press interest, with about 170 editorial pieces written in the first four months after the launch in Great Britain.

The campaign radically changed the Dove brand image with its culturally relevant message. Initial publicity generated more than 650 million media impressions in the United States, estimated to be worth more than $21 million in free media exposure.

Moreover, the definition of beauty portrayed in advertising really seems to be changing. When asked about the images in Dove ads, 76 percent said women in the ad are beautiful, and 68 percent said, "It made you think differently about the brand."

Advertising Age named the Dove's "Evolution" Web film as one of its best non-TV campaigns of the decade. The viral film earned more than 6 million hits and lots of mentions in the national press on shows like *Good Morning America* and *The View*, which translates to about $150 million worth of media time. Although the video drew some criticism, overall the response was overwhelmingly positive. The play, *Finding Body and Soul*, won a Festival of Media award. Beautiful.

Key Points Summary

1. **What is a media plan and what is the role of media research in developing media plans?** A media plan identifies how a brand can connect with its customers and other stakeholders in effective ways that resonate with the target audience. Media researchers gather, sort, and analyze the data used by media planners in making their planning decisions.

2. **What are the four steps in media planning and why are they important?** Step one identifies the media use patterns of the target audience and the times and places where they would be more receptive to brand messages. Step two states the media objectives in terms of reach and frequency. This step includes selecting the most appropriate media and developing a media mix that reaches the target audience in various ways. The third step is to develop media strategies that fine-tune the plan in terms of the reach/frequency relationship, geography, scheduling and timing, size and position in a media vehicle, and the way media vehicles are weighted in terms of their impact for this audience and brand situation. The final step is to use media metrics to analyze and predict the effectiveness (impact) and cost efficiency of the plan.

3. **How do IMC and global marketing affect media plans?** IMC focuses on contact points where brand experiences contribute to brand perceptions. IMC contact point planning is complex and uses multiplatform and multichannel programs. Global marketing programs need to be supported by media planning and buying across multiple countries and regions.

4. **What are the responsibilities of media buyers?** Media buyers have inside information about the media industries that they feed back into the planning. Their responsibilities as buyers include providing information to media planners, selecting media vehicles, negotiating rates, monitoring the media plan's performance, evaluating the effectiveness of the media buy, and handling billing and payments.

Words of Wisdom: Recommended Reading

Azzaro, Marian, *Strategic Media Decisions,* 2nd ed., Chicago: The Copy Workshop, 2008.

Katz, Helen, *The Media Handbook: A Complete Guide to Advertising Media Selection, Planning, Research, and Buying,* 2nd ed., Mahwah, NJ: Erlbaum, 2009.

Kelley, Larry, and Donald Jugenheimer, *Advertising Media Planning: A Brand Management Approach,* 2nd ed., Armonk, NY: M. E. Sharpe, 2008.

Sissors, Jack, and Roger Baron, *Advertising Media Planning,* 6th ed., New York: McGraw-Hill, 2002.

Key Terms

aperture, p. 461

average frequency, p. 456

bleed-throughs, p. 477

brand development index (BDI), p. 459

carryover effect, p. 462

category development index (CDI), p. 459

closings, p. 477

consolidated services, p. 479

continuity, p. 462

continuous strategy, p. 462

cost per point (CPP), p. 467

cost per thousand (CPM), p. 466

designated marketing area (DMA), p. 452

earned media, p. 466

effective frequency, p. 457

flighting strategy, p. 462

frequency, p. 456

frequency distribution, p. 457

frequency quintile distribution analysis, p. 457

gross rating points (GRPs), p. 463

heavy-up schedule, p. 459

image transfer, p. 474

lead time, p. 461

make goods, p. 477

measured media, p. 452

media flow chart, p. 462

media mix, p. 458

media objectives, p. 455

media plan, p. 452

media strategy, p. 458

multichannel, p. 478

optimization, p. 468

out-of-register color, p. 477

pass-along readership, p. 467

preferred positions, p. 476

program preemptions, p. 477

pull strategy, p. 463

pulsing strategy, p. 462

push strategy, p. 463

reach, p. 455

share of voice, p. 452

targeted cost per thousand (TCPM), p. 466

targeted rating points (TRPs), p. 464

targeted reach, p. 456

unbundling media services, p. 479

value-added media services, p. 476

wasted reach, p. 456

wearout, p. 462

weighting, p. 463

Review Questions

1. Explain the differences between media planning and media buying.
2. What is aperture, and how is it used in media planning?
3. How are gross impressions and gross rating points calculated?
4. What are some of the strategic considerations that determine the level of reach? Level of frequency?
5. Explain the differences among continuous, flighting, and pulsing schedules.
6. Explain the differences between GRPs and TRPs. How are they used to estimate the impact of a media plan?
7. Explain the differences among CPMs, TCPMs, and CPPs. How are they used to estimate the cost efficiency of a media plan?
8. In what ways do IMC and global marketing plans add complexity to media planning?
9. What do media buyers do?

Discussion Questions

1. You have just begun a new job as a media planner for a new automobile model from General Motors. The media planning sequence will begin in four months, and your media director asks you what data and information you need from the media research department. What sources should you request? How would you use each of these sources in the planning function?
2. The marketing management of McDonald's restaurants has asked you to analyze the aperture opportunity for its breakfast entrees. What kind of analysis would you present to management? What recommendations could you make that would expand the restaurant's nontraditional, as well as traditional, media opportunities.
3. In performing an aperture analysis, choose one of the following products: video games (Nintendo, for instance), men's cologne (such as Axe), computer software (such as PhotoShop), or athletic shoes for aerobics (Reebok, for ex-

ample). For the brand you selected, analyze the marketing situation and give your intuitive answers to the following questions:
   a. How does aperture work for this product?
   b. Which media vehicles should be used to maximize and leverage the prospect's media aperture?
   c. Explain how the timing and duration of the advertising can improve the aperture opportunity.
4. *Three-Minute Debate* You have been hired as a media consultant for the Women's Health Services Project campaign outlined in this chapter's sample media plan. You and another member of your team disagree on whether the plan should be focused more on reach or frequency. Working with a small team of your classmates, explain and justify your point of view to your class.

Take-Home Projects

1. *Portfolio Project* You have been asked to develop a media plan for a new reality show that you have created. Focus on the Internet as a primary medium for this launch. Go to both *www.google.com/adsense* and *http://searchmarketing.yahoo.com*. Indicate how you would use the information provided by these sites in developing your media plan for this new reality TV show. Write a one- to two-page report.

2. *Mini-Case Analysis* Outline the key decisions in the Dove "Real Beauty" campaign. What were the media strategies that contributed to the success of this campaign? Dove's Men+Care personal care product line was mentioned in this chapter. Using your "Real Beauty" analysis as a model, develop a proposal for a media plan for this men's line.

Team Project: The BrandRevive Campaign

In Chapters 11, 12, and 13, you developed ideas about various types of media that might be used in your BrandRevive project. Now let's pull everything together in a media plan for your brand.

- Use the four steps discussed in this chapter as an outline and develop your team's ideas for each section of the plan.

- Prepare a pie chart that shows the budget allocation percentages you recommend for each media vehicle; also prepare a flow chart that shows the scheduling you would recommend for your brand.

- Present and explain your media plan in a PowerPoint presentation that is no longer than three slides.

Hands-On Case

The Century Council

Read the Century Council case in the Appendix before coming to class.

1. What target market insights led to the development of The Stupid Drink media plan? Do you agree with The Stupid Drink campaign team that the closer they can get to the underage binge drinking on college campuses, the better chance they have of having a positive influence? Why or Why not?

2. Since binge drinking is a national problem, should the media plan use only national media instead of campus by campus plan? Why or why not?

Evaluation of Effectiveness

It's a Winner

Campaign:
*SkiPass Dynamic
Pricing*

Company:
SkiStar

Agency:
In-house

CHAPTER KEY POINTS

1. Why and how is marketing communication evaluation conducted?
2. Can you list and explain the stages of message evaluation?
3. What are the key areas of media evaluation?
4. How are IMC tools, campaigns, and programs evaluated?

SkiStar SkiPass

In March 2010, SkiStar, Sweden's largest hospitality brand, struck a deal with the RCI holiday exchange network. SkiStar Vacation Club Fjällhotell and SkiStar Vacation Club Snötorget are located in the Swedish ski resort of Sälen, offering some of Sweden's best skiing and snowboarding. The deal marked SkiStar's first entrance into the vacation ownership market; they had already established themselves as an Alpine ski resort brand with a 43 percent share of the total Scandinavian ski pass sale market. They also owned 10 resorts, a number of ski schools, and rental developments.

The new SkiStar Vacation Club would allow customers to purchase their favorite weeks in Sälen, but with the RCI connection, customers could exchange these for sauna holidays in Finland or sunshine holidays in the Canaries. RCI had built up a network of some 4,000 resorts. This was not RCI's first entry into the Swedish market; they already had 17 resorts signed up to the network and a total of over 250 ski locations around the world.

U.S.-based Wyndham Exchange and Rentals is the owner of RCI and some 30 other brands around the world. They are considered to be the world leader in vacation exchange and rentals. Collectively, their network has some 3.8 million members across 100 countries. They supply access to 85,000 vacation properties around the world from villas to city apartments, from private clubs and resorts to yachts.

The primary purpose of SkiStar's marketing and sales strategy is to steadily increase the number of alpine skiers at their destinations. Each of the destinations is clearly profiled and they are designed to cater to specific groups of customers. SkiStar coordinates sales via a single telephone number and a website, which has three main objectives: first, to encourage cross-selling opportunities, such as equipment hire; second, to ensure that customer service levels are maintained at a high level; and third, to coordinate the operations of the business to maximize efficiency.

A key goal of the marketing and advertising efforts is to encourage advance sales before the start of the season, in effect, to pre-sell across the year to even out cash flow and lower their risks. SkiStar's website has been particularly effective in this respect as it has led to a drop in business costs (sales costs) and it has registered many potential customers, providing SkiStar with a large customer database.

The tie-in between SkiStar and RCI is part of a growing trend in the ski market with a number of notable cross-border collaborations, alliances, and acquisitions. In France, for example, the Compagnie des Alps owns ski resorts in Italy and in Switzerland. The collaboration between SkiStar and RCI made perfect business sense as the ownership of most ski resorts is highly fragmented, many of them owned by fairly small, family-run businesses.

In Sweden, although SkiStar is very large, other ski resort companies, such as the Strömma Group, own resorts in Hemavan-Tärnaby and Riksgränsen. There is a noticeable trend toward fewer and larger companies, with the purpose of achieving economies of scale, greater coordination of operations, and the ability to build a brand and market it to customers. In this way, SkiStar is following this trend. By operating in different geographical locations and attracting specific customer target groups across the year, many of these difficulties can be overcome.

SkiStar has also taken a broader approach. The acquisition of new ski resorts, investments in existing ones, and the establishment of ski rental accommodations (working with RCI) and ski schools are all aimed at increasing overall sales volume.

However, this approach has brought with it some problems. With acquisition, SkiStar inherited outdated and incompatible customer databases that had to be consolidated and interlinked with their existing databases. The eventual consolidation, however, led to large savings for the business and a far more effective customer relationship management system alongside an opportunity to fully integrate their marketing communications across the whole of the database. The cost of maintenance and the management of bookings were streamlined by the whole process.

The inherited systems meant that one customer could have as many as four customer IDs, one for each destination that they had skied at in the past. There was no integrated booking system, so customers had to call all destinations for information and prices. In the new system, all customers were given one ID, which was independent of skiing destinations.

In addition, the entire booking data from the customer database is now analyzed once a day. This allows SkiStar to detect peak demands and adjust prices, and reposition staff. This has gradually allowed further integration of systems. The call centers can now access all data and the systems are now interlinked and working together as one unit. The system has proved effective for both the business and the customers. Customers can book online or over the telephone, they can receive targeted marketing messages, and the consumer database is far more functional.

The net result of the work led to the creation of the SkiPass, which took advantage of SkiStar's ability to target personalized e-mails to all of the customers in the consolidated database. In effect, the system rewarded the customer financially for early booking and commitment. The earlier the booking, the lower the cost per customer, very much in the same way that low-cost airlines price their seats using a dynamic pricing model. The dynamic pricing system is in operation until mid-December each year; after that the SkiPass prices are fixed according to the time of the year that the customer wishes to ski. To drive sales through their website, SkiStar guarantees that their SkiPass will always be cheapest on their own website.

By integrating their databases, enhancing customer relationship management and marketing, and making it easier to book and pay for ski passes, SkiStar is now able to deliver highly personalized, targeted, and automated multichannel customer communications, which has substantially improved its customer experience and has led to a steady increase in sales. SkiStar has been able to closely manage its customer data and understand the individual life cycles of each customer. The systems also allow them to understand individual behaviors and preferences. Their link-up with RCI was just one part of this journey.

The result cemented SkiStar as the leading provider of Nordic skiing holidays. You can find out more about what they achieved by turning to the end of the chapter and reading the *It's a Wrap* feature.

Sources: www.rci.com; www.skistar.com; http://corporate.skistar.com; www.rciventures.com.

Throughout this book you've read about the effectiveness of advertising. We've emphasized that effective campaigns do more than win awards for creativity. They work hard to achieve the campaign's communication and marketing goals, as does the SkiStar SkiPass initiative. As you will see in this chapter, there are many ways to evaluate the effectiveness of various aspects of an advertising and marketing communication program. Specifically, four categories of work get evaluated in advertising and marketing communication programs—the message execution, the media, the campaign, and the other marketing communication areas and their synergistic effect as part of an IMC program. This chapter discusses the basic concept of the evaluation of effectiveness and then examines those four areas.

IMPACT: DOES IT WORK?

What makes a marcom message effective? The fact that people like it—or the fact that it moves people to some kind of action? The classic campaign for Avis is an example of one that works on both levels—people like it and it drove the company to record sales levels. When advertising works—when marketing communication is effective—it has impact and generates a response of some kind from its target audience. The critical phrase—"as intended"—means there are multiple objectives and, therefore, multiple ways to evaluate the effectiveness of marketing communication campaigns and programs.

Let's just consider advertising to begin with. Many executives feel advertising works only if it produces sales. Syracuse University Professor John Philip Jones, who has written many books and articles on the topic, estimates that of the $500 billion spent annually on advertising globally, only 41 percent—less than half—produces sales.[1] Jones contends that "advertising must generate an immediate jolt to sales before it can be expected to produce any further effect."[2] Simon Broadbent, another leading figure in effectiveness research, disagreed with Jones's short-term sales focus and suggested instead that advertising should emphasize long-term brand building.[3]

Determining advertising effectiveness based on sales can be difficult because of the impact of other marketing mix factors. For example, an article in *Business 2.0* reported that an ad for the Six Flags amusement park was a smash success in viewer surveys. However, because attendance at the company's 31 theme parks

Avis is only No.2 in rent a cars. So why go with us?

We try harder.
(When you're not the biggest, you have to.)
We just can't afford dirty ashtrays. Or half-empty gas tanks. Or worn wipers. Or unwashed cars. Or low tires. Or anything less than seat-adjusters that adjust. Heaters that heat. Defrosters that defrost.

Obviously, the thing we try hardest for is just to be nice. To start you out right with a new car, like a lively, super-torque Ford, and a pleasant smile. To know, say, where you get a good pastrami sandwich in Duluth.
Why?
Because we can't afford to take you for granted.
Go with us next time.
The line at our counter is shorter.

CLASSIC
According to *Advertising Age*, the Avis "We Try Harder" campaign was one of the top 10 in advertising history. It was the ultimate simple idea that conveyed a great idea that was truthful and believable. The strategy—to state strongly a self-effacing underdog position—also tapped into people's sympathy for underdogs. The copy defined what it means to try harder (and what a leader in the car rental business should be providing)—clean ashtrays, full gas tanks, wipers that work, washed cars, heaters and defrosters that work—and the lines at the counter are shorter. It also subtly suggested the problems you might find with #1—Hertz. Created by the legendary Doyle Dane Bernbach agency in 1962 when Avis's market share was only 11 percent, the campaign drove a turnaround for the company. Four years later, Avis's market share was 35 percent and the campaign got credit for a 300 percent increase in business.

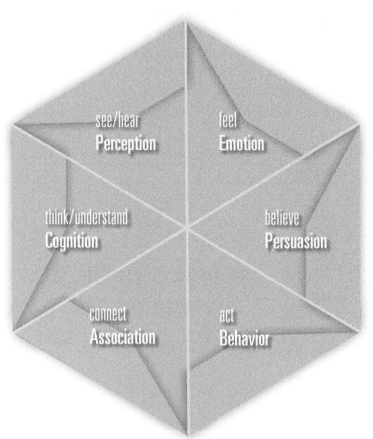

FIGURE 19.1
The Facets of Effects Model

fell after the campaign instead of increasing, it must be deemed ineffective. But sales are not the only reason brands advertise: one of the major objectives of advertising is to create higher levels of brand awareness. Perhaps the Six Flags awareness level increased, but the reason people didn't come to the parks has to do more with the lack of new attractions or maybe an external factor such as an increase in the price of gas. Does that mean the advertising is ineffective?

It's our view that marketers intend for their messages to accomplish a variety of goals, such as build a brand relationship, recruit volunteers or donations, or entice people to visit a website, which is why the other 60 percent of ads studied by Jones may be effective in their own way. That's why this book uses the Facets Model of Effects to broaden the way we evaluate message effectiveness.

Evaluating Effectiveness

The most important principle in this chapter—possibly in this book—is a well-known maxim: "If you can't measure it, you can't manage it."

Some evaluation is informal and based on the judgment of an experienced manager. There is always a need for the intuitive analysis of experienced professionals. The important thing, however, is to recognize early in the planning stage the need for a formal evaluation mechanism, as Professor Mark Stuhlfaut explains. Evaluation should be "planned in" to any campaign. Evaluation determines the success of a marketing communication, but it also feeds back into the ongoing brand communication plan. Figure 19.2 illustrates that process, and Professor Stuhlfaut's *A Matter of Principle* features builds on the idea of a cycle beginning and ending with research.

In addition to intuition and judgment, measurement that tracks consumer response is also needed and can be built into a campaign plan as structured feedback, such as response cards and calls. Often, however, the evaluation effort involves a more formal research project, which also needs to be part of the campaign planning.

Personal insights into what makes an ad great are important, but why do we also need formal evaluation? The first reason is that the stakes in making an advertising misstep are high. By the time an average 30-second commercial is ready for national television, it has cost about $200,000 in production costs. If it is run nationally, its sponsor can invest several million dollars in airtime. The second reason is advertising optimization, or reducing risk by testing, analyzing, tracking brand performance, and making changes where possible to increase the effectiveness of the advertising. The third reason is to learn what works and what doesn't—in other words, to identify best practices so a brand's advertising continues to improve.

Types and Stages of Evaluation

Evaluation is done through testing, monitoring, and measurement. Testing is used to predict results, monitoring tracks performance, and measurement evaluates results. In other words, for major campaigns a sample of the ads is typically tested before they run as a way to predict effectiveness. Ideally, the results of preliminary evaluative research should be available before large sums of money are invested in finished work or in media buys.

As a campaign unfolds, the performance is tracked to see whether any elements need to be changed. Sales may fall, or they may not increase as rapidly as expected. Is the advertising at fault? The results, the actual effects, are measured after the ad or campaign runs. Diagnostic research also is used in all three stages to deconstruct an ad to spot message problems. Four types of research are used in evaluation:

1. **Developmental research** through pretesting estimates the likelihood that an ad idea will work or that one idea is better than another.
2. **Concurrent research** using tracking studies and test marketing monitors the way the campaign is unfolding and how the messages and media are working.
3. **Post-testing research** evaluates impact after the campaign is over or after the ad ran. Postcampaign research encompasses benchmark or baseline studies to gauge movement. These can be research company norms, or they can be based on previous campaigns by this brand.
4. **Diagnostic research** deconstructs an ad to see what elements are working or not working. Researchers who evaluate commercials use frame-by-frame or moment-by-moment analysis to identify strengths and weaknesses in an ad.

Facets: Measuring Responses

Most advertisers would be happy if evaluation could simply tell them how much the advertising contributed to their sales effort. That's difficult for a number of reasons. Factors other than advertising affect sales (e.g., pricing, distribution, product performance, competition), and that makes it hard to isolate advertising to determine its impact. Furthermore, advertising effects tend to be delayed, so it's difficult to link the advertising seen at one time to a purchase made days or weeks later. Exceptions are direct-response advertising and ads carrying promotional offers good for only a limited time.

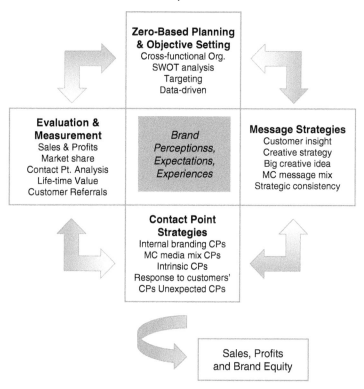

IMC Brand Optimizer Model

FIGURE 19.2

IMC Brand Optimizer Model

This IMC model created by Professor Tom Duncan illustrates that evaluation is a circular process—IMC plans start by gathering information and move through the various steps in the planning process to come back to the last step in the process, which is again gathering information. This time, however, information is gathered to determine what works and what doesn't. That information feeds back into the process and the organization learns from the results.

Usually advertising is measured in terms of its communication effects—the mental responses to a message, which become *surrogate measures* for sales impact. Such factors as awareness of the advertising, purchase intention, preference, and liking all suggest that the advertising message can make a positive contribution to an eventual purchase decision. According to research professionals at Ipsos ASI, one of the largest U.S. providers of advertising pretesting, "Ads work best when they engage viewers' interest, when consumers enjoy watching them, when they are relevant, and when they tell their story in a unique and interesting way."[4] Those are some of the dimensions of effectiveness, but others also are important, as we know from our discussion of how advertising works in Chapter 4.

On the other hand, some ads don't work, and it is just as important to understand why that happens. Some confuse the audience or fail to get attention or connect with consumers. In many cases, people can't remember the brand. In some cases, the ad can even boomerang, an effect mentioned in a feature on antidrug ads in Chapter 4. The same problem was noted with anti-smoking ads when the American Legacy Foundation announced that a study of smoking prevention ads by the tobacco industry actually increased the likelihood that teens would try smoking.[5]

Good evaluation objectives are based on a model of human response to an advertisement that identifies key effects. We developed the Facets Model of Effects in Chapter 4 as a guide for both setting objectives and evaluating effectiveness. Table 19.1 groups the key factors of effectiveness and then matches them to the types of research questions advertisers can use to determine effectiveness.

Principle

Good evaluation plans, as well as effective professional work, are guided by a model of how people respond to advertising.

A MATTER OF PRINCIPLE

Completing the Cycle

Mark Stuhlfaut, *Assistant Professor, University of Kentucky*

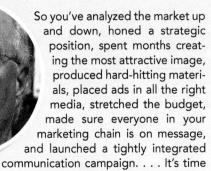

So you've analyzed the market up and down, honed a strategic position, spent months creating the most attractive image, produced hard-hitting materials, placed ads in all the right media, stretched the budget, made sure everyone in your marketing chain is on message, and launched a tightly integrated communication campaign. . . . It's time to sit back and enjoy the afterglow . . . right?

Not quite. You're job isn't finished until you've properly evaluated the results. Why? There are three very good reasons: (1) you need to find out what worked in the campaign, what didn't, and what could have worked better to solve any problems now; (2) a comprehensive evaluation provides valuable information that will serve as input for the next planning cycle; and (3) managers of marketing communication need to responsibly demonstrate the effectiveness of their efforts to clients and corporate management—you owe it to them to prove that their investment of resources in your programs and their trust in you were worth it.

Where do you start? A good beginning is to go back to the campaign's goals to see if they were met, which brings back the importance of having clear, measurable, and attainable objective statements.

What standards should you employ to know if you've succeeded? Sales data? They're one indicator, but too many intervening factors make tying marketing communication to sales figures difficult and not very meaningful. Therefore, other measures, such as the levels of awareness, comprehension, importance, and brand preference, are more useful for communication managers to determine whether the campaign was effective.

A thorough review takes more than a few quick surveys. Sure, you'll want to conduct quantitative and qualitative research to get feedback from consumers or customers. But you should also contact all the key stakeholders in the market—such as company sales personnel, distributors, dealers, editors, broadcasters, consultants, and other friendly third parties (FTPs)—to see if their communication needs were satisfied by the campaign. Include these important people in your evaluation, and you'll not only gain helpful information, you'll build strong relationships for the future.

The best evaluation techniques aren't something you add on to a campaign; they're something you build in to every phase of the process. Assess alternative positions early in the campaign's development. Compare different concepts in the rough layout stage. The earlier you test, the cheaper it is, and the better chance you have to get it right.

It's easy to say you don't have the time or the money to evaluate the campaign's elements. But consider the cost of not getting it right. The effort made to evaluate the effectiveness of the campaign before and after launch will pay off in the long run.

The SkiStar SkiPass dynamic pricing launch is an example of how a model of effects can be developed for a specific campaign and used to drive not only the planning of the effort, but also the evaluation of its effectiveness. One of the goals to a successful ski season and to assist cash flow is to lock in revenue as early as possible. This can happen in multiple ways. For SkiStar's ski resorts, linking up with the RCI holiday exchange network, consolidating the databases, and streamlining the contact choices for customers all contribute to a more efficient system. SkiStar's market share of season ticket sales provide a surge of revenue going into the season, particularly if they are advanced sales (encouraged by dynamic pricing). Destination skiers provide incremental revenue throughout the season by booking vacations and purchasing the lion's share of daily lift tickets, lodging and dining sales, ski school lessons, and rentals.

WHAT IS MESSAGE EVALUATION?

Copytesting is a general term that describes various kinds of research used at different stages in the advertising development process—before, during, and after an ad or campaign has run. Before we talk about specific types of studies, consider first the various copytesting services and the factors they feel are important to evaluate.

Table 19.1   Effectiveness Research Questions

Effect	*Research Questions*
Perception	
Awareness/noticed	Which ads do you remember seeing?
	Which ads were noted?
Attention	What caught your attention?
	Did the ad stand out among the other ads and content around it?
	What stood out in the ad?
Recognition (aided)	Have you seen this ad/this campaign?
	Sort elements into piles of remember/don't remember.
Relevance	How important is the product message to you? Does it speak to your interests and aspirations?
Emotional/affective	What emotions did the ad stimulate?
	How did it make you feel?
Liking/disliking	Do you like this brand? This story? The characters (and other ad elements)?
	What did you like or dislike about the brand? The ad?
Desire	Do you want this product or brand?
Cognition	
Interest	Did you read/watch most of it? How much?
	Did it engage your interest or curiosity?
	Where did your interest shift away from the ad?
Comprehension/ confusion	What thoughts came to you? Do you understand how it works? Is there anything in the ad you don't understand? Do the claims/product attributes/benefits make sense?
	Do you have a need for this brand or can it fulfill a need for you?
Recall (unaided)	What happened in the commercial? What is the main message? What is the point of the ad?
Brand recall/linkage	What brand is being advertised in this ad?
	[In open-ended responses, was the brand named?]
Differentiation	What's the difference between Brand X and Y?
Association	When you think of this brand, what (products, qualities, attributes, people, lifestyles, etc.) do you connect with it?
	Do you link this brand to positive experiences?
Personality/image	What is the personality of the brand? Of whom does it remind you? Do you like this person/brand personality?
	What is the brand image? What does it symbolize or stand for?
Self-identification	Can you see yourself or your friends using this brand?
	Do you connect personally with the brand image?
Persuasion	
Intention	Do you want to try or buy this product/brand?
	Would you put it on your shopping list?
Argument/ counterargument	What are your reasons for buying it? Or for not buying it—or its competing brand(s)? How does it compare to competitors' brand(s)?
	Did you argue back to the ad?
Believability/ conviction	Do you believe the reasons, claims, or proof statements?
	Are you convinced the message is true? The brand is best?
Trust	Do you have confidence in the brand?
Behavior	How many people buy, try, call, send, click, visit, attend, inquire, volunteer, donate, advocate, or whatever the desired action?
	What is the rate of change?

Copytesting

Copytesting companies have different specialties that focus on different effectiveness dimensions. The most successful of these companies have conducted enough tests that they have developed **norms** for common product categories. In other words, after they pretest an ad, they can compare its score with scores from comparable ads. Norms allow the advertiser to tell whether a particular advertisement is above or below the average for the brand or its product category. Without norms the advertiser would not know whether a score of 23, for example, is good or bad.

Most of these companies have also developed diagnostic methods that identify strong and weak points of the ad. Here is a list of some of the more prominent companies and the types of tests they provide:

* *Ameritest:* brand linkage, attention, motivation, communication, flow of attention and emotion through the commercial
* *COMSCORE ARSgroup:* persuasion, brand/ad recall, communication
* *Ipsos ASI:* recall, attention, brand linkage, persuasion (brand switch, purchase probability), communication
* *Mapes & Ross:* brand preference change, ad/brand recall, idea communication, key message delivery, like/dislike, believability, comprehension, desire to take action, attribute communication
* *Millward Brown:* branding, enjoyment, involvement, understanding, ad flow, brand integration, feelings about ad, main stand-out idea, likes/dislikes, impressions, persuasion, new news, believability, relevance
* *RoperASW:* overall reaction, strengths and weaknesses, understanding, clutter busting, attention, main message, relevance, appeal, persuasiveness, motivate trial, purchase intent.

Now let's consider how the services of such companies and the research they conduct can be used at various points in the development and evaluation of a marketing communication effort. This outline is based on the Facets Model of Effects that we first introduced in Chapter 4.

Message Development Research

Deciding what facts to convey in marketing communication is never easy. Research is needed to develop and test alternative message strategies. Planners conduct research with members of the target audience to develop the message strategy and test the relative effectiveness of various selling premises—hard sell or soft sell, informational or emotional, and so forth. Insights into consumer motivations and purchasing decisions help solve the often-difficult puzzle of selecting the most relevant information and motivating promise as well as the emotional appeal that best engages the audience.

Concept Testing   Advertising and other marketing communication messages usually incorporate a Big Idea, a creative concept that is attention getting and memorable. Research in **concept testing** compares the effectiveness of various message strategies and their creative ideas. This testing often relies on a *key concept card*, which is an artist's drawing of the visual idea with a sentence underneath that captures the essence of the idea. A researcher may use a pack of three, five, or more idea cards or rough layouts to elicit consumer responses in a mall or through discussions in a focus group.

An example of effective concept testing that was used in a campaign's development is Volvo's GLBT campaign, which was the first campaign of its kind to receive an Advertising Research Foundation (ARF) David Ogilvy award. Witeck-Combs Communications in collaboration with Prime Access, Inc., developed a set of concepts and rough ad executions representing a range of GLBT-specific imagery and copy. Ford and Volvo managers selected their top three choices from the group of proposed ad ideas. The messages were tested to assess the constructs of branding, communication, and persuasion, including the concept of consumer connection, or whether the ad makes consumers feel closer to the brand. These constructs were measured in four ways—cognitive, behavior, emotional, and aspirational dimensions.

Pretesting   Another type of evaluative research, called **pretesting**, helps marketers make final go/no-go decisions about finished or nearly finished ads. Pretesting differs from concept testing or message strategy research, which reveals the strengths and weaknesses of different versions of a concept or approach as marketers develop them. Pretesting assesses the strength of the finished message and predicts how well it will perform.

In terms of print advertisements, the ideas to be tested are often full mockups of the ad. In television, advertisers can test the commercials as storyboard ideas or **photoboards** (still photos arranged as a storyboard), but more often commercials are in the form of **animatics** (drawings or still photos shot on videotape synchronized with a rough version of the audio track). Advertisers can show these versions of the commercial to individuals, to focus groups, or in a theater testing situation. They follow the viewing of the advertisement with a survey, a more open-ended interview, or a set of questions for a group discussion.

Diagnostics   Many advertisers and agencies are moving away from copytesting methods that rely on single scores to evaluate an ad and turning to methods that are more focused on diagnosing strengths and weaknesses. The reason is that they believe an advertisement is too complex to be reduced to one factor and one simple score. Instead they are using research methods designed to diagnose the strengths and weaknesses of their advertising ideas to improve the work while it is still in development or to learn more from the ad to improve subsequent advertisements.

In theater tests for TV commercials, for example, respondents may have a black-box device and can press a button to record different types of responses—indicating what they liked or didn't like or how long they paid attention by letting up on the button when their attention shifts.

Moment-by-moment tests of commercials provide an analysis of the impact of the internal logic of the commercial. The Ameritest company, whose work is described in the *A Matter of Practice*, looks at two dimensions of moment-by-moment tests: a *Flow of Attention* measure and a *Flow of Emotion* measure. The procedure involves showing a **clutter reel,** a group of commercials that includes the test commercial, competitors' commercials, and other ads, and conducting interviews afterward. The Ameritest method uses a **picture sort** to diagnose the viewer's attention to and emotional engagement with different elements in the commercial. The viewers receive a deck of key frames from the commercial and sort them into images they remember seeing and ones they don't remember. Then they sort them into five categories from strong positive to strong negative. The researchers tabulate the sets to depict the flow of impact for both attention and emotion. In particular, they want to identify and analyze key moments in the commercial such as the solution to a problem or the introduction of the brand and analyze them in terms of viewers' attention and emotion.[6] The *A Matter of Practice* box takes you through this analysis.

During Execution: Concurrent Testing

Concurrent testing takes place while the advertising is running. There are three primary techniques: coincidental surveys, attitude tests, and tracking studies. The first two assess communication responses; tracking studies evaluate actual behavior.

The **coincidental survey** technique is most often used with broadcast media. Random calls are made to individuals in the target market. By discovering what stations or shows people are tuned to, the researcher can determine whether the target audience has seen/heard the ad and, if so, what information or meaning the audience members now have of the brand. This technique can be useful in identifying basic problems. For example, several years ago Pepsi discovered that the use of Madonna as a spokesperson was a terrible mistake.

In Chapter 4 we discussed the relationship between an attitude—a favorable or unfavorable disposition toward a person, brand, idea, or situation—and consumer behavior. This relationship is the basis of *attitude tests*. Researchers survey individuals who were exposed to the ad, asking questions about the spokesperson, the tone of the ad, its wording, and so forth. Results that show strong negative attitude scores may prompt the advertiser to pull an ad immediately. A favorable attitude indicates that people are more likely to purchase a brand than if they have an unfavorable attitude.

Tracking Studies   Studies that periodically (generally every three or six months) measure top-of-mind brand awareness (first brand mentioned) are called **tracking studies.** These studies can

Principle
Advertising effects are too complicated to be reduced to a single score.

Finding Moments of Truth

Charles E. Young, *President, Ameritest*

The most powerful search engine of all is the human eye, which scans advertising film, television commercials, and Web videos, continuously deciding on an unconscious level whether the visual information streaming toward it is important enough to let into consciousness. Because our conscious minds have limited bandwidth or workspace, much of the imagery that advertisers are trying to communicate to consumers is ignored or deleted by our preconscious eye-brain filters as so much visual spam.

Ameritest's Picture Sorts® is a set of nonverbal research tools that have been developed for the Internet to survey the right-brained scanning and sorting processes involved in visual communication. These tools make use of the power of still photographs to capture an instant of time and store our fleeting emotions.

By sorting a randomized deck of pictures taken from the ad itself—which is like the visual vocabulary of the film—the ad researcher can reconstruct consumers' moment-by-moment attention and emotional response to an ad they just saw. Three different sorting exercises enable the advertiser to perform the equivalent of putting on 3-D glasses to see advertising through the eyes of its target audience.

The Flow of Attention® graph, the first of three measurement dimensions, is like a visual spell-checker that the researcher can use to analyze whether or not a piece of advertising film or Web video has been put together well according to principles of proper film syntax or good visual grammar. The Flow of Attention graph reveals the hidden structure of audience attention to moving pictures, which, like music, follows a rhythmic beat of cognitive processing. The beat, or focal points of attention, is where the most important information in an ad, like the brand identity, is conveyed.

From the emotional hook at the beginning, to the turning points in a story, to the surprise ending of a funny commercial, engaging the emotions of consumers is essential to motivating them. The Flow of Emotion® graph measures not only the volume of emotions pumping through ad film but also reveals which of four archetypal dramatic structures is being used in the creative design. Knowing this structure tells the advertiser when the timing is exactly right to first introduce the brand in the ad, which might be at the beginning, or somewhere in the middle, or not until the end of a commercial.

The Flow of Meaning® tool shows the researcher where key communication points or brand values are being cued visually. Meaning is created when thought and emotion come together, in a few memorable and emotionally charged moments in a commercial when memories are being created. Because there are three distinct memory systems in the mind, branding moments come in three flavors: (1) images that convey concepts or rational ideas go into our knowledge, or semantic, memory system; (2) images that evoke emotions go into our emotion, or episodic, memory system; and (3) images that rehearse or mirror the behavior the advertiser is trying to influence go into our action, or procedural, memory system (where memories of how you ride a bike or play a violin are stored). Taken together, this learn–feel–do imaging process is how the long-term work of advertising is performed, building a brand's image.

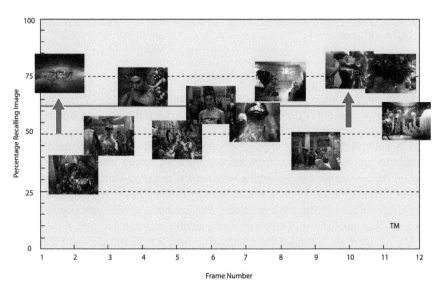

This diagram demonstrates the flow of attention across a commercial for Unilever's Thermasilk. The selected still frames represent those places in the commercial where the attention is high (above the red line) or low (below the red line). Note the highest attention points, which are indicated with the red arrows. In this commercial, that tight shot of the face is the "moment of truth," the most highly attended to frame in this execution.

also measure unaided and aided awareness of an ad and trial and repeat purchases. They sometimes ask the same questions of competing brands.

Tracking studies show how a marketer's brand is performing over time, especially after changes are made in the marketing communication. Because several different measures are taken, findings can indicate if there is an attention-getting problem, a recall problem (saw message but can't remember what it said), a trial problem (remembered the advertising but not moved to try the brand), or a repeat problem (tried the brand but have not repurchased for some reason).

Brand tracking is an approach that tracks the performance of the brand rather than or in addition to the advertising. The assumption is that with fragmented media and an abundance of high-quality but similar products, it is more important to track the brand because it reflects the quality of the customer's brand relationship. That's at the heart of the SkiStar SkiPass campaign. Instead of focusing on attributes and claims about a product, this research identifies how customers are involved with the brand and whether they are more favorably disposed toward it than toward other brands. As Peppers and Rogers point out, you also need a centralized customer database that allows you to track customer activity across channels.[7]

This analysis as depicted in Figure 19.3 is also based on the factors identified in the Facets Model of Effects.

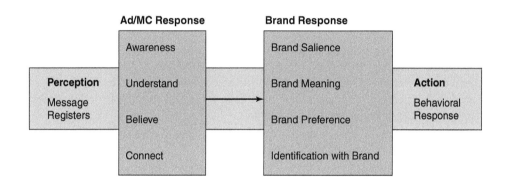

FIGURE 19.3
Tracking Brand Response

Brand tracking studies generally use sets of brand-related questions, but Bain & Company, a highly respected consulting firm, is promoting the use of a single-question test to track attitudes to a brand. Called *net promoter*, it tracks the response to a simple question: "How likely is it that you would recommend us to a friend or colleague?"[8] Another single measure is **brand penetration,** which is the number of customers who purchase the brand relative to the total population in the market.[9]

Although these single measures are useful as a broad indication of brand effectiveness, the other questions found in brand tracking studies, such as those about awareness and credibility, for example, are particularly important in an IMC program because they provide diagnostic information about areas of marketing communication that might need to be changed or refined.

Because spending information enters the analysis, much of the focus of tracking studies is on the target market, the selection of media vehicles, the schedule, the marketing communication mix, and the media mix. Account planners use several methods to collect tracking data, such as the attitude tests discussed earlier and wave analysis, consumer diaries, and pantry checks:

- *Wave Analysis* Wave analysis looks at a series of interviews during a campaign. The tracking begins with a set of questions asked of a random sample of consumers on a predetermined date. After the person is qualified as hearing or seeing the ad, the researcher asks a series of follow-up questions. The answers serve as a benchmark and allow adjustments in the message content, media choice, and timing. Perhaps two months later, the researcher makes another series of random calls and asks the same questions. The second wave is compared with the first until management is satisfied with the ad's market penetration and impact.
- *Consumer Diaries* Sometimes advertisers ask a group of representative consumers to keep a diary during a campaign. The consumers record activities such as brands purchased, brands used for various activities, brand switches, media usage, exposure to competitive promotions,

and use of coupons. The advertiser can then review these **consumer diaries** and determine factors such as whether the message is reaching the right target audience and whether the audience is responding to the message as intended. One common unfavorable finding from consumer diaries is that no attitude or behavioral change occurred because of exposure to the campaign.

- *Pantry Checks* The **pantry check** provides much of the same information as the diary method but requires little from the consumer. A researcher goes to homes in the target market and asks what brands or products they have purchased or used recently. In one variation of this procedure, the researcher counts the products or brands currently stocked by the consumer. The consumer may also be asked to keep empty packages, which the researcher then collects and tallies.

Test Markets   A **test market** might serve to evaluate product variations, as well as elements of a campaign or a media mix. These are generally conducted in two or more markets with the same number of similar markets chosen to act as controls. In the control markets the researcher can either (1) run no advertising or (2) continue to run the old ad. The new advertising (or product variation) is used in the test cities. Before, during, and after running the advertising, marketers compare sales results in the test cities. Some cities, such as Buffalo, Indianapolis, and San Antonio, are considered excellent test markets because their demographic and socioeconomic profiles are representative of either the United States or a particular target market. Furthermore, they are relatively isolated as media markets so the advertising impact is less likely to be affected by what is happening in other markets.

The possibilities for isolating variables in test markets are almost limitless. Researchers can increase the frequency of advertising or try a different media schedule, for example. They can see whether an ad emphasizing brand convenience will stimulate sales to two-career families. They can try an ad that plays up the brand's fiber or vitamin content or compare the effectiveness of a two-for-one promotion versus a cents-off coupon.

Post-Testing: After-Execution Research

Another evaluation method is post-testing, which occurs after the marketing communication has been used to determine if it met its objectives. The most common evaluative research techniques account planners and advertising researchers use include memory tests, persuasion tests, direct-response counts, frame-by-frame tests, in-market tests such as test markets, and brand tracking.

Some of these more traditional post-testing methodologies were discussed in Chapter 6, however, there is another type called **heuristics** that is relevant for certain types of post-testing evaluation. Harley Manning, vice president for customer experience at Forrester Research, describes heuristics as a type of expert review that Forrester uses to evaluate the performance of websites in terms of brand attributes (information provided) and user descriptions and goals as measured against "a valid set of rules (heuristics) that identify known types of user experience flaws." Manning explains that Forrester uses that type of expert-review research to gauge how well the sites served consumers (keep the brand promise).

The idea is that advertising—and other types of marketing communication messages—vary in the way they affect people, so the measurements also must be different.

Breakthrough: Attention   Most advertising is evaluated in terms of its ability to get and keep attention. This is a simple concept but difficult to measure. Similar to pretesting, some researchers use instantaneous tracking in a theater setting where viewers with a keypad indicate what they watch and don't watch—or rather what interests them and doesn't interest them. The Ameritest methodology asks respondents who have just watched a collection of ads to indicate which ones interested them.[10] Another firm's method asks viewers to rate how enjoyable the ad is, which confounds the attention score with a liking response. Other methodologies use noted scores for print ads or ask viewers to recognize the concept of a commercial and attach it to a brand.

Engagement Tests   Interest in a commercial is determined by concentration and excitement. **Eye-tracking** research is a mechanical technique that traces **saccadic eye movement**, the path the eye takes in scanning an ad. Because scanning involves a lot of stops and starts and revisits, this complex map of how a visual is scanned identifies what first caught the viewer's attention—the visual point of entry—and where it moved to next. It also records those elements the eye kept revisiting either to focus on because they were appealing visuals or because they needed more study. It also shows what elements didn't get noticed at all. The e-Motion system from the New Jersey–based firm PreTesting Group identifies eye fixations but also the amount of vibrations in the retina. The vibration is very minute, but it does indicate a level of excitement—the more the retina vibrates, the more interested the viewer.[11]

Understanding and Comprehension Tests   These tests are used as part of the diagnostic effort, but it is particularly important in post-testing to determine if consumers understood the message. Another comprehension problem can emerge from creative strategies that are engaging, but ask consumers to puzzle out the meaning. Ambiguity is sometimes used particularly because it is engaging, but it can also be a risky strategy, one that benefits from testing. An example is a billboard for a British beer brand John West, which is given a dramatic touch by making the rings on top of the can look like rings of rippling water cast from a fishing bobber.

A beautifully done image for John West, a British beer, uses a simple photograph of the top of a can. It takes on new meaning when the can's rings are associated with the rings in water from a fishing bobber. The question is do people get the association and understand the larger meaning of "Relax with a Can of John West."

Memory Tests   Memory tests are based on the assumption that an advertisement leaves a mental residue with the person who has been exposed to it; in other words, the audience has learned something. One way to measure an advertisement's effectiveness, then, is to contact consumers who saw the ad and find out what they remember. Memory tests fall into two major groups: recognition tests and recall tests.

One way to measure memory is to show the advertisement to people and ask them whether they remember having seen it before. This kind of test is called a **recognition test**. In a **recall test**, respondents who have read the magazine are asked to report what they remember from the ad about the brand. In aided recall tests, the interviewer may go through a deck of cards containing brand names. If the respondent says, "Yes, I remember seeing an advertisement for that brand," the interviewer asks the interviewees to describe everything they can remember about the ad. Obviously recall is a more rigorous test than a recognition test.

Similarly, a TV commercial is run on network television within a regular prime-time program. The next evening, interviewers make thousands of random phone calls until they have contacted about 200 people who were watching the program at the exact time the commercial appeared. The interviewer then asks a series of questions, such as the following:

- Do you remember seeing a commercial for any charcoal briquettes?
- *If No* Do you remember seeing a commercial for Kingsford Charcoal briquettes? (memory prompt)
- *If Yes to Either of the Above* What did the commercial say about the product? What did the commercial show? What did the commercial look like? What ideas were brought out?

The first type of question is called an **unaided recall** question because the particular brand is not mentioned. The second question is an example of **aided recall**, in which the specific brand name is mentioned. The answers to the third set of questions are written down verbatim. The test requires that the respondent link a specific brand name, or at least a specific product category, to a specific commercial.

Brand Linkage Tests   Testing for brand linkage is basically a test of memorability, however, the important aspect of this measure is not whether the message is remembered, but whether it

Pacific Life uses an image of a leaping whale to reflect its image of a confident insurance company that excels in its market.

associates the brand with the memory. If the commercial fails to establish a tight connection between the brand name and the selling message, the commercial will not get a high recall score. This is also called a test of "brand linkage." The long-running Pacific Life campaign with its image of a leaping humpback whale is a good example of a visual that serves as a strong brand reminder and associates the brand with strength and performance.

Emotion Tests Advertising is just beginning to move into this area of research. There are several ways to get at the emotional response. Ameritest uses photo sorts with still frames from commercials to identify the positive and negative moments that touch people's emotions.[12] Other researchers are wiring up viewers of television ads to monitor brain activity using a functional magnetic resonance imaging (fMRI) machine. The fMRI images identified ads from the 2007 Super Bowl that produced anxiety, fear, anger, and insecurity, as well as positive feelings.[13]

Likability Tests A study by the Advertising Research Foundation (ARF) compared a variety of different copytesting methods to see if any of them were better able to predict sales impact. Surprisingly, it wasn't awareness, recall, communication, or persuasion measures that won out but rather **likability tests.** Likability, however, is not easy to measure because it's difficult to know if the consumer likes the ad, the brand, or some other factor, such as the person giving the test. A number of the copytesting companies offer a likability score, but they suggest it needs to be interpreted relative to other consumer responses. Questions that try to evaluate likability investigate factors such as these: personally relevant, important to me, stimulates interest or curiosity, creates warm feelings, enjoyable, entertaining, and fun.

Persuasion Tests Another evaluative research technique is a **persuasion test,** or attitude change test. The basic format is to ask consumers how likely they are to buy a specific brand. Next they are exposed to an advertisement for that brand, usually as part of a collection of brands. After exposure, researchers again ask them what they intend to purchase. The researcher analyzes the results to determine whether *intention to buy* has increased as a result of exposure to the advertisement. This test is sometimes referred to as an **intend-to-buy** or **motivation test.** The validity of a persuasion test depends in part on whether participants in the experiment represent a good sample of the prospects the advertiser is trying to reach. A dog food advertiser, for example, would not be interested in responses from people who do not own dogs.

Inquiry Tests A form of action response, **inquiry tests** measure the number of responses to an advertisement. The response can be a call to a toll-free number, an e-mail or website visit, a coupon return, a visit to a dealer, an entry in a contest, or a call to a salesperson. Inquiry tests are the primary measurement tool for direct-response communication, but they also are used to evaluate advertisements and sales promotions when the inquiry is built into the message design. Inquiry tests also are used to evaluate the effectiveness of alternative advertisements using a split-run technique in magazines, where there are two versions of the magazine printed, one with ad A and the other with ad B. The ad (or direct-mail piece) that pulls the most responses is deemed to be the most effective.

Scanner Research

Many retail outlets, especially drug, discount, and food stores, use electronic scanners to tally up purchases and collect consumer buying information. When you shop at your local Safeway, for example, each product you buy has an electronic bar code that conveys the brand name, the product code, and its price. If you are a member of Safeway's frequent buyer program and have a membership card that entitles you to special promotional offers, the store can track your purchases.

Scanner research is also used to see what type of sales spikes are created when certain ads and promotions are used in a given market. Both the chain and the manufacturers of the brands are interested in this data. The regional Safeway system may decide to establish a consumer panel so it can track sales among various consumer groups. In **scanner research,** you would be asked to join a panel, which might contain hundreds of other customers. You would complete a fairly extensive questionnaire and be assigned an ID number. You might receive a premium or a discount on purchases for your participation. Each time you make a purchase, you also submit your ID number. Therefore, if Safeway runs a two-page newspaper ad, it can track actual sales to determine to what extent the ad worked. Various manufacturers who sell products to Safeway can do the same kind of testing. The panel questionnaire also contains a list of media that each member reported using, so media performance can also be evaluated.

Scanner research reads the information from a shopper's identification card and records that along with product information. Many retail outlets use electronic scanners to track sales among various consumer groups.

Using scanner data and the cooperation of local cable networks, researchers are closer to showing a causal relationship between advertising/promotion and sales because of **single-source research.** Single-source research companies, such as A. C. Nielsen, arrange to have test commercials (and sometimes test newspaper ads) delivered to a select group of households (HHs) within a market, comparing it to a control group of HHs. The purchasing behavior of each group of HHs is collected by scanners in local stores. Because advertising is the only manipulated variable, the method permits a fairly clear reading of cause and effect. Data collected in this way are known as *single-source data* because advertising and brand purchasing data come from the same HH source.

Syracuse University Professor John Philip Jones, who spent many years at J. Walter Thompson (JWT), has used single-source data from JWT combined with Nielsen TV viewing data to prove that advertising can cause an immediate impact on sales. His research has found that the strongest campaigns can triple sales, while the weakest campaigns can actually cause sales to fall by more than 50 percent.[14]

Although fairly expensive, single-source research can produce dependable results. Advertisements are received under natural conditions in the home, and the resulting purchases are actual purchases made by consumers. One drawback, besides cost, is the three to six months required to set up and run this test. Critics also say that single-source research is better for short-term immediate sales effects and doesn't capture very well other brand-building effects.

MEDIA EVALUATION

Advertising has little chance to be effective if no one sees it. Analyzing the effectiveness of the media plan is another important part of evaluation. Did the plan actually achieve reach and frequency objectives? Did the newspaper and magazine placements run in the positions expected and produce the intended GRP and CPM levels? In other words, did the advertisers get what they paid for?

A classic case of the power of media, particularly the repetition of commercials, is the "Please Don't Squeeze the Charmin" campaign that began in 1964. Because it dominated the airwaves for 20 years, it was hugely visible and built incredible brand awareness—awareness that led Charmin to dominate its category. It and its brand character, the comical grocer Mr. Whipple, was not only one of the best remembered campaigns, but also one of the most parodied campaigns ever made because the Whipple character was so goofy. Yet, it made Charmin one of the most successful brands in the history of Procter & Gamble. So what do you think: Does it make sense to use an irritating campaign with a lot of repetition in order to build brand awareness and memory? Could this strategy work in our time? What would an IMC planner say about this strategy?

Evaluating Audience Exposure

For major campaigns, agencies do post-buy analyses, which involve checking the media plan against the performance of each media vehicle. The critical question is whether the reach and frequency objectives were obtained.

Verifying the audience measurement estimates is a challenge. Media planners are working sometimes with millions of dollars, and they can't afford to get it wrong. We discussed how various media channels measure their audiences. For print, services such as the Audit Bureau of Circulations (ABC), Experian Simmons (formerly known as SMRB), and Mediamark (MRI+) provide data. Likewise for broadcast, Arbitron, RADAR, and A. C. Nielsen provide audience monitoring. Initially media planners use these estimates to develop a media plan, and media buyers use them later to verify the accumulated impact of the media buy after the campaign has run.

Media planning oversight is usually handled in-house by the media buyer, but it can also be contracted by the advertiser to independent companies who specialize in conducting media audits of the agency's media planning and buying operations. Nissan and Procter & Gamble are examples of companies that have hired outside media-auditing firms to confirm the execution of their media plans.

As the job gets more complex, media planners are being asked to prove the wisdom of their recommendations in an area where the data they use are sometimes suspect or unreliable, particularly if there are problems with the media measurement companies' formulas and reporting systems. Nielsen, for example, has been subject to much criticism for its television ratings.

Another issue is the impact of video recorders and DVRs. What do viewers see and remember as they skip or fast forward through commercials? Tests have shown that viewers do remember some of the spots, or at least the brands. The easiest to recall were ones that had been seen before. Other characteristics of successful ads have the brand's logo in the middle of the screen and leave it on the screen for more seconds than in a normal TV commercial. It also helps if the action isn't too fast with many screen changes. Simple commercials are easier to see and remember when zipping.[15]

To better understand the problems in media evaluation, let's look at two areas where media performance is hard to estimate: out-of-home media and new media, including the Internet.

Out-of-Home Media   As you would expect, accurately measuring the mobile audience for outdoor advertising is challenging. Traffic counts can be gathered, but the problem is that traffic does not equal exposure. Just because a car drives by a board doesn't mean that the driver and/or passengers see it, particularly since some outdoor boards are more attention getting than others, as the "road rage" board illustrates.

New Media   Similarly, the measures of effectiveness used to evaluate offline campaigns don't seem to transfer well to the online world. Is the website visitor or banner ad viewer similar to a member of the print or broadcast audience? The online industry hasn't been able to establish online equivalencies for GRPs and CPMs and is still trying to define what makes an effective Internet ad and to develop a system that accurately measures online effectiveness. At the heart of the problem is the question of what exactly is to be measured and how that equates to other media: readers, viewers, visitors, hits, click-throughs, or minutes spent with a site? Web-analytic firms are developing more sophisticated tracking programs to measure user activity in terms of Web pages visited, time spent, and click-throughs.

Alternative media, such as word of mouth, social media, and guerilla marketing campaigns, are even harder to measure and media planners search for reliable indicators of exposure numbers and buzz from these new sources that equate to the performance of traditional mea-

DO YOU GO INTO REVERSE EVERY TIME YOU DRIVE?

Don't drive like a dipstick.

This outdoor board from the United Kingdom attracted attention because of its interesting visual but also because of its challenging idea. Research based on traffic counts find it difficult to account for the emotional impact of messages like these.

sured media. Research company Millward Brown has designed a metric for online word of mouth (WoM) to track and analyze sentiments expressed on social networks, blogs, and chat rooms.[16] Procter & Gamble has created TREMOR, which develops buzz campaigns, but is also used to design analysis techniques to track measurable business results for WoM campaigns.

An example of using new media analytical tools to assess performance comes from the Taco Bell "Drive-Thru Diet" campaign, which promoted the fast-food chain's "Fresco" menu. Although the campaign wasn't presented as a weight-loss program, it generated a significant amount of buzz questioning the strategy. According to Zeta Buzz, a firm that tracks postings on blogs, message boards, and social media, Taco Bell's buzz rating dropped six points—the volume of postings increased but the tone was much more negative, which indicated the strategy was backfiring.[17]

Another interesting experiment was conducted by Boston University college students and the Mullen ad agency using Twitter to get near-instantaneous feedback on how viewers were reacting to Super Bowl ads. The project was designed "to use a new medium to comment on an old medium," according to Mullen's chief creative officer.[18]

ROI and Media Efficiency

Advertisers continue to improve how they measure *advertising ROI* (return on investment, which means the costs of creating and running the advertisement versus the revenue it generates). Another way to look at it is the cost-to-sales ratio.

Since the dollar impact for advertising—and public relations, especially—is difficult to measure, ROI is hard to calculate. The campaigns must be carefully designed not only to increase sales, but also to ensure that advertisers can isolate the impact of the message and verify that the advertising caused the increase in sales. ROI is easier to calculate for direct marketing (because there are fewer variables between the message and the sales) and for sales promotion (because there is an immediate response, which is easier to link to the message).

One question related to ROI is this: How much spending is too much? That is, how do you determine whether you are overadvertising or underadvertising? That's one of the key reasons to use test marketing. If a campaign is launched in several different, but matched, cities at different levels of media activity, a comparison of the campaign results (sales or other kinds of trackable responses) can determine the appropriate level and type of media spending.

Wearout   The point where the advertising, because it has been seen multiple times, no longer stimulates much of a response is called **wearout**. This is also the point where recall stabilizes or declines and irritation levels increase because people are tired of hearing or seeing the same ad.

Wearout is a combination of creative impact and media buying. The more intrusive or the less interesting the creative technique, the higher the level of irritation. It's like a joke: you may pay attention the first couple of times you hear it, but then it gets "old." Other types of advertising are less prone to wearout. Good jingles, for example, can be repeated almost endlessly. The more people like to hum along, the less likely there will be a wearout problem.

The issue is how long and how much is needed to create the necessary impact. John Philip Jones, who has done extensive research into effectiveness issues, argues that research supports higher continuity. He recommends spreading the budget out and adding weeks to the media schedule as much as possible.[19] Another way to evaluate such decisions is through media optimization models.

Media Optimization   One of the biggest challenges in media planning is media efficiency—getting the most for the money invested. You may remember from Chapter 14 that media planners operate with computer models of **media optimization**—or the optimum media performance—that are used in making decisions about media selection, scheduling, and weights (amount of budget). Models are always theoretical, so one result of postevaluation is that the actual performance of a plan can be compared with the results projected by the media planner's model. The goal of media optimization is to optimize the budget—to get the most impact possible with the least expenditure of money. That is the critical finding derived from the comparison of performance with projections. In addition to meeting the reach and frequency objectives, was the media plan efficient?

A new dimension to the efficiency question comes from a program by media company Starcom to measure the effectiveness of various media used by client Applebee's. The objective was to develop a model that compares the value of video ads, both on-air and online, across a number of NBC properties. The model will establish the relative value of the ads and also interaction across channels.[20]

EVALUATING IMC TOOLS, CAMPAIGNS, AND PROGRAMS

Evaluation is the final and, in some respects, most important step in an advertising campaign because it determines whether the campaign effort was effective. A campaign evaluation will assess the campaign's performance in terms of its message and media objectives. It employs either internal performance data or results from an outside research organization that monitors brand performance, such as Gallup-Robinson, Decision Analyst Inc., and Millward Brown. The important thing to remember in planning an evaluation program is that evaluation has to be built into the marketing communication plan from the very beginning.

An IMC campaign employs various marcom tools, such as sales promotion, public relations, direct marketing, events and sponsorships, personal sales, packaging, point of purchase (PoP), and specialties. You'll find that most of these areas have their own metrics by which performance is measured.

Even though an IMC campaign is evaluated in terms of its overall impact on a brand, the pieces of the mix may also be evaluated to determine the effectiveness of their performance. Advertising may be the most visible; however, other marketing communication tools, such as sales promotion, are better at getting people to respond with an immediate purchase, and public relations is particularly strong at building credibility. Let's look briefly at these other marketing communication areas in terms of their evaluation.

Marcom Tools

Principle
Advertising is particularly effective in accomplishing such objectives as creating exposure, awareness, and brand image and delivering brand reminders.

As Table 19.2 illustrates, marketers can use the Facets Model of Effects to identify the objectives commonly associated with the various marketing communication areas as well as the types of measures used to evaluate performance. The idea is that certain marketing communication functions, such as public relations and sales promotion, do some things better than other areas. Therefore, in an integrated plan, we would use the best tool to accomplish the desired effect. In Table 19.2, the main effects are located in the first column, with a collection of surrogate measures identified in the second column (this list is not inclusive, it's just a sample). The last column lists the communication tool or tools that may be most appropriate for achieving the objective.

Advertising   How do you describe effective advertising? You've been watching it for most of your life. One brand manager's answer to that question is presented in the *Practical Tips* at *www.pearsonglobaleditions.com/ moriarty*. An examination of Table 19.2 shows that advertising is particularly effective in accomplishing a number of objectives, such as creating exposure, awareness, and a brand's image. It is also good at providing brand reminders to the customer and encouraging repurchases. The preceding discussions about copytesting, message development research, concurrent testing, post-testing, and the evaluation of media cover the most common advertising methodologies. Many of these research methods are used by other marcom areas, but they all are derived initially from advertising.

Evaluation doesn't just happen at the end of a campaign or after the ad is run. It has to be planned into the campaign from the very beginning as this planning meeting illustrates.

Direct Response   The objective of direct-response communication is to drive a transaction or generate

Table 19.2   Message Effectiveness Factors

Key Message Effects	Surrogate Measures	Communication Tools
Perception	Exposure	Adv media; PR, PoP
	Attention	Adv; sales promo (SP), packaging; PoP
	Interest	Adv; SP; PR, direct; PoP
	Relevance	Adv; PR; direct; PoP
	Recognition	Adv; PR, packaging; PoP, specialties
Emotional/Affective	Emotions and liking	Adv; SP, Packaging; PoP
	Appeals	Adv; PR; sales; events/spnsrshps
	Resonate	Adv; PR; events/spnsrshps
Cognition	Understanding	Adv; PR; sales; direct
	Recall	Adv; SP; PR, PoP, specialties
		Adv; PR; packaging
Association	Brand image	Adv; PR; events/spnsrshps
Persuasion	Attitudes	Adv; PR; direct
	Preference/intention	Adv; PR; sales; SP
	Credibility	PR
	Conviction	PR; sales; direct
	Motivation	Adv; PR; sales; SP
Behavior	Trial	SP; sales; direct, PoP
	Purchase	SP; sales; direct
	Repeat purchase	Adv; SP; sales; direct, specialties

some other type of immediate behavioral response, such as a donation or visit to a dealer. What makes this marketing communication tool so attractive to marketers is that response is so easily measurable. Some advertisements request direct response via a toll-free number, a mail-in coupon, a website or e-mail address, or an offer embedded in the body copy. Instead of depending on consumers' memories, measures of a message's persuasive abilities, or some other indirect indication of effectiveness, the advertiser simply counts the number of viewers or readers who request more information or buy the product.

Principle
Direct-response communication drives action and that makes it highly measurable.

In some ways, direct response mechanisms are the easiest marketing communication tool to evaluate both in terms of message effectiveness and in terms of ROI efficiency—the sales-to-cost ratio. The efficiency of a direct-response offer is measured in terms of responses per thousand (RPM). To calculate the RPM, use the following formula:

$$\frac{\text{Total responses}}{\text{Total mailed}} \times 1{,}000 = \text{RPM}$$

This calculation lets you compare the response rate of alternative mailings. For example if one mailing of 15,000 pulled 750 responses, then the RPM was 50 per 1,000. If a different mailing of 12,000 pulled 800 responses, then the RPM was 66 per 1,000, making it a more effective offer.

Sales Promotion   Sales promotion programs for packaged goods and other products that use distribution channels need to evaluate both the impact of consumer (or end-user) direct promotions and promotions targeted at retailers and other channel members. You will recall the discussions of promotional allowances offered to retailers who agree to feature a brand in their ads or provide special in-store display and price discounts. These are measured by proof of performance such as copies of store ads and pictures of in-store displays. One responsibility of the sales force is to do store checks to verify that stores are doing what they promised. Promotions that contain a response device, such as coupons, have a built-in evaluation measure.

As for consumer promotions, the following evaluation measures are the most popular:

Measure	% Used
Sales	46
Response rates	20
Awareness	10
Other mix	9
Redemption rates	4

Principle

Proof of performance, various types of responses to promotional tactics, and payout planning provide built-in evaluation measures for promotions.

The efficiency of a sales promotion offer can be evaluated in terms of its financial returns more easily than advertising. We compare the costs of a promotion, called a **payout analysis,** to the forecasted sales generated by the promotion. A **break-even analysis** seeks to determine the point at which the total cost of a promotion exceeds the total revenues generated, identifying the point where the promotion is not wise to do. Figure 19.4 depicts this analysis.

Principle

Ultimately, public relations efforts are evaluated in terms of opinion change and relationship tracking.

Public Relations   The evaluation of public relations examines the success of getting a message out to a target audience in terms of *output* (materials produced and distributed) and *outcomes* (acceptance and impact of the materials). Outcomes can be measured in terms of changes in public opinion and relationship tracking. The output evaluation is conducted by asking questions such as these: How many placements (news releases that ran in the media) did we get? How many times did our spokesperson appear on talk shows? How much airplay did our public service announcements receive or how much and what kind of buzz are Twitters generating? The results are presented in terms of counts of minutes, mentions, or inches.

Content analysis also helps determine the favorability of the coverage, share of voice, and issue and competitor coverage. Ongoing public opinion tracking studies ask these questions: Has there been a change in audience knowledge, attitudes, or behavior (e.g., pretesting versus posttesting)? Can we associate behavior change (e.g., product trial, repeat purchase, voting, or joining) with the public relations effort? The most common measures of output and outcomes in public relations are summarized here:

Output Objectives Achieved

- *Production* Number of PR messages, such as news releases or brochures, generated.
- *Distribution* Number of media outlets (TV stations, newspapers) receiving PR products.
- *Coverage* Number and size of clips, column inches, or minutes of time or space.
- *Impressions* Media placements multiplied by circulation or broadcast reach.
- *Advertising Value* Equivalent ad costs for time or space.
- *Content Analysis* Positive or valence (whether the story or mention seems to be more positive or negative), key messages (the idea in the story), sources, and prominence.

Outcome Objectives Achieved

- *Awareness* Aided and unaided recall.
- *Attitudes* Perceptions, preferences, and intent to buy.
- *Behavior* Did target do what you wanted them to do?

The search for methods to tie public relations activities to bottom-line business measures, such as ROI (return on investment), is like the quest for the Holy Grail. PR practitioners would like to demonstrate ROI because it would provide even more support for the importance of PR effects. A surrogate ROI measure can be based on shareholder value, which can be seen as a company or brand's reputation capital. For example, research conducted on companies with the most effective employee communication programs has determined that they provide a much higher total return to shareholders. Recently Web-based analytical tools are making it possible to connect earned media results to online business goals, such as generating website traffic, sales leads, revenue, and donations for nonprofit organizations.[21]

Website Evaluation Evaluating the communication effects of website advertising is still a new game. Some performance indicators are traffic volume, such as **page views** or the simple number of visitors to a site. Banner advertising and other online ads are evaluated using **click-through rates,** and the one thing the industry has learned is that this form of advertising is decreasing in effectiveness. One problem is that people who have little or no interest in the product may click on the banner by accident or curiosity. Because this type of advertising is sold by **pay-per-click (PPC),** the advertiser has to pay regardless of the reason for the click. Pop-up banners can get more attention, but they are also seen as more irritating.

Instead of click-through rates, some advertising uses a **cost-per-lead** metric that records how well the click-through generates prospects, an attempt to get at ROI. The most important metric for Internet advertising, however, is **conversion rate,** which is the percentage of visitors to a site who complete a desired action, such as playing a game, signing up for a newsletter, or buying something. Of course, online sales are an important measure of a website's effectiveness.

The more sophisticated conversion rate services not only measure how well the site generates action but also how customers navigated the site. This information is obtained by tracking where they come from, what search terms they used, how they move around within the website, and where they go when they leave. It gives a more comprehensive picture of the path visitors and customers use in navigating a site.

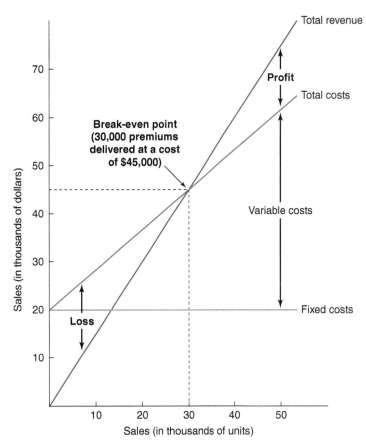

FIGURE 19.4

A Sales Promotion Break-Even Analysis

At the break-even point, where 30,000 premiums are delivered at a cost of $45,000, the sales revenues exactly cover, but do not exceed, total costs. Below and to the left of the break-even point (in the portion of the diagram marked off by dashed lines), the promotion operates at a loss. Above and to the right of the break-even point, as more premiums are sold and sales revenues climb, the promotion makes a profit.

Forrester Research has been developing methods for evaluating websites for years. The company tracks effectiveness of website performance in terms not only of making a brand promise, but in terms of also delivering easy-to-find and use information. Harley Manning, a Forrester vice president, reported that his company's research has found that "on average sites did a better job of making the brand promise than they did of meeting customer needs." Manning explains how this research is used to evaluate good and bad performing websites in *The Inside Story.* (Check Forrester's website at *www.forrester.com.*)

Special Advertising Situations

The various types of advertising identified in Chapter 18 are evaluated using many of the tools discussed previously; however, they each have their own particular objectives that affect how they are evaluated.

The primary objective of *retail advertising* is to generate store traffic. The results of traffic-building promotions and advertising are simple counts of transactions as well as the change in sales volume of brands receiving promotional support. Participation counts can be used to estimate the pull of special events. Loyalty is evidenced through participation in frequent buyer programs and measured in terms of registration, store visits, and average purchases per visit.

In *B2B marketing,* a common form of evaluation is a count of sales leads based on response devices such as calls, e-mails, and cards returned to the advertiser. Another common B2B objective is *conversion,* similar to the conversion rate in the online discussion; this refers to the number of leads that turn into customers who make a purchase. Conversion rates, which are percentages of the leads, are also calculated for most marketing communication tools used in support of B2B programs.

THE INSIDE STORY

How Web Sites Build Brands (Or Don't)

Harley Manning, *Vice President and Research Director, Customer Experience, Forrester Research, Inc.*

Brand is at or near the top of the priority list for companies doing business on the Web. In one Forrester survey, decision makers at 148 companies rated building the brand as the second most important goal for their business-to-consumer sites. The same group said that when considering new content and features for their sites, building the brand was as important as supporting customer goals.

So if online brand building is so important, how can companies make sure that their websites build their brands? To answer that question, we started by interviewing brand strategists at seven of the largest interactive agencies, including Razorfish and Tribal DDB Worldwide. We also talked to marketers at two companies that we respect for their brand management expertise: Johnson & Johnson and Procter & Gamble.

We found broad agreement that websites serve two equally critical functions: *They are both a communication medium and a delivery channel. In other words, consumers expect sites to not just make the brand promise but also to keep that promise by providing value in the form of detailed product information that's easy to find and use.*

As a result of our initial research, we created a methodology that grades how well sites make the brand promise and keep the brand promise. Our approach is a type of heuristic evaluation, sometimes referred to as an expert review. Standard heuristic evaluations date from the late 1990s and depend on three factors: detailed user descriptions, relevant user goals, and a valid set of rules (or heuristics) that identify known types of user experience flaws. We stuck with that approach to gauge how well the sites served consumers (i.e., kept the brand promise).

To measure how well sites make the brand promise, we created a variation on the standard expert review methodology. Instead of starting with user descriptions and goals, we begin by identifying the *brand attributes of the site* we intend to grade. We do this by looking at their annual reports and the public statements made by their executives. Then we collect above-the-line collateral ranging from annual reports to magazine ads to TV commercials. This preparation lets us check sites for cross-channel consistency of logos, colors, typography, and layout as well as consistency with intended brand attributes such as "reliable" or "innovative" (two of the most common).

We've been using this methodology now for about four years. During that time we've spotted a number of interesting trends. For one, websites on average do a poor job of building either major aspect of brands online: in an analysis of more than 150 reviews we found that only 8% of sites passed both halves of our test.

We also found that, *on average, sites did a better job of making the brand promise than they did of meeting customer needs.* Sixty sites passed our tests for making the brand promise but only 17 did an adequate job of serving customers' goals. For example, sites from companies as diverse as Nike, Edward Jones, BP, and Coca-Cola excel at online copy and imagery, but fall flat on user experience basics like providing the right content or making that content easy to read via easily legible text.

Like other types of advertising, *nonprofit organizations* need to communicate efficiently and effectively, particularly as they are stewards who must ensure that limited funding is used effectively and efficiently. Evaluation of communication for foundations and nonprofit organizations is an emerging field, and challenges to assessing effectiveness are many. Activities and behaviors being measured are complex and campaigns are often a multi-phase effort. There are no standard and widely accepted guidelines for communication evaluation for the nonprofit sector. Nonetheless, measuring success of a campaign begins with setting objectives and evaluating the progress toward achieving the objectives.[22]

International marcom is difficult to evaluate because of market differences (e.g., language, laws, cultural norms) and the acceptability of various research tools. There may also be incompatibilities among various measurement systems and data analysis techniques that make it difficult to compare the data from one market with similar data from another market. An international evaluation program for advertising should focus, at least initially, on pretesting because unfamiliarity with different cultures, languages, and consumer behaviors can result in major miscalculations. Pretesting helps the advertiser correct major problems before miscommunication occurs. To evaluate the global/local question, the best approach is to test two ads that are both based on the global advertising strategy: a locally produced version of the advertising and an original ad produced locally.

Campaign and Program Evaluation

While it is ideal to know how each marketing communication function has performed, the reality in most campaigns is that a variety of functions and media are used to reach and motivate customers to respond. Time is a factor as well. We mentioned in the beginning of this chapter that there is a debate about advertising's ability to impact short-term sales results as well as long-term branding.

University of Southern California Professor Gerard Tellis reminds us that advertising not only has *instantaneous* effects (consumer responds immediately) but also *carryover* effects (delayed impact).[23] Any evaluation of campaign effectiveness needs to also be able to track both types of effects over time. Differential effects also complicate the ongoing evaluation of IMC programs that operate with a 360-degree total communication philosophy, although tracking may be easier in some ways because the evaluation is continuous.

The Synergy Problem   The problem with evaluating campaigns—particularly IMC campaigns—is estimating the impact of synergy. Intuitively we know that multichannel communication with messages that reinforce and build on one another will have more impact than single messages from single sources; however, that can be difficult to prove. As Bob Liodice, CEO of the Association of National Advertisers, observes, "there is no single, consistent set of metrics that transcends discipline-centric measurements."[24]

If the campaign planning is well integrated, which means each specialty area cooperates with all others in message design, delivery, and timing, then there should be a synergistic effect. This means that the overall results are greater than the sum of the individual functional areas if used separately.

A number of studies have attempted to evaluate IMC impact by comparing campaigns that use two or three tools to see what is gained when more message sources are added to the mix. For example, a study by the Radio Ad Effectiveness Lab reported that recall of advertising is enhanced when a mix of radio and Internet ads are used rather than just website advertising alone.[25] A study published in the *Journal of Advertising Research* developed a multidimensional approach based on evaluation of four factors including unified and consistent communication, strategic consistency in targeting (different messages for different audiences), database communication, and relationship programs.[26] Such studies of both the platforms and components of IMC are beginning to tease out the effects of synergy, but they are a long way from evaluating the effects of a total communication program.

The most common way of measuring a campaign's total impact is the brand tracking approach mentioned previously. As various ingredients in the campaign are added and taken away, changes in tracking study results can show the effects and help identify what combinations of marketing communication functions and media work best for a brand. In other words, has the brand become stronger on critical dimensions of the image, such as personality and positioning cues, because of the campaign?

A complication in evaluating programs is the need to consider other messages and contact points beyond traditional marketing communication. As we have said, in a 360-degree total communication program, brand experiences, such as those involved with customer service and WoM, may be even more important than traditional marketing communication. *A Principled Practice* feature by Professor Keith Murray demonstrates how these unconventional message effects can be measured.

Connecting the Dots   The challenge in campaign and program evaluation is to pull everything together and look at the big picture of campaign performance rather than the individual pieces and parts. One of the first places to start is defining the objectives—all the various effects—and then adequately and realistically measure the campaign's performance against those objectives. Here's an example that demonstrates how evaluation methods can be matched to the original campaign objectives.

Effie award winner UPS wanted to reposition itself by broadening its package delivery image.[27] Although UPS owned ground delivery, it lost out to Federal Express in the overnight and international package market. UPS knew from its customer research that to break out of the "brown and ground" perception, the company had to overcome the inertia of shipping managers who use UPS for ground packages and FedEx for overnight and international. The company also had to shift the perception of senior executives from a company that handles packages to a strategic partner in systems planning. From these insights came three sets of objectives that focused on

A PRINCIPLED PRACTICE

Can a Broken Guitar Really Hurt United?

Keith Murray, *Associate Dean, College of Business, Bryant University*

It's been a YouTube hit and made the e-mail rounds for a long time—the "United Breaks Guitars" video. It's the story of a musician who made a trip on United Airlines (UA) and was compelled to "check" his Taylor guitar as baggage— which is how UA came to be vulnerable to the charge that, in the handling of it, they damaged the instrument.

When asked to make it right—to pay for fixing the Taylor guitar—UA declined.

The musician, Dave Carroll, responded by writing a ballad about the experience and posting it on YouTube and the Internet. (See it at *www.youtube.com/watch?v=5YGc4zOqozo*.)

A lot of people viewed the clip; it's catchy and tells the story in an amusing way. People have sent it to their friends . . . and friends have sent it to their friends, which has led now to literally millions of people seeing it! You can also see a CBS report about the incident at *www.youtube.com/watch?v=PGNtQF3n6VY&feature=related*.

So was UA smart to ignore this incident? In other words, did UA really "save" the $1,200 it would have taken to fix the guitar in the first place?

It seems clear that UA might have been short sighted. If you "do the numbers," you come to the conclusion that UA may have paid a much higher price than it realized!

The table following shows how much money might have been—and is still being?!!—lost by UA from 8 million people (in 2010) seeing the YouTube clip and deciding *against* using UA. It gives various levels of impact from 1 to 10 percent. It also com-

pares the percent of this lost revenue against UA's sales revenue in 2008.

# of $500 Trips NOT Taken in a Year	Percent of Viewers Influenced by YouTube Videos to NOT Patronize UA in a 12-Month Period			
	1%	2%	5%	10%
One trip	$30M	$60M	$150M	$300M
% '08 revenue	0.15	0.31	0.78	1.56
Two trips	$60M	$120M	$300M	$600M
% '08 revenue	0.31	0.63	1.56	3.13

What the calculations show is compelling. If only 1 percent of those who learned of the broken Taylor guitar were affected by the story, then UA only lost somewhere between $30 million and $60 million. However, if the negative influence is higher, then UA could arguably have forgone as much as half a *billion* dollars, or about 3 percent of its annual sales! In any case, all of these figures stand in stark contrast to the $1,200 asked for by Mr. Carroll in the first place!

This gets to the real point of the story: If UA (or any company) has a flawed system to handle and remedy customer complaints—in other words, if UA has customer service "issues" that produce unsatisfactory results for customers—then it can pay a very high price for its poor service. And the damage is exponential, because the average person tells about 10 people about a bad brand experience—all of which has a chilling effect on patronage by those who hear such tales of woe!

These numbers show the huge impact of failure to pay attention to customer complaints and service system problems. Can one little broken Taylor guitar—and all the other little failures each day—affect a mammoth company like United Airlines? You bet.

breaking through awareness, breaking the inertia trance, and breaking the relevance trance. Here's how the campaign performed on those objectives. Notice the mix of perception, image, and behavioral measures.

Objective 1: Breaking through Awareness

- Awareness of the Brown campaign outpaced *all* past UPS advertising measured in the 10-plus-year history of its brand tracking study.
- Among those aware of the campaign, correct brand linkage to UPS was 95 to 98 percent across all audiences (compared to a historical average of 20 to 40 percent for past UPS advertising).

- "What Can BROWN Do for You?" has taken hold in popular culture. For instance, the tagline was mentioned in both *Saturday Night Live* and *Trading Spaces* shows.

Objective 2: Breaking the Inertia Trance

- With shipping decision makers, the brand showed steady and significant gains in key measures like "Helps my operation run more smoothly," "Dynamic and energetic," and "Offers a broad range of services."
- International shipping profitability increased 150 percent, and overnight volume spiked by 9.1 percent after the campaign ran. The targeted companies' total package volume increased by 4.39 percent.
- From the start of the campaign in March to the year-end, annual ground shipping revenue grew by $300 million.
- The campaign was a hit in terms of response with a 10.5 percent response rate and an ROI of 1:3.5. In other words, every dollar spent on the campaign generated $3.5 dollars in revenue.

Objective 3: Breaking the Relevance Trance

- For the first time in the 10-plus-year history of the brand tracking study, UPS leads FedEx in all image measures among senior-level decision makers. All significant brand image measures continued upward.
- Among senior decision makers, the biggest gains were in key measures like "For people like me," "Acts as a strategic partner to my company," "Helps in distribution and supply chain operations," and "Provides global competitive advantage."
- At the start of the campaign, annual nonpackage (supply chain) revenue was approximately $1.4 billion. By the end of the year, nonpackage revenue had almost doubled to $2.7 billion.

Bringing It All Together   Beyond connecting the objectives to the measurements, advertisers continue to search for methods that will bring all the metrics together and efficiently and effectively evaluate—and predict—brand communication effectiveness. A small Florida agency, Zimmerman Advertising, positions itself specifically on that issue. It promises to deliver long-term brand building as well as short-term sales. The president explains, "The biggest problem marketers face today is connecting advertising to retail sales." To help determine the impact of its ads on sales, Zimmerman measures ad response immediately using a toll-free number and proprietary software that tracks sales to specific ads.[28]

The giant media research company, Nielsen, has undertaken a project to find the links in its various marketing metrics. In particular, the company wants to connect its Nielsen Media Research TV ratings with its A.C. Nielsen retail scanner and consumer panel data. Then it wants to mix in data from its Nielsen/NetRatings for online advertising and Nielsen Buzzmetrics online-buzz measurement system.[29] This is just one example of how important it is to connect the dots to draw an accurate picture of consumer response to marketing communication.

Ultimately, the goal is to arrive at holistic, cross-functional metrics that are relevant for integrated communication, a task undertaken by Dell Computers and its agency DDB. Given Dell's direct-marketing business model, the company had extensive call and order data in its database. DDB helped organize the collection of detailed marcom information, which made it possible to begin linking orders to specific marcom activities. This new marcom ROI tracking system made it possible for Dell to recognize a 3 percent gain in the efficiency of its marketing communication. As the metrics system became more sophisticated, it also began to move from a reporting and metrics evaluation engine to a strategic tool providing deeper insights into consumer behavior.[30]

Many pieces are still missing in the evaluation of advertising, not to mention more complex IMC programs. Research think tanks are struggling to find better ways to measure consumers' emotional connections to brands and brands' relationships with their customers[31] and how those connections and relationships are affected by various types of marketing communication messages. But let's end with an inspirational video called "Life Lessons from an Ad Man." It's a little old, but Rory Sutherland makes a good point about having fun even as you contemplate how marketing communication creates intangible value for brands. See it at: *www.ted.com/talks/rory_sutherland_life_lessons_from_an_ad_man.html*.

IT'S A WRAP

SkiStar Managing Decentralized Campaigns

In this final chapter we have reviewed various methods of evaluating the effectiveness of a campaign. No campaign uses all of them, but all successful campaigns have to do some kind of evaluation in order to determine success. SkiStar is an example of an IMC program that carefully monitors its marketing communication messages.

SkiStar's head of marketing and sales, Mathias Lindstrom, highlighted the importance of using automated marketing solutions to enable the company to target the right offer to the right customer at the right time. This fulfilled the cardinal elements of the marketing mix with the fourth dimension, place, being the virtual world of SkiStar's website.

By being able to understand and then act on their customers' preferences and interests, not only was the business able to cater to the specific needs of each customer, but they were able to personalize all of their marketing messages. This in turn meant that SkiStar could foster loyalty among its customers and make their resorts the ones of choice each time. SkiStar uses Portrait Campaign Manager, a software package that enables them to focus on customer retention and cross-selling opportunities, monitor and control marketing campaigns, and conduct real-time evaluations of their effectiveness.

Given the fractious nature of the market, the system allows SkiStar to achieve more with fewer resources. They can run decentralized and complex marketing campaigns at specific target markets and make them profitable. Another direct result of this was the development of the new SkiPass, which is valid for all SkiStar destinations during the season. The new SkiPass was launched for the 2010–2011 season and designed to cater to customers who were looking for a broader range of experiences across SkiStar's portfolio of resorts.

The latest available set of sales figures covers the 2009–2010 season. By late November 2009, the volume of bookings showed an 8 percent improvement compared to 2008–2009, which had been a record year. Some 78 percent of all planned accommodation sales had already been booked. Overall, there had been an increase in sales at the five main resorts: Sälen was up 10 percent; Vemdalen, Trysil, and Hemsedal all up 9 percent; and Åre up 2 percent.

Key Points Summary

1. **Why and how is marketing communication evaluation conducted?** Marketing communication evaluation is used to test, monitor, measure, and diagnose the effectiveness of marcom messages. The factors tested are the key effects outlined in a model of advertising effectiveness.

2. **Can you list and explain the stages of message evaluation?** Message evaluation is conducted before (pretesting), during (tracking), and after (post-testing) an ad or campaign has run. Diagnostic evaluation can be conducted at all three stages.

3. **What are the key areas of media evaluation?** Media evaluation begins by verifying the media exposure in terms of

the achievement of the reach and frequency objectives, as well as the audience measurement reports of the media used. Media ROI evaluations consider questions such as how much is enough, particularly in terms of advertising wearout.

4. **How are IMC tools, campaigns, and programs evaluated?** A campaign's performance is assessed in terms of how well it meets its message and media objectives. IMC plans also assess the performance of the various marketing communication tools, as well as the synergistic effect of the elements working together.

Words of Wisdom: Recommended Reading

Davis, John, *Measuring Marketing: 103 Key Metrics Every Marketer Needs,* Hoboken, NJ: John Wiley, 2007.

Jones, John Philip, *When Ads Work: New Proof That Advertising Triggers Sales,* 2nd ed., Armonk, NY: M. E. Sharpe, 2007.

Noble, Paul, and Tom Watson, *Evaluating Public Relations: A Best Practice Guide to Public Relations Planning, Research, and Evaluation,* Philadelphia: Kogan Page, 2007.

Tellis, Gerard, *Effective Advertising,* Thousand Oaks CA: Sage, 2004.

Young, Antony, and Lucy Aitken, *Profitable Marketing Communications: A Guide to Marketing Return on Investment,* Philadelphia: Kogan Page, 2007.

Young, Charles, *The Advertising Research Handbook,* Seattle, WA: Ideas in Flight, 2005.

Key Terms

aided recall, p. 617	cost-per-lead, p. 625	motivation test, p. 618	recall test, p. 617
animatics, p. 613	developmental research, p. 609	norms, p. 612	recognition test, p. 617
brand penetration, p. 615	diagnostic research, p. 609	page views, p. 625	saccadic eye movement, p. 616
break-even analysis, p. 624	eye-tracking, p. 616	pantry checks, p. 616	
click-through rates, p. 625	heuristics, p. 616	payout analysis, p. 624	scanner research, p. 619
clutter reel, p. 613	inquiry tests, p. 618	pay-per-click (PPC), p. 625	single-source research, p. 619
coincidental survey, p. 613	intend-to-buy test, p. 618	persuasion test, p. 618	test market, p. 616
concept testing, p. 612	likability tests, p. 618	photoboards, p. 613	tracking studies, p. 613
concurrent research, p. 609	media optimization, p. 621	picture sort, p. 613	unaided recall, p. 617
consumer diaries, p. 616	moment-by-moment	post-testing research, p. 609	wave analysis, p. 615
conversion rate, p. 625	tests, p. 613	pretesting, p. 612	wearout, p. 621

Review Questions

1. Why do marketers evaluate their advertising and marketing communication programs?

2. This chapter suggests that evaluation is most useful when based on a model of advertising response. Why is that so?

3. Why are diagnostic research methods becoming more important?

4. What is a tracking study and how is it used? A test market?

5. What is single-source research, and how does scanner data relate to it?

6. What is media efficiency, and how does that relate to ROI?

7. Why is an IMC campaign difficult to evaluate?

Discussion Questions

1. Many creative people feel that formal copytesting research doesn't do justice to their ideas. In particular, they feel that research results are designed to reward cognitive approaches and don't do a good job of evaluating brand image ads and emotional ads. From what you have read in this chapter about copytesting, why do they feel that way? Do you believe that is a legitimate criticism of copytesting?

2. Most clients want a quick and easy answer to the question of whether the ad works. Advertising professionals, however, tend to believe that a one-score approach to copytesting is not appropriate. Why do they feel that way? If you were helping an agency prepare for a presentation on its copytesting results, what would you suggest the agency say to explain away the idea that you can evaluate an ad with a single test?

3. *Three-Minute Debate* You are hiring a research consulting company to help a client evaluate the effectiveness of its advertisements. One of the consultants recommends using focus groups to evaluate their effectiveness. Another consultant suggests that focus groups aren't very effective for post-testing and recommends other measures. Which viewpoint do you believe is most insightful?

4. Explore the websites of two copytesting companies, such as Ameritest (*www.Ameritest.net*), Ipsos ASI (*www.ipsos.com*), Millward Brown (*www.millwardbrown.com*) or the ARS Group (*www.ars-group.com*), and compare the services they offer. If you were looking for a company to pretest a campaign for a cosmetic product, which one would you prefer? Why?

Take-Home Projects

1. *Portfolio Project* Put together a portfolio of 10 ads for a set of product categories targeted to a college audience. Set up a focus group with participants recruited from among your friends and ask them to look at the ads. In a test of unaided awareness, ask them to list the ads they remember. Identify the top performing ad and the bottom ad in this awareness test. Now ask the focus group participants to analyze the headline, the visual, and the brand identification of each ad. How do the two ads compare in terms of their ability to get attention and lock the brand in memory?

2. *Mini-Case Analysis* Reread the chapter opener about SkiStar. Explain what is meant when we say the point of this campaign is to build a brand relationship. How did this campaign succeed in that objective? How was effectiveness determined for the SkiPass? If you were on the marketing team and were asked to develop a broader set of evaluation tools, what would you recommend and why?

Team Project: The BrandRevive Campaign

This is it. You're now at the last steps in the development of a campaign for your BrandRevive client.

* First, develop an evaluation proposal for your campaign. How would you measure the effectiveness of your campaign ideas?
* Finally, bring all your ideas together as a complete campaign. From everything you've done in the preceding chap-

ters, as well as the evaluation proposal you just drafted after reading this final chapter, synthesize and consolidate your best ideas. Compose a campaign presentation of no more than 30 PowerPoint slides. This is a showcase presentation, so give your team a title and create a title for your campaign. Practice and present it to your class. Good luck and good work.

Hands-On Case

The Century Council

Read the Century Council case in the Appendix before coming to class.

1. If you worked for the Century Council, how would you pretest this campaign prior to using it across the country and spending a full $10 million on it?

2. How did "The Stupid Drink" team evaluate their progress step by step through the campaign development process?

3. If you worked for the Century Council, how would you evaluate the market success of "The Stupid Drink" campaign from year to year?

CHAPTER 5

Developing Creative Work 1

6 Advertising Design

Theoretical Frameworks and Types of Appeals

HYUNDAI MOTOR COMPANY

A Small Start-up Becomes a Powerful Player

In 1946, Ju-Yung Chung established the Hyundai Auto Service company in Seoul, South Korea. The name Hyundai translates to "modern" in English. The Hyundai logo has an oval shape designed to express the company's desire to expand globally, with the stylized "H" symbolizing two people (the company and the customer) shaking hands.

Over the next 50 years, the company developed its first domestic model, the Pony. The small automobile was tested, certified, approved, and exported to Europe. Eventually, versions of the Pony, including a pick-up truck, were sold in Canada. The Pony was replaced with an upgraded vehicle, the Hyundai Excel, which met all of the requirements for export into the United States in 1985. Four years later, the Hyundai Sonata was introduced.

At first, Hyundai products met with a great deal of skepticism. The company found its offerings being lumped together with low-quality exports from other countries in the minds of some U.S. consumers. The Yugo, produced in Yugoslavia, had reached U.S. shores at about the same time. At the low point, comedian Jay Leno made a joke about the Hyundai suggesting that buying a tank of gas doubled the value of the car.

In the next two decades, the company earned both respect and market share. The Hyundai Accent replaced the Excel and became especially popular in Australia. Following setbacks due to the financial crisis in Asia in the 1990s, Hyundai began to evolve under the leadership of a new chairman, Mong-Koo Chung, who replaced many top executives in the company with engineers. His goal was to compete with then-industry-leader Toyota on the basis of quality.

Mong-Koo's "zero defect mantra" became a major success. In 1998, Hyundai ranked among the worst in terms of initial defects. The change in quality level was "astounding," says Chance Parker, executive director at J.D. Power, which evaluates product quality. "We really haven't documented that

CHAPTER OBJECTIVES

After reading this chapter, you should be able to answer the following questions:

1 How can the hierarchy of effects model and a means–ends analysis help an advertising creative design better commercials?

2 How can leverage points and taglines increase advertising effectiveness?

3 What roles do visual and verbal images play in advertisements?

4 What are the seven main types of advertising appeals?

5 How can fear be used to create an effective advertisement?

6 How can humor be used to create an effective advertisement?

7 Why does sex play such a prominent role in advertising?

8 How can music, rationality, and scarcity be used to increase advertising effectiveness?

9 What are the primary areas of concern in international advertising?

level of turnaround in that period of time. They've adopted a quality mentality they didn't have before." *Consumer Reports* rated the 2004 Sonata the most reliable car in America for 2004, with only 2 problems per 100 vehicles. Likewise, Hyundai rose to second place in J.D. Power and Associates' 2004 survey of initial car quality, tied with Honda and trailing only Toyota.

These changes meant that by the mid-2000s Hyundai had become an established alternative to other models that were available in the United States. Much of the growth was attributed to the "America's Best Warranty Program," which featured a 10-year, 100,000-mile powertrain protection program, longer than any other company in the industry. The program also carried a 5-year, 60,000-mile new vehicle limited warranty. Both warranties strongly reinforced the company's claims of quality.

In 2008, the company took another turn in response to the dramatic plunge in economic conditions in the United States and worldwide.

Hyundai developed the "Hyundai Assurance Program," which included the warranty program; 24/7 roadside assistance; and, most important, a purchase clause that stated, "If, in the next year you lose your income, we'll let you return it (the car)," in hopes of selling or leasing cars to those worried about job security.

Currently, Hyundai operates two manufacturing plants in the United States, one in Alabama and a second in Michigan. The organization's reach has become global, both in the automotive and in other industries. Potential Hyundai dealers must exhibit high levels of professionalism in the automobile industry and powerful commitments to service. What was once a small start-up in a far away country has become a powerful player in the U.S. auto market and beyond.[1]

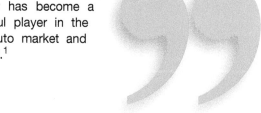

OVERVIEW

Which advertising message made the biggest impression on you in the past 5 years? Was it funny, sexy, or emotional? Was it something shown during the Super Bowl? In a recent Adweek Media and Harris Interactive survey, the majority of consumers (55 percent) said that advertisements were somewhat or very interesting. Only 13 percent replied that ads were not interesting at all. When making purchase

▲ By featuring a celebrity, this advertisement seeks to convince consumers of the importance of drinking milk.

decisions, 6 percent of the respondents said advertisements were "very influential," and 29 percent viewed them as "somewhat influential." Contrary to popular opinion, advertising does influence younger consumers. Nearly half of 18- to 34-year-olds in the survey reported that they were influenced in some way by advertising, compared to 37 percent for 35- to 44-year-olds, and 28 percent for consumers age 45 and older.[2]

This poll emphasizes the importance of designing an interesting and influential advertising campaign, which can be one of the most challenging elements of an integrated marketing communications program. A successful advertising campaign results when people do more than just enjoy what they see; it also changes their behaviors and attitudes. At the least, viewers should remember the good or service, so that the next time they make purchases the company or brand comes to mind.

Chapter 5 described the overall advertising management program. The advertising agency is led by an account executive who makes the pitch for the account and works with creatives, media planners, and media buyers. In this chapter, the focus is on the actual message design. This work will be completed by the agency's creative staff.

A message design process will be based on the creative brief that was prepared by the client in conjunction with the account executive. It takes into consideration the media to be utilized. By combining all of these elements, the creative can design effective advertisements.

This chapter covers two major topics. The first part details three theoretical approaches to advertising design:

- The hierarchy of effects model
- Means–end theory
- Visual and verbal imaging

The second part reviews the major advertising appeals. Many of these may seem familiar. The advertising agency's creative team selects the appeal with the best chance of conveying a message that achieves the desired outcome. Several steps are taken before beginning the process of creating an advertising campaign. The activities are summarized by the creative brief.

THE CREATIVE BRIEF

Figure 6.1 outlines the elements of the creative brief, which provides the background for the creative work. An effective advertising message begins with understanding the *objective* of the ad and the *target audience*. The advertising group agrees on the *message theme*, which is the outline of the key ideas the commercial conveys. The account executive or client provides *support* and documentation for the advertising theme or claim. Finally, the creative considers any *constraints* to be included. After completing these steps, the creative prepares the advertisement.

FIGURE 6.1 ▶
The Creative Brief

- The objective
- The target audience
- The message theme
- The support
- The constraints

ADVERTISING THEORY

In developing an advertising campaign, three theoretical approaches might aid in the design process. The hierarchy of effects model and a means–end chain can both assist in developing the leverage point. A *leverage point* moves the consumer from understanding a product's benefits to linking those benefits with personal values. A third theoretical perspective involves the visual and verbal images present in an advertisement.

Hierarchy of Effects

The **hierarchy of effects model** helps to clarify the objectives of an advertising campaign. The model outlines six steps a consumer or a business buyer moves through when making a purchase:

1. Awareness
2. Knowledge
3. Liking
4. Preference
5. Conviction
6. The actual purchase

These steps are sequential. A consumer spends a period of time at each one before moving to the next. Thus, before a person develops a liking for a product, she must first know about the product. Once the individual has the knowledge and develops liking for the product, the advertiser tries to influence the consumer to favor a particular brand or company.

The hierarchy of effects approach helps a creative understand how a consumer reaches a purchase decision. Some of the theory's assumptions have been questioned. For one, these six steps may not always constitute the route taken by a consumer. A person may make a purchase (such as an impulse buy) and then later develop knowledge, liking, preference, and conviction. Also, a shopper may purchase products when little or no preference is involved, because a coupon, discount, or purchase incentive caused him to choose one brand instead of another. At other times, the individual might not even remember the name of the brand he purchased. This may be the case with commodity products such as sugar or flour or even clothing purchases such as socks and shirts.

The major benefit provided by the hierarchy of effects model is that it identifies the typical steps consumers and businesses take when making purchases. Building brand loyalty involves all six steps. Logically, a customer cannot be loyal to a brand without first being aware of it. The customer typically also will not be loyal to a brand without sufficient knowledge. Then, the purchaser must like the brand and build a strong preference for it. Finally, the customer experiences the conviction that the particular brand is superior to the others on the market. The components of the hierarchy of effects approach highlight the responses that advertising or marketing communication should stimulate, in both consumers and business-to-business customers.

The hierarchy of effects model features similarities with theories about attitudes and attitudinal change, including the concepts of cognitive, affective, and conative elements. The *cognitive* component is the person's mental images, understanding, and interpretations of the person, object, or issue. The *affective* component contains the feelings or emotions a person has about the object, topic, or idea. The *conative* component consists of the individual's intentions, actions, or behavior. The most common sequence that takes place when an attitude forms is:

Cognitive → Affective → Conative

Any combination of these components is possible, which parallel the six-step hierarchy of effects process. Advertising may follow the steps or be different and highly successful because of how it captures an individual's attention in some unique way. As a general guideline, cognitive-oriented ads work best for achieving brand awareness and brand knowledge. Affective-oriented advertisements are better at inspiring liking, preference, and conviction.

1 How can the hierarchy of effects model and a means–ends analysis help an advertising creative design better commercials?

FIGURE 6.2 ▶
Personal Values

- Comfortable life
- Equality
- Excitement
- Freedom
- Fun, exciting life
- Happiness

- Inner peace
- Mature love
- Personal accomplishment
- Pleasure
- Salvation

- Security
- Self-fulfillment
- Self-respect
- Sense of belonging
- Social acceptance
- Wisdom

▼ This is a conative-oriented advertisement for Campbell's Mega Noodle, because it encourages consumers to try the new soup by offering them a coupon.

Conative-oriented ads are normally best suited to facilitating product purchases or other buyer actions.

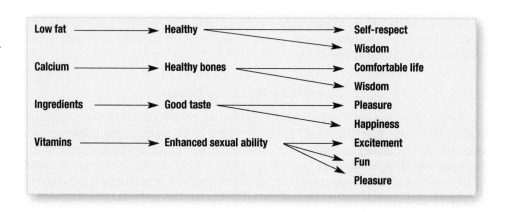

Source: Courtesy of Campbell Soup Company.

Means–End Theory

The second theoretical approach available to creatives is the **means–end chain**, which suggests that an advertisement should contain a message, or *means,* that leads the consumer to a desired end state. These *end* states are personal values (see Figure 6.2). A means–end chain should start a process in which viewing the ad leads the consumer to believe that using the product will help achieve one of the personal values.

Means–end theory forms the basis of the **Means–End Conceptualization of Components for Advertising Strategy (MECCAS)** model.[3] The MECCAS model suggests using six elements in creating ads:

- The product's attributes
- Consumer benefits
- Leverage points
- Taglines
- Personal values
- The executional framework

The MECCAS approach moves consumers through the six elements. The attributes of the product are linked to the specific benefits consumers can derive. These benefits, in turn, lead to the attainment of a personal value. Using the elements in Figure 6.3 and the milk advertisement shown in this section, the product attribute calcium is linked with the benefits of being strong and healthy. The personal value the consumer obtains from healthy bones may be feeling wise for using the product. The leverage point in the advertisement

FIGURE 6.3 ▶
Means–End Chains for Milk

Low fat	→ Healthy	→ Self-respect
		→ Wisdom
Calcium	→ Healthy bones	→ Comfortable life
		→ Wisdom
Ingredients	→ Good taste	→ Pleasure
		→ Happiness
Vitamins	→ Enhanced sexual ability	→ Excitement
		→ Fun
		→ Pleasure

arises from the connection between the benefit of health and the personal value of feeling wise. The white mustache and the text in the advertisement remind the viewer that drinking milk is healthy. In this case, preventing osteoporosis in women becomes the key selling point.

The MECCAS approach can be applied to business-to-business advertisements. Members of the buying center may be influenced by personal values, organizational values, and corporate goals. In the advertisement for Greenfield Online on page 164 and the means–end chain in Figure 6.4, each attribute is linked to the benefits business customers can obtain. Although not explicitly stated, the personal values of members of the buying center choosing Greenfield Online might include job security for making good decisions, self-fulfillment, wisdom, and social acceptance by other members of the buying group.

Leverage Points

Both the hierarchy of effects model and the means–end chain approach include leverage points. A leverage point moves the consumer from understanding a product's benefits to linking those benefits with personal values. To construct a quality leverage point, the creative builds the pathway that connects a product benefit with the potential buyer's value system.

In terms of the hierarchy of effects model, the initial level of awareness begins the process of exposing consumers to product benefits. As the viewer moves through the six stages, she eventually develops the conviction to buy the product. At that point, the benefit has indeed been linked with a personal value. In the milk advertisement used to illustrate the means–end chain, the leverage point presented in the phrase "There's one person I won't be" is tied to the copy message "a woman with osteoporosis." The copy explains that because milk contains calcium (the product attribute), it helps women maintain health bones (the product benefit). Making the decision to drink milk to prevent osteoporosis connects to the personal values of wisdom and seeking a healthy lifestyle.

In the Greenfield Online business-to-business advertisement, the leverage point is the picture of an old-fashioned woman using an old telephone sandwiched between the headline "Are you still buying marketing research done the old-fashioned way?" and the first sentence of the copy explaining that companies can "Do it better on the Internet." The picture presents an excellent mental image of marketing research conducted the old-fashioned way and the opportunities Greenfield Online can provide.

There's one person I won't be.

A woman with osteoporosis. So it's bloody marvelous that fat free milk has the calcium to help prevent it. Thank goodness there's enough to go around.

got milk?

Source: Courtesy of Bozell Worldwide, Inc.

▲ A "Got Milk?" advertisement illustrating the use of a means–end chain.

② How can leverage points and taglines increase advertising effectiveness?

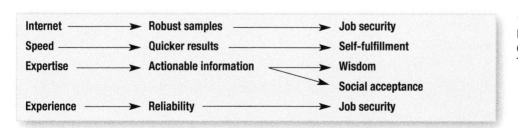

Internet	→	Robust samples	→	Job security
Speed	→	Quicker results	→	Self-fulfillment
Expertise	→	Actionable information	→	Wisdom
				Social acceptance
Experience	→	Reliability	→	Job security

◀ **FIGURE 6.4**
B-to-B Means–End Chain for Greenfield Online

ARE YOU STILL BUYING MARKETING RESEARCH DONE THE OLD-FASHIONED WAY?

Do it better on the Internet with the company that pioneered online marketing research.

Our panel of more than one million consumers from all across the Internet is the largest of its kind. It produces robust samples of any demographic or lifestyle you choose. You'll get richer, more actionable information quicker than you can say dot com.

Join the Research Revolution!™ Contact the world's most experienced Internet marketing research company for studies online, on time, on target and on budget.

www.greenfield.com 888.291.9997

Greenfield Online
Leading the Research Revolution®

▲ A Greenfield Online business-to-business advertisement illustrating the use of a means–end chain.

The means–end chain and MECCAS approaches are based on the product's attributes and its benefits to the consumer. The leverage point message links these attributes and benefits to consumer values. In the ad itself, the executional framework is the plot or scenario used to convey the message designed to complete the linkage. Chapter 7 presents executional frameworks in detail.

An effective leverage point can also be associated with an attitudinal change, especially when the cognitive → affective → conative sequence exists. As the attitude forms, the individual first understands, then is moved emotionally, and then takes action. A leverage point helps the viewer move through these three stages, tying cognitive knowledge of the product to emotional and personal values.

Creatives spend considerable amounts of time designing ads with powerful leverage points. Various types of appeals become the tools creatives use to help consumers make the transition from awareness of a product's benefits to incorporating them with personal values.

Taglines

The key phrase of an advertisement is the **tagline**. It should be something memorable that identifies the uniqueness of a brand or conveys some type of special meaning. "Just Do It" has been Nike's tagline for many years. Other well known taglines are identified in Figure 6.5.

Taglines carry over from one advertisement to others. They provide consistency across various advertising platforms. Consumers often remember taglines and identify them with specific brands. A catchy tagline identifies a brand and then stays with it over successive campaigns. In order to bring freshness to a campaign, company marketers occasionally tweak or modify a tagline. For instance, Allstate's tagline "You're in good hands with Allstate" became "Are you in good hands?" BMW modified the tagline "Sheer driving pleasure" to "The ultimate driving machine."

In other instances, a completely new tagline may be developed. To make the Oscar Mayer brand more contemporary, the company's marketing personnel and its agency, mcgarrybowen, created a new tagline. Oscar Mayer was known for trust, nostalgia, heritage, jingles, bologna, hot dogs, and kids. The image needed to be freshened, made more contemporary, and reach adults as well as kids. The Oscar Mayer marketing team wanted to take the brand to a place that was energetic, culturally relevant, and that captured the

FIGURE 6.5 ▶
Taglines Used by Various Brands

- American Express—"Don't leave home without it."
- Avis—"We try harder."
- Bounty—"The quicker picker-upper"
- Capital One—"What's in your wallet?"
- CNN—"The most trusted name in news"
- Energizer—"It keeps going, and going, and going."
- Hallmark—"When you care enough to send the best"

- John Deere—"Nothing runs like a Deer."
- Maxwell House—"Good to the last drop"
- Nokia—"Connecting people"
- Office Depot—"Taking care of business"
- Target—"Expect more. Pay less."
- UPS—"What can Brown do for you?"
- Wal-Mart—"Save money. Live better."

spirit of everyday food making people feel good. Real joy, real moments, real friendship, real emotion, and real people were at the forefront. The idea was that Oscar Mayer is "good mood food." This good mood feeling is visually conveyed in the Oscar Mayer ad in this section, in which marketing brainstorming sessions and music collaboration led to the campaign tagline "It doesn't get better than this."[4]

Verbal and Visual Images

Another theoretical approach to advertising design focuses on the decision the creative makes about the degree of emphasis given to the visual part of an advertisement versus the verbal element. Most major forms of advertising contain both visual and verbal or written elements. A visual ad places the greatest emphasis on the picture or visual element of the ad. A verbal or written ad places more emphasis on the copy.

Visual images often lead to more favorable attitudes toward both the advertisement and the brand. Visuals tend to be more easily remembered than verbal copy. They are stored in the brain as both pictures and words. This dual-coding process makes it easier for people to recall the message. Further, verbal messages tend be stored in the left side of the brain only; images are usually stored in both the left and right sides of the brain.

The advertisement for the Nicole Chair by Thomasville on the next page illustrates the power of visual imagery. Created by The Richards Group, it conveys the chair is "so you" that the design of the chair would be something you would be proud to wear as clothes. The imagery of the chair fabric matching a dress makes the message more powerful.

Visual images range from concrete and realistic to highly abstract. A concrete visual displays something recognizable, such as a person, place, or thing. In an abstract image, the subject becomes more difficult to recognize. Concrete pictures instill a higher level of recall than abstract images. Concrete pictures are dual-coded, allowing the image to be stored in the brain with both a visual and verbal elements. Viewers process an advertisement with a picture of spaghetti as both a picture and as a verbal representation of the restaurant. Ads with concrete images also tend to lead to more favorable attitudes than those with no pictures or abstract pictures.[5]

Radio advertisers often seek to create visual images for the audience. Pepsi produced a commercial in which listeners could hear a can being opened, the soft drink being poured, and the sizzle of the carbonation—an excellent example of creating a visual image. If consumers visualize an image in their imaginations, the effect may be greater than an actual visual. A visual image requires less brain activity than using one's imagination. The secret is getting the person to think beyond the advertisement and picture the scene being simulated.

Visual Esperanto

Visual imagery is widely used in international marketing. Global advertising agencies try to create **visual Esperanto**, the universal language that makes global advertising possible for any good or service. Visual Esperanto advertising recognizes that visual images are more powerful than verbal descriptions. Visual images are more likely to transcend cultural differences.[6] To illustrate the power of a visual image compared to a verbal account, think of the word *exotic*. To some, exotic means a white beach in Hawaii with young people in sexy swimsuits. To others, it may be a small cabin in the snow-capped mountains of Switzerland. To others still, exotic may be a close-up of a tribal village in Africa. The word exotic can vary in meaning. At the same time, a picture of a couple holding hands in front

Put a little O-M-G in your B-L-T.

Our bacon is naturally hardwood smoked for hours. And able to spread L-O-Ls all around.

it doesn't get better than this

▲ An advertisement for Oscar Mayer using the new tagline "It doesn't getter better than this."

3 What roles do visual and verbal images play in advertisements?

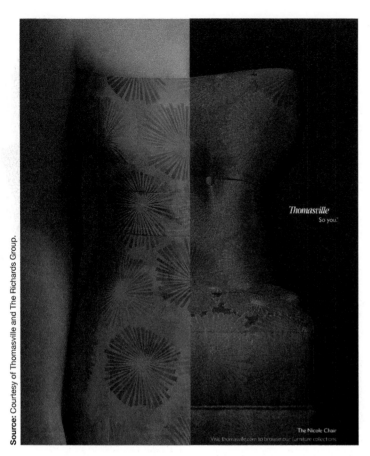

Source: Courtesy of Thomasville and The Richards Group.

Thomasville
So you.

The Nicole Chair
Visit thomasville.com to browse our furniture collections

▲ This advertisement for the Nicole Chair by Thomasville illustrates the power of visual imagery.

of Niagara Falls has practically the same meaning across all cultures as does the advertisement for Oscar Mayer shown on page 167. The image of the young couple looking at each other and eating from opposite ends of the hotdog conveys a similar meaning across multiple cultures.

Finding the appropriate image constitutes the most important task in creating visual Esperanto. The creative looks for the image that conveys the intended meaning or message. Brand identity can be emphasized using visuals rather than words. Then the creative uses words to support the visual image. For example, the creative may decide that a boy and his father at a sports event illustrate the priceless treasure of a shared family moment. In Mexico, the setting could be a soccer match instead of a baseball game in the United States. The specific copy (the words) can then be adapted to another country. Identifying an image that transcends cultures is the difficult part of inspiring visual Esperanto. Once a universal image has been found, creatives in each country represented take the image and modify it to appeal to the local target audience.

Business-to-Business

In the past, creatives designing business-to-business advertisements relied heavily on the verbal element rather than on visuals. The basis of this approach was the belief that business decisions are made in a rational, cognitive manner. In recent years, more business ads have incorporated strong visual elements to heighten the emotional aspects of making a purchase.

In summary, the three theoretical models provide useful ideas for the advertising creative. Each suggests a sequence to be followed as during the preparation of an advertisement. The endpoint will be reached when the viewer remembers the products, thinks favorably about it, and looks for that product when making a purchase decision. Various kinds of advertising messages, or appeals, can be utilized to reach such key advertising objectives.

TYPES OF ADVERTISING APPEALS

4 What are the seven main types of advertising appeals?

Throughout the years, advertisers have employed numerous advertising approaches. Of these, seven **advertising appeals** have achieved the most success. Normally one of these types of appeals will be featured in an advertisement (see Figure 6.6).

The type of appeal chosen should be based on a review of the creative brief, the objective of the advertisement, and the means–end chain to be conveyed. A number of factors will be considered, including the product being sold, the personal preferences of the advertising creative and the account executive, as well as the wishes of the client. The team also identifies appeals that are *inappropriate*. Advertising experts know that certain appeals are less successful in certain circumstances. For example, sexual appeals are not very effective for items not related to sex. The advertising team tries to ensure that the appeal represents the

FIGURE 6.6 ▶
Advertising Appeals

- Fear
- Humor
- Sex
- Music

- Rationality
- Emotions
- Scarcity

best option for the brand, target audience, and the message, to whatever degree is possible.

FEAR

Advertisements featuring fear appeals are commonplace. Life insurance companies focus on the consequences of not having a life insurance policy when a person dies. Shampoo and mouthwash ads invoke fears of dandruff and bad breath, which can make a person a social outcast. Fear is used more often than most realize.

Advertisers employ fear appeals because they work. Fear increases viewer interest in an advertisement and the ad's persuasiveness. Many individuals remember advertisements with fear appeals better than they do warm, upbeat messages.[7] Consumers who pay more attention to an advertisement are more likely to process the information it presents, which makes it possible to accomplish the advertisement's main objective.

The *behavioral response model* explains the way fear works (see Figure 6.7) in advertising.[8] As shown, various incidents can lead to negative or positive consequences, which then affect future behaviors.

Severity and Vulnerability

In developing fear advertisements, the creative includes as many aspects of the behavioral response model as possible. A business-to-business advertiser offering Internet services tries to focus on the **severity** of downtime if a company's Internet server goes down. Another ad describes the firm's **vulnerability** by showing the high probability that a company's server will crash. The Service Metrics advertisement on the next page features a picture of a blindfolded man ready to step into a manhole to illustrate the danger of e-business pitfalls. The advertisement attempts to cause business leaders to believe their companies may be vulnerable. Service Metrics can help them identify these potential problems before they turn into disasters.

Response Efficacy

To further understand the model, consider a young man who has taken up smoking and sees an ad for the Nicoderm CQ patches, which help a person quit smoking. The man

▲ The visual used in this ad contains visual Esperanto, because the meaning easily transfers across other cultures and nationalities.

5 How can fear be used to create an effective advertisement?

◄ **FIGURE 6.7**
The Behavioral Response Model

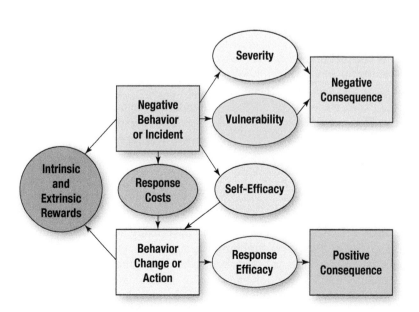

What you can't see about your e-business performance can hurt.

How's your site?

Let Service Metrics™ remove the blindfold. We measure Web site performance from your customer's perspective, revealing potential problems before they become e-business pitfalls. With Service Metrics, you can see exactly where you stand. We don't just help you compete, we give you an unfair advantage.

SERVICE METRICS™
an Exodus Communications Company

The Best Measure of Performance™
www.servicemetrics.com

▲ A fear appeal in a business-to-business advertisement.

considers three things in evaluating the advertisement and making a decision to purchase Nicoderm CQ.

Intrinsic and extrinsic rewards are the first factor. Intrinsic rewards come from gaining social acceptance by quitting and feeling healthier. Extrinsic rewards may include saving on the cost of cigarettes as compared to the price for Nicoderm CQ.

Response costs are the second factor considered. When an individual who smokes gains acceptance by his peers, smoking becomes rewarding and there is less incentive to quit. If smoking creates such intrinsic value, then quitting becomes even more difficult. A man who quits smoking becomes more likely to gain weight and lose the friends who continue to smoke. The higher the perceived costs, the less likely the decision to quit smoking becomes.

Self-efficacy constitutes the third factor. In this situation, self-efficacy relates to the man's confidence in his ability to stop smoking. Many individuals have tried and failed. The smoker must believe that Nicoderm CQ can truly help him quit, giving him the final edge needed.

The combination of intrinsic and extrinsic rewards, response costs, and the degree of self-efficacy contribute to the smoker's *response efficacy*. The decision to purchase Nicoderm CQ with the idea of stopping smoking will be based on the conclusion that doing so will have net positive consequences. The person concludes he will fit in with family and friends, feel better about himself, improve his health, and is capable of quitting smoking.

Appeal Strength

When using fear, another factor will be the strength of the appeal. Most advertisers believe a moderate fear level is most effective. A low level of fear may not be noticed, and the fear level may not be convincing in terms of severity or vulnerability. An advertisement with a fear level that is too strong can also backfire, because the message only generates feelings of anxiety. This leads the viewer to avoid watching the commercial, by changing the channel or muting the sound.[9] Consequently a fear appeal's goal should be to make it powerful enough to capture a viewer's attention and to influence her thinking, but not so scary that she avoids the advertisement.

Fear ads match well with certain types of goods and services, especially products that eliminate problems or threats to a consumer's sense of personal security. Account executives, creatives, and company leaders decide when fear represents a good approach or if some other type of appeal offers greater promise.

HUMOR

6 How can humor be used to create an effective advertisement?

Clutter remains a significant problem in every advertising medium. Capturing a viewer's attention is difficult. Even after grabbing the audience's attention, keeping it becomes even more challenging. Humor has proven to be one of the best techniques for cutting through clutter, by getting attention and keeping it. Consumers, as a whole, enjoy advertisements that make them laugh. Something that is funny has intrusive value and attracts attention.[10]

Humor is used in about 30 percent of television and radio advertisements.[11] Humorous ads often win awards and tend to be favorites among consumers. In a *USA Today* consumer survey of the most likeable advertising campaigns for 2006, humor was a key ingredient.[12]

For 27 years, Anheuser-Busch chose humor to advertise the Bud Light brand. Humorous ads included "Spuds McKenzie," "Yes I am," "I love you man," and "Real Men of Genius." As Bud Light's target market began to grow older, the marketing department decided to attract a new set of younger consumers. The decision was made to depart from humorous commercials and show young consumers that Bud Light was not your dad's beer. The "Drinkability" campaign was born. Sales dropped by 3 percent. It was the first decline in Bud Light's 27-year history. As a result, Anheuser-Busch dropped the "Drinkability" theme for Bud Light and returned to humor.[13]

Humorous ads achieve success for three reasons. Humor causes consumers to: (1) watch, (2) laugh, and, most important, (3) remember. In recall tests, consumers most often remember humorous ads. The best results occur when the humor connects directly with the product's benefits. The advertisement should link the product's features with the advantage to customers and personal values in a means–end chain.

Advantages of Humor

Humorous ads pique viewer interest, which makes gaining consumer consideration of the advertisement's message easier. A funny ad captures the viewer's attention, leading to improved comprehension and recall of the advertising message and tagline. Advertising research indicates that humor elevates people's moods. Happy consumers often associate a good mood with the advertiser's products. In essence, humor helps fix the brand in the consumer's cognitive structure with links to positive feelings.

Problems with Humor

Although a funny advertisement can capture the viewer's attention, cut through clutter, and enhance recall, humorous ads can also go wrong. A Snickers commercial that ran during a recent Super Bowl featured two mechanics eating from opposite ends of the same candy bar until they accidentally ended up kissing. The two men responded in disgust by ripping out their own chest hairs. The outcry for some groups was loud enough that it was immediately pulled.[14]

Advertisers should not allow the humor overpower the message. Humor fails when consumers remember the joke but not the product or brand. In other words, the advertisement was so funny that the audience forgets or does not catch the sponsor's name. Humorous advertisements can also fail in terms of accomplishing advertising objectives.

To avoid these problems, the humor used in an advertisement should focus on a component of the means–end chain. The humor should relate either to a product's attributes, a customer benefit, or the personal value obtained from the product. The most effective ads are those in which the humor incorporates all three elements.

International Usage

Some evidence suggests that humor is universal; however, there are particular executions of humor that may not be. Forms of humor are often rooted in various cultures, yet humor may not transfer from one culture to another. Not all audiences experience a humorous ad in the same way. Advertisers should pretest commercials before they are launched in other countries to ensure the message will be liked and will be considered funny rather than offensive.

Humor ads appear in a number of countries. A humorous ad developed for McDonald's in Singapore had the highest recall rate (90 percent) of all other commercials released during the month it ran. In Germany, Ford deviated from traditional ads that concentrated on promoting product quality and value to humor. One advertisement features a pigeon sitting on tree branch with a Ford Ka parked nearby. The bird swoops down to bomb the car, but at the last minute the car hood springs up and knocks the bird out. The advertisement was first shown on Ford's U.K. Web site. Word about the ad quickly spread until more than 1 million people had visited the Web site to see the ad. German dealers

FIGURE 6.8 ▶
Reasons for Using Humor in Ads

- Captures attention.
- Holds attention.
- Often wins creative awards.
- High recall scores.
- Consumers enjoy ads that make them laugh.
- Evaluated by consumers as likeable ads.

requested the ad so they could show it on television. The feedback and popularity of the ad in the United Kingdom caused Ford's marketing managers to agree to run the ad in Germany. The ad resonated with young, affluent buyers, which Ford had been trying to reach. The new ad was seen as witty, gutsy, and edgy, which worked well with Ford's theme of projecting the Ka as a stylish car.[15]

Humorous ads can be difficult to design. One cynic once noted that there are only 12 funny people in the United States. Humor that doesn't work often creates a negative image for the company. Humor that does work can bring great success to a company and provide great dividends in terms of brand equity. Figure 6.8 summarizes the major reasons for using humor.

7 Why does sex play such a prominent role in advertising?

▼ An advertisement for Old Orchard featuring a sensuality appeal.

SEX

Sexual appeals are often used to break through clutter. Advertisements in the United States and other countries contain more visual sexual themes than ever. Nudity and other sexual approaches are common. Sexual themes in ads, however, do not sell the way they used to. Sex no longer has shock value. Today's teens grow up in societies immersed in sex. One more sexually oriented ad captures little attention. Currently, many advertisers are shifting to more subtle sexual cues, suggestions, and innuendos.[16] Sexuality has been employed in advertising in the five ways listed in Figure 6.9.

Forever on the lips, never on the hips.

Exceptionally great taste – with 75% less carbs, calories and sugar. Introducing Old Orchard LoCarb juice cocktails – nine delicious blends sweetened with Splenda® no-calorie sweetener – the perfect juice for a low-carb, low-sugar lifestyle.

www.oldorchardjuice.com **ORCHARD** We make apple interesting.™

Subliminal Approaches

Placing sexual cues or icons in advertisements in an attempt to affect a viewer's subconscious is the subliminal approach. In an odd paradox, truly subliminal cues are not noticed, which means they do not create any effects. Consumers pay little attention to ads already. A subliminal message that registers only in the viewer's subconscious does not work. If it did, there would be no need for stronger sexual content in advertising.

Sensuality

Many women respond more favorably to a sensual suggestion than an overtly sexual approach. An alluring glance across a crowded room can be sensual and draw attention to a product. Many view sensuality as being more sophisticated, because it relies on the imagination. Images of romance and love can be more enticing than raw sexuality.

Sexual Suggestiveness

A sexually suggestive advertisement hints that sex is about to take place. The Bijan advertisement in this section features Bo Derek. The ad states, "Bo Derek is wearing Bijan Eau de Parfum and nothing else," a sexually suggestive message.

FIGURE 6.9 ▶
Sexuality Approaches Used in Advertisements

- Subliminal techniques
- Sensuality
- Sexual suggestiveness
- Nudity or partial nudity
- Overt sexuality

Recently, Pine-Sol used suggestiveness to advertise a household cleaner. In several television ads, shirtless, muscular men are shown mopping the floor while the female watches or fantasizes. Diane Amos, who has been featured in Pine-Sol ads for the last 16 years and also appears in this new series of ads featuring men, says "We would all like our husbands to mop. . . . It can be fun, it can be sexy, and women like it clean."[17]

Nudity or Partial Nudity

Products that have sexual connotations, such as clothing, perfume, and cologne, may feature a degree of nudity. Some ads are designed to solicit a sexual response. Others are not. In 1987, underwear companies were first allowed to use live models in television advertisements. The first commercials were modest and informational, emphasizing the design or materials used in the undergarment. The first Playtex bra commercials using live models drew strong criticism from organizations such as the American Family Association. Currently, advertisements for undergarments go much further and involve superstars, such as actress Jennifer Love Hewitt who appeared in television and print ads for the Hanes All-Over Comfort bra and the Perfect Panty. The campaign even included an online element with footage from the photo shoots, a "bad bra toss" game, and a blog about bad bra moments.[18]

Decorative Models

A common sexual approach in advertising is to place **decorative models**, or individuals in advertisements to adorn products as a sexual or attractive stimuli. The models serve no

▲ A Bijan perfume advertisement using the sexual suggestiveness approach.

▲ An advertisement for Benetton featuring partial nudity.

FIGURE 6.10 ▶

Factors to Consider
Before Using
Decorative Models

- The presence of female (or male) decorative models improves ad recognition, but not brand recognition.
- The presence of a decorative model influences emotional and objective evaluations of the product among both male and female audiences.
- Attractive models produce a higher level of attention to ads than do less attractive models.
- The presence of an attractive model produces higher purchase intentions when the product is sexually relevant than if it is not sexually relevant.

other purpose than to attract attention. In the past, commercials for automobiles, tools, and beer often used female models dressed in bikinis standing by the products. A number of studies were conducted to determine how effective decorative models are. The basic conclusions are listed in Figure 6.10.[19]

Overt Sexuality

Using overt sexuality in ads for sexually oriented products is normally accepted, but it often becomes controversial when used for other types of products. When Procter & Gamble launched a television advertising campaign for Dentyne, eyebrows were raised. The commercial showed two teens in a living room. The girl pops a piece of Dentyne Fire bubble gum into her mouth and then rips off her blouse and jumps on her boyfriend. At first the parents stare in shock. Then, the mom tries a piece of Dentyne Fire and promptly jumps on the dad. The controversy centered on whether the ad promoted teenage sexuality by suggesting that parents should openly display sexual feelings and desires.[20]

▼ A Guess advertisement with a male and a female model.

Source: Courtesy of Guess?, Inc.

Are Sex Appeals Effective?

Numerous studies have examined the effectiveness of sexual appeals and nudity in advertising. Almost all of them conclude that sex and nudity do increase attention, regardless of the gender of the person in the advertisement or the gender of the audience. Normally, the attention is greater for opposite-sex situations than same-sex situations, for both males and females viewing the opposite gender. To encourage both genders to pay attention to its ads, Guess often features a male and female in a sexually provocative setting in an advertisement.

Attracting Attention

Although sexually oriented ads attract attention, brand recall for ads using a sex appeal is lower than those using other types of appeals. It appears that although people watch the advertisement, the sexual theme distracts them from noticing the brand name.[21]

Sexually oriented advertisements are often rated as more interesting. Those ads deemed to be highly controversial in terms of sexual content are rated as more interesting by both males and females. The paradox, however, is that although the controversial ads are more interesting, they fail to increase the transmission of information. Respondents are less likely to remember any more about the message.[22]

Physiological Arousal

Advertisements using overt sexual stimuli or containing nudity produce higher levels of physiological arousal responses. These arousal responses have been linked to the formation of both affective and cognitive responses. If the viewer is male and the sexual stimulus is female, such as a nude female in an ad for cologne, then the viewer tends to develop a strong feeling toward the ad based on the arousal response his body experiences. Female viewers of male nudity in an advertisement often experience the same type of response, although the arousal response may not be as strong.

Cognitive Impressions

The cognitive impression made on viewers of a sexually oriented ad depends on whether the viewer feels the advertisement is pleasant or offensive. When the viewer likes the ad, it results in a positive impression of the brand. When the viewer thinks the ad is in poor taste, negative feelings and beliefs about the brand often emerge. When sex works, it increases sales. An ad that does not may inspire negative feelings toward the brand.[23]

Societal Trends

In determining the level of sex appeal to feature in an advertisement, the advertising team considers society's view and level of acceptance.[24] Just as economies go through cycles, attitudes toward sex in advertising experience acceptance fluctuate.

The use and acceptance of sexual themes in advertising had swung to a high level of tolerance in the early part of the 2000s, until the Super Bowl of 2004. The public reaction to Janet Jackson's breast-baring halftime show sent ripples all the way to Madison Avenue. Shortly afterward, Victoria's Secret dropped its TV lingerie fashion show. Abercrombie & Fitch killed the company's quarterly catalog, which had been strongly criticized for featuring models in sexually suggestive poses. Anheuser-Busch dropped some of its risqué ads.[25] The trend continued into the next year. When ads for Super Bowl 2005 were unveiled, few used sexual appeals.

The pendulum may now be slowly swinging back toward greater acceptance of sexually oriented ads, but it has not reached the pre-2004 level yet. A recent Calvin Klein ad featuring actress Eva Mendes in the nude in a provocative pose for its Secret Obsession fragrance was rejected by the major networks in the United States, but accepted by television stations in Europe. A less-provocative version had to be created for the United States, and it was not shown until after 9:00 P.M.[26]

The use of sex in advertising will continue. Advertisers should carefully determine the level and the type of sexuality to use and the target audience. What will work at one particular point in time may not work at another.

Disadvantages of Sex Appeals

One major criticism of sexually based advertising is that it perpetuates dissatisfaction with one's body. Females in print advertisements and models in television advertising are often thin. The key to success seems to be the thinner the better. As advertising models have gotten thinner, body dissatisfaction and eating disorders among women have risen. Research indicates that women feel unhappy about their own bodies and believe they are too fat after viewing advertisements showing thin models. Still, ads with thin models are more likely to convince women to purchase a product.[27]

Thin male models have an effect on men, but in reverse. Many men worry they are not muscular enough and are too thin or too fat. It does not make any difference whether the male is viewing a male model or a female model in advertisements.[28]

▼ An advertisement for Stetson directed to women using a sex appeal.

Source: Courtesy of J.B. Stetson Company.

Some companies have begun to feature real women of different shapes and sizes, such as Dove's "Campaign for Real Beauty." The campaign has garnered international attention, won several major advertising awards, and achieved a healthy growth in sales. The approach struck a responsive chord with many women.

Sex Appeals in International Advertising

What is deemed appropriate or acceptable in terms of sexual appeal varies across countries. In Chile, a campaign featuring nude celebrities touting the benefits of drinking milk was launched. The ad's producers stated, "Chile is a country of stuffed shirts, so this campaign is going to shake them up, and at a relatively low cost, thanks to nudity." The Chilean Dairy Federation believed that the ads would promote the idea of rebellion to Chilean youth. As more Chilean kids travel the world and see teens with green and blue hair and body piercings, public nudity will become more associated with freedom. Despite opposition by conservatives, the "naked" milk campaign aroused the attention of Chilean young people, and milk sales grew.[29]

Religions, cultures, and value systems determine the levels of nudity, sexual references, and gender-specific issues that are permitted in a country. Muslim nations tend to reject any kind of nudity and any reference to sexuality and other gender-related issues. They also do not permit any type of advertising for personal goods, such as female hygiene products, contraceptives, or undergarments. Any hint of sexuality or display of the female body is strictly forbidden.

In many Middle Eastern countries, sex and gender issues are taboo subjects. Sexual appeals are not used in advertising, and even sexually related products are difficult to advertise. In response, Procter & Gamble hosted a call-in TV show directed toward young girls in Egypt. The show's panel contained health experts, and topics ranged from marriage to menopause. The call-in show was followed up with a TV talk show called *Frankly Speaking* about feminine hygiene. The goal of the show was to tackle some of the more sensitive issues facing young Egyptian girls. Although the show discussed what happens during puberty, it was P&G's policy not to discuss sexuality. P&G sponsored the show and the primary product advertised was P&G's Always feminine sanitary pads.[30]

In other countries, standards regarding sexually oriented advertising are more permissive but sometimes confusing. In France, sex is everywhere. Advertisers can feature seminude or completely nude models in advertisements if they can be justified; a relationship must exist between the product and the nude model. It does not take much of a justification in France, where sex is viewed as healthy, innocent, and natural. One difference in France, however, is that sex and humor are not mixed. The French do not see sex as silly or funny.[31]

The problem with the stereotyping of females in ads takes a different twist in other countries. For example, in Saudi Arabia and Malaysia women must be shown in family settings. They cannot be depicted as being carefree or desirable to the opposite sex.[32]

In general, the use of sex to make products more appealing is a legitimate tactic for many companies, products, and advertising firms. The goal should be to use sex in an interesting manner that is germane to the product, and within the ethical standards of the region.

▼ An example of an effective sexual appeal promoting milk.

I'm here in the middle of Times Square to show off my best feature. My bones. What's my secret? Milk. It helps give bones the calcium they need to stay strong. And since they grow until about age 35, I'd say that's news worth putting on display.

got milk?

From there, taste and other more personalized standards serve as guides. The U.S. milk industry advertisement shown in this section has been very effective. Although the model is wearing a swimsuit, it is germane to the product. The advertisement seeks to persuade women that milk not only is good for healthy bones, but that it also enhances one's appearance. By telling women that bones continue to develop until the age of 35, the ad reinforces a reason to consume milk.

MUSICAL APPEALS

Music can be an extremely important advertising ingredient. It connects with emotions, memories, and other experiences. Music can be intrusive; it gains the attention of someone who previously was not listening to or watching a program. It may provide the stimulus that ties a particular musical arrangement, jingle, or song to a certain product or brand. As soon as the tune begins, consumers know what product is being advertised because they have been conditioned to tie the product to the music. For example, the Intel "tune" is widely recognized by numerous consumers.

Music gains attention and increases the retention of information when it becomes strongly intertwined with the product. Even when consumers do not recall the ad message argument, music can lead to a better recall of an advertisement's visual and emotional aspects. Music can also increase the persuasiveness of an argument. Subjects who compared ads with music to identical ads without music almost always rated those with music higher in terms of persuasiveness.[33]

Musical memories are often stored in long-term recall areas of the brain. Most people can remember tunes even from their childhood. Figure 6.11 lists some popular songs now being used in commercials. Several decisions are made when selecting music for commercials, including the following:

- What role will music play in the ad?
- Will a familiar song be used, or will something original be created?
- What emotional pitch should the music reach?
- How does the music fit with the message of the ad?

Music plays a variety of roles in advertisements. Sometimes the music is incidental. In others, it becomes the primary theme. An important decision involves selecting a familiar tune as opposed to creating original music. Writing a jingle or music specifically for the advertisement occurs more often. Background or mood-inducing music is usually instrumental, and advertisers often pay musicians to write music that matches the scenes in the ad.

An alternative method used by some advertising agencies is to send the creative brief to interested musicians and ask them to compose and pitch a song. The mcgarrybowen advertising agency used the approach when selecting a song for the new Oscar Mayer campaign. The creative brief was sent to approximately 60 musicians. Each was asked to compose a song he or she felt expressed the emotions conveyed in the brief. Both the Oscar Mayer marketing team and mcgarrybowen decided that the song "It Doesn't Get Better Than This" composed and sung by Joy Williams best brought the emotions of the new Oscar Mayer campaign to life.

8 How can music, rationality, and scarcity be used to increase advertising effectiveness?

- "Revolution" by Beatles (Nike)
- "Real Love" by John Lennon (JCPenney)
- "We're All in This Together" by Ben Lee (Kohl's)
- "Hush" by Deep Purple (Jaguar)
- "Just Fine" by Mary J. Blige (Chevrolet)
- "I'm in the Mood for Love" by Brenda Lee (Victoria's Secret)
- "Thriller" by Michael Jackson (Sobe)
- "Da Ya Think I'm Sexy?" by Rod Stewart (Chips Ahoy)
- "Eyes on Me" by Celine Dion (Celine Dion Sensational)

◄ **FIGURE 6.11**
Popular Songs Used in Ads

Who needs bread?

Our Deli Fresh meats are sliced, packed, and sealed at the peak of freshness. So they're great in a sandwich or just by themselves.

it doesn't get better than this

▲ The song "It Doesn't Get Better Than This" was written and sung by Joy Williams for the television ads in the Oscar Mayer campaign.

Advantages of Musical Appeals

Using a well-known song in an advertisement creates certain advantages. The primary benefit is that consumers already have developed an affinity for the song. Brand awareness, brand equity, and brand loyalty become easier to develop when consumers are familiar with the music. This occurs when consumers transfer an emotional affinity for the song to the product. One variation is to purchase an existing song and adapt the ad to the music.[34] Using popular songs may be expensive. The price for the rights to a very popular song can be in the range of six to seven figures.[35] The Internet company Excite paid $7 million for the rights to Jimi Hendrix's song "Are You Experienced," and Microsoft paid about $12 million for "Start Me Up."[36]

Alternate Methods

An alternative method of developing music has emerged, primarily because of the Internet. More cooperation now exists between musicians and marketers. Some musicians view advertisements as a way to get their songs heard. Marketers see an opportunity to tie a new, exciting song to a product. Many consumers are also interested in finding out who performs the music in various ads. The Internet provides the opportunity not only to find out, but also to post it for others to enjoy on sites such as YouTube. When an ad only contains part of the song, many firms place entire tuned on company Web sites or on YouTube so that individuals can download them.

Occasionally, a song written for a commercial will crack Billboard's Top 100 list. Jason Wade, a singer in the band Lifehouse, had never written a song for a commercial before. After viewing a copy of the 60-second commercial for Allstate Insurance produced by Leo Burnett Agency, Wade wrote a song entitled "From Where You Are." The commercial promoted Allstate's safe-driving program for teenagers. After the commercial aired, the song was made available on iTunes. Within 2 weeks, sales were high enough for the song to reach number 40 on Billboard's charts.[37]

RATIONAL APPEALS

A rational appeal follows the hierarchy of effects stages of awareness, knowledge, liking, preference, conviction, and purchase. A creative designs the advertisement for one of the six steps. An ad oriented to the knowledge stage transmits basic product information. In the preference stage, the message shifts to presenting logical reasons that favor the brand, such as the superior gas mileage of an automobile. A rational advertisement should lead to a stronger conviction about a product's benefits, so that the purchase eventually will be made.

Rational appeals rely on consumers actively processing the information presented in the advertisement. The consumer must pay attention to the commercial, comprehend the message, and compare the message to knowledge embedded in a cognitive map. Messages consistent with the current concepts in the cognitive map strengthen key linkages. New messages help the person form cognitive beliefs about the brand and establish a new linkage from her current map to the new product.

A business customer who sees a Kinko's advertisement about videoconferencing services already may have the company in his cognitive structure. The customer may have used Kinko's in the past but was not aware that the company offers videoconferencing.

When Kinko's has been established in this person's cognitive map, creating a new linkage to entice the customer to try its videoconferencing services becomes easier.

Media Outlets

Print media and the Internet offer the best outlets for rational appeals. Print and Internet ads allow readers greater opportunities to process copy information. They can pause and take time to think about the written content. Television and radio commercials are short, which makes it difficult for viewers to process message arguments. Also, if television viewers miss a television commercial they do not have the opportunity to see it until the ad is broadcast again.

Business-to-Business

Print media are used extensively for business-to-business messages. These advertisers take advantage of print's ability to feature rational appeals. Many advertising account executives believe trade publications are the best way to reach members of the buying center. Those in the industry read trade publications carefully. Placing an advertisement in a trade publication means the firm has an excellent chance of hitting its primary target market. Further, trade publications allow advertisers the opportunity to convey more details to potential buyers.

Buying center members who scan trade journals while in the information search stage of the buying process are likely to notice the ad, read it, and process the information. Buying center members who are not looking for information about the particular product will probably ignore the same ad. Magazines do not have intrusion value and readers can easily skip or ignore an advertisement. A rational appeal usually presents a primary appeal with no strong peripheral cues to attract the reader's attention.

Product Attributes

Conventional advertising wisdom suggests that rational appeals are well suited for high-involvement and complex products. High-involvement decisions require considerable cognitive activity, and consumers spend more time evaluating the attributes of the individual brands. Thus, a rational appeal should be the best approach to reach them. For some consumers, however, emotions and feelings even influence high-involvement decisions. For instance, life insurance involves both rational and emotional elements. Various insurance companies can use both in seeking to influence consumers.

In general, rational appeals are effective when consumers have high levels of involvement and are willing to pay attention to the advertisement. Message arguments and product information should be placed in the copy. Consumers can then more fully absorb information.

A rational appeal is superior to other appeals in developing or changing attitudes and establishing brand beliefs. This will be mainly true when a consumer has a particular interest in the product or brand. Otherwise, the consumer often ignores an ad using a rational appeal.

EMOTIONAL APPEALS

Emotional appeals are based on three ideas (see Figure 6.12). First, consumers ignore most advertisements. Second, rational appeals go unnoticed unless the consumer is in the market for a particular product at the time it is advertised. Third, and most important, emotional advertising can capture a viewer's attention and create an attachment between the consumer and the brand.

- Consumers ignore most ads.
- Rational appeals generally go unnoticed.
- Emotional appeals can capture attention and foster an attachment.

◀ **FIGURE 6.12**
Reasons for Using Emotional Appeals

Ever been to the intersection of
ROAD TRIP WITH THE GIRLS and
**ALL THAT MONEY I BROUGHT TO VEGAS
STAYED IN VEGAS?**

I'M THERE

We can't help you win at blackjack,

but we can help you make up for some of your losses.

You can save an average of $369*

just by letting State Farm®

take care of your auto insurance.

Call, click or visit a State Farm Agent now and

get a quote, because **Like a good neighbor,**

State Farm is there.

State Farm.
statefarm.com®

▲ An advertisement for State
Farm with an emotional appeal.

Brand Loyalty

Most creatives view emotional advertising as the key to brand loyalty. Creatives want customers to experience a bond with the brand. Visual cues in advertisements are important in emotional appeals. The visual elements of the New Balance ad on the next page contribute to a feeling or mood of serenity. Also, peripheral cues, such as the music and the actor, are crucial. Although individuals develop perceptions of brands based largely on visual and peripheral stimuli, it does not happen instantly. With repetition, perceptions and attitudinal changes emerge. Figure 6.13 displays some of the more common emotions presented in advertisements.

Godiva used an emotional appeal in its latest advertising campaign entitled "the golden moment." Created by Lipman Agency, the campaign focused on the emotional appeal of giving, sharing, or eating Godiva chocolates. According to Laurie Len Kotcher (Chief Marketing Officer and Senior Vice-President for Global Brand Development of Godiva Chocolatier), "When you give the gold box, receive the gold box, eating something from the gold box, there is something special about that moment."[38]

Business-to-Business

Emotional appeals are being used more frequently in business-to-business advertising. In the past, only 5 to 10 percent of all business-to-business ads featured emotional appeals. Today, the figure has risen to nearly 25 percent. A magazine advertisement created by NKH&W Advertising Agency for a product to treat racehorses switched from a rational appeal to an emotional appeal. The target market was veterinarians. In the past, an advertisement would have opened with such ad copy as "For swelling in joints use . . ." The emotional ad shows the horse thinking, "I will prove them wrong. I will run again. I will mend my spirits."[39]

The underlying principle for changing to more emotional business-to-business ads is that emotions can be part of every type of purchase decision. Members of the buying center consider product information in making decisions but, at the same time, they are likely to be affected by emotions. Although a member of the buying center may try to minimize the emotional side of a purchase, the person is still likely to be affected. The affective component of attitudes is just as important as the cognitive component. In the past, business-to-business advertisers tended to ignore the affective element.

FIGURE 6.13 ▶
Emotions Used in
Advertisements

● Trust	● Protecting loved ones
● Reliability	● Romance
● Friendship	● Passion
● Happiness	● Family bonds
● Security	● with parents
● Glamour–luxury	● with siblings
● Serenity	● with children
● Anger	● with extended family members

Media Outlets

Television remains one of the best media for emotional appeals. Television offers advertisers intrusion value and can utilize both sound and sight. Models in the ads can be "real people." Facial expressions convey emotions and attitudes. Consumers learn about a particular product and develop attitudes based on these experiences. Television ads also are more vivid, more lifelike, and often create dynamic situations that pull viewers in. Music can be incorporated to make the commercial more dramatic. Peripheral cues are important components of emotional appeals. The cues (such as music and background visuals) also capture the viewer's attention.

Emotional ads are widely featured on the Internet. Many of the same benefits for television are found online. The use of streaming video, animation, and software such as Photoshop make it possible to create engaging emotional ads.

Emotions are tied with humor, fear, music, and other appeals to make a compelling case for a product. The same ad can influence a consumer both emotionally and rationally. The creative selects the most appropriate emotional appeal for the product and company.

I trade sweat for strength.

I trade sleep for sunrises.

I trade doubt for belief.

I trade my walking for nothing.

achieve new balance

Source: Courtesy of New Balance Athletic Shoes Inc. Photographed by Paul Wakefield.

▲ New Balance uses visual elements in this advertisement to create an emotional appeal of serenity and peace.

SCARCITY APPEALS

Scarcity appeals urge consumers to buy a particular product because of a limitation. It can be a limited number of the products available or, more often, that the product will be made available for only a limited time. When there is a limited supply of a product, the perceived value of the product may increase. For the Olympics, General Mills introduced USA Olympic Crunch cereal and Betty Crocker Team USA desserts for a limited time.[40] McDonald's, Wendy's, and Burger King offer sandwiches (McRib, Hot N' Spicy Chicken, Dollar Whoppers) for limited-time periods throughout the year. The scarcity concept is also used for musical compilations, encouraging consumers to buy a CD because of its limited availability. By making sure it is not available in retail stores, marketers increase its scarcity value.

A scarcity appeal may be tied to other promotional tools. For example, a manufacturer will advertise a limited price discount offer to retailers who stock up early for Christmas or some other holiday season. Contests and sweepstakes also run for limited times. Encouraging consumers to take action is the primary benefit of a scarcity appeal. Creatives normally receive information about scarcity issues in the creative brief or from the account executive who has consulted with the company.

INTERNATIONAL IMPLICATIONS

Many of the international implications of both advertising theory and the various types of appeals have already been described in this chapter. In summary, leverage points lead to customer values. These values may be influenced by the culture or country in which the consumer lives. Therefore, advertisements should be constructed in ways that express those values.

Advertising appeals should be adapted to cultural differences. As a small example, fear of body odor often sells products in the United States. In other cultures, body odor does not carry the same meaning. Sexual appeals, as noted, must be adjusted to fit the

9 What are the primary areas of concern in international advertising?

!INTEGRATED CAMPAIGNS IN ACTION

Philadelphia Cream Cheese

Sales of Philadelphia Cream Cheese had been stagnant for several years, because most United States consumers only use the product to spread on bagels or as the main ingredient in cheesecake. In other countries, cream cheese is viewed as a more general product that can be spread on crackers, bread, and in cooking other items. Consequently, the opportunity exists to increase U.S. Philadelphia Cream Cheese consumption by suggesting new uses for the product.

To spur sales in the United States, Kraft Vice-President of Marketing Howard Friedman worked with the advertising agency mcgarrybowen to create a new campaign. The primary thrust of the campaign was to expand usage of the product and to increase the buy rate among medium and low users of cream cheese. mcgarrybowen designed a series of ads using an emotion appeal. Television, video, print, and digital ads were produced.

The campaign focused on two target markets: (1) women aged 25 to 44 with some college, incomes over $45,000, and low-skill cooking ability and (2) women older than age 45 with some college, incomes over $75,000, and high-skill cooking ability. In addition to the print and broadcast ads, the campaign focused on providing recipes online submitted by consumers through a contest entitled "Real Women of Philly." The grand prize was $125,000 and an appearance on television on a cooking show.

Your instructor has additional information about the ads, visuals, and displays used in this campaign.

▲ An advertisement for Philadelphia Cream Cheese developed by the mcgarrybowen agency.

laws and customs of a region. Musical tastes vary, as do perceptions of rationality and scarcity. Emotions may be stronger in some cultures, whereas in others people are much more reserved.

An international company or a firm seeking to expand into additional countries should adapt and adjust both the theoretical approach and type of appeal in order to create effective advertisements. Finding universal themes, such as visual Esperanto, may be a great help to the international advertising creative.

66 SUMMARY

Developing effective advertisements represents a key ingredient in integrated marketing communications efforts. The advertising team should define the objective of the ad, the target audience, the message theme used, the type of support needed, and any constraints that apply. Then, a creative works within the context of key advertising theories in selecting the correct media and designing the leverage point and message appeal that work effectively within each medium.

Three important theoretical approaches drive the development of many advertisements. The hierarchy of effects model suggests consumers move through a series of stages as they are persuaded to make a purchase: (1) awareness, (2) knowledge, (3) liking, (4) preference, (5) conviction, and (6) the actual purchase. Although the process probably is not a lock-step model that every buyer follows, the hierarchy of effects approach does provide important information about which mental issues to account for in various advertising campaigns. The hierarchy of effects model can be combined with the three main elements present in attitudes: (1) cognitive, (2) affective, and (3) conative components. Ads are designed to influence affective feelings, cognitive knowledge, or conative intentions to act or behave based on an attitude. A means–end chain displays the linkages between a means to achieve a desired state and the end or personal value at issue. Advertisers can select personal values that mesh with the key characteristics of the target market and then construct ads designed to provide them the means to achieve these ends by purchasing the good or service. These ideas help the creative develop a leverage point to move the buyer from understanding the product's benefits to incorporating those benefits with his or her personal values.

Visual and verbal issues should also be considered in the formation of an ad. Concrete visual images are easily recognized and recalled. Abstract images may be linked with values or emotions the product creates or the feeling the buyer should experience that may be associated with the product or company. Visual elements are key components in almost every form of advertising. Verbal elements must reach the more rational, central route of the audience's mental processing procedures.

Beyond these components, advertising creatives must form messages using one (or more) of the seven major appeals: (1) fear, (2) humor, (3) sex, (4) music, (5) rationality, (6) emotions, or (7) scarcity. Just as there are logical combinations of media, there are logical combinations of these appeals for various messages. Often, music provides the backdrop for messages invoking fear, humor, sex, and emotions. Humor can be linked with sex, music, rationality (by showing how being illogical is silly or funny), and scarcity. Rationality combines with fear in many commercials. Designing a message argument that takes advantage of the various characteristics of these appeals breaks through clutter, and convinces the audience to buy the item involved will be the creative's goal. Mismatches of message tactics are to be avoided, such as combining sex with humor in France, as was mentioned earlier.

Business-to-business ads often appear in print and many times include rational approaches in the copy because the purchase decision variables are more complex. At the same time, many advertisers have recently discovered that emotional ads can be effective, which expands business-to-business advertising into other venues, such as television, radio, and the Internet.

The process of designing ads for international markets is quite similar to that for domestic ads. The major difference is careful consideration of local attitudes and customers, with due care given to the language, slang, and symbols of the area. For example, Sega recently discovered that its product's name is slang for "masturbation" in Italian, after a major advertising campaign had started. These types of mistakes are to be avoided.

KEY TERMS

hierarchy of effects model   A marketing approach suggesting that a consumer moves through a series of six steps when becoming convinced to make a purchase: (1) awareness, (2) knowledge, (3) liking, (4) preference, (5) conviction, and (6) the actual purchase.

means–end chain   An advertising approach in which the message contains a means (a reasoning or mental process) to lead the consumer to a desired end state, such as a key personal value.

Means–End Conceptualization of Components for Advertising Strategy (MECCAS)   An advertising approach that suggests using five elements in creating ads: (1) the product's attributes, (2) consumer benefits, (3) leverage points, (4) personal values, and (5) the executional framework.

tagline   A catchy, easy-to-remember phrase in an ad used to make the key point and reinforce the company's image to the consumer.

visual Esperanto   A universal language that makes global advertising possible for any good or service by recognizing that visual images are more powerful than verbal descriptions.

advertising appeals   Approaches to reaching consumers with ads. The seven major appeals are: (1) fear, (2) humor, (3) sex, (4) music, (5) rationality, (6) emotions, and (7) scarcity.

severity   Part of the fear behavioral response model that leads the individual to consider how strong certain negative consequences of an action will be.

vulnerability   Part of the fear behavioral response model that leads the individual to consider the odds of being affected by the negative consequences of an action.

decorative models   Models in an advertisement whose primary purpose is to adorn the product as a sexual or attractive stimulus without serving a functional purpose.

REVIEW QUESTIONS

1. What are the five main elements of a creative brief? How do they affect the choice of advertising appeals?

2. What are the six stages of the hierarchy of effects model? Do they always occur in that order? Why or why not?

3. How are the three components of attitude related to the hierarchy of effects model?

4. In a means–end chain, what are the means? The ends? How do they affect advertising design?

5. What is a leverage point? How are leverage points related to the hierarchy of effects model, attitudinal changes, and means–end chains?

6. What is a tagline?

7. Why are visual elements in advertisement important? What is the relationship between visual and verbal elements? Can there be one without the other?

8. What is visual Esperanto?

9. What are the seven most common types of advertising appeals?

10. What are the advantages and disadvantages of fear appeals in advertising?

11. When does humor work in an ad? What pitfalls should companies avoid in using humorous appeals?

12. What types of sexual appeals can advertisers use?

13. When are sexual appeals most likely to succeed? To fail?

14. What should international advertisers consider when thinking about using sexual appeals?

15. Name the different ways music can play a role in an advertisement. Explain how each role should match individual appeals, media, and other elements in the design of the ad.

16. What are the advantages and disadvantages of rational appeals? Which media do they best match?

17. How can emotions accentuate advertisements? Why are they being used more often in business-to-business advertisements?

18. What is scarcity? How do scarcity ads lead to buyer action?

CRITICAL THINKING EXERCISES

Discussion Questions

1. Develop a means–end chain similar to the one in Figure 6.3 for each of the following branded products:

   a. Benetton clothes

   b. Stetson cologne

   c. New Balance shoes

   d. Oscar Mayer deli meats

2. Evaluate the balance of visual and verbal elements of five advertisements shown in this chapter. Which is predominant? Which images are considered appropriate for international advertising because they display visual Esperanto characteristics?

3. Watch one of your favorite television shows. Record all of the television commercials in one commercial break (at least seven ads). Identify the appeal used in each one. Were the ads effective? Why or why not?

4. Locate a print ad or television ad that features a fear appeal. Using the behavioral response model in Figure 6.7, identify various elements in the ad that correspond with the components in the model. Some of the elements will require thinking beyond what is visually or verbally present in the ad itself.

5. Hardee's and Carl's Jr. recently used a television commercial featuring a schoolteacher dancing on top of her desk while a room full of guys performed a rap song entitled "I Like Flat Buns." The song seemed appropriate because the ad was for the Patty Melt on a flat bun. Instead, the ad received considerable flack because the sexy blonde schoolteacher was wearing a short, tight skirt. Teachers' associations complained that it was inappropriate because it was a "sexually exploitive assault" on teachers, students, and schools.[41] Do you agree or disagree?

6. Using magazines that you normally read, locate at least one print ad for each of the appeals except music. Discuss the quality of each advertisement and its best and worst aspects. For each ad, present another possible appeal and how it could be used. What personal values and customer benefits does each advertisement present?

7. Locate five television commercials or find five print advertisements that use sex appeals. Identify which of the five ways sexuality was used. Evaluate each ad in terms of the appropriateness and effectiveness of the sex appeal.

8. For each of the following products and target markets, discuss which appeal you think would be the best. Explain why you think it would be effective. Briefly describe a print or television ad that you think would be effective.

   a. Senior citizens—soup

   b. Females, ages 25–40, with children—hot dogs

   c. College students—jeans

   d. Males, ages 25–40, married with children—life insurance

INTEGRATED LEARNING EXERCISES

1. Greenfield Online is one of the leading online research firms. Access the Web site at **www.greenfield central.com**. What types of products does the company offer? How would this information help a creative in developing an advertisement for Greenfield Online? How would this information assist an advertising agency in understanding the target audience for an advertisement?

2. Examine Figure 6.3 and then access the following Web sites for the milk industry. What differences do you see in the Web sites? Who do you believe is the intended audience for each Web site?

   a. **www.gotmilk.com**

   b. **www.whymilk.com**

   c. **www.bodybymilk.com**

3. Visit the following Web sites. Identify which type of appeal each site uses. Evaluate the quality of that appeal. What other appeals can be used to make the site more appealing? Discuss the balance of visual and verbal elements on the Web site and ad.

   a. Service Metrics (**www.servicemetrics.com**)

   b. Hyundai Motors, USA (**www.hyundaiusa.com**)

   c. Skechers (**www.skechers.com**)

   d. Bijan Fragrances (**www.bijan.com**)

   e. Guess (**www.guess.com**)

   f. Oscar Mayer (**www.oscarmayer.com**)

   g. Liz Claiborne (**www.lizclaiborne.com**)

4. Access an online database search engine through your library. Pick one of the appeals listed in the chapter. Find at least three different articles that discuss the appeal. Write a report based on your findings.

STUDENT PROJECT

Creative Corner

It is time to try your creativity with a television advertisement. Borrow a camcorder and develop a 30- or 45-second television spot for one of the following products, using the suggested appeal. Be sure to develop a means–end chain prior to creating the advertisement. If you do not have access to a camcorder, then develop a magazine ad.

a. Denim skirt, sex appeal

b. Tennis racket, humor appeal

c. Ice cream, emotional appeal

d. Vitamins, fear appeal

e. Golf club, rational appeal

f. Spring break trip package, scarcity appeal

g. Restaurant, music appeal

CASE 1   ECKO ENTERPRISES

It is a safe bet to guess that the majority of people over 40 years old have not heard of Marc Ecko or Ecko Enterprises. He was born as Marc Milecofsky and grew up south of New York City in Lakewood, New Jersey. His parents were real estate agents. Ecko has two sisters, one of whom is his twin, Marci. The name Ecko is the result of a family story. When Ecko's mother was pregnant with Marci, the doctor informed her of an "echo" on an ultrasound, which turned out to be Marc.

The world of hip hop belongs to a new generation, one with its own unique form of clothing, known to many as "urban apparel." Ecko Enterprises was formed in 1993 when three friends began creating T-shirt fashions using cans of spray paint. By 2004, the company reported sales of nearly $1 billion. Items from Ecko Enterprises and the Ecko Unlimited brand are sold in more than 5,000 department and specialty stores domestically and in over 45 countries internationally. There are now 30 Ecko Unlimited full-price company annex stores, 16 of which are located outside of the United States. The Ecko Unlimited clothing line often features the stark silhouette of a rhinoceros on T-shirts, baggy jeans, and other products.

Ecko's company competes with firms that rely on the "cred" (credibility) that comes from being a performer, such as the Sean John line featuring P. Diddy, Rocawear from Jay-Z and Damon Dash, and Phat Fashions offered by Russell Simmons. Marc Ecko, in contrast, is simply a fan of the music who grew up living in suburban neighborhoods. Although he is sometimes described as a "former graffiti artist," the reality is that his company was formed while he was studying at Rutgers University to become a pharmacist.

A variety of products are featured through Ecko Unlimited, Marc Ecko Formalwear, and Eckored Kids, including outerwear, footwear, watches, eyewear, underwear, belts, bags, hats, small leather goods, and formal wear. The Marc Ecko Cut & Sew brand is a contemporary menswear line consisting of casual and dress separates designed to blend street-inspired edginess with more sophisticated designs and fabrics. Cut & Sew offers semi-tailored separates, sweaters, urban spa-inspired active wear, woven shirts, and premium denim.

A newer brand, the G-Unit Clothing Company, is an independent venture operated by Ecko and multiplatinum-selling artist 50 Cent. The G-Unit line includes items for men, women, boys, and girls. It features denim, T-shirts, fleece, outerwear, hats, and sportswear. Also, Marc Ecko Enterprises formed an exclusive U.S. and Canadian licensing agreement with Avirex Ltd. to introduce a sportswear collection. The line carries a full collection of apparel, including fashion denim, tees, knits, and outerwear. Other licensing agreements have been formed with Geoffrey Allen, Skechers, Paul D'Avril, Inc., Kid Headquarters, and Viva International.

The company also offers skateboards and skater-influenced clothing and accessories through the Zoo York label. The brand was launched in 1993 and is now part of the MEE line, which is the East Coast's largest action sports company. Ecko also publishes *Complex Magazine*, a bimonthly urban lifestyle publication with a circulation of 325,000. Another new venture is Contents Under Pressure, a game developed in partnership with Atari, Inc. The game features stories and characters in a futuristic universe in which graffiti plays a key role.

▲ Ecko Enterprises began by selling its unique form of clothing, known as "urban apparel."

Source: Thinkstock Royalty Free.

Urban apparel can be viewed as a form of "lifestyle merchandising." Ecko was able to translate his own enthusiasm for hip hop into something new and different in the fashion world. By placing ads in hip-hop magazines such as *The Source* and *Vibe,* the Ecko rhino grew based on relationships with a wide range of maverick recording artists, including Talib Kweli and the Beatnuts. Although many retailers feared the urban look, Federated Department Stores, the owner of Macy's and Bloomingdale's, became an enthusiastic seller of Ecko Unlimited.

Russell Simmons, founder of Phat Fashions and the godfather of hip-hop culture, was quoted as saying, "Marc is a very, very creative designer. He's got more edge than most." Simmons describes Ecko's line as having an "alternative" quality or a "more suburban edge." In other words, the Ecko brands were able to gain market among the hip-hop audience. The next issue becomes, as the hip-hop generation ages and new fads and fashions emerge, will Ecko Enterprises be able to continue to grow and succeed?

1. Which of the models presented in this chapter best explains a consumer's purchase of a fashion product created by Ecko Enterprises? Explain.

2. Examine Ecko Enterprises' Web site at **www.marceckoenterprises.com**. Pick one of the brands

and develop a means–end chain that could be used by a creative to develop an advertising campaign.

3. Of the seven advertising appeals, which would work best for Ecko Enterprises' products? Why? Would combinations of appeals be useful for this company? If so, which ones?

4. Pick one of the appeals discussed in the chapter and one of the brands sold by Ecko Enterprises and then develop a print advertisement. Describe your target audience in terms of demographics and psychographics.

Source: Rob Walker, "Cul-de-sac Cred," *New York Times Magazine*, July 10, 2005.

LIGHTING UP KINDLE

The world of book publishing and book reading is currently undergoing radical changes that are largely being driven by new technologies. Authors who previously found themselves shut out of traditional publishing can now use the Internet to distribute their books on topics ranging from self-help to political ideology.

After the initial wave of e-book releases, including one by well-known author Stephen King, changes in consumer book-purchasing patterns slowed. Noted New York literary agent Peter Rubie believed that the secret was mobility. He stated that "as soon as someone can carry an e-book to the beach without needing a laptop, the industry is going to change."

That day may have arrived. In late 2007, Jeff Bezos, the founder and CEO of Amazon.com, announced the release of a revolutionary new product—the Kindle. The Kindle is a wire-less, portable reading device that offers instant access to more than 90,000 books, blogs, magazines, and newspapers. The technology behind the Kindle is the same as that contained in cell phones, which means that users do not need to find a Wi-Fi hotspot to use it. The Kindle weighs 10.3 ounces and can carry 200 books at any time. Readers can download books, magazines, blogs, and newspapers from any location.

The device offered a variety of new features. For example, if a person does not know the meaning of a word in a text, the word can be highlighted and then found in an instant dictionary. Links to other sources, such as Wikipedia, are also available.

The great benefit of Kindle to authors is that their books remain available in perpetuity. No longer will a book go "out of print." Each book download costs the reader about $10.00, and the author receives a royalty, just as in the past. For some authors, an additional benefit is the ability to revise a book over time, because the entire content is digital rather than print.

The Kindle debuted with some buzz, despite its hefty price tag ($400). Bezos appeared on *Charlie Rose*, and several newspaper and magazine articles about the product created some publicity. The company will need to build on that early momentum, because it clearly did not generate the same kind of interest as the MP3 player or the iPhone. Further, competition soon became available in the form of the Sony Portable Reading System.

Author Kevin Maney summarized the Kindle this way: "It's too early to tell whether this is the book's future. The Kindle isn't even set up to do all that just yet. But it is the first e-book reader built to be wirelessly connected to the Internet at all times. It's the first system that shows that living, connected books—some combination of traditional books and Wikipedia—are possible. And, in fact, that's the first reason to think that e-books could evolve into something other than paper books." Consumers will undoubtedly decide the rest.

▼ Portable readers can download books, magazines, blogs, and newspapers from any location.

Source: Shutterstock.

1. As an advertising executive who is working with a creative, which advertising theory do you think best fits the release and subsequent advertising for Kindle?

2. What should be the leverage point in a commercial for Kindle?

3. What type of advertising appeal, or sets of appeals, should be used in promoting Kindle?

4. What should be the headline of a Kindle ad? Why?

5. Design a print ad promoting Kindle. Identify which appeal you used and explain why you chose it.

Sources: www.amazon.com (accessed January 5, 2008); Kevin Maney, "A Book That Never Ends?" *USA Today*, December 6, 2007, p. 19A.

7 Advertising Design
Message Strategies and Executional Frameworks

DOVE

Social and Fashion Advertising

A recent advertisement, titled "Onslaught" was created for Dove products. The commercial opens with the words "A Dove film" and shows a close-up of a smiling, innocent, red-headed girl for nearly 20 seconds. With music featuring a modern sound and the words "Here it comes" frequently repeated in the background, cuts from various pseudo-advertisements display slinky, fashionable, beautiful models. The attributes needed to reach such a status are mentioned, among them "younger, smaller, lighter, thinner, tighter, softer." "It works" is highlighted again and again by the advertising pitchwomen. The inevitable pathway to yo-yo dieting, eating disorders, and various forms of cosmetic surgery follows.

Finally, as a group of young girls around the age of 10 cross a street, the commercial closes with the words, "Talk to your daughter before the beauty industry does." The compelling message does not mention Dove soap or any of its product features. Instead, it offers a strong indictment of the social pressures young girls and young women face.

Advertising and marketing to women and girls may be at a crossroad. Clearly, pressures to grow up more quickly, to look older at a younger age, and to fit in socially drive a great deal of product design and what is called *age-compression marketing.* Some responsible parents and those who offer social commentary are pushing back with the essential message, "Let girls be girls."

Complaints about body image issues are not new. In the 1960s, a young supermodel named Twiggy captured international attention by looking girlish and paper thin. Television programs and a movie remake of *Lolita* stirred additional controversy and debate. The Disney Channel's *Hannah Montana* once again highlighted the mega-power associated with marketing to young girls. The *Hannah Montana* stage show that traveled across the United States resulted in price gouging and

CHAPTER OBJECTIVES

After reading this chapter, you should be able to answer the following questions:

1 How are the three main types of message strategies used to increase advertising effectiveness?

2 How do the main types of executional frameworks help to deliver quality advertising messages?

3 What types of sources or spokespersons can be used in advertisements or commercials?

4 What characteristics are most important when selecting a source or spokesperson?

5 What process is used to create advertisements?

6 What are the principles of advertising effectiveness?

7 How are advertising programs adjusted to fit international circumstances?

Source: Author Supplied Image.

CHAPTER 7

pages called "Campaign for Real Beauty" for young girls and "Dove Pro-Age" for older women. Visitors can make charitable contributions to the Dove Self-Esteem fund through the Web site. Clearly, this division of the company is tapping into an emotion held by many women, especially mothers.

Time cynically notes that Dove is owned by Unilever, which "advertises its Axe Body Spray to men using a lingerie-and-stiletto-clad rock band called Bom

ticket scalping, sending ticket prices into the hundreds of dollars. One side of Hannah, of course, is the glamorous world of a rock star.

Dove's "Onslaught" advertisement sends a competing message. The Dove Web site includes

Chicka Wah Wahs," and then asks, "What do we tell our daughters about that?"[1]

OVERVIEW

Designing messages to effectively reach a target audience constitutes the essence of integrated marketing communications. Many of these messages are quite personal. They are designed to change or shape attitudes. They should be remembered and lead to a short- or long-term action.

Marketing messages travel in two ways. First, a personal message can be delivered through a personal medium. A sales representative closing a deal, shaking the hand of the buyer, giving a reassuring tap on the shoulder, and smiling while talking delivers a message in an intimate, warm, personal fashion. Clearly, personal media (e.g., sales reps, repair department personnel, customer services representatives) are part of the overall IMC program.

Marketing messages also travel through the various forms of advertising media. Most of these are *impersonal*. Televisions are indifferent as to what appears on the screen. Radios deliver any sound that can be transmitted. Computer screens are nothing more than special-purpose television screens. The challenge to the advertising agency, the company, and especially the creative is to design a personal message, even one being delivered by an impersonal medium. The message should engage the buyer and influence her to recall and purchase the product. Also, many marketers and advertising agencies seek tangible, measurable results.

This chapter first focuses on the main three types of message strategies. Each may be used to help convince the consumer to make a purchase, either through reason, emotion, or an action-inducing advertisement. Second, the major types of executional frameworks are explained. These forms of advertising presentations help the creative prepare original, convincing, and memorable messages. Third, the four types of sources or spokespersons that appear in various advertisements are described and the criteria used to select them are reviewed. Finally, the principles of effective advertising campaigns are presented. Advertisements that are effectively combined with other elements of the promotions mix can lead to a strong company image reflecting a clear IMC theme.

MESSAGE STRATEGIES

1 How are the three main types of message strategies used to increase advertising effectiveness?

The **message theme** outlines the key ideas in an advertisement. It is a central part of the creative brief. The message theme can be created using a number of message strategies. A **message strategy** is the primary tactic or approach used to deliver the message theme. The three broad categories of message strategies are:[2]

1. Cognitive strategies
2. Affective strategies
3. Conative strategies

The categories represent the components of attitudes, as described earlier. Figure 7.1 identifies the various forms or approaches from each category.

Cognitive Strategies

A **cognitive message strategy** presents rational arguments or pieces of information to consumers. The ideas require cognitive processing. The advertisement's key message describes the product's attributes or benefits. Customers can obtain these benefits by purchasing the product.[3]

A cognitive message strategy advertisement should influence a person's beliefs and/or knowledge structure by suggesting any one of a wide variety of potential product benefits. Foods may be described as healthy, pleasant tasting, or low calorie. A tool can be shown as durable, convenient, or handy to use. A drill press machine used in a manufacturing operation may be portrayed as being more reliable or faster than the competition's machines. Cognitive message strategies clearly present these benefits to customers. The five major forms of cognitive strategies are:

1. Generic messages
2. Preemptive messages

FIGURE 7.1 ▶
Message Strategies

- Generic
- Preemptive
- Unique selling proposition
- Hyberbole
- Comparative

- Resonance
- Emotional
- Action-inducing
- Promotional support

3. Unique selling proposition
4. Hyperbole
5. Comparative advertisements

Generic Messages

When an advertisement directly promotes the product's attributes or benefits without any claim of superiority, it sends a **generic message**. This works best when a firm is the brand leader and dominates the industry. A generic message makes the brand synonymous with the product category. Campbell's Soups can declare "Soup is good food" without making any claim to superiority. The company leads the industry. When most consumers think of soup, they think of Campbell's, which sells 69 percent of all cans sold each year.[4] Nintendo uses a similar approach because the company dominates the game-console category with a 47 percent market share.[5]

▲ An advertisement for Marion State Bank using a generic message strategy.

Generic message strategies are seldom found in business-to-business advertisements, because few firms dominate an industry to the extent of Campbell's or Nintendo. Intel is the major exception. The company controls 80 percent of the microchip market.[6] The generic message "Intel inside" has been repeated for years.

Generic message strategies can stimulate brand awareness. The advertiser may try to develop a cognitive linkage between a specific brand name and a product category, such as Skechers and sporty footwear. The advertisement may contain little information about the product's attributes. Instead, it attempts to place the brand in a person's cognitive memory and cognitive map.

Preemptive Messages

A claim of superiority based on a product's specific attribute or benefit with the intent of preventing the competition from making the same or a similar statement is a **preemptive message**. Crest toothpaste is known as "the cavity fighter," which preempts other companies from making similar claims, even though all toothpastes fight cavities. An effective preemptive strategy occurs when the company is first to state the advantage. Competitors that say the same thing become viewed as "me-too" brands or copycats.

Unique Selling Proposition

An explicit, testable claim of uniqueness or superiority that can be supported or substantiated in some manner is a **unique selling proposition (USP)**. The Bonne Bell advertisement shown in this section features a unique selling proposition aimed at teenagers. The message that Bonne Bell Lipshade is "your 1 and only, 1 handed, sleek sweep flipstick!" stresses a unique product feature.

Hyperbole

An *untestable* claim based on some attribute or benefit is **hyperbole**. When NBC states that it has America's favorite comedies, the claim is hyperbole. It does not require substantiation, which makes this cognitive strategy quite popular.

Comparative Advertising

The final cognitive message strategy, a **comparative advertisement**, allows an advertiser to directly or indirectly compare a product to the competition's. The advertisement may or may not mention the competitor by name. An advertiser can simply

▼ An advertisement for Bonne Bell featuring a unique selling proposition.

present a "make-believe" competitor with a name such as "Brand X." This approach, however, may not be as effective as making a comparison using the actual competitor's name. To provide protection from lawsuits, company leaders make sure any claim concerning the competition can be clearly substantiated.

AT&T and Sprint compare rates. VISA notes that many merchants will not accept American Express. In the business-to-business sector, shipping companies compare delivery times and accuracy rates.

Comparative ads offer the advantage of capturing the consumer's attention. When comparisons are made, both brand awareness and message awareness increase. Consumers tend to remember more of what was said about a brand than when the same information is presented in a noncomparative ad format.

Believability and consumer attitudes represent the negative side of comparative ads. Many consumers consider comparative ads to be less believable. They view the information about the sponsor brand as exaggerated and conclude that the information about the comparison brand probably is misstated to make the sponsor brand appear superior.

Another danger of comparative ads occurs when consumers develop negative attitudes toward the advertisement, which can then be transferred to the sponsor's product. This becomes more likely when the sponsor runs a *negative comparative ad* about the competition's product. Research suggests that negative comparative ads typically result in lower believability of the advertising claim and may result in less favorable attitudes toward the brand.[7] In psychology, the concept of *spontaneous trait transference* suggests that when someone calls another person dishonest, other people tend to consider the speaker to be less than honest. A comparative advertisement that criticizes the competition's brand based on a particular attribute may lead viewers to also attribute the deficiency to the sponsor brand. The transference becomes more likely when the consumer purchases the comparative brand, not the sponsored brand.[8]

Company leaders carefully choose an appropriate comparison firm and are cautious when using a negative comparison format. The comparison brand must be viewed as a viable competing brand. Actual product attributes and customer benefits are noted, without stretching the information or providing misleading information. When actual differences exist, comparative advertising works well. Comparisons consisting of hype and opinion with no substantial differences are less likely to succeed. Misleading comparisons can cause the Federal Trade Commission (FTC) to investigate. The majority of complaints filed with the FTC are about potentially misleading comparison advertisements.

Comparing a brand with a low market share to the market leader works well, because viewers concentrate more carefully on the advertisement's content and message. Comparing a high-market share brand with another high-market share brand may not be as effective. In these cases, a better strategy may be to simply make the comparison without naming the competitor.

Several years ago, Avis was in 10th place in market share in the rental car industry. A series of commercials compared Avis to the market leader, Hertz, mentioning the Hertz name specifically. Most consumers now believe Avis provides the same level of quality as Hertz.[9]

The five cognitive message strategies are based on rational logic. Messages are designed to make sure consumers pay attention to the ad and take the time to cognitively process the information. In terms of attitudes, the sequence of *cognitive* → *affective* → *conative* represents the rational approach. The cognitive message strategy first presents consumers with rational information about a good, service, or company, and then leads them to develop positive feelings about the same product or company.

Affective Strategies

Advertisements that invoke feelings or emotions and match those feelings with the good, service, or company use **affective message strategies**. These messages attempt to enhance the likeability of the product, recall of the appeal, or comprehension of the advertisement. Affective strategies elicit emotions that, in turn, lead the consumer to act, preferably by buying the product, and subsequently affecting the consumer's reasoning process.

An emotion such as love can be featured in order to convince consumers that Cheerios is a superior breakfast cereal for loved ones. Consumers can be told that Cheerios offers a rational choice. Company advertisements then mention the cereal's positive effect on cholesterol levels, as shown in the Cheerios ad in this section. The photo of three generations of a family is combined with the words "Your heart has better things to do than deal with heart disease." Family memories and emotions are combined with the product's heart-smart feature. Affective strategies fall into two categories: (1) resonance and (2) emotional.

Resonance advertising connects a product with a consumer's experiences in order to develop stronger ties between the product and the consumer. The use of music from the 1980s takes Echo Boomers back to that time. Any strongly held memory or emotional attachment becomes a candidate for resonance advertising.

Emotional advertising attempts to elicit powerful emotions that eventually lead to product recall and choice. Many emotions can be connected to products, including trust, reliability, friendship, happiness, security, glamour, luxury, serenity, pleasure, romance, and passion.

Emotional appeals are employed in both consumer-oriented and business-to-business ads. Members of the buying center in a business are human. They do not make purchasing decisions based solely on rational thought processes. Emotions and feelings also affect choices. When the product's benefits are presented using an emotional framework, the advertisement will normally be more effective, even in business-to-business ads.[10]

Affective strategies may help develop a stronger brand name. Affective advertisements can cause consumers to like the brand, have positive feelings towards it, and eventually purchase the item. Cognitive beliefs about the brand then follow. This approach relies on the attitude development sequence of *affective → conative → cognitive*. For some products, affective advertisements are effective because there are no real tangible differences among the brands. Skechers Sport Footwear uses an affective strategy in the advertisement in this section. It depicts social acceptance and the idea that Skechers shoes make you a part of the in-crowd, thus trying to create positive feelings toward the Skechers Sport brand.

Conative Strategies

Conative message strategies are designed to lead directly to some type of consumer response. They can support other promotional efforts, such as coupon redemption programs, Internet "hits" and orders, and in-store offers such as buy-one-get-one-free. The goal of eliciting behaviors can be found in any advertisement for old television programs that seeks to persuade viewers to call a toll-free number to purchase the DVDs. These ads typically encourage quick action by stating that the DVD cannot be purchased in stores and will be available for only a limited time.

Your Heart Has Better Things To Do Than Deal With Heart Disease

Eating heart-healthy whole grain oat foods like Cheerios as part of a low-fat diet, may be a good way to lower your cholesterol and reduce your risk of heart disease. So make health a habit for your heart, body and soul. And let your heart do something it's better at...holding your family together.

Cheerios

"The One and Only Cheerios"

▲ A Cheerios advertisement utilizing a resonance affective message strategy.

▼ An advertisement for Skechers Sport Footwear using an emotional message strategy.

FIGURE 7.2 ▶
The Hierarchy of Effects Model
and Message Strategies

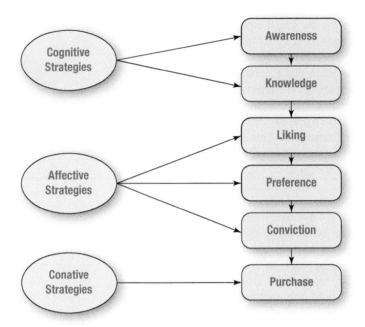

FIGURE 7.2 ▶
The Hierarchy of Effects Model
and Message Strategies

Action-inducing conative advertisements create situations in which cognitive knowledge of the product or affective liking of the product may come later (after the actual purchase) or during product usage. For instance, a point-of-purchase display can be designed (sometimes through advertising tie-ins) to cause people to make *impulse buys.* The goal is to make the sale, with cognitive knowledge and affective feelings forming as the product is used. The attitude sequence for conative message strategies is *conative → cognitive → affective.*

Promotional support conative advertisements are tied in with other promotional efforts, including coupons, phone-in promotions, or a sweepstakes that a consumer enters by filling out the form on the advertisement or by going to a particular retail store.

Cognitive, affective, and conative strategies can be matched with the hierarchy of effects approach, which suggests that consumers pass through a series of stages, from awareness to knowledge, liking, preference, conviction, and, finally, to the purchase. As shown in Figure 7.2, each message strategy can highlight a different stage of the hierarchy of effects model.

Choosing the right message strategy often becomes the key ingredient in creating a successful advertising program. To be effective, the message strategy should match the leverage point and executional framework. These should mesh with the media to be utilized. The creative and the account executive remain in constant contact throughout the process to be certain all of these advertising ingredients remain consistent.

EXECUTIONAL FRAMEWORKS

❷ How do the main types of executional frameworks help to deliver quality advertising messages?

An **executional framework** signifies the manner in which an ad appeal will be presented. It should be chosen in conjunction with an advertising appeal and message strategy. The common types of appeals include fear, humor, sex, music, rationality, emotions, and scarcity. Each can be matched with the appropriate executional framework. Figure 7.3 displays the various frameworks.

FIGURE 7.3 ▶
Executional Frameworks

- Animation
- Slice-of-life
- Dramatization
- Testimonial
- Authoritative
- Demonstration
- Fantasy
- Informative

Animation

Animation has become an increasingly popular executional framework, and its use has risen dramatically. The growing sophistication of computer graphics programs makes new and exciting animation technologies available. Successful films such as *Up* and *Bee Movie* continue to create a great deal of interest in animation advertising. Animation can be featured in television spots and in Internet advertising. It is also used in movie trailers. Single shots of animated characters, such as *Dora the Explorer*, are placed in print ads.

One exciting animation technique, *rotoscoping*, is the process of digitally painting or sketching figures into live sequences, which makes it possible to present both live actors and animated characters in the same frame.[11] The creative can also merge or modify various live scenes. As advertising executive Stan Richards noted, "The opportunities are great, because, we are at a point where, anything that we can think of, we can do. We've never had that before. There is a cost consequence. A lot of that digital production is expensive, but those costs are coming down. Within a few years, those costs will be half of what they are now."[12]

For years, animation was rarely used in business-to-business advertising. Many advertising leaders had negative views of it, believing animation appealed to children but not to businesspeople. These views have changed. Business ads shown on television now take advantage of high-quality graphics to illustrate a product's uses with animation.

Slice-of-Life

In slice-of-life commercials, advertisers provide solutions to the everyday problems consumers or businesses face. The format was made famous by Procter & Gamble during the early days of television advertising. Slice-of-life commercials show the common experiences, and especially the problems, people encounter, and a product is introduced to solve the problem. The most common slice-of-life format has four components: encounter, problem, interaction, and solution (see Figure 7.4). In some ads, the actors portray the dilemma or problem and solve the problems themselves. In others, a voice-over explains the benefits or solution to the problem that the good, service, or company provides.

Slice-of-life executions also appear in business-to-business advertisements, such as the MessageMedia ad shown on page 195. The encounter begins with the potential female customer's problem that the "average single female breaks up with 4.3 men, avoids 237 phone calls, and ignores approximately 79 red lights per year." The interaction occurs through the copy "What are the chances she'll read your e-mail

▲ A Green Giant advertisement using animation.

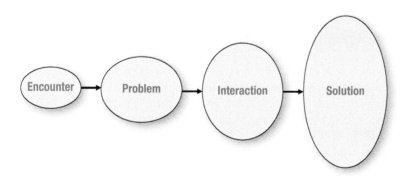

◄ **FIGURE 7.4**
Components of a Slice-of-Life Ad

▲ One of a series of advertisements created by Pink Jacket Creative for the Snoring Center using animation characters and a slice-of-life approach.

message?" The solution to this problem is Message-Media's "E-messaging campaign."

Business-to-business advertisements often utilize the slice-of-life method because it allows the advertiser to highlight the ways a product can meet business needs. A typical business-to-business ad begins with a routine business experience, such as a sales manager making a presentation to the board of directors. Then, a projector being used does not have a clear picture. The ad offers the solution: a projector from Sony. The presentation is made with great clarity, and the board of directors accepts the customer's bid for the account. As with all slice-of-life commercials, a disaster has been avoided and a happy ending results instead.

Slice-of-life executions are possible in most media, including magazines or billboards, because a single picture can depict a normal, everyday situation or problem. Finding an image that tells the entire story, with the product being the solution, will be the challenge.

Dramatization

A dramatization is similar to the slice-of-life executional framework. The same format in which a problem is first presented and then a solution appears is used. The difference lies in the intensity and story format. Dramatization presents a higher level of excitement and suspense to tell the story. A dramatization story normally builds to a crisis point leading to a suspenseful climax.

An effective and dramatic advertisement can be difficult to create, because the drama must be completed in either 30 or 60 seconds. Building a story to a climactic moment is challenging given such a short time period. The early "What's in Your Wallet" advertisements for Capital One credit cards did manage to create the appropriate level of excitement. The ads were later replaced with humorous executions. Not all dramatic execution styles can accomplish a high enough level of suspense to make them successful. The slice-of-life framework often offers a better approach.

Testimonials

The testimonial type of executional framework has been successful for many years, especially in the business-to-business and service sectors. When a customer tells about a positive experience with a product, it is a testimonial. In the business-to-business sector, testimonials from current customers add credibility to the claims being made. In many business buying situations, prospective vendors are asked for references. Testimonials provide references in advance. Further, most buyers believe what others say about a company more than they believe what a company says about itself. Testimonials offer greater credibility than self-proclamations.

Testimonials also are an effective method for promoting services. Services are intangible; they cannot be seen or touched, and consumers cannot examine them before making decisions. A testimony from a current customer can be an effective method of describing the benefits or attributes of the service. Most consumers talk to other people when selecting services. Choosing a dentist, an attorney, or an automobile repair shop leads customers to ask friends, relatives, or coworkers. A testimonial advertisement simulates this type of word-of-mouth recommendation.

Testimonials can enhance company credibility. Endorsers and famous individuals do not always have high levels of credibility, because consumers know they are being paid for their endorsements. In testimonials, everyday people, often actual customers, are the main characters. At other times, they are paid actors who look like everyday consumers.

Authoritative

When using the authoritative executional framework, the advertiser seeks to convince viewers that a given product is superior. One form is **expert authority**. These ads employ a physician, dentist, engineer, or chemist to state the particular brand's advantages compared to other brands. Firms also can feature less recognized experts such as automobile mechanics, professional house painters, nurses, and aerobics instructors. These individuals can talk about the brand attributes that make the product superior.

Many authoritative advertisements include some type of scientific or survey evidence. Independent organizations such as the American Medical Association undertake a variety of product studies. Quoting the results generates greater credibility. Survey results are less credible. Stating that four out of five dentists recommend a particular toothbrush or toothpaste is less effective, because consumers do not have details about how the survey was conducted or even how many dentists were surveyed (5 or 500). In contrast, an American Medical Association statement that an aspirin a day reduces the risk of a second heart attack is highly credible. A company such as Bayer can take advantage of the finding by including the information in the company's ads. The same holds true when a magazine such as *Consumer Reports* ranks a particular brand as the best.

Authoritative advertisements have been widely incorporated into business-to-business sector ads, especially when scientific findings support a company's product claims. Independent test results are likely to have a more profound influence on members of the buying center, especially if they are actively looking for rational information to help them make decisions.

The authoritative approach assumes consumers and business decision makers rely on cognitive processes when making purchase decisions and that they will pay attention to an ad and carefully think about the information conveyed in it. The approach works well in print ads, because the buyers take the time to read the claim or findings presented in the advertisement.

Authoritative advertisements perform well in specialty magazines and on specific Web sites. In a hunting magazine, an expert sportsman can discuss the superiority of a particular gun and the readers are individuals with an interest in hunting. Brides observe the endorsements of wedding experts in bridal magazines and Web sites. Readers notice these specialized messages, and the claims have greater credibility. The same will be true in business-to-business magazines. Trade journals in the business world are similar to specialty magazines in the consumer world.

Demonstration

A demonstration execution shows how a product works. A demonstration offers an effective way to communicate the benefits of a product to viewers. One recent advertisement featured a new form of dust cloth that could be attached to a handle or used separately. The demonstration highlighted the product's multiple uses by cleaning a television screen, a wooden floor, a saxophone, and light fixtures. Consumers were being shown how to use the product while at the same time hearing about its advantages.

Business-to-business ads often present demonstrations. They allow a business to illustrate how a product can meet the specific needs of another business. For example,

Source: Courtesy of MessageMedia.

▲ A business-to-business advertisement for MessageMedia containing a slice-of-life execution.

▲ An authoritative execution combined with a humor appeal.

▼ A Jantzen advertisement utilizing a fantasy execution.

GoldTouch, Inc. can demonstrate the InstaGold Flash System, which deposits a bright and uniform gold surface finish on products, such as jewelry, through a nonelectrical current process of immersion plating. Such demonstrations can be offered via television ads or flash media ads on the Internet.

Demonstration ads are well-suited to television and the Internet. To a limited extent, the print media can feature demonstrations, especially when a series of photos outlines the sequence of product usage.

Fantasy

Fantasy executions lift the audience beyond the real world to a make-believe experience. Some are meant to be realistic. Others are completely irrational. The most irrational and illogical ads are often more clearly recalled. Fantasies can deal with anything from a dream vacation spot or cruise ships to a juicy hamburger or an enticing DiGiorno pizza. The Jantzen ad in this section encourages consumer fantasies. People are encouraged to share their fantasies by contacting Jantzen.

The most common fantasy themes involve sex, love, and romance. According to some marketing experts, raw sex and nudity in advertisements are losing their impact. Instead, advertisers feature a softer, more subtle presentation of sex. Fantasy fits nicely with target audiences that have a preference for a tamer presentation of sexuality. Instead of raw sex and nudity that may be offensive, fantasy takes them into a world of romantic make-believe.

The perfume and cologne industries often employ fantasy executions. In the past, the most common theme was that splashing on a certain cologne caused women to flock to a man. For women, the reverse was suggested. Although used extensively, these ads were not particularly effective because people did not believe them. Currently, perfume advertisers tend to portray the product as enhancing a couple's love life or making a man or woman feel more sensuous.

Television fantasy ads for cruise lines show couples enjoying romantic, sensuous vacations together; swimming; jet skiing; and scuba diving. The cruise becomes more than just a vacation—it is a romantic fantasy trip. Fantasy ads also can show people experiencing the thrill of winning a major sports event or sharing a common product (e.g., beer, pizza) with a beautiful model. The billboard for Kickapoo Casino on the next page uses a fantasy approach by suggesting that hitting the jackpot at the casino will also yield three beautiful girls for the male in the ad. Effective fantasies can inspire both recall and action.

The business-to-business advertising field does not use fantasy a great deal, primarily because of fear that members of a buying center will not take it seriously. Some advertising creatives have been able to feature a fantasy in a business-to-business advertisement by showing a product helping the buyer achieve an unrealistic result or outcome. For example, being promoted from janitor to president because of the correct choice of a cleaning product would be a fantasy aimed at people using or purchasing janitorial supplies.

Informative

Informative advertisements present information to the audience in a straightforward manner. Agencies prepare informative messages extensively for radio commercials, where only verbal communication is possible. Informative ads are less common in television and print, because consumers tend to ignore them. With so many ads bombarding the consumer, it takes more than just the presentation of information to capture someone's attention.

▲ This billboard for the Kickapoo Casino uses a fantasy approach.

Consumers who are highly involved in a particular product category pay more attention to an informational ad. Business buyers in the process of gathering information for either a new buy or a modified rebuy will notice an informative advertisement. If the business is not in the market for a particular product, buying center members pay less attention to the advertisement. Thus, informative ads tend to work best in high-involvement situations. Many advertisers believe that business buyers desire detailed information to make intelligent buying decisions. As a result, the informative framework continues to be a popular approach for business-to-business advertisers.

Correct placement of an informative advertisement is vital. An informative advertisement about a restaurant placed on a radio station just before noon will be listened to more carefully than one that runs at 3:00 P.M. An informative ad about a diet product in an issue of *Glamour* that has a special article on weight control or exercising will be noticed more than if it is placed in the fashion section of the magazine. An informative business ad featuring a new piece of industrial equipment works well next to an article about the capital costs of equipment. Informative ads may have limited uses but become more effective when placed properly.

Beyond these types of executional frameworks, the creative selects the other ingredients, including music, copy, color, motion, light, and the size of a print ad. Almost any of these executional frameworks can be used within the format of one of the various appeals. A slice-of-life can depict fear, as can a dramatization. Informative ads may be humorous, but so can animations. Testimonials or demonstrations are rational or emotional, and so forth. As the advertisement comes together, one element remains: the choice of a source or spokesperson.

SOURCES AND SPOKESPERSONS

One final issue remains for the creative, the company, and the account executive. Selecting the ideal **source and spokesperson** to use in an advertisement will be critical. Figure 7.5 identifies four types of sources and spokespersons.

③ What types of sources or spokespersons can be used in advertisements or commercials?

Celebrity Spokespersons

Of the four types, celebrity spokespersons are the most common, even though their appearances in ads have been declining. According to the research firm Millward Brown, only around 6 percent of advertisements now feature celebrity endorsements.[13]

Companies use a celebrity endorser when the person's stamp of approval enhances the product's brand equity. Celebrities can also help create emotional bonds with brands. Transferring the bond that exists between the celebrity and the audience to the product being endorsed is the objective. A bond transfer will often be more profound for younger consumers. A MediaEDGE survey revealed that 30 percent of 18- to 34-year-olds would try a product promoted by a celebrity. The survey also indicated that younger people are 50 percent more likely than older consumers to recommend a celebrity-endorsed product to others. Older consumers are not as likely to be influenced by celebrity endorsements. Less than 14 percent reported that they would try a celebrity-endorsed product. Still, many advertisers believe that celebrity endorsements improve brand awareness and help define the brand's personality.[14]

▼ This advertisement contains an informative execution to convey the message that products people use every day are made with the petroleum ingredients processed by Calumet.

FIGURE 7.5 ▶
Types of Sources and
Spokespersons

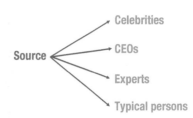

Athletes constitute a significant component of the celebrity endorsers. Some, such as Danica Patrick, earn more from endorsements than they do from their sports. Top athletic endorsers include Phil Mickelson, Dale Earnhardt, Lebron James, Kobe Bryant, Shaquille O'Neal, and Payton Manning, and, until recently, Tiger Woods. The top two female athletic endorsers are Danica Patrick and Maria Sharapova. The two top retired athlete endorsers are Michael Jordan and Cal Ripken, Jr.[15]

Agencies also use celebrities to help establish a brand "personality." The objective is to tie the brand's characteristics to those of the spokesperson. Elizabeth Taylor's love of the finer things in life can be attached to her line of scents and perfumes. A brand personality emerges after the brand has been established. The celebrity helps to define the brand more clearly. Using celebrities for new products does not always work as well as for already established brands.

Additional Celebrity Endorsements

Three additional variations of celebrity endorsements are: (1) unpaid spokespersons, (2) celebrity voice-overs, and (3) dead-person endorsements. *Unpaid spokespersons* are celebrities supporting a charity or cause by appearing in an ad. These types of endorsements are highly credible and can entice significant contributions to a cause. Politicians, actors, musicians, and athletes all appear in these ads. A recent campaign featured a number of musicians plus former Presidents Bush and Clinton in an effort to raise money for Haiti after its devastating earthquake.

▼ The milk industry employs a number of celebrities in the "Got Milk?" campaign.

Many celebrities also provide *voice-overs* for television and radio ads without being shown or identified. Listeners often respond to the ads and try to figure out who is reading the copy. This adds interest to the advertisement. Agencies may use a voice-over because the celebrity provides a quality voice to the advertisement even when individuals listening to the ad do not recognize the voice. According to advertising executive Stan Richards, "We use Hollywood actors quite a bit. It's largely not for their celebrity, we're not interested in that. Our voice for Home Depot is Ed Harris, who is a terrific actor. I don't think anybody in the world knows it's him, but he can take a script and bring it to life."[16] One negative of voice-overs is that they can be a distraction if the consumer becomes focused on identifying the speaker rather than hearing the content of the ad.

A *dead-person endorsement* occurs when a sponsor uses an image or past video or film featuring an actor or personality who has died. Dead-person endorsements are somewhat controversial but are becoming more common. Bob Marley, Marilyn Monroe, John Wayne, John Lennon, Elvis Presley, and many others have appeared in ads and have even become spokespersons for products after dying. Michael Jackson may become the next major dead-person endorser.

Your bones may be in jeopardy.

One in five
osteoporosis victims
is male. Luckily, fat free
milk has the calcium bones
need to help beat it.
Beating your Harvard Ph.D.
opponents? Well, that's
another story.

got milk?

ALEX TREBEK IS/FOR NATIONAL FLUID MILK PROCESSOR PROMOTION BOARD

CEO Spokespersons

Instead of celebrities, advertisers can use a CEO as the spokesperson or source. Michael Dell has appeared as the spokesperson for Dell. A highly visible and personable CEO can become a major asset for the firm and its products. Many local companies succeed, in part, because their owners are out front in small-market television commercials. They then begin to take on the status of local celebrities.

Experts

Expert sources include physicians, lawyers, accountants, and financial planners. These experts are not celebrities or CEOs. Experts provide backing for testimonials, serve as authoritative figures, demonstrate products, and enhance the credibility of informative advertisements.

Typical Persons

Typical persons are one of two types. The first includes paid actors or models who portray or resemble everyday people. The second is actual, typical, everyday people. Wal-Mart has featured store employees in freestanding insert advertisements. Agencies also create "man-on-the-street" types of advertisements. For example, PERT shampoo recently prepared ads showing an individual asking people if they would like to have their hair washed. Dr. Scholl's interviews people about foot problems that might be resolved with cushioned shoe inserts.

Real-people sources are becoming more common. One reason for this is the overuse of celebrities. Many experts believe that consumers have become bored by celebrity endorsers and that the positive impact today is not as strong as it was in the past. One study conducted in Great Britain indicated that 55 percent of the consumers surveyed reported that a famous face was not enough to hold their attention. [17]

Source: Courtesy of U.S. Marines.

▲ An advertisement for the U.S. Marines with a typical person spokesperson.

Source Characteristics

In evaluating sources, most account executives and companies consider several characteristics. The effectiveness of an advertisement that utilizes a spokesperson depends on the degree to which the person has one or more of the characteristics listed in Figure 7.6.

4 What characteristics are most important when selecting a source or spokesperson?

◄ **FIGURE 7.6**
Characteristics of Effective Spokespersons

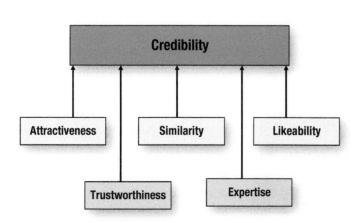

Credibility

Credibility is derived from the composite of attractiveness, similarity, likeability, trustworthiness, and expertise.[18] Credibility affects a receiver's acceptance of the spokesperson and the message. A credible source is believable. Most sources do not score highly on all four attributes, yet they need to score highly on multiple characteristics to be viewed as credible. Celebrities may be more likely to possess at least an element of all characteristics. A CEO, expert, or typical person probably lacks one or more of them.

Attractiveness

Two forms of attractiveness are: (1) physical characteristics and (2) personality characteristics. Physical attractiveness is usually an important asset for an endorser. Bijan used Michael Jordan's and Bo Derek's physical attractiveness to promote lines of menswear, perfume, and jewelry. Advertisements with physically attractive spokespersons fare better than advertisements with less attractive people, for both male and female audiences. At the same time, the attractiveness of the spokesperson's personality will also be important to many consumers. This personality component helps viewers form emotional bonds with the spokesperson. If the spokesperson appears to have a sour personality, even if physically beautiful, consumers are less likely to develop an emotional bond with the individual and the product.

Similarity

Closely related to attractiveness is the concept of similarity. Consumers are more inclined to be influenced by a message delivered by a person who is somehow similar. For example, a "stay-at-home" mom may be more influenced by an advertisement that starts out with a woman saying, "Since I made the decision to stop working and care for my family full-time . . ." Similarity allows the viewer to identify with the spokesperson. Sometimes this may involve the fantasy of identifying with a rich person buying a BMW. At other times *identification* comes from the belief that the source has similar beliefs, attitudes, preferences, or behaviors or faces the same or a similar situation as the customer. Female fans are able to identify with Anna Roberts as the "new face of horse racing" because many females have enjoyed horseback riding and have dreamed of winning a famous horse race. Identification was also gained because most jockeys are males. Anna Roberts immediately gained similarity and identification with female fans.

▼ Attractiveness can be a valuable source characteristic.

Bijan suits Bo...
(and vice versa!)

bijan

menswear
perfume
jewelry

Designer Bijan dresses Bo Derek!

Bijan 699 Fifth Avenue New York   420 N. Rodeo Drive Beverly Hills...

Likeability

Closely related to the personality components of attractiveness and similarity is likeability. Consumers respond positively to spokespersons they like. Viewers may like an actor or the character played by the actor in a movie. An athlete gains likeability if he plays on the consumer's favorite team. Other individuals are likeable because they support the favorite charities of consumers. Consumers who do not like a particular spokesperson are inclined to transfer that dislike to the product. It may not be an automatic transfer, because consumers recognize that endorsers are paid spokespersons. This explains why most companies who used Tiger Woods quickly dropped him as an endorser in 2010. The worry was that his endorsement would have a negative impact on attitudes toward the brand.

Trustworthiness

A celebrity may be likeable or attractive but may not be viewed as trustworthy. Trustworthiness represents the degree of confidence or the level of acceptance consumers place in the spokesperson's message. A trustworthy spokesperson helps consumers believe the message. Likeability and trustworthiness are highly related. People who are liked tend to be trusted, and people who are disliked tend not to be trusted. According to E-Poll Market Research, celebrities ranking the highest in terms of trustworthiness, awareness, and appeal included James Earl Jones, Tom Hanks, and Michael J. Fox.[19] See Figure 7.7 for a complete list.

▲ An advertisement for Louisiana Downs featuring the female jockey Anna Roberts.

Expertise

The final characteristic advertisers look for when examining sources is expertise. Spokespersons with higher levels of expertise are more believable. Richard Petty and Jeff Gordon are experts when automobile products and lubricants are advertised. Often when expertise is desired in an ad the advertising agency opts for the CEO or a trained or educated expert in the field. American Express features Maria Barraza, a small-business owner and designer, to promote its Small Business Services. Expertise can be valuable in persuasive advertisements designed to change opinions or attitudes. Spokespersons with high levels of expertise are more capable of persuading an audience than someone with zero or low expertise.[20]

Matching Source Types and Characteristics

The account executive, ad agency, and corporate sponsor, individually or jointly, may choose the type of spokesperson. They can choose a celebrity, CEO, expert, or typical person, and the specific individual should have the key source characteristics.

Celebrities

In terms of trustworthiness, believability, persuasiveness, and likeability, celebrities tend to score well. These virtues increase when the match between the product and celebrity consists of a logical and proper fit. Phil Mickelson endorsing golf merchandise is a good fit, as is Anna Roberts endorsing horse racing. Companies can be creative when making matches. The match of boxer George Foreman to his Lean Mean Grilling Machine has been a great success.[21] Some celebrities have become almost as famous for their advertising appearances as for an acting or athletic career. Danica Patrick has signed endorsement contracts with Honda, Secret, Boost Mobile, Pepsi, and, most recently, Go Daddy, possibly gaining as much notoriety from endorsements as she has from competing in races.[22]

Several dangers exist when using celebrities. Any negative publicity about a celebrity caused by inappropriate conduct may damage credibility. Michael Vick's arrest and conviction for dog fighting created considerable negative press. Hanes brands dropped Charlie Sheen because of domestic violence charges filed against him. Although advertisers like celebrity endorsers because of the potential they have for developing an attraction to their brands, they have to weigh the positive benefits against the potential risks.[23]

The potential for negative publicity has led some advertisers to use deceased celebrities. Companies have concluded that there is no need to risk bringing embarrassment or

1. James Earl Jones	6. Sally Field
2. Tom Hanks	7. Ron Howard
3. Michael J. Fox	8. Will Smith
4. Mike Rowe	9. Bill Cosby
5. Morgan Freeman	10. Denzel Washington

◄ **FIGURE 7.7**
The 10 Most Trusted Celebrities

Source: Adapted from Lacey Rose, "The 10 Most Trusted Celebrities," *Forbes.com* (www.forbes.com/2010/01/25/most-trusted-celebrities-business-intertainment) January 25, 2010.

▲ Michael Jordan is a rare celebrity who can endorse multiple products and maintain a high level of credibility.

injury to themselves or the brand. It is also a reason that more ads use cartoon characters. Practically everyone likes cartoons.

A second danger of using celebrities occurs when they endorse too many products, which can tarnish their credibility. Consumers know celebrities are paid, which detracts from believability. When a celebrity endorses a large number of products, consumers' evaluations of that person's credibility decline. Some advertising research indicates that when a celebrity endorses multiple products it tends to reduce likeability as well as consumer attitudes toward the brand.[24]

As a result, careful consideration should be given to the choice of a celebrity. The individual cannot simply be famous. The person should possess as many of the key source characteristics as possible, match the good or service being advertised, not be "spread too thin" or overexposed, and promote a positive image that can be transferred to the good, service, or company.

CEO

A CEO or other prominent corporate official may or may not possess the characteristics of attractiveness and likeability. CEOs should, however, appear to be trustworthy, have expertise, and maintain a degree of credibility. A CEO is not a professional actor or model. It might be difficult for the CEO to come across well in a commercial.

Companies must be aware of the trustworthiness issue. For example, many times the owner of a local auto dealership represents it as the spokesperson. The primary problem is that many consumers view used-car salespeople as untrustworthy. Other local business owners may be highly trustworthy, such as restaurant owners, physicians, and eye care professionals.

Advertising creatives and account executives carefully consider asking a CEO or business owner to serve as a source. They first must be convinced that the individual has enough of the source characteristics to promote the product and gain the consumer's interest and trust.

Experts

First and foremost, experts should be credible. The advertising agency seeks an expert who is attractive, likeable, and trustworthy. Experts are helpful in promoting health care products and other high-involvement types of products. Recent research indicates that experts are more believable than celebrities for high-technology products, and, as a result, the use of an expert reduces a consumer's level of perceived risk in purchasing the product, which means they are the most helpful when consumers or businesses perceive high levels of risk involved in a purchase.[25] When selecting an expert spokesperson, agency leaders should be certain that the person has valid credentials and will be able to clearly explain a product's benefits. Doing so will reduce the level of perceived risk.

Typical Persons

Advertisements with typical persons are sometimes difficult to prepare, especially when they use real persons. Typical-person sources do not have the name recognition of celebrities. Consequently, advertisers often use multiple sources within one advertisement to build credibility. Increasing the number of sources makes the ad more effective. Hearing three people talk about a good dentist will be more believable than hearing it from only one person. By using multiple sources, viewers are motivated to pay attention and process its arguments.[26]

Real-person ads present a double-edged sword. On the one hand, trustworthiness, similarity, and credibility rise when the source is bald, overweight, or has some other physical imperfections. This can be especially valuable when the bald person promotes a hair replacement program or the overweight source talks about a diet program. On the other hand, attractiveness and likeability may be lower.

Special K cereal created a series of ads featuring real women that the company encountered when conducting consumer research into fitness and weight-loss goals. In one spot, the woman "wants to stop using my arms to hide my stomach;" in another the woman wants to hear four little words: "Have you lost weight?" In another ad, the mother wants to show a young daughter "that mommy feels confident," and the voice-over conveys, "Be victorious— take the Special K Challenge." According to Jose Alberto Duenas, Vice-President for Cereal Marketing at Kellogg, "If you want to make a connection, you have to give consumers a chance to take part in the spotlight. Authenticity is what we're looking for."[27]

Using customers in ads can be difficult, because they will flub lines and look less natural on the screen. These difficulties with actual customers and employees lead many ad agencies to turn to professional models and actors to portray ordinary people. Professional actors make filming and photographing much easier. Also, the agency is in the position to choose a likeable, but plain, person. The desired effects (trustworthiness, similarity and credibility) are often easier to create using professional actors and models.

In general, the advertising agency wants to be certain that the source or spokesperson has the major characteristics the advertisement requires. Likeability would be important when creating a humorous appeal. In a rational or informational ad, expertise and credibility are crucial, especially in business-to-business ads. In each case, trying to include as many of the characteristics as possible when retaining a spokesperson will be the goal.

▲ This Jockey advertisement features an older typical-person model.

CREATING AN ADVERTISEMENT

Figure 7.8 illustrates the process a creative uses in preparing an advertisement. The work begins with the creative brief, which outlines the message theme of the advertisement, as well as other pertinent information. Using the creative brief blueprint, the creative develops a means–end chain, starting with an attribute of the product that generates a specific customer benefit and eventually produces a desirable end state. This means–end chain forms the foundation on which all other decisions will be made.

Following the development of the means–end chain, the creative selects a message strategy, the appeal, and the executional framework. The creative suggests or chooses a source or spokesperson at this point, because the choice usually affects other creative decisions. Development of the leverage point that moves the consumer from the product attribute or consumer benefit to the desired end state is usually undertaken after the creative begins work on the advertisement. The type of leverage point depends on the message strategy, appeal, and executional framework.

Although certain combinations tend to work well together, the creative has an almost infinite number of options when preparing an advertisement or campaign. For

5 What process is used to create advertisements?

FIGURE 7.8 ▶
Creating an Advertisement

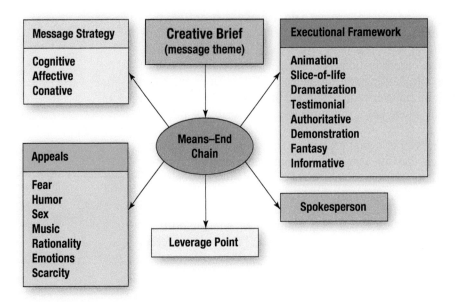

example, if the creative wants to present a cognitive message strategy, the most logical appeal is rationality. The creative could, however, use fear, humor, sex, music, or even scarcity. An emotional approach would be the one appeal that would not work. The emotional part of the advertisement tends to overpower the cognitive message being sent to the viewer.

When the creative decides to employ humor with a cognitive strategy, other logical and illogical combinations emerge. In terms of an executional framework, the dramatization and authoritative approaches tend not to work as well with humor. The other executional frameworks are viable. This flexibility allows a variety of advertisements to emerge from a single means–end chain. The best combination depends on the creative's expertise and experience as well as her judgment regarding the ideal way to accomplish the client's advertising objectives.

ADVERTISING EFFECTIVENESS

6 What are the principles of advertising effectiveness?

Producing effective ads requires the joint efforts of the account executive, creative, account planner, and media planner. Working independently can produce some award-winning ads, but often they will not be effective advertisements that meet a client's objectives. One major difficulty ad agencies face is producing a commercial that stands out among the thousands of competing messages. An advertisement that breaks through the clutter has won half the battle. Finding ways to lead consumers to react to the ad in the desired manner is what remains.

An effective advertisement accomplishes the client's objectives. Making sure the commercial accomplishes the IMC objectives is the challenge. The seven basic principles of advertising effectiveness, shown in Figure 7.9, should be followed.

FIGURE 7.9 ▶
Principles of Effective
Advertising

- Visual consistency
- Campaign duration
- Repeated taglines
- Consistent positioning—avoid ambiguity
- Simplicity
- Identifiable selling point
- Create an effective flow

Visual Consistency

Repeatedly seeing a specific image or visual display helps to embed it in long-term memory. Visual consistency is important because most customers spend very little time viewing an advertisement. In most cases, an individual makes just a casual glance at a print advertisement or a cursory glimpse at a television commercial. Visual consistency leads the viewer to move the message from short-term to long-term memory. Consistently used logos and other long-standing images help place the brand or company in the consumer's mind. People remember Nike because of the visually consistent use of Swoosh. The Prudential Rock emblem is well established in the minds of many consumers.

Campaign Duration

The length or duration of a campaign becomes important because consumers often do not pay attention to advertisements. Using the same advertisement for an appropriate period of time helps embed the message in the consumer's long-term memory. Account executives give careful thought to how long to run an advertisement. The ad should be changed before it becomes stale and viewers become bored with it; however, changing ads too frequently impedes retention. Reach and frequency affect the duration of a campaign. Higher frequency usually leads to a shorter duration. Low reach may be associated with a longer duration. In any case, typical campaigns last about 6 months, but there are exceptions.

Source: Courtesy of Loeffler Ketchum Mountjoy.

Source: Courtesy of Loeffler Ketchum Mountjoy.

▲ Notice the visual consistency present in these two advertisements for tourism in North Carolina.

Repeated Taglines

Visual consistency combined with consistent taglines can be a powerful approach. The advertisement may change, but either the visual imagery or the tagline remains the same. The U.S. Army has promoted the tagline "Be all that you can be" for many years, and the Marines are known as "The few. The proud. The Marines." Taglines help consumers tie the advertisement into current knowledge structure nodes that already exist in their minds. Figure 7.10 contains some of the more common taglines.

Consistent Positioning

Maintaining consistent positioning throughout a product's life makes it more likely that a consumer will place the product in a cognitive map. When the firm emphasizes quality in every advertisement, it becomes easier to tie the product into the consumer's cognitive map than if the firm stresses quality in some ads, price in others, and convenience in a

1. A diamond is forever.	6. Look Mom, no cavities.
2. Be all you can be.	7. The ultimate driving machine.
3. Can you hear me now?	8. What can Brown do for you?
4. Don't leave home without it.	9. We try harder.
5. Just do it.	10. You deserve a break today.

◀ **FIGURE 7.10**
Which Taglines Can You Identify?

third campaign. Inconsistency in positioning makes the brand and company more difficult to remember. Consistent positioning avoids ambiguity, and the message stays clear and understandable.

Simplicity

Simple advertisements are easier to comprehend than are complex ads. A print ad with a short tagline and limited copy will be much easier to read than one that is overloaded and complex. Consequently, advertisers should resist the temptation to describe all of a product's attributes in a single commercial. Although this practice is more prevalent in business-to-business print advertisements, it should be avoided there as well. Also, consumer ads on radio or television spots can be verbally overloaded, forcing the announcer to talk faster. Doing so is usually ineffective, because the listener receives too much information in a short time period.

The principle of simplicity applies to Internet advertising. The primary reason is load time. Individuals surfing the Internet will not wait more than a few seconds for something to load; if it does not load quickly, they move on to another site.

Identifiable Selling Point

An identifiable selling point places emphasis on three words: (1) identifiable, (2) selling, and (3) point. The advertisement should stress a selling point (price, quality, convenience, luxury) that is easily *identifiable* to the viewer of the ad. The advertisement should *sell* a product's benefits as much as the product itself. Also, the concept is a selling *point,* not selling points. The best advertisements emphasize one major point and do not confuse the viewer by presenting too many ideas. An advertisement's primary goal is to fix the product into the viewer's cognitive map through establishing new linkages or strengthening current linkages. An identifiable selling point helps reach that goal.

Create an Effective Flow

In order to create an effective flow, a print ad should move the reader's eye to all of the key points in the ad. In a television ad, the points to be made should flow in a manner that leads the consumer to the appropriate action or conclusion. Ads without flow confuse the consumer or are simply tuned out.

Beating Ad Clutter

Overcoming clutter constitutes a major challenge when creating an effective advertising campaign. The presence of a competitor's advertisement within the same medium or time slot makes the ad clutter problem worse. A recent survey of television advertising revealed that during prime-time programming 42 percent of the ads shown had one or more competitors advertised during the same hour. Research suggests that an advertisement's effectiveness will be significantly reduced when a competitor's advertisement runs during the same time slot.[28]

One method advertisers use to overcome this brand interference is repetition. Repeating an ad can increase brand and ad recall. In advertising studies, repetition effectively increases recall when no competitor ads are present. When competitor ads are present, repetition does not help the competitive ad interference problem and does not stimulate greater recall.

Variability Theory

Mere repetition of an advertisement does not always work. Some advertisers have begun to emphasize the principles present in **variability theory**,[29] which suggests that variable encoding occurs when a consumer sees the same advertisement in different environments. These varied environments increase recall and effectiveness by encoding it into the brain through various methods. Creatives can generate the effect by varying the situational context of a particular ad. For example, the MasterCard campaign uses various settings to convey the same basic message, "There are some things money can't buy. For everything else, there's MasterCard." Varying the context of the ad increases recall and is an effective method for overcoming competitive ad interference.[30]

▲ These two advertisements for St. Patrick's use variability theory concepts to help beat clutter.

Using a Second Medium

Using two media to convey a message generally is more effective than repeating an advertisement within the same medium. An advertisement placed in more than one medium reduces competing ad interference. In other words, an ad that appears on television and in magazines works better than one that appears only on television. Consumers seeing an advertisement in a different medium are more likely to recall the ad than if it is always seen in only one medium.

Clutter remains a difficult problem in advertising. Creatives who are able to capture the attention of the audience and transmit messages successfully are in great demand. Companies constantly experiment with various approaches to reach audiences. When a program works, the advertising firm and its client have a great deal to celebrate.

INTERNATIONAL IMPLICATIONS

Many common themes and messages translate well across cultures. The major challenge is making sure that the message strategy and form of executional framework match the tendencies and preferences in a region. For example, some cultures tend to be more rational in their decision-making processes, whereas others favor more emotional approaches. This may, in turn, affect the selection of a message strategy in a given nation.

Comparison ads are less common in other countries, due to both social and cultural differences as well as legal restrictions. Advertisers should be aware of these issues. For example, in many European countries comparative advertising is illegal. In Japan, it is not illegal, but it runs against the society's cultural preferences. In Brazil, the advertising

7 How are advertising programs adjusted to fit international circumstances?

industry is so powerful that any attempt to create a comparative advertisement has been challenged and stopped. Often, international consumers not only dislike the advertisements, but often transfer that dislike to the company sponsoring the ad.[31]

The message strategy chosen affects the execution. For instance, the slice-of-life execution has become popular in Japan in recent years. The slice-of-life style is suited to Japan's soft-sell approach to marketing. A more hard-sell attitude may be used in the United States. Japanese advertising tends to be more indirect, and the slice-of-life approach allows advertisers to present a product in a typical everyday situation. Benefits can be presented in a positive light without making brazen or harsh claims and without directly disparaging the competition.[32]

Other patterns and changes in preferred forms of executions can be discovered by watching local media and reading about trends in magazines and trade journals in the country involved. While maintaining an overall message and idea, the advertiser must adjust to social customs present in a region.

! INTEGRATED CAMPAIGNS IN ACTION

The Soap Opera

The Soap Opera is a one-location laundry that offers 24/7 self-service washers and dryers as well as a fluff and fold service. With the fluff and fold service, customers drop off their laundry and The Soap Opera's staff wash, iron, and fold the clothes. The Soap Opera is located in Ruston, Louisiana, near the campus of Louisiana Tech University.

The owners of The Soap Opera met with Emogen Marketing to discuss the feasibility of a marketing campaign. The objective of the campaign was to increase awareness of the fluff and fold service, particularly among college students. With limited funds, Emogen Marketing crafted a campaign entitled "Why do your own laundry?" that involved a 1-day, on-campus event; creation of a Facebook page; posters on campus bulletin boards; in-store registration for a $50 gift card; and a series of newspaper ads in the student newspaper.

Illustration was a central execution theme in the campaign. It was used in newspaper ads, on the posters, and in displays for the 1-day, on-campus event. One display featured a mannequin dressed as a typical college student doing laundry at the entrance to the student center with the bubble question, "Why do your own laundry?" It was supported by props of a washing machine, a box of laundry detergent, and 20 pieces of clothing strung out on a laundry line. In another display, a mannequin dressed as a Soap Opera employee was rigged with video cameras and a microphone, allowing Emogen staff to interact with students in the style of *Candid Camera*.

During the month following the ad campaign, sales increased by almost 25 percent at The Soap Opera, making it the highest monthly sales in over 20 years of operation. The sales increase held steady for a full year after the promotion. In addition, brand name recognition and brand awareness both increased substantially for The Soap Opera.[33]

▲ Illustration was a key component of The Soap Opera campaign.

Your instructor has additional information about the ads, visuals, and displays used in this campaign.

SUMMARY

Advertising is the process of transmitting a personal message through one or more impersonal media. The message should reflect the image that occurs throughout an IMC program. Three types of message strategies are present in advertisements. Cognitive strategies emphasize rational and logical arguments to compel consumers to make purchases. Affective strategies are oriented toward buyer emotions and feelings. Conative strategies are linked to more direct responses, behaviors, and actions. These strategies should be integrated with various types of appeals through the media selected for the campaign.

Executional frameworks tell the story in the ad. Animation has become more sophisticated and provides many new creative approaches in the design of ads. The slice-of-life approach and dramatizations are problem-solving types of ads, leading the consumer to something better by using the product. Testimonials are rendered by individuals who have realized the benefits of a product. An authoritative expert can build consumer confidence in a product or company. Demonstrations show how products can be used. A fantasy takes people away from the real world to a make-believe place. This makes the product more exotic and desirable. Informative ads render basic information about the product. Each execution can be used effectively to persuade consumers and business-to-business buyers to consider a company's offerings.

Celebrities, CEOs, experts, and typical persons can be chosen to be "out front" in the advertisement. Each has advantages and disadvantages. The marketing team selects sources or spokespersons based on the individual's attractiveness, similarity, likeability, trustworthiness, expertise, or credibility. The more of these characteristics that are present, the better off the advertiser will be.

Effective advertising campaigns are based on the seven principles of visual consistency, sufficient campaign duration, repeated taglines, consistent positioning, simplicity, presentation of an identifiable selling point, and creation of an effective flow. Creatives and account executives incorporate these principles into the advertising campaign to enhance the odds of success. Clutter can be overcome by repeating ads and showing them in various media.

Many consider advertising design to be the most glamorous part of the advertising industry, and in many ways it is. The other side of the glamour coin is hard work and the constant pressure to perform. Many people think being a creative is a burnout-type of job. At the same time, those who have proven track records of success are well rewarded for their efforts. Utilizing the principles presented in this chapter can be a key to success in the highly competitive and exciting business of advertising design.

KEY TERMS

message theme   The outline of the key idea(s) that the advertising program is supposed to convey.

message strategy   The primary tactic used to deliver the message theme.

cognitive message strategy   The presentation of rational arguments or pieces of information to consumers.

generic messages   Direct promotions of product attributes or benefits without any claim of superiority.

preemptive messages   Claims of superiority based on a specific attribute or benefit of a product that preempts the competition from making the same claim.

unique selling proposition (USP)   An explicit, testable claim of uniqueness or superiority that can be supported or substantiated in some manner.

hyperbole   Making an untestable claim based upon some attribute or benefit.

comparative advertisement   The direct or indirect comparison of a good or service to the competition.

affective message strategies   Ads designed to invoke feelings and emotions and match them with the good, service, or company.

resonance advertising   Attempting to connect a product with a consumer's experiences to develop stronger ties between the product and the consumer.

emotional advertising   Attempting to elicit powerful emotions that eventually lead to brand recall and choice.

conative message strategy   Advertisements that are designed to lead directly to some type of consumer response.

action-inducing conative advertisements   Advertisements that create situations in which cognitive knowledge of the product or affective liking of the product follow the actual purchase or arise during usage of the product.

promotional support conative advertisements   Ads designed to support other promotional efforts.

executional framework   The manner in which an ad appeal is presented.

expert authority   When an advertiser seeks to convince viewers that a given product is superior to other brands in some authoritative manner.

sources and spokespersons   Persons in the advertisement who make the actual presentation.

variability theory   A theory stating that when a consumer sees the same advertisement in different environments, the ad will be more effective.

REVIEW QUESTIONS

1. Name the three types of message strategies creatives can use. How are message strategies related to the message theme?

2. What types of goods or services best match cognitive message strategies? List the five types of cognitive approaches.

3. When will an affective message strategy be most effective? What two types of affective messages can creatives design? Give an example of each.

4. What is the primary goal of a conative message strategy?

5. How is an executional framework different from an ad appeal? How are they related?

6. List as many uses of animation-based advertisements as possible. What forms of animation are possible with the available technology?

7. How are slice-of-life and dramatization executional frameworks similar? How are they different?

8. How are authoritative and informational executional frameworks similar? How are they different?

9. What types of testimonials can advertisers use? Give an example of each.

10. Which media are best for demonstration-type ads?

11. What kinds of products or services are best suited to fantasy-based executional frameworks? What products or services are poor candidates for fantasies?

12. Identify the four main types of sources or spokespersons. What are the advantages and disadvantages of each?

13. List the key criteria used when selecting a spokesperson.

14. Identify the tactics available to overcome clutter. How does variability theory assist in this process?

15. What issues are present when adapting an advertising program to an international audience?

CRITICAL THINKING EXERCISES

Discussion Questions

1. Select five advertisements from a magazine. Identify the message strategy, appeal, and executional framework in each. Did the creative select the right combination for the advertisement? What other message strategies or executional frameworks could have been used?

2. Watch five television advertisements. Identify the message strategy, appeal, and executional framework each uses. Did the creative select the right combination for the advertisement? What other message strategies or executional frameworks could have been used?

3. Studies involving comparative advertisements as compared to noncomparative advertisements produced the following findings.[34] Discuss why you think each statement is true. Try to think of comparative ads you have seen that substantiate these claims.

   a. Message awareness was higher for comparative ads than for noncomparative ads if the brands were already established brands.

   b. Brand recall was higher for comparative ads than for noncomparative ads.

   c. Comparative ads were viewed as less believable than noncomparative ads.

   d. Attitudes toward comparative ads were more negative than those toward noncomparative ads.

4. The marketing team for Charles Schwab wants to develop an advertisement with the message theme that Charles Schwab understands the needs of individual consumers and can design an investment strategy to meet each person's particular needs. Which type of message strategy should Schwab choose? Why? Based on the message strategy chosen, which executional framework should the company use? Why? What type of source or spokesperson should

Schwab use? Why? Would the type of media being used for the advertisement affect the message strategy choice? Explain your answer.

5. A resort in Florida wants to develop an advertisement highlighting scuba diving classes. The target market will be college students. Discuss the merits of each of the following approaches. In your opinion, which one would be the best? Why? Describe a television ad that could be created using the strategy you chose.

   a. Hyperbole cognitive message strategy, humor appeal, and demonstration execution

   b. Emotional message strategy, emotional appeal, and slice-of-life execution

   c. Conative message strategy, scarcity appeal, and informative execution

   d. Emotional or resonance message strategy, sex appeal, and fantasy execution

   e. Comparative message strategy, fear appeal, and testimonial execution

6. Name three influential commercial spokespersons. For each one, discuss the five characteristics used to evaluate spokespersons and their overall level of credibility. Next, make a list of three individuals who are poor spokespersons. Discuss each of the five evaluation characteristics for each of these individuals. What differences exist between an effective and a poor spokesperson?

7. Find a copy of a business journal, such as *BusinessWeek* or *Fortune,* or a trade journal. Also locate a copy of a consumer periodical such as *Glamour, Time, Sports Illustrated,* or a specialty magazine. Look through an entire issue. What differences between the advertisements in the business journal and consumer journals are readily noticeable? For each of the concepts that follow, discuss specific

differences you noted between the two types of magazines. Explain why the differences exist.

   a. Message strategies

   b. Executional frameworks

   c. Sources and spokespersons

8. Identify an advertisement that uses each of the following executional frameworks. Evaluate the advertisement in terms of how well it is executed. Also, did the appeal and message strategy fit well with the execution? Was the ad memorable? What made it memorable?

   a. Animation

   b. Slice-of-life

   c. Dramatization

   d. Testimonial

   e. Authoritative

   f. Demonstration

   g. Fantasy

   h. Informative

INTEGRATED LEARNING EXERCISES

1. Current as well as past Super Bowl ads are available at **www.superbowl-ads.com**. Access the site and compare Super Bowl ads for the last several years. What types of message strategies were used? What types of executions were used? Who and what types of endorsers were used? Compare and contrast these three elements of ads.

2. Most advertising agencies provide examples of advertisements on company Web pages. The goal is to display the agency's creative abilities to potential clients. Using a search engine, locate three different advertising agencies. Locate samples of their work. Compare the ads produced by these three agencies in terms of message appeals, executions, and spokespersons. What similarities do you see? What differences do you see? Which agency, in your opinion, is the most creative? Why?

3. Access the following Web sites. For each, identify the primary message strategy used. Does the site use any sources or spokespersons? What type of appeal is being used? For each Web site, suggest how the site could be improved. Explain how the change would improve the site.

   a. Georgia–Pacific (**www.gp.com**)

   b. Playland International (**www.playland-inc.com**)

   c. MGM Grand (**www.mgmgrand.com**)

   d. The Exotic Body (**www.exoticbody.com**)

   e. CoverGirl (**www.covergirl.com**)

   f. Dove (**www.dove.com**)

   g. Skechers (**www.skechers.com**)

4. Access the following Web sites. For each, identify and evaluate the primary executional framework used. Is it the best execution, or would another execution work better? Does the site use any sources or spokespersons? What type of appeal is being used? For each Web site, suggest how the site could be improved. Explain how the change would improve the site.

   a. Kellogg's Frosted Flakes (**www.frostedflakes.com**)

   b. Bonne Bell (**www.bonnebell.com**)

   c. MessageMedia (**www.message-media.com.au**)

   d. Jantzen (**www.jantzen.com**)

   e. Jockey International (**www.jockey.com**)

STUDENT PROJECT

Creative Corner

For a number of years, LendingTree.com used the tagline "When banks compete, you win." In the mid-2000s, when the housing market tumbled, mortgage companies faced financial problems, and consumers defaulted on home mortgages, LendingTree.com changed its approach. The company developed new ads and modified the Web site to educate consumers about "smart borrowing." Other financial and mortgage companies followed suit. JPMorgan Chase asserted "Whether you are saving money, looking for a loan, or managing a business, you can always depend on Chase." Astoria Federal Savings promoted its longevity, telling consumers it had been in business "more than 118 years" and using phrases such as "We're part of your community" and "We're here when you need us."[35]

The marketing department for First National Bank intends to promote its home mortgage business. They are not sure about which creative message strategy to use, which execution would work best, and which appeal to use. They would also like to use some type of spokesperson, but they are not sure which of the four types would be the most effective. They also realize they cannot afford a famous celebrity.

Based on the information provided, design a print advertisement for the local newspaper for First National Bank. Describe a television campaign for the bank. Before launching into these two creative assignments, identify and justify your choice of creative message strategy, executional framework, appeal, and spokesperson.

CASE 1

BLACK-EYED MARKETING

If Black Eyed Peas band member will.i.am wasn't in music, "He'd be the best ad executive on Madison Avenue," says Randy Phillips, president and CEO of the concert promoter AEG Live. "I've never seen anyone more astute at dealing with sponsors' and companies' needs and understanding their brands." The Black Eyed Peas have been able to move beyond the status as a high-energy band into the world of corporate sponsorship without missing a beat.

Marketers love the Black Eyed Peas for the diverse ethnicity of the band's members, writes the *Wall Street Journal*. The band's corporate backers include Coors, Levi's, Honda, Apple, Verizon, and Pepsi. The advertisement featuring the group's song "Hey Mama" and dancing silhouettes that was used to help launch Apple's iTunes store gained almost iconic status.

What makes this group of musicians such an effective set of spokespeople? Part of the appeal is the group's global fan base and the Pea's fetching party anthems, with powerful dance beats, crazy special effects, and repetitive hooks that are integrated into numerous party mixes. As one critic noted, the band achieves the nearly impossible—making both kids and their parents feel cool at the same time.

Beyond the glitz and glitter of the shows, the group gives careful thought to its marketing. Oftentimes, will.i.am pitches concepts to corporate sponsors himself, using "decks" that sum up the Peas' package, frequently in PowerPoint form. He reports, "I consider us a brand. A brand always has stylized decks, from colors to fonts. Here's our demographic. Here's the reach. Here's the potential. Here's how the consumer will benefit from the collaboration."

There was a time when rock and roll was nearly synonymous with rebellion. Bands with corporate ties would be viewed as sell outs. For companies such a move would seem too risky; especially if the band's fans felt betrayed. Over the years, music has become less threatening, as Baby Boomers near retirement age.

The economics of music have also changed. Downloading and pirating CDs is commonplace. Bands can no longer count on record sales to make money. Many younger bands now look for other sources of income and publicity. The Peas were among the fastest learners of the industry's new math. Even now, however, the band hears complaints that they are merely shills. "You have to take the criticism, and sometimes it hurts a lot," says band member Stacy Ferguson, who is also known Fergie.

Currently, many top-name musicians and groups have corporate sponsors. Cooperative advertisements promote the brand, the band, and often a tour. The Rolling Stones began the movement when the group's "Tattoo You" tour was sponsored by Jovan Musk cologne. Even groups that at first resolutely avoided corporate tie-ins, such as U2, have changed. U2 developed a relationship with Apple that included commercials featuring the song "Vertigo." The band helped with BlackBerry commercials and had a sponsored tour with the brand.

The Black Eyed Peas continues to expand their corporate connections. A concert in Times Square promoted Samsung's new line of 3D televisions, which led to a meeting with *Avatar* director James Cameron, who agreed to direct a feature film

Source: Shutterstock.

▲ The Black Eyed Peas use marketing to enhance the band's image and presence.

about the Peas. The 3D film incorporates concerts, travel footage, and narrative themes about technology, dreams, and the brain.

According to will.i.am, all corporate partnerships are equally important. The band lends its music at relatively small charges in exchange for exposure. "It wasn't about the check," says former manager Seth Friedman.

The efforts have paid off. The Black Eyed Peas have performed at an NFL season-kickoff show, New Year's Eve in Times Square, the Grammys, a Victoria's Secret fashion show, and the season opener for *The Oprah Winfrey Show*, for which they summoned a flash mob of synchronized dancers to downtown Chicago. As will.i.am puts it, "I get the credit from the brands. They know. I used to work with the marketing people and the agencies, now I work with the CEOs of these companies."

1. Discuss each of the source characteristics in terms of the Black Eyed Peas serving as a spokesperson for a product. Would it make a difference as to what type of product the Black Eyed Peas were endorsing? Explain.

2. What types of brands or products are best suited to endorsements by the Black Eyed Peas? By rock bands in general? What about country music artists?

3. If you were going to design a television advertisement for a concert for the Black Eyed Peas, what would be your target market? What message strategy and executional framework would you use? Why? Describe your concept of an effective television ad.

4. Suppose the Black Eyed Peas were contracted to perform at your university. Design a print ad for your local student newspaper. Discuss the message strategy and execution you used and why you used it.

5. What types of brands or products would not be suited to endorsements by groups such as the Black Eyed Peas?

Source: John Jurgensen, "The Most Corporate Band in America," *Wall Street Journal Online* (**www.wsj.com**, accessed April 14, 2010).

SOUTH AUSTRALIAN FOOD MARKETING

CASE 2

The South Australia (SA) Food Center was established by the South Australian government in 2008 to provide practical advice to food businesses in the state. Approximately 300 businesses have already taken advantage of the agency's expertise. South Australia's major export markets are Japan, the United States, and Hong Kong. Its main exports are products meat, seafood, fruit, and cheese. The SA Food Center aims to promote South Australia's food businesses through *Food Talk* (an online magazine), Food-e-News (e-mail news updates), and the Premier's Food Awards (awards for South Australian food producers).

South Australian food producers work hard to make sure that their brand is exciting to consumers, focusing on factors such as packaging and labeling. However, like many businesses, they fall short in effectively marketing their products. SA Food Center encourages food producers to promote their brands by not only informing consumers about their availability, but to highlight what is special about a particular product. The key aim of the SA Food Center is to create a collaborative partnership with industry and government, in order to ensure a thriving South Australian food industry. One such result of this work came from Charlie's Group Limited.

▲ Thanks to the collaboration between SA Food Center and Charlie's Group Limited, South Australian fruit growers have seen a boost in sales.

South Australian fruit growers received a considerable boost from Charlie's Group Limited, the manufacturers of Charlie's and Phoenix Organics (smoothies and organic beverages). Charlie's, which was established in 1999, operates in New Zealand, Australia, Asia, the Pacific, the Middle East, and India. It has a major production facility in South Australia. Charlie's was able to gain entry into 750 Coles supermarket stores across Australia. Eleven Charlie's drinks are offered, including the brand-leading Spirulina Smoothie. The deal with the supermarket was so big that Charlie's needed to squeeze an additional 4 million lemons each year, a 300 percent increase, just to meet the demand. Coles supported the new brand roll-out with in-store marketing programs, and Charlie's launched a new advertising campaign. All of this was great news for South Australia's fruit growers.

Even foods such as mushrooms are not forgotten when the SA Food Center promotes South Australian produce. The SA Food Center promotes many events, including annual food festivals and shopping appearances alongside celebrity chefs and media personalities. The South Australian mushroom industry has three major campaigns a year. Mushroom Madness recognizes the best mushroom retailer in each state in Australia. The Mushroom Mania program involves some 2,000 restaurants across Australia in an effort to promote mushrooms as a healthy eating option when dining out. BBQ Mushrooms, fronted by the enthusiastic TV chef Fast Ed, encourages consumers to use mushrooms for outdoor meals. The industry also runs major advertising campaigns, targeting families, grocery buyers, and chefs. Growers also support the Mushroom Lovers' Club, which sends out regular newsletters to consumers, and Mushroom Farm Walks, where South Australian chefs are encouraged to visit mushroom farms to understand the mushroom-growing process. This well-supported program is indicative of the activities of the SA Food Center.

1. What type of message strategy should SA Food Center utilize? Should it be the same for all of the brands and in all of the markets (will there be strength in the unity of a South Australia brand)?

2. What leverage point makes the most sense for South Australian food producers' advertising?

3. What type of executional framework should be used in traditional advertisements aimed at consumers?

4. What type of executional framework should be used for print advertisements aimed at business-to-business sales? Why might it differ from ads aimed at consumers?

5. Should the SA Food Center use a spokesperson? If so, which one of the four types should be used?

Sources: Safe Food Centre (**www.safoodcentre.com.au**, accessed November 16, 2010); Charlie's Group (**www.charliesgroup.co.nz**, accessed November 6, 2010).

Source: © Olga Lyubkin–Fotolia.com.

CHAPTER 6

Developing Creative Work 2

9 Copywriting

It's a Winner

Campaign:	Company:	Agency:	Awards:
"The Habana Campaign"	The Star	DDB South Africa	2010 ADreach Cannes Award

1. What basic style of writing is used for advertising copy?
2. Which copy elements are essential to a print ad?
3. How can we characterize the message and tools of radio advertising?
4. What is the best way to summarize the major elements of television commercials?
5. How is Web advertising written?

The Right Message to the Right Audience
Time and Time Again

The winner of the 2010 ADreach Cannes Award was an innovative campaign created by Greg Watt and Martin Sing as art directors, Gareth Lessing as creative director, and Kenneth van Reenen as the copywriter, all from DDB South Africa. The campaign was designed for *The Star* newspaper. The ad campaign focused on the South African national rugby team, the Springboks, and some of its top players. It was given the title "The Habana Campaign" after Bryan Habana who had scored a record equaling eight tries (scores) during the Rugby World Cup in 2007.

The copywriter's idea was to mimic a live commentary featuring the Springbok players. The simple, yet effective, set of street pole advertisements read "Burger Passes to Habana," "Habana Passes to Fourie," then "Fourie Finds a Gap," and "Fourie Scores a Try." The final poster, which also featured *The Star* logo, stated "The Most Up-to-Date Sporting News." The idea was to maximize the repetitive message opportunities of street pole advertising to target consumers who want access to the very latest news and sports reports.

Street pole advertising has to be eye catching and succinct. The street poles are placed on high traffic volume routes across South Africa. They are double-sided panels that allow for specific directional messages for either commuters or pedestrians. ADreach claims that the street poles offer 24-hour brand exposure because they also incorporate illumination for night viewing.

ADreach itself is the third largest outdoor media company in South Africa, with over 40,000 advertising signs across the country. In championing the Habana campaign, they hope to show that cost-effective advertising solutions are available in outdoor media.

DDB is a worldwide agency that has been consistently ranked very highly by the advertising industry and has topped many creative polls. Bill Bernach was the founder of the group, arguably one of the most influential creative forces in advertising. His style, continued to this day by the group, aims to incorporate humor and striking images. In 2009, total advertising revenues for the group were estimated at $1.1 billion.

For DDB South Africa, the 2010 award was just the latest in a string of wins. In 2009, they won the Ad Agency of the Year at the seventh annual AdReview

Awards in Johannesburg. The judges noted that although DDB South Africa was very small compared to some of its competitors, creatively it was very effective. In no small part was this due to the skills of its copywriters.

Kenneth van Reenen had been the copywriter for one of the agency's most publicized campaigns: The Energizer campaign. The Energizer campaign was the Cannes Lion Press Grand Prix print winner in 2008. This campaign showed children getting into trouble because the batteries in their electric toys had failed. The copywriting headline was "Never Let Their Toys Die. The World's Longest Lasting Battery. Energizer." The advertising ran from June 2008 and the brief was to increase the sales of Energizer lithium batteries over the Christmas period. The target audience was parents.

The Energizer campaign had been selected from 28,000 entries from 85 countries. The effectiveness of the campaign was such that the Energizer brand hit national retail market leadership in South Africa for the first time in its 10 years of trading in the country. Other awards for that campaign included the 2008 Creative Circle Magazine of the Year, a 2008 Gold Clio, and a 2008 One Show Merit. The ads and copy were designed for maximum effect, showing worrying scenarios that could develop if children's Christmas toys stopped working.

Creative ideas and copywriting from agencies such as DDB South Africa continue to extend the importance of outdoor advertising in South Africa; it is a thriving marketing opportunity for brands and one that clearly has a definitive impact on consumers.

Print advertising and particularly street pole advertisements can be somewhat controversial. In the *It's a Wrap* feature at the end of the chapter, we look at why in countries such as South Africa the debate about outdoor advertising is ongoing.

Sources: http://streetpoleads.co.za; www.biz-community.com; www.canneslions.com; www.theloerieawards.co.za; www.jom.co.za.

Words and pictures work together to produce a creative concept. However, the idea behind a creative concept in advertising is usually expressed in some attention-getting and memorable phrase, such as "Curiously Strong Mints" for Altoids or "Eat Mor Chikin" for Chick-fil A. Finding these "magic words" is the responsibility of copywriters who search for the right way to warm up a mood or soften consumer resistance. They begin with the strategy outlined in the previous chapter, which is usually summarized in a creative brief. Then, working with an art director, and perhaps a creative director, the creative team searches for Big Ideas, in the form of magic words and powerful visuals that translate the strategy into a message that is attention getting and memorable. This chapter describes the role of the copywriter as part of this team and explains the practice of copywriting in print, broadcast, and Internet advertising.

WHAT IS THE LANGUAGE OF COPYWRITING?

Some creative concepts are primarily visual, but intriguing ideas can also be expressed through language; and a truly great Big Idea will come to life in the interaction between the words and pictures. For example, a long-running campaign for the NYNEX Yellow Pages illustrates how words and pictures work together to create a concept with a twist. The campaign used visual plays on words to illustrate some of the headings in its directory. Each pun makes sense when the visual is married with the heading from the directory but neither the words or the pictures would work on their own. One commercial in the series included three train engineers with overalls, caps, and bandannas sitting in rocking chairs in a parlor and having tea to illustrate the "Civil Engineering" category; a picture of a bull sleeping on its back illustrates the category "Bulldozing."

Although advertising is highly visual, words are crucial in four types of advertisements:

1. *Complex* If the message is complicated, particularly if it is making an argument, words can be more specific than visuals and can be read over and over until the meaning is clear.
2. *High Involvement* If the ad is for a high-involvement product, meaning the consumer spends a lot of time considering it, then the more information the better. That means using words.
3. *Explanation* Information that needs definition and explanation, like how a new wireless phone works, is best delivered through words.
4. *Abstract* If a message tries to convey abstract qualities, such as justice and quality, words tend to communicate these concepts more easily than pictures.

The Copywriter

The person who shapes and sculpts the words in marketing communication is called a **copywriter.** *Copy* is the text of an ad or the words people say in a commercial. A successful advertising copywriter is a savvy marketer and a literary master, sometimes described as a "killer poet." Many copywriters have a background in English or literature. They love words and search for the clever twist, the pun, the powerful description, the punch, the nuance, as well as the rhyme and rhythm of speech. They use words that whip and batter, plead, sob, cajole, and impress. They know the meanings, derivations, moods, and feelings of words and the reverberations and vibrations they create in a reader's mind. A classic ad, titled "The Wonderful World of Words," expresses this fascination. A house ad for the business-to-business agency Marsteller Inc., it was written by Bill Marsteller, another advertising legend. He also was co-founder of public relations agency Burson-Marsteller. Here is an excerpt from this ad:

> "Human beings come in all sizes, a variety of colors, in different ages, and with unique, complex and changing personalities.
>
> So do Words.
>
> There are tall, skinny words, and short, fat ones, and strong ones and weak ones, and boy words and girl words.
>
> For instance, title, lattice, latitude, lily, tattle, Illinois, and intellect are all lean and lanky. While these words get their height partly out of t's and l's and i's, other words are tall and skinny without a lot of ascenders and descenders. Take, for example, Abraham, peninsula and ellipsis, all tall.
>
> Here are some nice short-fat words: hog, yogurt, bomb, pot, bon-bon, acne, plump, sop and slobber."

In addition to having an ear for the perfect phrase, copywriters listen to the way people talk and identify the tone of voice that best fits the target audience and the brand. An example comes from an all-copy ad for British Airways. Set up like a poem with definite rhythm and alliteration, the copy block begins and ends with the airlines initials, but in between it lyrically interprets what "upgrading" to BA means to a passenger:

CLASSIC
The NYNEX ads feature puns based on Yellow Pages category headings. This ad, which is directed to media buyers, uses that same creative Big Idea with a visual pun on the heading "Amusement Devices" in the directory.

__Be a guest not a__
__passenger.__ We believe
The way you fly is
just as important
as where you fly.
It's not simply
about getting

a seat, it's about
getting service.
Not just food
but a meal. Not
just something
to watch but
something worth

watching. In short,
it's about upgrading
flying for every
passenger on
every plane. Now
there's an ideA.

Source: Courtesy of British Airways plc.

Like poets, copywriters may spend hours, even days, crafting a paragraph. After many revisions, others read the copy and critique it. It then goes back to the writer, who continues to fine-tune it. Copywriters must have thick skins as there is always someone else reading their work, critiquing it, and asking for changes. Versatility is a common trait of copywriters. They can move from toilet paper to Mack trucks and shift their writing style to match the product and the language of their target audience.

As Professor Mallia suggested in the Part III opener, copywriters can rejoice because the power of words remains strong even with new visual media. She says, "The power of words doesn't rest in their volume, but in their clever combination. In fact, the fewer the words, the more important every single one becomes—and the more critical copywriting talent becomes." The skill, she explains, is to "distill a thought down to its most concise, precise, and unexpected expression. That's the reason the craft isn't about to disappear anytime soon, and great copywriters will always be in demand. Think 'Got Milk?' and 'Think different' and see true mastery of the craft. Each tagline is just two words but rich in meaning and power."

The Art and Science of Names

The most important word selection in marketing communication is the brand or corporate name. Low-cost airline JetBlue was originally founded in 1999 as New Air but its founders realized it needed a more distinctive name. They considered naming it Taxi and painting the planes yellow, but backed off because of negative associations with New York City taxis and questionable service. JetBlue has been a good choice because it states the business (jet = airlines), as well as sky (blue) with its calming connotations.

Many brand names are made up, but it's not just names that are created by marketing communicators. The "uncola" position was created for 7-Up and more recently the True Value hardware chain has proclaimed itself "masters of all things hardwarian," a phrase that suggests mastery of a traditional art or skill.

There is a science to letters, as well as words. Research has determined that letters with a hard edge like T or K suggest effectiveness (Kodak, Target, Tide); X and Z relate to science (Xcel, Zantac, Xerox); C, L, R, P, and S are calming or relaxing (Cialis, Lexus, Puffs, Revlon, Silk); and Z means speed (Zippo, Ziplock, *Zappos.com*). In the erectile dysfunction category, Lilly's drug Cialis is derived from *ciel,* the French word for sky and was chosen because it is a smooth, soft sound that connotes a sense of intimacy. In contrast, Pfizer's Viagra evokes the power of Niagara Falls.[1]

Advertising Writing Style

In almost all situations, advertising has to win its audience, no small task given that it usually competes in a cluttered environment and the audience is generally inattentive and uninterested. For that reason, the copy should be as simple as possible—think 'The Most Up-to-Date Sporting News.' DDB's single line of copy is succinct and single-minded, meaning that it has a clear focus and conveys only one selling point.

As the YMCA ad demonstrates, advertising writing is tight. Every word counts because both space and time are expensive. Ineffective or overused words and phrases—such as *interesting, very, in order to, buy now and save, introducing, nothing less than*—waste precious space.

Copy is usually written in a conversational style using real people language. The legendary David Ogilvy, founder of the advertising agency that bears his name, Ogilvy & Mather (O&M), explained his view many years ago of advertising as conversation:

I always pretend that I'm sitting beside a woman at a dinner party, and she asks me for advice about which product she should buy. So then I write down what I would say to her. I give her the facts, facts, facts. I try to make it interesting, fascinating, if possible, and personal—I don't write to the

I COMMIT TO BEING HARD ON THE OUTSIDE AND SOFT ON THE INSIDE. NOT THE OTHER WAY AROUND.

SHOWCASE

Part of a membership drive campaign, this ad demonstrates how a copywriter plays with language to deliver a selling point succinctly and with style.

Copywriter Lara Mann is a graduate of the University of Florida advertising program. Her work was nominated for inclusion in this book by Professor Elaine Wagner.

crowd. I try to write from one human being to another. . . . And I try not to bore the poor woman to death, and I try to make it as real and personal as possible.[2]

(You can listen to David Ogilvy talking about his views on advertising at *www.youtube.com/watch?v=0kfsnjcUNiw*)

Copywriters try to write the way the target audience thinks and talks. That often means using personal language and direct address. For example, an ad for Trojan condoms makes a pointed argument on a touchy subject for its young, single target audience. Combining headline with body copy, it reads as a dialogue:

> *I didn't use one because I didn't have one with me.*
> *Get real.*
> *If you don't have a parachute, don't jump, genius.*

How to Write Effective Copy

Copywriters revise copy seemingly a hundred times to make it as concise as possible. The tighter the writing, the easier it is to understand and the greater its impact. Simple ads avoid being gimmicky, full of clichés, or too cute; they don't try too hard or reach too far to make a point. The following list summarizes some characteristics of effective copy:

Principle
Effective copy is succinct, single-minded, and tightly focused.

- *Be Succinct* Use short, familiar words, short sentences, and short paragraphs.
- *Be Single-Minded* Focus on one main point.
- *Be Specific* Don't waste time on generalities. The more specific the message, the more attention getting and memorable it is.
- *Get Personal* Directly address your audience whenever possible as "you" rather than "we" or "they."
- *Keep a Single Focus* Deliver a simple message instead of one that makes too many points. Focus on a single idea and support it.
- *Be Conversational* Use the language of everyday conversation. The copy should sound like two friends talking to each other, so don't shy away from incomplete sentences, thought fragments, and contractions.
- *Be Original* To keep your copy forceful and persuasive, avoid stock advertising phrases, strings of superlatives, brag-and-boast statements, and clichés.
- *Use News* News stories are attention getting if . . . if . . . they announce something that is truly newsworthy and important. (In contrast, Post Shredded Wheat ran an ad with the headline "Beware of New" in which it bragged about its original recipe that it had been using for 117 years.)
- *Use Magic Phrases* Phrases that grab and stick add power and memorability. In comparing its paper towels with the cheaper competition, Bounty asked "Why use more when you can use less?"
- *Use Variety* To add visual appeal in both print and TV ads, avoid long blocks of copy in print ads. Instead, break the copy into short paragraphs with subheads. In TV commercials, break up television monologues with visual changes, such as shots of the product, sound effects, and dialogue. The writer puts these breaks in the script while the art director designs what they will look like.
- *Use Imaginative Description* Use evocative or figurative language to build a picture in the consumer's mind.
- *Tell a Story—with Feeling* Stories are interesting and they have a structure that keeps attention and builds interest. But most importantly, they offer an opportunity to touch emotions. An ad about two brothers, one with cancer and the other who became inspired to become a radiation oncologist, told their story as they confronted the rare cancer and turned to the Memorial Sloan-Kettering Cancer Center to help defeat the illness.

Tone of Voice   To develop the right **tone of voice,** copywriters write to the target audience. If the copywriter knows someone who fits the audience profile, then he or she may write to that person as if they were in a conversation as the Trojan ad demonstrated. If the writer doesn't know someone, one trick is to go through a photo file, select a picture of the person who fits the description, and write to that "audience member."

So You Think You Want to Create a Funny Ad?

Fred Beard, *Professor, Gaylord College of Journalism and Mass Communication, University of Oklahoma*

These parting words of British actor Sir Donald Wolfit should give anyone thinking of creating a funny ad second thoughts: "Dying is easy, comedy is hard."

Writing a funny, effective ad is especially hard when you consider that the ad must make people laugh at the same time it accomplishes an advertising objective—an increase in attention, recall, favorable attitudes, or an actual purchase. If you're still not deterred, keep in mind that funny ads work best when the following circumstances apply:

1. *Your goal is to attract attention.* Decades of research and the beliefs of advertising creative professionals match up perfectly on this one.
2. *Your goal is to generate awareness and recall of a simple message (think Aflac).* Most advertising creatives agree that humor works best to encourage recall of fairly simple messages, not complex ones.
3. *Your humor is related.* Did you ever laugh at an ad and forget what it was advertising? Creatives will tell you humor is a waste of money if it isn't related to a product's name, uses, benefits, or users.
4. *Your goal is to get the audience to like your brand.* Research shows people often transfer their liking of funny ads to the brand.

5. *You expect the audience to initially disagree with your arguments.* An ad's humor can distract people from arguments they disagree with, encouraging them to lower their perceptual defenses, accept the message, and be persuaded by it.
6. *Your target audience is men, especially young ones.* Creative professionals say younger male audiences respond best to humor, and research confirms men favor more aggressive humor.
7. *Your audience has a low need for cognition (NFC) or a high need for humor (NFH).* People with a low NFC don't enjoy thinking about things—they prefer emotional appeals like humor. People with a high NFH seek out humor. If your audience is low NFC and high NFH, you can't miss.
8. *You have good reasons for using the broadcast media.* By far, the majority of creatives believe humor works best in radio and TV ads.
9. *You're advertising a low-involvement/low-risk product or service.* Academic researchers and creative professionals agree funny ads seem to work best for routine purchases people don't worry about too much.
10. *Your humor is definitely funny.* Research shows if an ad's humor fails, not only will there be no positive outcomes, it could even produce negative responses.

Molson Beer won awards for a commercial it created, called "The Rant," which mirrors the attitude of many Canadians. The commercial starts softly with an average Joe character disassociating himself from Canadian stereotypes. As he talks, he builds up intensity and at the end, he's in a full-blown rant ending with the line *"My name is Joe, and I am Canadian"* at the top of his voice. The commercial was so successful it was played at events all around the country.

Humor is a type of writing that copywriters use to create entertaining, funny ads. The idea is that, if the humor works, the funny copy will lend a positive aura to a brand. It's particularly important to master funny writing if you are trying to reach an audience that's put off by conventional advertising, such as young males. The *Practical Tips* box provides some suggestions on how to use humor in advertising copy.

The newest game in choosing a tone of voice is for brand avatars. If you were to talk with eBay or MTV, what would that brand's avatar sound like? You get computerized voices when you call most companies, but some organizations have moved away from the easily recognized computer voice to a voice that better reflects the brand's personality. So think about the way your brand sounds to customers as another dimension of styling the tone of voice for a brand or company.

Grammar and Adese   Copywriters also are attuned to the niceties of grammar, syntax, and spelling, although sometimes they will play with a word or phrase to create an effect, even if it's grammatically incorrect. The Apple Computer campaign for the Macintosh that used the slogan "Think different" rather than "Think differently" caused a bit of an uproar in Apple's school market. That's why copywriters think carefully about playing loose with the language even if it sounds right.[3]

In contrast to the good practices in copywriting we've been describing, there are also some things to avoid. Meaningless words (*really, very, that, a lot*) or words made meaningless by overuse (*free, guarantee, opportunity*) are to be shunned in business writing and advertising according to a feature on advertising writing on MSNBC.[4]

Formulaic advertising copy is one problem that is so obvious that comedians parody it. This type of formula writing, called **adese,** violates all the guidelines for writing effective copy that we've been describing. It is full of clichés (as easy as pie), superlatives and puffery (best in class), stock phrases (buy now; free trial offer), and vague generalities (prices too low to advertise). For example, consider this copy; can you hear yourself saying something like this to a friend?

> *Now we offer the quality that you've been waiting for—at a price you can afford. So buy now and save.*

For more advertising clichés, check this website: *www.the-top-tens.com/lists/most-overused-advertising-cliches.asp.*

The pompous overblown phrasing of many corporate statements doesn't work—it doesn't get attention; it's not memorable; it doesn't get read. We call it **your-name-here copy** because almost any company can use those words and tack a signature on the end. For example, a broadband company named Covad started off an ad like this:

> *Opportunity. Potential. These are terms usually associated with companies that have a lot to prove and little to show for it. But on rare occasion, opportunity can be used to describe a company that has already laid the groundwork, made the investments, and is well down the road to strong growth.*

It's all just platitudes and clichés—and any company could use this copy. It isn't attention getting and it doesn't contribute to a distinctive and memorable brand image. That's always a risk with company-centered copy, which doesn't say anything that relates to the customer's needs, wants, and interests. It just doesn't work.

Another type of adese is **brag-and-boast copy,** which is "we" copy written from the company's point of view with a pompous tone, similar to the Covad ad. Consider a print ad by Buick. The ad starts with the stock opening, "Introducing Buick on the move." The body copy includes superlatives and generalities such as "Nothing less than the expression of a new philosophy," "It strikes a new balance between luxury and performance—a balance which has been put to the test," and "Manufactured with a degree of precision that is in itself a breakthrough." Because people are so conditioned to screen out advertising, messages that use this predictable style are easy to ignore—or parody if you're a comedian.

The Strategy Imperative   We said in the beginning of this chapter that the creative team begins with the strategy statement from the client or the creative brief from agency planners. That means even beautiful writing has to also make the strategy sing. As Susan Gunelius, author of *Kick-Ass Copywriting in 10 Easy Steps* explains, "Copywriting is about creating perceived needs among a specific audience."[5] If it doesn't move the audience and deliver on the objectives, then it's not effective copywriting.

Furthermore, the writing not only has to be strategic, the claims also have to be tested and meet basic requirements of truth, as the *A Principled Practice* feature explains.

HOW IS COPY CREATED FOR PRINT?

A print piece, such as an advertisement or brochure, is created in two pieces: a copy sheet and a layout. Even though they work together to create a creative concept, we'll discuss copy in this chapter and layout in the next chapter.

The two categories of copy that print uses are display copy and body copy (or text). **Display copy** includes all elements that readers see in their initial scanning. These elements—headlines, subheads, call-outs, taglines, and slogans—usually are set in larger type sizes than body copy and are designed to get attention and to stop the viewer's scanning. **Body copy** includes the elements that are designed to be read and absorbed, such as the text of the ad message and captions.

A PRINCIPLED PRACTICE

Check Those Claims

You should be able to believe the advertising from trusted major brands such as General Mills and Kellogg's.

A high-profile case made headlines in 2009 when the Food and Drug Administration challenged Cheerios' long-running cholesterol-reduction claims. For years, Cheerios boxes have included the lines *"You can Lower Your* Cholesterol *4% in 6 weeks"* and *"Clinically proven to lower cholesterol."* The FDA believes this is a claim that puts it in the drug category. The FDA allows the more general claim of reduced heart disease but doesn't allow specific rates of risk reduction, which is more appropriate for drugs. If the FDA prevails, General Mills may face enormous marketing and packaging costs to rectify the questionable claim. There's even an issue with the language on the brand's website.

In defense of the Cheerios' claim, General Mills responded that "the clinical study supporting Cheerios' cholesterol-lowering benefit is very strong." General Mills points to 25 years of clinical proof that Cheerios can help lower cholesterol and, therefore, is heart healthy. The FDA, in fact, in 1997 granted Cheerios the first food-specific health claim for the fiber in oatmeal and its heart-healthy benefits.

Kellogg's was challenged by the Federal Trade Commission in 2009 for television advertising that said children's attentiveness improved nearly 20 percent for those who ate Frosted Mini-Wheats compared to those who skipped breakfast. It's probably true that kids who eat breakfast pay more attention in school, but the FTC said that only half of the children studied showed more attentiveness and of those only 11 percent had an improvement of 20 percent in their attentiveness. Kellogg's agreed to settle the charges.

Kellogg's Coca Krispies has been challenged for bragging on the package that the sugary cereal "helps support your child's immunity." San Francisco's city attorney wrote to Kellogg's demanding the claim be substantiated. He says, "I am concerned that the prominent use of the immunity claims to advertise a sugar-laden, chocolate cereal like Cocoa Krispies may mislead and deceive parents of young children."

Similarly a drink mix enhanced with vitamins A, C, and E claims that it will help "maintain a healthy immune system," even though the *Chicago Tribune* says there is no scientific evidence to back up this claim.

So are consumers being led astray by health claims on food packages, websites, and advertising? Should health claims for packaged foods be banned? And what is a copywriter to do if a marketing director asks for health claims. What kind of support would you like to see before you are comfortable writing this kind of copy?

Sources: Julie Deardorff, "Should Health Claims on Food Be Banned?" *www.pressofAtlanticCity.com*, October 26, 2009; Dan Mitchell, "San Francisco Goes after Crazy Cereal Health Claims," The Big Money website, October 30, 2009, *www.thebigmoney.com*; "Kellogg to Settle FTC Charges of False Advertising," *The New York Times*, April 20, 2009, *www.nytimes.com*; Donna Byrne, "When Is Breakfast Cereal a 'Drug?' When It's Cheerios," Food Law Prof Blog, May 13, 2009, http://lawprofessors.typepad.com/foodlaw/health_claims/; "FDA Warns General Mills: Cheerios Is a Drug," *The Wall Street Journal*, May 12, 2009, http://blogs.wsj.com; "Quaker Celebrates 25 Years of Clinical Proof," *PR Newswire*, November 17, 2008, *www.prnewswire.com*.

We have suggested that ad copy should be succinct but some respected copywriters, such as David Ogilvy and Howard Gossage, were successful in writing long copy ads that intrigued their audiences. Gossage, a legendary San Francisco ad man played with humorous ideas, as well as words. One ad for Eagle Shirtmakers asked, "Is this your shirt?" A following line said, "If so, Miss Afflerbach will send you your [Eagle logo picture] label." The idea, which is explained in the body copy, is that Eagle makes shirts for various shirtmakers, so you can contact "Miss Afflerbach" for the official logo to add to your shirt. If you're interested in more of Gossage's tongue-in-cheek ads, check a collection compiled by the LA Creative Club at *www.lacreativeclub.com/gossage.html* or get his book, *The Book of Gossage* from the Copy Workshop (*www.adbuzz.com/copyworkshop_catalog.pdf*).

No one ad uses all of the copy elements; however, they are all used in different ads for different purposes. The most common tools in the copywriter's toolkit are listed in Table 9.1.

How to Write Headlines

The **headline** is a key element in print pieces. It conveys the main message so that people get the point of the message. It's important for another reason. The headline works with the visual to get

Table 9.1 The Copywriter's Toolkit

- *Headline* A phrase or a sentence that serves as the opening to the ad. It's usually identified by larger type or a prominent position and its purpose is to catch attention. In the Corporate Angel Network ad, for example, the headline is "Cancer Patients Fly Free."

- *Overlines and Underlines* These are phrases or sentences that either lead into the headline or follow up on the thought in the headline. They are usually set in smaller type than the headline. The purpose of the overline is to set the stage, and the purpose of the underline is to elaborate on the idea in the headline and serve as a transition to the body copy. The underline leads into the body copy as demonstrated in the DuPont ad: "Find food that helps prevent osteoporosis."

- *Body Copy* The text of the ad. It's usually smaller-sized type and written in paragraphs or multiple lines. Its purpose is to explain the idea or selling point.

- *Subheads* Used in longer copy blocks, subheads begin a new section of the copy. They are usually bold type or larger than the body copy. Their purpose is to make the logic clear to the reader. They are useful for people who scan copy and they help them get a sense of what the copy says. The Corporate Angel Network ad uses subheads.

- *Call-Outs* These are sentences that float around the visual, usually with a line or arrow pointing to some specific element in the visual that they name and explain. For example, Johnson & Johnson once ran an ad that used call-outs as the main pieces of the body copy. The head read: "How to bathe a mommy." Positioned around a picture of a woman are short paragraphs with arrows pointing to various parts of her body. These call-outs describe the good things the lotion does for feet, hands, makeup removal, moisture absorption, and skin softening.

- *Captions* A sentence or short piece of copy that explains what you are looking at in a photo or illustration. Captions aren't used very often in advertising because the visuals are assumed to be self-explanatory; however, readership studies have shown that, after the headline, captions have high readership.

- *Taglines* A short phrase that wraps up the key idea or creative concept that usually appears at the end of the body copy. It often refers back to the headline or opening phrase in a commercial. For example, see the line, "Need a lift? Just give us a call. We'll do the rest," in the Corporate Angel Network ad.

- *Slogans* A distinctive catch phrase that serves as a motto for a campaign, brand, or company. It is used across a variety of marketing communication messages and over an extended period of time. "What happens in Las Vegas stays in Las Vegas" is a tourism slogan that hints at the pleasures you don't enjoy at home.

- *Call to Action* This is a line at the end of an ad that encourages people to respond and gives information on how to respond. Both ads—Corporate Angel Network and DuPont—have response information: either an address, a toll-free phone number, an e-mail address, or Web address.

attention and communicate the creative concept. This clutter-busting Big Idea breaks through the competitive messages. It comes across best through a picture and words working together, as the DuPont ad illustrates. The headline carries the theme ("To Do List for the Planet") and the underline ("Find food that helps prevent osteoporosis") makes a direct connection with the visual.

People who are scanning may read nothing more, so advertisers want to at least register a point with the consumer. The point has to be clear from the headline or the combination of headline and visual. That's particularly true with outdoor boards. Researchers estimate that only 20 percent of those who read the headline in advertising go on to read the body copy, so if they take away anything from the ad, it needs to be clear in the headline.

Headlines need to be catchy phrases, but they also have to convey an idea and attract the right target audience. Tobler has won Effie awards for a number of years for its clever headlines and visuals. For Tobler's Chocolate Orange, the creative concept showed the chocolate ball being smacked against something hard and splitting into orange-like slices. The headline was "Whack and Unwrap." The next year the headline was "Smashing Good Taste," which speaks to the candy's British origins and to the quirky combination of chocolate and orange flavors. The headline and visual also tell consumers how to "open" the orange into slices—by whacking it.

Agencies copytest headlines to make sure they can be understood at a glance and that they communicate exactly the right idea. Split-run tests (two versions of the same ad) in direct mail pieces have shown that changing the wording of the headline while keeping all other elements constant can double, triple, or quadruple consumer response. That is what experts, such as ad legend David Ogilvy, state that the headline is the most important element in the advertisement.[6] Because headlines are so important, some general principles guide their development and explain the particular functions they serve:

Principle
Good headlines interrupt readers' scanning and grab their attention.

- *Target* A good headline will attract only those who are prospects—there is no sense in attracting people who are not in the market. An old advertising axiom is "Use a rifle, not a shotgun." In other words, use the headline to tightly target the right audience.
- *Stop and Grab* The headline must work in combination with the visual to stop and grab the reader's attention. An advertisement by Range Rover shows a photo of the car parked at the edge of a rock ledge in Monument Valley with the headline, "Lots of people use their Range Rovers just to run down to the corner."
- *Identify* The headline must also identify the product and brand and start the sale. The selling premise should be evident in the headline.
- *Change Scanning to Reading* The headline should lead readers into the body copy. For readers to move to the body copy, they have to stop scanning and start concentrating. This change in mind-set is the reason why only 20 percent of scanners become readers.

Headlines can be grouped into two general categories: direct action and indirect action. **Direct-action headlines** are straightforward and informative, such as "Keep Your Body Strong," which is one in a series of "Healthy People" posters for Johnson & Johnson. The copy associates the health of your body with the health of nature. It closes with a line that pulls these two thoughts together: "Your body is just like nature. Keep it strong with daily physical activity and bring your planet to balance." Note how this structure of the message is consistent in the "Mind" and "Spirit" posters.

Direct-action headlines are highly targeted, but they may fail to lead the reader into the message if they are not captivating enough. **Indirect-action headlines** are not as selective and may not provide as much information, but may be better at drawing the reader into the message and building a brand image.

Here are some common types of direct-action headlines:

- *Assertion* An assertion is a headline that states a claim or a promise that will motivate someone to try the product.
- *Command* A command headline politely tells the reader to do something.
- *How-to Heads* People are rewarded for investigating a product when the message tells them how to use it or how to solve a problem.
- *News Announcements* News headlines are used with new-product introductions, but also with changes, reformulations, new styles, and new uses. The news value is thought to get attention and motivate people to try the product.

SHOWCASE

Michael Dattolico designed a series of posters for Johnson & Johnson to use in promoting its "Healthy People" initiative. These two advise you to keep "your mind flowing" and "your spirit pure."

A graduate of the University of Florida, Dattolico's work was nominated for inclusion in this book by Professor Elaine Wagner.

Here are some common types of indirect-action headlines:

- *Puzzles* Used strictly for their curiosity and provocative power. Puzzling statements, ambiguities, and questions require the reader to examine the body copy to get the answer or explanation. The intention is to pull readers into the body copy.
- *Associations* These headlines use image and lifestyle to get attention and build interest.

An ad for the Motorola Talk About™ two-way radio demonstrates the problem of bad reception in the headline: "Help, I Think I Need a Tourniquet!" That headline then draws us into the underline which makes the point that, if the reception isn't clear, the headline can sound like "Well, I think I'll eat a turnip cake!" This headline, which played with the similar sounds of words, and other curiosity-provoking lines are provocative and compel people to read on to find out the point of the message. Sometimes these indirect headlines are called "blind headlines" because they give so little information. A **blind headline** is a gamble. If it is not informative or intriguing enough, the reader may move on without absorbing any product name information, but if it works as an attention getter, it can be very effective.

How to Write Other Display Copy

Next to the headline, **captions** have the second highest readership. In addition to their pulling power, captions serve an information function. Visuals do not always say the same thing to every person; for that reason, most visuals can benefit from explanation. In addition to headlines, copywriters also craft the **subheads** that continue to help lure the reader into the body copy. Subheads are considered display copy in that they are usually larger and set in different type (bold or italic) than the body copy. Subheads are sectional headlines and are also used to break up a mass of "gray" type (or type that tends to blur together when one glances at it) into a large block of copy.

Taglines are short catchy phrases and particularly memorable phrases used at the end of an ad to complete or wrap up the creative idea. An ad from the Nike women's campaign used the headline "You are a nurturer and a provider. You are beautiful and exotic" set in an elegant script. The tagline on the next page used a rough, hand-drawn, graffiti-like image that said, "You are not falling for any of this."

Slogans, which are repeated from ad to ad as part of a campaign or a long-term brand identity effort, also may be used as taglines. To be successful, these phrases have to be catchy and memorable, although many corporate slogans fall back into marketing language or clichés and come across as leaden ("Total quality through excellence," "Excellence through total quality," or "Where quality counts"). Wells Fargo, for example, uses "Together we'll go far," which is not distinctive, could be used by any company, and says nothing about Wells Fargo or its business. Accenture uses "High performance. Delivered." which also is nondistinctive and not very memorable.

The best ones have a close link to the brand name: "With a name like Smucker's, it has to be good," "America runs on Dunkin'," and "Ford Tough." "Finger lickin' good" for KFC doesn't use the brand name, but still is highly recognizable because it connects with the product (fried chicken) and has been in use since 1952. That's another characteristic of a good slogan, it is enduring—slogans are rarely changed. A true classic, Maxwell House's "Good to the last drop," has been used since 1915 and Morton Salt's "When it rains, it pours" has been around since 1914.

Of course, they also have to be original as Wisconsinites found out when the official state slogan was changed to "Live Like You Mean It." The state spent some $50,000 on the new slogan and then later discovered that it had previously been used as the tagline in a Bacardi Rum campaign.[7]

Consider the distinctiveness and memorability of the following slogans

TEST YOURSELF

Match the Company with Its Slogan:

1. Together we can prevail
2. Imagination at work*
3. A mind is a terrible thing to waste*
4. Know How
5. A business of caring
6. Melts in your mouth, not in your hands*
7. Always surprising
8. We deliver for You*
9. Inspire the next
10. When you care enough to send the very best*
11. Where patients come first
12. Can you hear me now?*
13. For successful living
14. Inspiration comes standard
15. When it absolutely, positively has to be there overnight*
16. What can brown do for you?*

a. Merck
b. Bristol-Myers Squibb
c. Hallmark
d. Swatch
e. Hitachi
f. Verizon
g. Cigna
h. FedEx
i. Diesel
j. UPS
k. Canon
l. Chrysler
m. U.S. Postal Service
n. M&Ms
o. United Negro College Fund
p. GE

Answers to Companies: 1. 1:b Bristol-Myers Squibb; 2:p GE*; 3:o United Negro College Fund*; 4:k Canon; 5:g Cigna; 6:n M&Ms*; 7:d Swatch; 8:m USPS;* 9:e Hitachi; 10:c Hallmark*; 11:a Merck; 12:f Verizon*; 13:i Diesel; 14:l Chrysler; 15:h FedEx*; 16:j UPS.*

Study the slogans in the matching activity. Which ones did you get and which ones stumped you? Note that eight of the companies are identified with an asterisk. Those eight have been recognized by *Adweek* as winning slogans and have been celebrated as part of the magazine's annual Advertising Week. In your view, why were they selected for this honor, and what makes them different from the others on the list that have not been honored in this way?

One of America's favorite slogan winners according to *Adweek* is the "Don't Mess with Texas" anti-litter slogan. Created in 1986 by Austin-based GSD&M for the Texas Department of Transportation, the award-winning social-marketing campaign built around this slogan features billboards, print ads, radio and TV spots, and a host of celebrities (Willie Nelson, Stevie Ray Vaughan, Matthew McConaughey, George Foreman, and LeAnn Rimes, among others) who take turns with the tough-talking slogan that captures the spirit and pride of Texans. One billboard, for example, warns, "Keep Your Butts in the Car." The *dontmesswithtexas.org* website, where you can see all these ads, including the commercials, also has been featured by *Adweek* as a "Cool Site."

Copywriters use a number of literary techniques to enhance the memorability of subheads, slogans, and taglines. These are other techniques copywriters use to create catchy slogans:

- *Direct Address* "Have it your way"; "Think small."
- *A Startling or Unexpected Phrase* Twists a common phrase to make it unexpected, as in the NYNEX campaign: "If it's out there, it's in here."
- *Rhyme, Rhythm, Alliteration* Uses repetition of sounds, as in the *Wall Street Journal*'s slogan, "The daily diary of the American Dream."
- *Parallel Construction* Uses repetition of the structure of a sentence or phrase, as in Morton Salt's "When it rains, it pours."
- *Cue the Product* Maxwell House's "Good to the last drop"; John Deere's "Nothing runs like a Deere"; Wheaties' "Breakfast of Champions"; "Beef. It's What's for Dinner."
- *Music* "In the valley of the Jolly, ho-ho-ho, Green Giant."
- *Combination* "It's your land, lend a hand," which is the slogan for Take Pride in America. (*Rhyme, rhythm, parallel*)

How to Write Body Copy

The body copy is the text of the ad, and its primary role is to maintain the interest of the reader. It develops the sales message, states the argument, summarizes the proof, and provides explanation. It is the persuasive heart of the message. You excite consumer interest with the display elements, but you win them over with the argument presented in the body copy, assuming the ad uses body copy or an overt selling premise.

Consider the way the copy is written for this classic ad that comes from the award-winning Nike women's campaign. Analyze the argument the copywriter is making and how the logic flows to a convincing conclusion. The *A Matter of Principle* box explains the logic and message strategy behind the Nike's women's campaign, which focuses on self-awareness.

A magazine is not a mirror. Have you ever seen anyone in a magazine who seemed even vaguely like you looking back? (If you have, turn the page.) Most magazines are made to sell us a fantasy of what we're supposed to be. They reflect what society deems to be a standard, however unrealistic or unattainable that standard is. That doesn't mean you should cancel your subscription. It means you need to remember that it's just ink on paper. And that whatever standards you set for yourself, for how much you want to weigh, for how hard you work out, or how many times you make it to the gym, should be your standards. Not someone else's.

The "Let Me Play" ad is a more recent version of the sentiment expressed in the "Mirror" ad copy. Nike launched the Let Me Play Fund in support of this campaign after racist and sexist comments about the Rutgers University women's basketball team by radio shock jock Don Imus. In response to his offensive comments, Nike ran a full-page ad in *The New York Times* than opened with "Thank you, ignorance" followed by "Thank you for moving women's sports forward."

The Principle of Truth

Jean Grow, *Associate Professor, Marquette University*

"It wasn't advertising. It was truth. We weren't selling a damn thing. Just the truth. And behind the truth, of course, the message was brought to you by Nike."
—Janet Champ, *Nike*

The creatives who produced early Nike women's advertising (1990–1997) were an amazing trio of women (Janet Champ, copywriter, and Charlotte Moore and Rachel Manganiello, art directors). Their work was grounded in the principle of truth, fueled by creativity, and sustained by nothing less than moxie.

"Nike in 1990 was not the Nike of today," Manganiello said. There was always this "political stuff about big men's sports. And, you know, (it was like we were) just kind of siphoning off money for women. So, in some ways we couldn't be as direct as we sometimes wanted to be." However, being direct and being truthful are not always the same thing. And truth for the Nike women's brand, and for themselves, was what these women aspired to.

Living the principle of truth, and trusting their gut, is what defined their work ethic and ultimately the women's brand. Moore explained, "I would posit that market research has killed a lot of advertising that was based on effective human dialogue, because it negates faith in intuition. Guts. Living with your eyes open."

To launch the women's brand within the confines of the male parent brand was no easy assignment. The creative team members began with their "gut" and with their "eyes open." They created campaign after campaign that moved the needle, but each time the approval process was a test of their principles, with meetings that were more than tinged with gender bias.

"We were almost always the only women in the room, and they killed the stuff because it scared them," said Champ. "But we always came back. And they let us do what we wanted, as long as we didn't 'sully' the men's brand . . . and as long as women's products kept flying off the shelves, they were happy."

As time went on, their instincts and principles earned them respect. According to Champ, "We told them, pretty much, that we believed in it and they had to run it and trust us, and they sighed, once again. They were soooooo tired of hearing me say that. And they ran it and they were SHOCKED at what a nerve it touched."

In trusting their guts—in telling the truth—they created award-winning campaigns and exceeded marketing expectations. "As creative people," Moore said, "we had found our home and our voice, and we'd found the most fertile ground for the brand."

In the end, truth and the willingness to "trust your gut" are what make great brands and create fertile ground for others. When you consider the terrifically truthful Dove campaign, I suggest we owe a debt of gratitude to the women of early Nike women's advertising, who stood for truth nearly 20 years ago. I only wish we would see more truthful work. That however might take a truthful acknowledgment that women still make up less than a quarter of all advertising creative departments. In the end, truthful work depends on making a commitment to increasing the number of women in creative departments. To have guts. To live with ones eyes wide open.

There are as many different kinds of writing styles as there are product personalities, but there are also some standard approaches:

- *Straightforward* Factual copy usually written in the words of an anonymous or unacknowledged source.
- *Narrative* Tells a story in first person or third person.
- *Dialogue* Lets the reader "listen in" on a conversation.
- *Explanation* Explains how something works.
- *Translation* Technical information, such as that written for the high-tech and medical industries, which must be defined and translated into understandable language.

Two paragraphs get special attention in body copy: the **lead paragraph** and the **closing paragraph.** The lead, the first paragraph of the body copy, is another point where people test the message to see whether they want to read it. Notice in the copy from the Nike women's campaign how the first lines work to catch the attention of the target audience: "A magazine is not a mirror."

Closing paragraphs in body copy serve several functions. Usually, the last paragraph refers back to the creative concept and wraps up the Big Idea. Direct action messages usually end with a **call to action** with instructions on how to respond. A Schwinn bicycle ad that is headlined "Read poetry. Make peace with all except the motor car," demonstrates a powerful and unexpected ending, one that is targeted to its youthful audience:

> *Schwinns are red, Schwinns are blue.*
> *Schwinns are light and agile too.*
> *Cars suck. The end.*

Print Media Requirements

The media in the print category—from newspapers and magazines to outdoor boards and product literature—all use the same copy elements, such as headlines and body copy. However, the way these elements are used varies with the objectives for using the medium.

Newspaper advertising is one of the few types of advertising that is not considered intrusive because people consult the paper as much to see what is on sale as to find out what is happening in City Hall. For this reason, the copy in newspaper advertisements does not have to work as hard as other kinds of advertising to catch the attention of its audience. Because the editorial environment of a newspaper generally is serious, newspaper ads don't have to compete as entertainment, as television ads do. As a result, most newspaper advertising copy is straightforward and informative. The writing is brief, usually just identifying the merchandise and giving critical information about styles, sizes, and prices.

Magazines offer better quality ad production, which is important for brand image and high-fashion advertising. Consumers may clip and file advertising that ties in with the magazine's special interest as reference information. This type of magazine ad can be more informative and carry longer copy than do newspaper ads.

This ad from the "Let Me Play" campaign ad reflects Nike's strategy of talking to women about sports in a way that reflects their attitudes and feelings.

Copywriters also take care to craft clever phrasing for the headlines and the body copy, which, as in the Nike women's campaign, may read more like poetry.

Directories that provide contact information, such as phone numbers and addresses, often carry display advertising. In writing a directory ad, copywriters advise using a headline that focuses on the service or store personality unless the store's name is a descriptive phrase such as "Overnight Auto Service" or "The Computer Exchange." Complicated explanations don't work well in the Yellow Pages either, because there is little space for such explanations. Putting information that is subject to change in an ad can become a problem because the directory is published only once a year.

Posters and outdoor boards are primarily visual, although the words generally try to catch consumers' attention and lock in an idea, registering a message. An effective poster is built around a creative concept that marries the words with the visual. For the Coffee Rush chain, Karl Schroeder created a series of posters to change consumers' perceptions that the shop was merely a drive-through for fast, cheap coffee. Schroeder's team did this by promoting a line of cold drinks with captivating names such as Mango Guava and Wild Berry.

One of the most famous billboard campaigns ever was for a little shaving cream company named Burma Shave. The campaign used a series of roadside signs with catchy, cute, and sometimes poetic advertising copy aimed at auto travelers. Some 600 poems were featured in this campaign, which ran for nearly 40 years, from 1925 to 1963, until the national interstate system and fast roads made the signs obsolete.[8] (To read more about Burma Shave, go to *www.eisnermuseum.org/ _burma_shave/signs_of_the_times.html* or check the collection at *www.sff.net/people/teaston/ burma.htm.*) On the Burma Shave signs the product was always a hero:

> *If you think*   *My job is*
> *she likes*   *keeping faces clean*
> *your bristles*   *And nobody knows*
> *walk bare-footed*   *de stubble*
> *through some thistles*   *I've seen*
> *Burma Shave*   *Burma Shave*

More recently, the city of Albuquerque used the Burma Shave format to encourage drivers to reduce their speeds through a construction zone. Today, a construction zone is about the only place where traffic moves slowly enough to use a billboard with rhyming copy.

Through this maze of machines and rubble
Driving fast can cause you trouble
Take care and be alert
So no one on this road gets hurt.

In contrast to the Burma Shave signs, the most important characteristic of copywriting for outdoor advertising is brevity. Usually, a single line serves as both a headline and product identification. Often the phrase is a play on words. A series of black-and-white billboards in the Galveston-Houston area, recruiting priests for the Roman Catholic diocese, features a Roman collar with witty wording such as "Yes, you will combat evil. No, you don't get to wear a cape." Others are more thoughtful: "Help wanted. Inquire within yourself." Some experts suggest that billboard copywriters use no more than six to seven words. The copy must catch attention and be memorable. For example, a billboard for Orkin pest control showed a package wrapped up with the word Orkin on the tag. The headline read, "A little something for your ant."

Sometimes called **collateral materials** because they are used in support of an advertising campaign, product literature—brochures, pamphlets, flyers, and other materials—provides details about a product, company, or event. They can be as varied as hang tags in new cars or bumper stickers. Taco Bell's little messages on its tiny taco sauce packages are an example of clever writing in an unexpected place with messages like: "Save a bun, eat a taco," "Warning! You're about to make a taco very happy," and "My other taco is a chalupa."

Typically, product literature is a heavy copy format, or at least a format that provides room for explanatory details along with visuals; the body copy may dominate the piece. For a pamphlet with folds, a writer must also consider how the message is conveyed as the piece is unfolded. These pieces can range from a simple three-panel flyer to a glitzy multipage, full-color brochure.

HOW IS COPY WRITTEN FOR RADIO?

Ads that are broadcast on either radio or television are usually 15, 30, or 60 seconds in length, although 10- and 15-second spots may be used for brand reminders or station identification. This short length means the commercials must be simple enough for consumers to grasp, yet intriguing enough to prevent viewers from switching the station. That's why creativity is important to create clutter-busting ads that break through the surrounding noise and catch the listener's attention.

Because radio is a transitory medium and listeners are often in the car or doing something else, the ability of the listener to remember facts (such as the name of the advertiser, addresses, and phone numbers) is difficult. That's why copywriters repeat the key points of brand name and identification information, such as a phone number or address. Radio is pervasive in that it surrounds many of our activities, but it is seldom the listener's center of attention and is usually in the background. Radio urges the copywriter to reach into the depths of imagination to create a clutter-busting idea that grabs the listener's attention or a catchy tune that can be repeated without being irritating.

Radio's special advantage, referred to as **theater of the mind,** is that in a narrative format the story is visualized in the listener's imagination. Radio copywriters imagine they are writing a musical play that will be performed before an audience whose eyes are closed. The copywriter has all the theatrical tools of voices, sound effects, and music, but no visuals. How the characters look and where the scene is set come from their listeners' imaginations.

As an example of theater of the mind, consider a now-classic commercial written by humorist Stan Freberg for the Radio Advertising Bureau. The spot opens with an announcer explaining that Lake Michigan will be drained and filled with hot chocolate and a 700-foot mountain of whipped cream. The Royal Canadian Air Force will fly overhead and drop a ten-ton maraschino cherry, all to the applause of 25,000 screaming extras. The point is that things that can't be created in real life can be created by radio in the imagination of listeners.

The Radio Advertising Bureau has used the slogan "I saw it on the radio" to illustrate the power of radio's ability to evoke rich images in the listener's mind. Research indicates that the use of imagery in radio advertising leads to high levels of attention and more positive general attitudes toward the ad and its claims.[9] Even though we're talking about imagery, it is produced by the copywriter's masterful use of the tools of audio as discussed next.

Tools of Radio Copywriting

Print copywriters use a variety of tools—headlines, body copy, slogans, and so forth—to write their copy. In radio advertising, the tools are the audio elements the copywriter uses to craft a commercial: voice, music, and sound effects.

Voice   The most important element in radio advertising is the human voice, which is heard in songs, spoken dialogue, and announcements. Most commercials use an announcer either as the central voice or at the closing to wrap up the product identification. The voices the copywriter specifies help listeners "see" the personalities in the commercial. The copywriter understands that we imagine people and what they are like based on their voices. Dialogue uses character voices to convey an image of the speaker: a child, an old man, an executive, a Little League baseball player, a rock singer, and so forth. Copywriters specify voices for commercials based on the evocative qualities they contribute to the message. Chicago radio announcer Ken Nordine's voice was once described as sounding like warm chocolate; singer Ray Charles was described as having a charcoal voice.

Radio advertising relies on conversational style and vernacular language. A good radio copywriter also has an ear for distinctive patterns of speech. Two of the most famous jingles ever written used children singing about Oscar Mayer meats. The "Bologna Song" used a little child singing: "My bologna has a first name, it's O-S-C-A-R. My bologna has a second name, it's M-A-Y-E-R." The second big hit also used kids singing: "Oh I wish I were an Oscar Mayer Weiner. That is what I'd truly like to be. 'Cause if I were an Oscar Mayer Wiener, everyone would be in love with me."

Spoken language is different from written language. We talk in short sentences, often in sentence fragments and run-ons. We seldom use complex sentences in speech. We use contractions that would drive an English teacher crazy. Slang can be hard to handle and sound phony, but copy that picks up the nuances of people's speech sounds natural. In radio advertising, speaking style should match the speech of the target audience. Each group has its own way of speaking, its own phrasing. Teenagers don't talk like 8-year-olds or 50-year-olds.

Principle

Radio copywriters try to match their dialogue to the conversational style of the target audience.

Music   Similar to movie scriptwriters, radio copywriters have a sense of the imagery of music and the role it plays in creating dramatic effects. Music can be used behind the dialogue to create mood and establish the setting. Any mood, from that of a circus to a candlelit dinner, can be conveyed through music. The primary use of music is a **jingle,** which is a commercial in song, like the Oscar Mayer songs. Radio copywriters understand the interplay of catchy phrases and "hummable" music to create little songs that stick in our minds. Anything consumers can sing along with helps them remember and get involved with the message.

Advertisers can have a piece of music composed for a commercial or borrow it from previously recorded songs. Numerous music libraries sell *stock music* that is not copyrighted. A custom-made jingle created for a single advertiser can cost $10,000 or more. In contrast, many *jingle houses* create "syndicated" jingles made up of a piece of music sold to several different local advertisers in different markets around the country for as little as $1,000 or $2,000.

One of the most famous jingles of all time was the song "I'd like to teach the world to sing" produced for Coca-Cola in 1969 by its agency, McCann-Erickson. A great example of a jingle that was an instant hit worldwide, it later was recorded as a pop song without the Coke reference and sold millions of copies. Called "Hilltop," the TV commercial shows young people singing "I'd like to buy the world a Coke" on a hilltop in Italy. Surveys continue to identify it as one of the best commercials of all time. It is still run by Coke on special occasions and the sheet music continues to sell more than 30 years after the song was first written. You can read more about this famous commercial on *www.thecoca-colacompany.com/heritage/cokelore_hilltop.html.* Click through to "Hilltop" to hear the commercial.

Sound Effects   The sound of seagulls, automobile horns honking, and the cheers of fans at a stadium all create images in our minds to cue the setting and drive the action. The Freberg "Lake Michigan" commercial for the Radio Advertising Bureau used **sound effects (sfx)** to make a commercial attention getting and memorable. In the original commercial, which demonstrated the power of the "theater of the mind," listeners were asked to imagine the draining of Lake Michigan, which then is filled with hot chocolate and a 700-foot mountain of whipped cream. Then imagine the Royal Canadian Air Force flying overhead and dropping a ten-ton cherry to the applause of 25,000 screaming extras. All of this was conveyed through sound effects and an announcer telling the story. The point is that radio is more powerful than television in creating images in your mind. Sound effects can be original, but more often they are taken from *sound-effects libraries* available on CDs or online.

The Practice of Radio Copywriting

The following guidelines for writing effective radio commercials address the distinctive characteristics of radio advertising:

* *Keep It Personal* Radio advertising has an advantage over print—the human voice. The copy for radio ads should use conversational language—as if someone is "talking with" the consumer rather than "selling to" the consumer.
* *Speak to Listeners' Interests* Radio offers specialized programming to target markets. Listeners mostly tune in to hear music, but talk radio is popular, too. There are shows on health, pets, finance, politics—whatever interests people. Copywriters design commercials to speak to that audience interest and use the appropriate music and tone of voice.
* *Wake Up the Inattentive* Most people who are listening to the radio are doing something else at the same time, such as jogging, driving, or fixing breakfast. Radio spots are designed to break through and capture attention in the first three seconds with sound effects, music, questions, commands, or something unexpected.
* *Make It Memorable* To help the listener remember what you are selling, commercial copy should mention the name of the product emphatically and repeat it. An average of three mentions in a 30-second commercial and five mentions in a 60-second commercial are recommended, as long as the repetition is not done in a forced and/or annoying manner. Copywriters use taglines and other key phrases to lock the product in consumers' memories.
* *Include Call to Action* The last thing listeners hear is what they tend to remember, so copywriters make sure the product is it. In radio that's particularly important since there is no way to

show a picture of the product or the label. Those last words communicate the Big Idea in a way that serves as a call to action and reminds listeners of the brand name at the close of the commercial. "Got Milk?" is not only a highly memorable slogan, it's also a strong call to action.

- *Create Image Transfer* Radio advertisements are sometimes designed to link to a television commercial. Called **image transfer,** the visuals from the TV version are re-created in a listener's mind by the use of key phrases and ideas from the TV commercial.

Planning the Radio Script

Copywriters working on a radio commercial use a standard **radio script** format to write the copy to certain time blocks—all of the words, dialogue, lyrics, sound effects, instructions, and descriptions. The instructions and descriptions are to help the producer tape the commercial so that it sounds exactly as the copywriter imagined. The script format usually has the source of the audio written down the left side, and the content—words an announcer reads, dialogue, and description of the sound effects and music— on the right. The instructions and descriptions— everything that isn't spoken—are typed in all-capital letters. You may also see a script written in paragraph form with the instructions in parentheses. Note how the tools of radio are used in the LATCH child safety commercial.

HOW TO WRITE TELEVISION COPY

Television copywriters understand that it is the moving image—the action—that makes television so much more engaging than print. The challenge for the writer is to fuse the images with the words to present not only a creative concept, but also a story, as the Frontier Airlines commercials discussed in the previous chapter do so well.

One of the strengths of television is its ability to reinforce verbal messages with visuals or reinforce visuals with verbal messages. As Ogilvy's Peter Hochstein explains,

The idea behind a television commercial is unique in advertising. The TV commercial consists of pictures that move to impart facts or evoke emotion, and selling words that are not read but heard. The perfect combination of sight and sound can be an extremely potent selling tool.[10]

Viewers watching a program they enjoy often are absorbed to a degree only slightly less than that experienced by people watching a movie in a darkened theater. Storytelling is one way that copywriters can present action in a television commercial more powerfully than in other media. Television's ability to touch our emotions and to show us things—to demonstrate how they look and work—make television advertising highly persuasive. Effective television commercials can achieve this level of audience absorption if they are written to maximize the dramatic aspects of

---

AD COUNCIL / US DEPARTMENT OF TRANSPORTATION
LATCH Campaign – :60 Radio
ZRAG-11804R
"Bookstore"
1BON-08-0033
04/30/08 – Produced
07/1/08 – Final Mix
07/15/09 – Expiration Date

Checker:	I can help the next customer over here.
Woman:	Oh… thank you…hi.
Checker:	Wow, that's a lot of books! Let's see…*"How To Keep Your Child Safe."*(beep) *"Child-Proofing Your Home."* (beep) *"Child-Proofing Your Yard."* (beep) *"Child-Proofing Your In-Laws' Home and Yard."* (beep) I'm guessing you have a little one at home?
Woman:	Yeah.
Checker:	Well, it looks like you must take good care of her.
Woman:	Oh. Thank you.
Checker:	Now let's see… *"Parent's Guide To Safe Toys"* (beep) That's a really good one. *"Parent's Guide To Safe Foods."* (beep) *"Parents Guide To Safe Safety Products."* (beep) *"Parents' Guide To Parenting Guides"* (beep) … *"Don't Throw The Baby Out With The Bath Water And Other Safety…"*(continues under.)
VO:	Of all the things you can read about keeping your child safe, the most important is attached to the back of their car seat. Read the instruction manual and learn to use the LATCH system. It makes it easier to be sure your child's car seat is installed correctly.
Checker:	*"Parent's Guide To Telling Other Parents How To Raise Their Kids"* (beep)…
VO:	To learn more, go to safercar.gov. Anchor. Tether. LATCH. The next generation of child safety. A message from the US Department of Transportation and the Ad Council.

SHOWCASE

In his *The Inside Story* in Chapter 5, Trent Walters explained the strategy behind the LATCH campaign for car-seat safety. This commercial uses a sound effect—the beep of the cash register— to punctuate the idea that parents are highly concerned about the safety of their children.

Walters is a graduate of North Texas State University and he was nominated by Professor Sheri Broyles.

Principle
In great television commercials, words and pictures work together seamlessly to deliver the creative concept through sight, sound, and motion.

moving images and storytelling. These are just a few of the techniques used in television advertising. Here are more:

Technique	*Message Design*
• *Action* When you watch television, you are watching a walking, talking, moving world that gives the illusion of being three dimensional.	• Good television advertising uses the effect of action and motion to attract attention and sustain interest. Torture tests, steps, and procedures are all actions that are easier to present on TV than in print.
• *Demonstration* Seeing is believing. Believability and credibility—the essence of persuasion—are high because we believe what we see with our own eyes.	• If you have a strong sales message that lends itself to demonstration, such as how-to messages, television is the ideal medium for that message.
• *Storytelling* Most of the programming on television is narrative, so commercials use storytelling to take advantage of the medium's strengths.	• TV is our society's master storyteller because of its ability to present a plot and the action that leads to a conclusion in which the product plays a major role. TV can dramatize the situation in which a product is used and the type of people using it.
• *Emotion* The ability to touch the feelings of the viewer makes television commercials entertaining, diverting, amusing, and absorbing. Real-life situations with all their humor, anger, fear, pride, jealousy, and love come alive on the screen. Humor, in particular, works well on television.	• Emotional appeals are found in natural situations with which everyone can identify. Hallmark has produced some tear-jerking commercials about the times of our lives that we remember by the cards we receive and save. Kodak and Polaroid have used a similar strategy for precious moments that are remembered in photographs.

Tools of Television Copywriting

Television copywriters have two primary toolkits: visual and audio. Both words and pictures are designed to create exactly the right impact. Because of the number of visual and audio elements, as well as the many ways they can be combined, a television commercial is one of the most complex of all advertising forms. It is also an ideal form for storytelling. Copywriters who write scripts for television commercials are masters of the emotional moment as researcher Charles Young explains in the *A Matter of Practice* feature.

Video and Motion   When we watch a commercial, we are more aware of what we're seeing than anything else. Copywriters keep in mind that visuals and motion, the silent speech of film, should convey as much of the message—the Big Idea—as possible. Likewise, emotion, which is the effect created by storytelling, is expressed convincingly in facial expressions, gestures, and other body language. Because television is theatrical, many of the copywriter's tools, such as characters, costumes, sets and locations, props, lighting, optical and computerized special effects, and on-screen graphics, are similar to those you would use in a play, television show, or movie.

Audio   As in radio, the three audio elements are music, voices, and sound effects, but they are used differently in television commercials because they are connected to a visual image. The copywriter may have an announcer speak directly to the viewer or engage in a dialogue with another person, who may or may not be on camera. The copywriter writes the words they will say and blocks out on paper how this "talk" happens. A common manipulation of the camera–announcer relationship is the **voice-over,** in which an announcer who is not visible describes some kind of action on the screen. Sometimes a voice is heard **off camera,** which means you can't see the speaker and the voice is coming from the side, behind, or above.

How the Emotional Pivot Works in a Story

Charles Young, *Founder and CEO, Ameritest*

To investigate the power of emotional engagement in a video, we studied the structure of a six-minute film of Susan Boyle, who turned in a surprising 2009 performance on *Britain's Got Talent*. Employing the same research techniques we use to analyze television commercials, we found that this YouTube video is built on a standard dramatic structure that we commonly see in advertising, one that we call an "emotional pivot." (You can watch it on YouTube at *www.youtube.com/watch?v=9lp0IWv8QZY.*)

Good storytellers understand that with a pivot structure, the emotional impact is particularly strong because the valence of the emotion changes from initially negative to positive, which creates the strongest possible contrast between what the audience feels at the beginning of the story and what they feel at the end.

Here's how we identified the emotional pivot in the *Britain's Got Talent* video featuring a rather frumpy Scottish woman named Susan Boyle. Using a photo sort of still frames from the video, we track the flow of emotion throughout the six-minute video. In the graph, you can see strong negative emotions at the beginning of the video shown with strong spikes in the red line. This reflects the entrance on stage of this rather overweight and middle-aged Scottish woman. The rolled eyes and sideway glances of disbelief from the lead judge Simon Cowell reinforce this negative first impression.

Then toward the middle, the green (positive) line begins to rise rapidly and the red (negative) line fades away as emotions turn, or pivots, on frame 18 as Susan begins to sing. As her beautiful voice fills the room, the judges and the audience are transformed.

Finally, positive emotions rise to a sustained, high volume of intensity for the rest of the video. It ends with the entire studio audience—and even one of the judges—on their feet cheering wildly.

At the pivot point—the boundary between these two states of emotion—lies the most dramatic, brand-creating moment of this piece of film. So in frame 18 when Susan first begins to sing, we are able to pinpoint the actual moment of a birth of a new star—or brand, in advertising terms.

In storytelling, this is the moment when a gap opens up in the mind of an audience—a break between what the audience expected to see, and what just happened. The mind of the audience is forced to turn in a new direction. As their personal interpretations of the event are recalculated, audience members build a new mental model of realty to make sense of what they are seeing. Unexpectedly, the ugly duckling just turned into a swan!

Interestingly, when we tested a shorter version of the video with the "negative set-up" removed, we found the emotional response to the singing was just as positive, but when we interviewed respondents, it was obvious that something was lost. This shorter version was much less likely to be rated as "unique," "involving," "entertaining," or "inspirational." In other words, changing the narrative to an uninterrupted flow of positive emotions diminished the impact. Ironically, the Susan Boyle story would be different—and she might not be a star—without Simon Cowell's display of cynicism at the beginning.

You can watch this video on YouTube. Search for "Susan Boyle I dreamed a Dream."

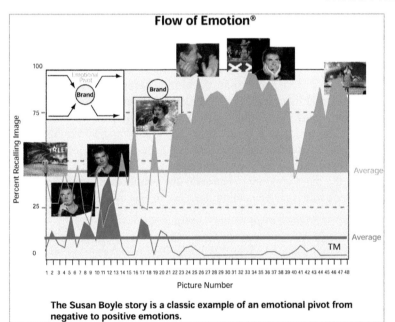

Flow of Emotion®

The Susan Boyle story is a classic example of an emotional pivot from negative to positive emotions.

Dialogue, both in radio and television, is an interesting challenge for copywriters who try to keep the words natural and the interaction interesting. In the Frontier Airlines talking animals commercials, for example, the repartee between the characters is as important to the message as the words themselves. Note how the dialogue between Jack the Rabbit and Larry the Lynx bounces back and forth in the "Leather Seats" commercial. Also note the brand identity text in the middle. This structure is called a "donut" because it uses an attention-getting idea to open and close with brand copy embedded in the middle.

Jack the Rabbit:	I'll tell you, Lar, the tarmac never looked better.
Larry the Lynx:	I'll say.
Jack:	New planes. New cities. New leather seats.
Larry:	Pretty exciting stuff, huh?
Jack:	Hey, uh, Larry, what's leather made from?
Larry:	Cowhide.
Jack:	Oh. So that's why there are no cows on the tails of our planes.
Larry:	It'd be creepy.
GRAPHIC:	New planes. New cities. New leather seats.
[MUSIC UNDER]	A whole different animal. *FrontierAirlines.com.* Frontier.
Larry:	Wanna moment of silence for the cows?
Jack:	Sure.
Both:	That's enough.
Jack:	Wanna grab a burger?
Larry:	I'm starving.

Source: Courtesy of Frontier Airlines and Grey Worldwide.

Music is also important in most commercials. Sometimes it is just used as background; at other times, the song is the focus of the commercial. In recognition of the role of music in advertising, Universal Music released a CD in 2001 called "As Seen on TV: Songs from Commercials," a collection of tunes that have become popular—or resurrected—thanks to their use in TV commercials. Included among the 20 songs are "Mr. Roboto" by Styx, "Right Here, Right Now" by Fatboy Slim, "Lust for Life" by Iggy Pop, and "Got to Give It Up" by Marvin Gaye. All of these songs have been used effectively in a television commercial. Clash's "London Calling" song became the theme for a highly successful sales event for Jaguar.

Other TV Tools   The creative tools examined next are the setting, casting, costumes, props, and lighting—all of which the copywriter must describe in the script. The setting, or **set,** is where the action takes place. It can be something in the studio, from a simple tabletop to a constructed set that represents a storefront or the inside of a home, or it can be a computer creation layered behind the action. Commercials shot outside the studio are said to be filmed **on location,** which means the entire crew and cast are transported somewhere away from the studio.

For many commercials, the most important element is the people, who are called **talent.** Finding the right person for each role is called **casting.** People can be cast as:

- *Announcers* (either onstage or offstage), presenters, introducers.
- *Spokespersons* (or "spokes-animals," such as the Geico Gecko and the Frontier talking animals).
- *Character Types* (old woman, baby, skin diver, police officer).
- *Celebrities,* such as Catherine Zeta-Jones and the Black Eyed Peas.

Costumes and makeup can be an important part of the story depending on the characterizations in the commercial. Of course, historical stories need period costumes, but modern scenes may also require special clothing such as golf outfits, swimsuits, or cowboy boots. Makeup may be important if you need to change a character from young to old. The copywriter must specify all of these details in the script. The director usually manipulates the lighting, but the copywriter might specify special lighting effects in the script. For example, you might read "Intense bright light as though reflected from snow" or "Light flickering on people's faces as if reflecting from a television screen."

Copywriters might also have to specify the commercial's **pace**—how fast or slowly the action progresses. Some messages are best developed at a languid pace; others work better when presented at an upbeat, fast pace. Research has found that the pace of TV commercials has been steadily getting faster since the mid-20th century. Why do you suppose that might be?

Planning the TV Commercial

Copywriters must plan how long the commercial will be, what shots will appear in each scene, what the key visual will be, and where and how to shoot the commercial. Other key decisions the copywriter must consider in planning a commercial are the length, number of scenes, and key frames. The common lengths of TV commercials are 10, 15, 20, 30, and 60 seconds. The 10-, 15-, and 20-second lengths are used for reminders and product or station identification. The 60-second spot, which is common in radio, has almost disappeared in television because of the increasing cost of airtime. The most common length for a TV commercial is 30 seconds.

Scenes and Key Frames   A commercial is planned in **scenes**—segments of action that occur in a single location. A scene may include several shots from different angles. A 30-second commercial usually is planned with four to six scenes, but a fast-paced commercial may have many more. Because television is a visual medium, the message is often developed as a **key visual** that conveys the heart of the concept. The **key frame** is the shot that sticks in the mind and becomes the image viewers remember when they think about the commercial. Copywriter Lara Mann describes a campaign she worked on for the Florida Film Festival. The campaign used television commercials but they were supported by posters with key frames from the commercials. The TV tagline "Where Will It Take You?" appears on the posters to express the thought that the Film Festival takes you to some exotic locations.

Copywriters need to answer many questions when planning a television spot. How much product information should there be in the commercial? Should the action be fast or slow? Is it wise to defy tradition and create unusual, even controversial ads as Crispin Porter + Bogusky did with Old Navy's SuperModelquins? How intrusive should the ad be?

Every producer and director will respond to these questions differently, depending on personal preferences and the advertising objectives. Nevertheless, these general principles as outlined by Drewniany and Jewler in their creative strategy book and earlier editions of their book are relevant for most effective television commercials:[11]

- *What's the big idea* you need to get across? In 30 seconds you barely have time to do much more than that. Alternative concepts are also tested as key visuals in developing the idea for the commercial. For each idea, a card with the key visual drawn on it is given to a respondent, along with a paragraph that describes the concept and how it will be played out in the commercial.
- *What's the benefit* of that big idea, and who does it benefit? Connect the big idea back to the target audience.
- *How can you turn that benefit into a visual element?* This visual is what sticks in people's minds.
- *How can you gain the interest* of viewers at the beginning? The first three seconds are critical.
- *How can you focus on a key visual,* a scene that encapsulates your entire selling message into one neat package?
- *Is the commercial single-minded?* Tell one important story per commercial. Tell it clearly, tell it memorably, and involve your viewer.
- *Is the product identified and shown* in close-up at the end?

Scripts, Storyboards, and Photoboards   Two documents are used to plan commercials: a television script prepared by the copywriter and a storyboard drawn by the art director. Similar to a radio script, a **television script** is the written version of the commercial's plan. It contains all the words, dialogue, lyrics (if important to the ad message), instructions, and descriptions of the details we've been discussing—sets, costumes, lighting, and so forth. For television commercials that use dialogue, the script is written in two columns, with the audio on the right and the video on the left.

The key to the structure of a television script is the relationship between the audio and the video. The dialogue is typed as usual, but the instructions and labels are typed in all-capital letters. The video part of the script includes descriptions of key frames, characters, actions, and camera movements in the commercial. Sometimes the script is in a two-column format with the video instructions on the left and the audio in the right column.

A **storyboard,** which is a visual plan or layout of the commercial, is drawn (by hand or on the computer) to show the number of scenes, composition of the shots, and progression of the action. The script information usually appears below the key images. Its purpose is to guide the filming. A **photoboard** uses photographic stills instead of art to illustrate the progression of images. It's created from the still photos or frames from the filming and is used to present to clients. (See the Frontier commercial in Chapter 8.)

HOW DIFFERENT IS COPYWRITING FOR THE INTERNET?

The Internet is more interactive than any other mass medium. Not only do viewers initiate the contact, they can send e-mail on many websites. This makes Web advertising more like two-way communication, and that's a major point of difference from other advertising forms. As a result, the Web copywriter is challenged to attract people to the site and to manage a dialogue-based communication experience. In addition to targeting messages to audiences, Web advertisers have to be prepared to listen and respond to those audiences. That's a major shift in how Web marketing communicators think about advertising.

Principle
To write great copy for the Web, copywriters must think of it as an interactive medium and open up opportunities for dialogue with the consumer.

It is true, however, that there are forms of Internet advertising that look like more traditional ads, such as **banners,** sidebar ads, and pop ups. E-mail and video ads, as well as mobile ads on smart phones, all require variations of traditional copywriting techniques. Most of these formats end with a link to the sponsor's website where the user can participate in a more interactive experience.

In this complicated, fast-changing medium, there aren't a lot of rules. In fact, marketing communication that uses text messaging and Twitter may even throw out the rules of spelling with vowel-free words. Cell-phone company Motorola follows that trend in naming new products such as RAZR, PEBL, and RCKR.

For banners and other formats that look like advertising and seek to attract someone to a company's website, verbosity is a killer. In that situation, no one wants to read a lot of type online. That means Web copywriters have to be able to write everything from catchy phrases for banners to copy that works like traditional advertisements, brochures, or catalogs. A basic principle, however, is that good writing is good writing, whether it is being done for traditional advertising media or for the Web.

Websites

The challenge for Web advertisers is to understand the user's situation and design messages that fit their needs and interests. However, the Web is an information medium and users come to it, in some cases, for reference information—formats that look a lot like catalogs, or even encyclopedias. Corporate or organizational websites are designed to provide information, as well as image cues, so strategies that organize information and package it for easy accessibility are important. **Key words** are used to help *visitors or surfers* (rather than readers, listeners, or viewers) search for the site online, as well as within the site for the information they need.

Creativity is also valued both to entice visitors, but also to keep them actively involved with the site. For example, the "Don't Mess with Texas" anti-litter website mentioned early as an *Adweek* favorite invites visitors into the campaign with advertising materials, testimonials, letters, special events, and involvement programs. It uses colorful animation to create action and spark interest. The language reflects the tough-talking slogan. For example, one section asks, "Who wants to live in a pig sty?" and "Why swim in an ashtray?" Check it out at *http://dontmesswithtexas.org*.

Banners

The most common form of online advertising is small banner ads containing text, images, and perhaps motion **(animation).** Banners in this small format have to be creative to stand out amidst the clutter on a typical Web page and, similar to outdoor advertising, they have to grab the surfer's attention with few words. Effective banners arouse the interest of the viewer, who is often browsing through other information on the computer screen. The key to stopping surfers is vivid graphics, motion, and clever phrases. It is critical to make the site easy to navigate. In general, the copywriter uses these strategies for grabbing surfers and turning them into longer-staying visitors:[12]

1. *Offer a deal* that promises a discount or a freebie as a prize.
2. *Use an involvement device* such as a challenge or contest.
3. *Change the offer frequently,* perhaps even daily. One of the reasons people surf the Internet is to find out what's happening now. Good ads exploit "nowness" and "newsiness."
4. *Keep the writing succinct* because most surfers have short attention spans and get bored easily.
5. *Focus surfers' attention* by asking provocative questions or offering knowledge they can use.
6. *Use the advertisement* to solicit information and opinions from users as part of your research. Reward surfers for sharing their opinions with you by offering them three free days of a daily horoscope or something else they might find fun or captivating.

Sometimes banners provide brand reminder information only, like a billboard, but they usually also invite viewers to click on the banner to link to an ad or the advertiser's home page. The effectiveness of such efforts is monitored in part by the number of **click-throughs.** Their creators make banners entertaining by using multimedia effects such as animation and sound, interactivity, emotional appeals, color, and provocative headlines. One mistake copywriters sometimes make, however, is to forget to include the company name or brand in the banner or ad. Surfers should be able to tell immediately what product or brand the banner is advertising. Effective banner ads satisfy the need for entertainment, information, and context (a link to a product), and often use promotional incentives, such as prizes or gifts, to motivate visitors to click through to the sponsor's website[13] to drive action.

Internet Ads

Similar in some ways to traditional advertising, Internet ads are designed to create awareness and interest in a product and build a brand image. In terms of creating interest, good copywriting works well in any medium, including the Internet. The "Ocean Speaks" ads in *The Inside Story* at *www.pearsonglobaleditions.com/moriarty* illustrates how the same writing style can transfer from print to the Internet and maintain a consistent brand personality. The scuba diving industry wanted to revive interest in the sport of scuba, both with current divers and potential newcomers. The objective of this striking campaign was to move people from print to the company's website.

Art director Chris Hutchinson explains, "We created a campaign in the literal voice of the ocean. The Ocean irreverently compares itself to the dull world up above and invites people to come down for a visit. Instead of using traditional beauty shots of scuba diving, we commissioned surreal organic underwater scenes." The ads were featured in *Archive,* an international collection of the best advertising, television, and poster images.

In contrast to the Ocean speaking campaign, Burton Snowboards uses copy that speaks in the voice of the product's user, but the copy also creates an association with a distinctive brand and user personality.

It also uses its corporate mission statement as copy that speaks in the same tone of voice. This is another creative website. Check it out at *www.burton.com*.

LESSONS ABOUT COPYWRITING

As discussed throughout this chapter, the copywriter's job is to find a memorable way to express the creative concept. All of a copywriter's talent will do no good if the audience cannot understand the "magic words." Understanding the words, as well as the creative idea, is particularly complicated in global brand communication.

Writing for a Global Brand

Language affects the creation of the advertising, which is a problem for global campaigns. English is more economical than many other languages. This creates a major problem when the space for copy is laid out for English and one-third more space is needed for French or Spanish. However, English does not have the subtlety of other languages such as Greek, Chinese, or French. Those languages have many different words for situations and emotions that do not translate precisely into English. Standardizing the copy content by translating the appeal into the language of the foreign market is fraught with possible communication blunders. It is rare to find a copywriter who is fluent in both the domestic and foreign language and familiar with the culture of the foreign market.

Headlines in any language often rely on humor or a play on words, themes that are relevant to one country, or slang. Because these verbal techniques don't cross borders well, copywriters remove them from the advertising unless the meaning or intent can be re-created in other languages. For this reason, international campaigns are not literally translated word by word. Instead, a copywriter usually rewrites them in the second language. An ad for a Rome laundry shows how a poor translation can send the wrong message: "Ladies, leave your clothes here and spend the afternoon having a good time."

Although computer words and advertising terms are almost universally of English derivation, some languages simply do not have words equivalent to other English expressions. Since 1539 the French have had legislation to keep their language "pure" and now have a government agency to prevent words, especially English words, from corrupting the French language. The words *marketing* and *weekend,* unacceptable to the French government agency, are translated literally as "study the market" (or "pertaining to trade") and "end of the week," respectively.

Experience suggests that the most reasonable solution to the language problem is to use bilingual copywriters who understand the full meaning of the English text and can capture the essence of the message in the second language. It takes a brave and trusting international creative director to approve copy he or she doesn't understand but is assured is right. A **back translation** of the ad copy from the foreign language into the domestic one is always a good idea, but it seldom conveys a complete cultural interpretation.

The most recent announcement on the global stage is the opening up of the Internet to non-Roman letters, such as those used in Chinese, Korean, and Arabic. It's a challenge to develop translations for these languages so that a posting can be read in its original language, as well as in Roman letter alphabets, but the technology is making that possible.

Looking Ahead

The most important enduring principle is that in a Big Idea the meaning emerges from the way the words and images reinforce one another. We've explored the practices and principles of copywriting. In the next chapter we'll introduce the role of the art director and explain the important role of visual communication.

IT'S A WRAP

Outdoor Advertising in South Africa

A survey carried out by TNS Research Surveys in 2010 indicated that outdoor advertising was more visible to consumers than television and print advertising. Although advertising and marketing creative copywriters enjoy the challenge of creating simple and effective campaigns using tightly written and designed copy, there is still debate in South Africa about outdoor advertising. It is often criticized as being responsible for littering the environment, distracting drivers, and obstructing vision.

However, in South Africa, despite recession fears, the outdoor advertising market, including billboards and other forms of out-of-home (OOH) advertising, grew by an estimated 8.8 percent according to research carried out by PriceWaterhouseCoopers in late 2010. The value of the market was also estimated to be worth $212 million. In a survey on behalf of Primedia Unlimited, projections culminating in a 9.1 percent growth would see the market increase in value to around $282 million by 2014.

The Out of Home Media South Africa (OHMSA) organization is the recognized trade association for outdoor advertising in the country. The OHMSA recognizes that many outdoor advertising operators are not compliant with its code or local by-laws and that many of the sites are actually unapproved. Their own system is based on speed of traffic. In areas where traffic is slow moving, the sites have to have a distance of 200 meters between them, and the distance increases with higher speed zones.

In South Africa, advertising is regulated in all cities and controlled in residential and suburban areas. According to the executive director of OHMSA, Les Holley, the biggest problem is ensuring that media owners adhere to regulations and approval processes and do not overpopulate areas with outdoor advertising. A prime example of the effectiveness of OHMSA is that until recently, the route into Sun City had over 200 out-of-home advertising sites. Today it has around 40.

Key Points Summary

1. **What basic style of writing is used for advertising copy?** Words and pictures work together to shape a creative concept; however, it is the clever phrases and "magic words" crafted by copywriters that make ideas understandable and memorable. Copywriters who have an ear for language match the tone of the writing to the target audience. Good copy is succinct and single-minded. Copy that is less effective uses adese to imitate a stereotyped style that parodies advertising.

2. **Which copy elements are essential to a print ad?** The key elements of a print ad are the headlines and body copy. Headlines target the prospect, draw the reader's attention, identify the product, start the sale, and lure the reader into the body copy. Body copy provides persuasive details, such as support for claims, as well as proof and reasons why.

3. **How can we characterize the message and tools of radio advertising?** Radio commercials are personal and play to consumers' interests. However, radio is primarily a background medium. Special techniques, such as repetition, are used to enhance retention. The three audio tools are voice, music, and sound effects.

4. **What is the best way to summarize the major elements of television commercials?** The elements of TV commercials are video and audio tools. Television commercials can be characterized as using action, emotion, and demonstration to create messages that are intriguing as well as intrusive.

5. **How is Web advertising written?** Internet advertising is interactive and involving. Online advertising has primarily focused on websites and banners, although advertisers are using new forms that look more like magazine or television ads. Banners and other forms of online advertising have to stand out amid the clutter on a typical Web page and arouse the viewer's interest. Good writing is still good writing, even online.

Words of Wisdom: Recommended Reading

Applegate, Edd, *Strategic Copywriting,* New York: Rowman & Littlefield, 2005.

Bayan, Richard, *Words that Sell: The Thesaurus to Help You Promote Your Products, Services, and Ideas*, rev. ed., New York: McGraw-Hill, 2006.

Bly, Robert, *The Copywriter's Handbook*, 3rd ed., Sand Springs, OK: Holt, 2006.

Gossage, Howard, *The Book of Gossage*, Chicago: The Copy Workshop, 2006.

Gunelius, Susan, *Kick-Ass Copywriting in 10 Easy Steps*, Irvine, CA: Entrepreneur Press, 2008.

Higgins, Denis, *The Art of Writing Advertising: Conversations with Masters of the Craft*, New York: McGraw-Hill, 2003.

Klauser, Anne Henriette, *Writing on Both Sides of the Brain: Breakthrough Techniques for People Who Write*, New York: HarperCollins, 1987.

Shaw, Mark, *Copywriting: Successful Writing for Design, Advertising, and Marketing*, London, UK: Laurence King Publishing, 2009.

Sugarman, Joseph, *The Adweek Copywriting Handbook: The Ultimate Guide to Writing Powerful Advertising and Marketing Copy from One of America's Top Copywriters*, Hoboken, NJ: Wiley, 2006.

Key Terms

adese p. 293
animation, p. 310
back translation, p. 312
banners, p. 310
blind headline, p. 297
body copy, p. 293
brag-and-boast copy, p. 293
call to action, p. 300
call-outs, p. 295
captions, p. 298
casting, p. 308

click-throughs, p. 311
closing paragraph, p. 300
collateral materials, p. 302
copywriter, p. 289
direct-action headline, p. 296
display copy, p. 293
headline, p. 294
image transfer, p. 305
indirect-action headline, p. 296
jingle, p. 304
key frame, p. 309

key visual, p. 309
key words, p. 310
lead paragraph, p. 300
off camera, p. 306
on location, p. 308
overlines, p. 295
pace, p. 309
photoboard, p. 310
radio script, p. 305
scenes, p. 309
set, p. 308

sound effects (sfx), p. 304
storyboard, p. 310
subheads, p. 298
talent, p. 308
television script, p. 309
theater of the mind, p. 303
tone of voice, p. 291
underlines, p. 295
voice-over, p. 306
your-name-here copy, p. 293

Review Questions

1. What is adese, and why is it a problem in advertising copy?

2. Describe the various copy elements of a print ad.

3. What is the difference between direct-action and indirect-action headlines? Find an example of each and explain how it works.

4. What qualities make a good tagline or slogan?

5. What is the primary role of body copy, and how does it accomplish that?

6. One principle of print copywriting is that the headline catches the reader's eye, but the body copy wins the reader's heart and mind. Find an ad that demonstrates that principle and explain how it works.

7. Explain the message characteristics of radio advertising. What does "theater of the mind" mean to a radio copywriter? What are the primary tools used by the radio copywriter?

8. What are the major characteristics of TV ads? Describe the tools of television commercial copywriting.

9. Discuss how Internet advertising is written.

Discussion Questions

1. Creative directors say the copy and art must work together to create a concept. Consider all of the ads in this chapter and the preceding chapters and identify one that you believe best demonstrates that principle. Explain what the words contribute and how they work with the visual.

2. A principle of TV message design is that television is primarily a visual medium. However, very few television commercials are designed without a vocal element (actors or announcers). Even the many commercials that visually demonstrate products in action use an off-screen voice to provide information. Why is there a need to use a voice in a television commercial?

3. What do we mean by *tone of voice,* and why is it important in advertising? Find a magazine ad that you think has an appropriate tone of voice for its targeted audience (the readers of that particular magazine) and one that doesn't. Explain your analyses of these two ads.

4. Select a product that is advertised exclusively through print using a long-copy format. Examples might be business-to-business and industrial products, over-the-counter drugs, and some car and appliance ads. Now write a 30-second radio and a 30-second TV spot for that product. Present your work to the class, along with an analysis of how the message design changed—and stayed the same—when you moved from print to radio and then to TV.

5. Critique the following (choose one):

   a. Jingles are a popular creative form in radio advertising. Even so, there may be as many jingles that you don't want to hear again as there are ones that you do. As a team, identify one jingle that your group really dislikes and another one that you like. Analyze why these jingles either work or don't work and present your critique to your class.

   b. As a team, surf the Web and find one banner ad that you think works to drive click-throughs and one that doesn't. Print them out and prepare an analysis that compares the two banner ads and explains why you think one is effective and the other is not. Present your critique to your class.

6. *Three-Minute Debate:* Your professor has set up a debate between the advertising sales director of the campus news-

paper and the manager of the campus radio station, which is a commercial operation. During the discussion the newspaper representative says that most radio commercials sound like newspaper ads, but are harder to follow. The radio manager responds by claiming that radio creativity works with the "theater of the mind" and is more engaging than newspaper ads, which mostly feature price copy and sales. In a team of two or three, pick one of these positions, and build your case by finding examples of ads in both print and radio that support your viewpoint.

Take-Home Projects

1. *Portfolio Project:* In Chapter 6's Three-Minute Debate, your team was asked to consider the research needed for a new upscale restaurant chain that focuses on fowl—duck, squab, pheasant, and other elegant meals in the poultry category. Now your creative team is being asked to develop the creative package for the restaurant chain. A specialty category, this would be somewhat like a seafood restaurant. You have been asked to develop the creative package to use in launching these new restaurants in their new markets. Develop the following:

   - The restaurant's name
   - A slogan for the restaurant chain
   - A list of five enticing menu items
   - A paragraph of copy that can be used in print to describe the restaurant
   - The copy for a 30-second commercial to be used in radio.

2. *Mini-Case Analysis:* The Habana campaign was very successful. Explain how the concept works. Then explain how the theme line defines the brand and reinforces the brand position. What other factors have made it a winner? Pretend you are assigned to this account and you need to come up with an idea for a new outdoor board execution. Describe your idea in a one-page proposal to turn in to your instructor.

Team Project: The BrandRevive Campaign

Review the message strategy you created in the last chapter for your BrandRevive campaign, as well as the Big Idea you developed as a team. The next step is to translate that strategy and Big Idea into copy. Normally you would be working in a copywriter and art director team, but because we have to introduce first one—copywriting—then the other—art direction, we'll focus in this step of the project on the language.

- Develop a slogan to use with your campaign, one that delivers on your strategy, but at the same time is attention getting and memorable—something that has the potential to move into popular culture.
- Write the copy for a print ad that would run in a magazine targeted to the audience you have selected.
- Write the copy for a radio spot that uses "theater of the mind" techniques.
- Write the copy for a television commercial that uses dialogue.
- Present your copy package in a two-page handout for your class and a PowerPoint presentation that is no longer than three slides. In the presentation explain and justify your copy decisions.

Hands-On Case

The Century Council

Read the Century Council case in the Appendix before coming to class.

1. The case briefly discusses the tonality of the communications. Write a one-page direction to the creative team explaining what the tonality should be and giving rationale for your recommendation. Keep in mind the target audience, your client (The Century Council) and the potential seriousness of the consequences of binge drinking on college campuses.

2. Write a one page instruction for finding your personal stupid drink that you would give to all freshmen arriving on campus.

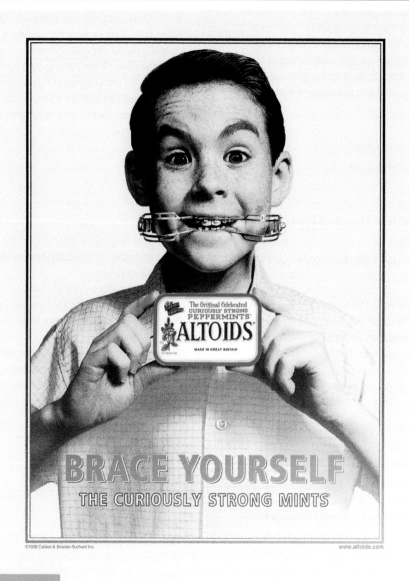

It's a Winner

Campaign:	Company:	Agencies:	Awards:
"Curiously Strong Mints"	Kraft Foods; Wm. Wrigley Jr. Co. (which became a subsidiary of Mars)	Leo Burnett, Publicis & Hal Riney, BBDO Chicago	Two Kelly Awards, including the Grand Prize, two One Show prizes, three Clios, the New York Festival Grand Prix

1. What is the role of visual communication in marketing communication messages?
2. How can we define *layout* and *composition*, and what's the difference between the two?
3. How are art and color reproduced in print media?
4. What are the steps in planning and producing video?
5. What are the basic techniques of Web design?

A Strong Mint with a Curious Past

Shortly after the United States fought for its independence from England, Smith Kendon created in 1780 a revolutionary British product designed to relieve intestinal discomfort. It's name: Altoids. Today we know Altoids as a "curiously strong mint" designed to fight bad breath. The story about how Altoids came to be the top-selling mint in the United States parallels the evolution of its brand personality.

Advertising as far back as the 1920s plugged the "curiously strong" mint-flavored lozenges, but Altoids was largely unknown in the United States until Kraft Food purchased it in 1995 and turned its advertising over to the Leo Burnett agency.

Kraft inherited a product that came in a distinctive, Old World–looking red-and-white metal tin emblazoned with the slogan, "The Original Celebrated Curiously Strong Peppermints." The Burnett creatives adapted that phrase and captured the brand essence with its campaign's wry slogan: "The Curiously Strong Mint."

The campaign tone features a type of amusing, rather British self-deprecation, as if the brand doesn't take itself seriously. That approach struck a nerve with the largely cynical, sometimes sarcastic Generation X and Y males who have been the brand's most loyal fans.

Burnett's memorable ads from this classic campaign have featured a muscle builder with the line "Nice Altoids," a 1950s teenager with oversized braces and the headline "Brace Yourself," and a stern-looking nurse carrying the little red-and-white Altoids tin with the headline "Now This Won't Hurt a Bit." Another ad proclaimed, "No Wonder the British Have Stiff Upper Lips."

As you probably know, the Altoids brand has expanded to include new flavors, from cinnamon and wintergreen to ginger and sours (in a round tin), as well as gum and strips. No longer do we think of Altoids for its medicinal qualities.

Change is an inevitable fact of life. Not only did the product come to mean something different to consumers over time, brand ownership has changed hands and so have the agencies that manage the marketing communication.

Altoids was a winner for Kraft, so much so that it sold the brand in 2004 to Wm. Wrigley Jr. Co. for the minty fresh sum of $1.46 billion. The new owner then awarded the Altoids advertising account to Publicis & Hal Riney. In late 2008, Mars bought Wrigley, and moved the account to BBDO Chicago. How does a brand maintain a consistent personality amid changing ownership and agencies?

The success of a brand's advertising is based on more than the humor of a single campaign—especially as ownership of a brand shifts. Altoids ads have an iconic look. Most feature an intriguing headline that is only a few words long in all capital letters and a drop shadow outline. Many of the ads are laid out on a plain, mint green background with a double rule border—a great retro look that reflects the package design, which reinforces the brand identity.

Although BBDO Chicago has recently dropped the "Curiously Strong" theme, replacing it with "A Slap to the Cerebellum," it kept some of the elements from the previous campaign. Steffan Postaer, one of the Leo Burnett creatives whose ideas resulted in Altoids award-winning work, did not agree entirely with the approach that BBDO took. But he said this of the new campaign: "You can still see the brand's DNA in the language and typography as well as in the tone and manner." Other efforts include "Brainstorm," a branded entertainment collaboration with Fox Mobile Studios.

See for yourself what you think gives a campaign continuity by looking at past and current advertising at *www.altoids.com/ad-gallery.do*. Then in the *It's a Wrap* section at the end of the chapter, see how well the advertising has performed over time for this intense, extreme, and curiously strong mint.

Sources: www.wrigley.com; www.altoids.com; http://godsofadvertising.wordpress.com/2008/03/13/my-altoids-can-beat-up-their-altoids; Rita Chang, "Altoids Pokes Fun at Itself with 'Brainstorm,'" www.adage.com, September 21, 2009.

This ad offers a visual pun, playing on the product name and the slang "nice 'toids." Pairing the unexpected—the hunk's deltoid muscles and the product—helps create a memorable association.

The visual consistency and wry humor in the Altoids campaign go far beyond the ability of words to describe things. The quirky images communicate ideas about the brand personality, as well as the feelings and sense of humor of the brand's target market. This chapter is about the visuals used in advertising—how they are designed and what they contribute to the meaning of the ad. First we review some basic ideas about visual impact, both in print and broadcast, and the role of the art director. Then we consider print art production and video production and end with a discussion of the design of Internet advertising.

WHY IS VISUAL COMMUNICATION IMPORTANT?

What makes Altoids so visually remarkable? Does the product grab your attention? How does the visual build brand personality? Is it interesting? Do you remember it?

The success of Altoids breath mints is primarily a result of the consistent graphic presentation of the brand in its marketing communication. The visual consistency is not only apparent in the design of the package and the ads; it also reflects the history of the brand as a quirky old British lozenge.

The Altoids ads use association to create curiosity, but also to reflect the meaning of the slogan. "Nice Altoids" builds on a unique connection between the sound of "deltoids" and the brand name. We've also reproduced an ad used to launch the Altoids Cinnamon line, which continues to build on the brand position but modifies it slightly to read "curiously hot" rather than "curiously strong." A firewalker tiptoeing across a patch of the little white mints visually reinforces a truth about the product—the Cinnamon Altoids are hot enough to tickle your toes.

In effective advertising, both print and television, it's not just the words that need to communicate the message—the visuals need to communicate, too. The visuals normally work with the words to present the creative concept. An example of a simple story told totally through the visuals is the Best of Show award for a One Show competition that showcased a British campaign for Volkswagen. It featured a gently humorous 30-second commercial built around the low price of the VW Polo. Bob Barrie, when he was president of The One Club, an association for people in the creative side of advertising, explained that it was possibly the quietest, most understated TV spot entered in the show. The idea was simple: A woman sits at her kitchen table. Her scanning of the newspaper—and her hiccups—stop abruptly as she discovers an ad for the VW Polo with its "surprisingly ordinary" price.[1]

Visuals do some things better than words, such as demonstrate something. How would you demonstrate, for example, the smallness of a computer chip or a new miniature hard drive? IBM did it through a visual analogy—showing its hard disk drive inside half an eggshell next to a newborn chick.

Even radio can evoke mental pictures through suggestive or descriptive language and sound effects. The effective use of visuals in advertising can be related to a number of the effects we have outlined in our Facets Model of Effects:

1. *Grab Attention* Generally visuals are better at getting and keeping attention than words.
2. *Stick in Memory* Visuals persist in the mind because people generally remember messages as visual fragments, or key images that are filed easily in their minds.
3. *Cement Belief* Seeing is believing, as the IBM chick ad demonstrates. Visuals that demonstrate add credibility to a message.
4. *Tell Interesting Stories* Visual storytelling is engaging and maintains interest.
5. *Communicate Quickly* Pictures tell stories faster than words, as the IBM chick visual illustrates. A picture communicates instantly, while consumers have to decipher verbal/written communication word by word, sentence by sentence, line by line.
6. *Anchor Associations* To distinguish undifferentiated products with low inherent interest, advertisers often link the product with visual associations representing lifestyles and types of users, as the "Nice Altoids" ad demonstrates.

ALTOIDS CINNAMON
THE CURIOUSLY STRONG MINTS
curious? altoids.com

SHOWCASE

This ad for Altoids Cinnamon shows a firewalker tiptoeing across a patch of the mints. This Altoids "Cinnamon" ad builds on a truth about the product. The cinnamon candies are curiously hot. Just stepping on them would be an experience. You see the ad. You smile. You associate the message with a product attribute. Just maybe you remember the brand when you're in the checkout line.

This Altoids "Cinnamon" ad, which won a Gold Pencil from the One Show, was submitted by the Leo Burnett copywriter and art director team of Andy Dao (top) and Matt Miller, both of whom graduated from the advertising program at the University of Colorado. Their work was nominated for inclusion in this book by Professor Brett Robbs.

Visual Impact

In most marketing communication, the power to get attention primarily lies with the visual. The excitement and drama in a television commercial is created through moving images. But it is an intriguing idea that grabs attention and remains in memory. This is particularly so for larger impact formats, such as posters and outdoor boards.

A provocative outdoor board for the Italian women's apparel firm, No-l-ita, certainly got people's attention, but it also raised ethical issues. The billboard raised a furor in Italy because

Principle
The visual's primary function in an advertisement is to get attention.

IBM used a chick and an egg to demonstrate the smallness of its hard disk drive, which is about the size of a large coin.

it showed shocking pictures of a naked anorexic woman. The image was shot by Oliviero Toscani, the former photographer/art director for Benetton, who stirred up emotions over his photos for that clothing brand by depicting a dying AIDS victim, death-row inmates, and a nun and priest kissing. Professor Edoardo Brioschi explains the issues with these images of anorexia in the *A Principled Practice* feature.

In general, print designers have found that a picture in a print ad captures more than twice as many readers as a headline does. Furthermore, the bigger the illustration, the more the message grabs consumers' attention. Ads with pictures also tend to pull more readers into the body copy; initial attention is more likely to turn to interest with a strong visual. People not only notice ad visuals, they remember ads with pictures more than those composed mostly of type. Both the believability factor and the interest-building impact of a visual story are reasons why visuals are anchored so well in memory.

Big Ideas that capture attention can be puzzling, shocking, or funny. An example is found in the "Welcome" doormat poster used with a twist by Columbia Sportswear. A Vonage campaign for its Web-based phone service uses videos of people doing silly things to illustrate its message: "That people do really stupid things. Like pay too much for home phone service." The commercials show a man cutting down a tree that falls on his car and a man on a treadmill who loses his footing and falls off. The stunts seem to defy credibility but, in fact, they are actual footage from the reality TV show *America's Funniest Home Videos*.[2] Attention, interest, memorability, believability—these factors help explain the visual impact of advertising messages.

Visual Storytelling

In visual storytelling the images set up a narrative, as the YMCA ad demonstrates, that has to be constructed by the reader or viewer. In television, for example, the commercial begins and ends with visual elements that establish the scene and the conclusion. Visual storytelling is important even for abstract concepts such as "empowered," "inspired," and "inventive," which were the focus of commercials in the PBS "Be More Inspired" campaign. In the "Be more empowered" commercial, a goldfish makes its escape from its little round bowl in an apartment and jumps from a puddle to a bottle to a river where it works its way upstream accompanying giant salmon who are leaping up waterfalls in their annual migration.

In another commercial in the series titled "Be more inspired," a composer agonizes over the right notes and eventually hits a point of total frustration. As he looks out the window, he sees a group of birds sitting on a set of five power and telephone wires that are conveniently aligned to look like a music staff. From the bird's positions he crafts a tune that becomes the theme for his composition. PBS used these clever little visual stories to present itself as a creative force that inspires people to use their imaginations.

The point is that creative people and art directors in particular design images that tell stories and create brand impressions. The art—the image or visual elements—in a marketing communication message can touch emotional buttons. Research by professor Karen Mallia, a regular contributor who wrote an essay for our Part 3 opener, suggests that not only are images moving, they also are becoming increasingly dramatic and controversial. She has studied the use of religious imagery in marketing communication and observes that "the change in tenor is best illustrated with the use of priests in advertising."

In 1975, Xerox's "Brother Dominick" spot starred a sweet, earnest monk invoking a "miracle" in duplicating 500 illuminated manuscripts. Fast-forward to 1991, when Benetton shocked the world with a priest and nun kissing. In 2005, Stella Artois' "Skating Priests" award-winning spot used surreal, almost sinister humor as you realize that a group of priests would rather see their fellow priest drown than lose a beer. In 2006, Pirelli tire launched a worldwide campaign with "The Call," a 20-minute Web film starring John Malkovich as a priest called upon to exorcise a car, and Naomi Campbell as the devil.

Mallia concludes that "The Call" with its dramatic tone brings a new level of darkness to advertising featuring priests. What do you think? Are images like these effective? Should religious images be avoided or are there times when they are relevant or appropriately dramatic?

A PRINCIPLED PRACTICE

An Imperative: Respect the Dignity of the Person

By Edoardo Teodoro Brioschi, *Università Cattolica del Sacro Cuore, Milan, Italy*

I believe that there exist certain ethical principles that apply to business activities and those include principles for marketing communication activities. Specifically I'm concerned about the protection of the dignity of the person. A case in obvious conflict with this principle is the use in an advertisement of an image of a woman suffering from an illness: acute anorexia. This is the case in the "No-Anorexia No-l-ita" campaign for an Italian brand of youth apparel.

The woman we see presented in the ad is, in fact, practically a living skeleton. The message shows the image of a naked woman suffering from anorexia posing with her gaze turned to the observer. (The model is 27-year-old French actress named Isabelle Caro who is five feet, five inches tall and weighs 70 pounds.) Both front and back views of her poses were used on outdoor boards and in the daily press during Milan fashion week, as well as in other big cities such as Rome and Naples.

The advertiser claimed that by presenting the images in this way it sought to make specific reference to a drama experienced by young women: anorexia: "We want to keep young people informed about this terrible illness so that, by seeing the effects, the young will not take the same risk."

The body that self-regulates the advertising industry in Italy (Istituto di Autodisciplina Pubblicitaria—the Italian Self-Regulation Institute) examined the No-l-ita "No Anorexia" campaign and judged this message to be in conflict with its Code of Self-Regulation. It summoned the advertiser, Flash & Partners, producer of the No-l-ita brand, for a specific hearing to discuss the case.

As a number of experts testified, anorexia is a complex illness. It follows that, whatever the factor causing the pathology, the behavior at risk is not due to ignorance of its effect. Hence the principle "If you know the results you will avoid them" is not valid. In fact, this pathology unfortunately derives from deep drives, probably including biochemical imbalances, which cannot be overcome or rectified by an advertisement that simply displays its devastating effects.

Therefore, this advertising was banned. In fact, the message in question uses the physical devastation of the naked body of a young woman for commercial purposes—for the purpose of marketing the firm's products—and in so doing it offends her dignity and debases the personal and social drama caused by this type of pathology.

On this question there was a more general observation by this jury, the highest judicial organ of the Italian Self-Regulation Institute. It notes that promotional campaigns dealing with such delicate areas as health and prevention call for extreme caution in their conduct, requiring scientific preparation and justifying a preventive screening by the bodies responsible for advertising self-regulation.

Brand Image

We've talked in previous chapters about the important role marketing communication plays in the creation of a brand image. Much of that contribution comes from the visual elements—the symbolic images associated with the brand and the elements that define the brand, such as the trademark and logo. A classic brand symbol, for example, is the target graphic used by the Target store. The association with the brand name is immediately clear and the brand meaning, that Target is a store where you can go to get what you are looking for, also adds to the identity of the retailer.

YOUR KIDS TRYING TO TELL YOU SOMETHING?

A **logo,** which is the imprint used for immediate identification of a brand or company, is an interesting design project because it uses typography, illustration, and layout to create a distinctive and memorable image that identifies the brand. Think of the cursive type used for Coca-Cola, the block letters used for IBM, and the apple with a bite out of it (in both rainbow stripes and white) for Apple computers. Also check out the logo designs by Michael Dattolico.

Brand icons are characters associated with a brand, such Mr. Peanut, Chester the Cheetah, Uncle Ben, and Ronald McDonald. If they are effective, they become an enduring symbol of the brand. Initially the character is designed to reflect the desired brand personality. The Jolly Green Giant is an imaginary and kind friend who encourages kids to eat their vegetables. Over time, however, they may need to be updated as the Betty Crocker image has been a number of times. The trade magazine *Adweek* celebrates brand icons and annually inducts winners into its Madison Avenue Advertising Walk of Fame event every fall. Check these out at *www.adweek.com*.

Package design is another area where brand image is front and center. Sometimes the brand link is in the shape of the packaging as in the distinctive grandmotherly Mrs. Butterworth syrup bottles (see an example at *www.mrsbutterworthsyrup.com*). It may also be in the stylistics as we have shown with Celestial Seasonings tea boxes (see Chapter 2). The package design also accommodates strategic elements with positioning statements, flags that reference current campaigns, recipes, and pricing announcements. During the Great Recession, a number of manufacturers found that new packaging with retro designs appealed to consumers. Check out the Ritz crackers, Oreo cookies, and Corn Flakes brands, among others.

There's always a tension in advertising between doing something over the top that's creative and attention getting and being responsible to the brand image, the strategy, and society. The acceptability of a wacky image in an ad depends, in part, on its targeting, but it also depends on judgment and intuition. Our ethics discussions in this book often focus on the appropriateness of an image and how it reflects on the brand.

For example, an ad for Vaseline Intensive Care Lotion shows a conference room with a speaker and a group of businesspeople—both men and women—paying careful attention to the presentation. In the foreground is a happy woman in a business suit with her back to the speaker and her colleagues. Her legs are up on the table and she's caressing them. Unfortunately she's also a black woman. The headline reads: "Nothing keeps you from handling your business." So does Vaseline Intensive Care want us to know that if black women use their product, they become totally clueless in a business meeting? The point is that what appears to the creative team to be a dynamite visual may, on reflection, send a number of contrary messages.

Environmental Design

Remember we have said that everything communicates and that includes the design of the environment in which goods and services are offered for sale. The architectural design and interior ambiance of a store contribute to its brand personality. If you have been in a Polo store or Polo

section in a department store, you might remember some of the details of the environment that make the space different from, say, a Sears department, not to mention a Nike or Patagonia store. Nike stores have even been described as retail theater with displays and spaces that showcase not only the shoes and apparel, but also the sports with which they are associated.

Think about the last time you went to a sit-down restaurant versus your experiences in fast-food places. What's the difference in the way these spaces are designed both inside and outside? Think about the colors and surfaces and types of furniture. Graphic designer Amy Niswonger has been following the redesign of McDonald's interiors and explains what she has observed in *The Inside Story*.

WHAT IS ART DIRECTION?

The person most responsible for creating visual impact, as well as the brand identification elements, is the art director. The art director is in charge of the visual look of the advertisement, both in print and TV, and how it communicates mood, product qualities, and psychological appeals. The art director and copywriter team usually work together to come up with the Big Idea, but the art director is responsible for bringing the visual side of the idea to life.

Specifically, art directors make decisions about whether to use art or photography in print and film or animation in television and what type of artistic style to use. They are highly trained in graphic design, including art, photography, typography, the use of color, and computer design software. Although art directors generally design the ad, they rarely create the finished art. If they need an illustration, they hire an artist. Newspaper and Web advertising visuals are often **clip art** or **click art,** images from collections of copyright-free art that anyone who buys the clip-art service can use.

In addition to advertising, art directors may also be involved in designing a brand or corporate logo, as well as merchandising materials, store or corporate office interiors, and other aspects of a brand's visual presentation, such as shopping bags, delivery trucks, and uniforms. Karl Schroeder's team at Coates Kokes in Portland, Oregon, even designed an ad to be painted on the wall of a building using the distinctive artwork in the SeaPort Air campaign, which we showcased in Chapter 7.

The Designer's Toolkit

One of the most difficult problems that art directors—and those who work on the creative side of advertising—face is to transform a creative concept into words and pictures. During the brainstorming process, both copywriters and art directors are engaged in **visualization,** which means they are imagining what the finished ad might look like. The art director, however, is responsible for translating the advertising Big Idea into a visual story. To do this, the art director relies on a toolkit that consists of illustrations or animation, photos or film shots, color, type, design principles, layout (print), and composition (photography, video, or film), among other visual elements.

Illustrations and Photos   When art directors use the word *art*, they usually mean photographs and illustrations, each of which serves different purposes in ads. For instance, photography has an authenticity that makes it powerful. Most people feel that pictures don't lie (even though they can be altered). For credibility, then, photography is a good medium.

The decision to use a photograph or an illustration is usually determined by the advertising strategy and its need for either realism or fanciful images. Generally a photograph is more realistic and an illustration (or animation in television) is more fanciful, as the Sony illustration shows. Illustrations, by definition, eliminate many of the details you see in a photograph, which can make it easier to understand their meaning since what remains are the "highlights" of the image. This ease of perception can simplify the visual message because it can focus attention on key details of the image. Illustrations

SHOWCASE

The distinctive illustration style from the SeaPort Air campaign was used to paint an ad on the side of a multistory building in Tillamook, Oregon.

A graduate of the University of Oregon advertising program, Karl Schroeder was nominated by Professor Charles Frazer.

THE INSIDE STORY

Loving McDonald's New Look

Amy Niswonger, *President, Little Frog Prints*

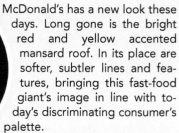

McDonald's has a new look these days. Long gone is the bright red and yellow accented mansard roof. In its place are softer, subtler lines and features, bringing this fast-food giant's image in line with today's discriminating consumer's palette.

With the addition of a new design and set of healthier food choices, McDonald's is updating its image from kiddy classic to a destination for all ages. In the past few years, the company has achieved success both in updating its look and feel and expanding its target market without losing core customers. How is this possible you might ask? BRAND EQUITY.

Without hesitation, most people in any country in the world can recognize a McDonald's sign instantly from a great distance. The Golden Arches are an icon, with enormous brand equity attached. For more than fifty years the red and yellow color scheme has been a mainstay among the 30,000+ worldwide locations, and not until recently has it strayed from this design.

Due to its overwhelming worldwide presence through advertisements, endorsements, and other marketing venues, McDonald's has built such a powerful brand—and volume amount of brand equity—that it could dramatically alter its environmental design without taking a hit to its market share. You, as the customer, inherently understand that the Big Mac is still the Big Mac; it's just served now in a hipper, cooler location.

Brand equity, it's a powerful tool. Those who have it love it. Those who don't strive desperately to achieve it.

When you walk into the new McDonald's, you will immediately notice plasma screen TVs, pendant lighting, comfortable armchairs, and perhaps the boldest new feature: WiFi Internet access. At first, you might even mistake the place for a Starbucks or even Panera Bread. That's part of the strategy, as McDonald's is now focusing on creating a specific type of customer experience, not just offering a convenient grab 'n go meal.

The new meaning of "I'm lovin' it" means more than a happy meal. It's an invitation to the customer to come in, eat, enjoy the environment, and stay for a while.

Note: Amy Niswonger is a graphic designer and professor who owns her own design studio. A graphic design and marketing graduate of Miami University in Oxford, Ohio, she was named Most Promising Minority Student by the American Advertising Federation (AAF). She was nominated by Connie Frazier, AAF chief operating officer.

---

also use artistic techniques to intensify meanings and moods, making illustrations ideal for fantasy (think about comic books and animated films). Photos convey a "seeing is believing" credibility. Photographs, of course, can also evoke fanciful images. For example, the Maxell "500 Plays" ad uses visual symbolism to represent a blast of sound.

It is also possible to manipulate a photograph and turn it into art, a technique that brought recognition to Andy Warhol, among others. This practice has become popular with the advent of the Internet and the availability of easy-to-find digital images, some of which are copyrighted.

Recently that technique was used to create a political poster and, at the same time, a legal nightmare for the artist, Shepard Fairey, as discussed in the *A Matter of Principle* feature. Recognized as one of the most important political images of recent years, the Obama HOPE poster raises questions about fair use of manipulated images, something everyone has to think about when they find images online and want to reuse them in marketing communication projects.

Another issue involving digitized images in a global environment revolves around the ability of software programs, such as Photoshop, to manipulate specific content within a photo. Microsoft fell into a hole in 2009 when its website in Poland used a clumsy Photoshop application to turn a black man white. The original image had been used on Microsoft's U.S. website and featured diverse genders and people of many colors. However, on the Polish website where, presumably, there are fewer people of color, the artist chose to paste a white man's head on the body of a black man. Microsoft has apologized, of course, but the fiasco ran wild on news sites and blogs.[3]

Color   In addition to photos and illustrations, another important visual element that art directors manipulate is color, as the Sony ad shown earlier illustrates. Color attracts attention, provides realism, establishes moods, and builds brand identity. Art directors know that print ads with color, particularly those in newspapers, get more attention than ads without color. Most ads—print, broadcast, and Internet—are in full color, especially when art directors use photographs.

Color is particularly important in branding. An example comes from Pepsi's rivalry with Coke in China. Coke, of course, has always used a red can and logo and Pepsi traditionally uses a blue can. For the Beijing 2008 Olympics, Pepsi, which is an official Olympics sponsor, brought out a

Obama's HOPE Poster Hangs on a Question of Fair Use

Graphic designer, illustrator, and graffiti street artist Shepard Fairey got more attention than he intended when his widely recognized Barack Obama "HOPE" poster from the 2008 presidential election was challenged for illegal use. The posters were seen everywhere including a painted version on the side of a building in Denver, Colorado, where Obama received his Democratic nomination. In 2009, the U.S. National Portrait Gallery added the original HOPE poster to its permanent collection.

Fairey claims he found the original Obama photo using a Google Image search. The problem is that the iconic portrait with its social realism style was eventually found to have been constructed from a copyright-protected image taken by Mannie Garcia while on assignment for the Associated Press. AP claims ownership of the image and wants credit, as well as compensation. The complication is that Garcia also believes he owns the copyright and supports Fairey's use of the image. Fairey believes his use of the image follows the legal definition of fair use and doesn't infringe on AP's copyright.

In U.S. copyright law, *fair use* permits limited use of copyrighted material to advance knowledge or criticism. A creative use is permitted if it transforms the original to advance art. Fair use means, however, the original image can't simply be copied and questions arise if the new image is criticized as derivative, rather than as a new artistic statement.

This artistic requirement is the source of the conflicting interpretations that surround the Obama HOPE poster. Fairey, who has built his career on recycling familiar images, claims that he dramatically changed the original image; AP and even some art critics say the manipulation isn't dramatic enough to be considered a new work of art.

So is it plagiarism, a blatant copy, or is it a street-culture conversion that transforms the original image into an important piece of political art? What do you think? And what principles would you recommend to help art directors avoid fair use issues, particularly with the easy availability of digital images?

Sources: "Shepard Fairey, Obama Poster Artist in Legal Battle with AP, Makes Major Admissions in Case," *Editor & Publisher,* October 16, 2009, www.editorandpublisher.com; "Protecting AP's Intellectual Property: The Shepard Fairey Case," Associated Press, October 20, 2009, www.ap.org/prights/fairey.html; "The Shepard Fairey-AP Case: A Clearer Picture," *Los Angeles Times,* November 1, 2009, www.latimes.com.

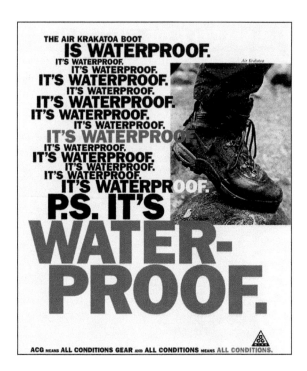

The layout for the Dunham boot ad shown here speaks in a quiet voice about the beauty of nature. Even though it's a boot ad, it projects an elegance that reflects an appreciation for nature and a serene outdoor scene (footprints in the snow). The ACG "Air Krakatoa" ad with an asymmetrical layout uses spot color effectively in the copy. Note how the layout "shouts," in contrast to the soft tone of the Dunham boot ad.

red can. The marketer defended itself saying the new can was more appealing to Chinese consumers and mirrors the color of the country's flag. Critics wonder if the dueling cans will just cause confusion among Chinese consumers who are slowly building loyalty to these Western brands.[4]

The use of black and white is also an important choice in image design because it lends a dignity and sophistication to the visual, even if it's a boot as the Dunham ad demonstrates. A historical effect can be created by shooting in black and white or by using a sepia tone, which can make the images look like old prints that have been weathered by time. When realism is important to convey in an ad, full-color photographs may be essential. Some products and ad illustrations just don't look right in black and white—pizza, flower gardens, and nail polish, for instance.

In print, designers also use **spot color,** in which a second color in addition to black (a black-and-white photo or illustration with an accent color) is used to highlight important elements. The use of spot color is highly attention getting, particularly in newspaper ads. The ACG ad uses red spot color to accent the product and key words.

Color also can help an ad convey a mood. Warm colors, such as red, yellow, and orange, convey happiness. Pastels are soft and often bring a friendly tone to a print ad. Earth tones are natural and no-nonsense. Cool colors, such as blue and green, are aloof, calm, serene, reflective, and intellectual. Yellow and red have the most attention-getting power. Red may symbolize alarm and danger as well as warmth. Black communicates high drama and can express power and elegance. Note that these color associations are culturally determined and uses like these are common in Western countries, but may not be effective in other cultures. White, for example, is the color of death in many Asian countries.

Principle

Type has a functional role in the way it presents the letters in words so they can be easily read, but it also has an aesthetic role and can contribute to the meaning of the message through its design.

Typography Not only do art directors carefully choose colors, they also specify the ad's **typography**—the appearance of the ad's printed matter. In most cases, good typesetting does not call attention to itself because its primary role is functional—to convey the words of the message. Type or lettering, however, also has an aesthetic role, and the type selection can, in a subtle or not so subtle way, contribute to the impact and mood of the message, as the ACG boot ad demonstrated.

Ad designers choose from among thousands of typefaces to find the right one for the ad's message. Designers are familiar with type classifications, but it is also important for managers and other people on the creative team to have some working knowledge of typography to understand what designers are talking about and to critique the typography and make suggestions. Figure 10.1 summarizes many of the decisions an art director makes in designing the type, such as these:

- The specific typeface, or **font**
- The way capitalization is handled, such as all caps or lowercase

a)

A Font

14 pt
ABCDEFGHIJKLMNOPQRSTUV
abcdefghijklmnopqrstuvwxyz
1234567890

Type has an aesthetic role in an ad. Art directors choose a serif or sans serif font, as well as a font's size and style, to support the tone of the advertising message.

Serif (top) and Sans Serif (bottom)

ABCDEFGHIJKLMNOPQRSTUVWXYZ ABCD
ABCDEFGHIJKLMNOPQRSTUVWXYZ ABCD

All caps (top), lower case (middle), and u&lc (bottom)

THIS IS TIMES ROMAN IN ALL CAPS.
this is times roman in lower case.
This is Times Roman in Upper and Lower Case.

Typeface variations

This is set in a light typeface.
This is set in a normal weight.
This is set in a boldface.
This is set in italic.
This is set in an expanded typeface.
This is set in a condensed typeface.

b)

This is justified text. This is justified text. This is justified text. This is justified text. This is justified text. This is justified text. This is justified text. This is justified text. This is justified text. This is jus-tified text.

          This is centered text. This is
               centered text.

This is left aligned text. This is
left aligned text.

                    This is right aligned text. This
                    is right aligned text.

Where the type sits on the ad and how it relates to the margin has an effect on the ad's overall look.

c)

6 Point
ABCDEFGHIJKLMNOPQRSTUVWXYZABCDEFGHIJKLMNOPQRSTUVWXYZABCDEFGHIJKLMNOPQRSTUVWXYZABCDEFG
abcdefghijklmnopqrstuvwxyzabcdefghijklmnopqrstuvwxyzabcdefghijklmnopqrstuvwxyz   1234567890

12 Point
ABCDEFGHIJKLMNOPQRSTUVWXYZABCDEFGHIJKLMNOPQ
abcdefghijklmnopqrstuvwxyzabcdefghijklmnopqrstuvwx 1234567890

18 Point
ABCDEFGHIJKLMNOPQRSTUVWXYZAB
abcdefghijklmnopqrstuvwxyzabc 1234567890

Here is a set of different sizes for the Times Roman typeface.

d)

THIS IS CAPITAL LETTERS.   **This is reverse type letters.**

This is ornamental type letters.

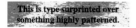

Research has shown that some typography presentations, such as those shown here—all cap letters, reverse type, overly ornamental type, and surprinted type—can hinder the reading process, which creates a legibility problem.

FIGURE 10.1
The Art of Type

- Typeface variations that come from manipulating the shape of the letterform
- The edges of the type block and its column width
- The size in which the type is set (vertical height)
- **Legibility,** or how easy it is to perceive the letters.

Generally speaking logos are designed to last for a long time, but sometimes brands change the design and typography in an attempt to modernize the look or match the mood of the country. An example comes from the Great Recession period when a number of major brands, such as Kraft and Walmart, among others moved from their all-cap presentations to lower case. The idea was to make their logos look softer and less stiff.[5]

Design Principles

The arrangement of the pieces in a print ad or video shot is governed by basic principles of design. The design has both functional and aesthetic needs—the functional side makes the visual message easy to perceive; the aesthetic side makes it attractive and pleasing to the eye.

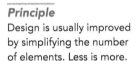

Principle
Design is usually improved by simplifying the number of elements. Less is more.

These design principles guide the eye by creating a visual path that helps the viewer scan the elements. For example, dominant elements that are colorful or high in contrast (big versus small, light versus dark) catch the viewer's attention first. How all of the elements come together is a function of the unity and balance of the design. Direction or movement is the way the elements are positioned to lead the eye through the arrangement. Simplicity is also a design principle, one that is in opposition to visual clutter. In general, the fewer the elements, the stronger the impact, an idea expressed in the phrase "less is more." Another saying is KISS, which stands for "Keep It Simple, Stupid." The Frontier "Caribou" ad is a powerful image because of its use of a simple horizontal photo across a two-page spread.

Let's look at how these design principles are used in print layout and in the composition of a picture or photograph.

With over 300 non-stops daily, crossing the country has never been easier.   FRONTIER. A whole different animal.

Sometimes the most powerful images are the simplest in structure—just a wide horizontal landscape with a swimming caribou leaving a trail in the water and a plane flying above him. Notice how the antlers point to the Frontier plane with a caribou on its tail. The whole composition is designed to pull your eye to the right and then up.

Print Layout

For print advertising, once art directors have chosen the images and typographic elements, they manipulate all of the visual elements on paper to produce a layout. A **layout** is a plan that imposes order and at the same time creates an arrangement that is aesthetically pleasing.

Different layouts can convey entirely different feelings about a product. For example, look at the two ads for work boots. The ACG "Air Krakatoa" boot ad screams "waterproof!" signaling the boots' ability to stand up to the most serious weather conditions. In contrast, the ad for the Dunham boot looks like a work of fine art. The difference between the two campaigns clearly lies with the visual impact that comes from the layouts as well as the imagery.

Types of Layouts   Here are some common types of ad layouts an art director might use:

- *Picture Window* A common layout format is one with a single, dominant visual that occupies about 60 to 70 percent of the ad's space. Underneath it is a headline and copy block. The logo or signature signs off the message at the bottom. The Altoids ads are of this style.
- *All Art* The art fills the frame of the ad and the copy is embedded in the picture. The Frontier "Caribou" ad is an example.
- *Panel or Grid* This layout uses a number of visuals of matched or proportional sizes. If the ad has multiple panels all of the same size, the layout can look like a window pane or comic strip panel. The Dunham boot ad uses two side-by-side panels.
- *Dominant Type or All Copy* Occasionally, you will see layouts that emphasize the type rather than the art, or even an all-copy advertisement in which the headline is treated as type art, such as the ACG ad. A copy-dominant ad may have art, but it is either embedded in the copy or placed in a subordinate position, such as at the bottom of the layout.
- *Circus* This layout combines lots of elements—art, type, color—to deliberately create a busy, jumbled image. This is typical of some discount store ads or ads for local retailers, such as tire companies.
- *Nonlinear* This contemporary style of layout can be read starting at any point in the image. In other words, the direction of viewing is not ordered, as in the "What a Ride" ad for Schwinn. This style of ad layout works for young people who are more accustomed to nonlinear forms.

This ad for Schwinn bicycles uses a plumbing drain motif to convey the industrial-strength features of the bike. It is a nonlinear design in that it doesn't matter where you start reading and what you read next. The text is carried in callouts that point to different visual elements in the layout.

Layout Stages   The stages in the normal development of a print ad may vary from agency to agency or from client to client. Figure 10.2 shows the six-stage development of an Orly nail polish ad. This ad went through **thumbnail sketches,** which are quick, miniature preliminary sketches; **rough layouts,** which show where design elements go; **semicomps** and **comprehensives,** which are drawn to size and used for presentation either in house or to the client; and **mechanicals,** which assemble the elements in their final position for reproduction. The final product that is used for actual production of the ad is a high-resolution computer file.

Composition

We've been talking about layout, which is a term used to describe how the elements in print (headline, art, tagline, etc.) are arranged. **Composition** refers to the way the elements in a picture are

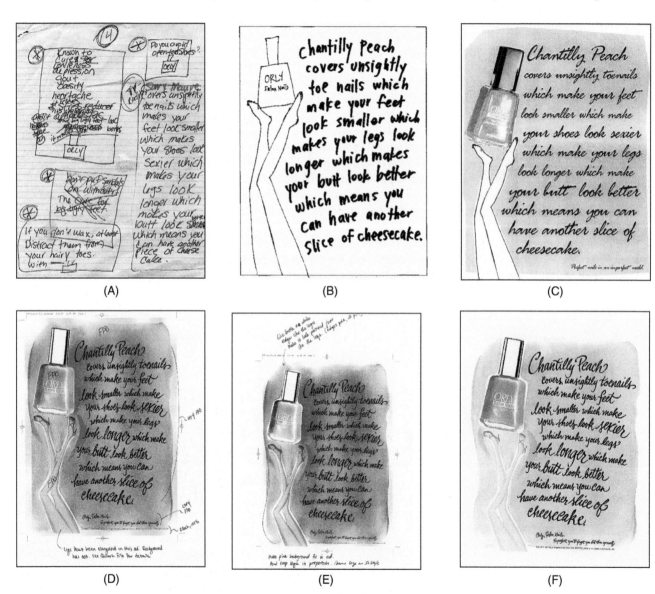

FIGURE 10.2

Orly "Chantilly Peach" Creative Process

(A) Thumbnail Sketches These ideas for Orly were developed by the creative team late at night over Diet Coke and Chinese chicken salad. **(B) Rough Layout** Transitioning to legs and painted toenails, the layout begins to give some glamour and personality to the product. **(C) Semicomps** Type, color, and tagline are still not finalized, but layout is more complete. **(D) Comprehensives** Tagline approved. The illustrator has added more glitz to the layout. **(E) Mechanicals** The digital file before retouching. Client still made small changes at this stage, but had approved the ad's layout and copy. **(F) Final High-Resolution Film** The film house had to retouch, creating separate files for the legs and background image so that the proportion of the leg illustration would be correct.

arranged (think a still-life painting) or framed through a camera lens (think a landscape photo or movie scene). Photographers and **videographers** (people who shoot a scene using a video camera) handle composition in two ways: (1) they may be able to place or arrange the elements in front of their cameras and (2) they may have to compose the image by manipulating their own point of view if the elements can't be moved. In other words, they move around to find the most aesthetic way to frame an image that isn't movable, such as a scene or landscape, as well as to catch different lighting situations, such as bright sun and shade or shadow.

Similar to the way layouts are developed by using sketches, video images are also drawn and presented as **storyboards,** which are sketches of the scenes and key shots in a commercial. The art director imagines the characters and setting as well as how the characters act and move in the scene. The art director sketches in a few key frames the visual idea for a scene and how it is to be shot and how one scene links to the scenes that follow. In addition, the storyboard sketches also reflect the position and movement of the cameras recording the scene, a description of which is spelled out both in the script and on the storyboard. The "Coffee Ambush" storyboard details the action in a commercial for McDonald's new McCafé line of specialty coffees. We'll explain more about the commercial in the production section that follows.

WHAT DO YOU NEED TO KNOW ABOUT PRODUCTION?

Art directors need to understand print media requirements and the technical side of production because these factors affect both the look of the printed piece and its cost. Marketing communication managers also need to understand some of these basics in order to critique ideas and evaluate them in terms of cost and feasibility.

Print Media Requirements

Different media put different demands on the design and production of advertising. Newspapers and directories, for example, are printed at high speed on an inexpensive, rough-surfaced, spongy paper called **newsprint** that quickly absorbs ink on contact. Newsprint is not a great surface for reproducing fine details, especially color photographs and delicate typefaces. Most newspapers offer color to advertisers, but because of the limitations of the printing process, the color may not be perfectly **registered** (i.e., all of the color inks may not be aligned exactly, creating a somewhat blurred image). For that reason, ads such as the Oklahoma City ads are specifically designed for high-contrast, black-and-white printing. These work well for both newspaper and directory ads.

Magazines have traditionally led the way in graphic print production because their glossy paper is a higher grade than newsprint. Excellent photographic and color reproduction is the big difference between newspapers and magazines. Magazine advertisements are also able to take advantage of more creative, attention-getting devices such as pop-up visuals, scent strips, and computer chips that play melodies when the pages are opened. An Altoids ad that launched Altoids chewing gum, for example, ran in magazines with a novel print production technique. It showed a box of Altoids chewing gum on one page, and a singed logo burnt onto the cartoon on the opposite page.

The key to an effective poster or outdoor board is a dominant visual with minimal copy. Because billboards must make a quick and lasting impression from far away, their layout should be compact with a simple visual path. The Institute for Outdoor Advertising (IOA) recommends these tips for designers:

- *Graphics* Make the illustration an eye-stopper.
- *Size* Images in billboards are huge—a 25-foot-long pencil or a 43-foot pointing finger. The product or the brand label can be hundreds of times larger than life.
- *Colors* Use bold, bright colors. The greatest impact is created by maximum contrast between two colors such as dark colors against white or yellow.[6]

High-contrast graphics are the key to good reproduction in a newspaper. The art in these ads simulates an old wood engraving.

- *Figure/Ground* Make the relationship between foreground and background as obvious as possible. A picture of a soft drink against a jungle background is hard to perceive when viewed from a moving vehicle at a distance. The background should never compete with the subject.
- *Typography* Use simple, clean, uncluttered type that is easy to read at a distance by an audience in motion. The industry's legibility research recommends avoiding all-capital letters, fanciful ornamental letters, and script and cursive fonts.
- *Product Identification* Focus attention on the product by reproducing the label or package at a huge size.
- *Extensions* Extend the frame of the billboard to expand the scale and break away from the limits of the long rectangle.
- *Shape* For visual impact, create the illusion of three-dimensional effects by playing with horizons, vanishing lines, and dimensional boxes. Inflatables create a better 3-D effect than most billboards can, even with superior graphics. Made of a heavyweight, stitched nylon, inflatables can be freestanding, or they can be added to outdoor boards as an extension.
- *Motion* Add motors to boards to make pieces and parts move. Disk-like wheels and glittery things that flicker in the wind create the appearance of motion, color change, and images that squeeze, wave, or pour. Use revolving panels, called *kinetic boards*, for messages that change.

Print Art Reproduction

In general, there are two types of printed images: line art and halftones. A drawing or illustration is called **line art** because the image is solid lines on a white page, as in the Oklahoma City ads. Photographs, which are referred to as **continuous tones** or **halftones,** are much more complicated to reproduce because they have a range of gray tones between the black and white, as shown in Figure 10.3.

FIGURE 10.3

Line Art and Halftone Art
An example of a figure reproduced as line art (left) and as a halftone (right).

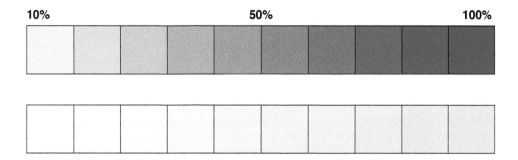

FIGURE 10.4

Screen Values and Tint Blocks
This shows the range of tint values that can be produced by different screens that represent a percentage of the color value.

Printers create the illusion of shades of gray in converting photos to halftones by shooting the original photograph through a fine **screen,** which converts the image to a pattern of dots that gives the illusion of shades of gray—dark areas are large dots that fill the screen and light areas are tiny dots surrounded by **white space.** The quality of the image depends on how fine the screen is: Newspapers use a coarse screen, usually 65 lines per inch (called a 65-line screen), whereas magazines use fine screens, which may be from 120 up to 200 or 300 lines per inch.

Screens are also used to create **tint blocks,** which can either be shades of gray in black-and-white printing or shades of color. A block of color can be printed solid or it can be screened black to create a shade. These shades are expressed as a range of percentages, from 100 percent (solid) down to 10 percent (very faint). Figure 10.4 gives examples of screens in color.

Color Reproduction   It would be impossible to set up a printing press with a separate ink roller for every hue and value in a color photo. How, then, are these colors reproduced?

Full-color images are reproduced using four distinctive shades of ink called **process colors,** in order to produce **four-color printing.** These colors are *magenta* (a shade of pinkish purple), *cyan* (a shade of bright blue), *yellow,* and *black.* Printing inks are transparent, so when one ink overlaps another, a third color is created and that's how the full range of colors is created. For example, red and blue create purple, yellow and blue create green, yellow and red create orange. The black is used for type and, in four-color printing, adds depth to the shadows and dark tones in an image. The process printers use to reduce the original color image to four halftone negatives is called **color separation.** Figure 10.5 illustrates the process of color separation.

Digitization   If an ad is going to run in a number of publications, there has to be some way to distribute a reproducible, duplicate of the ad to all of them. The duplicate material for **offset printing** is a slick proof of the original mechanical. More recently, **digitization** of images has been used to distribute reproducible images. This is also how computers now handle the color reproduction process. These digitized images can be transmitted electronically to printers across a city for local editions of national newspapers, or by satellite for regional editions of magazines and newspapers such as *USA Today.* Agencies also use this method for transmitting ad proofs within the agency network and to clients.

Digitization makes it possible to create some spectacular effects in out-of-home advertising. Some outdoor boards have become digital screens complete with changing and moving images. A new technique in transit advertising comes from Atlanta where the city's buses are wrapping their sides with something called "glow skin." The ads use electroluminescent lighting to make the ads glow at night and appear to jump off the sides of the buses.[7]

Binding and Finishing

Art directors can enhance their ads and other printed materials by using a number of special printing effects. For example, USRobotics, a maker of minicomputers, once used a small brochure the actual size of a Palm Pilot to demonstrate its minicomputer's size. The shot of the Palm Pilot was glued to a photo of a hand. As the ad unfolded, it became a complete product brochure that visually demonstrated the actual size of the minicomputer.

Other mechanical techniques include:

- **Die Cutting** A sharp-edged stamp, or die, is used to cut out unusual shapes. A common **die-cut** shape you're familiar with is the tab on a file folder.

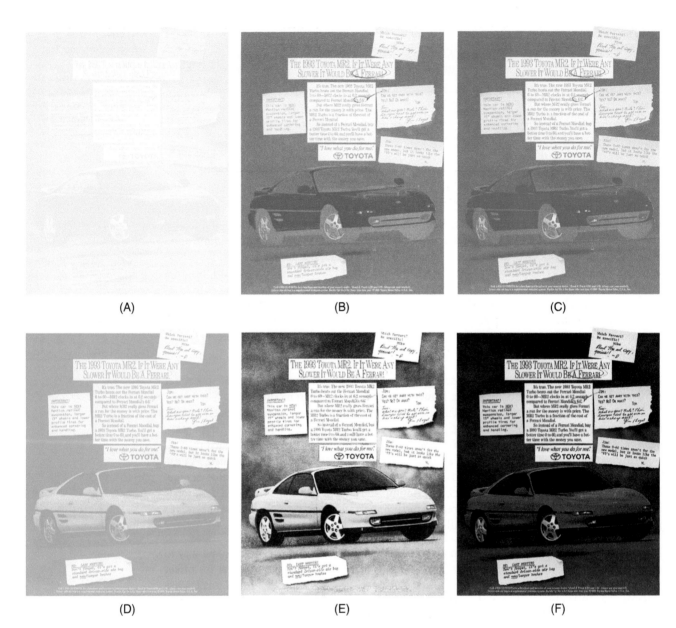

FIGURE 10.5

The Color Separation Process
These six photos illustrate the process of creating four-color separations: (A) Yellow plate. (B) Magenta plate.
(C) Yellow and magenta combined plate. (D) Cyan plate. (*Note:* After cyan is added, there would also be combined
plates showing cyan added first to yellow, then to magenta, then to the combined yellow and magenta plates. These
steps were left out to simplify the presentation.) (E) Black plate. (F) Finished art with all four process colors combined.

- *Embossing or Debossing* The application of pressure to create a raised surface (**embossing**)
  or depressed image (**debossing**) in paper.
- *Foil Stamping* The process of **foil stamping** involves molding a thin metallic coating (silver, gold) to the surface of an image.
- *Tip-Ins* A **tip-in** is a separate, preprinted ad provided by the advertiser that is glued into a
  publication as the publication is being assembled or bound. Perfume manufacturers, for example, tip in samples that are either scratch-and-sniff or scented strips that release a fragrance when pulled apart.

Another example of a nifty production trick is illustrated in the ad for Specialized Bikes using a "see-through" technique. The graphic elements are separated and printed on the front and

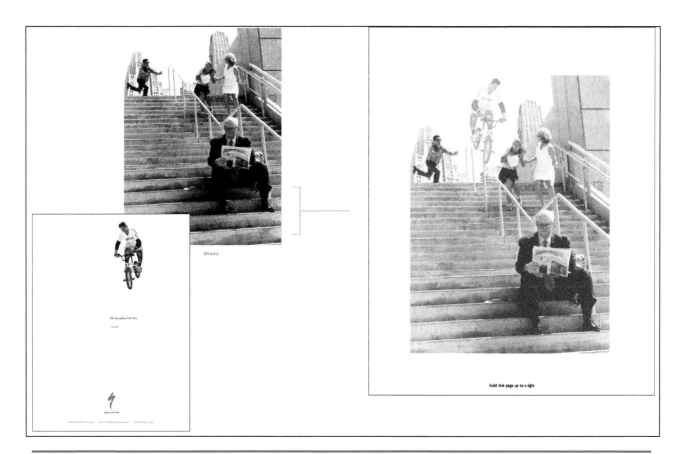

back of a page. When you look at the ad you see people in the foreground going about their business but in the background a faint image shows a daredevil bike rider jumping from one building to another or riding on a handrail going down the middle of a set of steps.

WHAT DO YOU NEED TO KNOW ABOUT VIDEO PRODUCTION?

Where does an art director start when putting together a video for a commercial, a video news release, or some other kind of corporate film or video? Lara Mann gives you a look inside the production of a television commercial in the *A Day in the Life* feature.

Obviously the first consideration is the nature of the image. The art director can arrange for filming on a constructed set or in a real location or choose to use **stock footage**—previously recorded images, either video, still slides, or moving film. Typical stock footage files are shots from a satellite, historical scenes such as World War II battles, or a car crash. Animation, stop motion, and 3D are other film production techniques that can be used instead of using stock footage or live filming.

Working within the framework of the creative strategy, art directors create the look of the TV commercial. The look of the award-winning "Cat Herders" commercial that the Fallon agency created for Electronic Data Systems (EDS) was a parody of the American West, much like a John Ford movie, with horses, craggy-faced cowboys who acted as cat wranglers, and stampeding animals (the cats).

A Copywriter's View of TV Production

Lara Mann, *Senior Copywriter, Draft FCB*

As a copywriter at an ad agency, a typical day for me involves a few meetings, a little presenting, a fair amount of concepting, some writing, and more than one trip to the coffee bar. Some of it's challenging. All of it's exciting. But once I've sold a campaign to a client, that's when the real fun begins.

Just between you and me, when I first started out I didn't even know shooting television was part of my job description. They never covered that in school. Director reels? Location scouting? Huh?

Now that I've been around the block (on a tricycle), I can confidentially tell you that coming up with ideas is only half of a copywriter's job. The members of the creative team have to shepherd their idea through all stages of production to make sure their vision is fully realized—or something like that.

First, we're assigned a producer, who will send us director's reels. We pick a director, pack our bags, and grab the next plane out of town. Once on location, we spend the next few days scouting scenes, casting the talent, selecting wardrobe, finding props, and reviewing the director's shooting boards. These tend to be long days, followed by long nights at the hotel watering hole.

Then the shoot begins. My partner and I will either sit in "video village" along with our client and account team, or off to the side with our own little monitor so we can keep track of the action. Should we see an issue (and there are sure to be many), we grab the ear of our producer, who will then tell the line producer, who will then tell the director. This is called the "chain of command" and helps the shoot run smoothly.

After the shoot has wrapped (yes, someone will yell, "That's a wrap!"), we pack up and head back to town, where we will then begin putting the footage together with the help of a talented editor. And so ends another exciting day in the world of advertising.

That's a wrap.

Note: Lara Mann, a graduate of the University of Florida, works for DraftFCB in Chicago. She was nominated by Professor Elaine Wagner.

Other graphic elements such as words, product logos, and still photos are digitized or computer generated right on the screen. A **crawl** is a set of computer-generated letters that appear to be moving across the bottom of the screen. All of these effects are designed or specified by the art director.

Sophisticated computer graphics systems, such as those used to create the *Star Wars* special effects, pioneered the making of artistic film and video advertising on computers. Computer graphic artists brag that they can do anything with an image. They can look at any object from any angle or even from the inside out. One of the most creative video techniques is called **morphing,** in which one object gradually changes into another. Photographs of real objects can change into art or animation and then return to life. Computer graphics specialists use computer software to create, multiply, and manipulate video images. (That's how 50 cats can be made to look like hundreds in the EDS "Herding Cats" commercial.)

Filming and Editing

Most local retail commercials are simple and inexpensive, and they are typically shot and taped at the local station. The sales representative for the station may work with the advertiser to write the script, and the station's director handles the taping of the commercial.

Creating a national TV commercial is more complex and requires a number of people with specialized skills. The ad agency crew usually includes the copywriter, art director, and producer. The producer oversees the production on behalf of the agency and client and is responsible for the budget, among other things. The director, who is the person responsible for filming the commercial, is usually someone from outside the agency. This person takes the art director's storyboard and makes it come to life on film.

The producer and director make up the core of the production team. The commercial's effectiveness depends on their shared vision of the final commercial and the director's ability to bring it to life as the art director imagined it. In the case of the "Cat Herders" commercial, the director was chosen by the agency because of his skill at coaxing naturally humorous performances from nonprofessional actors. In this commercial he worked with real wranglers on their semi-scripted testimonials about their work with kitties.

The following list summarizes the responsibilities of broadcast production personnel:

Who Does What in Broadcast Production?

Copywriter	Writes the script, whether it contains dialogue, narrative, lyrics, announcements, descriptions, or no words at all.
Art Director	In TV, develops the storyboard and establishes the look of the commercial, whether realistic, stylized, or fanciful.
Producer (can be an agency staff member)	Takes charge of the production, handles the bidding and all production arrangements, finds the specialists, arranges for casting talent, and makes sure the expenses and bids come in under budget.
Director	Has responsibility for the actual filming or taping, including how long the scene runs, who does what, how lines are spoken, and how characters are played; in TV determines how the camera is set up and records the flow of action.
Composer	Writes original music and sometimes the lyrics as well.
Arranger	Orchestrates music for the various instruments and voices to make it fit a scene or copy line. The copywriter usually writes the lyrics or at least gives the arranger some idea of what the words should convey.
Editor	Puts everything together toward the end of the filming or taping process; evaluates how to assemble scenes and which audio elements work best with the dialogue and footage.

The Process of Producing Videos

As we said earlier there are a number of ways to produce a message for a video, such as a television commercial. Let's look at these production choices.

Typically the film is shot on 35-mm film or videotape and then digitized, after which the editor transfers the image to videotape for dissemination, a process called **film-to-tape transfer.** Digital technology is changing the process. Eventually films will transfer to hard drives, eliminating the use of videotape. Art directors work closely with editors who assemble the shots and cut the film to create the right pacing and sequence of images as outlined in the storyboard.

Obviously the Big Idea for the "Cat Herders" ad created some real production challenges. In the spot, the Fallon art director decided that the metaphor of herding cats meant that the cats had to swim across a river, but was that even possible? Here's how it was done: The trainers taught a few cats that weren't adverse to water to swim by starting them out in one-quarter inch of water in a child's swimming pool and then gradually adding water to the pool until it was deep enough for the cats to swim. The "river" was actually a small pool warmed by a portable heater—Art Director Dean Hanson described it as "a little kitty Jacuzzi." Multiple copies of the swimming kitties were made and manipulated using computer graphics until an entire herd had been created. And that's how this famous scene came about—a creation of Hanson's unlikely vision of a herd of cats swimming across river.

The Fallon agency was given the impossible task of creating a commercial that illustrated the EDS positioning statement: "EDS thrives on defeating complexity." It translated that language into a popular phrase used in the Silicone Valley culture— "It's like herding cats." To bring that idea to life, the Fallon team filmed a team of rugged cowboys herding thousands of cats.

SHOWCASE

Karl Schroeder says he really hadn't considered stop motion before but it was perfect for this assignment for Metro Recycling and arguably the only solution for this recycling concept. Everything was shot in a studio and composited in the computer.

A graduate of the University of Oregon advertising program, Karl Schroeder was nominated by Professor Charles Frazer.

Animation   The technique of **animation** traditionally meant drawing images on film and then recording the images one frame at a time. Cartoon figures, for example, were sketched and then resketched for the next frame with a slight change to indicate a small progression in the movement of an arm or leg a facial expression. Animation is traditionally shot at 16 drawings per second. Low-budget animation uses fewer drawings, so the motion looks jerky. The introduction of computers has accelerated the process and eliminated a lot of the tedious hand work.

Animation is similar to illustration in print in that it abstracts images and adds a touch of fantasy and/or mood to the image. As Karl Schroeder, a copywriter with Coates Kokes in Portland, Oregon, explains about a project his team worked on for a recycling center: "What was nice about it, when you consider that the spots needed to appeal to EVERYONE who recycles in the area, was that it [animation] got us away from casting racially ambiguous, hard-to-pin-an-age-on talent."

Animation effects can also be used to combine animated characters, such as the little green Geico Gecko, with live-action figures, or even with other animated characters. The famous Aflac duck was created as a collaboration between Warner Brothers and the Aflac agency, the Kaplan Thaler Group in New York. More advanced techniques, similar to those used in movies like *Avatar, Up*, and the *Shrek* series, create lifelike images and movement. A technique called "mental ray" was used in a Levi Strauss ad featuring 600 stampeding buffalo. Mental ray is so good it not only created lifelike images but even added realistic hair on the animals.[8]

Stop Motion   A particular type of animation is **stop motion,** a technique used to film inanimate objects like the Pillsbury Doughboy, which is a puppet. The little character is moved a bit at a time and filmed frame-by-frame. Schroeder describes how he and his art director settled on the stop-motion technique for two commercials that changed residential recycling behavior in his community. He says that in developing a concept for commercials, he'll usually think of live-action film first. When he does consider animation, it's usually achieved with computer graphics or illustrations. But for these two recycling spots, here's how the stop-action effects were created:

> Both spots have three layers. All of the foreground elements, from the glass bottles to the yellow bins, are actual objects. The animator painstakingly moved each item frame by frame. Furthermore, each frame was shot twice. Normally you'd only need to shoot each frame once. But because we were shooting in front of a green screen and because we were using glass bottles (which reflect), we had to shoot each frame twice, one in front of the green screen and the second in front of a "natural background." So now with two sets of images (as if all this weren't enough work), next up was to clip out the bottles that had the alien green reflection (from the green screen) and drop in the bottles that sported the natural reflections from the other shots, again frame-by-frame.
>
> The next layer is more straightforward, featuring the house and yard. The third layer has the sky and clouds (which move if you look closely). Since the plastic bag spot didn't have glass, it was a little simpler but otherwise followed the same process. Lastly, we didn't want the logo, tag, and info to be tacked on at the end against a black background. Instead, we integrated the information by animating it against a tight shot of our yellow bin. The effect is much less jarring and better unites the "business" with the rest of the spot.

The same technique is used in **claymation,** which involves creating characters from clay and then photographing them one frame at a time. Both have been popular with art directors who create advertising where fantasy effects are desired, although new computer effects also are simplifying these techniques.

3-D Filming   3-D is a type of film production that creates the illusion of depth using a special motion picture camera and projection hardware. Viewers also have to wear special glasses. The 3-D technique has been around for many years but only with the big success of the movie Avatar did it achieve wide popularity. ESPN launched a 3-D Channel in 2010 for the World Cup broadcast and persuaded major advertisers such as Procter & Gamble and Sony to experiment with 3-D spots on the new channel.

Music and Action   Specifying the music is usually done as part of the copywriting; however, matching the music to the action is an art director or producer's responsibility. In some cases, as in high- production song-and-dance numbers, the music is the commercial. Other times, it is used to get attention, set a mood, and lock the commercial into memory.

For example, a recent JanSport commercial for its Live Wire Euphonic Pack, a backpack with built-in earphones and volume controls, cries out for a musical demonstration. The unlikely song picked for the spot, which targets the MTV crowd, was "Do-Re-Mi" from the 1959 *Sound of Music* musical. You might wonder why the creative team at the DDB Seattle agency would choose such a piece. Actually the rendition is not from the early recording but rather an ethereal, techno-pop version. The stick-in-the-head lyrics match the action on screen in a contemporary version of the classic story boy meets girl, boy loses girl, boy finds girl.[9]

The TV Production Process

For the bigger national commercials, the steps in the TV production process fall into four categories: message design, preproduction, the shoot, and postproduction. Figure 10.6 shows the steps in the process.

Preproduction   The producer and staff first develop a set of **production notes,** describing in detail every aspect of the production. These notes are important for finding talent and locations, building sets, and getting bids and estimates from specialists. In the "Cat Herders" commercial, finding the talent was critical. Some 50 felines and their trainers were involved in the filming. Surprisingly, different cats have different skills—some were able to appear to be asleep or motionless on cue, while others excelled as runners or specialized in water scenes.

Once the bids for production have been approved, the creative team and the producer, director, and other key players hold a **preproduction** meeting to outline every step of the production process and anticipate every problem that may arise. Then the work begins. The talent agency begins casting the roles, while the production team finds a location and arranges site use with owners, police, and other officials. If sets are needed, they have to be built. Finding the props is a test of ingenuity, and the prop person may wind up visiting hardware stores, secondhand stores, and maybe even the local dump. Costumes must be made, located, or bought.

The Shoot   The director shoots the commercial scene by scene, but not necessarily in the order set down in the script. Each scene is shot, called a **take,** and after all the scenes in the storyboard have been shot they are assembled through editing. If the director films the commercial on videotape, it is played back immediately to determine what needs correcting. Film, however, has to be processed before the director can review it. These processed scenes are called **dailies. Rushes** are

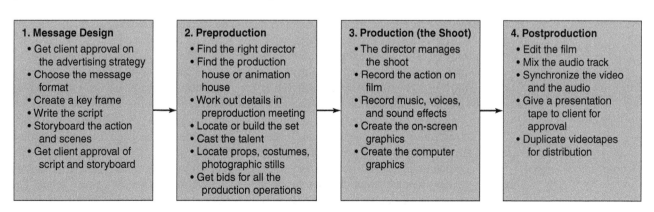

FIGURE 10.6

Video Production Process

In general, there are three steps in the production of a video after agreement is obtained on the message strategy.

rough versions of the commercial assembled from **cuts** of the raw film footage. The director and the agency creative team, as well as the client representative, view them immediately after the shoot to make sure everything's been filmed as planned.

The film crew includes a number of technicians, all of whom report to the director. For both film and video recording, the camera operators are the key technicians. Other technicians include—and you've probably seen these terms in movie credits—the **gaffer,** who is the chief electrician, and the **grip,** who moves props and sets and lays tracks for the dolly on which the camera is mounted. The **script clerk** checks the dialogue and other script details and times the scenes. A set is a busy crowded place that appears, at times, to be total confusion and chaos.

The audio director records the audio either at the time of the shoot or, in the case of more high-end productions, separately in a sound studio. If the sound is being recorded at the time of shooting, a **mixer,** who operates the recording equipment, and a *mic* or *boom* person, who sets up the microphones, handle the recording on the set. In the studio audio is usually recorded after the film is shot so the audio has to be synchronized with the footage. Directors often wait to see exactly how the action appears before they write and record the audio track. However, if the art director has decided to set the commercial to music, then the music on the audio track may be recorded before the shoot, as in the "Do-Re-Mi" audio track, and the filming done to the music.

Occasionally the footage will be shot live to catch natural reactions by the participants, such as the Burger King "Freak Out" commercials described in the opening story for Chapter 1. Another example comes from Boston University where an advertising class starred in a McDonald's McCafé spot called the "Coffee Ambush," as described in the *A Matter of Practice* feature.

In some rare cases, an entire commercial is shot as one continuous action rather than individual shots edited together in postproduction. Probably the most interesting use of this approach is "Cog," an award-winning commercial for the Honda Accord that shows the assembly of pieces of the car piece by piece. It begins with a rolling transmission bearing, and moves through valves, brake pedals, tires, the hood, and so forth, until the car drives away at the end of the commercial. It's tempting to think it was created through computer animation, but the Honda "Cog" commercial was filmed in real time without any special effects. It took 606 takes for the whole thing to work—that's 606 run-throughs of the sequence! One of the most talked-about spots ever made, the publicity given to the commercial was probably even more valuable than an advertising buy. The "Cog" commercial won a Grand Clio (a creative award show), as well as a Gold Lion at the Cannes Advertising Festival. Altogether, it picked up no fewer than 20 awards from various UK and international organizations. The spot can be seen at *www.ebaumsworld.com/flash/play/734.*[10]

Postproduction   For film and video, much of the work happens after the shoot in **postproduction**—when the commercial begins to emerge from the hands and mind of the editor. The objective of editing is to assemble the various pieces of film into a sequence that follows the storyboard. Editors manipulate the audio and video images, creating realistic 3-D images and combining real-life and computer-generated images. The postproduction process is hugely important in video because so many digital effects are being added to the raw film after the shoot. In the "Cat Herders" commercial, Fallon could not film the cats and horses at the same time because of National Humane Society regulations. The director had to film the horses, background, and kitties separately. An editor fused the scenes together during postproduction, editing seamlessly to create the illusion of the elaborate cat drive.

Another goal of **video editing** is to manipulate time, which is a common technique used in commercial storytelling. Condensing time might show a man leaving work, then a cut of the man showering, then a cut of the man at a bar. The editor may extend time. Say a train is approaching a stalled car on the tracks. By cutting to various angles it may seem that the train is taking forever to reach the car—a suspense tactic. To jumble time, an editor might cut from the present to a flashback of a remembered past event or flash forward to an imagined scene in the future. All of these effects are specified by the art director in the storyboard.

The result of the editor's initial work is a **rough cut,** a preliminary edited version of the story that is created when the editor chooses the best shots and assembles them to create a scene. The editor then joins the scenes together. After the revision and reediting have been completed, the editor makes an **interlock,** which means the audio and film have been assembled together. The final version with the sound and film mixed together is called an **answer print.** The answer

BU Ad Class Ready for Its Close-Up

Tom Fauls, *College of Communication, Boston University*

It can be quiet, even sleepy, during summer term. So it's no surprise students cue up for caffeine before class. But in August 2009, some Boston University (BU) College of Communication advertising students had a different kind of coffee encounter.

It started a few weeks earlier when Redtree Productions contacted BU officials and later BU professors Judy Austin and Tom Fauls. Working with agency Arnold Worldwide, Redtree was planning a TV shoot for McDonald's McCafé brands.

The concept was developed by Arnold creatives, including a BU alumna. It required a theatre-style hall filled with students expecting a cognitive anthropologist speaking on consumer-brand relationships. After a preproduction meeting at Redtree, Austin and Fauls, both of whom had worked on McDonald's ads at different agencies, invited their students to attend an optional 9 a.m. lecture by Robert Deutsch.

They didn't mention that the lecture would be (1) intentionally boring, (2) interrupted after 10 minutes by uniformed McDonald's workers with McCafé drinks, and (3) entirely captured on tape by cameras hidden behind a faux blackboard.

On the way in, signs said the lecture would be taped and no non-water drinks were allowed. The room was already partially filled with other students who were really paid extras. But the unsuspecting real students were asked to fill the front rows.

Minutes after the coffee was distributed, Arnold and Redtree producers emerged to reveal all and ask students to stay for close-ups and product hero shots, pictures of the products being marketed. Students then toured the substantial mobile production facilities in the alley behind the auditorium.

The final edit opens with a sleepy lecture hall shifting dramatically with up-tempo music as stunned ad students perk up to McCafé lattes and the realization they're in the middle of a real TV shoot.

In the end, students involved in the "Coffee Ambush" spot learned a little cognitive anthropology and a whole lot about broadcast campaigns and video production.

These photos provided by Professor Fauls record the experience of shooting the McDonald's "Coffee Ambush" ad in class. After the initial surprise entrance of the McCafé servers (you can see them on the right), this photo shows the Redtree crew emerging to capture close-ups. This second shot shows how the normal blackboard was replaced with a version modified to let cameras shoot through one-way mirror panels.

print is the final version printed onto a piece of film. For the commercial to air on hundreds of stations around the country, the agency makes duplicate copies—a process called **dubbing.** The dubbed copies are called **release prints.**

WHY STUDY WEB DESIGN?

Web design includes creating ads that run on the Web as well as the website itself. Banner ads are designed more like outdoor boards than conventional print ads because their small space puts intense requirements on the designer to make the ad communicate quickly and succinctly, and yet attract attention and curiosity to elicit a click-through response. You can check out banner ads online at *http://thelongestlistofthelongeststuffatthelongestdomainnameatlonglast.com/banner.html.*

Designers know that Web pages, particularly the first screen, should follow the same layout rules as posters: The graphics should be eye catching without demanding too much downloading time; type should be simple, using one or two typefaces and avoiding ALL CAPs and letter spacing, which can distort words. Because there is often a lot to read, organizing the information is critical. In terms of legibility, black type on a high-contrast background usually is best; all of the design elements—type and graphics—should be big enough to see on the smallest screen.

What makes Web design different from print designs is the opportunity to use motion, animation, and interactive navigation. While attention getting, these can also be irritating. Professor Mallia, who wrote the Part III opener, reminds us that online ads can succeed or fail because of their design, as well as their copy. She explains, "Visual tactics like rollovers and motion often annoy more than attract." She also points out that copy is important in Web design, "Experts find it's the copy that often gets the clickthrough—because it offers something the reader wants to *read* more about." So even in the highly visual online world, it's still important for the art and copy to work together to attract attention and build interest.

A fascinating website was created for a get-out-the-vote site aimed at young people during the 2008 election. Check out this website at *www.thingsarefine.org* and watch how the American flag falls apart on the opening page followed by the cynical admonition: "Don't vote. Things are

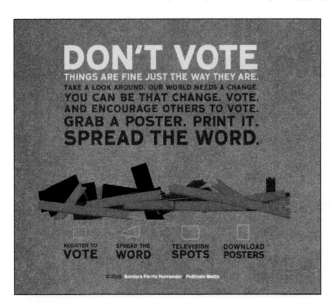

fine just the way they are." The site also has great posters that viewers can download for free, companion public service commercials, and links to sites that a committed viewer could use to remind friends to vote and invite them to visit the site.

Usually the illustrations are created by artists but sometimes for low-budget projects, the illustrations and photos are obtained from clip-art services, or rather click art, such as that provided by *www.dreamstime.com* or *www.1StopPictures.com.* Actually, any image can be scanned and manipulated to create a Web image, which is causing copyright problems for artists and others who originally created the images, as explained with the Obama HOPE story earlier in the chapter. Because of the magic of digitizing, Web pages can combine elements and design styles from many different media: print, still photography, film, animation, sound, and games.

The combination of interactive navigation, live streaming video, online radio, and 360-degree camera angles creates Web pages that may be more complex than anything you see on TV, which is why ease of use is a factor in website design. The following discussion in the *Practical Tips* feature describes research on the best and worst site design practices conducted by Forrester Research, a company that specializes in monitoring the effectiveness of Internet marketing communication.

Web designers use a completely different toolbox than other types of art directors. Animation effects, as well as sophisticated navigation paths, are designed using software programs such as Flash, Silverlight, Director, Blender, Squeak,

The Best and Worst Website Designs

Harley Manning, *Vice President and Research Director, Customer Experience, Forrester Research, Inc.*

Over the years Forrester has graded the quality of user experiences on over 1,300 websites with a technique called *heuristic evaluation*. Today, variations on this methodology are used by virtually every interactive design agency and testing lab to judge the effectiveness of sites. It's also used in house by many companies, including UPS and Johnson & Johnson.

To identify some of the best and worst examples of Web design each year, we grade sites in each of four industries. Most recently we graded the sites of the four largest auto insurers, discount retailers, running shoe manufacturers, and online travel agencies. When we published the results we kicked up quite a storm because we named names. Here are two key results from Forrester's research into the best and worst of site design in 2009:

- The online travel agency category came out best overall, earning the highest high score (Expedia) and ending up with the highest average score. What's more, three of the four sites received positive grades while only one (Priceline.com) earned a negative score.
- The footwear manufacturer sites we graded laid claim to the cellar, with both the lowest high score

(New Balance) and the lowest low score (Puma). In contrast to the online travel agencies, only one site received a positive grade.

So what explains the relatively poor showing of footwear manufacturer sites versus travel agency sites?

One reason is that online travel agencies' business success ties directly to the quality of customer experience on their sites: When customers can't easily plan and book a trip, it shows up immediately in lost sales. This feedback loop drives industry site designers to quickly find and fix problems like inadequate product information, confusing menus, and poor reliability.

In contrast, managers of footwear manufacturer sites have a conflicted agenda: they simultaneously seek to build the softer aspects of brand, drive store traffic, and enable online sales (which remains a small part of their business). This results in a disjointed and often confusing array of micro sites with inconsistent navigation and information, capped off by overly stylized text and graphics that add to shopper frustration. So when Web traffic logs show visitors wandering aimlessly around their sites, it's hard to tell whether the prospects are fascinated or just plain lost.

Check out Forrester's website at *www.forrester.com*.

Note: The information was contributed by Harley Manning, a master's degree graduate of the advertising program at the University of Illinois. He was nominated by the late Kim Rotzell, former dean of the College of Communication.

---

and nonlinear editing tools such as Premier, FinalCut, and AfterEffects. It's such a rapidly changing design world that it's difficult to keep track of the most recent innovations in Web design software. The use of animation effects and streaming video has made websites look more like television and film. The *A Matter of Practice* box explains how this tool is best used.

An example of a good website design is *www.crewcuts.com*, which was designated as the Best Website by the Internet Professional Publishers Association. It's hard to convey here why the site is effective because of the animation, so check out *www.crewcuts.com*. For more examples of excellence in website design and reviews of the top websites, check out:

www.webaward.org

www.worldbestwebsites.com

www.100bestwebsites.org

www.imarvel.com

www.topsiteslinks.com

www.time.com (look for "50 Best Websites" annual review)

www.webbyawards.com

www.clioawards.com

www.oneclub.com

Action and Interaction

Web advertisers are continuing to find ways to bring dramatic action to the small screen to make the imagery more engaging. For example, Ford used a banner on the Yahoo! home page with the familiar Ford oval and a bunch of little black birds on a wire. Then three of the birds flew down to the middle of the page and started pecking at what looked like birdseed, uncovering an image of the new Explorer. The link read: "Click to uncover the next territory." Those who did click probably expected a pop-up image, but instead the page shook, the birds scattered, and a big red Ford Explorer drove up to the front of the screen, replacing most of the content. It was a surprising, highly involving, and effective announcement of the vehicle.

Because users can create their own paths through the website, designers have to make sure that their sites have clear **navigation.** Users should be able to move through the site easily, find the information they want, and respond. Navigation problems can really turn off viewers. Eye-tracking research (studies that use a camera to follow eye movement when looking at a page or screen) has found that if the navigation is cluttered or unclear, viewers will give up and move on to some other site.[11] Ideally, users who visit a site regularly should be able to customize the site to fit their own interests and navigation patterns.

Online video has also expanded the avenues for action on the small screen on minicomputers, personal digital assistants, and cell phones. Web video is becoming a new business opportunity for businesses that want to use videos to display their products. The secret is to plan these videos specifically for a small screen and not just try to use regular television or film images because the screen is just a fraction of the size of a television and a lot of the detail in an image can get lost.[12]

If a site is well designed, people may want to interact with the organization sponsoring the site. For example, Texture/Media, a Boulder, Colorado, Web design firm, created a seven-episode series over five months that detailed the journey of two men attempting to climb the Meru Sharksfin summit in India, for client Marmot Mountain Works. Called ClimbMeru.com, it chronicled the team's training and trip and hosted contest giveaways that helped gather information about Marmot's customers. Texture/Media's objective with its award-winning websites is to make the consumer a participant in its brand stories.

Looking Ahead

This is the last chapter in Part 3 on the design of the message. We introduced creative thinking and the creation of creative briefs; then we discussed copywriting and in this chapter we have provided you with a brief introduction to art direction and design. Next we turn to Part 4 and the chapters that discuss how messages are delivered—both to and from the target audience and other key stakeholders.

ALTOIDS®   IT'S A WRAP

Keeping the Altoids
Brand in Mint Condition

As a product's owners change hands, the new owners are smart to recognize the value of the brand's heritage. The Altoids campaign has a strong, consistent look strengthened by the continuing presence of the distinctive Altoids tin. Repetition of the look is the key to brand recognition.

The brand is recognizable because it builds on the principle that the more times viewers see an ad with a consistent format, the more likely they are to remember the product. Another lesson to be learned from the curiously strong mint: Even though campaigns change, sometimes brands have accrued valuable equity in the previous work that needs to be maintained and protected.

The "Curiously Strong Mints" campaign is one of the most awarded and successful campaigns. The advertising has garnered multiple awards, including a long string of Kelly Awards for magazine advertising, One Show creative prizes, and multiple Clios. It won an international effectiveness award when it received the New York Festival's Grand Prix award. The Magazine Publishers of America (MPA) bestowed its $100,000 Grand Prize Kelly Award for outstanding magazine advertising for the Altoids "Burn Through" campaign, which launched Altoids gum.

The low-cost, edgy campaign has also been a business builder. The brand had virtually no presence in 1995 when Kraft bought it, but by 2000 it dominated the extreme mint market with a 25 percent share. Altoids now is the number one selling mint in the United States. Although it is difficult to predict how the current generation of edgy campaigns will fare, the "Brainstorm" branded entertainment effort shows promise. The trailer alone was viewed more than 100,000 times. Its creators expect to attract 2.5 million views over a six-month period.

What makes Altoids advertising a winner? The memorability and extendability of a curiously strong idea.

Key Points Summary

1. **What is the role of visual communication in marketing communication messages?** Visual communication is important in advertising because it creates impact—it grabs attention, maintains interest, creates believability, and sticks in memory. It also tells stories and creates brand images.

2. **How can we define *layout* and *composition*, and what's the difference between the two?** A layout is an arrangement of all of a print price's elements. It gives the reader a visual order to the information in the layout; at the same time, it is aesthetically pleasing and makes a visual statement for the brand. Principles that designers use in print advertising include direction, dominance, unity, white space, contrast, balance, and proportion. Composition is the way the elements in a picture are arranged, either through placement or by manipulating the photographer's viewpoint.

3. **How are art and color reproduced in print media?** Illustrations are treated as line art and photographs are reproduced through the halftone process by using screens to break down the image into a dot pattern. Full-color photos are converted to four halftone images, each one printed with a different process color—magenta, cyan, yellow, and black—through the process of color separation.

4. **What are the steps in planning and producing video?** Videos are planned using scripts and storyboards. TV commercials are shot live, shot on film or videotape, or created "by hand" using animation, claymation, or stop action. There are four stages to the production of videos—message design (scripts and storyboards), preproduction, the shoot, and postproduction.

5. **What are the basic techniques of Web design?** Web advertising can include ads and banners, but the entire website can also be seen as an advertisement. Art on Web pages can be illustrations or photographs, still images as well as moving ones, and may involve unexpected effects such as 360-degree images. When designers plan a Web page, they need to consider navigation—how people will move through the site. They also need to consider how to incorporate elements that allow for interaction between the consumer and the company that operates the site.

Words of Wisdom: Recommended Reading

Alessandri, Susan W., *Visual Identity*, Armonk, NY: M. E. Sharpe, 2009.

Beaird, Jason, *The Principles of Beautiful Web Design*, Melbourne, Australia: Sitepoint Books, 2007.

Cyr, Lisa L., *Innovative Promotions That Work: A Quick Guide to the Essentials of Effective Design*, Glouster, MA: Rockport, 2006.

Golombisky, Kim, and Rebecca Hagen, *White Space Is Not Your Enemy*, Burlington, MA: Elsevier, 2010.

Landa, Robin, *Advertising by Design: Creating Visual Communications with Graphic Impact*, Hoboken, NJ: John Wiley, 2004.

Morioka, Noreen, and Sean Adams, *Logo Design Workbook: A Hands-On Guide to Creating Logos*, Gloucester, MA: Rockport, 2004.

Samara, Timothy, *Design Elements: A Graphic Style Manual*, Glouster, MA: Rockport, 2007.

White, Alex, *Advertising Design and Typography*, New York: Allworth Press, 2007.

White, Alex, *Thinking in Type: The Practical Philosophy of Typography*, New York: Allworth Press, 2005.

Williams, Robin, *The Non-Designer's Design Book: Design and Typographic Principles for the Visual Novice*, 3rd ed., Berkeley, CA: Peachpit Press, 2008.

Williams, Robin, and John Tollett, *The Non-Designers Web Book*, 3rd ed., Berkeley, CA: Peachpit Press, 2006.

Key Terms

animation, p. 340	dubbing, p. 344	mixer, p. 342	script clerk, p. 342
answer print, p. 342	embossing, p. 336	morphing, p. 338	semicomps, p. 332
claymation, p. 340	film-to-tape transfer, p. 339	navigation, p. 346	spot color, p. 328
click art, p. 324	foil stamping, p. 336	newsprint, p. 333	stock footage, p. 337
clip art, p. 324	font, p. 328	offset printing, p. 335	stop motion, p. 340
color separation, p. 335	four-color printing, p. 335	postproduction, p. 342	storyboards, p. 333
composition, p. 332	gaffer, p. 342	preproduction, p. 341	take, p. 341
comprehensives, p. 332	grip, p. 342	process colors, p. 335	thumbnail sketches, p. 332
continuous tone, p. 334	halftones, p. 334	production notes, p. 341	tint blocks, p. 335
crawl, p. 338	interlock, p. 342	registered, p. 333	tip-in, p. 336
cut, p. 342	layout, p. 331	release prints, p. 344	typography, p. 328
dailies, p. 341	legibility, p. 330	rough cut, p. 342	video editing, p. 342
debossing, p. 336	line art, p. 334	rough layouts, p. 332	videographer, p. 333
die-cutting, p. 335	logo, p. 323	rushes, p. 341	visualization, p. 324
digitization, p. 335	mechanicals, p. 332	screen, p. 335	white space, p. 335

Review Questions

1. Explain why visual impact is so important in advertising.

2. What are the responsibilities of an art director?

3. Compare the use of black and white, spot color, and full color in terms of visual impact.

4. Explain the aesthetic role of typography. Find an ad that illustrates how type can add meaning to the message.

5. List the design principles and explain each one.

6. What's the difference between line art and halftones?

7. What does the phrase *four-color printing* mean? What are the four process colors? What does the phrase *color separation* mean, and how does that work?

8. Explain the following video terms:
   - stock footage
   - crawl
   - morphing
   - animation
   - stop motion
   - claymation

9. Explain the four steps in the video production process.

10. Draw up a list of guidelines to use in designing a website.

Discussion Questions

1. One of the challenges for designers is to demonstrate a product whose main feature cannot be seen by the consumer. Suppose you are an art director on an account that sells shower and bath mats with a patented system that ensures that the mat will not slide (the mat's underside is covered with tiny suction cups that gently grip the tub's surface). Brainstorm some ways to demonstrate this feature in a television commercial. Find a way that will satisfy the demands of originality, relevance, and impact.

2. One approach to design says that a visual image in an ad should reflect the image of the brand. Find a print ad that you think speaks effectively for the personality of the brand. Now compare the print ad with the brand's website. Does the same design style continue on the site? Does the site present the brand personality in the same way as the print ad?

3. Working in a team choose one of the following design critique problems:

   a. **Print** What principles govern the design of a magazine ad? Collect two sample ads, one you consider a good example of effective design and one that you think is not effective. Critique the two ads and explain your evaluation based on what you know about how design principles work in advertising layouts. Make suggestions for how the less effective ad could be improved.

   b. **Television** As a team, find a television commercial that you thought was creative and entertaining. Then find one that you think is much less creative and entertaining. Analyze how the two commercials work to catch and hold your attention. How do the visuals work? What might be done to make the second commercial more attention getting? You can also use online sources to find commercials at *www.adcritic.com* and at *www.badads.org*.

4. You have been asked to design a Web page for a local business or organization (choose one from your local community). Go to *www.flickr.com* or *www.1StopPictures.com* and choose a visual to illustrate the website by trying to match the personality of the organization to a visual image. Then

identify the primary categories of information that need to be included on the page. Develop a flowchart or map that shows how a typical user would navigate through the site. What other image could you find at *www.1StopPictures.com* that might be used on inside pages to provide some visual interest to this business's online image? Now consider interactivity: How could this site be used to increase interactivity between this company and its customers? Create a plan for this site that includes the visual elements and a navigation flowchart.

5. ***Three-Minute-Debate*** Your team is assigned to a new client who has a new hand lotion for men, one that is designed to help men whose hands take a beating in their jobs.

One of your colleagues, a photographer, believes the only way to visualize the product and its use in an ad is through photography. Another colleague, an artist, argues that there are times when art is a much better way to illustrate a product than photography and that this production is a good example. Analyze the differences between using an illustration and using a photograph. What are their roles, and how do they create different types of effects? Are there certain product categories where you would want to use an illustration instead of a photograph and vice versa? Which would work best for this new product? Develop a quick presentation for your class that explains which approach you would use for this assignment.

Take-Home Projects

1. ***Portfolio Project:*** Select a product that is advertised exclusively through print. Examples of such products are business-to-business and industrial products, school supplies, many over-the-counter drugs, and some food items. Your objective is to develop a 30-second television spot for this product. Develop a creative brief (see Chapter 8) to summarize the ad's strategy. Brainstorm about ways to develop a creative idea for the commercial. Then write a script and develop a storyboard to present your idea for this product. In the script include all the key decisions a producer and director would make.

2. ***Mini-Case Analysis:*** Summarize the creative strategy behind Altoid's "Curiously Strong Mints" campaign. Explain the critical elements of both the copy and the visuals. The brand management team has proposed developing a new (sugar-free) line of cough drops. How would you adjust this strategy to appeal to this new market? Design a launch ad that presents your copy ideas and a new visual. Accompany the ad with a statement that explains your thinking.

Team Project: The BrandRevive Campaign

Visit once again the BrandRevive message strategy your team created for Chapter 8, as well as your copy ideas that you developed in Chapter 9. Go online and review the advertising and package/store design (if appropriate) for your brand. Now consider how to marry the strategy and words with a new visual image. Should it be retro or use some other stylistic cues? Describe the new "look" you propose in a strategy statement. If you are unable to illustrate the look, then compile similar images and styles either from other print media or online to use as examples to help explain what you propose.

- Mock up, as best you can, a prototype product package, store, shopping bag, or other signature item that conveys the new look.

- Develop a series of thumbnails for a launch ad for your new campaign. Then choose the best idea and develop, as best you can, a full-page magazine ad for this launch.
- Design the accompanying website—or at least the home page—that takes your new look online.
- For each of these three pieces, write a paragraph that describes the impression you intend to create.
- Present and explain your new look in a two-page document and in a PowerPoint presentation that is no longer than three slides.

Hands-On Case

The Century Council

Read the Century Council case in the Appendix before coming to class.

1. Write a design memo that describes the "look" of The Stupid Drink campaign. What elements would you make mandatory

(e.g., typeface, colors, etc.) and which would you allow individual campuses to personalize in their own colors?

2. The Century Council is never identified as a sponsor of The Stupid Drink campaign. Is that the right thing to do? Why or Why not?

CHAPTER 7

Media Channels 1

Media Basics

It's a Winner

Campaign:	Company:	Agencies:	Award:
"Axe Detailer: The Manly Shower Tool"	Unilever	Bartle Bogle Hegarty with Mindshare and Edelman Integrated Marketing Services	Gold Effie Winner, New Product or Service Category

CHAPTER KEY POINTS

1. How do media work in marketing communication and how is the industry organized?

2. How would you describe the key strategic media concepts?

3. Why and how is the media landscape changing?

Getting Dirty Boys Cleaner

Let's start with the problem. You have a great product, but you need to reach an audience that's reluctant to be persuaded by traditional advertising techniques. How do you convince more young guys who like Axe products to throw away their bars of soap and start using Axe Shower Gel?

A little background first. Unilever's personal care brand Axe led the way in getting young men to use scented body sprays. Launched in 2002 in the United States, Axe deodorant body sprays captured the attention of its audience and soon became the top male deodorant brand in the country. (Did guys even know they needed scented body sprays before then?)

Expanding its line in men's grooming products with the shower gel represented a great opportunity for Unilever, who, along with its ad agency, Bartle Bogle Hegarty, wanted to grab the attention of the 18- to 34-year-old male audience. It ran the successful and award-winning "How Dirty Boys Get Clean" campaign, which you may have seen.

Axe reached its core audience with that campaign by creating an emotional approach that worked particularly well in the broadcast media. The big idea behind the campaign was that Axe Shower Gel would do more than clean guys physically; it would help clean their spirits as well. The campaign's creative work communicated the "dirty message." The agency chose media to reach and captivate the audience, amplifying the message in situations where guys might be having "dirty thoughts."

To reach these guys, TV commercials ran on programs like *Baywatch*, *The Real World*, and *Aqua Teen Hunger Force*. Print ads were placed in *Maxim*, *Playboy*, and the *Sports Illustrated* swimsuit issue. Axe also turned up at two of the largest spring break destinations for college guys where they encountered shower gel messages everywhere—on bar posters, hotel shower curtains, floor stickers, and bus wraps. The *www.theaxeeffect.com* website also entertained the guys.

After that campaign had run its course, Axe realized it needed to figure out how to get more of the target 18- to 34-year-old guys to switch from bars to shower gel. The "Aha!" moment for the next campaign emerged from research that indicated a correlation between using a loofah and satisfaction with shower gel's cleansing power. Without a scrubber, they just weren't using the shower gel, and although they said they used loofahs, shower ethnography (a bit tricky, don't you imagine?) showed that in reality, they were using fluffy, soft, girlie poufs. Not the macho image you'd expect.

The key to this campaign was to create a new shower tool soft enough for the guys' private parts and tough enough for them to feel clean for their women. Axe brilliantly created a scrubber that looked like a car tire and drawing from car culture, gave it a cool, masculine name, the Detailer. Carrying the idea to the max, the idea developed into a concept that appealed to the target audience: Guywash.

To demonstrate Guywash to the target audience, BBH used the storytelling power of cinema and TV. Furthermore, they capitalized on the interactivity of digital media to let guys try the Detailer. The "Dirty Night Determinator" on the website prescribed a personalized scrub routine for whatever dirty situations the guys might encounter. Girls could use Facebook to send a "gift" to "dirty" guys. Free Detailers were sent to anyone who requested one on the brand page. These media were supported by local-area promotions, in-store Detailer "technicians" who guided them to the section of the store, and point-of-purchase efforts that turned shopping into an experience.

You will find more about the marketing effects of Axe's shower gel campaign at the end of the chapter in the *It's a Wrap* section.

Sources: "Axe Detailer: The Manly Shower Tool," Effie Awards Brief of Effectiveness, *www.nyama.org;* "How Dirty Boys Get Clean," *www.nyama.org;* Michael Bush, "Unilever Wins Two Awards for Axe, Dove Media Campaigns," April 20, 2009, *www.adage.com;* "Mindshare Wins Bet Localisation at Valencia Festival of Media," April 20, 2009, *www.mindshareworld .com; www.theaxeeffect.com.*

The lesson that the Axe campaign teaches about media is that smart marketing requires creative thinking about how to connect with the audience in this complex media environment. What else has Axe done to reach guys? Read how Axe has made use of branded entertainment in *The Animated Axe Effect in City Hunters* later in this chapter (p. 373). This chapter and the three that follow explain the media side of marketing communication—the story you don't see, the backstory about how various ways to deliver a message are selected.

WHAT DO WE MEAN BY MEDIA?

When we talk about **media,** we are referring to the way messages are delivered to target audiences and, increasingly, back to companies, as well as among audience members themselves. Media is the go-between[1] step in the communication model—the way messages are sent and returned by the source and receiver, that is, the company or brand and its customers.

It's helpful to remember that the basis for most media historically was as a way to present the news to the public—and advertising made presenting the news possible because it supported the costs of producing and distributing print or broadcast media. Of course, some revenue is derived from subscriptions, but in the United States the bulk of the media revenue comes from advertising.

As a result, over the years the word *media* has been associated with advertising, leading many to think that media are used only or primarily for advertising. Nothing could be further from the truth! As Kelley pointed out in the Part 4 opener, advertising may not provide adequate financial support for the new media forms and all media are looking for new revenue streams in order to stay in business.

Media Classifications

The plural noun *media* is an umbrella term for all types of print, broadcast, out-of-home, and Internet communication. The singular noun *medium* refers to each specific type (TV is a medium, for example). A **media vehicle** is a specific TV program (*60 Minutes, The Simpsons*), newspaper (*The Washington Post, Chicago Tribune, El Nuevo Herald*), magazine (*Woman's Day, GQ*), or radio station or program (NPR's *All Things Considered*, Rush Limbaugh's talk show). When a company "buys media," it is really buying access to the audiences of specific media vehicles. The form that those "buys" take is "space" (print, outdoor boards, Internet) and "time" (radio and TV).

Media, particularly those used in advertising, are referred to as **mass media**, the communication channels through which messages are sent to large, diverse audiences. A mass medium reaches many people simultaneously and it uses some technological system or device to reach them (as opposed to personal communication). The size of the audience is the reason why we refer to radio and television as **broadcasting media**—they cast their audio and visual signals broadly to reach mass audiences.

In contrast, **niche media** are communication channels through which messages are sent to niche segments—identifiable groups of people with a distinct common interest, such as the Hispanic market served by *El Nuevo Herald*. *Advertising Age* and *Adweek*, for example, are a subsegment of the more general business magazine category. They reach the professional advertising industry niche. The distinction between mass and niche is not based necessarily on size. The *AARP Magazine*, for example, which targets baby boomers age 50+, is a niche publication and yet it is the world's largest circulation magazine.[2]

Two other categories of media refer to the way the media transmit the messages. **Addressable media**, such as the Internet, mail, and the telephone, are used to send brand messages to specific geographic and electronic addresses. They are particularly helpful in keeping in touch with current customers or with brand communities. *Interactive media*, such as the phone and Internet, allow two-way communication between companies and customers, as well as between and among consumers.

Another term you'll see in media plans is **measured media**, which refers to the ability of media planners to analyze the cost of a media buy relative to the size of the medium's audience. Metrics are available for traditional media either from the medium itself or from external auditing agencies, but these figures are much harder to find for new and nontraditional media because the auditing procedures for these new media have yet to be developed.

The media landscape, according to TNS Media Intelligence, a reporting service that tracks advertising spending, uses the following categories:[3]

- *Television* network, cable, syndication, spot (local), Hispanic
- *Radio* network, national spot, local
- *Newspapers* national, local, Hispanic
- *Magazines* consumer, B2B, Sunday, local, Hispanic, international
- *Internet*
- *Outdoor*
- *Branded Entertainment*

All marketing communication messages other than personal conversations are carried by some form of media. In other words, media are not just a concern of advertising planners. Integrated marketing communication (IMC) media convey messages, such as brand publicity and sales promotion offers, as well as direct-response messages and loyalty incentive programs. Furthermore, these messages are two way in that they are carried to and from companies and consumers.

All of this means that the face of mass media is changing. Professor Don Jugenheimer in the *A Matter of Principle* feature analyzes the principles of change that are remaking the media landscape.

Ethnic media are a type of niche media. *El Nuevo Herald* is an example of a successful newspaper targeted at an ethic group, in this case the Spanish-speaking consumers in Miami and South Florida.

Principle
All marketing communication messages, other than personal conversations, are carried by some form of media.

The Dynamics of the Changing Media Environment

Donald Jugenheimer, *Principal and Partner, In-Telligence Inc.*

Mass media are changing rapidly. Several trends that are in operation simultaneously are dramatically reshaping the face of mass media:

1. **Convergence** involves the digitization of the media, in which all of the mass media save and transmit information through the same digital forms, as well as the integration of the media to work through and with each other.
2. **Interactivity** means that audience members can send messages back and forth to the media and to each other.
3. **Engagement,** or holding onto the audience through the media using give-and-take messaging, also involves interactivity.
4. Commoditization results when many types of products are similar. Customers think that most airlines are pretty much alike, and most banks offer the same services and hours of operation. The advertising media are similar, too, with broadcast television, cable television, TiVo, and DVD programming all regarded alike by viewers.
5. Cadence reflects the pace of today's life. Things move ever faster, attention spans are shorter, and audiences want to spend less time with advertisements.
6. **Personalization** allows advertisers and others to appeal directly to an individual's interests and needs.
7. Networking brings related messages and offers to audience members, based on their past and present behavior.

What happens when we all get all of our news, entertainment, and information exchanges through our cell phones or over the Internet? What will be the role of the "older" media? What is coming next? Few saw the Internet coming, and there are bound to be significant changes in future media as well.

What Do Media Do?

All marketing communication areas, such as sales promotion, public relations, and direct marketing, use a variety of media to deliver messages to customers. We know from the communication model presented in Chapter 4 that messages move through *channels of communication.* So in this sense, media *deliver* messages. In traditional mass media this is a one-way process from the source (the advertiser) to the receiver (consumers).

In another sense, media are *interactive* because they offer opportunities for dialogue and two-way conversation. The media of marketing communication deliver messages to and from customers and move messages back and forth through channels. This refines the concept of delivery to include receiving and listening, as well as delivering messages. Jugenheimer explains further, "Now we can respond, ask questions, and even place orders for products or services. This interactivity can involve more than the Internet; we can gain interactivity on the telephone, through text messaging on cell phones, and while playing video games."

Media also offers opportunities for *engagement,* a media buzzword that refers to the captivating quality of media that the audience finds engrossing, such as the "wire dancers" on the Windows Vista outdoor board. Certainly this can apply to television commercials and cinema advertising, but it can also be applied to print and Internet ads—anything on which readers concentrate. Media experts describe engagement as the closeness of fit between the interests of viewers and the relevance of the media content.[4] This is how media open the door of the critical "perception" step in the Facets Model of Effects that we introduced in Chapter 4.

Media are also contact points in that they *connect* a brand with the audience and ultimately *touch* their emotions, as well as *engage* their minds. The difference between delivery and connection is significant. To deliver means "to take something to a person or place"; to connect means "to join together." Delivery is the first step in connecting: it opens the door to touching a customer in a meaningful way with a brand message. Beyond conventional mass media, IMC connection media also include personal experiences with events, salespeople, and customer service, as well as word-of-mouth messages from people who influence us—all of which may become imbued with emotions leading to strong personal feelings about a brand.

The Evolution of Media Roles

People in our contemporary society live in a world of media-delivered news and information, which traditionally has been supported by advertising. Over several hundred years, media have evolved from print, to radio, then television, and now the Internet. Newspapers, magazines, and posters provided the visual dimension of communication; radio added an audio dimension. Television enabled messages to be heard and seen with moving images. Today we have the Internet, which has basically combined television and the computer, thus providing the added dimension of interactivity. We can summarize these changes in technology as eras:

The Print Era Ink and print images reproduced as newspapers, magazines, and posters.

The Broadcast Era Visual and audio information in the form of radio and television programs originally transmitted through air waves but now also distributed by cable and satellite.

The Digital Era Electronic information transmitted through the Internet but, like broadcasting, now also distributed through cable and satellite.

Wire dancers on an oversized billboard brought the Microsoft logo to life for the launch of the Vista operating system—an example of a highly engaging use of outdoor advertising.

It's useful to remember that this Digital Era is quite recent. The first website went on line in 1991; the social networking sites of MySpace and Facebook went on line in 2003 and 2004, respectively; and Twitter only arrived in 2006. In contrast, the first newspaper ad appeared in the early 1700s, the first radio station went on the air in 1897, and television became popular in the United States in the 1940s.

Every technological advance has threatened the older media whose managers feared their medium was on the edge of extinction. In fact, the media adjusted to their new circumstances by emphasizing what they do best—newspapers and magazines deliver information in depth, radio delivers music and other programs tailored to listeners' tastes, and television brings entertainment to the living room. The new media take on some of the characteristics and roles of the old at the same time that they add to the richness of the communication experience. Television, for example, has news shows and advertising that sound a lot like radio news programs and both radio and television use news formats—and advertising—that they adopted from print.

Principle
Every technological advance has threatened older media, and every new medium is launched in the footprints of its predecessor media.

A more serious shift, however, is occurring in the 21st century as computers and the Internet personalize media and bring changes unlike any ever encountered in the history of media. Internet-based communication can do everything that the traditional media identified as their distinctive features and offers most of the communication dimensions of its media ancestors.

The only "medium" that is even more multidimensional than the Internet is personal selling. A salesperson can not only show, tell, and interact, but most importantly, can instantly create customized content. Internet sites can quasi-create content by compiling customer data from which information can be computed, such as creating a selection of customer preferences (Amazon's suggested books) or provide predetermined answers to FAQs (frequently asked questions).

Personalization is the answer to the commoditization point Jugenheimer included in his list of media trends. Another medium that delivers personalization is **word-of-mouth,** which

Principle
Word of mouth delivers personalization, as well as a high level of persuasion.

A MATTER OF PRACTICE

People Really Enjoy Their Large-Screen Televisions

Michael McNiven, *Assistant Professor, Rowan University and* Dean Krugman, *Professor, University of Georgia*

Televisions with screens of 40 inches or more are commonly referred to as large-screen TVs. The larger sets with a rectangular 16 × 9 aspect ratio—used on movie screens and in DVDs—are rapidly replacing the traditional 4 × 3 box-shaped screen. The large sets are a viable and high-quality television innovation that continues to gain prominence in the television marketplace. Annual total sales exceed 30 million sets per year and there is no indication that the tremendous growth of large-screen television adoption will decline. Projected worldwide unit sales for large-screen TVs in 2010 was close to 61 million units.

Larger wide-screen televisions coupled with digital reception represent a significant change from the past in how television fare is delivered to viewers. The combination of digital programming, wider screens, and larger television displays marks a historic and pivotal entrance into the new era of the 21st-century television industry. People report that the changes in television dramatically improve the viewing process.

Large-screen owners are more likely to be married, have teenagers and older children in the home, live with more people, and earn more money. Family entertainment is a major reason for purchasing the sets, which produces a larger, fuller family experience. In addition, large-screen owners are more likely to view event programming (such as sports and movies) and to play video games, which has become a family and/or multiplayer activity.

The large-screen television experience is found by consumers to be enjoyable, easy to watch, and to approximate a theater-like atmosphere. Lifelike pictures and compelling sound often help viewers feel like they are being transported to the location of the content. In most cases large-screen televisions are part of a cluster of television technologies including such items as video games, digital video recorders (DVRs), and cable/satellite distribution.

The synergies of the home television cluster provide dramatically enhanced viewing and entertainment experiences. The increased viewing experience has a social component. In addition to more family viewing, larger screen televisions are used for friend and visitor entertaining, providing an important social component.

---

has emerged as a powerful new force in marketing communication because of its inherent persuasiveness—you tend to believe what you hear from a friend, family member, or other important influencer in your life.

Although new media tend to launch themselves by adapting the forms of the media that preceded them, the older media also adapt by adopting some of the advances of new media. Nearly every media vehicle, for example, now has one or more (most have more) websites—and that creates *convergence*. Jugenheimer notes, "Newspapers have websites, advertisements can be transmitted by e-mail, and television programs can be downloaded into iPods." Furthermore, catalogs are on line, radio is on line, video is on computers, and cell phones and books are electronic.

Television, for example, is not just limited to viewing programs, but has become the center of the digital living room with viewers enjoying new experiences, such as games and exercise via their Wii players and other video games that now can be seen on the TV screen. The *A Matter of Practice* feature explains how consumers are converting their TVs into new multimedia centers.

The Media Industry

The modern media landscape includes up to 200 television channels in some markets, a huge number of special-interest publications, millions of websites, and new and novel media forms that weren't even imagined 20 years ago, such as ads on conveyer belts at airports or brands stamped into the sand at the beach. The Jeep trailer shows how designer Michael Dattolico designed a painted vehicle for one of his clients.

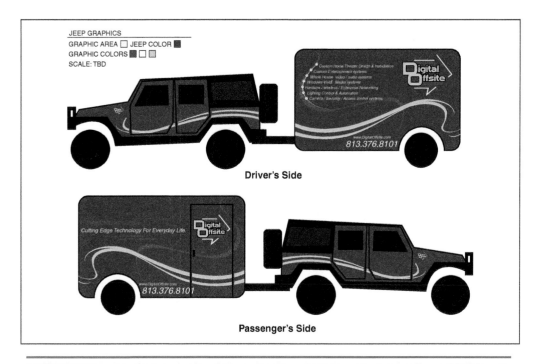

Driver's Side

Passenger's Side

SHOWCASE

The Jeep graphics designed by Michael Dattolico for a technology client turned a vehicle into a moving billboard.

Dattolico graduated from the advertising program at the University of Florida and was nominated by Professor Elaine Wagner.

Traditional mass media advertising is a huge industry with almost $141 billion in advertising spending.[5] Media research organization Kantar Media monitors advertising expenditures and provided the data used in Figure 11.1 Although advertising expenditures declined as a result of the Great Recession of the late 2000s, the greatest growth was in online advertising.

The recession, combined with the explosion of online media, seriously hurt traditional media. Even though they still dominate in terms of dollars, all traditional media saw decreases in their ad revenues. This was partly because of an overall decline in media advertising but also because marketers were increasingly turning to the Internet for visibility at less cost.

Newspapers were the biggest losers because of the shift of classified advertising to online sites and the ease with which readers could get news online. Many major papers closed; others were reduced in size, staff, and news coverage. Magazines suffered, as well. Revenues for broadcast were down with traditional radio and television companies seeing red ink. The bright spot during the recession was the cable television sector. *Advertising Age* reported at the end of 2009 that 11 of the top 100 media firms had filed for bankruptcy during the year with print dominating the list.[6]

Key Media Players

In terms of jobs and career opportunities in media, there are professionals who both sell and buy media. It is important that you understand the difference. First let's look at the professionals who sell space or time in media.

- **Media salespeople** work for a specific vehicle, such as a magazine or local television station, with the objective of building the best possible argument to convince media planners to use the medium they represent. A media salesperson is responsible for assembling packets of information, or **sales kits,** on the medium he or she represents, which usually means compiling profile information about the people who

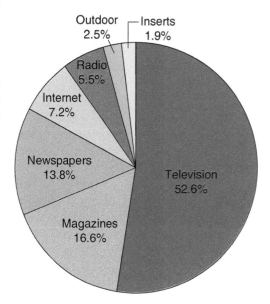

FIGURE 11.1

The Media Landscape

Source: Kantar Media. Based on January–March 2010 (% Share). Used with permission.

watch, listen, or read the medium, along with the numbers describing audience size and geographical coverage. Currently media conglomerates prevail. CBS, for example, created a coordinated ad-selling division, called CBS RIOT, which stands for radio, Internet, outdoor, and television. The new division was designed to serve primarily local markets and offers **cross-media** (also called **multichannel**) integrated deals. Disney is reorganizing its ad sales to deliver a similar cross-media ad sales program for its kids' media properties.[7]

- **Media reps** or **brokers** are people (or companies) who sell space (in print) and time (in broadcast) for a variety of media. If an agency wants to buy space in all of the major newspapers in the West, for example, the agency's buyer could contract with a media rep firm whose sales rep and brokers handle national sales for all those newspapers. This allows the media buyer to place the buy with one order.

On the buying side, media planners, buyers, and researchers work primarily for agencies, although they can also be found working for marketers who handle their own media work in house. Their challenge is to determine the best way to deliver a message, which is called **media planning.** The job functions are as follows:

- **Media researchers** compile audience measurement data, media costs, and availability data for the various media options being considered by the planners.
- **Media planners** develop the strategic decisions outlined in the media plan, such as where to advertise geographically, when to advertise, and which type of media to use to reach specific types of audiences.
- **Media buyers** implement the media plan by contracting for specific amounts of time or space. They spend the media budget according to the plan developed by the media planner. Media buyers are expected to maintain good media supplier relations to facilitate a flow of information within the fast-changing media marketplace. This means there should be close working relationships between planners and buyers, as well as media reps, so media planners can tap this source of media information to better forecast media changes, including price and patterns of coverage.
- Media buying companies, mentioned briefly in Chapter 1, are independent companies that specialize in doing media research, planning, and buying. They may be a spin-off from the media department in an advertising agency, but because they are now independent companies, they work for a variety of clients. They consolidate media buying to get maximum discounts from the media for the volume of their buys. They then pass on some of this saving to their clients.

WHAT ARE THE FUNDAMENTALS OF MEDIA STRATEGY?

Media placement is often the largest single cost item in a marketing communication budget, especially for consumer goods and services. Procter & Gamble, for example, spent more than $2 billion on measured media in 2009, although for the first time P&G lost its leadership position as the top U.S. advertiser to Verizon, the telecom giant, which suffered less during the Great Recession than P&G.[8] Because of the huge amount of money spent on measured media, as well as nontraditional media, decisions about how the money is to be spent are carefully analyzed and justified in the media planning process.

The Media Plan

Principle

The goal of media planning is to maximize impact while minimizing cost.

The challenge marketing communicators face is how to manage all of the media opportunities and yet maximize the efficiency of budgets that are inevitably too small to do everything the firm would like to do to reach every current and potential customer. All of this decision making comes together in a **media plan,** which identifies the best media to use to deliver an advertising message efficiently to a targeted audience. The goal is to balance message impact and cost—maximizing impact while minimizing cost.

The media plan is a subsection within a marcom plan and has its own objectives, strategies, and tactics. It is also developed in tandem with message planning, the topic of Chapter 8. Figure 11.2 shows these relationships, but this time with an emphasis on media planning. We'll introduce

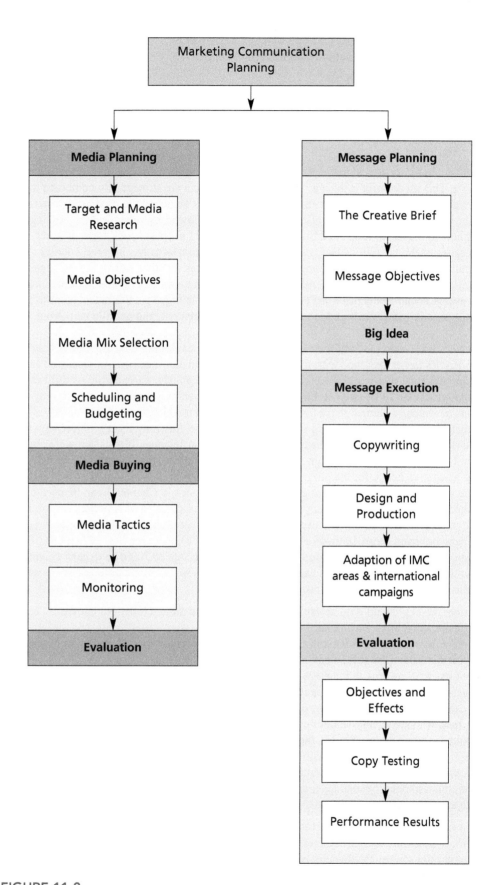

FIGURE 11.2
Marketing Communication Planning
Media and message planning activities are interrelated and work in parallel.

some of the basic media planning concepts here in this chapter but Chapter 14 on media planning and buying will explain these activities in much more detail.

Key Strategic Media Concepts

Now let's consider some of the basic components in media strategy and planning. You will need to be familiar with these terms to understand the review of media forms discussed in this chapter and the chapters that follow.

Media Mix   In most cases a media plan will include more than one medium, and therefore is a *media mix*. This **media mix** is the way various types of media are strategically combined to create a certain kind of impact. For example, the campaign that launched the iPod used posters and magazine ads to create awareness of the new product, followed by television advertising that showed how to use the product, and billboards that reminded people to look for it in stores.

Because of the breadth of IMC plans, the term **multiplatform** has become popular to describe multichannel and multimarketing communication areas. In other words, in IMC plans you will find, in addition to traditional measured media advertising, a variety of other tools being used, such as events, social media (such as Facebook and Twitter), branded entertainment (such as films or video games in which the brand is the hero), product placement, and guerilla marketing.

Targets and Audiences   One of the biggest challenges in developing a media plan is matching the advertiser's target audience with the audience of a particular medium. As discussed in *The Inside Story* feature at *www.pearsonglobaleditions.com/moriarty*, an example of tight targeting comes from the University of Florida where the university's student advertising agency, Adwerks, developed a campaign for the university's student travel program based on posters and flyers that were designed to reach a student audience. The Adwerks team's objective was to increase sign-ups in order to meet the required number of participants. If trips that were close to full didn't reach a certain level of sign-ups then there was the potential for unhappy participants, creating a negative image for the program.

Principle
Media planners match the target audience with the audience of a particular medium.

The same terms that are used to describe target audiences in Chapter 5 can be used to describe media audiences. A major study by the Newspaper Association of America, for example, grouped media audiences into four useful categories by generation: traditionalists (born before 1946), baby boomers (born 1946–1964), Gen X (1965–1976), and Gen Y (1977–1994).[9] Since this study, Millenials (born in the late 1990s into the first decade of 2000) have been commonly added to the list of media audiences categorized by generation. Dramatic differences are seen in the media experiences of these audience groups:

- *Traditionalists* grew up with newspapers, magazines, and radio. (*Note:* No television; no cell phone, computers, or Internet.)
- *Boomers,* who are in their 50s and 60s, always had those three types of media, but also grew up with television (but still no cell phones, computers, or Internet).
- *Gen Xers,* who are now in their 30s and 40s, grew up not only with the media of the preceding generations, but also with tape recorders, Walkman portable radios, video games, VCRs, and cable TV (still no cell phones, computers, or Internet).
- *Gen Yers,* who are twenty-somethings, had all the above media, but also grew up with the computer, as well as satellite TV, the Internet, CDs, and cell phones. (*Note:* Now, finally, we have a generation that grew up with computers and cell phones.)
- *Millennials,* the most recent generation, have grown up with DVDs, TiVo, satellite radio, iPods, smart phones, Second Life, and more recently they have witnessed the introduction of MySpace, Facebook, and Twitter.

The media planners' challenge is to know which media best reach which audiences, whatever their ages. In a classic example of targeting, the market for the launch of the iPod, for example, was a technologically sophisticated young adult. The target market also needed to have enough discretionary income to buy the product. That audience profile led initially to a target of innovators, people who are into cool gadgets and who love music. Now where do you find those people? One place to start was with posters in subways and other urban sites. The campaign also used outdoor boards, print media, and TV commercials in ways that would generate buzz. A key strategy was to get people talking about this new gadget. Eventually the price dropped and the market widened to include both college and high school students after the initial launch.

The Basis for the Buy

Decisions about which media to use are based on the profile of the audience that reads, views, listens, or visits a medium. Media sales reps provide their own data, but research by account planners also uncovers media use patterns that help make these decisions.

Media planners use a variety of terms to identify and measure audiences. The terms are easy to confuse, so let's explain some here before we begin talking about specific characteristics of traditional media forms in the following chapters.

- *Exposure* Media effects all begin with **exposure.** We know from the discussion in Chapter 4 that the first step in making an impact is perception—you have to be exposed to a message before any other effect is possible. Exposure is similar to circulation for television in that it's a rough estimate of the number of households watching a program. However, just because the television is on doesn't mean you are paying any attention to the program, let alone the advertising that surrounds it. Exposure, in other words, doesn't equate to readership or viewership. At the most basic level, however, media planners estimate the number of exposures delivered by a media mix.
- *Impressions* An **impression** is one person's opportunity to be exposed one time to an ad in a specific vehicle. Impressions can be added up as a measure of the size of the audience either for one medium (one insertion in print) or for a combination of vehicles in a media mix.
- *Circulation* Impressions are different from **circulation,** because impressions (at least in print) estimate the readership or rather the opportunity to be exposed (delivery to the household or a newsstand purchase), rather than just the circulation, which refers to copies sold.
- *Gross Impressions* Circulation doesn't tell you much about the actual exposure of a print ad. A magazine may have a circulation of 1 million, but it might be read on average by 2.5 people per issue. This means impressions for that issue would be 2.5 million. If the ad ran in three consecutive issues, then the estimate of total impressions, called **gross impressions,** would be 7.5 million. Similarly, the number of viewers watching a program might be greater than the number of households reached since there may be more than one viewer watching and the commercial may be repeated several times in a program. Media planners add up all those watching and multiply that times the number of placements to estimate gross impressions for TV.
- *Ratings* Gross impression figures become very large and difficult to work with, which is why the television and radio industries use **ratings** (percentage of exposure), which is an easier measurement to work with because it converts the raw figure to a percentage of households. When you read about a television show having a rating of 20.0 that means that 20 percent, or one-fifth of all the households with televisions, were tuned in to that program. *Note:* One rating point equals 1 percent of the nation's estimated 1,114,000 TV homes; that's why planners describe this program as having 20 **rating points,** or percentage points. A 20 rating is actually a huge figure, since the fragmentation of cable has diversified television watching and made it very difficult to get 20 percent of the households tuned to any one program.
- *Share* A better estimate of impressions might be found in a program's **share of audience,** which refers to the percent of viewers based on the number of sets turned on. The share figure is always larger than the rating, since the base is smaller. For example, the 2010 Super Bowl got a rating of 45 (45 percent of all households with television), but its share was 68, which means 68 percent of all televisions turned on were tuned to the Super Bowl.[10]

Reach and Frequency The goal of most media plans is to reach as many people in the target audience as often as the budget allows. **Reach** is the percentage of the media audience exposed at least once to the advertiser's message during a specific time frame. When we say that a particular media vehicle, such as the Super Bowl, has a wide reach, we mean that a lot of people are watching the program. When we say it has a narrow reach, such as the *El Nuevo Herald,* we mean that a small percentage of the newspaper audience is reading that publication. The idea for the iPod launch was to reach not just everyone who likes music, but specifically to target technologically sophisticated people who are also opinion leaders (whose thoughts on innovations like the iPod would influence many others).

Equally as important as reach is **frequency,** which refers to the number of times a person is exposed to the advertisement. There's a rule of thumb that you have to hear or see something three times before it makes an impact. That's the reason frequency of repetition is so important in many

Principle

Exposure doesn't equate to readership or viewership; just because the television is on doesn't mean anyone is paying attention to it.

Principle

The goal of most media plans is to reach as many people in the target audience as often as the budget allows.

advertising campaigns. Different media have different patterns of frequency. Radio commercials, for example, typically achieve high levels of frequency because they can be repeated over and over to achieve impact. Frequency is more difficult to accomplish with a monthly magazine because its publication—and an ad's appearance in it—is much more infrequent than a radio broadcast.

Most media plans state both reach and frequency objectives and the media mix is designed to accomplish both of those goals. You may remember the discussion in Chapter 6 of the lamb market in Iceland. The objective was to reposition lamb to meet the budget concerns of recession-stressed consumers. Let's revisit that case with more information about the campaign's media plan, which demonstrates how different media are chosen based on consumer use and the ability of the various media to deliver either reach or frequency.

You may remember that focus groups were used by the H:N Marketing Communication agency in Reykjavik, Iceland to uncover key consumer insights about lamb—principally that consumers were not buying pricey prime lamb cuts and didn't know how to cook the more budget-priced cuts. Other information uncovered in that research was useful in identifying key media characteristics of the target market. In particular, Ingvi Logason's research found the following:

* The target group members are the largest consumers of TV in the country.
* Close to 100 percent of the target group has high-speed Internet access and are frequent users of the Internet at work and at home.
* Iceland most likely has the highest penetration of Facebook users in the world: 94 percent of the population in the age group of 25- to 40-year-olds (the lamb industry's target group) have Facebook accounts.

Logason explained that his agency created "an interactive media plan that would connect with our target group in settings where they could be engaged in the ads. We would connect with them on their leisure time where they worked, at home, and in social settings." The plan used both television and Facebook. He explains, "The strength of self-dissemination and friend referrals on Facebook made sure the ad recipes traveled far and wide with recommendation that the person posting the recipe liked it. A strong connection was created between viral ads, the Lamb industry's website, and a Facebook group interested in lamb."

Traditional media, such as television, were also used but the interactive media "allowed us to focus on reach in the TV media buy while we were able to obtain high frequency through viral media." Additional activities included sponsoring TV cooking shows, placing the product in TV shows (cooking and other), and gathering various lamb recipes already online and linking them to the Facebook site. Logason reported that media measurements showed that the unorthodox media mix reached its target for both reach (mostly through TV) and frequency (mostly through viral activities).

Intrusiveness   Because of the high level of commercial message clutter, companies in the past have valued all of the help they can get in attracting attention to their messages. **Intrusiveness**— the ability of a medium to grab attention by being disruptive or unexpected—is the primary strategy for countering clutter. Kelley in the Part 4 opener pointed out that in the new media world, engagement will replace interruption. But still, most media use intrusiveness to some degree as a way to grab the attention of inattentive media consumers.

<aside>
Principle
The more intrusive a medium, the more it can be personalized, but also the more costly it is to use.
</aside>

Media, as well as messages, vary in their degree of intrusiveness. The most intrusive medium is personal selling because the sales representative's presence demands attention. Likewise a phone call is also demanding and a loud voice or sound on television can be irritating. The least intrusive media are print media because users choose when and to what extent to use these media and attend to them. The more intrusive a medium, generally speaking, the more it can be personalized, but also the more costly it is to use, which is why personal selling is so much more costly than mass media. Admittedly, the word *intrusive* has negative connotations. If a message is too disruptive or irritating, it may not help build a positive brand relationship.

There are ways to minimize intrusiveness. One is to choose media whose target audience is intrinsically interested in the product category. Research has shown that one of the benefits of specialized magazines is that readers enjoy learning about new products from the advertising. To have visibility without being intrusive is one of the reasons why product placements and events are popular. Giving customers opt-in or opt-out options for receiving brand information digitally means that when messages are sent, they are not unexpected and therefore less likely to be seen as intrusive.

HOW IS THE MEDIA ENVIRONMENT CHANGING?

As we said at the beginning of this chapter, marketing communication media are in an incredible state of flux, partially because of the introduction of the computer and the Internet, but also because of the way people choose to spend their time. Bruce Bendinger, formerly a creative director and now publisher of advertising books, analyzes the changing media environment in the *A Matter of Practice* feature.

IMC and Media

We have talked about the connection role of media. A dimension that is particularly important in IMC is creating, sustaining, and strengthening brand *relationships* over time. Relevant messages delivered through media that drive positive experiences create value for consumers. This value adds up over time and emerges as loyalty—the ultimate goal of relationship marketing programs.

Relationship marketing, a concept that originated with public relations, shifts the focus from the objective of getting a one-time purchase by a target to the maintenance of long-term involvement from all of the firm's critical stakeholders, whether employees, distributors, channel members, customers, agencies, investors, government agencies, the media, or community members. All stakeholders are seen as communicators who can send either positive or negative messages about the brand; therefore, it is important to keep in contact with them and keep them informed about brand programs (see Figure 11.3).

Channels to Contact Points

We have used the term *traditional media* in several places in recognition of the fact that the definition of media is changing. We've also mentioned *contact points*. These redefinitions are derived from technological change, from new patterns of consumer media use, and from changing business practices, particularly the introduction of the IMC perspective in marketing communication planning.

The thinking about contact points is an IMC-based idea that has redefined and broadened our understanding of media as a message delivery system. **Contact points** are the various ways

A MATTER OF PRACTICE

Thoughts about Media Evolution and Revolution

Bruce Bendinger, *Owner, The Copy Workshop*

The economic and recession issues aside, what's going on, simply put, is the evolution of our media—and our media usage. Marshall McLuhan offered some insights—as does history.

When we shifted to books, we had more than an increased appetite for ink and paper. We had the Reformation, the 30 Years' War, and a few years later, the American Revolution—all driven by the printing press. It's no accident that one of the most important (and most successful) individuals in the Colonies was a printer —Benjamin Franklin.

Moving right along, in *The World Is Flat*, Thomas Friedman quotes somebody who said "the printing press turned us into readers, the Xerox turned is into

publishers. Television turned us into viewers, the Internet is turning us into broadcasters."

The change in media usage in society is profound. It isn't just broken business models (my father was classified ad manager for a newspaper, a major cash cow, now gone to electronic pastures), it's brand new behaviors, and maybe more.

In that context, a Media Revolution, everything that's going on is . . . well, no surprise.

For you students, you're living in the middle of a recession/depression. But don't get recessed and depressed.

Rather think that you're living in the middle of a Media Revolution—and get excited—and start thinking the kinds of thoughts we'll all need to be having as we work our way into a rather interesting new age.

Long Live the Media Revolution!

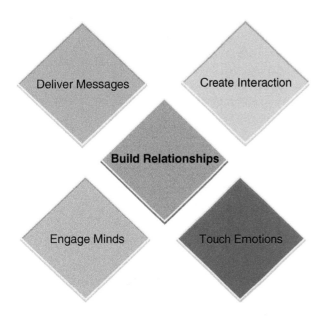

FIGURE 11.3
The Roles of IMC Media

a consumer comes in contact with a brand. This view of media moves from traditional advertising media (print, broadcast, outdoor) and the media of various marketing communication functions (press releases, events, promotional materials, sponsorships) to experiential contacts that in previous advertising-dominated media plans weren't generally considered to be media, such as word of mouth and customer service.

These opportunities are found in a huge variety of vehicles including everything from the traditional advertising media—newspapers and magazines, outdoor boards and posters, radio, and television—but also the Internet, telephone, directories, packages and labels, signs and building designs and ads painted on buildings, company trucks and cars, corporate letterhead and business cards, as well as all of the media of promotion, such as inflatables and airplane banners, and specialty items, such as calendars, coffee mugs, T-shirts, pens, refrigerator signs, and mouse pads, to name a few. The list is endless and can only be identified by studying the lives of customers to spot the points where they come in contact with a brand—or an opportunity for a brand experience or brand conversation.

In Chapter 7 we introduced the seventh principle of IMC: *All contact points deliver brand messages.* Another way to express the contact point idea in terms of our discussion here is: *Everything that delivers a message to a stakeholder about a brand is a contact point.* Contact point management, then, becomes the new way marketing communication planners develop systems of message delivery—and that includes both to and from all key stakeholders.

We also call them brand **touch points** in recognition of the impact these personal experiences can have on stakeholder feelings about a brand. A touch point is a brand experience that delivers a message that touches emotions leading to positive and negative judgments. A **critical touchpoint (CTP)** is one that connects the brand and customer on an emotional level and leads to a yes or no decision about a brand relationship.[11] The SAS lighted board placed in airports to reach SAS's business clients highlights the importance of these new brand connection opportunities.

Sometimes referred to as **experiential marketing,** touch-point strategies and programs use events and store design, among other means, to engage consumers in a personal and involving way. Some would argue that every brand contact is an experience; however, in experiential marketing the goal is to intensify active involvement beyond the more passive activity of reading, viewing, and listening to traditional media. The idea is to connect with consumers in ways that create higher levels of engagement, as well as lasting bonds with a brand.

Packaging   It's not a new function, but **packaging** is receiving increased attention as a key contact point. A package is both a container and a communication vehicle, and it works in the store and in the home or office. In particular, it is the last ad a customer sees before making the decision to buy a brand, as the Pepperidge Farm shelf photo illustrates. Although the focus of this discussion is primarily on packaging for goods, don't forget that services also are packaged in terms of such things as uniforms, other aspects of personal appearance, décor, and delivery vehicles.

The package is an important communication medium. Even if you can't afford a big advertising budget, you've got a chance to grab shopper attention if your product has a compelling image on the shelf." In an attempt to win over undecided consumers at the point of purchase, many manufacturers create innovative, eye-catching packages. Although the industry has never developed a standard for measuring impressions from a shelf, advertisers are aware of the billboarding effect of a massed set of packages, a practice that Pepperidge Farm uses to good effect. Once on the shelf at home or in the office, it is a constant brand reminder.

When the package works in unison with other marketing communication, it not only catches attention and presents a familiar brand image, it can communicate critical information and tie back to a current campaign. The package serves as a critical reminder of the product's important benefits at the moment the consumer is choosing among several competing brands.

Sometimes, the package itself is the focus of the advertising, particularly if there is a new size or innovation, such as Coca-Cola's introduction of a new bottle made from plant materials that is more compostable than plastic.[12] In sum, packaging is a constant communicator, an effective device for carrying advertising messages, and a strong brand reminder.

Packages can also deliver customer benefits. For example, recipes for Quaker Oats' famous Oatmeal Cookies, Nestlé's Tollhouse Cookies, Chex Party Mix, and Campbell's Green Bean Bake all started as promotional recipes on the product's packaging and turned into long-time favorites in homemakers' recipe boxes. There is even a website for these classic recipes (*www.backofthebox.com*) that features more than 1,500 recipes found on packaging.

Another use of packaging is found on milk cartons where cause-marketing campaigns, as well as other cross-promotions, have appeared. Missing children have been featured since the 1980s, but more recently ads on the half-pints given to school children act as tiny billboards promoting children's products such as kids movies. Larger milk cartons sold in stores promote local brands and sports teams, cereals, cookies, Honey Maid graham crackers, and Duncan Hines brownies.[13]

Packaging offers a way to deal with an ethical issue that bedevils some marketers—product ingredient and health effects labeling. A number of categories, such as household cleaners, have been challenged by consumers about the chemicals in their products. Steve Israel, a New York legislator, believes the problem can be addressed with mandatory labeling legislation. Tobacco companies are also being targeted, particularly in Europe where they are required to use a large part of the package for warning labels. Legislation has proposed that warning labels cover the top half of the front and back of cigarette packs and include frightening images, such as diseased lungs.[14]

Word of Mouth   Buzz is important because it means people are talking about a brand. This buzz may be the most important factor in consumer decision making because the recommendations of others are highly persuasive—more so than any advertisement. Given the engaging work of its agency, Crispin Porter + Bogusky, Burger King is often lauded as the "king of buzz." Tia Lang, interactive director at BK, says "Social media is very important in today's environment and we think generating buzz is a positive result in and of itself."

Pepperidge Farm, with its consistent design and distinctive brand image, dominates cookie shelves because of the power of its consistent design across all the brand's variations.

Principle
A package is the last ad a customer sees before making a decision on which brand to buy.

Principle
The goal of buzz-builder
strategies is to get the
right people saying the
right things about
the brand.

She explained that "We have done some innovative campaigns that have helped lead to 20 consecutive quarters of positive sales."[15]

A study of media use by the BIGresearch firm that polled 15,000 consumers found that the most influential form of media is word of mouth.[16] The goal is to get the right people talking about the brand and having them say things in support of the brand strategy. Some media plans are specifically designed to generate excited talk about something new, particularly if the strategies can reach influential or early adopters whose opinions are valued by others. One idea is that buzz is best generated by disrupting common patterns of thinking, or schemas. In other words, we talk about things that surprise and don't fit into our standard mental models.[17]

Viral Communication   An online version of buzz, viral communication describes the way a message spreads on the Internet. **Viral marketing** strategies are designed to create a groundswell of demand for a brand. However, the spread of messages depend totally on consumers creating buzz through their own e-mails and mentions on blogs, Facebook, YouTube, and Twitter. Brands can instigate the viral process, but not control it. An example comes from a McDonald's Filet-O-Fish special promotion that runs every year during Lent. In a parody of the "Big Mouth Billy Bass" gag gift, a fish hanging mounted on a plaque in a garage sings, "Give me back that Filet-O-Fish." The outlandish video has been viewed on YouTube more than a million times and has spawned ads and even a ring tone.[18]

One of the first viral hits was Burger King's "Subservient Chicken" which would respond to commands to do things like tap dance or do exercises. The site urged visitors to "tell their friends." Praised as possibly the most popular marketing website of all time, the site quickly registered half a billion hits in the first couple of weeks, as well as a big increase in sales of BK's chicken sandwiches. The creative team explained that BK's advertising was generally seen as boring and the "Subservient Chicken" was intended to make BK more edgy and fun. See the site and the story behind its complicated execution at *www.barbariangroup.com/portfolio/burger_king_subservient_chicken*.

A worry for planners is that viral messages can also spread negative stories or even be used to organize a boycott against a brand. As Simon Clift, Unilever's chief marketing officer, explains, "No matter how big your advertising spending, small groups of consumers on a tiny budget might hijack the conversation."[19]

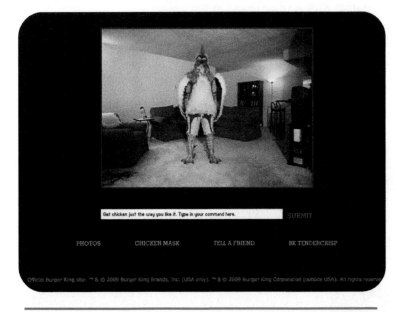

Get chicken just the way you like it. Type in your command here.   SUBMIT

PHOTOS   CHICKEN MASK   TELL A FRIEND   BK TENDERCRISP

Official Burger King site: ™ & © 2009 Burger King Brands, Inc. (USA only). ™ & © 2009 Burger King Corporation (outside USA). All rights reserved

CLASSIC
With the line, "Get chicken just the way you like it," Burger King's agency, Crispin Porter + Bogusky, launched the "Subservient Chicken" interactive video website for Burger King. Play with the "Subservient Chicken" (*www.cpbgroup.com/awards/subservientchicken.html*) and see if you think it is captivating. Why would it have been so popular at the time it was introduced?

Customer Service   It's not a new business function, but it is new to marketing communication planners who, in the past, were seldom involved in planning or monitoring this critical connection with customers. **Customer service** represents a company's attitude and behavior during interactions with customers. These interactions send some of the most impactful brand messages that customers receive. If the interactive experience is positive, it will strengthen the customer relationship; if it is negative, it can weaken or even destroy a customer's brand relationship.

The importance of customer service as a contact point that delivers positive (or negative) brand experiences is reflected in a campaign by online retailer Zappos.com that demonstrates to customers how its customer service representatives make it easy to order or return merchandise. Called "zappets," the puppet-like characters in the ads are based on actual Zappos.com employees, whom the company calls its "customer loyalty team."

Because customers have so many choices of brands and shopping outlets, how a company treats customers can be the major reason for choosing one over the others. Why has Southwest Airlines been so successful when competitors have faced bankruptcy? The primary reason is customer service. Marketing communication planners don't "manage" customer service in most companies, but they can monitor the messages that are being sent at this critical touch point.

New Consumer Media Use Patterns

Consumers' use of media is changing as fast as the technology. It used to be that most American audiences were involved with three television networks, a newspaper, and one or two magazines. The modern media landscape includes up to 200 television channels in some markets, a huge number of special interest publications, millions of websites, and new and novel media, such as Kindle, iPad, and Twitter, that hadn't even been imagined five years ago. Here are other trends:

- Media consumers are active, in control, and entertained.
- Lives are media focused.
- Personal life has become public.
- Global has become local.

Rather than controlling media choices, consumers are much more in control of their own media and designing their own media landscapes—from video games to Twitter. The people formerly known as "audiences" are creating their own content, a practice we have referred to as *consumer-generated content,* such as the homemade videos and commercials seen on YouTube and personalized audio listening courtesy of the iPod and other MP3 players. Entertainment has become as much of a driving force for modern digital media as news was for traditional media.

Two major changes in media use patterns are media-driven lives and media multitasking. In their youthful days the traditionalists' and baby boomers' lives were dominated by work and family activities. In contrast, more recent generations spend more time with media of all kinds, and those channels are more intertwined with their family, work, and leisure time. People not only spend more time with media, they use more than one medium at a time.[20]

Traditionally most media involved a solitary experience—reading a paper or listening to radio, for example, but another transformation is the creation of truly social media. First there were blogs, then MySpace and Facebook, then Twitter—all of which made personal space public. The immediacy and intimacy of a phone conversation has exploded into millions of interactions via Twitter. (Think about this: if you can send 1 million tweets, are you broadcasting? You probably don't know the 1 million recipients—so has Twitter become a form of mass media?)

It used to be that global media were limited in number and generally media were limited by national boundaries—most media, particularly newspapers, radio, and television, were primarily local. The Internet changed all that. You can be on an island in Indonesia and still text about your experiences to friends back home. Most travelers from Western countries are connected to their media wherever they are in the world. Some countries, such as China, try to control the Internet access of their citizens, but most people are able to travel the world of the Web logging into sites without consideration of where they are or where the site comes from.

New and Alternative Forms of Contact

This is the most creative time in the history of commercial media. We talk about new, converging, and emerging media—older media are converging with new media and new forms are being created faster than we can learn how to use them. We also use the term *nontraditional media* to refer to alternative forms of contact, such as product placement, video games, and guerilla marketing. Melissa Lerner, a specialist

ACTUAL CALL WITH ZAPPOS.COM

Zappos.com celebrates its customer service representative in a campaign that reiterates the company's value propositions, "Happy to help. 24/7" by showing how its employees—albeit in sock puppet form—interact with customers.

Principle
If an interaction is positive, it can strengthen a customer–brand relationship; if negative, it can weaken or destroy a brand relationship.

Principle
Entertainment is as much of a driving force for modern digital media as news was for traditional media.

Place/Affinity Based
Place-Based Broadcast:
Airport TV
In-Store TV/Radio
Mall TV
Physician/Pharmacy TV
Theatre Radio

Affinity-Based:
Bar/Restaurant Media
Cinema
C-Store Media
College Media
Day Care Center Media
Gas/Service Station Media
Golf Media
Health Club Media
In-Flight Media
In-Office Building Media
In-School Media
In-Stadium Media
In-Store Media
Leisure Media
Physician Media
Ski Media
VIP Airline Lounge Media
Wild Posters

Alternative/Guerrilla
Alternative:
Aerial Media
Custom Media
Event Sponsorships
Experiential Media
Interactive Kiosks
Naming Rights
Projection Media
Sampling
Specialty Media
Sports Sponsorship
Travel Affinity Sponsorships
New Technology

Guerrilla Media:
Coffee Cups/Sleeves
Graffiti Murals
Mobile Media (i.e. AdVans)
Pizza Boxes
Street Teams
Umbrellas
Deli Bags

FIGURE 11.4

Nontraditional Media

New-media specialist Melissa Lerner says, "Clients are demanding more unique plans and ideas than ever before because impact and engagement help them to become trendsetters in their respective industries." She describes these as exciting "never done before" campaigns.

Lerner earned a B.S. in Business and Economics from Lehigh University.

in new-media planning who formerly worked at WOW, a division of Kinetic Worldwide, described nontraditional media as including merging media and digital enhancements, place-based, branded environments, and guerilla executions (see Figure 11.4). She observes, "There is nothing better than working on a nontraditional media concept that comes to fruition and generates exciting PR and buzz within a marketplace."

The search for nontraditional media—that is, new ways to reach target audiences—is particularly important for advertisers trying to reach the elusive youth market, since teens are often the first to experiment with new media forms. In some ways, this search for innovative ways to deliver messages is just as creative as the message concepts developed on the creative side of advertising. That's why one of the principles of this book is that the media side can be just as creative as the creative side of advertising.

Guerilla Marketing A really hot area of alternative marketing communication is **guerilla marketing,** which uses the power of involvement to create memorable brand experiences. This place-based strategy creates unexpected personal encounters with a brand, such as painted messages on streets or costumed brand characters parading across a busy intersection creating excitement, as well as buzz about a brand.

The idea is to use creative ways to reach people where they live, work, and walk to create a personal connection and a high level of impact. If it works, the encounter gets talked about, creating a buzz moment. Sears used computer-equipped Segways on Michigan Avenue in Chicago to launch its online layaway program. Wireless carrier Vodaphone used holographic ads featuring Portuguese soccer players dribbling balls for the opening of one of its concept stores in Portugal.

A form of guerilla marketing you're probably familiar with are the sign holders hired by local businesses to promote their stores or special marketing events. Most sign holders simply stand and wave or do little dances to catch drivers' attention, but there is an art form in sign spinning, similar to break dancing, that calls for athletic prowess and dramatic moves to present an involved choreography. Also called "human directionals," they specialize in street corner advertising.

More about matching wits than matching budgets, guerilla marketing has limited reach but high impact. For example, Sony Ericsson Mobile Communications Ltd. hired actors to create buzz about a new mobile phone that is also a digital camera. The actors pretended to be tourists who wanted their picture taken, thus allowing consumers to try the product. As a typical guerilla marketing campaign, it only reached those who encountered the actors. Sometimes a guerilla marketing campaign will generate publicity that extends the impact.

Product Placement For years we have been exposed to **product placement,** in which a brand appears in a television program, movie, or even in print as a prop. With product placement, a company pays to have verbal or visual brand exposure in a movie or television program. George Clooney's movie *Up in the Air,* for example, prominently features American Airlines and Hilton Hotels as "integrated marketers." Media analysts estimate that Apple Computer and Pontiac each received over $25,000 in media value through placements in the television series *24.*[21]

Product placement has become important because it isn't as intrusive as conventional advertising, and audiences can't zap the ads, as they can for television advertising using the remote control or a DVR. At the same time, it may make the product a star—or at least be associated with a star. Sometimes the product placement is subtle as when a particular brand of aspirin is shown in a medicine chest or a character drinks a particular brand of beverage. In other cases, the brand is front

These painted stairs at the Denver Pavilions and the entertainment complex in downtown Denver is an example of guerilla marketing. It is also a "captive ad" because it is unavoidable for people walking up the stairs.

and center. That happened with the prominent role of a BMW Z28, which became a star in the James Bond movie *The World Is Not Enough.* The movie placement, in fact, was the car's launch vehicle.

Television programs have also gotten into the product placement game. Both the Coca-Cola brand and the Ford Motor brand have been embedded into the successful talent show *American Idol,* and the Target bulls-eye is frequently seen as part of the action sets and props on *Survivor.*

The greatest advantage of product placement is that it demonstrates product use in a natural setting ("natural" depending on the movie) by people who are celebrities. It's unexpected and, if it's an obvious use, may catch the audience when their resistance to advertising messages may be dialed down. It's also good for engaging the affections of other stakeholders, such as employees and dealers, particularly if the placement is supported with its own campaign.

The biggest problem is that the placement may not be noticed. There is so much going on in most movies that unless you can overtly call attention to the product, its appearance may not register. A more serious problem occurs when there is not a match between the product and the movie or its audience. Another concern is that advertisers have no idea whether the movie will be a success or failure as they negotiate a contract for the placement. If the movie is a dud, what does that do to the brand's image?

Another problem is an ethical one—when is a product placement inappropriate? For example, some pharmaceutical marketers have found that a product "plug" can be a way around the FDA's requirements on the disclosure of side effects. Public policy critics warn that it's not just drugs; the problem exists for weapons, alcohol, tobacco, and gambling, among other product categories that raise social concerns. Product placement has been called "stealth advertising," by the Writers Guild of America who argued that "millions of viewers are sometimes being sold products without their knowledge . . . and sold in violation of governmental regulations."[22] What do you think? Should there be more controls over product placement?

Video Games   Marketers and media planners have been frustrated trying to reach young people with traditional ads on mainstream media. That has led to an increased focus on Internet advertising, but also on unusual media that are clearly the province of young people, such as video games. Now a global multibillion-dollar industry, the video game business is developing as a major new medium for advertisers to target 12- to 34-year-old males, although girls are getting into the act as well, and Wii is bringing in an older adult audience of both men and women with its sports and exercise programs. The iPad made the video game market mobile. Video games offer opportunities for advertising, but also for product placement.

Guitar Hero: Smash Hits is an Activision video game released in 2009. The game basically has the same content as the older versions of *Guitar Hero,* except that it only has songs

released on previous *Guitar Hero* games that are supposed to be fan favorites and the most fun to play, so in that way *Smash Hits* is like the video game version of a "Greatest Hits" album. Diego Contreras, interactive art director at Crispin Porter + Bogusky explained the thinking behind an online promotion for *Smash Hits:* "We divided the songs in nine categories such as Best Scream, Best Shred (guitar solo), and Song of the Year. On the site, each category had a fun video with humorous voice-overs calling out the nominees, in the same fashion as the Oscars or the MTV Music Awards." Check out the site at *http://smashhits.guitarhero.com.*

Marketing communication opportunities will be mined both by creating online games as well as placing products within games. For example, games feature product placements for Puma athletic shoes, Nokia mobile phones, and Skittles candies, among others. Volkswagen of America bought a placement on Sony Computer Entertainment's *Gran Turismo 3* car-racing game. These questions remain: How are game players responding to ads in games and when does it make sense to incorporate branded content in games? Are some brands more acceptable or appropriate than others?

Branded Entertainment   Similar to product placement, the use of the media of entertainment to engage consumers with brands is referred to as **advertainment** or **branded entertainment.** In some cases, companies may produce films for the Internet where the brand is integrated into the storyline, such as an award-winning and ground-breaking series of mini-films for BMW, titled "The Hire." You may remember Geico's popular cavemen characters who became a television program.

We introduced the Altoids story in the last chapter. Primarily a print campaign in the past, Altoids has also moved with the times and created a video series of branded entertainment called "Brainstorm," created in conjunction with Fox Mobile Studios. Targeted at young, hip, urban audiences, these edgy videos are about an advertising agency as it tries to develop a new campaign for the curiously strong mint. Time will tell how successful this effort is as it puts the story behind Altoids on the small screen.

Similar to television programs with recurring episodes in a developing story, **webisodes** have created a new form of Web advertising. Fallon Worldwide created the original experiment in this new format for its client BMW. Known as the "BMW films," the series consisted of high-action mini-movies by well-known action movie directors (John Woo, Guy Ritchie, and Ang Lee), all of which featured various BMW models in starring roles. This practice has become particularly popular in China where increasingly marketers are building plots around their products, particularly lifestyle products that expose viewers to visions of how the newly rich should enjoy their healthy incomes.[23]

An example of branded entertainment is described in *The Inside Story* feature, which explains how an animated program was created for the male-grooming brand Axe. It took almost three years and more than 100 people in four different continents to produce the program titled *City Hunters*. The creative team was composed of award-winning screenwriters, novelists, and creatives under the direction of the Catmandu Branded Entertainment company. The integrated launch campaign featured a special edition package with *City Hunters* characters. The 360-degree promotional effort for the show included:

The Animated Axe Effect in City Hunters

Sonia Scappaticci, *New Business Director, Catmandu Branded Entertainment*

Branded entertainment has become something of a buzzword. Perhaps because global marketers are beginning to understand that the 30-second spot is not the whole answer to creating brand positioning and value.

Unilever's Axe brand has consistently created adventurous advertising that has helped position it as the world's top male-grooming brand. When Unilever launched into the branded entertainment realm in Latin America, it was very specific in its goal: to create a TV show for the Axe brand that was fresh, attractive, relevant, and, most important of all, that would help the brand's positioning to go even further. It had to be unlike anything ever seen before. High ratings at any cost were not the objective, but rather creating a show that would be watched by the right target and would live up to the Axe brand standards.

The result was *City Hunters*, an animated show that launched on the Fox Network in Latin America. Because Axe is about the mating game, the show had to be created in a universe where sensuality and seduction were always in the air. Character designs where commissioned to legendary Italian comic artist Milo Manara, famous for his sexy female drawings. It is the story of a master, an apprentice, and a secret society called the "X Lodge," whose members are experts in the art of seduction. The main characters are Dr. Lynch, a retired bon vivant rumored to have been one of the inventors of the original Axe fragrance in the 1970s, and Axel, a street-

smart young man who doesn't have trouble meeting women—just understanding them. According to the story, "The Axe Effect" is the compilation of more than 2,000 years of the study of women.

Until not so long ago, it would have been unimaginable to believe a network was going to pay the advertiser in order to co-produce a branded entertainment show. However, when we approached Fox with the *City Hunters* project, it was an instant match. For starters, the show was an animation, enabling it to be easily adaptable to different markets. Second, the format of the show made sense. The series of 10 short films could be aired in sets of two as a regular half-hour show, but could also be broadcast individually if needed.

In terms of results, *City Hunters* premiered as a weekly show in Argentina, where is was first aired, as Fox's number one show of the year (male viewers ages 18 to 24), reaching similar ratings as hit shows like *24* and *Nip/Tuck*. It was then aired in all of Latin America to similar top rating results. There are thousands of blog postings about the show. We also received a lot of media coverage from consumer magazines that index heavy with our target market, like *Rolling Stone* and *Playboy*. However, most importantly, the special-edition *City Hunters* packaging was a success and sold out immediately, even though it was priced higher that the regular product.

Sonia Scappaticci graduated from Michigan State University in 2000 with a B.A. in advertising. While at MSU, she was named one of the 25 Most Promising Minority Students in Communication by AAF and Advertising Age. She was nominated by Professor Carrie La Ferle.

- *Launch Parties* Celebrities and models depicted the show's characters.
- *Website* A dedicated website featured all of the show's info.
- *Text Messaging* Mating game tips were sent by the show's main character.
- *Interactive Billboards* Consumers could text a message that would change the image in the billboards.
- *In-Store Video Trailers* Special displays and flat screens were used to promote the show.
- *Sweepstakes* Prizes such as iPods were given away with a complete *City Hunters* season, merchandising, etc.

Mobile Marketing   The phone is the classic example of how media are shape shifting. Telephones, of course, started as a hard-wired home and office device connected by phone lines. With the development of satellite-based and broadband telecommunication, the cell phone has become the all-purpose personal communication tool. **Smart phones,** such as BlackBerry, the iPhone, and Google's Nexus One, are high-end cell phones that have computing and photographic capabilities and can access the Internet, as well as do all of the old telephone functions. The iPad is a hybrid that has some of the capabilities of smart phones. It combines some of the features of a laptop or notebook computer, with an e-reader (books, newspapers, magazines), a video viewer, and a video game player.

The most versatile of all media, the smart cell phones provide music, movies, photography, video games, personal conversation, shopping, and access to all the news and information available on the Internet. The leaders in the development of these new tools have been Scandinavian countries and Japan; the United States is just catching up with these high-tech countries that have been using smart phones for years.

Messages on mobile phones usually look like small banners tucked into the corner of a Web page or text messages that can resemble spam. Mobile marketing agency AdMob and Google have designed more visual ads, some even showing maps with a retailer's location or apps that allow users to watch a commercial between levels in a video game.[24]

Cell phones also launched new product lines such as graphic faceplates and specialty ring tones. Female teenagers were leaders in exploring **text messaging (TM)** on their cell phones and teaching others (their parents, older siblings, teachers). **Instant messaging (IM),** in which two people chat via their computers, has been used more for business, as has the Bluetooth technology, which keeps businesspeople in touch with their companies and clients wherever they are.

In addition to becoming essential communication, information, and entertainment tools in most people lives, cell phones also open up new avenues for commercial communication. **Mobile marketing** is the strategy based on reaching people on the run via their cell phones. It refers to the use of wireless communication (WiFi) and GPS locational devices to reach people on the move with geotargeting capabilities. The Mobile Marketing Association (MMA) defines *mobile marketing* as the use of wireless media, primarily cellular phones and personal digital assistants (PDAs), such as RIM's BlackBerry. But mobile marketing is more than just cell phones and PDAs; it also includes laptop computers and even portable game consoles as vehicles that can deliver content and encourage direct response within a cross-media communication program. Mobile marketing includes instant messaging, video messages and downloads, and banner ads on these mobile devices. The MMA reported that U.S. advertising expenditures on mobile marketing increased by more than 20 percent in 2009 and predicted similar increases during the 2010s.[25]

It is possible, for example, to send text messages or voice mail with news about special sales to people's cell phones or PDAs that use wireless technology (such as Bluetooth) when these customers are in the vicinity of a favorite store or restaurant. If a cell phone user, for example, registers with a favorite store, then that store can contact the user when he or she is in the neighborhood. These calls can announce special deals or invite the customer in for a taste test or some other type of promotion. If the call is not an opt-in message, then it can be intrusive and irritating. The phones can also be used to contact a store. Pizza Hut and Papa John's customers, for example, can use their smart phones to place orders and, by dragging and dropping toppings onto virtual pizzas, they can create their own personal pizza. Domino's features a simulated photographic version on its website that can be customized.[26]

Although IM/TM advertising—primarily in the form of product notices—is big in Japan, it's still seen as an invasion of privacy in the United States. Even with the huge increase in texting, particularly by 18- to 24-year-olds (95 percent use texting), it's a puzzle for marketers because, as *Advertising Age* reported, "it is very much a permission-based channel of communication."[27]

As in other forms of advertising, the way to be less intrusive is to be more relevant and offer opt-in options. Teens may permit advertising if it offers them information they want, such as news about music, games, sports, cosmetics, and fashion. In Japan, a bar code can be sent for a free sample or some other promotion. Like a free coupon, it can be redeemed when a cashier scans the code.

The emerging area of mobile marketing helps companies connect with customers in new ways and new places.

Branded Apps   An *app*, short for *application,* is a piece of software than runs on your computer, cell phone, or social networking site. Thousands of apps are available that serve as links to other sites or provide some kind of immediate service, such as weather reports or current news. The number of iPhone apps now exceeds 100,000. The Google Droid operating system was launched with a Google Map app as a point of competitive advantage.

Marketers are particularly interested in **branded apps,** which are generally free but prominently linked to a brand. For example, REI has an app for snow reports. Zippo has a free virtual lighter for iPhones that looks and acts like a real lighter. You can jerk the phone to open or close the Zippo and a little button let's you light it with a simple flick. The point is strictly brand identification but there is a bit of utility in using a cell phone for that Zippo moment in concerts when people hold up their lights—in this case, images of a Zippo on their iPhones. It's almost a toy but the engagement with the brand has made the Zippo app one of the more popular ones.[28]

Other apps offer more utility. Banks, for example, let you check balances, pay bills, make transfers, and locate branches—and with the GPS navigation capability in some smart phones, the app can even plot a route. A Starbucks app features a Starbucks location finder. Kraft's app, iFood Assistant, which is one of the few that comes with a price tag, provides recipes, cooking instruction videos, meal shopping lists, and store locators. CNN also offers a functional app that provides a 24-hour news feed with video for a one-time fee of $1.99.

The launch of Apple's App Store propelled the development of thousands of branded apps. The concept is showcased in some of Apple and AT&T's full-page ads in publications that show the iPhone with a suite of apps accompanied by callouts that explain what the apps do. You can check out the App Store at *www.apple.com/iphone/apps-for-iphone/phone.*

Other New Media   We have said before that media needs creative ideas just as much as the creative side does. There is a continual search for a novel way to get consumers engaged with a brand.

As we mentioned in the discussion of mobile marketing, **streaming videos** from professional media companies—including television programs and movies—are joining homemade creations like those from YouTube and appear not only on personal computers, but also on smart phones, such as iPhones. Nintendo is now adding Netflix as streaming video to its Wii video game console.[29] These creations can be as engaging as anything on conventional television. For example, CBS has created a cell phone app video game of *America's Next Top Model* where viewers can play with animated versions of the show, pick dresses, and experiment with the stars' makeup. (See it at *http://topmodel.pressokentertainment.com.*) Skype software has continued to innovate with international Internet-based phone service.

Another innovation using streaming video is the **viral video.** Technology has made it possible for interesting videos from a variety of sources (ads, films, YouTube) to be sent from one friend to another in a vast network of personal connections. *Advertising Age* keeps track of the most watched viral videos, such as the various episodes in the Mac vs. Microsoft battle of operating systems. *AdAge* reports that one of the more entertaining videos is for an unlikely company name Microbilt, which provides a risk management service for small and medium businesses. Rhett & Link is a team of YouTubers who created a microsite, *www.ilovelocalcommercials.com,* to promote themselves as ad creators. They sponsored a contest to get nominations for other local businesses who would then win equally engaging videos created by this geek team. Check out the site to see their self-promotion, as well as some of their creations, all of which have been distributed as viral videos.[30]

But innovation isn't focused only on digital forms. A YouTube video that captured a lot of attention showed tiny banners on flies that flitted around with their miniscule billboards—probably the ultimate in guerilla marketing. This Big Media Idea came from the German agency Jung von Matt. Check it out at *www.youtube.com/ watch?v=nVxTAz67SAI.*

Flies are the most unlikely of all media, but they were enlisted by German publisher Eichborn as a form of flying banners at the annual Frankfurt Book Fair.

Other new media include ads by Visa on stadium trays used at the Super Bowl concession stands, opening the door for a whole new medium.[31] Here's a review of the advantages and limitations of some of the new and nontraditional media we've discussed in this chapter.

Nontraditional Media Advantages and Limitations

Medium	Advantages	Limitations
Packaging	Stimulates point-of-purchase decision making Last ad a potential customer sees In-home is brand reminder on shelf Billboarding effect can dominate shelf Reinforces brand advertising Delivers product information Packaging costs are required, conveying promotional message is a bonus	Cluttered environment Shelf space may be limited Can get inconvenient placement—such as bottom shelf Limited space needs simple message Needs system for ROI evaluation
Guerilla Marketing	Engages people at unexpected places Highly involved Creates high level of excitement Generates buzz	Small reach Needs publicity
Product Placement	Harder to dismiss as advertising Opportunity for high visibility in natural setting Opportunity for brand reminder	May be overlooked Vehicle may not match the brand's positioning Not as much control over brand's presentation Hard to control targeting Hard to measure effectiveness
Branded Entertainment	The program or game is a vehicle for the brand Can reach new-media savvy audiences Harder to dismiss than advertising Takes advantage of power of film and engaging storylines More control over brand presentation than product placement More time to develop brand personality Opportunity for repetition	Viewers may resent the commercialization of programs/games Needs marketing support Effectiveness measures are still in development
Mobile Marketing	Goes everywhere the target goes Opportunity for location-based message The most personal of all media—also the most social Reaches the technologically savvy	Small screen Unwanted messages can be irritating Hard to type messages on small keyboard Effectiveness measures are still in development Needs technological literacy
Branded Apps	Opportunity for continuing brand contact Engages attention Links social media and their users to brands Provides utility functions for brands Strictly opt-in	Started free, but now some are charging which creates irritation On cell phone, limited by small screen size Opportunity for tracking use

Looking Ahead

We started out by noting that the media environment is going through lots of shifts and we ended by detailing some of those changes. With this brief introduction to the basics of marketing communication media, as well as the new and nontraditional forms of media, we turn now in the next chapter to a review of traditional media—print, outdoor, and broadcast—and the characteristics that make them different from other media forms.

Axe Cleans Up

As you read throughout this chapter, reaching consumers in a complex and rapidly changing media environment challenges advertisers to think creatively. Those who will be successful in advertising break through the clutter and deliver messages that are relevant to the consumer. The Axe campaigns you read about in the case opener, "How Dirty Boys Get Clean" and "Axe Detailer: The Manly Shower Tool," demonstrate how marketing contributed to making Axe the top male shower brand in the United States.

After the Detailer was introduced, sales exceeded expectations. For example, the number of units sold per Walmart store per week more than doubled that of other shower gel products. The campaign was so successful, many stores had trouble keeping Axe Shower Gel on the shelves. Share of market increased as well, peaking with the communication activity. Tracking studies indicated that the Detailer campaign achieved the goals of communicating the correct branding and teaching something about the product.

Demonstrating another way to clean up, Axe has won many advertising awards, including an Effie and two Bronze Lions from the Cannes International Advertising Festival.

If you read "The Animated Axe Effect in *City Hunters*" in this chapter you realized that Axe is a global brand. You read about Axe's efforts to create branded entertainment. Other award-winning work is occurring across the globe. Mindshare won "best localization" for its multinational work at the Valencia Festival of Media in Spain for a campaign that centered around the concept that "men should be as irresistible as chocolate" to women. To give you an idea about how this worked, French girls gave guys "nibbles and licks" on a social networking site, while in Belgium, luxury chocolate love tokens were distributed. Portuguese guys were coaxed into buying chocolate, seducing girls, and possibly winning a visit to the Chocolate Pleasure Mansion. These sparkling efforts show the extent to which creative ideas can be applied to a variety of media and contexts, all to achieve the same effect—to sell the product.

Key Points Summary

1. **How do media work in marketing communication and how is the industry organized?** Media send and return messages to and from the company or brand and its customers—in other words, they make connections. Media deliver messages and also offer opportunities for interaction; they also touch emotions, engage minds, and build brand relationships. Media has evolved technologically from print to broadcasting and now the Internet. Marketing communication is evolving to include more Internet-based media. Types of media include mass and niche media, as well as addressable, interactive, and measured media. Key players both sell and buy media space and time; they include media salespeople and reps, media researchers, media planners, and media buyers.

2. **How would you describe the key strategic media concepts?** A media plan, which is prepared by a media planner, is a document that identifies the media to be used to deliver an advertising message to a targeted audience both locally and nationally. A media mix is the way various types of media are strategically combined in an advertising plan. Reach is the percentage of the media audience exposed at least once to the advertiser's message during a specific time frame, and frequency is the number of times a person is exposed to the advertisement.

3. **Why and how is the media landscape changing?** More media are available to today's audience as the concept of media channels is redefined to mean contact points and touch points, which include experiences, word of mouth, viral communication, and customer service, in addition to traditional media. Media use is changing with consumers spending a lot more time with media and multitasking more as they are engaged with media. As media have become more social, people's personal lives have gone public and global is the new local. Media forms are also changing with new ways to reach people being included in marketing communication plans, such as packaging, product placement, guerilla marketing, video games, branded entertainment, mobile marketing, branded apps, and a variety of other new media.

Words of Wisdom: Recommended Reading

Azzaro, Marian, *Strategic Media Decisions,* 2nd ed., Chicago: The Copy Workshop, 2008.

Davis, Scott, and Philip Kotler, *The Shift: The Transformation of Today's Marketers into Tomorrow's Growth Leaders,* San Francisco CA: John Wiley & Sons, 2009.

Garfield, Bob, *The Chaos Scenario,* Nashville, TN: Stielstra Publishing, 2009.

McConnell, Ben, and Jackie Huba, *Citizen Marketers: When People Are the Message,* Chicago: Kaplan Publishing, 2007.

Warner, Charles, and Joseph Buchman, *Media Selling: Broadcast, Cable, Print, and Interactive,* Ames: Iowa State Press, 2004.

Key Terms

addressable media, p. 355
advertainment, p. 372
branded apps, p. 375
branded entertainment, p. 372
broadcasting media, p. 355
brokers, p. 360
circulation, p. 363
contact points, p. 365
convergence, p. 356
critical touchpoint (CTP), p. 366
cross-media, p. 360
customer service, p. 368
engagement, p. 356

experiential marketing, p. 366
exposure, p. 363
frequency, p. 363
gross impressions, p. 363
guerilla marketing, p. 370
impression, p. 363
instant messaging (IM), p. 374
interactivity, p. 356
intrusiveness, p. 364
mass media, p. 355
measured media, p. 355
media, p. 354
media buyer, p. 360
media mix, p. 362

media plan, p. 360
media planners, p. 360
media planning, p. 360
media reps, p. 360
media researchers, p. 360
media salespeople, p. 359
media vehicle, p. 355
mobile marketing, p. 374
multichannel, p. 360
multiplatform, p. 362
niche media, p. 355
packaging, p. 366
personalization, p. 356
product placement, p. 370

ratings, p. 363
ratings points, p. 363
reach, p. 363
relationship marketing, p. 365
sales kits, p. 359
share of audience, p. 363
smart phones, p. 373
streaming video, p. 375
text messaging (TM), p. 374
touch point, p. 366
viral marketing, p. 368
viral video, p. 375
webisode, p. 372
word-of-mouth, p. 357

Review Questions

1. Trace the evolution of media forms and explain how the new Digital Era is different from previous media environments.

2. Explain the roles of media salespeople, media planners, media buyers, and media researchers.

3. What is a media mix and how does the mix differ for an IMC campaign?

4. What is the difference between reach and frequency?

5. What is the difference between media channels, contact points, and touch points?

6. In what ways are consumer media patterns changing and how does that affect marketing communication.

7. Why have product placement, guerilla marketing, and branded entertainment become popular?

Discussion Questions

1. You are the media planner for an agency handling a small chain of upscale furniture outlets in a top-50 market that concentrates most of its advertising in the Sunday supplement of the local newspaper. The owner is interested in using new media to reach its upscale target market. What would be your recommendations to the furniture store owner?

2. Since his freshman year in college, Phil Dawson, an advertising major, has waited tables at Alfredo's, a small family-operated restaurant featuring excellent Italian food and an intimate atmosphere. The restaurant has relied on its Yellow Pages ads to generate business. The owner asks Phil for advice on what other contact points are important and how he

should use them in his admittedly low-budget marketing communication plan. What should Phil recommend?

3. *Three-Minute Debate* This chapter makes the argument that traditional advertising is declining in importance. A classmate argues that these media are still the most important and largest item in most marketing communication plans. If you are the marketing manager for the Segway personal transportation device, would you devote the largest percentage of your budget to traditional or nontraditional media? Take one side or the other of this argument and work with a small group of your classmates to argue your point of view.

Take-Home Projects

1. *Portfolio Project* Collect a set of three traditional media ads that also have online versions. Compare the original with the online version and analyze the differences. What does the traditional medium offer that is not available online, and what does the online version add to the offerings of the original medium.

   Write a one- or two-page report on how these vehicles might better position themselves as advertising media. What are their strengths and how should they position themselves in a competitive media marketplace?

2. *Mini-Case Analysis* Reread the Axe story at the beginning of this chapter. What was the problem this brand faced and how did that affect the media planning? What were the objectives of both the initial campaign and its follow-up? What was the Big Idea that drove the second campaign and how did that affect the media mix. Do you think this effort was driven by reach or frequency? Considering all of the new media reviewed in this chapter, what other media might Axe use in the next year of this campaign?

Team Project: The BrandRevive Campaign

For your BrandRevive campaign, revisit the research your team did on your brand's category or market and, specifically on the brand's target customer. What did you find out about their media use?

- What more do you need to know in order to develop a comprehensive media plan? What other research would be useful?
- From what you found out in your consumer research, what traditional media do you think are important to deliver this brand's message?

- How many different contact points can you identify for this brand? What are its touch points, the critical experiential points of contact that really affect people's attitudes and feelings about the brand?
- What nontraditional media do you think would be useful? In particular, how can you better engage your brand's customers with the brand?

Present and explain your analysis in a two-page document and a PowerPoint presentation that is no longer than three slides.

Hands-On Case

The Century Council

Read the Century Council case in the Appendix before coming to class.

1. Explain the concepts of reach and frequency in relation to The Stupid Drink Campaign. How did the team attempt to reach their target consumer at the right moment?

2. Which element of The Stupid Drink media plan do you believe would be most impactful on your campus? Why? Which would be least impactful? Why?

3. If you were asked to execute The Stupid Drink campaign on your campus, what advertising medium might you add to strengthen the plan? Why?

12 Traditional Media

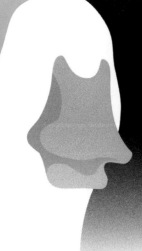

youdontknowquack.com

It's a Winner

Title:	**Client:**	**Agency:**	**Awards:**
"You Don't Know Quack"	American Family Life Assurance Company	Zimmerman Agency of Tallahassee, Florida; previously Linda Kaplan Thaler	Gold Effie; selected by online voters, Aflac duck icon enshrined on Madison Avenue's Advertising Walk of Fame

CHAPTER KEY POINTS

1. What key points should marketers know to make effective decisions about advertising in newspapers and magazines?
2. What factors do marketers consider when making out-of-home media advertising decisions?
3. How do radio and television work as marketing communication media?
4. How do marketers use movies and other video formats for marketing communication?

Quacking through Clutter

Geico. Allstate. Nationwide. Met Life. Many insurance companies are begging for your attention. You've probably never heard of the American Family Life Assurance Co., nor are you likely to be familiar with its primary service: supplemental workplace medical insurance, a type of insurance that is used by people to help cover the many loopholes and deductibles in their primary insurance coverage.

Then again, if you are like 94 percent of U.S. consumers, maybe you *have* heard of the company. In its advertising, it calls itself "Aflac."

Introduced in 2000, the long-running Aflac campaign featuring the quacking duck was the brainchild of the New York agency that bears its owner's name, Linda Kaplan Thaler. Almost all ads feature a white duck desperately screaming "Aflac!" at unsuspecting people who presumably need supplemental insurance. Alas, the duck's audience never quite seems to hear him. Most of the ads contain a fair amount of slapstick, usually at the expense of the duck, whose exasperated-sounding voice originates with former *Saturday Night Live* cast member Gilbert Gottfried.

The campaign has been enormously successful. Since its inception, brand name awareness increased from 12 percent to more than 90 percent. *Ad Age* has named a commercial featuring the duck as one of the most recalled ads in the country. Forbes named Aflac one of the Top 25 Power Brands in the United States in 2004. By 2004, sales of the multibillion-dollar corporation had increased by 20 percent.

What a bargain. By one account, Aflac spent a poultry, scratch that, paltry sum of $45 million on television advertising annually. Compare that to McDonald's $680 million annual ad budget, which supports Ronald McDonald, or Energizer, whose company has plunked down about $1 billion on its Bunny advertising during the past 35 years. So, the duck has been quite a bargain in terms of getting attention.

The spokesfowl is not without his problems, however. It seems that the duck gets all the attention. Everyone knows it as an advertising icon, but customers don't know what it sells. The next generation of ducky advertising is addressing that very problem.

Aflac has switched agencies to Zimmerman in Tallahassee, Florida, part of the Omnicom Group, who is building on the brand's identity by using the duck to transform brand identification into brand education. The agency is using both new and traditional media. If you looked, you would have seen the duck on billboards in Times Square along with this odd Web address: *youdontknowquack.com*. The multimedia campaign featured newspaper ads and television commercials during the Winter Olympics to direct people to another Web address for more information. It also featured full-page ads in newspapers, such as the *Wall Street Journal*.

The ad was a teaser ad in that the sponsor was unidentified (unless the duck gave it away). The ad relied on reader curiosity to get people to visit the Aflac site, which opened with a quiz that tested common knowledge. On television the announcer says, "If all you know about us is . . ." when he's interrupted by the duck quacking, "Aflac!" The announcer then continues, ". . . then you don't know quack. To find out all the ways Aflac's got you covered, visit *knowquack.com*."

The efforts to build the brand continue with variety of 45 elements in addition to the traditional print, outdoor, and TV already mentioned, including a Facebook and YouTube presence, trivia questions on TV, a line of duck clothing, a Quack energy drink, video clips called "duckumentaries," commercials on NBC's Winter Olympics, and a NASCAR race car showing the duck's image and using the "You Don't Know Quack" theme.

Turn to the *It's a Wrap* section at the end of the chapter to learn more about how this effective campaign got consumers to know more about Aflac than quack.

Sources: Aflac Corporate Citizenship Report 2009, www.aflac.com/us/en/docs/investors/CSRReport.pdf; Susan Vranica, "Creativity on the Cheap: Aflac Duck's Paddle to Stardom," the *Wall Street Journal*, July 30, 2004; Stuart Elliott, "Not Daffy or Donald, But Still Aflac's Rising Star," the *New York Times*, April 22, 2009, *www.nytimes.com*; Stuart Elliott, "Aflac Is Leaving Its Agency, and Taking the Duck," the *New York Times*, January 22, 2010, *www.nytimes.com*; Rupal Parekh, "Brand Awareness Was Only Half the Battle for Aflac," *http://adage.com*, June 22, 2009; James Wisdom, "Case Study: A Marketing Icon's Facebook Journey," October 13, 2009, imediaconnection.com; Noreen O'Leary, "Aflac Spots 'Quack' Wise," January 22, 2010, *www.adweek.com*; "Aflac Case Study," March 3, 2010, kaplanthaler.com.

The Aflac campaign has been successful because of its use of television to dramatize a funny situation where the Aflac duck tries to get the attention of people needing supplemental insurance. More recently it has used print and outdoor advertising with strong duck graphics to announce a new strategy that proclaims "You Don't Know Quack" about what Aflac offers. These teaser ads are designed to drive traffic to the website where you can find everything you need to know about supplemental insurance.

In this chapter, we explore the uses, structure, audiences, and advantages and disadvantages of traditional media such as print, which includes newspapers and magazines; out-of-home media; and finally broadcast media, which includes radio and television. We also review film and video formats that are used in campaigns.

WHAT ARE THE KEY PRINT MEDIA CHARACTERISTICS?

Print media vehicles include newspapers, magazines, brochures, and other printed surfaces, such as posters and outdoor boards. Although it is true that magazines and newspapers, especially, have expanded their message delivery online, billions of dollars are still spent on traditional print media. That is what this section is all about.

Principle
Print media generally provide more information, rich imagery, and a longer message life than other media forms.

In terms of impact, print media generally provide more information, rich imagery, and a longer message life than broadcast media. It's an information-rich environment so, in terms of our Facets of Effects Model, print media are often used to generate cognitive responses. If you want someone to read and understand something new, then a newspaper or magazine ad is useful because readers can take as much time as they need.

Consumers also find that reading a print publication is more flexible than watching or listening to broadcast because they can stop and reread, read sections out of order, or move through the publication at their own speed and on their own time. They can also save it and reread. Because the print message format is less fleeting than broadcast and more concrete, people tend to spend more time with print and absorb its messages more carefully. Print can be highly engaging when targeted toward audiences that have a special interest in the publication's content, such as women and women's magazines.

Print has the ability to engage more of the senses than other media because it can be both tactile (different types of paper and other surfaces) and aural (smell). Magazines, for example, have long offered scratch 'n' sniff ads, particularly for perfume, and that's becoming more common in newspapers. Newspapers have announced the availability of aromatic ads, so the smell of coffee may waft from your morning newspaper sometime soon.

Newspaper Basics

Newspapers' primary function is to carry news, which means that marketers with news to announce, such as a special sale or new product, may find newspapers to be a comfortable environment. Studies have consistently found that people consider many ads—that is, commercial information—to be news, too, and they read newspapers as much for the ads as they do for the news stories.

Principle
A basic principle of newspaper publishing is that people read newspapers as much for the ads as they do for the news stories.

Marketers trying to reach a local market use newspapers because most newspapers (other than *USA Today* and the *Wall Street Journal)* are identified by the geography of the city or region they serve. The *New York Times* serves the New York region, but it also has a national circulation, particularly for its Sunday edition. Local papers are struggling to survive but their readers still value them for their coverage of local politics, education, crime, sports stories, local events, church news, and local people features.

Retailers like to place ads and press releases in daily newspapers because their **lead time** (the advance time needed to produce a publication) is short—just a few days. Food stores, for example, can change offers and pricing quickly depending on product availability. Also, because most newspapers are local, retailers aren't paying to reach people who live outside their shopping area.

Newspapers can be categorized according to their publication frequency, such as dailies, weeklies, and Sunday editions. In addition, business and organizational newspapers are available to trade and membership groups.

Although newspapers go to a mass audience, they offer **market selectivity,** which allows them to target specific consumer groups. Examples of market selectivity are special-interest newspapers (e.g., for coin collectors); ethnic editions, such as *El Nuevo Herald;* special-interest sections (business, sports, lifestyle); and advertising inserts delivered only to particular zip codes or zones. Newspapers also exist for special-interest groups, religious denominations, political affiliations, labor unions, and professional and fraternal organizations. For example, *Stars & Stripes* is the newspaper read by millions of military personnel. The *Wall Street Journal* and the *Financial Times* are considered specialty newspapers because they concentrate on financial business.

The Newspaper Industry   A $59 billion industry, newspapers remain an important medium, although newspaper readership has been declining for years, particularly among young people. Complicating the readership problem, the recession of the late 2000s brought double-digit percentage declines in advertising that caused a rash of newspaper closures.

A beautifully designed illustration using painted hands illustrates the idea of worldwide coverage for telecom giant AT&T.

Newspapers are third to television in terms of advertising revenue. The two largest U.S. newspapers, *USA Today* and the *Wall Street Journal,* continue to be leaders, although circulation has eroded for them, as well as for many local newspapers. To balance the budget, Dow Jones, the owner of the *Wall Street Journal,* has sold six newspapers, cut *WSJ* staff and costs, including reducing the page size, and increased its emphasis on its other media and Internet publishing opportunities to reduce its dependence on print ad revenue. The *WSJ*, however, is one of few newspapers to gain circulation during the recession.[1] *USA Today* reported a 17 percent drop in circulation in 2009, which threatens its number one position. The biggest problem it faces is a travel slump, which has hurt *USA Today's* hotel circulation.

Other sources of revenue besides advertising include reader subscriptions and single-copy sales at newsstands. Circulation is the primary way newspapers' reach is measured and compared with the reach of other media. *USA Today's* circulation is different from other daily newspapers in that it is targeted to travelers and its primary sales consist of single-copy sales and bulk sales to hotels, rather than subscriptions. Subscriptions, however, have been a problem as readers have migrated to online versions and dropped their print subscriptions.

Newspapers are chasing revenue in a number of new areas, in addition to online sales. The *New York Times*, for example, sells a variety of classy items in its *New York Times* store. The merchandise is similar to that found in museum stores, such as art glass, music boxes, and old ship models. It has also started the *New York Times* Knowledge Network and offers a variety of online courses for personal and career development.

A more serious change was announced by the *Dallas Morning News* (*DMN*). The changes revolved around a reorganization that would see section editors (sports, entertainment, real estate, automotive, travel, among others) reporting to sales mangers. Die-hard journalists were horrified at the thought of the editorial side being merged with advertising because of implications for news objectivity and independence. The *DMN* executives, however saw it as a way to grow the business by better meeting advertisers' business development needs.[2]

Newspaper Ad Sales   Mirroring the circulation patterns, newspaper advertising can be described as national or local (retail), as well as classified and online. Newspaper advertising is sold based on the size of the ad space and the newspaper's circulation. The charges are published on a **rate card,** which is a list of the costs for advertising space and the discounts given to local advertisers and advertisers who make volume buys. National advertisers pay a higher rate.

Most advertising sales are handled locally by the sales staff of the newspaper; however, newspaper representatives (called "reps") sell space for many different newspapers. This saves an advertiser or its agency from the need to make a multitude of buys to run a national or regional campaign in newspapers. The system is known as **one-order, one-bill.** The Newspaper National Network (*www.nnnlp.com*) is a partnership of newspaper companies that place ads in some 9,000 newspapers. Google has also gotten into this business, allowing advertisers to buy ads in daily newspapers through its website.

Until the 1980s national advertisers shied away from using newspapers, not only because of the buying problem, but also because each paper had its own peculiar size guidelines for ads, making it difficult to prepare one ad that would fit every newspaper. In the early 1980s, the American Newspaper Publishers Association and the Newspaper Advertising Bureau introduced the **standard advertising unit (SAU)** system to solve this problem. The latest version of the SAU makes it possible for newspapers to offer advertisers a great deal of choice within a standard format. An advertiser can select one of the 56 standard ad sizes and be assured that its ad will work in every newspaper in the country.

Another alternative that allows national advertisers to pay the local rate is cooperative (co-op) advertising with a local retailer. **Co-op advertising** is an arrangement between the advertiser and the retailer whereby the retailer buys the ad and the manufacturer pays half—or a portion depending on the amount of space the manufacturer's brand occupies.

Types of Newspaper Advertising   Three types of advertising are found within the local newspaper: retail/display, classified, and supplements—and most of these are found online, as well as in the print form of the newspaper.

- *Display* The dominant form of newspaper advertising is **display advertising.** Display ads, such as the Aflac ads, can be any size and can be placed anywhere in the newspaper except

the editorial page. The *Wall Street Journal* made headlines in late 2006 when it announced it would add a "jewel-box" ad space to the lower right corner of its front page (think an ad the size of a CD case). Display ads can even be found in the classified section. Display advertising is further divided into two subcategories: *local (retail)* and *national (brand)*. Advertisers who don't care where their display ads run in the newspaper pay the **run-of-paper (ROP) rate**. If they want more choice over the placement, they can pay the **preferred-position rate**, which lets them select sections in which the ad will appear.

- *Classified* Two types of **classified advertising** include advertising by individuals to sell their personal goods and advertising by local businesses. These ads are arranged according to their interest to readers, such as "Help Wanted" and "Real Estate for Sale." Classified ads have represented approximately 40 percent of total newspaper advertising revenue in the past, but local online services, such as Craigslist, have almost destroyed newspaper classified advertising. That has created a huge bottom-line problem for local newspapers.
- *Supplements* Newspaper **supplements** are magazine-style publications inserted into a newspaper, especially in the Sunday edition, that are either syndicated nationally or prepared locally. Syndicated supplements, such as *Parade* and *USA Weekend,* are provided by an independent publisher that sells its publications to newspapers throughout the country. A **freestanding insert (FSI)** is the set of advertisements, such as the grocery ads, that are inserted into the newspaper. These preprinted advertisements range in size from a single page to more than 30 pages and may be in black and white or full color. This material is often printed elsewhere and then delivered to the newspaper. Newspapers charge the advertiser a fee for inserting a supplement. FSI advertising is growing in popularity with retail advertisers for three reasons: (1) it allows greater control over the reproduction quality of the advertisement, (2) it commands more attention than just another ad in the paper, and (3) advertisers can place FSIs in certain newspapers that are delivered to certain neighborhoods, or even certain people.

Newspaper Readership Measurement   Nearly half of all adults receive home delivery of a Sunday or weekday newspaper; delivery levels are highest in small- and medium-sized cities and lowest in rural locations and larger metropolitan areas. Historically, newspaper reading tends to be highest

These are examples of business-to-business newspaper display ads for Aflac that ran in the *Wall Street Journal.* They address business managers with a message about making the supplemental insurance available to their employees.

among older people and people with a higher educational and income level. It is lowest among people in their late teens and early twenties and among lower education and lower income groups.

Newspaper readership tends to be selective, with a greater percentage reading specific sections rather than the whole paper. Business and professional newspapers, such as *Ad Age,* have particularly high readership levels. Newspapers measure their audiences in two ways: circulation and readership. Readership is always a larger number than circulation because when a paper is delivered to a home or office, it is often read by more than one person. This type of information facilitates the media planner's ability to match a certain newspaper's readership with the target audience. Agencies obtain objective measures of newspaper circulation and readership by subscribing to one or both of the following auditing companies:

Principle
Readership is always larger than circulation because a newspaper is often read by more than one person.

- **The Audit Bureau of Circulations (ABC)** The ABC is an independent auditing group that represents advertisers, agencies, and publishers. This group verifies statements about newspaper *circulation* and provides a detailed analysis of the newspaper by state, town, and county. ABC members include only paid-circulation newspapers and magazines.
- **Simmons-Scarborough** Simmons-Scarborough Syndicated Research Associates provides a syndicated study that annually measures *readership* profiles in approximately 70 of the nation's largest cities. The study covers readership of a single issue and the estimated unduplicated readers for a series of issues.

Magazine Basics

The more than 6,000 magazines published in the United States appeal to every possible interest. Most magazines aim at niche markets with a focus on a particular hobby, sport, age group, business category, and profession. These special-interest publications generally have small circulations but there are exceptions. The number-one magazine in terms of circulation is *AARP, The Magazine,* which is sent free to anyone over age 50.

Principle
People spend more time with magazines because the ads and articles usually are more relevant to their interests.

The Magazine Publishers Association (MPA) estimates that more than 90 percent of all American adults read at least one magazine per month, and the average reader spends 44 minutes reading each issue. Furthermore, 80 percent of these readers consider magazine advertising "helpful as a buying guide." In general, media planners know that people tend to pay more attention to magazine advertising and stories, including publicity articles, than to television because they are concentrating more on the medium and the messages are generally more relevant to their interests. Readers also spend more time reading a magazine than they do reading a newspaper, so there is a better opportunity to provide in-depth information.

Quality of reproduction is one of the biggest strengths of magazines. It allows the advertiser's products and brand image to be presented in a format superior to the quality of newspapers. Food companies especially like the ability to make their products look appetizing.

Health of the Magazine Industry The magazine industry hasn't suffered as much from the recession and changing media environment as newspapers have. Although single-copy sales were down at the end of 2009, these sales make up a small slice (2 percent) of magazine circulation. More importantly, circulation from subscriptions was basically stable—down only 1 percent.[3] The "Power of Print" ad by a group of magazine publishers compares the lasting quality of print with the ephemeral nature of Web content.[4]

Despite the high risks associated with the magazine business, new publications continue to emerge, especially those that target business markets and

In these [ ] times of ours, you might think that [ ] don't read magazines. That the overwhelming [ ] of the online world has swept them right out of [ ]. But it's not true at all. From through their [ ] years, folks are reading magazines [ ] than they were just a few years ago. Sure, there's a [ ] being spent online. But there's also a lot of [ ] being spent on magazines, with nearly 300 million paid subscriptions.

MAGAZINES
The Power of Print

This campaign by a group of magazine publishers makes the case that magazines are an effective advertising medium even in the Age of the Internet.

growing market segments such as computer users, skateboarders, and scrapbookers. But the greatest growth area is in online magazines, called **zines,** and the online versions of traditional printed magazines. For the Oscars, for example, *People* magazine (*www.people.com*), *Vanity Fair* (*www.vanityfair.com*), and *Entertainment Weekly* (*www.ew.com*) dedicated sections of their websites to this event, piggybacking on the immense viewership—second only to the Super Bowl—the Oscars capture.

Given the growth of zines, magazines are trying to figure out their new future with both hard and online copies. One of the most interesting dilemmas is *Wired* magazine, the publication that has been on the cutting edge for the digital community. Owned by Conde Nast, it's a small-circulation publication at the giant magazine publisher; its

Advertisers look at the audience, geographic coverage, demographics, and editorial diversity of magazines as criteria for using them in a media plan.

website, however, is the most popular of all Conde Nast sites. So issues about the digital future sometimes read like arguments for the print magazine's future. The question the editors debate is this: What happens to the website if Conde Nast decides to eliminate the print version?[5]

Meredith, the giant publisher of magazines such as *Better Homes & Gardens* and *Ladies Home Journal,* is searching for new revenue with custom publishing, e-mail, social media, and mobile campaigns for major marketers who are also its advertisers. For Kraft Foods Meredith publishes Spanish-language magazines, designs Kraft's website, and coordinates weekly e-mail blasts that feature recipe ideas. It also built Kraft's iFood Assistant, an app for cell phones that includes recipes, how-to videos, and shopping lists.[6]

Types of Magazines   The focus of audience interest is the main factor used when classifying magazines. The two main types of audiences that magazines target are consumer and business audiences. **Consumer magazines** are directed at people who buy products for personal consumption. Examples are *Newsweek, Time,* and *People,* which are general-interest publications. However, the largest growth area for consumer magazines is for special-interest publications aimed at narrow or niche audiences.

Business magazines target business readers; they include the following types of publications:

- *Trade magazines* aimed at retailers, wholesalers, and other distributors; *Chain Store Age* is an example.
- *Industrial magazines* aimed at manufacturers; an example is *Concrete Construction.*
- *Professional magazines* aimed at physicians, lawyers, and other professionals; *National Law Review* targets lawyers, and *MediaWeek* targets advertising media planners and buyers.
- *Farm magazines* aimed at those working in agriculture; *Farm Journal* and *Feed and Grain* are examples.
- *Corporate publications* are produced by companies for their customers and other stakeholders. Airline magazines are a good example.

Business magazines are also classified as vertical or horizontal publications. A **vertical publication** presents stories and information about an entire industry. *Women's Wear Daily,* for example, discusses the production, marketing, and distribution of women's fashions. A **horizontal publication** deals with a business function that cuts across industries, such as *Direct Marketing*. In terms of vehicle selection, a number of factors influence how media planners fit magazines into their media mix:

- *Geography* Many magazines have a national audience, but some cater to certain sections or regions of the country or have regional editions. The area covered may be as small as a city (*Los Angeles Magazine* and *Boston Magazine*) or as large as several contiguous states (the

Principle

If you want to start a successful magazine, create a special-interest publication aimed at a narrow or niche audience.

southwestern edition of *Southern Living Magazine*). Geographic editions help encourage local retail support by listing the names of local distributors in the advertisements. Most national magazines also offer a zone edition that carries different ads and perhaps different stories, depending on the region of the country.

- *Demographics* Demographic editions group subscribers according to age, income, occupation, and other classifications. Some magazines for example, publish a special "ZIP" edition for upper-income homes sent to subscribers who live in specific zip codes and who typically share common demographic traits, primarily based on income. *Newsweek* offers a college edition, and *Time* sends special editions to students, business executives, doctors, and business managers.
- *Editorial Content* Each magazine emphasizes a certain type of editorial content. The most widely used categories are general editorial (*Reader's Digest*), women's (*Family Circle*), shelter (*House Beautiful*), business (*Forbes*), and special interest (*Ski*).
- *Physical Characteristics* Media planners and buyers need to know the physical characteristics of a magazine because ads containing various elements of words and pictures require a different amount of space. The most common magazine page sizes are 8 1/2 × 11 inches and 6 × 9 inches. Ads running in *Reader's Digest,* which is a 6 × 9 format, allow for fewer visuals and little copy.
- *Ownership* Some magazines are owned by publishing companies (*Glamour, Brides, Vanity Fair,* and *The New Yorker* are owned by Condé Nast), and some are published by organizations such as AARP. Some magazines are published by consumer companies, such as Kraft's *Food & Family,* that sell ads and carry stories and ads for many of their own products.
- *Distribution and Circulation* Magazine revenues come from advertising, subscriptions, and single-copy sales. According to the MPA, advertising in general contributes 55 percent of magazine revenue and circulation is 45 percent (subscriptions 32 percent; single-copy sales 13 percent).[7]

Controlled versus Uncontrolled Circulation **Traditional delivery,** called **controlled circulation,** is through newsstand purchases or home delivery via the U.S. Postal Service. These are measured media and their circulation or sales can be determined. **Nontraditional delivery,** referred to as **uncontrolled circulation,** means that the magazine is distributed free to specific audiences. Generally speaking, uncontrolled (free) circulation magazines have lower readership and therefore also lower ad costs. They may also be sponsored by a company and sent to key stakeholders as part of a corporate communication program. In addition to mail, other nontraditional delivery methods include hanging bagged copies on doorknobs, inserting magazines in newspapers (such as *Parade* magazine), delivering through professionals' offices (doctors and dentists), direct delivery (company magazines or those found on airplanes), and electronic delivery, which is being used by organizational and membership publications, such as university alumni magazines.

Magazine Ad Sales Like newspapers, magazine ad costs are based on the size of the ad and the circulation of the magazine. Media planners and buyers analyze a magazine's circulation so they can assess circulation potential and determine whether the audiences that best match a campaign's target will be reached. In deciding in which magazines to place ads, advertisers need to consider factors such as format and technology.

Although the format may vary from magazine to magazine, all magazines share some format characteristics. For example, the inside front and back cover pages are the most costly for advertisers because they have the highest level of exposure compared to all the other pages in a magazine. The inside back cover is also a premium position.

Normally, the largest unit of ad space that magazines sell is the **double-page spread,** in which two ad pages face each other. A double-page ad must jump the **gutter,** the white space running between the inside edges of the pages, meaning that no headline words can run through the gutter and that all body text is on one side or the other. A page without outside margins, in which the ad's ink extends to the very edge of the page, is called a **bleed.** Magazines sometimes offer more than two connected pages (four is the most common number) that fold in on themselves. This kind of ad is called a **gatefold.** The use of multiple pages that provide photo essays is an extension of the gatefold concept.

Another popular format is a special advertising page or section that looks like regular editorial pages but is identified by the word "advertisement" at the top. The content is usually an article about a company, product, or brand that is written by the corporation's publicity department. The idea is to mimic the editorial look in order to acquire the credibility of the publication's articles. Multiple-page photo essay ads are more common in magazines such as *Fortune* and *BusinessWeek;* these magazines may present, for example, a 20-page special section for businesses in a foreign country.

Finally, a single page or double page can be broken into a variety of units called *fractional page space* (for example, vertical half-page, horizontal half-page, half-page double spread, and checkerboard in which an ad is located in the upper left and the lower right of a double-page spread).

Technology   New technologies have enabled magazines to distinguish themselves from one another. For example, *selective binding* and *ink-jet imaging* allow publishers to personalize issues for individual subscribers. Selective binding combines information on subscribers kept in a database with a computer program to produce magazines that include special sections for subscribers based on their demographic profiles. Ink-jet imaging allows a magazine such as *U.S. News & World Report* to personalize its renewal form so that each issue contains a renewal card already filled out with the subscriber's name, address, and so on. Personalized messages can be printed directly on ads or on inserts ("Mr. Jones—check out our new mutual fund today").

Time Inc. and Lexus hoped to revitalize the magazine business with a new venture called *Mine* and a new approach to personalized marketing communication. Its philosophy was customization, similar to what Lexus offers its upscale customers, but in this print publication, it's the ads that are customized—"Hello (name of customer)," as well as the selection of articles from Time Inc.'s portfolio of publications. The idea for the experiment came from Team One, the Lexus agency.

Satellite transmission, along with computerized editing technology, allows magazines to print regional editions with regional advertising. This technology also permits publishers to close pages (stop accepting new material) just hours before press time (instead of days or weeks as in the past) so that advertisers can drop up-to-the-minute information in their ads. Sophisticated database management lets publishers combine the information available from subscriber lists with other public and private lists to create complete consumer profiles for advertisers.

Magazine Readership Measurement   Magazine rates are based on the **guaranteed circulation** that a publisher promises to provide. Magazine circulation is the number of copies of an issue sold, not the readership of the publication (called readers-per-copy). A single copy of a magazine might be read by one person or by several people, depending on its content. *Time* magazine turned the industry upside down when it announced in 2007 that it would trim its rate base (average circulation level) by almost 20 percent to 3.25 million from 4 million. (In July, 2010 it continues to hold circulation at 3.4 million.)[8] More importantly, it also offered advertisers a figure for its *total audience,* which it estimates at 19.5 million.

Several companies attempt to verify the circulation of magazines, along with the demographic and psychographic characteristics of specific readers. As with newspapers, the Audit Bureau of Circulation is responsible for verifying circulation numbers. Created in 1914, the ABC audits subscriptions as well as newsstand sales and also checks the number of delinquent subscribers and rates of renewal. MediaMark, which provides a service called MRI, is the industry leader in magazine readership measurement. MRI measures readership for many popular national and regional magazines (along with other media). Reports are issued to subscribers twice a year and cover readership by demographics, psychographics, and product use. The Simmons Market Research Bureau (SMRB) provides psychographic data on who reads which magazines and which products these readers buy and consume. Other research companies such as Starch and Gallup and Robinson provide information about magazine audience size and behavior.

One problem with these measurement services is the limited scope of their services. MRI, for example, only measures about 210 magazines. That leaves media buyers in the dark regarding who is actually seeing their ads in magazines not covered by MRI's research. Without the services of an objective (outside) measurement company, advertisers must rely on the data from the magazines themselves, which may be biased.

One interesting change in magazine measurement is the move, which is supported by the MPA, to quantify the "experience" of reading the magazine, rather than just the circulation and readers-per-copy. A major study to pilot test this concept was conducted by the MPA, the Northwestern University Media Management Center, and the American Society for Magazine Editors (ASME). The study identified a set of 39 types of experiences that people report having with their magazines. More importantly, the study found that the more engaged people were in the magazine experience, the more impact the advertising had.[9]

Directories

Newspapers and magazines are important print media types, but directory advertising is another form that is particularly effective at driving specific types of consumer responses. Directories are books like the **Yellow Pages** that list the names of people or companies, their phone numbers, and their addresses. In addition to this information, many directories publish advertising from marketers who want to reach the people who use the directory. Corporations, associations, and other organizations, such as non-profits, also publish directories either in print or online that include members, as well as other stakeholders. These are often provided as a service to members as part of a corporate communication program.

Directory advertising is designed to get attention, communicate key information about the organization, reinforce the company's brand image and position, and drive behavior, the hardest of all facets of advertising effects to achieve. The Terminix ads illustrate how this complex set of objectives was accomplished by the winner of a student advertising competition. The Terminix judges commented that Tran's ads were "terrific examples of creating an unexpected visual without distracting from the main message." The judges explained that "this visual coupled with the explicit copy points (all presented in a clean, accessible layout) differentiate (in a very positive way) Terminix from its directory competitors." Tran's package included a large directory ad, a small directory ad, and an Internet directory ad.

One of the biggest advantages of advertising in directories is that if people have taken the initiative to look for a business or service, then the listing is reaching an audience already in the market for something and ready to take action. Directory advertising doesn't have to create a need because it is a number one shopping aid as reflected in the classic Yellow Pages slogan: "Let Your Fingers Do the Walking." That's why directory advertising's biggest advantage is **directional advertising**: it tells people where to go to get the product or service they want. If you are going to move across town and you want to rent a truck, you will consult the local phone book. As the *A Matter of Principle* feature explains, directory advertising is the main medium that prospects consult once they have decided to buy something they need or want.

A MATTER OF PRINCIPLE

Directories: The Medium You Trust the Most

Joel Davis, *Professor, School of Journalism & Media Studies, San Diego State University*

Which advertising medium satisfies all four of the following criteria?: It is specifically designed to reach consumers when they are thinking about a purchase, it is a medium in which consumers voluntarily seek out ads, its monthly reach exceeds the monthly reach of search engines, and it is the most frequently mentioned medium when consumers are asked by the Forrester media research company, "Which media do you trust a lot?"

The answer is the Yellow Pages—both print and online.

The Yellow Pages continue to connect sellers with consumers in its traditional print format. However, as both consumers and media change, the Yellow Pages have expanded their reach through a variety of approaches. Online yellow pages such as Yellowpages.com and Superpages (*www.superpages.com*) reach a broad online population, while other more narrowly focused approaches reach additional consumers, for example:

- AT&T Interactive's partnership with Yahoo allows Yahoo's Yahoo Local division to use advertiser content from Yellowpages.com.
- Superpages' new Twitter channel allows users to receive addresses and phone numbers via tweets.

Regardless of how the Yellow Pages reaches a consumer, the majority of Yellow Pages usage is motivated by consumers' needs, which in turn are the results of commonly and infrequently occurring life events.

There are two types of commonly occurring events: anticipated and unanticipated. Anticipated events are those that occur without surprise in the normal course of daily activities. These events may occur frequently, such as having a car's oil changed or ordering office supplies, or they may occur less frequently, such as the decision to build a fence or order flowers.

Unanticipated events are those that take you by surprise, for example, the need to repair a roof or respond to flood damage. Yellow Pages usage increases whenever one of these events occurs. The relationship between these events and Yellow Pages usage is reflected in the most commonly used headings, which typically relate to these types of events. The most frequently referenced headings include restaurants, physicians, pizza, auto parts and dealers, and plumbing contractors.

Infrequently occurring events also motivate Yellow Pages usage. In any given year, many individuals and families undergo a major life event, such as marriage, birth of children, or change in jobs. Regardless of the nature of the event, the presence of the event itself causes a need for assistance or information, and the Yellow Pages are one source of information individuals turn to in an attempt to satisfy problems that arise as a result of a life-related event. Yellow Pages usage more than doubles when these events occur: child getting married, birth of a child, youngest child leaves home, personal marriage, separation, or divorce. Given that these events occur only once (or a few times) in an individual's life, the Yellow Pages provide an opportunity to reach consumers who have an immediate need to satisfy, but who have not yet developed strong loyalty to businesses or services that can be used to satisfy their need.

The biggest change for this medium is the advent of online directory information, as well as the decline in landline phones because of the growth of cell phone usage. Directories are expensive to print so it is becoming harder for phone companies to justify the costs of community-wide distribution of the residential books. Some directory providers are using an "opt-in" program for those customers who prefer the book to the computer, but the Yellow Pages and business White Pages are still in business.[10]

The key difference between directory advertising and brand-image advertising is this: directory advertising reaches prospects, people who already know they have a need for the product or service, whereas brand-image advertising seeks to create a need and attractive personality for a brand. Almost 90 percent of those who consult the Yellow Pages follow up with some kind of action.

In addition to the Yellow Pages, an estimated 7,500 directories cover all types of professional areas and interest groups. For example, the *Standard Directory of Advertisers and Advertising Agencies* (known as the Red Book) not only lists advertisers and agencies, it also accepts advertising targeted at those who use the directory. *The Creative Black Book,* another directory used by advertising professionals, also takes ads for photographers, illustrators, typographers, and art suppliers. Most of the directories have been transformed into an electronic version accessible through the Internet.

Principle

The principle behind directory advertising is that it is directional—it tells people who already are in the target market where to go to get the product or service they want.

Other Print Media

At this time, we don't know what Kindle and its other e-book siblings will offer to advertisers, although there's sure to be some angle. But books, even in print, have been and are being used as promotional tools. A number of marketing communication agencies have published books, for example, that focus on the thoughts of their founders and the philosophies of their agencies: Crispin Porter + Bogusky and *Hoppla*, Leo Burnett's *Leo*, DDB's *Bill Bernbach Said,* and Ogilvy and Mather's *Ogilvy on Advertising.* More recently a bank in Brazil presented 120 reasons why people should be customers of Banco Bradesco—one reason per page. The book is at the center of the bank's customer acquisition program.[11]

The biggest change, however, may be coming in the form of the iPad, which may turn out to be the electronic savior of newspapers and magazines because its technology permits a larger page layout than ebooks. *Wall Street Journal* ads, for example, helped launch the iPad with an appeal to download the WSJ for iPad from the iTunes App Store. Publishers hoped the new device would restore ad revenue they had lost to online publications.[12]

WHAT ARE THE OUT-OF-HOME MEDIA CHARACTERISTICS?

Out-of-home advertising includes everything from billboards to hot-air balloons. That means ads on public spaces, including buses, posters on building walls (barn roofs in the old days), telephone and shopping kiosks, painted and wrapped cars and semi-trucks, taxi signs and mobile billboards, transit shelters and rail platforms, airport and bus terminal displays, hotel and shopping mall displays, in-store merchandising signs, grocery store carts, shopping bags, public restroom walls, skywriting, in-store clocks, and aisle displays. Even tall, highly visible grain silos have been recycled into huge Coke cans in Emporia, Kansas; a 50-foot fiddle in Green Island, Iowa; and a beer can in Longmont, Colorado. And don't forget blimps and airplanes towing messages over your favorite stadium.

In addition to being one of the most creative vehicles for delivering brand messages, as the LATCH billboard demonstrates, out-of-home media is also a big and growing segment of the media industry. Although total spending on out-of-home media is hard to determine because of the industry's diversity, this category ranks second only to the Internet as the fastest growing marketing communication industry.[13]

Why is it such a growth area? Out-of-home advertising's defining characteristic is that it is situational: it can target specific people with specific messages at a time and place when they may be most interested. A sign at the telephone kiosk reminds you to call for reservations at your favorite restaurant, a sign on the rail platform suggests that you enjoy a candy bar while riding the train, and a bus card reminds you to listen to the news on a particular radio station. As mass media has decreased in impact, *place-based forms,* such as outdoor, have become more attractive to many advertisers.

Principle
Out-of-home advertising is situational in that it targets people at specific locations.

Outdoor Advertising

One of the growth areas in the out-of-home category is **outdoor advertising,** which refers to billboards along streets and highways, as well as posters in other public locations. Of the nearly $6 billion spent on traditional outdoor advertising, billboard ads accounted for approximately 60 percent; street furniture, such as signs on benches, and transit ads brought in the rest.

An advertiser uses outdoor boards for two primary reasons. First, for national advertisers, this medium can provide reminders to the target audience, as the Olympus sign illustrates. A second use for billboards is directional; it acts as primary medium when the board is in proximity to where a brand is available. The travel and tourism industries are major users of billboards directing travelers to hotels, restaurants, resorts, gas stations, and other services.

Size and Format   In terms of size and format, there are two traditional kinds of billboards: printed poster panels and painted bulletins. **Printed posters** are created by the advertiser or agency, printed, and shipped to an outdoor advertising company. The prepasted posters are then applied in sections to the poster panel's face on location, much like applying wallpaper. They come in two sizes based on the number of sheets of paper used to make the image: 8 sheet (5 × 11 feet) and 30 sheet (12 × 25 feet). The other kind is the **painted outdoor bulletin,** which differ from posters in that they are normally created on site and vary in size or shape, although their standard size is 14 × 48 feet. They can be painted on the sides of buildings, on roofs, and even natural structures, such as the side of a mountain. Designers can add **extensions** to painted billboards to expand the scale and break away from the limits of the long rectangle. These embellishments are sometimes called **cutouts** because they present an irregular shape.

Outdoor LED boards are brightly lit plastic signs with electronic messaging. These signs come in a variety of sizes, colors, and brightness. Another innovation for billboards, electronic posters, and kiosks is the use of **digital displays.** Digital displays use wireless technology, which allows them to be quickly changed to reflect an advertising situation (a tire company could advertise all-weather tires during snowy conditions) or the presence of a target audience member. Mini USA invited some owners of its Mini cars to join a pilot test of a new program called Motorby. The drivers provide some basic information and agree to participate. They are given special key fobs that trigger Mini billboards to deliver personal messages. This was an experiment and discontinued because of costs, but it illustrates the ideas marketers are exploring to reach people on the go.

Outdoor boards are also getting into green marketing. Many are already solar powered. WePower, a clean energy company, is promoting the idea of fitting the approximately 500,000 billboards on U.S. highways with wind turbines. The company estimates these boards could power approximately 1.5 million homes.[14]

Because of the very short time consumers are normally exposed to a traditional billboard message (typically, three to five seconds), the message must be short and the visual must be very attention getting. No more than 8 to 10 words is the norm. An example of an unusual billboard with immense attention-getting power is the Microsoft Vista billboard with wire dancers that appeared in New York (see page 357 in Chapter 11). A similar spectacular featured two live players on wires playing a game of (vertical) soccer in the Adidas "Football Challenge" outdoor board that captivated audiences in Japan.

The *Practical Tips* box identifies key features of outdoor media and provides suggestions on how to design effective attention-getting messages for this "gigantic canvas." A good example of the power of a strong message comes from the LATCH public service campaign that we introduced in Chapter 4. It demonstrates the key point that a number of young children are not secure in their car seats. How many of the points in the *Practical Tips* box are demonstrated in this outdoor board?

Outdoor: An Effective Brand Communication Medium

James Maskulka, *Associate Professor of Marketing, Lehigh University*

In a recent campaign, the outdoor industry proclaimed, "Outdoor is not a medium. It's a large." In the contemporary view of outdoor, it is not just complementary but an integral part of a multiplatform advertising campaign and a viable alternative for establishing a brand's image, in addition to building brand awareness. Here are some tips on how to plan for and use outdoor advertising for maximum effectiveness:

1. **Frequency of Exposure** The successful execution of a transformational advertising strategy to build brand image requires frequent exposure over an extended time period—a primary benefit of outdoor.

2. **Brand Image Touch-Up** "Great brands may live forever," according to famous adman Leo Burnett, but even great brands may need image updating. This is the area where outdoor may have its greatest relevance to branding. Shifting a brand's image in response to changing consumer lifestyles guarantees that the brand remains relevant. The dynamic imagery of outdoor is an important tool in brand touch-ups.

3. **The Power of the Visual** Certain brand advertisers, such as those handling fashion and food, use visually driven creative as the brand's *raison d'être*. The campaigns must have consistent production values from market to market, a benefit offered by national outdoor campaigns.

4. **A Friend in the Neighborhood** Rather than building a brand on attributes and differentiation, brands with strong philosophies and attitudes build on relationships with consumers. Outdoor delivers consistent exposure of brand personality cues to targeted customers who relate to the brand.

5. **Brand Image Build-Up** The 30-day posting period is long enough so that these exposures can be seen as repositories of long-term brand image leading to favorable consumer attitude accumulation. It's like making a deposit in a bank and watching your wealth grow.

6. **Speaking the Language of Consumers** Brands increasingly serve as a form of consumer communication shorthand. The compact information of outdoor advertising matches consumers' limited processing time. To illustrate, a billboard combined with a vinyl-wrapped car and reinforced by a transit ad or a taxi poster reaches the time-starved consumer with much less investment in personal processing time.

7. **Clarity of Focus** Usually the shorter the outdoor ad copy, the more effective the message. The outdoor message imposes a creative and disciplined brand communication lexicon that ensures ongoing reinforcement of the brand message.

8. **A Gigantic Canvas** Successful outdoor advertisers see billboards as "a gigantic canvas" on which the brand advertiser can create "mega art"[15] that links the brand with relevant icons and symbols. Some of the most important slogans and images in advertising have been captured on billboards.

Source: Adapted from "Outdoor Advertising: The Brand Communication Medium," Outdoor Advertising Association of America (OAAA) special report, November 1999; the original can be found at *www.oaa.org*; Herbert Graf, "Outdoor as the Segue Between Mass & Class," *Brandweek*, July 20, 1999: 19.

Outdoor Ad Sales The cost of outdoor advertising is based on the percent of population in a specified geographical area exposed to the ad in one day. This is typically based on a traffic count—that is, the number of vehicles passing a particular location during a specified period of time, called a **showing**. If an advertiser purchases a "100 showing," the basic standard unit is the number of poster boards in each market that will expose the message to 100 percent of the market population every day. If three posters in a community of 100,000 people achieve a daily exposure to 75,000 people, the result is a 75 showing. Conversely, in a small town with a population of 1,200 and one main street, one board may produce a 100 showing. As you can see, the number of boards required for a 100 showing varies from city to city.

Advertisers can purchase any number of units (75, 50, or 25 showings daily are common quantities). Boards are usually rented for 30-day periods, with longer periods possible. Painted bulletins are bought on an individual basis, usually for one, two, or three years.

On-Premise Signs

Retail signs that identify stores have been with us throughout recorded history and are today the most ubiquitous form of brand communication. Signs are found on small independent businesses, restaurants and chains like Starbucks, hospitals, movie theaters, and other public facilities like zoos and large regional shopping centers. In this complex environment an effective sign may be relatively simple, like McDonald's giant M, or more complex, like those found on the strip in Las Vegas with their large illuminated and animated visual extravaganzas.

Some on-premise signs also act like billboards. American Eagle Outfitters, for example, has a 15,000-square-foot sign above its Broadway store in New York City. The sign has 12 panels and operates 18 hours a day. The company hired ABC Regional Sports and Entertainment to handle sales for the panels.[16]

Out-of-home advertising, such as this on-premise sign from Las Vegas, is a highly creative medium, as well as the second fastest growing medium after the Internet. Every building, every store, needs a sign.

Posters

Posters are used on kiosks, bulletin boards, the sides of buildings, and even vehicles. In London, daily hand-lettered posters have been used for centuries to announce newspaper headlines, and the walls of the subway or Tube stations in London are lined with posters advertising all kinds of products, but particularly theater shows. The iPod was launched in London with walls of posters that Tube riders encountered coming up or down the escalators. The walls were papered with the distinctive silhouetted images against their neon backgrounds. The repetition of the images created a strong billboarding effect.

Empty storefronts in prime downtown locations and major thoroughfares have become the latest venue. With their large expanse of window space, these abandoned retail stores have become a frugal way to deliver a big message during the recession. Landlords may charge as little as $500 a month in comparison to comparable spots on a billboard that might cost $50,000.[17]

Special structures called **kiosks** are designed for public posting of notices and advertising posters. Kiosks are typically located in places where people walk, such as a many-sided structure in a mall or near a public walkway, or where people wait. The location has a lot to do with the design of the message. Some out-of-home media serve the same function as the kiosk, such as the ad-carrying bus shelter. The series of posters for Dallas-based Texins Activity Center were contributed by Michael Dattolico.

Transit Advertising

Transit advertising is mainly an urban mass advertising form that places ads on vehicles such as buses and taxis that circulate through the community as moving billboards. Some of these use striking graphics, such as the designs on the sides of the Mayflower moving trucks. Transit advertising also includes the posters seen in bus shelters and train, airport, and subway stations. Most of these posters must be designed for quick impressions, although people who are waiting on subway platforms or bus shelters often study these posters, so here they can present a more involved or complicated message than a billboard can.

There are two types of transit advertising: interior and exterior. **Interior transit advertising** is seen by people riding inside buses, subway cars, and taxis. **Exterior transit advertising** is mounted on the side, rear, and top exteriors of these vehicles, so pedestrians and people in nearby cars see it. Transit advertising is reminder advertising; it is a frequency medium that lets advertisers get their names in front of a local audience who drive a regular route at critical times such as rush hour.

Painted vehicles is another type of transit advertising. It started in 1993, when PepsiCo paid Seattle in return for permission to wrap six city buses with its logo. More recently recession-weary drivers have been tempted to sign up to have their cars and trucks wrapped with ads for brands such as Jamba Juice and Verizon in exchange for monthly payments.

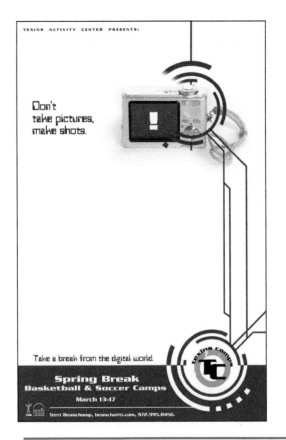

Using Print and Out-of-Home Media Effectively

This review of print and out-of-home advertising should be helpful in explaining when and why various types of media are included in a media mix. To summarize these key decisions, consider using newspaper advertising for messages that include an announcement of something new. Newspapers are also good for targeting local markets. Magazines are great for targeting people with special interests. They also have great production values and are good for messages that either focus on brand image or need space for a more complete explanation.

Outdoor advertising targets audiences on the move and provides directional information. Outdoor messages are also good for brand reminders. Directory ads catch people when they are shopping. The following table summarizes the advantages and limitations of these various media:

Print and Out-of-Home Media Advantages and Limitations

	Advantages	*Limitations*
Newspapers	Good for news announcements	Short life span
	Good market coverage	Clutter
	Good for comparison shopping	Limited reach for certain groups
	Positive consumer attitudes	Poor production values
	Good for reaching educated and affluent consumers	
	Flexibility—geographic; scheduling	

	Advantages	*Limitations*
Magazines	High production values	Long lead times—limited flexibility
	Targets consumers' interests—specialized audiences	Lack of immediacy
	Receptive audience	High cost
	Long life span	Sometimes limited distribution
	Format encourages creativity	
	Good for brand messages	
	Good for complex or in-depth messages	
Directories	Directional: Consumers go to directories for shopping information	Lack of flexibility—can be a long time before a change can be made
	Trusted	Competitive clutter and look-alike ads
	Inexpensive	Low production quality
	Good ROI of 1:15—every dollar spent on an ad produces $145 in revenue	
	Flexible in size, colors, formats	
	Long life	
Out-of-Home Media	Good situational medium	Traffic moves quickly
	Directional	Can't handle complex messages—designs must be simple
	Brand reminder medium	May be easy to miss (depending on location)
	High-impact—larger than life	Some criticize outdoor ads as "polluting" the landscape
	Least expensive	Transit lacks the size advantage of other outdoor media
	Long life	

WHAT ARE BROADCAST MEDIA CHARACTERISTICS?

When we speak of **broadcast media,** we are discussing media forms that transmit sounds or images electronically. These include radio, television and other video forms, and movie advertising. (The Internet and other digital new media will be discussed in the next chapter.) Print is a static medium bought by amount of space (column inches) and circulation; in contrast, broadcast media are dynamic and bought by amount of time (seconds, minutes) and their audience size. Broadcast media messages are fleeting, which means they may affect the viewer's emotions for a few seconds and then disappear, in contrast to print messages, which can be revisited and reread.

What that means, in terms of our Facets of Effects Model, is that broadcast is more entertaining, using both drama and emotion to attract attention and engage the feelings of the audience. Radio is a talk, news, or music-driven medium, where advertisements can also engage the imagination to create stories in the mind. In contrast, television has movie-like qualities that bring stories to life and create powerful brand imagery. You can see that in the images from the LATCH "Slow Motion" public service commercial. TV can make believers of people who see something demonstrated. Both radio and television use music for emotional impact and to intensify memory of the message through the repetition of tunes and sounds.

Radio Basics

The United States has more than 10,000 commercial radio stations, and most of them, except for the new Internet stations, have a limited geographical reach. In recent years the radio industry's growth has been slow.

The Structure of the Radio Industry   Traditional radio stations are found on the AM/FM dial and most serve local markets. Other options for radio listeners include public radio, cable and satellite

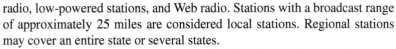

radio, low-powered stations, and Web radio. Stations with a broadcast range of approximately 25 miles are considered local stations. Regional stations may cover an entire state or several states.

Radio networks are groups of affiliated stations. The network system produces programs and distributes them to their **affiliates** who contract with the system. Some of the networks include ABC Radio, Clear Channel Communications, CNN Radio Network, the Fox Sports and Fox News networks, and others that deliver special-interest programming, such as talk radio.

Local **public radio** stations are usually affiliates of National Public Radio (NPR) and carry much of the same programming, although they have to buy or subscribe to the NPR services. For that reason, some local public radio stations might carry a full range of NPR programming, while others that are less well funded may only carry a partial list of NPR programs.

Public radio stations are considered noncommercial in that they rely on listener support for most of their funding. In recent years, however, they have slowly expanded their corporate sponsorship messages. Although public television is losing market share to the many new cable competitors, public radio is growing relative to its competitors. Likewise, corporate underwriting (or sponsorship) has increased along with the audience size because public radio is one of the few media that can deliver an audience of well-educated, affluent consumers.

The radio industry in the United States includes several other broadcast forms:

- *Cable Radio* Launched in 1990, **cable radio** technology uses cable television receivers to deliver static-free music via wires plugged into cable subscribers' stereos. The thinking behind cable radio is that cable television needs new revenue and consumers are fed up with commercials on radio. The service typically is commercial free with a monthly subscription fee.
- *Satellite Radio* The newest radio technology is **satellite radio.** It can deliver your favorite radio stations, regardless of where you are in the continental United States. Sirius and XM satellite radio introduced their systems in 2002. The two companies merged in 2007 as Sirius XM Radio and had some 18 million subscribers in 2009. For a monthly fee, the system allows you to access more than 100 channels.
- *LPFM* If you're a college student, you probably have a **low-power FM (LPFM)** station on your campus. These nonprofit, noncommercial stations serve a small market, with a reach of three to five miles.
- *Web Radio* Web radio provides **webcasting,** which is audio streaming through a website. There are two formats—one is a streaming version of an offline station and the other is Internet-only radio. Web radio offers thousands of stations as well as highly diverse radio shows that play mostly to small select audiences. Radio has been the slowest of all media to make the online version a revenue source with only 2.4 percent of revenue coming from online. In contrast, newspapers get 7 percent and television brings in 3.4 percent of its revenue from online.[18]

Some of the lines between these forms are blurring. For example, some commercial radio networks with special-interest programming, such as the liberal talk radio network Air America, are asking listeners to donate to keep the programs on air, similar to the way public radio is financed.

The Radio Audience The reason advertisers like radio is that it is as close as we can come to a universal medium. Virtually every household in the United States (99 percent) has at least one radio and most have multiple sets. And almost everybody listens to radio at some time during the day.

A $20 billion industry, radio is tightly targeted based on special interests (religion, Spanish language, talk shows) and musical tastes. In other words, radio is a highly segmented advertising medium. About 85 percent of the radio stations are focused on music. Program formats offered in a typical market are based on music styles and special interests, including hard rock, gospel, country and western, top-40 hits, soft rock, golden oldies, and nonmusic programs such as talk radio and advice, from car repair to finances to dating. Talk radio host Rush Limbaugh is generally acknowledged to have the largest audience with estimates of his audience ranging from 14 million to 25 million.[19]

Recent research has provided some findings that bode well for radio. One study, for example, found that radio listeners are far less likely to change the dial during ads than are television viewers. An unexpected 92 percent listen through the four- and six-minute commercial pods. The percent is even higher for in-car listeners. The study also found a high level of loyalty among listeners for their favorite station.[20]

Principle
Media planners use radio for tight targeting of narrow, highly segmented markets.

Dayparts   Advertisers considering radio are most concerned with the number of people listening to a particular station at a given time. Radio audiences are grouped by the time of day when they are most likely to be listening, and the assumption is that different groups listen at different times of the day. The typical radio programming day is divided into five segments called **dayparts** as follows:

Morning Drive Time   6–10 A.M.

Midday   10 A.M.–3 P.M.

Evening Drive Time   3–7 P.M.

Evening   7 P.M.–midnight

Late Night   midnight–6 A.M.

The **morning drive time** segment is the period when the most listeners are tuned in to radio. This drive-time audience is getting ready for work or commuting to work, and radio is the best medium to reach them.

Measuring the Radio Audience   The radio industry and independent research firms provide several measures for advertisers, including a station's **coverage,** which is similar to circulation for print media. This is simply the number of homes in a geographic area that can pick up the station clearly, whether those homes are actually tuned in or not. A better measure is station or program **ratings,** which measures the percent of homes actually tuned in to the particular station. Factors such as competing programs, types of programs, and time of day or night influence the circulation figure.

The Arbitron Ratings Company estimates the size of radio audiences for more than 250 markets in the United States. Arbitron has been using a seven-day, self-administered diary. A new technology Arbitron is rolling out called the Portable People Meter (PPM) is a pager-size device that detects codes embedded in the audio programming regardless of where the device—whether traditional radio, computer, or cell phone—is located. The device has been found to be quite effective at predicting audience interest, even leading to some major format changes such as when WRFF in Philadelphia switched from a Spanish-language talk show format to alternative rock after new PPM data revealed that rock music was more popular with the WRFF audience.

Radio Advertising   The first radio commercials hit the air in 1922 in New York and advertised a real estate firm. These early ads were highly successful for many of the same reasons that keep radio popular today with advertisers. The radio listening experience is unlike that of any other media, creating both challenges and opportunities for radio advertisers. It can be a more intimate experience, because we tend to listen to it alone, particularly for people wearing headphones. In cars, where many people listen to radio, it offers advertisers something close to a captive audience. And it's relatively inexpensive both to produce commercials and buy airtime. Check out the Radio Ranch website, *www.radio-ranch.com* for a look behind the scenes of radio commercial production.

Media planners use radio to deliver a high level of frequency because radio commercials, particularly **jingles,** which are commercials set to music, lend themselves to repetition. Barry Manilow was awarded an Honorary CLIO Award recognizing his long career as a jingle writer. One of his best known is the catchy Band-Ad jingle, "I am stuck on Band-Aid brand cuz Band-Aid's stuck on me." Hear this classic at *www.youtube.com/watch?v=_7MtLNK02lI.*

Radio can also engage the imagination more than other media because it relies on the listener's mind to fill in the visual element. Many radio ads use drama, especially **public service**

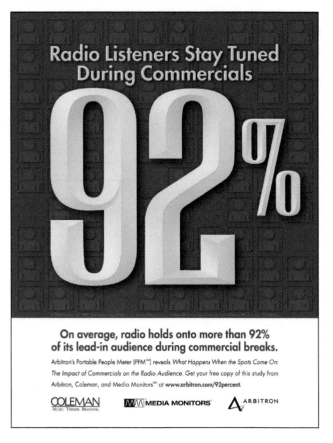

Radio Listeners Stay Tuned During Commercials

92%

On average, radio holds onto more than 92% of its lead-in audience during commercial breaks.

Arbitron's Portable People Meter (PPM™) reveals *What Happens When the Spots Come On: The Impact of Commercials on the Radio Audience.* Get your free copy of this study from Arbitron, Coleman, and Media Monitors™ at www.arbitron.com/92percent.

COLEMAN |\/|\/|\/| MEDIA MONITORS   ARBITRON

Arbitron is one of several major audience-rating services in the advertising industry. It estimates the size of radio audiences for more than 250 U.S. markets.

Principle
Radio advertising has the power to engage the imagination and communicate on a more personal level than other forms of media.

announcements (PSAs), which are spots created by agencies that donate their time and services on behalf of some good cause. PSAs run for free on radio and TV stations. Check out the Ad Council's website (*www.adcouncil.org*) for a collection of these types of spots. You can also check out the radio spots from the Ad Council's LATCH campaign that we introduced in Chapter 4.

Radio advertising is divided into three categories: network, spot, and local. Network revenues are by far the smallest category, accounting for approximately 5 percent of total radio revenues. Local advertising revenues account for approximately 75 percent, and national spot advertising makes up the remainder. In addition to local, let's consider the categories of national radio buys:

- *Network Radio Advertising* Network advertising can be bought from national networks that distribute programming and advertising to their affiliates. A **radio network** is a group of local affiliates connected to one or more national networks through telephone wires and satellites. The five major radio networks are Westwood One, CBS, ABC, Unistar, and Clear Channel. The largest network by far is Clear Channel, with more than 1,200 stations. Satellite transmission has produced important technological improvements that also make it easier to distribute advertising to these stations. Many advertisers view network radio as a viable national advertising medium, especially for food and beverages, automobiles, and over-the-counter drugs.
- *Spot Radio Advertising* Spot advertising lets an advertiser place an advertisement with an individual station rather than through a network. Although networks broadcast blocks of prerecorded national advertisements, they also allow local affiliates open time to sell spot advertisements locally. (*Note:* National media plans sometimes buy spots at the local level rather than through the network, so it is possible to have a national spot buy that only reaches certain markets.) Thanks to the flexibility it offers the advertiser, **spot radio advertising** makes up nearly 80 percent of all radio advertising. In large cities, 40 or more radio stations may be available. Local stations also offer flexibility through their willingness to run unusual ads, allow last-minute changes, and negotiate rates. Buying spot radio and coping with its nonstandardized rate structures can be cumbersome, however.
- *Syndicated Radio Advertising* This is the original type of radio programming that plays on a large number of affiliated stations, such as the Paul Harvey show, which is broadcast on some 1,200 stations. Program **syndication** has benefited network radio because it offers advertisers a variety of high-quality, specialized, and usually original programs. Both networks and private firms offer syndication. A local talk show may become popular enough to be "taken into syndication." Advertisers value syndicated programming because of the high level of loyalty of its audience.

The growth of network radio has contributed to an increase in syndicated radio, creating more advertising opportunities for companies eager to reach new markets. In fact, syndication and network radio have practically become interchangeable terms.

Using Radio Effectively   We have seen that radio is highly targeted and that makes it a great tool for reaching audiences through specialized programming, such as talk shows and musical interests. Radio advertising messages tend to have a higher level of acceptance than television because radio listeners are more loyal to their favorite programs and stations. The Radio Advertising

Bureau (RAB) promotes radio as having a dynamic consumer engagement that can be measured using audience metrics of reach, relevance, and receptivity.

Although radio may not be a primary medium for most businesses, it does have excellent reminder and reinforcement capability and is great about building frequency through repetition, particularly if the message can be delivered through a jingle. It also sparks the imagination because of its ability to stimulate mental imagery through the *theater of the mind*, which uses humor, drama, music, and sound effects to tell a story. It also brings the persuasive power and warmth of a human voice. A good example is the series of Tom Bodett's Motel 6 commercials by the Dallas-based Richards Group. Listen to them at *http://adland.tv/search/node/Motel%206*.

To maximize the impact of a radio spot, timing is critical and depends on understanding the target audience's aperture, which is particularly important in radio with its "drive-time" daypart. **Aperture** means knowing when the target audience is most likely to be listening and responsive. Restaurants run spots before meals; auto dealerships run spots on Friday and Saturday, when people are free to visit showrooms; and jewelry stores run spots before Christmas, Valentine's Day, and Mother's Day. For fast-food franchises, radio buys at the local level supplement national television. Radio acts as a reminder, with spots concentrated during morning drive time, noon, and evening drive time. The messages focus on the location of local restaurants and special promotions. Radio is also flexible and allows for easy changes to schedules. For example, a local hardware store can quickly implement a snow-shovel promotion the morning after a snowstorm.

A disadvantage of radio is that it plays in the background for many of our activities. Although the radio is on, the multitasking listener may not really be listening to or concentrating on the message. Listeners tend to tune in and tune out as something catches their attention, which is why effective radio advertising is designed to "break through" the surrounding clutter. Generally radio ad clutter is lower than television clutter, which averages 15 to 20 minutes per hour of commercials versus 10 to 15 minutes on radio. Also, the lack of visuals on radio can be a problem for products that need to be demonstrated.

Television Basics

Television has become a mainstay of society with, on average, some 280 million sets in use in the United States. Television approaches the universality of radio with 98 percent of American households having one or more television sets. In over half of U.S. households, the TV is on "most" of the time. The U.S. television audience, however, is highly fragmented, tuning in to 100 or more different channels. Nielsen Media Research estimates that the average U.S. household has the set on more than five hours a day.[21]

Television is primarily an entertainment medium although a recent trend, called "behavior placement," is experimenting with moving TV programs into social behavior modification. For example, a segment of *The Office* turned one of the actors into a superhero obsessed with recycling. Scripting positive behaviors into TV shows is seen as a way to model positive behaviors and influence viewers.[22]

Television's use also expanded with the introduction of the Wii, which makes the home TV screen a facilitator in exercise programs, as well as games. As computers begin to use TV screens to project their content, this cross-channel merger will open up entirely new uses for home TVs.

The heavy use of television by children is of concern to parents and early childhood experts. Recent studies found that U.S. children spend an average of nearly four hours a day watching television, DVDs, and videos. Furthermore, three-fourths of sixth graders have a TV in their bedroom. Advertisers are happy to hear that kids haven't totally abandoned TV programming for games and the Web, but these numbers are still worrisome for critics of children's programming and advertising.

Television advertising is embedded in programming, so most of the attention in media buying, as well as in the measurement of television advertising's effectiveness, is focused on the performance of various shows and how they engage their audiences. During the Golden Age of television in the 1950s and 1960s, the three networks virtually controlled the evening viewing experience, but that dominance has shrunk in recent years. The following table shows **prime-time** viewing over the years, as well as the drastic drop in percentage of people watching the leading shows during those years.

Years	Top Show (Percentage of Audience)
1952–53	67 *I Love Lucy* (CBS)
1962–63	36 *Beverly Hillbillies* (CBS)
1972–73	33 *All in the Family* (CBS)
1982–83	26 *60 Minutes* (CBS)
1992–93	22 *60 Minutes* (CBS)
2002–03	16 *CSI* (CBS)
2007–08	16 *American Idol* (Fox)

Source: Adapted from James Poniewozik, "Here's to the Death of Broadcast," Time, March 26, 2009: 62.

Principle

Television advertising is tied to television programming and the ad's effectiveness is determined by the popularity of the television program.

Some programs are media stars and reach huge audiences—the Super Bowl is a good example. In 2010 the Saints vs. Colts game became the most watched telecast ever with an average audience of 106.5 million viewers in the United States, and some 51.7 million households tuned in.[23] Others reach small but select audiences, such as *The News Hour with Jim Lehrer* on PBS. As discussed in the *A Matter of Practice* feature, a surprise hit has been the retro *Mad Men* with its stories about the 1950s advertising industry. It's not a huge ratings hit, but is popular with its loyal fan base because of its dramatic power and ability to engage audiences emotionally with the characters, their stories, and the historical period.

In an interesting experiment with television costs and revenue, in early 2010 NBC moved Jay Leno from his late-night time slot to a 10:00 p.m. time (EST) five nights a week. The network gambled that his show would be cheaper to produce than the scripted programs that characterize prime time. Of course, his program would probably also have lower ratings, but the trade-off was worthwhile given the lower program costs. What that decision ignored was the importance of those scripted shows with their higher ratings to the local affiliates who get a share of the revenue from those shows. The lower ratings also hurt their revenue stream from both national and local advertising. Even worse, the Leno show ended up being a weaker "lead-in" for the local stations' 11:00 p.m. newscasts. So what seemed to be a savvy business decision played havoc with the budgets of more than 200 affiliates and six months later the network moved Leno back to his 11:30 p.m. slot. Even though the network made money by saving on production costs, it created a firestorm of complains from affiliates who lost ratings and advertising revenues.[24]

The economic model of broadcast television is generally based on an advertising-supported model, at least for the traditional networks. The model relies on producing programs that attract a large audience that advertisers want to reach. Advertising, plus revenue from the programs that are syndicated after they go off air, has supported network TV since its beginnings, although that model is in serious trouble with the development of cable and the splintering of the viewing audience.

Structure of the Television Industry   To better understand how television works, let's first consider its structure and programming options. Then we'll look at television as an advertising medium, the way it connects with its audience, and its advantages and disadvantages. The key types of television delivery systems include network, subscription (cable and satellite), pay programming, local and public television, and syndication.

Network Television   A **broadcast network** is a distribution system that provides television content to its affiliated stations. Currently, there are four national, over-the-air television networks in the United States: the American Broadcasting Company (ABC), the Columbia Broadcasting System (CBS), the National Broadcasting Company (NBC), and Fox Broadcasting. The big three networks' hold on the viewing audience has dropped from 75 percent in 1987 to less than 30 percent. When Fox is included, networks still only capture less than half of the audience. The networks suffered in the recession except for Fox, which, in 2010 made more money than the evening newscasts of NBC, ABC, and CBS combined.[25]

Each network has about 150 affiliates. The network sells some commercial time to national advertisers and leaves some open for the affiliates to fill with local advertising. Affiliates pay their

Mad Men: Advertising at the Intersection of Social Change

Bruce Vanden Bergh, Professor, Michigan State University

Advertising is a fascinating business because it sits somewhat precariously at the intersection of societal change as it constantly adjusts to people's changing desires in an effort to sell products, services, and ideas ostensibly to make their lives better. That is what makes the advertising agency portrayed in the TV drama *Mad Men* such a great prism through which to view one of the most socially tumultuous eras of the 20th century, the 1960s. The show starts in the early 1960s in the New York City office of Sterling Cooper, a small conservative advertising agency inhabited by a caste of iconic characters, each of whom represents his or her own subculture's struggle to find its place and identity in a rapidly changing world.

The central character in the show is Don Draper who, with all of his Hollywood leading-man good looks, is the brilliant creative director of Sterling Cooper. His knack for conjuring up winning ideas just at the point the client is ready to walk out of the room is illustrated by his day-saving idea to say that Lucky Strikes are "toasted" to avoid the federal government's scrutiny of the health hazards of smoking even as he and his colleagues indulge in the habit.

Don Draper is as troubled as he is handsome. His troubles are manifold. He has created a false identity for himself that gives him the freedom to create the life he thinks he wants unfettered by a past. However, this still leaves him empty in ways he cannot fully satisfy by chasing women, drinking, smoking, or making money. He avoids serious commitment like the plague, including working without a contract. Thus, he always has one foot out the door should he want to escape from his responsibilities.

The central cast that surrounds Don Draper presents us with other struggles and changes to come in our country at the time. Joan Holloway is the office manager who knows how to get what she wants from the secretarial pool and the men at the office. However, she is still playing by and manipulating the old rules of power, which for her are based on beauty and sex appeal. Peggy Olson, on the other hand, rises out of the secretarial pool to become a copywriter with a keen sense of the changes going on in society and how to harness them in her copy and ideas. Salvatore Romano is an art director awakening to the fact that he is gay in a world not yet ready to accept that revelation. Peter Campbell is a young, ambitious account executive who never seems quite sure of himself and his relationships at the office, with his parents, or with his wife. Paul Kinsey gives us a glimpse of the impending civil rights crisis by dating a woman of color and participating in the early stages of the movement. Finally, there is Roger Sterling, one of the agency's principals, who marries a 20-year-old as his way of dealing with his senior status and denying his mortality.

Mad Men also is illuminating in the way it uses changes in the advertising agency business itself to demonstrate that change is an opportunity for some really forward-looking thinking and creative problem solving. This is best demonstrated when the ad agency McCann-Erickson is going to buy a British agency, PPL, that also happens to own Sterling Cooper. While PPL has allowed Sterling Cooper to operate somewhat autonomously, the McCann deal threatens to relegate Don and his colleagues to "midlevel cogs." Don, Roger, and others devise a scheme to get fired to void their contracts with McCann so they can start a new agency with key people (Joan, Peggy, Peter, Roger, and others) and clients from the old Sterling Cooper.

All of this happens in December of 1963 against the backdrop of the assassination of John F. Kennedy, which casts a dark cloud over the country and appears to dash the feeling of hope and a new vitality JFK promised the younger generation. Don Draper, who seemed personally unaffected by the assassination, renews his passion for advertising just three weeks later. This renewal comes complete with a new respect for Peggy and Peter because he now realizes that he needs them more than they need him at the new agency.

One of the paradoxes of *Mad Men* is that while the characters indulge in the unhealthy use of tobacco and alcohol, they appear much more secure in their world than we are in ours. Our world has become more complicated and the advertising business has become as fragmented as has our society. We no longer have just three big TV networks that can deliver large audiences for our ads. We no longer smoke as much, but that has been replaced by overeating. Old problems get solved and new ones arise. Creativity, however, has survived the times intact. It appears to be the common denominator that has helped the very flawed characters of *Mad Men* to change and survive.

For recaps on Mad Men episodes and videos, check out the *TV Guide* site, *www.tvguide.com/tvshows/mad-men/289066.*

respective networks 30 percent of the fees they charge local advertisers. In turn, affiliates receive a percentage of the advertising revenue (12 to 25 percent) paid to the national network. This advertising is the primary source of affiliate revenues.

Subscription Television   Cable is the most familiar example of **subscription television,** which means that people sign up for service and pay a monthly fee. Subscription television is a delivery system that carries the television signal to subscribers. **Cable television** is a form of subscription TV. It has grown into a national network of channels that provide highly targeted special-interest programming options. The impact of cable programming has been to fragment the audience and make it difficult to reach a large, mass audience. Cable has become a significant threat to the financial health of the networks. Viewing time for cable also has increased as the quality of the programming has improved and advertisers have found that "narrowcasting," which uses cable's special-interest programs to reach more tightly targeted audiences, can be even more efficient than mass broadcasting. The Cabletelevision Advertising Bureau found that ad-supported cable has taken over the lead from the broadcast networks.[26] Satellite television is similar to cable in that it's just a competing delivery system.

Some of the best programming in recent years, such as the award-winning *Sopranos* show, have been produced by cable channels. Oprah Winfrey rocked the industry when she announced she was leaving NBC to set up her own cable channel that would carry her programs.

Cable programming comes from independent cable networks and independent **superstations.** These networks include Cable News Network (CNN), the Disney Channel, the Entertainment and Sports Programming Network (ESPN), and a group of independent superstations whose programs are carried by satellite to cable operators (for example, WTBS-Atlanta, WGN-Chicago, and WWOR-New York).

Another form of subscription television is **satellite television.** Direct broadcast television services became available in the United States in the 1990s. Dish Network and DirecTV provide the equipment, including the satellite dish, to access some 125 national and local channels. Satellite television is particularly useful for people who live in rural areas without local or over-the-air service.

Pay Programming and On-Demand Programming   Pay programming and on-demand programming are available to subscribers for an additional monthly fee. This type of programming offers movies, specials, and sports under such plans as Home Box Office, Showtime, and The Movie Channel. Pay networks do not currently sell advertising time.

Local Television   Most local television stations are affiliated with a network and carry both network programming and their own programs. **Independent stations** are local stations not affiliated with networks. Costs for local advertising vary, depending on the size of the market and the demand for the programs carried. For example, a major station in Houston may charge local advertisers $2,000 for a 30-second spot during network prime time. This same time slot may cost $50 in a smaller town. Most advertisers for the local market are local retailers, primarily department stores or discount stores, financial institutions, automobile dealers, restaurants, and supermarkets. Advertisers buy time on a station-by-station basis. National advertisers sometimes buy local advertising on a city-by-city basis, using **spot buys.** They do this to align the buy with their product distribution, to "heavy-up" a national schedule to meet competitive activities, or to launch a new product in selected cities. Even some cable channels are attempting to localize their programming

Principle
Cable programming has fragmented the television audience and makes it difficult for advertisers to reach a large, mass audience.

to gain ground in this market. ESPN, for example, which dominates national and international sports viewing, is testing the use of local websites to report on hometown sports teams.

Public Television   Although many people still consider **public television** to be commercial free, the FCC allows the approximately 350 Public Broadcasting System (PBS) stations some leeway in airing commercial messages, called program **underwriting.** The FCC says these messages should not ask for a purchase or make price or quality comparisons. PBS is an attractive medium for advertisers because it reaches affluent, well-educated households. In addition, PBS still has a refined image, and PBS advertisers are viewed as good corporate citizens because of their support for noncommercial TV. Current FCC guidelines allow ads to appear on public television only during the local 2.5-minute program breaks. Each station maintains its own acceptability guidelines. Some PBS stations accept the same ads that appear on paid programming. However, most PBS spots are created specifically for public stations. Some PBS stations will not accept any commercial corporate advertising, but they do accept noncommercial ads that are "value neutral"—in other words, ads that make no attempt to sell a product or service.

Syndication   An important revenue stream for networks and cable channels, such as HBO, that produce original programming is syndication. As in radio programming, television syndication refers to content providers that sell their programs to independent firms and other cable channels to replay as reruns. Some of the most popular first-run programs, such as *House* and *Law & Order,* are valuable properties and move quickly into syndication.

New Technology and Innovative Television   New technology is having an impact on programming options, as well as on distribution patterns and systems. Innovations, such as high-definition TV and interactive TV, expand advertising opportunities.

High-definition TV (HDTV) is a type of TV standard that delivers movie-quality, high-resolution images. All over-the-air stations broadcast their programming in an HDTV format. It's been a struggle, however, getting enough HDTV programming broadcast to build demand on the consumer side. As stations upgraded their equipment and moved to HDTV by 2009, the increased availability of HDTV programming made it necessary for consumers to upgrade to HDTV sets.

Say you're watching your favorite program and a commercial comes on for a product that interests you. A button pops up on the screen that you can click with your remote and you are asked questions about whether you want more information, a coupon, or to give some other response. Cable and DVRs are making **interactive television** feasible. The technology requires that advertisers give their ads to TiVo, for example, where codes are embedded. The ads are then distributed to TV and cable networks. When the ad airs, the digital video recorder boxes pick up the coding and turn on the interactive component for that subscriber. Axe used it to show young men how to use its body spray. The ad featured a motocross champion performing a motorbike stunt. While doing a back flip, the star ripped off his shirt and sprayed Axe from armpit to armpit. Viewers were then asked to go to a different channel to learn the move. Other features included videos and Web pages that can be navigated by using the remote control.

Interactive television also opens up the opportunity for **addressable television,** which is a type of television that makes it possible for individual homes to receive targeted and personalized advertising. The ability to address ads to different homes through cable and other subscription services is becoming more feasible. Several cable companies are experimenting with technology that would make addressability feasible, particularly for local video-on-demand programming. Cablevision provides viewers with a remote control they can use to request samples or promotional offers to be sent to their homes. It's also a lead-generation opportunity and the cable company boasts a high conversion rate tracking the number of viewers who click a second time to actually make an order.[27]

A number of researchers are testing the feasibility of bringing **3-D television** to living rooms by improving on current technology and its use of special glasses. One technology involves a set-top box, and 3-D sets are being tested by Japanese and Korean electronics rivals; Sony and ESPN are particularly focused on this new market.[28] British Sky Broadcasting is proposing a special 3-D television channel that will provide content for these new sets. In the United States several 2010 Super Bowl ads were filmed in 3-D. The logistics are difficult but 3-D may finally be on its way to home television sets.

Principle

If you want to reach an otherwise difficult-to-reach target—the well-educated, affluent household—one way to do it is to underwrite public television programming.

With TiVo, you'll never have to watch bad TV again. Unless, of course, you really like watching bad TV.

Hey, it's your time. Spend it watching whatever you want to. You tell TiVo what shows you like, and TiVo takes care of it. Records 'em all, no questions asked (or judgments rendered), so you can watch 'em later, like after you finish dinner.

TiVo DVRs are like VCRs, but with a hard disk and without the hassles of videotape. It hooks up to cable, satellite or antennae and digitally records up to 60 hours of your favorite stuff.* And it's very easy. Just buy the box ($399), subscribe to the TiVo service, and call it a night—whatever kind of night you like. Still say you can live without it? Ask any TiVo subscriber.

Order now to get Free Shipping and a 30-Day Money-Back Guarantee at www.tivo.com/MH07 or call 1-877-BUY-TIVO (289-8486) Code: MH07.

Season Pass™	Control Live TV	WishList	Series2 DVR
Choose your favorite shows and the TiVo service will automatically record every episode, wherever it airs.	With TiVo you can pause, rewind, and slo-mo live TV.	Got a favorite actor? Special hobby? The TiVo service will find and record programs based on your interests.	Now, up to 60 hours recording time.

DVR technology poses a challenge for advertisers since it enables consumers to bypass commercials.

Traditional forms of network television are being threatened by **online video.** After Comcast bid to buy NBC, one of the ideas floated by the new management team involved subscription fees for NBC—hoping to make the previously ad-supported network more like premium cable. The new combined media and entertainment company also considered bringing the cable-TV subscription model to the Web and its online video programming.[29]

Another technology that is having a profound effect on television programming and the way people watch television is the **digital video recorder (DVR),** such as TiVo. DVR systems allow users to record favorite TV shows and watch them whenever they like. The technology makes it possible to record the programming without the hassles of videotape, letting users pause, do instant replays, and begin watching programs even before the recording has finished. This capability is known as **time-shifting.**

DVRs are a threat to marketers because it allows consumers to zip past commercials completely. It also is forcing advertisers to rethink the design of their ads, recognizing that they have 3 to 4 seconds, at best, to win the attention of button-happy viewers. It also raises the issue of how advertisers should respond. Some are experimenting with new ways to send messages that immediately engage attention. Coca-Cola and TiVo, for example, have created ads that appear on screen as a small text box when viewers pause a show.[30]

Advertisers and television executives are alarmed over the increasing popularity of time-shifting technology. It calls into question audience measurement numbers: If 20 percent of the audience is recording *24* on Monday night only to watch it Saturday morning commercial free, then is the Monday night measurement accurate? The DVR industry estimates that viewers zip past (fast forward through) about 6 percent of TV commercials—an estimated waste of some $5 billion in ad spending—and predicts that by the end of 2011, about 16 percent will suffer that fate. [31]

A Nielsen study, however, found that viewers are not zipping through commercials as much as advertisers feared. To further understand this pattern, TiVo has also announced that it is considering a service that will provide second-by-second data about which programs the company's subscribers are watching and which commercials they are skipping.

Measuring the Television Audience   A great number of advertisers consider television their primary medium. Can television deliver a target audience to advertisers effectively? What do we really know about how audiences watch television? Is it a background distraction? Do we switch from channel to channel without watching any single show? Or do we carefully and intelligently select what we watch on television?

Television viewers are sometimes irritated by the intrusiveness of advertising and are not reluctant to switch channels or zip through commercials on prerecorded programs. Clutter is part of the problem advertisers face and the audience has become very good at avoidance, unless the ads are intrusive or highly engaging. The Super Bowl is one of the few programs where viewers actually watch commercials. Nielsen has found that the average drop in viewing between the game and the commercials was less than 1 percent. CBS says that the typical drop during a normal program is approximately 5 percent.[32]

A. C. Nielsen is the research company that dominates the television measurement industry. **Exposure** is television's equivalent to circulation. Exposure measures households with sets turned on, a population referred to as **households using television (HUT).** But a HUT figure doesn't tell you if anyone is watching the program. Remember from Chapter 11 that we defined an **impression** as one person's opportunity to be exposed one time to an ad. Like print, the impressions from television—the number of viewers exposed to a program—might be greater than the number of households reached since there may be more than one viewer watching and the commercial may be repeated several times in a program or during a time period. We add all of these impressions up and call them **gross impressions.**

For television programs, the exposure is estimated in terms of number of viewers. The 2010 Super Bowl was watched by 106 million people, making it the most watched telecast ever, surpassing the viewership of the 1983 M*A*S*H final episode. Following those programs, the 1996 Dallas vs. Pittsburgh Super Bowl game drew 97 million viewers and the 2007 Super Bowl featuring the Chicago Bears and Indianapolis Colts, attracted some 93 million viewers.

- *Ratings* These gross impression figures become very large and difficult to work with, which is why the television industry, similar to radio, uses ratings (percentage of exposure) instead. Ratings are an easier measurement to work with because they convert the raw figure to a percentage. When you read about a television show having a rating of 20 that means that 20 percent, or one-fifth of all households with televisions, were tuned in to that program. Note that one rating point equals 1 percent of the nation's estimated 114 million TV homes; that's why planners describe this program as having 20 **rating points,** or percentage points. A 20 rating is actually a huge figure, since the fragmentation of cable has diversified television watching and made it very difficult to get 20 percent of the households tuned to any one program.

- *Share* A better estimate of impressions might be found in a program's **share of audience,** which refers to the percent of viewers based on the number of sets turned on during a specific broadcast period. The share figure for a particular program is always larger than its rating, since the base is smaller. For example, if the Super Bowl gets a rating of 40 (40 percent of all households with television), its share would be 67 if the total HUT was 60 percent. In other words, the Super Bowl has 2/3 (40 divided by 60 = 67) of all households that have their television sets turned on during the Super Bowl.

Independent rating firms, such as A. C. Nielsen, provide the most commonly used measure of national and local television audiences. Nielsen periodically samples a portion of the television viewing audience, estimates the size and characteristics of the audiences watching specific shows, and then makes these data available, for a fee, to advertisers and ad agencies, which use them in their media planning.

Nielsen's calculations are based on audience data from about 5,000 measurement instruments, called **people meters,** which record what television shows are being watched, the number of households that are watching, and which family members are viewing. The recording is done automatically; household members indicate their presence by pressing a button. These are placed in randomly selected households in the 210 television markets in the United States. The company also uses viewer diaries mailed out during the **sweeps** period, which are quarterly periods when more extensive audience data and demographics are gathered. About 1 million diaries are returned each year.

Nielsen continues to add people meters in its top markets to track local viewing patterns. Meters are used only to determine what show is being watched, and not the specific demographics of who is watching it. Demographic data come from diaries. A new locally based meter system would allow Nielsen to identify the age, race, and sex of viewers on a nightly basis. Note that these ratings are based on programs, and are not measures of specific advertisements.

One interesting finding from an analysis of ratings is that even in this age of DVRs, the lead-in show does matter. Fox's *American Idol*, for example, has been a strong lead-in to other Fox shows such as *Fringe*. Another Nielsen finding during the recent recession is the power of ethnic media. For example, the number one TV station in Los Angeles isn't one of the networks, it's Spanish-language KMEX. And it's not just LA's top station, Nielsen ranks it as the number one station in the United States with viewers ages 18 to 49.[33]

Something not measured by all of these metrics is the dedication of a program's superfans. When NBC proposed dropping *Chuck*, fans launched a campaign on Facebook, Twitter, and TV blogs in defense of their favorite program. Realizing the significance of the attachment, Subway jumped in as an ally. To demonstrate the marketing power of ChuckTV.net, a consumer-generated campaign called "Finale & Footlong" urged fans to buy foot-long sandwiches from Subway to eat as they watched the season finale. The effort was successful, and NBC announced it would renew the show.[34]

Television Advertising

The first television commercial aired in 1941 when Bulova bought time on a New York station before a Phillies vs. Dodgers game.[35] Television is used for advertising because it works like the movies—it tells stories, engages the emotions, creates fantasies, and can have great visual impact. Because it's an action medium, it is also good for demonstrating how things work. It brings brand images to life and adds personality to a brand. An example of the dramatic, emotional power of television comes from one of the greatest commercials of all time. Called "Iron Eyes Cody," the Ad Council PSA was created as part of an environmental campaign. It shows a Native American paddling a canoe through a river ruined by trash. A close-up shows a tear from his eye.

Advertising Sales   The first decision in designing a television ad is determining its length, which is usually 10, 15, 30, or 60 seconds. The most common length is 30 seconds because for most advertisers, the 60-second spot is considered too expensive. The 10-second ad is like a billboard and simply announces that a program is "brought to you by . . ." the advertiser. ESPN is experimenting with these "mini-mercials" and offering in-house produced ads that combine an advertiser's message with the lead-in to a show. For example, in an Asics spot, a runner returns home and turns on his TV, which shows the ESPN "SportsCenter" logo with its theme song.[36]

Long-form ads, which are of various lengths, are seen on late-night TV as "infomercials," when the cost of broadcast time is much lower than at other times of day. Late-night infomercials have been the venue for direct-response television with its promise of how-to-do-it tools and vegetable cutters, as well as get-rich investing. An interesting variation is found in rural India where traveling performers present live infomercials from mobile stages to a large and growing population of international brand-focused customers. Late-night informercial products like Snuggies and the Windshield Wonder that clean the insides of car windows are also showing up in retail stores, such as Walmart, Target, and Bed Bath & Beyond.[37]

The actual form of a television commercial depends on whether a network, local, or subscription service schedule is used.

- *Sponsorships* In program **sponsorships,** the advertiser assumes the total financial responsibility for producing the program and providing the accompanying commercials. The *Hallmark Hall of Fame* program is an example of a sponsored program. Sponsorship can have a powerful effect on the viewing public, especially because the advertiser can control the content and quality of the program as well as the placement and length of commercials. However, the costs of producing and sponsoring a 30- or 60-minute program make this option too expensive for most advertisers. Several advertisers can produce a program jointly as an alternative to single sponsorship. This plan is quite common with sporting events, where each sponsor receives a 15-minute segment.
- *Participations* Sponsorships represent less than 10 percent of network advertising. The rest is sold as **participations,** where advertisers pay for 10, 15, 20, 30, or 60 seconds of commercial time during one or more programs. The advertiser can buy any time that is available. This approach, which is the most common one used in network advertising today, provides a great deal more flexibility in market coverage, target audiences, scheduling, and budgeting. Participations do not create the same high impact as sponsorships, however. Finally, the "time avails" (available time slots) for the most popular programs are often bought up by the largest advertisers, leaving fewer good time slots for small advertisers.

The price of a commercial is based on the rating of the surrounding program (note the rating is for the program, not the commercial). The price is also based on the daypart during which the commercial is shown. The following table shows the Television Standard Dayparts. The most expensive time block is prime time.

- *Spot Announcements* The third form a television commercial can take is the **spot announcement.** Spot announcements are commercials that appear in the breaks between programs, which local affiliates sell to advertisers who want to show their ads locally. Commercials are sold on a station-by-station basis to local, regional, and national advertisers. However, local buyers dominate spot television. PSAs are also distributed to stations for local play based on the station's time availability.

Standard Television Dayparts

Early morning	M–F 7–9 A.M.
Daytime	M–F 9 A.M.–4:30 P.M.
Early fringe	M–F 4:30–7:30 P.M.
Prime access	M–F 7:30–8 P.M.
	M–S 8–11 P.M.
	Su 7–11 P.M.
Late news	M–Su 11–11:30 P.M.
Late night	M–Su 11:30 P.M.–1 A.M.
Saturday morning	Sa 8 A.M.–1 P.M.
Weekend afternoon	Sa–Su 1 P.M.–7 P.M.

Note: All times are Eastern Standard Time (EST).

Media sales operations are trying to encourage advertising through various types of partnerships and cooperative advertising strategies. We have already mentioned ESPN's "mini-mercials," which embed a brand's reminder ad in the opening of a sports program. Another example comes from Campbell's Soup and CBS, which partnered in an advertising campaign that paired various shows with different types of Campbell soups.

Effectiveness of Television   Television is used because of the reach it delivers. You may remember from our previous discussions of our Facets of Effects Model that one of the most important effects is awareness. A recent study of viewers conducted by the Yankelovich research company for the Television Bureau of Advertising tracked the impact of television from awareness, which it measured at 80 percent, through various decision-making stages for 15 product categories ending at 53 percent for transactions. The study compared TV and the Internet and determined that television had more impact, particularly at the awareness stage.[38]

Television advertising also makes a strong visual and emotional impact. The interaction of sight, sound, color, motion, and drama creates a stronger emotional response than most other forms of advertising media. In Chapter 4 we mentioned *engagement,* which certainly applies to TV. Television is particularly good at creating messages that can be highly engrossing. Even with TiVo, people still sit through advertisements and use online search engines to seek out advertising that is relevant to them.[39] Television is also good for delivering messages that require action, movement, and demonstration, such as the messages created for Avista Utilities in Portland, Oregon. When it comes to energy efficiency, Karl Schroeder explains, every little bit adds up—using energy-efficient bulbs, cleaning the coils on a refrigerator, using Energy Star appliances, and other environmental practices. To spread this idea and empower customers, the messages demonstrate different actions folks can take to improve the efficiency of their home.

Television has drawbacks, as well. The commercial breaks between programs can be difficult time slots for advertisers because there is a great deal of clutter from competing commercials, station breaks, and public service announcements. Commercial breaks also tend to be the time when viewers take a break from their television sets. Research has found that the best position is at the beginning and the end of the commercial break—the spots in the middle have only a quarter of the impact.

The downside of large reach to a mass audience is **wasted reach**—communication directed at an audience that may not fit the advertiser's target market. Cable television is much more

Principle
If you are going to use television, design a message that takes advantage of its visual and emotional impact.

Principle
As the number of commercial messages increases, the visibility and persuasiveness of television advertising diminishes.

targeted than network and spot television, so it has less waste. Disinterest is another problem because people are often inclined to **zip** (fast forward) or **zap** (change channels) commercials if they don't have a DVR.

Another big drawback is that television advertising is expensive relative to other media, both for time and production costs. (*Note:* Television is "expensive" in terms of dollar amounts even though it is relatively cheap in terms of gross impressions because its audience is so much larger than that of other media.) A 30-second, prime-time spot averages about $185,000, and most advertisers would want to run a commercial multiple times. That average, however, doesn't mean much because costs vary considerably for a highly rated prime-time show versus a lower rated program. Production costs are higher than ads in other media, as well. They include filming the commercial (several thousand to several hundred thousand dollars) and paying the talent—writers, directors, and actors. When celebrities are used, the price tag can be millions of dollars for the campaign budget.

Another problem is clutter, and its stepchildren, intrusiveness and irritation. In the past, the National Association of Broadcasters (NAB) restricted the allowable commercial time per hour to approximately 6 minutes, but the Justice Department overturned this restriction and the number of commercials has increased significantly (up to 20 minutes per hour of programming). As the number of commercials increases, the visibility and persuasiveness of television advertising diminishes. As clutter has increased, advertisements are becoming more intrusive to grab attention from a disinterested and irritated audience. The high irritation level is what has led viewers to mute and zap commercials.

OTHER VIDEO FORMATS

Radio and television dominate broadcast, but other broadcast forms also carry advertising and marketing communication messages. We'll discuss film trailers and other video formats here.

Movie Trailers and Disc Ads

Movie theaters, particularly the large chain theaters, sell time at the beginning of their film showings for commercials, called **trailers.** Most of these trailers are previews advertising upcoming films, but some are national commercials for brands, ads for local businesses, public service announcements, or other forms of sponsored programs. These messages can be targeted to a certain extent by the nature of the film and the rating, such as G or PG. Some films, such as *Shall We Dance,* draw an audience that is heavily female, while action films, such as the *Matrix* series, draw more males.

Movie trailers are one of the fastest growing types of advertising because of advances in digital technology. According to the Cinema Advertising Council, in-theater advertising is a $500 million industry.[40] The cost of the trailer is based on the number of theaters showing the spot and their estimated monthly attendance. Generally the cost of a trailer in a first-run theater is about the same as the cost of a 30-second television spot in prime time. The reason trailers are valued by marketers is that they play to a captive audience with their attention on the screen, not reading or talking to other people. The attention level is higher for these ads than for almost any other form of commercials. But the captive audience dimension is also the biggest disadvantage of movie advertising because people who have paid $6 to $10 for a ticket resent the intrusion. They feel they paid for the ticket so they shouldn't have to pay with their time and attention to watch commercials.

DVD, Blu-ray, and other video distribution systems also place ads before their movies and on the cases. The targeting strategy is the same as that for theater ads, called *trailers,* where the ad is matched to the movie audience. Unlike the theaters, rental videos tend to carry more brand advertising than movie previews. Even some billboards are now equipped to run mini-movies and ads electronically. The job search company *Monster.com* has been successful with trailers that replay as electronic signboard messages in public spaces—another example of media convergence with video appearing as out-of-home media.

Promotional Videos

Promotional video networks run sponsored programs and commercials, such as the channels you see in grocery stores, doctor's offices, and truck stops that distribute commercials by video or satellites. The pioneer in this arena is Channel M, which markets customized in-store video programming to such companies as Payless Shoes and Kampgrounds of America.

Marketers, such as General Electric and Pepsi, are experimenting with short video clips—both live-action and animated—that can be watched free on the video-on-demand service available to Time Warner cable customers. The shorts can also be seen on the GE website (*www.ge.com/imaginationtheater*), as well as on sites like MySpace, Google Video, and YouTube. Finally, videos and DVDs are used for product literature, as well as in public relations for video news releases (VNRs) to the media.

Using Broadcast and Video Effectively

Now that we have reviewed television and radio media, as well as other film and video formats, we can summarize how to use broadcast media effectively. The following table summarizes advantages and limitations of these media and provides guidelines for broadcast media decisions.

The Cinema Advertising Council (CAC) is an organization devoted to advertising in movies. This ad was placed in *Advertising Age* to reach media buyers and remind them of the power of cinema advertising to target particular groups of moviegoers.

Broadcast and Video Media Advantages and Limitations

	Advantages	*Limitations*
Radio	• Pervasiveness; in most every home and car • Reaches specialized target audiences • Reaches them at critical apertures (morning and evening drive time) • Offers high frequency; music (jingles) can be repeated more easily than other forms of advertising • Flexible, easy to change • Good for local tie-ins and promos • Mental imagery can be highly engaging • Audience less likely to switch channels when ads come on	• Listener inattentiveness; may just be on in the background • Lack of visuals • Clutter • May have buying difficulties for local buys • Lack of control: talk show content is unpredictable and may be critical
Television	• Pervasiveness; in most every home • High level of viewing • Reaches a mass national audience although can be targeted by programs • High impact: has audio, video, motion, music, color, high drama • Cost efficient	• Clutter—cable offers a large number of channels • High production costs • Wasted reach • Inflexibility; can't easily make last-minute changes • Intrusiveness—some audience resistance to advertising leads to zipping and zapping

Broadcast and Video Media Advantages and Limitations

	Advantages	*Limitations*
Movies	• Captive audience • No need for intrusiveness because audience can't do multitasking • High impact	• Audience resistance is high; hates being a captive audience • Expensive; needs high-value production

Looking Ahead

This chapter has provided an overview of traditional media, their characteristics, and their strengths and weaknesses. But, in truth, traditional media hardly exist any more. An interview on public radio's NPR headlined, "In a 24/7 World, What Is a Magazine?" began with this line: "It's hard to know what a magazine is these days." Is it paper? Is it a website? Martin Sorrell, head of WPP, the world's largest communication company (125 firms including Ogilvy & Mather and JWT advertising agencies) asks: "How do you define a newspaper or a magazine?" He observes, "I doubt free-to-air television or, in particular, newspapers and magazines, will ever be the same again."[41] This is one of the key points of change that Kelley pointed out in his essay in the Part 4 opener. He observes that all media, including the traditional ones, will have some type of digital and interactive component and this will only make media selection more challenging.

Not only are these traditional media formats changing, so are the ads that appear in them. CBS promoted its fall season with ads in the magazine *Entertainment Weekly* that contained video clips of its new programs. Similar to musical greeting cards, the technology used a flexible, thin, plastic screen that was activated when the two-page ad was opened. The videos also included a Pepsi Max ad inside the CBS ad. An executive at Time Warner, publisher of *EW*, observed, "It we can efficiently put video into magazines, think about the possibilities it would open up."[42]

So let's move on to the exciting and equally fast-changing world of digital media, which are generating even more new opportunities for marketing communication. The next chapter will review the dynamic world of online communication.

IT'S A WRAP

Aflac's Duck Spreads Its Wings

How effective is the Aflac duck? The Kaplan Thaler Group succeeded in creating a campaign that led to a 94 percent awareness of Aflac and an increase of 55 percent in U.S. sales during the first three years of the campaign, followed by double-digit growth in the following years. This campaign earned a Gold Effie for the duck who successfully communicated the brand personality as well as the honor of being voted one of the best-known brand icons.

Will the next generation of this ad campaign be as effective as a new agency uses the duck to challenge consumers to find out more about the company? Stay tuned.

In the meantime, you can learn much from these campaigns featuring the celebrated odd duck. This case demonstrates that even in a changing media environment that puts much emphasis on the Web and social media, traditional media are often critical to a campaign's effectiveness. Traditional media helped drive consumers to Aflac's website. All components of the campaign worked together to educate consumers about the brand, to increase brand comprehension, and have a little fun.

Also, you can learn that even as campaigns evolve, it's important to stay true to the brand. According to James Wisdom, senior manager of new media for Aflac, the message in social media, like that in the traditional media, has to "straddle a fine line between lighthearted quips and corporate messaging."

Wisdom said, "We work very hard to stay true to the Aflac Duck as he has been defined in the past, while defining his personality going forward."

As the campaign takes flight, watch as our fine-feathered friend continues to show his plucky, rock star personality and build his vocabulary beyond the one word he knows best, "Aflac."

Key Points Summary

1. **What key points should marketers know to make effective decisions about advertising in newspapers and magazines?** Newspapers are great for announcements of news. They also provide local market coverage with some geographic flexibility, plus an interaction with national news and the ability to reach shoppers who see the paper as a credible source. Magazines reach special-interest audiences who have a high level of receptivity to the message. People read them slowly, and they have long life and great image reproduction. However, magazines require long lead times, have a low level of immediacy and limited flexibility, and generally do not reach a broad mass market.

2. **What factors do marketers consider when making out-of-home media decisions?** Out-of-home media includes everything from billboards to hot-air balloons. A common out-of-home medium is outdoor advertising, which refers to billboards along streets and highways as well as posters. Outdoor is a high-impact and directional medium; it's also effective for brand reminders and relatively inexpensive with a long life. Other forms of out-of-home media include on-premise signs, posters, and transit advertising.

3. **How do radio and television work as marketing communication media?** The traditional radio stations are found on AM and FM and primarily serve local markets. AM and FM are only the beginning of the radio listener's options, which

also include public radio, cable and satellite radio, low-powered stations, and Web radio. Radio dramas engage the imagination, but radio is primarily a music-driven medium, which serves audiences defined by their musical tastes. Listeners can have a very intimate relationship with radio and can be quite loyal to their favorite stations, but radio also serves as background.

Television is useful as a marketing communication medium because it works like a movie with story, action, emotions, and visual impact. TV audiences are fragmented, often irritated by advertising, and prone to avoidance. Audiences are measured in terms of ratings and share. TV's greatest advantage is that it is pervasive and cost efficient when reaching a large number of viewers. Because of the special-interest aspect of cable programming, it is good at reaching more narrowly targeted audiences.

4. **How do marketers use movies and other video formats for marketing communication?** Movie theaters sell time for advertisements before their films. Marketing communication messages are also carried on discs, such as DVDs and Blu-ray, as well as in lobbies and other public spaces. Video-generated commercials, sponsored programs, and announcements can also be seen in supermarkets, transit stations, and waiting rooms for professional services such as doctors' offices.

Words of Wisdom: Recommended Reading

Aitchison, Jim, *Cutting Edge Radio: How to Create the World's Best Radio Ads for Brands in the 21st Century,* Upper Saddle River, NJ: Pearson Education, 2002.

Hassett, James, *AdverSelling: How to Build Stronger Relationships,* Burlington, MA: The Avertraining Group, 2005.

Prooth, Victor, and Shelly Ng, *"Radio Advertising Does Not Work." Says Who?* Chicago: American Mass Media Corp, 2006.

Weyland, Paul, *Successful Local Broadcast Sales,* New York: American Management Association, 2008.

Winicki, Michael, *Killer Techniques to Succeed with Newspaper, Magazine, and Yellow Pages Advertising,* Big Noisy Publishing, 2005.

Key Terms

3-D television, p. 405

addressable television, p. 405

affiliates, p. 398

aperture, p. 401

bleed, p. 388

broadcast media, p. 397

broadcast network, p. 402

cable radio, p. 398

cable television, p. 404

classified advertising, p. 385

consumer magazines, p. 387

controlled circulation, p. 388

Review Questions

1. Explain how newspapers vary based on frequency of publication, format and size, and circulation.

2. Explain how newspaper readership is determined and measured.

3. How is magazine readership measured?

4. Explain how advertising impact is measured for outdoor advertising.

5. What is the greatest advantage of outdoor advertising? Directory advertising?

6. How can radio be used most effectively, and what are the advantages and limitations of advertising on radio?

7. How can television be used most effectively, and what are the advantages and limitations of advertising on television?

8. What are trailers and how are they used as an advertising form?

9. How can movie advertising be used most effectively, and what are its advantages and limitations?

Discussion Questions

1. You are the media planner for an agency handling a small chain of upscale furniture outlets in a medium-sized metro market that concentrates most of its advertising in the Sunday supplement of the local newspaper. The client also schedules display ads in the daily editions for special sales. Six months ago a new, high-style metropolitan lifestyle magazine approached you about advertising for your client. You deferred a decision by saying you'd see what reader acceptance would be. Now the magazine has shown some steady increases. If you were to include the magazine on the ad schedule, you'd have to reduce the newspaper advertising somewhat. What would be your recommendation to the furniture store owner?

2. A new radio station is moving into your community. Management is not sure how to position the station in this market and

has asked you to develop a study to help make this decision. What key research questions must be asked and what research methods would you recommend using to get more information about this market and the new station's place in it?

3. You are the media planner for a cosmetics company introducing a new line of makeup for teenage girls. Your research indicates that television advertising might be an effective medium for creating awareness about your new product line. In exploring this idea, how do you design a television advertising strategy that will reach your target market successfully? What programs and times do you choose? Why? Would you consider syndicated television? Why or why not?

4. You have been asked to advise on where advertising should be placed for a new restaurant in town that specializes in

low-fat and low-carb healthy food. Consider newspaper, magazine, outdoor, directory, and local radio and television advertising. Evaluate each medium in terms of its strengths and weaknesses and how well it connects with the people you think would be the target market for this restaurant. What more do you need to know to determine the appropriateness of these media for this restaurant? In your response, begin by stating your advertising goals and your target audience profile, then state what you might or might not accomplish by advertising in each print medium.

5. *Three-Minute Debate* You are a major agency media director who has just finished a presentation to a prospective client in convenience food marketing where you recommend increasing the use of local radio and television advertising in spot markets. During the Q and A period, a client

representative says: "We know that network television viewers' loyalty is nothing like it was ten or even five years ago because so many people now turn to cable, VCRs, and the Web. There are smaller audiences per program each year, yet television time costs continue to rise. Do you still believe we should consider commercial television as a primary medium for our company's advertising?" Another member of the client team questions whether broadcast is effective given the clutter on both radio and television with long commercial pods. "Why shouldn't we decrease our use of broadcast advertising?" How would you answer? Working in a team of classmates, develop an argument either in support of increasing or decreasing the use of broadcast advertising for this client. Prepare a presentation to give in class that explains your team's point of view.

Take-Home Projects

1. *Portfolio Project* You have been asked by the director of your school's student union to make a chart of all the traditional media serving your market to use in promoting the center's 50th anniversary events. Develop a profile for each medium giving the key characteristics, such as type of programming (for broadcast), the type of audience reached, the products commonly advertised, and the appropriateness of this medium as an advertising vehicle for the center's special celebration. At the end of your media analysis,

identify the top three that you would recommend and explain why.

2. *Mini-Case Analysis* Aflac has been an award-winning campaign for years. Explain how its media use has contributed to its success. In particular, describe the changes in the new strategy and how the media mix has evolved. If you were a member of the team planning the next year's campaign, what changes would you recommend? What other media might be useful?

Team Project: The BrandRevive Campaign

Review the strengths and limitations of the various types of print, out-of-home, and broadcast media discussed in this chapter in terms of your BrandRevive campaign.

- Review your previous audience research to develop some insight into your target's media use.
- Go through the lists of strengths and limitations, as well as the discussions in the text for each traditional medium we discussed in this chapter and analyze if that medium is or isn't appropriate for this BrandRevive project. Give each

medium a score of from 1 to 10 with 10 being an excellent medium to use and 1 being the least appropriate.

- From your analysis, make a prioritized list beginning with the medium that you think is the most appropriate. For each of your top two traditional media write a one-paragraph recommendation that explains and justifies your thinking.
- Convert your key findings to a PowerPoint presentation that is no longer than three slides. Prepare and practice to give this presentation to your class.

Hands-On Case

The Century Council

Read the Century Council case in the Appendix before coming to class.

1. Which advertising medium do you believe would be more impactful in The Stupid Drink campaign; television or outdoor stadium boards? Why?

2. The Stupid Drink campaign ignores college radio. Why do you think the media planners thought this was the correct choice? How could they prove it?

3. In choosing colleges to advertise at, The Stupid Drink team choose "ranked" party schools. Do you agree with that methodology of targeting? Why or Why not?

CHAPTER 8

Media Channels 2: Digital Media

Chapter 9
Marketing communications using digital media channels

Chapter at a glance

Main topics

Case studies

Learning objectives

After reading this chapter, the reader should be able to:

- Distinguish between the different types of digital media channels
- Evaluate the advantages and disadvantages of each digital media channel for marketing communications
- Assess the suitability of different types of digital media for different purposes

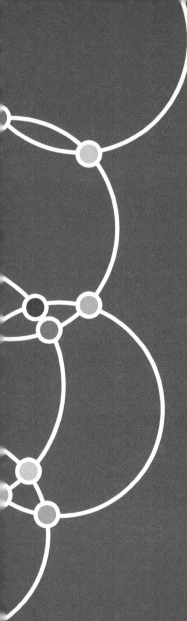

Questions for marketers

Key questions for marketing managers related to this chapter are:

- Which digital communications media should we select for different types of market?
- What are the success factors for using digital media that will make our campaigns more effective?

**Scan code
to find the
latest updates
for topics in
this chapter**

Links to other chapters

Related chapters are:

- Chapter 1 introduces the main options for communications with digital media.
- Chapter 8 reviews how to plan campaigns which use digital media channels. The section towards the end of the chapter on 'Selecting the right mix of digital media communications tools' in 'Step 5. Budgeting and selecting the digital media mix', is particularly relevant.
- Chapter 10 also considers the measurement of communications effectiveness.

Introduction

Digital marketing managers use many different **digital media channels**, such as affiliate, e-mail, social and search engine marketing, to attract visitors to their website. They also have options such as display advertising and widget marketing for communicating brand values to visitors of third-party websites. Traditional communications disciplines such as advertising, direct mail and PR remain important in generating awareness and favourability about brands and in encouraging visits to a companies online presence.

Choosing the most effective digital communications techniques and refining them to attract visitors and new customers at an efficient cost is now a major marketing activity, both for online business and multichannel businesses. In this chapter, we explain the differences between the different digital media options and review the strengths, weaknesses and success factors for using the communications techniques.

How is this chapter structured?

This chapter is structured around the six main digital media channels we have identified in Table 9.1 (Figure 1.9 on page 28 portrays a graphical summary). To enable easy comparison of the different techniques and to assist with assignments and revision, we have structured each section the same way:

- *What is it?* A description of the digital media channel.
- *Advantages and disadvantages?* A structured review of the benefits and drawbacks of each channel.
- *Best practice in planning and management.* A summary of the issues such as targeting, measurement and creative which need to be considered when running a campaign using each digital channel. This expands on the coverage given in the previous chapter on these issues.

As you read each section, you should compare the relative strengths and weaknesses of the different techniques and how consumers perceive different options in terms of trust (Activity 9.1). In the final section, we summarise their strengths and weaknesses for different applications.

Table 9.1	Summary of different digital media channels	
Digital media channel	**Description**	**Different communications techniques**
Search engine marketing (SEM)	Gaining listings in the search engine results pages of the major search engines, Google, Bing, YouTube and popular country-specific engines. Also includes advertising on third-party publisher sites which are part of the search display networks	• Search Engine Optimisation (SEO) listing in the natural listing which does not attract a fee per click. Based on on-page optimisation and link-building • Pay-per-click (advertising) sponsored listings using Google AdWords for example
Online public relations (E-PR)	Maximising favourable mentions of your company, brands, products or websites on third-party sites such as social networks or blogs that are likely to be visited by your target audience. Also includes monitoring and, where necessary, responding to negative mentions and conducting public relations via a site through a press centre or blog, for example	• Syndicating content (e.g. press releases), gaining positive mentions, managing reputation on third-party sites, particularly forums and social networks • Use of owned media – own company feeds, blogs and feeds • Blogger and influencer outreach for earned media

Table 9.1	Continued	
Online partnerships including affiliate marketing	Creating and managing long-term arrangements to promote your online services on third-party websites or through e-mail communications. Different forms of partnership include link building, affiliate marketing, aggregators such as price comparison sites, online sponsorship and co-branding	• Commission-based affiliate marketing • Creating long-term partnership relationships such as sponsorship, link-building or editorial
Interactive display advertising	Use of online display ads such as banners and rich media ads to achieve brand awareness and encourage click-through to a target site	• Site-specific media buys • Use of ad networks • Behavioural targeting
Opt-in e-mail marketing	Using legal, permission-based e-mailing to prospects or customers who have agreed to receive e-mails from an organisation. E-mails to communicate with prospects can be rented from a publisher or other list owner or companies can build up their own 'house list' containing customer or prospect details	• Acquisition e-mail activity including list rental, co-branded campaigns, advertising on e-newsletters • Retention and growth activity, e.g. house list for e-newsletters and customer e-mail campaigns • Automatic or event-triggered e-mail campaign activity
Social media marketing including viral and electronic word-of-mouth marketing	Social media marketing and viral marketing is effectively online word of mouth – compelling brand-related content is shared, forwarded or discussed electronically or discussed offline to help achieve awareness and, in some cases, drive response. Strong link with online PR activity	• Branded presence or advertising within social network • Creating 'viral agents' or compelling interactive content • Encouraging amplification of viral messages • Using customer advocacy effect • Widget marketing

The importance of each of these digital media channels in driving visitors will vary from company to company, but to give you an indication of how important they are on average see Digital marketing insight 9.1. You can see why search engine marketing is an important channel and this is why we start our coverage in this chapter with this. You can also see that direct traffic is high reflecting the importance of visits driven by traditional channels or visits from e-mail or social networks that are not being tracked separately. You can also see that links from other sites are also quite significant.

Digital marketing insight 9.1   How balanced is your referrer mix?

One approach to determining the most appropriate mix of digital media channels is this compilation across all sites that use the web analytics tool Google Analytics to measure site effectiveness (See Chapter 10 for a description of how these tools work). Figure 9.1 shows the average mix of referrers across sites tracked by Google Analytics.
This is a summary of the different terms in the pie chart:

- *Search engine* – this groups both natural and paid search (AdWords).
- *Referral* – this is traffic from other sites which have direct links to a site.

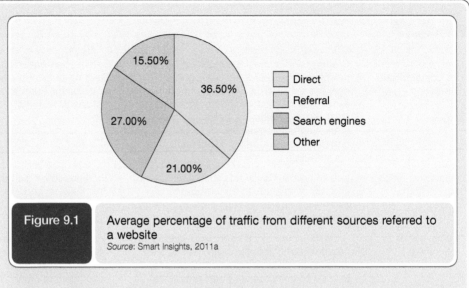

Figure 9.1	Average percentage of traffic from different sources referred to a website

Source: Smart Insights, 2011a

- *Direct* – direct traffic results from URL type ins, bookmarks or when e-mail marketing isn't tracked by marketers adding specific link tracking to their e-mail so that they show up in analytics. These days direct traffic will also include non-browser traffic from visitors clicking on apps for reading social messages like Hootsuite or Tweetdeck or other mobile apps linking to a site.
- *Other* – campaigns include AdWords when linked to the Google Account and any other campaigns like affiliates, display ads and e-mail campaigns when these have had marketing campaign tags attached. In this compilation AdWords is included under search engines.

Digital marketing in practice   The Smart Insights Interview

Kate Webb, online marketing manager at Vision Express, explains how the multichannel retailer prioritises its use of social media to meet business goals.

The Interview

Q. How big an impact has the increase in popularity of social media with consumers had on Vision Express?

Kate Webb: It's had quite an impact in terms of time and resource, especially in the early days. As a company we're relatively new to social media; we've only been active for just over a year. We spent a lot of time during the first three to six months listening, watching and learning what consumers were saying about our brand/looking for from our brand, in order to decide on how we should communicate, and where – which platforms.

During this time we have seen both our follower/fan numbers grow, but more importantly the engagement with our customers is increasing and we feel that our customers are really starting to converse with us as a brand.

Since being involved in social media we have seen an increase in the number of customers who mention us directly, or seek us out, rather than simply mentioning our brand name in passing conversation. To us this is an important development in building our customer relationship.

At Vision Express our social media activities are based on engaging with our existing customer base; we want to improve on relationships, or continue offline relationships, with our customers, online. In the optical industry we have a long purchase cycle, on average our customers come back to us every two years, so it is a long period during which to maintain our social media relationships.

We have found that for probably about one to two per cent, of our customer base, social media is their main point of contact with us. The type of communication varies between the different social media platforms, for example we find that Twitter is more of a customer service tool, whilst Facebook is a fun and engaging platform, suitable for promotional outreach.

There is still progress to be made, especially as social media grows and platforms are developed/changed, but we're confident we're on the right track to providing the same high level of service, that our customers get in our stores, online.

Q. What do you see as the key parts of a social media strategy that require management?

Kate Webb: I find that too often businesses think that social media is just about posting messages about the company on Twitter or Facebook, or getting an agency in to handle everything for them. But the key to making social media work, for me, is to have a strong strategy behind it, and to manage that strategy.

For me the key areas of focus in this strategy should be:

- *Brand/business persona*: I feel it's key to define a persona or personality for your business and to identify how you want to position your brand on social media, is the brand/business fun/funky, calm/serious, sensitive/nurturing or brash/loud? You need flexibility to evolve this over time as your relationship with customers grows.
- *Which platforms*: There are hundreds of social media platforms that we could all be involved in, so it's key to identify which platforms support your business objectives, and which ones you are going to get involved with. Otherwise resources and communication will simply be spread too thinly.
- *Goals/objectives*: It is important to ensure that your social media objectives or goals are aligned with that of your organisation. What is it that you want to achieve via social media. For Vision Express, our three critical goals are to:
  - Add value and service to our online customers, via informative dialogue, responsive customer service and feedback. This also works as a 2-way path, in that we then pass onto our store network all/any feedback we have received from our online customers.
  - Engage with our online customers, and build relationships with them. In order to do this effectively, we are working towards a one customer view database, which will enable us to match social media activity to in-store activity by our customers, thus enabling us to provide a tailored approach in our conversations.
  - Build brand awareness and consumer knowledge about our service offering. We want our customers to understand our company, and to recognise our values, ethics and personality, online & offline.
- *Analytics/results*: Be this sentiment or engagement levels, reporting on results/analytics needs to be regular, managed and analysed in order to adapt future strategy.
- *Technology advancements*: Social media platforms are changing all the time. Because of this it is imperative that we understand and gain knowledge of how these advancements/changes will affect our business's social media presence going forward. For example the development of Facebook's iframes in March this year, opened up a great opportunity for us to integrate our websites core offers into our Facebook page.

Q. How should a company assess the relevance of different social media opportunities to prioritise their focus?

Kate Webb: Having clear objectives and a clear strategy will help. Enabling you, on a case by case basis, to identify what social media opportunities work for which promotion/aspect of the business.

It's important for any business/brand not to spread their actions/activities too thinly, identify where the majority of your customers are and focus on engaging well with your customers on a few platforms.

As well as identifying which platforms to be active on, it's important to also understand to what extent you work with these platforms, does your business need/require interactive apps or games? Or is simple communication the key to your social media engagement.

I feel it is also important to identify where social media fits in with your overall online and offline presence, and ensure that it complements your other activities. Recently I have seen an increase in brands advertising both online and on TV their Facebook and Twitter presences, but not their website? To me, a brands website should take precedence, and social media presences should complement the website messaging and be aimed at engaging customers with the website.

If through doing these engagement activities we acquire customers, then great, but this isn't our primary focus.

Q. What advice would you give to a company starting a social media listening/ reputation management initiative?

Kate Webb: Listen, listen and listen some more. Social media isn't about who shouts the loudest, it's about engaging in conversation with your customers/prospective customers and about keeping them informed.

There are some free tools which you can use at the very beginning, such as Tweetdeck or Hootsuite, but bear in mind these are often limited to either one platform, or to scheduling outreach messages only.

If you are really serious about social media, and I think companies need to be these days, you need to enlist a social media monitoring platform, which will enable you to listen to what consumers are saying about your brand across micromedia (Twitter/ Facebook), blogs and forums.

You won't be able to respond to all consumer mentions, due to forum rules, but you can at least listen and feed this back into the business, so you can modify activities, or continue doing popular ones! Start small, don't overstretch your resources, and be realistic about the amount of time/resource and money social media can take up.

A few key things to remember are once you start talking, you need to continue the commitment to maintain the conversations, and ensure you gain inter-company awareness, there is nothing worse than talking to a customer via Twitter, and then having them go into store to be presented with 'We're on Twitter? I didn't know that'.

You will also need to get to know your customers, the ideal solution here is to integrate social media activities into your core customer database, so you have one customer view, but this can take time, money and resource. In the interim, the better social media monitoring tools these days are offering engagement platforms, which allow you to add notes and assign tasks, so you can build up a reasonable knowledge of your social media customers.

Q. Where do you think the responsibilities for managing social media marketing in a company should lie? How is it managed at Vision Express?

Kate Webb: By spending our first three to six months listening to what our customers were saying about our brand and what they were looking for from our brand, we managed to identify that our social media activities needed to be part of the whole business, not just an 'add-on' to our marketing activities.

It is important that social media activities have management 'buy-in' in any business. It needs to be integrated into core business activities if it is going to work properly. To integrate these activities into different departments correctly requires management support, the management structure need to understand why/how/who social media impacts on and affects both internally and within our customer base.

As a result, so far, we've integrated social media into a couple of key departments within the business, with the online marketing team as social media 'owners', in that we will identify the next strategic steps, bring in agency support, provide understanding of new developments and report on analytics and progress.

We have involvement from our customer care team, who respond on a day-to-day basis to customer enquiries/queries and feedback. We integrate social media into our marketing planning activities from the out-set, identifying whether a promotion is suitable for social media and if so, which platform it suits best, and we have our product department involved to provide a great level of product information and advice

To have social media as purely a marketing tool/activity will restrict a business in providing the right level of customer care, and will lead to sporadic/untimely and unfocused outreach.

Activity 9.1   ## How do consumers rate communications

Figure 9.2 shows consumer ratings of different forms of advertising. Review the alternatives and then discuss the implications for a marketer using these communications channels.

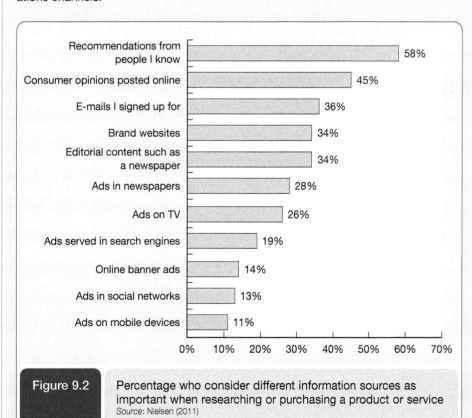

Figure 9.2 — Percentage who consider different information sources as important when researching or purchasing a product or service
Source: Nielsen (2011)

Search engine marketing

Search engine marketing (SEM)
Promoting an organisation through search engines to meet its objectives by delivering relevant content in the search listings for searchers and encouraging them to click through to a destination site. The two key techniques of SEM are *search engine optimisation (SEO)* to improve results from the natural listings, and *paid-search marketing* to deliver results from the sponsored listings within the search engines.

Search engine marketing (SEM) is vital for generating quality visitors to a website as suggested by Figure 9.1. We all now naturally turn to a search engine when we are seeking a new product, service or entertainment. The main options include Google, Bing, the Google-owned YouTube, which is the second largest search engine by volumes of searches in many countries or other regional search engine. We also turn to search when we are familiar with a brand, shortcutting site navigation by searching for a brand, appending a brand name to a product or typing a URL into Google, which is surprisingly common, accounting for over 50 per cent of paid search expenditure according to Atlas (2007). This is known as **navigational (or brand) search**. Given the obvious importance of reaching an audience during their consideration process for a product or when they are locating a brand, search engine marketing (SEM) has become a fiercely competitively area of digital marketing.

There are two main types of SEM that are quite distinct in the marketing activities needed to manage them, so we will study them separately, although in practice they should be integrated:

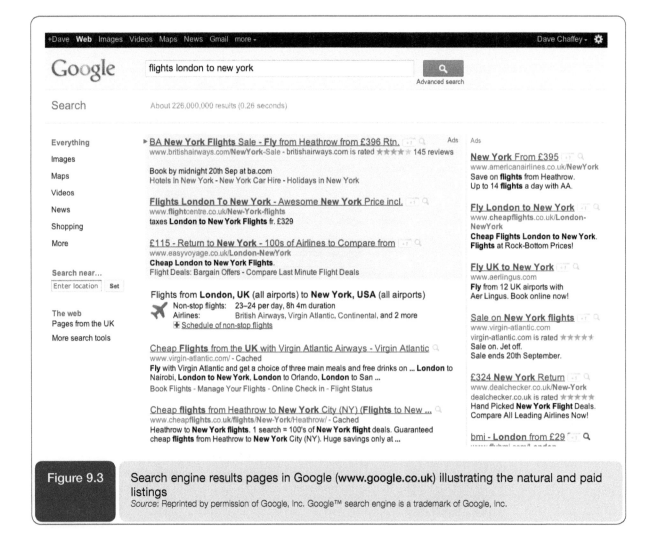

Figure 9.3   Search engine results pages in Google (**www.google.co.uk**) illustrating the natural and paid listings
Source: Reprinted by permission of Google, Inc. Google™ search engine is a trademark of Google, Inc.

1 **Search engine optimisation (SEO)** involves achieving the highest position or ranking practical in the **natural or organic listings** shown in Figure 9.3 as the main body of the **search engine results pages (SERPS)** across a range of specific combination of keywords (or keyphrases) entered by search engine users.

As well as listing pages which the search engine determines as relevant for the search performed based on the text it contains and other factors, such as links to the page, the SERPs also contain other tools which searchers may find useful. Google terms these tools part of a strategy known as **universal search** for blended search. For example, Figure 9.3 shows a link to a price comparison service.

2 **Paid search (pay-per-click) marketing (PPC)** is similar to conventional advertising; here a relevant text ad with a link to a company page is displayed when the user of a search engine types in a specific phrase. A series of text ads usually labelled as 'sponsored links' are displayed above, or to the right of, the natural listings as in Figure 9.3. Although many searchers prefer to click on the natural listings, a sufficient number do click on the paid listings (typically around a quarter or a third of all clicks) such that they are highly profitable for companies such as Google and a well-designed paid search campaign can drive a significant amount of business for companies. There are also opportunities to create awareness and response from pay-per click ads displayed on third-party sites as we will see in the section on paid search marketing.

The importance of effective search engine marketing is suggested by Figure 9.4 which shows that generating the highest rankings for a company in the search engine results pages (SERPs) can generate many more visits because of a higher clickthrough rate. Note that click-through rate according to position will vary dramatically by type of keyword such as brand or generic keyword, but this research is based on 10,000 keywords across 250 B2C and B2B companies. To use search marketing effectively it's important to understand common customer behaviours, read Digital marketing insights 9.2.

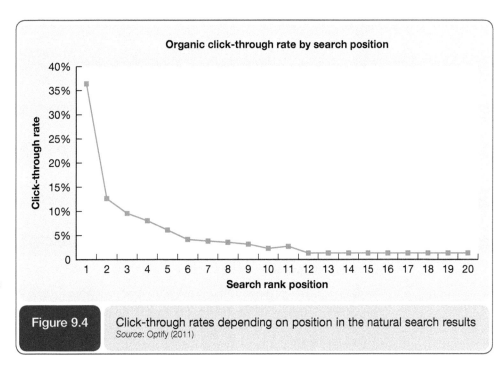

Figure 9.4   Click-through rates depending on position in the natural search results
Source: Optify (2011)

Digital marketing insight 9.2	Understanding consumer search engine behaviour

Search marketing firm Performics (2010) researched search preferences for a panel of 5000 users. The type of information they use search engines to find is shown in Figure 9.5. You can see this includes both information for online and offline purchase.

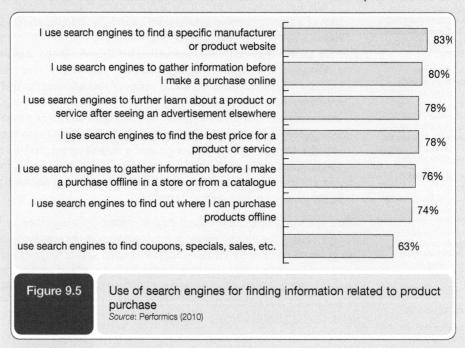

I use search engines to find a specific manufacturer or product website	83%
I use search engines to gather information before I make a purchase online	80%
I use search engines to further learn about a product or service after seeing an advertisement elsewhere	78%
I use search engines to find the best price for a product or service	78%
I use search engines to gather information before I make a purchase offline in a store or from a catalogue	76%
I use search engines to find out where I can purchase products offline	74%
use search engines to find coupons, specials, sales, etc.	63%

Figure 9.5 Use of search engines for finding information related to product purchase
Source: Performics (2010)

- More than three-quarters of respondents search to learn more about a product or service after seeing an ad elsewhere.
- Searchers are tenacious – if at first they don't succeed, they will modify their search and try again (89 per cent), try a different search engine (89 per cent), and go through multiple search results pages if necessary (79 per cent).
- 43 per cent at least occasionally view or click on sponsored video ads.
- Nearly two-thirds know the difference between natural and sponsored search results, with those age 18–29 most likely to be aware of the difference.
- 92 per cent click on the sponsored results, although many don't acknowledge this when asked.

Source: Performics (2010)

What is SEO?

Robots or spiders
Spiders are software processes, technically known as robots, employed by search engines to index web pages of registered sites on a regular basis. They follow or crawl links between pages and record the reference URL of a page for future analysis.

Improving positions in the natural listings is dependent on marketers understanding the process whereby search engines compile an index by sending out spiders or robots to crawl around sites that are registered with that search engine (Figure 9.6). The figure shows that the technology harnessed to create the natural listings involves these main processes:

1 *Crawling*. The purpose of the crawl is to identify relevant pages for indexing and assess whether they have changed. Crawling is performed by **robots** (bots) that are also known as **spiders.** These access web pages and retrieve a reference URL of the page for later analysis and indexing.

Although the terms 'bot' and 'spider' give the impression of something physical visiting a site, the bots are simply software processes running on a search engine's server which request pages, follow the links contained on that page and so create a series of page references with associated URLs. This is a recursive process, so each link followed will find additional links which then need to be crawled.

2 *Indexing.* An index is created to enable the search engine to rapidly find the most relevant pages containing the query typed by the searcher. Rather than searching each page for a query phrase, a search engine 'inverts' the index to produce a lookup table of documents containing particular words.

The index information consists of phases stored within a document and also other information characterising a page such as the document's title, meta description, PageRank, trust or authority, spam rating, etc. For the keywords in the document, additional attributes will be stored such as semantic markup (<h1>, <h2> headings denoted within HTML), occurrence in **link anchor text**, proximity, frequency or density and position in document, etc. The words contained in link anchor text 'pointing' to a page are particularly important in determining search rankings.

3 *Ranking or scoring.* The indexing process has produced a lookup of all the pages that contain particular words in a query, but they are not sorted in terms of relevance. Ranking of the document to assess the most relevant set of documents to return in the SERPs occurs in real time for the search query entered. First, relevant documents will be retrieved from a runtime version of the index at a particular data centre, then a rank in the SERPs for each document will be computed based on many ranking factors, of which we highlight the main ones in later sections.

Link anchor text
The text used to form the blue underlined hyperlink viewed in a web browser defined in the HTML source. For example, a link: Visit Dave Chaffey's Digital Marketing site is created by the HTML code: <A href="http://www.smartinsights.com">Visit Dave Chaffey's Digital Marketing site</A>.

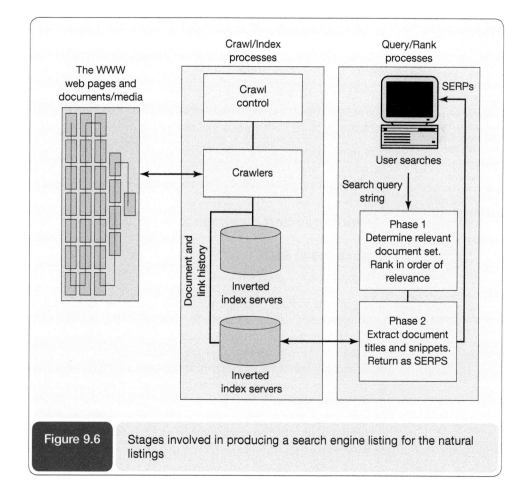

| Figure 9.6 | Stages involved in producing a search engine listing for the natural listings |

4 *Query request and results serving.* The familiar search engine interface accepts the searcher's query. The user's location is assessed through their IP address and the query is then passed to a relevant data centre for processing. Ranking then occurs in real time for a particular query to return a sorted list of relevant documents and these are then displayed on the search results page.

Search engine ranking factors

Google has stated that it uses more than 200 factors or signals within its search ranking algorithms. These include positive ranking factors that help boost position and negative factors or filters which are used to remove search engine spam from the index where SEO companies have used unethical approaches such as automatically creating links to mislead the Google algorithms.

The two most important factors for good ranking positions in all the main search engines are:

On-page optimisation
Writing copy and applying markup such as the <title> tag and heading tag <h1> to highlight to search engine relevant keyphrases within a document.

Backlink
Hyperlink which links to a particular web page (or website). Also known as an inbound link. Google PageRank and Yahoo! WebRank are methods of enumerating this.

External link building
A proactive approach to gain quality links from third-party sites.

Internal link architecture
Structuring and labelling links within a site's navigation to improve the results of SEO.

Social graph
A term popularised by Facebook in 2007 when describing its Facebook platform. The social graph describes the relationship between individuals linked through social networks and other connections such as email or personal contact.

- *Matching between web page copy and the key phrases searched.* The main factors to optimise on are keyword density, keyword formatting, keywords in anchor text and the document meta-data including page title tags. The SEO process to improve results in this area is known as **on-page optimisation**. We will cover some of details of best practice for this process in a topic later in this section.
- *Links into the page (inbound or* **backlinks**). Google counts each link to a page from another page or another site as a vote for this page. So pages and sites with more external links from other sites will be ranked more highly. The quality of the link is also important, so if links are from a site with a good reputation and relevant context for the keyphrase, then this is more valuable. Internal links are also assessed in a similar way. The processes to improve this aspect of SEO are **external link building** and **internal link architecture.**

With the growing importance of sharing of links through social media the search engines now use the number of social mentions to a page and across a site to determine ranking positions (Smart Insights, 2010). For example, a representative of Bing said of assessment of Twitter:

> We take into consideration how often a link has been tweeted or retweeted, as well as the authority of the Twitter users that shared the link.

The implications of this are that if companies can get influencers with a larger influence to recommend their content or offers through social networks this can have the dual effect of reaching more people through their **social graph** and improving rankings.

Advantages and disadvantages of SEO

Advantages of SEO

The main benefits of SEO are:

- *Significant traffic driver.* Figure 9.1 showed that search marketing can attract a significant proportion of visitors to the site IF companies are successful in implementing it.
- *Highly targeted.* Visitors are searching for particular products or services so will often have a high intent to purchase – they are qualified visitors.
- *Potentially low-cost visitors.* There are no media costs for ad display or click-through. Costs arise solely from the optimisation process where agencies are paid to improve positions in the search results.
- *Dynamic.* The search engine robots will crawl the home page of popular sites daily, so new content is included relatively quickly for the most popular pages of a site (less so for deep links).

Disadvantages of SEO

Despite the targeted reach and low cost of SEO, it is not straightforward as these disadvantages indicate:

- *Lack of predictability*. Compared with other media SEO is very unreliable in terms of the return on investment – it is difficult to predict results for a given investment and is highly competitive.
- *Time for results to be implemented*. The results from SEO may take months to be achieved, especially for new sites.
- *Complexity and dynamic nature*. The search engines take hundreds of factors into account, yet the relative weightings are not published, so there is not a direct correlation between marketing action and results – 'it is more of an art than a science'. Furthermore the ranking factors change through time. See for example, SEOmoz (2011a) for the latest updates.
- *Ongoing investment*. Investment needed to continue to develop new content and generate new links.
- *Poor for developing awareness in comparison with other media channels*. Searchers already have to be familiar with a brand or service to find it. However, it offers the opportunity for less well-known brands to 'punch above their weight' and to develop awareness following click-through.

For these reasons, investment in paid search may also be worthwhile.

Best practice in planning and managing SEO

In this section we will review six of the main approaches used to improve the results from SEO. You will see that SEO is a technical discipline and that the techniques used change through time. For this reason SEO is often outsourced to a specialist SEO agency, although some companies believe they can gain an edge through having an internal specialist who understands the company's customers and markets well. You will see, though, that some of the on-page optimisation techniques recommended in this section are relatively straightforward and it is important to control brand and proposition messages. Content editors and reviewers within a company therefore need to be trained to understand these factors and incorporate them into their copywriting.

1 Search engine submission

While some unscrupulous search marketing companies offer to register you in the 'Top 1000 search engines', in reality registering in the top 5–10 search engines of each country an organisation operates in will probably account for more than 95 per cent of the potential visitors. Most existing companies will be automatically included in the search index since the search engine robots will follow links from other sites that link to them and do not require submission services.

Search engine submission
The process of informing search engines that a site should be indexed for listing in the search engine results pages.

For new companies, achieving **search engine submission** is now straightforward – for example, in Google there is an 'Add a URL' page (e.g. **www.google.com/addurl.html**), but it is more effective to get existing sites to link to a new site which the robots will follow. Unfortunately it can take time for a site to be ranked highly in search results even if it is the index: Google allegedly places new sites in a review status sometimes referred to as the *Google sandbox effect*. However, Google search engineers deny the existence of this and explain it is a natural artifact produced by new sites having limited links, history and so reputation. Either way, it is important to remember this constraint when creating startup companies or separate unlined microsites for a campaign since you may have to rely on paid search to gain SERPS visibility.

2 Index inclusion

Index inclusion
Ensuring that as many of the relevant pages from your domain(s) are included within the search engine indexes you are targeting to be listed in.

Although a search engine robot may visit the home page of a site, it will not necessarily crawl all pages or assign them equal weight in terms of PageRank or relevance. So when auditing sites as part of an SEO initiative, SEO agencies will check how many pages are included within the search engine index for different search engines. This is known as **index inclusion**.

Potential reasons for not gaining complete index inclusion include:

- Technical reasons why the search robots do not crawl all the pages, such as the use of SEO-unfriendly content management system with complex URLs.
- Pages identified as spam or of less importance or considered to be **duplicate content** which are then contained in what used to be known as the supplemental index in Google which don't rank so highly. In these cases it is sometimes best to use a specific 'canonical' meta tag which tells the search engine which the primary page is. If you are a multinational company with different content sites for different countries, then it is challenging to deliver the relevant content for local audiences with use of regional domains tending to work best.

Duplicate content
Different pages which are evaluated by the search engine to be similar and so don't rank highly, even though they may be for distinct products or services.

Companies can check the index inclusion through:

- Reviewing web analytics data which will show the frequency with which the main search robots crawl a site.
- Using web analytics referrer information to find out which search engines a site's visitors originate from, and the most popular pages.
- Checking the number of pages that have been successfully indexed on a site. For example, in Google the search 'inurl:www.smartinsights.com' or 'site:www.smartinsights.com' lists all the pages of Dave's site indexed by Google and gives the total number in the top-right of the SERPs.

3 Keyphrase analysis

Keyphrase (keyword phrase)
The combination of words users of search engines type into a search box which form a search query.

The key to successful search engine marketing is achieving **keyphrase** relevance since this is what the search engines strive for – to match the combination of keywords typed into the search box to the most relevant destination content page. Notice that we say 'keyphrase' (short for 'keyword phrase') rather than 'keyword' since search engines such as Google attribute more relevance when there is a phrase match between the keywords that the user types and a phrase on a page. Despite this, many search companies and commentators talk about optimising your 'keywords' and, in our opinion, pay insufficient attention to keyphrase analysis.

Key sources for identifying the keyphrases your customers are likely to type when searching for your products include your market knowledge, competitors' sites, keyphrases from visitors who arrive at your site (from web analytics), the internal site search tool and the keyphrase analysis tools such as the Google Keyword Tool listed at **www.smartinsights.com/search-engine-optimisation-seo**. When completing keyphrase analysis we need to understand different qualifiers that users type in. Here are examples of common types of qualifiers for 'car insurance':

- *comparison/quality* – compare car insurance
- *adjective* (price/product qualifiers) – cheap car insurance, woman car insurance
- *intended use* – high mileage car insurance
- *product type* – holiday car insurance
- *vendor* – churchill car insurance
- *location* – car insurance UK
- *action request* – buy car insurance.

According to the Google Keyword tool for a single month in 2011, for searches completed in the UK, the most popular exact phrases related to car insurance were:

- car insurance: 550,000
- cheap car insurance: 201,000

- car insurance quotes: 110,000
- compare car insurance: 49,500
- cheapest car insurance: 40,500
- car insurance comparison: 40,500
- temporary car insurance: 33,100
- car insurance groups: 27,100
- short-term car insurance: 27,000
- car insurance for young drivers: 22,200
- classic car insurance: 22,200

These data suggest the importance of ranking well for high-volume keyphrases such as 'cheap car insurance' and to consider products and services that target a need such as 'temporary' or 'short-term insurance'.

4 On-page optimisation

Although each search engine has its own algorithm with many weighting factors that change through time, fortunately there are common factors in the match between search terms entered and the occurrence of the words on the page that influence search engine rankings.

Occurrence of search term in body copy

The number of times the keyphrase is repeated in the text of the web page is a key factor in determining the position for a keyphrase. Copy can be written to increase the number of times a word or phrase is used (technically, keyphrase density) and ultimately boost position in the search engine. Note though that search engines carry out checks that a phrase is not repeated too many times such as 'cheap flights... cheap flights... cheap flights... cheap flights... cheap flights... cheap flights... cheap flights... cheap flights...' or the keyword is hidden using the same colour text and backgound and will not list the page if this keyphrase density is too high or it believes 'search engine spamming' has occurred. Today, other ranking factors like anchor text of backlinks pointing to the page from other sites are much more important.

In its guidance for Webmasters, Google states:

> Google goes far beyond the number of times a term appears on a page and examines all aspects of the page's content (and the content of the pages linking to it) to determine if it's a good match for your query.

These other factors include:

- frequency (which must be not too excessive, i.e. less than 2–4 per cent)
- occurrence in headings <h1>, <h2>
- occurrence in anchor text of hyperlinks
- markup such as bold
- density (the number of times)
- proximity of phrase to start of document and the gap between individual keywords
- alternative image text (explained below)
- document meta-data (explained below).

Alternative image text

Graphical images can have hidden text associated with them that is not seen by the user (unless graphical images are turned off or the mouse is rolled-over the image) but will be seen and indexed by the search engine and is a minor ranking factor, particularly in images linking to other pages. For example, text about a company name and products can be assigned to a company logo using the 'ALT' tag or attribute of the image tag as follows:

```
<img name="Logo" src="logo.gif" alt="Car insurance">
```

Document meta-data

'Meta' refers to information 'about' the page whichcharacterises it. The three most important types of meta-data are the document <title> tag, the document 'descriptions' meta tag and the document 'keywords' meta tag. These need to be unique for each page on a site(s) otherwise the search engine may assess the content as duplicate and some pages may be downweighted in importance. Let's look at it in a little more detail:

1   *The document title.* The <title> tag is arguably the most important type of meta-data since each search engine places significant weighting on the keyphrases contained within it AND it is the call-to-action hyperlink on the search engine results page (Figure 9.3). If it contains powerful, relevant copy you will get more clicks and the search engine will assess relevance relative to other pages which are getting fewer clicks.

2   *The 'description' meta tag.* A meta tag is an attribute of the page within the HTML <head> section which can be set by the content owner. It doesn't directly affect ranking, but shows the information which will typically be displayed in the search engine results page. If it is absent or too short relevant 'snippets' will be used from within the body copy, but it is best to control messages and this can help identify the page as unique to prevent duplicate content problems. So, the page creator can modify this to make a stronger call-to-action in the search engine listings as in this case:

    <meta name="description" content="Direct Line offers you great value car insurance by cutting out the middleman and passing the savings directly on to you. To find out if you could save, why not get a car insurance quote? Breakdown Cover Insurance also available.">

    To see how relevant and unique your <title> and meta descriptions are, use the Google 'site': syntax with a keyphrase – this will return all the pages on your site about a particular topic. For example:

    <seo site:smartinsights.com>

    To view meta tags for a site, select View, Source or Page Source in your browser.

3   *The 'keywords' meta-tag.* The meta keywords meta-tag is used to summarise the content of a document based on keywords. Some unscrupulous SEOs can still be heard to say to potential clients ('we will optimise your meta tags'). But this is not significant today since the keywords meta tag is relatively unimportant as a ranking factor (Google has never used them), although these keywords may be important to internal search engines. For example:

    <meta name="keywords" content="Car insurance, Home insurance, Travel insurance, Direct line, Breakdown cover, Mortgages personal loans, Pet insurance, Annual holiday insurance, Car loans, uk mortgages, Life insurance, Critical illness cover">

5   External linking

Boosting externals links is vital to SEO in competitive markets – on-page optimisation is insufficient, although it is less easy to control and often neglected. The founders of Google realised that the number of links into a page and their quality was a great way of determining the relevance of a page to searchers, especially when combined with the keyphrases on that page (Brin and Page, 1998). Although the Google algorithm has been upgraded and refined continuously since then, the number and quality of external links is still recognised as the most important ranking factor and this is similar for other search engines. As we mentioned above, links shared through social media are now also used as ranking factors.

Generally, the more links a page has from good quality sites, the better its ranking will be. **PageRank** helps Google deliver relevant results since it counts each link from another site as a

PageRank
A scale between 0 to 10 used by Google named after Google founder Larry Page which is used to assess the importance of websites according to the number of inbound links or backlinks.

vote. However, not all votes are equal – Google gives greater weight to links from pages which themselves have a high PageRank and where the link anchor text or adjacent text contains text relevant to the keyphrase. It has been refined to identify sites that are 'authority sites' or hub sites for a particular type of search. For keyphrases where there is a lot of competition, such as 'car insurance', the quantity and quality of inbound links will be more important than keyphrase density in determining ranking.

While natural links will be generated if content is useful, a proactive approach to link-building is required in competitive markets. Chaffey and Smith (2008) recommend these steps to help boost your external links.

1 *Identify and create popular content and services.* By creating more valuable content and then showcasing them within your navigation, or grouping it within a few pages such as a 'Useful Resources' or a more extensive 'Resource Centre', you can encourage more people to link to your content naturally, or approach them and suggest they link or bookmark not only to the home page, but directly to the useful tools that have been created.

2 *Identify potential partner sites.* There are several options to find partner sites. It is helpful to try to identify the types of sites that you may be able to link with, for example:

   • directories of links (often less valuable)
   • traditional media sites
   • niche online-only media sites
   • trade associations
   • manufacturers, suppliers and other business partners
   • press release distribution sites
   • bloggers including customers and partners
   • social networks.

   Note: The section on online PR later in this chapter has more guidance on approaches for link-building.

3 *Contact partner sites.* A typical sequence is:
   • Step 1 – write e-mail encouraging link (or phone call to discuss from someone inside the company will often work best).
   • Step 2 – follow-up link.
   • Step 3 – setup links.

6 Internal link structures

Many of the principles of external link building can also be applied to links within sites. The most important principle is to include keyphrases used by searchers within the anchor text of a hyperlink to point to relevant content. It's also important to consider how to increase the number of internal links to pages which you want to rank well. A meshed structure with lots of interlinks can work better than a simple hierarchy.

PageRank varies for pages across a site. The home page is typically highest, with each page deeper within the site having a lower PageRank. There are several implications of this. First, it is helpful to include the most important keyphrases you want to target on the homepage or at the second level in the site hierarchy. Second pages that feature in the main or secondary navigation (text link menus referencing the keyphrase in the anchor text are best) are more likely to rank highly than pages deeper in the site that don't have many internal backlinks because they are not in the menu. Third, you need to review whether there are pages deeper within the site which feature products or services that are important, and which you need to rank for.

To summarise the complexities of SEO, see the compilation of the most important ranking factors based on a panel of experts defined by SEOMoz (2011b) Google Search Engine Ranking Factors.

Paid search marketing

Although SEO has proved a popular form of digital marketing, paid search marketing is still of great relevance since it gives much more control on the appearance in the listings subject to the amount bid and the relevance of the ad.

Each of the main search engines has its own paid advertising programme:

- Google Adwords (**http://adwords.google.com**)
- Microsoft Bing and Yahoo! adCenter (**http://adcenter.microsoft.com**)

What is paid search marketing?

We explained the principles of paid search marketing or sponsored links in the introduction to the section on search engine marketing . Although we said that the main model for paying for sponsored listings in the search engines is pay-per-click marketing, we have called this section paid search marketing since there are, increasingly, other options for payment on what is known as the content network.

Paid search content network

Display(or content) network
Sponsored links are displayed by the search engine on third-party sites such as online publishers, aggregators or social networks. Ads can be paid for on a CPC, CPM or a CPA basis. There are also options for graphical or video ads as well as text-based ads.

Contextual ad
Ad relevant to page content on third-party sites brokered by search ad networks.

Trusted feed
An automated method of putting content into a search engine index or an aggregator database.

Quality score
An assessment in paid search by Google AdWords (and now other search engines) of an individual ad triggered by a keyword which, in combination with the bid amount, determines the ranking of the ad relative to competitors. The primary factor is the click-through rate for each ad, but quality score also considers the match between the keyword and the occurrence of the keyword in the text, historical click-through rates, the engagement of the searcher when they click-through to the site and the speed at which the page loads.

Paid listings are also available through the **displaynetwork** of the search engines such as Google Adsense and Yahoo! Content Match. These **contextual ads** are automatically displayed according to the page content. They can be paid for on a CPC, CPM or CPA (pay-per-action) basis and include not only text ads but also options for graphical display ads or video ads. Google generates around a third of its revenue from the content network, so there is a significant amount of expenditure on the network.

Trusted feeds

Trusted feeds or paid for inclusion is no longer significant to search advertising for most organisations, so we will only cover them briefly. In trusted feeds used by Yahoo!, the ad or search listings content was automatically uploaded to a search engine from a catalogue or document database for inclusion in the search results. A similar approach is used by retailers to include their products in Google Product Search (see documentation for Google Merchant Blog for the latest techniques). Another related option is to advertise in RSS feeds.

What controls position in paid search?

In early pay-per-click programs, the relative ranking of sponsored listings was typically based on the highest bidded cost-per-click for each keyword phrase. So it was a pure auction arrangement with the cost-per-click dependent on the balance of the extent of competition in the marketplace against the revenue or profit that can be generated dependent on conversion rates to sale and retention. The variation in bid amounts for clients of one search bid management tool are shown in Table 9.2.

Contrary to what many web users may believe, today it is not necessarily the company which is prepared to pay the most per click who will get top spot. The search engines also take the relative click-through rates of the ads dependent on their position (lower positions naturally have lower click-through rates) into account when ranking the sponsored links, so ads which do not appear relevant, because fewer people are clicking on them, will drop down or may even disappear off the listing. The analysis of CTR to determine position is part of the **quality score**, a concept originally developed by Google but now integrated as part of the Microsoft Bing and Yahoo! search networks.

The quality score

Understanding the quality score is the key to successful paid search marketing. You should consider its implications when you structure the account and write copy. Google developed

Table 9.2	Variation in cost-per-click in different categories for US paid search campaigns	
Category	**CPC ($)**	
All finance	2.03	
Travel	0.48	
Automotive	0.53	
Retail	0.43	

Source: Efficient Frontier (2011)

the quality score because they understood that delivering *relevance* through the sponsored links was essential to their user's experience, and their profits. In their AdWords help system, they explain:

> The AdWords system works best for everybody; advertisers, users, publishers and Google too when the ads we display match our users' needs as closely as possible. We call this idea 'relevance'.

> We measure relevance in a simple way: Typically, the higher an ad's quality score, the more relevant it is for the keywords to which it is tied. When your ads are highly relevant, they tend to earn more clicks, move higher in Ad Rank and bring you the most success.

A summary formula for the Google quality score is:

> Quality score = (keyword's click-through rate, ad text relevance, keyword relevance, landing page relevance and other methods of assessing relevance)

So, higher click-through rates achieved through better targeted creative copy are rewarded as is relevance of the landing page (Google now sends out AdBots-Google to check them out). More relevant ads are also rewarded through ad text relevance, which is an assessment of the match of headline and description to the search term. Finally, the keyword relevance is the match of the triggering keyword to the search term entered.

If you have ever wondered why the number of paid ads above the natural listings varies from none to three, then it's down to the quality score – you can only get the coveted positions for keywords which have a sufficiently high quality score – you can't 'buy your way to the top' as many think.

Advantages and disadvantages of paid search marketing

Paid search listings, or sponsored links, are very important to achieve visibility in search engines when an organisation is in a competitive market given the competition to appear on the first page of the natural listing for target keyphrases.

As a result, many companies with an established paid search programme may generate more visits from paid search than SEO, although this wouldn't be true for companies that are class leaders in SEO.

Advantages of paid search marketing

The main benefit of paid search marketing are:

- *The advertiser is not paying for the ad to be displayed.* As we explained at the start of Chapter 8, wastage is much lower with paid search compared to traditional advertising. Cost is only incurred when an ad is clicked on and a visitor is directed to the advertiser's website. Hence it's a cost-per-click (CPC) model! However, there are increasingly options for paid search marketing using other techniques – Google also offers CPM (site targeting) and CPA (pay-per-action) options on its content network where contextual ads are displayed on third-party sites relevant to the content on a page.
- *PPC advertising is highly targeted.* The relevant ad with a link to a destination web page is only displayed when the user of a search engine types in a specific phrase (or the ad appears on the content network, triggered by relevant content on a publisher's page), so there is limited wastage compared to other media. YouTube users can also be targeted through Google's 'promoted video' PPC option. Users responding to a particular keyphrase or reading related content have high intent or interest and so tend to be good-quality leads.
- *Good accountability.* With the right tracking system, the ROI for individual keywords can be calculated.
- *Predictable.* Traffic, rankings and results are generally stable and predictable in comparison with SEO.
- *Technically simpler than SEO.* Position is based on combination of bid amount and quality score. Whereas SEO requires long-term, technically complex work on page optimisation, site re-stucturing and link building.
- *Remarketing.* Google offers retargeting through cookies placed on the searchers computer to display ads on the content network after someone has clicked on a paid search ad as a reminder to act. These can be effective in boosting the conversion rate to lead or sale.
- *Speed.* PPC listings get posted quickly, usually in a few days (following editor review). SEO results can take weeks or months to be achieved. Moreover, when a website is revised for SEO, rankings will initially drop while the site is re-indexed by the search engines.
- *Branding.* Tests have shown that there is a branding effect with PPC, even if users do not click on the ad. This can be useful for the launch of products or major campaigns.

Disadvantages of paid search marketing

However, there disadvantages to be managed:

- *Competitive and expensive.* Since pay-per-click has become popular, some companies may get involved in bidding wars that drive bids up to an unacceptable level. Some phrases such as 'life insurance' can exceed £10 per click.
- *Inappropriate.* For companies with a lower budget or a narrower range of products on which to generate lifetime value, it might not be cost effective to compete.
- *Requires specialist knowledge.* PPC requires a knowledge of configuration, bidding options and of the reporting facilities of different ad networks. Internal staff can be trained, but they will need to keep up-to-date with changes to the paid search services.
- *Time consuming.* To manage a PPC account can require daily or even hourly checks on the bidding in order to stay competitive. This can amount to a lot of time. The tools and best practice varies frequently, so keeping up-to-date is difficult.
- *Irrelevant.* Sponsored listings are only part of the search engine marketing mix. Many search users do not click on these because they don't trust advertisers, although these are mainly people involved in marketing!

Best practice in planning and managing paid search marketing

With PPC, as for any other media, media buyers carefully evaluate the advertising costs in relation to the initial purchase value or lifetime value they feel they will achieve from the average customer. As well as considering the cost-per-click (CPC), you need to think about the conversion rate when the visitor arrives at your site. Clearly, an ad could be effective in generating click-throughs or traffic, but not achieve the outcome required on the website such as generating a lead or online sale. This could be because there is a poor-incentive call-to-action or the profile of the visitors is simply wrong. One implication of this is that it will often be more cost effective if targeted microsites or landing pages are created specifically for certain keyphrases to convert users to making an enquiry or sale. These can be part of the site structure, so clicking on a 'car insurance' ad will take the visitor through to the car insurance page on a site rather than a home page.

Table 9.3 shows how cost-per-click can differ between different keywords that on generic (e.g. 'car insurance') and specific (e.g. 'women's car insurance'). It also shows the impact of different conversion rates on the overall CPA. The table also shows the cost of PPC search in competitive categories and why companies will strive to maximise their quality score to help reduce costs.

The cost per customer acquisition (CPA) can be calculated as follows:

$$\text{Cost per acquisition} = \frac{100}{\text{conversion rate \%}} \times \text{cost–per–click}$$

Given the range in costs, two types of strategy can be pursued in PPC search engine advertising. If budget permits, a premium strategy can be followed to compete with the major competitors who are bidding the highest amounts on popular keywords. Such a strategy is based on being able to achieve an acceptable conversion rate once the customers are driven through to the website. A lower-cost strategy involves bidding on lower-cost, less popular phrases. These will generate less traffic, so it will be necessary to devise a lot of these phrases to match the traffic from premium keywords.

Table 9.3	Examples of cost-per-click and CPA figures				
Keywords	**Clicks/day**	**Avg. CPC**	**Cost/day**	**CPA @ 25% conversion**	**CPA @ 10% conversion**
'car insurance'	1323	€15.6	€20,640	€62	€156
'cheap car insurance'	199	€14.6	€2905	€58	€146
'woman car insurance'	4	€11.6	€46	€46	€116

Optimising pay-per-click

Each PPC keyphrase ideally needs to be managed individually in order to make sure that the bid (amount per click) remains competitive in order to show up in the top of the results. Experienced PPC marketers broaden the range of keyphrases to include lower-volume phrases. Since each advertiser will typically manage thousands of keywords to generate click-throughs, manual bidding soon becomes impractical.

Some search engines include their own bid management tools, but if an organisation is using different pay-per-click schemes, it makes sense to use a single tool to manage them all. It also makes comparison of performance easier too. Bid management software such as Acquisio (**www.acquisio.com**) and WordStream (**www.wordstream.com**) can be used across a range of PPC services to manage keyphrases across multiple PPC ad networks and optimise the costs of search engine advertising. The current CPC is regularly reviewed and your bid is reduced or increased to maintain the position you want according to different strategies and ROI limits, with amounts capped such that advertisers do not pay more than the maximum they have deposited.

As more marketers have become aware of the benefits of PPC, competition has increased and this has driven up the cost-per-click (CPC) and so reduced its profitability.

Although pay-per-click marketing does not initially appear as complex as search engine optimisation, in reality, there are many issues to consider. For example, the Econsultancy (2008b) guide to pay-per-click marketing identifies these paid search strategy issues which paid search marketers and their agencies must address.

1   Targeting

- *Search ad network strategy*. Which of the search networks mentioned above do you use? Which are used in different countries?
- *Content network strategy*. How do you treat the content network? Do you disable it? Create separate campaigns? Target specific sites using the Placement tool? Develop different creative? Use placement targeting in Google?
- *Campaign structure strategy*. Campaign structure is important to ensure that searches using a specific search term trigger the relevant ad creative. Are AdGroups small enough to deliver a message relevant for the keyphrase entered?
- *Keyword matching strategy*. How is creative targeted using the combination of broad match and negative match, phrase match and exact match?
- *Search-term targeting strategy*. What are the strategies for targeting different types of keyphrases such as brand, generic, product-specific and different qualifiers (cheap, compare, etc.)?

2   Budget and bid management

- *Budgeting strategy*. Is budget set as maximum cost-per-click (CPC) at the appropriate level to deliver satisfactory return on investment? Is daily budget sufficient that ads are served at full delivery (always present)?
- *Listing position strategy*. Which positions are targeted for different keywords?
- *Bidding strategies*. What is the appropriate maximum cost per click for different target keywords and campaigns to maximise effectiveness?
- *Dayparting strategy*. Are ads delivered continuously through the day and week or are different certain days and times targeted (e.g. office hours, evening after ad breaks)?
- *Bid management tool strategy*. Is a tool used to automate bidding? Which?

3   Creative testing and campaign optimisation

- *Ad creative and copy strategy*. How are the 95 characters forming ad headlines, description and creative used to encourage click-through (and reduce click-through from unqualified visitors if necessary)? Is alternative copy tested? How are ads tested?
- *Destination or landing page strategy*. How are landing pages improved?
- *Campaign review and optimisation strategy*. What is the workflow for reviewing and improving success? Which reports are used? How often are they reviewed? By who? Which tests are used? What are the follow-ups?
- *Specialist and innovative paid search techniques*. These include local, international, pay-per-call, mobile search.

4 **Communications integration.**

- *SEO integration strategy.* How is SEO integrated with paid search to maximise ROI?
- *Affiliate integration strategy.* How is affiliate marketing integrated with paid search to maximise ROI?
- *Marketing campaign integration strategy.* How is budget and creative changed during offline campaigns?

Beware of the fake clicks!

Whenever the principle of PPC marketing is described to marketers, very soon a light bulb switches on and they ask, 'So we can click on competitors and bankrupt them?' Well, actually, no. The PPC ad networks detect multiple clicks from the same computer (IP address) and say they filter them out. However, there are techniques to mimic multiple clicks from different locations, such as software tools and even services where you can pay a team of people across the world to click on these links. It is estimated that in competitive markets one in five of the clicks may be fake. While this can be factored into the conversion rates you will achieve, ultimately this could destroy PPC advertising so the search engines work hard to eliminate it.

Online public relations

What is online public relations (e-PR)?

Public relations (PR)
The management of the awareness, understanding and reputation of an organisation or brand, primarily achieved through influencing exposure in the media.

Digital media have become a very important element of **public relations (PR)**. Mike Grehan, a UK search engine marketing specialist, explains (Grehan, 2004):

> Both online and off, the process is much the same when using PR to increase awareness, differentiate yourself from the crowd and improve perception. Many offline PR companies now employ staff with specialist online skills. The web itself offers a plethora of news sites and services. And, of course, there are thousands and thousands of newsletters and zines covering just about every topic under the sun. Never before has there been a better opportunity to get your message to the broadest geographic and multi-demographic audience. But you need to understand the pitfalls on both sides to be able to avoid.

Online PR activity is closely associated with improving results from many of the other communications techniques described in this chapter, in particular SEO (link-building), partnership marketing and social media marketing. Furthermore, online PR has witnessed much innovation of Web 2.0-based approaches such as blogs, feeds, social networks and widgets which we will explore in this section.

But let's start with an understanding of traditional public relations – itself somewhat intangible. As you will know, 'PR' and 'public relations' are often used interchangeably. Unfortunately, PR is also an abbreviation for 'press release' or 'press relations'. Of course, the scope of PR is much wider than press releases. On its website, the UK Institute of PR defines PR as follows:

> Public relations is about reputation – the result of what you do, what you say and what others say about you. Public relations is the discipline which looks after reputation, with the aim of earning understanding and support and influencing opinion and behaviour. It is the planned and sustained effort to establish and maintain goodwill and mutual understanding between an organisation and its publics [its target audience including potential customers and stakeholders].

From a marketing communications and traffic building perspective, the main activities we are interested in are media relations which are used to influence potential customers. While websites are important tools for promoting investor relations and CSR (corporate social responsibility), this is not our main focus here.

Online public relations (e-PR)
Maximising favourable mentions of your company, brands, products or websites on third-party websites which are likely to be visited by your target audience. Online PR can extend reach and awareness of a brand within an audience and will also generate backlinks vital to SEO. It can also be used to support viral or word-of-mouth marketing activities in other media.

Online PR or e-PR leverages the network effect of the Internet. Remember that Internet is a contraction of 'interconnected networks'! Mentions of a brand or site on other sites are powerful in shaping opinions and driving visitors to your site. The main element of online PR is maximising favourable mentions of an organisation, its brands, products or websites on third-party websites which are likely to be visited by its target audience. Furthermore, as we noted in the section on search engine optimisation, the more links there are from other sites to your site, the higher your site will be ranked in the natural or organic listings of the search engines. **Online influencer outreach** is now an important activity to identify companies or individuals with a strong online following and then using these contact to influence their audience. Minimising unfavourable mentions, for example monitoring and influencing conversations in blogs and social networks through **online reputation management,** is also an aspect of online PR.

Mini Case Study 9.1   Renault use influencer outreach to support the growth

In 2010, Renault launched a new range of zero emission vehicles. Renault's objective was to get people talking about the range, and especially the star model, the TWIZY. Renault wanted to create links with opinion leaders sensitive to the automotive sector but also to ecology and new technologies.

To reach influencers and help spread the word about the new model, Agency BuzzParadise organised a special meeting at an international event, LeWeb. The idea was for Renault to use this platform to set up viral advertising aimed at a target sensitive to technological advances. Invitations were sent to 13 bloggers from France, Germany, Great Britain, Italy and Spain writing about High-Tech, Trends, Innovation and Scientific themes. These partners met for a conference session and to tests of vehicles in the ZE range.

As a result, 22 articles were created across the blogs and, through these, 900,000 exposures to the message were generated. This increased visibility for Renault and its TWIZY in the European blogosphere, social networks (Facebook, Twitter) and SEO (Google). The amplification effect of a relatively small number of bloggers is illustrated well by this reach figure. But it's worth remembering that visibility on blogs and social networks like this is usually ephemeral, meaning that the message is only visible for a short time within the blogosphere. So other techniques are also needed to give a more sustained delivery of messages and reminders to the audience. This is where traditional advertising and remarketing through displaying advertising to those who have already visited a company microsite play an important role.

Source: Buzz Paradise (2010), PR 2.0 for Renault, Case study: http://www.buzzparadise.com/case-studies/pr-2-0-event-for-renault-le-web-2010/

Differences between online PR and traditional PR

Online influencer outreach
Identifying online influencers such as bloggers, media owners or individuals with a large online following in the social networks and then approaching them to partner together to communicate with their audience.

Online reputation management
Controlling the reputation of an organisation through monitoring and controlling messages placed about the organisation.

Ranchhod *et al.* (2002) identify four key differences between online PR and traditional PR which are fundamentals of online PR that remain true today.

1 *The audience is connected to organisations.* Previously, there was detachment – PR people issued press releases which were distributed over the newswires, picked up by the media, and then published in their outlets. These authors say:

> The communication channel was uni-directional. The institutions communicated and the audiences consumed the information. Even when the communication was considered a two-way process, the institutions had the resources to send information to audiences through a very wide pipeline, while the audiences had only a minuscule pipeline for communicating back to the institutions.

2 *The members of the audience are connected to each other.* Through publishing their own blogs, social profiles or e-newsletters or contributing to reviews or discussions on others, information can be rapidly distributed from person to person and group to group.

Consumers will also have their own conversations about their needs and brands which will shape brand perception and purchase intent. The authors say:

> Today, a company's activity can be discussed and debated over the Internet, with or without the knowledge of that organisation. In the new environment everybody is a communicator, and the institution is just part of the network.

3 *The audience has access to other information.* Often in the past, the communicator was able to make a statement that it would be difficult for the average audience member to challenge – the Internet facilitates rapid comparison of statements. The authors say:

> It takes a matter of minutes to access multiple sources of information over the Internet. Any statement made can be dissected, analysed, discussed and challenged within hours by interested individuals. In the connected world, information does not exist in a vacuum.

4 *Audiences pull information.* Today this is often known as inbound marketing. Previously there were limited channels in terms of television and press. Today there are many sources and channels of information – this makes it more difficult for the message to be seen. The authors say:

> Until recently, television offered only a few channels. People communicated with one another by post and by phone. In these conditions, it was easy for a public relations practitioner to make a message stand out.

For the marketer or PR professional, managing PR, the main differences are:

- *Less easy to control.* There are many more places a brand can be discussed online, such as in blogs and forums, compared to traditional media where there are a smaller number of media outlets with news filtered through journalists and other editorial staff.
- *More options to create their own stories.* Since a company will have its own site, press centre, feeds and blogs, it is possible to bypass other media owners to some extent. Many companies have now created a 'social media newsroom'.
- *Need for faster response.* It is often said that 'bad news travels fast'. This has been facilitated online and a 'blogstorm' can soon arise where many bloggers are critical of a brand's action. Rapid response teams are needed. Some brands have created a social media command centre as part of a **social media governance** process based on **social media listening**. To see examples of social media governance policies in a range of sectors, see **www. socialmediagovernance.com**.
- *Easier to monitor.* Since Google and online reputation management tools index many pages, it is arguably easier to identify when a brand is discussed online.

Social media governance
A definition of how companies should respond to social mentions that may give rise to leads or reputational damage.

Social media listening
The process of using monitoring tools to review mentions of a brand and related keywords within social networks and other online sites.

Advantages and disadvantages of online public relations

Advantages of online public relations

The advantages of the proactive online public relations techniques which seek to build a buzz around a campaign or to gain favourable mentions and links on third-party sites are:

- *Reach.* E-PR can be a relatively low-cost method of directly reaching a niche audience or a mass audience if the brand is amenable to stories that are of interest to publishers. This is often the case for new online brands and startups such as Zopa (**www.zopa.com**). If buzz around an online campaign orchestrated through online PR is successful then additional reach and impact may also be generated by traditional media such as TV, print and radio.
- *Cost.* The costs for online PR are the agency or internal staff fees for developing the online PR plan, concepts and content. Since there are no media placement costs, this can be cost effective.

Mini Case Study 9.2	Dell and Gatorade launch social media command centres

In 2010/2011 Dell and Gatorade (Figure 9.7) independently launched 'social media command centres'. Watch the videos (available from the links for this chapter) to see how they planned to use them for reputation managing and reviewing the impact of social media.

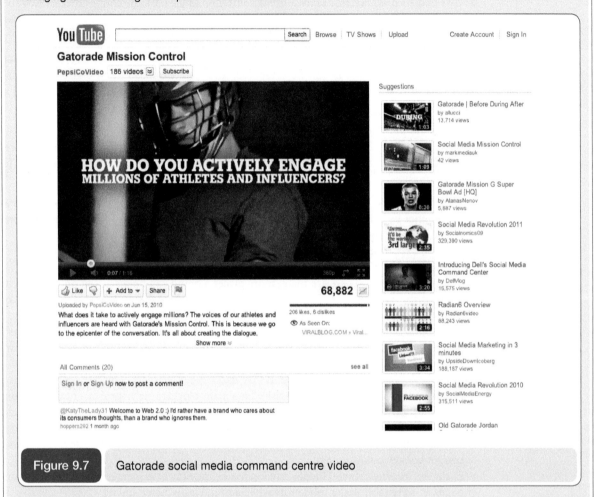

Figure 9.7	Gatorade social media command centre video

Clearly, these are big brands, what does this mean for smaller organisations? Some have even questioned their relevance for larger companies calling them white elephants. These are some implications of the need for social media listening highlighted by the approach of these big brands:

1 Put in place free or paid listening tools.
2 Use free tools initially to check the volume of conversation. If it's not significant, you probably don't need a 'mission control centre', but you should use a free tool to monitor your brand and respond appropriately – it's not just about monitoring the negatives as some seem to think, it's about reaching out to potential partners and collaborators too.
3 Set up social governance policies.
4 Find a method such that you can follow-up on potential partnership options – remember that Partnerships is the 8th P in the marketing mix.
5 Integrate your social media monitoring and reporting with other business and campaign reporting and web analytics systems.

Source: SmartInsights.com (2011b)

- *Credibility.* Independent comments that are made by a person independent from a company are considered more authentic and can so help raise trust about an online provider such as a retailer (see Figure 9.2). You can see that personal recommendations are particularly important and seem to be trusted more than content sites giving reviews and opinions (although these are still given credence by many web users).
- *Search engine optimisation.* E-PR can help generate backlinks to a site which are favourable for SEO, often from large sites such as online newspapers or magazines which have good link equity.
- *Brand-enhancement and protection.* Favourable stories can enhance the reputation of a brand among its target audience and amplification through influencers can help reach a new audience. But since unfavourable media mentions may damage a brand, so monitoring and response to these is a necessity for most brands.

Disadvantages of online public relations

The main disadvantage of e-PR is that it is not a controlled discipline like online advertising techniques such as pay-per-click marketing or display advertising where the returns generated will be known for a given expenditure. In other words, it could be considered a high-risk investment.

Many marketers are also wary of creating blogs or forums on their sites which may solicit negative comments. However, there are counter-arguments to this, namely that it is best to control and be involved with conversations about a brand on the site rather than when it is less controlled on third-party sites. For example, brands such as Dell (**www.ideastorm.com**) and Honda enable web users to make comments about their brands so this shows they are listening to customer comments and gain valuable sentiment that can feed into new product development ideas.

Best practice in planning and managing online public relations

In this section we will review the different types of online PR activities and techniques to improve results from these activities. The main activities that can be considered to be specifically involved with online PR include:

- communicating with media owners online (influencer outreach)
- link building
- web 2.0 content including blogs, podcasting, RSS feeds and widgets
- managing how your brand is presented on third-party sites
- creating a buzz – online viral marketing.

Communicating with online media owners (influencer outreach)

Forming relationships with publishers of media online gives a way to expand the reach of a brand. These influencers may include traditional journalists, but as we saw in Mini Case Study about Renault, bloggers or celebrities.

Journalists can be influenced online through a press-release area or social media newsroom on the website; creating e-mail alerts about news that journalists and other third parties can sign up to; news stories or releases submitted to online news feeds. Examples of feeds include PR Newswire: (**www.prnewswire.com**), Internetwire (**www.internetwire.com/iwire/home**), PressBox (**www.pressbox.co.uk**), PRWeb (**www.prweb.com**), Business Wire (**www.businesswire.com**). Press releases also can be written for search engine optimisation (SEO) since they will link back to the site.

An increasing number of journalists rely on blogs and feeds for finding sources for stories rather than traditional press releases, so engaging influencers through these is also important. Charles Arthur (**www.charlesarthur.com**), contributor to the *Guardian* in a posting 'Why I'm not reading PR e-mails to get news stories any more', says:

I'm not going to read things that are obviously press releases because the possibility of it just being annoying or irrelevant is too great; I'm going to go to my aggregator instead, because I've chosen every feed there for its potential interest. I pay more attention to my RSS feeds because they're sources I've chosen, rather than the e-mails I get from PR companies.

Link building

Link building
A structured activity to include good quality hyperlinks to your site from relevant sites with a good page rank.

Reciprocal link
Link agreed between yourself and another organisation.

Link building is a key activity for SEO. It can be considered to be an element of online PR since it is about getting your brand visible on third-party sites and creating backlinks related to your site.

Link building needs to be a structured effort to achieve as many quality links into a website as possible from referring websites (these commonly include **reciprocal links** which tend to be less valuable from an SEO perspective than one-way links). We have also seen that your position in the search engine results pages will be higher if you have quality links into relevant content on your site (not necessarily the home page).

McGaffin (2004) provides a great introduction to implementing a structured link building programme. The main principle of link building is as follows, McGaffin says: 'Create great content, link to great content and great content will link to you.' He describes how you should review existing links, link to competitors, set targets and then proactively enquire to suitable site owners for links.

Digital marketing insight 9.3 | Reviewing the links into a site

You can use the syntax link:site in Google to see examples of links into a page on a site as judged by Google, e.g. **site:www.smartinsights.com**. But note that this also includes internal links and is not comprehensive. A better option to display links is the SEOmoz Site Open Site Explorer tool (**www.opensiteexplorer.com**). For alerts of new links or new mentions on other sites, Google's own alerts (**www.google.com/alerts**) are useful tools.

Web 2.0 atomised content

Web 2.0 concept
A collection of web services that facilitate interaction of web users with sites to create user-generated content and encouraging behaviours such as community or social network participation, mashups, content rating, use of widgets and tagging.

Blog
An online diary or news source prepared by an individual or a group of people. From 'Web log'. Business blogs are created by an organisation for communication to their audiences.

Many specialist online PR techniques such as blogs, podcasting and RSS feeds, are collectively referred to as **Web 2.0** which we introduced in the first chapter. Web 2.0 represents a revolution in web usage where previously passive consumers of content become active contributors. In Web 2.0 the web itself is merely a platform for interacting with content.

Blogs and blogging

Blogs give an easy method of regularly publishing web pages as online journals, diaries or news or events listings. Many blogs provide commentary or news on a particular subject; others function as more personal online diaries. A typical blog combines text, images and links to other blogs, web pages and other media related to its topic. The capability for readers to leave comments in an interactive format is an important part of many blogs. Feedback (trackback) comments from other sites are also sometimes incorporated. Frequency can be hourly, daily, weekly or less frequently, but several updates daily is typical.

There are many free services which enable anyone to blog (for example **www.wordpress.com** and **www.blogger.com**. The blogging format enables the content on a website to be delivered in different ways. For example, the SmartInsights blog has a lot of rich content related to Internet marketing which can be delivered in different ways:

Figure 9.8	Smart Insights blog (**www.smartinsights.com**) showing content available from within a category of 'social media marketing'

- *By topic* (in categories or topics to browse) – example, social media marketing category (Figure 9.8).
- *By tag* (more detailed topics – each article will be tagged with several tags to help them appear in searches) – example, 'B2B' or 'case studies'.
- *By author* (features from different columnists who can be internal or external). Guest posting is an effective method for both guest author and blog to increase reach.
- *By time* (all posts broken down by the different methods above are in reverse date order).

Tagging and folksonomies

Tagging
Users or web page creators categorise content on a site through adding descriptive terms. A common approach in blog posts.

A defining characteristic of Web 2.0 is **tagging** whereby users add their own metadata to content they produce, consume and share. On Flickr (**www.flickr.com**) and Del.icio.us (**del. icio.us**) for example, any user can attach tags to digital media items (files, bookmarks, images). The aggregation of tags creates an organic, free-form, 'bottom-up' taxonomy. The information architect Thomas van der Wal coined the term or 'folksonomy' derived from the idea of a 'folk-taxonomy' (Fitzgerald, 2006). **Folksonomies** are flat (that is, they have no hierarchy, and show no parent–child relationships) and, critically, are completely uncontrolled. A key implication of their lack of structure is that they do not support functions such as drill-down searching and cross-referencing.

Folksonomy
A contraction of 'folk taxonomy', a method of classifying content based on tagging that has no hierarchy, i.e. without parent–child relationships.

Social bookmarking

Social bookmarking
Web users keep a shared version of favourite sites ('Favorites') online. This enables the most popular sites in a category to be identified.

Sites like Digg, Google, Reddit, StumbleUpon and Del.icio.us allow users to store, organise, search and manage favourite web pages on the Internet rather than on their PC. With such **social bookmarking** systems, users save links to web pages that they want to remember and/ or share on bookmark hosting sites. These bookmarks are usually public but can be saved privately, shared only with specified people or groups, shared only inside certain networks, or some other combination of public and private domains.

Podcast
Individuals and
organisations post online
media (audio and video)
which can be viewed in
the appropriate players
including the iPod which
first sparked the growth in
this technique.

Podcasts are related to blogs since they can potentially be generated by individuals or organisations to voice an opinion either as audio (typically MP3) or less commonly currently as video (video podcasts). They have been successfully used by media organisations such as the BBC which has used them for popular programmes such as film reviews or discussions and for live recordings such as the Beethoven symphonies that received over 600,000 downloads in June 2005 alone. Virgin Radio has also used podcasting, but cannot broadcast music (due to copyright restrictions), only the presenters! A big challenge for achieving visibility for podcasts is that content can only currently be recognised by tags and it is difficult to assess quality without listening to the start of a podcast. All the main search engines are working on techniques to make searching of voice and video content practical. In the meantime, some start-ups such as Odeo (**www.odeo.com**) and Blinkx (**www.blinkx.com**) are developing solutions.

In a business-to-business context, network provider Cisco (**www.cisco.com**) has used video podcasts for its Interaction network, which is used to sell the benefits of its services to small and medium businesses.

Photo, video and slide sharing sites

Photo sharing sites which are popular include Flickr (a Yahoo! service), Picasa (a Google service), Photobucket, Webshots Community, Kodak Gallery, ImageShack and SnapFish. These again rely on tagging to enable users to find related shots they are interested in and can be used to create mashups using widgets to embed the object into a blog or other site (see below for explanation of these terms). Some online campaigns for high-involvement products such as cars or holidays now invite customers to submit their own pictures via services such as Flickr to build ongoing interest in a campaign.

Video sharing sites include YouTube, Google Videos, Jumpcut, Grouper, Revver, Blip.TV, VideoEgg and Daily Motion. These sites have very similar features to photo sharing sites but some add more features in the form of subscriptions to channels and offer code to embed the players on social networks or blogs.

Another way of sharing content important in professional B2B markets is through slide sharing sites such as Scribd and SlideShare.net.

Really Simple Syndication feeds

**Really Simple
Syndication feed (RSS)**
Blog, news or other
content is published by
an XML standard and
syndicated for other sites
or read by users in RSS
reader software services.
Now typically shortened
to 'feed', e.g. news feed
or sports feed.

Really Simple Syndication (RSS) is closely related to blogging where blog, news or any type of content such as a new podcast is received by subscribers using a feed reader. It offers a method of receiving news in a feed that uses a different broadcast method from e-mail, so is not subject to the same conflicts with spam or spam filters. Many journalists now subscribe to RSS feeds from sources such as the BBC (**http://news.bbc.co.uk/2/hi/help/3223484.stm**) which publishes RSS feed for different types of content on its site.

RSS is now being used to syndicate not just notices of new blog entries, but also all kinds of data updates including stock quotes, weather data and photo availability. Today, RSS is arguably important for integration of content shared from a blog through to social networks like Google, Facebook and LinkedIn

Mashups

Mashup
Websites, pages or
widgets that combine the
content or functionality
of one website or data
source with another to
create something offering
a different type of value
to web users from the
separate types of content
or functionality.

Mashups (a term originally referring to the pop music practice, notably hip-hop, of producing a new song by mixing two or more existing pieces) are sites or widgets that combine the content or functionality of one website with another to create something offering a different type of value to web users from the other types of content or functionality. In practice they provide a way of sharing content between sites and stitching together sites through exchanging data in common XML-based standards such as RSS.

Examples of mashups include:

- Chicagocrime.org took police data for crime incidents and plotted them on street maps from Google Maps so that visitors could check in advance whether it was the sort of place you might get mugged, and when.

- Housingmaps.com combines Google Maps with Craigslist apartment rental and home purchase data to create an interactive housing search tool.
- Personal content aggregators such as Netvibes (**www.netvibes.com**), iGoogle (**www.google. com/ig**) or Pageflakes (**www.pageflakes.com**) often incorporate news stories from feeds and other data such as the latest e-mails or social network alerts. These are effectively a personal mashup.

Social networks

Social network
A site that facilitates peer-to-peer communication within a group or between individuals through providing facilities to develop user-generated content (UGC) and to exchange messages and comments between different users.

We have described **social networks** in more depth in other chapters, including Chapters 1, 2 and 6. From an online PR perspective, social networking sites can be valuable in these ways:

- They can be used to assess the 'Zeitgeist', i.e. what current trends and opinions are being discussed which can then be built into PR campaigns.
- They can assist in recommendations about brands and products. For example, Hitwise research (Hitwise, 2007) suggests that a high proportion of visits to fashion retail stores such as Top Shop were preceded by usage of social networks, suggesting that some visits are prompted by discussions.
- They can be used to solicit feedback about product experiences and brand perception, either by explicit requests or observing what is discussed. *New Media Age* (2008) quotes Miles Sturt, head of customer experience satisfaction at Nokia, saying buzz research can have an impact on the next model the company makes, rather than the one after:

Widget
A badge or button incorporated into a site or social network space by its owner, with content or services typically served from another site making a widget effectively a mini-software application or web service. Content can be updated in real time since the widget interacts with the server each time it loads.

> It gives us feedback on new handsets within three or four weeks, instead of the four to six months it takes to sit people down for market research interviews. That's important because our product teams start working on a refresh of a model straight after launch, so they can apply feedback to the next version of a handset rather than wait a few months for conventional market research that may have to wait for the launch after that.

But, as we note in the section on managing reputation, it is important to monitor comments and respond as appropriate.

Widgets

Widgets are different forms of tools made available on a website or on a user's desktop. They are a relatively new concept associated with Web 2.0. They either provide some functionality, like a calculator, or they provide real-time information, for example on news or weather.

Site owners can encourage partners to place them on their sites and this will help educate people about your brand, possibly generating backlinks for SEO purposes and also engaging with a brand when they're not on the brand owner's site. Widgets offer partner sites the opportunity to add value to their visitors through the gadget functionality or content, or to add to their brand through association with you (co-branding).

Widgets are often placed in the left or right sidebar, or in the body of an article. They are relatively easy for site owners to implement, usually a couple of lines of Javascript, but this does depend on the content management system.

The main types of widgets are:

- *Web widgets.* Web widgets have been used for a long time as part of affiliate marketing, but they are getting more sophisticated by enabling searches on a site, real-time price updates or even streaming video.
- *Google gadgets.* Different content can be incorporated into a personalised Google 'iGoogle' homepage.
- *Desktop and operating system gadgets.* Microsoft Windows and Apple Operating systems provide dashboard gadgets which make it easier to subscribe to information updates.
- *Social sharing widgets.* These encourage site visitors to share content they like, effectively voting on it. Share buttons provided by the networks or aggregators like AddThis.com

or ShareThis.com are now an essential part of many sites to assist in 'viral amplification'. Figure 9.9 gives an example where you can see how the popularity of different sharing services varies in different countries.

- *Facebook applications.* Facebook have created an API known as the Facebook platform (application programming interface) to enable developers to create small interactive programs that site owners can add to their sites to personalise them. Charitable site Just Giving has a branded app with several hundred users.

Atomisation

Atomisation
Atomisation in a Web 2.0 context refers to a concept where the content on a site is broken down into smaller fundamental units which can then be distributed via the web through links to other sites. Examples of atomisation include the stories and pages in individual feeds being syndicated to third-party sites and widgets.

Atomisation is a way of summarising a significant trend in Web 2.0 which incorporates some of the marketing techniques we have reviewed here such as posts on social networks, feeds and widgets.

In a Web 2.0 context atomisation describes how the content on a website can be broken down into smaller 'content objects' which are then shareable and can potentially be aggregated together with other content to provide content and services valuable for other site owners and visitors.

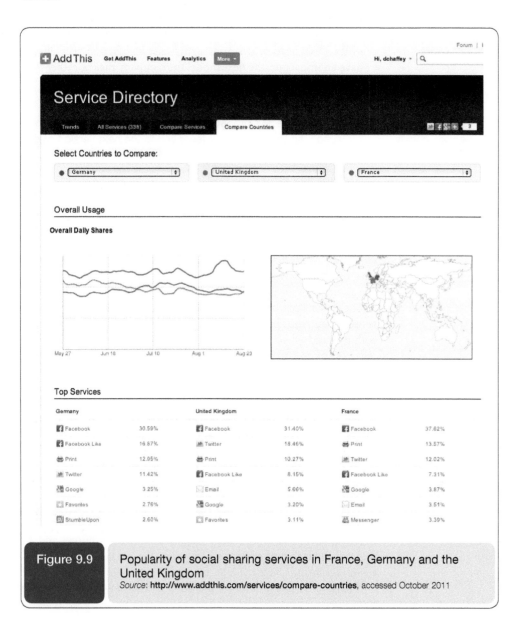

Figure 9.9	**Popularity of social sharing services in France, Germany and the United Kingdom**
	Source: **http://www.addthis.com/services/compare-countries**, accessed October 2011

For site owners, options to consider for the application of atomisation include:

- Providing content RSS feeds in different categories through their content management system. For example, the BBC effectively provides tens of thousands of newsletters on their site at the level of detail or granularity to support the interest of their readers i.e. separate feeds at different levels of aggregation, e.g. sport, football, premier league football or a fan's individual team.
- Sharing social updates, images, videos or whitepapers. These can be embedded from specialist sites like Flickr, YouTube or Scribd using widgets made available by the site owner.
- Separating out content which should be provided as data feeds of new stories or statistics into widgets on other sites. For example, UK retail statistics widget dashboard for iGoogle created by Google.
- Development of web services which update widgets with data from their databases. A classic example is the Just Giving widget (**www.justgiving.com**) where money raised by a charity donor is regularly updated.
- Creating badges which can be incorporated within blogs or social networks by their fans or advocates. The membership body CIPD does this well through their 'link to us' programme (**www.cipd.co.uk/absite/bannerselect.htm**) which encourages partners to add banners or text links to their site to link with the CIPD site. Similiarly, Hitwise encourages retailers to link it through its Top 10 Award programme (an award for the Top 10 most popular websites across each of the 160+ Hitwise industries by market share of visits).

Online partnerships including affiliate marketing

We showed in Chapter 5 that partnerships are an important part of today's marketing mix. The same is true online. Resources must be devoted to managing your online partners. Many large organisations have specific staff to manage these relationships. In smaller organisations partnership management is often neglected, which is a missed opportunity. There are three key types of online partnerships which need to be managed: link building (covered in the previous section), affiliate marketing and online sponsorship. All should involve a structured approach to managing links through to a site. The main and most important form of partnership marketing for transactional e-commerce sites which we review in this section is affiliate marketing. We also review options for online sponsorship. Other forms of digital marketing communications reviewed in this chapter, which are often free in terms of the visitors generated, can also be considered as partner marketing, for example online PR, link-building and use of Web 2.0 syndication.

Affiliate marketing

Affiliate marketing
A commission-based arrangement where referring sites (publishers) receive a commission on sales or leads by merchants (retailers or other transactional sites). Commission is usually based on a percentage of product sale price or a fixed amount for each sale (CPA or cost per acquisition), but may also sometimes be based on a per-click basis, for example when an aggregator refers visits to merchants.

Affiliate marketing divides marketers and agencies as to its value. The discussion revolves around the value of affiliate marketing in generating incremental sales. There is no doubt that affiliates can generate more sales at a controlled cost, the question is whether these sales would have occurred anyway if a brand is well known. For example, Amazon has an affiliate programme but it could be argued that its brand is so well known and it has such a large customer base that it would receive most sales anyway. However, Amazon has run its programme for over ten years and although it has reduced commissions, it is still running and is used to promote new product offerings such as music downloads.

What is affiliate marketing?

Affiliate marketing is the ultimate form of marketing communications since it is what is known as a 'pay-per-performance marketing' method – it's a commission-based arrangement where the merchant only pays when they make the sale or get a lead. Compare this to the wastage with traditional advertising or direct mail! It can also drive a volume of business in a range of sectors – many banks, travel companies and online retailers get more than 10% of their sales from a well-run affiliate marketing programme. It's not so suitable though for business products or lower-priced consumer products since it will not be sufficiently profitable for the affiliates, and it may be difficult to recruit sufficient affiliates.

Figure 9.10 summarises the affiliate marketing process. You can see that when a visitor to an affiliate site (who may be an online publisher or aggregator) clicks through to a merchant site, this prospect will be tracked through a cookie placed on the visitor's PC. If the prospect later transacts within an agreed period, usually 1, 7, 30, 60 or 90 days, the affiliate will be credited with the sale through an agreed amount (percentage of sale or fixed amount).

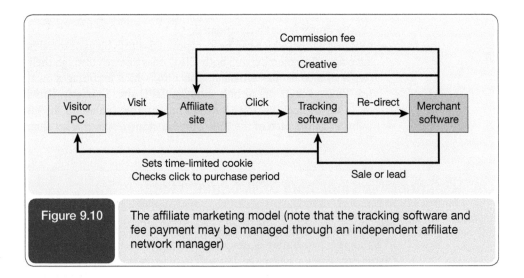

Figure 9.10   The affiliate marketing model (note that the tracking software and fee payment may be managed through an independent affiliate network manager)

Digital marketers need to be selective in choosing the right forms of affiliate marketing – not all may be desirable. These are the options of affiliate marketing models for you to consider.

- *Aggregators.* These are the major comparison sites like Kelkoo, USwitch and Moneysupermarket. These aren't strictly affiliates since some, such as Kelkoo and Shopzilla, charge on a cost-per-click, but USwitch and Moneysupermarket have a CPA model as well. Google Product Search (formerly Froogle) uses a similar model, but is a free option for retailers to submit a feed for which products may then be featured in the top of the Google SERPs.
- *Review sites.* For example CNet software or hardware reviews, or maybe startups like Reevoo or Review Centre. These all link to merchants based on cost-per-click or cost-per-acquisition deals.
- *Rewards sites.* These split the commission between the reward site and their visitors. Examples are GreasyPalm or QuidCo.
- *Voucher code sites.* MyVoucherCodes or Hot UK Deals are typical. If you have some great deals to entice first-time shoppers you should generate business, although many search by well-known brand.
- *Über-bloggers.* Martin Lewis's MoneySavingExpert.com is an incredibly popular site due to his PR efforts and great content. Although he has no ads, he is an affiliate for many sites he recommends.
- *Everyone else.* They don't tend to be high volume super-affiliates like all the above, but they're collectively important and you can work them via affiliate networks like Commission Junction or Tradedoubler. They often specialise in SEO or PPC.

Advantages and disadvantages of affiliate marketing

Advantages of affiliate marketing

Many of the benefits of affiliate marketing are closely related to search engine marketing since affiliates are often expert at deploying SEO or PPC to gain visibility in the search results pages. The main benefits of affiliate marketing are:

- *SERPS visibility*. Gain more visibility in the paid and natural listings of the SERPs (increase 'share of search' page).
- *Reach different audiences*. Can use different affiliates to target different audiences, product categories and related phrases.
- *Responsiveness to marketplace changes*. Affiliates may be more responsive than your in-house or agency teams in terms of algorithm changes for SEO or changes in bidding approaches for PPC. They are also great at identifying gaps in your search strategy. For example, they may be quicker at advertising on new products, or may use keyphrase variants that you haven't considered.
- *Target generic phrases in SERPs*. Enables you to reach customers through generic phrases (e.g. 'clothing') at a relatively low cost if the affiliates secure better positions in natural listings.
- *Increase reach in SERPs*. Increase the reach of your brand or campaign since affiliate ads and links featuring you will be displayed on third-party sites.
- *Generate awareness*. Can be used to generate awareness of brand or new products for which a company is not well known.
- *Diversity risk*. Use of affiliates reduces the risk caused by temporary or more fundamental problems with your SEM management or other digital marketing programmes.
- *Pay-per-performance*. The costs of acquisition can be controlled well.

Disadvantages of affiliate marketing

But there can be substantial drawbacks to an affiliate marketing programme which arise from the fact that your affiliates are mainly motivated by money. It follows that some of them may use unethical techniques to increase their revenue. Potential disadvantages are:

- *Incremental profit or sales may be limited*. You may be cannibalising business you would have achieved anyway.
- *Affiliates may exploit your brand name*. This is particularly the case where affiliates exploit brand names by bidding on variations of it (for example 'Dell', 'Dell Computers' or 'Dell laptop') or by gaining a presence in the natural listings. Here there is already awareness. It is important to prevent this and many affiliate programmes exclude brand bidding, although affiliates can have a role in displacing competitors from the listings for brand terms.
- *May damage brand reputation*. Your ads may be displayed on sites inconsistent with your brand image, such as gambling or pornography sites. Alternatively, creative may be out-of-date which could be illegal.
- *Programme management fees*. If using an affiliate network to manage your campaigns they may take up to 30% of each agreed affiliate commission as additional 'network override'.
- *Programme management time*. Affiliate marketing is founded on forming and maintaining good relationships. This cannot be done through the agency alone – marketers within a company need to speak to their top affiliates.

Best practice in planning and managing affiliate marketing

In this section we will review how affiliate networks can be used to improve the results from affiliate marketing and the main controls on affiliate marketing, i.e. commission, cookie periods and creative. It is important that these parameters are clearly defined in the affiliate agreement to reduce the likelihood of abuse.

Affiliate networks

Affiliate network
Third-party brokers also known as affiliate managers who manage recruitment of affiliates and infrastructure to manage a merchant's affiliate programme in the form of links, tracking and payment of a range of affiliates.

To manage the process of finding affiliates, updating product information, tracking clicks and making payments many companies use an **affiliate network** or affiliate manager such as the US/European networks Commission Junction (**www.cj.com**), Link Share (**www.linkshare.com**) or Trade Doubler (**www.tradedoubler.com**, mainly European). Since the affiliate network takes a cut on each sale, many merchants also try to setup separate relationships with preferred affiliates, often known as 'super affiliates'.

Since many of the important affiliates are members of more than one affiliate network programme, it is usually found that it is not worthwhile for a merchant to join more than two affiliate networks. They also need to be careful that several affiliates are not credited for multiple sales since this quickly becomes unprofitable for the merchant.

Affiliate marketing is often thought to apply solely to e-retailers where the affiliate is paid if there is a purchase on the merchant site. In fact, payment can occur for any action which is recorded on the destination site, for example through a 'thank you' post-transaction page after filling a form. This could be a quote for insurance, trial of a piece of software or registration for download of a paper. However, the majority of affiliate activity is within consumer sectors such as travel, finance and retail rather than business-to-business.

The value of affiliate networks in managing the relationships between merchants and publishers is such that it is rare for merchants to bypass them and so avoid the network override, although Amazon is one example of a merchant with their own programme.

Commission

In affiliate marketing, it is vital that commission is set at such a level that it incentivises affiliates to preferentially promote a merchants' products, while at the same time being profitable.

Earnings per click (EPC)
A relative measure of the effectiveness of a site or section of a site in generating revenue for the site owner through affiliate marketing for every 100 outbound clicks generated.

The affiliates or publishers are naturally obsessive about their **earnings per click (EPC)**. This is average earnings per click and is usually measured across 100 clicks.

EPC is a crucial measure in affiliate marketing since an affiliate will compare merchants on this basis and then usually decide to promote those with the highest EPC, which will be based on the commission levels and the conversion rates to sale for different merchants.

A merchant will set commission levels according to a product's awareness level within a merchant's portfolio of products or how much they feel they need to promote them. It will also be worth increasing commissions when there is a favourable promotion on a product since affiliates will then promote it, knowing that their EPC is more likely to increase. Less well-known products or newly launched products will often have more favourable commissions. For example at the time of writing, Tesco.com used affiliates for different products with different commission as follows:

- e-diets commission from £12 on 1–9 sales to £20 on 61+ sales
- wine at 2 per cent on lowest tier to 3 per cent on the Gold tier of sales of >£2500
- grocery and utilities – flat fee of £5 for first-time purchase only.

Cookie expiry period

Affiliates' EPC will also depend on the cookie expiry period agreed on the time between a visitor clicks the affiliate link and the sale is accredited to the affiliate. Common times are 7, 30 or 90 days. A longer cookie period will result in a higher EPC. Prussakov (2011a) recommends that 60 to 90 days is often best to incentivise affiliates in competitive markets with a longer decision-making period. Merchants don't typically want to pay multiple affiliates for a single sale. Instead, it is usually the last referring affiliate that is credited or a mix between the first and last. So a good tracking system is required to resolve this. Prussakov (2011b) uses the data presented in Figure 9.11 to argue that the majority purchase within a shorter-period, so a longer period gives a better incentive without adversely affecting profitability.

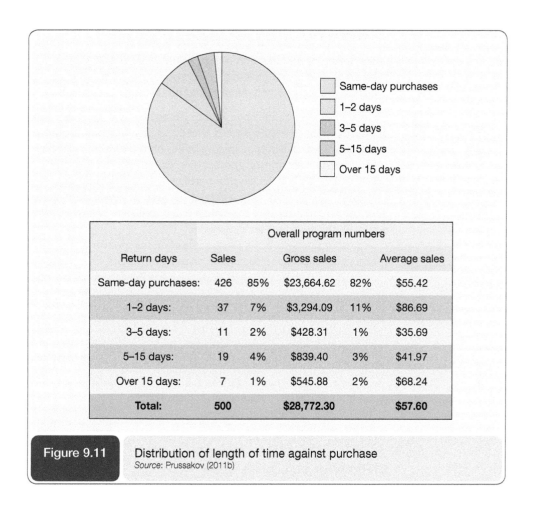

	Overall program numbers				
Return days	Sales		Gross sales		Average sales
Same-day purchases:	426	85%	$23,664.62	82%	$55.42
1–2 days:	37	7%	$3,294.09	11%	$86.69
3–5 days:	11	2%	$428.31	1%	$35.69
5–15 days:	19	4%	$839.40	3%	$41.97
Over 15 days:	7	1%	$545.88	2%	$68.24
Total:	**500**		**$28,772.30**		**$57.60**

Figure 9.11   Distribution of length of time against purchase
Source: Prussakov (2011b)

Creative and links

Managing the creative which affiliates use to promote a merchant is a challenge since creative needs to be up-to-date in line with different promotions or it may be misleading, or even illegal. So this needs to be monitored by the affiliate manager. Many merchants now provide live product feeds to affiliate networks in order to keep their promotions and product pricing up-to-date.

There are risks of brand damage through affiliates displaying creative on content which a merchant might feel was not complementary to their brand (for example, a gambling site). This needs to be specified in the affiliate agreement – sites need to be reviewed carefully before affiliates are permitted to join a specific programme and additional sites used by each affiliate should be monitored.

Another form of brand or trademark abuse is when an affiliate bids on a merchant's brand name such that they may receive credit for a sale when a prospect was already aware of the merchant, as explained in Chapter 3 in the legal section. The limits of this should also be specified within the affiliate agreements and monitored carefully.

Online sponsorship

Online sponsorship is not straightforward. It's not just a case of mirroring existing 'real-world' sponsorship arrangements in the 'virtual world', although this is a valid option. There are many additional opportunities for sponsorship online which can be sought out, even if you don't have a big budget at your disposal.

Ryan and Whiteman (2000) define online sponsorship as:

> the linking of a brand with related content or context for the purpose of creating brand awareness and strengthening brand appeal in a form that is clearly distinguishable from a banner, button or other standardised ad unit.

For the advertiser, online sponsorship has the benefit that their name is associated with an online brand that the site visitor is already familiar with. So, for users of a publisher site, with whom they are familiar, sponsorship builds on this existing relationship and trust.

Paid-for sponsorship of another site, or part of it, especially a portal, for an extended period is another way to develop permanent links. Co-branding is a lower-cost method of sponsorship and can exploit synergies between different companies. Note that sponsorship does not have to directly drive visitors to a brand site – it may be more effective if interaction occurs on the media owner's microsite.

A great business-to-business example of online sponsorship is offered by WebTrends which sponsors the customer information channel on ClickZ.com (**www.clickz.com/experts**). They combined this sponsorship with different ads each month offering e-marketers the chance to learn about different topics such as search marketing, retention and conversion marketing through detailed white papers and a 'Take 10' online video presentation by industry experts which could be downloaded by registered users. The objective of these ads was to encourage prospects to subscribe to the WebTrends WebResults e-newsletter and to assess purchase intent at sign-up enabling follow-up telemarketing by regional distributors. WebTrends reported the following results over a single year of sponsorship:

- list built to 100,000 WebResults total subscribers
- 18,000 Take 10 presentations
- 13,500 seminar attendees.

Co-branding and contra-deals

Co-branding of sites or e-mails are closely related to online sponsorship. These **contra-deals**, as they are sometimes referred to, typically occur where there is an association between two brands and they are complementary but not competitive.

For example, one online publisher may offer subscribers the chance to sign-up with newsletters from a another company, a process known as 'co-registration'.

Co-branding can be a cost-effective form of online marketing, but specific resource such as 'online partnership manager' has to be put in place to set up and manage the relationships between partners. This will often be part of an affiliate manager's role.

Interactive display advertising

What is display advertising?

Display advertising involves an advertiser paying for an advertising placement on third-party sites such as publishers or social networks. The process usually involves **ad serving** from a different server from that on which the page is hosted (ads can be served on destination sites in a similar way). Ad serving uses a specialist piece of software, possibly mounted on an independent server such as Doubleclick (now owned by Google). In 2008, Google launched its free ad manager service (**www.google.com/admanager**) to help site owners sell, schedule, optimise revenue, serve ads and measure directly-sold and network-based inventory.

Advertising is used on a range of sites in order to drive traffic to an organisation's **destination site**, or alternatively a **microsite** or nested ad-content on the media owner's site or on the destination site. The destination page from a banner ad will usually be designed as a specifically created direct-response page to encourage further action. For example, the nappy

Co-branding
An arrangement between two or more companies who agree to jointly display content and perform joint promotion using brand logos, e-mail marketing or banner advertisements. The aim is that the brands are strengthened if they are seen as complementary. Co-branding is often a reciprocal arrangement which can occur without payment as part of a wider agreement between partners.

Contra-deals
A reciprocal agreement in the form of an exchange where payment doesn't take place. Instead services or ad space to promote another company as part of co-branding occurs.

Display advertising
Display ads are paid ad placements using graphical or *rich media ad units* within a web page to achieve goals of delivering brand awareness, familiarity, favourability and purchase intent. Many ads encourage interaction through prompting the viewer to interact or rollover to play videos, complete an online form or to view more details by clicking through to a site.

Ad serving
The term for displaying an advertisement on a website. Often the advertisement will be served from a web server different from the site on which it is placed.

Destination site
The site reached on click-through.

Microsite
A small-scale destination site reached on click-through which is part of the media owner's site.

Run-of-site
Cost per 1000 ad impressions. CPM is usually higher for run-of-site advertisements where advertisements occur on all pages of the site.

Results-based payment
Advertisers pay according to the number of times the ad is clicked on.

supplier Huggies placed an advertisement on a childcare site that led the parents clicking on this link to more detailed information on Huggies contained on the site and encouraging them to opt-in to a loyalty programme.

Display advertising is still colloquially known as banner advertising, but practitioners such as the trade body, the Internet Advertising Bureau (**www.iab.net** and **www.iabuk.net**), media owners such as publishers, advertisers and their agencies now commonly refer to 'display advertising'. This reflects the increasing range of ad formats we will discuss below.

Purchasing ad placements

When media is purchased, it is either purchased on a specific site such as *The Times* or *New York Times*, or it is purchased across several sites, which are known as an ad network.

Display advertising is purchased for a specific period. It may be purchased for the ad to be served on:

- the **run-of-site** (the entire site)
- a section of site
- according to keywords entered on a search engine.

Traditionally, the most common payment is according to the number of customers who view the page as a cost-per-thousand (CPM) ad or page impressions. Typical CPM is in the range £10–£30. Other options that benefit the advertiser if they can be agreed are per click-through or per action such as a purchase on the destination site. Although initially media owners were able to control charging rates and largely used a per exposure model with the increase in unused ad inventory, there has been an increase in **results-based payment** methods particularly within ad networks.

Advantages and disadvantages of display advertising

Robinson *et al.* (2007) have noted that the two primary goals of online display advertising are first, using display adverts as a form of marketing communication used to raise brand awareness; and second, as a direct response medium focused on generating a response. Cartellieri *et al.* (1997) refer to a wider range of goals for online campaigns including:

- *Delivering content.* This is the typical case where a click-through on a banner advertisement leads through to a destination site giving more detailed information on an offer. This is where a direct response is sought. Today ads often embed videos or whitepapers to deliver content directly within the ad.
- *Enabling transaction.* If a click-through leads through to a merchant such as a travel site or an online bookstore this may lead directly to a sale. A direct response is also sought here.
- *Shaping attitudes.* An advertisement that is consistent with a company brand can help build brand awareness.
- *Soliciting response.* An advertisement may be intended to identify new leads or as a start for two-way communication. In these cases an interactive advertisement may encourage a user to type in an e-mail address or other information.
- *Encouraging retention.* The advertisement may be placed as a reminder about the company and its service and may link through to on-site sales promotions such as a prize draw.

These objectives are not mutually exclusive, and more than one can be achieved with a well-designed ad campaign.

Advantages of online advertising

- *Direct response.* Display advertising can generate an immediate direct response via click-through to a website enabling transaction for retail products for example.

- *Indirect response.* We will see in the section on the disadvantages of display advertising that click-throughs are so low that it suggests display advertising is not worthwhile. However, the indirect response should not be underestimated. This is where viewers of an ad later visit a website or search on the brand or category. Research by OPA Europe (2010) showed that for members sites, one third exposed to display advertising conducted searches for the advertised brands while 42 per cent visited advertised brand sites. Note that these results are for well-known brands and control figures were not presented to show the uplift compared to those non exposed.

- *Enhancing brand awareness and reach.* The visual imagery of a display ad can generate awareness about a brand, product or need. This is less practical in search engine marketing where searchers are already seeking a specific brand, product or need, although there are opportunities to make searchers aware of other, unknown suppliers. We also saw at the end of Chapter 8 that **XMOS (cross-media optimisation studies)** showed that online was useful for reaching audiences whose consumption of traditional media has decreased.

- *Media-multiplier or halo effect.* Repeated exposure to ads online, particularly in association with other media, can increase brand awareness and ultimately purchase intent. Furthermore, practitioners report a **media multiplier or halo effect** of buying online ads which can help increase the response rates from other online media. For example, if a web user has been exposed to banner ads, this may increase their response to paid search ads and may also increase their likelihood of converting on a site since brand awareness and trust may be higher. Attribution modelling, which we introduced in Chapter 8, can help determine the contribution of display ads as shown in Digital marketing insights 9.2.

This is suggested by research reported by MAD (2007) in the travel market which involved asking respondents what their response to an online ad that appealed to them would be. Surely it would be a click? In fact the results broke down as follows:

- search for a general term relating to the advertisement (31 per cent)
- go straight to advertisers site (29 per cent)
- search for the advertiser's name (26 per cent)
- click on banner to respond (26 per cent)
- visit a retail store (4%).

Of course, this methodology shows us reported behaviour rather than actual behaviour, but it is still significant that more than twice as many people are being driven to a search engine by banner advertising than by clicking directly on the banner! The research concludes that paid search marketing needs to be optimised to work with banner advertising, by anticipating searches that are likely to be prompted by the banner and ensure a higher rank for search results. For example, a brand featuring a Cyprus holiday offer will generate generic search terms like 'package holiday Cyprus' rather than brand searches.

Abraham (2008) has also shown that online ads can stimulate offline sales. For one retailer with a turnover of $15 billion, research showed that over a three-month period, sales increased (compared to a control group) by 40 per cent online and by 50 per cent offline among people exposed to an online search – and display – ad campaign promoting the entire company. Because its baseline sales volumes are greater in physical stores than on the Internet, this retailer derived a great deal more revenue benefit offline than the percentages suggest.

- *Achieving brand interactions.* Many modern display ads comprise two-parts – an initial visual encouraging interaction through a rollover and then another visual or application encouraging interaction with a brand. This enables advertisers to calculate an interaction rate (IR) to assess the extent to which viewers interact with a brand ad.

- *Targeting.* Media buyers can select the right site or channel within a site to reach the audience (e.g. a specialist online car magazine or review site or the motoring channel within an online newspaper or TV channel site). Audiences can also be targeted via their profile through serving personalised ads, or ad in e-mail if visitors have registered on a site.

Behavioural re-targeting options is used in an ad network to preferentially serve an ad to someone who seems to have an interest in a topic from the content they consume.

XMOS (cross-media optimisation studies)
Research designed to help marketers and their agencies answer the question 'What is the optimal mix of advertising vehicles across different media, in terms of frequency, reach and budget allocation, for a given campaign to achieve its marketing goals?' The mix between online and offline spend is varied to maximise campaign metrics such as reach, brand awareness and purchase intent.

Media multiplier or halo effect
The role of one media channel on influencing sale or uplift in brand metrics. Commonly applied to online display advertising, where exposure to display ads may increase click-through rates when the consumer is later exposed to a brand through other media, for example sponsored links or affiliate ads. It may also improve conversion rates on destination sites through higher confidence in the brand or familiarity with the offer.

Effectively the ad follows the viewer around the site. For example, if someone visits the car section of a site, then the ad is served to them when they view other sections of the site. Re-targeting can work across an ad-network too and can even be sequential, where the messages are varied for an individual the more times they are exposed to the ad. Search re-targeting offers the option to display an ad after a visitor has searched on a particular term such as a car marque. Tracking of individuals is achieved through use of cookies.

- *Cost.* There are opportunities to buy online media at a cheaper rate compared to traditional media, although this is less true in focused, competitive markets such as financial services where there is limited premium inventory for media buyers to purchase.

   Ad networks from suppliers such as Blue Lithium or 24-7 Media give advertisers the options of advertising across a network of sites to reach a particular demographic, e.g. female 18–25, but at a lower cost than media buys on a specific site since the actual site used for the ad placement isn't known (hence these are sometimes known as '*blind network buys*'). Lower CPMs are achievable and in some cases CPC or CPA payment options are available. Site owners such as publishers use ad networks since it gives them a method of gaining fees from unused ad inventory which has not sold at premium rates.

- *Dynamic updates to ad campaigns.* In comparison with traditional media, where media placements have to be bought weeks or months in advance, online ads are more flexible since it is possible to place an advertisement more rapidly and make changes during the campaign. Experienced online advertisers build in flexibility to change targeting through time. Best practice is to start wide and then narrow to a focus – allow 20 per cent budget for high-performing ad placements (high CTR and conversion).

Demand Side Platforms (DSPs)
A service that enables ads to be managed across multiple ad networks and ad exchanges through a single interface designed for managing reporting and performance.

Real-time bidding (RTB)
Bids for buying ads against keywords can be managed in real-time in conjunction with a DSP.

   A major change in the use of online advertising is through what are known as **Demand Side Platforms (DSPs)** that use an approach called **real-time bidding (RTB)**. The purpose of these is to exploit efficiencies through using technology to automatically bid on the most cost-effective ad inventory in an auction. Since individuals are tracked across different sites they can be targeted according to their interests shown by content view using a technique known as behavioural targeting. However, it is unclear whether privacy concerns such as those we covered in Chapter 3 will prevent this in future.

   In an iMediaConnection (2003) interview with ING direct VP of marketing, Jurie Pieterse, the capability to revise creative is highlighted:

   > Another lesson we learned is the importance of creative. It's critical to invest in developing various creative executions to test them for best performance and constantly introduce new challengers to the top performers. We've also learned there's no single top creative unit – different creative executions and sizes perform differently from publisher to publisher.

- *Accountability.* As we will discuss later in the section, it is readily possible to measure reach, interaction and response to ads. However, it is more difficult to measure brand impact.

Disadvantages of online advertising

- *Relatively low click-through rates.* When discussing online ads, many web users will state they ignore ads and find them intrusive. Published click-through rates support this, with most compilations showing response rates of around 0.1 to 0.2 per cent, but with rich media formats such as video ads attracting higher click-through rates. This phenomenon is known among practitioners as banner blindness (see for example, Nielsen (2007)). The first 468×68 pixel banner ad was placed on Hotwired in 1995 and the call-to-action 'Click here!' generated a click-through of 25 per cent. Since then, the click-through rate (CTR) has fallen dramatically with many consumers suffering from 'banner blindness' – they ignore anything on a website that looks like an ad. Remember though, that for reasons such as awareness generation and the media multiplier effect, digital marketers should not dismiss online advertising as ineffectual based on click-through rates alone.

- *Relatively high costs or low efficiency.* When the low response rates are combined with relatively high costs of over £10 per thousand, this makes online ads an inefficient medium.
- *Brand reputation.* Brands can potentially be damaged in the consumers' mind if they are associated with some types of content such as gambling, pornography or racism. It is difficult to monitor precisely which content an ad is served next to when millions of impressions are bought across many sites, this is particularly the case when using ad networks.

Best practice in planning and managing display ad campaigns

In this section we will review how measurement, targeting and creative can be used to improve the results from display ad campaigns.

Measurement of display effectiveness

Different terms are used for measuring banner ad effectiveness. Each time an advertisement is viewed is referred to as an advertisement or **ad impression – page impressions** (page views) are other terms used. Since some people may view the advertisement more than one time, marketers are also interested in the **reach**, which is the number of unique individuals who view the advertisement. This will naturally be a smaller figure than that for ad impressions. Cost of ads is typically based on **CPM** or cost-per-thousand *(mille)* ad impressions as with other media. However, the popularity of CPC search advertising and CPA affiliate deals mean that these are options too.

As with other digital media, direct response to ads is measured through click-through rate. **Interaction rate (IR)** is a form of measurement that is unique to display ads. It refers to the many ads which encourage the site visitor to interact through a prompt to 'rollover' and another Flash creative will be loaded which may offer a clear brand message rendered in large font, a response form such as an insurance quote or a request to obtain a SIM or a game or poll. The engagement of the ad campaign for different placements can then be assessed through the interaction rate which will typically be ten times higher than the click-through rate if the targeting, offer and creative is right.

When payment is made according to the number of viewers of a site it is important that the number of viewers be measured accurately. To do this independent **website auditors** are required. The main auditing body in the UK is the Audit Bureau of Circulation Electronic, ABCelectronic (**www.abce.org.uk**).

There is much discussion about how many impressions of an advertisement an individual has to see for it to be effective. Novak and Hoffman (1997) note that for traditional media it is thought that fewer than three exposures will not give adequate recall. For new media, because of the greater intensity of viewing a computer screen, recall seems to be better with a smaller number of advertisements compared with old media. The technical term for adequate recall is **effective frequency**.

When a user clicks on the advertisement, he or she will normally be directed to further information, viewing of which will result in a marketing outcome. Usually the user will be directed through to part of the corporate website that will have been set up especially to deal with the response from the advertisement. When a user clicks on an advertisement immediately this is known as a **click-through**, but adserving systems (using cookies) also measure **view-through** which indicates when a user views an ad and subsequently visits a website within a defined period, such as 30 days. This increases overall response, but it should be borne in mind that users may have visited the site in response to other stimuli.

Interactive ad formats

As well as the classic 468 × 60 rotating GIF banner ad which is decreasing in popularity, media owners now provide a choice of larger, richer formats which web users are more likely to notice. Research has shown that message association and awareness building are much higher for flash-based ads, rich-media ads and larger-format rectangles (multipurpose units, MPUs)

Page and ad impressions
One page impression occurs when a member of the audience views a web page. One ad impression occurs when a person views an advertisement placed on the web page.

Reach
Reach defines the number of unique individuals who view an advertisement.

CPM
The cost of placing an ad viewed by 1000 people.

Interaction rate (IR)
The proportion of ad viewers who interact with an online ad through rolling over it. Some will be involuntary depending on where the ad is placed on screen, so it is highly dependent on placement.

Website auditors
Auditors accurately measure the usage of different sites in terms of the number of ad impressions and click-through rates.

Effective frequency
The number of exposures or ad impressions (frequency) required for an advertisement to become effective.

Clickthrough
A clickthrough (ad click) occurs each time a user clicks on a banner advertisement to direct them to a web page that contains further information. The click-through rate is expressed as a percentage of total ad impressions, and refers to the proportion of users viewing an advertisement who click on it. It is calculated as the number of click-throughs divided by the number of ad impressions.

View-through
Indicates when a user views an ad and subsequently visits a website.

Interstitial ads
Ads that appear between one page and the next.

Overlay
Typically an animated ad that moves around the page and is superimposed on the website content.

and skyscrapers. Other online ad terms you will hear include **interstitials** (intermediate adverts before another page appears) and the more common **overlays** (formerly more often known as *superstitials* or *overts*) that appear above content and, of course, *pop-up windows* that are now less widely used because of their intrusion. Online advertisers face a constant battle with users who deploy pop-up blockers or less commonly ad-blocking software, but they will persist in using rich-media formats where they generate the largest response.

Interactive ad targeting options

Online ads can be targeted through placing ads:

- *On a particular type of site (or part of site)* which has a specific visitor profile or type of content. So a car manufacturer can place ads on the home page of Handbag.com to appeal to a young female audience. A financial services provider can advertise in the money section of the site to target those interested in these products. To reach large mass-market audiences, advertisers can place an ad on a large portal home page such as MSN which has millions of visitors each day (sometimes known as a 'road-block' if they take all ad inventory).
- *To target a registered user's profile.* A business software provider could advertise on the FT to target registrants' profiles such as finance directors or IT managers.
- *At a particular time of day or week.*
- *To follow users' behaviour.* **Behavioural ad targeting** is all about relevance – dynamically serving relevant content, messaging or ad which matches the interests of a site visitor according to inferences about their characteristics. These inferences are made by anonymously tracking the different types of pages visited by a site user during a single visit to a site or across multiple sessions. Other aspects of the environment used by the visitor can also be determined, such as their location, browser and operating system. For example, FT.com using software from Revenue Science can identify users in eight segments: Business Education, Institutional Investor, Information Technology, Luxury and Consumer, Management, Personal Finance, Travel and Private Equity. The targeting process is shown in Figure 9.12. First the ad serving system detects whether the visitor is in the target audience (media optimisation), then creative optimisation occurs to serve the best ad for the viewer type.

Behavioural ad targeting
Enables an advertiser to target ads at a visitor as they move elsewhere on the site, visit other sites on an ad network return to the site, thus increasing the frequency or number of impressions served to an individual in the target market.

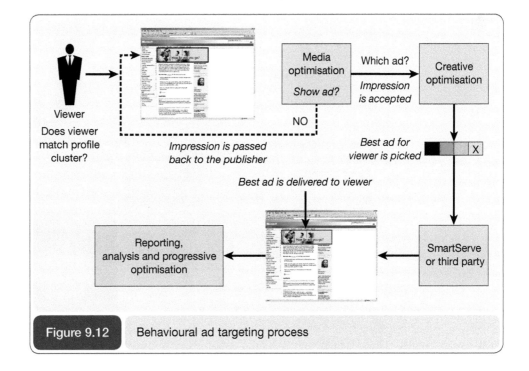

| Figure 9.12 | Behavioural ad targeting process |

In 2010 behavioural targeting became available through Google's Adwords platform as Remarketing which made it available to many more advertisers.

Ad creative

As with any form of advertising, certain techniques will result in a more effective advertisement. Robinson *et al.* (2007) conducted research on the factors which increased click-through response to banner ads. The main variables they (and previous studies they reference include):

- banner size
- message length
- promotional incentive
- animation
- action phrase (commonly referred to as a call-to-action)
- company brand/logo.

Their research indicated that the design elements which made the most effective banner ads included a larger size, longer message, absence of promotional incentives and the presence of information about casino games. Surprisingly, the inclusion of brand name was not favourable in increasing click-through, although, as we noted, this may be because the ad generates a subsequent search on the brand. Please note that this study was restricted to online gambling ads.

Anecdotal discussions by the authors with marketers who have advertised online indicate the following are also important and worth considering:

- *Appropriate incentives are needed to achieve click-through.* Banner advertisements with offers such as prizes or reductions can achieve higher click-through rates by perhaps as much as 10 per cent.

Figure 9.13   Banner blog (www.bannerblog.com.au) ad review site

- *Creative design needs to be tested extensively.* Alternative designs for the advertisement need to be tested on representatives of a target audience. Anecdotal evidence suggests that the click-through rate can vary greatly according to the design of the advertisement, in much the same way that recall of a television advertisement will vary in line with its concept and design. Different creative designs may be needed for different sites on which advertisements are placed. Zeff and Aronson (2001) note that simply the use of the words 'click here!' or 'click now' can dramatically increase click-through rates because new users do not know how banners work!
- *Placement of advertisement and timing need to be considered carefully.* The different types of placement options available have been discussed earlier in the chapter, but it should be remembered that audience volume and composition will vary through the day and the week.

Different styles of ad creative can be viewed by visiting the Ad Gallery of an ad serving company such as Tangozebra (**www.tangozebra.com**) or Eyeblaster (**www.eyeblaster.com**), or an ad review site such as Banner Blog (**www.bannerblog.com.au**, Figure 9.13) which features ads from many countries.

Opt-in e-mail marketing and mobile text messaging

We have grouped email marketing with text messaging since these are both 'push media' which share much in terms of their applications for prospect and customer communications. In this coverage we concentrate on e-mail marketing since mobile marketing was covered in Chapter 3.

What is e-mail marketing?

When devising plans for e-mail marketing communications, marketers need to plan for:

Outbound e-mail marketing
E-mails are sent to customers and prospects from an organisation.

Inbound e-mail marketing
Management of e-mails from customers by an organisation.

- **Outbound e-mail marketing**, where e-mail campaigns are used as a form of direct marketing to encourage trial and purchases and as part of a CRM dialogue.
- **Inbound e-mail marketing**, where e-mails from customers, such as service enquiries, are managed (this was discussed in Chapters 3 and 5 and isn't discussed further in this chapter).

The applications of outbound e-mail marketing communications broadly break down into customer acquisition and retention activities. e-mail activities within organisation tend to focus on customer acquisition as these ratings (on a 5-point scale) on the relative merits of different applications of e-mail by Chittenden and Rettie (2003) suggest:

- customer retention (4.5)
- sales promotion (4.4)
- gathering customer data (3.0)
- lead generation (3.0)
- brand awareness (2.7)
- customer acquisition (2.1).

Opt-in e-mail options for customer acquisition

For acquiring new visitors and customers to a site, there are three main options for e-mail marketing. From the point of view of the recipient, these are:

- *Cold e-mail campaign.* In this case, the recipient receives an opt-in e-mail from an organisation that has rented an e-mail list from a consumer e-mail list provider such as Experian (**www.experian.com**), Claritas (**www.claritas.com**) or IPT Limited (**www.myoffers.co.uk**)

or a business e-mail list provider such as Mardev (**www.mardev.com**), Corpdata (**www. corpdata.com**) or trade publishers and event providers such as VNU. Although they have agreed to receive offers by e-mail, the e-mail is effectively cold. For example, a credit card provider could send a cold e-mail to a list member who is not currently their member. It is important to use some form of 'statement of origination', otherwise the message may be considered spam. Cold e-mails tend to have higher CPAs than other forms of online marketing, but different lists should still be evaluated.

- *Co-branded e-mail.* Here, the recipient receives an e-mail with an offer from a company they have a reasonably strong affinity with. For example, the same credit card company could partner with a mobile service provider such as Vodafone and send out the offer to their customer (who has opted in to receive e-mails from third parties). Although this can be considered a form of cold e-mail, it is warmer since there is a stronger relationship with one of the brands and the subject line and creative will refer to both brands. Co-branded e-mails tend to be more responsive than cold e-mails to rented lists since the relationship exists and fewer offers tend to be given. The Digital marketing insight gives an example of where email marketing is used to increase awareness as part of an integrated campaign combined with display advertising.

- *Third-party e-newsletter.* In this visitor acquisition option, a company publicises itself in a third-party e-newsletter. This could be in the form of an ad, sponsorship or PR (editorial) which links through to a destination site. These placements may be set up as part of an interactive advertising ad buy since many e-newsletters also have permanent versions on the website. Since e-newsletter recipients tend to engage with them by scanning the headlines or reading them if they have time, e-newsletter placements can be relatively cost effective.Viral marketing, which is discussed in the next main section, also uses e-mail as the mechanism for transferring messages.

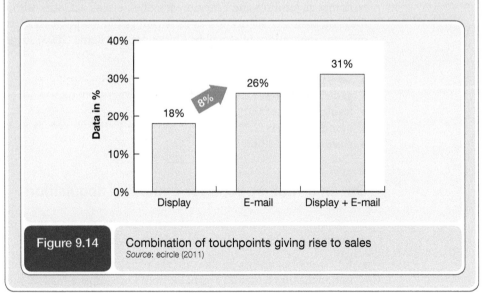

Digital marketing insight 9.4   **SEAT combine e-mail with display advertising to increase awareness**

This study analysed the advertising effectiveness of e-mail marketing and display advertising, looked at responses from over 1000 consumers to SEAT Ibiza ST campaigns. It used a classic 'hold out' approach where different respondents were reached through different combinations of media:

Figure 9.14   Combination of touchpoints giving rise to sales
Source: ecircle (2011)

- contact through an e-mail campaign
- contact with display advertising
- contact with both campaign channels.

The main results from the campaign which showed the integrated benefits of the campaign were:

1 The combination of display and e-mail advertising improves advertising recall by 13 per cent compared with just display advertising (Figure 9.14)
2 E-mail increases disposition to buy in 47 per cent of cases and is therefore ideal for increasing conversions
3 Spending power as a target group – by using e-mail you can precisely reach your target group
4 E-mail allowed the required reach of advertising to be reached three times more quickly than display advertising

Source: eCircle (2011)

Opt-in e-mail options for prospect conversion and customer retention (house list)

Opt-in
An individual agrees to receive e-mail communications.

House list
A list of prospect and customer names, e-mail addresses and profile information owned by an organisation.

E-mail is most widely used as a prospect conversion and customer retention tool using an **opt-in house list** of prospects and customers that have given permission to an organisation to contact them. For example, Lastminute.com has built a house list of over 10 million prospects and customers across Europe. Successful e-mail marketers adopt a strategic approach to e-mail and develop a contact or touch strategy which plans the frequency and content of e-mail communications as explained in Chapters 4 and 6. Some options for in-house e-mail marketing include:

- *Conversion e-mail.* Someone visits a website and expresses interest in a product or service by registering and providing their e-mail address, although they do not buy. Automated follow-up e-mails can be sent out to persuade the recipient to trial the service. For example, betting company William Hill found that automated follow-up e-mails converted twice as many registrants to place their first bet compared to registrants who did not receive an e-mail.
- *Regular e-newsletter type.* Options are reviewed for different frequencies such as weekly, monthly or quarterly with different content for different audiences and segments. These are commonly used to update consumers on the latest products or promotions or business customers on developments within a market
- *House-list campaign.* These are periodic e-mails to support different objectives such as encouraging trial of a service or newly launched product, repeat purchases or reactivation of customers who no longer use a service.
- *Event-triggered.* These tend to be less regular and are sent out perhaps every three or six months when there is news of a new product launch or an exceptional offer.
- *E-mail sequence.* Software can send out a series of e-mails with the interval betweene-mails determined by the marketer.

Advantages and disadvantages of e-mail marketing

Advantages of e-mail marketing

We saw in Chapter 6 that permission-based e-mail is an effective tool for building relationships with customers online. Despite the increase in spam, such that the vast majority of e-mails are spam or viruses (most estimates exceed 80 per cent), e-mail can still drive good response levels, particularly for house lists (retention e-mail marketing). Opt-in email communications provide a controlled push message which encourages response. An example of the continued power of e-mail marketing campaigns is shown in Figure 9.15. This shows research from GSI (2011) for the combination of touchpoints that can be attributed to sale from a single day, 29 November 2010, known in the US as 'CyberMonday' from 15GSI retail e-commerce sites. Since this is a known peak-day for sales, retailers are active in driving visitors to the site.

Owing to these advantages, in many countries such as the volume of e-mail marketing exceeds direct mail volumes. However, no one is suggesting direct mail will disappear immediately since it will typically have a higher impact than e-mail marketing and the two work best when integrated.

The main advantages of e-mail marketing are:

- *Relatively low cost of fulfilment.* The physical costs of e-mail are substantially less than direct mail.
- *Direct response medium encourages immediate action.* E-mail marketing encourages click-through to a website where the offer can be redeemed immediately – this increases the likelihood of an immediate, impulsive response. For this reason, it is one of the best methods of attracting existing customers to return to a site (it's a push media).
- *Faster campaign deployment.* Lead times for producing creative and the whole campaign lifecycle tends to be shorter than traditional media.
- *Ease of personalisation.* It is easier and cheaper to personalise e-mail than for physical media and also than for a website.

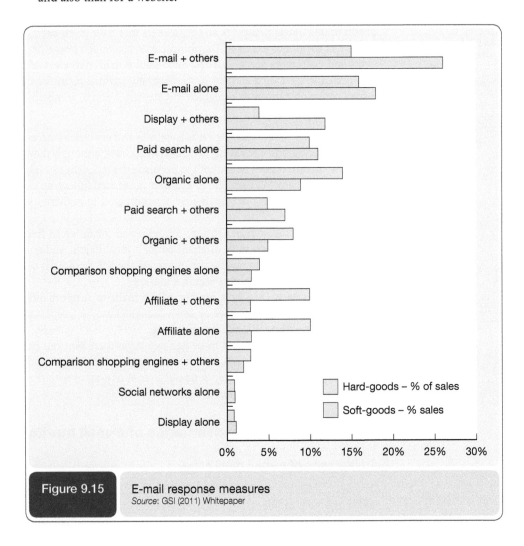

Figure 9.15	E-mail response measures
	Source: GSI (2011) Whitepaper

- *Options for testing.* It is relatively easy and cost effective to test different e-mail creative and messaging.
- *Integration.* Through combining e-mail marketing with other direct media that can be personalised, such as direct mail, mobile messaging or web personalisation, campaign response can be increased as the message is reinforced by different media.

Disadvantages of e-mail marketing

Some of the disadvantages of e-mail marketing which marketers need to manage as they run their campaigns so that they are closely related to best practice are:

- *Deliverability.* Difficulty of getting messages delivered through different Internet service providers (ISPs), corporate firewalls and web mail systems.
- *Renderability.* Difficulty of displaying the creative as intended within the in-box of different e-mail reading systems.
- *E-mail response decay.* E-mail recipients are most responsive when they first subscribe to an e-mail. It is difficult to keep them engaged.
- *Communications preferences.* Recipients will have different preferences for e-mail offers, content and frequency which affect engagement and response. These have to be managed through communications preferences.
- *Resource intensive.* Although e-mail offers great opportunities for targeting, personalisation and more frequent communications, additional people and technology resources are required to deliver these.

Best practice in planning and managing e-mail marketing

In this section we will review how measurement, targeting and creative can be used to improve the results from e-mail marketing.

E-mail service providers

E-mail service providers (ESPs)
Provide a web-based service used by marketers to manage their e-mail activities including hosting e-mail subscription forms, broadcast and tracking.

E-mail service providers (ESPs) are a popular method companies use to manage their e-mail marketing. ESPs provides a web-based service used by marketers to manage their e-mail activities with less recourse to an agency. Rather than buying software that you host and manage on your server, the software is effectively used on a subscription basis, with a cost based on number of e-mails sent and runs on another company's server. The ESP manages four key capabilities including hosting of forms for managing e-mail subscriptions and landing pages, the broadcast tools for dispatching the e-mails and a database containing the prospect or customer profiles. They also provide tracking of effectiveness as shown by the example in Figure 9.16.

Measuring e-mail marketing

Figure 9.16 shows that the key measures for e-mail marketing are:

- *Delivery rate* (here indicated by 'non-bounce rate'). E-mails will bounce if the e-mail address is no longer valid or a spam filter blocks the e-mail.
- *Open rate.* This is measured for HTML messages through downloaded images. It is an indication of how many customers open an e-mail, but is not accurate since some users have preview panes in their e-mail readers which load the message even if is deleted without reading, and some e-mail readers such as Outlook Express now block images by default (this has resulted in a decline in open rates through time). Open rates for particular types of e-mail address, e.g. Hotmail.com, is also an indication of deliverability problems.
- *Click-through or click rate.* This is the number of people who click through on the e-mail of those delivered (strictly unique clicks rather than total clicks). You can see that response rates are quite high at around 10%.

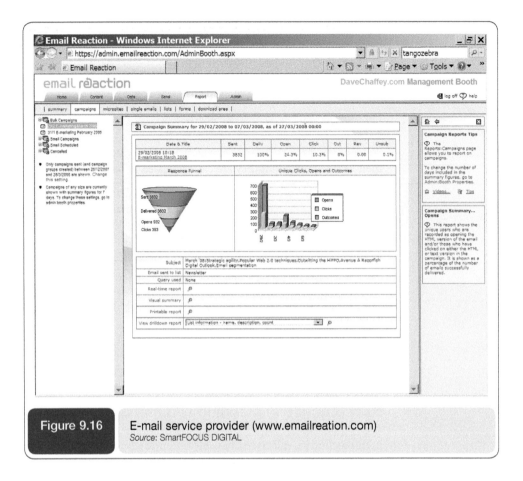

Figure 9.16	E-mail service provider (www.emailreation.com)
	Source: SmartFOCUS DIGITAL

Additionally, and most important, are the marketing outcomes or value events (Chapter 8) such as sales and leads achieved when an e-mail recipient clicks through to the website. Retailers will also have additional methods of comparing e-mail campaigns such as revenue/profit per e-mail or thousand e-mails and average order value (AOV).

E-mail marketing success factors

Effective e-mail marketing shares much in common with effective direct e-mail copy. Chaffey (2006) uses the mnemonic CRITICAL for a checklist of questions that can be used to improve the response of e-mail campaigns. It stands for:

- *Creative.* This assesses the design of the e-mail including its layout, use of colour and image and the copy (see below).
- *Relevance.* Does the offer and creative of the e-mail meet the needs of the recipients? This is dependent on the list quality and targeting variables used.
- *Incentive (or offer).* The WIFM factor ('What's in it for me?') for the recipient. What benefit does the recipient gain from clicking on the hyperlink(s) in the e-mail? For example, a prize draw is a common offer for B2C brands.
- *Targeting and timing.* Targeting is related to the relevance. Is a single message sent to all prospects or customers on the list or are e-mails with tailored creative, incentive and copy sent to the different segments on the list? Timing refers to when the e-mail is received: the time of day, day of the week, point in the month and even the year; does it relate to any particular events? There is also the relative timing – when it is received compared to other marketing communications – this depends on the integration.

- *Integration.* Are the e-mail campaigns part of your integrated marketing communications? Questions to ask include: are the creative and copy consistent with my brand? Does the message reinforce other communications? Does the timing of the e-mail campaign fit with offline communications?
- *Copy.* This is part of the creative and refers to the structure, style and explanation of the offer together with the location of hyperlinks in the e-mail.
- *Attributes (of the e-mail).* Assess the message characteristics such as the subject line, from address, to address, date/time of receipt and format (HTML or text). Send out Multipart/ MIME messages which can display HTML or text according to the capability of the e-mail reader. Offer choice of HTML or text to match users' preferences.
- *Landing page (or microsite)* – These are terms given to the page(s) reached after the recipient clicks on a link in the e-mail. Typically, on click-through the recipient will be presented with an online form to profile or learn more about them. Designing the page so the form is easy to complete can affect the overall success of the campaign.

A relevant incentive, such as free information or a discount, is offered in exchange for a prospect providing their e-mail address by filling in an online form. Careful management of e-mail lists is required since, as the list ages, the addresses of customers and their profiles will change, resulting in many bounced messages and lower response rates. Data protection law also requires the facility for customers to update their details.

Practical issues in managing e-mail marketing

Two of the main practical challenges for e-mail marketers or their agencies to manage are **deliverability** and **renderability**.

Deliverability
Refers to ensuring e-mail messages are delivered and aren't blocked by spam filters because the e-mail content or structure falsely identifies a permission-based e-mail as a spammer, or because the sender's IP address has a poor reputation for spam.

E-mail marketers have to ensure their e-mails are delivered given the increase in efforts by ISPs and web-e-mail companies to reduce spam into their end-users in-boxes due to the volume of spam. E-mail marketers do not want to be identified as a 'False positive' where permission-based e-mails may be bounced or placed into junk-mail boxes or simply deleted if the receiving system assesses that they are spam.

Web-based e-mail providers such as Hotmail and Yahoo! Mail have introduced standard authentication techniques known as Sender ID and Domain Keys which e-mail marketers should use to make sure the e-mail broadcaster is who they say they are and doesn't spoof their address as many spammers do. E-mail providers also assess the reputation of the e-mail broadcasters using services such as SenderScore (**www.senderscore.org**) based on the number of complaints and quality of e-mails sent.

Renderability
The capability of an e-mail to display correctly formatted in different e-mail readers.

It is also important that e-mail marketers do not use keywords in their e-mails which may identify them as spam. For example, e-mail filter such as Spam Assassin (**www.spamassassin. org**) have these types of rules which are used to assess spam:

- SUB_FREE_OFFER
- SUBJECT_DRUG_GAP_VIA
- TO_ADDRESS_EQ_REAL
- HTML_IMAGE_RATIO_04
- HTML_FONT_BIG

- Subject starts with 'Free'
- Subject contains a gappy version of 'viagra'
- To: repeats address as real name
- BODY: HTML has a low ratio of text to image area
- BODY: HTML tag for a big font size

Although the word 'free' in a subject line may cause a problem, this is only one part of the signature of a spam, so it may still be possible to use this word if the reputation of the sender is good.

Renderability refers to how the e-mail appears in different e-mail readers. Often images are blocked by readers in an effort to defeat spammers who use the fact that images are downloaded as the user views the e-mail to detect that the e-mail is a valid address. So e-mails that are only made up of images with no text are less likely to be effective than hybrid messages combining text and images. Formatting can also differ in different readers, so designers of e-mails have to test how e-mails render in common e-mail readers such as Hotmail and Yahoo! Mail.

A further challenge is trying to achieve ongoing engagement with list members. Some approaches that are commonly used include:

- Develop a welcome programme where over the first three to six months targeted automatically-triggered e-mails to educate subscribers about your brand, products and deliver targeted offers.
- Use offers to re-activate list-members as they become less responsive.
- Segment list members by activity (responsiveness) and age on list and treat differently, either by reducing frequency or using more offline media.
- Follow-up on bounces using other media to reduce problems of dropping deliverability.
- Best practice when renting lists is to request only e-mails where the opt-in is within the most recent six to nine months when subscribers are most active.

List management

E-mail marketers need to work hard to improve the quality of their list as explained in Chapter 6. DMA (2008) report that companies often fail to collect the most recent address with UK companies having e-mail addresses for only 50 per cent of their database. Respondents believed that the data and its selection accounted for over half of a campaign's success. The creative and offer are still considered significant while timing is viewed as having the least impact, accounting for just 10 per cent of the success of an e-mail campaign. The report noted that the majority of respondents gather new e-mail addresses through organic website traffic with offline (paper-based) activity accounting for 40 per cent and telemarketing for 31 per cent.

Mini Case Study 9.3	Beep-beep-beep-beep, that'll be the bank then – driving sales through mobile marketing

Say and Southwell (2006) creators of the text message banking system at First Direct (part of the HSBC Group, describe how if mobile marketing is carefully used with a trusted brand it can be effective. Their use of mobile marketing started in 2001 with product offer campaigns encouraging mobile users to log-on to the bank, call the contact centre or receive a direct mail pack for more information. Since there was a delay between requesting a direct mail pack and receiving one, a more responsive mechanism was for customers who replied to a text message with their e-mail address to immediately receive an e-mail with a link to a website featuring more information and an application form.

First Direct also use mobile short codes within their offline advertising encouraging those who read ads in newspapers about a product, for example, to follow-up on them immediately.

Short codes were also used for promotions. In one example, a 'text to win TXT2WIN' approach was used where customers were sent an e-mail or a direct mail pack with information about a new Internet Banking Plus account aggregation service plus details of a prize draw to win a holiday or ticket to a football match. To enter the competition, customers were asked to review an online demonstration, find an answer to a question, and text the answer to a shortcode number with their name, postcode and e-mail address.

The campaign objectives and results (in brackets) were to:

- capture 5000 mobile phone numbers from customers (200% of plan)
- acquire 3000 e-mail addresses (176% of plan)
- raise awareness about the new service (31,000 customers view demonstration)
- create 1000 new registrations (576% of plan).

This case shows the need for text message marketing to be carefully integrated with other direct channels such as web, e-mail and phone. It also shows the importance of capturing and maintaining up-to-date customer details such as e-mail addresses and mobile phone numbers.

Source: Say and Southwell (2006).

Mobile text messaging

We have concentrated our coverage on e-mail marketing in this section since the amount of marketing investment and levels of activity in e-mail marketing is much higher than mobile text messaging because it seems that receiving permission-based e-mails is more acceptable than receiving what may be perceived as an intrusive text message on a mobile device. Additionally, it enables more complex, visual messages to be delivered. However, Rettie *et al.* (2005) in an analysis of 26 text marketing campaigns (5401 respondents) demonstrated surprising levels of effectiveness. Her team found that overall acceptability of SMS advertising was 44 per cent, significantly higher than the acceptability of telemarketing and found relatively high response rates and brand recall compared to direct mail and e-mail marketing.

Social media and viral marketing

Social media marketing
Monitoring and facilitating customer-customer interaction and participation throughout the web to encourage positive engagement with a company and its brands. Interactions may occur on a company site, social networks and other third-party sites

Social media marketing is an important category of digital marketing which involves encouraging customer communications on a companies own site, or social presences such as Facebook or Twitter or in specialist publisher sites, blogs and forums. It can be applied as a traditional broadcast medium, for example companies can use Facebook or Twitter to send messages to customers or partners who have opted in. However to take advantage of the benefits of social media it is important to start and participate in customer conversations. These can be related to products, promotions or customer service and are aimed at learning more about customers and providing support so improving the way a company is perceived.

We've seen throughout this book that the opportunities of communicating with customers through social network sites, online communities and interactions on company sites are so great today that a social media strategy has become a core element of e-business strategy. Yet creating a social media or customer engagement strategy is challenging since it requires a change in mindset for the company since they may have to give up some control on their messaging to enable them to communicate with customers effectively. The change in approach required is clear from a movement that originated in the USA in 1999, known as the Cluetrain manifesto (**www.cluetrain.com**). The authors, Levine *et al.* (2000), say:

> Conversations among human beings sound human. They are conducted in a human voice. Most corporations, on the other hand, only know how to talk in the soothing, humorless monotone of the mission statement, marketing brochure, and your-call-is-important-to-us busy signal. Same old tone, same old lies. No wonder networked markets have no respect for companies unable or unwilling to speak as they do. Corporate firewalls have kept smart employees in and smart markets out. It's going to cause real pain to tear those walls down. But the result will be a new kind of conversation. And it will be the most exciting conversation business has ever engaged in.

Of course, more than a change in mindset is required – to achieve change on this scale requires senior management sponsorship, investment and changes to processes and tools as described in the next chapter on change management.

You can see that the Cluetrain manifesto is a call-to-action encouraging managers to change their culture and provide processes and tools to enable employees of an organisation to interact with and listen to customer needs in a responsible way.

Developing a social media communications strategy

When developing a social media strategy there seems to be a tendency for managers to turn straight to the tools they'll be using – should we start with Twitter or Facebook, or should we create a blog? This is the worst possible way to develop strategy, indeed it's not strategy, it's tactics! Strategy development for social media should be informed by demand analysis of customer channel adoption and the commercial potential of the approach.

Customer adoption of social media tools will vary according to customer segments and markets. So it's important to start by completing a marketplace analysis as described in Chapter 2 to see which social tools and engagement techniques are most effective for the target audience.

Next, the commercial benefits of social media need to be reviewed and goals defined. Some marketers will see social media primarily as a way of gaining new customers through the viral effect of social media as existing customers or contacts discuss or recommend your content or products. For others, the benefits may be centred more around how recommendations, reviews and ratings can increase conversion rate. Public relations specialists will want to listen to the conversations for positive and negative sentiment about brand and then seek to manage this by increasing the positives and managing the negatives. Finally, social media can be viewed as a customer engagement and retention tool. Here social media are used to deliver customer service or are used as alternative channel to email marketing to inform customers about new product launches or promotions.

POST is a useful framework for businesses to apply to help them develop a social media strategy summarised by Forrester (2007). POST is a simplified version of the SOSTAC framework introduced at the start of this chapter:

- *People*. Understanding the adoption of social media within an audience is an essential starting point. The Forrester social media profiling tool shows how usage varies for different demographic groups: **http://www.forrester.com/Groundswell/profile_tool.html.**
- *Objectives*. Set different goals for different options to engage customers across different aspects of the customer lifecycle from customer acquisition to conversion to retention. Josh Bernoff of Forrester recommends, 'Decide on your objective before you decide on a technology. Then figure out how you will measure it.'
- *Strategy*. How to achieve your goals. Bernoff suggests that because social media are a disruptive approach you should imagine how social media will support change. He says: 'Imagine you succeed. How will things be different afterwards? '*Imagine the endpoint and you'll know where to begin.*'
- *Technology*. Finally, decide on the best social media platforms and tools to achieve your goals; we reviewed the options for building communities and generating awareness through social networks at the end of Chapter 6.

Viral marketing

Viral marketing
Online viral marketing, or buzz marketing, is a form of electronic word-of-mouth marketing. Brands and promotions are discussed and awareness of them transmitted in two main forms, either as passalong e-mail or discussion in a social network.

Social media marketing can often be assisted through **viral marketing** that harnesses the network effect of the Internet and can be effective in reaching a large number of people rapidly as a marketing message is rapidly transmitted in the same way as a natural virus or a computer virus. It is effectively an online form of word-of-mouth communications which is sometimes also known as 'buzz marketing'. The two main forms of online viral marketing are through passalong-e-mails or discussions within social networks. When planning integrated campaigns, it is important to note that the online viral affect can be amplified through offline media mentions or advertising either on TV and radio or in print.

Word-of-mouth (WOM) marketing
According to the Word-of-Mouth Marketing Association it is giving people a reason to talk about your products and services, and making it easier for that conversation to take place. It is the art and science of building active, mutually beneficial consumer-to-consumer and consumer-to-marketer communications.

Word-of-mouth (WOM) marketing is an established concept closely related to viral marketing, but broader in context. The Word-of-Mouth Marketing Association (**www.womma.org/ wom101**) explain how WOM can be harnessed:

Word-of-mouth can be encouraged and facilitated. Companies can work hard to make people happier, they can listen to consumers, they can make it easier for them to tell their friends, and they can make certain that influential individuals know about the good qualities of a product or service.

They go on to explain that all word-of-mouth marketing techniques are based on the concepts of customer satisfaction, two-way dialogue and transparent communications. The basic elements are:

- educating people about your products and services
- identifying people most likely to share their opinions
- providing tools that make it easier to share information
- studying how, where and when opinions are being shared
- listening and responding to supporters, detractors and neutrals.

WOMMA identify different approaches for facilitating WOM. The ones that are most relevant to online marketing are:

- *Buzz marketing.* Using high-profile entertainment or news to get people to talk about your brand.
- *Viral marketing.* Creating entertaining or informative messages that are designed to be passed along in an exponential fashion, often electronically or by e-mail.
- *Community marketing.* Forming or supporting niche communities that are likely to share interests about the brand (such as user groups, fan clubs and discussion forums); providing tools, content and information to support those communities.
- *Influencer marketing.* Identifying key communities and opinion leaders who are likely to talk about products and have the ability to influence the opinions of others.
- *Conversation creation.* Interesting or fun advertising, e-mails, catch phrases, entertainment or promotions designed to start word-of-mouth activity.
- *Brand blogging.* Creating blogs and participating in the blogosphere, in the spirit of open, transparent communications; sharing information of value that the blog community may talk about.
- *Referral programmes.* Creating tools that enable satisfied customers to refer their friends.

Positive WOM is believed to increase purchase intent. For example, Marsden *et al.* (2005) found that brands such as HSBC, Honda and O2 with a greater proportion of advocates measured through Net Promoter Score (NPS, Chapter 6) tended to be more successful. They recommend ten ways to encourage word-of-mouth, most of which can be facilitated online:

- *Implement and optimise referral programmes.* Reward customers for referring new customers, and reward the referee as well as the referrer.
- *Set up brand ambassador schemes.* Recruit brand fans as ambassadors who receive exclusive merchandise/offers to share with their contacts.
- *Use tryvertising.* A combination of 'try' or 'trial' and 'advertising', this is a twist on product sampling. The idea is that rather than provide free samples or trials to anyone in a target market, tryvertising involves sampling on a selective and exclusive basis to lead users – ideally with new products or services before they become widely available.
- *Use causal marketing.* Associate your brand with a good cause that builds on brand values (e.g. Nike anti-racism in sport).
- *Measure your Net Promoter Score (NPS).* Track your NPS (see page 338 for further details) at all brand touchpoints to find out what you are doing right, and what needs to be improved.
- *Start an influencer outreach programme.* Reach out to the 10% who tell the other 90% what to try and buy with special offers and programmes.
- *Harness the power of empowered involvement.* Create advocacy – let your lead clients, customers or consumers call the shots on your innovation and marketing with VIP votes and polls.
- *Focus innovation on doing something worth talking about.* Do something new that delivers an experience that exceeds expectations.

In an online context, word-of-mouth marketing is important since there is great potential for facilitating electronic word-of-mouth. It is very important for online marketers to understand how WOM can be generated and influenced since research, such as that conducted by Forrester (2007) quoted in the section on online public relations, shows that recommendations from friends, family or even other online consumers are trusted and are a major consideration in product and supplier selection.

E-mail forwarding or passalong viral marketing

Before the growth of social networking, e-mail forwarding was the main source of online viral activity. For example, research quoted by Dee *et al.* (2007) showed that for a US sample, around 60 per cent of web users frequently forwarded on by e-mail anything they think may be of interest to friends, family or colleagues. Today, social media are more important for the viral affect, but the methods to facilitate propagation of messages through email marketing should still be asssessed.

Chaffey and Smith (2008) distinguish between these types of viral e-mail mechanisms:

- *Passalong e-mail viral.* This is where e-mail or word-of-mouth alone is used to spread the message. This is classic viral marketing such as those showcased on the New Media Age Viral Chart (**http://www.nma.co.uk/resources/viral-brand-chart**) which involve an e-mail with a link to a site such as a video or an attachment. Towards the end of a commercial e-mail it does no harm to prompt the first recipient to forward the e-mail to interested friends or colleagues. The dramatic growth of Hotmail, reaching 10 million subscribers in just over a year, was effectively down to passalong as people received e-mails with a signature promoting the service. Word-of-mouth helped too. This mechanism is what most people consider to be viral, but there are the other mechanisms that follow too.
- *Web-facilitated viral (e-mail prompt).* Here, the e-mail contains a link/graphic to a web page with 'e-mail a friend' or 'e-mail a colleague'. A web form is used to collect the e-mail address to which the e-mail should be forwarded, sometimes with an optional message. The company then sends a separate message to the friend or colleague.
- *Web-facilitated viral (web prompt).* Here it is the web page such as a product catalogue or white paper which contains a link/graphic to 'e-mail a friend' or colleague. A web form is again used to collect data and an e-mail is subsequently sent.
- *Incentivised viral.* This is distinct from the types above since the e-mail address is not freely given. This is what we need to make viral really take off. By offering some reward for providing someone else's address we can dramatically increase referrals. A common offer is to gain an additional entry for a prize draw. Referring more friends gains more entries to the prize draw. With the right offer, this can more than double the response. The incentive is offered either by e-mail (the second option above) or on a web page (the third option). In this case, there is a risk of breaking privacy laws since the consent of the e-mail recipient may not be freely given. Usually only a single follow-up e-mail by the brand is permitted. So you should check with the lawyers if you are considering this.
- *Web-link viral.* But online viral isn't just limited to e-mail. Links in discussion group postings or blogs which are from an individual are also in this category. Either way, it's important when seeding the campaign to try to get as many targeted online and offline mentions of the viral agent as you can.

Social network-related viral marketing

Dee *et al.* (2007) also note the importance of social networks in influencing perceptions about brands, products and suppliers. Their research shows large differences in gender and age on the types of products discussed, but recommendations on restaurants, computers, movies and vehicles are popular in all categories.

Microsoft (2007), which part owns Facebook, has developed these approaches for taking advantage of social networking either through buying ad space, creating a brand space or brand channels that enable consumers to interact with or promote a brand:

- *Understand consumers' motivations for using social networks.* Ads will be most effective if they are consistent with the typical lifestage of networkers or the topics that are being discussed.
- *Express yourself as a brand.* Use the web to show the unique essence of your brand, but think about how to express a side of the brand that it is not normally seen.

- *Create and maintain good conversations.* Advertisers who engage in discussions are more likely to resonate with the audience, but once conversations are started they must be followed through.
- *Empower participants.* Social network users use their space and blogs to express themselves. Providing content or widgets to associate themselves with a brand may be appealing. For example, in the first six months of launching charity donation widgets, 20,000 have been used online and they became one of the biggest referrers to the JustGiving website and driving more people to fundraising pages to make donations (JustGiving, 2007).
- *Identify online brand advocates.* Use reputation management tools to identify influential social network members who are already brand advocates. Approach the most significant ones directly. Consider using contextual advertising such as Microsoft content ads or Google AdSense to display brand messages within their spaces when brands are discussed.
- *The Golden Rule: behave like a social networker.* Microsoft recommend this simple fundamental principle which will help the content created by advertisers to resonate with social networkers: behave like the best social networkers through:
  - being creative
  - being honest and courteous (ask permission)
  - being individual
  - being conscious of the audience
  - updating regularly.

Advantages and disadvantages of social media and viral marketing

The advantages and disadvantages of viral marketing are shared with those with online PR as covered earlier in the chapter. However, it can be argued that the risk in investment in viral marketing is higher since it is difficult to predict the success of a particular viral agent.

Advantages of social media and viral marketing

The main advantage of social media and viral marketing is that an effective viral agent can reach a large audience in a cost-effective way. We have also seen how consumers rate the opinions of their peers, friends and family highly, so they can be highly influential. Kumar *et al.* (2007) have discussed the potential value that can be generated through customer referrals in several case studies. Within social networks, major influencers can help spread the message more widely.

Disadvantages of social media and viral marketing

The main disadvantage of viral marketing is that this is a high-risk marketing communications technique, since it requires significant initial investment in the viral agent and seeding. However, there is no guarantee that the campaign will 'go viral', in which case the investment will be wasted.

With marketing within social networks it is challenging to engage audiences when they are socialising with their contacts and may not wish to interact with brands. It is also difficult to find the right types of content which will engage audiences and they will share with their contacts. Seeding to key influencers can help with distributing content, but seeding is a time-consuming specialist activity.

Of course, although positive viral marketing can spread rapidly, so can negative sentiments about a company, which we referred to in the section on online reputation management (see page 506).

Best practice in planning and managing viral marketing

Much discussion of practice in viral and word-of-mouth marketing centres around how and who to reach to achieve influence. Some, such as Malcom Gladwell and Seth Godin in their popular books *The Tipping Point and Unleashing the Idea virus* have suggested that influentials are important. Godin (2001) writes about the importance of what he terms 'the ideavirus' as a marketing tool. He describes it as 'digitally augmented word-of-mouth'. What differences does the ideavirus have from word-of-mouth? First, transmission is more rapid, second, transmission tends to reach a larger audience, and third, it can be persistent – reference to a product on a service. Godin emphasises the importance of starting small by seeding a niche audience he describes as a 'hive' and then using advocates in spreading the virus – he refers to them as 'sneezers'. Traditionally, marketers would refer to such a grouping as 'customer advocates' or 'brand loyalists'.

Others believe that the role of influencers in achieving word-of-mouth can be overstated. Balter and Butman, in their book, *Grapevine*, say:

> Everybody talks about products and services, and they talk about them all the time. Word-of-mouth is NOT about identifying a small subgroup of highly influential or well-connected people to talk up a product or service. It's not about mavens or bees or celebrities or people with specialist knowledge. It's about everybody.

While the influencers will have a greater impact, academics, Watts and Dodds (2007) concur, arguing that the 'influentials hypothesis' is based on untested assumptions and in most cases does not match how diffusion operates in the real world. They comment that 'most social change is driven not by influentials, but by easily influenced individuals influencing other easily influenced individuals'.

The role of social media in influencing consumers is discussed further in Chapter 2 in the section on consumer behaviour (see page 89).

To make a viral campaign effective, Justin Kirby of viral marketing specialists DMC (**www. dmc.co.uk**) suggested these three things are needed (Kirby, 2003):

- *Creative material – the 'viral agent'*. This includes the creative message or offer and how it is spread (text, image, video).
- *Seeding*. Identifying websites, blogs or people to send e-mail to start the virus spreading. Seeding can also be completed by e-mail to members of a house list or renting a list with the likely audience.
- *Tracking*. To monitor the effect, to assess the return from the cost of developing the viral agent and seeding.

Today, these factors are still relevant within online PR campaigns although we talk about 'shareable social objects' rather than 'viral agent' and 'influencer outreach' rather than 'seeding'.

Offline promotion techniques

The importance of offline communications in driving visitors to a website is well-known by site owners who find that greater levels of investment in offline advertising using TV, print or radio results in a greater numbers of direct visitors to websites (Figure 9.1). This can be tracked by web analytics which shows an increase in searches containing the brand or campaign name or the web address or direct visitors who enter the site URL into the address bar.

Research has identified that there is a clear correlation between investment in offline advertising and visits to a website. For example, Hitwise (2006) found in a study of brands including BSkyB, Orange and the AA that searches on brand terms and URLs increased when offline media investment was combined with online. For example, when Sky's media campaign included both online and offline advertising (in September to November of 2005) the strongest result was achieved online with searches for the Sky brand increasing +20% and searches for the Sky URL more than doubling. When offline ran without the integration of online in March 2006, the same lift in searches was not evident. This research also shows the need for significant offline spend with Sky spending around 20 per cent online with print, TV and radio still remaining significant (see Figure 9.17).

The linkage between advertising and search has also been investigated by Graham and Havlena (2007) who additionally studied the role of advertising in generating word-of-mouth discussion online. They found 'strong evidence that advertising does stimulate increased visitation to the websites of advertised brands – an indicator of consumer interest and involvement with a brand'.

Online website promotion techniques such as search engine marketing and banner advertising often take prominence when discussing methods of traffic building. But we start with using offline communications to generate site visitors since it is one of the most effective techniques to generate site traffic and the characteristics of offline media are such (Figure 8.6, page 439) that they often have a higher impact and are more creative, which can help explain the online value proposition. **Offline promotion** refers to using communications tools such as advertising and PR delivered by traditional media such as TV, radio and print in order to direct visitors to an online presence.

Despite the range of opportunities for using new online communications tools, traditional communications using offline media such as TV, print and direct mail and others shown in Figure 1.10 (page 30) remain the dominant form of investment in marketing communications for most. Even organisations which transact a large proportion of their business online continue to invest heavily in offline communications. EConsultancy (2008a) research into advanced adopters showed that even here the average expenditure on digital media channels as a proportion of communications budget was only 23 per cent. Consider the travel sector where both travel suppliers such as BA, Thomson and easyJet and intermediaries such as Expedia and Opodo transact an increasing proportion of their sales online, but are still reliant on offline communications to drive visitors to the web to transact.

Offline promotion
Using traditional media such as TV, radio and print to direct visitors to an online presence.

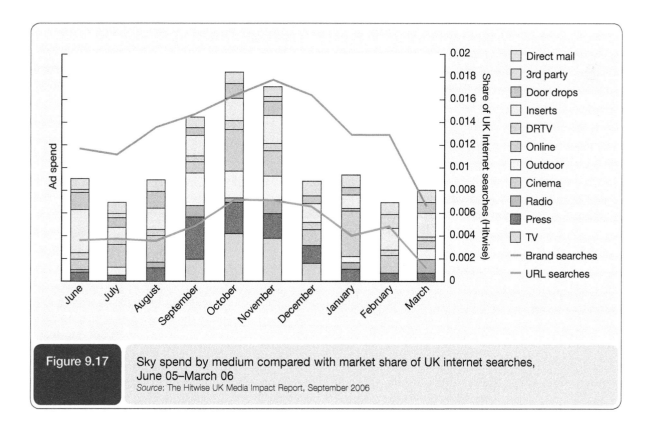

Figure 9.17 Sky spend by medium compared with market share of UK internet searches, June 05–March 06
Source: The Hitwise UK Media Impact Report, September 2006

When the web analytics data about referring visitors is assessed, for most companies who are not online-only businesses, we find that over half the visitors are typically marked as 'No referrer'. This means that they visited the site direct by typing in the web address into the address bar in response to awareness of the brand generated through real-world communications (others may have bookmarked the site or clicked through from a search engine).

So offline communications are effective at reaching an audience to encourage them to visit a site, but are also useful as a way of having an impact or explaining a complex proposition as, Mini Case Study 9.4 shows.

Advantages and disadvantages of using offline communications to support e-commerce

Offline communications work; they are effective in achieving four critical things:

- *Reach* – since newspaper, TV and postal communications are used by virtually all consumers.
- *Brand awareness* – through using high-impact visuals.
- *Emotional connection* – with brand again through visuals and sounds.
- *Explanation* – of the online value proposition for a brand.

A further benefit is that for any given objective, integrated marketing communications received through different media are more effective in achieving that objective. We mentioned this cumulative reinforcement effect of integrated marketing communications when referring to the 4 Cs of coherence, consistency, continuity and complementarities earlier in the chapter. Having said this, the disadvantages of using offline communications to encourage online channel usage compared to many online communications tools are obvious. In general the disadvantages of offline communications are:

- *Higher cost.* Return on investment tends to be higher for online communications such as search engine optimisation, pay-per-click marketing or affiliate marketing.
- *Higher wastage.* The well-known expression about 'half my advertising is wasted, but I don't know which half' may be true about offline marketing, but it isn't true online if the right tracking processes are in place.
- *Poorer targeting.* Targeting by behaviour, location, time, search keyword, site and site content is readily possible online. This tends to be more targeted compared to most offline media (apart from direct marketing).
- *Poorer accountability.* It is straightforward to track response online – offline it is expensive and error-prone.
- *Less detailed information.* The detailed information to support a decision can only be cost-effectively delivered online.
- *Less personalised.* Although direct mail can be personalised, personalisation is more straightforward online.
- *Less interactive experience.* Most offline communications are one-way – interaction is possible online with the right creative.

Incidental and specific advertising of the online presence

Incidental offline advertising
Driving traffic to the website is not a primary objective of the advert.

Specific offline advertising
Driving traffic to the website or explaining the online proposition is a primary objective of the advert.

Two types of offline advertising can be identified: incidental and specific. Reference to the website is **incidental offline advertising** if the main aim of the advert is to advertise a particular product or promotion and the website is available as an ancillary source of information if required by the viewer. Traditionally, much promotion of the website in the offline media by traditional companies has been incidental – simply consisting of highlighting the existence of the website by including the URL at the bottom of an advertisement. Reference to the website is **specific offline advertising** if it is an objective of the advert to explain the proposition of the website in order to drive traffic to the site to achieve direct response. Here the advert will highlight the offers or services available at the website, such as sales promotions or online customer service. Many state 'Visit our website!!', but clearly a more specific strapline can be developed which describes the overall proposition of the site ('detailed information and product guides to help you select the best product for you') or is specific to the campaign ('we will give you an instant quote online, showing how much you save with us').

Offline response mechanisms

The different response mechanics such as web response and URL strategy which we discussed in Chapter 8 in the section on campaign response mechanisms have to be used to maximise response since this helps to direct potential customers to the most appropriate content on the website. Different URLs are also useful for measuring the response of offline media campaigns since we can measure the number of visitors arriving directly at the URL by entering the domain name.

Public relations

Public relations can be an important tool for driving traffic to the website if changes to online services or online events are significant or if a viral campaign is discussed online. The days of the launch of a website being significant are now gone, but if a site is re-launched with significant changes to its services, this may still be worthy of mention. Many news-papers have regular features listing interesting entertainment or leisure sites or guides to specific topics such as online banking or grocery shopping. Trade magazines may also give information about relevant websites.

Jenkins (1995) argues that one key objective for public relations is its role in transforming a negative situation into a positive achievement. The public relations transfer process he suggests is as follows:

- from ignorance to knowledge
- from apathy to interest
- from prejudice to acceptance
- from hostility to sympathy.

These are, of course, goals of online PR which was discussed in more detail earlier in this chapter.

Direct marketing

Direct marketing can be an effective method of driving traffic to the website. As mentioned earlier, a web response model can be used where the website is the means for fulfilling the response, but a direct mail campaign is used to drive the response. Many catalogue companies will continue to use traditional direct mail to mail-out a subset of their offering, with the recipient tempted to visit the site through the fuller offering and incentives such as competitions or web-specific offers.

Other physical reminders

Since we all spend more time in the real rather than the virtual world, physical reminders explaining why customers should visit websites are significant. What is in customers' hands and on their desk top will act as a prompt to visit a site and counter the weakness of the web as a pull medium. This is perhaps most important in the B2B context where a physical reminder in the office can be helpful. Examples, usually delivered through direct marketing, include brochures, catalogues, business cards, point-of-sale material, pens, postcards, inserts in magazines and password reminders for extranets.

Word-of-mouth marketing

It is worth remembering that, as we stated in the section on viral and word-of-mouth marketing, word-of-mouth plays an important role in promoting sites, particularly consumer sites where the Internet is currently a novelty. Opinion Research Corporation International, ORCI (1991), reported on a study among US consumers that showed that the typical Internet consumer tells 12 other people about his or her online shopping experience. This compares with the average US consumer, who tells 8.6 additional people about a favourite film and another 6.1 people about a favourite restaurant! It has been said that if the online experience is favourable then a customer will tell 12 people, but if it is bad they will tell twice as many, so word-of-mouth can be negative also. Parry (1998) reported that for European users, word-of-mouth through friends, relatives and colleagues was the most important method by which users found out about websites, being slightly more important than search engines and directories or links from other sites.

Activity 9.2 — Selecting the best digital media channel mix techniques

Suggest the best mix of online (and offline) promotion techniques to build traffic for the following situations:

1 Well-established B2C brand with high brand awareness.
2 Dot-com start-up.
3 Small business aiming to export.
4 Common B2C product, e.g. household insurance.
5 Specialist B2B product.

Case Study 9 — Innovation at Google

In addition to being the largest search engine on Earth, mediating tens of billions of searches daily, Google is an innovator. All online marketers should follow Google to see the latest approaches it is trialling.

Google's mission

Google's mission is encapsulated in the statement 'to organise the world's information ... and make it universally accessible and useful'. Google explains that it believes that the most effective, and ultimately the most profitable, way to accomplish its mission is to put the needs of its users first. Offering a high-quality user experience has led to strong word-of-mouth promotion and strong traffic growth.

Further details on the culture and ethics of Google is available at http://www.google.com/intl/en/corporate/tenthings.html. Notable tenets of the Google philosophy are:

1 Focus on the user and all else will follow.
2 It's best to do one thing really, really well.
3 You can make money without doing evil.

Putting users first is reflected in three key commitments in the Google SEC filing:

1 *We will do our best to provide the most relevant and useful search results possible, independent of financial incentives. Our search results will be objective and we will not accept payment for inclusion or ranking in them.*
2 *We will do our best to provide the most relevant and useful advertising. Advertisements should not be an annoying interruption. If any element on a search result page is influenced by payment to us, we will make it clear to our users.*
3 *We will never stop working to improve our user experience, our search technology and other important areas of information organisation.*

In the SEC filing, the company explains 'how we provide value to our users':

> We serve our users by developing products that quickly and easily find, create, organise, and share information. We place a premium on products that matter to many people and have the potential to improve their lives.

Some of the key benefits which are explained are: *Comprehensiveness and Relevance; Objectivity; Global Access; Ease of Use; Pertinent, Useful Commercial Information; Multiple Access Platforms and Improving the Web.*

The range of established Google services is well known and is listed at **http://www.google.com/options/**. Google's commitment to innovation is indicated by these more recent additions:

- Google+ announced 2011 – the social network to rival Facebook?
- Google TV (announced 2010) as part of a partnership agreement with Sony.
- Nexus One Phone using the Google Android mobile operating system launched in January 2010 (**www.google.com/phone**).
- Google Mobile advertising (although Google has offered text ads for some time, the 2009 acquisition of AdMob enables improvements in sophistication of this approach).
- Google Chrome OS (a lightweight operating system announced in 2009 and targeted initially at Netbooks).
- Google Chrome (a browser announced as a beta in 2008 and a full product for Windows in 2009).

For 2009, Google spent around 12 per cent of its revenue in research and development, an increase from less than 10 per cent in 2005, and a larger amount than Sales and Marketing (8.4 per cent).

Google revenue models

Google generated approximately 99 per cent of its revenues in 2007 and 97 per cent in 2008 and 2009 from its advertisers, with the remainder from its enterprise search products where companies can install search technology through products such as the Google Appliance and Google Mini.

Google AdWords, the auction-based advertising program, is the main source of revenue. Advertisers pay on a 'pay-per-click' cost basis within the search engines and someother services, but with cost-per-thousand payment options available on Google Networks members' web sites. Google has introduced classified style ad programmes for other media, including:

- Google Audio Ads (ads are placed in radio programmes)
- Google Print Ads
- Google TV Ads
- Google Promoted Video Ads within YouTube, user-initiated click-to-play video ads.

Google's revenues are critically dependent on how many searches it achieves in different countries and the proportion of searchers who interact with Google's ads. Research by ComScore (2008) suggests around 25 per cent of searches result in an ad click where sponsored search results are included (around 50 per cent of searches). Google is also looking to increase the number of advertisers and invests heavily in this through trade communications to marketers. Increased competition to advertise against a search term will result in increased bid amounts and so increased revenue.

International revenues accounted for approximately 53 per cent of total revenues in Q4 2009, and more than half of user traffic came from outside the US. In Q4 2009, 12 per cent of ad revenue was from the UK alone.

31 per cent of Google's revenue is from the Network of content partners who subscribe to the Google Adsenseprogramme.

Risk factors

Some of the main risk factors that Google declares include:

1 New technologies could block Google ads. Ad-blocking technology could, in the future, adversely affect Google's results, although there has not been widespread adoption of these approaches.
2 Litigation and confidence loss through click fraud. Click fraud can be a problem when competitors click on a link, but this is typically small-scale. A larger problem is structured click fraud where site owners on the Google content network seek to make additional advertising feeds.
3 Index spammers could harm the integrity of Google's web search results. This could damage Google's reputation and cause its users to be dissatisfied with products and services.

Google says:

> There is an ongoing and increasing effort by 'index spammers' to develop ways to manipulate our web search results. For example, because our web search technology ranks a web page's relevance based in part on the importance of the web sites that link to it, people have attempted to link a group of web sites together to manipulate web search results.

On 31 December 2009, Google had 19,835 employees. All of Google's employees are also equity holders, with significant collective employee ownership. As a result, many employees are highly motivated to make the company more successful. Google's engineers are encouraged to spend up to 10 per cent of their time identifying new approaches.

You can find updates on this case study by searching at **www.smartinsights.com** for 'Google Marketing updates'. For further reading, try Bala and Davenport (2008) – see Further Reading at the end of this chapter.

Question

Explain how Google generates revenue and exploits innovation in digital technology to identify future revenue growth. You should also consider the risk factors for future revenue generation.

Source: SEC, 2008

Summary

1 Online promotion techniques include:
   - *Search engine marketing* – search engine optimisation (SEO) improves position in the natural listings and pay-per-click marketing features a company in the sponsored listings of a search engine or on the display network
   - *Online PR* – including techniques such as influencer outreach, link building, blogging, and reputation management.
   - *Online partnerships* – including affiliate marketing (commission-based referral), co-branding and sponsorship.
   - *Online advertising* – using a range of formats including banners, skyscrapers and rich media such as overlays.
   - *E-mail marketing* – including rented lists, co-branded e-mails, event-triggered e-mails and ads in third-party e-newsletters for acquisition, and e-newsletters and campaign e-mails to house lists.
   - *Social media marketing* – engaging audiences on different social networks and on a company's own site through sharing content and developing great creative concepts which are transmitted by online word-of-mouth or viral marketing.
2 Offline promotion involves promoting the website address, highlighting the value proposition of the website and achieving web response through traditional media advertisements in print or on television.
3 Interactive marketing communications must be developed as part of integrated marketing communications for maximum cost effectiveness.
4 Key characteristics of interactive communications are the combination of push and pull media, user-submitted content, personalisation, flexibility and, of course, interactivity to create a dialogue with consumers.
5 Objectives for interactive communications include direct sales for transactional sites, but they also indirectly support brand awareness, favourability and purchase intent.
6 Important decisions in the communications mix introduced by digital media include:
   - the balance between spend on media and creative for digital assets and ad executions;
   - the balance between spend in traditional and offline communications;
   - the balance between investment in continuous and campaign-based digital activity;
   - the balance of investment in different interactive communications tools.

Table 9.4 provides a summary of the strengths and weaknesses of the tools discussed in this chapter.

Table 9.4	Summary of the strengths and weaknesses of different communications tools for promoting an online presence

Promotion technique	Main strengths	Main weaknesses
Search engine optimisation (SEO)	Highly targeted, relatively low cost of PPC. High traffic volumes if effective. Considered credible by searchers	Intense competition, may compromise look of site. Complexity of changes to ranking algorithm
Pay-per-click (PPC) marketing	Highly targeted with controlled cost of acquisition. Extend reach through content network	Relatively costly in competitive sectors and low volume compared with SEO
Trusted feed	Update readily to reflect changes in product lines and prices	Relatively costly, mainly relevant for e-retailers. No longer widely available.
Online PR	Relatively low cost and good targeting. Can assist with SEO through creation of backlinks	Identifying online influencers and setting up partnerships can be time-consuming. Need to monitor comments on third-party sites
Affiliate marketing	Payment is by results (e.g. 10% of sale or leads goes to referring site)	Costs of payments to affiliate networks for setup and management fees. Changes to ranking algorithm may affect volume from affiliates
Online sponsorship	Most effective if low-cost, long-term co-branding arrangement with synergistic site	May increase awareness, but does not necessarily lead directly to sales
Interactive advertising	Main intention to achieve visit, i.e. direct response model. But also role in branding through media multiplier effect	Response rates have declined historically because of banner blindness
E-mail marketing	Push medium – can't be ignored in user's inbox. Can be used for direct response link to website. Integrates as a response mechanism with direct mail	Requires opt-in for effectiveness. Better for customer retention than for acquisition? Inbox cut-through – message diluted among other e-mails. Limits on deliverability
Social media marketing, viral and word-of-mouth marketing	With effective viral agent, possible to reach a large number at relatively low cost. Influencers in social networks significant	Difficult to create powerful viral concepts and control targeting. Risks damaging brand since unsolicited messages may be received
Traditional offline advertising (TV, print, etc.)	Larger reach than most online techniques. Greater creativity possible, leading to greater impact	Targeting arguably less easy than online. Typical high cost of acquisition

Exercises

Self-assessment exercises

1 Briefly explain and give examples of online promotion and offline promotion techniques.
2 Explain the different types of payment model for banner advertising.
3 Which factors are important in governing a successful online banner advertising campaign?
4 How can a company promote itself through a search engine?
5 Explain the value of social media marketing.
6 How can online PR help to promote a new product?
7 How should websites be promoted offline?
8 What do you think the relative importance of these Internet-based advertising techniques would be for an international chemical manufacturer?
   (a) display advertising
   (b) paid search marketing
   (c) affiliate marketing.

Essay and discussion questions

1 How should companies evaluate the relevance and effectiveness of the digital media channels discussed in this chapter to their organisation?
2 Discuss the merits of the different models of paying for banner advertisements on the Internet for both media owners and companies placing advertisements.
3 Explain the factors that control the position of a company's products and services in the search engine results pages of a search engine such as Google.
4 Compare the effectiveness of different methods of online advertising including display advertisements, paid search marketing and affiliate marketing.

Examination questions

1 Give three examples of digital media channels and briefly explain their communications benefits.
2 Describe four different types of site on which online display advertising for a car manufacturer's site could be placed.
3 Click-through is one measure of the effectiveness of online advertising.
   (a) What is 'click-through'?
   (b) Which factors are important in determining the click-through rate of a banner advertisement?
   (c) Is click-through a good measure of the effectiveness of online advertising?
4 What is meant by co-branding? Explain the significance of co-branding.
5 What are 'meta tags'? How important are they in ensuring a website is listed in a search engine?
6 Name three alternative types of e-mail marketing that can be used for customer acquisition.
7 Briefly evaluate the strengths and weaknesses of affiliate marketing for a well-known retailer.
8 Which techniques can be used to promote a website in offline media?

References

Abraham, M. (2008) The off-line impact of online ads, *Harvard Business Review*, April, 86(4), 28.

Atlas (2007) Paying for navigation: the impact of navigational behavior on paid search, Research report by Nico Brooks, Director, Search Strategy, Published at: (**www.atlas solutions.com**).

Balter, D. and Butman, J. (2005) *Grapevine: The New Art of Word-of-Mouth Marketing*, Portfolio, New York.

Berthon, P., Lane, N., Pitt, L. and Watson, R. (1998) The World Wide Web as an industrial marketing communications tool: models for the identification and assessment of opportunities, *Journal of Marketing Management*, 14, 691–704.

Brin, S. and Page, L (1998) The anatomy of a large-scale hypertextual web search engine, *Computer Networks and ISDN Systems*, April, 30(1–7), 107–17, published at: **http://www-db.stanford.edu/~backrub/google.html**.

Cartellieri, C., Parsons, A., Rao, V. and Zeisser, M. (1997) The real impact of Internet advertising, *McKinsey Quarterly*, No. 3, 44–63.

Chaffey, D. (2006) *Total E-mail Marketing*, 2nd edn. Butterworth–Heinemann, Elsevier, Oxford.

Chaffey, D. and Smith, P.R. (2008) *E-marketing Excellence*, 3rd edn. Butterworth–Heinemann Elsevier, Oxford.

Chittenden, L. and Rettie, R. (2003) An evaluation of e-mail marketing and factors affecting response, *Journal of Targeting, Measurement and Analysis for Marketing*, March, 11(3), 203–17.

ComScore (2008) Why Google's surprising paid click data are less surprising, by Magid Abraham, 28 February, published at: **http:www.comscore.com/blog/2008/02/why_googles_surprising_paid_click_data_are_less_surprising.html**.

Dee, A., Bassett, B. and Hoskins, J. (2007) Word-of-mouth research: principles and applications, *Journal of Advertising Research*, December, 47(4), 387–97.

DMA (2008) UK National Client Benchmarking Report, published at: **www.dma.org.uk**.

Ecircle (2011) Display versus email. The SEAT Ibiza campaign illustrating how to effectively allocate your online advertising budgets. Research study published March.

EConsultancy (2008a) *Managing Digital Channels Research Report*, Dave Chaffey, available from: **www.e-consultancy.com**.

EConsultancy (2008b) *Paid Search Marketing, Best Practice Guide*, Dave Chaffey, available from: **www.e-consultancy.com**.

Efficient Frontier (2011) CPCs a strong month for finance, but weak for travel, 6 April, a blog post by Dr.Siddharth Shah: **http://blog.efrontier.com/insights/2011/04/march-2011-cps-a-strong-month-for-finance-but-weak-for-travel.html**

Fitzgerald, M. (2006) 'The Name Game: tagging tools let users describe the world in their own terms as taxonomies become folksonomies', *CIO Magazine*, 1 April.

Forrester (2007) Consumer Trends Survey North America – leveraging user-generated content, January, Brian Haven.

Gladwell, M. (2000) *The Tipping Point: How Little Things Can Make a Big Difference*, Little Brown.

Godin, S. (2001) *Unleashing the Ideavirus*, available online at: **www.ideavirus.com**.

Graham, J. and Havlena, W. (2007) Finding the 'missing link': advertising's impact on word of mouth, web searches, and site visits, *Journal of Advertising Research*, December, 47(4), 427–35.

Grehan, M. (2004) Increase your PR by increasing your PR. Article in *E-marketing News e-newsletter*, November. Source: **www.e-marketing-news.co.uk/november.html#pr**.

GSI (2011) The Purchase Path of Online Buyers. SucharitaMulpuru, March. Whitepaper published at http://www.gsicommerce.com/purchasepath/.

Hitwise (2006) UK media impact report, Analyst Heather Hopkins. Available online at: www.hitwise.com.

Hitwise (2007) Social networks can drive traffic – case study of ASOS and TopShop, blog posting by analyst Heather Hopkins, 1 March: http://weblogs.hitwise.com/heather-hopkins/2007/03/social_networks_can_drive_taf.html.

iMediaConnection (2003) Interview with ING Direct VP of Marketing, Jurie Pietersie: www.mediaconnection.com/content/1333.asp.

Jenkins, F. (1995) *Public Relations Techniques*, 2nd edn. Butterworth–Heinemann, Oxford.

JustGiving (2007) Justgiving Widget version 2.0, blog posting, 24 July: http://justgiving.typepad.com/charities/2007/07/justgiving-widg.html.

Kirby, J. (2003) Online viral marketing: next big thing or yesterday's fling? *New Media Knowledge*, published online at: www.newmediaknowledge.co.uk.

Kumar, V., Petersen, J. and Leone, R. (2007) How valuable is word of mouth? *Harvard Business Review*, October, 85(10), 139–46.

Levine, R., Locke, C., Searls, D. and Weinberger, D. (2000) *The Cluetrain Manifesto*, Perseus Books, Cambridge, MA.

MAD (2007) How online display advertising influences search volumes, published 4 June, MAD Network (*Marketing Week*), Centaur Communications: http://technology-weekly.mad.co.uk/Main/InDepth/SearchEngineMarketing/Articles/f66d813eeab74e93ad8f252ae9c7f02a/How-online-display-advertising-influences-search-volumes.html.

Marsden, P. Samson, A. and Upton, N. (2005) Advocacy drives growth, *Brand Strategy*, Dec 2005/Jan 2006, Issue 198.

McGaffin, K. (2004) Linking matters: how to create an effective linking strategy to promote your website, published at: www.linkingmatters.com.

Microsoft (2007) Word of the web guidelines for advertisers: understanding trends and monetising social networks. Research report available from: http://advertising.microsoft.com.

New Media Age (2008) Measuring Buzz. By Sean Hargrave, 17 January.

Nielsen, J. (2007) Banner blindness: old and new findings, Jakob Nielsen's Alertbox, published online, 20 August: http://www.usit.com/alertbox/ banner-blindness.html.

Nielsen (2011) State of the Media: Advertising Spend and Effectiveness. Q1 2011 summary published at: http://www.nielsen.com/us/en/insights/reports-downloads/2011/advertising-spend-effectiveness-q1-2011.html?status=success

Novak, T. and Hoffman, D. (1997) New metrics for new media: towards the development of web measurement standards, *World Wide Web Journal*, 2(1), 213–46.

OPA Europe (2010) The Silent Click. Building brands online in Europe: http://www.opa-europe.org/news/press-releases/265.

Optify (2011) The changing face of SERPS: organic clickthrough rate, whitepaper published Spring: http://www.optify.net/wp-content/uploads/2011/04/Changing-Face-of-SERPS-Organic-CTR.pdf.

ORCI (1991) Word-of-mouth drives e-commerce. Survey summary, May. Opinion Research Corporation International: www.opinionresearch.com.

Parry, K. (1998) *Europe gets wired. A survey of Internet use in Great Britain, France and Germany, Research Report 1998*. KPMG Management Consulting, London.

Performics (2010) Search engine usage study: 92% of searchers click on sponsored results, press release: http://www.performics.com/news-room/press-releases/Search-Engine-Usage- Study-92-Percent/1422.

PRCA (2005) Website definition of PR. The Public Relationships Consultants Association, www.prca.org.uk.

Prussakov, E. (2011a) *A Practical Guide to Affiliate Marketing. Quick Reference for Affiliate Managers and Merchants*. Self-published.

Prussakov (2011b) Back to Affiliate cookie duration return days question, blog post by Geno Prussakov, 12 September: http://www.amnavigator.com/blog/2011/09/12/back-to-affiliate-cookie-duration-return-days-question/.

Ranchhod, A., Gurau, C. and Lace, J. (2002) Online messages: developing an integrated communications model for biotechnology companies, *Qualitative Market Research: An International Journal*, 5(1), 6–18.

Rettie, R., Grandcolas, U. and Deakins, B. (2005) Text message advertising: response rates and branding effects, *Journal of Targeting, Measurement & Analysis for Marketing*, June, 13(4), 304–12.

Robinson, H., Wysocka, A. and Hand, C. (2007) Internet advertising effectiveness: the effect of design on click-through rates for banner ads, *International Journal of Advertising*, 26(4), 527–41.

Ryan, J. and Whiteman, N. (2000) Online advertising glossary: sponsorships. ClickZ Media Selling channel 15 May.

Say, P. and Southwell, J. (2006) Case study: Beep-beep-beep-beep, that'll be the bank then — Driving sales through mobile marketing, *Journal of Direct, Data and Digital Marketing Practice*, 7(3), 262–5.

SEC (2008) Annual report filing on form 10–K to US Securities and Exchange Commission (SEC) for Google Inc., 15 February.

SEOMoz (2011a) Google Algorithm Change History page: http://www.seomoz.org/google-algorithm-change.

SEOMoz (2011b) Google search engine ranking factors, published at: www.seomoz.org/article/search-ranking-factors.

Smart Insights (2010) 'Official': Facebook and Twitter DO influence natural search rankings. Author: Chris Soames, December 2010.

Smart Insights (2011a) Blog post: How balanced is your traffic mix? Author: Dave Chaffey. 4 July: http://www.smartinsights.com/digital-marketing-strategy/customer-acquisition-strategy/how-balanced-is-your-traffic-mix/.

Smart Insights (2011b), Social media command centres, blog post: 13 July. Author: Dave Chaffey. http://www.smartinsights.com/analytics-conversion-optimisation-alerts/social-media-command-centers/: http://www.smartinsights.com/search-engine-optimisation-seo/seo-strategy/customer-acquisition-strategy/facebook-twitter-influence-natural-search-rankings/.

Watts, D. and Dodds, S. (2007) Influentials, networks and public opinion formation, *Journal of Consumer Research* 34(4), 441–58.

Zeff, R. and Aronson, B. (2001) *Advertising on the Internet*, 3rd edn. Wiley, New York.

Further reading

Bala, I. and Davenport, T. (2008) Reverse engineering google's innovation machine, *Harvard Business Review*, April, 86(4), 58–68.

Fill, C. (2009) *Marketing Communications – Interactivity, Communitiesand Content*, 5th edn. Financial Times/Prentice Hall, Harlow. The entire book is recommended for its integration of theory, concepts and practice.

Novak, T. and Hoffman, D. (1997) New metrics for new media: towards the development of web measurement standards, *World Wide Web Journal*, 2(1), 213–46. This paper gives detailed, clear definitions of terms associated with measuring advertising effectiveness.

Weblinks

General digital media channel-related e-mail newsletters and portals

- **ClickZ Experts** (www.clickz.com/experts). Has columns on e-mail marketing, e-mail marketing optimisation and e-mail marketing case studies.
- **Econsultancy.com** (www.econsultancy.com). Best practice sections on different e-communications tools and newsletter features interviews with e-commerce practitioners.
- **Marketing Sherpa** (www.marketingsherpa.com). Articles and links on Internet marketing communications including e-mail and online advertising.
- **Smart Insights** (www.smartinsights.com) Advice on best practice and the latest updates on digital marketing edited by Dave Chaffey.

E-mail-related advice sites

- **Direct Marketing Association UK** (www.dma.org.uk). Best practice guidelines and benchmarks of response rates.
- **E-mail Experience Council** (www.emailexperience.org). A US organisation with compilations of practical tips on e-mail marketing.

Affiliates and aggregator advice sites

- **A4UForum** (www.a4uforum.co.uk). Used by affliates to discuss approaches and compare programmes.
- **Affiliate marketing blog** (http://blog.affiliatetip.com). Practical tips and the latest developments from affiliate Shawn Collins.
- **AM Navigator** (www.amnavigator.com/blog). Advice on managing affiliate programmes from Geno Prussakov).
- **Comparison Engines** (www.comparisonengines.com). A blog focusing on developments in shopping comparison intermediaries.

Internet advertising research sites

- **AtlasSolutionsInstitute** (http://www.atlassolutions.com). Microsoft owned ad-serving and tracking provider with research about consumer behaviour and optimising ad effectiveness.
- **Doubleclick** (http://www.doubleclick.com/insight/research). Google owned ad-serving and tracking provider with research about consumer behaviour and optimising ad effectiveness.
- **EyeBlaster** (www.eyeblaster.com) is one of the main providers of rich media ad-serving technologies. Its galleries have good examples.
- **iMediaConnection** (www.imediaconnection.com). Media site reporting on best practice in online advertising.
- **US Internet Advertising Bureau** (www.iab.net). The widest range of studies about Internet advertising effectiveness. In UK: www.iabuk.net.
- **Tangozebra** (www.tangozebra.co.uk) is a UK-based provider of ad-serving technology which showcases many of the most recent ad campaigns by industry category.
- **World Advertising Research Centre** (www.warch.com). Mainly subscription service, but some free resources.

Search-engine-related links

- **Google Webmaster tools** (www.google.com/webmasters). Provides a useful set of tools for sites verified by their owners including index inclusion, linking and ranking for different phrases in different locations.
- **Dave Chaffey's keyword suggestion tools** (www.davechaffey.com/seo-keyword-tools). The latest version of a range of free and paid tools for natural and paid search.
- **Reputation management** (www.davechaffey.com/online-reputation-management-tools).
- **Search Engine Watch** (www.searchenginewatch.com). A complete resource on SEO and PPC marketing. See Search Engine Land (www.searchengineland.com) for more commentary.
- **Webmasterworld** (www.webmasterworld.com). A forum, where search practitioners discuss best practice.

Viral marketing/Word-of-mouth research sites

- **Mashable** (www.mashable.com). Site focusing on developments and statistics related to social networks.
- **Viral and Buzz Marketing Network** (www.vbma.net). A European-oriented community of academics and professionals for discussion of the applications of connected marketing
- **Word-of-mouth marketing association** (www.womma.org). A US-oriented community of word-of-mouth marketing specialists.
- **O'Reilly Radar** (http://radar.oreilly.com). Commentary on the development of Web 2.0 approaches technologies from publishers O'Reilly, whose founder Tim O'Reilly coined the term Web 2.0.

CHAPTER 9

Global Advertising and Public Relations

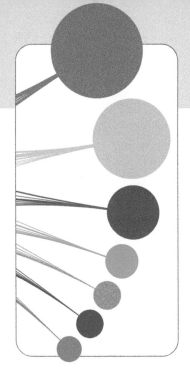

13

Global Marketing Communications Decisions I: Advertising and Public Relations

CASE 13-1

The Gulf Oil Spill: BP's Public Relations Nightmare

It's not hard to figure out what keeps BP executives awake at night. The catastrophic explosion on the Deepwater Horizon oil-drilling platform in the Gulf of Mexico in April 2010 killed 11 workers and allowed millions of gallons of oil to spill into the waters off the Louisiana coast. Numerous efforts to stop the leak failed. As an estimated 30,000 barrels of oil leaked from the stricken well each day, Deepwater Horizon became the worst oil spill in U.S. history, surpassing the 1989 Exxon Valdez accident

in Alaska. As one newspaper noted in mid-2010, "BP has become public enemy number-one in the U.S."

BP, which was once known as British Petroleum, is the leading producer of gas and oil in the United States. Forty percent of its shareholders are in the United States. Ironically, in 2000, BP implemented an ecology-themed corporate identity campaign keyed to the theme "Beyond Petroleum." As the disaster unfolded, oil-contaminated oyster beds and fishing grounds threatened the

Exhibit 13-1 Thousands of workers took part in a massive cleanup effort as oil washed ashore in Louisiana, Mississippi, Alabama, and Florida. One year after the spill, tar balls were still washing up on coastal beaches. The Gulf Coast Claims Facility was responsible for distributing $20 billion to individuals and businesses affected by the spill. Although economic repercussions are still being felt, fisheries have reopened and the shrimp catch has rebounded.
Source: Craig Ruttle/Alamy.

livelihoods of thousands of fishermen. Images of oil-soaked brown pelicans were widely circulated by the media. Hotels owners in Alabama, Florida, Louisiana, and Mississippi faced the prospect of fewer tourists as tar balls began to wash up on beaches.

While engineers struggled around the clock to plug the leak, BP tried to reassure the public that it was doing everything possible. Full-page print ads declared, "We will get it done. We will make this right." Even so, critics pounced on early comments by BP CEO Tony Hayward that the environmental impact of the spill would likely be "very, very modest." BP was also embarrassed over revelations that some photos of the spill operation posted on the company's Web site had been digitally altered.

As the crisis continued into the summer months, the rhetoric on both sides of the Atlantic escalated. U.S. President Barack Obama declared that he wanted to find out "whose ass to kick." In a televised address from the Oval Office, President Obama asserted that he would hold BP accountable. BP's board of directors canceled the company's dividend and pledged $20 billion in aid to those impacted by the spill. For more on BP's response to the Deepwater Horizon spill, see Case 13-1 at the end of the chapter.

Advertising, public relations, and other forms of communication are critical tools in the marketing program. Marketing communications—the promotion P of the marketing mix—refers to all forms of communication used by organizations to inform, remind, explain, persuade, and influence the attitudes and buying behavior of customers and others. The primary purpose of marketing communications is to tell customers about the benefits and values that a company, nation, product, or service offers. The elements of the promotion mix are advertising, public relations, personal selling, and sales promotion.

Global marketers can use all of these elements, either alone or in varying combinations. BP's experience in the aftermath of the Deepwater Horizon oil spill highlights the critical importance of public relations to any entity—be it a nation or a business enterprise—that finds itself spotlighted on the world stage. This chapter examines advertising and public relations from the perspective of the global marketer. Chapter 14 examines sales promotion, personal selling, event marketing, and sponsorships. As you study these chapters, remember: All the communication tools described here should be used in a way that reinforces a consistent message.

LEARNING OBJECTIVES

1 Define *global advertising* and identify the top-ranked companies in terms of worldwide ad spending.

2 Explain the structure of the advertising industry and describe the difference between agency holding companies and individual agency brands.

3 Identify key ad agency personnel and describe their respective roles in creating global advertising.

4 Explain how media availability varies around the world.

5 Compare and contrast publicity and public relations and identify global companies that have recently been impacted by negative publicity.

Global Advertising

The environment in which marketing communications programs and strategies are implemented varies from country to country. The challenge of effectively communicating across borders is one reason that global companies and their advertising agencies are embracing a concept known as **integrated marketing communications (IMC)**. Adherents of an IMC approach explicitly recognize that the various elements of a company's communication strategy must be carefully coordinated.[1]

---

[1] Thomas R. Duncan and Stephen E. Everett, "Client Perception of Integrated Marketing Communications," *Journal of Advertising Research* (May–June 1993), pp. 119–122; see also Stephen J. Gould, Dawn B. Lerman, and Andreas F. Grein, "Agency Perceptions and Practices on Global IMC," *Journal of Advertising Research* 39, no. 1 (January–February 1999), pp. 7–20.

For example, Nike has embraced the IMC concept. Trevor Edwards, Nike's vice president for global brand and category management, notes:

> We create demand for our brand by being flexible about how we tell the story. We do not rigidly stay with one approach. . . . We have an integrated marketing model that involves all elements of the marketing mix from digital to sports marketing, from event marketing to advertising to entertainment, all sitting at the table driving ideas.[2]

Advertising is one element of an IMC program. **Advertising** may be defined as any sponsored, paid message that is communicated in a nonpersonal way. Some advertising messages are designed to communicate with consumers in a single country or market area. Regional or pan-regional advertising is created for audiences across several country markets, such as Europe or Latin America. **Global advertising** may be defined as messages whose art, copy, headlines, photographs, taglines, and other elements have been developed expressly for their worldwide suitability. Companies that have used global themes include McDonald's ("I'm lovin' it"), IBM ("Solutions for a small planet"), De Beers ("A diamond is forever"), BP ("Beyond Petroleum"), and Vodafone ("Your voice"). In Chapter 10, we noted that some global companies simultaneously offer local, international, and global products and brands to buyers in different parts of the world. The same is true with advertising: A global company may use single-country advertising in addition to campaigns that are regional and global in scope.

A global company possesses a critical marketing advantage with respect to marketing communications: It has the opportunity to successfully transform a domestic advertising campaign into a worldwide one. Alternatively, it can create a new global campaign from the ground up. The search for a global advertising campaign should bring together key company and ad agency personnel to share information, insights, and experience. McDonald's "I'm lovin' it" tagline is a case in point; it was developed after global marketing chief Larry Light called a meeting of representatives from all of McDonald's ad agencies. Global campaigns with unified themes can help to build long-term product and brand identities and offer significant savings by reducing the cost associated with producing ads. Regional market areas such as Europe are experiencing an influx of standardized global brands as companies align themselves for a united region by making acquisitions and evaluating production plans and pricing policies. From a marketing point of view, there is a great deal of activity going on that will make brands truly pan-European in a short period of time. This phenomenon is accelerating the growth of global advertising.

The potential for effective global advertising also increases as companies recognize and embrace new concepts such as "product cultures." An example is the globalization of beer culture, which can be seen in the popularity of German-style beer halls in Japan and Irish-style pubs in the United States. Similarly, the globalization of coffee culture has created market opportunities for companies such as Starbucks. Marketing managers also realize that some market segments can be defined on the basis of global demography—youth culture or an emerging middle class, for example—rather than ethnic or national culture. Athletic shoes and other clothing items, for instance, can be targeted to a worldwide segment of 18- to 25-year-old males. William Roedy, global chairman of MTV Networks, sees clear implications of such product cultures for advertising. MTV is just one of the media vehicles that enable people virtually anywhere to see how the rest of the world lives and to learn about the latest electronic gadgets and fashion trends. As Roedy has noted, "Eighteen-year-olds in Paris have more in common with 18-year-olds in New York than with their own parents. They buy the same products, go to the same movies, listen to the same music, sip the same colas. Global advertising merely works on that premise."[3]

According to data compiled by ZenithOptimedia and eMarketer, worldwide advertising expenditures in 2010 totaled $450 billion. Because advertising is often designed to add psychological value to a product or brand, it plays a more important communications role in marketing consumer products than in marketing industrial products. Frequently purchased, low-cost products generally require heavy promotional support, which often takes the form of reminder advertising. Consumer products companies top the list of big global advertising spenders. Procter & Gamble,

[2]Gavin O'Malley, "Who's Leading the Way in Web Marketing? It's Nike, Of Course," *Advertising Age* (October 26, 2006), p. D3.
[3]Ken Wells, "Selling to the World: Global Ad Campaigns, After Many Missteps, Finally Pay Dividends," *The Wall Street Journal* (August 27, 1992), p. A1.

Unilever, L'Oréal, and Nestlé are companies whose global scope can be inferred from the significant proportion of advertising expenditures outside the home-country markets.

Advertising Age magazine's ranking of global marketers in terms of advertising expenditures is shown in Table 13-1.[4] The top 100 advertisers spent $107.6 billion in 2009. The United States is the world's top advertising market, with $151 billion spent on major media in 2010. This figure represents a recovery of sorts; as the recession deepened in 2009, U.S. advertising spending fell by about 12 percent. A close examination of Table 13-1 provides clues to the extent of a company's globalization efforts. For example, packaged-goods giants Procter & Gamble and Unilever spend significant amounts in all major world regions. By contrast, the table shows that the geographic scope of France's Peugeot Citroën is largely limited to Europe, with additional presence in Asia and Latin America.

Global advertising also offers companies economies of scale in advertising as well as improved access to distribution channels. Where shelf space is at a premium, a company has to convince retailers to carry its products rather than those of competitors. A global brand supported by global advertising may be very attractive because, from the retailer's standpoint, a global brand is less likely to languish on the shelves. Landor Associates, a company specializing in brand identity and design, recently determined that Coke has the number one brand-awareness and esteem position in the United States, number two in Japan, and number six in Europe. However, standardization is not always required or even advised. Nestlé's Nescafé coffee is marketed as a global brand, even though advertising messages and product formulation vary to suit cultural differences.

TABLE 13-1 **Top 25 Global Marketers by Ad Spending, 2009 ($ millions)**

Company/Headquarters	Worldwide	United States	Asia*	Europe	Latin America
1. Procter & Gamble (United States)	$8,678	$2,838	$1,777	$3,004	$341
2. Unilever (United Kingdom, Netherlands)	6,033	864	1,632	2,340	578
3. L'Oréal (France)	4,559	890	748	2,605	115
4. General Motors Corp. (United States)	3,268	2,214	112	663	126
5. Nestlé (Switzerland)	2,615	844	261	1,229	135
6. Coca-Cola Co. (United States)	2,442	406	602	1,057	181
7. Toyota Motor Corp. (Japan)	2,305	836	818	503	27
8. Johnson & Johnson (United States)	2,250	1,296	250	567	29
9. Reckitt Benckiser (Great Britain)	2,236	473	209	1,297	117
10. Kraft Foods (United States)	2,117	791	146	925	124
11. McDonald's (United States)	2,075	874	365	690	40
12. Ford Motor Co. (United States)	2,057	1,098	40	612	128
13. Volkswagen (Germany)	1,937	258	99	1,448	94
14. Pfizer (United States)	1,827	1,518	110	124	31
15. Sony Corp. (Japan)	1,714	793	222	613	20
16. GlaxoSmithKline (United Kingdom)	1,630	798	143	530	93
17. Danone Group (France)	1,621	129	52	1,228	159
18. Mars Inc. (United States)	1,586	462	278	716	22
19. PepsiCo (United States)	1,454	630	279	210	117
20. Walt Disney Company (United States)	1,440	1,095	29	276	1
21. PSA Peugeot Citroën (France)	1,426	0	24	1,324	73
22. Walmart Stores (United States)	1,423	1,174	0	154	59
23. Time Warner (United States)	1,412	1,204	8	165	2
24. Deutsche Telekom (Germany)	1,396	513	0	863	21
25. Henkel (Germany)	1,371	75	28	1,214	10

*Asia includes Australia and New Zealand.
Source: Adapted from "Top 100 Global Marketers," *Advertising Age* (December 6, 2010), p. 11.

---

[4]To be included in the rankings, companies must report media spending on at least three continents.

Global Advertising Content: Standardization Versus Adaptation

Communication experts generally agree that the overall requirements of effective communication and persuasion are fixed and do not vary from country to country. The same is true of the components of the communication process: The marketer is the source of the message; the message must be encoded, conveyed via the appropriate channel(s), and decoded by a member of the target audience. Communication takes place only when the intended meaning transfers from the source to the receiver. Four major difficulties can compromise an organization's attempt to communicate with customers in any location:

1. The message may not get through to the intended recipient. This problem may be the result of an advertiser's lack of knowledge about appropriate media for reaching certain types of audiences.
2. The message may reach the target audience but may not be understood or may even be misunderstood. This can be the result of an inadequate understanding of the target audience's level of sophistication or improper encoding.
3. The message may reach the target audience and may be understood but still may not compel the recipient to take action. This could result from a lack of cultural knowledge about a target audience.
4. The effectiveness of the message can be impaired by noise. *Noise*, in this case, is an external influence, such as competitive advertising, other sales personnel, or confusion at the receiving end, that can detract from the ultimate effectiveness of the communication.

The key question for global marketers is whether the *specific* advertising message and media strategy must be changed from region to region or country to country because of environmental requirements. Proponents of the "one world, one voice" approach to global advertising believe that the era of the global village has arrived and that tastes and preferences are converging worldwide. According to the standardization argument, people everywhere want the same products for the same reasons. This means that companies can achieve significant economies of scale by unifying advertising around the globe.

Advertisers who prefer the localized approach are skeptical of the global village argument. Instead, they assert that consumers still differ from country to country and must be reached by advertising tailored to their respective countries. Proponents of localization point out that most blunders occur because advertisers have failed to understand—and adapt to—foreign cultures. Ad industry veteran Nick Brien is currently CEO of Interpublic Group's McCann Worldgroup global agency network. As Brien observed in the late 1990s, the local/global debate does not necessarily have to be framed as an "either/or" proposition:

> As the potency of traditional media declines on a daily basis, brand building locally becomes more costly and international brand building becomes more cost effective. The challenge for advertisers and agencies is finding ads that work in different countries and cultures. At the same time as this global tendency, there is a growing local tendency. It's becoming increasingly important to understand the requirements of both.[5]

Nils Larsson, an external communications executive at IKEA, echoes Brien's view, but leans more towards the localized side of the debate:

> If we could find one message on a global basis it could be effective, but so far there are different needs in different countries. We have been in Sweden for 60 years and in China for only 4 or 5 so our feeling is that retail is local. It is important to take advantage of local humor, and the things on people's minds.[6]

And consider this quote from Michael Conrad, the chief creative officer at Leo Burnett Worldwide:

> I can think of very few truly global ads that work. Brands are often at different stages around the world, and that means there are different advertising jobs to do.[7]

---

[5]Meg Carter, "Think Globally, Act Locally," *Financial Times* (June 30, 1997), p. 12.
[6]Emma Hall and Normandy Madden, "IKEA Courts Buyers with Offbeat Ideas," *Advertising Age* (April 12, 2004), p. 1.
[7]Vanessa O'Connell, "Exxon 'Centralizes' New Global Campaign," *The Wall Street Journal* (July 11, 2001), p. B6.

During the 1950s, the widespread opinion among advertising professionals was that effective international advertising required assigning responsibility for campaign preparation to a local agency. In the early 1960s, this idea of local delegation was challenged repeatedly. For example, Eric Elinder, head of a Swedish advertising agency, wrote: "Why should three artists in three different countries sit drawing the same electric iron and three copywriters write about what, after all, is largely the same copy for the same iron?"[8] Elinder argued that consumer differences between countries were diminishing and that he would more effectively serve a client's interest by putting top specialists to work devising a strong international campaign. The campaign would then be presented with insignificant modifications that mainly entailed translating the copy into language well suited for a particular country.

As the 1980s began, Pierre Liotard-Vogt, then-CEO of Nestlé, expressed similar views in an interview with *Advertising Age:*

> *Advertising Age:* Are food tastes and preferences different in each of the countries in which you do business?
>
> *Liotard-Vogt:* The two countries where we are selling perhaps the most instant coffee are England and Japan. Before the war they didn't drink coffee in those countries, and I heard people say that it wasn't any use to try to sell instant coffee to the English because they drink only tea and still less to the Japanese because they drink green tea and they're not interested in anything else.
>
> When I was very young, I lived in England and at that time, if you spoke to an Englishman about eating spaghetti or pizza or anything like that, he would just look at you and think that the stuff was perhaps food for Italians. Now on the corner of every road in London you find pizzerias and spaghetti houses.
>
> So I do not believe [preconceptions] about "national tastes." They are "habits," and they're not the same. If you bring the public a different food, even if it is unknown initially, when they get used to it, they will enjoy it too.
>
> To a certain extent we know that in the north they like a coffee milder and a bit acid and less roasted; in the south, they like it very dark. So I can't say that taste differences don't exist. But to believe that those tastes are set and can't be changed is a mistake.[9]

The "standardized versus localized" debate picked up tremendous momentum after the 1983 publication, noted in earlier chapters, of Professor Ted Levitt's *Harvard Business Review* article, "The Globalization of Markets." Recently, global companies have embraced a technique known as **pattern advertising**. This is analogous to the concept of global product platforms discussed in Chapter 10. Representing a middle ground between 100 percent standardization and 100 percent adaptation, a pattern strategy calls for developing a basic pan-regional or global communication concept for which copy, artwork, or other elements can be adapted as required for individual country markets. For example, ads in a European print campaign for Boeing shared basic design elements, but the copy and the visual elements were localized on a country-by-country basis.

Much of the research on this issue has focused on the match between advertising messages and local culture. For example, Ali Kanso surveyed two different groups of advertising managers, those adopting localized approaches to advertising and those adopting standardized approaches. One finding was that managers who are attuned to cultural issues tended to prefer the localized approach, whereas managers less sensitive to cultural issues preferred a standardized approach.[10] Bruce Steinberg, ad sales director for MTV Europe, discovered that the people responsible for executing global campaigns locally can exhibit strong resistance to a global campaign. Steinberg reported that he sometimes had to visit as many as 20 marketing directors from the same company to get approval for a pan-European MTV ad.[11]

As Kanso correctly notes, the long-standing debate over advertising approaches will probably continue for years to come. Kanso's conclusion: What is needed for successful international

---

[8]Eric Elinder, "International Advertisers Must Devise Universal Ads, Dump Separate National Ones, Swedish Ad Man Avers," *Advertising Age* (November 27, 1961), p. 91.

[9]"A Conversation with Nestlé's Pierre Liotard-Vogt," *Advertising Age* (June 30, 1980), p. 31.

[10]Ali Kanso, "International Advertising Strategies: Global Commitment to Local Vision," *Journal of Advertising Research* 32, no. 1 (January–February 1992), pp. 10–14.

[11]Ken Wells, "Selling to the World: Global Ad Campaigns, After Many Missteps, Finally Pay Dividends," *The Wall Street Journal* (August 27, 1992), p. A1.

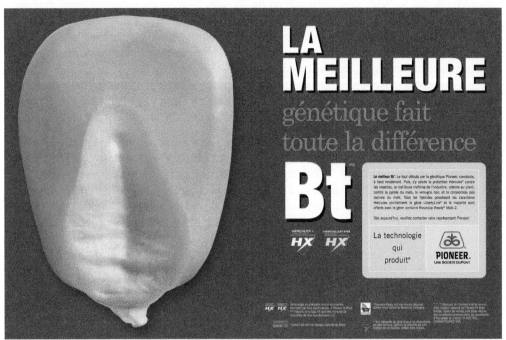

advertising is a global commitment to local vision. In the final analysis, the decision of whether to use a global or localized campaign depends on recognition by managers of the trade-offs involved. A global campaign will result in the substantial benefits of cost savings, increased control, and the potential creative leverage of a global appeal. It is also true that localized campaigns can focus on the most important attributes of a product or brand in each nation or culture.

As a practical matter, marketing managers may choose to run *both* global *and* local ads rather than adopt an "either/or" stance. For example, marketing and advertising managers at Pioneer Hi-Bred International frequently use both global and localized advertising executions. It is management's belief that some messages lend themselves to straight translation, whereas others need to be created in a way that best suits the farmers, marketplace, and style of the particular country or region. Of the ads shown in Exhibit 13-2, the top ad is for the United States; the ad at the bottom was created for Québec.

The question of *when* to use each approach depends on the product involved and a company's objectives in a particular market. The following generalizations can serve as guidelines:

- Standardized print campaigns can be used for industrial products or for high-tech consumer products. Examples: Apple's iPhone and iPad.
- Standardized print campaigns with a strong visual appeal often travel well. Example: Chivas Regal ("This is the Chivas Life"). Similarly, no text appears in the assembly instructions for IKEA furniture. Picture-based instructions can be used throughout the world without translation.
- TV commercials that use voiceovers instead of actors or celebrity endorsers speaking dialogue can use standardized visuals with translated copy for the voiceover. Examples: Gillette ("The best a man can get"); GE ("Imagination at work"); UPS ("We ♥ Logistics").

Advertising Agencies: Organizations and Brands

Advertising is a fast-paced business, and the ad agency world is fluid and dynamic. New agencies are formed, existing agencies are dismantled, and cross-border investment, spin-offs, joint ventures, and mergers and acquisitions are a fact of life. The industry is also very mobile, as executives and top talent move from one agency to another. The 20 largest global **advertising organizations** ranked by 2010 gross income are shown in Table 13-2. The key to understanding the table is the word *organization*; most of the firms identified in Table 13-2 are umbrella corporations or holding companies that include one or more "core" advertising agencies, as well as units specializing in direct marketing, marketing services, public relations, or research. A close inspection of the table reveals that IBM has gotten into the advertising business. Not surprisingly, IBM Interactive (ranked 18) is a digital specialist.

As shown in Figure 13-1, the family tree of Omnicom Group is quite complex. The group includes three core global agency networks: DDB Worldwide Communications, BBDO

TABLE 13-2 Top 20 Global Advertising Organizations

Organization and Headquarters Location	Worldwide Revenue 2010 ($ millions)
1. WPP Group (London)	$14,416
2. Omnicom Group (New York)	12,543
3. Publicis Groupe (Paris)	7,175
4. Interpublic Group of Cos. (New York)	6,532
5. Dentsu (Tokyo)	3,600
6. Aegis Group (London)	2,257
7. Havas (Suresnes, France)	2,069
8. Hakuhodo DY Holdings (Tokyo)	1,674
9. Acxiom Corp. (Little Rock, Arkansas)	785
10. MDC Partners (Toronto/New York)	698
11. Alliance Data Systems Corp.'s Epsilon (Plano, Texas)	613
12. Groupe Aeroplan's Carlson Marketing (Minneapolis)	593
13. Daniel J. Edelman (Chicago)	544
14. Sapient Corp.'s SapientNitro (Boston)	515
15. Asatsu-DK (Tokyo)	484
16. Media Consulta (Berlin)	408
17. Cheil Worldwide (Seoul)	386
18. IBM Corp.'s IBM Interactive (Chicago)	368
19. Grupo ABC (Sao Paulo)	362
20. Photon Group (Sydney)	334

Source: "World's Top 50 Agency Companies," *Advertising Age* (April 25, 2011), p. 26.

FIGURE 13-1

**Omnicom Group
Family Tree**

Source: Advertising Age.

Worldwide, and TBWA Worldwide. Omnicom's other agencies provide services in various specialty areas such as media buying, public relations, digital services, and direct marketing. Omnicom generates about 43 percent of annual revenues from advertising and media; public relations accounts for 9.5 percent, and customer relationship management (CRM) for 38 percent. Specialty services such as health care advertising account for the remaining 9.5 percent of revenues.

Table 13-3 presents the rankings of individual agencies (agency "brands") by 2010 worldwide income. Most of the agency brands identified in Table 13-3 are *full-service agencies*: In addition to creating advertising, they provide other services, such as market research, media buying, and direct marketing. The agencies listed in Table 13-3 are all owned by larger holding companies.

TABLE 13-3 Top 10 Global Advertising Agency Brands

Agency	Estimated Worldwide Revenue 2010 ($ millions)
1. Dentsu (Dentsu)	$2,494
2. McCann Erickson Worldwide (Interpublic)	1,438
3. BBDO Worldwide (Omnicom)	1,210
4. DDB Worldwide (Omnicom)	1,149
5. JWT (WPP)	1,149
6. TBWA Worldwide (Omnicom)	1,082
7. Hakuhodo (Hakuhodo DY Holdings)	1,028
8. Publicis (Publicis)	1,023
9. Y&R (WPP)	987
10. Leo Burnett Worldwide/Arc (Publicis)	877

Source: Adapted from "Advertising Agencies: World's Top 10," *Advertising Age* (April 25, 2011), p. 30.

Selecting an Advertising Agency

Companies can create ads in-house, use an outside agency, or combine both strategies. For example, Chanel, Benetton, H&M, and Diesel rely on in-house marketing and advertising staffs for creative work; Coca-Cola has its own agency, Edge Creative, but also uses the services of outside agencies such as Leo Burnett. When one or more outside agencies are used, they can serve product accounts on a multicountry or even global basis. It is possible to select a local agency in each national market or an agency with both domestic and overseas offices. Like Coca-Cola, Levi Strauss and Polaroid also use local agencies.

Today, however, there is a growing tendency for Western clients to designate global agencies for product accounts to support the integration of the marketing and advertising functions; Japanese companies are less inclined to use this approach. For example, in 1995, Colgate-Palmolive consolidated its $500 million in global billings with Young & Rubicam. That same year, IBM consolidated its ad account with Ogilvy & Mather for the launch of the "Solutions for a small planet" global campaign. Similarly, Bayer AG consolidated most of its $300 million consumer products advertising with BBDO Worldwide; Bayer had previously relied on 50 agencies around the globe. Agencies are aware of this trend and are themselves pursuing international acquisitions and joint ventures to extend their geographic reach and their ability to serve clients on a global account basis. In an effort to remain competitive, many small independent agencies in Europe, Asia, and the United States belong to the Transworld Advertising Agency Network (TAAN). TAAN enables member agencies to tap into worldwide resources that would not otherwise be available to them.

The following issues should be considered when selecting an advertising agency:

- *Company organization.* Companies that are decentralized typically allow managers at the local subsidiary to make ad agency selection decisions.
- *National responsiveness.* Is the global agency familiar with local culture and buying habits in a particular country, or should a local selection be made?
- *Area coverage.* Does the candidate agency cover all relevant markets?
- *Buyer perception.* What kind of brand awareness does the company want to project? If the product needs a strong local identification, it would be best to select a national agency.

Despite an unmistakable trend toward using global agencies to support global marketing efforts, companies with geocentric orientations will adapt to the global market requirements and select the best agency or agencies accordingly. Western agencies still find markets such as China and Japan to be very complex; similarly, Asian agencies find it just as difficult to establish a local agency presence in Western markets.

As noted later in the chapter, advertising professionals face escalating pressure to achieve new heights of creativity. Some critics of advertising complain that agencies sometimes try to create advertising that will win awards and generate acclaim and prestige rather than advertising that serves clients' needs. The search for fresh answers to promotion challenges has prompted

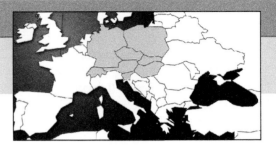

→ THE CULTURAL CONTEXT

Smokers Fume About Limits on Tobacco Advertising

According the World Health Organization (WHO), 5 million people die each year as a direct result of consuming tobacco products. A total of 172 countries are signatories to the Framework Convention on Tobacco Control (WHO FCTC), which aims to reduce global tobacco production as well as the consumption of tobacco products. The treaty entered into force in February 2005.

Even before the WHO FCTC, policymakers in various countries had taken steps to reduce the extent to which tobacco companies could promote their products and brands. In China, tobacco advertising has been banned from television and radio since 1994; the ban also extends to newspaper, magazine, and cinema ads. With a population of 1.3 billion people, including one-third of the world's smokers, China is a massive potential market for cigarette manufacturers at a time when Western markets are shrinking. The ban was part of China's first law regulating advertisements. The WHO asked Chinese leaders to launch antismoking campaigns and impose tougher controls on cigarette smuggling and higher taxes on domestic cigarette producers. China agreed to ratify the WHO FCTC.

The EU spends about €16 million ($21 million) annually on antismoking initiatives. A tobacco ad ban proposal was introduced in mid-1991 with the aim of fulfilling the single-market rules of the Maastricht Treaty. The directive would have prohibited tobacco advertising on billboards as of July 2001; newspaper and magazine advertising was slated to end by 2002, with sports sponsorship banned by 2003 (such "world-level" sports as Formula One racing would be excluded until 2006). Not surprisingly, tobacco companies and advertising associations opposed the proposed ban. The European Commission justified the directive on the grounds that various countries had, or were considering, restrictions on tobacco advertising and that there was a need for common rules on cross-border trade.

Prior to the directive's implementation date, however, the German government took the issue to the European Court of Justice (ECJ). The Germans argued that the directive was illegal because tobacco advertising is a health issue; thus, the directive could only be adopted if the member states agreed unanimously. The EU's advocate general concurred with the German government. On October 5, 2000, the court ruled that the directive prohibiting tobacco ads should be annulled. A revised directive concerning cross-border tobacco advertising was adopted in December 2002; it went into effect in August.

However, the German government challenged the new directive at the ECJ on the grounds that it would restrict single-country print advertisements for local cigarette brands. Germany's argument, that most media operate on a local or national basis, was dismissed by the ECJ. Even as Germany set about complying with the ban, a retailer's association asserted that some 40,000 jobs would be lost across Germany after the ban was implemented.

For RJ Reynolds International, Philip Morris International, B.A.T., and other tobacco marketers, the receding threat of a pan-European ban on tobacco ads comes as welcome news. The industry spends between $600 million and $1 billion on advertising in the EU annually. An EU ban would have hurt them most in the countries where they compete with entrenched state tobacco monopolies, namely, France, Italy, and Spain.

Tobacco companies in Central Europe face the prospect of tougher marketing regulations as countries in the region work to meet requirements for entry into the EU. In Lithuania, authorities began to enforce the country's 3-year-old tobacco advertising ban on May 1, 2000; some newspapers printed blank pages in protest. Jurga Karmanoviene, media director for Saatchi & Saatchi Lithuania, interprets the enforcement as evidence that the government is sending a signal that it is beginning to meet EU requirements. Similar developments are occurring in Poland, Hungary, Bulgaria, and Romania.

Sources: Enda Curran, "Australia Plans to Get Tougher on Tobacco," *The Wall Street Journal* (April 8, 2011), p. B2; Cailainn Barr, "Cigarette Factories Suck in €1.5 Million of Funds," *Financial Times* (December 2, 2010), p. 8; Rita Rubin, "Smoking Warnings More Graphic Elsewhere," *USA Today* (December 9, 2010), p. 13A; Farai Mutsaka, "Zimbabwe Enemies United on Tobacco," *The Wall Street Journal* (November 13–14, 2010), p. A8; Hugh Williamson, "Germany to Stub Out Most Tobacco Adverts," *Financial Times* (June 13, 2006); Geoffrey A. Fowler, "Treaty May Stub Out Cigarette Ads in China," *The Wall Street Journal* (December 2, 2003), pp. B1, B6; Joyce-Ann Gatsoulis, "EU Aspirants Shake Up Tobacco Marketing Scene," *Advertising Age International* (July 2000), p. 15; Tony Koenderman and Paul Meller, "EU Topples Tobacco Ad Rules," *Advertising Age* (October 9, 2000), pp. 4, 97; Juliana Koranteng, " EU Ad Ban on Tobacco Under Fire as Illegal," *Advertising Age* (July 10, 2000), pp. 4, 49; "Australia's Ad Ban Is Fought," *The New York Times* (June 7, 1994), p. 19; Marcus Brauchli, "China Passes Law in Move to Prohibit Ads for Tobacco," *The Wall Street Journal* (October 31, 1994), p. B10; Lili Cui, "Mass Media Boycott Tobacco Ads," *Beijing Review* (June 6, 1994), p. 8; "Tobacco Adverts: Fuming," *The Economist* (February 5, 1994), pp. 60–61.

some client companies to look to new sources for creative ideas. For example, McDonald's historically relied on American agencies for basic creative direction. However, Larry Light, McDonald's global marketing chief, staged a competition that included agencies from all over the world. A German agency devised the "I'm lovin' it" tagline.[12] Leo Burnett China's ideas included a hand signal for the McDonald's global campaign. As Light noted, "China just blew our minds. We didn't expect that kind of expression and joy. Our expectation was for more conservatism, much less individuality, and more caution."[13]

---

[12]Erin White and Shirley Leung, "How Tiny German Shop Landed McDonald's," *The Wall Street Journal* (August 6, 2003), pp. B1, B3.

[13]Geoffrey A. Fowler, "Commercial Break: The Art of Selling," *Far Eastern Economic Review* (October 30, 2003), pp. 30–33.

Creating Global Advertising

As suggested earlier in the discussion of the adaptation versus standardization debate, the *message* is at the heart of advertising. The particular message and the way it is presented will depend on the advertiser's objective. Is the ad designed to inform, entertain, remind, or persuade? Moreover, in a world characterized by information overload, ads must break through the clutter, grab the audience's attention, and linger in their minds. This requires developing an original and effective **creative strategy**, which is simply a statement or concept of what a particular message or campaign will say. Advertising agencies can be thought of as "idea factories"; in industry parlance, the Holy Grail in creative strategy development is something known as the **big idea**. Legendary ad man John O'Toole defined the *big idea* as "that flash of insight that synthesizes the purpose of the strategy, joins the product benefit with consumer desire in a fresh, involving way, brings the subject to life, and makes the reader or audience stop, look, and listen."[14] In his book about Subaru of America, Randall Rothenberg describes the big idea in the following way:

> The Big Idea is easier to illustrate than define, and easier to illustrate by what it is not than by what it is. It is not a "position" (although the place a product occupies in the consumer's mind may be a part of it). It is not an "execution" (although the writing or graphic style of an ad certainly contributes to it). It is not a slogan (although a tagline may encapsulate it).
>
> The Big Idea is the bridge between an advertising strategy, temporal and worldly, and an image, powerful and lasting. The theory of the Big Idea assumes that average consumers are at best bored and more likely irrational when it comes to deciding what to buy.[15]

Some of the world's most memorable advertising campaigns have achieved success because they originate from an idea that is so big that the campaign offers opportunities for a seemingly unlimited number of new executions. Such a campaign is said to have *legs* because it can be used for long periods of time. The print campaign for Absolut Vodka is a perfect example: Over the course of two decades, Absolut's agency created hundreds of two-word puns on the brand name linked with various pictorial renderings of the distinctive bottle shape. Other campaigns based on big ideas include MSN ("Life's better with the butterfly") and MasterCard ("There are some things in life money can't buy"). In 2003, McDonald's executives launched a search for an idea big enough to be used in multiple country markets even as the company faced disapproval in some countries from consumers who link it to unpopular U.S. government policies (see Case 1-2).

The **advertising appeal** is the communications approach that relates to the motives of the target audience. For example, ads based on a **rational appeal** depend on logic and speak to the audience's intellect. Rational appeals are based on consumers' needs for information. The Pioneer Hi-Bred ads inform farmers about the attributes of pest-resistant seed varieties that will boost yields (see Exhibit 13-2). By contrast, ads using an **emotional appeal** may tug at the heartstrings or tickle the funny bone of the intended audience and evoke a feeling response that will direct purchase behavior. For example, a recent global campaign for IKEA, the Swedish home furnishings retailer, positioned houses as homes: "It's a place for love . . . a place for memories . . . a place for laughter. Home is the most important place in the world."[16]

The message elements in a particular ad will depend, in part, on which appeal is being employed. The **selling proposition** is the promise or claim that captures the reason for buying the product or the benefit that ownership confers. Because products are frequently at different stages in their life cycle in various national markets, and because of cultural, social, and economic differences that exist in those markets, the most effective appeal or selling proposition for a product may vary from market to market.

Effective global advertising may also require developing different presentations of the product's appeal or selling proposition. The way an appeal or proposition is presented is called the **creative execution**. In other words, there can be differences between *what* one says and *how* one says it. Ad agency personnel can choose from a variety of executions, including straight sell, scientific evidence, demonstration, comparison, testimonial, slice of life, animation, fantasy, and

---

[14]John O'Toole, *The Trouble with Advertising* (New York: Random House, 1985), p. 131.
[15]Randall Rothenberg, *Where the Suckers Moon* (New York: Vintage Books, 1995), pp. 112–113.
[16]Suzanne Vranica, "IKEA to Tug at Heartstrings," *The Wall Street Journal* (September 18, 2007), p. B6.

dramatization. The responsibility for deciding on the appeal, the selling proposition, and the appropriate execution lies with *creatives*, a term that applies to art directors and copywriters.

Art Direction and Art Directors

The visual presentation of an advertisement—the "body language"—is a matter of **art direction**. The individual with general responsibility for the overall look of an ad is known as an *art director*. This person chooses graphics, pictures, type styles, and other visual elements that appear in an ad. Some forms of visual presentation are universally understood. Revlon, for example, has used a French producer to develop television commercials in English and Spanish for use in international markets. These commercials are filmed in Parisian settings but communicate the universal appeals and specific benefits of Revlon products. By producing its ads in France, Revlon obtains effective television commercials at a much lower cost than it would have paid for commercials produced in the United States. PepsiCo has used four basic commercials to communicate its advertising themes. The basic setting of young people having fun at a party or on a beach has been adapted to reflect the general physical environment and racial characteristics of North America, South America, Europe, Africa, and Asia. The music in these commercials has also been adapted to suit regional tastes, ranging from rock 'n' roll in North America to bossa nova in Latin America to the high life in Africa.

 EMERGING MARKETS BRIEFING BOOK

Localizing Ad Executions in China

A creative challenge presented to Ogilvy & Mather in China illustrates the relationship between creative strategy, appeal, and execution. The client, Coca-Cola's Fanta, wanted a national TV ad that would communicate to consumers that Fanta is an antidote to everyday pressures on Chinese youth. This was the overall creative strategy; in other words, what the message should say. What type of appeal would be appropriate? Not surprisingly, soft drinks lend themselves especially well to emotional appeals; that was the appeal Ogilvy & Mather preferred.

The next step was to choose a specific execution. Soft drink marketers often utilize slice-of-life and fantasy executions, usually injected with an element of fun or humor. As Jeff Delkin, Ogilvy's regional business director in Shanghai, notes, for a U.S. ad the creative strategy could be executed with a teen's fantasy or images of revenge on a mean teacher. However, in China it is not acceptable to challenge or undermine the position of authority figures. The completed ad shows that drinking Fanta can create a fun experience in a classroom. When a student opens a can of Fanta, oranges begin to rain down. The teacher catches the oranges and juggles them—much to the delight of the students.

Another example is a Nike campaign created by Wieden & Kennedy in China. Nike's "Just Do It" ads typically showcase famous athletes and sports heroes and are legendary for their inspirational appeals. The selling proposition is universal—Nike is a "cool" brand. However, a localized execution of a Nike ad that featured Chinese superstar Wang Zhizhi did not connect with consumers; they prefer to draw inspiration from the world's best players rather than a national star who has yet to prove himself in the global arena. Nike tried a different execution with the theme "Chamber of Fear" featuring NBA star LeBron James defeating a kung fu master. This spot was banned after consumer complaints.

In 2006, Nike launched a new campaign that featured Chinese youth who had overcome personal obstacles to excel at sports. Young people were encouraged to share their stories at Nike stores or on a Nike Web site. Web site visitors were able to view short, 3- to 4-minute films featuring Chinese youth playing sports in well-known locales. Shortened versions of the clips were used as TV ads. As Jesse Lin, Wieden's managing director in Shanghai, said, "China's younger generation is in the midst of forming its own style, mixing together Chinese elements and influences they've absorbed from the West, but they don't think they need to learn from the West. Nike realized this and wants to be a part of this new generation, rather than telling them what to do."

McDonald's used a localized campaign for the Chinese launch of the Quarter Pounder sandwich; ironically, the campaign came as the fast-food giant removed menu items such as an Asian-style chicken or beef wrap with rice created to appeal to Chinese tastes. Beef is considered a luxury, upscale item in China; beef also is perceived to boost energy and heighten sex appeal. In Chinese, the word *beef* connotes manliness, strength, and skill. Television commercials for the Quarter Pounder have sex appeal: They include close-ups of a woman's neck and mouth juxtaposed with images of fireworks and spraying water. The voice-over says, "You can feel it. Thicker. You can taste it. Juicier."

The McDonald's print ads also conveyed sexual innuendo. One execution featured a "beauty shot" of a Quarter Pounder with an extreme close up of a woman's mouth in the background. The copy read, "Part of your body will be excited. You will feel 100 percent of the beef." As Jeffrey Schwartz, the head of McDonald's Chinese operations, explained, "Our customers are young, modern, and bilingual. If we're not edgy in communications, out front in technology, this consumer is going to blow right by us."

Sources: Gordon Fairclough and Janet Adamy, "Sex, Skin, Fireworks, Licked Fingers—It's a Quarter Pounder Ad in China," *The Wall Street Journal* (September 21, 2006), pp. B1, B2; Geoffrey A. Fowler, "Commercial Break: The Art of Selling," *Far Eastern Economic Review* (October 30, 2003), p. 32; Normandy Madden, "Nike Drops Its American Idols," *Advertising Age* (March 20, 2006), p. 12.

The global advertiser must make sure that visual executions are not extended inappropriately into certain markets. In the mid-1990s, Benetton's United Colors of Benetton campaign generated considerable controversy. The campaign appeared in scores of countries, primarily in print and on billboards. The art direction focused on striking, provocative interracial juxtapositions—a white hand and a black hand handcuffed together, for example. Another version of the campaign, depicting a black woman nursing a white baby, won advertising awards in France and Italy. However, because the image evoked the history of slavery in the United States, that particular creative execution was not used in the U.S. market.[17]

Copy and Copywriters

The words that are the spoken or written communication elements in advertisements are known as **copy**. *Copywriters* are language specialists who develop the headlines, subheads, and body copy used in print advertising and the scripts containing the words that are delivered by spokespeople, actors, or hired voice talents in broadcast ads. As a general rule, copy should be relatively short and avoid slang or idioms. Languages vary in terms of the number of words required to convey a given message; thus the increased use of pictures and illustrations. Some global ads feature visual appeals that convey a specific message with minimal use of copy. Low literacy rates in many countries seriously compromise the use of print as a communications device and require greater creativity in the use of audio-oriented media.

It is important to recognize overlap in the use of languages in many areas of the world (e.g., the EU, Latin America, and North America). Capitalizing on this, global advertisers can realize economies of scale by producing advertising copy with the same language and message for these markets. The success of this approach will depend in part on avoiding unintended ambiguity in the ad copy. Then again, in some situations, ad copy must be translated into the local language. Translating copy has been the subject of great debate in advertising circles. Advertising slogans often present the most difficult translation problems. The challenge of encoding and decoding slogans and taglines in different national and cultural contexts can lead to unintentional errors. For example, the Asian version of Pepsi's "Come alive" tagline was rendered as a call to bring ancestors back from the grave.

Advertising executives may elect to prepare new copy for a foreign market in the language of the target country or to translate the original copy into the target language. A third option is to leave some (or all) copy elements in the original (home-country) language. In choosing from these alternatives, the advertiser must consider whether the intended foreign audience can receive and comprehend a translated message. Anyone with knowledge of two or more languages realizes that the ability to think in another language facilitates accurate communication. To be confident that a message will be understood correctly after it is received, one must understand the connotations of words, phrases, and sentence structures, as well as their translated meaning.

The same principle applies to advertising—perhaps to an even greater degree. A copywriter who can think in the target language and understands the consumers in the target country will be able to create the most effective appeals, organize the ideas, and craft the specific language, especially if colloquialisms, idioms, or humor are involved. For example, in southern China, McDonald's is careful not to advertise prices with multiple occurrences of the number four. The reason is simple: In Cantonese, the pronunciation of the word *four* is similar to that of the word *death*.[18] In its efforts to develop a global brand image, Citicorp discovered that translations of its slogan "Citi never sleeps" conveyed the meaning that Citibank had a sleeping disorder such as insomnia. Company executives decided to retain the slogan but use English throughout the world.[19]

Cultural Considerations

Knowledge of cultural diversity, especially the symbolism associated with cultural traits, is essential for creating advertising. Local country managers can share important information, such as when to use caution in advertising creativity. Use of colors and man–woman relationships

---

[17]Janet L. Borgerson, Jonathan E. Schroeder, Martin Escudero Magnusson, and Frank Magnusson, "Corporate Communication, Ethics, and Operational Identity: A Case Study of Benetton," *Business Ethics: A European Review* 18, no. 3 (July 2009), pp. 209–223.

[18]Jeanne Whalen, "McDonald's Cooks Worldwide Growth," *Advertising Age International* (July–August 1995), p. I4.

[19]Stephen E. Frank, "Citicorp's Big Account Is at Stake as It Seeks a Global Brand Name," *The Wall Street Journal* (January 9, 1997), p. B6.

→ STRATEGIC DECISION MAKING IN GLOBAL MARKETING

Adidas Hopes Beckham Will Score with Americans

Adidas enjoys a reputation as the leading sports brand in the world of soccer. Recently, the German company has intensified its efforts to increase its lead over archrival Nike. Chief executive Herbert Hainer has described soccer as the "heart and soul" of Adidas. In 2008, the company's sales revenues from soccer-related products reached a record €1.3 billion ($1.8 billion).

In the key U.S. market, soccer superstar David Beckham was at the center of a splashy new promotional campaign. Beckham has been a worldwide Adidas endorser for more than a decade. Following Beckham's highly publicized move from the Real Madrid to the Los Angeles Galaxy, he signed a 5-year, $250 million contract with Adidas (see Exhibit 13-3). Beckham was featured prominently in a variety of media, including billboards and prime-time television ads. Adidas executives expected Beckham's endorsement to lead to increased sales of a variety of branded merchandise. As Stephen Pierpoint, vice president for brand marketing at Adidas, said, "The U.S. market has a real opportunity to grow. Football [soccer] has always been a core sport for Adidas. We hope David will be the catalyst for growth."

The 2010 World Cup was critical to Adidas's marketing plans. The company supplies shoes and other gear to 12 of the 32 teams, at an annual cost of about €85 million. Adidas also supplied the official soccer balls and uniforms for officiating crews. The opening match featured South Africa and Mexico, the two teams whose branded merchandise are top sellers for Adidas. The American team's successes in the first two rounds raised awareness and interest in the sport. What does Adidas expect in the way of return on investment? In addition to sales revenues, the company will conduct marketing research to determine consumer awareness and attitudes toward the brand.

Nike has also made its presence known. Several years ago, the Oregon-based company paid $200 million to sponsor the Brazilian team. However, Nike's attempts to "ambush" Adidas at the World Cup centered on a 3-minute advertisement titled "Write the Future." The ad first appeared on Facebook in May 2010; Nike then bought airtime during the World Cup broadcasts.

Sources: Joseph D'Hippolito, "Beckham Returns, Fans Turn," *The New York Times* (March 22, 2011), p. B10; Tim Bradshaw, "The Force Is with Adidas," *Financial Times* (July 1, 2010); James Wilson, "Adidas Prepares for World Cup Shoot-Out," *Financial Times* (June 8, 2010); David Owen, "Brand Beckham Kicks off Soccer's American Appeal," *Financial Times* (March 20, 2007), p. 7.

Exhibit 13-3 Former New Orleans Saints running back Reggie Bush holds an "American" football as soccer legend David Beckham prepares to kick off. Both athletes endorse Adidas; in 2006, Bush was fined several thousand dollars for wearing Adidas cleats during a preseason football game. The reason? The NFL has partnership agreements with Nike and Reebok; players aren't allowed to wear other shoe brands.
Source: REUTERS/Adidas/HO/Landov.

can often be stumbling blocks. For example, in Japan intimate scenes between men and women are in bad taste; they are outlawed in Saudi Arabia. Veteran adman John O'Toole offers the following insights to global advertisers:

Transplanted American creative people always want to photograph European men kissing women's hands. But they seldom know that the nose must never touch the hand or that this rite is reserved solely for married women. And how do you know that the woman in the photograph is married? By the ring on her left hand, of course. Well, in Spain, Denmark, Holland, and Germany, Catholic women wear the wedding ring on the right hand.

When photographing a couple entering a restaurant or theater, you show the woman preceding the man, correct? No. Not in Germany and France. And this would be laughable in Japan. Having someone in a commercial hold up his hand with the back of it to you, the viewer, and the fingers moving toward him should communicate "come here." In Italy it means "good-bye."[20]

Ads that strike viewers in some countries as humorous or irritating may not necessarily be perceived that way by viewers in other countries. American ads make frequent use of spokes-people and direct product comparisons; they use logical arguments to try to appeal to the reason of audiences. Japanese advertising is more image oriented and appeals to audience sentiment. In Japan, what is most important frequently is not what is stated explicitly, but rather what is implied. Nike's U.S. advertising is legendary for its irreverent, "in your face" style and relies heavily on celebrity sports endorsers such as Michael Jordan. In other parts of the world, where soccer is the top sport, some Nike ads are considered to be in poor taste, and its spokespeople have less relevance. Nike has responded by adjusting its approach; as Geoffrey Frost, former director of global advertising at Nike, noted over a decade ago, "We have to root ourselves in the passions of other countries. It's part of our growing up."[21] Some American companies have canceled television ads created for the Latin American market portraying racial stereotypes that were offensive to persons of color. Nabisco, Goodyear, and other companies are also being more careful about the shows during which they buy airtime; some very popular Latin American programs feature content that exploits class, race, and ethnic differences.[22]

Standards vary widely with regard to the use of sexually explicit or provocative imagery. Partial nudity and same-sex couples are frequently seen in ads in Latin America and Europe. In the U.S. market, network television decency standards and the threat of boycotts by conservative consumer activists constrain advertisers. Some industry observers note a paradoxical situation in which the programs shown on U.S. TV are frequently racy, but the ads that air during those shows are not. As Marcio Moreira, worldwide chief creative officer at the McCann-Erickson agency, noted, "Americans want titillation in entertainment but when it comes to advertising they stop being viewers and become consumers and critics."[23] However, it is certainly not the case that anything goes outside the United States. Women in Monterrey, Mexico, recently complained about billboards for the Playtex unit of Sara Lee Corporation that featured supermodel Eva Herzegova wearing a Wonderbra. The campaign was created by a local agency, Perez Munoz Publicidad. Playtex responded by covering up the model on the billboards in some Mexican cities. French Connection UK made waves in the United States recently with print ads that prominently featured the British company's initials; that is, FCUK. Public outcry prompted the company to tone down the ads by spelling out the name.

Food is the product category most likely to exhibit cultural sensitivity. Thus, marketers of food and food products must be alert to the need to localize their advertising. A good example of this is the effort by H.J. Heinz Company to develop the overseas market for ketchup. More than 20 years ago, marketing managers at Heinz formulated a strategy that called for adapting both the product and advertising to target country tastes.[24] In Greece, for example, ads show ketchup pouring over pasta, eggs, and cuts of meat. In Japan, they instruct Japanese homemakers on using ketchup as an ingredient in Western-style food such as omelets, sausages, and pasta. Barry Tilley, London-based general manager of Heinz's Western Hemisphere trading division, says Heinz uses focus groups to determine what foreign consumers want in the way of taste and image. Americans like a sweet ketchup, but Europeans prefer a spicier, more piquant variety. Significantly, Heinz's foreign marketing efforts are most successful when the company quickly adapts to local cultural preferences. In Sweden, the made-in-America theme is so muted in Heinz's ads that "Swedes don't realize Heinz is American. They think it is German because of the name," says Tilley. In contrast to this, American themes still work well in Germany.

---

[20]John O'Toole, *The Trouble with Advertising* (New York: Random House, 1985), pp. 209–210.
[21]Roger Thurow, "Shtick Ball: In Global Drive, Nike Finds Its Brash Ways Don't Always Pay Off," *The Wall Street Journal* (May 5, 1997), p. A10.
[22]Leon E. Wynter, "Global Marketers Learn to Say 'No' to Bad Ads," *The Wall Street Journal* (April 1, 1998), p. B1.
[23]Melanie Wells and Dottie Enrico, "U.S. Admakers Cover It Up; Others Don't Give a Fig Leaf," *USA Today* (June 27, 1997), pp. B1, B2.
[24]Gary Levin, "Ads Going Global," *Advertising Age* (July 22, 1991), pp. 4, 42.

Kraft and Heinz are trying to outdo each other with ads featuring strong American images. In one of Heinz's TV ads, American football players in a restaurant become very angry when the 12 steaks they ordered arrive without ketchup. The ad ends happily, of course, with plenty of Heinz ketchup to go around.[25]

Much academic research has been devoted to the impact of culture on advertising. For example, Tamotsu Kishii identified seven characteristics that distinguish Japanese from American creative strategy:

1. Indirect rather than direct forms of expression are preferred in the messages. This avoidance of directness in expression is pervasive in all types of communication among the Japanese, including their advertising. Many television ads do not mention what is desirable about the brand in use and let the audience judge for themselves.
2. There is often little relationship between ad content and the advertised product.
3. Only brief dialogue or narration is used in television commercials, with minimal explanatory content. In the Japanese culture, the more one talks, the less others will perceive him or her as trustworthy or self-confident. A 30-second advertisement for young menswear shows five models in varying and seasonal attire, ending with a brief statement from the narrator: "Our life is a fashion show!"
4. Humor is used to create a bond of mutual feelings. Rather than slapstick, humorous dramatizations involve family members, neighbors, and office colleagues.
5. Famous celebrities appear as close acquaintances or everyday people.
6. Priority is placed on company trust rather than product quality. Japanese tend to believe that if the firm is large and has a good image, the quality of its products should also be outstanding.
7. The product name is impressed on the viewer with short, 15-second commercials.[26]

Green, Cunningham, and Cunningham conducted a cross-cultural study to determine the extent to which consumers of different nationalities use the same criteria to evaluate soft drinks and toothpaste. Their subjects were college students from the United States, France, India, and Brazil. Compared to France and India, the U.S. respondents placed more emphasis on the subjective, as opposed to functional, product attributes. The Brazilian respondents appeared even more concerned with the subjective attributes than the Americans were. The authors concluded that advertising messages should not use the same appeal for these countries if the advertiser is concerned with communicating the most important attributes of its product in each market.[27]

Global Media Decisions

The next issue facing advertisers is which medium or media to use when communicating with target audiences. Media availability can vary from country to country. Some companies use virtually the entire spectrum of available media; Coca-Cola is a good example. Other companies prefer to utilize one or two media categories. In some instances, the agency that creates advertising also makes recommendations about media placement; however, many advertisers use the services of specialized media planning and buying organizations. Omnicom's OMD Worldwide, the Starcom Media Vest Group unit of Publicis, and WPP's MindShare Worldwide are three of the top media specialists.

The available alternatives can be broadly categorized as print media, electronic media, and other. Print media range in form from local daily and weekly newspapers to magazines and business publications with national, regional, or international audiences. Electronic media include broadcast television, cable television, radio, and the Internet. Additionally, advertisers

[25]Gabriella Stern, "Heinz Aims to Export Taste for Ketchup," *The Wall Street Journal* (November 20, 1992), p. B1.

[26]C. Anthony di Benedetto, Mariko Tamate, and Rajan Chandran, "Developing Creative Advertising Strategy for the Japanese Marketplace," *Journal of Advertising Research* (January–February 1992), pp. 39–48. A number of studies have compared ad content in different parts of the world, including Mary C. Gilly, "Sex Roles in Advertising: A Comparison of Television Advertisements in Australia, Mexico, and the United States," *Journal of Marketing* (April 1988), pp. 75–85; and Marc G. Weinberger and Harlan E. Spotts, "A Situation View of Information Content in TV Advertising in the U.S. and UK," *Journal of Advertising* 53 (January 1989), pp. 89–94.

[27]Robert T. Green, William H. Cunningham, and Isabella C. M. Cunningham, "The Effectiveness of Standardized Global Advertising," *Journal of Advertising* (Summer 1975), pp. 25–30.

may utilize various forms of outdoor, transit, and direct mail advertising. Globally, media decisions must take into account country-specific regulations. For example, France bans retailers from advertising on television.

Global Advertising Expenditures and Media Vehicles

Each year, more money is spent on advertising in the United States than anywhere else in the world. As noted previously, U.S. ad spending in 2010 totaled $151 billion. To put this figure in perspective, consider that 2010 ad spending in Japan, the second largest advertising market, totaled approximately $43 billion. In addition, as one might expect, the largest per capita ad spending occurs in highly developed countries. However, much of the current growth in advertising expenditures—as much as one-third—is occurring in the BRIC countries. Russia alone represents a $7.8 billion advertising market; ad expenditures are growing at about 30 percent annually, compared with a rate of 4 or 5 percent in the United States and Europe. The WPP Group recently announced an alliance with Video International, Russia's largest ad agency.[28]

Worldwide, television is the number one advertising medium; with estimated ad revenues of $176 billion in 2008, television captured slightly more than one-third of global expenditures. Newspapers rank second on a worldwide basis, accounting for about 27 percent of advertising spending. However, media consumption patterns vary from country to country. For example, television is the number one medium in both the United States and Japan. By contrast, newspapers are the leading medium in Germany; television ranks second. In Germany, outlays for newspaper advertising surpass those for television by a ratio of two to one. In real terms, television spending in the EU increased by 78 percent between 1990 and 2000, compared with 26 percent for newspapers and 11 percent for magazines during the same period. This trend is likely to continue as digital broadcasting gains acceptance in Europe.

Television is also important in the Latin American market. In Brazil, expenditures on television advertising are nearly three times higher than those for newspapers. The availability of media and the conditions affecting media buys also vary greatly around the world. In Mexico, an advertiser that can pay for a full-page ad may get the front page, whereas in India paper shortages may require booking an ad 6 months in advance. In some countries, especially those where the electronic media are government owned, television and radio stations can broadcast only a restricted number of advertising messages. In Saudi Arabia, no commercial television advertising was allowed prior to May 1986; currently, ad content and visual presentation are restricted.

Worldwide, radio continues to be a less important advertising medium than print and television. However, in countries where advertising budgets are limited, radio's enormous reach can provide a cost-effective means of communicating with a large consumer market. Also, radio can be effective in countries where literacy rates are low. One clear trend that is gaining traction throughout the world: Spending on CRM and Internet advertising is gaining ground at the expense of TV and print.

> "The U.S. online advertising market is much bigger than Europe's, but it is a crowded market and the room for growth is shrinking. In Europe, online advertising is growing much faster and portals like Yahoo want to tap into that."[29]
>
> Jupiter Research

Media Decisions

The availability of television, newspapers, and other forms of broadcast and print media varies around the world. Moreover, patterns of media consumption differ from country to country as well. In many developed countries, for example, newspapers are experiencing circulation and readership declines as consumers devote more time to new media options such as the Internet. In India, by contrast, print media are enjoying a revival as redesigned newspaper formats and glossy supplements lure a new generation of readers. India is home to nearly 300 daily newspapers, including the *Times of India* and the *Hindustan Times*; the price per copy is only 5 rupees—about 10 cents. Additional critical factors in India's media environment include the lack of penetration by cable television and the fact that only about 4 million Indians currently subscribe to an Internet service.[30] By contrast, billboards are the medium of choice in Moscow. As Thomas L. Friedman has pointed out, Moscow is a city built for about 30,000 cars; during the past decade, the number of cars has grown from 300,000 to 3 million.[31] The result is massive

[28]Guy Chazan, "Moscow, City of Billboards," *The Wall Street Journal* (July 18, 2005), p. B1.

[29]Dan Bilefsky, "Yahoo Tightens Control in Europe and Asia," *The New York Times* (November 8, 2005), p. C18.

[30]John Larkin, "Newspaper Nirvana? 300 Dailies Court India's Avid Readers," *The Wall Street Journal* (May 5, 2006), pp. B1, B3.

[31]Thomas L. Friedman, "The Oil-Addicted Ayatollahs," *The New York Times* (February 2, 2007), p. A19.

traffic jams and commuting delays; affluent businesspeople spend hours in traffic and have little time to read the newspaper or watch TV.

Even when media availability is high, its use as an advertising vehicle may be limited. For example, in Europe, television advertising is very limited in Denmark, Norway, and Sweden. Regulations concerning content of commercials vary; Sweden bans advertising to children younger than 12 years of age. In 2001, when Sweden headed the EU, its policymakers tried to extend the ban to the rest of Europe. Although the effort failed, Sweden retained its domestic ban. This helps explain why annual spending on print media in Sweden is three times the annual spending for television.[32]

As noted earlier, cultural considerations often affect the presentation of the advertising message. One study comparing the content of magazine advertisements in the United States with those in the Arab world found the following:

- People are depicted less often in Arabic magazine ads. However, when people do appear, there is no difference in the extent to which women are depicted. Women appearing in ads in Arab magazines wear long dresses; their presence generally is relevant to the advertised product.
- U.S. ads tend to have more information content; by contrast, brevity is considered a virtue in the Arab world. Context plays a greater role in interpreting an Arab message than in the United States.
- U.S. ads contain more price information, and are more likely to include comparative appeals than Arabic ads.[33]

Public Relations and Publicity

Public relations (PR) is the department or function responsible for evaluating public opinion about, and attitudes toward, the organization and its products or brands. Public relations personnel also are responsible for fostering goodwill, understanding, and acceptance among a company's various constituents and publics. Like advertising, PR is one of four variables in the promotion mix. One of the tasks of the PR practitioner is to generate favorable **publicity.** By definition, publicity is communication about a company or product for which the company does not pay. (In the PR world, publicity is sometimes referred to as *earned media*, and advertising and promotions are known as *unearned media.*)

PR professionals also play a key role in responding to unflattering media reports, crises, or controversies that arise because of company activities in different parts of the globe. In such instances, especially if company's reputation is on the line, it is good PR practice to respond promptly and provide the public with facts (see Exhibit 13-4). The basic tools of PR include news releases, newsletters, media kits, press conferences, tours of plants and other company facilities, articles in trade or professional journals, company publications and brochures, TV and radio talk show interviews, special events, social media, and corporate Web sites.

Caterpillar's recent activities in China are a textbook example of the power of public relations. The Chinese market for industrial machinery is booming because the government is spending billions of dollars on infrastructure improvements. Caterpillar hopes to sell giant wheel tractor-scrapers that are more efficient to operate than the hydraulic excavators and trucks currently in use. However, a business intelligence team that contacted 100 customers and dealers across China found low levels of awareness and acceptance of Caterpillar's machines. Survey respondents were not persuaded by data from other countries about the machines' cost savings. To gain traction, Mike Cai, Cat's man in China, staged product demonstrations—road shows— around the country. "Word-of-mouth is the best form of publicity for the construction industry in China," he says. Scott Kronick, president for Ogilvy Public Relations Worldwide/China, agrees. "Chinese customers are being introduced to a lot of products and services for the first time, so you can't advertise something that's intangible," he said. Reporters from the local and

---

[32]John Tylee, "EC Permits Sweden to Continue Child Ad Ban," *Advertising Age* (July 11, 2003), p. 6.
[33]Fahad S. Al-Olayan and Kiran Karande, "A Content Analysis of Magazine Advertisements from the United States and the Arab World," *Journal of Advertising* 29, no. 3 (Fall 2000), pp. 69–82. See also Mushtag Luqmani, Ugur Yavas, and Zahir Quraeshi, "Advertising in Saudi Arabia: Content and Regulation," *International Marketing Review* 6, no. 1 (1989), pp. 59–72.

Exhibit 13-4 Because of its size and presence in more than 200 countries, the Coca-Cola Company is often the target of antiglobalization protests. The Indian villagers shown here were protesting the company's water consumption in areas severely affected by drought. Coca-Cola chairman and CEO E. Neville Isdell has responded to this type of negative publicity by guiding the company toward greater transparency in its global operations. Isdell also wants to make sure that the public perceives Coke as a global leader in corporate social responsibility. To do this, he is forging relationships and partnerships with nongovernmental organizations (NGOs).
Source: Raveendran/Getty Images, Inc. AFP.

national media were invited to the demonstrations; in one instance, China Central Television ran a story that featured a clip of the tractor-scraper at work.[34]

Senior executives at some companies relish the opportunity to generate publicity. For example, Benetton's striking print and outdoor ad campaigns keyed to the "United Colors of Benetton" generated both controversy and wide media attention. Richard Branson, the flamboyant founder of the Virgin Group, is a one-man publicity machine. His personal exploits as a hot-air balloon pilot have earned him and his company a great deal of free ink. The company does employ traditional media advertising; however, as Will Whitehorn, Virgin's head of brand development and corporate affairs, noted, "PR is the heart of the company. If we do things badly, it will reflect badly on the image of the brand more than most other companies." At Virgin, Whitehorn says, "Advertising is a subset of PR, not the other way around."[35]

Not surprisingly, social media's importance as a PR tool is growing at many companies. PR professionals point to increasing consumer "engagement with the brand" on Facebook, Twitter, and other Web 2.0 platforms. Consider, for example, that as of mid-2011 Adidas Originals had 9.3 million Facebook fans, and Heineken had 1.5 million fans. FedEx's "I am FedEx" Facebook page features "Team Member Stories from FedEx." This communication channel allows the company's 285,000 employees to share stories about their work and home lives. Joe Becker, an executive at Ketchum Digital, believes that the conversations that take place on Facebook can be leveraged as content that can be used to enhance the FedEx brand. He says, "The primary goal is about enabling employees to tell and create stories, which influences public opinion about the brand."[36] Another advantage: Because visitors to social media sites can immediately click on a link to an e-commerce site, it is easy to track return on investment (ROI). We discuss social media in more detail in Chapter 15.

As noted earlier, a company exerts complete control over the content of its advertising and pays for message placement in the media. However, the media typically receive many more press releases and other PR materials than they can use. Generally speaking, a company has little control over when, or if, a news story runs; nor can the company directly control the spin, slant, or tone of the story. To compensate for this lack of control, many companies utilize **corporate advertising** that, despite the name, is generally considered part of the PR function. As with "regular" advertising, a company or organization identified in the ad pays for corporate

---

[34]Jason Leow, "In China, Add a Caterpillar to the Dog and Pony Show," *The Wall Street Journal* (December 10, 2007), p. B1.

[35]Elena Bowes, "Virgin Flies in Face of Conventions," *Ad Age International* (January 1997), p. I.

[36]Matthew Schwartz, "Metrics of Success: PR's New Numbers," *Advertising Age* (November 29, 2010), p. S14.

TABLE 13-4 Negative Publicity Affecting Global Marketers

Company or Brand (home country)	Nature of Publicity
Sony (Japan)	Hackers attacked PlayStation online gaming network, compromising user data.
BP (Great Britain)	Massive oil spill in the Gulf of Mexico off the coast of Louisiana.
Apple (United States)	Suicides by employees at Chinese supplier Foxconn Technologies; injuries due to exposure to toxic chemicals at plant that makes glass screens for iPhone.
Google (United States)	Self-censorship of Chinese search engine.
Toyota (Japan)	Massive product recalls and quality issues.
Nike (United States)	Since the mid-1990s, Nike has been responding to the criticism that its subcontractors operate factories in which sweatshop conditions prevail. Filmmaker Michael Moore featured an interview with Nike CEO Phil Knight in the antiglobalization documentary *The Big One*.

advertising. However, unlike regular advertising, the objective of corporate advertising is not to generate demand by informing, persuading, entertaining, or reminding customers. In the context of integrated marketing communications, corporate advertising is often used to call attention to the company's other communications efforts. In addition to the examples discussed in the following pages, Table 13-4 summarizes several instances of global publicity involving well-known firms.

Image advertising enhances the public's perception of a company; creates goodwill; or announces a major change, such as a merger, acquisition, or divestiture. In 2008, for example, Anheuser-Busch InBev placed full-page ads in the business press to announce their merger. Global companies frequently use image advertising in an effort to present themselves as good corporate citizens in foreign countries. BASF uses advertising to raise awareness about the company's innovative products that are used in the automotive, home construction, and pharmaceutical industries. Similarly, a campaign from Daimler AG announced an eco-friendly

Exhibit 13-5 Daimler AG is one of the world's leading producers of diesel automobiles. This corporate image advertisement is not about the company's cars per se; rather, it is about the company's ongoing efforts to create more eco-friendly diesel fuels to power its cars.

The ad positions Daimler both as an innovator and as a responsible corporate citizen. Because the message and the associated image have worldwide appeal, this ad lends itself to an extension strategy.

Source: Courtesy of Daimler Corporation.

fuel called Sun Diesel (see Exhibit 13-5). In **advocacy advertising**, a company presents its point of view on a particular issue. Consider the following examples of advocacy advertising:

- Japan's Fuji Photo Film asked its advertising agency to develop an advocacy campaign for the United States. At the time, Fuji was embroiled in a trade dispute with Kodak. Fuji had also invested more than $1 billion in U.S. production facilities and had won a long-term photofinishing contract with Walmart. The campaign was designed to appeal both to Walmart and to the giant retailer's customers; as a Walmart spokesman said, "We've long said we buy American when we can. The more people understand how American Fuji is, the better."[37]
- In 1995, the American International Automobile Dealers Association (AIADA) hired Hill & Knowlton to create a PR campaign designed to convince then-President Bill Clinton, Congress, the media, and the general public that a proposed plan to impose a 100 percent tariff on 13 luxury cars was ill-advised. The campaign's central message was that foreign automakers account for a good number of U.S. jobs that would be jeopardized if the sanctions were enacted. Nissan and other companies also sent position papers and information packets to dealers and the media. Interviews with representatives from auto dealers were carried by both print and electronic media. Within a few weeks, the Clinton administration announced that the United States and Japan had reached an agreement. No sanctions were imposed, and the AIADA was able to claim an important PR victory.

Sometimes a company generates publicity simply by going about the business of global marketing activities. As noted in Table 13-4, Nike and other marketers have received a great deal of negative publicity regarding alleged sweatshop conditions in factories run by subcontractors. Today, Nike's PR team is doing a better job of counteracting the criticism by effectively communicating the positive economic impact Nike has had on the nations where it manufactures its sneakers (see Exhibit 13-6).

Any company that is increasing its activities outside the home country can utilize PR personnel as boundary spanners between the company and employees, unions, stockholders, customers, the media, financial analysts, governments, or suppliers. Many companies have their own in-house PR staff. Companies may also choose to engage the services of an outside PR firm. During the past few years, some of the large advertising holding companies discussed previously have acquired PR agencies. For example, Omnicom Group bought Fleishman-Hillard, WPP

Exhibit 13-6 When making public appearances, Nike chairman Phil Knight and other executives frequently defend labor practices and policies in the Asian factories where the company's shoes are made. In the late 1990s, a protester filed a lawsuit against Nike alleging that the company's public assertions about working conditions constituted false advertising. Attorneys for Nike argued that statements made by executives constitute free commercial speech, are part of a public policy debate, and are protected by the First Amendment. *Source:* Chuck Kennedy/ Newscom.

---

[37]Wendy Bounds, "Fuji Considers National Campaign to Develop All-American Image," *The Wall Street Journal* (October 1, 1996), p. B8.

Group acquired Canada's Hill & Knowlton, and Interpublic Group bought Golin/Harris International. Other PR firms, including the London-based Shandwick PLC and Edelman Public Relations Worldwide, are independent. Several independent PR firms in the United Kingdom, Germany, Italy, Spain, Austria, and the Netherlands have joined together in a network known as Globalink. The purpose of the network is to provide members with various forms of assistance such as press contacts, event planning, literature design, and suggestions for tailoring global campaigns to local needs in a particular country or region.[38]

The Growing Role of PR in Global Marketing Communications

Public relations professionals with international responsibility must go beyond media relations and serve as more than a company mouthpiece; they are called upon to simultaneously build consensus and understanding, create trust and harmony, articulate and influence public opinion, anticipate conflicts, and resolve disputes.[39] As companies become more involved in global marketing and the globalization of industries continues, company management must recognize the value of international PR. Today the industry faces a challenging business environment with a mixture of threats and opportunities. Many PR firms saw revenues and profits decline in 2009 as a result of the global recession. At the same time, the recession has also increased the demand for PR services. Edelman Worldwide chief Richard Edelman recently noted that PR's status as a key input to corporate decision making has been improving. Edelman says, "We used to be the tail on the dog."[40]

Europe has a longstanding PR tradition; for example, the Deutsche Public Relations Gesellschaft (DPRG) recently commemorated its 50th anniversary. Many European PR practitioners and trade associations, including the DPRG, are members of the Confédération Européenne des Relations Publiques (www.cerp.org). The UK-based International Public Relations Association (www.ipra.org) has an Arabic Web site, an illustration of the way PR's importance is recognized in all parts of the world. An important factor fueling the growth of international PR is increased governmental relations between countries. Governments, organizations, and societies are dealing with broad-based issues of mutual concern, such as the global recession, trade relations, the environment, and world peace. The technology-driven communication revolution that has ushered in the Information Age makes public relations a profession with truly global reach. Smartphones, broadband Internet connectivity, social media, satellite links, and other channel innovations allow PR professionals to be in contact with media virtually anywhere in the world.

In spite of these technological advances, PR professionals must still build good personal working relationships with journalists and other media representatives, as well as with leaders of other primary constituencies. Therefore, strong interpersonal skills are needed. One of the most basic concepts of the practice of PR is to know the audience. For the global PR practitioner, this means knowing the audiences in both the home country and the host country or countries. Specific skills needed include the ability to communicate in the language of the host country and familiarity with local customs. A PR professional who is unable to speak the language of the host country will be unable to communicate directly with a huge portion of an essential audience. Likewise, the PR professional working outside the home country must be sensitive to nonverbal communication issues in order to maintain good working relationships with host-country nationals. Commenting on the complexity of the international PR professional's job, one expert notes that, in general, audiences are "increasingly more unfamiliar and more hostile, as well as more organized and powerful . . . more demanding, more skeptical and more diverse." International PR practitioners can play an important role as "bridges over the shrinking chasm of the global village."[41]

How PR Practices Differ Around the World

Cultural traditions, social and political contexts, and economic environments in specific countries can affect public relations practices. As noted earlier in the chapter, the mass media and the written word are important vehicles for information dissemination in many industrialized countries.

---

[38]Joe Mullich, "European Firms Seek Alliances for Global PR," *Business Marketing* 79 (August 1994), pp. 4, 31.
[39]Karl Nessman, "Public Relations in Europe: A Comparison with the United States," *Public Relations Journal* 21, no. 2 (Summer 1995), p. 154.
[40]"Good News: Other Firms' Suffering Has Bolstered the PR Business," *Economist* (January 14, 2010).
[41]Larissa A. Grunig, "Strategic Public Relations Constituencies on a Global Scale," *Public Relations Review* 18, no. 2 (Summer 1992), pp. 127–136.

In developing countries, however, the best way to communicate might be through the gong man, the town crier, the market square, or the chief's courts. In Ghana, dance, songs, and storytelling are important communication channels. In India, where half of the population cannot read, writing press releases will not be the most effective way to communicate.[42] In Turkey, the practice of PR is thriving in spite of that country's reputation for harsh treatment of political prisoners. Although the Turkish government still asserts absolute control as it has for generations, corporate PR and journalism are allowed to flourish so that Turkish organizations can compete globally.

Even in industrialized countries, PR practices differ. In the United States, the hometown news release comprises much of the news in a small, local newspaper. In Canada, in contrast, large metropolitan population centers have combined with Canadian economic and climatic conditions to thwart the emergence of a local press. The dearth of small newspapers means that the practice of sending out hometown news releases is almost nonexistent.[43] In the United States, PR is increasingly viewed as a separate management function. In Europe, this perspective has not been widely accepted; PR professionals are viewed as part of the marketing function rather than as distinct and separate specialists in a company. In Europe, fewer colleges and universities offer courses and degree programs in public relations than in the United States. Also, European coursework in public relations is more theoretical; in the United States, PR programs are often part of mass communication or journalism schools and there is more emphasis on practical job skills.

A company that is ethnocentric in its approach to public relations will extend home-country PR activities into host countries. The rationale behind this approach is that people everywhere are motivated and persuaded in much the same manner. This approach does not take cultural considerations into account. A company adopting a polycentric approach to PR gives the host-country practitioner more leeway to incorporate local customs and practices into the PR effort. Although such an approach has the advantage of local responsiveness, the lack of global communication and coordination can lead to a PR disaster.[44]

The ultimate test of an organization's understanding of the power and importance of public relations occurs during a time of environmental turbulence, especially a potential or actual crisis. When disaster strikes, a company or industry often finds itself thrust into the spotlight. A company's swift and effective handling of communications during such times can have significant implications. The best response is to be forthright and direct, reassure the public, and provide the media with accurate information.

China's ongoing trade-related friction with its trading partners highlights the need for a better PR effort on the part of the Chinese Foreign Ministry. Some sources of this friction have been discussed in earlier chapters, such as estimates that Chinese counterfeiting of copyrighted material costs foreign companies billions of dollars annually or that 98 percent of the computer software used in China is pirated. Such revelations reflect poorly on China. As Hong Kong businessman Barry C. Cheung noted in the mid-1990s, "China lacks skills in public relations generally and crisis management specifically, and that hurts them."[45] Part of the problem stems from the unwillingness of China's Communist leaders to publicly explain their views on these issues, to admit failure, and to accept advice from the West.

Summary

Marketing communications—the promotion *P* of the marketing mix—includes advertising, public relations, sales promotion, and personal selling. When a company embraces **integrated marketing communications (IMC)**, it recognizes that the various elements of a company's communication strategy must be carefully coordinated. **Advertising** is a sponsored, paid message that is communicated through nonpersonal channels. **Global advertising** consists of the same advertising appeals, messages, artwork, and copy in campaigns around the world.

[42]Carl Botan, "International Public Relations: Critique and Reformulation," *Public Relations Review* 18, no. 2 (Summer 1992), pp. 150–151.

[43]Melvin L. Sharpe, "The Impact of Social and Cultural Conditioning on Global Public Relations," *Public Relations Review* 18, no. 2 (Summer 1992), pp. 103–107.

[44]Carl Botan, "International Public Relations: Critique and Reformulation," *Public Relations Review* 18, no. 2 (Summer 1992), p. 155.

[45]Marcus W. Brauchli, "A Change of Face: China Has Surly Image, but Part of the Reason Is Bad Public Relations," *The Wall Street Journal* (June 16, 1996), p. A1.

The effort required to create a global campaign forces a company to determine whether or not a global market exists for its product or brand. The trade-off between standardized and adapted advertising is often accomplished by means of **pattern advertising**, which can be used to create localized global advertising. Many advertising agencies are part of larger **advertising organizations**. Advertisers may place a single global agency in charge of worldwide advertising; it is also possible to use one or more agencies on a regional or local basis.

The starting point in ad development is the **creative strategy**, a statement of what the message will say. The people who create ads often seek a **big idea** that can serve as the basis for memorable, effective messages. The **advertising appeal** is the communication approach—rational or emotional—that best relates to buyer motives. **Rational appeals** speak to the mind; **emotional appeals** speak to the heart. The **selling proposition** is the promise that captures the reason for buying the product. The **creative execution** is the way an appeal or proposition is presented. **Art direction** and **copy** must be created with cultural considerations in mind. Perceptions of humor, male–female relationships, and sexual imagery vary in different parts of the world. Media availability varies considerably from country to country. When selecting media, marketers are sometimes as constrained by laws and regulations as by literacy rates.

A company utilizes **public relations (PR)** to foster goodwill and understanding among constituents both inside and outside the company. In particular, the PR department attempts to generate favorable **publicity** about the company and its products and brands. The PR department must also manage corporate communications when responding to negative publicity. Important PR tools include interviews, media kits, press releases, social media, and tours. Many global companies make use of various types of **corporate advertising**, including **image advertising** and **advocacy advertising**. Public relations is also responsible for providing accurate, timely information, especially in the event of a crisis.

Discussion Questions

1. In what ways can global brands and global advertising campaigns benefit a company?
2. How does the "standardized versus localized" debate apply to advertising?
3. What is the difference between an advertising appeal and creative execution?
4. Starting with Chapter 1, review the ads that appear in this text. Can you identify ads that use emotional appeals? Rational appeals? What is the communication task of each ad? To inform? To persuade? To remind? To entertain?
5. When creating advertising for world markets, what are some of the issues that art directors and copywriters should take into account?
6. How do the media options available to advertisers vary in different parts of the world? What can advertisers do to cope with media limitations in certain countries?
7. How does public relations differ from advertising? Why is public relations especially important for global companies?
8. What are some of the ways PR practices vary in different parts of the world?

CASE 13-1 CONTINUED (REFER TO PAGE 406)

The BP Oil Spill: The Assignment

BP was not the only global company with a PR problem in 2010. Japanese automaker Toyota found itself under fire for quality issues, and Wall Street investment firm Goldman Sachs was fined more than $500 million for securities fraud. As PR specialist Howard Rubenstein noted, "These were real reputational implosions. In all three cases, the companies found themselves under attack over the very traits that were central to their strong global brands and corporate identities."

BP chief executive Tony Hayward became a lightning rod for America's anger and frustration about the spill. At times, Hayward appeared in public in pinstriped suits; his attire was in stark contrast to the overalls worn by shrimp-boat operators and others whose livelihoods were threatened by the spill. Some of Hayward's public statements appeared insensitive. For example, *The Guardian*, a British newspaper, quoted him as saying, "The Gulf of Mexico is a very big ocean. The amount of oil and the volume of dispersant we are putting into it is tiny in relation to the total water volume." Critics also pilloried Hayward for two other statements he made during a television interview. "There's no one who wants this thing over more than I do," he said. "I want my life back."

Some industry observers wondered whether the rhetoric directed against BP was motivated in part by the perception that the company is British. Global companies must ensure that they have successfully positioned themselves as diverse entities with representation from the various markets in which they have operations. As brand consultant Wally Olins noted, the BP disaster "shows you need people at, or near, the top of the business who can speak the language and use the style of the countries in which they operate." In this regard, many observers agreed that both BP and Hayward himself came up short.

Crisis management practitioners are in wide agreement that in times of crisis it is imperative for company spokespersons to tell the truth and to take responsibility. Failure to do so can result in lost credibility. Rubenstein is especially critical of BP in this regard. The company's early assessment of the spill was that very little oil was leaking into the Gulf; these reports were contradicted by estimates from specialists outside BP. Also, BP tried to pin blame for the blowout on contactors. Rubenstein said, "It was one of the worst PR approaches I've seen in my 56 years of business. They tried to be opaque. They had every excuse in the book. Right away they should have accepted responsibility and recognized what a disaster they faced. They basically thought they could spin their way out of catastrophe. It doesn't work that way."

Another point of view is that some corporate crises are so monumental that traditional PR approaches will simply not suffice. Eric Dezenhall is a communications strategist who holds this view. According to Dezenhall, BP's attempts to win over the American public were bound to be futile as long as the oil was leaking. Dezenhall says, "Two things that are very hard to survive are hypocrisy and ridicule. It's the height of arrogance to assume that in the middle of a crisis the public yearns for chestnuts of wisdom from people they want to kill. The goal is not to get people not to hate them. It's to get people to hate them less."

Hoping to regain some credibility in Washington, BP assembled a team of consultants and lobbyists to help it prepare for congressional testimony and respond to government inquiries. The team included James Lee Witt, former director of the Federal Emergency Management Agency (FEMA). BP also tapped Hilary Rosen, a partner in the Brunswick Group public relations firm, for assistance. Some observers were dismayed that people with political connections would agree to be on BP's payroll. Robert Weissman, president of the Public Citizen Action Network, asked, "Do these people go to bed at night and think, 'I hope I get to wake up in the morning and represent a corporate criminal?'" In response to such criticism, Donna Brazile, a Democratic strategist, noted, "This is an enormous challenge and it doesn't matter who they hire to contain the spill, clean up the mess and compensate those who have lost so much."

Although the crippled well was finally shut down in August 2010, BP faces the prospect of criminal and civil suits that will likely keep the company in court for many years. For example, the U.S. government could prosecute BP for violating the Clean Water Act or the Refuse Act. Also, because the spill coincided with spawning and nesting season for the Gulf's wildlife, the Migratory Bird Treaty Act could also be the basis for legal action. Thousands of private lawsuits are also pending. BP has established a $20 billion compensation fund; BP's lawyers hope that individuals whose livelihoods were harmed by the spill will apply to the fund rather than go to court. Finally, there is the prospect of shareholder suits from investors who have seen the value of their BP holdings plummet in the wake of the crisis.

Discussion Questions

1. Some industry observers think that BP should not have spent money on print and TV ads to reassure the American public. Do you agree or disagree? Explain.
2. On October 1, 2010, an American, Bob Dudley, replaced Tony Hayward as chief executive of BP. Does this change surprise you?
3. How might the advice from BP's lawyers differ from the advice BP receives from PR professionals?
4. What factor(s) will affect whether BP's corporate reputation can be repaired?

Sources: Peter S. Goodman, "In Case of Emergency: What Not to Do," *The New York Times* (August 22, 2010), p. C1; Michael Peel, "Eagles and Vultures," *Financial Times* (July 2, 2010), p. 5; Mimi Hall, "BP Enlists Washington Elite to Help Image," *USA Today* (July 1, 2010); Morgen Witzel and Ravi Mattu, "The Perils of a Tarnished Brand," *Financial Times* (June 23, 2010); Stefan Stern, "Can Too Strong a National Identity Harm the Business?" *Financial Times* (June 16, 2010), p. 10; Ed Crooks, "BP's Disaster Manager," *Financial Times* (May 1–2, 2010), p. 7.

CASE 13-2
Marketing Pepsi's New Healthy Option in the United Kingdom

In February 2008, PepsiCo launched its new healthy option, Pepsi Raw, in the United Kingdom. PepsiCo states that the product is made from natural ingredients and contains no artificial preservatives, colorings, flavorings, or sweeteners. In 2009, Pepsi Natural, which is almost identical to Pepsi Raw, was launched in the United States.

The launch of Pepsi Raw was a major move, because it was the first time that PepsiCo had added a new drink to its product line in more than 10 years. PepsiCo claims that by simply replacing the high fructose corn syrup with cane sugar it has been able to drive down the calorie content of a 300-milliliter bottle from 120 calories to around 90. Traditional Pepsi uses high fructose corn syrup, artificial flavorings, caffeine, citric acid, phosphoric acid, and natural flavorings. Pepsi Raw, in contrast, is formulated from apple extract, caramel coloring, coffee leaf, tartaric acid from grapes, cane sugar, gum Arabic from acacia trees, and sparkling water. The two major differences between the Pepsi Raw and regular Pepsi is that Pepsi Raw is paler and less fizzy. Pepsi claims that it is offering the drink in response to consumer demand for a premium, yet more natural, soft drink.

Initially, Pepsi Raw was launched in bars and clubs. The venues were carefully selected in seven cities: London, Manchester, Glasgow, Brighton, Birmingham, Leeds, and Liverpool. After the

PepsiCo and Coca-Cola are the two cola market leaders in the United Kingdom with a combined market share of 60 percent. Each time one of them launches a new inititative or product line, the other counters it to retain its market position.
Source: © Irochka.

success of the initial launch, the product was rolled out across the UK. PepsiCo focused its national launch of the new brand in up-market chains such as Waitrose, supported by sampling and promotional activity. Its launch in the larger retail market was supported by a $2.4 million integrated campaign created by Abbott Mead Vickers BBDO.

One of the innovative ideas used in marketing the new product was the inclusion of a Twitter tag on Pepsi Raw cans. In a message on the can, consumers were invited to log on to the microblogging Web site and share their thoughts on the soda in 140 characters or less. The Twitter campaign was launched in May 2008. The @PepsiRaw campaign was part of a major sampling drive, which included 1.4 million cans across the United Kingdom. The idea was created by the digital agency Graphico DMG. The purpose of the initiative, which also featured a Pepsi Raw Facebook page, was to increase PepsiCo's dialogue with consumers. The Facebook page featured a competition and downloadable coupons. By early June 2008, Pepsi Raw had attracted 150 Twitter fans (and more than 1,000 by November 2009) and 1,250 Facebook fans (and nearly 2,000 by November 2009). Over 95 percent of the Pepsi Raw tweets were positive.

For its conventional print advertising campaign, Pepsi Raw used the concept of "stripped-back cola," showing naked people in front of a cityscape. On city buses, the advertising featured the tagline "Natural Born Cola."

Pepsi Raw is targeted at a sophisticated urban market and was created to provide consumers with a choice of premium cola, complementing the existing PepsiCo range with a more subtle-tasting cola and distinctive brand image. Graphico DMG was given a clear brief, with Pepsi Raw positioned as a "stripped back" cola. PepsiCo wanted Graphica DMG to make that proposition live and breathe online. The agency's solution was to dovetail the campaign with the fact that the product was going to be introduced to consumers in a limited number of bars and clubs in the United Kingdom. The agency created a Web site that started with a visually appealing short film that could also be run in the bars and clubs. The film was, in fact, an animated dance sequence. Everything in the film was stripped back to the essentials to mirror the product. Bar codes of light suggested dancing figures; the idea was to challenge the viewer to fill in the gaps in what they were seeing. The film was shot using technology more closely associated with sports science. The dancers wore reflective nodes, which were picked up by the cameras. Each of the nodes was triangulated, meaning that the movement of the dancers rather than the dancers themselves was recorded in 3D. Animators then worked to create the bodies of the dancers and inserted a light source.

Packaging was another key issue. The packaging was designed to complement Pepsi Raw as a natural, up-market drink. A glass bottle with an old-fashioned crimped crown cap was used. The packaging was received positively, so much so that it helped to accelerate the rollout to the home market.

The UK cola market is estimated to be worth more than $9.7 billion per year. The market is dominated by Coca-Cola and PepsiCo, who have been fierce rivals for more than a hundred years. Coca-Cola remains the most valuable grocery brand in the United Kingdom. In the UK, PepsiCo's sales revenue from its cola beverages rose from $349 million in 2006 to $410 million in 2008, increasing its market share from 11 percent to 12 percent. Coca-Cola saw its sales revenues rise from $1,520 billion in 2006 to $1,575 billion in 2008, increasing its market share from 47 percent to 48 percent.

Advertising spending is not necessarily the only reason behind the disparity in the sales and market share of Coca-Cola compared to PepsiCo. However, in 2008 Coca-Cola spent nearly $57 million on advertising in the United Kingdom. Over the same period, PepsiCo spent just under $18 million.

The two cola giants seem set for another major advertising and marketing war, this time in the natural sugar market. In 2008, just as PepsiCo was launching Pepsi Raw, Coca-Cola announced a partnership with U.S. conglomerate Cargill to create a stevia-based product called Truvia. PepsiCo beat its rival to market with its version, PureVia. Both are based on stevia, an all-natural, plant-based sweetener, which is some 300 times sweeter than sugar. According to Lou Imbrogno, the senior vice president of Pepsi Worldwide Technical Operations, its version is more natural and extracted from the stevia plant leaf and is not synthetic in any way. Both companies believe that this is the way forward for artificial sweeteners.

Each new product launch and advertising campaign simply reignites the so-called "Cola Wars" between the two main cola producers, and Pepsi Raw is just the latest move in this hundred-year battle for dominance.

Discussion Questions

1. Why might PepsiCo be willing to launch this brand in the United Kingdom rather than its home market, the United States?
2. Why was the positioning and ultimately the correct choice of advertising so important to this product's success?
3. To what extent might it be the case that PepsiCo's relative sales turnover and market share is simply a reflection of its relatively small advertising budget compared to its larger rival, Coca-Cola?

Sources: Graphico New Media Limited, Digital Marketing Group plc., www.graphicodmg. co.uk (accessed December 26, 2011); Britvic, www.britvic.com (accessed December 26, 2011); PepsiCo, www.pepsi.co.uk (accessed December 26, 2011); Pepsi Raw, www. pepsiraw.co.uk (accessed December 26, 2011).

CHAPTER 10

Organisation and Role of Public Relations

CHAPTER 1

Lee Edwards

Public relations origins:
definitions and history

Learning outcomes

By the end of this chapter you should be able to:

■ identify the key definitions of public relations used in practice today

■ recognise the debates around the nature of public relations and what it means

■ understand the origins of public relations in the science of public opinion

■ describe the key features of the history of public relations in the United States, Britain and Germany

■ understand the social and cultural dynamics that led to the emergence of the profession in these countries.

Structure

■ Public relations definitions

■ Public opinion: justifying public relations

■ Business, politics and public relations: country case studies

Introduction

What is public relations (PR)? And when did PR begin? This chapter briefly reviews why it has proved so difficult to define PR work or reach a universally agreed definition of what the job entails. It then outlines what is known about the emergence of PR as a modern occupation, drawing primarily on the histories of the United States, Britain and Germany (further references to the European evolution are discussed in Chapter 7). The discussion of both definitions and histories reflects the social nature of the profession; PR is a product of the economic and political circumstances of its time and evolves according to the needs of these broader environments. At the same time, its historical ties to advertising and propaganda continue to provide fertile ground for debate about its ethical and professional merit (see Chapters 3 and 15).

PR is now a global occupation and implemented in many corners of the world in different ways. However, written histories of PR reflect the dominance of the United States on the academic field of public relations and tend to focus on its origins in the United States rather than in other countries (McKie and Munshi 2007). Exceptions include the comprehensive account of PR in Britain by Jacquie L'Etang (L'Etang 2004b), discussed in this chapter and *The Global Public Relations Handbook* (Sriramesh and Verčič 2003), which offers a range of 'potted' histories of PR in a number of countries. Moreover, and as L'Etang (2004b) points out, despite the current dominance of women in the profession (see Chapter 3), written histories tend to be his-stories, delivered through the eyes of the men who were at the top of the profession during its emergence. Women who worked in PR in its early years would in all probability have taken a different view of developments. These issues should be taken into account when reading this chapter. There is much still to be said and understood about the emergence of this modern-day profession (see also Chapter 3).

Public relations definitions

Public relations (PR) is used in a huge range of industries and in each one slightly different skills and competencies have emerged among practitioners. As a result, there is no one universally agreed definition of PR (Grunig 1992; L'Etang 1996; White and Mazur 1996; Moloney 2000). The likelihood is that if you ask three practitioners and three academics to define PR, all six answers will be different in some way. In part, this is because the profession is still young. It certainly gives lots of scope for debate, as described in the following section, which outlines some of the most common views of PR among academics and practitioners (Cutlip et al. 2006). See Activity 1.1.

Academic definitions of public relations

Harlow (1976) found 472 different definitions of PR coined between 1900 and 1976. He built his own definition from these findings, offering:

> *Public relations is a distinctive management function which helps establish and maintain mutual lines of communication, understanding, acceptance and cooperation between an organisation and its publics; involves the management of problems or issues; helps management to*

Activity 1.1

Defining public relations

With a group of friends, write down your definition of PR. Now think about how you arrived at that definition:

- Is it based on your experience of PR and what you observe PR practitioners doing?

- Is it based on what you read about PR in the newspapers?

- Is it based on what your tutors have told you about PR?

Now compare your definitions:

- How different are they?

- What do they have in common?

- What are the differences and why do you think they exist?

Each of you will have different thoughts about what should and should not be included in the definition. See if you can agree on a common set of ideas, then test them on other friends and see how far they agree or disagree.

Picture 1.1 This chapter will consider the historical evolution of public relations and its practice. Debates continue as to whether this should include press agents such as the UK's well-known publicist Max Clifford (*source*: David Dyson/Camera Press)

keep informed on and responsive to public opinions; defines and emphasises the responsibility of management to serve the public interest; helps management keep abreast of and effectively utilise change; serving as an early warning system to help anticipate trends; and uses research and ethical communication techniques as its principal tools. (Harlow 1976: 36)

This definition contains overall goals, processes and tasks of PR, and positions the profession firmly within the organisation, as a management role. It covers most aspects of PR, but is somewhat long-winded and other researchers have tried to simplify things by separating tasks from strategy.

Grunig and Hunt (1984: 6), for example, went to the opposite extreme from Harlow and defined PR in one sentence as 'the management of communication between an organisation and its publics', which Grunig later

refined as 'an organisation's managed communications behaviour' (Grunig 1997, cited in Grunig, Grunig and Dozier 2006: 23). Grunig (1992) argues that this definition allows for differences in practice between practitioners in different contexts, but still includes important elements, such as the management of communication and the focus on external relationships. Kitchen (1997) is even briefer with his definition, suggesting that PR can be defined as 'communication with various publics', although he does add to this by arguing that PR is an important management function and has a strategic role to play.

Other definitions focus on 'ideal' communications practices: two-way communications and building positive relationships between organisations and their publics. Some include its strategic importance to organisations and recognise its influence on reputation (Hutton 1999; Grunig and Grunig 2000). Cutlip et al. (2000: 6) combine these aspects and suggest: 'Public relations is the management function that establishes and maintains mutually beneficial relationships between an organization and the publics on whom its success or failure depends.'

White and Mazur (1996: 11) offer a definition based on the goals of PR: 'To influence the behaviour of groups of people in relation to each other. Influence should be exerted through dialogue – not monologue – with all the different corporate audiences, with public relations becoming a respected function in its own right, acting as a strategic resource and helping to implement corporate strategy.'

Key debates on definitions

All these definitions highlight the fact that PR is about managing communication in order to build good relationships and mutual understanding between an organisation and its most important audiences (Gordon 1997). However, it is important to recognise that they do incorporate underlying assumptions that presume its main function is to promote the organisation's interests, and some writers have objected to this. Botan and Hazelton (1989), for example, argue that such definitions tend to present a view of PR as a neutral communications channel and only partially reflect actual practice, in which the main job of a PR officer is to manipulate public opinion for the benefit of organisations. McKie and Munshi (2007) echo this view and argue that the idea of PR as a profession overemphasises the organisational and technical aspects of PR work, with the desired outcomes of status, professional 'territory' and financial reward all serving to de-prioritise the interests of less advantaged social groups.

If we look at the views of PR held by the general public, most people think of PR as a means by which people are persuaded to think or behave in a particular way (Kitchen 1997; Cutlip et al. 2006). Botan and Hazelton (1989), Kitchen (1997) and Cutlip et al. (2006) all emphasise that popular usage of the term PR is often a synonym for deception and that everyday understanding of PR is usually determined by the visible results of PR activity (e.g. media coverage). However, the idea of *persuasion* has been left out of academic definitions, despite recognition of its importance in the profession's history, as we will see later in this chapter (see also Chapter 13 for further explorations of persuasion). Some academics point this out and argue that we should explicitly recognise the fact that PR is biased in favour of commercial interests. They define PR in terms of its social effects. L'Etang (1996), for example, suggests that the narrow focus of traditional definitions, which begin and end with the interests of the organisation, blinds practitioners and academics to the social and political costs and benefits of PR.

Moloney (2000: 6) agrees with L'Etang that PR is too multifaceted to be incorporated into a single definition, but that its effect on society demands extensive investigation regardless. His view is that PR is about power and 'manipulation against democracy' (p. 65) because it is so often used to support government and commercial interests at the expense of other interests. In so far as he uses definitions, he suggests that PR can be defined differently as a 'concept' ('communications management by an organisation with its publics'), as a practice ('mostly dealing with the media') and in terms of its effects on society ('a category of persuasive communications done through the mass media or through private lobbying by groups to advance their material or ideological interests'). See Activity 1.2.

Definitions are important because they shape people's expectations of what PR could or should be about. If they overemphasise the interests of organisations over individuals, or the privileged over the less powerful, then

Activity 1.2

Key debates

Why do you think academics disagree about definitions of PR? Is it because they don't understand PR or because they have different views about its contribution to society? Summarise, in your own words, the key debates between different PR definitions. How would you explain these definitions to your friends and family?

Activity 1.3

Public relations and social awareness raising

The journey of the Olympic Torch to Beijing in 2008 was marked by pro-Tibet protests in every major city, aimed at highlighting China's human rights abuses in Tibet. Look up references to the 'Olympic Torch Relay 2008' on the Internet. How much of the coverage was about the torch's journey and how much comment was made about China's activities in Tibet? Based on this, how successful do you think the protestors were at raising the issue of Tibet's human rights in the context of the Olympics?

people will assume that PR can serve only these interests. In fact, while privileged groups may be able to invest more resources in public relations, there are many examples of public relations strategies being applied effectively by 'minority' groups or individuals to challenge governments and corporations. When considering public relations, then, your definition should recognise the breadth of possible contexts for activity and recognise the social benefits of PR as a tool to increase discussion about matters that might otherwise be ignored. See Activity 1.3.

Practitioner definitions of public relations

Practitioner definitions of PR tend to be more based in the reality of the day-to-day job, often use the term 'public relations' interchangeably with other terms such as organisational communication or corporate communication (Grunig 1992; Hutton 1999) and often include concepts of persuasion and influence. Grunig, Grunig and Dozier (2006) acknowledge that many practitioners still associate PR with media relations, although some do recognise its potential as a management function guiding interaction with publics. You could argue that this kind of flexibility means simply that practitioners have difficulty explaining exactly what their job entails – and indeed, this seems to be the case.

In 1978, the First World Assembly of Public Relations Associations in Mexico defined PR as 'the art and social science of analyzing trends, predicting their consequences, counselling organizational leaders, and implementing planned programs of action which will serve both the

Picture 1.2 The 1978 'Mexican Statement' has defined public relations as 'the art and social science of analyzing trends, predicting their consequences, counselling organizational leaders, and implementing planned programs of action which will serve both the organization and the public interest' (*source*: Jon Arnold Images/Alamy)

organization and the public interest' (Newsom et al. 2000: 2). The definition offered by the Public Relations Society of America, coined in 1988, is similarly broad: 'Public relations helps an organization and its publics adapt mutually to each other' (Public Relations Society of America 2004).

More recent definitions have been more detailed. In a survey by the former Department of Trade and Industry (DTI) and the UK Chartered Institute of Public Relations (CIPR), PR was defined as 'influencing behaviour to achieve objectives through the effective management of relationships and communications' (Department of Trade and Industry and Institute of Public Relations 2003: 10). This definition is an attempt to combine the idea of managed communications with exercising influence on relationships and achieving mutual understanding, to incorporate as broad a range of activity as possible.

The CIPR defines PR as: 'About reputation – the result of what you do, what you say and what others say about you. Public relations is the discipline which looks after reputation, with the aim of earning understanding and support and influencing opinion and behaviour. It is the planned and sustained effort to establish and maintain goodwill and mutual understanding between an organisation and its publics' (Institute of Public Relations 2004).

Some practitioners disagree with this definition because it leads with the concept of reputation and they do not believe this is the primary focus for PR programmes. However, the Public Relations Consultants Association (PRCA) in the UK has also adopted the CIPR definition for use by its members (Public Relations Consultants Association 2004) and it is included in some UK-based text and practitioner books on PR (e.g. Gregory 1996; Harrison 2000; Genasi 2002). Given this consistency, we can assume that this formal definition is the one most regularly referred to by practitioners in the UK (see Think about 1.1).

Think about 1.1   **Academics vs practitioners**

Academics and practitioners have come up with very different definitions of PR. From the summary above, consider the following questions with a group of friends:

- What are the main differences between the definitions of academics and practitioners?

- Why do you think such differences exist?

- Is there a right or wrong definition? If so, why?

- Which definition do you think is most appropriate for PR and why?

Feedback

Consider the interests of the people creating the definitions. For example, are they trying to build theories about how PR works or are they trying to simply describe what it does? Who is the audience for the definition and how might the audience affect what is included?

Public opinion: justifying public relations

The practice of using communication to influence the public is hundreds of years old, with its roots in ancient civilisations, including the Greek and Roman Empires. Throughout history, governments, monarchs and powerful institutions such as the Roman Catholic Church have used communication and information to generate support for their cause among the populace (Grunig and Hunt 1984; Cutlip et al. 2006). But it was the emergence of the concept of public opinion that eventually formed the scientific justification for using PR and communications techniques in this way.

Nowadays, the term public opinion is used frequently in the media, by government and by PR practitioners almost without thinking. However, as it emerged from the philosophical traditions of the eighteenth and nineteenth centuries, it was a hotly debated topic and the context in which it is used today only emerged in the early years of the twentieth century. The concept of public opinion became relevant in the mid-eighteenth century, accompanying the emergence of fledgling democratic states. Rousseau, the French philosopher, is generally credited with first coining the term, in 1744, and its use quickly became more extensive as discussions continued about how democracies should and could incorporate the views of the populations they were supposed to govern (Price 1992).

Two basic conceptions of public opinion have dominated the evolution of the term: public opinion as an abstract, *collective view*, emerging through rational discussion of issues in the population; and public opinion as an *aggregate view*, the sum total of individual opinions of the population governed by the democratic state (Pieczka

1996). There are limitations to both these views – for example, who is included in, and who is excluded from, the term 'public'? To what extent does the rational debate required for the 'collective' view really take place and does everyone have equal access to the debate? If not, then 'public opinion' may only be the view of a select number of individuals who bother to engage in discussions. Alternatively, if public opinion is interpreted as an aggregate of individual opinions, then what happens to minority views that are swamped by majority concerns? Where do they find expression?

Many writers have expressed concern about the inherent nature of the individual – more interested in, and persuaded by, emotional arguments and events than logic and politics. If the democratic state is supposed to take public opinion as its guide for what is important to the population, then an emotional public is not necessarily going to provide the best information. Finally, researchers on public opinion in the twentieth century expressed reservations about the ability of the public to understand the complexities of modern democracies and argued that it was the job of communications channels such as the media to simplify politics and government so that the public could understand matters of importance to them (Lippmann 1922).

The end of the nineteenth and turn of the twentieth century saw a rise in interest in the social and behavioural characteristics driving publics and public opinion, while philosophical debates took a back seat. Particularly important in this development was the emergence of social research techniques – and in particular survey research – that enabled 'public opinion' on particular issues to be defined and quantified. This also resulted in the gradual dominance of the aggregate view of public opinion over the collective view (researching an abstract concept on the basis of concrete individual opinions made no scientific

Activity 1.4

Surveys and public opinion

PR practitioners often use surveys as a means of making a particular topic newsworthy. For example, you might see an article announcing the latest findings on levels of debt incurred by students taking a degree or the amount of alcohol drunk each week by men and women in their early twenties. Take a look at the newspapers for the past two weeks and find an example of a survey that has created some 'news' about a particular topic and consider the following questions:

Q To what extent do the views expressed in the survey findings correspond to your own views?

Q How do your views differ and why do you think that might be?

Q Would you support governments or organisations taking action based on these survey findings (for example, making new laws to limit alcohol consumption or reducing student fees)? Why/Why not?

Q Has the news story changed your view of the issue being discussed? Why/Why not?

Feedback

Consider the motivations of the organisations carrying out the survey (they are usually mentioned in the news article). What motivations might they have for being associated with a particular issue? What kind of influence are they hoping to have on general views of the matter being researched?

sense and so the approach had to be rejected). As a result, public opinion nowadays is interpreted most frequently as the view of the majority and we often see survey statistics in the media that suggest we all think in a particular way about a particular matter (see Activity 1.4).

As literacy levels and the media industry have expanded in modern states, the ability to quantify public opinion through research has also opened up new routes for it to be influenced. While the idea of influencing the public to cater to the interests of governments and elites is not new, the challenge to do so became more urgent in the twentieth century as a result of concerns about the public's ability to understand complex issues based on their own independent research (Price 1992).

Mass communication methods, and particularly the media, offered ready-made channels to communicate

messages about such issues in a manageable format to an increasingly literate population. Public opinion became inseparable from communication and, as we will see from the case studies outlined below, PR practitioners in business and government were not slow to understand this logic and take advantage of the rapidly growing media industries to put their views across in logical and emotional forms that could influence individuals who were fundamentally open to persuasion (Ewen 1996).

Business, politics and public relations: country case studies

Wherever PR is practised, its history is tied to its social, political and economic context. This chapter outlines the history of PR in only three countries: the United States, Britain and Germany. PR practices elsewhere are shaped and constrained by the forces that caused them to emerge in the first place. Therefore, the accounts in this chapter should not be treated as a definitive history of the profession, but as case studies of countries where PR has reached a recognised level of sophistication and professionalism. Accounts of public relations in other countries have been given elsewhere and students should refer to *The Global Public Relations Handbook* (Sriramesh and Verčič 2003) for an excellent starting point. For further discussion on the international aspects of PR practice, see Chapter 7.

The United States: private interests in public opinion

Many PR textbooks written by US scholars include a brief overview of PR history in that country (Grunig and Hunt 1984; Wilcox et al. 1992; Cutlip et al. 2000, 2006). For the most part, they focus on the role of key companies and figures including Ivy Lee, P.T. Barnum and Edward Bernays in defining the practice and techniques of PR (Cutlip 1994). In addition to these texts, Ewen (1996) provides a useful overview of the broad social context for understanding the emergence of PR in the United States.

The first widespread use of PR in the United States was in the service of politics. Cutlip et al. (2000, 2006) chart the use by American Revolutionaries during the War for Independence (1775–1782), of techniques commonly used today, including symbols, slogans, events, agenda setting (promoting certain topics to influence the themes covered by the media) and long-term campaign development (see Mini case study 1.1).

Mini Case Study 1.1
Early US public relations in practice

During the early nineteenth century, presidential campaigns included a press secretary for the first time and there was general recognition of the need for public support of candidates if they were to be successful. In the commercial world, banks were the first to use PR to influence their publics, while later in the century large conglomerates such as Westinghouse Electric Corporation set up their own PR departments.

In the late nineteenth century, recognition of the social impact of poor business practices on the working populace in the United States led to the emergence of 'progressive publicists' – individuals and groups arguing through the media for social reform in order to counter the negative effects of enterprise. Perhaps the first to recognise the need for formal publicity in order to support a cause, they couched their arguments in rational terms with the intent to appeal to public opinion and generate support for their cause. The resulting '**reform journalism**', pressing for social change, gained momentum and the issues raised could no longer be ignored by businesses.

The benefits of the reform movement depended on your perspective; business leaders regarded reform journalism as '**muckraking**', overstating the case against business and ignoring much of the social good it provided. The fear was that too much reform journalism might incite social disorder. As a result, from these very early days, businesses used communication to try and counter this tendency and establish social control by proposing and communicating ideas through the media that would unite the public and stabilise opinions (Ewen 1996). Increasing levels of literacy, combined with the advent of mass communication channels in the form of a rapidly expanding newspaper industry and new technologies such as the telegraph and wireless, meant that media relations quickly became established as a major tool for both sides of the debate.

By the turn of the century a number of individual PR consultancies had set up, catering mainly to private sector interests trying to defend themselves against the muckrakers. Clients included railroad companies, telecommunications companies, Standard Oil and companies interested in lobbying state and federal governments (Cutlip et al. 2006). Communications, largely media-based, tended to

be practised by organisations in crisis rather than on an ongoing basis and most businesses hired journalists to combat media on their own terms. As a result, the PR practised was predominantly press agentry (see Chapter 8), using the media to influence public opinion (Grunig and Hunt 1984).

It was in this environment that Ivy Lee emerged as the first formal and widely recognised PR practitioner. Making his mark as a publicity agent for the Pennsylvania Railroad, he argued that businesses had to build bridges to a sceptical public if they were to establish understanding and buy in to their practices. If they did not, their legitimacy would be called into question and their operations constrained more by public opinion than by good business principles. He put this into practice by opening up communications for the Railroad and being the first to issue press releases to keep journalists up to date with events (Ewen 1996; Cutlip et al. 2006).

Lee embraced the principles of accuracy, authority and fact in communications, formalising this in his Declaration of Principles in 1906. He suggested that these principles would generate the best arguments for convincing public audiences. However, corporations were slow to adopt this level of transparency and while their communications may have been accurate in principle, their practices were still shrouded in secrecy. Indeed, Lee's definition of 'fact' was frequently interpreted by him and his employees as information that could *become* fact in the public's mind as a result of a persuasive argument. As a consequence, 'muckraking' and the debate over reform continued (Ewen 1996).

The importance of communication was given two additional sources of credibility at the turn of the century, both of which eventually contributed to the wider take-up of PR as a business function. First, increases in disposable income and disposable goods created a new category of public – the consumer. Consumers had a new and very personal interest in the successful functioning of business and organisations were quick to exploit the potential for uniting their consumer base through advertising and PR.

Second, social psychology emerged and gained credibility as the science of persuasion. It provided a scientific basis for the arguments in favour of using PR to create a general public 'will' by shaping press coverage of a particular issue. The underlying objective, echoing the original motives behind reform journalism, was to rationalise irrational public opinion through the power of ideas and argument.

Edward Bernays, nephew of Sigmund Freud and regarded by many in the United States as the father of modern PR, was heavily influenced by social psychology and reflected this in his two books: *Crystallizing Public Opinion* (1923) and *Propaganda* (1928). Originally an arts journalist who used his PR career as a publicist for the arts, Bernays wrote books that were practitioner focused, case study based, backed up by insights from the social sciences into how the public mind could be controlled through persuasive techniques (see Chapter 13, p. 257 on persuasion). This combination of practical tactics substantiated by scientific argument was extremely powerful and an increasing number of practitioners, many of whom had gained expertise in propaganda during the war years and subsequently joined the PR profession, were heavily influenced by his ideas (Ewen 1996).

Bernays and Lee were not the only influential practitioners at this time: Theodore Roosevelt's sophisticated use of the press during his presidential campaigns left a significant legacy for subsequent political PR practice, while Henry Ford, Samuel Insull and Theodore Vail all implemented impressive PR strategies for the motor, electricity and telecommunications industries (Cutlip et al. 2000, 2006).

By the 1930s, commercial, non-commercial entities and government routinely implemented PR strategies, and their popularity was enhanced by the multiplication of outlets as the newspaper industry expanded and commercial radio started broadcasting. Techniques became more sophisticated as social research, which neatly divided populations into manageable groups with predictable characteristics, enabled specific targeting of communications. Increasingly, images were combined with words to increase the emotional pull of rational arguments, an important aspect of communication that continues today (Ewen 1996).

However, the advent of the Depression in the 1930s, when millions of Americans lost their jobs and savings, again called into question the ethics of business and the degree of social good it provided. The myth of a prosperous America full of happy consumers belied the reality experienced by hundreds of thousands of normal American families forced on to the breadline. Perhaps not surprisingly, businesses communicated much less vigorously during this period – but it was not the end of PR. Under the leadership of President Franklin D. Roosevelt, the federal government used communications to promote recovery strategies including social enterprise. Roosevelt focused strongly on personal communication, integrating strategic messages with the power of charismatic and credible leadership – a highly persuasive technique.

The result was a shift in public opinion towards an ethos of social good – a movement that businesses quickly realised they had to align themselves with to remain credible in light of such economic hardship. For the first time, companies joined together in industry associations and societies, in order to generate stronger and more unified messages promoting social progress as a result of

free enterprise. Business, it was argued, was inherently in the public interest. Perhaps the most obvious demonstration of this was at the World Fair in 1939, which included representatives from all types of businesses, symbolised democracy and forged an idealistic link between business and the greater public good. The advent of the Second World War helped the business sector to recover further from the Depression and reinforce its positive image (Ewen 1996).

During the Second World War, PR was used widely by the armed forces and emerged as the discipline that could promote American interests and identity overseas. Wartime PR also made extensive use of advertising to generate popular support for the conflict, a combination still used today in marketing and communications strategies.

In the immediate aftermath of war, the overall theme of commercial PR remained welfare capitalism, rather than unfettered free enterprise. However, the origins of PR as an essentially manipulative discipline were never far away, despite this apparent nod to public interest. In 1955, Bernays published *The Engineering of Consent*, underpinning PR as a discipline that could shape and mould public opinion, rather than engage and have a dialogue with individual groups. Television, the ultimate visual medium with a correspondingly large capacity to influence viewers on an emotional level, increased the level of commercial interest in mass media, and the manipulation of opinion once more dominated the PR industry.

In subsequent years, the PR industry was characterised by an increasing number of associations promoting sector-based interests, the consolidation of the consultancy industry, increasing amounts of literature, including the first *Public Relations Journal*, established in 1944 by PR baron Rex Harlow, and academic training for the profession. Harlow was also a key figure in the establishment of the Public Relations Society of America in 1947. Table 1.1 shows key historical publications in American PR.

Author	Title	Year
Ivy Lee	*Declaration of Principles*	1906
Edward Bernays	*Crystallizing Public Opinion*	1923
Edward Bernays	*Propaganda*	1928
Rex Harlow	*Public Relations Journal*	1944
Edward Bernays	*The Engineering of Consent*	1955

Table 1.1 Key publications in the early years of American public relations

Britain: public interest in private opinions

While commercial interests adopted and drove the development of PR in the United States, it was the public sector, and local government in particular, that was the driving force behind the early use of PR in Britain (see Chapter 29). As noted in the introduction, little has been written about the history of PR in Britain, with the exception of Jacquie L'Etang's (2004b) professional history. Her book forms the basis for much of the discussion that follows.

In the same way as the business sector in the United States began to use public relations as a means of protecting itself against attacks from the reformists, local governments in Britain found themselves looking to PR techniques to reinforce the importance of their role in the face of potential central government cutbacks during the 1920s and 1930s. Local communities and businesses did not understand what the role of local government was and regarded it as a bureaucratic irritant rather than a valuable service. As a result, the focus of much early PR in Britain was on the presentation of facts to persuade the public – genuine truths about what local government contributed to the public good. It was assumed that the power of truth would persuade both the public and central government to be more supportive of local officials and policies. As early as 1922, the local government trade union, the National Association of Local Government Officials (NALGO), recommended that all local councils include a press or publicity division in their makeup (L'Etang 2004b).

While central government did not make so much use of communications strategies in peacetime, the development of PR was also closely linked to the use of propaganda during the two world wars. Truth, here, was not so critical but its sacrifice was justified in light of the need to win at all costs. The need to unite a population under one cause did create opportunities to persuade using other messages and means. One of these was the British Documentary Film Movement, inspired by John Grierson, who focused on using film to educate the public on matters of public interest. Visual communications were thus used to present 'truth', in the form of a rational argument, in a compelling fashion (L'Etang 2004b). See also Box 1.1.

The propaganda industry during both world wars spawned many post-war practitioners, individuals seeking a new profession in a world where propaganda was no longer required. In addition, many wartime journalists were left jobless once peace broke out, and frequently went into PR. In the years following the Second World War, the commercial sector in Britain woke up to the possibilities of communication and the industry started to expand more rapidly. Almost 50 years after the first US consultancies,

Box 1.1

Documentary film in UK public relations

Documentary film was one of the most popular forms of both internal and external communication in both the public sector and corporations between the 1930s and the late 1970s. Under the influence of Stephen Tallents, state-sponsored film units were attached to the Empire Marketing Board, the Post Office (GPO), the Ministry of Information during the Second World War and, following the war, the Central Office of Information. One of the most famous documentaries of this early period was *Night Mail* (1936) made for the GPO, scripted by the poet W.H. Auden and with music composed by Benjamin Britten. The nationalisation of key industries after the war led to other public sector film units being set up for internal training and external promotion. Examples of these are British Transport Films (BTF) and the National Coal Board Film Unit.

Corporate film units were connected to Dunlop and ICI, but it is the Shell Oil Film Unit that is regarded as one of the most celebrated of the Documentary Movement. The films were often released into cinemas and while many were indirectly related to the company's activities (Shell's first film was *Airport* (1934)), the themes were more general, thus exerting a subtle influence on the public. Another group of films made by the Shell Oil Film Unit were educational and unrelated to oil. These films covered topics such as traditional rural crafts, the evolution of paint, and the environment. When film was replaced by video in the 1980s, Shell continued as one of the key players in the audio-visual communications industry.

Source: adapted from www.screenonline.org.uk/film/id/964488/index.html (British Film Institute)

Mini Case Study 1.2

Basil Clarke – Britain's first public relations consultant?

Basil Clarke was a former *Daily Mail* journalist who founded his own consultancy, Editorial Services, in 1926, following a career in several government ministries where he directed public information. Editorial Services was founded jointly with two practising consultants, R.J. Sykes of London Press Exchange (LPE) and James Walker of Winter Thomas. Basil Clarke is credited by some as the 'father' of PR in Britain, partly because of his government track record and partly because he drafted the Institute of Public Relations' first code of practice.

Source: L'Etang 2004a

the first UK consultancies were established and in-house practitioners in commercial organisations became much more common (L'Etang 2004b). See Mini case study 1.2.

Perhaps because of the early influence of public sector bureaucracy, PR practitioners were quick to organise themselves as a group in Britain, first under the auspices of the Institute of Public Administration and subsequently as an independent Institute of Public Relations (IPR). The IPR was established in 1948 under the leadership of Sir Stephen Tallents – a career civil servant and a keen supporter of publicity and propaganda from his tenure as Secretary of the Empire Marketing Board in the 1920s and 1930s, where he used communications to promote the reputation of the British Empire and its products among its trading partners. As the first Public Relations Officer in Britain, he joined the Post Office in 1933 and then moved to the BBC in 1935. Throughout his professional life, he used the widest range of tools at his disposal to promote the interests of his employer to the public, including radio, telegraph, film and, of course, newspapers. He was also a strong advocate for recognition of the publicity role as a profession in itself, with a specific and unique skills base. This was reflected in the Institute's immediate role as a lobbying body to encourage recognition of PR as a separate profession (L'Etang 2004b).

The IPR also served as a body through which practitioners could share their expertise and establish standards

for their rapidly expanding number. The vast majority of its founding members came from the public sector and subsequently set up the first interest group within the Institute, focusing in particular on the need to recognise PR as an important role in local government (L'Etang 2004b).

This early institutionalisation of the profession means that, in many ways, the presentation of PR in Britain has been heavily influenced by the efforts of the IPR as the industry body. Key themes emerging from early years of PR practice have permeated the approach taken by the Institute, including: the importance of truth as the 'ideal' PR tool; the conception of PR as a public service; and the potential for PR to be used as a means for promoting freedom, democracy and, in particular, the British way of life – this last being particularly influenced by institutions such as the British Council using PR in this way. In addition, the IPR conceptualised PR very broadly, specifically extending the definition of communications beyond pure media relations (L'Etang 2004b).

The emergence of PR consultancies in the 1950s, often based on editorial services and media liaison, confirmed the existence of PR as a distinct profession, separate from its cousins marketing and propaganda – although these boundaries were often blurred. Indeed, although the IPR was intent on maintaining a broad conception of communications in its definition of the profession, the reality was that the ex-journalists entering the profession could provide a unique, easily identifiable service on the back of their media expertise that did not overlap with advertising or other marketing disciplines and therefore served the profession well.

The IPR, dominated by in-house and public sector practitioners, had difficulty catering to the specific interests of independent consultancies. One particular concern included the maintenance of professional standards and reputation across a wide range of small organisations. In light of this, a specific consultancy association, the Society of Independent Public Relations Consultants (SIPRC), was created in 1960 and worked closely with the IPR. However, the SIPRC itself was poorly defined and eventually folded. Subsequently, in 1969, the Public Relations Consultants Association was set up and still exists alongside the IPR today (L'Etang 2004b).

By the 1970s, then, the British PR industry had established itself as an identifiable body with a national institute and increasing numbers of practitioners. Standards of practice, areas of competence and the range of services provided were all discussed and developed. With this institutional basis in place, the next phase of development was driven by commercial interests. A rapid expansion, particularly in the consultancy sector, took place in the

1980s and continued in the 1990s. It was initially driven by deregulation and privatisation programmes for state-owned companies under the Conservative government during the 1980s.

Deregulation opened up opportunities for private sector operators in two ways: first, as consultants to lucrative public sector accounts such as the NHS and, second, as professional lobbyists on behalf of the bidding companies (Miller and Dinan 2000). Privatisation during the 1980s and early 1990s of national utilities, including oil, gas, water and telecommunications, prompted extensive use of PR consultants by government departments. Persuading the public to buy shares in the new companies required more than standard Government Information Service briefings to standard media. Sophisticated techniques were needed to create sound marketing strategies, build public perceptions of the value of the opportunity and then per-suade them actually to buy shares in the new companies (Miller and Dinan 2000; Pitcher 2003).

These programmes were highly successful: by the early 1990s and the completion of the privatisation pro-grammes, 12 million members of the British public owned shares (Pitcher 2003). Media headlines were generally positive and company reputations began on a high. The newly privatised companies were the first to recognise the value of PR and continued the use of consultancies after their initial flotation (Miller and Dinan 2000).

The knock-on effects of this for the financial sector were considerable. From now on, listed companies had to communicate with the general public as well as with the privileged few who had previously made up their target audience. Communications had to be simpler and reach a wider range of people. In-house practitioners – if there were any – turned to consultants for support and the new specialism of investor relations was born (Miller and Dinan 2000; Pitcher 2003).

Deregulation of professions such as law and account-ing, as well as the financial services industry, also created new opportunities for the PR industry by prompting the companies concerned to market themselves and com-municate directly with their customers. For most, the concept of talking to the 'man in the street' was unknown and the newly expert PR consultancies were able to pro-vide valuable support and advice (Miller and Dinan 2000). Increasing numbers of mergers and acquisitions in these new markets have underpinned the growth of PR during the last two decades, with communications strategies often the deciding factor between success or failure (Davis 2000; Miller and Dinan 2000).

The growth in PR that these processes prompted eased off in the early 1990s, but the social and economic environ-ment continued to encourage PR activity. The 1980s had seen the (right of centre) Conservative government con-

sistently emphasise the virtue of individual rights over community responsibilities – home ownership rather than council tenancy, share ownership rather than taxes. By the end of the decade, this mentality had become embedded in Britain; private interests were automatically regarded as superior to social concerns. In this environment, PR was used by groups and individuals to justify their decisions by making their voices heard above the general cacophony of the market (Moloney 2000).

The key characteristics of this evolution are reflected in the nature of PR in Britain today, particularly in the debates around PR's use of truth, the ethics and morality of the profession, the justification for using PR in terms of mutual benefit rather than one-sided advantage, and the ongoing blurring of boundaries between marketing, propaganda and PR. Moreover, the fluidity of movement between journalism and PR has also given rise to the ongo-ing relationship between the two professions – there is plenty of antagonism despite the symbiotic relationship. Also of interest are the contrasts with the United States, where commercial interests drove an early and clear focus on the principles of free enterprise, situating private sector PR clearly in the capitalist arena. Federal government use of communications during the Depression and two world wars also helped establish the legitimacy of PR and, com-bined, these factors resulted in much faster development of the formality, size and sophistication of the profession than was the case in Britain.

Germany: industrialists, politics and critique

As with most countries outside the United States, informa-tion on the development of the PR industry in Germany is not widely available. Baerns (2000) and Nessmann (2000) offer the most comprehensive overviews so far. PR-type activities in Germany emerged considerably earlier than in the United States or Britain and were accompanied by critical analysis from social commentators suspicious of its potential to dominate public communication. The dynamics that shaped its emergence were similar to those elsewhere: industrialisation; new forms of technology; changing political environments, increasing levels of liter-acy; urbanisation; and the emergence of the mass media (Nessmann 2000).

Nessmann (2000) argues that PR as an activity first emerged in Germany in the early eighteenth century, although it was not formally termed PR until the mid-twentieth century. Practical applications of media relations can be seen with the systematic news office of Frederick the Great (1712–1786), Napoleon's mobile printing press that he used to circulate favourable stories about his

Mini Case Study 1.3
The first public relations stunt

In 1851, German steelmaker Krupp executed what was perhaps the first PR 'stunt' when it transported a two-ton block of steel to the Great Exhibition in London, an effort that generated significant publicity and recognition for the company across the world. Krupp remained at the forefront of communicative efforts among German industrialists, along with other conglomerates including Siemens, Henkel, Bahlsen and AEG. Each recognised the value of media relations, circulating reports about their activities to the media on a regular basis, while Krupp established the first formal press office in a German company in 1893.

military campaigns and his practice of monitoring foreign news coverage to check how his image was developing abroad. State media relations can be traced back to 1807, while in the mid-nineteenth century German industrialists were already recognising the importance of the views of the general public as well as of their own employees as sources of social legitimacy in the rapidly industrialising economy (see Mini case study 1.3).

The German state also cottoned on relatively early to the value of PR, with a press department set up in the Foreign Ministry in 1871 (the year the German Reich was founded). The freedom of the press was first established through the Reichspressegesetz (Reich press law) passed in 1874, the Navy commissioning its own press officers in 1894 and the first municipal press office set up in Magdeburg in 1906 (Nessmann 2000). Otto von Bismarck, the Chancellor of the German Reich, understood the power of the media and under his rule the press expanded – although he also made efforts to control and influence journalists and editors (Bentele and Wehmeier, 2003). Similarly to Britain, colonisation also shaped the development of PR, although its use in Germany was more to persuade internal audiences of the wisdom of expanding the Reich, rather than promoting German culture to those in the colonised nations (Bentele and Wehmeier, 2003).

From an academic perspective, this early development of PR practice was accompanied from the mid-nineteenth century by an increasingly critical view of PR among academics, as an exploitative medium used primarily by political and commercial groups, even as the need for it as a source of legitimacy for such organisations was also acknowledged. At around the same time, a debate emerged in relation to the German media about the separation of clearly labelled advertising materials from unbiased editorial contributions (Baerns 2000). This debate revolved around the need for the press to retain its credibility by separating advertising from journalism, so that its legitimacy as an information-carrying channel for the general public could be sustained. In fact, the debate continues today and Baerns (2000: 245) points out that as recently as the 1990s, the German press council issued guidelines that stated: 'The credibility of the press as a source of information demands particular care in dealing with public relations texts.' While Baerns points out that these statements have not necessarily led to a black-and-white distinction between advertising, PR materials and 'pure' journalism in the modern media, the existence of the debate does highlight the cultural dynamics that frame PR practice in Germany.

As in the United States and Britain, the First World War brought with it new opportunities for press relations and propaganda by the state and businesses. This growth in the practice and understanding of the discipline led to a corresponding flourishing of the profession in the postwar years. During the Third Reich, however, the sophistication of new PR techniques was relegated to the back seat while Adolf Hitler used propaganda techniques and press censorship to cement his regime (Bentele and Wehmeier, 2003).

Following the Second World War and the end of the Nazi regime, PR as a profession was revitalised. The term PR finally came into general use in the 1950s, when the influence of the US occupation in West Germany resulted in both linguistic and practical adoption of the term and its modern practice. The German Public Relations Association (Deutsche Public Relations Gesellschaft, DPRG) was founded in 1958 and the industry once again expanded rapidly in the newly democratic state. As elsewhere, genuine two-way communications emerged as consumers became more demanding of organisations in the 1970s and 1980s (Bentele and Wehmeier 2003). See Table 1.2.

Table 1.2 Periods of German public relations (*source*: Bentele and Wehmeier 2003: 200)

Periods of German Public Relations	
Pre-history: Official press politics, functional public relations, development of instruments	
Period 1 (mid-19th century–1918) Development of the occupational field.	Development of the first press offices in politics and firms, war press releases under the conditions of censorship, first public campaigns.
Period 2 (1918–1933) Consolidation and growth.	Fast and widespread growth of press offices in different social fields: economy, politics, municipal administration
Period 3 (1933–1945) Media relations and political propaganda and the Nazi regime.	Party-ideological media relations within political propaganda. National and party-related direction and control of journalism, media relations and inner relations.
Period 4 (1945–1958) New beginning and upturn.	Postwar development, upturn and orientation to the American model starting in the early 1950s, development of a new professional self-understanding under the conditions of democratic structures (public relations defined as distinct from propaganda and advertisement), fast development of the professional field predominantly in the economic sphere.
Period 5 (1958–1985) Consolidation of the professional field in the Federal Republic of Germany and establishment of a socialist public relations in the German Democratic Republic (GDR).	Development of a professional self-consciousness, 1958 foundation of the professional association DPRG, which initiated private training programmes. Simultaneous with the developments in West Germany, a type of socialist public relations developed in the GDR from the mid-1960s.
Period 6 (1985 – present) Boom of the professional field and professionalisation.	Strong development of public relations agencies, professionalisation of the field, beginning and development of academic public relations education improvements in the training system, scientific application and enhancement of the instruments; development of public relations as a science.

Summary

The histories presented here highlight the social nature of PR. It is a profession that applies the value of communication to situations where it is required. In the United States, the private sector has been the most active force driving the development of the profession, while in Britain, first the public then the private sector have resulted in the industry we see today. In other countries, such as Germany, different cultural and social dynamics affect the practice, popularity and implementation of communications and will shape the PR industry in different ways.

Perhaps because communications techniques can be so widely applied, definitions of PR are various. While the general principles of using relationship management and dialogue in order to exert influence on target audiences are evident in most definitions, controversy exists about other aspects of the profession – such as reputation management – and whether they are core to its practice. These debates are unlikely to disappear in the near future. Whether they relate to the relative youth of the profession, the fast changing world in which it operates and the correspondingly rapid changes in the demands made on it, or simply the complexity of the practice itself, the reality is that the social nature of PR will always mean that it differs from one context to the next. Practitioners need to establish the principles that are most appropriate in their personal and professional situation and operate accordingly. The chapters in this book outline some of the issues that they will need to consider: personal and professional ethics, the sector in which they operate, the specialism they choose and the audiences they target.

Bibliography

Baerns, B. (2000). 'Public relations and the development of the principle of separation of advertising and journalistic media programmes in Germany' in *Perspectives on Public Relations Research*. D. Moss, D. Verčič and G. Warnaby. London: Routledge.

Bentele, G. and S. Wehmeier (2003). 'From literary bureaus to a modern profession: The development and current structure of public relations in Germany' in *The Global Public Relations Handbook*. K. Sriramesh and D. Verčič. Mahwah, NJ: Lawence Erlbaum Associates, pp. 199–221.

Bernays, E. (1923). *Crystallizing Public Opinion*. New York: Boni and Livenight.

Bernays, E. (1928). *Propaganda*. New York: H. Livenight.

Bernays, E. (1955). *The Engineering of Consent*. Norman, OK: University of Oklahoma Press.

Botan, C.H. and V. Hazelton (1989). *Public Relations Theory*. Hillsdale, NJ: Lawrence Erlbaum Associates.

Cutlip, S.M. (1994). *Public Relations: The Unseen Power. A history*. Hillsdale, NJ: Lawrence Erlbaum Associates.

Cutlip, S.M., A.H. Center and G.M. Broom (2000). *Effective Public Relations*; 8th edition. Upper Saddle River, NJ: Prentice Hall.

Cutlip, S.M., A.H. Center and G.M. Broom (2006). *Effective Public Relations*; 9th edition. Upper Saddle River, NJ: Prentice Hall.

Davis, A. (2000). 'Public relations, business news and the reproduction of corporate power'. *Journalism* **1**(3): 282–304.

Department of Trade and Industry and Institute of Public Relations (2003). *Unlocking the Potential of Public Relations: Developing Good Practice*. London: European Centre for Business Excellence.

Ewen, S. (1996). *PR! A Social History of Spin*. New York: Basic Books.

Genasi, C. (2002). *Winning Reputations: How to be Your Own Spin Doctor*. Basingstoke: Palgrave.

Gordon, J.C. (1997). 'Interpreting definitions of public relations: Self assessment and a symbolic interactionism-based alternative'. *Public Relations Review* **23**(1): 57–66.

Gregory, A. (1996). *Public Relations in Practice*. London: Kogan Page.

Grunig, J.E. (1992). *Excellence in Public Relations and Communication Management*. Hillsdale, NJ: Lawrence Erlbaum Associates.

Grunig, J.E. and L.A. Grunig (2000). 'Public relations in strategic management and strategic management of public relations: theory and evidence from the IABC excellence project'. *Journalism Studies* **1**(2): 303–321.

Grunig, J.E., L. Grunig and D. Dozier (2006). 'The Excellence Theory' in *Rhetorical and Critical Perspectives of Public Relations*. C. Botan and V. Hazelton (eds). Mahwah, NJ: Lawrence Erlbaum Associates.

Grunig, J.E. and T. Hunt (1984). *Managing Public Relations*. New York: Holt, Rinehart & Winston.

Harlow, R.F. (1976). 'Building a definition of public relations'. *Public Relations Review* **2**(4).

Harrison, S. (2000). *Public Relations: An Introduction*. London: Thomson Learning.

Hutton, J.G. (1999). 'The definition, dimensions and domain of public relations'. *Public Relations Review* **25**(2): 199–214.

Institute of Public Relations (2004). *What is Public Relations?* London: Institute of Public Relations.

Kitchen, P.J. (1997). *Public Relations: Principles and Practice*. London: International Thomson Business Press.

L'Etang, J. (1996). 'Public relations as diplomacy' in *Critical Perspectives in Public Relations*. J. L'Etang and M. Pieczka. London: International Thomson Business Press.

L'Etang, J. (2004a). 'Public relations and democracy' in *Handbook of Corporate Communication and Public Relations: Pure and Applied*. S.M. Oliver. London: Routledge.

L'Etang, J. (2004b). *Public Relations in Britain: A history of professional practice in the 20th century*. Mahwah, NJ: Lawrence Erlbaum Associates.

Lippmann, W. (1922). *Public Opinion*. New York: Harcourt Brace Jovanovich.

McKie, D. and D. Munshi (2005). 'Global public relations: a different perspective', special issue. *Public Relations Review* **30**(4).

McKie, D. and D. Munshi (2007). *Reconfiguring Public Relations: Ecology, Equity and Enterprise*. Abingdon, Oxon: Routledge.

Miller, D. and W. Dinan (2000). 'The rise of the PR industry in Britain 1979–98'. *European Journal of Communication* **15**(1): 5–35.

Moloney, K. (2000). *Rethinking Public Relations: The Spin and the Substance*. London: Routledge.

Nessmann, K. (2000). 'The origins and development of public relations in Germany and Austria' in *Perspectives on Public Relations Research*. D. Moss, D. Verčič and G. Warnaby. London: Routledge.

Newsom, D., J.V. Turk and A. Scott (2000). *This is PR*. Belmont, CA: Wadsworth.

Pieczka, M. (1996). 'Public opinion and public relations' in *Critical Perspectives in Public Relations*. J. L'Etang and M. Pieczka. London: International Thomson Business Press.

Pitcher, G. (2003). *The Death of Spin.* Chichester: John Wiley & Sons.

Price, V. (1992). *Public Opinion.* Newbury Park, CA: Sage.

Public Relations Consultants Association (2004). 'What is PR?' London: Public Relations Consultants Association.

Public Relations Society of America (2004). *About Public Relations.* New York: Public Relations Society of America.

Sriramesh, K. and D. Verčič (2003). *The Global Public Relations Handbook.* Mahwah, NJ: Lawrence Erlbaum Associates.

White, J. and L. Mazur (1996). *Strategic Communications Management: Making Public Relations Work.* Harlow: Addison-Wesley.

Wilcox, D.L., P.H. Ault and W.K. Agee (1992). *Public Relations: Strategies and Tactics.* New York: Harper-Collins.

CHAPTER 2

Anne Gregory

Management and organisation of public relations

Learning outcomes

By the end of this chapter you should be able to:

- describe the principal external influences that contextualise public relations activity overall
- analyse this external environment, select those factors relevant to any particular organisation and evaluate their impact using appropriate theories and analytical tools
- identify the principal internal influences that affect the status and nature of public relations activity
- identify the relevant underlying theories
- provide an evidence-based rationale for proposing an appropriate public relations structure for typical organisations
- describe, justify and evaluate the roles, location and tasks of public relations specialists within organisations and their relationship with other functional and line departments
- speculate on the future role of public relations specialists, building realistic scenarios from current evidence.

Structure

- Importance of context
- External environment
- Internal environment
- Systems theory
- Location of public relations in organisations
- Future of the public relations department

Introduction

The way each organisation manages, structures and undertakes its public relations (PR) activity is unique; that is because every organisation is unique. A single-issue pressure group has a focused purpose and its range of target publics is often very specific. A large government department, such as the UK's Department of Health, touches the lives of every citizen in a variety of ways, from prenatal ultrasound scanning to childhood and adult illnesses, through to terminal care. Some business enterprises operate in tiny niche markets in one country while others operate in numerous markets on a global scale.

PR is used by some organisations in a very narrow way, typically to support sales and marketing activity. An example is a small restaurant promoting its menus, prices and opening hours to students through the local media. Other organisations use PR in a whole host of ways, for example, a large retailer such as Wal-Mart will develop relationship programmes with financial analysts, government officials and politicians, the local community, employees, consumers and suppliers.

Sometimes PR is a standalone function; sometimes it is located within marketing or human resources. A number of large enterprises now have their senior PR person on the board with all other communication disciplines, including marketing reporting to them (Gregory and Edwards, 2004).

PR also operates under a number of guises: corporate communication, corporate affairs, public affairs, communication management, public relations, reputation management ... the list seems to expand almost every year.

This chapter examines the range of factors that influence the way PR is managed and organised in different types of organisation. It also points to some current societal and regulatory developments which will affect the way public relations is conducted in the future – a future that is full of opportunity and growth.

Importance of context

Organisations do not exist in isolation. Business history is littered with companies that did not spot changing industry trends quickly enough and adapt – Olivetti used to make superb typewriters, but where is it now? Other companies such as Nike and McDonald's have been held to account by activist groups over their production activities in the developing world; activism is now a part of modern life in developed societies.

Public relations means what the words imply. It is about the relationships organisations have with various publics, both internal and external. Those publics comprise people who are, in turn, affected by developments and trends in society. The environment in which organisations operate is dynamic. Society is changing: new issues and trends arise, some of them very quickly. For example, corporate social responsibility was not such a well-recognised issue for many large organisations even 10 years ago (see Chapters 6 and 17).

Similarly, organisations themselves are changing. The workforce is different – for example, there are more women and part-time workers – and attitudes are different. Because people are empowered in their lives outside work, for example, in having more choices about where they live and the lifestyles they lead, they are no longer willing to remain disempowered at work (Smythe 2007). Furthermore, organisations are much more accountable to external publics who want to know what they stand for,

how they conduct themselves, and the impact they have on society and the environment.

Given the critical role that public relations has in 'establish[ing] and maintain[ing] goodwill and mutual understanding between an organisation and its publics' (CIPR 2004), it is clear that careful consideration has to be given to both the external and internal contexts in which it operates. This will, of course, vary between different organisations, depending on the nature of their business, their size, their sphere of operation and their culture.

External environment

The external environment is vitally important for organisations because it determines the future. Smart organisations constantly scan the external environment to identify emerging issues. Having spotted these issues early, precious time is bought for the organisation to adjust itself to those issues, to engage with them and to influence their development.

The external environment can be divided into two main areas: the 'macro' and the 'task' environment.

Macro environment

This environment might be described as containing the 'big picture' issues over which the organisation has no control. These are the issues that emerge from the actions of gov-

Picture 2.1 Public relations activity ranges from consumer and business to business sales support to government communications during times of conflict such as war. The 'allied forces' commander at a press conference in Kabul, Afghanistan (*source*: Syed Jan Sabawoon/EPA Photos)

ernments, economic and societal trends, and from scientific and technological developments. Sometimes called the 'remote' or 'societal' environment, the macro environment originates beyond, and usually irrespective of, any single organisation's operating situation (Steyn and Puth 2000).

To make sense of this, environmental analysts examine the macro environment under a series of headings. The most well-known analytical tool is PEST, which segments the overall environment into four topic areas – Political, Economic, Social and Technological. Figure 2.1 presents some examples of subjects that could come under each of these areas. What is important about these subjects is the impact they might have on existing relationships or what they reveal about the need to develop a relationship. The identification of these subjects could present public

Political	Economic
Employment legislation Trade legislation Change of government Political alliances between nations	Interest rates Levels of employment Value of the currency Energy costs
Social	Technological
Lifestyle changes Social attitudes Demographic changes Purchasing habits	New technologies Access to technology Cost of research and development Impact of new technologies on work practices

Figure 2.1 Example of a PEST analysis

relations issues for an organisation (see Chapter 18 for further discussion).

Increasingly, the limitations of PEST fail to do justice to the complex modern environment. An extension of PEST is EPISTLE, which includes the four existing elements of PEST, but also gives consideration to Information, Legal and the green Environment. The 'information' heading invites special consideration for its ability to empower people via technologies such as mobile personal devices, although it must be remembered that people who are deprived of relevant information will become disenfranchised and unable to engage in debate effectively. The legal environment is becoming increasingly complex. Organisations need to be aware not only of national regulations, but also of transnational legislation such as EU law. Furthermore, non-binding but moral undertakings carried out by nations such as the various climate change agreements often lead to national protocols. Finally, the green environment is the cause of increasing concern and no analysis of the macro environment would be complete without reference to environmental concerns.

Clearly, different organisations will be impacted in different ways by these macro issues. An arms manufacturer will be very susceptible to political shifts (e.g. arms export bans to particular countries) and a clothes manufacturer needs to be acutely aware of social trends (e.g. consumer preferences based on changing lifestyles). However, a careful eye needs to be kept on all areas because they will affect the longer term issues that organisations, and therefore PR, will need to address.

It is important to understand trends emerging from the political, economic, technological and social environments and how these various trends interact with each other. While there are literally hundreds of issues and trends in the wider environment, it is worth picking out a few for special mention. The themes of globalisation, information, pluralism and consumerism/individualism and, of course, the news media, are selected here because of their relevance to PR.

Globalisation

PR people who work for global organisations will understand the need to communicate across timelines, cultures, languages and different communication delivery systems. But even if the organisation is local, what it does may have global impacts and attract global attention. A local clothes store may buy stock from an intermediary who is supplied by a manufacturer who damages the environment in a developing country.

Organisations also need to be sensitive about what they put on their website for national audiences, as websites may be accessed by people from other cultures who may take great offence at what is said – for example, encouragement to drink alcohol may offend cultures where alcohol is frowned on.

Information and information technology

This is connected to the theme of globalisation. The fact that information can be sent and accessed immediately across time and geographical boundaries brings great opportunities, but also can provide threats for the professional communicator. Activists can organise quickly and misinformation can spread worldwide at the click of a mouse or telephone button. Contrariwise, organisations can engage with stakeholders in innovative ways. They can provide information instantly and research topics thoroughly without relying on physical information resources such as reference libraries. All this bring pressures for organisations and communicators that need to be geared for action 24/7 (24 hours a day, seven days a week). See Mini case study 2.1.

It also needs to be remembered that there are still many communities that do not have access to these technologies, which also need to be catered for (see Chapter 24 and, in particular, the debate surrounding the 'digital divide').

Pluralism

It is thought that **pluralism** – that is a plural (diverse) society – offers the most favourable conditions for democracy and protection against totalitarianism (Kornhauser 1960). Within a highly industrialised and urbanised society such as in Britain, for example, the merging of values and ideals, together with understanding and accepting different cultures and alternative views, are taken as a sign of advancing civilisation. But at the same time it increases uncertainty and insecurity as people question religious beliefs and authority norms. Counter to this, the rise of nationalism, fundamentalism and activism can pose a threat

to these liberalising forces (Herriot and Scott-Jackson 2002). Stepping among and around the tensions involved is a great challenge for professional communicators. They have to assert or defend a particular position without offending anyone. They have to consider their role in conflict resolution and dialogue, especially if one party refuses to accept any compromise. For example, reconciling pro- and anti-abortion lobbyists can be seen as a major challenge.

Consumerism and individualism

In consumer societies, people know their rights. Expectations are rising all the time and many organisations feel beleaguered by the demands placed on them. Similarly, some would say that in an attempt to replace the old certainties, people in developed societies are becoming ever more consumerist and very individualistic (Ritzer 2004). In place of church and community, they are seeking to associate with like-minded others in pursuance of their own tastes and values. The number of pressure groups, non-governmental organisations (NGOs), special interest associations and clubs of all kinds, many supported by the new technologies that facilitate global affiliations, is burgeoning.

Professional communicators have to deal with knowledgeable, assertive individuals and groups. For example, in Britain, the parents' lobby for healthier school dinners (given prominence by the celebrity chef Jamie Oliver) encouraged the then Prime Minister Tony Blair to make election promises to improve food quality in schools. This has led to an ongoing campaign by the UK government to improve the quality of school food through the work of the School Food Trust (DCSF, 2008).

News media

The news media, comprising newspapers and broadcast channels, have been revolutionised over the last few years (see also Chapter 4). Global news businesses owned by powerful groups and individuals, often with their own political agendas, are setting the political backdrop and leading public opinion in a way that simply was not the case in the last century (Hargreaves 2005; Evans, 2008). Furthermore, the demand for 24/7 news, along with the increasing amounts of space that journalists have to cover without a matching increase in personnel, means that the media are becoming increasingly dependent on sources with their own biases – often PR professionals. An environment where 'PRisation of the media' (Moloney 2000; 2006) is becoming more prevalent could be regarded as advantageous for the public relations industry. But is that good for the public interest? Some would say (e.g. Gregory 2003) that the press should be free to challenge vested interests and that there should be a distance between PR people and journalists. For example, it is suggested that in the financial area the relationships between financial PR specialists and journalists are too cosy and the media have

Mini Case Study 2.1
Asian tsunami disaster

The tsunami in the Indian Ocean struck on 26 December 2004, the day after Christmas Day in Christian countries and traditionally a national holiday. When news emerged in the early morning of 26 December, the public relations staff in the US headquarters of a number of hotel chains were still in bed. They had to react quickly with few support mechanisms available. Technology meant that they could communicate relatively quickly with concerned families via websites, semi-automated helplines, email and social networks.

Think about 2.1   **The macro environment**

What other macro or global trends do you think are important? What might be the implications for PR professionals? How might you communicate with rural communities in developing countries that do not have access to the Internet or mobile phones?

Feedback

For further details of global trends read J. Naisbitt and P. Aburdene (1991) *Megatrends 2000*, London: Pan with Sidgwick and Jackson. Also *'think-tanks'* such as Demos and research companies, for instance Ipsos/MORI, undertake futures research in a range of subjects.

not been as challenging of some corporate activities as they should be because they are dependent on key PR sources for their information (Stauber and Rampton, 2002). There are some balancing factors which help to mitigate some effects of the 'PRisation of the media', notably the rise of citizen journalism. See Think about 2.1.

Another trend to take into account is that younger people are turning away from traditional media formats such as the large terrestrial broadcasts and newspapers and accessing online sources of news (Loughrey 2007). This, compounded by a drop in advertising revenues to the traditional media (Edelman 2006), is leading to significant changes as those media outlets struggle for readers and funds. The implications of this for PR are obvious: as channels fragment and readership fragments too, the PR

practitioners will need to become adept at working with discrete publics who may share little in common with each other.

Task environment

Apart from the links to the macro external environment, organisations are also affected by things closer to home, termed the 'task environment'. These factors are more within their control and usually relate to groups of individuals (publics) who have quite definable characteristics, such as customers or shareholders.

Esman (1972) has divided those publics into four categories that are characterised by their relationship with an organisation (see Figure 2.2).

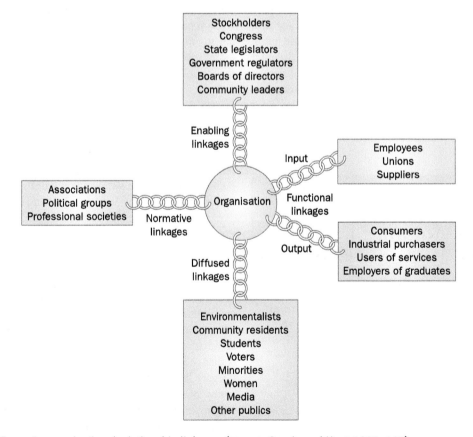

Figure 2.2 Esman's organisational relationship linkages (*source*: Grunig and Hunt 1984: 141)

The following may help to explain how these linkages work:

- *Enabling* linkages connect the organisation to those who have the power and resources to allow it to exist.

- *Functional* linkages either provide some kind of input to the organisation or consume its outputs.

- *Normative* linkages are to peer organisations.

- *Diffused* linkages are to those who have no formal relationship with the organisation, but may take an interest in it.

Chapter 11 gives more detail on the nature of publics, but it is worth making the point here that there has been a shift away from the idea of the organisation as an autonomous monolith accountable to no one but its shareholders (as espoused by Friedman 1970) towards the notion of organisations as stakeholding communities. Freeman (1984) first articulated this in a systematic way, arguing that organisations were defined by the relationship they had with their stakeholders. Stakeholders are not just those groups that management believe to have a legitimate interest in the organisation, but those groups who decide for themselves that they will take a stake in the organisation. The actions of activist groups have made this a living reality for many organisations. For example, in Britain, Huntingdon Life Sciences is a firm that breeds animals for experiments. The premises have been lobbied by activist groups for many years, to the point where special security measures have had to be taken both for the property and for employees, some of whom have been seriously threatened with violence and have had their own cars and homes damaged.

Stakeholding theory has itself progressed. In the 1990s the idea of the corporate community emerged and in the new century, Halal (2000) encouraged organisations to recognise that stakeholders can collaborate with them in problem solving. The role of the organisation is to pull together the economic resources, political support and special knowledge of all stakeholding groups (see Activity 2.1).

Internal environment

As well as being profoundly affected by external factors, the way communication is organised is shaped by the nature of the enterprise itself and the type of operation it undertakes. The kind of enterprise will determine the balance of PR activities and their relative priority. Here are just some of the factors that should be considered.

Sector

If the organisation is located in a stable, well-established industry sector such as furniture manufacturing, it is likely that pre-planned and sustained PR activity can be maintained. Fast growing and turbulent sectors such as IT will require quick, **reactive**, as well as proactive, programmes. That is not to say that activity should not be planned, but an inbuilt capability to react to the fast moving market is a key requirement.

Different sectors require different types of programme. The emphasis in the confectionary sector is likely to be in marketing communication, whereas local authority work is more likely to focus on community involvement. Furthermore, work for a government department, indeed any work for the public or not-for-profit sector, requires communication professionals to be aware of the need for accountability to the public who pay taxes. Work in the private sector means that shareholders and the profit motive are significant and this creates different priorities for communication.

Size

Small organisations usually have small, multifunctional PR departments. Public relations services could even be totally outsourced to a PR consultancy. It may be, that PR is only part of the responsibilities of a single individual, such as a sales, marketing or general office manager. Such individuals may be part of the management team and their activities will be seen as critical to the success of the organisation.

Large organisations may well have large PR departments with several PR specialists taking on a whole raft of activities.

Activity 2.1

Stakeholding

Who are the stakeholders for a university? How would you describe the linkages between a university and its:

- students
- lecturers
- administrators
- governors
- local communities
- local and central government education departments?

They may or may not work in standalone PR departments and they may or may not be part of management.

Stage of organisational development

PR activity is often dictated by the stage of development that the organisation has reached. When the organisation is at *startup* stage, most suppliers, customers and employees will be well known. Thus PR effort is often face to face and the emphasis is on growth. Hence marketing communications, which is aimed at supporting the sales of goods and services (see 'Public relations tasks' section later, p. 29) will be very important.

When companies reach maturity, it is probable that they will undertake the full range of PR activity. Offering public shares in the company may be under consideration, which will require financial PR. The organisation may want to influence government regulation affecting its sector or processes, in which case it may engage a public affairs consultancy (see Chapter 22). It will probably want a strong corporate identity and may have a well-developed corporate social responsibility (CSR) programme including active community relations (see Chapters 6 and 17 for more on CSR and community relations activities). See Table 2.1 for PR activity structure at various points in an organisation's lifecycle.

Culture

One of the most significant influences in determining how the PR function is organised is the culture of an organisation.

Table 2.1 Example of how PR activity may be structured at various stages of the organisational lifecycle

	Startup	Growth	Maturity	Decline
Public relations orientation	Marketing communication	Marketing communication Internal communication	Marketing communication Community relations Internal communication Financial public relations Public affairs	Marketing communication Investor relations Internal communication
Examples of public relations activity	Face-to-face ■ meetings ■ presentations ■ social events Printed literature ■ product/service brochures ■ corporate brochure ■ business cards Website Social media Media relations ■ news releases ■ press conferences	Merchandise Joint promotions Media relations ■ news releases ■ press conferences ■ facility visits ■ features ■ exclusives Internal communication ■ briefings ■ noticeboards ■ emails	Corporate social responsibility programme ■ educational support ■ charity giving ■ employee volunteering ■ community projects Investor relations ■ city analysts briefings ■ shareholder liaison ■ financial press Issues management ■ government lobbying Internal communication ■ intranet ■ employee conferences ■ newsletters ■ project groups	Crisis management Mergers and acquisitions Internal communication ■ working with HR to handle layoffs and redundancies or new working arrangements Marketing communication ■ customer retention Supplier relations ■ retention
Staffing	Public relations undertaken as part of marketing duties	Public relations specialist or consultancy	Public relations department and consultancy if required	Specialist public relations staff and specialist consultancies

Note: This chart is progressive: all the activities undertaken at an earlier stage in the lifecycle will also be undertaken at a later stage.

There are many definitions of *organisational culture* but a commonly articulated view is that it is 'the set of conscious and unconscious beliefs and values, and the patterns of behaviour (including language and symbol use) that provide identity and form a framework of meaning for a group of people' (McCollom 1994, cited in Eisenberg and Riley 2001, pp. 306–7). Culture, in other words, is a shorthand term for ways in which people think and behave within an organisation. Leaders of organisations, too, can make a difference, in that they can attempt to define and shape *corporate culture* – how they want people to think and behave. Leaders, in turn, will be affected by their *national cultures*, which will have specific characteristics – for example, strong individualism has been identified as a characteristic of American culture (Hofstede and Hofstede 2004). (Chapter 16, which focuses on internal communication, goes into culture in more detail, but it is also important to mention it here.)

As a broad generalisation, most successful private sector organisations tend to be *entrepreneurial* (often led by an **entrepreneur**), whereas many public sector organisations are *systematised* (Grunig and Grunig 1992). No value judgements are being made here – the culture is driven by the nature of the organisation and the job of work that needs to be done. Business enterprises have to make money in a competitive environment. Their PR functions will tend to be proactive, seeking to exploit competitive advantage and supporting the profit-making activities in the firm.

Public sector organisations are characterised by a service mission. They are usually social enterprises concerned with supporting the lives of citizens. Making money is not their priority, although they need to demonstrate that they spend it wisely in the service of the community. They react to the requirements of their publics and act in predictable, dependable ways. Their PR departments are often concerned with providing information or engaging their publics in dialogue, therefore a systematised and interactive mode of operation is appropriate (see Chapter 29).

However, it would be a mistake to think that public bodies are never entrepreneurial in character, whatever their mission. There is some highly creative and proactive work in the public sector as evidenced by the numerous awards they win (see www.cipr.uk/lgg/index.htm). Equally it would be a mistake to assume that all successful private sector organisations are unbureaucratic: the banking industry offers a good example of bureaucratic organisation.

From all the foregoing it can be seen that both external and internal influences are critical to the way PR is organised. Yet, it can be observed that there is often little systematic review of these factors. PR structures are often placed in a particular location in the organisation at a point in time and remain there until there is a major,

Activity 2.2

Different organisations

Research two organisations within the same sector that appear to you to have different characters. Why are they so different? Sectors that provide useful organisational comparisons are:

- the motor industry, e.g. Chrysler and BMW
- clothes retailing, e.g. TopShop and Benetton
- supermarkets, e.g. Carrefour and Aldi or Wal-Mart and Morrisons
- airlines, e.g. Cathay Pacific and Virgin.

Go to company websites and look at media stories about the companies to help with your comparisons.

Feedback

Points of difference may include country of origin, leadership style, price/target market, age of organisation and product design. Manifestations of cultural difference may be evident in kinds of advertising, colours used, attitudes of staff, layout of stores, company initiatives and after-sales service.

normally externally driven, incident – such as a crisis – that prompts a radical review of PR's worth and position (Gregory and Edwards 2004). See Activity 2.2.

Systems theory

It is clear that organisations are not free-floating bodies unaffected by what is around them. They are affected by and in turn affect the environment in which they operate. One of the theories used by PR academics (Grunig and Hunt 1984; Cutlip et al. 2006) to explain this is **systems theory** (a detailed overview and critique of systems theory and PR is given in Chapter 8). Systems theory describes organisations as a set of subsystems that affect each other and jointly interact with the external environment. Organisations have to adjust and adapt as they change from within and as the environment changes. They form part of a social system that consists of individuals or groups (publics) such as suppliers, local communities, employees, customers and governments who all interact with it. PR is there to develop and maintain good relationships with these publics, to help the organisation achieve its objectives.

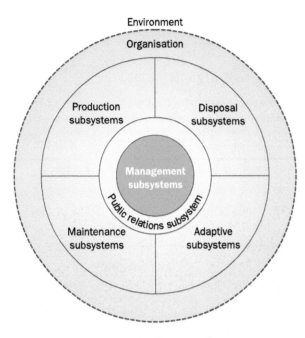

Environment

Organisation

Production subsystems

Disposal subsystems

Management subsystems

Public relations subsystem

Maintenance subsystems

Adaptive subsystems

Figure 2.3 Organisational subsystems (*source*: Grunig and Hunt 1984: 9)

So which subsystem does PR fit into? When considering this question Grunig and Hunt (1984) have turned to the work of organisational theorists who describe organisations as having typically five subsystems (see Figure 2.3).

The following may help explain Figure 2.3:

■ *Production* subsystems produce the products or services of an organisation.

■ *Maintenance* subsystems work throughout the organisation encouraging employees to work together – human resources, for example.

■ *Disposal* subsystems encompass the marketing and distribution of products and services.

■ *Adaptive* subsystems help the organisation adjust to its changing environment, such as the strategic planning role.

■ *Management* subsystems control and direct all the other subsystems and manage any conflicting demands that they might have. They also negotiate between the requirements of the environment (for example, demand for a particular product) and the survival needs of the organisation (supply of that product). Usually the board and senior management of the organisation undertake this responsibility.

Taking a systems perspective, it can be seen that PR professionals have a *boundary-spanning* role. They work at the boundaries within organisations, working with all

the internal subsystems by helping them to communicate internally. They also help these subsystems with their external communication by both providing expert advice on what and how to communicate and by helping them with implementation. For example, PR may work closely with marketing (disposal subsystem) on product support and with senior management (management subsystem) on investor relations.

Location of public relations in organisations

Apart from all the external and internal considerations just discussed, the location of PR within an organisation depends on a variety of other factors: the position of the most senior practitioner; the tasks allocated to the function; and how it is situated in relation to other functions.

Position of the senior practitioner

The position of the PR *senior practitioner* provides a good indication of how the function is regarded within organisations. Grunig and Hunt (1984) say that public relations can be seen as valued when the function is within the 'dominant coalition' – in other words, the group of people who determine 'what the organisation's goals should be'. Certainly, an aspiration of PR professionals over many decades has been to obtain a place on the board of organisations. Undoubtedly progress has been made towards this goal. Now all the UK's FTSE 100 companies have PR departments (CIPR 2004) and there are indications that more senior practitioners are being appointed to board positions (Gregory and Edwards 2004; CIPR 2005).

Work done by Moss et al. (2000, 2005) and Moss and Green (2001) in Britain and Toth et al. (1998) in the United States has identified an alternative senior role: that of *senior adviser*. The senior adviser is not actually on the board, but reports directly to the CEO or chair of the board and holds a special position of power and influence. A good (if controversial) example of this is Alastair Campbell, Communications Director to the then UK Prime Minister Tony Blair until 2003. Campbell did not occupy a Cabinet position, but he was clearly a powerful figure constantly alert to the communication issues surrounding government policy and decision making and advising the Prime Minister directly. Another, less well-known, example of a senior adviser is Will Whitehorn who supported Richard Branson during Virgin's period of expansion during the 1990s and 2000s.

Picture 2.2 Alastair Campbell was the then UK Prime Minister's Communications Director until 2003 and although he did not occupy a Cabinet position, he was a powerful figure constantly alert to the communication issues surrounding government policy and decision making (*source*: © Reuters/Corbis)

Board level and senior adviser communicators will usually take a research-based approach to PR. They will know their publics' views and be well informed of all the issues likely to affect the organisation. Their role will be to counsel and advise senior managers. They will also know the business intimately and be good at business as well as at communication. See Think about 2.2.

Think about 2.2

Top PR practitioners

Why do you think more PR practitioners are achieving senior positions within organisations? Has education played a part in this development? Or is it the ever-changing communication demands of the modern world?

Public relations roles

Research undertaken by US researchers Broom and Smith (1979) and Dozier and Broom (1995) identifies two dominant PR roles:

■ The *communication manager*, who plans and manages PR programmes, advises management, makes communication policy decisions and oversees their implementation.

■ The *communication technician*, who is not involved in organisational decision making but who implements PR programmes, such as writing press releases, organising events and producing web content. Technicians usually do not get too involved in research or evaluation: they are the 'doers'.

The communication manager role itself divides into three identifiable types:

■ The *expert prescriber*, who researches and defines PR problems, develops programmes to tackle these problems and then implements them, sometimes with the assistance of others.

■ The *communication facilitator*, who acts as communication broker, maintaining two-way communication between an organisation and its publics, liaising, interpreting and mediating.

■ The *problem-solving process facilitator*, who helps others solve their communication problems, acts as a counsellor/adviser on the planning and implementation of programmes. This role can be fulfilled by specialist consultancies as well as the in-house person.

Two other roles, sitting between the manager and technician are also noted:

■ *Media relations role*, a highly skilled job requiring profound knowledge and understanding of the media. This is not just about the dissemination of messages, but a crucial function where the needs of the media are met in a sophisticated way. This is a role often fulfilled by a senior journalist who has made the crossover to public relations.

■ *Communication and liaison role*, meaning the individual who represents the organisation at events and meetings and creates opportunities for management to communicate with internal and external publics.

The classification into manager and technician roles does not mean that lines are fixed. Most PR professionals perform a mix of manager and technician work, but the point is that one role will tend to predominate. Entry-level practitioners are normally entrusted with technical tasks at the initial stages of their career. As practitioners become more experienced they may move on to the manager role. (A fuller discussion of these roles can be found in Chapters 3 and 8.)

Of course, there is enormous variety within these roles. A technician employed for their writing skills may be involved in a range of work, such as writing press releases,

speech writing, writing for the web, or may be involved in just one job, for example producing the house journal.

The communication manager may be responsible for the full PR programme or, if they work for a large corporate organisation, they may be responsible for one specialist area such as government or investor relations.

Public relations tasks

Fombrun and Van Riel (2006) divide corporate communication, as they label it, into three areas:

■ *Management communication* is communication by management aimed at developing a shared vision, establishing and maintaining trust in the leadership, managing change, and empowering and motivating employees. Fombrun and Van Riel regard management communication as the responsibility of all managers. They may have a communication expert to help them with developing effective communication, but Fombrun and Van Riel warn against the danger of thinking that hiring an expert absolves management of its overall responsibility.

■ *Marketing communication* is aimed at supporting the sale of goods and/or services. This will include advertising, sales promotion, direct mail, personal selling, online and mobile marketing as well as market-orientated public relations – or publicity, as they call it. Typically this includes media relations and events, too.

■ *Organisational communication* is a host of communication activities usually at a corporate level, not all of which will be necessarily located in the PR department, which include public affairs, environmental communication, investor relations, labour market communication, corporate advertising, internal communication and PR.

Such a division along *functional* lines is often reflected in the structure of PR departments. Figure 2.4 shows a

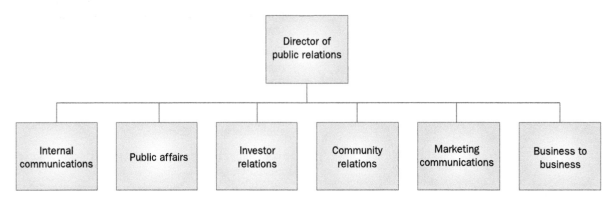

Figure 2.4 PR department structured in functions

Writing and editing	Special events
Print and broadcast news releases, feature stories, newsletters, correspondence, website/online media, shareholder/annual reports, speeches, brochures, AV scripts, advertisements, product and technical materials	Arranging and managing news conferences, conventions, openings, ceremonies, anniversaries, fund-raising events, visiting dignitaries, contests, awards, facility visits

Writing and editing

Print and broadcast news releases, feature stories, newsletters, correspondence, website/online media, shareholder/annual reports, speeches, brochures, AV scripts, advertisements, product and technical materials

Media relations and placement

Contacting news media, magazines, supplements, trade publications and freelancers to get them to publish material about the organisation. Responding to media requests

Research

Gathering information about public opinion trends, issues, political climate, legislation, media coverage, special interest groups and other concerns relating to stakeholders. Online searches. Designing research, surveys and hiring research firms

Management and administration

Programming and planning with other managers, determining needs, prioritising, defining publics, setting goals and objectives, developing strategy and tactics, administering personal budgets and managing programmes

Special events

Arranging and managing news conferences, conventions, openings, ceremonies, anniversaries, fund-raising events, visiting dignitaries, contests, awards, facility visits

Speaking

Gaining speaking platforms, coaching others, speaking to groups

Production

Of multimedia, artwork, typography, photography, layout, DTP, AV, either personally or by other specialists

Training

Media training and public appearance, preparation for others, coaching others in writing and communication skills. Helping introduce change in culture, policy, structure and process

Contact

Liaising with media, community, internal and external groups. Listening, negotiating, managing conflict, mediating, meeting and entertaining guests and visitors

Counselling

Advising management on social, political and regulatory environments, crisis avoidance and management, working with others on issues management

Figure 2.5 Cutlip and colleagues' categorisation of public relations work (*source*: Cutlip, Scott M., Center, Allen H., Broom, Glen M., *Effective Public Relations*, 8th Edition, © 2000, pp. 36–37. Adapted by permission of Pearson Education, Inc., Upper Saddle River, NJ)

typical functional structure. In such a structure an individual or group will look after all the activities falling within the area, whether these are media relations, sponsorship, events or individual relationships.

Cutlip et al. (2000) choose to categorise PR work along *task* lines. They list 10 elements (see Figure 2.5) that summarise what PR practitioners do at work.

Figure 2.6 is an example of a PR department structured on task lines.

An obvious danger of both these approaches is that the specialist individuals or teams become function or task orientated and lose the overall picture of organisational priorities. The job of the manager is to ensure this does not happen. One way in which this is approached in

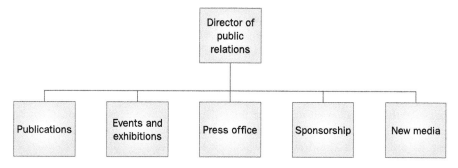

Figure 2.6 PR department structured by tasks

consultancies is to put together project teams for accounts as they are won. These comprise functional and task experts drawn from across the consultancy who work on other cross-functional/task accounts concurrently.

Many in-house teams use a mixture of functional and task teams. For example, it is not unusual to have a press office that serves all the functional teams simply because this is a particular type of expertise and it would be inefficient to have a press specialist based in each team. It could also be dangerous since different functional teams could give out different messages reflecting their own priorities, rather than the overall and coordinated view of the corporate organisation.

Because they are part of the support function of an organisation, PR departments and people will operate with all other departments, offering support and advice as required. This is part of the boundary-spanning role described earlier and fits in very well with the systems theory approach. However, organisations are complex and some areas of responsibility do not always fit neatly into functional departments. For example, internal communication is sometimes based in PR, sometimes in marketing and sometimes in human resources (HR). Again, some departments seem to have less well-defined boundaries than others and PR is a good example of this.

There are two main departments where there is potential for both close cooperation and 'turf' or territorial disputes – marketing and HR. The legal department is a third area that requires special attention.

Marketing

The relationship between PR and marketing can be a fractious one (for more on this debate see Chapter 27). For decades there have been non-productive arguments about whether PR is a part of marketing or vice versa. There are misconceptions on both sides.

For many marketing people PR is all about getting free 'publicity' in the media to support the promotion of products and services to consumers. However, PR – as this book amply demonstrates – is much more than that; it is about building relationships with numerous stakeholders, using a whole range of channels and techniques. As the idea of organisations as networks of stakeholding communities gains credence in the business world (Freeman 1984; Halal 2000), there is growing recognition that PR, with its particular skills in relationship building, has a role far beyond marketing communication (Rogers 2007).

This is a sentiment that is not missed by marketers either. Marketing is broadening its remit to include the internal 'customer' and other (non-profit) relationships, bringing to bear its considerable knowledge base and expertise in managing consumer relationships to other stakeholders. For example, the 'corporate branding' debate

in marketing circles recognises that organisations have many stakeholders and that if a whole organisation is to gain support, then all stakeholders, not just customers, will need to be addressed (Balmer and Gray 2003; Gregory 2007).

However, marketing has some way to go in adjusting its basic philosophy. Marketing assumes that there is a 'profit' in any exchange relationship – the organisation comes out as the net beneficiary. The notion of relationships being of value in themselves is one of the key tenets of PR and is a point of major difference between the disciplines.

However, as the two functions develop it is inevitable that the distinction between them will blur. Indeed, many organisations now have a single communication function integrating all aspects of the organisation's communication, often headed by a board-level director who can be either a marketing or a PR professional – sometimes both.

Human resources or personnel

As the section earlier indicated, Van Riel regards organisational communication and internal communication as part of the overall corporate communication remit. It is evident that the PR and HR/personnel functions should and must work in a collaborative way to communicate with employees. For example, where there is a reorganisation, a merger, an acquisition or layoffs, HR must play the lead role in renegotiating employees' contracts, terms and conditions and location. However, PR is vital to communicating these kinds of change in an appropriate and timely way and in helping to maintain morale.

HR is sometimes the host department for internal communication. Irrespective of its physical location, PR's involvement in strategic communication objectives, together with its knowledge of communication techniques and content, are good reasons for close collaboration.

HR and PR departments both regard employees as one of their most important stakeholders. Recruiting and retaining employees is being increasingly recognised by CEOs as vitally important (Smythe 2007) because as 'knowledge' becomes the differentiator adding value to organisations, the collective 'knowledge' of its workforce becomes increasingly precious (see also Chapter 16).

Legal

Organisations in crisis or under threat turn to their legal departments for advice. Lawyers are naturally cautious and their instinct is to keep quiet and say nothing that might incriminate an individual or make the organisation liable in any way. However, today's organisation is held to account for what it does not say and do as well as for what it actually says and does. Stakeholders value transparency and honesty. It is imperative, therefore, that lawyers and PR professionals work closely together, each contributing

Think about 2.3   Marketing and PR relationship

Why do you think there is tension between the marketing and public relations disciplines? Have you been aware of this tension on work experience or placements? Is it reflected in the attitudes of tutors for these subjects?

Feedback

Marketing sees PR as only marketing communications and as a 'cheap option'. It does not appreciate that placing material in the media is more difficult than paying for advertising. Further, it does not appreciate the skill involved in media relations. Neither does it recognise the range of stakeholding relationships that PR practitioners need to manage and maintain.

PR sees marketing as being powerful because of the size of budgets. It does not think that customer focus is all important, as marketing people do. It considers encroachment on PR territory as a threat. (For more information, read Hutton 2001.)

---

their particular knowledge and skills to manage issues, crises and risks.

Battles for ascendancy among specialist functions are essentially futile. What matters is that the interests of the organisation and its publics are well served. That is best done by fellow professionals working together to fulfil that common aim (see Think about 2.3 and Activity 2.3).

Activity 2.3

The public relations department

Choose an organisation that you have easy access to, in either the public or private sector. Find out where PR is located, how it is structured and what tasks are undertaken. What have you learned from this exercise?

Future of the public relations department

New directions in PR are discussed at the end of this book, but it is worth pointing out a number of developments that are likely to impact on the structure of the PR function of the future and may enhance the role of PR within organisations.

Regulatory issues

Reforms to reporting conventions in Britain will require companies to report on a range of non-financial factors, such as the company's interactions with stakeholders, their treatment of employees and their environmental policies. The EU Directive on Information and Consultation, which demands that larger companies consult with employees on a range of issues, provides PR with large opportunities. PR professionals are ideally positioned to collect the data for these activities and to report on them.

Risk management and stakeholder interest

Risk management, along with reputation management, is becoming more important to CEOs (Murray and White 2004). Risk management is intimately bound up in relationship building with important stakeholders.

Technology

As technology develops, practitioners will need to become more adroit at using it with many more specialist technician roles being created to exploit new ways of communicating with stakeholders. At the same time, the impact of these new technologies will need deeper consideration at a strategic level. For example, how will organisations manage the requirement for on-demand, tailored information from potentially millions of stakeholders on a global basis 24/7, 365 days a year? See Activity 2.4.

Activity 2.4

The public relations industry

From your reading and research around the topics discussed in this chapter, conduct an EPISTLE analysis of the PR industry. What are the key issues for PR?

Summary

This chapter has sought to describe and discuss some of the key factors and theories that influence the management and organisation of PR. It is a function subject to many external and internal influences. It is a subtle discipline, significantly affected by organisational culture and by the power and influence that it is allowed to exercise. However, PR is not shaped only by organisa-tions; it helps to shape them too. Communication-aware organisations are very different from those that are not. The PR function can be a dynamo of energy and change within organisations. Smart organisations embrace what the PR discipline has to offer through its knowledge of relationship building and stakeholder management and its sophisticated use of communications techniques and channels. Less smart organisations will be left behind.

Bibliography

Balmer, J.M.T. and E.R. Gray (2003). 'Corporate brands: What are they? What of them?'. *European Journal of Marketing* 37(7/8): 972–997.

Broom, G.M. and G.D. Smith (1979). 'Testing the practitioner's impact on clients'. *Public Relations Review* 5(2): 47–59.

CIPR (2004). www.ipr.org.uk/direct/news.asp?v1=factfile accessed 10 July 2004.

CIPR (2005). 'The economic significance of public relations'. Report commissioned by CIPR from the Centre for Economics and Business Research Ltd. London: GDR.

CIPR/DTI (2003). 'Unlocking the potential of public relations'. Joint Report of the Chartered Institute of Public Relations and Department of Trade and Industry. London: CIPR.

Cutlip, S.M., A.H. Center and G.M. Broom (2000). *Effective Public Relations*, 8th edition. Upper Saddle River, NJ: Prentice Hall.

Cutlip, S.M., A.H. Center and G.M. Broom (2006). *Effective Public Relations*, 9th edition. Upper Saddle River, NJ: Prentice Hall.

DCSF (2008). 'Funding boost for the school food revolution'. www.dcsf.gov.uk/pns/DisplayPN.cgi?pn_id=2008_0026 accessed 14 March 2008.

Dozier, D.M. and G.M. Broom (1995). 'Evolution of the managerial role in public relations practice'. *Journal of Public Relations Research* 7(2): 17.

Edelman, R. (2006). 'The communication revolution'. Speech given to Public Relations Society of America Conference, *Towards a Global Public Relations Model*, New York, 2 June.

Eisenberg, E.M. and P. Riley (2001). 'Organizational culture' in *The New Handbook of Organizational Communication: Advances in theory, research and methods*. F.M. Jablin and L.L. Puttnam (eds). Thousand Oaks, CA: Sage.

Esman, M.J. (1972). 'The elements of institution building' in *Institution Building and Development*. J.W. Eaton (ed.). Beverley Hills: Sage.

Evans, H. (2008). 'Broadcasting house'. BBC Radio 4 broadcast, 16 March.

Fombrun, C.J. and C.B.M. Van Riel (2006). *Essentials of Corporate Communication*. London: Routledge.

Freeman, R.E. (1984). *Strategic Management: A stakeholder approach*. Boston, MA: Pitman.

Friedman, M. (1970). 'The social responsibility of business is to increase its profits'. *The New York Times Magazine*, 13 September.

Gregory, A. (2003). 'Public relations and the age of spin'. Inaugural lecture at Leeds Metropolitan University, 26 March.

Gregory, A. (2007). 'Involving stakeholders in developing corporate brands: the communication dimension'. *Journal of Marketing Management* 23: 59–73.

Gregory, A. and L. Edwards (2004). 'Patterns of PR: Public relations management among Britain's "most admired" companies'. Report for Eloqui Public Relations. Leeds: Leeds Metropolitan University.

Grunig, J.E. and L.A. Grunig (1992). 'Models of public relations and communication' in *Excellence in Public Relations*. J.E. Grunig (ed.). Mahwah, NJ: Lawrence Erlbaum Associates.

Grunig, J.E. and T. Hunt (1984). *Managing Public Relations*. New York: Holt, Rinehart & Winston.

Halal, W.E. (2000). 'Corporate community: A theory of the firm uniting profitability and responsibility'. *Strategic Leadership*, 28(2): 10–16.

Hargreaves, I. (2005). *Journalism: A very short introduction*. Oxford: Oxford University Press.

Herriot, P. and W. Scott-Jackson (2002). 'Globalisation, social identities and employment'. *British Journal of Management* 13: 249–257.

Hofstede, G. and G.J.H. Hofstede (2004). *Cultures and Organizations: Software of the mind*, 2nd edition. New York: McGraw-Hill.

Hutton, J.G. (2001). 'Defining the relationship between public relations and marketing: Public relations' most important challenge' in *The Handbook of Public Relations*. R.L. Heath (ed.). Thousand Oaks, CA: Sage.

Kornhauser, W. (1960). *The Politics of Mass Society*. London: Routledge.

Loughrey, P. (2007). 'Future screens: local and national'. Lecture at Leeds Metropolitan University, 4 December.

McCollom, M. (1994). 'The cultures of work organizations'. *Academy of Management Review* 19: 836–839.

Moloney, K. (2000). *Rethinking Public Relations*. London: Routledge.

Moloney, K. (2006). *Rethinking Public Relations*, 2nd edition. London: Routledge.

Moss, D.A. and R. Green (2001). 'Re-examining the manager's role in public relations: What management and public relations research teaches us'. *Journal of Communication Management* 6(2): 18–132.

Moss, D.A., G. Wamaby and A. Newman (2000). 'Public relations practitioner role enactment at the senior management level within UK companies'. *Journal of Public Relations Research* 12(4): 227–308.

Moss, D.A., A. Newman and B. De Santo (2005). 'What do communication managers do? Defining and refining the core element of management in a public relations/communication context'. *Journalism and Mass Communication Quarterly* 82(4): 873–890.

Murray, K. and J. White (2004). 'CEO views on reputation management: A report on the value of public relations. as perceived by organisational leaders'. London: Chime PLC.

Naisbitt, J. and P. Aburdene (1991). *Megatrends 2000*. London: Pan with Sidgwick and Jackson.

Ritzer, G. (2004). *The Globalisation of Nothing*, 2nd edition. Thousand Oaks, CA: Pine Forge Press.

Rogers, D. (2007). 'Global current trends bode well for PR'. *PR Week*, 9 March.

Smythe, J. (2007). *The CEO – The Chief Engagement Officer*. London: Gower.

Stauber, J. and S. Rampton (2002). *Toxic Sludge is Good for You: Lies, Damn Lies and the Public Relations Industry*. Monroe, ME: Common Courage Press.

Steyn, B. and G. Puth (2000). *Corporate Communication Strategy*. Sandown: Heinemann Publishers (Pty).

Toth, E.L., S.A. Serini, D.K. Wright and A.G. Emig (1998). 'Trends in public relations roles: 1990–1995'. *Public Relations Review* 24(2): 53–175.

CHAPTER 11

Planning Public Relations 1

CHAPTER 9
Anne Gregory

Public relations as planned communication

© Getty Images

Learning outcomes

By the end of this chapter you should be able to:

- debate why planning is important for public relations programmes
- identify what research is required to underpin sound programmes
- determine appropriate programme objectives
- select and justify chosen strategy and tactics
- determine required timescales and resources
- evaluate the effectiveness of the campaign and review future direction.

Structure

- Why planning is important
- Systems context of planning
- Approaches to the planning process
- Analysis
- Setting objectives
- Identifying publics
- Messages or content
- Strategy and tactics
- Timescales and resources
- Evaluation and review

Introduction

Successful public relations (PR) programmes do not just happen. They are the result of sound research, meticulous planning and careful implementation. This does not rule out the impromptu or the reactive, but these are exceptions.

Research among Britain's 'most admired companies' (Gregory and Edwards 2004) shows that up to 70% of their communication activity is pre-planned. The majority of the remaining time is spent making the most of unexpected opportunities and reacting to events such as a major media story, and some time is spent in crisis management. But once these incidents are dealt with, the planned approach is resumed.

Planning will not make a poorly conceived programme successful in achieving its objectives, but planning makes it more likely that a programme will be well conceived in the first place. By ensuring that plans are targeted at the right people, use the right channels of communication and say the appropriate things at the right time, all within agreed timescales and budget, the foundations for success are laid.

Planning PR is not overly complicated but time, effort and knowledge of the planning process is required.

This chapter provides an overview of the planning process. It will introduce each of the stages involved in planning PR programmes and examine some of the theories that underlie the process. Other chapters will discuss some elements of the planning process in more depth (for example, Chapter 10 on research and evaluation). These chapters and further reading will be highlighted throughout this chapter.

Why planning is important

Within the many definitions of PR that were discussed in Chapter 1, planned or managed communication is frequently mentioned as a defining characteristic of the discipline. Planning for PR programmes provides a framework that can stimulate thinking; it acts as a prompt for problem solving and it releases creativity while ensuring it is focused and purposeful.

There are a number of very practical reasons for planning PR activity:

- planning focuses effort – by eliminating unnecessary and low-priority work

- planning improves effectiveness – by ensuring the planner works to achieve agreed objectives from the outset

- planning encourages the long-term view – by requiring the planner to look to the organisation's future needs, preparing it for change and helping it manage future risks

- planning assists proactivity – setting the agenda means planners can be proactive and 'on the front foot'

- planning reconciles conflicts – putting together a comprehensive PR plan means that potential difficulties and conflicts have to be thought through in the planning stage

- planning minimises mishaps – thinking through potential scenarios means that most eventualities can be covered and contingency plans put in place

- planning demonstrates value for money – planners can show they have achieved programme objectives within budget, and past achievements also help the planner argue for future resourcing.

So why doesn't everyone plan everything? The following suggests why practitioners are sometimes reluctant to plan, despite the arguments outlined above:

- lack of time – planning is time consuming and ongoing work cannot be suspended while it is done

- plans are out of date as soon as they are written – business and particularly communication is conducted in an ever-changing and dynamic environment, so planning has little point

- planning raises unrealistic managerial expectations – too many factors that are outside the planner's control to guarantee results

- plans are too rigid and stifle the impromptu and opportunistic – flexibility of response is a crucial strength of the communication function

- plans are a block to creativity – the approach is formulaic and encourages formulaic activities

- plans always reflect the ideal, not the real – it makes it appear that communication work can be tightly controlled and all ambiguities 'planned out'. The reality of doing PR work, say some practitioners, is not like that.

See Think about 9.1.

Think about 9.1

Planning

Which argument do you find more persuasive: the arguments for planned activity or against? Why? Would these arguments apply to planning a birthday party? Or a study project, such as a dissertation?

Picture 9.1 Effective public relations planning might help avert media stories like this where shoppers overwhelmed a newly opened London store (*source*: Johny Green/PA/Empics)

Systems context of planning

PR planning is located within the positivist framework and maps across very well to the systems view of organisations (see Chapter 8 for more discussion of systems theory). The 'open system' view of an organisation is an important concept for PR planning, because an open system assumes that the organisation is an organism or 'living entity with boundaries, inputs, outputs, "through-puts", and enough feedback from both the internal and external environments so that it can make appropriate adjustments in time to keep on living' (McElreath 1997).

Cutlip et al. (2006) present an open systems model of PR that clearly identifies how all these systems characteristics map on to the planning process (see Figure 9.1). So, for example, 'input' refers to actions taken by, or information about, publics. These inputs in turn are transformed into goals (aims) and objectives that underpin the desired relationships with publics. By contrast, a 'closed system' approach might neglect to take account of information about publics and thus the planner might formulate aims and objectives in isolation.

Scope of PR planning

Systematic planning can be applied to PR activity over a period of several years, such as the Full Stop campaign to prevent child abuse conducted by the UK's National Society for the Prevention of Cruelty to Children (NSPCC), or to short-focused campaigns, such as the launch of a new service, or even to a single activity, such as a press conference.

When discussing the role of the communication planner, Windahl et al. (1992) embrace a wider interpretation of planning programmes or 'campaigns'. Informal communication, which is initiated to begin a dialogue for its own sake, is legitimate and may be 'planned'. It will have a purpose and will involve different publics. For example, key opinion formers may be invited by a university to a hospitality event such as an annual dinner. This occasion may not have a specific planned outcome other than a belief that interpersonal communication is in itself a valuable process which helps people work together in a more cooperative way. This dialogue helps build relationships and a sense of community around the university.

Furthermore, the type of work that planners undertake can be extremely varied. Some planners work for large

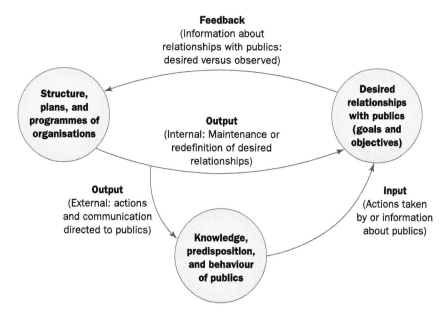

Figure 9.1 Open systems model of public relations (*source*: Cutlip, Scott M., Center, Allen H., Broom, Glen M., *Effective Public Relations*, 8th Edition, © 2000, p. 244. Reprinted by permission of Pearson Education, Inc., Upper Saddle River, NJ)

organisations on large communication projects. For example, government communicators may work on nationwide initiatives such as the one to encourage healthy eating in schools (DCSF 2008) or voting in EU elections, while those working for large corporations may work on global corporate identity initiatives. However, some planners work on quite small projects, for example running an open day for a local charity or volunteering to work with local communities and activists to protest about a local road scheme.

Windahl et al. (1992) also point out that communication initiatives can start at the bottom of an organisation as well as the top. For example, a small department may begin a series of sporting events to build informal communications in the team, which eventually widens out into a company-wide and company-supported programme of activities.

This chapter takes the systemic approach to planning, outlined earlier, as its basis. The next step therefore is to examine some of the existing planning approaches.

Approaches to the planning process

The planning process is ordered and enables the PR planner to structure their approach around certain key aspects (see Figure 9.2). It is helpful to see it as answering six basic questions:

- What is the problem? (Researching the issue.)
- What does the plan seek to achieve? (What are the objectives?)
- Who should be talked to? (With which publics should a relationship be developed?)
- What should be said? (What is the content or message?)
- How should the message be communicated? (What channels should be used for dissemination?)
- How is success to be judged? (How will the work be evaluated against the objectives?)

Marston (1979) provided one of the best-known planning formulae for PR which is encapsulated in the mnemonic RACE – **R**esearch, **A**ction, **C**ommunication and **E**valuation. American academics Cutlip et al. (2006) articulate the PR planning process as in Figure 9.2.

Gregory (2000) has expanded PR planning into a sequence of steps that add further detail to the process (see Figure 9.3).

All planning processes follow a basic sequence, whether they are for the strategic management of an organisation or for PR (see Figure 9.4 and Think about 9.2). The approach advocated here is known as 'management by objectives' (MBO), which means:

- setting objectives and targets
- participation by individual managers in agreeing unit (i.e. department) objectives and criteria of performance
- review and appraisal of results (Mullins 1989: 254).

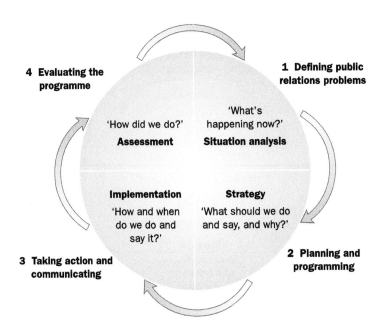

Figure 9.2 Cutlip and colleagues' planning model (*source*: Cutlip, Scott M., Center, Allen H., Broom, Glen M., *Effective Public Relations*, 8th Edition, © 2000. Reprinted by permission of Pearson Education, Inc., Upper Saddle River, NJ.)

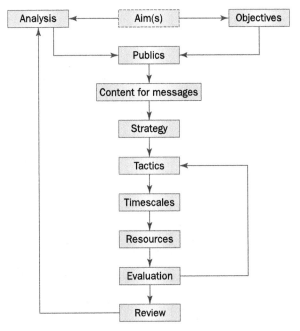

Figure 9.3 Gregory's planning model (*source*: Gregory 2000: 44)

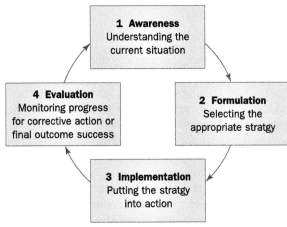

Figure 9.4 Basic business planning model

Although, ideally, the PR practitioner would undertake analysis of the situation before determining objectives, in practice they are often given objectives by their managers. Such an objective might be to help overturn proposed legislation. In these circumstances it is still vital that the

The MBO system can be integrated into strategic-level corporate planning, at unit level (as in a PR department) and at the individual level where there is a review of staff performance in a given role (Mullins 1989).

Gregory's planning model in Figure 9.3 provides a sequence of activities and captures the essence of the planning approaches outlined. It will be used to examine the steps of the planning process in detail. However, first it is important to explain the structure of the first part of the diagram.

Think about 9.2

Planning processes

Look at the PR planning processes and models described so far. What are the main similarities between them?

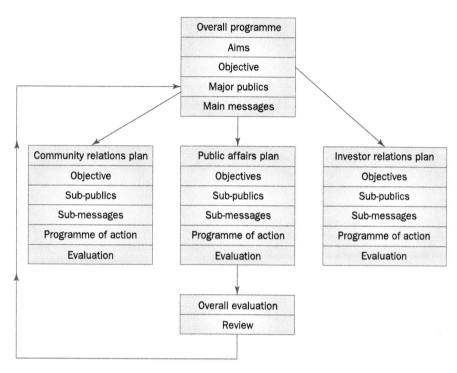

Figure 9.5 Framework for multi-project public relations plans (*source:* adapted from Gregory 2000: 46)

objectives themselves are scrutinised to see if they are appropriate. For example, an organisation may wish to resist the introduction of a stringent piece of environmental legislation because it will be expensive to implement and thereby affect shareholder dividends. However, on investigation, the PR practitioner may discover that: stakeholders are very much in favour of the legislation; competitor companies will support it; and the company will be out of line if it persists. In this situation the PR practitioner may recommend that the proposed campaign is abandoned.

The 'aim' element is in a dotted box because sometimes a campaign has a single, simple objective that does not need an overarching aim. If the programme is particularly large, it may be necessary to break down the whole into a series of projects that follow the same basic steps. Each project will have its own specific objectives, publics and content or messages, but this needs to be incorporated into a larger plan which provides a coordinating framework with overall aims, objectives and the message content guidance so that the individual projects do not conflict. (See Figure 9.5.)

Two things need to be borne in mind at this stage. First, the planning template could be seen to encourage a very rigid and undynamic approach. Sometimes practitioners have to move very rapidly in response to unpredictable events. Of course, practitioners must respond to the unplanned. However, even in these circumstances, the template can be used as a checklist to ensure that all the

essential elements have been covered. Second, the degree to which any element of the planning process is followed will vary according to the requirements of the task in hand. For example, a full analysis of an organisation's external environment (see also Chapter 2 for an explanation of EPISTLE) will not be required to run an effective open day for families because any key issues will be relatively easy to identify. However, if a major programme is planned, such as the introduction of new rules for building environmentally friendly housing, then a full analysis is certainly required, since research about lifestyles, demographics, technological advances and environmental impacts may need to be undertaken to identify and understand the full range of issues which have to be borne in mind by the PR planner.

The rest of this chapter explores each stage of the planning process in turn.

Analysis

Analysis is the first step of the planning process. The point of analysis, sometimes called 'situation analysis' is to identify the issues or specific problems on which to base the programme. Without identifying the key issues the programme will not have a clear rationale. For example, if the core issue identified for action is that the organisation is seen to be unfriendly towards family carers, there is no point in aiming a recruitment campaign at potential employees, such as women returning to work, without addressing the reasons why the organisation is not an employer of choice for them.

Analysing the environment

This analysis of the external and internal environment is called 'environmental monitoring' by Lerbinger (1972), a phase that is now generally called 'environmental scanning' in the PR literature (e.g. Grunig et al. 2002).

This analysis may seem more appropriate to the identification of strategic business issues than communication issues. However, PR practitioners need to be alert to the wider environmental issues because it is these that will force some sort of action from the organisation. Action always has communication implications. Indeed, one of the major contributions that PR can make is to maintain an environmental scanning brief on behalf of their organisation. This 'early warning' of issues allows organisations to manage future risks and is a key strategic input at senior management level. In the light of these emerging issues, organisations can make adjustments to their own strategy and actions to align themselves to new realities. (See also Chapter 18.)

Furthermore, issue spotting helps organisations contribute sensibly to public debate at an early stage and hence influence the outcome. Pressure groups, for example, will spot issues early to influence public debate. In one case, the intervention of environmental and human rights activists at a formative stage in the debate led to the stalling of plans to build dams in disputed areas in India.

Given the speed at which activists can galvanise action via the Internet and mobile technologies, even the most astute PR practitioners can get the briefest or even no warning of an impending issue. However, most issues develop more slowly and some forward thinking and good intelligence gathering can help predict many of them.

The main questions to be asked when undertaking this kind of analysis are:

- What are the environmental factors that affect this organisation (identified from the EPISTLE analysis)?

- Which ones are of most importance now?

- Which will become the most important in the next four years?

From this it will be possible to derive a list of the main issues that will affect the organisation. These will differ depending on the country, the industry sector and the particular circumstances the organisation operates in.

It is important to identify whether some of these issues are linked. For example, social and technological changes are often connected: the lifestyle of many people has been significantly transformed by mobile phone technology. As well as current issues, it is vital to identify the long-term forces for change. For example, concerns about obesity in developed economies will have a profound effect on the drinks, confectionary and fast food industries in the coming decade. Many organisations, from governments to financial and leisure companies, will need to respond to changing demographics that will see the average age of the population rising in many developed countries, with profound effects on the nature of health, welfare and educational provision and on the taxation system that supports them.

Having identified the broader environmental issues that affect the organisation and over which it has little control, it is then necessary to look at the organisation itself and those things over which it has greater control. A classic way to undertake this internal analysis is to use a technique called SWOT. The first two elements, **s**trengths and **w**eaknesses, are particular to the organisation and can usually be changed by it – although all organisations are to a certain extent captive to their own history and culture. However, it is in the organisation's power to address its strengths and weaknesses. The third and fourth, **o**pportunities and **t**hreats, are generally external to the organisation and can be derived from wider environmental analysis (see Chapter 2), but are usually related to those factors that have a direct impact on it. The four elements of SWOT can be seen as mirror segments in a quadrant. An example of a SWOT analysis is given in Figure 9.6.

Analysing publics

Having analysed the environment and the organisation and identified the key issues, it is then essential to look at

Strengths	**Weaknesses**
Good capital reserves Leading-edge products Loyal customer base Good reputation for service delivery Committed employees	Risk averse in investment Limited product line Ageing customer base Bureaucratic Limited skills base
Opportunities	**Threats**
New market opportunities in Russia Potential to acquire competitors Tax breaks if offices relocated	Potential political instability Danger of being overstretched Loss of loyal employee base

Figure 9.6 Example of SWOT analysis

Mini Case Study 9.1

Sea Fish Industry Authority

Identifying stakeholders

Identifying stakeholders is often a complex business. Figure 9.7 is a stakeholder map of the Sea Fish Industry Authority, a trade body based in Scotland.

The inner circle shows the priority stakeholders with the outer rings showing those with progressively less stake in the organisation.

The Sea Fish Industry Authority (Seafish), established in 1981, works across all sectors of the UK seafood industry to promote quality seafood. Its research and projects are aimed at raising standards, improving effi-

ciency and sustainability and ensuring that the entire industry develops in a viable way.

Seafish is the UK's only cross-industry seafood body working with fishermen, processors, wholesalers, seafood farmers, fish friers, caterers, retailers and the import/export trade. It works closely with some 100 trade bodies across the UK. As an executive non-departmental public body (NDPB), sponsored by the four UK government fisheries departments and funded primarily by a levy on seafood landed, farmed or imported, it is accountable to all these stakeholders, as well as to those who provide it with grant assistance for individual project work. Seafish must demonstrate to all these groups that its services offer good value for money.

Mission statement

Seafish works with the seafood industry to satisfy consumers, raise standards, improve efficiency and secure a sustainable future.

---

the organisation's publics and discover what their attitudes are towards the organisation itself, to the wider issues identified by the EPISTLE (see Chapter 2) and SWOT processes or to the particular issue that management have asked the PR department to address. (See Mini case study 9.1.)

Cutlip et al. (2006) suggest that research can be informal or formal. Informal or exploratory research methods may involve the use of any of the following:

■ Personal contacts – these could be at public meetings (e.g. for shareholders or community) or trade shows.

■ Key informants – these can be experts, editors, journalists, politicians.

■ Focus groups – for example, informal discussion groups of employees, groups of consumers or a cross-section of the public. Focus groups can be more structured, however, and use an independent moderator to elicit discussion around key themes.

■ Advisory committees, panels or boards – many non-profit organisations have these to gauge responses to ideas.

■ Ombudsman/woman – this is someone (usually independent) appointed by an organisation to identify and detect problems.

■ Call-in telephone lines (e.g. helplines) – these can be set up with varying degrees of success; however, they do signal that the organisation is 'listening'.

■ Mail analysis – this involves examining letters to identify comments and criticisms.

■ Online sources – monitoring chatrooms, and websites and social networks are an important source of intelligence.

■ Field reports – these come from people such as the salesforce who can serve as a useful early warning system for potentially difficult situations.

Chapter 10, on research and evaluation, goes into detail about how to conduct research, including the range of formal social scientific methods that can be employed, but it is important to mention here that the analysis stage of the planning process makes use of all the available information and intelligence on which PR programmes are based. This preparation work is vitally important in answering the first basic question, 'What is the problem?'

(For an example of a campaign based on solid research, see Case study 9.1 on BT's 'Better World' campaign at the end of this chapter.)

If the PR professional discovers that a key public hold a view different from that of the organisation on an issue, then there are two choices. Either the organisation must change to bring itself into line with what the public expects – for example, it may need to change its transport policy so that the local community is no longer disturbed by rogue parking. Or the organisation may wish to persuade its publics to a particular point of view. For example, it may seek to persuade people living around a chemical plant that the fume emissions genuinely are harmless. If key publics are opposed because they simply do not have relevant or accurate information, that can easily be remedied.

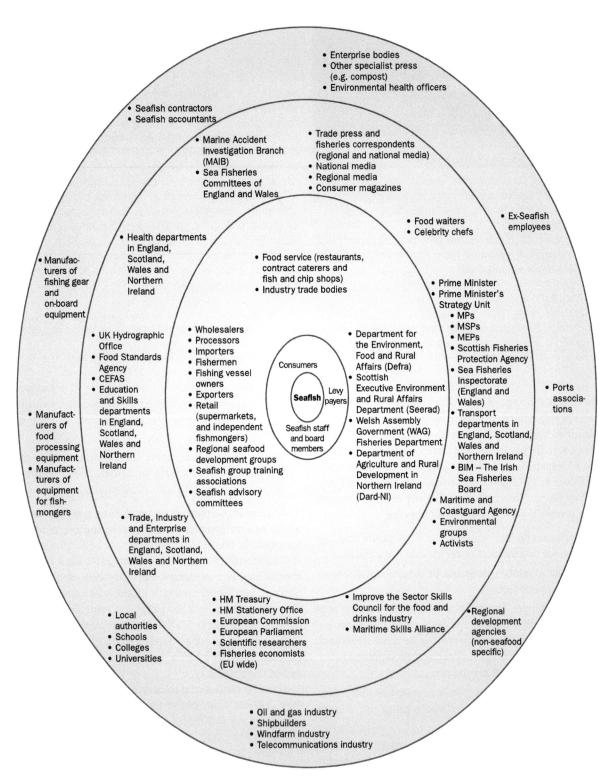

Figure 9.7 Stakeholder map of the Sea Fish Industry Authority (produced by Kirsty Innes MCIPR on behalf of the Sea Fish Industry Authority (Seafish))

If the problem is more complex, for example, the fumes are harmless as long as filtered through specially installed chimney baffles, the safety baffles have to be in place before communication can do its job.

As this last example indicates, sometimes PR practitioners are asked to solve problems that are not just communication problems. So the planner must analyse the situation to see if they are amenable to communication solutions. Windahl et al. (1992) say that a communication problem can be defined in one of two ways: first, the problem arises from the *lack of* or the *wrong sort of communication*. For example, it may be that a child vaccination is not being taken up because it has been publicised only to doctors, not to parents, and because it has been described by its technical name, not its popular name. Second, the problem is a communication problem if it can be solved by *communication alone*. In this example, if parents are given the required information (*lack of* communication problem solved) and the popular name is used (*wrong sort* of communication problem solved), it is likely that vaccination uptake will increase.

Often what are regarded as 'communication problems' are a mixture of communication and other issues and the PR practitioner must be able to separate them. For example, if the uptake of child vaccinations was also being affected by suspicion about side-effects, or if they were only available at certain clinics, then there is more than a communication problem. Some other measures such as independent clinical opinion or wider distribution of the vaccine may be needed to stimulate use.

There are occasions when no amount of communication will assist in solving a problem. For example, no amount of excellent communication (e.g. consultations) will make citizens happy to have a rubbish dump sited next to them. The best that can be hoped for is limited protest, as long as the organisation takes into account as many as possible of the citizens' suggestions for making the operation of the dump more acceptable – for example: ensuring it operates within specified hours, that any vermin are effectively dealt with and that smells are eradicated.

Thus it can be seen that analysis not only identifies the issue, but also points to what needs to be done and the precise contribution that PR can make to its resolution.

Setting objectives

To set realistic objectives it is necessary to know the size and nature of the communication task. Research among publics will have uncovered their knowledge, attitudes and behaviour on any particular topic, which will provide the starting point. The planner then needs to decide what movement is required, if any: a legitimate objective may be to confirm existing attitudes or actions. Objectives are usually set at one of three levels (Grunig and Hunt 1984; Cutlip et al. 2006), as shown in Table 9.1.

According to Grunig and Hunt (1984), three things should be borne in mind that will make the achievement of objectives easier:

1 The level of effect (or outcome) should be chosen with care. If the communication planner wants to introduce a new or complex idea, it would be sensible to set cognitive objectives first, rather than hoping for conative effects from the start.

2 Choose target publics with advocacy in mind. Research should have identified those who already support the organisational policies or who could be easily enlisted (more on this in Chapter 10). They can then act as advocates on behalf of the organisation.

3 Organisations can change too. Sometimes minor adjustments in the organisation's stance can elicit a major, positive response from publics.

Generally speaking it is much more difficult to get someone to *behave* in a certain way than it is to prompt them to *think* about something, the notable exception being over hot issues (see Chapter 13).

Cutlip et al. (2006) warn that PR programme objectives all too often describe the tactic instead of the desired outcome

Table 9.1 Objectives set at one of three levels	*Cognitive* (means related to thoughts, reflection, awareness)	Encouraging the target public to *think* about something or to create awareness. For example, local government might want the local community to be aware that it is holding a housing information day. The whole community will not need the service, but part of local government's reason for making them aware is so that they know what a proactive and interested local council they have
	Affective (means related to feelings, emotional reaction)	Encouraging the target public to form a particular attitude, opinion or feeling about a subject. For example, a pressure group may want moral support for or against gun ownership
	Conative (means related to behaviour, actions or change)	Encouraging the target public to *behave* in a certain way. For example, the local hospital may use television to ask for emergency blood donors following a major incident

Table 9.2 Examples of objectives

Issue	Objective for strategic programme	Objective for tactical campaign
Company viewed as environmentally irresponsible	Demonstrate environmental credentials	Promote company recycling scheme in local media
After-sales service perceived as slow and unresponsive	Create awareness of customer service facilities	Publicise guaranteed repair service and 24-hour customer helpline
Proposed legislation will damage environmentally sensitive areas	Change proposed legislation by lobbying government	Galvanise local pressure groups into action

for a particular public. In the 'employee' public example below, a tactical objective would be to issue the corporate plan. However, the objective that focuses on the desired outcome for employees is 'to ensure awareness of the new corporate plan'. This is the PR objective where the effort is focused on confirmation or change in knowledge, attitude or behaviour among those publics communicated with.

All objectives should be SMART: **s**pecific, **m**easurable, **a**chievable (within the planner's ability to deliver), **re**sourced and **t**ime bound. Examples of SMART objectives follow. Note that the desired outcome for each public is highlighted in bold.

Employees: *Ensure every employee is aware* of new corporate plan by 10 November and, three weeks later, can list three priorities for next year.

Community: Use sponsorship of 20 local junior football teams to *promote more positive opinion about company among parents.*

Corporate: Change legislation on taxation of charity giving within two years by *influencing voting behaviour of government ministers via a lobbying campaign.*

Trade: Double amount of coverage in trade media in one year *to overcome lack of awareness among key suppliers.*

Consumer: Increase face-to-face contact with consumers by 20% in 18 months to *counter perception of company being remote.*

Apart from setting SMART objectives, there are four prerequisites for objective setting that will ensure that they are organisationally relevant and deliverable (Gregory 2000):

■ Ally the PR objectives to *organisational objectives*. If the corporate objective is to grow the company by acquiring other companies, then PR activity must be focused on that.

■ Ensure the objectives are *PR* objectives. Employee satisfaction cannot be achieved through communication

if the main problem is poor working conditions. The source of the problem must be removed first and this is a management issue.

■ Promise what is *achievable*. It is better to set modest objectives (e.g. cognitive objective) and meet them than to over-promise (e.g. set behavioural objectives) and fail.

■ Work to *priorities*. This way the more important areas of the plan will be achieved. If the planner is then required to work on other things, the least important things can be removed from the plan. Likewise, if there are budget cuts, again the least important activities can be forgone.

As stated earlier, programmes and campaigns can be large or small. Similarly, objectives apply to both large and small programmes and campaigns. They can also be applied in strategic or tactical programmes or campaigns. The examples in Table 9.2 show how. Note how the tactical objectives do not go into detail of the specifics of the tactical approach.

Setting sound objectives is fundamental to PR planning. They define what the outcomes of the programme should be, they support the strategy, set the agenda for action and are the benchmark against which the programme will be evaluated. Their importance cannot be overstated. (See Activity 9.1.)

Activity 9.1

Evaluating objectives

Go to the Chartered Institute of Public Relations website (http://www.cipr.co.uk/prideawards/casestudies/index.html). Look at some of the award-winning entries and analyse the objectives. Are they genuine objectives? Are they SMART?

Identifying publics

The section on objectives answered the second basic question in planning programmes, 'What does the plan seek to achieve?' This next section answers the third, 'Who should we talk to?' Chapter 11 is devoted to audiences, publics and stakeholders so this section will be relatively brief.

Research for the proposed programme will have identified the key publics (see section on analysis). Sometimes the key publics are apparent to the planner. If the planned programme is to support a product launch, then existing and potential customers will be a priority. However, groups are often not homogenous. It is incorrect to assume that all-embracing groups such as the *local community* comprise individuals who are similar or who will act in the same way. Within these groups there will be the 'active', 'aware', 'latent' and 'apathetic' publics that Grunig and Repper (1992) discuss (explained in Chapter 11). They will have very different interests and concerns. It is likely that many individuals will belong to more than one stakeholding or public category too. Employees of an organisation may well be partners in a community relations campaign, or consume their organisation's products or services; they may even be shareholders.

There are many ways in which stakeholders and publics can be segmented and the type of campaign will determine the best way to do that. For example, if a government wants to introduce a new benefit targeted at lower-income families, it makes sense to segment stakeholders by income and where they live. A charity wanting to start up a coun-

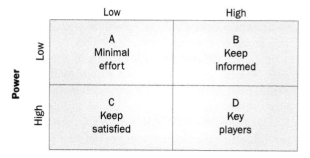

Figure 9.8 Power/interest matrix (*source*: adapted from Mendelow 1991, cited in Johnson and Scholes 2002: 208)

selling service for refugees may wish to segment by ethnicity; a leisure company wanting to set up Saturday morning clubs for children will segment by age. (See Box 9.1.)

The practitioner has to decide the most appropriate ways to undertake the segmentation of stakeholders. Then it is important to move from the general to the particular. Broad categories must be divided into discrete groups. This could be done on the basis of the communication effort required for each group or on the basis of their power and influence.

The power/interest matrix (Figure 9.8) is used in strategic planning and can be readily transferred to the communication context. It categorises stakeholders depending on the amount of power they have to influence others and the level of interest they may have in a particular issue. Clearly the more power and interest they have, the more likely their actions are to impact on the organisation, so the support of this group is crucial. Johnson, Scholes and Whittington (2007) point out that power comes from a number of sources including status in or outside the organisation, the ability to claim resources (for example, investors money or internal budget), and the symbols of power that individuals have (for example use of titles).

It is possible, even desirable at times, that stakeholders in one segment should move to another. For example, powerful institutional investors often reside in segment C. It may be in times of crisis that the communicator will want to move them to segment D so that they can use their power and influence with others to support the organisation.

Similarly, just because a stakeholding group appears not to have much interest or power does not mean that it is not important. It may be desirable to stimulate local community groups located in segment B because they in turn are connected to more interested and powerful stakeholders, such as employees, in segment D.

By plotting stakeholders and publics in the power/interest grid it is possible to identify who the key blockers and facilitators of communication are likely to be and to react to this, for example, through more information or dialogue. It is also feasible to identify whether some stakeholders and publics should be repositioned (as above) and who should be maintained in their position.

It is informative to map stakeholders in a number of ways. For example, not only can current position and desired position be mapped, but a useful exercise is to map how stakeholders might move in relation to a developing issue and whether or not this is desirable, preventable or inevitable. Communication strategies can then be devised that accommodate these movements.

Once categorised according to a suitable method, the groups need to be prioritised and the amount of communication effort devoted to them apportioned. Figure 9.9 shows an example of how this might be done for a luxury wallpaper manufacturer.

The number of publics that are communicated with and the depth of that communication is likely to be limited by either a financial or time budget. However, it is import-

Grouping	Percentage of communication effort apportioned
Corporate	**20**
Shareholders (active)	8
Shareholders (latent)	2
Investment analysts	5
Financial press (active)	5
Customers	**30**
Large do-it-yourself retailers	10
Specialist wholesale decorating suppliers	6
Specialist retail outlets	6
Trade press	7
Trade exhibition organisers	1
Consumers	**15**
Consumer press	10
TV and radio specialist programme producers	5
Suppliers	**10**
Raw materials	
Major suppliers	6
Minor suppliers	4
Employees	**15**
Executives	2
Supervisors	2
Shopfloor workers	4
Designers and salesforce	3
Trade union leaders	2
Pensioners	2
Community	**10**
Neighbours	6
Schools	4

Figure 9.9 Prioritisation of effort for luxury wallpaper manufacturer

ant that all the key 'gatekeepers' or leaders of active groups are identified. They may well interpret information for others, act as advocates on the organisation's behalf and catalyse action. Key individuals may belong to more than one group, so PR activity needs to be coordinated to ensure that there are no conflicting objectives, messages or tactics.

Messages or content

The fourth basic question is, 'What should be said?' Traditionally, PR people have focused on messages. Heath (2001) says this could be explained partly because many practitioners have come from a journalistic background, where 'getting the story' out is seen as important. This has led to a focus on 'message design and dissemination to achieve awareness, to inform, to persuade – even manipulate' (Heath 2001: 2).

There are many kinds of campaign where messages are critically important, especially in public information campaigns. So, a country's health department that wants to inform the public about aspects of healthcare often uses memorable messages. Similarly, road safety messages are encapsulated in slogans such as 'Don't drink and drive'.

Messages are important for four main reasons:

1   Messages assist the awareness and attitude-forming process. Publics who can repeat a message they have seen or heard are demonstrating that it has been received. They are also likely to have a view on it.

2   Messages demonstrate that the communication channels have been appropriate and that the message reached the recipient.

3   Messages are essential in the evaluation process. Messages intended for the media can be evaluated through media content analysis. If the same messages are picked up and repeated by the target public (e.g. through survey research), it demonstrates that the communication has been, at least in part, effective. What publics do with that assimilated message is the other half of the story.

4   Summarising an argument down to its bare essentials in a key message such as 'eat five fruits and vegetables every day' helps focus management minds and imposes discipline on woolly thinking.

However, messages have limitations. They indicate one-way communication: the originator simply checks to see if their communication has been received. If an organisation genuinely wants to enter into a *dialogue* with publics where the outcome will be mutually determined, messaging is not so appropriate. For example, if a new organisation wants to discuss with its employees what its values and goals should be, dialogue is required. Where dialogue is part of the overall purpose of communication, simplistic approaches to messaging are inappropriate. (For more on dialogue see relationship management theory in Chapter 8.)

How then can programmes that involve dialogue be evaluated if messages are one of the ways to measure communication effectiveness? The obvious answer is: by the quality of the relationship that results from the dialogue and the level of mutual cooperation and support. More on this later in the chapter.

Messaging or dialogue initiation is often undervalued or reduced to simple statements, but it is very important. It is the point of contact, providing the meaning between an organisation and its publics. It is 'given' by the organisation, and 'received' by its publics and vice versa. Once mutually understood and internalised it can be said that the meaning of the message or dialogue is mutually 'owned'. If messages are poorly conceived and the way they are conveyed poorly executed, it can be the end of the communication process. There are four steps in determining how to frame messages:

1   Take existing articulated perceptions that encapsulate the issue or problem. For example, it may be that the organisation is regarded as an old-fashioned employer.

2   Define what realistic shifts can be made in those perceptions. If working practices and policies have been completely overhauled, this needs explaining.

3   Identify realistic elements of persuasion. Work on the basis of fact. For example, the organisation may have introduced a crèche and family-friendly work practices. The number of women managers may have increased by 25%; the organisation may have achieved Investors in People status and won a major training award. All these facts demonstrate that the organisation is not an old-fashioned employer, and should form the platform for programme content. However, facts are rarely enough. People are not just rational beings, so it is important to add human emotion to these facts. People associate more readily with other people and their experiences rather than to purely factual information. For example, providing case studies from employees that people can relate to in a human way and which illustrate how the organisation operates as a social as well as an economic unit adds warmth and depth.

4   Ensure that the message or content is deliverable and credible through PR activity rather than via advertising or direct mail.

See Box 9.2.

The integrity of the message is affected by a range of factors that can determine whether it is taken seriously or not, such as:

- format – should words or pictures be used?

- tone – serious or light-hearted?

- context – is it a day when there is bad news for the business or the country?

- timing – is it controllable and if so, has the most auspicious time been chosen?

- repetition – can the message be repeated often enough to be remembered, but not so often as to breed contempt?

- credibility – is what you are saying believable and is the organisation that is communicating trusted?

Sometimes, circumstances dictate the format of the message and the medium in which it should be conveyed. For example, stock market information has to be provided in a prescribed form and a product recall dictates that advertising is used to get the message out quickly, in the required media and in an unmediated way.

Messages and content are key components of effective communication campaigns. Vague content leads to confusion and wasted effort. Carefully thought-through content is vital to understanding and dialogue – and essential to relationship building. (See Activity 9.2.)

Strategy and tactics

Strategy

The fifth basic question, 'How should the message be communicated?' falls into two parts: strategy and tactics. The temptation for the PR planner is to move immediately to tactics because in many ways it is easier to think of a raft of ideas than it is to think about the rationale behind them. Implementation – where the tactics are put into action – is often the most exciting part of the planning process, and the most obviously creative. However, an underpinning strategy provides coherence and focus and is a clear driving force. It is the framework that guides the menu of activities. As Windahl et al. (1992: 20) state, communication planning 'should include both systematic and creative elements. Both are essential to information/communication work.'

There is much discussion on the meaning of 'strategy'. Most books on strategic planning, for example Steyn and Puth (2000), who have applied strategy specifically to communication, provide several definitions and this in itself indicates that there is an issue around precise definitions. Strategy is described as: the 'overall concept, approach or general plan' (Cutlip et al. 2000: 378); the coordinating theme or factor; the guiding principle, or purpose; and 'the big idea', the rationale behind the programme. If an articulated strategy satisfies one or more of these elements it will be broadly satisfactory.

Strategy is dictated by, and springs from, the issues arising from the analysis of the problem and it is the foundation on which tactics are built. Tactics are the 'events, media, and methods used to implement the strategy' (Cutlip et al. 2000: 378). In the three examples in Figure 9.10, the first shows how strategy can describe the nature of, and summarise the tactical campaign for, a simple, single objective campaign. The second example is for a conceptual proposition, while the third is for a slogan-driven campaign encapsulating a key theme. All are equally valid.

Tactics

It is obvious that tactics should be linked to, and flow from, strategy. Indeed, having got the strategy correct, tactics should flow easily and naturally. Strategy should guide brainstorming and be used to reject activities that do not support the strategic intent or the programme objectives. There should be a clear link between objectives, strategy and tactics.

A level of caution is required when planning the tactics of a programme. It is easy for the practitioner to allow creative ideas to take over while ignoring the key aim and objectives. The aim is to get a programme that reaches the right people in sufficient numbers and that has the right level of impact to do the job required, all within acceptable costs and timescales. Sometimes that can be done with a single activity – for example, the international Live 8 concerts on 2 July 2005 stimulated global awareness of developing countries' indebtedness overnight.

More usually a raft of complementary tactics over a period of time is required. These will vary depending on the nature of the programme, so the practitioner will need to draw from a palette of tactics as appropriate. For example, if a company wants to launch new and highly visual products such as a range of expensive household accessories, it is important that tactics are selected that will show how these products look and feel. In this case, a range of tactics might include displays at exhibitions, product samples provided to journalists to encourage placement in the consumer media, DVDs and websites showing the products in use, in-store demonstrations, brochures and high-quality posters.

In a different situation, for example, if the campaign involves lobbying over some aspect of financial legislation, quite different tactics, such as research reports, seminars, opinion-former briefings, one-to-one meetings with members of parliament (MPs), would be more appropriate.

When designing the tactical elements of a campaign, two questions should be asked:

	Example 1	**Example 2**	**Example 3**
Objective	Publicise new product	Establish organisation as thought leader	Encourage people to exercise
Strategy	Mount media relations campaign	Position as industry-leading think-tank	Drive home health policy through memorable message
Tactics	Press conference, press releases, exclusives, features, competition	Research reports, speaker platforms, information resource facility, online helpline, sponsorship of awards, etc.	Media campaign, posters, competitions, bus adverts, website, schools programme, etc.

Figure 9.10 Different types of strategy

1 Is the tactic *appropriate*? Will it reach the target publics? Will it have the right impact? Is it credible and influential? Does it suit the content in terms of creative treatment and compatibility with other techniques used?

2 Is the tactic *deliverable*? Can it be implemented successfully? Is there sufficient budget? Are the timescales correct? Are there the right people and expertise to implement it?

Figure 9.11 is a sample menu of activity that can be used in campaigns. (See also Chapter 3 on the role of the practitioner, and Activity 9.3.)

Media relations
Press conference
Press release
Articles and features
One-to-one briefings
Interviews
Background briefings/materials
Photography
Video news releases
Website
Email
Advertising (PR led)
Corporate
Product
Direct mail (PR led)
Annual report
Brochures/leaflets
Customer reports
External newsletters
General literature
(also multimedia material)
Exhibitions
Trade and public
Literature
Sampling
Demonstrations
Multimedia
Conferences
Multimedia
Literature
Hospitality
Community relations
Direct involvement
Gifts in kind
Sponsorship
Donations
Special events
AGMs
SGMs
Special occasions
Customer relations
Media relations
Direct mail
Advertising
Internet
Exhibitions
Retail outlets
Sponsorship
Product literature
Newsletter

Internal communication
Videos
Briefings
Newsletters
Quality guides
Compact disk interactive
Email
Intranet

Corporate identity
Design
Implementation

Sponsorship
Sport
Arts
Worthy causes

Lobbying
One-to-one briefings
Background material
Videos
Literature
Group briefings
Hospitality
CDs
Audio cassettes

Research
Organisations
Public relations programmes
Issues monitoring
Results monitoring

Crisis management
Planning
Implementation

Liaison
Internal (including counselling)
External

Financial relations
Annual report
Briefing materials
One-to-one briefing
Media relations
Hospitality
Internet
Extranet

Figure 9.11 A selection of public relations activities

Public relations tactics

Bearing in mind the content of this section, list the tactics you would use to promote engagement rings. Then list the tactics you would use to encourage the customers of a utility company to pay online.

Feedback

To promote engagement rings, the tactics might include, for example, special shop openings (e.g. after office hours) targeted at couples to enable people to view and try on the rings. The shops would play romantic music, there would be champagne on offer and subtle lighting. This would be the sensory component. Feature articles written for the local press would need to be more factual but would seek to stimulate interest in the shop openings. Photography will be an important part of the media effort. Timing, of course, would be around festive or traditionally romantic occasions such as New Year and St Valentine's day.

Box 9.3

Checklist for a press facility visit

1 Draw up invitation list
2 Alert relevant departments
3 Select visit hosts
4 Book catering
5 Issue invitations
6 Prepare display materials
7 Write speeches
8 Prepare media packs
9 Brief visit hosts
10 Follow up invitations
11 Prepare visit areas
12 Collate final attendance list
13 Rehearse with visit hosts
14 Facilitate visit
15 Follow up

Timescales and resources

Time

Time is a finite commodity and the life of a PR practitioner is notoriously busy. Furthermore, PR often involves the cooperation of others, and getting them to observe deadlines requires firmness and tact.

Deadlines can be externally imposed or internally driven by the organisation. Internal events may include the announcement of annual results, launching a new service or the appointment of a senior executive. External events may be major calendar dates, such as the Olympic Games, Chinese New Year or Thanksgiving.

To ensure deadlines are met, all the key elements of a project must be broken down into their individual parts and a timeline put against them. Check out Box 9.3, which contains a list of the main elements of a press facility visit.

Each of these elements will need its own action plan and timescale. Thus, preparing the visit areas may include commissioning display boards with photographs and text and a DVD player with commissioned DVD. That in turn will mean briefing photographers and printers, producers and film crew and getting content approved by senior management. It may also involve liaising with, for ex-

ample, the marketing department for product literature, organising cleaners and arranging for porters to move furniture and erect the displays.

Having split the project down into its individual tasks, it is then useful to use techniques such as critical path analysis (CPA) (see Figure 9.12). There are also software packages available to help with project planning tasks like this. If tasks have to be done to a short timescale, time-saving measures will have to be implemented, such as employing a specialist agency to help or using existing display material.

Once the project is complete, it is vital to undertake a post-event analysis to see how the task could be done more efficiently and effectively another time. Certainly the planner should make a checklist of all the things undertaken so that it can be used for future events.

An annual activity plan allows the peaks and troughs of activity to be identified so that they can be resourced accordingly (see Figure 9.13). The times when activity is less intense can be used for reviewing or implementing other proactive plans.

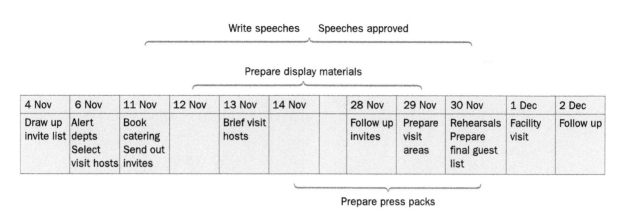

Figure 9.12 Example of critical path analysis

From this annual planner it is clear that June will be a pressurised month, so extra help may be needed. May, on the other hand, looks fairly quiet, so this may be an ideal time for a team event to review plans and prepare for the future.

Resources

There are three areas of resourcing that underpin PR work: human resources, implementation costs and equipment (Gregory 2000). Having the right staff skills and competencies as well as an adequate budget are critical to success. Skilled investor relations personnel, for example, are rarer and more expensive than general media relations staff (see Chapters 15 and 23 to gain an understanding of the skills involved in these areas). Generally speaking, a single practitioner with a few years experience can handle a broad-ranging programme of limited depth or a focused in-depth specialism, such as internal communication.

Ideally, the organisation decides its optimum communication programme, and resources it accordingly. The reality is usually a compromise between the ideal and the actual budget allocated (Beard 2001). However, it has to be borne in mind that PR is a relationship-driven activity and therefore people are more valuable than materials. Media relations work survives without expensive press packs. It cannot survive without people.

When considering the implementation costs of a programme, PR practitioners have a duty to be effective and efficient. So, for example, if an investor magazine is an appropriate medium, choices have to be made on the number of colours, quality of paper, frequency of publication, and so on. A full-colour, glossy, monthly magazine may be desirable, but would it be effective and efficient? On the other hand, a single-colour publication on cheap

paper, issued once a quarter, may fail to make investors feel important or be frequent enough to be meaningful.

There are more difficult decisions to be made requiring knowledge of media (see Chapter 15). Email distribution of press releases is cheap, but of variable effect. Writing and negotiating exclusives with media outlets is time intensive and expensive, but the effects may be more powerful. Deciding on what is the most effective and efficient solution will depend on the PR problem.

If budgets are restricted, it is important to think creatively about how a similar result can be obtained at a fraction of the cost. Joint ventures with complementary organisations, sponsorship and piggyback mailings (i.e. when one mailing such as an annual statement from a bank is used to include other information) should be considered. See Mini case study 9.2.

Sometimes it can be more effective and efficient to spend slightly more money. Run-ons (i.e. additional copies of a part or all of a publication) of a feature can provide a powerful promotional tool. Holding an employee conference off-site may cost more, but may guarantee their attention. Posting an analyst's briefing to other key shareholders may cost a little extra, but it may retain their support.

While not requiring excessive amounts of equipment to support their work, it is important that practitioners have the right technology to ensure quick and easy access to key stakeholders in a manner that is appropriate (Beard 2001).

Consultancy costs

If a PR consultancy is hired, it is worth noting that consultancy charges vary. Consultancies usually invoice fees, implementation costs and expenses. Fees can be charged in two ways. First, *advisory* fees, which cover advice, attending meetings, preparing reports, etc. Often this is billed at a fixed cost per month based on the amount of time

Activity	January	February	March	April	May	June	July	August	September	October	November	Decem
One-to-one editor briefings	Trade press × 2	Consumer press × 2	Trade press × 2	Consumer press × 2		Consumer press × 1	Trade press × 1		Consumer press × 2	Trade press × 2		Loca press
Advertorials with key journals		*The Grocer*		*Cosmopolitan*		*Sunday Times Magazine*		*Woman*		*Regional Consumer*		
News stories (including new products)	News story	Prepared foods	News story	Healthy options	News story	Summer fruits	News story	Barbeque foods	News story	Root veg	News story	Xmas goods
Seasonal themes			Spring promo			Outdoor life			Autumn promo			Winte warme
Competitions		Trolley dash		Holiday bargains		Picnic hampers		Kids' adventure		Freezer filler		Santa party
Exhibitions			Ideal Home	Local shows	Local shows	Great Yorkshire Show		Local shows	Local shows			

Figure 9.13 Annual media relations plan for a supermarket chain

Mini Case Study 9.2
3D mummy campaign

Being efficient and effective

Sometimes a little lateral thought and creativity can bring additional efficiency to PR campaigns. Portfolio Communications looked closely at the needs of an existing client to come up with an imaginative and cost-effective campaign.

The 3D mummy

Bringing a 3000-year-old Egyptian mummy to life was an award winning PR campaign by Portfolio Communications for supercomputing company SGI Silicon Graphics.

Portfolio's brief was to develop a campaign to popularise SGI's 3D visualisation technology, used by car designers, oil engineers and pharmaceutical companies to study large amounts of data in a visual, 3D format. The campaign needed to appeal to a broad set of media to reach the client's target audiences of ABC1 scientists, engineers and managers.

The campaign began by using a planning tool that contains information on all aspects of consumers' lifestyles. This revealed an excellent match between SGI's target audiences and their tendency to visit museums, with 42% of SGI's AB audience having visited a museum within the last 12 months. It also identified the key publications read by this audience, enabling careful targeting of the right publications for the campaign.

Portfolio approached The British Museum to explore ideas for applying the 3D technology to ancient antiquities. The collaboration saw a mummy recreated in 3D, a virtual unwrapping that was not only a world first, but also resulted in very exciting 3000-year-old discoveries.

The *Financial Times* was identified as a primary target publication read by both museum visitors and SGI customers. Armed with this information, Portfolio approached the *Financial Times* with an advance on the story and the campaign was then rolled out across print, broadcast and online media. The coverage achieved was widespread and included the *Financial Times*, *BBC 6 O'clock News*, BBC News 24, CNN and also key science media/programmes such as *Tomorrow's World*, *New Scientist*, Discovery Channel, *National Geographic* Channel and BBC Radio 4's *Material World*.

Above all, the huge success of the PR campaign showed The British Museum the potential in bringing the 3D mummy to the general public. The Museum went on to purchase SGI technology as part of a public exhibition called *Mummy: the inside story*.

Source: www.portfoliocomms/mummycase.htm

---

spent – a *retainer*. Sometimes it is billed on a project basis. Second, *implementation* fees are charged to undertake the agreed programme of work and are in addition to advisory fees. There is usually a mark-up fee on bought-in services such as print and photography where the consultancy bears the legal responsibility to deliver as contracted. The UK Public Relations Consultancy Association recommends a mark-up of 17.65% to cover things such as indemnity insurance. Value added tax (VAT) or other taxes may also be payable unless the consultancy is below a certain size.

It is important that planners maintain a careful watch on resources. It is a sign of good management if they are efficient and look for value-for-money solutions wherever possible. As an employee or consultant they will be judged on their ability to manage resources as well as being judged on programme effectiveness. Unfortunately, the creative services industry (of which PR is part) is not well known for its performance in this area.

Evaluation and review

Evaluation

Chapter 10 goes into detail about evaluation, but it is important to cover some basic principles here. PR is like any other business function. It is vital to know whether the planned programme has done what it set out to do and, if not, why not.

It needs to be stressed that evaluation is an ongoing process and should be considered at the objective-setting stage: it does not just happen at the end of the programme. All the planning approaches emphasise the importance of ongoing monitoring. Throughout its duration, practitioners will be regularly checking to see if the programme is on track. So, for example, media coverage will be evaluated monthly to see if the selected media are using the material supplied (e.g. feature articles or press releases) and to judge how they are using it.

When the programme is complete it will need to be evaluated to discover whether it has met its overall objectives. Sometimes that is relatively easy. For example, if the objective was to achieve a change in legislation and that has happened, then clearly it was successful. Sometimes the situation is rather more complicated. If the plan is to change societal attitudes towards people who have mental health problems, for example, it will take a long time: different publics will require different amounts and types of communicative effort; as a result the evaluation programme will need to be much more sophisticated and long term, employing formal social scientific research methods (see Chapter 10 for more detail).

Building in evaluation focuses effort, demonstrates effectiveness and efficiency and encourages good management and accountability. However, research shows that there is still a limited amount of evaluation done in the PR industry and it is fraught with debate and difference (Gregory and White 2008).

There are a number of principles that can help to make evaluation easier:

- Setting SMART objectives: if objectives are clear and measurable, then judging whether they have been achieved is relatively easy.

- Building in evaluation from the start: if objectives are set with evaluation in mind, the task is simpler.

- Agreeing measurement criteria with whomever will be judging success.

- Evaluating and monitoring as the programme progresses: using ongoing monitoring as a management information tool; examining tactics and channels if things are not developing as the planner intends; revising the strategy if this fails.

- Taking an objective and a scientific approach: the requirement to provide facts and figures about the programme means that the planner may need training in research methods or to employ specialists who are.

- Evaluating processes: the planner needs to make sure they are *managing* the programme well, within budget and to timescales.

- Establishing open and transparent monitoring processes, through, for example, monthly review reports.

Evaluation is contentious among PR practitioners. Fortunately, the UK Chartered Institute of Public Relations has produced a number of guides or toolkits that can help, but there is still some distance to go in agreeing a common standard. Work in America, published by the Institute for Public Relations in Florida, is focusing less on objective setting as the basis for evaluation and more on measuring the quality of relationships. Grunig and Hon's (1999) guide to measuring the quality of relationships indicates that judgements should be made on six key criteria: control, mutuality, trust, satisfaction, commitment, and exchange and commercial relationship. (For more on this, see Chapter 10.)

Review

While evaluation is both an ongoing and end-of-campaign process, a thorough review of all PR activity should be undertaken regularly, but on a less frequent basis, every 12 months or so. As part of this, the external and internal environment should be surveyed systematically to ensure that all issues have been captured and any new ones accommodated. Campaign strategies should be tested to see if they are still entirely appropriate. Certainly tactics should be reviewed to see if they need refreshing with any new creative input and to ensure that they are addressing the needs of the target publics.

Sometimes new internal or external issues or factors force a major review. For example: new regulations may be introduced by government; the organisation may have merged with another organisation; the chief executive may have retired; a well-organised pressure group may be raising important issues that require changes to the way the organisation operates; or there may be large budget cuts.

Where a major review is required, it is important to take a holistic approach. Programmes always need to be dynamic and flexible enough to embrace opportunities and challenges, but sometimes a fundamental reappraisal has to take place. If that is the case, all the stages in the planning process outlined in this chapter need to be taken again. It may be time consuming and demanding, but having done it the planners can be assured that they will have built the foundation for success. (See Case study 9.1.)

Case Study 9.1

The value of research: BT's 'Better World' campaign

BT's award-winning Better World campaign illustrates how correctly targeted and implemented research can help to define and sustain a PR-led social marketing campaign.

The search for a sustainable corporate social responsibility (CSR) programme began when MORI research revealed that BT's CSR reputation had hit a plateau. Thus BT embarked on a research and consultation process beginning with an assessment of CSR perceptions, and went on to identify a key social issue that has subsequently underpinned every strand of the campaign.

The early consumer research showed that companies should focus on areas where their role would be instantly understood and in line with the business. In the case of BT, this meant focusing on its core business area of communications. Research also revealed that a number of issues were of direct concern to BT's customer base; these included health, homelessness and young people. Thus a broad theme for a campaign around 'young people' and 'communications' was agreed.

BT then embarked on a phase of desk-top research to explore possibilities. A source book was created which contains information on over forty organisations active with young people and communications. Existing research on young people's views about this subject, research from organisations about how to include young people in consultation, information on children's rights and other campaigns around these areas was all included. In this phase the research identified a potential campaign theme of helping to give young people a voice.

BT spoke to a number of key organisations, including the UK Youth Parliament. They commissioned research from the Parliament and sought the views of 1,200 young people aged 7–16, exploring whether they felt they were being heard in today's society. Worryingly, 44% of the UK's youth believe that adults don't listen to them. The government is seen as the worst group of listeners by 56% of young people in the UK, followed closely by local councils at 47%. 80% of young people rate their friends as the best listeners followed by their parents (73%).

Adult opinion appears to back this up. Some 83% of adults say that it is very important to listen to children and young people, but only 57% agree that they do listen and act on what they hear. Significantly, the research also highlighted what happens when young people feel they are not listened to, and what could happen if adults did listen more. The findings identified some marked differences between the things that young people want to speak out about, and the issues adults think young people are interested in. The research showed that young people would like to be 'active citizens' and speak out on how to run schools, how to improve their local services and how the police should deal with their age group. Clearly there is a communications failure which BT believed it could help remedy.

This primary research, supported by statistics and research from UNICEF, UNESCO and I CAN, the communications charity, and ChildLine, led to the development of a campaign strategy focusing on three areas which became the campaign objectives. Planning and developing the objectives and the campaign itself took a full year and included robust consultation with stakeholders. The campaign itself had the support of BT's Chairman who signed off the strategy.

In developing the 'giving young people a voice' strategy for the campaign, it became clear that when BT went to consumer and employee groups, the wide concept of the campaign was hard to grasp. So, the example of ChildLine as a potential charity partner was used, and this had instant recognition and approval by the majority. BT made a strategic decision that while the campaign's longer-term aim was to give young people a voice, they should start where the need is greatest, with those children who desperately need to be listened to. Supporting ChildLine was an obvious starting point.

As a result of the research, three campaign objectives were developed:

- helping young people most in need to be heard and helped
- developing young people's communication skills by sharing information, knowledge, skills and tools
- helping young people to create real social change

Collaborating with youth organisations was seen to be key in developing the programme and in its sustained success. So BT invited the UK Youth Parliament to be part of the campaign's steering group and have established a partnership with them.

The research undertaken by the Parliament (mentioned earlier) and the other research material was collated

case study 9.1 (continued)

into a publication called 'Seen and Heard', the launch of which, by BT's Chairman, marked the start of the campaign. Apart from the research, the report also gave a number of case studies which illustrate the wide range of interests that young people have and the diverse areas in which they have a valuable contribution to make. The case studies demonstrate the positive role young people play in their local communities when they succeed in making their own voices heard – often against the odds. Direct action by young people is helping to address key social issues, and contributing to genuine social community development across the UK.

BT believe that promoting the research and case studies would uncover more positive stories and inspire adults and children, so they turned the report into an annual undertaking and extended it into an awards scheme: The Seen and Heard Awards.

Seen and Heard awards are judged by a panel of young people and in 2008 there were over 100 entries, including international nominations from countries including Canada, Ukraine, Nigeria, Sweden, India and Afghanistan.

So how have BT met the campaign objectives it has set for itself?

Objective one: helping young people most in need to be heard and helped
In support of this objective, BT have provided support for ChildLine in fundraising, technical support and helping them develop the organisation. In early 2006 ChildLine merged with the NSPCC, supported by BT. BT is now working with both charities to look at how new technologies can enable more young people to be heard, for example online counselling and use of text messaging. This is helping to reach difficult audiences, such as ethnic minorities and boys. So far around £6.3 million has been raised for ChildLine since 2003 – £2.2 million being raised in 2006/7, which is the largest amount ever raised for one charity. This has given the charity the resources to answer an additional 700 calls a day. On top of this BT has secured over £5 million of support in kind. BT has also helped ChildLine and the NSPCC successfully to lobby the government for tens of millions of pounds for services to children.

Objective two: to develop young people's communication skills by sharing information, knowledge, skills and tools
BT communications resources (DVDs and online teaching resources) in schools are produced to assist teachers and parents help young people develop their communications skills. The BT education website hosts content and information about improving communication skills and over 20,000 teachers are registered users. Three million pupils have use of BT's educational resources every year. The numbers of registrants on BT's education website has doubled in the last year and the numbers of online orders for BT's communication resources increased by 13.5% in the first 6 months of 2008.

In addition, in 2006/7 over 400,000 pupils participated in BT's communication skills road shows.

BT is also developing its partnership with I CAN, which is dedicated to improving communication skills with early years children. All this work is supported by a BT volunteering scheme, with over 3,000 volunteers supporting school visits and working with the charity partners.

Objective three: helping young people to create real social change
The partnership with the UK Youth Parliament in which BT supplies funding and strategic advice has enabled young people to campaign on issues that affect them. BT supported the 'Circles of Influence' event, which allowed young people to engage with government and businesses. In 2006/7, over 50 UK Members of Parliament were engaged in a series of parliamentary events.

BT have also been working with the BBC on a nationwide current affairs TV broadcast called 'Question Time', and for the first time the BBC allowed a young person on the panel of experts answering audience questions.

Up to the end of 2007 over 4,000 young people had participated in the BT Seen and Heard Awards scheme in which their contributions to social change were demonstrated.

Ongoing research with key stakeholders, with employees and with young people sustains the campaign. Since it was launched in 2002, a number of new initiatives have been introduced, all thoroughly researched beforehand. These continue to address the issue of young people being given a voice and to equip them to be confident and competent to make that voice heard, so that they can shape and positively contribute to local, national and international communities. Research not only continues to underpin the campaign, but BT constantly monitors employee awareness and involvement in the Better World campaign and investigates the impact on opinion formers to evaluate and improve its performance.

This multifaceted approach to research has defined BT's award-winning campaign from the outset and continues to guide its ongoing development.

Summary

This chapter has sought to show that *planning* communication is critical to PR success. Successful PR programmes do not just happen. Professional communicators plan. Planning puts them in control. It puts order and purpose into a busy and potentially chaotic and reactive working life. Seeing a planned PR programme come to life is exciting and rewarding. It also clearly demonstrates to organisational peers and employers that PR can make a real, measurable difference.

Bibliography

Beard, M. (2001). *Running a Public Relations Department*, 2nd edition. London: Kogan Page.

Cutlip, S.M., A.H. Center and G.M. Broom (2000). *Effective Public Relations*, 8th edition. Upper Saddle River, NJ: Prentice Hall International.

Cutlip, S.M., A.H. Center and G.M. Broom (2006). *Effective Public Relations*, 9th edition. Upper Saddle River, NJ: Prentice Hall International.

Davis, A. (2004). *Mastering Public Relations*. London: Palgrave.

DCSF (2008), 'Funding Boost for the School Food Revolution'. http://www.dcsf.gov.uk/pns/DisplayPN.cgi?pn_id=2008_0026, accessed 18 September 2008.

Freeman, R.E. (1984). *Strategic Management: A stakeholder approach*. Boston: Pitman.

Gregory, A. (2000). *Planning and Managing Public Relations Campaigns*, 2nd edition. London: Kogan Page.

Gregory, A. (2004). 'Scope and structure of public relations: A technology-driven view'. *Public Relations Review* **3**(30): 245–254.

Gregory, A. and L. Edwards (2004). 'Patterns of PR: Public relations management among Britain's "most admired" companies'. Report for Eloqui Public Relations, Leeds Metropolitan University.

Gregory, A. and White, J. (2008). 'Introducing the Chartered Institute of Public Relations work on research and evaluation' in B. Van Ruler, A. Tkalac Verčič and D.Verčič (eds). *Public Relations Metrics: Research and evaluation*. New York: Routledge.

Grunig, J.E. (1994). 'A situational theory of public: Conceptual history, recent challenges and new research'. Paper presented at the International Public Relations Research Symposium, Lake Bled, Slovenia.

Grunig, J.E. and T. Hunt (1984). *Managing Public Relations*. New York: Holt, Rinehart & Winston.

Grunig, J.E. and F.C. Repper (1992). 'Strategic management, publics and issues' in *Excellence in Public Relations and Communication Management*. J.E. Grunig (ed.). Hillsdale NJ: Lawrence Erlbaum Associates.

Grunig, J.E. and L.C. Hon (1999). 'Guidelines for measuring relationships in public relations'. http://www.instituteforpr.org/research_single/guidelines_measuring_relationships/.

Grunig, J.E., L.A. Grunig and D.M. Dozier (2002). *Excellent Public Relations and Effective Organizations*. Mahwah, NJ: Lawrence Erlbaum Associates.

Heath, R.L. (2001). 'Shifting foundations: Public relations as relationship building' in *Handbook of Public Relations*. R.L. Heath (ed.). Thousand Oaks, CA: Sage.

IPR (2004). 'Best practice in the measurement and reporting of PR and ROI'. www.ipr.org.uk/direct/news/roi_fullreport.pdf, accessed 15 July 2004.

Johnson, G., K. Scholes and Whittington, R. (2007). *Exploring Corporate Strategy*, 8th edition. London: Pearson Education.

Lerbinger, O. (1972). *Designs for Persuasive Communication*. Englewood Cliffs, NJ: Prentice Hall.

Maconomy (2004). 'Agency Profit Watch Survey'. London: Maconomy.

Marston, J.E. (1979). *Modern Public Relations*. New York: McGraw-Hill.

McElreath, M.P. (1997). *Managing Systematic and Ethical Public Relations Campaigns*. 2nd edition. Madison, WI: Brown and Benchmark.

Mendelow, A. (1991) Proceedings of 2nd International Conference on Information Systems. Cambridge, MA, cited in *Exploring Corporate Strategy*, G. Johnson and K. Scholes (2002).

MORI (2004). Corporate Social Responsibility Annual Report. London: MORI.

Mullins, L.J. (1989). *Management and Organizational Behaviour*, 2nd edition. London: Pitman.

Steyn, B. and G. Puth (2000). *Corporate Communication Strategy*. Sandown: Heinemann.

Windahl, S. and B. Signitzer (with J.E. Olson) (1992). *Using Communication Theory*. London: Sage.

CHAPTER 12

Planning Public Relations 2

CHAPTER 10

György Szondi and Rüdiger Theilmann

Public relations research and evaluation

Learning outcomes

By the end of this chapter you should be able to:

- identify the role of research and evaluation in public relations practice
- define and describe both quantitative and qualitative research approaches
- apply relevant research methods
- understand the different theoretical and practical approaches to evaluation in public relations.

Structure

- Context of research in public relations
- Designing research
- Qualitative vs quantitative research
- Research methods
- Designing research instruments
- Research applications
- Evaluation

Introduction

Research plays a crucial role for many different reasons in public relations (PR). First, it is an integral part of the PR planning process. Without research it is difficult to set communication objectives, identify publics or develop messages. Second, research is also undertaken to evaluate PR efforts. Evaluation has been one of the biggest and most talked about issues over many years for the entire PR industry. Evaluation helps practitioners understand and improve programme effectiveness through systematic measurement and proves the value of PR efforts to clients, management or other disciplines, such as marketing or integrated communications.

Research and evaluation can also reveal a lot about the current state of PR practice as well as contribute to the development of the PR theoretical knowledge base. Research findings have business benefits too and can facilitate attempts to show how PR can improve the bottom line. This chapter will explore the research process, the most commonly used research methods in PR and the theory and practice of evaluation. The principles of research approaches and methods would fill a book, therefore in this chapter only the basic principles will be discussed.

Context of research in public relations

Academic research aims to generate theories and models, to describe and analyse trends in PR. Academic journals, such as the *Journal of Public Relations Research* or *Public Relations Review,* are concerned with theory building and are among the major outlets of academic research. Another important contribution comes from students in the form of undergraduate and postgraduate dissertations and theses as part of a degree. The ability to understand and carry out systematic research highlights the importance of education. Practitioners with a degree in higher education are better equipped in the complex world of research as opposed to those who use only 'seat-of-the-pants' methods.

Research can have different purposes and origins. The primary purpose of research is to contribute to the existing body of knowledge in the field of PR, even if such research does not deal with the real problems of practice ('basic research'). But the purpose of research is also to answer questions that come out of practice or are imposed by a client ('applied research').

Nevertheless, if we use the term 'research' – either basic or applied – we always mean 'scientific' research, not 'informal', 'quick and dirty' or 'everyday-life research' – as it is often understood by practitioners. For example, Lindenmann (1990) reports results of a survey among PR professionals in which about 70% of the respondents thought that most research on the subject was informal rather than scientific (Cutlip et al. 2006; Gregory 2000).

In contrast to scientific research, informal research is based on subjective intuition or on the 'authority' of knowledge or 'tenacity', which refers to sticking to a practice because it has always been like that (Kerlinger 1986). It is subjective if information is gathered in an unsystematic way by talking to a couple of people, looking at guidelines ('Five Steps to do World Class Public Relations') or just based on feelings. Other examples of PR practice based on informal research are where:

- a practice might be considered as best practice because the senior manager of a well-known consultancy declares it to be the latest trend in PR (based on 'authority')

- an advisory committee, panel or board recommends it (based on 'authority')

- an organisation writes news releases in the same style they have used for the last 10 years ('tenacity' – 'it is the right way because we have always done it like that').

Scientific research is systematic and objective: it follows distinct steps and uses appropriate research design. In doing PR research we have to guide research by:

- defining the research problem (what to research)

- choosing a general research approach (qualitative or quantitative)

- deciding on research strategy (primary or secondary research)

- selecting the research method (survey, content analysis, focus group, etc.)

- deciding on the research instruments (questions in a questionnaire or categories in a content analysis)

- analysing the data (e.g. Wimmer and Dominick 2006).

See Think about 10.1.

Research and evaluation in public relations planning and management

Research is an integrated part of PR management, which means that it should be included in each step of the PR

To identify internal and external environmental factors, SWOT and PEST (or EPISTLE) analyses are often considered to be useful techniques (see Chapter 9). This might be conducted in a meeting in which practitioners of the in-house PR department gather and do a brainstorming session about the strengths, weaknesses, opportunities and threats of their organisation. But can this be considered as research? SWOT and PEST brainstorms may offer guidelines about what to research but they are not research in themselves. For example, to explore the weaknesses of an organisation, a focus group discussion might be conducted. Only by doing a SWOT or PEST analysis with proper research methods does it become research. Doing a SWOT or PEST analysis by subjective intuition might reveal interesting ideas but is not research.

planning process. This might sound controversial, since models such as the RACE model – **r**esearch, **a**ction, **c**ommunication and **e**valuation – suggest that research is only undertaken in the first and the last steps: 'research' and 'evaluation'. Nevertheless, this does not mean that research is limited to these steps; it is crucial in each step. The following four points refer to the four stages in the Cutlip et al. (2006) planning process shown in Chapter 9:

- using research to define PR problems
- using research to assess PR plans and proposals
- using research during programme implementation
- using research for programme impact.

Using research to define PR problems

Research findings such as problem definitions or identifying publics are key inputs for programme planning. For example, an organisation might have a bad image in the media and turn to a PR consultancy to address this problem. The consultancy is very likely to use research to find the reasons for the image problem, before developing a strategy to address it. This process can be defined as *problem definition* and *situation analysis* and should address the following research questions (see Chapter 9 for more detail):

- What are the internal and external environmental factors that affect the organisation?
- Who are the publics?
- What do they know? What do they think about key issues?
- How are public–organisation relationships characterised?
- What media do publics rely on or prefer for information?

Using research to assess PR plans and proposals

Before implementing a plan, its various elements can be tested through a variety of measures: expert assessment; using checklists as criteria; testing messages in focus group discussions; or in a survey among key publics. Initial identification of publics, messages, strategies or tactics included in the plan might be subject to assessment. The assessment might result in changes in the programme.

Using research during programme implementation

Process research aims at improving programme performance and takes place while the programme is in operation (in process). It is also referred to as *monitoring* or *formative* evaluation. It enables the PR practitioner to modify campaign elements, such as messages (too complicated, misunderstood, irrelevant), channels (inappropriate choice for delivering a particular message), or the chosen strategies and tactics. Research during implementation enables the practitioner to make corrections according to circumstances and issues that were not foreseen during the planning process, especially in the case of complex and long-term programmes. It can also document how the programme is being implemented, including the practitioner's own activity, resources allocated or timing of the programme.

Using research for programme impact

Finally, research is done to measure programme impact or effectiveness with respect to goals and objectives. Principles of programme evaluation will be discussed in the second half of the chapter.

Areas of research

Lerbinger (1977) offers a classification that defines areas of PR research less concerned with the process of programmes. He distinguishes four major categories of PR research as: environmental monitoring (or scanning); PR audits; communication audits; and social audits. Table 10.1 identifies these categories of research and defines the scope of each approach.

Table 10.1
Categories of
research and
their scope (*source*:
based on Lerbinger
1977: 11–14)

Categories of research	Scope of research
Environmental monitoring (scanning)	Issues and trends in public opinion Issues in mass media Social events which may have significant impact on an organisation Competitor communications analysis
Public relations audit	Assesses an organisation's public relations activities
Communication audits	All forms of internal and external communications are studied to assess their consistency with overall strategy as well as their internal consistency Narrower than a public relations audit
Social audits	Measures an organisation's social performance

Designing research

After identifying questions that help assess the initial situation, we have to decide how to research them. This demands a research plan that answers the following questions:

- What types of data are of interest?

- Which research approach should be followed: qualitative or quantitative research?

- Which research methods are appropriate?

- How should the research instruments be designed?

Type of data: primary or secondary research?

Information or data can be gathered in two basic ways: through primary or secondary research. Primary research generates data that are specific for the case under investigation. Primary data are directly retrieved ('in the field') from the research object through empirical research methods – interview, focus group, survey, content analysis or observation (Wimmer and Dominick 2006).

Secondary research or 'desk research', in contrast, uses data that have already been gathered, are available through different sources and can be analysed sitting at the desk as opposed to gathering data 'in the field' (Neumann 2003). The term 'secondary' implies that somebody else has already collected this information through primary research and documented the results in various sources. A specific type of secondary research is 'data mining', which is the exploration and analysis of existing data with reference to a new or specific research problem.

Data about size and composition of media audiences such as newspaper readership or television audiences are available to the practitioners and are published regularly. Table 10.2 is an example from the *Guardian*'s media supplement.

Secondary data are available from many different sources like libraries, government records, trade and professional associations, as well as organisational files. The following list includes some of the large UK and European datasets:

- Annual Employment Survey, which covers about 130,000 businesses (www.statistics.gov.uk)

- British Social Attitudes survey (www.natcen.ac.uk)

- Chartered Institute of Public Relations: posts useful resources of research on its website (www.cipr. co.uk)

- Eurobarometer, which monitors public opinion in member states on a variety of issues (enlargement, social situation, health, culture, information technology, environment, the euro, defence policy, etc.)

- Eurostat, the Statistical Office of the European Communities

- online research services such as LexisNexis (www. lexisnexis.com)

- population census, which is held every 10 years (www.census.ac.uk).

Caution must be taken when interpreting and using secondary research findings since they can reflect the views and interests of the sponsoring organisations. (See Activity 10.1.)

Table 10.2 UK national daily newspaper circulation excluding bulks, December 2007 (*source*: adapted from Guardian Unlimited, 1 April 2008, http://www.guardian.co.uk/media/table/2008/sep/05/abcs.pressandpublishing. Copyright Guardian Newspapers Limited 2008. Data from Audit Bureau of Circulations)

Title	Dec 2007	Dec 2006	% change
Daily Express	744,539	773,768	−3.78
Daily Mail	2,310,806	2,311,057	−0.01
Daily Mirror	1,494,114	1,540,917	−3.04
Daily Record	385,928	407,212	−5.23
Daily Star	726,465	750,374	−3.19
Daily Telegraph	873,523	899,493	−2.89
FT	449,187	437,720	2.62
Guardian	353,436	365,635	−3.34
Independent	228,400	238,756	−4.34
Sun	2,985,672	3,028,732	−1.42
Times	615,313	635,777	−3.22

Activity 10.1

Secondary research

You are commissioned by the Department of Health to design a PR campaign to raise awareness of obesity in the UK. You are interested in hard facts about this disease. What types of secondary sources would you turn to? Put together a small research report on the topic.

Feedback

Start with the following link: www.official-documents.co.uk.

Starting research

As a first step to start research in Case study 10.1, research questions must be developed. Key questions in the first stage of the planning process are:

1   What do residents know about the service?

2   What do residents think about recycling?

3   Are residents willing to recycle?

A next step is the question of which type of data to use to answer these questions. Primary or secondary research might be conducted. An example of secondary research would be to find and use research data that has been gathered by other city councils in the UK or use data from

Case Study 10.1

Research and evaluation: 'Bin There Done That'

The following case study on Westminster City Council's campaign about recycling will be used throughout the rest of the chapter.

Background

The improvement of doorstep recycling formed part of a new Westminster cleansing contract. Recycling was seen as a critical part of the cleansing service. Getting doorstep recycling right was seen as essential for the council to meet government targets by 2010. Large increases to landfill tax and costs of incineration also made the success of the new service vital.

Objectives

■ To change the behaviour of residents to increase take-up of service by one-quarter and thereby recycle a greater proportion of waste – from 30 tonnes per week to 50 tonnes per week

■ To position the authority as the leading recycling authority through raising the City Survey satisfaction rating from 43% to 60% for recycling

case study 10.1 (continued)

■ To increase awareness of recycling service among target audience to drive up usage to help us meet government targets for tonnage of recycled household waste by 2010

Planning and implementation
Audit
Westminster City Council's (WCC) in-house PR department examined its market extensively before committing to the final campaign. Quantitative research surveying 502 residents in July 2003 found that:

■ 60% of residents did not feel informed about the service

■ 98% said that recycling was important

■ 72% said they would recycle only if the council made it easier first.

To accurately target audience and message, WCC conducted two focus groups of Westminster residents drawn from across the borough in July 2003. One group recycled regularly and one had never recycled.

The focus group research found that there was a shocking lack of knowledge about WCC's recycling service, confusion over what materials could be recycled and an emphatic desire for the process to be made easy.

Two campaigns were market tested to the groups. Both groups unanimously opted for a 'we've made it easy, you make it happen' message.

Strategy
WCC had to vastly improve the information sent to households, providing clear, concise and accurate information about the types of material that could be recycled.

Its communications had to:

> Reinforce that the Council had made the service easier (a single bin for all goods), promote two way communications (a helpline and website were introduced), deliver strong messages that were easy to understand.

The Bin There Done That (BTDT) campaign was adopted after trialling a number of alternatives, as it met these criteria. The research had shown that messages must be clear, simple, easy and immediately recognisable as WCC. The campaign included:

■ a two-week teaser campaign (something's coming to your doorstep)

■ rollout of service information campaign (ways to recycle)

■ advertising campaign (Bin There Done That)

■ intensive field marketing follow-up campaign

■ follow-through information campaign.

Evaluation and measurement
Evaluation was ongoing. Trained council staff surveyed over 16,000 homes and as a result some new messages were adopted, e.g. how to order replacement bins that neighbours had stolen! Final evaluation compared the council's 2002/3 City Survey conducted by MORI with the 2003/4 MORI City Survey, a specially commissioned populus survey on communication messages and analysis of tonnages and rates of participation.

Results of analysis were then compared against objectives.

■ *Objective 1: change behaviour of residents to recycle a greater proportion of their waste – increase from 30 tonnes per week to 50 tonnes per week.* Tonnage for doorstep recycling increased from 30 tonnes per week to 85 tonnes per week.

After seeing the campaign, people were much more likely to recycle: 68% of those aware of the campaign now recycle whereas only 45% who were unaware chose to do so.

Of residents who were aware of the campaign, 73% thought that the council had made recycling easier for them. This is nearly twice as many (40%) as those who had not seen the campaign.

■ *Objective 2: position the authority as the leading recycling authority through raising City Survey satisfaction rating from 43% to 60% for recycling.* There was almost a 20% increase in satisfaction rating to 61% for the recycling service (City Survey 2002/3 to 2003/4). The Association of London Government Survey of Londoners 2003 found an increased satisfaction rating for recycling of only 7% across all London boroughs.

The City Survey 2003/4 found that residents felt more strongly about the importance of recycling. Recycling was the fourth most important service. In 2002/3 recycling did not even make an appearance in the list of top 10 services.

Residents also believed that recycling was the second 'elective' (voluntary) service that they most benefited from, behind libraries (53%) – recycling 35%. This shows an increase from 2002/3 of 25% (City Survey 2002/3 to 2003/4).

Of the public that were aware of the campaign, 84% thought it was a good idea to recycle compared with 70% who were unaware of the campaign (December 2003).

■ *Objective 3: increase take-up rate of service by one-quarter.* The increase in take-up for the doorstep recycling service has almost trebled – from 4,843 participants in May 2003 to 12,572 in December 2003.

Source: www.cipr.co.uk/member_area and Westminster City Council Communication Team

research in other countries about the acceptance of recycling. Nevertheless, the validity of such data would be questionable since the local situation, awareness and traditions would not have been considered. Therefore, it is more appropriate to conduct primary research.

Qualitative vs quantitative research

The question of whether to use qualitative or quantitative research methods is widely discussed in the academic and professional community. However, the answer depends on each research question: **qualitative** approaches are often used to explore areas about which no knowledge exists yet and results are expressed in words ('qualities'); **quantitative** approaches are used to deliver comparable, generalisable results, expressed in numbers ('quantities').

Picture 10.1 Research 'in the field': data gathering for public relations can require working with diverse publics and therefore in a wide range of settings (*source*: Jack Sullivan/Alamy)

Mini Case Study 10.1
Qualitative or quantitative?

The Inland Revenue (UK tax-gathering authority) is a public sector organisation that wants to research its image among employees, prior to developing a corporate identity programme. Since this is the first time that the internal image has been researched, not a lot of information is available about issues that are relevant in the eyes of the employees. Therefore, the first step might be to hold focus group discussions as a qualitative approach. The goal is to explore relevant features of the image. The second step would be to analyse the results of these focus groups to develop standardised questionnaires that are then distributed to all employees. The features of the image that were explored in the focus groups are assessed by the employees and provide a general view of the employees of their organisation.

Qualitative and quantitative research approaches are complementary and should be combined rather than used as alternatives. In research terms this is often described as the *mixed method* approach (Lindlof and Bryan 2002). Mini case study 10.1 gives an example.

Qualitative and quantitative approaches both have advantages and disadvantages, which are summarised in Table 10.3.

Westminster City Council's BTDT campaign is another good example of how qualitative and quantitative methods can be combined. The focus groups found that there was a lack of knowledge about the council's recycling service, confusion over what materials could be recycled and a huge motivation for the process to be made easy. Especially since the motivation of residents to recycle ('Are residents willing to recycle?', 'What might determine their willingness to recycle?') was rather an unexplored issue, it was appropriate to use a qualitative approach. The results of the focus groups could then be used in the survey that gave a representative overview of what Westminster residents know and think.

Research methods

The main research methods used in PR research and evaluation are:

Table 10.3
Advantages and disadvantages of quantitative and qualitative research techniques (*source*: adapted from Neumann 2003: 150)

		Potential advantages	Potential disadvantages
	Quantitative approaches	Generate comparable results Results can be generalised Can be guided by less experienced researchers (e.g. interviewers) Higher acceptance by clients	Quantitative methods can only find out what is put in through prepared questions or categories Can guide respondents into a rather irrelevant direction Do not allow deeper analysis of reasons
	Qualitative approaches	Provide insights into causes and motivations Explore information that is completely unknown or unpredicted	Time consuming and demand financial resources Demand qualified researchers Limited generalisation Results are influenced by researcher

- qualitative: intensive or in-depth interviews and focus groups
- quantitative: surveys and content analysis.

In the case of the BTDT campaign, focus groups or surveys were used as methods to research knowledge, attitudes and motivation of Westminster residents to behave in a certain way. But it is not always so obvious what the most appropriate method is, as Think about 10.2 demonstrates.

Intensive or in-depth interviews

Intensive interviews are a specific type of personal interview. Unlike surveys, they do not attempt to generalise answers. So when is it appropriate to use intensive interviews? Their main purpose is to explore attitudes and attitude-relevant contexts. The biggest advantage is the wealth of detail that they can provide. On the negative side, they are sensitive to interviewer bias. The answers might easily be influenced by the behaviour of the interviewer, so well-trained interviewers are needed to minimise the bias. Intensive interviews are characterised by:

- generally *smaller samples* of interviewees
- *open questions* that probe the reasons *why* respondents give specific answers: they elaborate on data concerning respondents' opinions, values, motivations, experiences and feelings
- being *customised* – or reactive – to individual respondents in so far as the order and/or wording of questions can be changed, or new questions added, during the interview depending on the answers given

---

Think about 10.2   Evaluation of a news release

After releasing a news story about new online services on behalf of its client, a large telecommunications provider, ABC PR consultancy discusses how to evaluate the outcome of this activity. Should it:

- measure the media coverage by monitoring media (newspapers, radio, TV, www) and analysing circulation numbers and readership figures using available media data, or
- conduct a representative survey among relevant publics?

Feedback

With the first suggestion, it can be very precisely tracked in which media the news has come up. Additionally, the media data provide figures on the number and type of reader (age, gender, education, income, etc.) who might have seen or read the news. But this is already the weak point in the evaluation: it remains unclear whether they have read the news, what they think about the news and whether they can recall the news.

Using a survey, in contrast, gives clear evidence of what people know and think about the online services of the telecommunications provider. But it remains rather vague as to where they have obtained their information. It might be that the information originates from sources other than the media coverage of the news release.

■ *non-verbal behaviour* of respondents being recorded and contributing to the results.

Focus groups

Focus group or group interviewing is like an intensive interview, with 6 to 10 respondents who interact with each other. Focus groups generate qualitative data. The interviewer plays the role of a moderator leading the respondents in a relatively free discussion about the topic. The interactions between the group members create a dynamic environment that gives respondents additional motivation to elaborate on their attitudes, experiences and feelings.

Main disadvantages are that groups can become dominated by a self-appointed group leader who monopolises the conversation. Focus groups depend heavily on the skills of the moderator who must know when to intervene to stop respondents from discussing irrelevant topics, probe for further information and ensure all respondents are involved in the discussion.

In the BTDT campaign, focus groups were not only conducted to explore attitudes of the residents; they were also used to test messages for the campaign. The use of focus groups helped the PR department to understand that the main criterion for residents doing recycling is convenience. If a survey were used as the only method, it could have provided misleading results. A survey would have measured positive attitudes of the residents about recycling. But why do only few practise it? The focus groups could explore and explain in-depth the gap between attitudes and behaviour: the inconvenience of recycling.

Box 10.1 gives some rules for conducting a focus group study.

Surveys

The survey among Westminster residents illustrates the kind of decisions that have to be taken when conducting a survey.

Which type of survey should be conducted?
Table 10.4 details the types of survey and their advantages and disadvantages. (See Activities 10.2 and 10.3.)

How many people should be interviewed and how will you select them?
Since most research cannot reach all members of a population (all units of consideration to be researched), a sample has to be drawn. There are various sampling designs that

---

Box 10.1

How to conduct a focus group study

There are 12 basic steps in focus group research:

1. Is a focus group study really appropriate?
2. Define the problem.
3. Decide who will moderate.
4. Determine the number of groups necessary.
5. Design a screening questionnaire for selecting a sample.
6. Recruit participants according to screening results.
7. Develop question guideline for the moderator.
8. Brief the moderator.
9. Select and brief focus group observers.
10. Prepare facilities and check catering arrangements.
11. Conduct the session.
12. Analyse the data and report findings.

Source: Broom and Dozier 1990; Wimmer and Dominick 2006

---

can be used to select the units of research. For example, in our case of the BTDT campaign, the population consists of all residents of Westminster from which a sample is drawn. The sample consists of 502 residents, which is a sufficient sample size to ensure validity of the results.

What do you want to measure?
Before developing a survey questionnaire, you need to decide what you want to measure. A basic distinction is to research awareness/knowledge/beliefs (cognitions), attitudes, behaviour.

In the BTDT campaign the key research questions cover these aspects:

■ What do residents know about the service (knowledge)?

■ What do residents think about recycling (attitudes)?

■ Are residents willing to recycle or what prevents them from recycling (motivation/behaviour)?

Table 10.4 Types of survey

Method	Requirements	Advantages	Disadvantages
Mail survey – self-administered questionnaires (self-explanatory)	Mailing list Reply envelope Cover letter (separate) Incentives Follow-up mailings	Anonymity Specific mailing lists available Low cost, little time to prepare and conduct Respondent convenience	Response rate Slow data collection Only standardised questions Response: only motivated respondents – not representative
Telephone survey	Telephone numbers Interviewers Training and instruction (manner of speaking, what to say . . .)	Interviewers can clarify questions Speed, costs Control, probing complex answers High response rates, completeness of questionnaires	Reach of respondents Limited use of scales, visual materials
Personal interview (face to face)	Interviewers and training	Interviewers can clarify questions Use of scales and visual materials	No anonymity Expensive Interviewer bias
Online surveys	Website Email list	Inexpensive Respondent convenience Anonymity	No control who is contacted Only Internet users Not representative Low response rates

---

Activity 10.2

Types of survey

In the BTDT campaign the sample consisted of 502 residents. But which type of survey would be the most appropriate method to collect data?

Consider and write down:

- How will respondents be reached?
- What might be the response rate?
- Think about cost and time effectiveness, too.

Activity 10.3

Developing a questionnaire

One key question in the BTDT campaign was to find out the attitudes of Westminster residents about recycling. Develop a short questionnaire to measure this.

Which instruments do you use?

Do you measure them directly or indirectly?

What are you going to ask?

The next step is to develop 'instruments for measurement', that is, framing the right kind of questions. The key research questions in the BTDT campaign indicate 'what' is to be measured, but they are not yet the questions that are used in a questionnaire. In general, the objects of research – in this case, knowledge, attitudes, behaviour – can be measured with various types of question and scale. Developing questions means to develop instruments that measure knowledge, attitude, etc. These concepts are *operationalised* through the questions (Wimmer and Dominick 2006). (See Glossary for definition of **operationalisation**.)

Are you going to measure attitudes or images?

Images or attitudes can be measured using a variety of different techniques and instruments. Instruments are the specific questions or scales with which attitudes are measured. The next section gives an idea about the instruments that can be used depending on the object (e.g. attitudes about fast food), the respondents and the situation. The instruments are either quantitative, with standardised scales, or qualitative, going more in depth and providing insights that are not generated by quantitative approaches.

Further instruments can be classified as direct or indirect. Direct instruments clearly reveal the purpose of the questioning, for example, 'Do you intend to recycle?' Indirect instruments are used when there is the danger that respondents might answer in a 'socially acceptable' manner or follow existing stereotypes in their answers, instead of revealing their real attitudes.

An example of the choice of the instrument influencing the results are surveys about fast food. Fast foods and restaurants serving them seem to have a rather negative 'image' among university students, according to many surveys, if they are directly asked about their attitudes. There seems, however, to be a gap between the results of surveys and the behaviour of the students, who constitute one of the biggest customer groups of fast food restaurants.

Designing research instruments

Quantitative instruments to measure attitudes or images

Semantic differential (Example 10.1) is one of the most frequently used instruments in image measurement. It consists of pairs of contrary items by which the object of interest (organisations, persons, advertisements, issues, etc.) is evaluated. This approach draws on semiotics, an approach to the study of words, signs and symbols, which

discovered that people tend to group objects in simple either/or categories. Cars, councils, celebrities, baked beans can all be assessed by asking people whether they think these things are either luxury or basic goods, for example. You can go on to ask if they are old/young, male/female, etc. These either/or polarities can be either descriptive-direct or metaphoric-indirect. Item pairs that are descriptive-direct are **denotative**, that is, they relate to the perceived functions of the subject. Metaphoric-indirect items are **connotative**, that is, they relate to the emotional or mental associations of the item being researched. It is useful to use either denotative or connotative items. For example, if you evaluate a car, then item pairs such as 'slow–fast', 'expensive–good value' are denotative. Pairs like 'female–male' or 'warm–cold' are rather connotative.

The advantage of semantic differentials is that it is a highly standardised instrument with which different objects can easily be compared. A disadvantage is that it might consist of items that are rather irrelevant to the respondent's attitude about an object. If the research object is new and unexplored, then the relevance of items can be unclear.

Likert scales (Example 10.2) ask how far a respondent agrees or disagrees with statements about an object. The statements should cover all relevant facets of the research object. Nevertheless, it remains open as to how relevant statements are for respondents in their attitude about the object.

In *rank ordering* (Example 10.3), respondents have to place research objects – often listed on separate cards – in order from best to worst. This can be combined with open, qualitative questions that ask what they most like/dislike about the objects. This explores which features are relevant for their assessment. A problem with rank orders is that each object is only evaluated in comparison with the others but not on an absolute scale. An advantage is that the object is assessed as a whole entity and leaves it to the respondents to decide which features determine their opinion.

The *Kunin scale* (Example 10.4) is an example of how to assess objects non-verbally, which is easy for children or elderly people to understand.

Example 10.2   ## Likert scale

How much do you agree with the following statement: 'BT is a progressive corporation'?
Please tick one box.

Strongly agree	Agree	Neither agree nor disagree	Disagree	Strongly disagree

Example 10.3   ## Rank order

In front of you there are 10 cards with telecommunications providers. Please put the card with the telecommunications provider you like the most in the first position, the one you like the second best in the second position, and so on.

Example 10.4   ## Kunin scale

Please mark how much you like Virgin Trains.

Example 10.5   ## Free associations

Question: Please write down everything that comes into your mind when you hear the words 'Royal Mail'.

Possible answers: post, expensive, conservative, reliable, etc.

Additionally, the respondents might be asked in a follow-up question to assess all their answers and state whether they consider them 'positive (+)', 'neutral (0)' or 'negative (–)'. This avoids subjective misinterpretations of the researcher:

Post (0), expensive (–), conservative (0), reliable (+)

Qualitative instruments to measure attitudes or images

Free associations (Example 10.5) are considered to be a qualitative instrument because the respondents are not guided by existing categories for their answers.

If there is a danger that respondents might not admit or even express their real opinions, it makes sense to use a *projective question technique* (Example 10.6). The respondent is asked to answer a question as if replying for somebody else. The respondent projects their real answers into that person.

In the *balloon test* (Example 10.7) as a *specific projective instrument* the respondent gets a drawing with two people and is asked to fill in the empty 'balloon'. The idea is that the respondent projects their thoughts into the person with the empty balloon.

Box 10.2 on page 210 provides an example of measuring relationships by surveys.

Example 10.6   **Projective question**

In your opinion, what do other people think about the Royal Mail?

Example 10.7   **Balloon test**

'I travel regularly with Virgin Trains'

Box 10.2

Using survey research to measure relationships

A typical research project for the study of relationships between an organisation and its publics is Hon and Grunig's (1999) measurement of relationships. So the research object is 'relationships'. Hon and Grunig specify 'successful relationships' as: control mutuality, trust, satisfaction, commitment, exchange relationship and communal relationship. The research method is conducting a survey.

In order to measure the concept 'relationship' they operationalise – 'make measurable' – the idea of relationship. They explore the six factors mentioned above by generating a list of statements for each factor, for respondents to agree or disagree with.

For example, the factor 'trust' is measured by statements:

- This organisation treats people like me fairly and justly.
- This organisation can be relied on to keep its promises.
- Whenever this organisation makes an important decision, I know it will be concerned about people like me.
- I feel very confident about this organisation's skills.
- I believe that this organisation takes the opinions of people like me into account when making decisions.

With these statements they conduct a survey among publics who evaluate their relationship with different organisations by how much they agree/disagree with each statement.

Source: Hon and Grunig 1999

Media content analysis

Media monitoring, collecting and counting press clippings, is widely used in public relations to track publicity. However, collecting data or output is only a first step in conducting a media content analysis. Only the systematic analysis of these materials according to a set of criteria can be considered as content analysis. 'Content analysis is a method to analyse media reality, verbal and visual output (content of newspapers, magazines, radio, television and web) which leads to inferences about the communicators and audience of these contents' (Merten 1995: 15).

Content analysis itself does not directly measure outcomes – for example, the image of an organisation in the mind of the audience – and might only be considered as an indicator of certain effects. Web logs, online newsgroups and chatrooms can be monitored, too. Computer-assisted content analysis uses specific software programs, which analyse frequencies of words or other categories. There are specialist research firms that offer services in this field (e.g. www.uk.cision.com).

In general, a content analysis is conducted in eight discrete steps (Wimmer and Dominick 2006).

Formulate the research question
Table 10.5 presents an overview of typical questions that can be answered by content analysis. The particular research question determines the further steps in the process of a content analysis.

Define a population
By defining the time period and the types of media (population) that will be analysed, the researcher sets the frame for the investigation.

For example, a content analysis might compare how fast food providers are covered in mass media. Since the general public might be considered a relevant audience, daily newspapers are defined as the population in question.

Select a sample from the population
As stated above, it is not possible to survey all members of a population all the time. So a smaller number of outlets and a specific period of time must be selected.

For example, the time period of the last half-year is the period in which the media coverage is analysed. Smaller newspapers reach fewer readers, so only the top five daily newspapers with the highest readership are selected.

Select and define a unit of analysis
There needs to be agreement about what exactly is being counted in the analysis. For example, each newspaper article in which the name of a fast food provider or the term 'fast food' is mentioned is a unit of analysis (in other words, not every mention of hamburger or of chips is counted).

Construct the categories of content to be analysed
The categories are determined by the research questions. In our example, this might be the rating of an article as 'positive/negative/neutral', the topic of the article, the sources quoted, etc. It is important to define indicators which determine what 'positive/negative/neutral' mean.

Establish a quantification system
The category system used to classify the media content is the actual measurement instrument. For each category, subcategories must be created. An example of a category might be 'corporate social responsibility'. Subcategories could be 'donations to charity', 'employee volunteering' and 'environmental policy'. The subcategories should be exhaustive, in that they cover all aspects of 'corporate social responsibility' that occur in the articles, and exclusive, which means that they should not overlap or denote the same.

Train coders and conduct a pilot study
To obtain valid results, different researchers, or coders, must assess the same article in the same way. A pilot study,

Table 10.5 Examples of questions researched through content analysis (*source*: adapted from Merten and Wienand 2004: 5)

Media	Issues and actors	Image
Which media/journalists dominate the media coverage?	Which issues dominate the media coverage?	Which image is portrayed?
How do media report about the organisation? (positive/negative/neutral)	Which actors dominate the media coverage?	Which factors dominate the image?
How many and which audiences are reached?	In the frame of which issues does the organisation and its representatives appear?	How is the organisation positioned in its sector?
		What do competitors do?

or trial run, can point out weaknesses in the categories or instructions for the coders. In practice, this will involve analysing a small sample of articles to test the instrument – the category system.

Code the content according to established definitions

Finally, all sample articles have to be assessed for each category and given a number for that assessment. The assessments are determined by the definitions associated with each category. For example, a mention of 'donations to charity' as a subcategory of 'corporate social responsibility' might be given a number code 1 to denote 'donations to charity'. Numbering like this helps with the data analysis, particularly across a wide range of categories and subcategories.

Research applications

Internet as a research tool and object

The Internet has become an increasingly important research object as well as a research tool. Research objects can be issues which are discussed in web logs or chatrooms. Another increasingly relevant issue is the measurement of the chatter and discussion about an organisation in cyberspace, which can be used to help understand an organisation's image or reputation. The same criteria used in analysing print and broadcast articles can be applied when analysing postings on the Internet, which is referred to as cyberspace analysis (Lindenmann 1997). Another output measure of cyberspace might be a review and analysis of website traffic patterns. For example, some of the variables that ought to be considered when designing and carrying out cyberspace analysis might include examining the requests for a file of website visitors, a review of click-throughs or flash-click streams, an assessment of home page visits, domain tracking and analysis and assessment of bytes transferred, a review of time spent per page, traffic times, browsers used and the number of people filling out and returning feedback forms (Lindenmann 1997).

The Internet also offers new opportunities to conduct research in online focus groups, online interviews or online surveys. Online focus groups can be conducted in 'real time' or in 'non-real time', or using a combination of both. It allows access to populations in disparate places and is highly cost effective. Nevertheless, the problem of participant verification (who is recruited as participant through the Internet) remains a problem in all forms of online research techniques (Mann and Stewart 2000).

Identifying publics: social network analysis

One tool that is used to identify relevant publics and opinion leaders, and to understand the communication flow and lines of influences within and between groups of people, is social network analysis (SNA) (Scott 2000). SNA is the mapping and measuring of relationships and flows between people, groups or organisations. It can be used for external and internal analysis (organisational network analysis) of relationships. But like a PEST (or EPISTLE) or SWOT analysis, the social network analysis is not a method itself. The network has to be explored, for example, through observation or interviews.

To understand the network, the location and context of the actors (people whose relationships are being observed) has to be evaluated first. For example, with whom does an actor interact? How many connections does an actor have? Is a person central in a network or peripheral? Is a person connected to well-connected or poorly connected people?

Of further interest in network analysis is:

- structural equivalence: which actors play similar roles in the network?
- cluster analysis: find cliques and densely connected clusters
- structural holes: find areas of no connection between actors that could be used for communication
- E/I ratio: find which groups in the network are open or closed to others (Scott 2000).

Communication audit

Communication audits assess the tangible and intangible communications resources of an organisation. A very formal and thorough audit may take months to complete. Communication audits examine:

- face-to-face communication
- written communication in the form of letters, memos and internal reports
- communication patterns among individuals, sections and departments
- communication channels and frequency of interaction
- communication content, its clarity and effectiveness
- information needs of individuals, sections or departments
- information technology
- informal communication, particularly as it affects motivation and performance

- non-verbal communication
- communication climate (Hamilton 1987: 4–5).

Evaluation

Importance of evaluation

Evaluation is the evergreen topic of the entire practice and one of the areas where both practitioners and academics have a vast common interest. In the UK, the Chartered Institute of Public Relations has initiated and coordinated research on evaluation and encouraged practitioners to evaluate their efforts in a systematic way by using a variety of methods.

Evaluating PR activities is essential for many reasons, including accountability, assessment of programme effectiveness and professionalism.

Evaluation is the systematic assessment of the impacts of PR activities. It is a purposeful process, carried out for a specific audience. Audiences include numerous parties that have an interest in the evaluation – the organisation, the PR practitioners involved, target publics and the evaluators themselves. (Sometimes an external agency, such as a media monitoring company, does media evaluation.) (See Activity 10.4.)

In a typical PR campaign, the following actors are present: the *organisation*, which can commission a *PR agency* to work on its behalf to reach and communicate with a variety of *publics* through the *media*. Figure 10.1 visualises the actors and their influences.

Out of these four actors, the emphasis has been on media, and print media evaluation still dominates the field of evaluation. Measuring effects on, and changes in, the targeted publics' knowledge, attitudes and behaviour in the form of outcome is also paramount. During the early

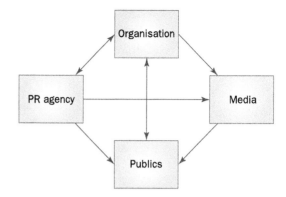

Figure 10.1 Actors and their influence

1990s the organisational dimension was emphasised, demonstrating how PR can add value to achieving organisational goals. Around the turn of the millennium a new dimension emerged, measuring relationship in the client/agency and client/publics contexts. Table 10.6 summarises the aims of evaluation according to orientations.

For an extensive evaluation, each of these orientations should be considered. However, the emphasis often remains on only one or two of these dimensions. Evaluation often serves as budget or action justification. In the media orientation approach the emphasis is on the quantity (how many articles were generated, how big is the circulation of the newspaper in which an article appeared) and quality of media coverage (negative, positive tone). (See Mini case study 10.2.)

PR practitioners overemphasise print media evaluation. Despite the fact that the world is moving more and more towards image-based communication, PR practice has been slow to embrace methods of evaluating TV and other types of image. Fathers4Justice is a pressure group in the UK whose aim is to highlight the problems of fathers separated from their children by divorce or relationship breakdown. They have performed 'stunts' to attract media attention to their issue by dressing up as children's or comic book characters. They have climbed government buildings, bridges and the Queen's London residence, Buckingham Palace, to create visually sensational, shocking images that can be easily transmitted into the living rooms of millions and grab attention. (See Activity 10.5.)

Dimensions of evaluation

PR evaluation can be:

- **formative, summative** or **goal-free evaluation**, depending on the time of intervention
- assessed at individual, programme, organisational and societal level, depending on the level of effectiveness.

Table 10.6
Orientations of public
relations evaluation

Orientation	Aim of evaluation	Levels
Media	Quantity and quality of coverage	Programme, societal
Publics	Effects on publics, how they have changed their knowledge, attitudes or behaviour as a result of public relations activities	Programme
Organisation	To demonstrate how public relations can contribute to achieving organisational goals	Organisational
Persuasion	Demonstrates return on investment (ROI) to clients or management; value of public relations; accountability of public relations professionals or departments	Individual, programme
Relationship	Client/agency, organisation/publics	Individual, organisational

Mini Case Study 10.2
The IKEA story in the media

The media reported extensively the chaotic opening of London's Edmonton IKEA store in February 2005. Beyond the negative headlines was an undercurrent of hostility towards the company. The IKEA consumer experience, deemed to come a poor second to low prices, was singled out for particular criticism: 'IKEA treats its customers so badly, a riot is the least it might have expected' wrote the *Guardian* (10 February 2005), cataloguing an absence of Internet ordering, insufficient stock, poor customer service and lengthy queues. Others accused it of irresponsibly stimulating demand with heavy advertising and special offers in a deprived area: 'Does it pay to advertise?' (*The Times*, 10 February 2005).

Figure 10.2 is a typical example of evaluating media coverage, counting how many times certain types of messages occurred and assessing the tone of the coverage.

Source: www.echoresearch.com

Activity 10.5

Measuring media stunts

Examine the Fathers4Justice campaign (visit their website: www.fathers-4-justice.org). How would you conduct content analysis of TV coverage of one of their campaigns?

Feedback

Quantity: how many times was the name of the pressure group mentioned? How long was the entire coverage? Was it a leading piece of news?

Quality: What was the context of the coverage? Who was interviewed? How did the newsreader comment on their actions (favourably or unfavourably)? Do you now understand their demands more clearly?

As we saw earlier, formative evaluation (or process research) takes places while the programme is still in operation. Summative evaluation aims at assessing outcomes and impacts as they take place towards the end of a programme or after its conclusion. Summative research evaluates results against objectives. This can be feasible only if SMART objectives have been set: specific, measurable, achievable, realistic and timebound (see Chapter 9).

Evaluation purposes and circumstances dictate which type of evaluation (summative, formative or goal free) is most appropriate in a given case. Bissland's (1990: 25) definition illustrates that in PR literature evaluation is frequently used as a summative activity: 'Evaluation is the systematic assessment of a program and its results. It is a means for practitioners to offer accountability to clients – and to themselves.'

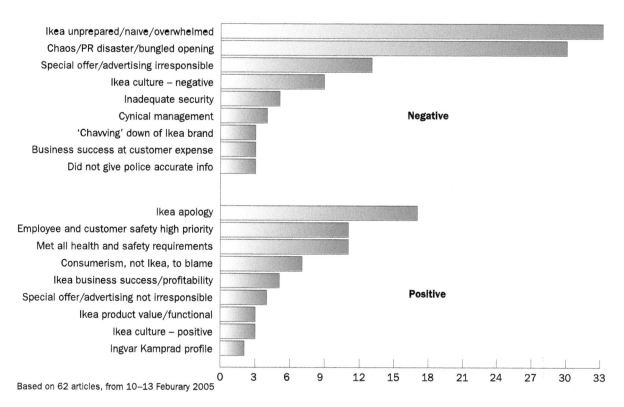

Figure 10.2 IKEA's image in the print media after opening a new store (*source*: a weekly snapshot review of 'messages in the news' prepared by Echo Research for trade journal *PR Week*; Echo Research, http://www.echoresearch.com)

Picture 10.2 Fathers 4 Justice using media stunts to raise their campaign's media profile (see: http://www.fathers-4-justice.org) (*source*: Alisdair Macdonald/Rex)

Box 10.3

Four categories of performance measure

Input: background information and research that informs initial planning.

Output: measures the result of PR activity such as media coverage or publicity (exposure to messages, quantifiable features such as number of press releases sent out, consultation sessions scheduled, telephone calls answered or audience members at speech events). Output measures are short term, concentrate on visible results and do not say anything about audience response.

Outcome: the degree to which PR activities changed target public's knowledge, attitudes and behaviour. It may take weeks, months or even years for these changes to occur.

Outtake: describes an intermediate step between output and outcome. It refers to what people do with an output but what might not necessarily be a specific outcome as a set objective of a campaign. Whereas outtake is related to the output, outcome is to be seen with reference to the objectives set. For example, people might remember the message (outtake) of a communication campaign but might not change their behaviour (outcome).

Source: adapted from Gregory 2000: 169–71

Levels of effectiveness

According to Hon (1997) effective PR occurs when communication activities achieve communication goals. She conceptualised effectiveness at four levels.

Individual practitioners

The first level is that of individual practitioners, measuring how effective they are at achieving whatever is expected of them. This is closely related to performance measurement, partly because consultancy practitioners work on a fee basis. Depending on the positions and experience, the hourly rate of consultancy practitioners can vary. Another dimension of the individual level is the quality and nature of relationship between the consultant and the client. Client/agency relationship has become the focus of many evaluation studies, moving beyond the simple programme evaluation level.

Programme level

The second level is the programme level. Effectiveness in PR is quite often synonymous with effectiveness at the programme level and this level is usually the focus of evaluation. The results of PR activity can be further assessed by means of four categories of performance measures: input, output, outcome and outtake. Box 10.3 summarises these measures. (See Think about 10.3.)

Organisational level

The third level of effectiveness is organisational level. The typical question at this level is, 'How do PR activities and

efforts contribute to achieving organisational goals, such as being the market leader or increase sales figures?' Assessing effectiveness at organisational level also includes the aggregates of different PR activities, as in the case of a multinational organisation, which has regional or national offices with their own PR plans and programmes. If PR objectives are not in line with organisational goals, it might be difficult to evaluate the programme at this level. Another issue at this level may be the difficulty of separating PR effects from other effects (advertising, direct mails).

Think about 10.3

Output or outcome evaluation

Legoland Windsor is a family theme park aimed at three to twelve-year-olds. To help build excitement, the park attempted to build the world's tallest Lego tower over the May Day bank holiday 2008. The campaign objectives were to:

■ achieve national press and broadcast coverage

■ increase visitors to the museum

Source: PR Week 18 July 2008, campaigns section – 'Lego builds fanbase one brick at a time', p. 25

How do you evaluate the campaign?

What are the output and outcome measures?

Article mentions versus headlines
Press set: UK newspapers

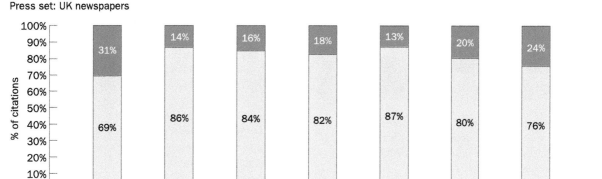

Figure 10.3 F4J grabbing headlines (*source*: Reputation Intelligence)

Societal level

As Hon noted, the final level of effectiveness is at the level of society. This level is usually examined from either a systems theory or a critical perspective (see Chapter 8). The systems theory approach asserts that PR plays a positive role in society; according to the critical perspective, PR activities have negative consequences on the society at large.

Evaluation methods

Earlier we discussed surveys, focus groups, interviews and content analysis as most frequently used methods to conduct research. They are used to evaluate PR programmes as well but there are other methods available for PR practitioners.

PR Week commissioned research in 1999 among 200 PR practitioners to gauge their attitudes and behaviour with regard to evaluation. About 60% of respondents said that they used media content analysis or press cuttings to evaluate their PR activities. The next most frequently used technique was opportunities to see (OTS), which is the number of occasions that an audience has the potential to view a message. The circulation numbers of the British daily newspapers presented in Table 10.2 includes these opportunities in the case of print media.

Surveys, focus groups and advertising value equivalents (AVEs) are also often used to evaluate PR programmes. AVE is the notional equivalent cost of buying editorial. It is a controversial method and practitioners are being discouraged from using this method because it compares advertising and PR (Watson and Noble 2005). However, national and international research confirms this method remains widely used by both in-house and consultancy practitioners. (See Box 10.4.)

Box 10.4

PR effects on societies

The effects and influences of PR practices on society at large can be broad and varied. PR can help to:

■ Maintain the trust in the political system (western democracies)

■ Integrate a society (after the collapse of the Soviet Union many Russians remained in the Baltic States and PR has been used to integrate Estonians, Latvians and Lithuanians with Russians)

■ Transform a society (Latin America) or economy (Eastern Europe)

■ Build nations (Malaysia, East Timor)

■ Disintegrate countries, regimes (e.g. Yugoslavia, or Hill and Knowlton's infamous case about using alleged Iraqi atrocities to mobilise public opinion for a war against Iraq in 1991)

Source: Szondi 2006: 20

Fathers4Justice (F4J) press coverage

On behalf of F4J, Reputation Intelligence, a research agency, analysed more than 10,000 articles from 330 UK newspapers published between 2000 and 2004. Media evaluation showed that:

- Articles on fathers' rights have increased by over 700% since F4J mounted its high-profile media campaign.
- F4J has engaged the politicians to speak on fathers' rights and encourage opposition parties to take up its fight.
- Compared to other political campaigning organisations, F4J is grabbing a high ratio of headlines to article mentions (see Figure 10.3, p. 217).
- F4J is well placed to turn this profile into clear messages on policy reform.

Source: Reputation Intelligence (2004)

Organisations do not always want to get publicity. In the case of a crisis, for example, the company may prefer minimal exposure to media. Nor is publicity the same as understanding – newspaper coverage may be extensive without clearly explaining the goals of those seeking publicity.

Evaluation guidelines

'Is it possible for those of us who work in the public relations field to ever develop generally accepted models or standards of public relations evaluation upon which everyone in the industry can agree?', asked Walter Lindenmann (1997: 391), a well-respected research specialist in the field.

The search for an objective, simple and effective methodology for evaluating PR programmes occupied much academic literature in the 1980s. Pavlik (1987: 65) commented that: 'Measuring the effectiveness of PR efforts has proved almost as elusive as finding the Holy Grail.' The search was over at the beginning of the 1990s, as Lindenmann (1993: 9) commented: 'There is no one simplistic method for measuring PR effectiveness . . . An array of different tools and techniques is needed to properly assess PR impact.'

Searching for a single and universal method was replaced by practitioners focusing on compiling an evaluation toolkit based on the best practice guidelines. In 1997 a 28-page booklet entitled *Guidelines and Standards for Measuring and Evaluating PR* was published by the

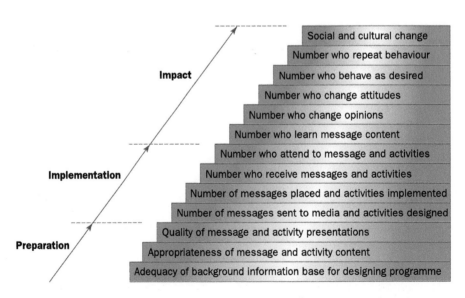

Figure 10.4 Stages and levels of public relations programme evaluation (*source*: Cutlip, Scott M., Center, Allen H., Broom, Glen M., *Effective Public Relations, 8th Edition*, © 2000, p. 437. Reprinted by permission of Pearson Education, Inc., Upper Saddle River, NJ)

Institute of Public Relations Research & Education in the USA. In Europe, two booklets were produced with a more focused purpose, covering how to prepare measurable goals and objectives prior to the launch of a campaign and how to measure PR outputs.

In the UK, a research and evaluation toolkit was compiled in 1999 utilising the findings of the above-mentioned *PR Week* survey on evaluation. This toolkit spells out the best reasons for employing research and evaluation in campaigns and gives guidance on how to set about it. The author of the toolkit argued that the UK is taking a leading position on research and evaluation. In 2003 the Institute of Public Relations published the 'IPR Toolkit: Media evaluation edition'.

Evaluation models

A number of evaluation models have been developed to serve as guidelines in terms of what to evaluate and how to evaluate. Most are three-stage models embracing a variety of techniques. Cutlip et al.'s 'stages and levels of public relations programme evaluation', represents different levels of a complete programme evaluation: preparation, implementation and impact (Figure 10.4). This first level assesses the information and planning, the implementation evaluation deals with tactics and activities while the impact evaluation provides feedback on the outcome.

Activity 10.6

Macnamara's model

Review the evaluation of the Bin There Done That campaign. What are the inputs, outputs and results that are measured in this campaign? What does it tell you about the extent or depth of evaluation?

Preparation evaluation assesses the quality and adequacy of information that was used to plan the programme. Some key publics might have been unidentified at the planning stage or some issues overlooked. This stage is very similar to the plan assessment we discussed earlier.

At the second level, implementation evaluation assesses the number of messages distribution and measures outputs. The final stage, the impact level, examines the extent to which the defined goals of the campaigns have been achieved. This level is primarily concerned with the changes in knowledge, attitudes and behaviour.

As the authors noted, the most common error in programme evaluation is substituting measures from one level for those at another (Cutlip et al. 2006).

Macnamara's (1992) model is similar but uses different terminology: inputs, outputs and results. (Output is usually the short-term or immediate results of a particular PR programme or activity.) This model lists evaluation methodologies that can be applied to each step, but for different steps different methodologies are required. The model is presented in a pyramidal form starting from inputs through outputs to results (see Figure 10.5; see also Activity 10.6).

Barriers and challenges to developing and using effective research in PR activities can be summarised as follows. Watson (1994) found that the barriers to evaluation uncovered in his survey were mirrored worldwide:

■ lack of time

■ lack of personnel

■ lack of budget

■ cost of evaluation

■ doubts about usefulness

■ lack of knowledge

■ can expose practitioner's performance to criticism

■ aversion to scientific methodology.

The challenge of the profession lies in overcoming these difficulties.

Summary

This chapter outlined the principles of research, which is a central activity in any PR programme. A variety of research methods have been presented that enable PR practitioners to conduct systematic and objective research, and scopes of research and evaluation have been outlined.

Since an organisation's public relations are related to other communication activities such as marketing communications, research must also be integrated with these areas. PR research and evaluation cannot be seen in isolation from an organisation's other communication research (see Chapter 25). If we talk about integrated communications, then we also have to talk about 'integrated communications research (and evaluation)'.

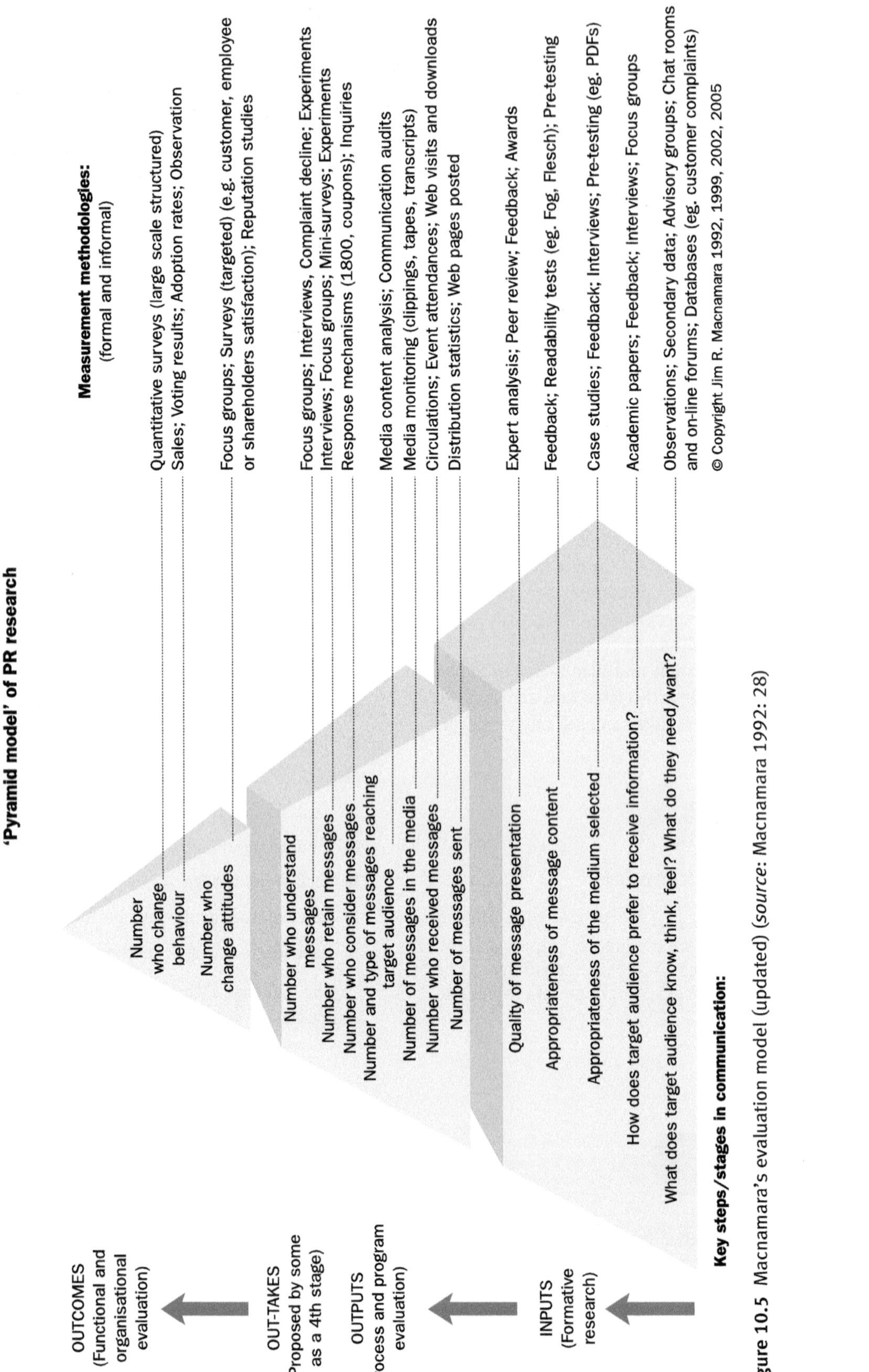

'Pyramid model' of PR research

Measurement methodologies:
(formal and informal)

Quantitative surveys ((large scale structured)
Sales; Voting results; Adoption rates; Observation

Focus groups; Surveys (targeted) (e.g. customer, employee
or shareholders satisfaction); Reputation studies

Focus groups; Interviews, Complaint decline; Experiments
Interviews; Focus groups; Mini-surveys; Experiments
Response mechanisms (1800, coupons); Inquiries

Media content analysis; Communication audits
Media monitoring (clippings, tapes, transcripts)
Circulations; Event attendances; Web visits and downloads
Distribution statistics; Web pages posted

Expert analysis; Peer review; Feedback; Awards

Feedback; Readability tests (eg. Fog, Flesch); Pre-testing

Case studies; Feedback; Interviews; Pre-testing (eg. PDFs)

Academic papers; Feedback; Interviews; Focus groups

Observations; Secondary data; Advisory groups; Chat rooms
and on-line forums; Databases (eg. customer complaints)

© Copyright Jim R. Macnamara 1992, 1999, 2002, 2005

OUTCOMES
(Functional and
organisational
evaluation)

Number
who change
behaviour

Number who
change attitudes

OUT-TAKES
(Proposed by some
as a 4th stage)

Number who understand
messages
Number who retain messages
Number who consider messages
Number and type of messages reaching
target audience

OUTPUTS
(Process and program
evaluation)

Number of messages in the media
Number who received messages
Number of messages sent

Quality of message presentation

Appropriateness of message content

Appropriateness of the medium selected

INPUTS
(Formative
research)

How does target audience prefer to receive information?

What does target audience know, think, feel? What do they need/want?

Key steps/stages in communication:

Figure 10.5 Macnamara's evaluation model (updated) (*source:* Macnamara 1992: 28)

Bibliography

Besson, N. (2008). *Strategische PR-Evaluation. Erfassung, Bewertung und Kontrolle von Öffentlichkeitsarbeit*, 3. Auflage. Wiesbaden: VS Verlag für Sozialwissenschaften.

Bissland, J.H. (1990). 'Accountability gap: evaluation practices show improvement'. *Public Relations Review* **16**(2): 25–26.

Broom, G.M. and D.M. Dozier (1990). *Using Research in Public Relations: Applications to program management*. Englewood Cliffs, NJ: Prentice Hall.

Cutlip, S.M., A.H. Center, G.M. Broom (2000) *Effective Public Relations*, 8th edition, p. 437. Pearson Education, Inc., Upper Saddle River, NJ.

Cutlip, S.M., A.H. Center and G.M. Broom (2006). *Effective Public Relations*, 9th edition. Upper Saddle River, NJ: Prentice Hall International.

Gregory, A. (2000). *Planning and Managing Public Relations Campaigns*, 2nd edition. London: Kogan Page.

Hamilton, S. (1987). *A Communication Audit Handbook – Helping Organisations Communicate*. London: Pitman.

Hon, L.C. (1997). 'What have you done for me recently? Exploring effectiveness in public relations'. *Journal of Public Relations Research* **9**(1): 1–30.

Hon, L.C. (1998). 'Demonstrating effectiveness in public relations: Goals, objectives, and evaluation'. *Journal of Public Relations Research* **10**(2): 103–135.

Hon, L.C. and J.E. Grunig (1999). *Measuring Relationships in Public Relations*. Gainesville, FL: Institute for Public Relations.

Kerlinger, F.N. (1986). *Foundations of Behavioral Research*, 3rd edition. Fort Worth, TX: Holt, Rinehart & Winston.

Kim, Y., J. Kim, J. Park and Y. Choi (1999). 'Evaluating media exposure: An application of advertising methods to publicity measurement'. *Corporate Communications* **4**(2): 98–105.

Lerbinger, O. (1977). 'Corporate uses of research in public relations'. *Public Relations Review* **3**(4):11–20.

Lindenmann, W.K. (1990). 'Research, evaluation and measurement: A national perspective'. *Public Relations Review* **16**: 3–15.

Lindenmann, W.K. (1993). 'An "effectiveness yardstick" to measure public relations success'. *PR Quarterly* **38**(1): 7–9.

Lindenmann, W.K. (1997). 'Setting minimum standards for measuring public relations effectiveness'. *Public Relations Review* **23**(4): 391–408.

Lindlof, T.R. and C.T. Bryan (2002). *Qualitative Communication Research Methods*. Thousand Oaks, CA: Sage.

Macnamara, J.R. (1992). 'Evaluation of public relations: The Achilles heel of the profession'. *International Public Relations Review* **15**(4): 17–31.

Mann, C. and F. Stewart (2000). *Internet Communication and Qualitative Research: A handbook for researching online*. London: Sage.

Merten, K. (1995). *Inhaltsanalyse. Einführung in Theorie, Methode und Praxis*. Opladen: Westdeutscher Verlag.

Merten, K. and E. Wienand (2004). 'Medienresonazanalyse'. Paper presented at the Redaktion und wissenschaftlicher Beirat der Pressesprecher Conference, Berlin, 7 May.

Neumann, P. (2003). *Markt- und Werbepsychologie Bd. 2. Praxis*. Gräfelfing: Fachverlag Wirtschaftspsychologie, 2nd edition.

Pavlik, J.V. (1987). *Public Relations: What research tells us*. Newbury Park, NJ: Sage.

Reputation Intelligence (2004) 'F4J heralds a new era in political campaigning: Media Report', http://bten.co.uk/fathers-4-justice.org/pdf/ReputationIntelligence_MediaReport_14Sept04_v4.pdf. accessed 25 September 2008.

Scott, J. (2000). *Social Network Analysis*. London: Sage.

Szondi, G. (2006). 'Re-Valuating Public Relations Evaluation – Putting Values at the Centre of Evaluation'. *Medien Journal* (4): 7–26.

Vos, M. and H. Schoemaker (2004). *Accountability of Communication Management – A Balanced Scorecard for Communication Quality*. Utrecht: Lemma Publishers.

Watson, T. (1994). 'Evaluating public relations: models of measurement for public relations practice'. Paper presented at the International Public Relations Symposium, Lake Bled, Slovenia.

Watson, T. (1997). 'Measuring the success rate: Evaluating the PR process and PR programmes' in *Public Relations Principles and Practice*. P. Kitchen (ed.). London: Thomson Business Press.

Watson, T. and P. Noble (2005). *Evaluating public relations*. London : Kogan Page.

Wimmer, R.D. and J.R. Dominick (2006). *Mass Media Research: An introduction*, 8th edition. Belmont, CA: Wadsworth.

CHAPTER 13

Consumer Public Relations

Public relations and the consumer

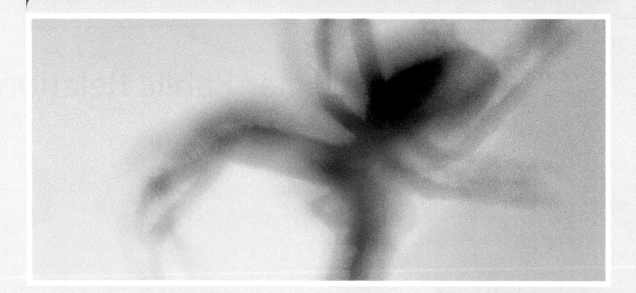

Learning outcomes

By the end of this chapter you should be able to:

- understand the term consumer public relations
- describe different types of consumer public relations activity
- appreciate the critical factors that drive successful consumer public relations campaigns
- understand how consumer public relations complements other communication disciplines
- appreciate the benefits that can be generated by a successful consumer public relations campaign
- apply the principles to real-life scenarios
- understand the challenges facing practitioners.

Structure

- What is consumer public relations?
- Tools and techniques
- The wonderful world of brands
- Key challenges
- Tomorrow's people

Introduction

The public relations (PR) and marketing landscape is changing. In a world of media fragmentation, information overload and a revolution in personal communication – not to mention the rise of the 'promiscuous' consumer – the conventional maxims of marketing are being challenged as never before. In this environment PR, which was once perceived as a rather lightweight addition to the marketing family, has proved that it can deliver results. Many marketing professionals now view PR as an effective way to win over the hearts and minds of consumers and its status in the marketing mix has grown accordingly. Some (Ries and Ries 2001) even argue that a seismic shift is underway, which will result in a diminished role for advertising in the future as companies look for more sophisticated ways to promote their products and services. Superbrands, such as Virgin and Amazon, have already placed PR at the forefront of their marketing strategies, as have a host of other companies, although it should be noted that the majority are still a long way from grasping even a slice of its full potential.

Whatever the level of acceptance and application, one thing is certain: consumer PR has moved from the fringes of marketing communication to a position of credibility and influence. While the lion's share of the marketing budget still tends to be spent elsewhere, the universe of consumer PR is expanding rapidly and it is a challenging and intoxicating place for a practitioner to be. It is a world of brands, buzz and creative advantage, all of which is driven by a simple business imperative: to sell their products and services companies must first get them noticed and into the minds of consumers. Only then can they start to forge lasting and productive relationships with their intended targets and it is at this stage of a campaign lifecycle that PR really comes into its own. The purpose of this chapter is to provide a greater appreciation of PR in a consumer marketing context and to demonstrate the advantages it has over other forms of communication. Attention will also be given to the strategic and intellectual rigour that is required to deliver an effective consumer PR campaign that makes a genuine difference by delivering tangible commercial results.

What is consumer public relations?

PR is a holistic discipline concerned with the complex relationships that exist between an organisation and those groups that can influence its reputation and affect the way it operates: employees, the local community, government, shareholders, financial institutions, regulators, suppliers and customers. As a result, PR campaigns can have many different objectives, such as:

- to help attract and retain staff
- to show that an organisation is environmentally responsible
- to change a piece of unfavourable legislation
- to educate people about an issue
- to demonstrate that the organisation is a worthy investment, a sound trading partner or the provider of quality products and services.

This breadth of outcomes means that every type of organisation – whether a company, charity or governing body – should be concerned with good PR practice in one form or another.

Clearly, PR does not focus only on the commercial activities of an organisation, and its remit extends beyond winning new customers and duelling with competitors in the highly pressurised world of modern capitalism. This chapter is, however, concerned specifically with this aspect of PR practice and will examine how organisations use the PR tools at their disposal to interact with consumers in a trading environment (how PR promotes transactions *between* businesses is discussed in Chapter 21). This commercial focus also excludes discussion of those PR campaigns in the public sector that are designed to educate citizens about issues such as smoking, recycling and taxation (see Chapter 29), as well as the recruitment and fundraising activities executed by charities.

The world we are concerned with here is where PR interfaces with **marketing** activities, such as advertising, to stimulate the sale of products and services in the free market economy. As the chapter unfolds it will become apparent that although the endgame of consumer PR in this context is to drive sales, its role is often more subtle and sophisticated than more direct forms of communication. By changing the attitudes and behaviour of consumers, PR can create a more favourable sales environment for a company and its products, so helping to facilitate the path to purchase.

Figure 20.1 illustrates this process by highlighting the stages a consumer can take on the **path to purchase**, the journey from initial awareness to purchase and consumption.

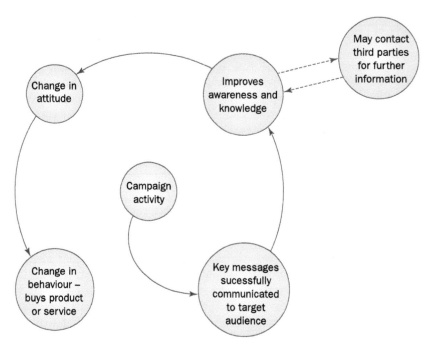

Figure 20.1 Path to purchase

Marketing mix

In developed countries it sometimes seems that everyone thinks they are a consumer PR expert (although they often mistake PR for **advertising**). After all, are we not all consumers and do we not all have valid views and opinions on the communication that is directed at us? It is true that as human beings we all use and consume goods and services to satisfy a complex range of needs. Every day we make countless decisions about the things we buy, from the cheap and mundane, to the expensive and exciting: everything from food, beer, clothing, bus and cinema tickets, to holidays, cars and mortgages. Indeed, it could be said that it is consumers – not companies – who exert the real power in the marketplace, as it is our individual buying decisions that determine the products that succeed and those that fail. It is not surprising, therefore, that most companies appear to be obsessively driven by the need to persuade consumers to buy their goods and services rather than those of their competitors.

It is increasingly appreciated in marketing circles and textbooks (e.g. Brassington and Pettitt 2006) that PR is a diverse practice that when successfully applied can grab attention, get people talking and move them to action. These are important attributes when the goal is to sell something to the man and woman in the street. In this context, PR has become a valuable part of what is known as the **marketing mix**, an often quoted term that refers to

the set of tools that a company has at its disposal to influence sales. The traditional formulation is popularly known as the 4Ps: product, price, place and promotion (Kotler 2003).

Promotion is the area that encompasses PR, as it is this part of the marketing equation that focuses on the messages that are designed to stimulate awareness, interest and purchase. To communicate these messages and to attract interest and awareness in their products and services, companies use a combination of disciplines – including advertising, **sales promotion**, **direct mail** and PR – to reach their desired audiences. When used in this way, PR should become a planned and sustained element of the wider *promotional mix*, working in tandem with other marketing activities to achieve maximum impact and with the potential to meet a range of objectives, such as:

- raising an organisation's profile
- redefining its image
- helping to promote its credibility in a new or existing market
- demonstrating empathy with a target audience
- launching a new product or service
- reinvigorating an existing product or service
- stimulating trial and purchase.

Building relationships

Underpinning a host of valid communication outcomes, helping an organisation to build positive and lasting relationships with consumers and those that influence them is the most important role that PR can play in marketing. While it can be argued that relationship building represents the Holy Grail for all disciplines in the promotional mix, the world we live in is changing. Mark Adams, a founder of high-tech PR firm Text 100 explains:

> Companies boast that they have relationships with their customers, while customers get more unwanted marketing rubbish in the post, and less of the face-to-face contact they really love. Ask them if they have a relationship with companies and they won't just laugh in your face – they'll probably spit. Relationship is being killed by corporate convenience and mass-producing. With it, customer trust and loyalty are becoming outdated concepts. It makes pure marketing sense for companies to spot this and aim to fix it. Those that do will achieve wondrous things. PR people are there to help do the fixing, to build relationships.

PR is increasingly showing itself to be a first among equals in the quest to connect with consumers. This is reflected in the growing preponderance of PR-led campaigns with marketing spend being diverted from advertising, direct mail and other budgets into what were once regarded as Cinderella activities. In short, the tools that PR professionals have at their disposal are increasingly seen to have the capacity to communicate with consumers in a way that other marketing disciplines cannot match.

Tools and techniques

Fit for purpose

Before discussing the individual tools and techniques that can make up a PR programme, it is important to stress that the key characteristics of the target audience play a big part in defining and shaping the strategy and tactics that are deployed in a campaign. Who do we need to talk to? How can we reach them? What are they interested in? What do we want them to do? By posing a series of simple questions it is possible to refine and sharpen the scope of the planned activity, ensuring a clinical rather than a wasteful, scatter-gun approach to the tools and techniques that are at the practitioner's disposal. (See also Chapter 9.)

For example, if the purpose of the campaign is to get young mothers to visit their local supermarket, a national media relations campaign might not have the same impact as activity targeted at a local newspaper. Or, if research shows that the same audience is concerned about their children walking to school, then a road safety sponsorship executed at local level may strike a chord and help to establish a positive relationship with the store. One of PR's great attributes is its flexibility as campaigns can be tailored to appeal to many audiences and modified to accommodate the requirements of different delivery channels, such as the media, events or sponsorship.

Media relations

Getting a journalist to write or talk on air about a company, product or service is an objective of many consumer PR campaigns. The persuasive power of editorial is much greater than paid-for advertising as the stories and features that appear in newspapers and magazines – as well as on radio and television – tend to be viewed by consumers as unbiased and objective. In contrast, advertising in the same media channels relies on paid-for space and therefore lacks the same credibility as coverage that has been created by an independent third party such as a journalist. Influencing this editorial process is a key task for the PR practitioner (see also Chapter 15). No advertisement or salesperson can convince you about the virtues of a product as effectively as an independent expert, such as a journalist, and if this opinion is then repeated to you by a friend, family member or colleague it has an even greater resonance. Indeed, most of us got to hear about Innocent, Goggle, easyJet, lastminute.com, Virgin and Amazon not through advertising but from news stories in the press, radio, TV and online, or through personal recommendation.

While the benefits of a successful media relations campaign are obvious, achieving the desired result is not so easy. As editorial coverage, by definition, cannot be bought and because someone else produces the finished article, the PR practitioner has no direct control over it (unlike an advertisement). In addition, although there are opportunities to write straightforward product press releases that achieve positive coverage (a glance at the 'best buy' features in lifestyle magazines or an examination of the motoring press will highlight good examples of product-focused editorial), most journalists tend to shy away from commercially driven stories and are certainly not receptive to what they see as **company propaganda**.

Furthermore, to reach many consumers a company needs to be featured in the general news sections of the media rather than in specialist editorial. In this environment, media relations campaigns have to incorporate an additional *news* hook to motivate a journalist to cover a story and this might involve independent research, a celebrity association, an anniversary, a great photograph or a new and surprising angle on a traditional theme. (See Activity 20.1, Mini case study 20.1 and Picture 20.2.)

Media stories

Take two daily newspapers – one quality paper and one popular or tabloid paper. Identify stories that you believe have been generated by an in-house PR department or agency to promote a product or service.

Feedback

Clues to stories with a PR source include: staged photographs accompanying the news item; results of research published on the date of the news item; anniversary of an event; book/film/CD published on the date of the news item.

In addition to traditional print and broadcast media, the contemporary PR practitioner is also faced with a new landscape of channels and content (see Chapter 15). In 2007 a report by the respected Arthur W. Page Society in the United States noted that:

With the development of 'Web 2.0' capabilities such as blogs, wikis, podcasts, content syndication and immersive virtual worlds, it is literally the case that any literate person today can become a global publisher for free in five minutes, drawing on a richer array of communications capabilities than William Randolph Hearst . . . ever dared to imagine. Content about your enterprise is not produced and distributed globally just by a corporation, or Communications or the press now, but by your employees, your partners, your communities – and your adversaries.

Ofcom, the UK's official communication regulator, also highlighted the structural and long-term implications of the changes that are underway. In its annual Communications Market Report it provided empirical evidence that showed how young people, in the quest for entertainment, are turning off their televisions and radios – as well as shunning newsstands – in favour of the Internet, mobile phones and MP3 players (*The Times*, 2006). As well as the World Wide Web, the advent of technology such as Sky+ means that, increasingly, consumers are creating their own media channels that they can control and edit without outside interference.

These technological developments, giving citizens media autonomy, self determination and new forms of self expression – as graphically illustrated by the blogging and social media phenomenon – have changed the rules of

Mini Case Study 20.1
Media relations driving sales – a fishy story

UK supermarket Morrisons agreed to donate a percentage of its takings from fish sales on National Sea Fish Day to the Royal National Mission for Deep Sea Fishermen. The objective set for the PR team was to develop a media relations campaign, targeting newspapers and radio stations within the catchment areas of Morrisons stores, in order to boost awareness of the initiative and encourage shoppers to visit their fish counter.

A number of potential story angles were researched before it was decided that the recently published link between fish consumption and increased brainpower provided the most media potential. Further research of GCSE performance in schools near Morrisons stores identified academic 'hot spots' and this was linked to higher than usual levels of fish consumption.

Photocalls were then held in Morrisons stores to support a fun and entertaining press pack that gave details

Picture 20.1 UK supermarket Morrisons agreed to donate a percentage of its takings from fish sales on National Sea Fish Day to the Royal National Mission for Deep Sea Fishermen.

of National Sea Fish Day and highlighted why fish is believed to boost brainpower. Favourable print and broadcast coverage appeared in all targeted areas and a significant amount of customer interest was generated at Morrisons fish counters.

Source: Used with kind permission of Morrisons (www.morrisons.co.uk)

Mini Case Study 20.2

Social media and word of mouth – Rumba Caracas

Diageo GB, part of the world's second largest drinks company, used social media to help seed its Venezuelan golden rum, Pampero. The campaign was targeted at independently-minded young males in the city of Leeds, the drink's first test market in the United Kingdom.

In the planning and research phase Diageo's PR consultancy researched the independent bar and lifestyle culture within the city and concluded that the target audience adopted brands quickest if they were also recommended by friends and opinion formers. The agency also discovered that the target group were Internet savvy and enjoyed new entertainment experiences. Consequently, a key element of the communications strategy was that the brand should be promoted to consumers through what would appear to be a series of independent events. With this in mind, the PR con-

sultancy created an event company called Rumba Caracas which became the public vehicle for the delivery of specific campaign activity. Its website (www.rumbacaracas.com) included a forward events calendar, a community exchange and blog space, as well as an interactive picture galley.

As part of a wider word-of-mouth campaign and to help bring Venezuela's vibrant and colourful art scene to life, a free graffiti jam was organised in Leeds, showcasing the skills of 25 artists. Working closely with some of the city's key lifestyle influencers, the event was promoted by Rumba Caracas through its own website, as well as MySpace, the online social media network. It was held in a series of disused dark arches under Leeds railway station, and local film students were hired to document the graffiti jam and their productions were set to Venezeulan music and seeded onto You Tube, under the auspices of Rumba Caracas and as part of an online viral campaign.

As a result of the campaign, Pampero's outlet listings in the city increased from 10 to 80, while its rate of sale rose by 160% in six months and, after a year, it had exceeded its target rate of sale in each outlet by an average of 25%.

Think about 20.1

- Do you think it is necessary for a parent/owner to be explicit about its relationship to a brand and declare its involvement in a campaign?

Think about 20.2

Events

- Can you think of a PR event, like one of those listed, that you have attended in the past year?

- What about the open day you may have attended at your current or other colleges or universities?

- What were the factors that made it a success or failure?

engagement so new communication solutions are being tried and tested by PR consultancies and in-house departments (see Mini case study 20.2).

Events

It is a common misconception that PR is only concerned with the generation of positive media coverage. Open days, workshops, roadshows, exhibitions, conferences and AGMs are all events that can provide a company with the opportunity to interact directly with consumers either on its home turf or out and about in the community, generating enhanced presence for the business and a forum for face-to-face, two-way communication. (See Think about 20.2.)

Sponsorship

Whether in sport, the arts or in support of a worthy cause, **sponsorship** is fundamentally about third-party endorsement and as such sits neatly under the PR umbrella (see also Chapter 26). If successfully managed to maximise opportunities – and this is where advertising and direct mail also play a role – sponsorship can provide a powerful

Picture 20.2 To create a news hook, companies use research, celebratory associations and great photographs to get the editor's attention. Quality Street is worldwide confectionery manufacturer Nestlé's second biggest selling brand. After redesigning the packaging, the company produced giant individual sweets from the selection and set up a roadshow featuring a giant motorised Quality Street tin.

platform from which to increase the relevance of a company and its products among key target audiences. By harnessing the emotions, qualities and values associated with the **sponsorship property** and perhaps providing some form of added value experience, a business can successfully stand out in a cluttered consumer market. (See Think about 20.3 and Mini case study 20.3.)

By discussing the different tools a practitioner has at their disposal, it soon becomes clear that a consumer PR campaign can have many dimensions, with media relations, event or sponsorship initiatives supporting one another in an integrated and imaginative programme of activity. Figure 20.2 (overleaf) seeks to show: the components that can make up a campaign; the different audience outtakes that can be generated; and the great potential for overlap and maximisation. For example, a sponsorship might be promoted through a media relations campaign and a series of events.

Think about 20.3

Sponsorship

For a sponsorship to be truly effective, does the sponsoring company need to have an obvious link with the property (for example, adidas and football)?

Can you think of an example of a successful sponsorship where there is no obvious connection between the core activities of the business and the sponsored property, such as Xerox and football?

If you were PR director of Coca-Cola, how would you justify its sponsorship of the Olympics? Is it about sporting performance, a particular lifestyle statement, credibility by association, or none of these?

Mini Case Study 20.3

Maximising a sponsorship – the Nationwide giant shirt

Nationwide Building Society was the official sponsor of the England football team. The aim of the sponsorship was to provide a platform for an integrated communications programme that would enhance the company's profile and consumer appeal in the highly competitive personal finance market.

In the run-up to the 2000 European Championships, Nationwide wished to achieve maximum impact so as to eclipse the activities of all other sponsors. The build-

ing society asked its agency to create a campaign that would not only dominate media coverage of sponsors but would also directly involve and excite England fans. The campaign focused on the production of the world's largest football shirt – measuring 30 metres by 20 metres, which became the centrepiece of a national roadshow and was signed with good luck messages by fans and celebrities.

Attendance at the roadshows exceeded 400,000 and the shirt was signed by 10,000 people, including celebrities such as Rod Stewart and Robbie Williams and the serving Prime Minister, Tony Blair. Media coverage generated through photocalls and press interviews exceeded £1.3 million and awareness of Nationwide as the England football team's sponsor trebled during the four-week campaign period.

Source: used with kind permission of Ptarmigan Consultants Limited and Nationwide Building Society

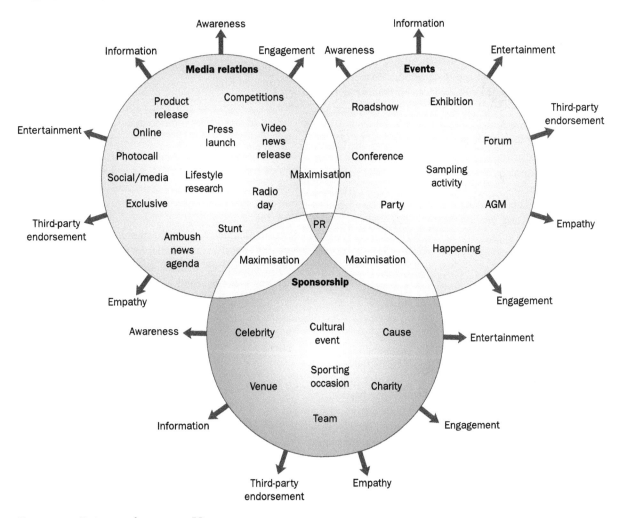

Figure 20.2 Universe of consumer PR

Something extra

The campaigns that have been described were not only concerned with generating awareness and presence but were also driven by the need to communicate a personality and set of values. If a company can communicate these qualities it may succeed in differentiating itself from the competition. (See Activity 20.2.)

By helping to project human qualities on to a company, product or service, PR can play an active role in the fascinating world of **brand** development. It is necessary to understand the role and power of effective branding more fully to appreciate the benefits that PR can generate within the context of a successfully executed consumer strategy.

The wonderful world of brands

Method in the madness

Our societies appear to be overflowing with brands. In popular culture everything and everybody seems to be referred to as a brand: pop stars, sportsmen, royalty, airlines, places, politicians – never mind the products that line the shelves in supermarkets or fill the shops on the high street. In one sense, everything can be legitimately called a brand because the term does apply to any label that carries some meaning or association. However, for the purposes of this chapter, it is necessary to apply a more structured definition in order to appreciate fully the role that PR can play in brand development.

Adam Morgan (1999) in his book *Eating the Big Fish* usefully defines a brand as an entity that satisfies all the following four conditions:

1 Something that has a buyer and a seller (e.g. David Beckham and Kylie Minogue but not the Queen). Morgan also makes the distinction that 'buying and selling' does not have to be a financial transaction to be of value to both sides.

2 Something that has a differentiating name, symbol or trademark (e.g. easyJet but not aeroplanes). Morever, it is differentiated from other similar products around it for reasons other than its name or trademark (e.g. the name of an elite military squad rather than the standard armed forces).

3 Something that has positive or negative associations in consumers' minds for reasons other than its literal product characteristics (e.g. Coca-Cola but not tap-water).

4 Something that has been created, rather than is naturally occurring (e.g. the Eiffel Tower, Taj Mahal or Nou Camp (Barcelona), but not Niagara Falls or the Amazon River).

(See also Chapter 25 and Think about 20.4.)

By studying different brand definitions, such as the one put forward by Morgan, it becomes apparent how brands can add resonance to a product or service. Successful brands offer consumers tangible and emotional benefits over other products, which consumers not only recognise but also desire, at both a conscious and subconscious level. (See the neuromarketing investigation into Coke and Pepsi in Chapter 13.) Furthermore, great brands usually take this appeal a stage further by focusing more on emotional than rational benefits and this ultimately manifests itself in a distinct and consistent personality running

Think about 20.5

Brands and their personalities

Think of five other brands and the personalities they try to project:

■ Do you admire these brands?

■ What attracts or repels you about each brand?

Think about different brands of the same product, e.g. mobile phones or record companies:

■ Do they carry different personalities?

■ How is that personality conveyed?

through all their marketing activities. (See Think about 20.5 and Mini case study 20.4.)

Emotional power of brands

It is not surprising that brand owners are increasingly turning to image and emotional marketing to win over consumers. In today's fast-paced economy, companies tend to copy any competitor's advantage until it is nullified, which is why emotional appeal assumes such importance and why companies such as Nike try to sell an attitude: 'Just Do It'.

The power of brands is also linked to an increasingly strong desire to express individuality through the ownership of goods and services that are perceived to be innovative, different and original. Indeed, psychologist David Lewis (Lewis and Bridger 2003: xiii) goes as far as to say that:

> For many New Consumers the purchase of products and services has largely replaced religious faith as a source of inspiration and solace. For an even larger group, their buying decisions are driven by a deep rooted psychological desire to enhance and develop their sense of self.

Given the emotional capital that is invested in some – if not all – purchasing decisions, PR can be used to demonstrate that a brand empathises with the worries, needs and aspirations of particular groups of people, allowing it to connect and align itself with consumers in an indirect but powerful association. From an implementation perspective, this is one of the reasons why many PR campaigns hook into lifestyle issues and popular culture, using celebrity association, the services of psychologists, anthropologists, fashion gurus, chefs, interior designers and a range

Mini Case Study 20.4

Communicating a brand personality – MINI roof gardens

After much anticipation, BMW launched the new MINI to the UK public in 2001, receiving mass plaudits from the motoring press. The PR challenge in subsequent years was to maintain awareness of the MINI brand in the post-launch phase – keeping consumers talking about the car by emphasising its 'cheeky' personality – while focusing on coverage in the non-motoring media.

A feature of the car that supported these objectives was the opportunity for owners to personalise their MINI, particularly through the various roof designs that could be ordered through MINI dealerships. As part of a sustained campaign, the first mobile rooftop gardens were commissioned by the PR team, using the expertise of one of London's top flower arrangers to create real mini gardens on top of two cars: one featuring a miniature maze, including a MINI toy car lost inside, and the other with a floral swirl of colours with a fully functioning fountain in the centre.

In keeping with the car's irreverent personality, the MINIs arrived unannounced at the Chelsea Flower Show on VIP/press day to ensure optimum media coverage, after which they drove around London to maximise brand presence. The MINI roof gardens were seen by thousands of people visiting the show and the story generated over 50 pieces of media coverage in the national and regional press, online, as well as a special live link to BBC's *10 O'clock News*.

Source: used with kind permission of MINI

Picture 20.3 Mobile rooftop gardens were commissioned by the PR team, using the expertise of one of London's top flower arrangers to create real mini gardens on top of two cars: one featuring a miniature maze, including a MINI toy car lost inside, and the other with a floral swirl of colours with a fully functioning fountain in the centre.

of other experts to add bite and relevance to their campaigns. (See Mini case study 20.5.)

Key challenges

Creativity is king

The biggest danger facing any consumer PR campaign is indifference. That is why companies seek to gain marketing advantage in the battle for hearts, minds and wallets through the application of superior creativity. The search for an idea that will make busy, preoccupied consumers stop and take notice of a brand is a perennial quest across

all communication disciplines. However, achieving '**standout**' recognition and reaching the right people with key messages is now more difficult than ever before.

Consumers are inundated with print, broadcast and electronic information. In the UK alone there are more than 3000 consumer magazines and 2800 local, regional and national newspapers, not to mention 600 radio and television stations, as well as a plethora of websites, blogs and social media platforms (see also Chapters 4 and 15 for more details on the media landscape). It is not surprising, therefore, that consumers have developed routines to protect themselves from information overload. Most direct mail gets thrown straight in the bin, we delete unsolicited emails, leave the room to make a cup of tea during commercial breaks and put the phone down on sales calls.

Mini Case Study 20.5

Plugging into lifestyle issues – The Kylie Generation

Lifestyle-oriented consumer PR was traditionally not a part of UK financial services firm Britannia Building Society's marketing mix. The press office handled media relations activity with the emphasis on targeting the personal finance pages with straightforward product and rate news. However, with a raft of modern and attractive competitors gaining an increased share of the mortgage market, Britannia saw the need to freshen its brand image in order to ensure its products and services were seen to be relevant by key target audiences. A brand-building campaign was required that would reach a young professional audience and reposition the building society as a consumer-focused organisation, in touch with modern lives and social changes.

A fun campaign hook, 'The Kylie Generation', was created that would appeal to a younger consumer audience by entertaining them as well as informing them about what Britannia had to offer. The campaign

declared the death of the then popular Bridget Jones theory – the curse of the 'desperate singleton' – and instead celebrated a new generation of professionals who, like Kylie Minogue (the Australian actress/singer), were opting to live alone, whether they were single or not. To ensure the story would make both the news and personal finance pages, research was commissioned that analysed the behaviour of the target audience, carefully intertwining lifestyle attitudes with their views on money and the home.

Britannia's story was featured in five national newspapers, including a full-colour, double-page centre spread in the *Daily Mirror* (including full commentary of Britannia's products, plus details of its telephone number and website) and the lead consumer story in the *Sun*, as well as 40 regional dailies across the country. Radio interviews featuring a Britannia spokesperson were also negotiated with local and regional stations. The story also ran on key consumer websites that met the required profile of the campaign's key target audience, including *GQ, Handbag, Femail* and *New Woman*, prompting over 3,500 online click-throughs to the Britannia website. The overall success of The Kylie Generation idea encouraged Britannia to invest in a series of additional lifestyle-focused PR campaigns.

Source: used with kind permission of Britannia Building Society

In this consumer counter-revolution, it is difficult to get anyone's attention and as Davenport and Beck (2001) point out, the glut of information is leading to what they call an attention deficit disorder. Indeed, it can appear as if businesses are allocating more and more money in pursuit of consumers who are increasingly likely to ignore what they have to say.

Most people want to be entertained or informed about the things that matter to them, not bludgeoned with seemingly random messages and images. To break through the barrier of indifference, PR campaigns need to include at least one of these elements to succeed and the great challenge is to think of an idea that will draw the audience to the brand. Being creative is about generating new and surprising ideas that will connect with the consumer, which is not always easy when confronted with a dull or second-rate product, a non-existent campaign budget, an uninterested media or disengaged target audience.

It is this climate of change and the need for creative advantage that has, for example, fuelled the growth of

guerrilla campaigns (Tench and Willis 2009). Levinson (1984) first coined the term guerrilla marketing in his book, *Guerrilla Marketing* and classified the activity as:

> An unconventional system of promotions on a very low budget by relying on time, energy and imagination instead of a big marketing budget.

As originally conceived, his work was a toolkit and manifesto for action that was designed to appeal to small rather than large organisations.

Since the 1980s, however, the term has entered the vernacular of the marketing profession and its meaning has mutated to the point where it has become a loose descriptor for a range of unconventional and non-traditional marketing methods that straddle the promotional mix, serving also to highlight how the divisions between different marketing disciplines have blurred in contemporary practice. Consequently, advertising agencies, PR consultancies and even so-called guerrilla marketing specialists promote their services using derivatives of the term such as:

- word-of-mouth marketing
- experiential marketing
- ambient marketing
- buzz marketing
- presence marketing
- undercover marketing
- viral marketing
- grass-roots marketing (also known as astro-turfing)
- alternative marketing
- anonymous marketing

Furthermore, as shown by the Pampero word-of-mouth case study earlier in this chapter (Mini case study 20.2), far from being associated with the marketing activities of small and medium-sized enterprises (SMEs), such activities are now part of the promotional arsenal of the world's largest businesses. In their desire to get people talking about their products and services, guerrilla marketing activities are being used by big corporations to either complement traditional techniques or as stand-alone campaigns when other strategies and tactics cease to become effective.

The sponsorship of guerrilla activity by big business has, in turn, influenced the character of the campaigns conceived and executed by PR practitioners. Unconventional tactics and media are being used to not only generate creative cut through – as originally conceived by those operating with limited budgets – but to deliberately mask the involvement of brand owners who are struggling with how to market to audiences which are rejecting their overtures. This, in turn, raises a number of ethical issues for practitioners and the brands they promote (Tench and Willis 2008).

Furthermore, guerrilla campaigns are no longer only delivered on a shoestring budget as originally conceived by Levinson. As Alex Wipperfurth (2005) notes:

> Brands like Starbucks and Red Bull – the leaders of the 'no marketing' school of thought – are spending hundreds of millions of dollars in non-advertising each year, creating the illusion for their passionate user base that success happened serendipitously.

Regardless of the type of PR activity and the creative ideas that are adopted, they must fit the brand – particularly its personality, values and ethics – as well as the strategic objectives of the campaign. It should never be forgotten that the umbilical cord that links a great idea to a successful outcome is a robust strategy driven by a set of clear objectives, executed in a professional and ethical manner (see Chapter 9 for planning and managing a campaign).

Adding value

As PR has gained more prominence in the marketing mix, so the stakes have generally risen in terms of campaign effectiveness and measuring value. It is one thing to create awareness, another to draw attention to a brand, but still another to trigger action. Sergio Zyman (2000: 4–5), former Chief Marketing Officer at the Coca-Cola Company, highlights the challenge in a typically forthright manner:

> Marketing has to move . . . consumers to action. Popularity isn't the objective. I don't want virtual consumption – the phenomenon that occurs when customers love your product but don't feel the need to buy it . . . the only thing I care about is real consumption. Convincing consumers to buy your products is the only reason that a marketer is in business and the only reason that a company should spend any money at all on marketing.

Measuring and evaluating the success of a campaign is fundamentally important. By its nature, PR cannot always be directly linked to a sale but, as discussed in Chapters 9 and 10, techniques can be deployed that illustrate how PR activity can influence consumer perception, attitude and behaviour, and ultimately create a more favourable sales environment for a brand and its products. (See Activity 20.3 and Mini case study 20.6.)

Elephant traps

As well as demonstrating how a carefully conceived and executed PR initiative can have a direct impact on a company's bottom line, Yorkshire Bank and the other case studies in this chapter also highlight that good campaigns must be built on solid foundations, such as in the bank's case, a genuinely innovative product offering.

Activity 20.3

PR-driven media stories

Look out for PR-driven stories in the media, particularly survey material, that has achieved nothing more than a solitary name check for the brand. Has this coverage caused you to think differently about the brand?

Contrast these campaign outputs with PR ideas that have moved you to action or positively changed your attitudes about a brand.

Yorkshire Bank is owned by National Australia Group (NAG) and has access to a number of financial services products that started their lives in the Australasian market. The Flexible Payment Mortgage (FPM) revolutionised the mortgage market 'Down Under' by offering customers daily rather than annual interest calculation, together with the ability to over- or underpay each month. When Yorkshire Bank first introduced the FPM to the UK market, it did not promote the product aggressively, which resulted in media indifference and low consumer demand for the product. The PR agency was asked to develop a campaign that would raise the product's profile and help establish the flexible mortgage as a mainstream home-buying product.

It was decided to position the FPM in the media as a product that could revolutionise the UK mortgage market, therefore helping to position Yorkshire Bank as a consumer champion. Daily interest calculation was the key theme of the campaign as research showed every other lender charged annually at that time, severely penalising mortgage holders. A shock figure of £13.5 billion was calculated to generate stand-out and highlight the total amount of interest that could be saved by all homeowners in one year if their lender changed to daily interest calculation. This research formed the cornerstone of the campaign.

The FPM campaign dominated financial services media coverage for weeks, netted Yorkshire Bank £130 million of mortgage sales in a six-week period (with no advertising support) and eventually led to over 40 mainstream lenders changing the way they charged interest, all to the benefit of the consumer.

Source: Yorkshire Bank

Digging for PR gold is rarely easy and finding an attribute to hook a campaign on is an important skill for all practitioners. At the same time, however, consumer PR is not about trying to turn a sow's ear into a silk purse. Both consumers and journalists can quickly see through vague or misleading claims about a product or service. Although a powerful tool in the appropriate context, PR is not a panacea that can unilaterally fix a brand that is rotten to the core. However, in the white heat of market competition, more and more companies are trying to emulate organisations such as Nike, BMW and Google to become so-called 'power' brands. Lots try but few succeed and companies can waste vast sums of money on marketing in a vain attempt to dress up their brand and products as something they are not. (See Think about 20.6.)

Tomorrow's people

Rise of the 'marketing refusenik'

The future is bright for consumer PR. Audience and media fragmentation means it is now difficult for marketers to harness a single communications medium to create and sustain a brand as television once did (see also Chapter 4 for a fuller discussion). At one time companies could reach a large slice of the public by advertising on one of a limited number of channels (for example, in the UK by advertising on the only independent channel, ITV); now they have to spread their budgets over dozens of media outlets. Furthermore, the process of cramming more advertising into traditional and online media, or even placing ads in new locations, often does nothing more than irritate consumers who are increasingly resisting mass message marketing, either because they are now immune to its effects, disillusioned with its intent or have simply 'tuned it out'. The rise of the '**marketing refusenik**' is inescapable.

PR is poised, therefore, to play an even bigger role in brand building, a point supported by marketing commentator Philip Kotler (2003: 145) who claims that advertising is losing some of its effectiveness: 'The public knows that advertising exaggerates and is biased. At its best, advertising is playful and entertaining; at its worst, it is intrusive and dishonest. Companies overspend on advertising and under spend on public relations.'

PR does not, however, represent a quick fix. Building a brand through PR takes time and large doses of creativity, but the results can be dramatic if the tools that practitioners use are in tune with the communications environment of the new century. As we have seen, the weapons in the PR armoury do not only grab attention but also promote word-of-mouth recommendation. This is particularly important given the growing tendency for consumers to opt out of mass message advertising and instead turn to family, friends, colleagues, neighbours and personal experts for ideas and information on a range of subjects. The buying decisions of these marketing refuseniks are increasingly the result of consultation and conversation within a universe of informal, interlocking networks. For example, brands such as Google and iPod have benefited hugely from positive one-to-one personal recommendation.

Clearly, a key challenge for brand owners is how to target and influence the growing number of people who have become disengaged from the marketing process. Figure 20.3 shows how PR can give brands access to consumers who have switched off to mass message marketing through the use of third-party editorial endorsement and positive word-of-mouth recommendations.

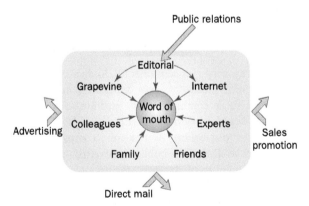

Figure 20.3 New challenges – the citadel of consumer culture

Person to person

In *The Influentials*, Keller and Berry (2003: 5–6) illustrate how Americans are now twice as likely to cite word of mouth as a better source of ideas and information than advertising on a host of different issues:

- restaurants to try
- places to visit
- prescription drugs to use
- hotels to stay in
- retirement planning
- saving and investing money
- purchasing computer equipment
- best brands
- best buys.

Keller and Berry (2003: 5–6) go on to note: 'There are few areas in which advertising outperforms word of mouth . . . Moreover, the person-to-person channel of word of mouth, particularly among friends and family, has grown in importance in recent decades.'

In this environment, the media are still regarded as a useful source of information and advice. Mobile communication, personal computers and the Internet have broadened the process still further, allowing people readily to research their options, communicate quickly with companies and other consumers, as well as build relationships with people who have similar interests to their own. In this diverse communications environment, PR's potential to harness third-party editorial endorsement – both online and offline – assumes an even greater importance than before, as does its ability to target and connect with individuals in a way that advertising cannot match.

The desire for word-of-mouth recommendation is nothing new, and turning consumers into brand evangelists has long been held up as a key benefit of PR. However, the need to focus strategically on generating positive word-of-mouth outcomes is more important than ever. Consumers are increasingly confident about what they hear from others and are increasingly ignoring the voice of vested interest that comes to them through direct and traditional media channels. The challenge for PR practitioners and brand owners is to adjust to this evolving landscape.

Such a task requires fresh thinking and even greater powers of creativity. The people who hold the key to endorsement are a discerning audience who are known to be sceptical of hype and mass marketing techniques. The rise of the marketing refusenik will continue and PR, having established itself as a viable partner in the marketing mix, should have an increasingly important role to play in shaping consumer attitudes and opinions.

Summary

This chapter has explored the terrain where PR interfaces with the world of consumer marketing. A place where the ultimate objective for companies is to stimulate the sale of goods and services in the face of relentless competition. PR campaigns are playing an increasingly active role in the marketing communications arena because of their potential either to harness third-party endorsement – through media relations and sponsorship – or to allow brands to engage directly with their intended audience – through events and other activities. These tools can change attitudes, build relationships and positively influence behaviour.

The attributes PR can bring to a campaign are growing in importance at a time when more established communication techniques are losing some of their effectiveness. However, it would be wrong to conclude that disciplines such as advertising are on the wane; in the complex communications environment of the twenty-first century, the very best campaigns tend to be integrated, multifaceted affairs, harnessing every tool at the marketer's disposal, including PR.

In return, PR not only has the ability to raise awareness of a product's benefits or key characteristics but can also help to give life and substance to a brand. The communication strategy of successful brands is often their defining characteristic and helps to establish a valuable point of difference in the market. PR, which is more subtle in its message delivery than either advertising or direct mail, can help to create and sustain a brand's personality and values, in ways that appeal to consumers.

To further develop the discipline in a marketing environment, PR practitioners must think creatively from both a strategic and tactical perspective. Grabbing the attention of consumers is increasingly difficult and PR must evolve in a professional and ethical manner to ensure that it continues to enhance its reputation in a commercial context.

Bibliography

Arthur W. Page Society Report (2007). *The Authentic Enterprise.* http://www.awpagesociety.com/site/about/annual_reports, accessed 25 January 2009.

Brassington, F. and S. Pettitt (2006). *Principles of Marketing*, 4th edition. Harlow: FT/Prentice Hall.

Davenport, T. and J. Beck (2001). *Attention Economy – Understanding the New Currency of Business.* Harvard, MA: Harvard Business School Press.

Greener, T. (1991). *The Secrets of Successful Public Relations.* Oxford: Butterworth-Heinemann.

Keller, E. and J. Berry (2003). *The Influentials.* New York: Free Press.

Knobil, M. (ed.) (2003). *Consumer Superbrands.* London: The Brand Council.

Kotler, P. (2003). *Marketing Insights from A to Z: 80 concepts every manager needs to know.* New York and Chichester: John Wiley & Sons.

LaSalle, D. and T. Britton (2003). *Priceless: Turning ordinary products into extraordinary experiences.* Harvard, MA: Harvard Business School Press.

Levinson, J. (1984). *Guerrilla Marketing: secrets for making big profits from your small business.* Boston, MA: Houghton Miflin.

Lewis, D. and D. Bridger (2003). *The Soul of the New Consumer.* London: Nicholas Brealey.

Mariotti, J. (1999). *Smart Things to Know About Brands and Branding.* Oxford: Capstone.

Morgan, A. (1999). *Eating the Big Fish: How challenger brands can compete against brand leaders.* New York and Chichester: John Wiley & Sons.

Profile (2000). 'The true religion of PR'. *Profile Magazine* April, Issue 5. London: IPR.

Ries, A. and L. Ries (2001). *The Fall of Advertising and the Rise of PR.* New York: HarperCollins.

Rosen, E. (2001). *The Anatomy of Buzz.* London: HarperCollins Business.

Tench, R. and P. Willis (2009). 'Creativity, deception or ethical malpractice – a critique of the Trumanisation of marketing public relations through guerrilla campaigns'. *Ethical Space: The International Journal for the Institute of Communication Ethics* (in print).

The Times (2006). 'Multi-tasking young spurn old media'. 11 August.

Wilmhurst, J. (1995). *The Fundamentals and Practice of Marketing.* Oxford: Butterworth-Heinemann.

Wipperfurth, A. (2005). *Brand Hijack, Marketing Without Marketing.* Penguin Group.

Zaltman, G. (2003). *How Customers Think.* Harvard, MA: Harvard Business School Press.

Zyman, S. (2000). *The End of Marketing As We Know It.* London: HarperCollins Business.

CHAPTER 14

Media Relations

Media relations

Learning outcomes

By the end of this chapter you should be able to:

■ critically evaluate the role of media relations within a democratic society and within public relations practice

■ identify the key purpose and principles of media relations activity

■ evaluate the factors that cause media relations activities to succeed or fail

■ identify the key trends in communications and the media

■ identify the ethical issues involved in media relations practice.

Structure

■ Role of media relations

■ Defining issue: advertising or public relations?

■ Media relations principles

■ Negotiated news: media relations in practice

■ Media partnerships

■ Old media, new media and me media

■ Media relations techniques

Introduction

Working with the media is what most people think of when they talk about public relations (PR). The image is of a press officer or celebrity PR consultant trying to get their client – be it a product (adidas eyewear) or a person (Victoria Beckham) – into the media spotlight through print and broadcast outlets. To some extent this is true. And it is true that one of the first things most of us do when we start working in PR is to write press releases for media distribution and cross our fingers hoping to get 'coverage'.

In defining the skills required for a career in PR, writing and media relations come high up the list of criteria. When employers are asked to list the skills and attributes required of applicants for jobs in PR, they usually name writing skills and knowledge of the media (Fawkes and Tench 2004). In other words, they are hiring people for a press office or media relations role. Media relations thus tends to be the most public and visible aspect of PR practice. Yet it is also often condemned as 'puffery', 'flackery' or 'spin'. This chapter will explore the role, function and ethics of media relations within PR practice and within a rapidly changing media landscape.

Role of media relations

In principle, PR practitioners should be 'media neutral' (to use the jargon of the day). That means they should have the skills and experience to choose the most suitable channels to reach target audiences with appropriate messages. These channels are many and include public meetings, newsletters and web pages, to name a few.

In practice, the channels controlled by an independent media tend in many societies to have significance beyond others available to the PR practitioner (see Chapter 4). This is explained by the reach and the credibility of the independent media and by the perceived value of editorial endorsement. The significance of media endorsement as a key source of influence has led PR to become synonymous in many eyes with media relations. This perception is misleading, but it is enduring.

This chapter explores the role of media relations within PR, in theory and in practice.

Defining issue: advertising or public relations?

Many students are confused at the start of their studies about the distinction between **advertising** and **public relations**. Identifying the differences between editorial and advertising is an important first step in understanding the media relations challenges faced by the public relations practitioner. Box 15.1 provides a snapshot of today's media newsroom and how PR plays an increasingly important role in shaping the news on our screens, in our newspapers, magazines and websites.

Advertising and PR may both seek the same goal: publicity, the process of making something known. Yet they use very different techniques to achieve this end. Lord Bell (chairman of Chime Communications who, as Tim Bell, was an advertising executive with Saatchi & Saatchi) is a British practitioner who has held senior roles in both fields. He describes the difference succinctly by defining advertising as 'the use of paid-for media to inform and persuade' and PR as 'the use of third-party endorsement to inform and persuade'. In other words, the advertiser controls the message (by paying for it) while the PR practitioner seeks to persuade other people ('third parties') to convey the message for them in a supportive way ('endorsement'). Typically, these other people will be journalists who have the power to confer editorial endorsement by reporting favourably on a product, a service, a person or an organisation.

The veteran Californian PR consultant and part-time PR lecturer Fred Hoar used memorably to describe advertising as 'pay for play' and PR as 'pray for play'. The point he was making is similar to Lord Bell's: the advertiser controls the message by paying for it, while the PR practitioner seeks to influence and persuade by force of argument or creative thinking, but cannot guarantee results.

As a means of informing and persuading, advertising offers more control over the process (although still much uncertainty over the outcome). Yet it is an expensive way of conveying messages to mass audiences so it is in effect restricted to organisations with the largest budgets. And, crucially, advertising lacks one thing that money cannot always buy: credibility.

When we see or hear an advertisement, we know what it is and what it is trying to do. The reader or viewer may tend to tune out (or throw out) the adverts, preferring to concentrate instead on the programme or the editorial

Box 15.1

The new landscape of media relations

Time: 24/7

Place: Media Newsroom

Location: Global

Personnel: Not as many as before

Outlets: Many more than before

New factor: Greater PR input

Welcome to the new landscape of media relations. The newsroom is a very good place to start when charting the rise in PR input. Some evidence is obvious. Greater reliance on technology; younger age profile; some ethnic diversity. More important is content. Look over the News Editor's shoulder at which stories are on the agenda for the hour, day, week, month. And then wonder how they got there.

A Cardiff University study into the state of British journalism and the influence of PR (2008) found that:

■ More journalists are required to do more with less time, a trend that increases the dependence on 'ready made' news and restricts the opportunity for independent journalism;

■ The content of domestic news stories in the UK's quality media is heavily dependent on 'pre-packaged news . . . 60% of press articles and 34% of broadcast stories come wholly or mainly from these "pre-packaged" sources'. ('Pre-packaged' refers to PR or

newswire services such as the Press Association (PA).);

■ 19% of newspaper and 17% of broadcast stories were found to be derived 'mainly or wholly' from PR material;

■ The news topics most influenced by PR sources were health, consumer/business news and entertainment/sport. (Lewis et al. 2008: 3)

One journalist was quoted: 'Today it's not uncommon to be knocking out 5 or 6 [stories] in a day – and when you're doing that you rely more on the wires and on PR than you did before.' A correspondent at the Press Association Agency elaborated further: 'I average about 10 a day . . . The main difference has been the growth in 24-hour news stations which need stories all day and night, so there is no peace for an agency journalist [. . .] I don't usually spend more than an hour on a story, otherwise I wouldn't be able to write so many' (Lewis et al. 2008: 49).

This marks the rise of an increasingly symbiotic relationship between media and PR. Fewer journalists with more space to fill; increasing economic constraints as media ownership is concentrated in fewer hands; and the move towards multi-platform transmission with the time and input pressures involved. File the web copy first; write the video/radio broadcast; then develop the full copy for the next day.

Nick Davies in his book *Flat Earth News* (2008) contends that there is a PR 'supply line' designed to sell an angle. Now, add to that the continuing development of a more professional cadre of PR professionals with their sights set on a more strategic role and, truly, there is a new landscape of media relations.

Source: Mike Hogan

content. As media channels and programmes have proliferated, more advertising placements are required to reach the same audience share. Yet the more adverts we are exposed to, the more we tend to tune them out, thus requiring more advertising placements to get the message through. So the paradox facing advertisers, articulated by Internet marketing author Godin (1999: 38), is: 'The more they spend the less it works. The less it works, the more they spend.'

Editorial endorsement may be considered more persuasive because it is not in the form of an advertisement. Critics who recommends a book or a film or a restaurant are, we believe, exercising their independent judgement.

We may have built up trust in their judgement by reading or listening to them over months or years and may have noted that they are not afraid to express a negative judgement when they feel it is merited. (See Think about 15.1.)

Yet the distinction between advertising and editorial is not always so clear cut. The UK's state-owned broadcaster, the BBC, is untypical among media organisations in receiving its funding from a licence fee and carrying no advertising. This frees its reporters to follow a noncommercial agenda. Yet most TV channels, newspapers and magazines are heavily dependent on advertising revenues, which typically come from a few big spenders. Would the media outlet be prepared to remain independent in the

Mini Case Study 15.1
Editorial independence

There was some controversy in Britain a decade ago when Microsoft, as part of its lavish publicity campaign for Windows 95 – on a scale never previously seen – negotiated to 'buy' *The Times* newspaper for a day. The then editor defended this decision on the grounds that (a) it benefited readers who would receive the newspaper for free on that day and (b) Microsoft had no control over the editorial content of the newspaper. Yet an article on the public scramble to be among the first to receive Windows 95 appeared on the front page of *The Times* that day, a very unusual prominence for a product as technical as a computer operating system.

face of pressure from one of its big advertisers? (See Mini case study 15.1.)

There are other ways in which the distinction between editorial and advertising can be blurred. One is in the hybrid form known as an '**advertorial**'. In this case, the space is bought as with conventional advertising, but used for articles and images purporting to be independent editorial coverage, often written by members of the regular editorial team. The articles are an attempt to 'soft sell' a product or service. Best practice guidelines require these to be clearly identified as an 'advertisement' or 'advertising feature' and to use typography and layout that is distinct from the regular editorial pages. But clearly the intention here is for an advertisement to masquerade as editorial and the potential exists for it to mislead the reader (see also Chapter 21 for the implication in business-to-business PR of this activity).

Another hybrid takes the form of a sponsored competition. In this case, the space will usually be given for free, provided that the prize or prizes are considered sufficiently valuable. This hybrid is thus closer to 'free editorial', although its text is usually unedited promotional copy supplied by the company behind the competition or its PR advisors.

Controversy persists over the practices of those publishers who seek to extract payment for editorial coverage. Their request is rarely as crude as a direct charge for inclusion, but rather it follows the formula of asking for payment for 'colour separation charges'. The defence of this practice is that editorial coverage is still gained on merit, but that the payment helps to offset the additional costs of printing a colour photograph in support of the story. Yet the advice of professional bodies such as the UK's Chartered Institute of Public Relations (CIPR) and the National Union of Journalists (NUJ) is to reject this practice. By, in effect, asking for payment for inclusion, the publication is revealing its lack of separation between advertising and editorial. In other words, it is not the sort of publication capable of providing editorial credibility, so the practitioner should move on to more worthwhile targets. Unfortunately, some practitioners feel the need of such 'soft' coverage in pursuit of a fat cuttings file to impress the boss or the client and are willing to pay for it.

This brings us to 'free advertising', a popular but misleading understanding of the purpose of media relations. Certainly, for it to be credible, editorial coverage will have been gained on merit and without payment for inclusion. To this extent alone it may be considered as 'free advertising'. Yet the lack of payment for inclusion does not make it a free process. Costs may be low compared to advertising, but they are not insignificant. Good media relations requires a skilled practitioner or team of practitioners to tune into the media's agenda, to develop relationships with appropriate journalists and editors, and to develop and deliver effective 'stories', images and comments to the right media at the right time and by the right means. All of this takes time and this has its cost.

But the main condemnation of 'free publicity' is that it confuses the role and purpose of editorial as distinct from advertising. It is not the job of a journalist to give 'free publicity' to a company, a product or a cause. Their job is

Think about 15.2

Journalists' antagonism

'Why do they (journalists) hate us?'

This is a question frequently asked of media relations practitioners from those seeking to understand the media's apparent hostility towards their organisations.

Feedback

To which the honest answer is: 'They're neither for you nor against you.'

It is, in fact, the journalist's job to be sceptical and independent. Would you rather you lived in a society with media controlled by the state or by big corporations?

And while some journalists find some PR practitioners courteous and helpful, others find they cannot get answers to urgent (especially negative) questions and blame all PR staff for these problems.

Box 15.2

The importance of media relations

The significance of media relations within corporate communications can be explained by several trends. As White and Mazur (1995) argue, these include the rise of consumer power, the proliferation of the media and a realisation that employees read papers and watch TV too.

There are two problems implicit in this. The first is that you have to attempt to manage the media or the media's agenda may hijack the organisation's purpose. The second is that channels of communication can rarely be neatly segmented. It is no longer possible to say one thing to one audience and a different thing to another in an age when employees may be shareholders, and shareholders may be customers. Media channels of communication reach all stakeholders. To manage or be managed by the media, which is it to be?

to inform and educate their readers, viewers and listeners through news and features they and their editors consider of interest. PR-originated stories have to be included on merit. The journalist's intention is not to provide free publicity, but if this arises from the feature or story, then so be it.

Although editorial coverage does not equate to advertising space, the practice of evaluating media relations outputs by calculating the '**advertising value equivalent**' (**AVE**) of press cuttings persists. At its crudest, this is a measure of the column inches or centimetres devoted to the client or the product and a calculation of the equivalent cost had that space been bought. Yet it is not possible to buy advertising on the BBC, one of the world's most credible media sources. So how can an advertising value equivalent be calculated in this case? And much major media coverage tends to be negative rather than positive, making a nonsense of the saying that 'there's no such thing as bad publicity'.

It is important that this debate does not give the impression that PR is still struggling to emerge from the shadow of advertising. For instance, some influential voices have championed the benefits of the editorial route. Ries and Ries (2002: xi) argue in their explicitly titled book *The Fall of Advertising and the Rise of PR*: 'You can't build a new brand with advertising because advertising has no credibility . . . You can launch new brands only with publicity or public relations.'

To be credible, the PR practitioner should seek to use media relations to gain editorial coverage in respected programmes and publications with a reputation for editorial independence. But for a *journalist* to be credible, they should only write or broadcast stories that are of interest to their audiences. These conflicting priorities explain the tension that will always exist between the PR agenda and the journalist's. (See Think about 15.2.)

Along with the misunderstanding about free advertising, the other demand frequently made of media relations specialists is to 'get me on the front page of tomorrow's paper'. To which there are two possible answers. First, 'I can do it, but I wouldn't recommend it' (there being more bad news stories than good on the news pages of the major newspapers). The other answer is 'No problem; it will cost you £50,000.' Completely controlled, unmediated messages require you to choose the advertising route. (See Box 15.2.)

Media relations principles

Most texts about media relations tend to focus on the 'how' rather than the 'why'. Yet it is important to ask what the objective of media relations activity should be.

Table 15.1 Two models of media relations (*source*: adapted from Grunig and Hunt 1984: 22)

	Publicity model	Relationships model
Purpose	Tomorrow's headlines	Mutual understanding
Characteristic	Short-term goals	Medium- to long-term goals
Nature of communication	One way	Two way
Communication model	Source to receiver	Dialogue of equals
Nature of research	Little; 'counting house'	Formative
Views media as	Channel	Public and channel
Where practised today	Sports, entertainment, product promotion	Corporate communications in regulated businesses and industry regulators
Who practised by	Junior PROs; experienced publicists	Senior public relations consultants; corporate communications advisors

Is it to get 'good' stories into the news or to keep 'bad' ones out?

David Wragg (Bland et al. 1996: 66–67) argues that: 'The purpose of press relations is not to issue press releases, or handle enquiries from journalists, or even to generate a massive pile of press cuttings. The true purpose of press relations is to enhance the reputation of an organisation and its products, and to influence and inform the target audience.'

US author and communications consultant Shel Holtz (2002: 157) goes further: 'Contrary to the apparent belief of many observers, the role of an organizational media relations department is not to make the company look good in the press, nor is it to keep the company out of the newspapers . . . Ideally, the job of the media relations department is to help reporters and editors do their jobs. That objective is entirely consistent with the broader goal of public relations, which is to manage the relationship between the organization and its various constituent audiences.'

This ideal contains the same contradiction as with Grunig and Hunt's (1984) model of two-way symmetric PR. Why should an organisation fund an activity that is not overtly aimed at pursuing its own interests? And the answer will be the same: the organisation's long-term interests should prevail over its desire for short-term publicity.

Since Grunig and Hunt's four models of PR begin explicitly with media relations (in the form of 'press agentry'), Table 15.1 presents two alternative models for media relations practice. (See Activity 15.1.)

The media have a significant role in helping citizens to make informed choices within democratic, consumer

Activity 15.1

The publicity or relationship approach?

Using the model presented in Table 15.1, go online and search the 'press office' or 'media centre' on company websites for different styles of news release. Which model do you think the releases fit into?

Feedback

Try looking at different types of company and organisation, perhaps big branded companies such as clothing, fashion or sports brands such as adidas or Nike. Then try service providers such as local councils or utility companies in your country, such as gas, electricity or water.

societies (see Chapter 5). Journalists are often the representatives of the general public – in parliaments, at the EU Commission, in the courts and at other major decision-making occasions where only small numbers of witnesses can be present. They report on matters that affect the wider population and that might otherwise go unrecorded. It is this important role that fuels the urge of the investigative journalist to uncover duplicity and wrongdoing by public figures or powerful organisations. It is also this role that enables journalists to believe that they are seekers after truth, in contrast to PR practitioners whose duty, as they perceive it, is to protect and promote their organisation's interests.

Yet the simplistic view that 'journalism is good, PR is bad' is hard to sustain. Most media organisations are private sector businesses that must also seek profits and competitive advantage (see Think about 15.3). Much newspaper journalism is highly selective and politically biased (this bias is acceptable where it is widely understood and where a choice of newspapers expressing a range of opinions is available to the citizen). Media organisations need to entertain as well as – or even more than – they need to inform.

Nevertheless, it is worth PR students and practitioners remembering that journalism has a proud history of uncovering abuses of power that organisations and/or governments wanted to keep secret.

While media channels and publications have continued to proliferate, there has not, in general, been a corresponding growth in the numbers of people working on the editorial side or in budgets for investigative journalism. This means that fewer journalists are writing and reporting more stories. As pointed out in Box 15.1, the time available for investigating and fact-checking stories is shrinking.

It is in this context that the media relations function becomes increasingly important. A journalist may have hours at most to research and write a story (particularly if working for the broadcast media, an online news site or a daily newspaper). Yet a press officer (or equivalent) should have had days to plan and research a news announcement or news release. This means that: the facts of the story should be clear and credible; it should have a strong angle (the reason why it is news); and it should contain interesting quotations from authoritative sources, some of whom may not be normally available to the press to interview. It should, if targeting television or radio, have a strong visual or aural appeal.

Where PR sources are credible, there should be less suspicion in the relationship with journalists, although there will rarely be a common agenda on both sides. Where PR sources are used by the media (either because they are credible or because they are entertaining), then the PR function can be said to be subsidising the newsgathering function of the media. (Outside the untypical worlds of sports and celebrity PR or the realm of the tabloid '**kiss and tell**' story, payment will never be asked or expected from the media for publication of a PR-originated story.) So PR gives the media stories for free (and free of copyright). If 'free advertising' is an unacceptable description of the purpose of media relations, then perhaps 'free editorial' might be a more useful perspective.

How influential is public relations on the news agenda?

At one extreme, the publicist Max Clifford has claimed to have broken more stories over the last 20 years than any journalist in Britain (interview in the *Guardian*, 13 December 2004). And many trade and technical titles are heavily dependent on PR sources for their editorial content and accompanying images (see also Chapter 21).

Several US surveys have indicated that around half of the news printed in the newspapers has had some involvement of PR people (Grunig and Hunt 1984; Cutlip et al. 2000). More recent UK research indicates a higher proportion of news stories to be heavily dependent on PR sources in some topics (see Box 15.1). Hardly a day goes by without some evidence of PR having some influence on the news agenda, whether it is a sponsored consumer survey, a stage-managed party political media briefing or news of a charity's national awareness day, week or month.

On the other hand, journalists are quick to present PR practitioners as gatekeepers who seek to withhold information, rather than as good sources of news and comment. Few journalists are willing publicly to admit to their close working relationships with PR contacts, although they will often acknowledge this in private.

Negotiated news: media relations in practice

Most forms of mass communications are paid for and the messages controlled by the sender. Examples include newsletters, advertising, corporate websites, sponsorships and many others.

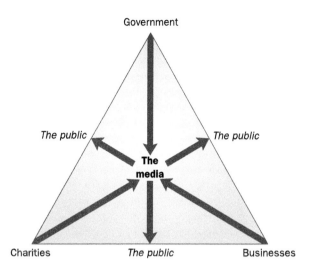

Figure 15.1 Communications through the prism of the media (*source*: Bailey 2005a)

Box 15.3

Some rules for effective media relations

1 Act as a service to the media: answer questions, return calls before deadline, provide information and context.

2 Accept the independence of the media: do not offer payment; do not ask for copy approval.

3 Disclose your interest (i.e. let the journalist know who you are representing).

4 Be as available to the media when the news is bad as when you have good news to promote.

One form of mass communications is uncontrolled and not paid for by the sender. It relies on an independent medium choosing to convey the news or message because of its perceived value or interest to the readers, viewers or listeners. This lack of control is the defining characteristic of media relations: it can make the practice infuriatingly imprecise and unscientific – but it means that those stories and messages that are published or broadcast gain value through editorial endorsement (see Figure 15.1).

The media are not essential for third-party endorsement: there are many instances when the critics have condemned a film or a musical only for the public to vote in its favour by flocking to the cinema or theatre – and the other way round. But in a society where most people gain news and views from the newspapers and the broadcast media, this will usually be the most effective route to generating opinions about a product or service. If really successful, a 'buzz' can be created by media coverage leading to word of mouth endorsement.

In recent years, many brands have come to prominence through this word of mouth effect rather than by more traditional advertising. Examples are drawn from: the Internet (Google); publishing (*Captain Correlli's Mandolin*, *Bridget Jones's Diary* and the Harry Potter books); toys and games (Tamagotchi, Furby).

Another way to view media relations is as a relationship between an organisation and the press. There are journalists who argue (partly for effect) that PR is, at best, unable to influence them and, at worst, an irritating distraction from their jobs. And there are those PR practitioners who argue – equally controversially – that media relations works best if its aim is to provide a service to the media (rather than being primarily a promotional channel for

their clients or organisations). Somewhere in between, most journalists rely on PR contacts to open doors, to provide information and pictures – and many are willing to accept hospitality. (See Box 15.3.)

Part of the media's frustration may come from a tacit acknowledgement of the power of PR. As media channels have proliferated and editorial budgets have been squeezed, the opportunity for investigative journalism has been restricted, leaving reporters more reliant on PR sources. This is very evident in the national and consumer press where most days PR-sponsored surveys make the news. (See Mini case study 15.2.)

The influence of PR is also evident in the well-trodden path from a career in journalism to a senior role in PR (very few make the journey in reverse, although some journalists find the PR role less easy than they had imagined and make a quick return). (See Think about 15.4.)

The concept of negotiated news is an important principle for media relations practice. It recognises that the media do not exist to report your client or organisation. Journalists are neither for you nor against you, but neutral intermediaries standing between you and the public. Give them something interesting to report and you have a good chance of making the news; push corporate platitudes in their direction and you will be filtered out of their news agenda. Persist in this and you may be blocked entirely.

Most PR practitioners, even the most junior, quickly come to understand the realities of dealing with a free and independent media (if only because of the many slights and setbacks they receive when pitching 'good news' stories to a seasoned reporter who is more attuned to digging for bad news). Yet they are caught in the middle,

Mini Case Study 15.2

Consumer survey in the news

J Sainsbury news release dated 4 March 2005

'Brighton is our banana borough, but Glasgow is our melon metropolis' – the headline of release from supermarket J Sainsbury about a consumer survey showing which fruits were preferred in which UK cities (www.j-sainsbury.co.uk/index.asp?PageID=31&subsection=&Year=2005&NewsID=518).

Reported by:

- Reuters, 4 March 2005: 'Brighton has healthiest eaters'

- *Daily Mirror*, 4 March 2005: 'Brighton, the fruit capital of Britain'

- *Daily Mail*, 4 March 2005: 'Brighton is the "healthiest" place in the UK'

- The *Sun*, 4 March 2005: 'Brighton loves its fruits'

NB: The *Sun*, the *Daily Mail* and the *Daily Mirror* are the three largest circulation daily newspapers in the UK.

Think about 15.4

A world without managed media relations

Is it possible to imagine a world without managed media relations?

Feedback

It may be, but it is hard to see how this would serve the interests of the media. There would be no press offices or PR consultancies to handle their enquiries (or to treat them as Very Important People). There would be no one to argue that an interview with a newspaper reporter should be given priority in the chief executive's diary over some other meeting. There would be no media accreditation or media facilities at large events, making it harder for journalists to attend and do their job. No news releases providing a factual summary of new products, policies or positions. No one to facilitate visits and to ensure that meetings are useful to both parties and that questions are answered and facts researched. Organisations, governments and charities would have no mechanisms for releasing information, as part of their accountability to society in general. The doors of people who matter would remain firmly closed to the press. There would be more suspicion of – and hostility towards – the media, not less.

often having to explain these realities to business managers or marketing managers who expect to exert control over the delivery of their messages. Managers who are willing to espouse the virtues of a free market can often seem appalled by the workings of a free press. Yet as former British Prime Minister Margaret Thatcher used to point out: 'You can't have a free society without a free press' (Ingham 2003).

Organisations have their own news agendas and their own internal discourse, while the media must remain alert to broader news events and agendas. Most of what the one does will never interest the other; the skill in media relations is in spotting the stories or the angles that can turn corporate news into media news or bring a corporate angle into a global news story (see Figure 15.2 and Mini case study 15.3, overleaf).

Negotiated news involves bringing an external perspective to internal news stories (an advantage a PR consultant may have over an in-house practitioner who may be too close to the organisation or to its management team to offer dispassionate advice) so that only objective and genuinely interesting news stories are issued.

Figure 15.2 Overlapping news agendas (*source*: Bailey 2005b)

The next negotiation takes place with the media. It may involve a decision on timing – there is a good time and a bad time to issue most news stories, although in a 24/7 (24 hours/seven days a week) media age you can no longer follow the old adage to make announcements 'early in the

Mini Case Study 15.3
Barclays Bank

A news release from Barclays, a UK bank, dated 6 March 2005, talks about the pressures on small business owners and calls on the Chancellor to 'give them back their sleep' as part of his spring budget. This refers to the annual statement on government taxation and expenditure from the Chancellor of the Exchequer, the UK government finance minister. The budget speech was given on 16 March 2005, so the Barclays news release was timed to anticipate pre-budget interest. It was reported by the *Sunday Times* newspaper on 6 March 2005 under the headline 'Revealed: owners who lose most sleep'.

day, early in the week and early in the month'. It may involve a decision on exclusivity (recognising that the media market is highly competitive). It will involve an understanding that the negotiations with a TV station and a national newspaper will be very different discussions. The one needs a visual story, the other a strong issue or theme. (It is not enough to announce Product X, but if Product X can credibly promise less housework, lower bills, greater health or happiness, then you may have a story.)

Many media relations programmes are built on the assumption that the flow of information will be one way and based only on the news the organisation wants to see in the public domain. Yet the more you are in the news, the more you should expect to become a media target. Organisations that have been very accessible to the media when they have good news to promote have an obligation to remain accessible when the news is bad (Shell UK is discussed in this context in both the crisis and community involvement chapters (Chapters 19 and 17 respectively) of this book. Relationships are a two-way thing.

Media partnerships

Media relations, as we have discussed, is a highly demanding and competitive area of PR practice and is constantly changing and evolving with new trends emerging all the time. One of the most prevalent trends in this area of practice, typified by an evermore competitive media environment with more publications and outlets but at the same time more organisations actively vying for their attention, is the rise of media relations by media partnership. This is where organisation and media are contractually bound in joint editorial, advertising and marketing relationships, from which they derive mutual benefit (see Case study 15.1).

Case Study 15.1

The evolution of the exclusive: media relations by media partnership

Building media partnerships is a practice that PR departments and consultancies worldwide are actively engaging in as the relationships often include guaranteed 'quality' editorial coverage in target media for their organisation or brand. This allows them to reach target audiences. As an example, between the summer of 2004 and the spring of 2005, UK PR firm Connectpoint PR (www.connectpoint.co.uk) negotiated media partnerships for clients ranging from luxury furniture, clothing and fast moving consumer goods (fmcg) companies to international sporting events with print, television, radio and online media partners. In total, over 25 indi-

vidual partnerships were negotiated during this period. Over the past few years one of the most successful examples of this that the agency has worked on is that of the Salford Triathlon ITU (International Triathlon Union) World Cup. (See Think about 15.5.)

What is the Salford Triathlon, ITU World Cup?

The only ITU triathlon world cup event in the UK, the Salford Triathlon ITU World Cup is one of the 15 scheduled international World Cup events staged by the ITU. The event attracts 150 elite athletes from around the world who compete for world ranking points. The event is one of a series of flagship events used by Salford City Council to assist in projecting positive images of the city. It is essential that high-volume media coverage projects a positive image of Salford in the international and national press. It is also important that the coverage profiles the event in the regional press to generate interest in the race and deliver value to the local government and other sponsors.

case study 15.1 (continued)

Picture 15.1 Salford Triathlon ITU World Cup 2003 elite women's swim start in the Quays at Salford, UK (*source*: courtesy of Connectpoint PR www.connectpoint.co.uk)

Since its inception in 2003, this event has, on average, generated annual UK press coverage worth over £13,000,000. Of this, the majority has been through the aforementioned media partnerships and carried key messages portraying Salford positively and mentioning event sponsors. This fact has helped to raise the profile of the event, derive value for sponsors and has raised the event's profile beyond its natural place in the UK sporting hierarchy, which is traditionally dominated by sports such as football (soccer), rugby and cricket.

However, this poses the question as to how the event has managed to secure these partnerships. The answer is quite simply that each of these partnerships offers editorial and marketing benefits that they perceive as equal to, or greater than, the costs involved. This can include such rights as exclusivity of broadcast rights. In the case of the BBC this has included the UK and beyond for news coverage. Also, there are features and stories for the various print and online partners for the marketing rights. With these the logos and details are included on local event outdoor advertising and event branding that is visible on television coverage and partnerships. Furthermore, for the media partners it also

delivers the opportunity to borrow from the event its brand attributes of sport, vitality, well-being, endurance and difference that the sport of triathlon possesses.

In return, the event receives guaranteed editorial levels, adverts without charge and competition spaces which deliver quality editorial, communicate key messages usually to a depth much greater than is possible without a partnership.

Specifically for the event, this exchange of value in 2004 comprised benefits to each party with respect to the four main partners, as can be seen in Table 15.2 (see also Think about 15.6 on p. 308).

As you can see, this partnership approach provides numerous benefits for both parties. However, this approach to media relations does have several potential pitfalls to watch out for. First, there is a significant chance that in partnering with one media outlet you alienate their competitors, who in turn could choose not to cover the event from even a news perspective. In

case study 15.1 (continued)

Media partners	Benefits to partner	Benefits to the event
Manchester Evening News	■ Category exclusivity (i.e. no other newspapers able to partner event) ■ Sponsorship package including: free entries, event branding, VIP programme, inclusion on all marketing materials and outdoor advertising ■ Dedicated features exclusive to partner ■ 24hr advance notification on all non-time-sensitive news stories ■ High-value prizes for reader competitions	■ Guaranteed media coverage, which in the end resulted in over 30 pieces of coverage, including three front-page pieces and three front pages of sport section stories ■ 6 free 1/4-page adverts worth over £10,000 ■ 2 free reader competitions with event sponsor branding ■ Promotion of event on posters on street vendor stands
Key 103 fm	■ Category exclusivity (i.e. no other radio stations able to partner event) ■ Sponsorship package including free entries, event branding, VIP programme, inclusion on all marketing materials and outdoor advertising ■ Dedicated features exclusive to partner ■ 24hr advance notification on all non-time-sensitive news stories ■ High-value prizes for listener competitions	■ Cash sponsorship ■ 350 30-second on-air read or event advert free of charge over 4 months ■ Guaranteed media coverage, which resulted in over 10 feature stories, plus 50+ news pieces broadcast ■ Roadshow at event with music provided by a DJ
220 Triathlon	■ Category exclusivity (i.e. no other Triathlon print media partner) ■ Sponsorship package including free entries, event branding, VIP programme and inclusion on all marketing materials ■ Dedicated features exclusive to partner ■ High-value prizes for reader competitions	■ 4 1/4-page adverts free of charge ■ 6 pages of feature editorial, accompanied by free advert ■ Preferential news editorial resulting in 10 individual pieces ■ 10 free subscriptions for event prizes
BBC Grandstand	■ Category exclusivity ■ Television rights for programming ■ Dedicated features exclusive to partner	■ Guaranteed 1hr national television broadcast of the event reaching over 3.5m viewers where sponsors receive high-value recognition and Salford portrayed positively

Table 15.2 Salford Triathlon ITU World Cup: benefits to media partners and organisers

the case of the triathlon, Key 103's principal competitors in the same regional radio market refused to cover the event, as they felt that all the benefits Key 103 received from the event gave them a potential commercial advantage due to the high-profile outdoor advertising campaign and event branding.

An additional pitfall that needs to be considered is the demand that such media partnerships will have on the resources (financial and time) for organisations or agencies. In the case of the triathlon, Connectpoint PR had a separate account director who managed the media partnerships, ensuring that sufficient exclusive stories were generated to satisfy all parties concerned. Lastly, it is also important to realise that the partnership may be adversely affected if the event is embroiled in scandal and the media partners as objective members of the media must cover the story that is adversely affecting the event. Fortunately for the Salford Triathlon this has not been a problem. (See Think about 15.7 on p. 308.)

case study 15.1 (continued)

It is undoubtedly true that in the case of the Salford Triathlon ITU World Cup, the media relations by media partnership approach has been extraordinarily successful, delivering a level of media coverage well beyond that which would be achieved under a traditional media relations model. This approach is one where both the media partner and event benefit significantly and for which careful planning can avoid potential pitfalls.

Manchester Evening News

Monday, July 26, 2004   www.manchesteronline.co.uk   30p

■ Great Britain's Michelle Dillon celebrates as she wins the women's elite race.   Picture: SEAN WILTON

Triathlon a triumph - now Salford goes for the world!
See M.E.N. Sport

M&S DOORS LOCKED AS RIVALS CLASH

Shoppers caught in demo fury

BY CARL PALMER

POLICE were forced to lock the front entrance of Manchester's huge Marks & Spencer store after clashes between rival protesters.

A confrontation between pro-Palestinian supporters picketing the Market Street store and defenders of Israel became so volatile that extra officers were drafted in to control the crowd.

One person was arrested in the worst clash since the Saturday pickets started three-and-a-half years ago.

Cordon

Mounted police kept the two sides apart and the front doors of the store were locked to protect customers. Police later closed one end of Market Street to traffic for safety reasons, and cordoned off other parts of the shopping area.

A number of people were warned about their behaviour. The demonstration began quietly at noon, but by 1.45pm when counter-protesters had increased the crowd to more than 80, the mood changed as the two sides chanted slogans at each other.

Shoppers had to walk in the road and squeeze past the crowd, who were block-

■ FACE TO FACE . . . A counter protester and police

ing the pavement. In a similar incident last week, a man was arrested when the two groups were caught in a heated exchange. This week one person was arrested but was later released without charge.

Hanoch Segal was one of the people led away by police.

A furious Mr Segal said: "We have ev-

ery right to protest peacefully but my partner, who has cancer, was pushed three times by police and treated appallingly. When her son tried to intervene to speak with her, and complained that someone had pushed him in the face, the police didn't want to know." The picket,

Turn to Page 5

INSIDE: DIARY 7; COMMENT 8; WORLD NEWS and WEATHER 10; CHECKOUT 20; POSTBAG 16; STARS, CROSSWORD 22

Picture 15.2 The media exclusive resulted in three front-page pieces on the Salford Triathlon ITU World Cup over the three days of the event (*source*: used with kind permission of the *Manchester Evening News*)

Think about 15.5 — The motivation for media partnerships

Why do you think the media would be willing to partner such an event and what types of media do you think would partner the event?

Feedback

The answer is that media partnerships deliver a benefit to the media partner that is equal to or even exceeds the perceived cost of the relationship. In the case of the Salford Triathlon ITU World Cup, partnerships were struck by the agency and organisers with:

- The *Manchester Evening News* (UK regional newspaper: circulation 158,143)
- Key 103 (UK regional radio station: listeners 623,000)
- *220 Triathlon* (UK national triathlon magazine: circulation 20,000)
- BBC Sport, *Grandstand* (UK national television: viewers 3,500,000)
- www.triathlon.org and www.trisalford.info (online media partner)
- International television distribution done via the ITU.

Think about 15.6

Adding new media partners

In future years, are there any additional media partners the event could add without causing conflict?

The answer is yes, one such example could be a lifestyle/sport magazine for men/women's fitness or health.

Think about 15.7

Crises and scandals

How might one use a media partnership to limit the damage of any potential scandals or negative stories while also ensuring the media partner's objectivity is not compromised?

Feedback

Damage limitation could be ensured by the organiser providing the partner with a steady stream of the organisation's side of the story and, in turn, the media partner reporting this side to balance its coverage. Additionally, the media partner could highlight the inaccuracies in other media coverage, in contrast to its own balanced approach. However, this approach cannot be relied on in a media environment where bad news traditionally sells.

Old media, new media and me media

It is time to declare an end to press relations and all its offshoots – press officers, press releases, press conferences, press packs. Using 'the press' as a collective noun for the media makes it easy to ignore all the radio stations, TV programmes and Internet news sites and weblogs that should also be considered in any media relations activity.

Yet many people are reluctant to move on. In part, this can be explained by the heavy emphasis in some sectors on specialist or trade publications (see Chapter 21) that as yet have no equivalent expression in the broadcast media and are often not even published online. In part, it stems from the need to hand a regular (preferably bulging) press cuttings file to the senior management team and to leave a copy in reception. Video and audio broadcasts are harder to capture and display, and monitoring and recording comments on thousands of ephemeral websites poses a considerable challenge. There are, however, companies that aim to provide this service to organisations.

The reality is that we live in a multimedia age – but then this has always been the case. The great age of mass circulation newspapers began in the late nineteenth century, alongside the arrival of mass adult literacy. Yet the phenomenon of the *Daily Mail* – the world's first tabloid newspaper – was preceded by the arrival of an electronic newswire service (Reuters). Radio broadcasts began in the 1920s, followed a decade later by television broadcasts. (See Box 15.4.)

The summary in Box 15.4 demonstrates the recent rapid developments in broadcasting, as well as other forms of communication and yet, despite the more recent arrival of broadband Internet access, the demand for television and radio has not diminished. In fact, from a UK

Box 15.4

Broadcast and media developments in the UK

In just over 20 years, the UK has gone from having three television channels (BBC1, BBC2 and ITV) to having many hundreds of digital channels as well as two more 'terrestrial' channels. Something similar has happened on the radio, with the arrival of commercial stations being followed by specialist digital channels.

Meanwhile, the Internet has become an everyday addition to work and home lives. Most media organisations now have a web presence: for example, the *Guardian*'s award-winning site (www.guardian.co.uk) does more than reproduce its print version, as it contains lengthy background reports, regular updates and other web-based features. The BBC site (www.bbc.co.uk) not only offers news and educational material, but also the possibility of listening to last week's radio broadcasts or even downloading programmes to any PC in the world.

'What is clear is that the story of the news media involves a process of evolution, in which old media are not replaced by new media, but modified by them' (Hargreaves 2003: 52).

Mini Case Study 15.4

The great GM food debate

In early 1999, genetically-modified (GM) food became a media talking point in the UK, characterised by tabloid newspaper headlines including the emotive phrase 'Frankenstein food' (e.g. *Daily Mirror* 16 February 1999) and by the equally powerful image of environmental activists in white coats digging up GM crops. According to the Parliamentary Office of Science and Technology report into this 'media storm', an influential factor in this was that several newspaper editors 'saw a clear opportunity to champion what they took to be the popular cause of resistance to GM crops and GM foods'. In other words, the media were not only reporting the news, they were also **setting the agenda** and leading public opinion. On this occasion, the 'media storm' led to a move against GM foods by food suppliers and retailers and the tactical retreat of biotechnology company Monsanto. As the parliamentary report concludes: 'The real lesson of the Great GM Food Debate is that in a democracy, any significant interest – science included – ignores the public at its peril.'

Source: www.parliament.uk/post/report138.pdf

If the trend appears to be towards broadcast and online media, then you should not overlook the resurgence and profitability of local and regional newspapers (for example, in Barcelona readers are loyal to *La Vanguardia* rather than the established national Spanish newspaper *El Pais*). They usually hold a local monopoly and provide the sort of local content that people most want and cannot get elsewhere (what's-on listings, local news and events, classified and job adverts). Depending on the title, they also often tend to pursue a more positive (and so PR-friendly) news agenda.

This multi-channel, multimedia landscape – coupled with long working hours and long commuting distances – makes it very difficult for advertising media buyers and PR practitioners to advise on the most effective means of reaching target audiences.

It was once so much simpler, at least for the advertisers. A commercial on the one TV channel that took advertising, if timed around the popular national **soap opera** *Coronation Street*, could be expected to reach half of all UK homes. Now, not only has the audience fragmented as it flits between hundreds of competing channels, but we have started to tune out advertisements (both psychologically and, depending on recording equipment, technically) because of their ubiquity and because we do not trust their messages.

This is where media relations comes into the equation. Although the PR practitioner faces the same questions as the media buyer (Who is watching the programme? Are they paying attention to it?), PR messages have more credibility than advertising messages because they come with an editorial endorsement. As the Chartered Institute of Public Relations (2005) tells us: 'Public relations is about reputation, the result of what you do, what you say, and *what others say about you*' (our italics). Editorial endorsement amounts to word of mouth recommendation ('what

perspective it is arguable that it has extended it, to judge from the expatriates who correspond with the BBC following its sports broadcasts or discussion programmes. It is possible to conclude that television did not kill radio off, any more than broadcasting killed off newspapers.

Picture 15.3 Genetically-modified (GM) food became a media talking point in the UK, characterised by tabloid newspaper headlines including the emotive phrase 'Frankenstein food' (*source*: © Darrell Gulin/Corbis)

others say about you'), but with the power to reach many thousands of ears.

Equally, others may not have good things to say about you. A programme or publication that is not beholden to its advertisers (the licence-fee-funded BBC in the UK, which carries no advertising, is particularly potent here) may be fearless in scrutinising corporate arrogance (*Watchdog*, BBC TV) and be critical of a new luxury car (*Top Gear*, BBC TV).

So the media relations practitioner should not only pursue and facilitate opportunities for positive publicity, but must be alert to the dangers of gaining a bad press. The journalist or reporter may have personal reasons for disliking a company or product or they may be responding to public concerns. The media may be in contact with a 'whistleblowing' employee unhappy for some reason with your organisation's practices.

Now, it seems, we are all media experts. Any '**wannabe**' seems to know how to get hold of publicist Max Clifford in order to 'sell their story'; individuals know to take their complaints to the media as well as to their MPs; and pressure groups and campaigning organisations are among the

most effective at creating photo opportunities pitching their side of the story (think about Greenpeace's activities worldwide as well as direct action campaigns in the UK such as Fathers4Justice, www.fathers-4-justice.org).

Access to the press and the public is no longer limited to the rich and powerful. Anyone with something to promote or criticise can set up a website to get their message across: one disgruntled customer of a bank or a retailer can become a talking point out of all proportion to their size, status or the merits of their arguments. This is the power of PR being turned on the traditional users of PR.

But even websites take some time and resources to set up and manage. The true voice of the man or woman on the street is beginning to be expressed through the much more accessible form of the **weblog**. These are at the other end of the spectrum from the mass media: they are micromedia projects usually reflecting the views of just one individual and often read by tiny numbers – but they are capable of being linked and repeated until the micromedium in turn becomes a mass media phenomenon. (See Think about 15.8, Box 15.5 and Think about 15.9, all overleaf.)

Think about 15.8   Weblogs

Should public relations practitioners add weblogs to their media lists?

Feedback

Yes and no. Yes, because many *webloggers* are influential individuals with detailed industry knowledge (many are themselves professional journalists). No, because you should handle them with particular care.

They are writing for their own interest and do not want to feel subject to any outside, commercial interests. By all means engage them in dialogue on their chosen topics, but beware of 'pitching' them with your own stories. You should certainly monitor the more influential weblogs covering your area (you can gauge the influence by a metric such as Google PageRank, a measure of other pages that link to this one in a form of online peer review).

Box 15.5

Citizen journalism

The news reporting of the London bombings of July 2005 initially relied heavily on citizen journalists (CJs). Pictures from the Tube, from the Russell Square bus and from the chaos on the street all came to our TV screens as a result of mobile phone cameras belonging to people at the scenes of the bombings. CJs are said to have started in many places but some claim that they grew out of the 1999 demonstrations in Seattle against a meeting of the World Trade Organisation (Saul 2005). Conscious that standard mediated coverage might not give enough scope for their anti-

globalisation arguments to be heard, the protestors set up a website and became their own reporters reaching out to a new audience without having to go through the editorial filtration process. This activity is now widespread with major corporations, such as McDonald's and Shell, on the receiving end of web-based criticism. The issues for the PR profession centre, to a degree, on how seriously a corporation takes the work . . . often hostile . . . of the CJ. Ignore it and hope it goes away; combat it and risk adding to the publicity; or try a mixture of the two. What is clearly vital is that communications departments monitor the work of the CJ sites so they are well prepared for rebuttal where appropriate. The level of engagement with the CJ will remain a delicate balancing act.

Source: Mike Hogan

Think about 15.9   Ethics and media relations

Media relations is surrounded by a minefield of ethical issues, such as:

- Should you offer hospitality, a gift or bribery?
- Should you ever offer payment for placement or offer one story to keep another out of the news?
- Just how close should you allow your relationships with journalists to become?
- Is it ever acceptable to lie?

Feedback

One guiding principle is to respect the independence of the media. If the hospitality is too lavish, could this be perceived as a form of bribery, one favour that expects

another in return? (In the USA, it is usual for media organisations to pay the travel and accommodation expenses of their journalists attending a media event; in Europe, they tend to travel at the expense of the organiser.)

A second guiding principle is to consider what would be best in developing longer term relationships, rather than aiming solely at tomorrow's news headline. If you over-promote this week's news, could you jeopardise your chances of success with the same people in future?

Likewise, if you lie about this week's stories, why should a journalist trust you next week? (See also Chapter 14.)

Media relations techniques

Boy meets girl. It is an old story and the fundamentals never change. But the techniques used are subject to the whims of fashion and technology. Each year, the popular press gets hold of a new 'love rat' who becomes the first celebrity caught 'dumping' his partner by fax, email or text message. It is the same story, only this time using different technology.

Media relations is similarly about relationships. The PR practitioner needs to find the appropriate ways to identify, meet and woo the media target and the relationship then needs to be *maintained*. Correspondence, phone, email, face to face are all valid forms for such communication, but each has its drawbacks.

The PR industry used to mass market the media with news releases sent by post. Then the fax took over as the communications device of choice. Now it is email. But each in turn has become discredited though overuse and misuse. Now all forms of mass marketing seem inappropriate and micro-targeting is in.

Some journalists will not open an email unless they recognise the sender; many do not welcome HTML messages complete with fancy fonts, logos and graphics; most do not open file attachments unless they have been specifically requested (they may contain viruses). To understand how they feel about inbox overload, consider how you feel about receiving 'spam' email offering you medication, plastic surgery, mortgages or university diplomas. Do you welcome it?

'Ring-rounds'

To understand how journalists feel about being 'cold called' by PR practitioners 'selling' their stories, consider how you respond to phone calls offering you insurance, double-glazing or a new kitchen when you are at home cooking a meal. Are you interested? Do you prolong the conversation? Or do you consider it kinder to end it as quickly as possible, even if it means being rude to the poor individual who is 'only doing a job'? That's just how many journalists feel about PR calls.

But the PR practitioner should be offering something of interest to them as professional journalists. In which case, the practitioner should prove their credentials (by, say, considering offering an 'exclusive' on the news story) and should not ever waste their time. Tabloid editors in the UK will always find time to take a call from Max Clifford because they trust him to have something interesting to say to them (as stated earlier, he is a publicist with a track record of providing sensational revelations about the lives, actions and activities of the powerful, rich and famous).

The media 'ring-around' is contentious territory. The boss or client is entitled to expect the practitioner to canvas journalists on the target media list for their interest in a particular story. But the shrewd PR practitioner will avoid phoning *after* the news release has been distributed. By the time the news has been distributed, it is already too late to phone: the call is most likely to antagonise the journalist. As such, it is bad media relations. The smart practitioner will prefer to call selected journalists *before* issuing the news release. Only at this point, before it has been distributed, is the news of potential interest to most media and the call at this point can prepare reporters to a potentially interesting story, which they may be able to write about early or exclusively – and so get ahead of their competitors.

Entertaining

PR practitioners used to entertain lavishly, organising press conferences in foreign cities and drinking fine wines over lunch. Now, journalists have to put in longer hours in their offices and can rarely afford the time for these 'junkets'. Working lunches tend to be accompanied by sparkling water, not champagne. The transparency demanded of those in public life is transmitting itself to journalists who are less able to accept gifts, travel and hospitality.

Press conferences

The set-piece press conference is much less common than those watching the evening television news might suppose. As with all good media relations, the decision to call a press conference should be taken by asking if it is in the interests of the media (rather than solely in the interests of corporate priorities). The answer will usually be to rule out press conferences on 'soft' stories such as most product launches, reserving this approach for 'hard' news events (often precipitated by a crisis; see Chapter 19).

Media contacts list

Media proliferation may have made it harder for PR practitioners to keep up with all the channels, programmes, websites and publications available to them, but it also raises new opportunities. While staff journalists may be working harder on a wider range of stories (and for more than one format), there is a growing army of **freelancers** struggling to make a living by supplying news and features to these programmes and publications. These freelancers will be much more receptive to ideas and offers from PR sources and can often be a more effective channel for pitching ideas to editors.

So, an effective media list should list not only publications and programmes, but also a number of different editorial contacts along with various ways to communicate (noting where possible the journalist's preferences). To the list should be added non-media influencers (e.g. industry analysts, webloggers, politicians, trade associations) that you also wish to keep informed.

Targeting your news story

The end of mass marketing in media relations teaches us another lesson. Rather than sending *all* your stories to *all* your media, you will have to select appropriate media for each story. Depending on the type of organisation you work for or represent, very few of your news events will merit national BBC news coverage; only a few will receive national newspaper coverage; most may be suitable for inclusion in a selection of trade, specialist and local publications.

This can bring unexpected benefits. The appearance of your spokesperson on local radio or in the local newspaper or specialist trade magazine will sometimes lead to requests for interviews from national newspapers or broadcasters. There is a 'food chain' that operates in news-gathering and it is in your interests to feed in your news where it is most likely to be consumed. The knock-on effect can often be beneficial, just as it can from offering one exclusive and then watching the news take on a life of its own.

News releases

The news release is the most visible tool used by the PR practitioner. Most journalists will tell you how little attention each one receives in the newsroom and many senior PR practitioners will tell you that they no longer use them (preferring instead to pitch each story personally to a selected journalist or reporter). The traditional printed release is also of less value to a TV newsroom than to a newspaper's news desk.

Yet the advent of the Internet and a more open and inclusive approach to stakeholder communications has given new life to this old tool. While journalists may claim to find them rarely newsworthy, an organisation's stakeholders may be keen to remain informed of its activities through the posting of regular news in its online press office. A company that has posted no news stories this year looks like a dead company; conversely, one that issues regular news updates and delivers consistent messages looks to be dynamic and well managed. In this way, the media relations function can now, in the Internet age, contribute to PR (and not just remain focused on media relations as the only way of reaching the public).

Space does not allow a comprehensive survey of media relations techniques. Instead, an analysis of the key trends should provide a template for understanding best practice (see Table 15.3, Box 15.6 and Activity 15.2).

Box 15.6

The rise of social media

Social media is an umbrella name pulling together blogs, wikis, online discussion fora or chat rooms and a host of other Internet communities. Facebook and MySpace social sites are well known and the video-sharing site YouTube is ranked as top of the league of the new generation community websites (Sweney, *Guardian*, 31 July 2006). Many organisations now recognise the opportunities presented by social media for targeting very specific markets and particularly youth markets. Britvic's television advertisement for the spring water brand Drench featuring the Thunderbirds puppet Brains dancing to a popular 90s club track created an online 'buzz'. The ad had more than two million hits on YouTube and a Facebook fan site was created. Britvic's communications department tracked the social media interaction with the Drench brand as part of its overall campaign evaluation (Gray, *PR Week*, 29 August 2008: 31).

The drawback in PR terms is that the content of social media is created by users and can often be thought to have an inbuilt credibility gap. The perceived strength of going through the traditional mediated channels is that credibility is said to be built in. Many, of course, take issue with this. Whatever the view of social versus mainstream media, that distinction is narrowing all the time. Leading the way is the *Daily Telegraph*, the first British newspaper to go for a newsroom which produces stories in print, audio and video with journalists expected to service all three outlets. In addition blogging by journalists is now common practice (one example is Robert Peston, the BBC's business editor), to the point where they ask for feedback from users and rehearse some very personal opinions.

Source: Mike Hogan

Table 15.3 'Old' and 'new' media relations techniques

'Old' PR	'New' PR
Press	Media
Emphasised 'good news'	Willing to discuss good and bad news
One-way channel	Emphasis on relationships
Mass marketing approach	Micro-targeting
Promotes products and services	Talks up issues, ideas and trends
Focused on print publications	Skilled in all media types
Press conferences favoured	Individual briefings and exclusives favoured
Addressed only the media	Aware of all stakeholders and publics

Activity 15.2

New technology in media relations

The CIPR Excellence awards provide good examples of current PR practice. Look at this year's entries or last year's award winners (at www.cipr.co.uk). How do they use new technology? How important was media relations to the campaign's success? Were there any startling new approaches worth remembering?

Feedback

As this chapter has shown, PR's use of the media is evolving all the time, as are the media channels and content themselves. The successful practitioner keeps an eye on current 'best practice' both to prevent being left behind and to create new ideas for the future.

Summary

This chapter has explored examples of how the media and media relations are used by organisations to achieve communications objectives. Differentiation has been established between the use of media relations and other forms of bought media space such as advertising. A link should also be made at this point to other chapters in the book that look at the broader issues of media context discussed (Chapter 4), the planning and management of campaigns (Chapter 9) as well as the research and evaluation chapter (Chapter 10), which also considers measuring PR's (and media relations') effectiveness.

Other factors have also been discussed, such as the role of new media channels – specifically the Internet and weblogs. These are emerging areas for the practice; students and practitioners should maintain a close eye on how they are being used in campaigns and how this might affect some of the public relations and communications models discussed in this chapter and other parts of the book.

Bibliography

Bailey, R. (2005a). 'Communications through the prism of the media'. Unpublished.

Bailey, R. (2005b). 'Overlapping news agendas'. Unpublished.

Bland M., A. Theaker and D. Wragg (1996). *Effective Media Relations*. London: Kogan Page.

Chartered Institute of Public Relations (2005). www.cipr.co.uk, accessed 23 March 2005.

Cornelissen, J. (2004). *Corporate Communications: Theory and practice*. London, Thousand Oaks, CA and New Delhi: Sage.

Cutlip, S.M., A.H. Center and G. Broom (2000). *Effective Public Relations*, 8th edition. Upper Saddle River, NJ: Prentice Hall.

Davies, N. (2008). *Flat Earth News*. London: Chatto and Windus.

Fawkes, J. and R. Tench (2004). 'Public relations education in the UK: A research report for the IPR'. Leeds Metropolitan University.

Gillmor, D. (2004). *We the Media: Grassroots journalism by the people, for the people*. Farnham: O'Reilly.

Godin, S. (1999). *Permission Marketing*. London: Simon & Schuster.

Gray, R. (2008). 'Unravel the webchatter'. *PR Week*, 29 August: 31.

Grunig J.E. and T. Hunt (1984). *Managing Public Relations*. New York and London: Holt, Rinehart & Winston.

Hargreaves, I. (2003). *Journalism: Truth or dare?* Oxford: Oxford University Press.

Holtz, S. (2002). *Public Relations on the Net*, 2nd edition. London: Amacom.

Ingham, B. (2003). *The Wages of Spin*. London: John Murray.

Lewis, J., A. Williams, B. Franklin, J. Thomas and N. Mosdell (2008). 'The Quality and Independence of British Journalism', Cardiff School of Journalism, Media and Cultural Studies. Report found at: http://www.mediastandardstrust.org/resources/mediaresearch/researchdetails.aspx?sid=12914, accessed 12 October 2008.

McCombs, M.E. and D.L. Shaw (1972). 'The agenda-setting function of mass media', *Public Opinion Quarterly* **36**(Summer): 176–187.

McQuail, D. (2005). *Mass Communication Theory*, 5th edition. London: Sage.

Ries, A. and L. Ries (2002). *The Fall of Advertising & The Rise of PR*. New York: HarperCollins.

Saul, J.R. (2005). *The Collapse of Globalism*. London: Atlantic Books.

Sweney, M. (2006). 'You Tube overtakes My Space'. *MediaGuardian* 31 July, http://www.guardian.co.uk/technology/2006/jul/31/news.newmedia, accessed on 12 October 2008.

White, J. and L. Mazur (1995). *Strategic Communications Management: Making public relations work*. London: Addison-Wesley.

CHAPTER 15

Corporate and Financial
Public Relations

CHAPTER 12

Daniel Löwensberg

Corporate image, reputation and identity

Learning outcomes

By the end of this chapter you should be able to:

- define organisational public relations and recognise it in practice
- define the various elements belonging to organisational public relations
- describe and understand the strategic process involved in the management of organisational public relations.

Structure

- Organisational public relations
- Organisational image
- Organisational reputation
- Organisational identity
- Personality and culture
- Organisational identity, strategy and process: two models

Introduction

Since the early twentieth century, organisations such as Shell, Mercedes-Benz and Michelin have harnessed the power of their visual identities to communicate their values to key audiences. But organisations communicate in more ways than through logos or visuals. Within this chapter we explore the related elements of image, reputation, identity and personality that make up the total communications of an organisation.

Corporate communications, corporate affairs, communications and public relations (PR): despite the discrepancies in job titles, their job functions are largely similar (Dolphin and Fan 2000). Although practitioners use these terms fairly interchangeably, the academic literature on communications often makes a distinction between the terms above, circumscribing their remits to specific areas (see Van Riel 1995; Balmer and Greyser 2003; Van Riel and Fombrun 2007 for accounts of the various perspectives and opinions to do with these terms and their meanings). This situation has led to a relative lack of perspective or a limited inclusion of the topics that form the core of this chapter in some of the PR literature. This could be misleading for those new to the field in that they might believe that the term 'communications' involves *only* the specific act of communication (for example, communicating with the media, prospective investors and other stakeholders). However, this is not the case if we refer to the definition of PR adopted by the Chartered Institute of Public Relations in the UK: 'Public relations practice is the planned and sustained effort to establish and maintain goodwill and mutual understanding between an organisation and its publics' (Gregory 1997: 14)

From the above, it is clear that the aims of PR are wide ranging and that a strategy (hence the word 'planned') is required for its correct implementation over time.

Successful communication strategies are used to attain healthy relationships between organisations and their stakeholders (or publics; see also Chapter 11). These communication strategies, if used effectively, are not 'just' isolated actions that are completely independent from one another. In every organisation, communication strategies need to be based on, and to share, sound common parameters to provide cohesion to the communications. In this way the risk of confusion and misinformation among the organisation's publics can be reduced.

Based on the implications and scope of the definition above, and to avoid misinterpretations, this chapter uses the term organisational public relations (or organisational PR) rather than corporate communications, corporate affairs and so on. An explanation for this decision is given below.

This chapter contains two major sections: the first one, 'Organisational public relations', explores the various terms commonly used in organisational PR; the second one, 'Organisational identity, strategy and process: two models', looks at the management process (the strategic element) involved in organisational PR.

Organisational public relations

The academic literature refers to the concepts of 'corporate public relations' (Gregory 1997) or 'corporate communication' (Van Riel 1995; Cornelissen 2008; Christensen et al. 2008)). They are worth closer examination. The meanings of PR and communication have been dealt with in earlier chapters and at the beginning of this chapter. So, what does the term 'corporate' add – what is meant by it?

When we think of organisations, we might think of them as lots of different sections and departments, such as sales, top management, accounting, production, marketing, human resources, research and development and so on, where these sections interact with one another to some degree. However, in order to understand the concept of 'corporate' we must adopt a different view, in which we look at an organisation as one body, as a whole, as if we were looking at a person. Human beings consist of many different elements, from organs to limbs to way of thinking. We tend not to think of people as parts, but as one entity: John, Marie, Klaus, the elderly lady in the bus, etc. It is the same with an organisation. Before considering its component parts, when you think 'corporate' you think of the organisation as one whole entity.

Let us extend the concept of corporate to 'corporate PR'. If corporate is to do with an organisation as a whole, you need to look at corporate PR (or corporate communication) in exactly the same way – the communication activities and PR of the whole organisation and not of just one of its sections (for example, the marketing department or the human resources section in isolation). Christensen et al. (2008: 3) view corporate communication simply as a 'mindset, an ambition to encompass all communications within one perspective'. Van Riel (1995: 26) defines the term corporate communication as follows:

Corporate communication is an instrument of management by means of which all consciously used forms of internal and external communication are harmonised as effectively and efficiently as possible, so as to create a favourable basis for relationships with groups, upon which the organisation is dependent.

Van Riel defines the specific aims of corporate communication as well as presenting it as a tool used by management to shape an organisation's *deliberate* communications with all its stakeholders. It is worth remarking on the deliberate nature of corporate communication since, as we will see later on, other forms of communication also play an important role in the relationship between an organisation and its stakeholders (or publics). He also uses the terms 'favourable relationships', which implies a reciprocity (or symmetric approach) between the organisation and its stakeholders. In order for the relationship to be favourable to all parties, it is imperative that the differences and discrepancies between them are eliminated or, at least, reduced to a minimum.

Using the term 'corporate' with reference to PR could be misleading in this age of globalisation, competition and takeovers, and of great financial and economic power wielded by a number of large companies, also known as corporations. The term 'corporate' could be seen as referring only to organisations that exist, among other things, to provide a dividend to their shareholders. This could make someone think that PR is only used by commercial firms. However, most organisations – from local and national governments, charitable organisations, educational institutions to pressure groups, charities and religious orders – engage actively in PR. To avoid any possible confusion, and with the aim of making it clear that PR can be used by a wide range of entities, we are going to replace 'corporate' by 'organisational' from now on in our terminology.

It is the all-encompassing nature of **organisational public relations**, and the proactive and symmetric managerial aspect it involves that suggest the following definition which is that organisational public relations affects an entire organisation and not just one (or a few) of its parts in isolation. It does so in a proactive way by deploying and managing strategies with the aim of reducing the gap between how the various internal and external publics of an organisation view it and how the organisation would like to be viewed by those publics.

It helps to think of organisational PR as an umbrella that covers the entire organisation. Every sector of the organisation is influenced by it. In 2001 Hatch and Schultz (2001: 136–137) in the *Harvard Business Review* argued that successful companies 'promote a corporate brand – a single umbrella that casts one glow over a panoply of products'. They built on this theme in their 2008 book on branding (Hatch and Schultz 2008) using examples of detailed case studies based on depth research with companies such as Lego, ING, Johnson & Johnson and Nokia.

Organisational PR is a management function that achieves its aims by providing a leitmotiv (a characteristic and coherent theme and style, or 'lead motive') that aims to inform and influence how *everyone* in the organisation acts, behaves and communicates.

Organisational image, reputation, identity and other such terms are often used informally as if they were synonymous. However, in the context of organisational PR each one has got a specific sense and it is important to agree on their meanings to avoid confusion.

Organisational image

As the word implies, image is a reflection. In this particular case, it is the reflection of an organisation in the eyes and minds of its publics. (See Activities 12.1 and 12.2.) See Glossary for one definition of **organisational image**.

Over time an individual might accumulate a number of different images of the same organisation.

It is important at this point to differentiate between product and corporate image (brands). Hatch and Schultz (2008: 8–9) argue the difference is in the scale of branding; the different target audiences; the origins of the brand; and in the length of the planning life cycle (see Table 12.1).

Activity 12.1

Organisational image

Think of the shop where you, your family or friends buy their groceries. Ask two or three of them what they thought of that shop last time they visited it. What were their answers? Next time you go there, ask two or three of the members of staff what they think of that shop on that day.

Feedback

Did you find any similarities or differences between the various answers? How did they compare? In other words, what were the images those different publics (e.g. an external public like the customers and an internal one, like staff) had of that shop? You may have come across differences depending on who you asked. However, they all referred to the same store – or *did* they? Yes and no. Strictly speaking it was the same store: they all referred to 'that' store, same address, same name . . . However, the picture (or image) was probably different in each case. What does this tell you about image?

Activity 12.2

Thinking again about organisational image

You could try repeating the exercise in Activity 12.1 on a different day, let's say a fortnight after you conducted the first one. You ask the same question about the shop to your friends and you also go to the shop and ask the question to the same members of staff (if you can find them again).

Feedback

How do the recent answers compare with the previous ones? Are there similarities or differences? What is your conclusion this time? Did you get *exactly* the same answer again from each individual? It is quite unlikely. So, in addition to saying that corporate image changes from individual to individual, we can also say that it changes in time.

Organisational reputation

Metaphorically speaking, we could think of the relationship between image and reputation in terms of photography. Organisational *image* could be equated with a photograph of an organisation taken at one moment in time by an individual; **organisational reputation** is when that individual collates all the photographs (or images) taken over

a period of time into an album and forms an opinion of the organisation by looking at the entire collection of photographs. (See Think about 12.1.)

So far we have established that image can be quite fickle. In what way is this relevant to an organisation? Organisations pay a great deal of attention to the image their publics hold of them. This has been stressed by some authors (Bernstein 1984) who argue that image should be considered as *true reality* by organisations. Does this sound a little strange at first? (See Think about 12.2.)

Organisational identity

We have seen how important image and reputation are and how much can depend on them. This leads organisations to want to influence the images and reputations their various stakeholders hold of them. To do this they use organisational identity. We will explore **organisational identity** in more detail now. When the term identity was applied in a corporate communications context for the first time, authors referred specifically to those visual elements organisations used to portray themselves to their publics. The main element here was the organisation's logotype (or 'logo', for short) – this was a visual emblem designed by the organisation with the aim of conveying a number of characteristics it wanted its publics to think of in relation to the organisation. Logos were also intended to help those publics recognise and differentiate the organisation from others. Organisations put a lot of thought and invest large sums of money in nurturing their logo,

Table 12.1
Differences between corporate and product branding (*source*: adapted from Hatch and Schultz 2008: 9)

	Product brand	Corporate brand
Scope and Scale	One product or service, or a group of closely related products	The entire enterprise, which includes the corporation and all its stakeholders
Origins of brand identity	Advertisers' imagination informed by market research	The company's heritage, the values and beliefs that members of the enterprise hold in common
Target audience	Customers	Multiple stakeholders (include employees, managers as well as customers, investors, NGOs, partners and politicians)
Responsibility	Product brand manager and staff, advertising and sales departments	CEO or executive team, typically from marketing, corporate communication, human resources, strategy and sometimes design or development departments
Planning horizon	Life of product	Life of company

Picture 12.1 The London Olympics logo
(*source*: Getty Images)

Think about 12.1

Organisational reputation

Think about your own experience at college or university. Before you chose to join your institution it would be fair to assume you had quite a positive image of it. However, now that you have been a student there for a while, you have accumulated different images of the institution over time. Maybe you found certain aspects that you were unhappy with, others that were unexpectedly good, and so on. Taking all those various images into account, would you say you are happy you joined that institution? Has your opinion about it changed radically? Please reflect on what you are now drawing on in order to answer these questions. You are considering an accumulation of different images and probably taking stock of the pluses and minuses to help you find the answer. In other words, you are considering the reputation *you* hold of the institution.

Think about 12.2

Corporate image once more

Is image reality? How do you feel about this? Do you agree or disagree?

Think back to the previous reflection about yourself and your image of your college or university before you enrolled. Whatever image you held of the college or university was a mental representation of what you thought was true about the institution and was strong enough to encourage you to apply. Had your perception not been regarded as reliable or truthful enough at the time, you might not have applied for a place. (Of course, if you ended up somewhere you did not want to study at, you would have had negative images of the place, which may have since been changed by experience.)

Now put yourself in the position of the college or university. The image prospective students hold of the institution is really important for the college/university. This image (or a sum of images, i.e. reputation) is the deciding factor taken into account by prospective new students when judging whether to apply or not. Since universities and colleges depend on these people for their survival, institutions take the images (and reputations) held by prospective students to be *real* factors – and devote a lot of time and resources to influencing those images in a positive way.

Figure 12.1 Organisations that have proactively managed their logos (*source*: Spaeth 2002 in www.identityworks.com; copyright Pepsico © 2001 Pepsico, Inc., used with permission; copyright 3com, used with permission)

making sure it conveys the right message and, where appropriate, adapting or changing the logo (see Figure 12.1) to fit in with changes in the environment (e.g. cultural tastes) or changes in the organisation itself (e.g. cases of mergers or acquisitions such as BP and Mobil Oil).

The pictures in Figure 12.1 are examples of organisations that take proactive steps and measures to influence their publics' images of the company or institution. In the case of PepsiCo, the company wanted to replace an old-fashioned logo with one that reflected more clearly its brands. To achieve this aim it used a variety of colours,

Activity 12.3

How organisations influence their image

Think of other ways in which organisations influence the image their publics hold of them. To help you do this, think of a large organisation you are familiar with, perhaps a clothes retailer, sports team or phone provider. Now make a list of the stakeholders of the organisation and next to each write the tactics that the organisation uses to influence them.

Such a list can be extensive and will probably contain some of the following:

- advertising
- community relations
- corporate colours and designs
- direct marketing
- events
- financial communications
- lobbying
- media relations
- newsletters
- personal selling
- relationship marketing
- sales promotion
- sponsorship
- staff training
- staff uniforms.

Think about 12.3

Unintentional factors in image change

Go back to the grocery store example from Activity 12.1 and consider possible unintentional factors that may have contributed to some of the customers' change in image of the store. These could have been elements to do with the service provided by an attendant – the person in question may have been affected by good or bad personal circumstances that influenced the way in which they treated a customer on a particular day. Maybe a delivery lorry was delayed by road repair works en route to the store, resulting in a shortage of stock of certain items a particular customer wanted to buy.

representing the colours of its divisions. The globe reflects the company's global scope. For 3Com it was a case of upgrading its logo to a more contemporary 3D design.

One of the common denominators among the items on the list in Activity 12.3 is that they are all **proactive** and therefore *deliberate*. They are premeditated actions and efforts by organisations to communicate with stakeholders and influence them. However, organisations also influence stakeholders' image through *unintentional* actions and factors outside their control or volition. (See Think about 12.3.)

There are many elements over which an organisation has no or little direct control; however, they play a very important role in the formation of image in a customer's mind. Taking this idea a little further, we can say that every organisation has an *organisational identity*, whether it is deliberate or not. Just by their existence organisations portray and send messages to their various stakeholders – and it is those messages that influence the stakeholders' image of the organisation.

What follows in Box 12.1 (overleaf) is a statement on organisational identity that was put together by an international group of academics.

The statement does not highlight the unintentional elements that are also a significant part of an organisation's organisational identity. In fact, the statement does not offer a definition of corporate identity – it simply states that every organisation has got a corporate identity. This is so because organisations exist within a societal context. Even by doing nothing an organisation conveys a message. Its stakeholders will still form an image of the organisation, however active or inactive that organisation happens to be.

The Strathclyde Statement (Balmer et al. 2003, in Balmer and Greyser 2003) places great emphasis on the proactive element of organisational identity. As such, identity is described as 'a strategic issue' that should be managed by organisations and that leads to a number of beneficial outcomes for the organisation.

There are very close links between the various concepts introduced so far in this chapter. It is the relationship between these concepts that creates a management function in organisations that has very specific responsibilities and aims. This management function is organisational PR.

When comparing the various perceptions (images and reputation) of an organisation held by the various stakeholders of that organisation – including the internal stakeholders (for example, the frontline staff, the dominant coalition or management, and so on), it is likely that a gap or dissonance between those perceptions will appear.

Also, dissonance (inconsistency or conflict) might exist between how the organisation would like to be perceived and how it is perceived in reality. The task of organisational PR is to reduce dissonances to a minimum. The

Box 12.1

The International Corporate Identity Group's (ICIG) statement on corporate identity: 'The Strathclyde Statement'

'Every organization has an identity. It articulates the corporate ethos, aims and values and presents a sense of individuality that can help to differentiate the organization within its competitive environment.

'When well managed, corporate identity can be a powerful means of integrating the many disciplines and activities essential to an organization's success. It can also provide the visual cohesion necessary to ensure that all corporate communications are coherent with each other and result in an image consistent with the organization's defining ethos and character.

'By effectively managing its corporate identity an organization can build understanding and commitment among its diverse stakeholders. This can be manifested in an ability to attract and retain customers and employees, achieve strategic alliances, gain the support of financial markets and generate a sense of direction and purpose. Corporate identity is a strategic issue.

'Corporate identity differs from traditional brand marketing since it is concerned with all of an organization's stakeholders and the multi-faceted way in which an organization communicates.'

Source: Balmer et al. in Balmer and Greyser 2003: 134

'tool' used by corporate PR to achieve this is organisational identity. Organisational PR strategies address the proactive and reactive actions and communications of the organisation as well as trying to minimise any negative unintentional ones. It is through doing this that organisational PR influences the images and reputations of the organisation's stakeholder. (See Activity 12.4.)

What shapes and influences an organisation's identity? In essence, the answer to this question is what the organisation is like, the way it simply 'is'. Using a metaphorical approach, some authors (Bernstein 1984; Meech 1996, among others) have likened organisations to human beings. They talk about an organisation's personality as being that factor that defines what the organisation is like.

Personality and culture

The concept of organisational personality is very difficult to pin down and define. Why? (See Activity 12.5.)

It is difficult to define your own personality (see Chapter 13 for more about personalities). In the case of an organisation it is more difficult still. What group of stakeholders would we use to find out the personality of an organisation? What would we find if we were to ask more than one group of stakeholders? The simple fact that there are so many different stakeholders might lead to different answers to our questions.

To make matters more complicated, the terminology used by academics can be confusing. In addition to 'personality' the term 'culture' is often used. **Organisational culture** (or corporate culture) is described by Trompenaars and Hampden-Turner as 'the way in which attitudes are expressed within a specific organisation' (1999: 7), offering a wide-angled and encompassing view of the term. The attitudes (and opinions) in an organisation are expressed through a variety of channels. Some are quite observable, like the different communications used, while some others are less so.

During the 1980s there was a strong tendency to look at organisational culture from a very prescriptive perspective,

Activity 12.4

Comparing images

Let's do a quick comparison . . .

Think of two or three airlines, like a long-established national carrier and a low-cost newcomer, for example, and the different images you have about them. Now think of the types of communication and actions that made you arrive at those images. What is the nature or style of their corporate identities? What makes them different? Is it their advertising campaigns? The friendliness of their staff? . . .

Activity 12.5

Defining personality

Take a few seconds and answer the following quickly.

What is your personality? Are you an extrovert or an introverted person? A bit conservative or maybe rebellious?

The point here is not to dwell on your type of personality (however tempting this might be!). Take a moment now to think about how you arrived at your answer. What made you say you are the way you defined yourself to be just now? How do you know *what* your personality is?

Feedback

It is highly likely that you know what your personality type is because someone else told you or maybe you read the information after completing a test. In other words, you may have found that the answer to the question is based on someone else's image of you.

namely that which represented the views of the dominant coalition or management (Parker 2000). For some, this is still the prevalent perspective today. Important elements that affect an organisation's culture are its aims, the mission statement, and the overall strategy (the organisational objectives and the type of tactics the organisation uses to achieve them). In some cases, the founder's or owner's personality spreads onto the organisation's culture. This phenomenon is quite typical in small organisations or businesses, but it can also happen in larger ones – the Virgin group of companies and the influence of its founder, Richard Branson, are a good example of the link

between the personality of a founder and the culture of an organisation (www.virgin.co.uk).

The managerial version of organisational culture is imposed on stakeholders through very explicit rules, mission statements, procedures, organisational PR, marketing communications, systems and styles of management (see Mini case study 12.1). However, there are other aspects of an organisation's culture that are often less obvious:

- the predominant types of communications (personal vs impersonal) used in the organisation

- the level of formality vs informality in communications and personal interactions (for example, do customers need to fill in endless forms and paperwork before their requests are actioned?)

- tacit 'rules' for promotion (for example, are promotion opportunities the same for men and women?)

- unstated expectations from staff by management (for example, are employees 'expected' to work long hours?) and many others.

The managerial approach to culture in organisations tends not to consider such aspects. This less overt area of culture is explored in more detail by the French approach to identity (Moingeon and Ramanantsoa 1997).

The 'iceberg' concept

The 'French school' likens the whole phenomenon of culture and identity to an iceberg, where the more 'obvious' elements are exposed while those elements that are more difficult to access and diagnose (rites, myths and taboos in an organisation) are 'under the surface'. The latter shape the internal dynamics of organisations and affect the organisation's identity and the image stakeholders have of the organisation.

Mini Case Study 12.1
Mission statements and straplines

Bayer

From Bayer's mission statement: 'Working to Create Value: Bayer is a global enterprise with core competencies in the fields of health care, nutrition and high-tech materials. Our products and services are designed to benefit people and improve their quality of life.'

Bayer's strapline in its global website: Bayer – Science For A Better Life

Source: www.bayer.com

Nestlé

From Nestlé's Business Principles: 'Since Henri Nestlé developed the first milk food for infants in 1867, and saved the life of a neighbor's child, the Nestlé Company has aimed to build a business based on sound human values and principles.'

Nestlé's strapline: Nestlé – Good Food, Good Life

Source: www.nestle.com

Those engaged in organisational PR must be aware that the invisible elements take a long time to be discovered and cannot be influenced or changed very easily. In a study of a merger of various French saving banks where employees from the various organisations were taken on by the new company, Moingeon (1999) found a number of elements, mainly feelings and perceptions among staff, that were covert (the submerged part of the 'iceberg'). Some of these were the nostalgia people felt for the warmth and friendliness of their 'old' organisation, the tensions that arose between staff from different 'old' companies, the view that power was not shared equitably between staff from the old organisations and the perception that a number of them had lost some level of autonomy as an individual after the merger. These feelings and perceptions are very real for those whom they affect and might have a degree of influence in the way these people behave and communicate among themselves and with other stakeholders – and, therefore, influence the organisational identity of the institution!

The managerial aspect of organisational personality will have a direct impact on the type and style of those ele-ments that are proactively planned by an organisation as part of its organisational identity activities.

However, the managerial aspect of the personality can also affect the reactive and unintentional elements of the organisational identity. This influence might be reflected, for example, in times of crisis for the organisation, when it is imperative that the organisation tries to remain operational. In other words, the organisation must keep running its 'business as usual'. In order to achieve this, members of staff may be expected to show cooperation by working longer hours or taking over duties that are not usually their own. In such situations staff need to rely on their own initiative. However, this might be very difficult for staff if, for example, they have been used to working under a very authoritarian management. This will affect their decisions and communications and, in doing so, shape the corporate identity the organisation is projecting towards stakeholders.

In addition to the managerial aspects, there are other elements that affect organisational personalities. These are articulated less formally but nevertheless are equally

Picture 12.2 Icebergs have hidden elements beneath the water's surface. The 'French school' likens culture and identity to an iceberg, they consist of visible and concealed elements. Schein (2004) argues three levels of organisational culture: *artefacts*, *values* and *assumptions* with the first being the only visible element of the iceberg metaphor

powerful and influential. Often the type of industry or activity will influence organisational culture. For example, if we think about the banking industry in the last decade or two, it is apparent that banks have changed radically in the way they do business with their customers and in the way they are perceived by them. One aspect of this change is reflected in the design of bank premises. Gone are the days when banks were intimidating, fortress-like, safe-looking buildings. Today banks are housed in open, airy buildings designed to give customers and staff a friendly feeling.

Another element that can influence an organisation's personality is its country of origin. The culture of the country of origin often impacts on the social ways in which people interact in the organisation. (See also Hofstede on national culture in Chapter 16.) Without wanting to reinforce national stereotypes, the culture of the country of origin is particularly influential in larger multinational organisations where it can shape behaviours, systems and, in general, the way things are done. For example, the former Swiss airline Swissair imposed the Swiss sense of punctuality on its staff around the world even in countries where the local customs related to punctuality were different. (See also Mini case study 12.2.)

We can conclude then that organisational culture is made up of a number of overt (open to view) and a number

Mini Case Study 12.2
Audi

One good illustration of how country of origin influences organisational identity is the case of the German car manufacturer Audi and its operations in some English-speaking countries around the world. In the UK, Audi has consciously incorporated a strapline in German, 'Vorsprung durch Technik' (advancement through technology), in its marketing communications activities. Similarly in South Africa, Audi is using 'Vorsprung, the spirit of Audi' in its communications. Why is Audi using the language of its own country where the majority of people do not speak German? Audi is 'borrowing' the image among consumers in the UK and South Africa that things German are of good technical quality and linking this perception with its products and brand – the association here is so strong that customers need not speak German to understand the message!

Source: www.audi.co.uk

Source: Advertising Archives

of covert (concealed) elements with an area of interface where the overt and the covert elements converge.

Organisational identity, strategy and process: two models

Organisational PR is a management function that uses strategies to achieve its aims and objectives. This way of working is similar to the strategic approach employed in any PR campaign.

Organisational identity management strategy

When reading books and journals about strategic management and also when discussing this topic with tutors and practitioners, we find that the specific words used to talk about strategic management are often very confusing – people employ terms like objectives, aims, strategy and so on very widely but often with different meanings. When we talk about strategy, do we mean a combination of dif-ferent tools to achieve an outcome? Or do we mean the overall process of management? What is the difference between aims and objectives? It is wise practice to clarify terminology before we talk strategy. The main purpose of the model in Figure 12.2 is to 'cut through the jargon' by using simple open-ended questions in order to clarify what the various words mean and to show what each stage in the model is about. The model is also a tool that reminds us of the different stages in a strategy and shows the relationships between the various elements that make up a strategic approach to organisational identity manage-ment within the realm of organisational PR. (See also Chapters 2 and 9 for more about strategic planning.)

Research

Research helps you identify and/or clarify issues from the environment in order to define and fine-tune your strategy. Research will help you find answers to specific questions, which may address a multitude of areas, depending on the PR task ahead. For example, through research you might be able to: define an aim (if this has not been provided); find out who the stakeholders are you need to target; get an indication as to what the best tactics are, and so on.

Aims

These provide you with the basic reason why you are going to engage in a particular communication strategy. Aims

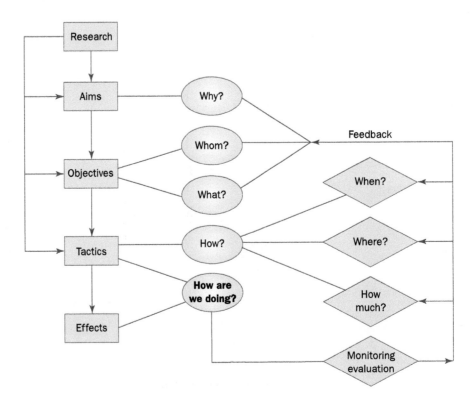

Figure 12.2 Organisational identity management strategy © Daniel Löwensberg, used with permission (*source*: based on Harrison 1995: 47–50)

tend to be broad in nature and reflect the organisation's mission statement or business principles.

Objectives

Objectives are very time-specific goals you can measure. In general, good objectives will be SMART (**s**pecific, **m**easurable, **a**chievable, **r**ealistic, **t**ime bound). The objectives will make it clear who needs to be addressed (stakeholders) and what you are going to convey (the messages).

Tactics

How are you going to achieve your objectives? What specific actions will you use? These could be several (for example, corporate advertising, media relations, and events). You will need to address questions of timing – when these actions are going to take place, where they are going to take place (you can consider both geographical locations and virtual ones, www) – and you will need to consider budgets (how much?).

Effects

How are we doing? The arrows link monitoring and evaluation with all the elements in the model. This is so because you need to establish your efficiency while deploying your tactics during the strategy and also to work out

whether your objectives and aims have been achieved at the end. The sort of questions you will ask are: Did we use the most resource-effective tactics? Do we need to change the publications we have targeted originally? Have we exceeded or fallen short of our planned objectives; if so, by how much? Are things happening on time? And so on. The 'how are we doing?' stage will help you correct any shortcomings while your strategy is ongoing and will also help you define your aims and objectives better for future projects (remember we all learn from experience . . .).

A word of advice about the model: it is intended to be a tool and as such you should feel free to adapt it to the circumstances in which you are going to use it. For example, you will need to decide the stages at which you will conduct research and what type of research you can afford. The number of objectives and tactics you decide to employ will be dependent on your professional judgement on the one hand, and, again, on the time and budget available on the other.

Organisational reputation process

The next model, 'Organisational reputation process' (Figure 12.3), addresses the relationship between the vari-

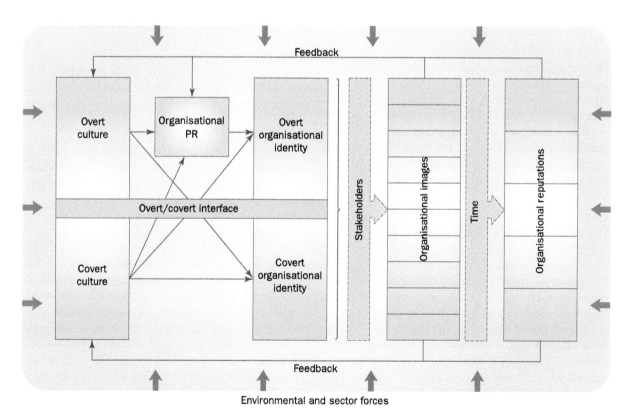

Figure 12.3 Organisational reputation process (*source*: © Daniel Löwensberg, used with permission)

ous elements focused on in this chapter, namely organisational culture, organisational PR, organisational identity, organisational image and organisational reputation. It places these elements in a process that consists of various stages. The model helps to understand which element has an influence on which other elements.

The model reminds communication practitioners of the elements that contribute to the formation of reputations. In addition, the model alerts them of the fact that the various phenomena involved do not happen in isolation and that we must always remember to look at the process as a 'whole' – very much in the same way as we discussed how to view organisations in the first section of this chapter.

Environmental and sector forces

The whole organisational reputation process is immersed within an environmental and sector of activity context. The environmental forces consist of factors related to politics, the economy, social contexts, technology, information technology and communications, national and international laws, the natural environment, and so on. Sector forces refer to the sector or type of activity or industry the organisation belongs to (for example, the hotel industry, the charity sector or the government). Environmental and sector forces can influence every stage and section of the model, as well as the process as a whole, including feedback.

Culture (overt and covert)

The starting point in the formation of organisational reputation is the organisation's culture – this concept includes the organisational personality, which has not been mentioned separately since it can be argued that culture and personality could be regarded as the same or are, at least, very closely interlinked and interdependent. The model highlights both cultural elements, the overt and covert ones, and how these have an influence on the next stages in the model.

Overt/covert interface

This is the overlap area between overt and covert cultural elements. Using the French analogy of an iceberg again, this area is the water surface. Like any water surface, the interface zone is not static meaning that the divide between overt and covert culture can fluctuate – what is overt for some stakeholders will be covert for some others, for example. Organisational PR professionals need to pay attention to the interface area. They need to discover covert cultural and identity elements in the organisation. In doing this, they will convert covert elements into overt ones for their own purpose and communication activities – otherwise the undiscovered covert elements could turn into barriers to the PR communication process.

Organisational public relations

This is the management function that operates in a proactive and deliberate way using strategies to achieve its goals (see Figure 12.3). Because of this it is placed in the overt section of the model. However, covert cultural elements will also have an influence on it.

Organisational identity (covert and overt)

The model shows that the organisational identity also has an overt and a covert aspect – some of its aspects are premeditated communications efforts by the organisation, while some others happen without the organisation being proactive or consciously involved in the communication. Organisational identity is affected by the overt and covert cultural aspects as well as by organisational PR strategies.

Stakeholders

These are the publics who are the receivers of the organisation's identity. They process the organisational identity and create organisational images in their minds.

Organisational images

There are many organisational images. They will vary from stakeholder to stakeholder and, within one stakeholder's mind, they will also be numerous and accumulate over time. Influences from environmental forces can be particularly relevant in the shaping of organisational images.

Time

Time is the factor that will allow for an accumulation of organisational images that will contribute to the formation of organisational reputations in the minds of stakeholders.

Organisational reputations

Similar to the case of organisational images, there are many organisational reputations. Reputations will vary from stakeholder to stakeholder, and will also be influenced to some degree by environmental forces.

Feedback

The organisation must put research tactics in place in order to obtain feedback from its stakeholders' perceptions (the organisational images and reputations). In addition to premeditated research tactics, feedback will also return to the organisation through unplanned channels (for example, gossip between internal and external stakeholders or unprompted opinions from customers). Feedback will, therefore, inform the overt culture of the organisation (for example, the business principles dictated by the dominant coalition) and organisational PR strategies, as well as elements of the covert culture. (See Case study 12.1 and Think about 12.4.)

Case Study 12.1

Vulcan's organisational reputation among employees

Vulcan Industries is a British manufacturer of high-quality cookers. At the time of the research the company had grown to approximately 800 employees who worked in a number of different sections, including engineering, marketing and management. The research looked at organisational culture in Vulcan and at its identity. Through a process of qualitative research it was discovered that the company had a number of issues in relation to its workforce and the image of the firm held by its employees. Some of these issues are going to be presented here to illustrate the validity and use of the organisational reputation model.

A message of a 'family-type organisation with a common language' (*overt culture*) was used by management in messages to staff (*organisational PR*) to convey a happy message (*overt identity*) to them. However, there were a number of rituals (*covert culture*) in the company that had an influence on the *covert identity* the firm

conveyed to staff. For example, there was a ritual by which people of one section would eat in a specific area of the refectory and never move to another section's area. This custom contradicted the 'friendly' *overt identity* promoted by management by promoting a perception of 'us and them' (*covert identity*) in the workforce. Also, the geographical location of offices and workshops (*overt culture*) and the quality of décor, which was more lavish in the 'white-collar' work areas and offices than in the workshop managers' offices (*overt culture*), contributed to the segregation (*covert culture*) in the firm. An illustration of the *overt/covert* interface area could be found in the divide (another ritual) that existed between old and new members of staff, which is a very personal matter and could vary from person to person. PR professionals need to recognise the existence of this ritual when implementing communication strategies that target these two stakeholder groups to avoid miscommunication.

One of the interesting findings in the research was that members of staff would report different images at different *times* to the researcher. At some moments in time, depending on the situation, they would reflect the 'family' overt identity while at some others they would reflect the fragmented nature of the covert identity.

Source: adapted from Parker 2000: 127–156

Think about 12.4   Vulcan case study

This abbreviated example shows the complexity inherent in the formation of organisational image and reputation in just one group of stakeholders. It also illustrates the importance of time and context, on the one hand, and the fact that organisational reputation in the minds of stakeholders is made up of many different images on the other.

Have you noticed any differences between the stated or overt culture of a workplace or university and the actual behaviour, practices and attitudes (covert culture)? How do you explain any gaps?

Summary

The main aims of this chapter were to introduce the concept of organisational PR, to define some of the terms used and also to present the strategic processes involved in this activity.

Organisational PR can be used by *any* type of organisation. Also, organisational PR acts like an umbrella covering every sector of the organisation and provides a sense of cohesion to its activities.

Image is a stakeholder's perception of an organisation at one moment in time. Stakeholders accumulate a number of images of an organisation over time. The aggregate of images forms the organisational reputation in the minds of the stakeholders.

Organisational identity consists of the sum total of proactive, reactive and unintentional activities and messages of organisations. Organisational PR uses the proactive and sometimes the reactive elements of identity as a tool to help reduce the dissonance that might exist between how the organisation would like to be perceived by its stakeholder and the actual image the stakeholder has of the organisation. Organisational PR uses a strategic approach in its management of the organisation's identities.

An important element that has an influence in an organisation's image and reputation is its own culture or personality. Organisational culture has two aspects: the overt ones – those that are easily recognisable and premeditated; the covert, often present as rituals or 'ways of doing things and behaving' that are not explicit. Both these elements of culture have a defining influence on the identities projected by the organisation and, therefore, will affect images and reputations of the organisation. Consequently, it is vital that professionals working in organisational PR are aware of both elements of organisational culture to produce effective communications in line with their strategies.

Bibliography

Balmer, J.M.T. and S.A. Greyser (2003). *Revealing the Corporation: Perspectives on identity, image, reputation, corporate branding, and corporate-level marketing.* London: Routledge.

Bernstein, D. (1984). *Company Image and Reality: A critique of corporate communications.* Eastbourne: HRW.

Christensen, L.T., M. Morsing and G. Cheney (2008). *Corporate Communications: Convention, Complexity and Critique.* Sage, London.

Cornelissen, J. (2008). *Corporate Communication: A Guide to Theory and Practice,* 2nd edition. Sage: London.

Dolphin, R. and Y. Fan (2000). 'Is corporate communications a strategic function?' *Management Decision* **38**(2): 99–106.

Gregory, A. (1997). *Planning and Managing a Public Relations Campaign: A step-by-step guide.* London: Kogan Page.

Harrison, S. (1995). *Public Relations: An introduction.* London: Routledge.

Hatch, M.J. and M. Schultz (2001). 'Are the strategic stars aligned for your corporate brand?' *Harvard Business Review* February: 128–134.

Hatch, M.J. and M. Schultz (2008). *Taking Brand Initiative: How companies can align strategy, culture and identity through corporate branding.* San Francisco: Josey-Bass.

Löwensberg, D. (2005). Unpublished.

Meech, P. (1996). 'Corporate identity and corporate image' in *Critical Perspectives in Public Relations.* J. L'Etang and M. Pieczka (eds). London: Thomson Business Press.

Moingeon, B. (1999). 'From corporate culture to corporate identity. *Corporate Reputation Review* **2**(4): 352–360.

Moingeon, B. and B. Ramanantsoa (1997). 'Understanding corporate identity: The French School of thought'. *European Journal of Marketing* **31**(5/6).

Parker, M. (2000). *Organizational Culture and Identity.* London: Sage.

Schein, E. (2004) *Organizational Culture and Leadership,* 3rd edition. San Francisco, CA: Josey-Bass.

Spaeth, T. (2002). *Honors to the Bold.* www.identityworks.com.

Trompenaars, F. and C. Hampden-Turner. (1999). *Riding the Waves of Culture: Understanding cultural diversity in business,* 2nd edition. London: Nicholas Brealey.

Van Riel, C.B.M. (1995). *Principles of Corporate Communication.* London: Prentice Hall.

Van Riel, C.M. and C. Fombrun (2007). *Essentials of Corporate Communication.* London: Routledge.

Financial public relations (FPR)

Learning outcomes

By the end of this chapter you should be able to:

■ define and describe financial public relations

■ identify who is involved in financial public relations practice

■ compare the practice of financial public relations in the UK and internationally

■ identify how financial public relations practice impacts on organisations

■ recognise emerging trends in financial public relations practice.

Structure

■ Overview of financial public relations

■ The landscape of the City: who's involved in financial public relations

■ Financial PR practice

■ Financial PR as strategic corporate marketing

■ Emerging issues and trends

Introduction

'How many public relations (PR) people does it take to change a light bulb? Don't know. I'll have to get back to you on that one.' An old joke, perhaps, but apposite until surprisingly recently. The typical London PR person of the 1980s did little more than hand out press releases and take journalists to lunch – and was more familiar with the Savoy's wine list than with his client companies' strategies. That has all changed. Lunch, this correspondent is happy to report, still definitely plays its part. But today's spin doctors are sharp-minded professionals, often indistinguishable from investment bankers and lawyers – and increas-ingly demanding to be paid like them. In America, financial PR (communicating companies' strategies to shareholders, analysts and the financial press) is still done largely in-house. But it is the top British agencies – Brunswick, Financial Dynamics, The Maitland Consultancy, Finsbury, Citigate Dewe Rogerson and Tulchan – which are showing that financial PR is becoming an industry in its own right. (The Economist, 2001: 74–75)

Financial PR, like so many areas of PR practice, has in the past been perceived to be nothing more than an *Absolutely Fabulous* (1990s' BBC television programme stereotyping a PR practitioner) world of champagne and caviar, with practitioners as bubbly as their preferred drink. However, as the extract above suggests, financial PR practice is now something much more complex, practised in the environments of domestic and international financial markets and the corporate world. Financial PR is a practice which for most people within and outside the PR industry remains a mystery shrouded in the complexities of these environments.

The following chapter aims to explore and illustrate for the reader the reality of financial PR practice, demystify its practices and culture, identify its body of knowledge and provide a glossary for its truly unique lexicon.

Overview of financial public relations

Financial PR is an area of PR practice which is often misconstrued. This confusion is only furthered when consulting the limited yet varied literature on the subject and largely results from what is an apparently fundamental difference in the practice of financial PR in the UK and the United States. This difference is evident in the literature on financial PR.

The US perspective on financial PR: an investor-focused approach

Financial PR in the United States has historically focused on investor relations (IR). Indeed the Public Relations Society of America's (**PRSA**), Financial Communications Section was until 1992 known as the Investor Relations Section (PRSA 2005). This positioning of financial PR as investor relations is reflected in key American PR texts such as Argenti's seminal text *Corporate Communications*, where the chapter on financial communications is called 'Investor Relations: A Random Walk Down Wall Street' (Argenti 1998: 143–166).

So what is IR? One definition is that offered by the Investor Relations Society (1997) where IR is referred to as 'the management of the relationships between a company with publicly traded securities [shares] and the holders or potential holders of such securities' (quoted in Marston and Straker 2001: 82). The definition draws out an American financial PR practice, which is focused on communicating solely with the shareholder (and potential shareholder). Although Argenti points out that the practice involves other intermediary stakeholders who are communicated with in order to reach the shareholder, he refers to these as 'buy-side' and 'sell-side' analysts, referring to financial publics that facilitate for shareholders either the purchase or sale of shares (Argenti 2005).

The British approach to financial PR

This US view of financial PR practice is fundamentally different from the UK perspective, most notably because in the UK IR is viewed as a practice separate from financial PR and is traditionally not handled by financial PR, but rather a company's nominated broker (Middleton 2002: 160). Within the American perspective the broker would be one of Argenti's 'sell-side' analysts.

The fundamental difference then is that American financial PR (IR) is focused on the shareholder whereas in the UK, as Middleton points out, financial PR is focused on 'raising awareness and building understanding amongst primarily the City's (financial exchanges) opinion formers who influence investors and potential investors, which she refers to as "third party" audiences or stakeholders' (Middleton 2002: 160). Further discussion on the reasons for this are introduced in Box 23.1. (See Activity 23.1.)

Picture 23.1 Frankfurt – home of the German stock exchange and the European Central Bank is one of the world's leading financial centres (*source*: Getty Images)

Box 23.1

The dollar difference

The US cityscape . . .

In reflecting on the stakeholders involved in financial PR we can start to uncover one of the major reasons for the differences in the practice of financial PR between the United States and the United Kingdom.

Differences lie both in the historical structure and the mindset of the US press (often referred to as the 'Fourth estate') versus those of the British press (Wikipiedia 2008a online). One senior international financial PR practitioner interviewed in the research for this chapter stated that the British financial media market has traditionally been much more competitive than the American market. Britain with its smaller geographic size, has numerous national newspapers (due to ease of national distribution) covering the financial activities of the City based solely in London. As a result of this competitive environment a tradition was forged in the media which has seen the 'press' more likely to print rumour (or, more often, interpretation of fact) and offer opinion in order to differentiate themselves from their competitors. This has resulted in financial PR practice in an environment where practitioners have been required actively to manage and influence the output of the financial press.

In contrast, the United States, due to its vast size, has historically seen 'one-paper towns' where newspapers do not operate in competitive markets. In this context the media reporting is much more objective, and focused more on the transmission of information from which opinions are formed, rather than the transmission of opinion and conjecture. It is important to remember that titles such as the *New York Times*, *Washington Post* and *LA Tribune* are only regional papers.

As a result the focus of US financial PR practice is in working less with the media, but rather more on the buyers and sellers of shares and their intermediaries. While this is a fundamental difference, it is also clear that in an evolving business world of global markets American financial PR practice is placing greater emphasis on media relations outside the USA.

Think about 23.1

Different approaches to financial PR

Before reading on, ask yourself, why do you think this core difference might exist? Jot down your thoughts and come back to them after you've read the remainder of the chapter and see whether or not you were correct.

Feedback

You may want to draw on theories about defining stakeholders and publics in Chapter 11 and professionalism in Chapter 14 for inspiration as to why these differences may exist.

Activity 23.1

Financial PR in different countries

Using the Internet and other reference materials examine and determine whether financial PR practice in the countries listed below resembles a UK or American approach.

1   Sweden
2   Australia
3   South Africa
4   Canada

Feedback

For example you may want to start by visiting the Internet sites of the professional bodies for PR in these various countries and examine the information available on financial communications.

1   Sweden: Swedish Public Relations Society (www.sverigesinformationsforening.se/in-english.aspx)
2   Australia: Public Relations Institute of Australia (www.pria.com.au)
3   South Africa: Public Relations Institute of Southern Africa (www.prisa.co.za)
4   Canada: Canadian Public Relations Society (www.cprs.ca)

Look for key words and themes in the information you find that might give you an insight into the practice of financial PR.

Why is financial PR so important?

Though at first examination we see a very different stakeholder focus of the US and UK practices of financial PR, what they both hold is that this corporate communication function (see Chapter 27) plays a fundamentally important role in any modern **listed** business.

Financial PR's increasing importance is reflected in the *Economist* statement: 'to keep share price up, it is no longer enough merely to have a strategy. The strategy also needs to be articulated smartly – as any manager at BT, Ford or Marconi will tell you.' (The *Economist* 2001: 75). Communication with financial communities about an organisation's position and future strategy is essential to the development of a good financial reputation, which in turn contributes to the overall reputation of an organisation. Good financial reputation is viewed by authors such as Deephouse (1997) and Roberts and Dowling (1997) as contributing to improved organisational performance and superior profitability, a view which is shared by the majority of academic and professional writers. (See Activity 23.2.)

Activity 23.2

Financial PR and reputation

With a partner or in a small group of peers, discuss why you think good financial PR is important both in terms of protecting an organisation's share price and in building reputation?

Feedback

You may find it beneficial to refer to Chapter 12 on reputation. Think of the shares as if you were buying them: what would be important to you and what might affect your purchase decision?

Think about 23.2

The benefits of financial PR

In what ways does good financial PR benefit an organisation?

Feedback

1   Assists in maintaining share price.
2   Assists in developing corporate reputation.
3   This, in turn, leads to greater performance and profitability.

The perceived worth of financial PR is valued like no other area of PR practice. Fees in excess of £1 million ($1.6 million) for financial PR services are not uncommon. The *Economist* points to the fact that Brunswick (financial PR) was first in 1995 to break the £1 million mark for the fee surrounding a single piece of work and in 2000 broke the £2 million fee mark (The *Economist* 2001: 75).

The landscape of the City: who's involved in financial public relations

By now it should be evident that financial PR has a clear role in contributing to organisational success by managing effective communication with key financial stakeholders and that differences in international financial PR reflect different priorities given to different stakeholders. What these difference stakeholders share is that they are all concerned with the activities of financial exchanges (e.g. Wall Street, Frankfurt or **the City**) in other words the exchange of money between 'people who have money and people who need money' (Middleton. 2002: 160). These two parties in the exchange reflect Argenti's discussion of the 'buy-side' and 'sell-side' of the City (Argenti 1998: 144).

Markets/exchange

These 'haves' and 'have-nots' of the financial world carry out their exchange of money on the global money markets/exchanges. This exchange is usually money (whether US dollars or pounds sterling or the euro) or in the majority of cases shares in companies, futures on agriculture crops, oil or other commodities (varying forms of securities). It is worth noting that practitioners normally communicate only with respect to activities of listed companies and the trading of their shares. Some of the main financial markets that you may have heard of are the London Stock Exchange based in the 'City' of London or the New York Stock Exchange, which can be found on New York's famous Wall Street. There are also important exchanges in Frankfurt, Germany (see Picture 23.1) and Tokyo, Japan, as well as in most national capital cities. When talking of these stock exchanges people often refer to the 'indexes' of companies that are part of the exchange when discussing overall sector or market performance (see Glossary: **stock market index**).

Looking at the exchange markets holistically, who is involved? Simply stated, it could be said that they are made up of three overarching categories of stakeholders:

1 those who regulate the exchange of money

2 those who exchange money

3 those who influence or communicate about the exchange of money.

Regulators

The regulation of the exchange of money is controlled at various levels internationally and nationally. Internationally regulators include the World Bank, the EU and the geographical areas covered by various trade agreements such as the North American Free Trade Agreement (**NAFTA**). Individual countries all impose regulations on the exchange of money. However, in the case of individual markets, national regulators control how the exchange of money on a market is conducted, as well as how information which can affect the prices of securities traded on the market is disseminated. In the UK, the regulator responsible for British securities markets is the Financial Services Authority (**FSA**). The American equivalent is the Securities and Exchange Commission (**SEC**) and in the European Union individual countries have their own regulators, though the Commission of European Securities Regulators (CESR) was established in 2001 to coordinate and advise regulators in a bid to ensure consistency in practice and implementation of European law.

Those involved in the exchange of money are institutional shareholders, private shareholders, private client brokers and investment and merchant banks.

Shareholders

Institutional shareholders (potential and current) Institutional shareholders are organisations that control collective sums of money that are being used for investment/wealth creation purposes and in turn invest this money into listed companies. This investment is normally to a level far beyond the capabilities of individual private shareholders, often possessing between 1–100% of an organisation's securities with a value often ranging into the billions of pounds or dollars in the case of larger listed companies. Often institutional shareholders are mutual funds, pension funds or insurance companies investing premiums.

Private shareholders (potential and current) Private shareholders are individuals. Like their institutional counterparts they are investing money with the aim of wealth creation, although in the majority of cases this investment is only a small fraction comparatively, much less than 1% of an organisation's value. However, exceptions to this rule exist in relation to the founders of private companies which become listed companies or, in rare cases, individuals such as Malcolm Glazer who in May 2005 purchased a controlling stake of 76% in Manchester United Football

Club. It should be noted that, with the continuing developments in communications technologies, individual shareholders are becoming ever more important.

Stockbrokers Stockbrokers are intermediaries who arrange on behalf of private investors the sale and purchase of shares. These intermediaries may also sometimes act as 'influencers' in this exchange of money, advising clients on when to sell shares and when to buy.

Investment and merchant banks Investment and merchant banks are organisations that play several roles in the City. First, these organisations often act on behalf of institutional shareholders and listed companies arranging the sale or purchase of securities, quite often at different times in the financial cycle of an organisation (this cycle is discussed later). Second, unlike stockbrokers, these same organisations often arrange the finance around purchases or sales for institutional shareholders or for listed companies looking to purchase another listed company. In both of these exchanges the investment banks represent the 'buy-side' member of the exchange while merchant banks represent the 'sell-side'. Furthermore, these two City organisations are required by law to interact directly with each other at any time, even when they are two divisions of the same overarching financial organisation. This is to ensure transparency in deals and to avoid one side gaining insider knowledge. Quite often the 'parent' organisation will even house the two divisions in separate buildings to ensure geographic space illustrating the practical separation.

Affecting these decisions are the analysts and the various forms of financial media.

Influencers

Analysts Analysts are individuals who often work for investment and merchant banks as well as stockbrokerages (collectives of stockbrokers) who research and analyse financial information on selected companies, usually within a specific industry sector (e.g. food, oils, transport, entertainment, etc.) and provide shareholders (current and potential) with comment and advice on the investment prospects. This information is published in documents referred to as 'research notes'. The commentary included usually surrounds recommendations about whether or not to buy, sell or hold on to a particular security.

The media/financial press Like the analysts, the media communicates as well as passes judgement on the performances and prospects of companies, and in turn influence stakeholders involved in the sale and purchase of shares. Making up this group of 'influencers' are:

- *The national financial and business print media*, which in the UK includes key titles such as the *Financial Times* newspaper (commonly referred to as the FT), the national business sections of the quality 'dailies' and 'Sundays' (traditionally the *Daily Telegraph*, *The Times*, the *Independent* and the *Guardian*) as well as magazines such as the *Investors Chronicle*. Outside the UK, key titles are the *Wall Street Journal* and *USA Today* in the United States and titles such as the *Economist* and *International Herald Tribune*, and *Le Figaro* and more internationally.

- The importance of *regional print media* should also be acknowledged with British titles such the *London Evening Standard* and the *Manchester Evening News* and US titles such as the *New York Times*, *Washington Post* and *Los Angeles Tribune*.

- *Radio and television* also play an important role in the financial media, providing an immediacy which extends beyond that of the print media. Some of the key radio and television media in the UK and Europe are BBC Radio 4, BBC24, BBC News (www.bbc.co.uk), SKY News and CNN Europe, with CNN and the major American radio and television networks such as CBS radio, CBS, ABC and NBC, CNBC television playing similar roles in the United States.

- A further media channel which is gaining more importance is the *Internet*. With its ability to make information at all levels instantaneously available to a large spectrum of stakeholders it is becoming the information stream of choice. The importance of the investor is underlined by the fact that the traditional financial print media have also established themselves as the leaders in the provision of financial news on the Internet with the *Financial Times* online at www.FT.com in the UK and the *Wall Street Journal* online at http://online.wsj.com in the United States. These, along with the rising trend of Internet billboard sites (visit www.executivelibrary.com to find the links to several great billboard sites) where individuals post their own views and questions and share them with others, are changing the shape of financial PR practice.

- **Wire services** are further financial media and interestingly they are usually the source from which all other media (including the Internet) receive their information due to their immediacy and ability to communicate price-sensitive information to a host of financial opinion formers and stakeholders. As will be discussed further in this chapter, this position as the main source of information is not accidental but ties to the regulations surrounding the practice of financial PR. As an example, in the UK the main wire services include the RNS, Reuters (www.reuters.co.uk), The Press Association (**PA**), AFX, Perfect Information, PR Newswire.

- *Other media*, which at times play roles as stakeholders in financial PR include, but are not limited to, trade media as well as – in the cases of unique high profile organisations – mainstream news media.

See Activity 23.3 and Activity 23.4.

Financial PR practice

While it might, at first seem that the practice of financial PR internationally differs fundamentally from country to country, this is not the case. Of course, the practice in each country has its own regulations with a unique lexicon and special occurrences, such as mergers and acquisitions and hostile takeovers (these will be discussed below); however, it is also characterised by repetitive and regimented cycles of communications, familiar across the globe.

One area, however, where a noticeable change has taken place is with respect to whether or not the financial PR is handled in-house or by a consultancy.

In-house vs consultancy

In the United States, financial PR has predominantly and traditionally been practised internally as 'most American companies of any size have big and experienced in-house teams', using agencies only to carry out specific transactions such as the special occurrences which are discussed below (the *Economist* 2001: 75). In the UK, however, according to several senior practitioners interviewed by the author and reinforced by the *Economist* article, financial PR is more commonly carried out by an external agency. This may be as a result of the competitive media environment and the need to be able to draw upon the kind of contacts and relationships a specialist consultant communicating frequently with specific journalists will have. With regard to the practice of Investor Relations (**IR**) in Europe, Marston and Straker found that 96% of the organisations they researched had an internal IR function which managed part or all of the organisation's IR, although of these, 45% still engaged an outside consultancy carrying IR functions (Marston and Straker 2001: 86–87).

Regulatory practice

Whether practised internally or externally, financial PR is subject to country-specific sets of guidelines and regulations that govern the practice. This is unlike most other PR functions. In the UK the regulations controlling this practice are in general laid out by the FSA (Financial Services Authority). These regulations are laid out in the FSA's *Purple Book* (previously *Yellow* and *Blue books*, among others). Since 2001 this book has served 'as a single handbook of rules and guidance for all authorised financial firms in the UK', often pointing firms to other more detailed

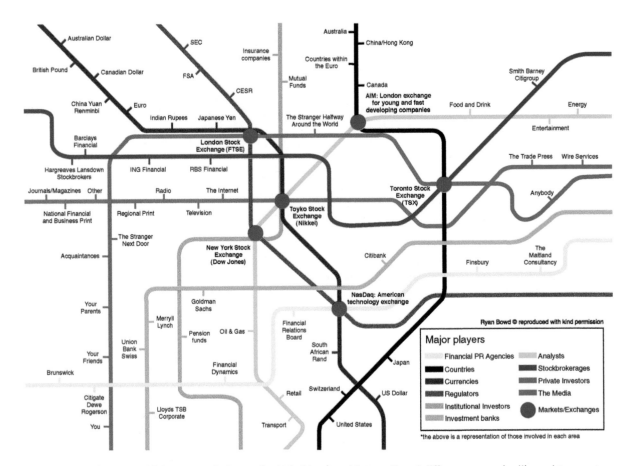

The following labels appear on the metro-style diagram:

Australian Dollar, SEC, Insurance companies, Australia, China/Hong Kong, Smith Barney Citigroup, British Pound, Canadian Dollar, FSA, Mutual Funds, Countries within the Euro, Canada, Food and Drink, Energy, China Yuan Renminbi, Euro, CESR, AIM: London exchange for young and fast developing companies, Entertainment, Barclays Financial, Indian Rupees, Japanese Yen, The Stranger Halfway Around the World, London Stock Exchange (FTSE), The Trade Press, Wire Services, Hargreaves Lansdown Stockbrokers, ING Financial, RBS Financial, Toronto Stock Exchange (TSX), Anybody, Journals/Magazines, Other, Radio, The Internet, National Financial and Business Print, Regional Print, Television, Toyko Stock Exchange (Nikkei), The Maitland Consultancy, The Stranger Next Door, New York Stock Exchange (Dow Jones), Citibank, Finsbury, Acquaintances, Goldman Sachs, Financial Relations Board, NasDaq: American technology exchange, Your Parents, Merrill Lynch, Pension funds, Oil & Gas, South African Rand, Japan, Union Bank Swiss, Financial Dynamics, Your Friends, Brunswick, Retail, Switzerland, US Dollar, Citigate Dewe Rogerson, Lloyds TSB Corporate, Transport, United States, You

Major players

- Financial PR Agencies — Analysts
- Countries — Stockbrokerages
- Currencies — Private Investors
- Regulators — The Media
- Institutional Investors — Markets/Exchanges
- Investment banks

*the above is a representation of those involved in each area

Ryan Bowd © reproduced with kind permission

Picture 23.2 The City, with its range of players (stakeholders) and international differences can be likened to a metro or tube system which sees money (equity) travel through various stations on rail lines. Different factors can influence the journey or movements of the equity each and every day of the year (*source*: Ryan Bowd)

sources of information on specific points of law (FSA 2008). The book and the FSA as a whole aim to create a 'marketplace that is run in an efficient, orderly and fair manner whilst ensuring that consumers receive a fair deal by being properly informed and appropriately protected' (FSA 2008).

As a result, a regimented structure has been established for when, or more specifically at what intervals and with what content (updates on financial results and details of projections on future results, etc.), organisations must regularly communicate with financial stakeholders. This process is often referred to as the 'financial calendar' (Gummer 1995: 51). Furthermore, the guidelines also specify how organisations must communicate when involved in extraordinary special occurrences such as:

- initial placing offers (IPO)
- first trading on an exchange
- when a company is subject to mergers and acquisitions or hostile takeovers

- when an organisation 'de-lists' from an exchange and removes its shares from public trading
- any other news which, might be considered '**price-sensitive information**'.

Internationally, it is important to note that regulations do vary and not all countries have either the same presentation format for regulations or the same regulations. In the USA, for example, regulations relevant to financial PR are found in a series of acts passed by the Congress and signed by the President. These include but are not limited to the Securities Act of 1933, the Securities Exchange Act of 1934 (and its 1964 amendment), the Investment Companies Act of 1940 and the Sarbanes-Oxley Act of 2002 (SEC 2008). This regulation provides for a fundamental difference between the US and UK financial calendars. For instance in the American financial calendar financial PR practice operates on an annual cycle of quarterly reporting rather than the British cycle, which operates on a cycle of mandatory reporting every six months.

Box 23.2

Getting it out on the wire

When financial information in the UK is communicated by an organisation it is distributed through a wire service to City stakeholders, particularly the influencers (such as the media and analysts), who then interpret it and pass on their views on the item to readers or clients.

The working practice has evolved as a result of regulation laid down by the FSA which stipulates that all financial communication must be released via a wire service first in order to ensure that all interested parties receive the information at the same time. This is done in order to ensure no individuals gain an unfair advantage over another party.

Until 15 April 2002 there was one authorised service which had to be used in the UK and that was the Stock Exchange's own Regulatory News Service (**RNS**). However, since this date the distribution of regulatory financial information to the City has been carried out in a competitive commercial system and there now exist six authorised wire services:

- Business Wire Regulatory Disclosure
- Newslink Financial
- PimsWire
- PR Newswire Disclose
- RNS
- Firstsight by Waymaker

Source: (adapted from FSA press release dated 12 April 2002: FSA/PN/037/2002, available on www.fsa.gov.uk

The financial calendar

According to Gummer the calendar of events is made up of the interim results, preliminary results, annual report and accounts and the annual general meeting (**AGM**) (Gummer 1995: 52–56).

Interim results

In the UK these are often referred to as the half-year results (whereas in the USA these are published three times in the year) and serve to provide shareholders and City with a 'health check' on the state of an organisation's financial results to that point of the year, also providing insight into their expectations for the next six months through a statement from the Chairman that will accompany a financial account of figures.

Preliminary results

As with the interim results, the preliminary results are a reporting to the City of the organisation's financial results and future prospects, though in this case it is the first reporting of the financial results for the year and, in turn, often ends up as a 'highlight of the financial year' (Gummer 1995: 53). These results are the City's first opportunity to see and judge whether the strategy of an organisation's management has been successful against their expectations. As a result, both for preliminary results or interim results, if an organisation feels it is unlikely to meet the expectations of its financial stakeholders it is common practice that in advance of the regulatory report-

ing they will issue what is referred to as a 'profits warning statement' via the regulatory wire services. This statement is released in order to soften the blow of poorer than expected results and minimise the impact from any resulting loss of confidence with 'City' audiences. These impacts can include the lowering of share price or a reduction/ loss of financial/organisational reputation, the latter can affect the confidence of suppliers and the ability of the organisation to secure finance – such as loans from lenders and more.

(It should also be noted at this point that with respect to both interim and preliminary results, the dates on which organisations report results vary with respect to the date of their initial listing (see below), so on any exchange on any given day multiple organisations will report their results.)

Annual report and accounts

An organisation's annual report is a document which presents an in-depth accounting of the year's financial results (confirming the preliminary results), as well as covering a variety of other topics of interest to their stakeholders. These include but are not limited to: the codes of business practice; ethical statement; corporate citizenship; and corporate governance and philanthropic activities (Bowd and Harris 2003: 22). This plethora of information is included as a result of both regulatory demand and stakeholder expectations, often tied in to the organisational CSR (see Chapter 6). Some larger organisations, such as Shell, publish separate CSR reports along with their annual report and accounts.

Activity 23.5

Reporting financial news

Over the coming days watch the financial news portion of your national television reporting (BBC, CNN Europe, CNBC, etc.) and read the financial sections of major papers. Look at how companies who posted results in line with City expectations are reported versus those who fail to hit their expectations.

Feedback

You will probably notice that in the current media environment organisations whose posted results have just met expectations are a non-story, worthy of only a brief mention; organisations who have exceeded expectations may receive slightly more coverage; but a company which has done poorly against its stakeholders' expectations receives a vast amount of coverage. This coverage may extend into features, as well as the examination of whole sectors in order to gauge whether or not other similar organisations will be likely to post comparable results.

It is important to note that all listed companies are required by law to produce an annual report within six months of their financial year end (date on which preliminary results must be released) and 21 days before their annual reports (Middleton 2002: 168).

The annual general meeting (AGM)

The final element of the annual cycle of the financial calendar is the annual general meeting which is an opportunity for investors (individual or institutional shareholders) to meet and ask questions of an organisation's management. They can also vote people onto – or off – the organisation's board of directors (such as chairman, secretary, etc.) as well as new company articles (regulations). As a result the AGM is potentially a chance for an organisation's shareholders to forge the direction for the coming year. However, apart from times of organisational crisis (brought on by a loss of investor confidence), in practice for most organisations the AGM is an anticlimax (Gummer 1995: 55). The meetings are often poorly attended and most motions have been voted on in advance by postal ballot and the decisions follow the wishes of the institutional shareholders.

Case study 23.1 places some of these activities into context. (See also Think about 23.3, 23.4 and 23.5.)

Case Study 23.1

Pace Micro Technology plc

It's a material world: the financial calendar and listings regulations

Pace Micro Technology plc is the world's largest dedicated manufacturer of digital set-top boxes, supplying major operators such as BskyB in the UK and Time Warner in the US. Based in West Yorkshire, Pace is a FTSE techMARK 100 company (one of the FTSE indices), trading its shares on the London Stock Exchange. The company's Head of Corporate Communications and Marketing retains a specialist consultancy to enhance Pace's financial PR capability at key times in the financial year, as is typical in UK financial markets. Citigate's in-depth knowledge of the City and other financial stakeholders helps Pace to anticipate how the markets are likely to react to communication of their results and other financial matters. As well as using the services of a City PR consultancy, the in-house communication team takes advice from brokers who guide them on the strict regulations governing disclosure of financial information.

It can be difficult to assess what is 'material' and how potentially price-sensitive information that must be announced to the Stock Exchange should be handled. The *Listing Rules* (set out by the UK listings authority (**UKLA**) which is part of the FSA) prescribe certain matters that must be announced to the market via the RNS (or approved alternative) as mentioned earlier, as well as large commercial deals, board appointments or departures and the like. Usually such announcements must be made without delay and there may be only a narrow window to agree the format of an announcement.

Pace's financial communication programme works on a six-monthly cycle, driven by the interim results in January and preliminary final results announced in July. The communications team has to factor in production of the annual report for August, prior to the preparation for the annual general meeting in September. Key stakeholders include institutional and private investors, analysts within the UK, Europe and the USA, and the national and international financial media, for

case study 23.1 (continued)

example the *Financial Times* and Reuters. Important other publics are major business customers who need to be assured of the stability of the business and, of course, staff who are particularly affected by the financial reporting in the local press.

Taking the interim results as an example, the head of corporate communication begins work on the chairman's report in November or early December, keeping track of redrafts as the messages are developed with the chief executive officer (CEO) and finance director, along with the brokers and City PR consultancy. In January the board meets to sign off the results, prior to the announcement of the Interims usually on a Monday, when Citigate then issues the information to the Stock Exchange. On results day information is sent out via a regulatory wire service at 7am, then Pace executives meet with analysts at 9.30am, the City press at 11.30am (often communication with national journalists is by phone, rather than face to face) and the trade press in the afternoon. The results presenta-

tion and supporting documentation produced by the communication team forms the basis of subsequent investor road shows led by the CEO. The cycle is repeated in depth when full results are announced in July.

Reflecting on the purpose of financial PR for his organisation, Pace CEO John Dyson says:

The most effective financial PR is actually about delivering business results. PR without substance is meaningless, but today analysts and the media demand continuous news and information. Lack of 'noise' can be misinterpreted, so it's vital that financial communication finds a healthy balance between delivering transparent and meaningful messages which meet regulatory requirements without creating exaggerated expectations of performance, either for the good or bad.

Source: courtesy of Jo Powell, Senior Lecturer,
Leeds Metropolitan University

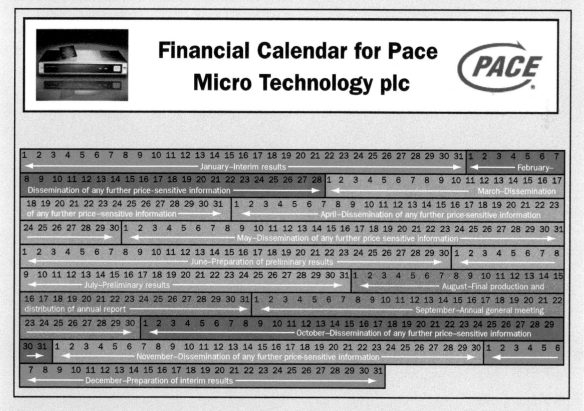

Picture 23.3 Putting the financial calendar into context: a graphic representation of Pace Micro Technology plc's financial year

Think about 23.3

PR for a listed company

PR for a listed company regularly involves managing information, which may be price sensitive. How can you be sure that what you are publicising to the trade and consumer press in way of new product development does not conflict with FSA rules?

Feedback

Consult FSA guidelines in the *Purple Book* on reporting and ensure you follow them prescriptively.

Think about 23.4

Skills of the FPR

What are the main capabilities and competencies required of a financial PR practitioner?

Feedback

You might want to refer to the sections on PR roles and practitioner skills (Chapters 3 and 14) as well as think about the particular skills required by financial PR practitioners.

Special financial events

In addition to the financial calendar and the communication of 'price sensitive information', there exist three principal types of special occurrence that a financial PR practitioner may have to deal with as part of the practice of financial PR:

1   initial placing offer (**IPO**)

2   mergers or acquisitions

3   hostile takeovers.

The first of these traditionally only involves one team of practitioners, whereas the other two activities will often involve multiple teams.

Initial placing offer

An initial placing offering (IPO) is when an organisation lists itself on an exchange in order to become a traded security which can be bought and sold. For most organisa-

Think about 23.5

How to use the financial calendar

After reading Case study 23.1, how might a financial PR practitioner carry out the individual elements in the financial calendar?

Feedback

Do you think they will run in a similar manner of preparation of materials, distribution, hosting meetings and briefings or will other elements be different? You might want to consult the FSA guidelines or Peter Gummer's (1995) chapter on financial PR, which offers a practical list of the financial PR's role in specific situations.

tions this is an incredibly important step that is undertaken for various reasons and if successfully handled can enable them to move from strength to strength. Julius Duncan, Associate Partner of Finsbury, one of the UK and Europe's leading financial PR consultancies, provides a practitioner's guide to IPOs covering the motivation to float, the process of flotation and some potential pitfalls for practitioners to watch out for in the process (see Case study 23.2).

Think about 23.6

An IPO

If you were acting as the financial PR for a company about to go through the IPO process, what could you do to try to minimise the potential for the pitfall described in Case study 23.2, where potential investors 'talk down' the share value of an organisation?

Feedback

One thing you could do is undertake an issues management programme for the IPO process and documentation to identify any potential issues or weaknesses that could be used against you and plan a communications strategy around each (see Chapter 18 on issues management). Often this will involve ensuring that you have brought this information to the City's attention prior to a third party doing so and, in the process of raising the information, effectively communicating why it is either a 'non-issue' or actually a positive for the organisation.

Case Study 23.2

A practitioner's guide to the IPO

The motivation for flotation

The primary reason an organisation floats on an exchange is to tap the public equity markets for funds. Companies that have previously been owned by private individuals, private equity companies or governments (in the case of privatisations in the 1980–90s) sell a stake in themselves on to a stock exchange of their choosing. This brings them an injection of equity (cash), known as the proceeds of the offer, which the company will use to further its strategy/development. This 'use of proceeds' is stated upfront by the company in its prospectus or 'listing particulars'. Typical uses are to restructure debt or pay out exiting shareholders. Other benefits of being on the public markets are heightened profile, the ability to use your quoted shares as currency in further deals, and the ability to use equity to attract and incentivise staff.

The process of flotation

Step 1

Once a company has decided it will pursue an IPO it will appoint legal and banking advisers to prepare the necessary paperwork and documents to go public. At the heart of this is the prospectus, or 'listing particulars', which set out every element of the business that is to be sold to investors and provides financial details on its past performance. A critical section of this document covers the 'risk factors' where the company must list every potential threat to its business and its prospects. The prospectus is a legally binding document and must be approved by the UKLA and finally 'stamped' to show that it has been approved.

Step 2

The floating company's banking advisers will then go out on the company's behalf to test the level of demand in the market for the company's stock: this process is called pre-marketing. This pre-marketing is based on research notes that are written by the analysts attached to the banks following meetings with the company and its management. From a communications perspective the initiation of pre-marketing is the most common time for the company to issue an 'intention to float' announcement outlining its plans and giving brief details on the business and its management.

Step 3

At the end of the pre-marketing period the company sets a 'price range' for its shares that sets a range for the company's valuation when it first floats. This price range will be communicated to the market by way of a statement and journalists will take a view on whether or not the IPO is attractively priced for investors.

Step 4

The management of the company then goes on what is known as an 'investor roadshow' to meet institutional investors in a gruelling series of face-to-face meetings, typically over a one- to two-week period. The banks then go out to these potential investors and find out if they wish to take up shares, and at what price. This is known as the 'book-building' process. Dependent on the level of demand in the book, the IPO will be priced. The intention is to get as high a price as possible. In instances where there is very high demand the price could be outside the top of the range; if there is low demand the range could be lowered or the IPO could be priced below the range. In the worst scenario the IPO is 'pulled' because the selling shareholder refuses to accept the lowered price that investors are willing to pay.

Step 5

In the instance that the float has been priced successfully the company proceeds to listing on the nominated exchange. The necessary logistics of assigning a ticker code to the new listed company and setting it up as a new stock on the exchange are handled by the company's banks and lawyers.

Step 6

Once this is complete the company commences its 'first day of dealing' and its life as a publicly listed company. From this stage on the company is exposed to a heightened level of scrutiny on the public markets, including constant journalist attention, and it must abide by the listing rules as outlined by the UKLA.

A few pitfalls to beware of during the course of an IPO

It is in potential investors' interests to 'talk down' the value of an IPO during the marketing process to enable them to buy the company more cheaply. This is often done through the press, and journalists are willing recipients of negative stories about valuation and the possibility of a deal being re-priced or failing.

Journalists tend to focus on the personal and colourful elements of the information in the prospectus. They are particularly keen to write about any significant payments to management or individuals selling shares. If this is the case for an organisation, it is necessary to explain in detail why these payments exist and communicate them proactively to journalists to gain their understanding.

Source: courtesy of Julius Duncan, past Associate Partner, Finsbury (Financial PR)

Mergers and acquisitions

Mergers and acquisitions are the second special occurrence a financial PR may have to regularly undertake for an organisation. Most company takeovers are carried out as 'friendly' transactions. These takeovers or mergers are carried out with the recommendation of the target company's board of directors. Under this friendly manner of execution the risk of failure is lessened, therefore the cost at which one can raise capital to buy a company is lower. Also, they do not have to offer a high premium to the market, and the advisor's bills will be less than if the situation were to be more complicated. This is an activity that the City expects most listed companies will engage in as part of their corporate strategic plan at some time (Middleton 2005: 169). It will see either one organisation merge with another resulting in a new company or will see a larger company 'swallow up' a smaller organisation. This process often involves one of the organisations raising money to finance the merger or acquisition to enable the shares of the other company to be purchased, this can be done via a rights issue (new shares being offered to the market/ exiting shareholders of the other company in the new company) or through loans from financial institutions to purchase the shares for cash. Additionally, it is often necessary for the shareholders of either one or both companies to be persuaded to agree with the proposed action, whether it is a merger or an acquisition. There are basic laws that govern the flow of information to the market and it is important to understand them fully before getting involved in a takeover. If you get it wrong you can be sent to jail. However, the basic rule is that all shareholders must be in full possession of the facts of the bid at the same time. This information is usually released in the offer document at the start of the buying process and 'new information' may not be added to it subsequently. (See Think about 23.7.)

Hostile takeovers and unsolicited advances

Hostile takeovers and unsolicited advances are the final of the three common special occurrences that PR practitioners will involve themselves in. Though financial PR practitioners perform many tasks for the institutions they work for, perhaps their role and importance is brought most firmly into focus during a company takeover. This is when the press is most interested in a company and where the messages, and in particular the sentiment surrounding a bid, really can make a difference to everybody's 'bottom line' (profitability). Financial institutions are well aware of this phenomenon and will pay a lot of money for professional media advice during this period.

An 'unsolicited' bid for a company is where financial PR gets most interesting. Here the bidder has not asked the directors of the target company for their support. They just go ahead and try and buy the company. Examples of this include Malcolm Glazer's bid for Manchester United plc. or Philip Green's attempt to buy Marks & Spencer. In both these situations the target company did not put itself up for sale – it became a target without wishing to be so. In both situations, however, the bidding parties wished to enter into negotiations with the target. In the Marks & Spencer case no formal offer was made for the company but there was significant media speculation surrounding the bid; handling this situation is the job of the financial PR practitioner.

The case of Manchester United offers interesting insight into whether a bid is 'hostile' or not. A bid becomes hostile if the board of the 'target' publicly rejects a bid. This situation is not at all common, but during the 1980s James Goldsmith and Tiny Rowlands carried out a number of so-called 'corporate raids'. Press speculation increases massively and, therefore, the job of the financial PR becomes time consuming and crucial to the success of the bid. In the case of Manchester United plc, the board never stated an outright rejection of the Glazer bid and therefore this bid must be deemed 'unsolicited'; then again, they did not welcome it either and press coverage surrounding the bid suggested it was 'hostile' even though it was not. These grey areas are becoming more common and the so-called 'half bid' situation is making a big difference to the way in which financial PRs do their job, and provides problems for the financial regulators. The situation can become even more complicated if another bidder becomes interested. This is called a 'competitive bid'. Competitive bids are very expensive for the buyer, so when other potential buyers are thinking of

---

Think about 23.7

Mergers, acquisitions and IPOs

In the process of a merger or acquisition, what do you think the role of the financial PR is? How different do you think it will be from the role the practitioner team plays in the IPO process?

Feedback

In these situations it is the role of the financial PR, working with the legal teams and banks involved, to communicate to both shareholders and 'buy-side' and 'sell-side' analysts to ensure shareholder support is won and the City expectations of the effects of the activity are managed effectively.

Box 23.3

Important 'trigger points' in takeover code

Note: % = percentage of shares owned

- **29.9%** – once a bidder has taken more than 29.9% of the stock of a listed company it must make a formal offer for the rest of the shares.

- **50% + 1** – you have effective control of the company; in reality you probably have control before this point is reached.

- **75%** – you can force a company to de-list with no regard for minority shareholders. You can change the rules of the company: to never pay a dividend, for example. At this point, most shareholders will sell their stakes in the company.

- **90%** – all minority shareholders must sell to the bidder.

Voluntary **de-listing** can occur when an organisation or its shareholders as a whole decide to de-list the organisation (assuming they are able to so) or if one shareholder acquires a majority so large that they are able to take an organisation into private ownership without the consent of the other shareholders. In the UK this level is set at 90% ownership of shares, where that shareholder triggers a compulsory sale of the remaining shares to themselves. With respect to the previous case of an organisation or all shareholders deciding to de-list, though rare, it does occur; one such case in the USA was where many small organisations de-listed in order to save the costs of meeting the reporting requirement of the Sarbanes-Oxley Act of 2002 (Miller and Frankenthaler 2004, online). The act introduced many new reporting regulations and as a result made the costs of reporting outweigh the benefits of being a publicly traded security.

An organisation can be de-listed from an exchange if it commits a severe breach of the 'listing rules' or is found to have repeatedly contravened the regulations, although this rarely occurs. Additionally, an organisation can be de-listed from an exchange if it no longer meets requirements to qualify for a listing. This can happen, for example, to companies traded on the US NASDAQ or New York Stock Exchanges if their share price trades for less than $1 per share for 30 consecutive trading days and they are unable to respond appropriately according to the respective 'listing rules'. (See Box 23.3.)

making a counter offer the financial PR must try to influence opinion.

The actual work carried out by the financial PR changes depending on the nature of the offer, whether one is working for the buyer or the seller and whether the offer is in cash (with no equity), stock (all equity), or a mixture. If the PR is working for a buyer they try to explain that the offer is 'full and fair' especially if it is a cash offer. If it is hostile they will highlight the limitations of the current management and feed journalists with evidence of the company's past underperformance. If the offer includes equity (stock) the PR may highlight how much better the new company will perform and that the value is in the interests of the shareholder.

The key point is that at no time may you produce 'new information', but bids can succeed or fail on the sentiment expressed around the marketplace – and financial PRs are crucial to this process.

Apart from the financial calendar, the communication of other price-sensitive information and the special occurrences discussed above, there is one other rare area of communications activity in financial PR: when an organisation de-lists from an exchange.

How is effectiveness measured in financial PR?

Given that, as this chapter has shown, financial PR has arisen from a variety of historic routes, contains fundamental differences in international practice, has to communicate with a wide range of stakeholders and covers highly regulated activities within the financial calendar, it may seem hard to measure its effectiveness.

Although its activities could be measured via the various techniques described in Chapter 10, financial PR tends to be solely evaluated on its net impact on the business. Middleton (2002) points to the main measure of financial PR being the share price of an organisation though others would probably widen this to include being on the winning side in takeovers or successfully achieving the desired price at flotation or enabling a merger to take place.

This emphasis on results is exemplified in Pace CEO John Dyson's quote where he says: 'The most effective financial PR is actually about delivering business results' (see Case study 23.1). In the *Economist* article that was quoted at the beginning of the chapter, Alan Parker, the founder of Brunswick (UK financial PR consultancy), is quoted as saying: 'retainers are the enemy of value . . . we want to be paid for results' (The *Economist* 2001: 75).

Emerging issues and trends

One of the trends which requires careful consideration is that of converging markets. The potential dangers of con-

vergence were seen in the final quarter of 2008 with the collapse of the worldwide banking system and attendant financial insecurity and recession. The UK recession was the first significant economic downturn for 15 years (BBC 2008a and *Financial Times* 2008). This crisis caused practitioners and financial PR audiences to consider the non-traditional role of the function in this changing landscape. Clea Bourne's study of the Northern Rock bank crisis in the UK (see Case study 23.3) raises several interesting points to ponder about the future and emerging issues and trends that may impact on financial PR practice (BBC 2008b). (See Think about 23.8.)

Case Study 23.3
A crumbling financial rock

Northern Rock

In September 2007, the UK witnessed its first run on a British bank in more than 100 years. Following an increase in the cost of borrowing in the global money markets, Northern Rock became insolvent and secretly approached the Bank of England for emergency credit. The secret talks were 'leaked' and the story broke on the BBC 1 *Ten O'Clock News*. Even as the Bank of England said it would stand by Northern Rock, hundreds queued to withdraw their money. Attempts by the **Chancellor of the Exchequer** to reassure savers served only to lengthen the queues.

Northern Rock was unable to recover from its losses. It was eventually nationalised costing the UK taxpayer billions of pounds. This single event became the UK's most dramatic indicator of the global financial crisis that began in the summer of 2007 and came to be known as the 'credit crunch'. The public's faith in the UK banking system faltered and the mishandled crisis

posed a serious setback for the newly-formed government of Prime Minister Gordon Brown.

For much of Northern Rock's history it was a small building society, prudently managed on behalf of its members. In 1997 Northern Rock demutualised, transforming itself from a building society to a bank run for the benefit of shareholders rather than members. Northern Rock grew rapidly over the next decade, becoming the largest mortgage lender and the fifth largest bank in the UK. It built a reputation as an aggressive, nimble organisation with a dynamic chief executive. The bank was popular in the media, receiving largely positive coverage. As its share price grew, its shareholders were increasingly happy.

But Northern Rock's success depended on a wide range of stakeholders, not just the people who owned its shares. It was particularly dependent on the lenders who make up the global credit markets – their decision to halt lending helped trigger the bank's crisis. Northern Rock also depended on its board of directors and executive team who devised the bank's novel business strategy based on riskier forms of mortgage lending. As the crisis unfolded, Northern Rock's future was eventually determined by a range of stakeholders including UK regulators and policymakers, thousands of customers and millions of taxpayers.

Source: courtesy of Clea Bourne (BBC 2008b)

Think about 23.8 — Northern Rock

The Northern Rock crisis presents a number of interesting PR questions:

1 Should more have been done to communicate the risks associated with Northern Rock's mortgages?

2 Did the bank's stakeholders truly understand the risks involved?

3 Should the bank, the regulators and the media have done more to explain the risks associated with Northern Rock?

4 Was PR effectively used to manage the Northern Rock crisis?

5 Is an organisation's survival always in the interest of its stakeholders?

Feedback

In response to the first question, Northern Rock's customers were taken by surprise when the bank became insolvent as a result of the global credit crunch. Whereas other banks financed their mortgage loans using their stockpile of reserves, Northern Rock financed its highly-competitive mortgage rates by borrowing money cheaply in the international credit markets. It was an innovative approach that enabled many people to own a home. As a publicly-listed company, Northern Rock's business strategy was well reported in the media.

Regarding questions 2, 3 and 4, the organisations involved – Northern Rock, the Financial Services Authority, the Bank of England and HM Treasury – all had in-house PR staff. There were also external PR advisors. Reports suggest that external PR advisors 'leaked' the story of Northern Rock's secret talks with the Bank of England to the media. Yet there seems to have been no joint communication plan for anticipating or managing such a crisis. The institutions involved were variously accused of exhibiting complacency in the face of crisis. In-house PR staff did not appear to have had 'a seat on the board' of their respective organisations, which may help to account for the inadequate communications response.

Finally, in response to question 5: PR practitioners often work to ensure the continued success and survival of organisations in the face of a crisis. But organisations do not exist forever even if they are consistently well run. Northern Rock was not well run, but it continues to survive (at the time of publication as a state-owned bank). Many of its employees were made redundant. Many of its mortgage customers were adversely affected – some eventually lost their homes. Shareholders were left with almost nothing. Meanwhile, the bank's nationalisation came at a huge cost to taxpayers. How many of Northern Rock's stakeholders might be better off had the bank been allowed to collapse?

Summary

This examination of financial PR has served to demystify the practice by defining what practitioners do, identifying who is involved, illustrating international differences and similarities in practice, introducing some of its unique lexicon and body of knowledge, and examining its impact on business. Furthermore the chapter has drawn out some of the trends that will need to be considered in future years.

One of the trends that it will be essential to consider is converging markets. This constant evolution of the global financial environments in which companies operate will see the practice continue to evolve, and practitioners will need to understand the dynamics involved. As with the metro/tube system map of who's involved in the City, if a practitioner fails properly to navigate the evolving system they will find themselves lost and their organisation derailed.

The potential pitfalls of this convergence made themselves readily apparent in the last quarter of 2008 with the worldwide banking collapse, financial insecurity and recession.

The impact of the credit crunch on the worldwide economic climate poses numerous questions and issues for the world of financial PR. For instance it demonstrates that working in finance and financial PR is a highly specialised vocation which brings significant rewards but also carries great risks, and the penalties for failure are extreme. It is imperative that PR practitioners are confident of their ground before getting involved. However, financial PR practices such as mergers and takeovers are highly testing and stimulating. If you do ever get involved, it is likely that the experience will take over your life and push all other matters to one side.

Bibliography

Allen, R.E. (ed.) (1984). *The Pocket Oxford Dictionary*, 7th edition. Oxford: Clarendon Press.

American Heritage Dictionary (2004). www.answers.com/wire+services&r=67, accessed 13 June 2005.

Argenti, P. (1998). *Corporate Communication*, 2nd edition. Boston, MA: Irwin McGraw-Hill.

Argenti, P. (2005). *Corporate Communication*, 4th edition. Boston, MA: Irwin McGraw-Hill.

BBC Newsonline (2008a). 'Recession fear as economy shrinks'. http://news.bbc.co.uk/1/hi/business/7686552.stm, accessed on 08/11/08.

BBC Newsonline (2008b). 'Timeline: Northern Rock Bank Crisis'. http://news.bbc.co.uk/1/hi/business/7007076.stm, accessed on 8 November 2008.

Bowd, R. and P. Harris (2003). 'CSR – A Schools Approach to an Inclusive Definition: Setting the scene for future Public Relations and communications research'. Conference Paper. BledCom 2003; 10th International Public Relations Research Symposium. Slovenia. 3–6 July.

Clarke, G. and L.W. Murray (2000). 'Investor relations: Perceptions of the annual statement'. *Corporate Communications: An International Journal* **5**(3): 144–151.

Cornellisen, J. (2008). *Corporate Communications: Theory and practice*, 2nd edition. London: Sage Publications.

Deephouse, D. (1997). 'The effect of financial and media reputations on performance', *Corporate Reputation Review* **1**(1/2): 68–72.

Dolphin, R. (2004). 'The strategic role of investor relations' in *Corporate Communications: An International Journal* **9**(1): 25–42.

The *Economist* (2001). 'The spin doctors get serious'. The *Economist*. 14 July 2001 **360**(8230): 74–75.

Financial Times (2008). In Depth; Global Financial Crisis; FT Microsite http://www.ft.com/indepth/global-financial-crisis, accessed online 25 November.

FSA (2008). The FSA Internet site: www.fsa.gov.uk accessed 18 November 2008.

Gummer, P. (1995). 'Financial Public Relations' in *Strategic Public Relations*. N. Hart (ed.). Basingstoke: Macmillan Press.

Hagg, C. and K. Preilholh (2004). 'The art of financial relations; reflection on strategic growth'. *Corporate Communications: An International Journal* **9**(1): 50–56.

Harrison, S. (2001). *Public Relations: An Introduction*, 2nd edition. London: International Thompson Business Press.

Investors Relations Society (1997). *Practice Guidelines*. UK: Investors Relations Society.

Marston, C. and M. Straker (2001). 'Investor relations: a European survey'. *Corporate Communications: An International Journal* **6**(2): 82–93.

Middleton, K. (2002). 'An introduction to financial public relations' in *The Public Relations Handbook*. A. Theaker (ed.). London: Routledge.

Miller, D. and M. Frankenthaler (2004). 'Voluntary delisting: a cost-efficient alternative to going private. Insights section, *Corporate & Securities Law Advisor* **17**(10): 7–12. www.bowne.com/newsletters/newsletter.asp?storyID=812, accessed 13 June 2006.

PRSA (2005). 'Section guidelines' www.prsa.org/_networking/fc/guidelines.asp?ident-fc6, accessed 27 May 2005.

Roberts, P. and G. Dowling (1997). 'The value of a firm's corporate reputation: How reputation helps attain and sustain superior profitability'. *Corporate Reputation Review* **1**(1/2): 72–75.

SEC (2008). www.sec.gov/about/whatwedo.shtml, accessed 18 November 2008.

Stone, N. (1995). The *Management and Practice of Public Relations*. Basingstoke, Hampshire: Macmillan Business Press.

Wikipedia (2008a). http://en.wikipedia.org/wiki/Fourth_Estate, accessed 18 November 2008.

Wikipedia (2008b). http://en.wikipedia.org/wiki/Stock_market_index, accessed 18 November 2008.

Wikipedia (2008c). http://en.wikipedia.org/wiki/Chancellor_of_the_Exchequer, accessed on 18 November 2008.

Acknowledgements

The author would like to thank Finsbury, one of the UK and Europe's leading financial PR consultancies for a significant amount of assistance from its directors to ensure the practical and real world context of this chapter.

Websites

The Australian: www.theaustralian.news.com.au
Australian Financial Review: www.afr.com
Bild: www.bild.de
Canadian Public Relations Society: www.cprs.ca
The Committee of European Securities Regulators: www.cesr-eu.org
Deutsche Börse Group: www.exchange.de
Dow Jones and Company: www.dowjones.com
Financial Relations Board: www.financialrelationsboard.com
Financial Services Authority: www.fsa.gov.uk
Financial Times: www.ft.com
Finsbury Group: www.finsbury.com
FTSE Group: www.ftse.com
Globe and Mail: www.globeandmail.com
Handelsblatt: www.handelsblatt.de
International Herald Tribune: www.iht.com
Le Figaro: wwww.lefigaro.fr
Le Monde: www.lemonde.fr
Mail and Guardian: www.mg.co.za
NASDAQ Stock Market Inc: www.nasdaq.com
National Post: www.nationalpost.com
NIKKEI (Nihon Keizai Shimbun, Inc): www.nikkei.co.jp
Pace Micro Technology plc: www.pacemicro.com
Public Relations Institute of Australia: www.pria.com.au
Public Relations Institute of Southern Africa: www.prisa.co.za
Reuters: www.reuters.co.uk
Swedish Public Relations Society: www.sverigesinformationsforening.se/in-english.aspx
TSX Group Inc: www.tse.com
US Securities and Exchange Commission: www.sec.gov
Wall Street Executive Library: www.executivelibrary.com
Wall Street Journal: http://online.wsj.com

CHAPTER 16

Crisis Public Relations

CHAPTER 19

Martin Langford

Crisis public relations management

Learning outcomes

By the end of this chapter you should be able to:

- define and describe crisis public relations
- recognise how crises occur
- identify the key principles of crisis public relations planning and management
- apply this understanding to simple, personally meaningful scenarios
- apply crisis public relations planning and management principles to real-life scenarios.

Structure

- Crisis public relations management: the context
- Crisis public relations management vs operational effectiveness
- Where do crises come from?
- Communicating *during* a crisis
- The Internet and public relations crisis management
- How to prepare for a crisis
- Key principles in crisis management

Introduction

Crisis public relations (PR) management is one of the most critical aspects of modern communications. Effective crisis management protects companies, their reputations and, at times, can salvage their very existence. A crisis is an event that disrupts normal operations of a company or organisation and, if badly managed, can ruin hard-won reputations in just days and even, in some cases, destroy companies (note the disastrous effects in 2008 of the 'credit crunch' on established banks and businesses

e.g. Lehman Brothers, Halifax Bank of Scotland (HBOS), AIG and others). The list of companies whose share price and market capitalisation have nose-dived because of badly managed crises would fill this entire book, let alone this chapter. In a crisis, there is always more than the immediate issue at stake.

This chapter will look at examples of effectively managed crisis situations as well as some of those badly handled crises. We will explore, in some detail, the characteristics of a crisis.

The key to PR crisis management is preparedness. It is vital to effective crisis management that a crisis is identified *before it happens* and, when it does, that it does not get out of control. In this 'information and communications' age, when a crisis does happen, it is crucial to understand the role communication plays and particularly the role of the Internet. In this chapter we will examine the key principles for managing *any* crisis situation using a variety of case studies of both good and bad practice.

Mini Case Study 19.1

Crisis snapshot – Andersen

In 2001 Andersen was one of the best known and respected auditing companies in the world. It was an established and trusted brand. As it became caught up in, and associated with, the problems arising from the Enron energy company crisis (Enron executives had been mismanaging the business and falsifying its financial performance), it saw its business and client base rapidly and drastically reduced. More than just being associated with Enron's mismanagement, Andersen was implicated in an attempted cover-up with reports of coded instructions to employees to 'clean out' Enron-related documents as US federal investigators prepared to launch an investigation. Andersen's board were quickly into a situation of 'last ditch rescue talks' seeking a merger with rival firms. Eventually, Andersen as a brand and as a commercially operating company was destroyed as a consequence of a poorly managed crisis.

Crisis public relations management: the context

PR crisis management literature is filled with lists of 'dos' and 'don'ts' together with countless checklists, for example Howard and Mathews (1985) include a 17-point crisis

plan in their media relations book. All these are helpful in describing and dissecting crises. Some of this planning relates to the preparations before a crisis has happened, but generally the lists and guidelines concern coping with the situation in a practical sense after a crisis has happened. Reference should be made to Chapter 18, which deals with issues management which is often closely associated with the crisis planning or preparation phase, i.e. defining and understanding the issues. Heath (1997) supports the link to crisis management and highlights how managing issues can help prevent a crisis. He states (1997: 289): 'If a company is engaged in issues management before, during, and after a crisis (in other words, ongoing), it can mitigate – perhaps prevent – the crisis from becoming an issue by working quickly and responsibly to establish or re-establish the level of control desired by relevant stakeholders.' In this chapter we will aim to build understanding by applying theoretical and practical models to crisis scenarios.

As a starting point it is important to define the area. Cornelissen (2008) describes crisis management as a point of great difficulty or danger to an organisation, possibly threatening its existence and continuity, that requires decisive change.

Seymour and Moore (2000: 10) use a snake metaphor to argue that crises come in two forms:

> The cobra – *the 'sudden' crisis – this is a disaster that hits suddenly and takes the company completely by surprise and leaves it in a crisis situation.*
>
> The python – *the 'slow-burning' crisis or 'crisis creep' – a collection of issues that steal up on the company one by one and slowly crush it.*

In 1989 Sam Black broke crises down into the 'known unknown' and the 'unknown unknown'. The former

Activity 19.1

Cobras and pythons

Spend some time thinking about (and researching) crises that have affected organisations and list them under the headings of cobras and pythons as described by Seymour and Moore.

Feedback

Now refer to Lerbinger's eight types of crisis (below) and classify your list under one of them.

includes mishaps owing to the nature of the organisation and its activities, e.g. manufacturing or processing and potential for spillage. The 'unknown unknowns' are events that cannot be predicted and that can come about from employees' behaviour, unconnected events or circumstances that are unpredictable. Before reading further, see Activity 19.1.

Lerbinger (1997) categorised eight types of crisis that he attributed to two causes: management failures or environmental forces. The eight categories are:

1   *natural* (for example, the Asian tsunami, which affected nations, governments, corporations, businesses and the lives and social infrastructure of millions)

2   *technological* (Mercedes 'A' Class car had a design fault and 'rolled over')

3   *confrontation* (Shell Oil whose petrol stations suffered a consumer boycott after the company wanted to sink an oil platform in the North Sea – the Brent Spar, see also Chapters 6 and 18)

4   **malevolence** (product tampering by a private citizen, like the Tylenol case detailed later, or direct action by animal rights campaigners, such as placing bombs under the cars of executives whose stores sell cosmetics tested on animals)

5   *skewed management values* (Barings Bank went out of business after managers were accused of turning a blind eye to 'rogue' trader Nick Leeson who hid details of his massive financial losses in the currency markets. An act repeated in 2008 by Jérôme Kervie when working for the French bank, Société Générale. See later in the chapter)

6   *deception* (examples include deceiving employees about the amount of money in pension funds after it has been used by executives to support the business, a UK case being that of Robert Maxwell and the Mirror Group of national newspapers)

7   *management misconduct* (Enron is one of the most shocking examples of this with both illegal and unethical practices rife in the senior management of the practice – see also Andersen, Mini case study 19.1)

8   *business and economic* (the late 1990s boom/bust in numerous small IT/technology companies is an example of how economic cycles can impact an organisation).

Fearn-Banks (2006) defines five stages of a crisis, outlined in Table 19.1.

Table 19.1
Fearn-Banks' five stages of a crisis (*source*: adapted from Fearn-Banks 2006)

	Stage	Features
1	Detection	The organisation is watching for warning signs or what Barton (1993) calls *prodromes* (warning signs)
2	Preparation/prevention	The organisation takes note of the warning signs and prepares plans proactively to avoid the crisis, or reactive ones to cope with the crisis if it comes
3	Containment	Taking steps to limit the length of the crisis or its effects
4	Recovery	This is the stage where effort is made to get back to the 'normal' operational conditions or effectiveness of the organisation
5	Learning	This is when the organisation reflects and evaluates the experience to consider the negative impacts for the organisation and any possible positive benefits for the future

Crisis public relations management vs operational effectiveness

However well a crisis is managed from an operational perspective, it is how an organisation communicates about the crisis that makes the real difference. There is evidence that good communication in a crisis situation can support or increase a company's reputation (British Midland, Tylenol, discussed later). Poor management or a lack of communication skills can have a powerful negative effect on a company's business.

Let us examine the case of the *Exxon Valdez* oil spill in March 1989. The spill took place in Alaska, one of the few true wildernesses in the world, and received a considerable amount of global media coverage. Even though the accident site was appropriately cleaned up (*operational effectiveness*), Exxon took far too long to address its stakeholders (see Chapter 11 for a definition of stakeholders) and, particularly, the media. As a result of this failure of communication, its reputation was substantially tarnished. Insult was added to injury when the CEO finally did talk to the media as he blamed them for exaggerating 'the public relations disaster' that was created around the spill. Exxon's stock market capitalisation dropped $3 billion in the two weeks after the *Exxon Valdez* oil spill in Alaska. (Seymour and Moore 2000: 157)

Seymour and Moore (2000) describe the 'association' or 'parenthesis' factor that lingers on after a crisis. In discussing the mass poisoning of Minimata Bay in Japan, caused by Chisso Corporation, when mercury was dumped into the sea over several decades, poisoning thousands of consumers who ate polluted fish, Seymour and Moore (2000: 157) write:

> For Chisso the hundreds of deaths and thousands of injuries represented a financial burden, aside from the fact that it would be linked with Minimata. The 'association factor' lingers on over other companies; Union Carbide and Bhopal; Exxon, the Exxon Valdez and oil spills; the Herald of Free Enterprise, ferry safety, and P&O.

Now, consider the frequently discussed case at Johnson & Johnson. Over 25 years ago Johnson & Johnson faced a potentially devastating crisis. Tylenol, the company's trusted and leading analgesic (pain reliever) was contaminated with cyanide by a member of the public. This action directly caused the deaths of six people in the Chicago area. Could anything worse happen to an over-the-counter product? Johnson & Johnson did not hesitate to

act and act quickly. For the first time in the history of any product, it issued a comprehensive product recall. It literally pulled off the shelves *all* the capsules throughout the USA – not just in the Chicago area where the deaths occurred. The potential financial consequences of losing a leading product, and the subsequent damage to its brand, could not be exaggerated. But, at the same time, it communicated exactly what it was doing, in a timely manner to *all* stakeholders – shareholders, employees, regulators, the police, press and consumers. How would it act next? How would it re-establish confidence in the product and the brand? How was anyone to trust a Johnson & Johnson product again? Could anyone with a grievance or grudge or another random 'madman' claim to have poisoned the product and effectively blackmail them?

Johnson & Johnson's next response was both direct and decisive. It introduced tamper-evident packaging. It was, in many ways, a very simple operational 'addition' in terms of production – a metal foil to visibly 'seal' the product plus two more physical barriers to entry. Its simplicity was its key. Now, without any doubt, all stakeholders could actually see that the product was safe. Johnson & Johnson acted swiftly and effectively both in terms of operation and communication. Even today Tylenol is seen as one of the best-managed crises and the brand (appropriately) is still a success around the world. This crisis was so well handled that Johnson & Johnson's reputation has actually benefited in the long term – Johnson & Johnson's words *and* actions were seen to be in accord. (See Activity 19.2.)

Activity 19.2

Crisis lessons

What could Exxon have done better in its situation – think in terms of actions and words? If you were an environmentalist, what would you want to know? If you had shares in the company, how would you react? If you were a news reporter, what would your agenda be?

The good . . .

What do you think are the key lessons from the Tylenol case that make this crisis, from over 25 years ago, still discussed so favourably? What do you feel the company got right? How did the company get it right?

Picture 19.1 Protests against Union Carbide following the Bhopal chemical plant disaster (*source*: © Reuters/Corbis)

Where do crises come from?

A spoonful of sugar

Leading crisis counsellors argue that over 50% of crises occur with products that are either ingested or swallowed – including food, drink and oral pharmaceuticals. We all eat and get ill – it is easy to understand how a damaged or defective foodstuff or pharmaceutical can be a major cause for concern. But the source of a crisis might not always be so subtle. A crisis can hit any organisation regardless of what or whom it represents. Whatever manufacturing process is employed or whatever information is disseminated, things can and will go wrong. The food dye scandals that hit the UK in early 2005 showed the extent of impending crisis, when potentially cancer-causing additives resulted in the recall of nearly 500 products (see Food Standards Agency, www.food.gov.uk/news/newsarchive/2005/ for further information).

It's not what you know, but who knows it

This is the information and communications age when highly confidential information somehow always escapes the bounds of its host organisation. Strictly confidential, paper-based hospital records have been found on rubbish dumps, and the hard drives of second-user computers have been found to contain sensitive company or even government information. On 18 October, 2007 HM Revenue and Customs (HMRC) sent via unregistered mail two unencrypted CDs containing the entire child benefit database to the National Audit Office, but they did not arrive. The data on the disks included name, address, date of birth, National Insurance number and bank details of 25 million people. HMRC chairman Paul Gray resigned as a consequence of the crisis. Police believed the CDs were thrown out as rubbish, but over 7 million UK families were asked to remain alert to fraudulent use of their details.

In today's climate it is nearly impossible to keep confidential information confidential. Any organisation should expect that what is known on the *inside* is just as well known on the *outside*.

You won't believe what so-and-so just told me

According to the Institute of Crisis Management, around a quarter of global crises are caused or triggered by employees/members of an organisation. Employees are a company's best asset when they are effectively motivated, remunerated and appreciated. But loyalty may turn – often when least expected. The disaffected employee or former employee taking some form of revenge can trigger a crisis – and when feelings are running high, their negative impact can be huge. One disaffected employee brought down the stock price of a leading healthcare firm by 35% by giving incorrect research information to a leading newspaper; how can we forget the one-man crisis caused by Nick Leeson who brought down the merchant bank Barings through his overzealous financial actions! These actions were well chronicled in a 1998 film, *Rogue Trader*.

On 24 January 2008 French bank Société Générale reported it had fallen victim to the activities of another rogue trading fraud and as a result lost almost €5 billion. The bank stated that these fraudulent transactions were conducted by Jérôme Kerviel, a trader with the company. After the initial investigation police stated they lacked evidence to charge him with fraud and charged him with abuse of confidence and illegal access to computers. Kerviel stated that his actions were known to his superiors as the transactions had been going on for over two years.

Seymour and Moore (2000: 142) outline the characteristics of rumours under crisis conditions:

- Accept that rumours always generate interest and are often more attractive than the facts.
- Silence – or a vacuum caused by lack of communication – will always be filled by rumour and speculation.
- Any organisation of 10 or more people will always have a series of rumours circulating.

Under these circumstances, rumour can contribute to and exacerbate already serious problems. Thus monitoring and **pickup systems** are required, especially when a company is facing or handling a crisis situation.

What are the real costs of a crisis?

With any crisis there are, as we have seen, clear financial costs involved in withdrawing a product, cleaning up after an industrial accident, oil spill, etc. However, compared to the damage that can be done to a reputation, these costs are minimal. Let's take a look at the *real* costs of a crisis.

Management distraction

Even when a crisis is handled well, key leaders or the leadership team are preoccupied for periods that can last from several days to several weeks and cannot manage the daily business. When a crisis hits, the people running an organisation have a crisis to handle!

Labour/employee concern

Employees will naturally be concerned about their own welfare, jobs and financial security. Too few companies communicate effectively with their employees during a crisis. Employees who are both well informed and motivated can be a powerful force in times of crisis. Without them, an organisation will not exist. With them, most things are possible.

Political backlash

Whether at country, EU or global level, crises sow discontent among regulators and 'the authorities' and the chances of regulatory or political pressure on or against an organisation are high. This may be driven by public reaction to the crisis.

Legal actions

We live in a 'do or sue' world. Crises encourage litigious behaviour in individuals, and injury or other compensation claims can inflict huge financial demands. In terms of litigation, an organisation must plan for the worst – and particularly so in the area of product liability.

Customer reactions

It is reassuring how forgiving customers can be, but only if they feel their concerns have been adequately addressed. When an organisation fails to communicate effectively with consumers, it is likely to see its support disintegrate and market share plummet often irretrievably.

Market confidence and reputation

This is the most significant cost of all. Rebuilding a reputation with stakeholders, such as shareholders, consumers and regulators, is not only costly, it can also take years to achieve. Again effective communication is key to reinforcing both public and market confidence. (See Activity 19.3 and Box 19.1.)

Communicating *during* a crisis

The examples and experiences described so far in this chapter dramatically demonstrate that today it is more and more evident why a company or organisation should

Crisis and reputation

In 2004 Shell was overoptimistic about its global oil reserves (oil stocks). This miscalculation resulted in the resignations of the head of exploration and the chairman. These revelations plus the two resignations had a substantial impact on share price and reputation for Shell. Think about the points just examined – how would you, as a trainee PR crisis manager, begin to piece together the full impact on Shell of its crisis? What should you be thinking about? Whom should you be thinking about? How does the future look? How has your reputation suffered? What is the way forward?

Feedback

You need systematically to research and answer questions such as these to build an accurate picture.

Crises in action – What *actually* happens and how does it feel?

The following description of a crisis is based on the experiences of a senior crisis consultant who describes what happens and how it feels.

There is a distinct pattern of events and behaviour that occurs during a crisis. Let's take a look at them.

Surprise!

Crises happen at the most inopportune times – Easter, Christmas, bank holidays or 8 o'clock on a Friday night after a week of hell, when you're enjoying a 'good night out'. It's almost guaranteed that if a crisis were to happen in Japan it will be during the Golden Week holiday, in China it will happen during Chinese New Year or over Thanksgiving in the USA. And the company is usually unaware of the situation until the issue is raised by someone else – be it a regulator, 'authority', key customer or media. Your mobile phone rings. You don't recognise the number, but it's a work phone, so you answer it. What next?

You're on your toes and you can guarantee that your briefcase is not where you left it and you can't find the number for the out-of-hours PR officer. You think you know what to say and the caller tells you they've got a deadline and whatever you say is going to be quoted. As you are thinking on your feet, so your organisation may feel they don't have enough information to deal with the crisis. What are the facts? Who has that information and how is it best understood and represented? Both you and your organisation feel there is an escalating flow of events. Within what may feel like moments, the media are talking about the situation, investment analysts are asking awkward questions and NGOs are getting involved. Everyone seems to be looking in on the organisation – you are in a goldfish bowl and everyone is peering in. It's highly probable that you and your organisation will feel a loss of control over the situation – there are so many different stakeholders and they want to know *right now* what has actually happened and what's being done, or going to be done, and said about it.

Roll down the shutters – crisis leads to drama

There is immense and intense scrutiny from outside the company. This can lead to a siege mentality where individuals feel everyone is *against them* and their organisation. This reaction invariably and rapidly leads to panic. 'I don't know what you're on about!' you tell the caller. 'I don't believe a word of it – you're just after a story. I suggest you go and pick on someone less gullible.' Once panic sets in rational decision making goes out of the window. But applying *rational* thinking to *irrational* events is exactly what's called for. 'Those are very serious allegations. It is not appropriate for me to comment immediately. I will return your call within 15 minutes. Before this time, I'm afraid I'm unable to comment.' What happens next?

communicate effectively at the onset of a crisis (see also the London bombings crisis, Case study 19.1). Yet many companies argue against it. Preparing for a crisis costs time, money and energy – and crisis preparedness training is often seen as an unnecessary luxury. Even when an organisation is urged to communicate about its situation by experienced crisis management counsellors, there is often a list of reasons why it cannot communicate, such as:

Case Study 19.1

The London bombings of 2005: a case in crisis communication management at Leeds Metropolitan University

In 2004 following the London suicide bombings of 7 July, Leeds Metropolitan University had to respond to a media frenzy as journalists tried to identify and reveal information about the bombers. The university's communications team were used to dealing with real and often unexpected situations that attracted media attention but never before on this scale.

During the afternoon of 12 July the world's media turned its attention to Leeds as the police hunt for suspects to the 7 July bombings closed in on a largely Asian community in Leeds. At this time the university's Head-ingley Campus was hosting in excess of 3,000 people each day during a four-day festival of graduation ceremonies, which included well-known names like Dame Kelly Holmes, Lucas Radebe, and Joe Simpson as well as Brendan Foster being installed as the new chancellor; there was already a media presence on campus.

At approximately 5pm on Tuesday 12 July, one of the university's communications team took a call from a jour-nalist suggesting that one of the London bombers was a student at Leeds Met. The journalist gave a name and the course they had studied and wanted a comment from the university. Data protection legislation meant the communications team could not comment, which gave crucial time to investigate and prepare for a situation.

The first crisis management team meeting took place the following morning, made up of the head of com-munications, head of security, a deputy vice-chancellor and a dean (the vice-chancellor himself was welcoming VIPs onto campus for the day's ceremonies).

With mobiles phones switched off, the crisis manage-ment team discussed the situation, the need for damage limitation, the key stakeholders, and the university's main concerns.

Main concerns and objectives

The main concerns were having the university's name associated with Muslim fundamentalism and the UK's

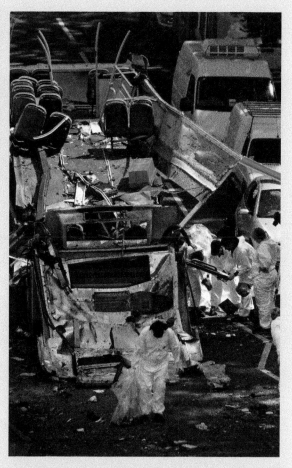

Picture 19.2 The London Bombings crisis is an example of how an organisation can get drawn into a crisis unexpectedly. This happened to Leeds Metropolitan University when it fell under the media spotlight after it was alleged by journalists that the bombers lived in Leeds and had met at the University (*source*: Corbis)

first home-grown suicide bombers; associations which could impact on the university's reputation and, ulti-mately, student numbers and subsequent funding. All these factors were crucial to the success of the univer-sity. Crisis management objectives therefore were to:

- manage the flow of information
- avoid distortion
- actively promote positive stories about the university
- identify and communicate with priority stakeholders
- operate on a 'business as usual' basis.

case study 19.1 (continued)

Stakeholders

Journalists

As well as responding to journalists' requests, the communications team called their contacts on the regional press to find out more – good relations with this stakeholder group meant that they could comfortably discuss the developing situation.

Vice-chancellor

Given the vice-chancellor's trust and knowledge in the university's communications team, he authorised them to use whatever resources they needed to best manage the situation.

Regional contacts

The communications team made calls to discuss developments with other stakeholders including the city council, further education colleges in the city, and the University of Leeds – all of whom were receiving similar requests from the media. Responses were discussed and the communications team gave advice.

Staff

An email was sent to all staff requesting that any calls from the press be referred to the communications team. A comprehensive staff induction informs all staff of the need to refer any calls from the press to the press office so this was simply reinforcing this message.

Students

Subsequent crisis management team meetings included representatives from the students' union and the president of the university's Islamic Society to reassure them that the names of individual students were not discussed with the media.

Community groups

The university learned of the number of displaced residents from the communities where the alleged bombers came from. The university offered its halls of residence and other facilities to support their needs during this period of uncertainty.

University governors

The head of communications advised the university's chancellor Brendan Foster and other key governors of the situation and assured them that the university was cooperating with the police investigation and managing the situation. The governors and chancellor in turn gave their support.

By the time the police confirmed the names of the bombers at 2pm, the communications team was able to confirm that at least one of the bombers had been a student at the university. The university's press statement led with offers of support to the community affected.

Newspaper coverage

Although Leeds Met was mentioned in many of the national and regional press it was never headline news; campus photographs were never shown; and much of the coverage was positive as the university was reported as having provided accommodation to displaced residents. Increased security on campus contributed to this. Following the initial 48 hours when the journalists were looking for any details they could regarding the bombers, more lengthy, considered and researched articles appeared in the national press regarding Muslim fundamentalism on university campuses. This led to further media enquiries by which time the university had been able to verify its actions in dealing with fundamentalism over the previous 10 years and identify the protocols and accessibility of campus facilities such as the prayer rooms and student groups.

Further coverage

Confident in its actions and 'policing' of facilities, the communications team decided that it was appropriate to provide some journalists with access to the vice-chancellor. Further national and regional features were published which were more considered and demonstrated transparency, corporate citizenship and ethical consideration of how to manage a large multicultural university. By way of contrast, the University of Leeds did not adhere to data protection laws when the media gave details of an Egyptian PhD student who was suspected of renting out the flat where the bombs were made. He was later cleared of any involvement but not before his photograph and personal details had appeared on the front page of every national newspaper, following details released by the university.

Conclusion

Leeds Met was quick to implement a damage limitation strategy, including tight security and being very tough with journalists. As a result, the university's coverage in the media was, on the whole, passing comment on one of the bomber's association with Leeds Met. Coverage was considerably less than that of the University of Leeds and other organisations in Leeds who, it may be considered, provided more detail and spokespeople with no security in place to reduce impact.

case study 19.1 (continued)

In 2006 Leeds Met was awarded 'gold' in the category of 'outstanding contribution to the local community award' and 'silver' in the 'university of the year' category at the prestigious *Times Higher Education* awards. In the same year Leeds Met recorded the highest percentage increase in student applications in the UK, when most universities were experiencing a decrease in applications following the introduction of tuition fees.

The university's relationship with the communities affected has gone from strength to strength. Many students continue to come from the ethnic minority communities in Leeds, students engage with these communities as part of the citizenship elements of their studies, and staff are engaged in research activities ranging from health inequalities, employment and skills audits, and delivery of courses within the communities to improve employability and aspirations.

Further information

Timeline

Wednesday 13 July 2005
Following a media report late on Tuesday 12 July that one of the bombers was a Leeds Met student a full search of Banner (the university's student database) took place on Wednesday 13 July at 8am revealing that all three suspected bombers' names matched records on Leeds Met's database (some names were spelt differently)

A crisis management team was scrambled to identify a damage limitation strategy: staff and security identified as priority as well as governors and students

By midday the University had eliminated all but one of its students, but without police confirmation a holding statement was issued

The University received over 50 media calls and security turned away at least five journalists/cameramen (BBC Radio 4's *Today* programme was escorted off the Headingley Campus a minimum of three times, with the *Daily Mail* and *Mirror* caught trying to access Fairfax Hall) – no access to a spokesperson or campuses was permitted; the brief holding statement was issued on request

All but the main access to the halls at Headingley campus were locked with security based at each of the main entrances to prevent journalists intruding

The university received mentions in at least 15 regional, national and international newspapers and websites

The (London) Metropolitan Police were contacted and they booked an appointment to visit the university the following morning

Other departments in the registrar's office supported the communications team, with a second team handling calls at the Civic Quarter and issuing the holding statement and a third team searching the website for media mentions

Vice-chancellor consulted on a number of occasions

Thursday 14 July 2005
The Metropolitan Police visited campus and spent approximately 2 hours with the head of communications, who gave an official statement and handed over records of one suspect and his best friend, while the Banner system was checked for approximately 8 names, with further requests throughout the day – the administrative team in Fairfax Hall were the main source of Banner searches, with the support of their senior management

The university received mentions in at least 20 regional, national and international newspapers and websites, including *Arab News* and the *New Zealand Herald*, plus regular radio and television mentions

The university received around 15 media calls and evicted a French cameramen from Civic Quarter, who returned with the head of human resources speaking to them

At 3.50pm a press statement issued by the Metropolitan Police confirmed the names of suspects, including a Leeds Met student Shezhad Tanweer. A further statement was issued confirming Shezhad Tanweer was a Leeds Met student and identifying the support the university was offering to the evacuated communities in Leeds

BBC television's *Look North's* 6pm bulletin and Radio Five Live reported that Leeds Met was providing accommodation for evacuated residents

The *Yorkshire Evening Post* also carried positive coverage of the University's graduations, including photographs of honorary doctorates and Kids@Uni (crèche scheme)

The use of the official statement with no further comment available seemed to reduce the amount of coverage Leeds Met received in the national media

case study 19.1 (continued)

University of Leeds and Thomas Danby issued statements that were shared among the press offices

Vice-chancellor consulted on a number of occasions

Friday 15 July 2005
The attention firmly shifted to the University of Leeds and Leeds City Council but the university was aware that it should be ready for other developments should they involve Leeds Met.

British press: brief mentions of Leeds Met in the *Daily Mail* and *Daily Mirror*; the *Mirror* mentioned that the prayer room at the University of Leeds was under scrutiny

International press: brief mentions in the *Brisbane Courier Mail* and *Newsday*, Long Island, New York

Local press: a variety of mentions including positive mentions from graduation and our community support

Fewer requests for the latest statement including GMTV who wanted to film the university providing support to evacuated residents

New statement sent out proactively to local contacts who the university had not cooperated fully with in the previous two days

Times Higher Educational Supplement requested interview with Professor Simon Lee (vice-chancellor)

Dr Max Farrar spoke to the *Independent on Sunday* about the issue in Leeds generally (asked not to speak about Leeds Met specifically)

The crisis management team continued to meet in the morning having met twice each day of the previous two days, with security still on full alert to evict journalists

Despite staff being advised not to speak to the press, reports came through of a member of staff in the School of Tourism and Hospitality Management speaking to the press with two 'hats' on – one as a member of the Muslim community in Leeds and as a Leeds Met employee. The head of communications spoke to him about not doing further statements, which he agreed to.

Some aggressive journalists still sought statements – one from the *Sunday Telegraph* persistent and rude.

Vice-chancellor consulted on a number of occasions

Saturday 16 July 2005
Leeds Met staff member quoted in the *Independent* saying: 'I can tell you categorically that at Leeds Metropolitan University and Leeds University there are no radical groups there. If there was a problem, I would report it. I've never had to.'

Over ten mentions in the media, including most of the broadsheets.

Reported in the *Sun* that Shezhad Tanweer was reportedly involved in a race-hate street murder but no evidence to take him to court.

Sunday 17 July 2005
The *Independent on Sunday* claimed Mohammed Sadique Khan and Hasina Patel met at Leeds Met (Saturday's *Independent* claimed they had met at Dewsbury College)

The *Sunday Telegraph* opinion (Niall Ferguson) said about Tanweer: 'He was not uneducated, assuming you regard a degree in sports science from Leeds Metropolitan University as education.'

The *Sunday Telegraph* ran a separate article with the headline 'Islamic extremism goes underground at British universities.'

Monday 18 July 2005
Two mentions in the *Yorkshire Post*, including some good press about Verity Jenning's thesis on 'Chavs'.

Some journalists were still requesting more on Shezhad Tanweer and Leeds Met's view on Muslim fundamentalism – including the BBC R4 *Today* programme

Looking forward

■ Continue to keep an eye on developments in the press

■ Downgrade but keep vigilant message to security

■ Promote positive messages – summer schools, Larkia, regional college network, Harrogate festival sponsorship, community work, graduation stories for the regional and local press, broader comment on the issues of integration and diversity

■ Some contacts in the regional press keen to generate positive stories.

Source: Laville (2008)

Think about 19.1

'No comment'– what happens when companies will not respond

If a company spokesperson refuses to comment, what is your reaction? What would you think if you were the journalist asking the question? or a customer of the company?

Feedback

The sequence of events may go something like this:

- The company chooses to say: 'No comment.'

- The media say: 'The company was unwilling to take part in this programme.'

- Consumers think: 'No smoke without fire.'
  'They're hiding something.'
  'Guilty!'

When an organisation does not take control of a crisis situation and fails to communicate immediately, the media will go to a whole range of *other* sources to get the information they need. Take a look at the following list – they are all readily available sources of information and 'expert' opinion in a crisis situation: the company website; the Internet; emergency services – police, ambulance, fire, coast guard, mountain rescue, etc.; hospital authorities; medical, scientific and other experts; former employees; directors; local authorities; government departments; government ministers and

other politicians; social services; neighbouring businesses, security, business and other analysts; academics; your customers and clients; charities and aid organisations; psychologists and 'disaster' counsellors; specialist writers and correspondents; freelance journalists; newspaper cuttings; film; picture libraries; public records; annual and other reports and directories; members of the public and 'eye witnesses'; competitor companies and organisations; trade unions and professional bodies and pressure groups and other NGOs.

The media will also talk to the company receptionist – the friendly face who's been on the front desk representing the organisation for the last 25 years. They'll speak to the night security officer or the person in company overalls who keeps the boiler going and is seen leaving the plant at 6 o'clock in the morning. They're loyal and dependable; they are the face of the company . . . But how much do they really know? How much do you think they know? Maybe they know more than you think. Have they been prepared for crisis situations – for the leading questions of journalists who might appear to be their best friend? They have a voice and the media will let them speak for themselves. If they are prepared appropriately, they too are an invaluable resource to a company.

- The need to assemble all the facts before it communicates.

- The desire to avoid panic, for instance it fears that by mentioning the individual brand, people will think the corporate brand is 'infected' as well.

- It does not have a trained spokesperson and is not going to put anyone up against a seasoned television interviewer such as Jeremy Paxman on the BBC's *Newsnight* (a late-evening 'hard' news programme).

- It has had other problems recently and cannot talk about this problem because it will impact on its overall corporate reputation.

- The issue of how to solve the crises – no one knows how to solve the problem at the outbreak of the crisis; every single crisis situation companies face, and their solutions, will be substantially different.

- The fear of revealing proprietary information or revealing competitive information that may give the company new competitive problems.

See Think about 19.1.

Talking to the media

The way a company communicates to the media is critical. Selecting a spokesperson or spokespeople is one of the most important decisions in the effective management of any crisis. Whoever acts as spokesperson should follow the proposed 5Cs model (Figure 19.1) to be effective. This is based on consultancy experience of senior crisis managers.

Figure 19.1 The 5Cs effective communication model

The sections of the 5Cs model in Figure 19.1 can be explained as follows.

Concern

Not to be confused with legal liability, concern is a simple human emotion. The organisation's spokesperson needs to show true concern about the problem, concern about what has happened and concern for the people affected now and in the future – including potential customers/ service users.

Clarity

Organisations need to talk with clarity. Starting from the early hours of the crisis, they need to have very clear messages. What the spokesperson says at the outset will be repeated throughout the duration of the crisis.

Control

When talking to the media, spokespeople must take control of the messages, the situation, the environment and the venue.

Confidence

The spokesperson must get the key messages across with confidence, but without appearing complacent or arrogant.

Competence

They must also demonstrate competence and reflect how, as the representative of the organisation, they will handle the crisis.

How will the media react?

In the first instance, the media will want to know the facts. Their first questions are likely to be those in Box 19.2.

Box 19.2

Typical first questions from the media

- What happened?
- What went wrong? Why?
- Who is to blame/accountable?
- What is happening right now?
- What are you doing to prevent it from happening again?

While these initial questions are generally predictable, how the media will act and how they will report a crisis should never be assumed. Everyone asks questions from 'their own perspective' and everyone, especially the news-hungry media, will have their 'own take' on the crisis situation. As well as general reporters, there may also be very well-informed specialist correspondents to consider. (See Activity 19.4.)

Activity 19.4

A crisis from a journalist's perspective

Put yourself in the position of a journalist being asked to report on a crisis scenario, say a major rail crash. How might you react as a journalist in a crisis? What might you want to know if you were in their situation? To whom would you want to speak? What do you need to get your story on the front page? How different would your questions be if you worked for the local paper or a transport publication?

Feedback

If you were in this situation, what kind of media coverage should you expect? You *could* experience the following:

- The initial media reports will be speculative, wrong, exaggerated, sensationalised, often very personalised, spiteful or hurtful – and possibly, even, right! Expect the media to 'round up' the scale of the problem simply because it makes for a better story. Expect the media to make a drama out of your crisis.

- Experts will be called in to comment on the problem. These 'specialists' in various 'fields of expertise' will discuss ideas of what went wrong and how it happened.

- An exclusive article, containing sensitive information that, of course, the organisation did not want to have made known.

- Someone will say this disaster has been waiting to happen.

- The timing will be wrong, the crisis team will be out of town, their deputies abroad or the spokesperson's mobile phone will have been stolen!

- Opinions and rumours will dominate media reporting – especially if the organisation does not respond effectively. Expect rumours to become fact and expect rumour to chase rumour.

The Internet and public relations crisis management

Since the days of the Tylenol crisis referred to earlier in this chapter, the media environment has changed dramatically. The once limited media market has become global and highly sophisticated. The impact the Internet has on crisis management today is enormous. The speed with which communications can be delivered is phenomenal and available to so many people – from home computers, via Internet cafés, through to corporate communications infrastructure. If something happens, someone somewhere will be giving their own, often live, version of events. From individuals, through online communities, adversarial organisations and NGOs, the Internet is very effective in putting a message out. It is impossible to censor the Internet – which is both its strength and its weakness – but it is a highly effective vehicle for the dissemination of information and opinion that may masquerade as information.

Seymour and Edelman (2004) describe the new challenges posed by the Internet:

> But when considering how to turn around a crisis today, management teams must accept that the media represent only part of an array of communication channels – albeit one of the most noisy and demanding. In a world dominated by low trust and the corrosive effects of cynicism, corporate voices can quickly be ignored, distorted or drowned out by the incessant noise that characterizes each and every crisis situation . . . Over the last ten years, crisis management and communications have been forced to develop in response to a series of technology and IT-driven changes. . . . At the same time single-issue groups and NGOs were recognizing the potential of the internet. Now it is possible for a small group to drive campaigns across the internet, while at the same time empowering individuals to express their opinions at the click of a mouse.

(See Box 19.3.)

The totally unregulated nature of the Internet thus gives organisations huge cause for concern. The Internet has become the new rumour mill where people can say anything they want or create websites that criticise specific organisations, companies and specific industries (see, for example, www.untied.com, which is dedicated to problems with United Airlines, or www.mercedes-benz-usa.com/, a site whose agenda is obvious!). On a basic level, we see viruses crippling so many of our computer systems, from worms to Trojans, and the average user gets increasingly concerned about losing control of their own com-

Box 19.3

Speed of the Internet in a crisis

The speed of spread of information and news in the new communication era is well illustrated by the Paddington/Ladbroke Grove accident in London on 5 October 1999.

At 08.06, Michael Hodder, the Thames Train driver, pulled out of the platform at Paddington Station.

At 08.11, having gone through three warning and stop signals, the Thames Train ploughed into the front of inbound GNER express train.

It took until 08.32 for the operational staff at Reading to establish from the controlling signal box at Slough that a serious accident had taken place involving one of their trains, that a serious fire had broken out (most unusual in train crash incidents) and that there were probably many injuries and even fatalities.

But if anyone had been on the Internet at 08.21 they would have been able to read 'breaking news' reports of a rail accident at Ladbroke Grove involving deaths, serious injuries and a severe fire.

puter. As technologies advance, so these viruses and the impact they have on our day-to-day lives become more apparent – they are, at best, an annoyance.

At a corporate level, there are a host of both technical and security issues that affect the operation and effectiveness of an organisation. Consider website tampering – where individuals can gain access to a company's website – a malicious individual or organisation can enter their views, enforce some new policies or give spurious comments, interfere with email and raise all manner of hoaxes. This costs a considerable amount of time and money and can become unmanageable. In September 2004, UK telephone company NTL had its systems sabotaged when a hacker changed the outgoing message on its customer service phone number to tell callers that NTL did not care about their problem and they should just get a life! One need only think back to the resources deployed for preparations for the 2000 new year (Y2K, the new millennium, when there was a fear that all computer systems would crash) to see how many companies chose to spend large sums of money on IT, rather than take any chances. The Gartner Group estimates that global spending on Y2K totalled $600 billion.

Direct face-to-face communication generally, and particularly during a time of crisis, is therefore a positive advantage – whether that be two individuals face to face in a TV interview or the CEO of a 'mega corp' (major multinational organisation) addressing their staff directly at a meeting.

How to prepare for a crisis

Crises do come as a surprise and at unexpected times, but any organisation – commercial or public sector – can prepare itself for the inevitable and every company should. Methods such as research in the form of crisis audits, preparing a crisis manual and conducting crisis simulations or training will ensure that organisations are better equipped to handle any crisis. (See Box 19.4.)

Crisis audit

The first step in preparation is to conduct an audit that assesses the current vulnerabilities and strengths of the company or organisation. The audit will research key areas, such as operations, marketing, employee relations, safety experts, environmental experts, government, legal and communications people. It will ask tough questions to determine the most likely scenario that could happen, assess how well prepared the company is to deal with it and whether it has all the necessary resources.

Box 19.4

Actions to prepare for a crisis

- Conduct a crisis audit.
- Prepare a crisis manual.
- Conduct regular crisis simulation training.

Activity 19.5

Doing a crisis audit

If you were conducting a crisis audit for your place of study or work, what would you need to know? Make a list of the key areas where something might go wrong. How could you find out whether your organisation has a crisis plan? What would you expect it to contain?

Feedback

The audit often shows companies a need for change. It might be an operational change, a change in how a product is labelled or how the company is marketed, or a change in what research is openly discussed with the regulator.

An educational organisation, for example, would have to consider potential problems originating from staff or students, such as scandals, court cases, exam results, protests. Some colleges and universities have also had crises due to outbreaks of meningitis, for example, which have led to clearer guidance to new students about symptoms and proper actions to take.

The audit results can then be used to identify the key trouble spots, identify which stakeholders would be affected and help management build scenarios to train a key crisis team with the techniques of effective crisis management. In addition to being able to train a crisis team, the assessment can help build a comprehensive system for managing crisis communications. (See Activity 19.5.)

Crisis manual

Another means of preparation is a crisis manual. A good crisis manual contains a simple system of rapid communications, basic messages and audience identification and should not be more than 10 pages long. Anything longer will not be used in a crisis. A well-prepared crisis manual can serve as a guide for many of the basic tasks, such as activating the crisis team and facilities, and allows more time for the crisis team to focus on the more critical issues (see Figure 19.2).

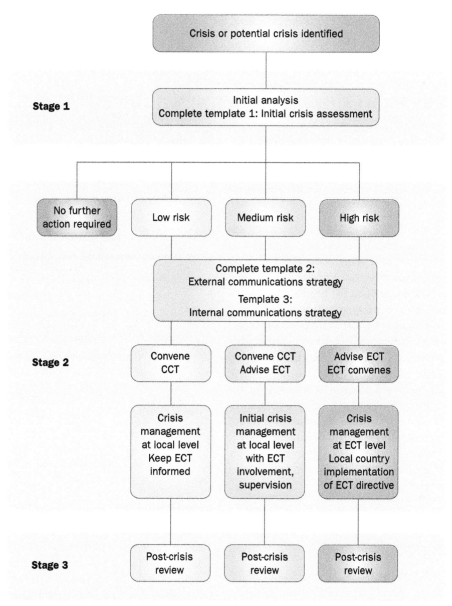

Key: ECT – External Communications Team; CCT – Crisis Communications Team

Figure 19.2 Crisis communications action plan

Crisis simulation and training

The final step in crisis planning is to conduct simulation training. Crisis simulation training is designed to create a real atmosphere of crisis. It integrates group and individual exercises, tests the skills of the spokesperson or spokespeople, tests the crisis plan and finally examines and evaluates the communications tools to find weak spots. Such exercises range from desktop exercises to full-blown global tests of the team. Repetition of crisis simulation and exercises are crucial to ensure that any weaknesses are addressed.

A useful method that can also help prepare a company is to incorporate debriefing sessions into the communications plan to make sure the team understands the emerging issues, what they are doing in terms of community relations and how they are working with the newest techniques in crisis management. They should also be aware of the importance of community and employee relations.

Today in the UK, just over one-quarter of companies (27%) research possible vulnerabilities but only 16% conduct regular crisis preparedness workshops (Webserve Solutions Ltd, www.webservesolutions.net). Those companies who have not prepared or trained will be rehearsing their crisis strategy in the middle of their first major crisis!

Ambassador L. Paul Bremer, former Chairman of the US National Terrorism Commission before he was assigned to his mission in Iraq, stated in an article in the *Harvard Business Review* April 2002:

> Before 9/11, a poll of CEOs in the US showed that 85% expected to manage a crisis during their time in office but only 50% admitted to having a plan. However 97% were confident that they could handle a crisis. This sounds to me like over-confidence. I hope that more businesses are taking a hard look at their plans.

There is no doubt that physical and IT aspects of plans – contingency plans, business continuity, security and business interruption – have come under closer scrutiny since the **9/11** tragedy. However, the main focus has been on operational factors and often the key aspects of communication readiness and planning have been neglected.

One of the hallmarks of a well-managed crisis is knowledge. A company is better prepared when it knows what its stakeholders think about the product, the brand and the corporation. Both Mattessons Walls (see the Peperami case, Case study 19.2) and Johnson & Johnson (in the Tylenol crisis covered earlier in the chapter) commissioned research throughout their situation to find out precisely what their key audiences were thinking. There is often a tendency to judge what the audience thinks on the basis of media headlines, which can lead to overreaction and mismanagement of a crisis.

Key principles in crisis management

To draw this chapter together and support students in understanding how to manage crisis PR situations, the following 10 key principles have been identified. These are based on the experience of leading crisis consultants (counsellors) over three decades and influenced by the analysis of crises in a range of international settings, with various commercial and non-commercial situations. These principles are summarised in Box 19.5 and described in further detail below.

Crisis management principles

Define the real problem

This is the most critical aspect of effective PR crisis management. Define both the short-term problem – address

---

Box 19.5

Ten key principles in public relations crisis management

1. Define the real problem.
2. Centralise or at least control information flow.
3. Isolate a crisis team from daily business concerns.
4. Assume a worst-case planning position.
5. Do not fully depend on one individual.
6. Always resist the combative instinct.
7. Understand why the media are there.
8. Remember all constituents (stakeholders).
9. Contain the problem.
10. Recognise the value of short-term sacrifice.

---

the situation right now – and the long-term problem to ensure the brand/corporation recovers in terms of both market share and reputation.

Centralise or at least control information flow

This applies to items of information both coming in and going out. If there is a multi-country issue, have one 'central place' as the focus. This, in very practical terms, will make communication within the organisation easier. If it is not feasible to have one centre, then all spokespeople must be rigorously trained so as to communicate the same message. Be aware of language sensitivities and terms of reference that may not translate readily from one language to another.

Isolate a crisis team from daily business concerns

Crises, as we have seen, are by their very nature all enveloping. While managing a crisis, the day job has to be put on hold. In the case of Tylenol, Jim Burke, Johnson & Johnson CEO, insisted he became the brand manager for Tylenol. He was able to delegate his many leadership tasks and this enabled him to focus on doing the right thing for Johnson & Johnson while relieving him of his day-to-day responsibilities.

Mini Case Study 19.2
Coca-Cola Belgium

Coca-cola representatives in 1999 acknowledged that the crisis described below was bigger than any worst-case scenario they could have imagined. They also publicly admitted that perhaps they had lost control.

Philippe L'Enfant, a senior executive with Coca-Cola Enterprises in 1999, in an interview on Belgian television said: 'Perhaps [we] lost control of the situation to a certain extent.'

The population of Belgium was still reeling from fears about mad cow disease and the presence of the carcinogen dioxin in animal feed when reports of schoolchildren being hospitalised after drinking Coca-Cola surfaced. More cases from other parts of Europe were found and Coca-Cola products were banned in several countries. While the public speculated as to the cause, ranging from rat poison to extortion, the company delayed full apologies and tried to deny the problem and its responsibility.

Coca-Cola sources speculated that the problem could be due to contaminated CO_2 and creosote-tinged pallets and were quoted as saying: 'It may make you feel sick, but it is not harmful.' Meanwhile, Coca-Cola was losing an estimated $3.4 million in revenue each day and 19% of consumers had 'reservations' about drinking Coke.

Coca-Cola most definitely had a crisis management strategy but it still found itself losing control.

Box 19.6
Key learning points from the Coca-Cola case

- Facts do not always rule – emotions, speculations/ rumours are strong complicating factors.

- Think 'outside in' – plan messages and actions based on stakeholders' perspectives. Here, Coca-Cola was caught out by a combination of extremely sensitive regulatory authorities and parents keen to protect their children.

- The CEO must be visible.

- Do not let other stakeholders shape your reputation.

- Call on your allies (these could be other producers or suppliers of materials or packaging).

- Message alignment and internal communications are key (to maintain consistency in messages circulating inside and outside the organisation).

- Regret, resolution and reform (demonstrate regret, find a resolution to the problem and how to reform what the company is doing).

- Be better prepared – think 'worst case', not just precedent.

Assume a worst-case planning position

Ensure the crisis team thinks about the worst-case scenario in terms of what could happen to the brand and to the organisation. More often than not, people estimate the worst from their own perspective, or what they are able to handle, rather than a true worst case. It is, therefore, important to brainstorm and get as much input from others as possible. (See Mini case study 19.2 and Box 19.6.)

Do not fully depend on one individual

The person managing the crisis must depend on the whole team for information, but never rely on information from just one individual. Some team members may have a vested interest in a particular area and want to protect their own or their department's reputation. It is important that the messages put out during a crisis are not subverted by the influence of one department over another. These subtleties can be worked out at a later date. There is usually more than one department's internal reputation on the line when a crisis hits.

Always resist the combative instinct

Do not go into battle with the media, NGOs, competitors or suppliers. An organisation must demonstrate it is in control during the crisis. The outcome of being combative could well destroy the brand or reputation. Words said in anger, or defence, may be temporarily satisfying, but they may not represent the best position for the crisis PR manager or the organisation. When Ronald Li, Chairman of the Hong Kong Stock Exchange suspended trading in 1987 in an attempt to defuse a run on the exchange, the crisis was made worse when he lost his cool with a journalist at the subsequent press conference. The journalist suggested that closing the exchange was outside Mr Li's legal powers. Mr Li responded by demanding his name and threatening to sue him. He actually ended up in prison himself (for unrelated charges of insider trading).

During the 2001 general election campaign in the UK, the Deputy Prime Minister John Prescott found out only too well the impact of a violent reaction from someone in the public eye. When a heckler threw an egg at Mr Prescott, it was not particularly newsworthy. But when Mr Prescott replied with a left-hook punch, it was in all the papers for days.

Understand why the media are there

The media are searching for a good story. They need focus, a 'cause and effect' – something that their audience will relate to. A firm can assert the facts as it sees them and thus defuse an 'on-the-face-of-it' story.

Remember all constituents (stakeholders)

It is not just the media that need fast and relevant responses during a crisis. The crisis plan has to take all the stakeholders into consideration. (See Activity 19.6.)

Contain the problem

Reduce the problem to as small a geographical area as possible to prevent it becoming a bigger problem – from local to national or national to international. In these days of the international media and the Internet, localising an issue is a major challenge. However, it should be an objective. For example, in the Peperami case (Case study 19.2), the affected batch was only being sold in the UK. Efforts to focus the problem led to the subsequent recall being limited to just the UK despite the product being widely available throughout Europe.

Recognise the value of short-term sacrifice

This might involve recalling the product or dismissing the person responsible for causing the problem.

The value of short-term sacrifice can be well illustrated by Case study 19.2 on Peperami (see also Case study 19.3).

Case Study 19.2
Peperami

In 1987 the UK Department of Health linked Peperami to an outbreak of salmonella poisoning, a notifiable illness in the UK. The decision was taken to recall affected products, but due to the packaging used for the product, the affected batch could not be precisely identified by consumers from the bar code. The recall was therefore extended to the whole of the UK.

Peperami dominated the salami-style meat snacks market, with 80% of market share and widespread product distribution across 40,000 outlets. Peperami could be found in a huge range of retail outlets, including supermarkets, corner stores, clubs and pubs.

Strategy

Peperami is just one of many meat products produced by Mattessons Walls and a key early priority was to limit the impact of the salmonella problem to the Peperami brand. Mattessons Walls was positioned as an importer and not a manufacturer, distancing Peperami from the parent company to stop a product problem becoming a major corporate problem. Meanwhile, it was crucial to share the facts in the case and communicate fully to all stakeholders.

Actions

A media control centre was set up, manned by experienced media relations people 24 hours a day, 7 days a week. A consumer telephone centre was also established with telephone operators given daily updates/briefings. Tracking research was initiated to determine exactly how consumers thought the crisis was being handled and analyse their perceptions of the Peperami brand, giving the management team crucial information on the impact it was having beyond the media reactions.

Employee statements were prepared for all Mattessons Walls employees and regular updates were given to Unilever, Mattesons Walls' parent company, to keep it up to date with developments.

During the recall and the time the product was off the market, each media relations executive worked with an individual health editor from each national newspaper and a member of the team was appointed to liaise with the Department of Health.

Result

Mattessons Walls received public commendation from the Department of Health for the way it had handled the situation, and research showed that more than 90% of consumers were impressed with the way the withdrawal was handled. Within three months of relaunch, Peperami's share of the salami snack foods market stood at 94%, a 14% increase, despite the introduction of a competitive product from a national supermarket's (Sainsbury) own label. (See Activity 19.7.)

Case Study 19.3
Melbourne Gas crisis

Finally, let us take a look at a crisis that puts all these key principles into perspective: the Melbourne Gas crisis that threw the entire state of Victoria, Australia, into chaos for a fortnight, but is remembered for being one of the best managed crises in Australian history.

Event

A major explosion at the Exxon refinery at Longford, Melbourne, on Friday 25 September 1998 destroyed part of the plant, killing two and injuring eight refinery workers and cutting gas supplies to factories, businesses and private homes across the state.

Effects

The state of Victoria was highly dependent on cheap gas and its population of more than 3 million was almost totally dependent on this one plant. Ninety-eight per cent of Victoria's gas customers would have no gas supply for the foreseeable future. Manufacturing industries stood down 150,000 employees and the estimated cost to industry was $A100 million a day. VENCorp, the distributor of gas for Victoria, invoked emergency powers to restrict gas use, and media reporting highlighted that millions of people faced the prospect of cold showers.

case study 19.3 (continued)

Strategy

Gas would only be available to emergency services and both VENCorp and the state government stressed in all communications that jobs were the first priority, not hot showers!

When the gas supply was ready to be restored, it constituted the biggest single gas relight programme in the world and both consumers and the system needed to be prepared to be protected from relighting accidents. The crisis team made editorial content and a multi-language brochure the focus of a safe relight communications programme. Operationally, when the supply was ready to be reintroduced, the odd/even house numbers would be used to phase gas supply in safely and particularly to protect the gas network.

Actions

Four thousand emergency service volunteers were used to turn off gas meters, and call centres were established which, at the crisis peak, received 131,561 calls a day. There was in-house coordination and development of call centre scripts and the top 10 frequently asked questions from the call centres were advertised daily in major media.

To ensure seamless communication, the communications team sat on the government gas supply emergency coordination committee and critical services working group, established a 24-hour media response centre manned by a team of 15 people and arranged twice-daily media briefings at 10am and 3pm. Key spokespersons were given media training.

A responsive and pre-emptive issues management programme was developed and as a key element of a safe relight programme, 2.3 million brochures were sent to all households and small businesses alongside a major print and television ad campaign.

Communicating with the ethnic communities was identified early as a challenge in Victoria; the brochure was translated into 20 languages and distributed, and an information line was set up offering interpreter services in 100 languages.

Assessment

When the gas supply was restored there were only 9 relight accidents and 12,000 appliance repairs. Alan Stockdale, Treasurer of Victoria, said at a government press briefing on Friday 9 October 1998:

> *I think every Victorian can take pride in the fact that our community has responded so well, and that the reconnection program, on the massive scale, is taking place in such a safe and orderly manner.*

> *We estimate that 1.1 million domestic customers, out of a total of 1.35 million, have been reconnected to the gas supply now.*

> *Eighty-five percent of domestic customers have been able to reconnect without assistance, indicating that the wide-ranging safety program has been very successful.*

> *I consider this to be the best-handled issue that I have seen since I have been interested in public affairs issues in this state.*

> *I have been told by many, including my wife, that this [holding up the brochure] was the first document of the kind that they have read and clearly understood what they needed to do and what they shouldn't do.*

> *This incident has been managed as well as it could have possibly been done – there is no higher praise than that.*

David Guthrie-Jones, Manager Communications VENCorp, said at an Australian Gas Association meeting on 16 November 1998:

> *So we called in communications experts, who sent an excellent team of experience and enthusiasm to help with our crisis communication strategy and implementation.*

> *I can tell you this. Having back-up communication or public relations consultants experienced in crisis management is absolutely crucial to the success of handling large scale emergencies . . . this is what helped make the difference between success and failure for us at the end of the day.*

Case Study 19.4

TeGenero

Event

Clinical trial of TGN1412 (intended for treatment of multiple sclerois, leukaemia and rheumatoid arthritis). Trial was conducted by research company Parexel on six volunteers in premises leased from Northwick Park Hospital. The clinical trial began on 13 March 2006 and all trial volunteers (excluding two who were given placebo) experienced inflammatory reactions within 90 minutes of receiving the antibody. Within 12 to 16 hours the participants were critically ill.

The TGN1412 crisis is a clear example that major crises can come out of nowhere and affect the smallest of companies. At the time of the crisis TeGenero employed just 15 people. The company had a portfolio of products in development but TGN1412 was by far the most advanced. In the development of TGN1412 the company had complied with the extensive regulatory requirements in order to proceed to a phase 1 clinical trial. This included responding to detailed questions to establish the appropriateness of the species of animal used in safety tests. The side effects were completely unexpected, there having been no evidence of risk in pre-clinical tests.

The events were immediately a lead media story mixing elements of tragedy, human interest and horror. The exposure was heightened following a powerful early interview with a girlfriend of one of the participants (who happened to be a BBC employee).

Stakeholders

All crises, by their very nature, involve a range of stakeholders. The clinical trial crisis included the added complexity of six separate parties linked to the condition of the volunteers: the hospital doctors treating them; Parexel who conducted the trial; TeGenero who developed the antibody; Medicines and Healthcare products Regulatory Agency (MHRA) who approved the trial; the local ethics committee who also approved the trial; and a German company who manufactured the antibody. There is always confusion in the early stages of a crisis; this complexity added to that.

In addition to these parties a great number of further stakeholders became involved including the family members of the volunteers, lawyers representing the volunteers, the management of the hospital, the pharmaceutical and biotechnology industry associations

and a range of politicians with various motivations (see range of issues below).

The waters were further muddied by the complexity of the information behind the trial. TGN1412 was an agonist monoclonal antibody, one of a relatively 'new breed' of treatments, and the effects on the volunteers appeared to be due to cytokine release syndrome – the immune system going into overdrive – but the facts were not clear and neither was it easy to establish these facts due to the condition of the volunteers. Many media questions sought information on the development of TGN1412, much of which was highly complex and indeed some of which was confidential.

Speculation and application of 'common sense'

Led by a selection of bio-technology experts speculation developed quickly as to what could have caused the side effects, and how they might have been predicted or even prevented (several investigations have concluded that, without the benefit of hindsight and following standard procedures, it is reasonable that the side effects were not predicted).

Alongside expert commentary were many analyses drawing on that most uncommon of things, common sense ('you should surely give doses one at a time?' – not the common practice; 'shouldn't it have been given to patients rather than healthy volunteers?' – again, not common practice for a treatment with such a pre-clinical profile). In this case the common sense was mixed with the benefit of hindsight.

Initial statements about how this was the first time such events had happened in a clinical trial for a very long time quickly developed into notions that the system was clearly deficient. The implication was that the 99.9% of trials which were safe were safe by chance, while this one trial was the real marker of the integrity of the approval system.

Range of issues and conflicting views on them

A wide range of issues were involved in the crisis:

- Animal testing – the events in the trial were used both as an example of why animal testing is flawed and as an example of why animal testing is essential

- Ethics of human trials – should volunteers be paid for their time? How would they be recruited otherwise?

case study 19.4 (continued)

- Would volunteers continue to come forward? (including a very personal interview with Margaret Hodge MP about how important such trials are)
- Are government institutions such as the MHRA 'up to the job' when facing powerful private companies? One journalist adapted the well-known phrase to say 'those that can do, those that can't regulate'. (When this question was asked it was overlooked that TeGenero could not be seen as an example of 'big pharma')
- The basic human interest in why these people had become involved in trials (student debt etc.) and whether they would recover.

It was quickly apparent that the implications of the events would bring implications for similar treatments in development (which would receive closer and costlier scrutiny) but also for clinical trials generally.

Actions

The immediate priority for the chief scientific officer of TeGenero was to work with the doctors treating the trial volunteers. However, he was also the main source of information to respond to media and other stakeholder questions. Such a small staff was immediately immensely stretched by the magnitude of the events and of the coverage.

A call centre was established to receive and process the large volume of calls.

An early decision was to communicate independently, rather than remain part of the Parexel response. It was important for TeGenero to present a face as quickly as possible to answer questions but also to show how truly devastated the company was, and how stunned by the events. Despite having received no previous media training the chief scientific officer conducted a press conference alone on the afternoon of the first day of media attention. Many people have been surprised to learn of the scientific officer's inexperience at handling the media having seen the press conference. Furthermore, at the time it was also unknown whether the events had been caused by incorrect conduct of the trial, by an error in the production of the drug being tested, or by TGN1412 itself.

Rebutting rumour was a major activity alongside providing information as it became available. On the first day it was widely reported that a dog had died in testing. TGN1412 had never been tested on dogs and in fact no animals had died as a result of being given TGN1412. Although the source of the rumour was never confirmed, some time later it was suggested that it traced back to a joke made by one of the volunteers to his girlfriend when discussing his participation in the trial. She had asked 'is it safe', to which he joked that only a dog had died.

Arguably a particularly interesting element of this crisis is the difference between the approaches of the two companies primarily involved. While TeGenero communicated quickly and openly (within limited resources), Parexel chose to offer only limited comment by written statements. In the short term this difference led to the main association being with TeGenero rather than Parexel. However, over time and particularly following TeGenero's insolvency, Parexel's refusal to communicate openly has left them in an exposed position with no history of engagement.

Some have argued that clinical research organisations do not need to pay close attention to their public profile but as the industry develops this may change, particularly as the ethics relating to recruitment come under future scrutiny.

Summary

There is no guaranteed recipe for successful crisis management but there are key ingredients: knowledge, preparation, calmness, control and communication will see an organisation secure the best possible outcome from a crisis. They may even help to find the opportunity that can come from a crisis (the characters that represent 'crisis management' in both Chinese and Japanese actually mean 'danger' and 'opportunity'). Preparing for the unexpected but inevitable ensures that any organisation can take the drama out of a crisis.

Bibliography

Baker, G.F. (2000). 'Race and reputation: Restoring image beyond the crisis' in *Handbook of Public Relations*. R.L. Heath (ed.). London: Sage.

Barton, L. (1993). *Crisis in Organisations: Managing communications in the heart of chaos*. Cincinati, OH: South Western.

Baskin, O. and C. Aronoff (1997). *Public Relations: The profession and the practice*. London: Brown & Benchmark.

Black, S. (1989). *Introduction to Public Relations*. London: Modino Press.

Bland, M. (1998). *Communicating Out of a Crisis*. London: Macmillan.

Bremer, P.L. (2002). 'Doing business in a dangerous world'. *Harvard Business Review* **80**(4), April: 22.

Cornelissen, J. (2008). *Corporate Communications: A guide to theory and practice*, 2nd edition. London: Sage.

Daniels, T., B. Spiker and M. Papa (1997). *Perspectives on Organizational Communication*, 4th edition. London: Brown & Benchmark.

Fearn-Banks, K. (2000). 'Crisis communication: A review of some best practices' in *Handbook of Public Relations*. R.L. Heath (ed.). London: Sage.

Fearn-Banks, K. (2006). *Crisis Communications: A casebook approach,* 3rd edition. Mahwah, NJ: Lawrence Erlbaum Associates.

Fearn-Banks, K. (2008). *Crisis Communication Student Workbook*, 3rd edition. London: Routledge.

Food Standards Agency (2005). www.food.gov.uk/news/newsarchive/2005, accessed 26 September 2008.

Harrison, S. (2000). *Public Relations – An Introduction,* 2nd edition. London: Thompson Business Press.

Hearit, K.M. (2000). 'Corporate apologia: When an organization speaks in defense of itself' in *Handbook of Public Relations*. R.L. Heath (ed.). London: Sage.

Heath, R.L. (1997). *Strategic Issues Management: Organizations and public policy challenges*. Thousand Oaks, CA: Sage.

Heath, R. L. (2004). *Handbook of Public Relations*. London, Sage.

Howard, C. and W. Matthews (1985). *On Deadline: Managing media relations*. Prospect Height, IL: Waveland Press.

Laune, J. (1990). 'Corporate issues management: An international view'. *Public Relations Review* **XVI**(1), Spring.

Laville, L. (2008). 'A crisis case study: The London Bombings 2005', unpublished. Leeds Metropolitan University

Lerbinger, O. (1997). *The Crisis Manager: Facing risks and responsibility*. Mahwah, NJ: Lawrence Erlbaum Associates.

Olaniran, B.A. and D.E. Williams (2000). 'Anticipatory model of crisis management: A vigilant response to technological crises' in *Handbook of Public Relations*. R.L. Heath (ed.). London: Sage.

O'Rourke, R. and B. Marsteller (1998). 'Managing in times of crisis'. *Corporate Reputation Review* **2**(1).

Regester, M. and J. Larkin (1997). *Risk Issues and Crisis Management*. London: Kogan Page.

Regester, M. and J. Larkin (2008). *Risk Issues and Crisis Management in Public Relations*. London: Kogan Page.

Reynolds, C. (1997). 'Issues management and the Australian gun debate'. *Public Relations Review* **23**(4), Winter.

Seitel, F. (2006). *The Practice of Public Relations*, 10th edition. London: Prentice Hall.

Seymour, M. and D.J. Edelman (2004). 'Fighting on all fronts'. *CEO Magazine* September.

Seymour, M. and S. Moore (2000). *Effective Crisis Management: Worldwide principles and practice*. London: Cassell.

Thill, J. and C. Bovee (1996). *Business Communication Today,* 4th edition. New York: McGraw-Hill.

Young, D. (1996). *Building Your Company's Good Name: How to create and protect the reputation your organization deserves*. New York: Amacon.

Zyglidopoulos, S. (1999). 'Responding to reputational crisis: A stakeholder perspective'. *Corporate Reputation Review* **2**(4).

Websites

Food Standards Agency: www.food.gov.uk
The *Daily Telegraph*: www.dailytelegraph.co.uk
The *Guardian*: www.guardianunlimited.co.uk

CHAPTER 17

Public Affairs

Public affairs

Learning outcomes

By the end of this chapter you should be able to:

- define public affairs and recognise it in practice
- understand the societal context in which it is done
- describe its key operating principles and methods
- judge the ethical consequences of public affairs.

Structure

- Scope of public affairs
- Public affairs defined
- Contexts of public affairs
- Public affairs: knowledge, skills and behaviour needed
- Ethics and public affairs

Introduction

Public affairs (PA) is a crucial and demanding specialism inside the broader field of public relations (PR). It can claim this status because it involves influencing governments and therefore affects the quality of a country's democracy. In liberal democracies which are market-oriented and capitalist, external PR for an organisation or group can be divided into two parts: dealing with markets; dealing with government, businesses, interest and pressure groups. Marketing PR communicates with the purchasers of goods and services, whether they are individual consumers or other businesses. Public affairs communicates with government and other external stakeholders affecting a company or an organisation on matters of public policy.

Public affairs is not just the preserve of big businesses talking to government about the very big issues of public policy, such as signing up to the proposed constitution of the European Union (EU) or joining the euro. It can be businesses talking among themselves trying to form a common front before they meet their national government or the European Commission about, say, food labelling. Consumer-facing companies also do PA, with The Body Shop being a long-established example through its campaigns to stop testing cosmetics on animals. Public affairs is not confined to commercial organisations; public sector bodies and charities need public affairs as well. For example, UK universities brief members of parliament and talk to the media about varying tuition fees for students, and Oxfam campaigns for better national coordination of emergency aid.

Interest and cause groups are also very active in PA. For example: the British Medical Association tells the media about its negotiations with the National Health Service over junior hospital doctors' hours of work; 60 Greenpeace campaigners demonstrate outside the headquarters of the UK supermarket Sainsbury's dressed as pantomime cows in protest against genetically modified feed allegedly given to milk cows; the Vatican lobbies the European Constitutional Convention to insert a clause about Christian heritage in the proposed EU constitution; the European Referendum Campaign organises support in over 30 countries for national votes on that constitution.

Finally, interests and causes rise and fall in the political agenda all the time. For example, concerns about workers' rights have increased since the death of Chinese cocklepickers in the north of England in 2004. Employers bringing in legal immigrants formed the Association of Labour Providers to lobby MPs and ministers and to talk to the media, in order to stop human rights abuses. The fashion house Gap monitored how clothes manufacturers treat their workers with a view to pressurising governments to set minimum standards.

Scope of public affairs

Public affairs (PA) can be conceptualised as the 'voice' that lets organisations and groups (big and small, commercial and non-profit, public and private, religious and secular, conservative and radical, permanent and temporary, national and local) in a country or in a larger political union talk to each other and to government – publicly and privately – about public policy at international, transnational, national, regional and local levels. (For a detailed explanation of how political organisations work, see Chapter 5.)

Public and private 'voices' are both used in PA practice. The first speaks through media relations mainly but also through corporate brochures, websites, conferences, event management, protests and demonstrations, while the latter is heard by senior officials, ministers, members of parliament (MPs), members of the European Parliament (MEPs), local councillors and officials in their offices when they make policy. The more powerful the organisation or group doing PA, the more likely it will use the private, office-based 'voice' of lobbying (see Mini case study 22.1).

The opposite is true with less powerful, 'outsider' organisations and groups.

For example, transnational companies such as Airbus Industries has guaranteed access to ministers and officials throughout the EU. It has 16 development and manufacturing sites in France, Germany, Spain and the UK and has sold 5,000 airplanes worldwide. Radical groups such as Reclaim the Streets and Stop the War in Iraq, however, are oppositional to capitalism and to core government policies and so are limited to doing their PA through protests, demonstrations and media relations. They are not invited to the prime minister's office or to the European Commission in Brussels. They are, both physically and metaphorically, 'outsider groups'.

While PA is a specialised part of PR, it is still closely connected with other parts of the PR discipline, It can be seen, for example, as the operations side of issues management (see Chapter 18). Opportunities and threats facing organisations or groups need first to be identified before there can be a PA response. For example, the Confederation of British Industry (CBI) needed to 'boundary scan' proposals by the United Nations (UN) to make multinational companies responsible for labour and human rights

Mini Case Study 22.1
Lobbying for a fairer tax

Lunn Poly (now Thomson), a large UK travel agency, along with the Association of British Travel Agents (ABTA) lobbied government to ensure that consumers paid the same rate of tax on travel insurance, whether it was bought from a bank/financial services company or a small family-owned travel agent. There was a hefty 50% difference in the tax rate, depending on where it was bought. These two lobbying partners wanted the support of the whole travel trade and so they linked up with the leading travel trade magazine, which published a feature on the advantages of the policy change for small agents. A fair tax helpline distributed information packs to these small businesses and encouraged them to write to their MPs, who then asked questions in the UK's House of Commons. A petition was organised and articles appeared in the national press and there were meetings with the Treasury. The lobbying goal of a single rate tax was achieved a year later and refunds for past overpayments were given to travel agencies.

abuse by their overseas customers, suppliers and host governments before it could lobby the UK government to block any such resolutions. Community relations (see Chapters 6 and 17) is another close cousin of PA. British Nuclear Fuels (BNFL) illustrates this through its engagement in active dialogue with its critics and the communities around its plants in north-west England. (See Activity 22.1 and Think about 22.1.)

Activity 22.1

Helping organisations to prosper

Look around your community and identify one business, one charity and one pressure group that you support. What public policies would help them prosper more? What should your government do to help them more? List three ways you could work with others to help.

Think about 22.1

Lobbying for change

Have you been a lobbyist without realising it? Have you been a member of a school or college student union (or council) and asked your teachers for rule changes? For extra computers? For more books?

Public affairs defined

If *public affairs* is a widely practised and challenging specialism inside PR, how is it defined? A good starting point – one that clarifies by separating things out – is to see it as the relations of organisations and groups not with markets but with government. White and Mazur (1995: 200) take this non-marketing focus and say that: 'Within public relations, public affairs is a specialised practice that focuses on relationships which will have a bearing on the development of public policy.'

It is very hard to find a definition of public affairs that does *not* centre on public policy. It is important to remember this when considering a variety of titles under which public affairs is conducted. Besides 'public affairs' departments, you will find 'corporate affairs', 'corporate communications', 'government relations' – all doing what we have defined as public affairs.

The focus on public policy extends, of course, to policy made by local councils, regional tiers of government, national governments and the EU. For example, businesses and environmentalists want to influence the route of high-speed railways through their villages and countryside, towns and cities, regions and national territories.

This chapter says throughout that public affairs is done by organisations and groups. Organisations include commercial businesses, state services such as hospitals, police, schools, and established voluntary bodies such churches, charities and trade unions. They have bureaucratic features – hierarchy, structure, managerialism, instrumental reasoning and legal foundations. Groups, contrariwise, are entities representing the interests and causes in society and have non-bureaucratic features – collegial decision making, where power is shared equally, unclear lines of command and control, open membership, uncertain legal status and a values orientation. However, it is best to see organisations and groups as two ends of a continuum, with established businesses at one end (e.g. Ford Motors, Mercedes-Benz) and groups of protestors (e.g. against more airport runways, against nuclear power) at the other, and with shades of fixity and fluidity in between. (See Think about 22.2.)

This organisation/group distinction largely matches an important characteristic noted by Grant (2000) – between 'insiders' and 'outsiders'. The former are those that

Think about 22.2

Public affairs

Can you think of three people from among family, friends or colleagues who have said: 'I don't like that new law'; 'they shouldn't make people do that'; or 'that's wrong and I want to change it'? What did they do about it? If they did nothing, why not? Do you agree with their judgements and actions?

Box 22.1

Public affairs for all – an accessible specialism

The skills needed to do public affairs can be learnt by residents' groups who are unhappy with student parking and partying near their homes and who want to protest to the university and the local council.

The same skills can be hired in by a large insurance company unhappy with a UK parliamentary select committee condemning the sale of endowment mortgages and wanting to deflect criticism. We can talk about citizens' PA and corporate PA.

government recognises as bodies to consult about policy and who want to be called on; the latter are those outside the government's network of advice seeking and who are happy or not happy to be excluded. An 'insider' example in the UK is the National Farmers' Union; an 'outsider' example is the fuel tax protest by Farmers' Action. Organisations tend to be on the inside and groups on the outside.

There is a cooperative aspect to the public affairs of many organisations and groups: they network to maximise support for their policy and they join industry- or activity-wide representative bodies that can speak with one 'voice' (e.g. the Confederation of British Industry (CBI) and the Trades Union Congress (TUC) in the UK). The Food and Drink Federation is the UK 'voice' for that industry and the British Dental Association speaks for dental practices around the UK. Cancer Research UK liaises with the Sunbed Association to promote good tanning practice in salons. Protestor groups use mobile phones to coordinate demonstrators.

All of this can be summarised as follows: public affairs is the PR specialism that seeks to influence public policy for the advantage of those doing it and it is undertaken by a wide range of businesses and public sector bodies as well as interest, pressure and cause groups. It is done by established bodies that work within the existing policy set-up and by those who seek to reform it. It is done by national and transnational bodies and by small groups of people making a local protest. Public affairs can work for the powerful and for citizens. (See Box 22.1.)

Contexts of public affairs

Pluralism

In what sort of environment is public affairs done? The answer is that public affairs is stimulated by the increased **pluralism** (publicly expressed differences of values, inter-

ests and behaviours) of the UK and much of Europe. This pluralism takes two forms and both involve an increased need for public affairs.

For example, since the 1960s, the UK has witnessed great, observable changes in personal behaviour by its citizens and in collective behaviour by voluntary groups. These changes derive principally from altered values regarding sex, lifestyle, the environment, race, consumption and religion. They, in turn, generate social pressure for acceptance and tolerance of individuals practising them. This pressure frequently leads to collective, group action by like-minded individuals to promote and defend their choices. Increased pluralism of values and groups has been associated with social movements such as feminism, gay rights, environmentalism, consumerism and multiculturalism. These movements are often distinguished by 'contentious collective actions' (Tarrow 1994), such as sit-ins, media events, petitions, demonstrations, all of which are designed to influence public opinion and government. Stonier (1989: 31) argues that 'social movements are of prime importance to the public relations practitioner'.

So what is the link between this accelerated pluralism and PA? The answer lies both in the individual's need to have their new values and behaviours accepted, or at least tolerated, by society and in the pressure on government to react to these changes in civil society. We cannot be openly gay if homosexuality is illegal: government is challenged to make same-sex acts legal. We cannot be free citizens if there is excessive security legislation against terrorist threats. We cannot be a sovereign consumer without

Picture 22.1 Much public affairs and lobbying has been done in the past in private. Less so today as professionals, workers, students and individuals seek more say about their roles at work and in society (*source*: Sipa Press/Rex)

Picture 22.2 Influencing government is at the heart of public affairs – here is a traditional British way (*source*: Tony Kyriacou/Rex)

knowing, say, food ingredients; one would be a dead sovereign consumer unless the government regulates for food safety. We cannot be an informed citizen about the environment if levels of river pollution are not monitored and published. Employees want workplace rights on health and safety and on pensions: only government can enforce minimum standards. Individuals and groups urge involvement by government, and representative, accountable government responds in a **liberal democracy**.

In this way, PA activities between organisations or groups and government express the concerns and hopes of the former and the policy responses of the latter. They are the conversations of a liberal democracy. This shift in UK society and in much of the EU to more individual expression and supportive voluntary groups is identified here as value pluralism and group pluralism of a civic kind. Brought together, they can be called *civic pluralism* (Moloney 2000, 2006).

In addition, a commercial variant of pluralism has come to the fore in the UK in approximately the same period. From the middle of the 1970s, it was noticeable that the climate of ideas about markets and business was shifting away from the collective and the planned towards the singular and the autonomous. This altered paradigm for the UK political economy has resulted in business and pro-market interests predominating over their ideological and material competitors. Mainstream political parties are more business friendly and, as a result, there is now in the UK a pronounced **commercial pluralism**. Without it, accelerated pluralism would not affect the lives of all the UK population. Tens of millions are affected by personal and civic value changes; all are affected by market and business changes. This commercial pluralism speaks when we hear calls for the abolition of farm subsidies and when the gaming industry lobbies for the use of credit cards in casinos.

In liberal, market economies, popularly elected governments react to changes in civil society (voluntary associations outside the family and government) and in the political economy (the wealth creation nexus in society). We are closer to those changes when we see them legislated for, and regulated by local, regional and national governments. Increasingly, however, the source of this legislation is further away from us at the EU level, and yet we often feel the consequences of legislation close to our homes and work (animal welfare in abattoirs, workplace rights for part-time employees). (See also Chapter 5.)

European context

Public affairs at the European level is made more complex by the number of interests and governmental institutions involved and it is likely that, because of the interrelated forces of EU expansion and closer integration, there will be more **lobbying** at this level. (See Chapter 5 for further discussion of European institutions.)

Cram (2001: 162) is not exaggerating when she writes 'it is generally recognised that the EU policy process is very complex', for she notes that 'no single actor has total control'. It is clear, however, that the Council of Ministers – representing the member states or countries of the European Union – has significant powers of veto (the right to reject something) over the European Commission, which proposes policy and regulates its enforcement, and over the European Parliament, which can scrutinise policy and budgets but not initiate legislation.

Around these European institutions is a great array of interest, cause and pressure groups, staffed and led by professional and citizen lobbyists. There are, for example, nearly 5,000 lobbyists accredited to the Parliament. To cut through this clamour for influence, the most effective way is to have the unconditional support of the lobbyists' national governments. With this support, organisations and groups have a direct route into the confidential power politics of the Council of Ministers. For example, UK private healthcare companies wanting new business in Europe are in a better position than British trade unionists wanting stronger rights to strike, because their national government supports business and market interests more than it does employee interests.

Lobbying within Europe

Without that national government support, the lobbyist is faced with a choice of various tactics. McGrath (2005) notes that successful European lobbyists start their work very early in the life of a new policy and congregate around the officials and consultative committees of the Commission. The reason is that the Commission develops new legislation by consensus building across 25 national governments, its own institutions and dozens of interest and cause groups. Officials, who are mostly lawyers and economists, are keen to have technical views on how policy will work in pan-European circumstances and this need for expert opinion is a point of influence for PA people. Facing these complexities, therefore, the Commission follows a snowball approach which favours early persuaders trying to steer the direction of policy, and ensures that most proposals backed by the Commission become law. Lobbyists for consumer and environmental protection and animal welfare will also keep close to the Parliament, which has a pronounced interest in these areas. But remember that national interests keep surfacing, for many MEPs will only see national public affairs personnel or those with an established public interest in their home state. In all these circumstances, the importance of personal contact is high and that of media relations relatively unimportant.

Personal influence and public affairs

Because of this importance, personal influence models of PR are relevant to public affairs, although it is an open question whether this is a positive or negative effect. Chen and Culbertson (2003: 27) note how in China *quanxhi* (personal networks of connections and friendship to acquire what is needed) pose 'challenges' including the possibility of corruption of public officials. Chay-Nemeth (2003) sees personal influence at work in Singaporean policy making. These comments illustrate how national cultures (see Hofstede on national cultures in Chapter 7) can influence PA and it is manifest that personal relationships do affect the course and outcome of European lobbying.

Many professional lobbyists mention their personal connections to indicate that they have access to powerful policy makers and it is undeniable that lobbying projects need the meeting of minds and values to be successful. There is, however, an important balance to be struck in these relationships to avoid illegality or favouritism. The UK saw such flawed relationships in sleazy 'cash for questions' incidents involving MPs in the early 1990s. The result was a damaged government and a public loss of confidence, in part restored by the Nolan Committee (1994) (see the ethics and public affairs section later in this chapter).

The 'public sphere' and public affairs

If corrupt personal relationships are the worst environment for PA and lobbying in a democracy, the ideal setting is the public sphere concept. This was developed by Jürgen Habermas, one of the most influential of European social philosophers since the Second World War in the middle of the last century. The 'public sphere' has two meanings: the historical one, which describes the emergence of middle-class public opinion in eighteenth-century England, France and Germany; the normative one, which describes how public opinion *should* be formed in civil society. It is the latter that concerns us here, for public affairs operates in the medium of public opinion and the conditions set by the public sphere offer an ideal – a gold standard – to aim for. Those conditions are threefold, stipulating that debate to form public opinion should be:

- rational
- open to all wanting to partake
- conducted in a disinterested way (Moloney 2000: 150–155).

(See also 'Ethics and public affairs', p. 454.)

Think about 22.3

Student issues and 'ideal' conditions for debate

To what extent do public debates on issues affecting students (for example, on tuition fees or student accommodation) meet Moloney's three conditions? How is public opinion formed? Do you feel able to put forward informed arguments and to participate in debate? How are public debates around these issues handled (e.g. by your student union/university)?

These are manifestly the conditions of perfection and thus beyond practice, but they are a constant reminder to working PA people and lobbyists about how to behave. Having defined public affairs and put it in national and European contexts, we can now explore how it is done. (See Think about 22.3.)

Public affairs: knowledge, skills and behaviour needed

The core skills needed in PA to operate successfully in the competitive environment of accelerated pluralism are lobbying (both in private and publicly) and media relations (see Chapter 15).

Lobbying is persuading public policy makers to act in the interests of your organisation or group (Moloney 1997). The first operational decision is to decide whether to lobby in private or publicly, or both. Three questions will help you decide. Do you know the decision makers? Is the matter to be lobbied on the current political agenda? Are you an 'insider' organisation or group? If the three answers are 'yes', then you should go the private route and avoid the media and public events. If the answers are 'no', then your lobbying may be best achieved by using the media and organising public events. (See Box 22.2 and Activity 22.2.)

Who are the lobbyists?

Because PA is an accessible activity, lobbyists are not only professionals but laypeople armed with the skills set out in this and the media relations chapters (Chapter 15). Professional lobbyists work inside organisations and groups as employees or in lobbying firms, which are usually small to

Before starting to think of lobbying tactics, consider this. Lobbying is a serious activity with costs, risks about outcomes and possible damage to reputation. It is also very time consuming, may last for years and involves mental, emotional and physical commitment. It may be more prudent not to use the lobbying 'voice' and instead to accept public policy as it is or is proposed. Remember that when you lobby, you can activate opposition and set up a competition for favourable policy that was not there beforehand. You could avoid this and seek to influence policy through membership of a political party.

Because public affairs seeks to influence public policy making, it deals with elected government and in so doing is in contact with the most powerful institution in a liberal democracy. The organisations and groups seeking change or the status quo are dealing with a

constitutional power, refreshed by periodic popular mandate, which can legislate and regulate in any area of the political economy and of civil society. Lobbyists should also remember that politicians are always asking themselves – privately – 'how many voters will support a "yes" or "no" decision?' This is not necessarily cynical if the politicians also have in mind the rights and wrongs of a decision and the public interest. We are, after all, a democracy that enshrines the principle of majority voting for decision making. So numbers do count.

For all these reasons, lobbying is a serious matter not to be undertaken lightly. Furthermore, while success can greatly improve circumstances, failure can make matters worse. For example, a trade union lobbying today to abolish a secret ballot of members before strike action would be seeking to overturn a piece of legislation very widely accepted as part of the current UK political settlement and would call into question the quality of its overall political judgement. And, finally, the odds of success are no more than even in the best of circumstances: for every successful lobby, there is invariably an unsuccessful one on the other side of the argument.

Activity 22.2

Government involvement in public issues

There is intense argument about what government should or should not allow, particularly on issues of personal morals such as abortion, age of consent, drugs. Can you list three examples of human behaviour, public or private, in which government should *not* be involved? Now list three examples where they should be involved.

Would you lobby or use the media to get the result you believed in?

---

medium-sized businesses (SMEs) offering their lobbying skills for hire. (These latter professionals are also called commercial lobbyists.) Professional lobbyists are usually graduates in politics or communications and have an intense interest in daily politics and policy development. They have often worked for MPs or for political parties as researchers. They often swap between employee and hired status. Their most distinguishing feature is that their main

skills concern lobbying rather than the subject matter being lobbied about. For example, a lobbyist hired to help supermarkets build out-of-town developments will know more about parliamentary and local government procedures than about the retail sector.

The lay (non-professional) lobbyists are often very knowledgeable and impassioned about the subject or cause for which they are lobbying (e.g. animal welfare, railway safety, inheritance tax, domestic violence) and this knowledge and concern leads them to develop lobbying skills. Their knowledge and passion means that their formal educational background is unimportant, as is their age. They are the local members of national organisations (e.g. speaking in the local media for the UK's National Pensioners' Convention) or the core members of a small and temporary grouping (e.g. getting speed bumps installed in a residential road). They make up what Edmund Burke, the eighteenth-century political philosopher, called the 'little platoons' in civil society (Burke 1969) – small groups of citizens who share common interests and give each other support. In the USA, they would be called 'grassroots' lobbyists (McGrath 2004). These lay lobbyists can be called citizen lobbyists, doing civic public affairs. Lattimer (2000) has written about the skills they need, as has Levine (1993).

One point of caution: like-minded people who share a strong belief or interest can become overenthused with their cause and can forget the hours, days, months, years needed to change policy decisions. So whether the lobbyist is a professional or an individual citizen, representing the rich and powerful or poor and neglected, the assumption should be that the desired objective will only happen – if it happens at all – after much planned, sustained and persuasive effort. Success invariably depends on a well-planned PA campaign, concentrating resources to achieve a predefined goal in a limited time and with a distinctive launch, middle and end. All campaigns, military as well as civilian, are risky, demanding ventures. (See Box 22.3, Case Study 22.1, and Think about 22.4 on p. 454.)

Skills set

The skills needed to lobby have been described by David Curry (1999), who was a UK minister and who therefore gives advice from an insider's point of view. Charles Miller (2000) has done the same but from the lobbyist's position. These skills can be summarised as two major categories:

Box 22.3

What do lobbyists do?

When employers advertise jobs in public affairs, they say things like:

- 'You will be responsible for the day-to-day management of our parliamentary relations and be working with a range of other stakeholders in communicating our key messages.'

- 'You will play a key role in the continuing development of socially responsible policies for the industry and communicating them to relevant audiences.'

- 'You will develop and implement public affairs strategies that promote our members' policies to government, parliament, other organisations and the public at large.'

Case Study 22.1

The story of consultancy lobbying and its growth in the UK

Since the early 1980s we have witnessed the formation of a new branch of the PR industry – lobbying consultancy. Lobbying is far from new – individuals and companies with their roots in PR and law have acted in the political arena on behalf of clients for many years. What set these new firms apart was that lobbying was their core activity and they offered across-the-board political advice to their clients. They are in effect 'lobbyists for hire' (Moloney 1996).

This boutique industry provides us with an excellent case study of a discrete PR sector. We can consider what factors have influenced its development that may illustrate the driving forces that can effect change. This case study tells the story of this industry and considers how external and internal factors have affected the nature of the consultancy lobbying business.

Pre-1980s

There have probably always been individuals and organisations that have offered their clients knowledge of politics and an ability to influence politicians. Since the Second World War, PR firms and legal advisors have offered such advice to paying customers (Finer 1966). But these organisations did not focus on this activity nor did they offer these services as the central core of their business. This may well have been because the post-war environment was one in which close connections existed between politicians, civil service mandarins and industry leaders. They were likely to have schooled together and socialised at the same 'gentlemen's clubs' (private members' clubs), therefore space for skilled communicators to practise and in particular offer 'access' simply did not exist.

By the 1970s these social relationships were starting to break down; with globalisation, more foreign organisations became interested in the UK. By the end of that decade a new breed of firms such as Ian Greer Associates (founded in 1969) were offering political advice to clients unfamiliar with the UK political establishment. Individuals, PR firms and lawyers acted on

case study 22.1 (continued)

behalf of mainly private sector clients, while others such as the large UK private sector companies, nationalised industries and the trade unions relied on their personal and directly sponsored relationships with politicians to secure political advantage.

1980s

By the early 1980s specialist PA companies like GJW appeared, fuelled by a round of privatisations and the interest of US companies wishing to gain a presence in the UK and Europe. Many US firms retained professional lobbyists at home and looked for similar advice in the UK. British firms followed suit and an era of tremendous growth began. PR companies and others set up formal lobbying operations in the UK to cash in; the number of firms and lobbyists in consultancy work increased year on year (see Figure 22.1).

Sectors such as property, health and defence turned to consultancy lobbyists for complementary advice hoping to gain political advantage. This new breed of professional firms, dominated by practitioners with Conservative party sympathies, had grown and was now catching the public eye and, increasingly, its tactics and motives were questioned. In response, the industry formed the Association of Professional Political Consultants (APPC) to represent their interests. Initially starting with five member firms, the APPC has grown ever since. There have always been more firms offering political consultancy than are members of the APPC, but they do represent a significant proportion of the industry. This is demonstrated by comparing the firms listed in the commercially available reference guides or 'political directories' that list contact details for lobbying firms and have been sporadically published. Although these directories are never a complete record, they do indicate a greater number of lobbying consultancies being available for hire between 1991 and 2002 (Atack 1990; Johnson 2002).

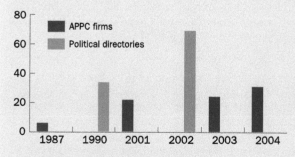

Figure 22.1 Growth of political consultancies (*source*: Milner 2005)

1990s

By the early 1990s well over 30 consultancies had been established. The largest of these were very successful and were becoming established with recognisable brands and steady income streams. This had two effects: first, it allowed practitioners to take on 'loss-leading' clients such as smaller charities; second, lobbying consultancies became takeover targets for larger communications groups looking to move into this space.

The number of consultants continued to expand into the hundreds and client lists grew as it became the norm for companies faced with an increasingly interventionist government to retain a lobbying consultancy. The dotcom bubble fuelled growth, but the initial dynamism of the young industry was fading as large privatisations slowed and lobbying firms themselves sold out. The industry came under particular scrutiny from political audiences and beyond as a series of scandals led to the Committee of Enquiry into Standards in Public Life, which investigated links between lobbyists and MPs. Yet the sector continued to grow.

By 1996/7 it became clear that the Labour party would form the next government and this regime change fuelled further expansion. Consultancies employed Labour specialists in response to nervous clients unsure of what a Labour government would mean for their businesses. Questions arose about the links between lobbyists and politicians, this time Labour links, yet again this had little impact on the success of these firms.

2000 on

Despite a general economic downturn in the early decade, consultancy lobbying continued to grow, only more slowly. New Labour policies were a driver of growth, freeing the political reins on government institutions (for example, industry regulators such as OFGEN) which started to turn to lobbyists for political advice, while increasing regulation forced greater interaction between government institutions and their potential clients and new directives on 'contracting out' helped consultancies.

By 2001 organisations were familiar with Labour, and started to build specialist lobbying capacities in-house on a scale not observed before, expanding the overall number of jobs available to lobbyists. Consultancies, although still hiring, did not expand as rapidly as in the 1980s and 1990s. Client numbers also grew slowly as did fee income (see Figure 22.2).

case study 22.1 (continued)

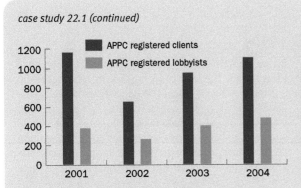

Figure 22.2 Steady growth of consultancies following the millennium (*source*: Milner 2005)

This is a simplified overview of the industry, but it illustrates the way in which markets may grow, stabilise or contract, depending on a number of external and internal influences. The next section considers four prime factors and their specific impact on the industry over time.

The economy

Comparing the FTSE indices with the growth experienced in the UK market, one would expect a close correlation. Clients are unlikely to hire external political help if they are under financial pressure. There are clearly exceptions to this rule (when a company's very existence depends on a political decision, for example) but we can see that the FTSE trends do indeed echo those experienced in the lobbying sector.

The FTSE100, FTSE250 and the FTSE All-Share Index record the combined share price performance of those companies which are registered on the London Stock Exchange (Figure 22.3). As such they act as an accurate guide to UK economic performance. The indices clearly record a general economic downturn in 2002/3. This directly correlates with a drop in the number of client relationships and lobbyists employed around that period. Commercial companies remain the mainstay of most lobbying firms and it is these relationships that are the most important to the financial success of a firm. The general economic environment plays a major role in determining business success. In consultancy lobbying, however, there are other external factors that are equally important.

Political environment

If the economy were the only driver in this market then why were there no comparable lobbying firms operating to any scale prior to the 1980s? Clearly, other factors influence this market.

Although close connections still exist today, society's 'players' are less likely to have the intimate relationships as before, therefore there is now space for skilled communicators to practise.

This is an example of how political affairs companies work within a very specific ecology, that of politics. Changes within that environment make real differences to the prospects for consultancies.

Westminster legislation and parliament

In October 2004 the government introduced new gambling legislation in the Houses of Parliament. Casino

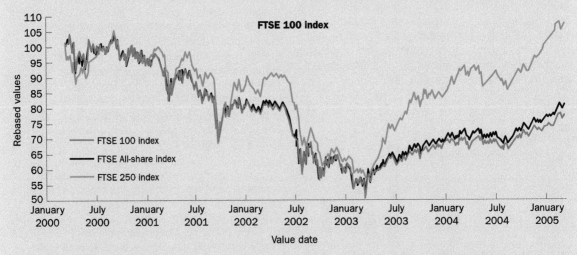

Figure 22.3 FTSE indices 2000–2005 (*source*: London Stock Exchange 2005 www.londonstockexchange.com)

case study 22.1 (continued)

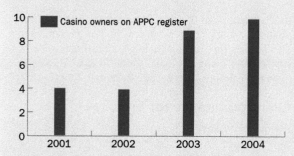

Figure 22.4 Casino industry growth recorded in APPC register (*source*: Milner 2005)

operators and their respective trade bodies required legal change in order to achieve scale in the UK. One would therefore predict a sudden presence in the APPC register (see Figure 22.4).

One can clearly observe that post-2003 (once intention to legislate was signalled), the number of casino organisations hiring lobbying firms doubled and for an industry with relatively few participants, this represented a significant percentage of the total number of casino organisations worldwide. This is a clear indication that legislation drives the lobbying market. Other activities of parliament such as select committees can drive clients to use lobbyists – the 2004 review of Pubcos by

the Trade and Industry Select Committee, for example, increased lobbying activity.

Many lobbying firms act as the secretariat of the all-party parliamentary groups. In January 2005, 301 such groups were registered with the Houses of Parliament (Vacher's Quarterly 2005).

Increasing size of government
More government institutions, increasing regulation and greater market intervention have helped consultancies to grow – there is simply more work to do. On the most basic level, the Scottish Parliament was passed into law in 1998; by 2004, 8 of the 22 listed APPC firms had offices in Edinburgh (Milner 2005).

From 1996 to 2003, 23,322 new regulations were enacted and over 100 new non-departmental public bodies had been created. As more organisations come into contact with regulation (and therefore government) the more likely they are to turn to lobbying firms for advice (House of Commons Library 2004).

A direct effect of the growth of government has been the number of public bodies that are employing lobbyists. Indeed, over a four-year period of study (2001–2004), government institutions have been second only to private companies as the most frequent user of commercial lobbyists (see Figure 22.5).

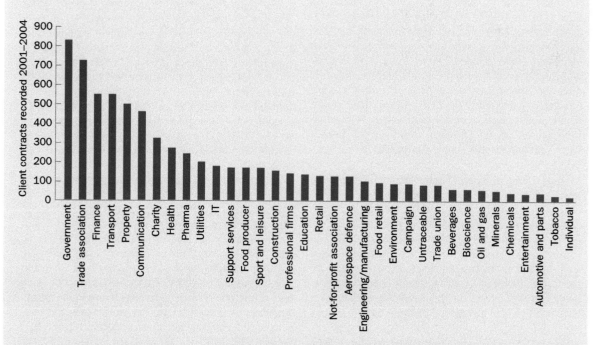

Figure 22.5 Most frequent users of commercial lobbyists 2001–2004 (*source*: Milner 2005)

case study 22.1 (continued)

Local government institutions from Edinburgh to Essex have hired APPC lobbyists over the past four years, and in large numbers. In the majority of cases it is difficult to assess motive as there is no geographic or party political pattern to the makeup of this group. In total, almost one-quarter of all recorded instructions between clients and lobbying consultancies in the period 2001–2004 were from government institutions and not-for-profit clients.

Government procurement

Although the size of government has clearly increased, there are equally a growing number of areas in which government is 'contracting out' to non-governmental organisations. Governments have always relied on private arms manufacturers, for example, but it would seem to be a practice that is moving into all types of new areas. Suppliers to government are most likely to hire lobbyists.

Supply side

One factor that is often overlooked is the role played by the lobbying industry participants themselves in choosing their clients. The UK lobbying industry still lacks real scale, therefore the individual prejudices of practitioners can have a significant effect on the client base.

Studies in the USA have uncovered the way lobbyists use their time. They have found that for one-third of the time lobbyists are at work they are involved in issues of personal political interest (Kersh 2002). Consultancy lobbying is cyclical in nature; this means lobbyists often find themselves with time to fill and if you are interested in politics, what better way of 'having fun' than in politics itself or on behalf of a client with whom you have an affinity. This type of activity can have a significant impact on a market (Loomis 2003).

There is a long tradition of commercial lobbying firms working for charitable organisations. Some charitable organisations are far better funded than private companies and no doubt pay lobbyists well for their time, but many do not. Working with highbrow charities will improve your networking or may enhance your image with your key audiences; working for a political party or candidate during an election clearly improves knowledge and arguably access. Whatever the reason, there is a long history of this type of philanthropy.

Since 1997 it has become more common for trade unions to use political lobbyists. At least 20 trade unions used commercial lobbyists between 2001 and 2005. Perhaps this is because of the increasing sophistication of the political campaigning of trade unions. This phenomenon also reflects the pre-eminence of Labour-sympathising lobbyists in the marketplace (post-1990s) wishing to have trade unions on their books (Milner 2005).

Client preference for in-house

A growing number of organisations are building their own in-house PA capacity. If you turn to the back of any issue of *PR Week* published between 2001 and 2004, you will observe many more advertisements for in-house lobbying positions than for consultancies and in-house-dominated informal practitioner groupings, such as 'PubAffairs' in Westminster, have seen their membership lists expand in recent times, from 10 practitioners in 2002 to 1,030 members in 2005 (Milner 2005).

This in-house growth does not seem to have diminished the number of lobbying firms being hired but it has increased the competition for lobbying talent. It has also changed the nature of the retained relationship for many consultants who now have to work alongside PR and legal departments far more regularly than in the past.

Conclusion

It is beyond doubt that the economy is a key factor determining consultancy success, but it is not the only one. Whether a change of government automatically drives a growth in the lobbying market is harder to fathom. By 1997 the Labour party had been out of power for many years, and businesses and other organisations were not familiar with them. With limited in-house provision, firms and organisations turned to consultancies. New governments do herald a plethora of new laws and parliamentary activity, therefore a change probably would influence growth. And, if patterns were to repeat themselves, a further change of government would bring a new generation of 'rain-makers' to the top to drive consultancies forward. Those lobbyists, in turn, influence the makeup of their client lists, but it is commercial clients that fund consultancies, effectively subsidising the work carried out on behalf of charities, political campaigns and others by lobbyists themselves. We also await a time when the size of government shrinks. This has not happened since the Second World War but perhaps it may in the future. Whatever the future holds, it seems likely that consultancy lobbying will remain a significant sector within the wider PR field.

Source: Milner (2005)

1   *Gaining access* involves: the knowledge and skills associated with work and social networking; identifying allies and opponents; knowing how to get the attention of policy makers.

2   *Making representations* is presenting your case clearly and briefly, persuasively, and accurately in terms of the wider interest. This is a key point – to persuade accountable politicians and officials to change policy, you have to align your interest with the wider, public interest. Moreover, underlying effective representation is knowledge of how policy is made in: political parties; ministries; the Prime Minister's Office; local authorities; and the EU. This knowledge includes the understanding that timing is vital in lobbying, because proposals are much easier to change than declared policy.

See Mini case study 22.2 and Think about 22.5.

Mini Case Study 22.2
Gaining access and making representations

The British Ceramic Confederation has 150 members who represent 90% of the UK pottery industry. As the trade association, it is the 'voice' of an important industry, has access to ministers and represents the industry's views on various issues. One such issue is how foreign counterfeit ceramics are threatening UK jobs and markets.

This example and the terms 'access' and 'making representations' highlight again the 'outsider' and 'insider' distinction, and draw attention to the power of business, the sensitivity of government to employment and trade issues and the importance of contacts.

It is usually impossible to know why your lobby succeeded or failed. This leads to another vital skill – patience. The readiness to 'play a long game' can make all the difference. There are so many variable factors influencing policy making that it is extremely difficult to say which are crucial to success or failure and when they will change. As an example of how policy priorities change, there is now more public money for anti-alcohol and anti-obesity campaigns. Because of this uncertainty, it is unwise to claim publicly that your lobbying tipped the balance and got the desired outcome. Besides, public boasting about changing the minds of politicians and public officials is not attractive in a democracy and may stir up opposition.

The difficulty of isolating the winning factors in a lobbying campaign leads to another warning to the lobbyist – do not believe that there is a winning formula. There is most definitely not. There is, however, a set of behaviours that have been associated in the past with successful lobbying. Moloney (1996), Curry (1999) and Miller (2000) outline many of these but they should be treated as guidelines – pointers suggested by experience – not recipes for guaranteed success. (See Box 22.5, Activity 22.3 and Mini case study 22.3.)

Ethics and public affairs

Because PA seeks to influence public policy in a democracy, it receives more scrutiny than any other PR specialism, and rightly so. The use of professional lobbyists on a hired basis, their relationship with MPs and ministers, the declaration of interests by lobbyists and politicians, and the use of entertainment and free gifts were all matters of public concern regarding UK lobbying in the late 1980s and early 1990s – leading to the Nolan Committee (1994) investigation into standards in public life. Today the responsible lobbyist in any country should be aware of the seven principles of public life recommended by Nolan (see

Box 22.4

One week in the life of a public affairs consultant

The practitioner diary of Richard Casofsky, public affairs account executive for Finsbury Public Relations Consultants

Monday

5am: My taxi arrives to take me to the office to get me there for 5.30. A House of Commons select committee has released government responses to its earlier report and I need to summarise these to present to our client by 7am.

9am: Begin to check the press and emails and to prepare for an 11.30am meeting with another client. This client is following the progress of a bill through parliament and it is my job to stay constantly in touch with any developments as they take place – we need to always be the client's first source of any new information.

3pm: Client meeting went well. I now need to draft the minutes and relevant action points ASAP to send on today. Also a number of points of detail need to be researched further to uncertainties that emerged during the meeting.

4pm: I get home early to compensate for the very early start.

Tuesday

8am: Check press and respond to emails. We're trialing a monitoring service to help us follow the progress of a bill and I am inundated with information – much of this is superfluous to the client's needs.

12pm: Phones have been very busy with our clients wanting to know our position on a controversial government White Paper. A brief team meeting is convened and we return each client call with our predictions and a simplified explanation of what the White Paper will mean to them.

3pm: Further team meeting to discuss strategy for preparing for a pitch for new business. With the team, I now need to begin speedy background research into the relevant sector and the related governmental departments. We (the account execs) are preparing a first draft of a PowerPoint presentation and an accompanying contact list.

Wednesday

9am: Check emails and answer the phone. The secretary is on leave today so we all need to muck in to spread her workload (answering phones mainly).

1pm: Have been spending the morning making calls to government departments trying to get hold of the government's draft priorities for health for the UK's presidency of the EU. This is for a pharmaceutical client. The sponsoring department doesn't wish to give out the information, so I try to get this from the part of the Cabinet Office that coordinates on all EU-related matters – not proving easy to get hold of this information.

6pm: Today has been busy with all the team managing their part of the research for the new business pitch in between regular daily tasks and constant ringing of phones . . .

7pm: Tonight is the company's anniversary party – there is a drinks party with clients from 7.30 to 9.30 and the team go out after the clients have left.

Thursday

9am: Hung over, I need to prepare 20 biogs of MPs to send to a client hosting an event at parliament. The MPs have been selected for having an interest in the client's business area. I also make a point of calling parliamentary offices to remind MP researchers of the event.

1pm: Lunch with a friend from when I was at university. He is now working as a press officer for the Conservatives [UK political party].

2pm: The remainder of the day is spent amending the presentation for the pitch we are working on.

8pm: Still in the office – manager has been out at meetings for most of the day and is only now catching up with his emails/work. I have just been given several tasks (finding recent press articles and past emails relating to a particular client issue) to complete before I leave the office.

Friday

10am: Today has been fairly quiet. We've been preparing a strategy document for Britain in Europe setting out the advantages the European Constitution would bring to British business.

2pm: Have been making calls to the Department for Culture, Media and Sport about the Gambling Bill. Preparing a briefing document for a client who is meeting a minister and his officials on Monday.

4pm: The rest of my day has been spent trying to understand the European Commission's recently updated merger policy for a briefing note to send to clients. The new Merger Regulation is very complex and this is proving to be a daunting task.

Source: Richard Casofsky

Box 22.5

How to lobby government – a checklist

- Define the matter to be lobbied.
- Define success and failure.
- Network with allies.
- Monitor opponents.
- Establish who the decision makers are.
- Decide whether to influence privately, publicly or both.
- Lobby before policy is decided.

- Write your case on one sheet of A4 paper.
- Gain access.
- Let your most powerful and persuasive person lobby.
- Socialise with decision makers.
- Consider joining/supporting the party in power.
- Be persuasive both on paper and in person.
- Be technical – don't challenge policy directly.
- Be knowledgeable about how policy is made.
- Lobby in the name of the public interest.
- Be discreet about whom you are lobbying.
- Plan public events if private lobbying is not working.
- Use the media when they add pressure.
- If you change policy, never take the credit – in public!

Activity 22.3

Understanding lobbying

- What is lobbying? Write down your own definition of lobbying.
- Write down what you think are the top three skills needed to lobby.
- Under what circumstances is a private lobby better than a public one? Write down an example.
- Do you think you have lobbying skills? List them.

Mini Case Study 22.3

Lobbying on student top-up fees

In the UK, two academic unions (AUT, NATFHE) and the National Union of Students mounted a short six-day joint campaign to remove all references to variable student top-up fees in the third reading of the 2004 Higher Education Bill. To succeed they needed to change the minds of three Labour MPs.

Branch officials in the regions were asked to contact all members, give them the briefing previously sent to MPs, urge them to write to their MPs and visit them in their surgeries. They were sent a template letter and told that the union websites provided briefings and supportive arguments. They were supported by the small number of vice-chancellors opposing variable fees who lobbied sympathetic members of both Houses of Parliament. The campaign lost because government business managers persuaded previously rebellious MPs to be loyal.

Box 22.6); these have set a 'gold standard' for behaviour by holders of public office.

Any scrutiny of public affairs asks three questions:

1 Who has access to public decision makers and under what conditions (private or publicly known access)?

2 What weight do policy makers give to representations made to them?

3 Have powerful interests more right of access to public policy makers than poor and marginal interests?

Concerns over access may be triggered by private meetings between officials and business people at the Prime Minister's Office or in Brussels when policy is developed. Critics say that their meetings should be publicly flagged up in advance and that a record of their contents made public later.

All these health warnings strengthen the need for caution when deciding whether or not to lobby. The caution

Box 22.6

Standards in public life – the Nolan principles

Professional and citizen lobbyists should be aware that holders of public office are expected to behave with:

- selflessness
- integrity
- objectivity
- accountability
- openness
- honesty
- leadership.

Box 22.7

Whether or not to lobby publicly?

An organisation or group would first ask itself:

- Is there easy access to councillors, MPs, senior civil servants and ministers?
- Is our policy position on the mainstream political agenda?

If the answers are 'no', you are halfway to doing a citizens' lobby.

The next stage has two more questions:

- Have we got many people who would support us publicly?
- Can we get media coverage?

If the answers are 'yes', a public lobbying strategy would be more effective.

has two aspects, one self-interested and the other principled – and both should be asked in the context of the Nolan principles. Do we help or harm the interests we represent when we do PA? Do we help or hinder the quality of our democracy when we lobby? (See Boxes 22.7 and 22.8, Case study 22.2 and Activity 22.4.)

Box 22.8

Public lobbying – action checklist

Influencing public policy makers is a 'numbers' game'. So can you:

- drum up support in public at a rally, protest, demo?
- organise a well-supported petition?
- get testimonials of support from celebrities, experts, losers and gainers?
- develop slogans?
- organise attention-seeking events over time?
- work cooperatively with enthusiasts?
- have an agreed script for your interest/cause and stick to it?
- develop a news sense?

Activity 22.4

Analysis of Case study 22.2 (see p. 458)

- Whom did the residents have to convince that their case was right?
- Rank in order of importance the tactics which brought about the result.
- Why do you think that the government supported the residents' case?

Case Study 22.2

A 'David and Goliath' public affairs battle on the English Channel

The primary definition of globalisation is the integration of markets across the world and it is a definition that foregrounds the role of ports. As international trade increases, ports expand and contract with changing patterns of demand. Examples are Felixstowe and Rotterdam, which have grown in tonnage and area occupied, unlike London and Amsterdam, which grew smaller or stopped trading.

Modern ports are capital intensive, take up large areas of land, generate jobs and markets for their suppliers, disturb their environments from ecological, physical and amenity perspectives and are the subject of national government policy. Most of these features came to the fore in 1997 when Associated British Ports, owners of Southampton port on the south coast of England, proposed a £745m expansion of the docks on the western side of Southampton Water, on a site known as Dibden Bay.

That proposed expansion, however, was the subject of intense debate in the city and surrounding communities. While Southampton City Council supported the new dock, opposition to it coalesced around the group known as Residents Against Dibden Bay Port (RADBP). Paul Vickers, who had a background in the petroleum industry, was its chairman. He led the group to a successful conclusion and here he describes the seven-year campaign that led the UK government to refuse planning permission for a new dock in the bay. It is a campaign that shows the benefits and costs of concerned citizens doing PA. He tells the story of the Dibden Bay incident by the English Channel.

Background

The proposal was for a container port at Dibden Bay, which is directly connected to the proposed New Forest National Park. The bay's foreshore is home to 50,000 rare birds and protected under the European Birds Directive, as well as being the strategic gap between the townships of Hythe and Marchwood. It would have been the UK's biggest port infrastructure project ever. One-third the size of Heathrow Airport London, it was to take 10 years to construct.

'The announcement provoked a public outcry. Associated British Port's (ABP) argument was that there was a national need for extra container capacity and that Dibden Bay was the only available site. The New Forest District Council soon organised a public meeting, which led to the formation of our group. We ran the campaign from 1997 up to and through the public inquiry, culminating on 20 April 2004 with the government's decision on the expansion.'

Gathering information

'At the outset, the ABP case appeared cut and dried and most organisations and institutions thought that the only option was to compromise and limit the damage. The European Directive provides no protection if there is deemed to be an overriding public need. Consequently it is possible to win the argument at a public inquiry and still have the decision go against you.

'From day one, RADBP set out to be a professional organisation. Whilst we would inevitably be accused of "nimby"-ism [i. e. "not in my back yard" (NIMBY) or property-owner self-interest], our plan was to be consistently articulate and accurate with facts and arguments. The first requirement was to gather data about the UK container port industry: the facts/story as put forward by ABP and the growth in container demand, etc. This was achieved by RADBP writing letters which were sent in the name of either the New Forest Council or the local MP. A letter on House of Parliament paper guarantees a reply! At the end of this period it was abundantly clear that ABP's case was flawed.'

Lobbying

'With as much information as possible, our next objective was to lobby all of those organisations which could potentially become opponents to the expansion proposal. At the outset, there were only two groups on our side (Royal Society for the Protection of Birds and New Forest District Council) but slowly and following presentations, leafleting and more letters from the MP, other groups began to doubt ABP. By 2000, we had become the coordinating group for the opposition and taken on the role of passing information between the groups, heading up the media campaign and vetting statements made by other groups to ensure accuracy and consistency. By now the media wanted to talk to us.'

The strategy

'This can be summarised as follows:

- maximise the opposition in advance of the formal planning application and the expected public inquiry

- sponsor alternative locations (to give the government a way out)

case study 22.2 (continued)

■ delay ABP as long as possible to allow alternative proposals to come forward (one of the ways of achieving this was to continuously put more and more questions into the public arena, so that ABP had to respond).'

Tactics

'Between 1997 and 2004 we used a number of different methods to get our message across. These included:

■ frequent leafleting

■ car stickers

■ letters to ABP's shareholders pointing out financial weaknesses in the proposed extension

■ information packs handed out at the ABP annual general meeting

■ getting the BBC to make a documentary on the project

■ persuading other interest and pressure groups to go public

■ media relations

■ and asking parliamentary questions.'

Winning the public affairs battle

'By 2000, the tide of expert and public opinion was moving against ABP. The turning point came at a decisive public presentation in January in the chamber of the New Forest District Council between us and ABP, when our case was much stronger. After this, ABP never appeared in public with us again. The same presentation was used extensively throughout 2000 to lobby support.'

Fighting the planning application

'The formal application was submitted by ABP in October 2000. By this time the opposition was extensive. Six and a half thousand individual objections went to the government in the six weeks allowed, a record for a planning application, and the official bodies and pressure groups that lined up with us came to 50.'

'By contrast, ABP only had the support of Southampton City Council.'

'Also by this time, our involvement with the possibility of building a container port on a redundant refinery site in Essex came to fruition with the decision by P&O Ports (a competitor of ABP) to go ahead with this project.

Furthermore, we had agreed with P&O that they would announce this project to coincide with ABP submitting their application. This allowed us to go to the media with the story that this development (the London Gateway project) was on a brownfield site and that Dibden Bay was a protected greenfield site.'

'ABP appeared to believe throughout that no one would turn down a project for the strategically important port of Southampton. The inquiry inspector organised a preliminary meeting in April 2001 to agree the scope and the management of the inquiry. We asked for two extra topics – financial viability and human rights – to be inserted, knowing that these were weak areas for ABP.'

'The inquiry was set to start in December that year, after everyone had submitted their evidence. In the intervening period, it was expected that ABP would fly barrage balloons in the bay to indicate the height of the cranes and the line of the 1.8-kilometre quay on the foreshore. But this did not happen, so we planned the event for the weekend immediately before the inquiry opened in order to maximise publicity. ABP, in the role of harbour master, tried to prevent us going ahead, but faced with the inevitable media coverage this would have given them, they relented.'

'The flying of the barrage balloons at 330 feet high over the length of the proposed quay in an unspoilt bay was a master stroke, as this was the first time the local population had seen anything visual to indicate the size and impact of the project.'

Giving the government a way out

'As I have said earlier, it is possible to win the inquiry and lose the political decision. We wanted therefore to ensure that the government had other container port expansion options besides Dibden Bay and to this end we also contacted Hutchinson Ports, the owners of Felixstowe (the largest UK container port) and Harwich. They were well aware that if Dibden Bay went ahead, it would severely affect their own business. They therefore decided to put in their own application for expansion in Harwich and they agreed to announce this on the day the inquiry opened to give us yet another media opportunity. This meant that the media story was now "why do we need Dibden when we can have London Gateway and also Harwich, neither of which involve such a large environmental impact as Dibden Bay?"'

case study 22.2 (continued)

Decision day: 20 April 2004

'The inquiry and the government denied the application to make Dibden Bay a port on a long list of grounds, not just the environmental issues, e.g. ABP failed on the two topics we inserted, financial viability and human rights. We had won a seven-year battle of public campaigning and private lobbying. It was incredibly hard work and needed sustained commitment but it showed that it is possible for a small group of determined citizens to succeed against a powerful company. Those who care can win.'

Endnote

From Paul Vickers' account, the outstanding feature of the residents' campaign was the result in their favour. Most pressure groups do not win their case so completely against well-resourced interests. The residents were a David to the Goliath of Associated British Ports in terms of the resources that could be devoted to a public affairs campaign. In this case, the residents spent £120,000 compared to ABP's estimated £45m. In terms of the 'insider' and 'outsider' distinction about relationships with government (see earlier in the chapter, p. 454), ABP provide much of the physical infrastructure which allows the UK to trade by sea, while the residents were a temporary and changing association of volunteers who had not worked together before and who were unknown to public policy makers. It is this imbalance of resource and status that is so striking about this case. The success of RADBP is reminiscent of the struggle between Greenpeace and Shell over Brent Spar in the mid-1990s. Indeed, the Dibden Bay incident may well be seen eventually to have had greater significance in environmental, political and public affairs terms.

For ABP, there was disappointment about the decision not to expand – a reminder that in public affairs work, there are always competing views. In a statement immediately afterwards, it said that the decision was 'extremely serious'. It added that: 'The decision not to give ABP's Port of Southampton the go-ahead for its expansion plans to handle growth in the UK's international trade will certainly result in a loss of job opportunities in the area and will have a worryingly adverse effect on the local and regional economies. The future shape of the port will now be significantly different to that of the expanded Port of Southampton which we had planned for.'

Source: Moloney and Vickers 2004

Summary

Public affairs is the much used PR specialism that seeks to influence public policy making through lobbying, done either privately or publicly, along with media relations, or by combining both routes. Lobbying is at the heart of public affairs and is often connected to the linked specialisms of issues management, community relations and sponsorship (Chapters 17, 18 and 26). It is conducted by the widest range of organisations and groups, from the largest companies to the smallest groups of citizens, all seeking to advance some interest or cause or right some wrong.

PA is done in a particular social, political and economic context, i.e. accelerated pluralism, where organisations and groups seek advantage for their values, behaviours and material interests over their competitors. They often act cooperatively with allies to achieve this. PA is the 'voice' of this competition for advantage.

There is a particular skills set required to do PA whether by professional lobbyists or laypeople. The core skills are those of identifying and analysing issues, building a case in response, getting access to decision makers, aligning private and public interests, persuading officials and politicians in your favour, and deciding on private and/or public routes of influence.

Public affairs can be a controversial activity and it should not be undertaken lightly. It touches on the quality of democracy by influencing elected representatives and officials. It is part of public life and should be conducted to the high standards established by the Nolan Committee.

Bibliography

Atack, S. (1990). *The Directory of Public Affairs and Government Relations*. London: Berkeley International Recruitment Consultants.

Burke, E. (1969, first published 1790). *Reflections On The Revolution in France*. London: Penguin.

Chay-Nemeth, C. (2003). 'Becoming professionals: A portrait of public relations in Singapore' in *The Global Public Relations Handbook*. K. Sriramesh and D. Verčič (eds). London: Lawrence Erlbaum Associates.

Chen, N. and H. Culbertson (2003). 'Public relations in mainland China: An adolescent with growing pains' in *The Global Public Relations Handbook*. K. Sriramesh and D. Verčič (eds). London: Lawrence Erlbaum Associates.

Committee on Standards in Public Life: Issues and questions (1994). London: HMSO (Dd 8389342) (the Nolan Committee).

Cram, L. (2001). 'Integration and policy processes in the European Union' in *Governing the European Union*. S. Bromley (ed.). London: Sage.

Curry, D. (1999). *Lobbying Government*. London: Chartered Institute of Housing.

Finer, S.E. (1966). *Anonymous Empire: A study of the lobby in Great Britain*, 2nd edition. London: Pall Mall Press.

Grant, W. (2000). *Pressure Groups, Politics and Democracy in Britain*, 2nd edition. Hemel Hempstead: Harvester Wheatsheaf.

Hansard (2004). Prime Minister's response to questions posted by Stephen O'Brian MP, July.

House of Commons Library (2004). Quoted in 'Reversing drivers in regulation: Big Government'. Conservative Party Paper Policy Document.

Johnson, J. (2002). *Directory of Political Lobbying 2002*. London: Politico's Publishing.

Kersh, R. (2002). 'Corporate lobbyists as political actors' in *Interest Group Politics*. A. Ciglar and B. Loomis. Washington, DC: CQ Press.

Lattimer, M. (2000). *The Campaign Handbook*, 2nd edition. London: Directory of Social Change.

Levine, M. (1993). *Guerrilla PR: How you wage an effective publicity campaign*. New York: HarperCollins Business.

London Stock Exchange (2005). www.londonstockexchange.com.

Loomis, B. (2003). 'Doing well, doing good and (shhh!) having fun: A supply-side approach to lobbying'. Paper presented at the American Political Science Association, Philadelphia.

McGrath, C. (2004). 'Grass roots lobbying: Marketing politics and policy "beyond the beltway"'. Paper presented at the Elections on the Horizon Conference, British Library, London, March.

McGrath, C. (2005). *Perspectives on Lobbying: Washington, London, Brussels*. Lampeter: Edwin Mellen Press.

Miller, C. (2000). *Political Lobbying*. London: Politico's Publishing.

Milner, K. (2005). 'Analysis of APPC records (lobbying in the UK)'. Unpublished report. Leeds: Leeds Metropolitan University.

Moloney, K. (1996). *Lobbyists for Hire*. Aldershot: Dartmouth Press.

Moloney, K. (1997). 'Government and lobbying activities' in *Public Relations Principles and Practice*. P. Kitchen (ed.). London: Thomson Business Press.

Moloney, K. (2000). *Rethinking PR: The spin and the substance*. London: Routledge.

Moloney, K. (2006). *Rethinking Public Relations: PR Propaganda and Democracy*, 2nd edition. London: Routledge.

Moloney, K. and P. Vickers (2004). Unpublished case study.

Stonier, T. (1989). 'The evolving professionalism: Responsibilities'. *International Public Relations Review* **12**(3): 30–36.

Tarrow, S. (1994). *Power in Movement*. Cambridge: Cambridge University Press.

Vacher's Quarterly (2005). *Dod's Parliamentary Communications*. March: 216–246.

White, J. and L. Mazur (1995). *Strategic Communications Management*. Harlow: Addison-Wesley.